Platzni W9-DDG-836

The Psychoeducational Assessment of Preschool Children

The Psychoeducational Assessment of Preschool Children

Second Edition

Bruce A. Bracken, Ph.D.,
Editor
Memphis State University

Allyn and Bacon
Boston   London   Toronto   Sydney   Tokyo   Singapore

Copyright © 1991 by Allyn and Bacon
A Division of Simon & Schuster, Inc.
160 Gould Street
Needham Heights, Massachusetts 02194

All rights reserved. No part of the material protected
by this copyright notice may be reproduced or utilized
in any form or by any means, electronic or
mechanical, including photocopying, recording, or by
any information storage and retrieval system, without
written permission from the copyright owner.

A previous edition was published © 1983 by Grune &
Stratton, Inc.

Library of Congress Cataloging-in-Publication Data

The Psychoeducational assessment of preschool children / Bruce A.
   Bracken, editor.—2nd ed.
      p. cm.
   Includes bibliographical references and index.
   ISBN 0-205-12520-4
    1. Child development—Evaluation. 2. Ability—Testing.
  3. Readiness for school. I. Bracken, Bruce A.
LB1115.P963 1991
372.12'6—dc20   91-43426
                                 CIP

Printed in the United States of America
10 9 8 7 6 5 4 3   97 96 95

To my principal instructor in the
area of preschool behavior,
Bruce A. Bracken Jr.,
and to his mother and my loving wife,
Mary Jo Bracken.

CONTENTS

PREFACE

The first edition of *The Psychoeducational Assessment of Preschool Children* was conceived in 1979 primarily to meet the needs of the editors and those persons assigned the task of teaching courses in preschool psychoeducational assessment. In preparation for our own teaching assignments, we noted that no broad-spectrum resource books were available to address the theoretical and practical issues, practices, and techniques that would guide students and practitioners toward the meaningful assessment of preschool children. In the late 1970s, the literature was quite limited, generally out-dated and tended to be focused on singular aspects of preschool assessment (e.g., specific instruments, developmental issues).

To acquaint practitioners with the idiosyncratic behavior of preschool children and address the pertinent issues related to the assessment of this unique population, the editors identified and invited a nationally prominent multidisciplinary team of professionals to write chapters that would serve as the foundation for sound psychoeducational assessment of preschool children for the decade to come. Since its publication in 1983, the first edition has become adopted nationally as the standard text in preschool assessment courses. Also, the first edition has continued to serve professionals as the only comprehensive preschool assessment text available.

As the decade of the 1980s elapsed many advancements in preschool assessment and education occurred. Public Law 99-457 brought with it the promise of appropriate assessment and remedial services for exceptional preschool children. Many of the out-dated, yet venerable, preschool assessment instruments, such as the WPPSI and the Vineland Social Maturity Scale, were revised and restandardized. Many new instruments were developed and added to the repertoire of those individuals who assess young children. New theoretical orientations expanded the focus of preschool assessment and combined assessment with instruction (e.g., curriculum-based assessment/intervention and dynamic assessment/intervention.) Nationally, universities increased their graduate and undergraduate offerings in early childhood regular and special education, assessment, and therapeutic interventions. Local, state, regional, and national professional organizations and institutions sponsored a truly amazing number and array of skill-building workshops.

Additionally, special topic newsletters were developed, thematic journal issues were published, and lists of consultants were developed and distributed to guide professionals toward sound practice with preschool clients. In light of these remarkable advances, it has been professionally and personally rewarding that the first edition was in the vanguard of this historical preschool movement.

The goal for the Second Edition was to incorporate the many advances and changes that occurred in the field and continue to serve as a catalyst for future advances in preschool assessment. The revision of the first edition was a major undertaking that resulted in the addition of several new chapters, the deletion of a few, the reworking and up-dating of all the content, and a complete synthesis of old knowledge and recent developments. A major advantage of the second edition is the inclusion of five instrument-specific cognitive assessment chapters that comprise the most complete professional resource compendium on preschool cognitive assessment published. Additionally, the inclusion of chapters devoted to family assessment, preschool screening, and intervention design broadened and rounded out the thematic content.

The second edition presents a chapter sequence that can be read in consecutive order to provide professionals with a thorough and somewhat sequential understanding of the issues and practices related to preschool assessment, or the chapter order can be reorganized to meet instructors' needs or course dictates. The order of the chapters has been arranged to facilitate the reader's development of a hierarchical knowledge base. The first two chapters present an historical perspective of academic advances in child study and the practical issues that surfaced from that line of inquiry. Chapters 3 and 4 are foundational procedural chapters that provide clinical insight into the procedures, practices, and environmental characteristics necessary for conducting sound psychoeducational assessments. Chapters 5 through 9 are instrument specific chapters dedicated to intellectual assessment, and Chapter 10 follows with the assessment of adaptive behavior. Chapters 12 through 16 represent specific content related to modes of information processing (i.e., reception and expression) and communication (verbal and manual), with two language chapters, two chapters on motor assessment, and two chapters on auditory and visual processing. Chapters 17 through 21 focus on special populations of children or noncognitive areas of assessment (e.g., multicultural, severely handicapped, and gifted children; social/emotional and neuropsychological assessment). Finally, the last three chapters are dedicated to special topics in preschool assessment (i.e., screening, family assessment, and intervention design).

The second edition continues to be appropriate for school, child clinical, and pediatric psychologists, early childhood educators and diagnosticians, speech and language pathologists, and other professionals who observe and assess preschool children. The second edition is appropriate for undergraduate and graduate courses devoted to the psychoeducational assessment of preschool children, related special topics courses, and as a "best practices" resource for the practicing professional. Given the legal, ethical, practical, and professional mandates facing those professionals who assess preschool children, it is hoped that the second edition will remain in the vanguard as a reliable guide and resource well into the 1990s.

I would like to extend my appreciation for the very helpful comments and suggestions made by an outside, prepublication reviewer, Dr. Doris Bergen, Department of Educational Psychology, the University of Miami of Ohio.

Bruce A. Bracken

ACKNOWLEDGMENTS

I would like to thank Ms. Karen Kuehn Howell for her diligent and careful indexing of this work, and her continual and faithful assistance in all my projects, especially during the editorial phase of the book.

I would also like to acknowledge the Department of Psychology's Center for Applied Psychological Research (CAPR), which is funded by the State of Tennessee. It is through the support of the CAPR that the necessary time and resources are made available to pursue works such as this.

CONTRIBUTORS

Andrés Barona
Department of Educational Psychology
Arizona State University
Tempe, Arizona

Ann E. Boehm
Department of School Psychology
Teachers College
Columbia University
New York, New York

Bruce A. Bracken
Department of Psychology
Memphis State University
Memphis, Tennessee

Diane N. Bryen
Temple University
Moorestown, New Jersey

David W. Barnett
Department of School Psychology and
  Counseling
University of Cincinnati
Cincinnati, Ohio

Marilyn F. H. Boyden
The Hospital for Sick Children
Toronto, Ontario, Canada

Karen T. Carey
California State University
Fresno, California

Edward J. Caropreso
Department of Pediatrics
Yale University School of Medicine
New Haven, Connecticut

Mark H. Daniel
American Guidance Service
Circle Pines, Minnesota

Colin D. Elliott
Centre for Educational Guidance & Special
  Needs
University of Manchester
Manchester, England

Barbara Ewer-Jones
Monroe County Community Schools
Indianapolis, Indiana

Rebecca R. Fewell
Department of Education
Tulane University
New Orleans, Louisiana

Diane Gallagher
HMS School
Philadelphia, Pennsylvania

Kathryn C. Gerken
Department of Educational Psychology
The University of Iowa
Iowa City, Iowa

Gretchen W. Guiton
The Psychological Corporation
San Antonio, Texas

James S. Gyurke
The Psychological Corporation
San Antonio, Texas

Patti L. Harrison
Department of Educational Psychology
University of Alabama
Tuscaloosa, Alabama

Stephen R. Hooper
Clinical Center for the Study of
*   Development and Learning*
University of North Carolina
Chapel Hill, North Carolina

Harry Ireton
University of Minnesota of Minneapolis,
*   Saint Paul*
Saint Paul, Minnesota

Randy W. Kamphaus
Department of Educational Psychology
University of Georgia
Athens, Georgia

Alan S. Kaufman
Department of Educational Psychology
University of Alabama
Tuscaloosa, Alabama

Michael F. Kelley
Education and Human Services
Arizona State University
Phoenix, Arizona

Robert Lichtenstein
Psychological Services
New Haven Public Schools
New Haven, Connecticut

Carol Schneider Lidz
School Psychology Department
Temple University
Philadelphia, Pennsylvania

Roy P. Martin
Department of Educational Psychology
University of Georgia
Athens, Georgia

R. Steve McCallum
Department of Educational and Counseling
*   Psychology*
University of Tennessee
Knoxville, Tennessee

Kathleen D. Paget
Department of Psychology
University of South Carolina
Columbia, South Carolina

Chandrakant P. Shah
Department of Preventive Medicine and
*   Biostatistics*
Faculty of Medicine
Universtity of Toronto
Toronto, Ontario, Canada

Elaine Surbeck
Division of Curriculum and Instruction
Arizona State University
Tempe, Arizona

E. Paul Torrance
Georgia Studies of Creative Behavior
University of Georgia
Athens, Gerogia

Zona R. Weeks
Department of Occupational Therapy
University of Indianapolis
Indianapolis, Indiana

Harriet G. Williams
Department of Physical Education
University of South Carolina
Columbia, South Carolina

1

History of Preschool Assessment

MICHAEL F. KELLEY
ELAINE SURBECK

Throughout the course of history, humans have proposed and analyzed theories about the nature of experience, particularly intelligent activity. Usually such discussion was reserved for the philosophers and politicians of the time; but as civilizations developed and human activity and awareness expanded, the social concern for education emerged. Such concern manifested itself in Europe and America during the nineteenth century.

As indicated by Goodenough (1949), prior to the nineteenth century the assessment of human ability was given little attention. The Chinese, however, used a formal examination system for civil servants as early as 1115 B.C. (DuBois, 1966). They recognized that performance on tests under controlled conditions yielded an estimate of ability for later performance on the job. Assessment issues such as the objectivity of the measure, anonymity of the applicant and the test examiners, the need for uniform testing conditions, and the importance of rank ordered scores were considered by the Chinese (Du Bois, 1966). Many of these issues did not surface in the West until much later.

Historians have shown that life during the eighteenth and nineteenth centuries was difficult for all but a few (Aries, 1962; De Mause, 1974). Those who suffered most were young children and individuals considered mentally deficient and insane. One of the central educational issues raised during the nineteenth century was the lack of any classification scheme for determining those who might benefit from a proper education and those who were considered uneducable (Goodenough, 1949). It was precisely the need for some form of classification of human ability that impelled the great scientists of France, England, Germany, and America to formulate the early versions of our present day assessment devices.

This chapter demonstrates how the early scientists' view of the nature of human development and mental activity influenced the subsequent preschool testing movement. As new concepts of intelligent activity were proposed and challenged, concomitant changes occurred in the instruments used to assess such ability. Eventually, methodological issues such as test validity and reliability, sampling techniques, and the use of elaborate statistical analysis emerged.

NINETEENTH CENTURY INFLUENCES ON PRESCHOOL ASSESSMENT

The contributions of the great philosophers and educators who lived prior to the twentieth century were instrumental in the formulation of early theories of mental activity and various concepts of intelligence (Goodenough, 1949). However, because preschool assessment didn't formally begin until the early twentieth century, the focus on the nineteenth century contributions will be limited. (For the contributions of the early philosophers and educators see Braun & Edwards, 1972; Osborn, 1975, and Ulich, 1945, 1947). Different issues were raised in countries around the world.

In France, the study and treatment of the insane and the mentally deficient received considerable attention from Esquirol, Itard, Sequin, and Binet. Their contributions included establishing the need for a classification system to diagnose mental retardation, experimenting with sensory training for the mentally deficient, and developing practical diagnostic classification systems for admission to special schools (Goodenough, 1949; Johnson, 1894).

In England, scientists were struggling with the assessment of mental ability. Galton constructed very simple tests of memory, motor, and sensory functions to differentiate between high and low achievers. Moreover, he advocated studying individual differences between twins, and was one of the first scientists to use quantitative methods in analyzing data (Anastasi, 1982), earning him the title "the father of mental testing" (Goodenough, 1949).

Charles Darwin suggested that the early behaviors of young children might provide relevant information concerning the ontogenesis of human development. Thus, numerous studies of infant behavior were conducted (Darwin, 1877; Preyer, 1882; Shinn, 1900; Stern, 1914, 1924). These early baby biographies were important to the preschool testing movement in that they demonstrated a sequence of early behavioral development and individual differences regarding the rate of development (Goodenough, 1949). Furthermore, the baby biographies extended the course of study to an age previously neglected. This resulted in a beginning awareness of the importance of infancy and the early childhood years to later develop-

ment. Indeed some of the protocols used in early preschool assessment devices to establish developmental sequences were derived, in part, from the work of the baby biographers.

In Germany, scientists such as Wundt and Cattell were directing their attention toward sensation, perception, and individual differences. Their efforts influenced the emerging testing movement by clearly demonstrating the need for uniform experimental procedures and, more importantly, the existence of age-related individual variation in performance (Goodenough, 1949). The issue of individual differences and instability in test performance among young children proves to be a continuing problem in preschool assessment.

In the United States, educators were beginning to recognize the need for accurate identification and classification of children and adults with special needs but they were hampered by the lack of discriminating assessment instruments. Virtually all of the tests constructed until that time were of a highly sensory nature, failed to differentiate individuals of various levels of ability, and were limited primarily to school-aged children and adults (Goodenough, 1949; Stott & Ball, 1965).

The activity of the scientists during the nineteenth century raised many issues concerning the assessment of children and adults. Questions of test validity that had a direct impact on the prevalent theories of mental development were raised. (The most prevalent theory was that mental ability was fixed genetically, unalterable from a environmental perspective). Methodological issues such as the need for controlled testing conditions, useful sampling techniques, and test reliability emerged during the latter part of the nineteenth century. Finally, how to assess the nonschool-age child began to emerge as a question of study (Senn, 1975).

EARLY TWENTIETH CENTURY INFLUENCES ON PRESCHOOL ASSESSMENT

The early twentieth century witnessed dramatic developments in technology, medicine, and the behavioral sciences. The major universities in the United States opened psychological clinics with the study of child development as their primary focus (Sears, 1975).

In France and the United States, the institution of compulsory school attendance laws resulted in school admission problems. Eventually, the governments of France and the United States commissioned groups of individuals to devise tests of mental ability that would assist in differentiating school-age children and allow for proper school placement (Goodenough, 1949).

THE BINET SCALES AND THEIR INFLUENCE ON PRESCHOOL ASSESSMENT

Alfred Binet and several of his colleagues were asked by the Paris Minister of Public Instruction to construct a means for identifying children in need of special education (Goodenough, 1949). Binet, who published numerous studies related to perception and reasoning, eventually became interested in qualitative differences in functioning displayed by young children and adults (Pollack & Brenner, 1969).

The commonly held belief of the time was that intelligence or mental functioning was a genetically fixed entity manifested behaviorally through the sensory functions of the body. Most of the early influential scientists argued for such a position and constructed sensory tests based on that premise. Binet was one of the first scientists to challenge that belief (Goodenough, 1949). He argued that complex mental functioning could not be determined by a simple test of sensory functioning. He suggested judgment, reasoning, and comprehension were more adequate dimensions of intellectual ability (Binet & Simon, 1905). With the assistance of Simon, Binet developed a 30-item test that was administered to a small sample of subnormal and normal children in Paris. The main objective of the test was to determine general mental development rather than simple sensory functioning. The items were arranged in order of difficulty and were scored on a pass/fail basis. Although by today's standards the 1905 scale was quite crude, several important methodological issues were raised by Binet and Simon (1905). They argued that tests of mental ability must be simple to administer and score, must have standard procedures to follow, and should provide

results that distinguish the retarded from the normal (Pinter, 1923).

In 1908, Binet and Simon reported the results of a second test series. They introduced the concept of "mental age" and described the test standardization procedures to determine item placement. In 1911, the year Binet died, a third revision was reported. The 1911 scale was a further refinement of the previous scale with new items added and some of the original items dropped because they did not measure general intelligence.

Numerous translations of the Binet scale appeared including English translations provided by Goddard in 1908 and 1910. Moreover, Goddard and his associates at Vineland Training School established test administration seminars for teachers and advocated the importance of early diagnosis (Goodenough, 1949). Kuhlmann (1912, 1914) published two versions of the Binet scales, and it was his second version that extended the test items down to 2 months of age. This was one of the first revised editions to test children younger than 3 years of age (Goodenough, 1949).

The Binet and Simon efforts, along with the subsequent revised versions of others, contributed greatly to the subsequent early testing movement and importantly to the emerging preschool assessment movement. These individuals challenged the widely held beliefs regarding the static nature of intelligent activity. Moreover, they described standardization procedures for item placement, discussed issues concerning test administration, and were aware of the difficulties in reporting meaningful test results (Goodenough, 1949).

CHILD STUDY MOVEMENT

In the United States, the child study movement of the early 1900s gained momentum under the leadership of G. Stanley Hall at Clark University. Several influential scientists (Kuhlmann, Goddard, Terman) studied under Hall; Arnold Gesell was another influential figure who was his student (Senn, 1975).

Because the vast majority of the tests developed in the early 1900s were for school-age children, it became increasingly apparent to those individuals at Cornell University (Pauline Park and Wilson Knapp), Yale University (Arnold Gesell), the University of Minnesota (John Anderson), the University of Iowa (Bird Baldwin), Teachers College, Columbia (Lois Meek), Merrill-Palmer Institute in Detroit (Edna Noble White), and the University of California at Berkeley (Herbert Stolz and Nancy Bayley) that additional revisions were needed for the preschool years. Lawrence K. Franks, through funding provided by the Laura Spelman Rockefeller Memorial, was instrumental in establishing institutes of child welfare for the study of child development in many of these universities. Thus, the preschool assessment movement began in earnest with the study of young children as the primary thrust.

During the years between 1920 and 1940, considerable time and effort went into formulating answers to three major questions in regard to preschool assessment. First, what are the characteristics of normal young children? Second, is intelligent behavior determined by heredity or environment? Third, what can be done to improve assessment devices designed to test the ability of young children? These questions were raised not only by the scientists and academicians of the time, but also by the public.

The statistics continued to reflect high infant and maternal mortality among the poor, and the World War I recruits displayed a strikingly poor educational and physical preparedness (Senn, 1975). Moreover, the proliferation of day care, nursery, and kindergarten facilities led to the realization that little was known about the overall development of young children (Sears, 1975).

The baby biographies written in the latter part of the nineteenth century represented the first real attempt at organizing and describing child growth and development. The vast majority of the early scientists and educators directed their attention toward school-age children and the mentally deficient. Although constrained by the theoretical perspective of genetically "fixed" mental ability, several important psychologists and educators of the early 1900s recognized the social and scientific need for relevant information regarding the growth and development of normal young children. (For review, see Sears, 1975, and Senn, 1975).

In 1916 Lucy Sprague Mitchell and several of her colleagues began a series of experiments at the Bureau of Educational Experiments (presently the Bank Street College of Education) in New York. The research conducted at the Bureau consisted of studying child development and experimental schools. Techniques of recording children's behavior and analyzing and interpreting the data in terms that displayed the interdependent complexities within each child became a primary focus. These efforts were in direct contrast to the work of John B. Watson and colleagues who chose to ignore the issue of context effects for the science of objective observation and measurement (Senn, 1975).

In addition to the work of Mitchell and her colleagues, the behavioristic work of both Thorndike (1921) and Watson (Watson & Watson, 1928) legitimized the study of children by demonstrating that the right stimuli and environment improved children's ability to learn. However, data regarding the typical pattern and sequence of normal behavior of young children were still unavailable. Although testing of school-age children was well established by 1910 (Goodenough, 1949), the preschool child received little attention until Burt (1921), Yerkes and Foster (1923), and Kuhlmann (1914) published versions of intelligence tests that extended downward into the preschool years. Unfortunately, these early tests were considered methodologically lacking in that standardization procedures were poor and reliability and validity data usually were not reported (Stott & Ball, 1965).

GESELL AND THE MATURATIONAL PERSPECTIVE

Perhaps the earliest significant interest in understanding the development of prechool-age children was shown at the Yale Clinic for Child Development. Exceptional children were observed in the Yale Clinic as early as 1911, but by 1916 Gesell had undertaken a project to explore developmental change and growth of normal children under 5 years of age. Operating under the belief that growth and development were biologically predetermined, Gesell (1925) and his colleagues argued for a maturational perspective that incorporated time-bound qualitative change in development. This theoretical viewpoint had support among scientists disenchanted with the views and experiments of Watson, and significantly influenced the child study movement and later de-bates about the impact of environment on intelligent activity (Senn, 1975).

Gesell (1925), a pediatrician by training, began his study with 50 "representative" children; they were examined at each of 10 age levels—birth, 4, 6, 9, 12, 18, 24, 36, 48, and 60 months. A psychological examination and an observational survey of the child's behavior at home were made at each level. Although little attention was paid to precise methodology, the initial results were presented as a "developmental schedule" and contained approximately 150 items in 4 areas: motor development, language development, adaptive behavior, and personal–social behavior. Gesell's work continued for more than 40 years. Several of the subsequently developed tests for infants and preschoolers used information derived from the Gesell profiles (Stott & Ball, 1965). Innovative techniques for observing children, such as the use of the one-way observation booth, were developed by Gesell.

While Gesell and his colleagues were gathering normative data on young children at the Yale Clinic, several other assessment instruments were being developed for use with infants and preschoolers. The most notable among these were the Merrill-Palmer Scale of Mental Tests (Stutsman, 1931), the Minnesota Preschool Scale (Goodenough, 1926), the California First Year Mental Scale (Bayley, 1933), and the Iowa Test for Young Children (Fillmore, 1936). (See Stott & Ball, 1965, and Brooks & Weinraub, 1976, for reviews.)

Although the reliability and validity data for these early scales would be considered questionable by contemporary standards, the formulation of these tests and their subsequent publication generated considerable research activity on their use as adequate measures (Goodenough, 1949); of central concern was test reliability, predictive validity, and stability of test scores. Moreover, individuals such as Kurt Lewin were proposing naturalistic observational approaches as scientific tools of investigation that would parallel laboratory approaches (Senn, 1975).

Although most of these early test developers did not focus on intelligence per se, they were concerned with the mental and physical growth of normal children. Influenced by the theory of maturation of Hall and Gesell, the underlying assumption made by the majority of the test developers and child developmentalists of this period

was that mental ability or intelligence was stable and unmodifiable (Stott & Ball, 1965). These assumptions of predetermined development and genetically fixed intelligence established the climate for perhaps one of the best known controversies in developmental psychology. This controversy was the prelude to major shifts in thinking about the nature of intelligent activity and concomitant preschool test construction.

WELLMAN-GOODENOUGH CONTROVERSY

With the formation of university child development laboratories in the United States, researchers were afforded sizable numbers of preschoolers on which to conduct studies of growth and development. Wellman and her colleagues at the Iowa Child Welfare Research Station administered intelligence tests to the preschool children enrolled in their program. Over a period of several years Wellman (1932b) observed an increase in the IQ's of the children and attributed these increases to the stimulating environment in the program. In 1932, Wellman (1932a) published the first of several articles (1932b, 1934, 1940) that challenged the fixed intelligence assumption so prevalent at the time. Several other investigators subsequently conducted longitudinal studies with young children and reported findings that suggested that environment could either increase or decrease IQ's (Crissey, 1937; Skeels, 1938; Skodak, 1939). The results of these studies were fiercely attacked by proponents of the fixed intelligence view (Stott & Ball, 1965).

Primary among those who vehemently disagreed with the view of modifiable intelligence were Simpson (1939) and Goodenough. Although Goodenough had earlier (1928) found IQ increases in a study of nursery school children, she dismissed the findings by concluding that the test (1922 Kuhlmann-Binet) was poorly standardized and that any changes in IQ could not be attributed to actual increases in intelligence. In a similar manner, Goodenough (1940) also dismissed the Wellman studies as poorly controlled and methodologically unsound. Finally, Goodenough and Maurer (1940) published another research report that compared IQ changes among nursery school children and nonnursery school children. The result displayed an average IQ gain of 4.6 points for both groups. Thus, as far as Goodenough was concerned, the notion that environment influenced mental development was not tenable. Lewis Termin had reached similar conclusions in his own research (Senn, 1975).

Controversy ensued throughout psychological circles. New studies were designed and conducted with environmentally deprived children (Bradway, 1945; McHugh, 1943). Eventually evidence that supported the conclusion that environment was, indeed, a factor in mental development began to accumulate. The evidence suggested a need for a reevaluation of the structure of intelligence (Stott & Ball, 1965), and the manner in which intelligent activity was assessed.

NEW DEVELOPMENTS AND REVISIONS

While the heredity–environment controversy was raging, Terman and Merrill published the 1937 revised edition of the 1916 Stanford-Binet. Additional items for the preschool child coupled with more elaborate and carefully designed standardization procedures, were introduced. The test incorporated more nonverbal items, had additional memory tests, reported high-reliability coefficients, and could be administered in either of two forms. The 1937 revision was criticized on several grounds (Flanagan, 1938; Krugman, 1939). It took longer to administer than previous editions, it still reflected mostly verbal ability, the standard error of measurement could not be determined, and the notion of one global IQ score did not accommodate the emerging conceptualization of multifactored approaches to intelligence.

Individuals (Hotelling 1933; Kelley 1935; Thurstone 1935) conducted factor analytic studies on the most widely used tests of the day and reported a number of recognizable group factors related to intelligence. These factors included verbal ability, numerical ability, mechanical ability, and attention. Thurstone (1938) reported six primary mental abilities: verbal-comprehension, word-fluency, space, memory, number, and induction. Thus, it became apparent that the global structure of intelligence was in need of reconceptualization.

The 1930s and 1940s represented a major turning point in the testing movement. The inherent limitations of the Stanford-Binet concept of global intelligence and the findings of primary mental abilities led Wechsler (1949) to develop the Wechsler Intelligence Scale for Children (WISC), which incorporated subtests to measure the various aspects of intelligence. Furthermore, the economic depression and World War II created the need for child care facilities (Osborn, 1975). Longitudinal research program investigations of the effects of environment on intelligence were conducted. Finally, the older intelligence scales underwent revision. Throughout the 1940s and into the 1950s the emphasis shifted from intelligence testing to the study of personality, social, and motoric factors related to general functioning.

THE YEARS 1940–1960

Although the previous 20 years had seen increased test construction for preschool-age children and infants, in the years 1940–1960 there was concern over the lack of predictive validity of the existing instruments (Stott & Ball, 1965). Numerous studies reported little correlation between infant and preschool assessment ratings with those gathered at later school-age years (DeForest, 1941; Escalona, 1950; Gallagher, 1953; Goodenough & Maurer, 1942; Mowrer, 1934). These results raised doubts about the generally accepted view of mental development as being genetically endowed and quantitative in nature (Stott & Ball, 1965). However, these doubts did not stop the designers of tests from continuing their test construction efforts.

NEW TEST DEVELOPMENTS

During the 1940s several tests were published for infant and preschool assessment. These included the Cattell Infant Intelligence Scale (Cattell, 1940), the Northwest Infant Intelligence Scale (Gilliland, 1948), the Leiter International Performance Scale (Leiter, 1948), and the Full Range Picture Vocabulary Test (Ammons & Ammons, 1948). (See Stott & Ball, 1965, for a description of each.) The Cattell scale and the Northwest test were devised to assess infant abilities while the Leiter scale and the Full Range Picture Vocabulary Test were concerned with the abilities of preschoolers 2 years of age and older.

The Leiter (1948) scale was devised as a nonlanguage mental test to be as culture fair as possible. This represented a significant advance in test construction because the Leiter scale proved to be more culture free than the widely accepted Stanford-Binet (Stott & Ball, 1965). However, this finding did not change public opinion; the Stanford-Binet continued to be the most widely used test of mental ability (Goodenough, 1949).

The Full Range Picture Vocabulary Test was novel in that it was a test with high reliability and validity. In addition, care was taken to standardize the test on a sample of preschoolers considered representative of the general population (Ammons & Holmes, 1949). One serious drawback in the standardization procedure, however, was the fact that the entire group of 120 "representative" children was Caucasian.

In 1949, Wechsler published the WISC. The WISC contained 12 subtests applicable to children between 5 and 15 years of age. The subtests included Arithmetic, Vocabulary, Similarities, Picture Completion, Block Design, Object Assembly, to name a few. Although the WISC was intended for use with children, its application for preschool-age children raised questions. Most of the criticism of the WISC was concerned with its level of difficulty for young children (Stott & Ball, 1965). In spite of this criticism, the WISC was listed as one of the five most frequently used tests to measure mental functioning in preschoolers (Stott & Ball, 1965). This downward extension of tests designed for school-aged children into the preschool years was a common practice.

During the 1950s two more tests were published; one for infants and the other for young children about to enter the first grade. The Griffiths Mental Development Scale (Griffiths, 1954) was designed to measure infant mental ability. Constructed under the premise that intelligence is general ability, Griffiths' test consisted of 260 items in 5 subscales. Although the test-retest reliability coefficient reported was .92 based on 52 cases, no predictive validity coefficients were reported (Stott & Ball, 1965).

The Brenner Gestalt Test (Brenner, 1959) was designed as a screening device to evaluate children's "readiness" for first grade. The tasks included copying dots, drawing a man, recognizing numbers, and copying sentences. The test correlated .81 with teacher ratings of children's functioning and was easy to administer.

Although the tests just mentioned were developed with far greater precision than their earlier counterparts, they still proved inadequate in predicting later mental development. Although factors such as test resistance (Rust, 1931) and individual temperament (Stutsman, 1931) were considered partly responsible for the lack of predictive validity, the idea that intelligence is qualitative in nature was gaining acceptance in the literature.

THEORETICAL REVISIONS REGARDING THE NATURE OF DEVELOPMENT

In the late 1940s and early 1950s Escalona (1950), Garrett (1946), and Piaget (1952), among others, proposed that mental development was qualitative in nature. Piaget (1952), in his classic work on the origin of intelligence in young children, postulated a fixed sequence of "structures" that were qualitatively different in composition yet functionally related in that each developed out of the earlier structure. Central to Piaget's theory was the importance of experience. To Piaget, mental development was dependent on the organism's active construction of the invariant aspects of the environment. Thus, the quality of the environment and the nature of the organism's activity were of vital importance. With the publication of *Intelligence and Experience* by J. McVicker Hunt (1961), and the pioneering replication research of Piaget's concepts by David Elkind (Senn, 1975), American psychologists were confronted with a new conceptualization of human experience and intelligent activity.

This alternative view of development coupled with multiple-factor analytical models of intelligence (Guilford, 1956, 1957, 1959) significantly altered the nature of test construction. No longer could intelligence be considered a general unitary ability. Instead, primary mental abilities were seen as constituting a part of intelligence (Stott & Ball, 1965). In addition, it was becoming increasingly apparent that an individual's level of functioning was not dependent solely on mental activity. With the popularization of Freudian theory, psychologists and educators began considering personal and social variables as important components of overall functioning.

The ideas proposed by Piaget (1952) and others (e.g., Escalona, 1950; Hunt, 1961) concerning the qualitative nature of development directly affected subsequent research and educational thought. Research studies demonstrated that the quality of the environment was an important factor in development (Bayley, 1954; 1955; Bradway et al., 1958; Dennis & Najarian, 1957). Educators began calling for social intervention and early education for the poor and for the children of working mothers (Frank, 1938; Hunt, 1964; Hymes, 1944). These ideas were, no doubt, a result of the successes of the war nurseries and child care centers established by the 1940 Lanham Act (Braun & Edwards, 1972). With the successful launching of the Russian spacecraft Sputnik in 1957, the federal government began providing additional education funds for science and math programs (Osborn, 1975). All of these factors contributed to the development of the compensatory early childhood education programs of the 1960s and 1970s. Unfortunately, the previously designed infant and preschool assessment instruments were considered too subjective, culturally outdated, of poor validity, and inadequate in characterizing a child's level of functioning (Stott & Ball, 1965). Hence, new assessment devices that would reflect current theoretical concepts of the qualitative nature of development, contain a child-oriented approach, and provide sufficient diagnostic applications were needed. The period of major developments in preschool assessment was underway.

THE YEARS 1960–1980

Until the 1960s the primary focus of the testing movement was the testing of school-age children and military inductees (Parker, 1981). Beginning in the early 1960s, remarkable growth occurred in the testing of preschool children. This was primarily because of the significant role the federal government began to play in education. The most influential events were the funding of the 1964 Maternal, Child Health and Mental Retardation Act, the 1964 Educational Opportunity Act, and the

1965 Elementary and Secondary Education Act (Osborn, 1975). These programs provided improved educational and social opportunities for the children of poor families.

Although the period of social and educational concern of the late 1950s and early 1960s generated a few privately funded intervention programs, Head Start and Follow Through programs were the most widely recognized educational experiments. These programs directed attention to the need for effective program evaluation and adequate preschool assessment instruments.

HEAD START AND TEST DEVELOPMENT

Program orientation and goals in the Head Start models usually reflected one of three philosophies: an emphasis on maturational principles that stressed a nurturant social–emotional environment; a behavioristic approach that emphasized highly structured didactic methods; or a cognitive–interactionist approach that focused on the child's construction of knowledge.

The original Head Start model programs varied in theoretical and instructional orientation, however, they were all required to establish the effectiveness of their program. Primarily through the efforts of Senator Robert Kennedy, a provision was made that federally funded programs have a performance-based evaluation design (Hoepfner et al., 1971). The continuation of funding was dependent on gains in intelligence scores, academic achievement, or some other measurable dimension. Because most of the measures discussed earlier were imprecise or inappropriate for young children (Stott & Ball, 1965) and often did not reflect program goals, many new measures were developed between 1965 and 1975. Some of the more notable included the McCarthy Scales of Children's Abilities (MSCA) (McCarthy, 1972), the Wechsler Preschool and Primary Scale of Intelligence (WPPSI) (Wechsler, 1967), and the Caldwell Preschool Inventory (CPI). The CPI formed the basis for curriculum objectives and was a forerunner of the criterion-referenced movement (Hoepfner et al., 1971).

With program evaluation as a central concern of early childhood education programs in the

1960s and 1970s, the majority of preschool assessment instruments were developed to measure the various goals of the programs. Thus, tests were devised to measure outcomes in the affective domain, the intellectual domain, the psychomotor domain, and the subject-achievement domain (Hoepfner et al., 1971). These developments represented a significant shift because overall functioning was seen as a composite of numerous skills, abilities, and aptitudes.

In reviewing several listings of contemporary preschool assessment instruments, one can see the impact of the Head Start movement on preschool test construction (Dykes et al., 1979, Frost & Minisi, 1975; Hoepfner et al., 1971). More than 200 assessment instruments were constructed and published during the years 1960–1980. In 1971, the Center for the Study of Evaluation, and the Early Childhood Research Center of the UCLA Graduate School of Education published a comprehensive evaluation guide of more than 120 preschool and kindergarten tests (Hoepfner et al., 1971). Their primary objective was to provide teachers, supervisors, and early childhood specialists with relevant information as to the validity, examinee appropriateness, administrative utility, and normed technical excellence of each test. Of 120 tests comprised of 630 subtests, only 7 subtests were rated as providing *good* validity. The ratings for examinee appropriateness and administrative utility were generally higher for most of the tests; however, the general ratings for normed technical excellence were either *poor* or *fair*.

Although additional preschool test construction has continued (Barnes, 1982; Dykes et al., 1979), there are still the age old measurement problems of inadequate test validity (content, construct, predictive) and inadequate standardization procedures. Such findings, coupled with recent views on the myth of measurement and the social implications of testing (Bersoff, 1973; Houts, 1977; Meisels, 1987; White, 1977) have raised concern about using test performance as the sole criterion for educational decision making. Indeed, recent concerns have been raised about the use of invalid and unreliable screening and readiness tests for early childhood education placement (Meisels, 1987; Shepard & Smith, 1986). These issues will be addressed later in this chapter.

IMPACT OF ADDITIONAL FEDERAL SUPPORT AND SPECIAL EDUCATION

With the appropriation of federal funds for Head Start, Follow Through, and the Education Acts, university undergraduate and graduate teacher training programs began to proliferate. In addition, the government saw the need for expanding personnel training grants to the field of special education. Prior to 1960, few universities were adequately staffed with professors for training special education personnel (Meyen, 1978). By 1975, 61 federal laws related to the handicapped had been passed (Weintraub et al., 1976), with Public Law (P.L.) 94-142 serving as the cornerstone.

P.L. 94-142 mandated a free and appropriate public education for handicapped children in the least restrictive environment possible. Included within the provisions were parental input and the requirement that an Individual Education Program (IEP) be developed and maintained for each handicapped child. Integral to the development of the IEP is the evaluation and diagnosis of each child's level of functioning. The assessment devices for special education range from informal behavioral checklists to standardized tests (Rotatori et al., 1990). In addition, the special education personnel rely on anecdotal information provided by parents and former teachers and observation of the child's behavior in the classroom. Once an adequate diagnosis of functional level has been ascertained, the instructional program is developed based on clearly stated educational objectives.

The mandate for IEPs holds for all exceptional children at various levels of functioning. These include the mentally retarded, hard of hearing, deaf, speech impaired, visually imparied, severely emotionally disturbed, and the gifted and talented. Moreover, with the passage of the 1986 Education of the Handicapped Amendments (P.L. 99-457), all handicapped preschoolers must be served educationally by 1991 or states risk losing portions of their federal funding. Furthermore, the identified handicapped preschoolers must be placed in the least restrictive environment possible, preferably with nonhandicapped peers (Weiner & Koppelman, 1987). This has led the vast majority of states to consider the creation of interagency agreements between Head Start centers and the public schools to serve handicapped preschool children.

Unfortunately, some states refuse to allow Head Start centers and local day care centers to contract with the state to provide handicapped preschoolers with special education services. They argue that Head Start and day care centers don't meet regular educational requirements (Weiner & Koppelman, 1987). Another problem centers around the public schools' definition of handicapped. By holding to stringent definitions of handicapping conditions and requiring significant assessment data, public schools are able to exclude some mildly to moderately handicapped preschool children from being served.

The burden falls on Head Start programs. Of central concern is the need for assessment tools capable of providing diagnostic and evaluative information for each of the handicapping conditions across all areas of functioning.

The federal government's involvement in establishing educational program guidelines for special education and providing substantial dollars for those programs has contributed significantly to the development of assessment devices for the early childhood years. Moreover, this involvement has helped to shape some very important legal parameters related to educational programs, testing, and to parents' rights to participate in the development of special educational programs.

The 1975 passage of P.L. 94-142 specifically established that a free, appropriate public education must be made available to all handicapped children between the ages of 3 and 21 years. This educational opportunity legislation mandated formal due process procedures for schools to follow. These included notice to parents and the children of educational programming changes, the right of the parents and the child to outside legal representation, the right to refuse placement without a full and individual evaluation of the child's educational status and needs, and the right to seek outside testing if desired (Prasse, 1983).

With regard to testing specifically, legislation (P.L. 94-142, Section 504 of the Rehabilitation Act of 1973), and court cases (Hobson vs. Hansen, 1967; Diana vs. State Board of Education, 1970; Guadalupe Organization, Inc. vs. Tempe School District No. 3, 1971; Covarrubias vs. San Diego Unified School District, 1971; Larry P. vs. Riles, 1979; PASE vs. Hannon, 1980) have mandated

some specific special educational assessment requirements. These include:

- Tests and accompanying materials/procedures must be void of racial and/or cultural bias
- Tests and accompanying materials/procedures must be valid and administered by trained personnel
- Tests and accompanying materials/procedures must be capable of assessing eductional need
- Appropriate educational programming for a child must not rely on a single assessment procedure as the sole criterion
- A multidisciplinary team or group of persons, including a teacher with specialized knowledge, must be a part of the evaluation
- The child must be assessed in all areas related to the suspected disability

Although these requirements relate to special education, the specific assessment requirements hold utility for preschool assessment. Moreover, they are in congruence with the American Psychological Association's (1985) standards for educational testing.

PUBLIC SCHOOL PRESCHOOL PROGRAMS AND THE DEVELOPMENTAL ASSESSMENT DEBATE

Considerable debate has been focused on the implementation of preschool programs within public schools (Strother, 1987). A number of national politicians and state legislatures are calling for increased investment in preschool education, while public commitment to early childhood education programs has grown considerably. Some of the major policy issues that must be struggled with include the matter of funding, where the programs should be located, and which children should be served, and by whom (Schweinhart, Koshel, & Bridgeman, 1987).

The issue of which children should be served has raised numerous concerns. It has been argued that preschool programs are most beneficial for economically disadvantaged children and those "at risk of school failure" (Schweinhart, Koshel, & Bridgeman, 1987). How one determines the "at risk of school failure'' child is currently at the center of a major debate in early childhood circles.

In a recent publication, *Uses and Abuses of Developmental Screening and School Readiness Testing,* Samuel Meisels (1987) has raised several important issues pertinent to preschool assessment. Specifically, Meisels argues that far too many children are being assessed with screening and readiness tests that have little or no validity and reliability data to support their use. As a result children are being labeled as developmentally immature or not ready for school placement. Meisels argues, ''Tests that exclude children from public education services or that delay their access to the educational mainstream . . . are antithetical to legal and constitutional rights to free education and equal protection. In addition, such tests and practices are incompatible with the belief systems, theoretical perspectives, and best practices of most early childhood educators (Meisels, 1987, p. 71).

Specifically, Meisels has challenged the use of the Gesell School Readiness Screening Test (Ilg & Ames, 1972), also known as the Gesell Preschool Test (Haines, Ames, & Gillespie, 1980). Although thousands of public and private schools have subscribed to the use of these tests, the Gesell tests have failed to display adequate psychometric properties of validity and reliability. Furthermore, the developers of the tests use a concept of developmental age that has never been tested empirically (Meisels, 1987).

The tests are derived from a theoretical perspective (maturational) that focuses on time as the most important variable in behavior change. Hence, from a Gesellian perspective young immature children need only time to develop. This leads to the claim that, ''perhaps 50% of school failures could be prevented or cured by proper placement based on a child's behavior age'' (Ames, Gillespie, Haines, & Ilg, 1979, p. 182). The Gesell Institute cites a study by Wood, Powell, and Knight (1984) to support its claim that the readiness assessments are predictive of school success. However, according to Meisels (1987) and Shepard and Smith (1986), for every child identified by the assessment as potentially ''at risk of school failure,'' a successful child was falsely identified.

In recent reviews of the Gesell Preschool and School Readiness Tests, Kaufman (1985), Naglieri (1985), and Bradley (1985) all have questioned the use of the tests. The concern is predominately related to the lack of sound psychometric properties and the potential of misuse and misinterpretation that could lead to serious placement problems. Unfortunately, as mentioned earlier, thousands of public and private school settings are using the Gesell tests with little or no apparent concern for the issues raised by Meisels (1987) and others.

A recent publication focusing on school readiness and kindergarten retention (Shepard & Smith, 1986), addresses the issue of assessing readiness. The authors state, ''Scientific knowledge underlying readiness assessment is such that none of the existing tests is sufficiently accurate to justify removing children from their normal peer group and placing them in special two-year programs. In part the lack of high correlations with later school success is caused by the instability of the very traits we are seeking to measure'' (Shepard & Smith, 1986, p. 83). Thus, extra-year schooling has not shown the achievement-related benefits that many thought would result. Any achievement differences that are shown tend to level off by the third grade (Shepard & Smith, 1986).

The Shepard and Smith (1986) findings are congruent with a study conducted by Kelley and Surbeck (1987). In this study, a small public school district was interested in examining the effects of a developmental kindergarten and first grade program. Specifically, the Early Prevention of School Failure Program (EPSF) was utilized to see if children who participated in an extra year of schooling benefited academically. Retention patterns also were examined. It should be noted that children are placed in the developmental kindergarten and/or first grade based on performance on a variety of tests (the Preschool Language Scale, Visual-Motor Index, Peabody Picture Vocabulary Tests, House-Tree-Person Test, Motor Activity Scale, Oral Language Test, Bilingual Syntax Measure) and input from parents, nurses, speech and language therapists, and classroom teachers. The placement cut-scores were established by the EPSF program staff in Peotine, Illinois (we were unable to obtain any data from the EPSF program staff explaining the placement cut-score process. Thus, we have no way of knowing the accuracy or dependability of the placement decisions).

Forty-two children enrolled in developmental kindergarten (DK) programs were compared to a random sample of 68 children enrolled in regular kindergarten (RK) programs. An examination of Visual Motor Index and Peabody Picture Vocabulary Test pre- and posttest scores and one year later Iowa Test of Basic Skills national percentile ranks showed that the extra year of schooling did not benefit the developmental kindergarten children. These results were in sharp contrast to the beliefs held by teachers and parents of both groups who responded to a survey. Indeed, 90% of the teachers (N = 11) and 76% of the parents (N = 100) believed that the EPSF program had helped the young children improve their academic performance.

To examine the retention question, 50 children at three grade levels (1, 2, and 3) placed initially in DK were compared to 237 children at the same 3 grade levels who were initially placed in RK. Retention rate and days absent were examined for differences. Using *t*-tests and chi-square statistics, the results displayed no significant differences for retention patterns or days absent. From grade 1 to 3 for the DK group, there was a steady decline in the percentage of children retained. The decline for the RK group was not as consistent over the same time frame. In second grade the percentage of retained RK children went up whereas the percentage for DK children continued to decline.

An examination of parent and teacher responses displayed a favorable picture for the EPSF program. Eighty percent of the teachers and 60% of the parents believed that the children were carefully and accurately identified when placed in developmental kindergarten. In addition, 60% of the teachers and 74% of the parents believed that the EPSF program improved parents' understanding of their child's educational strengths and weaknesses. Hence, although there might be few apparent academic effects on developmentally placed young children, the social and attitudinal influences as perceived by parents and teachers were quite evident in this study. From a policy perspective, the decision for maintaining developmental programs for this district should be based on the satisfaction of the parents and teachers and not on the academic performance of the children.

As discussed earlier, public school preschool programs for both handicapped and nonhandicapped young children are an emerging reality. Indeed, 28 states and the District of Columbia support early childhood education either through state funded prekindergarten programs, parent education programs, or expansion of Head Start programs (Strother, 1987). By 1991, all of the states must meet the educational needs of all handicapped 3 to 5 year old children. Thus, the need for adequate preschool assessment instrumentation devices is apparent because identification of disability will become the primary assessment task.

FUTURE ISSUES IN PRESCHOOL ASSESSMENT

The 1980s have emerged as the decade of the preschool child. New, long-term follow-up research on the effects of the High/Scope Perry Preschool Project has shown significant benefits of high quality early childhood programs for poor children (Berrueta-Clement et al., 1984). Moreover, new theoretical developments concerning the nature of intelligent behavior have emerged. Sternberg (1979) has attempted to compile the information processing components that constitute intelligent behavior. The goal is to identify explicitly the mechanisms involved in simple and complex problem solving. Gardner (1983) has proposed a multiple intelligences perspective that includes linguistic, musical, spatial, logical-mathematical, bodily-kinesthetic, and intra- and interpersonal forms. He argues that each of these forms of intelligence is relatively autonomous and independent of one another. These efforts might assist in furthering the development of appropriate preschool assessment devices.

In terms of test construction, Kaufman and Kaufman (1983) have developed the Kaufman Assessment Battery for Children (K-ABC). The K-ABC is designed to measure mental processing and achievement of children ages $2\frac{1}{2}$ to $12\frac{1}{2}$.

The Stanford Binet Intelligence Scale has been revised to produce a Fourth Edition (Thorndike, Hagen, & Sattler, 1986). This edition is designed to assess the intelligence of children, adolescents, and adults in an age range of 2 years through 24 years.

Additional preschool instruments include the Battelle Developmental Inventory (Newborg et al., 1984), the Bracken Basic Concept Scale (Bracken, 1984), the Early Screening Inventory (Meisels & Wiske, 1983), and the Peabody Picture Vocabulary Test Revised (Dunn & Dunn, 1981) to name a few.

Each of these tests serve appropriate functions yet also are fraught with limitations. Recently, Bracken (1987) examined many of the commonly used preschool instruments for their technical adequacy. In his study, Bracken examined the subtest internal consistencies, total test internal consistencies, test-retest reliabilities, subtest floors, item gradients, total test floor, and various forms of validity for each of the preschool instruments. By using these criteria, Bracken displayed the psychometric strengths and weaknesses of the various tests. He concluded ". . . preschool assessment below the age of 4 years seems to present the greatest psychometric problems. Selection of tests for use with low-functioning children below age 4 needs to be made with special care. As can be seen, many of these tests designed for preschool use are severely limited in floor, item gradient, and reliability, especially at the lower level." (Bracken, 1987, p. 325). The technical issues raised by Bracken (1987) along with continued theoretical developments regarding the nature of intelligent functioning will prove to be crucial in the future development of preschool assessment devices.

SUMMARY

Many of the issues (technical and theoretical) discussed here often were not considered in the early developmental years of preschool assessment. Although the primary concern in assessment initially was the identification of the mentally deficient, the tests were of a highly sensory nature, focused predominately on the school-age child, and proved incapable of discriminating various levels of functioning. With the development of the Binet scales and the subsequent construction of related instruments, interest began to shift to the younger child; the issues of simple test va-

lidity, reliability, standardization procedures, and the assessment of higher mental abilities were also of concern. Yet, many of the early tests and those that followed were constrained by a view that intelligence was static. This view of genetically fixed intelligence and performance was predominant until well into the 1950s; resultant test construction reflected this view. Eventually new theories were proposed that posited a qualitative dimension to intelligent activity. Hence, there was a decade of compensatory programs and educational intervention.

With millions of dollars in federal support, hundreds of new assessment instruments were constructed to measure the "whole child." Tests were developed to measure achievement, personality, cognitive functioning, adaptive behavior, and specific skills in a variety of areas including music and the arts. However, the majority of these assessment instruments continued to reflect questionable psychometric properties of validity and reliability as well as inadequate standardization procedures.

Today, with advances in cognitive psychology and psycholinguistic theories, coupled with research on the functioning of the brain, the need for additional preschool assessment instruments is apparent. Because the educational programs of the 1960s and the 1970s were mandated to operate under new social and educational conditions, it appears that diversity and variation in educational practice will necessitate changes in assessment techniques. Whereas in the past, large segments of the population under 5 years of age were typically ignored, current federal and state initiatives now require that the needs of children birth to 5 years must be addressed. Although the psychometric concerns for validity, reliability, standardization, and utility will continue to be important, it appears that the primary thrust will be how well the assessment instruments and processes assist in planning and evaluating educational programs for individuals. Because of the influential role that preschool assessment can play in the life of a young child, caution must be used in the weight that any one assessment device holds for program placement and planning. Concurrently, new approaches to psychoeducational assessment of preschool children must reflect the dynamic nature of the young child while respecting the inherent discontinuities in development that prove so difficult to measure.

REFERENCES

American Psychological Association. (1985). *Standards for educational and psychological testing*. Washington, D.C.: American Psychological Association.

Ames, L. B., Gillespie, C., Haines, J., & Ilg. F. (1979). *The Gesell Institute's child from one to six*. New York: Harper & Row.

Ammons, R. B., & Ammons, H. S. (1948). *The Full Range Vocabulary Test*. New Orleans; Authors.

Ammons, R. B., & Holmes, J. C. (1949). The Full-Range Picture Vocabulary Tests: III, Results for a preschool age population. *Child Development, 20*, 5–14.

Anastasi, A. (1982). *Psychological testing* (5th ed.). New York: Macmillan.

Aries, P. (1962). *Centuries of childhood*. New York: Knopf.

Barnes, K. E. (1982). *Preschool screening: The measurement and prediction of children at-risk*. Springfield, IL: Thomas.

Bayley, N. (1933). *The California First Year Mental Scale*. Berkley, Calif.: University of California Press.

Bayley, N. (1954). Some increasing parent-child similarities during the growth of children. *Journal of Educational Psychology, 45*, 1–21.

Bayley, N. (1955). On the growth of intelligence. *American Psychologist, 10*, 805–818.

Berrueta-Clement, J. R., Schweinhart, L. J., Barnett, W. S., Epstein A. S., & Weikart, D. P. (1984). *Changed lives: The effects of the Perry Preschool Program on youths through age 19*. Ypsilanti, Mich.: High/Scope Press.

Bersoff, D. N. (1973). Silk purses into sow's ears: The decline of psychological testing and a suggestion for its redemption. *American Psychologist, 28*, 892–899.

Binet, A., & Simon, T. (1905). Methodes nouvelles pour le diagnostic du niveau intellectuel des anormaux. *L'Annee Psychologique, 11*, 191–244.

Bracken, B. A. (1984). *Bracken Basic Concept Scale*. San Antonio, TX: The Psychological Corporation.

Bracken, B. A. (1987). Limitations of preschool instruments and standards for minimal levels of technical adequacy. *Journal of Psychoeducational Assessment, 5*, 313–326.

Bradley, R. H. (1985). Review of Gesell School Readiness Tests. In J. Mitchell, Jr. (Ed.), *The ninth mental measurements yearbook* (Vol. I). Lincoln, NE: The University of Nebraska Press.

Bradway, K. P. (1945). An experimental study of the factors associated with Stanford-Binet IQ changes from the preschool to the junior high school. *Journal of Genetic Psychology, 66*, 107.

Bradway, K., Thompson, C. W., & Cravens, R. B. (1958). Preschool IQ's after twenty-five years. *Journal of Educational Psychology, 49*, 278–281.

Braun, S., & Edwards, E. (1972). *History and theory of early childhood education*. Worthington, Ohio: Jones.

Brenner, A. (1959). A new gestalt test for measuring readiness for school. *Merrill-Palmer Quarterly, 6*, 1–25.

Brooks, J., & Weinraub, M. (1976). A history of infant intelligence testing. In M. Lewis (Ed.), *Origins of intelligence*. New York: Plenum Press.

Burt, C. (1921). *Mental and scholastic tests*. London: King.

Cattell, P. (1940). *The measurement of intelligence of infants and young children*. New York: Psychological Corporation.

Covarrubias vs. San Diego Unified School District. Civ. No. 70-394-S. (S.D. Cal., filed Feb. 1971).

Crissey, O. L. (1937). Mental development as related to institutional residence and educational achievement. *University of Iowa Studies in Child Welfare, 13*, 1.

Darwin, C. (1877). A biographical sketch of an infant. *Mind, 2*, 285–294.

DeForest, B. (1941). A study of the prognostic value of the Merrill-Palmer Scale of Mental Tests and the Minnesota Preschool Scale. *Journal of Genetic Psychology, 59*, 219–223.

De Mause, L. (1974). *The history of childhood*. New York: Psychohistory Press.

Dennis, W., & Najarian, P. (1957). Infant development under environmental handicap. *Psychological Monographs, 71* (7, Whole No. 436).

Diana vs. State Board of Education. C.A.N. C-70-37 R.F.P. (N.D. Cal., filed Feb. 3, 1970).

DuBois, P. (1966). A test dominated society: China, 1115 B.C.-1905 A.D. In A. Anastasi (Ed.), *Testing problems in perspective: Twenty-fifth anniversary volume of topical readings from the invitational conference on testing problems*. Washington, D.C.: American Council on Education, p. 29.

Dunn, L. M. & Dunn, L. M. (1981). *Peabody Picture Vocabulary Test-Revised*. Circle Pines, MN: American Guidance Service.

Dykes, J. K., Strickland, A. M., & Munyer, D. D. (1979). *Assessment and evaluation instruments for early childhood programs*. Gainsville, Fla.: Florida Educational Research and Development Council (Eric Document No. ED 171 378).

Escalona, S. K. (1950). The use of infant tests for predictive purposes. *Bulletin of the Meninger Clinic, 14*, 117–128.

Fillmore, E. A. (1936). Iowa Tests for Young Children. *University of Iowa Studies in Child Welfare, 22,* 4.

Flanagan, J. S. (1938). Review of *Measuring Intelligence* by Termin and Merrill. *Harvard Educational Review, 8,* 130–133.

Frank, L. (1938). The fundamental needs of the child. *Mental Hygiene, 22,* 353–379.

Frost, J., & Minisi, R. (1975). *Early childhood assessment list.* Highstown, N.J.: Northeast Area Learning Resource Center (ERIC Document No. ED 136 474).

Gallagher, J. J. (1953). Clinical judgment and the Cattell Intelligence Scale. *Journal of Consulting Psychology, 17,* 303–305.

Gardner, H. (1983). *Frames of mind: The theory of multiple intelligences.* New York: Basic Books.

Garrett, H. E. (1946). A developmental theory of intelligence. *American Psychologist, 1,* 372–378.

Gesell, A. (1925). *The mental growth of the preschool child: A psychological outline of normal development from birth to the sixth year.* New York: Macmillan.

Gilliland, A. R. (1948). The measurement of the mentality of infants. *Child Development, 19,* 155–158.

Goodenough, F. L. (1926). *Measurement of intelligence by drawings.* Chicago: World Book.

Goodenough, F. L. (1928). A preliminary report on the effects of nursery school training upon intelligence test scores of young children. *27th Yearbook of the National Society for the Study of Education,* pp. 361–369.

Goodenough, F. L. (1939). Look to the evidence: A critique of recent experiments on raising the IQ. *Educational Methods, 19,* 73–79.

Goodenough, F. L. (1940). New evidence on environmental influence on intelligence. *39th Yearbook of the National Society for the Study of Education* (Part I), pp. 307–365.

Goodenough, F. L. (1949). *Mental testing.* New York: Rinehart.

Goodenough, F. L., & Maurer, K. M. (1940). The mental development of nursery school children compared with that of non-nursery school children. *39th Yearbook of the National Society for the Study of Education* (Part II), pp. 161–178.

Goodenough, F. L., & Maurer, K. M. (1942). *The mental growth of children from two to fourteen years.* Minneapolis: University of Minnesota Press.

Goodenough, F. L., Maurer, K. M., & Van Wagenen, M. J. (1940). *Minnesota Preschool Scales: Manual of instructions.* Minneapolis: Educational Testing Bureau.

Griffiths, R. (1954). *The abilities of babies.* London: Univerity of London Press.

Guadalupe Organization, Inc. vs. Tempe School District No. 3. Civ. No. 71-435 (D. Ariz., filed Aug. 9, 1971).

Guilford, J. P. (1956). The structure of intellect. *Psychological Bulletin, 53,* 267–293.

Guilford, J. P. (1957). *A revised structure of intellect* (Report No. 19). Los Angeles: University of Southern California, Psychology Laboratory.

Guilford, J. P. (1959). Three faces of intellect. *American Psychologist, 14,* 469–479.

Haines, J., Ames, L. B., & Gillespie, C. (1980). *The Gesell Preschool Test manual.* Lumberville, PA: Modern Learning Press.

Hobson vs. Hansen. 209 F. Supp. 401 (D. D.C. 1967).

Hoepfner, R., Stern, C., Nummedal, S. G., et al. (1971). *CSE-ERIC preschool/kindergarten test evaluations.* Los Angeles: UCLA Graduate School of Education.

Hotelling, H. (1933). Analysis of a complex of statistical variables into principal components. *Journal of Educational Psychology, 24,* 417–520.

Houts, P. L. (Ed.). (1977). *The myth of measurability.* New York: Hart.

Hunt, J. McV. (1961). Intelligence and experience. New York: Ronald.

Hunt, J. McV. (1964). The psychological basis for using preschool enrichment as an antidote for cultural deprivation. *Merrill-Palmer Quarterly, 10,* 209–248.

Hymes, J. L. (1944). Who will need a post-war nursery school? *Kaiser Child Services Center Pamphlet for Teachers,* (No. 3).

Ilg, F. L., & Ames, L. B. (1972). *School readiness.* New York: Harper & Row.

Johnson, G. E. (1894). Contributions to the psychology and pedagogy of feebleminded children. *Pedagogical Seminars, 3,* 246–301.

Kaufman, A. S., & Kaufman, N. L. (1983). *Kaufman Assessment Battery for Children.* Circle Pines, MN: American Guidance Service.

Kaufman, N. L. (1985). Review of Gesell Preschool Test. In J. Mitchell, Jr. (Ed.), *The ninth mental measurements yearbook* (Vol. I). Lincoln, NE: The University of Nebraska Press.

Kelley, T. L. (1935). *Essential traits of mental life.* Cambridge, Mass.: Harvard University Press.

Kelley, M. F., & Surbeck, E. (1987). *Evaluation report of the Littleton School District Early Prevention of School Failure Program.* Tempe, AZ: Michael F. Kelley & Associates.

Krugman, M. (1939). Some impressions of the revised Stanford-Binet scale. *Journal of Educational Psychology, 30,* 594–603.

Kuhlmann, F. (1912). A revision of the Binet-Simon system for measuring the intelligence of children. *Journal of Psycho-Asthenics Monographs Supplement, 1*(1), 1–41.

Kuhlmann, F. (1914). *A handbook of mental tests.* Baltimore: Warwick & York.

Larry P. vs. Riles. 495 F. Supp. 96 (N.D. Cal. 1979).

Leiter, R. G. (1948). *International Performance Scale*. Chicago: Stoelting Co.

McCarthy, D. (1972). *The McCarthy Scales of Children's Abilities*. San Antonio, TX: The Psychological Corporation.

Meisels, S. J. (1987). Uses and abuses of developmental screening and school readiness testing. *Young Children, 42*(2), 4–6 – 68–73.

Meisels, S. J., & Wiske, M. S. (1983). *Early Screening Inventory*. New York: Teachers College Press.

McHugh, G. (1943). Changes in IQ at the public school kindergarten level. *Psychological Monographs, 55*, 2.

Meyen, E. L. (1978). *Exceptional children and youth: An introduction*. Denver: Love.

Mowrer, W. M. C. (1934). Performance of children in Stutman tests. *Child Development, 5*, 93–96.

Naglieri, J. A. (1985). Review of Gesell Preschool Tests. In J. Mitchell, Jr. (Ed.), *The ninth mental measurements yearbook* (Vol. I). Lincoln, NE: The University of Nebraska Press.

Newborg, J., Stock, J. R., Wnek, L., Guidubaldi, J., & Svinicki, J. (1984). *Battelle Developmental Inventory*. Allen, TX: DLM/Teaching Resources.

Osborn, D. K. (1975). *Early childhood education in historical perspective*. Athens, GA: Education Associates.

Parker, F. (1981). Ideas that shaped American schools. *Phi Delta Kappan, 62*(5), 314–319.

PASE vs. Hannon. No. 74-C-3586 (N.D. Ill., July 16, 1980).

Piaget, J. (1952). *The origins of intelligence in children* (M. Cook, trans.). New York: International University Press.

Pinter, R. (1923). *Intelligence testing*. New York: Holt.

Pollack, R. H., & Brenner, M. W. (1969). *The experimental psychology of Alfred Binet*. New York: Springer.

Prasse, D. P. (1983). Legal issues underlying preschool assessment. In K. D. Paget & B. A. Bracken (Eds.), *The psychoeducational assessment of preschool children*. Orlando, FL: Grune & Stratton.

Preyer, W. (1882). *The mind of the child*. New York: Appleton.

Rotatori, A. F., Fox, R. A., Sexton, J. D., & Miller, J. H. (Eds.), (1990). *Comprehensive assessment in Special Education: Approaches, procedures, and concerns*. Springfield, Illinois: Charles C. Thomas.

Rust, M. M. (1931). The effects of resistance on intelligence scores of young children. *Child Development Monographs*, (No. 6).

Schweinhart, L. J., Koshel, J. J., & Bridgman, A. (1987). Policy options for preschool programs. *Phi Delta Kappan, 68*(7), 524–529.

Sears, R. R. (1975). Your ancients revisited: A history of child development. In E. M. Heatherington (Ed.), *Review of child development research* (Vol. 5). Chicago: University of Chicago Press.

Senn, M. J. E. (1975). Insights on the child development movement in the United States. *Monographs of the Society for Research in Child Development, 40*(3–4, Whole No. 161).

Shepard, L. A., & Smith, M. L. (1986). Synthesis of research on school readiness and kindergarten retention. *Educational Leadership, 44*(3), 78–86.

Shinn, M. (1900). *The biography of a baby*. Boston: Houghton Mifflin.

Simpson, B. R. (1939). The wandering IQ: Is it time to settle down? *Journal of Psychology, 7*, 351–367.

Skeels, H. M. (1938). Mental development of children in foster homes. *Journal of Consulting Psychology, 2*, 33–34.

Skodak, M. (1939). Children in foster homes: A study of mental development. *University of Iowa Studies in Child Welfare, 16*, 1.

Stern, W. (1914). *The psychological methods of testing intelligence*. Baltimore: Warwich & York.

Stern, W. (1924). *Psychology of early childhood up to the sixth year of age*. New York: Henry Hal. (Originally published, 1914).

Sternberg, R. J. (1979). Intelligence research at the interface between differential and cognitive psychology: Prospects and proposals, In R. J. Sternberg & D. K. Detterman, (Eds.), *Human intelligence: Perspectives on its theory and measurement*. Norwood: Ablex.

Stott, L. H., & Ball, R. S. (1965). Infant and preschool mental tests: Review and evaluation. *Monographs of the Society for Research in Child Development, 30*(3, Whole No. 101).

Strother, D. B. (1987). Preschool children in the public schools: Good investment? Or bad? *Phi Delta Kappan, 69*(4), 304–308.

Stutsman, R. (1931). *Mental measurement of preschool children*. New York: World Book.

Terman, L. M., & Merrill, M. A. (1937). *Measuring intelligence*. Boston: Houghton Mifflin.

Thorndike, E. L. (1921). Intelligence and its measurement. *Journal of Educational Research, 12*, 124–127.

Thorndike, R. L., Hagen, E. P., & Sattler, J. M. (1986). *Stanford-Binet Intelligence Scale, Fourth Edition*. Chicago: Riverside.

Thurstone, L. L. (1935). *The vectors of the mind*. Chicago: University of Chicago Press.

Thurstone, L. L. (1938). *Primary mental abilities*. Chicago: University of Chicago Press.

Ulich, R. (1945). *History of educational thought*. New York: American Book.

Ulich, R. (1947). *Three thousand years of educational wisdom*. Cambridge, Mass.: Harvard University Press.

Watson, J. B., & Watson, R. R. (1928). *The psychological care of the infant and child*. New York: Norton.

Wechsler, D. (1949). *Manual for the Wechsler Intelligence Scale for Children*. New York: The Psychological Corporation.

Wechsler, D. (1967). *Wechsler Preschool and Primary Scale of Intelligence*. San Antonio, TX: The Psychological Corporation.

Weiner, R., & Koppelman, J. (1987). *From birth to five: Serving the youngest handicapped children*. Alexandria, VA: Capitol Publications Inc.

Weintraub, F. J., Abeson, A., Ballard, J., & La Vor, M. L. (Eds.), (1976). *Public policy and the education of exceptional children*. Reston, VA: Council for Exceptional Children.

Wellman, B. L. (1932). Some new bases for interpretation of the IQ. *Journal of Genetic Psychology, 41,* 116–126. (a)

Wellman, B. L. (1932). The effects of preschool attendance upon the IQ. *Journal of Experimental Education, 1,* 48–49. (b)

Wellman, B. L. (1934). Growth of intelligence under different school environments. *Journal of Experimental Education, 3,* 59–83.

Wellman, B. L. (1940). The meaning of environment. *39th Yearbook of the National Society for the Study of Education* (Part I), pp. 21–40.

White, S. H. (1977). Social implications of IQ. In P. Houts (Ed.), *The myth of measurability*. New York: Hart.

Wood, C., Powell, S., & Knight, R. C. (1984). Predicting school readiness: The validity of developmental age. *Journal of Learning Disabilities, 17,* 8–11.

Yerkes, R. M., & Foster, J. C. (1923). *The point scale for measuring mental ability*. Baltimore: Warwick & York.

2

Issues in the Assessment of Preschool Children

CAROL SCHNEIDER LIDZ

This chapter addresses issues relevant to psycho-educational assessment of preschool children. In some cases the issues apply to infant assessment as well, and infancy can be invoked as a point of reference in understanding preschool issues. The focus of this chapter is on assessment of children between the ages of 2 and 6 who might or might not be classifiable as handicapped.

In responding to some of the issues that apply to or are specific to the assessment of preschool children, the discussion leads to the questions:

- What is special about preschool children vis-à-vis psychoeducational assessment?
- Should preschool children be assessed?
- What are the strengths and weaknesses of the prevailing preschool assessment models and methods?
- What skills or abilities should be assessed in preschool children; that is, what are the appropriate targets of assessment?

WHAT IS SPECIAL ABOUT PRESCHOOL CHILDREN?

Depending upon one's point of view, related to the examiner's training, experience, and personality, assessment of preschool children can be either a delightful or frustrating endeavor. Characteristics of preschool children that many professionals find delightful include their spontaneity, lack of self-consciousness, and physical appeal. In fact, lack of self-consciousness and spontaneity often become significant diagnostic indicators of possible problems. To those who view preschool assessment as a frustrating experience, the child's spontaneity frequently is interpreted as unpredictability and unreliability; lack of self-consciousness is perceived as inaccessability to important sources of diagnostic information.

Although all living creatures can be philosophically described as "in process" or "becoming," the preschooler seems to be an accelerated case of process and development. Although rate of development is accelerated during the preschool years, there is a predictable developmental sequence during this time period. Thus, while young children might be highly individualistic on parameters such as temperament and growth rate, they appear more like each other at this stage than at any other. Infants and young children appear more closely bound to biological development than older children and adults, and this maturational tendency provides the theoretical foundation for many of the assessment procedures that have been devised for this population.

The spontaneity and lack of self-consciousness of the young child have implications for assessment procedures that are uniquely useful during these years, namely, play and observational techniques. The predictable and sequential nature of child development leads to the use of developmental tests that sample from the universe of developmental characteristic behaviors at each level.

Also specific to the young child is the difficulty of assessing children who are at the beginning stages of their language development. Limited language skills have at least two implications for assessment. First, language development itself becomes an important target of assessment as an indicator of developmental progress, as well as a precursor to cognitive functioning. Second, to circumvent the limitations posed by the child's limited language skills, assessors must rely heavily on behavior rating scales and third-party interviews of significant adults in the child's life to gain needed information.

Preschoolers have additional characteristics that create special challenges for the assessor, including fleeting attention, unresolved separation issues, and frequent lack of concern with pleasing the examiner or with achieving a correct answer or solution to problems (e.g., Gotts, 1979; Martin, 1986; Ulrey & Schnell, 1982). On the other hand, children who do not have separation problems might be pleased with the special attention provided by the examiner, and are unlikely to have developed negative reactions to psychologists. Instead of wishing to shrivel from sight when the psychologist approaches, the independent child might beg to be taken out of the classroom and feel rejected if overlooked or passed over.

Because of these unique characteristics of preschool children, it is especially important for examiners to be both flexible and patient. The examiner needs a wide repertoire of assessment procedures and must be able to capitalize on situations that occur spontaneously. The examiner must allot sufficient time for the assessment to elicit multiple samples of behaviors and productions to allow derivation of an accurate estimate of the child's current level of functioning.

SHOULD PRESCHOOL CHILDREN BE ASSESSED?

One might quite correctly anticipate that the answer to the question: Should preschool children be assessed? would in one form or another be a firm "yes." However, there are important issues to consider when undertaking the task of preschool assessment, and it is not an endeavor assumed lightly.

Those who object to or express anxiety about the assessment of young children generally are concerned with the issues and problems associated with early labeling and premature diagnoses. The concern with labeling implies that labels are potentially harmful, and concern about early identification or diagnosis raises issues of stability of behavior, accuracy of early predictions, and effectiveness of early intervention. Each of these issues is important; however, these issues can be summarized and addressed lightly in this chapter.

There has been considerable concern expressed in both popular and professional publications about the possible negative consequences of labeling (Hobbs, 1975; Mercer, Algozzine, & Trifiletti, 1979). In view of the history of poor predictive ability of tests for children below 3 years of age who are functioning above the retarded level (Dunst & Reingrover, 1981; Goodman & Cameron, 1978; Hunt, 1986; Simeonsson, Huntington & Parse, 1980; Stott & Ball, 1965), labeling is an important issue. Outcome predictions for low functioning children show greater reliability (DuBose, 1976; Vanderveer & Scheweid, 1974) than when the child is functioning above the retarded level. The preschool years for children between 3 to 5 years represent the transition period between poor and relatively good predictions of future cognitive level, but even these improved prediction rates are only moderate. For example, Clarke (1982) noted that the average correlation between IQ at ages 3 and 5 and adult IQ is .40. Part of the problem in early childhood diagnosis and prediction relates to the difficulties associated with assessing children at these ages (Goodwin &

Driscoll, 1980). If preschool children were stable responders (which frequently they are not) and the assessment tools reliable and valid (which frequently they are not) (Bracken, 1987), diagnostic labels might at least be valid descriptors of the child's current levels of functioning, if not good predictors of future levels of functioning.

There are those who would be satisfied with an accurate description of the child's current level of functioning (Busch-Rossnagel, Hawryluk, & Pavone-Kennedy, 1983; Palmer, 1983). However, it is difficult to defend the validity of identification and intervention on the basis of description alone, without prediction. If current behaviors are not indicative of later functioning, there is no justification for identifying a child as in need of treatment. Most writers in this area seem to agree that there is no justification for diagnosis without treatment. Conversely, there needs to be a reliable process for identifying children who are at risk for future difficulty and thereby render them eligible for intervention (Rolf & Hasazi, 1977). The challenge to accurate prediction has been to isolate and accurately assess significant "at risk" variables. All biological risk factors seem to interact with socioeconomic status (SES), and specifically with the mother's level of education (e.g., Kopp, 1983; Wilson, 1985). While there might be no clear justification for claiming that labels such as mental retardation are necessarily harmful (Guskin, Bartel & MacMillan, 1975), the need for justification of the long, complex, and expensive assessment process remains. Diagnosis must, at the minimum, result in enrollment in an effective treatment program.

Historically, the labeling process has assumed treatment implications (Gallagher & Bradley, 1972) that have not been realized fully in the educational setting. However, if a label is all that is produced from a complex and expensive diagnostic process, assessment becomes a relatively meaningless exercise. Attempts to increase the meaningfulness of preschool assessment have included advocacy of noncategorical diagnostic systems, where the child would be identified as being in need of intervention and labeled more generically with a term such as "at risk," "special need," or "developmental delay." Also, the follow-up intervention would be "custom made" to reflect the assessment team's detailed description

of the child's needs (MacMillan & Meyers, 1979; Smith & Schakel, 1986).

The only legitimate justification for assessment, at any age, is to anticipate and remediate problems as early as possible. Generally, the assumption that "the earlier the intervention, the better" has prevailed, despite the lack of clarity of research evidence to support this conclusion (Clarke, 1982; Hourcade & Parette, 1986; Mastropieri, 1987). However, there is evidence to support the observation that problems manifested during the preschool years often do not simply dissipate with time.

For example, Glueck and Glueck (1966) were able to predict with almost 85% accuracy which boys would become delinquent by age 17 from the behaviors and family interaction patterns observed in the children between the ages of $5\frac{1}{2}$ and 6 years. Kohn and Rosman (1972) reported a positive relationship between their interest-participation variable in preschool years and first and second grade achievement, while anger and defiance evident during preschool years was negatively associated with the first and second grade achievement of their male subjects. Murphy and Moriarty (1976) found a high correlation between "vulnerability" during preschool years and adult vulnerability (vulnerability was generally defined as success at coping with the environment, and specified for each age; for example, for infants, vulnerability involved feeding and digestive disturbances, developmental imbalances, inadequate attunement between mother and child). Richman, Stevenson, and Graham (1982) conducted a longitudinal study and found that 62% of the children who were rated as behaviorally disturbed at the age of 3 were still disturbed at age 8. Specifically, these authors found that early restlessness predicted later antisocial behavior, and that early fearfulness predicted later neurotic behavior; children with early language delays also had a high incidence of later behavior problems. The single most predictive variable evident during the preschool years was poor peer relationships. However, it also must be mentioned that the evidence is not totally in support of the stability of problem behaviors. Lytton, Watts, and Dunn (1986), in their seven-year longitudinal study of children between the ages of 2 and 9 found that social maladjustment was particularly related to environmental factors, and that the mother's child-rearing practices were more predictive of the child's later social adjustment than the child's early social behaviors.

With regard to assessment, there is some evidence that preschool tests have greater accuracy for high than for low test scores (Keogh, 1969; Rubin, Balow, Dorle, & Rosen, 1978), which allows the examiner to conclude with greater confidence that a child who does well on standardized measures will be more likely to succeed in the academic setting than the child who scores poorly will fail. This evidence is derived from single test scores, and prediction is more likely to increase with an increase in the sources of data on which decisions are based.

What, then, is the answer to the question of whether preschool children should be assessed? This question can be answered affirmatively if examiners used valid and reliable instruments capable of identifying children who are at risk educationally, and for whom professionals can prescribe an effective program of intervention. This is a large order, and professionals are only in the midstages of meeting each of these criteria.

ISSUES CONCERNING EXISTING MODELS AND PROCEDURES

The next issue to be discussed concerns the prevailing ideas and approaches involved in determining *how* preschool children should be assessed. Indeed, Goodwin and Driscoll (1980) proposed that the issue in early identification is more one of *how* than of *whether*. The issues concerning *what* skills and abilities are best assessed will be examined next. The existing repertoire of models and approaches includes a variety of norm-referenced, criterion-(or domain-)referenced, and curriculum-referenced tests. Emerging approaches include "dynamic" procedures and ecological models, as well as continuing interest in diagnostic classrooms as a setting for any or all of these. Within and overlapping these, we have developmental measures (which might be norm- or criterion-referenced) and a child-referenced approach. All of these assessment approaches relate to the general issue of "readiness."

Because of the biological/developmental link

and the grossly sequential nature of the young child's maturation, developmental measures are particularly popular among preschool examiners. Despite the prevalence of developmental scales and the popularity of this approach, there are many issues and problems related to developmental assessment that are worthy of consideration.

Developmental assessment assumes that:

- The variables assessed are the most important behaviors to note about the developing child
- There is continuity across these variables over time
- The individual's relative standing compared to other children her age remains stable over time
- Development of the observed variables follows a predictable, hierarchical, and sequential course
- Comparison of all children to the developmental norm is accurate and useful for predicting future development and for making and implementing remedial plans

Discussion of the first assumption, the appropriate targets of assessment, will be discussed in greater detail shortly. Suffice it to say, there are some serious questions raised regarding the appropriateness and meaningfulness of the characteristics currently targeted for assessment (Linn, 1986). Also, there has been criticism of most developmental measures because of their lack of theoretical base (Keith, 1987) and the poor translation of assessment results into meaningful treatments (e.g., Ramey, Campbell, & Wasik, 1982).

The issues of continuity and stability of traits or characteristics and of the individual's relative standing in the group are of central importance to the developmental model. Although claims have been made in this chapter about the stability of problem behaviors between preschool and later years, it is quite another issue to claim stability for each and every variable measured in attempts to assess normal development (Dunst & Rheingrover, 1981). The determination of which behaviors to include on these scales is derived from large group studies, and it remains difficult to interpret the applicability of results based on large groups to an individual undergoing assessment

(Flapan & Neubauer, 1970). As indicated previously, conclusions regarding successes can be made with more confidence than conclusions regarding failures. For example, because 80% of the children crawl before they walk, it is difficult to ascertain if children will necessarily show abnormal development without crawling. There are numerous documentations in the literature to substantiate rank order changes of individuals in response to a variety of situational effects (Dunst & Rheingrover, 1981; Mattick & Murphy, 1971), so developmental scales become uncertain indicators of an individual's relative placement in relation to chronological age peers.

There also is increasing complaint that, while comparison of handicapped individuals with normal developmental standards might delineate the degree an individual deviates from average, it provides little information about the developmental projectory of the handicapped child, or the effects of various handicapping conditions on development (e.g., Brooks-Gunn & Lewis, 1981; DuBose, 1981; Garwood, 1982). DuBose (1981) pointed out that neither Gesell nor Piaget observed or worked with handicapped children, and that there is a "shortage of documented developmental information" (p. 9) on these children. And, as is so often the case when reviewing or discussing assessment procedures, information is lacking regarding the implications of these measures for the treatment of handicapped children.

Furthermore, one might assume that if developmental age is a useful parameter of assessment under some circumstances, there would be agreement across major measures regarding these developmental age equivalents. However, Guralnick and Weinhouse (1983), in a review of developmental peer social interaction tests, reported wide variations in age equivalents attributed to social characteristics. For example, they noted that the age equivalents for parallel play ranged between 10 and 42 months, depending upon the test used.

Developmental measures have been used not only to describe the current functioning of the child in relation to a normative standard (and some, in relation to a developmental theory) and to identify domains for intervention, but they also have been used to determine the child's "readiness" for formal education or to move from one grade to another. The central assumption of the

"readiness" concept is that the individual maintains a steady state in relation to developmental course (e.g., once ready, always ready), but this approach has been most vulnerable in its implicit implication that "time for maturation" is a sufficient intervention for most developmentally unready children.

Perhaps the best known advocates of determination of readiness as a basis for school placement are found within the Gesell tradition. According to Ilg and Ames (1965), the basic tenets of this approach propose that:

- The child should be allowed to progress at his own pace
- The child functions best when placed with others progressing at a similar rate and functioning at a similar level
- Readiness for school is best determined by estimating the child's developmental (neuromaturational) level, or developmental age
- A child needs to be functioning at the developmental equivalent of 5 years old to be able to succeed in most American kindergartens, and should be developmentally 6 years or older to cope with first grade

A representative statement that expresses this approach is "many well-meaning but ill-informed parents and educators are pushing young children into our school systems too soon. Being bright and being ready to begin formal schooling are two very separate issues. When children enter school before they are developmentally ready to cope with it, their chances for failure increase dramatically" (Uphoff & Gilmore, 1986).

The major criticisms of the readiness approach have been that there is a lack of good evidence either to substantiate these claims or to document the reliability and validity of the measures used to estimate readiness. These criticisms are particularly poignant in view of the length of time the readiness philosophy and procedures have been advocated and implemented. The readiness approach also has been criticized for the apparent lack of explicit concern or elaboration regarding what to do about potentially handicapped children who might obtain low developmental scores, but do not progress in response to simple delay tactics. Finally, further criticisms include the questionable implicit assumption regarding the static nature of develoment that is overreliant on biological maturation and nonexplicit regarding the potential effects of experiences that enhance development, and the overemphasis of the readiness approach on a narrow concept of kindergarten as a criterion of readiness. Goodwin and Goodwin (1982) express some of these concerns in their statement, "Readiness is not always well defined . . . a child may be ready for one type of kindergarten but not for another, or ready for work in language but not in arithmetic" (p. 543).

A sample of some of the work that has been done in the area of readiness in general and Gesell testing in particular follows. In 1972 Kaufman and Kaufman studied the predictive validity of the Gesell Readiness Tests, a Piaget-based battery, and the Lorge-Thorndike Intelligence Test in relation to first grade achievement, as measured by the Stanford Achievement Test. They also looked at the predictive validity of teething in relation to first grade achievement, because this was a variable mentioned by the Gesell institute staff as another indicator of readiness. The results supported the predictive validity of both the Gesell and the Piaget-based tests, and found that IQ added little to these results, and teething added nothing. However, these authors concluded "The fact that the GSRT is an excellent predictor of [first grade] achievement does not imply that a bulk of the low-scoring children should be placed back into kindergarten or into transitional classes" (p. 533). They considered such placement decisions as separate issues.

Gredler (1978) examined the data available to date on the issue of readiness and made the following points: On the whole, socioeconomic status seems to be a more potent predictor of success in school than entry age. In Sweden, where school entry age is 7 years, first grade reading failure rate is 13%, similar to British estimates where children enter school one year earlier than Americans; an American study showed that of children who would have been eliminated from first grade if the entry date were changed from December 1 to September 1, 73% achieved reading grades of A, B, or C, and there was little difference on an achievement test between older and younger children; another study showed that early differences on a readiness test disappeared after four years in school; that is, there were no differences on achievement tests at the later date. Another study reported that children who were recommended for

retention but who were not retained because of parental refusal, outperformed those who were retained when assessed on a reading test in later grades. Gredler suggests that it is the school program that needs to adapt to the child's developmental level, rather than vice versa.

In a 1978 concurrent validity study, MacTurk and Neisworth reported results with a very small number of preschool children, including both handicapped and nonhandicapped, and found a high correlation between the Gesell Test and a criterion measure based upon the HICOMP Curriculum (a major frequently used preschool curriculum).

May and Welch (1984) pointed out that the assumption of developmental placement is that "behavior is a function of growth which is structured, orderly, predictable, and measurable by a single screening test . . . [and that] physical, social, emotional, and intellectual aspects of the child are interdependent; one should not be pushed ahead of the others" (p. 338). They found these assumptions to be contrary to contemporary ideas of early intervention, which advocate matching the program to the child's needs. In 1986, May reported the results of a study with 152 children who received Gesell testing before kindergarten, at the end of kindergarten, and at the end of first grade. The study examined the interrelationships of these scores, as well as their relationship with achievement and IQ in grades 3, 4, and 5. The only high correlations were between end of kindergarten Gesell and first grade achievement scores for some of the subjects; but even this accounted for only about 25% of the total variance. Prekindergarten Gesell scores were not related to later achievement (significant at a low level only for a small portion of the subjects). Interestingly, the grade 1 Gesell's predictive success was lower than the end of kindergarten Gesell scores.

Wood, Powell, and Knight (1984) reported the ability of the Gesell School Readiness Screening Test to discriminate between those who succeeded or failed in kindergarten (a discriminant validity study). These authors found developmental age (DA) (as derived from Gesell) to relate more strongly to achievement than chronological age (CA) and CA added nothing to the discriminant ability of DA. Developmental age alone accounted for about 22% of the variance.

Bear and Modlin (1987) reported their results of Gesell Preschool Test (GPT) administration to 88 Virginia pupils. They were administered the GPT prior to kindergarten entrance and at the end of kindergarten year. These authors sought to determine if the Gesell scores discriminated between children who were and were not promoted and they found that the Gesell scores did not discriminate between these groups. This study, however, is confounded by the fact that the teachers had access to the Gesell scores, as well as to achievement test results when they made their decisions, and they seemed to make their promotion decisions on the basis of reading and math test scores. However, this finding might tentatively suggest a lack of relationship between the Gesell and achievement scores.

It is not intended in this section to suggest that developmental assessment has nothing to contribute to the understanding of the preschool child, or that some preschool children are not helped by delaying entry to formal education. What is seen in the few studies reported is some documentation of low level, short-term predictive and discriminate validity of the Gesell tests. However, this is not sufficient reason to substantiate large scale administration of these measures, or base program decisions for individual children on these results alone.

The results of these studies also suggest poor long-term predictive validity, supporting Meisels' (1987) concerns about the lack of reliability and validity of the measures, and the insufficient justification for using these tests to exclude children from programs. Meisels further criticizes the Gesell norms as being based on white Connecticut children. In view of these many limitations, some authors agree with Meisels' statement, "Testing in early childhood and kindergarten should only be used to make better and more appropriate services available to the largest number of children . . . [and that] the use of exclusionary tests suggests that children should conform to school programs, rather than schools adjusting to the needs of children" (p. 71).

For assessment information to be useful, it is necessary to have a point of reference (Hamilton & Swan, 1981). To merely describe the child's performance does not allow us to draw conclusions or to derive recommendations. This need for a reference or standard of comparison brings up the next area for discussion: the existing models or approaches to the assessment of young children. Assessment tasks can be norm-referenced, criterion-(or domain-) referenced, child-referenced, or curriculum-referenced. Administration models can include standardized-static, diagnostic-teaching, or dynamic approaches. Specific procedures such as observations, rating scales, or play scales fall into one of these categories in most cases.

This is not the place for extensive elaboration on these various approaches; these elaborations are available to the reader from other sources (e.g., Lidz, 1981, 1987). Tests also can be purely empirically based, or theory based, and many tests represent a combination of these factors. Developmental tests, for example, are often norm-referenced and criterion-referenced and empirically based; however, empirical basis is a focus of criticism. If there is no logical relationship between items or tasks, and if there is no underlying hypothetical mechanism guiding the choice of items that appear on the test, there is little reason to expect the measure to be useful in the derivation of intervention strategies, even if the test is of proven predictive value (Garwood, 1982). Take as a hypothetical example, that the number of eyeblinks per minute at 6 months of age is predictive of 4 year ability to count; can one safely assume that a child who has a below average number of eyeblinks should be coached to increase the number, with the expectation that his or her 4 year old number concepts will be improved? The search for a causative connection between the two variables requires some theoretical basis for speculating that there is a relationship. This is a particular problem for preschool assessment where the strategy for deriving a preschool version of a cognitive measure is so often a downward extension of a model developed for older children or adults, without rethinking the measure in terms of the theoretical basis and characteristics of cognitive functioning of the younger child.

MAJOR ASSESSMENT APPROACHES

The various major assessment approaches and their strengths and weaknesses, as well as their applications and misapplications will be discussed shortly. Which approach is preferred is an issue related to the decision to be made. The appropriate approach is the one that yields data to facilitate the decision to be made. Therefore, no single apporach is appropriate for all cases.

Norm-referenced assessment

Norm-referenced measures compare the child's performance with the average performance of either age or grade peers. Items are selected on the basis of the item's ability to discriminate within these age or grade groups. In norm-referenced assessment, the instrument provides an estimate of the extent to which the child is able to do what the average child her age can do. The fact that the child might not be able to perform a task might be interpreted as an indication of poor progress, and possibly might be predictive of a slower rate of development in the future. Unless demonstrated otherwise through techniques such as biserial factor analysis or biserial correlations, in many cases, it is only the composite score (or scores) that are treated normatively, and there is no basis to assume the predictive validity of individual items. Therefore, it is not necessarily a legitimate use of the test to infer that a child who fails to draw a circle has problems with fine motor development and therefore should be taught to draw circles as a way of improving his fine motor coordination. Furthermore, unless the items have been demonstrated to have validity through the biserial techniques it also is not a legitimate practive to select items from a variety of tests to create a new measure and assume that the validity of the original tests then applies to the new measure. It would be necessary to validate this new assessment procedure.

Whether what is measured by these tests is the most appropriate or meaningful content in terms of either prognostications or prescriptions is another issue, and will be discussed later. Mattick and Murphy's (1971) comments apply to norm-referenced measures: "Tests may indeed point up lags, dysfunctions, distortions and certain patterns of cognitive behavior; they tell us little about their origin or their meaning to cognitive functioning outside of the testing situation" (p. 426).

Criterion-referenced and Curriculum-based tests

Criterion-referenced measures yield information regarding the child's level of mastery of a specific content domain (e.g., math, reading), and are best used for assessing what the child knows currently and what the child needs to learn next. Curriculum-based measurement is a subcategory of criterion-referenced measurement, and works under the assumption that the content domain assessed is a sample of a specific curriculum. Teacher-made tests are best characterized as curriculum-based measures. Although not often adhered to, particularly at the preschool level, there are standards and criteria that help define technical adequacy in this area of testing (Lidz, 1981), although, as Boehm and Sandberg (1982) point out, these procedures are not yet covered by the Standards for Educational and Psychological Tests. Curriculum-based measures are developed to reveal what a child knows now (within a particular domain), and what is the next instructional step in the curriculum. A good criterion-referenced measure provides an appropriate criterion by which to judge the effectiveness of instruction (Hunt & Kirk, 1974). Criterion-referenced tests do not, however, provide diagnostic information that reveal the reasons for the child's mastery or non-mastery, and they do not necessarily lead to instructional strategies.

Norm-referenced and criterion-referenced assessments can be obtained from a single instrument, thus yielding normative/comparative information, as well as outlining the specific content areas of strength and weakness. For handicapped children, however, sufficient sensitivity to growth and change still is lacking in most criterion-referenced measures because these children often progress in quite small increments, and often show their response to intervention in qualitative, rather than quantitative ways. Curriculum-based tests placed within a test-teach-test assessment model, as described by Bagnato, Neisworth, and Capone (1986), come much closer to allowing the teacher or diagnostician to derive implications for teaching strategies and interventions, *if* imaginatively applied. That is, information still is lacking concerning the quality and nature of the teaching strategies that are derived; furthermore, the specific criterion-referenced measures specified by the authors as useful to the test and retest portions of the model have not always demonstrated technical adequacy.

The hierarchical arrangement of items in a criterion-referenced or curriculum-based test suggests the existence of an inherent hierarchy of skills, where mastery of lower level skills is prerequisite to those occurring later. This hierarchical assumption is not the case for all subject matter (e.g., history, geography). Furthermore, what the criterion-referenced measure reveals regarding the child who is not progressing well is precisely that the child is not progressing well, as well as outlining the specifics of what the child does and does not know. This is useful information, but it is lacking in implications for remediation unless we can assume that repeated exposure is sufficient to overcome the lack of progress; this might be the case for many children, but is unlikely to suffice for many referred children. For most children, it is desirable to know they are not progressing, as well as what instructional efforts will facilitate their learning. Answers to the question of what will work might lie within the child's home experiences, temperamental predispositions, characteristics of neurological processing, history of past instruction, and so on. The answer to how we can induce change requires a more involved, interactional approach. Such an interactional approach is called diagnostic teaching if it involves specific academic content, and dynamic assessment if the focus is on general cognitive processing characteristics or metacognitive processes of the learner (Lidz, 1987).

Both criterion-referenced and dynamic approaches can be used in a child-referenced way. Child-referencing compares the child's current performance with her previous performance. The fact that many skills and abilities are emerging during the preschool years (Barnett, 1986) makes procedures such as dynamic assessment especially relevant, because the focus is on the child's responsiveness to intervention rather than on mastery of specific content.

Because children's responses can fluctuate not only in response to experiences external to the assessment, but also in response to situational effects within the assessment, an ecological model of assessment is particularly important. The ecological model involves awareness that responses are products of a number of possible sources (e.g., examiner, examinee, environment, history), as well as the need to view the child within the various contexts that might be relevant to the targets of the assessment.

Blom, Lininger, and Charlesworth (1987) pro-

vide a basic definition of the ecological approach, which they contend is more an issue of the examiner's attitude than technique. They suggest that the ecological model examines behavior as "the result of the interaction between the child and the environment and [assumes] that the problem does not solely reside in the child but in a mismatch between the child and the environment" (pp. 49–50). Such a view makes observational procedures especially valuable (e.g., Moskowitz, 1986), because observational procedures are ideally suited to sampling the child's behavior within a variety of environments.

TARGETS OF ASSESSMENT

The final major issue to be discussed concerns the *what* of preschool assessment; that is, what aspects of the child's functioning, environment, and experiences are to be assessed. Developmental measures have been successful in providing current descriptions of the child's functioning, for tracking developmental course, and for documenting and predicting the future of severely handicapped infants; however, these measures have a poor record of predicting the future outcomes of the child who is more moderately or midly at risk, or for providing guidelines for intervention for a child at any level of functioning (Diamond, 1987; McCall, Hogarty, & Hurlburt, 1972). Examiners often proceed as if developmental measures provide treatment implications; however, current circumstances only permit the inference that direct practice on the times of the test is an appropriate prescription for treatment. As Hamilton and Swan (1981) noted, the fact that one behavior precedes another does not necessarily indicate that the earlier behavior is a precursor of the later. This causative relationship needs to be established. Stott and Ball (1965) also suggested that one of the possible reasons for the poor predictive validity of existing measures was that they might be looking at the wrong variables. These authors specifically noted an overconcern with quantitative changes and underconcern with the qualitative aspects of development.

Valid preschool assessment requires the establishment of the precursors of later development. It is possible that such precursors do not exist; that is, the factors that make a difference to later development are in such different, obscure, or inaccessible forms during the child's younger years that determination of assessable precursors never will be accomplished. However, the literature suggests that the search has only recently begun, and a number of researchers are making significant progress.

If predictions are to be accurate, it is necessary to look beyond the variables that are limited to the child's functioning, and look to the situational influences as well (Marcovitch & Simmons, 1986). Socioeconomic status and, specifically, mother's educational level, are potent factors in the child's level of functioning and in predicting the future course of development (McCall et al., 1972). Even these factors can be considered distal to the more proximal variables involved in the specific interactions of the parent and the child; that is, it is not sufficient to state that more highly educated parents tend to have children who function at a higher cognitive level, but it is necessary to determine the specific variables associated with the higher level of education that relate to the child's cognitive development (Feuerstein, 1979, 1980). Feuerstein describes these variables in terms of Mediated Learning Experience (MLE). Hunt and Kirk (1974) found differences regarding "comparative observation with care, listening to the final syllables of words . . . taking care to comply with adult requests . . . delaying immediate responding . . . feeling responsibility for what happens" (p. 174) to discriminate between their Head Start and middle-class groups; these characteristics overlap considerably with the components of MLE as described by Feuerstein.

There are a number of precursor behaviors evident in the infant and the young child that show promise of predictive value. These might provide a more valid basis for intervention than what currently exists.

Meyers and Dingman's (1960) hypothesized factor domains of preschool abilities and ages of initial emergence provide an illustration of the difference between manifest preschool behavior and precursors. For example, the domain of perceptual speed, which first emerges as a factor at 18 months, is preceded at 1 month by visual pursuit movements, and at 5 months by recognition of parents. Preschool articulation and semantic fluency, which emerge as factors at $1\frac{1}{2}$ (articulation) and 2 years (fluency) are preceded by non-crying vocalization at 1 month and babbling at 6 months.

Bell, Weller, and Waldrop (1971) found significant relationships between newborn respiration rate, tactile threshold, and reaction to interruption of sucking and intensity of behavior in preschool years. However, this relationship was inverse; that is, high levels during infancy related to low intensity as a preschooler. Despite this relationship, these authors found that newborn behavior provided few cues to later development.

McCall and colleagues (1972), in reporting the results of their principal component analysis of the Fels longitudinal study sample, cited early infant vocalization as behavior that had positive predictive value in relation to later IQ, more so for girls than for boys. They found the following Gesell items to predict IQ successfully:

- At 12 months: "imitation of fine motor behavior and the learning of rudimentary social skills" (p. 741) is predictive of IQ for girls at $3\frac{1}{2}$, 6, and 10 years.
- At 18 months, verbal production, verbal comprehension, and extension of imitation of verbal and motor behavior is predictive of IQ for boys at $3\frac{1}{2}$ and for girls at $3\frac{1}{2}$, 6, and 10 years, and predictive of nonverbal behavior of boys at 13 years.
- At 24 months, verbal production and labeling, comprehension, fluent verbal production, and grammatical maturity was predictive of IQ for both boys and girls at most ages.

Murphy and Moriarty (1976) reported a positive association between an appropriately dependent relationship with mother during preschool years and later robustness" (for boys), and a negative association between infant "functional stability" and later anxiety (i.e., early lability is predictive of later anxiety). There also was a positive relationship between frequency of vocalization during infancy and preschool ability to "project conflict" and to grasp mature concepts. For boys, there was a positive association between sensory reactivity during infancy and preschool rivalry and supportive interaction with peers. Finally, these authors reported a positive association between being demanding in infancy and the later ability to control environmental impact and level of preschool maturity in perceptual concepts.

Dunst and Rheingrover (1981) cited early vocalization (for girls) and smiling in response to successful problem solving as behaviors that have research support for their association with cognitive functioning. Lewis (1975) and Brooks-Gunn and Lewis (1981) established a relationship between attention in infancy and later intellectual performance.

Sigman and coworkers (1986) reported the results of their longitudinal study of 93 medically at risk children, which found a negative relationship between attention (fixation time) in infancy and at 4 months and WISC-R IQ at 8 years. Further, they conclude that attention is an important precursor to later cognitive development and "infant attention measures appear to reflect individual differences in the rate and efficiency of visual processing" (p. 788) and "the early attention measures may also tap state control capacities that are precursors for information intake" (p. 791).

Hunt (1986) cited developmental rate changes during infancy, rather than levels per se, as good predictors of later cognitive functioning, and supported the view that family variables contribute significantly to cognitive development. She agreed with other investigators that ". . . most infants with future intellectual problems are virtually unpredictable during the first year" (p. 53).

Palisin's (1986) research supports the significance of attention span and persistance in 4- and 5-year-old children as concurrently strongly associated with achievement.

Messer and coworkers (1986) reported the results of their study of mastery behavior (task persistance), using scores from the McCarthy Scales as a criterion of preschool competence. These authors found significant relationships between the McCarthy scores and goal-directed behavior and exploratory behavior at 12 months. They also cited their previous research that revealed positive relationships between task persistance at 6 months and 12 month Bayley scores, and task persistance at 13 months and McCarthy scores at $3\frac{1}{2}$ years (for girls).

These studies have established connections between behaviors that are observable during infancy and preschool years. These investigators have considered behaviors such as attention, vocalization, task persistance, exploratory behavior, and level of attachment. The conclusions

often differ according to the gender of the subjects, and it might be necessary to search for precursors for girls and boys separately.

SUMMARY

This chapter has explored some of the central issues involved in the assessment of preschool children. It is reasonable to conclude that assessment of preschool children is a complex and difficult endeavor, and not one for which competence can be assumed from the average course of training for psychologists (Oakland & Zimmerman, 1986), even though these are the professionals most likely to have had some preparation in this area. It is agreed, along with Gotts (1979) that "The specific educational background and experience needed for early childhood assessment usually is not required of, or demonstrated by, persons who are primarily certified to perform assessment of school-age children" (p. 535). Gotts continues, ". . . early childhood assessment is too often carried out by persons who are in some sense legally eligible to assess children but who are not professionally qualified" (p. 536).

REFERENCES

Bagnato, S. J., Neisworth, J. T., & Capone, A. (1986). Curriculum-based assessment for the young exceptional child: Rationale and review. *Topics in Early Childhood Special Education, 6,* 97–110.

Barnett, D. (1986). School psychology in preschool settings: A review of training and practice issues. *Professional Psychology: Research and Practice, 17,* 58–64.

Bear, G. G., & Modlin, P. D. (1987). Gesell's developmental testing: What purpose does it serve? *Psychology in the Schools, 24,* 40–44.

Bell, R., Weller, G. M., & Waldrop, M. F. (1971). Newborn and preschooler: Organization of behavior and relations between periods. *Monographs of the Society for Research in Child Development, 36,* (1 & 2, Serial No. 142).

Blom, S. D., Lininger, R. S., & Charlesworth, W. R. (1987). Ecological observation of emotionally and behaviorally disordered students: An alternative method. *American Journal of Orthopsychiatry, 57,* 49–59.

Boehm, A. E., & Sandberg, B. R. (1982). Assessment

of the preschool child. In C. R. Reynolds and T. B. Gutkin (Eds.). *The Handbook of School Psychology*. NY: John Wiley & Sons, 82–120.

Bracken, B. A. (1987). Limitations of preschool instruments and standards for minimal levels of technical adequacy. *Journal of Psychoeducational Assessment, 5*, 313–326.

Brooks-Gunn, J., & Lewis, M. (1981). Assessing young handicapped children: Issues and solutions. *Journal of the Division for Early Childhood, 2*, 84–95.

Busch-Rossnagel, N. A., Hawryluk, M. K., & Pavone-Kennedy, M. (1983). Issues and considerations in the early identification of exceptional preschool children. *New Jersey Journal of School Psychology, 2*, 2–8.

Clarke, A. M. (1982). Developmental discontinuities: An approach to assessing their nature. In L. A. Bond and J. M. Joffe (Eds.). *Facilitating Infant and Early Childhood Development*. Hanover, NH: University Press of New England, 58–77.

Diamond, K. E. (1987). Predicting school problems from preschool developmental screening: A four-year follow-up of the Revised Denver Developmental Screening Test and the role of parent report. *Journal of the Division for Early Childhood, 11*, 247–253.

DuBose, R. F. (1981). Assessment of severely impaired young children: Problems and recommendations. *Topics in Early Childhood Special Education, 1*(2), 9–21.

DuBose, R. F. (1976). Predictive value of infant intelligence scales with multiply handicapped children. *American Journal of Mental Deficiency, 81*, 388–390.

Dunst, C. J., & Rheingrover, R. M. (1981). Discontinuity and instability in early development: Implications for assessment. *Topics in Early Childhood Special Education, 1*(2), 49–60.

Feuerstein, R. (1980). *Instrumental Enrichment*. Baltimore: University Park Press.

Feuerstein, R. (1979). *The Dynamic Assessment of Retarded Performers*. Baltimore: University Park Press.

Flapan, D., & Neubauer, P. B. (1970). Issues in assessing development. *Journal of the American Academy of Child Psychiatry, 9*, 669–687.

Gallagher, J. J., & Bradley, R. H. (1972). Early identification of developmental difficulties. In I. J. Gordon (Ed.). *Early Childhood Education: The Seventy-First Yearbook of the National Society for the Study of Education*. Chicago: University of Chicago Press, 87–122.

Garwood, S. G. (1982). (Mis)use of developmental scales in program evaluation. *Topics in Early Childhood Special Education, 1*, 61–69.

Glueck, E., & Glueck, S. (1966). Identification of potential delinquents at 2–3 years of age. *International Journal of Social Psychiatry, 12*, 5–16.

Goodman, J. F., & Cameron, J. (1978). The meaning of IQ constancy in young retarded children. *Journal of Genetic Psychology, 132*, 109–119.

Goodwin, W. L., & Driscoll, L. A. (1980). *Handbook for Measurement and Evaluation in Early Childhood Education*. San Francisco: Jossey-Bass.

Goodwin, W. L., & Goodwin, L. D. (1982). Measuring young children. In B. Spodeck (Ed.). *Handbook of Research in Early Childhood Education*. NY: The Free Press, 523–563.

Gotts, E. E. (1979): Early childhood assessment. In D. A. Sabatino and T. L. Miller (Eds.). *Describing Learner Characteristics of Handicapped Children and Youth*. NY: Grune & Stratton, 531–566.

Gredler, G. P. (1978). A look at some important factors in assessing readiness for school. *Journal of Learning Disabilities, 11*, 284–290.

Guralnick, M. J., & Weinhouse, E. (1983). Child-child social interactions: An analysis of assessment instruments for young children. *Exceptional Children, 50*(3), 268–271.

Guskin, S. L., Bartel, N. R., & MacMillan, D. L. (1975). Perspective of the labeled child. In N. Hobbs (Ed.). *Issues in The Classification of Children*. San Francisco: Jossey-Bass.

Hamilton, J. L., & Swan, W. W. (1981). Measurement references in the assessment of preschool handicapped children. *Topics in Early Childhood Special Education, 1*(2), 41–48.

Hobbs, N. (1975). *The Futures of Children*. San Francisco: Jossey-Bass.

Hourcade, J. J., & Parette, H. P., Jr. (1986). Early intervention programming: Correlates of progress. *Perceptual and Motor Skills, 62*, 58.

Hunt, J. McV., Kirk, G. E. (1974). Criterion-referenced tests of school readiness: A paradigm with illustrations. *Genetic Psychology Monographs, 90*, 143–182.

Hunt, J. V. (1986). Developmental risk in infants. *Advances in Special Education, 5*, 25–59.

Ilg, F. L., & Ames, L. B. (1965). *School Readiness: Behavior Tests Used at the Gesell Institute*. NY: Harper and Row.

Kaufman, A., & Kaufman, N. (1972). Tests built from Piaget's and Gesell's tasks as predictors of first grade achievement. *Child Development, 43*, 521–535.

Keith, T. Z. (1987). Assessment research: An assessment and recommended interventions. *School Psychology Review, 16*, 276–289.

Keogh, B. K. (1969). The Bender Gestalt with children: Research implications. *Journal of Special Education, 3*, 15–21.

Kohn, M., & Rosman, B. L. (1972). Relationship of preschool social-emotional functioning to later intellectual achievement. *Developmental Psychology, 6,* 445–452.

Kopp, C. (1983). Risk factors in development. In M. Haith and J. Campos (Eds.). Infancy and the biology of development (Vol. 2, pp. 1081–1188). In P. Mussen (Ed.). *Manual of Child Psychology.* NY: Wiley.

Lewis, M. (1975). The development of attention and perception in the infant and young child. In W. M. Cruikshank and K. P. Hallahan (Eds.). *Perceptual and Learning Disabilities in Children (Vol. 2).* Syracuse: NY: Syracuse University Press.

Lidz, C. S. (1981). *Improving Assessment of School Children.* San Francisco: Jossey-Bass.

Lidz, C. S. (Ed.) (1987). *Dynamic Assessment: An Interactional Approach to Evaluating Learning Potential.* NY: Guilford.

Linn, R. L. (1986). Educational testing and assessment: Research needs and policy issues. *American Psychologist, 41,* 1153–1160.

Lytton, H., Watts, D., & Dunn, B. E. (1986). Stability and predictability of cognitive and social characteristics from age 2 to age 9. *Genetic Psychology Monographs, 112,* 363–398.

MacMillan, D., & Meyers, C. E. (1979). Educational labeling of handicapped learners. In D. C. Berliner (Ed.). *Review of Research in Education (Volume 7).* American Educational Research Association.

MacTurk, R. H., & Neisworth, J. T. (1978). Norm-referenced and criterion based measures with preschoolers. *Exceptional Children, 48*(1), 34–39.

Marcovitch, S., & Simons, J. N. (1986). Social and behavioral problems in the preschool years. *Advances in Special Education, 5,* 121–146.

Martin, R. P. (1986). Assessment of the social and emotional functioning of preschool children. *School Psychology Review, 15*(2), 216–232.

Mastropieri, M. A. (1987). Age at start as a correlate of intervention effectiveness. *Psychology in the Schools, 24,* 59–62.

Mattick, I., & Murphy, L. B. (1971). Cognitive disturbances in young children. In J. Hellmuth (Ed.). *Cognitive Studies, 2: Deficits in Cognition.* NY: Brunner/Mazel, 280–323.

May, D. (1986). Relationships between the Gesell School Readiness Test and standardized achievement and intelligence measures. *Educational and Psychological Measurement, 46,* 1051–1059.

May, D., & Welch, E. (1984). Developmental placement: Does it prevent future learning problems? *Journal of Learning Disabilities, 17,* 338–341.

McCall, R. B., Hogarty, P. S., & Hurlburt, N. (1972). Transitions in infant sensorimotor development and prediction of childhood IQ. *American Psychologist, 27,* 728–748.

Meisels, S. J. (1987). Uses and abuses of developmental screening and school readiness testing. *Young Children, 42,* 4–9 and 68–73.

Mercer, C. D., Algozzine, B., & Trifiletti, J. J. (1979). Early identification issues and considerations. *Exceptional Children, 46,* 52–54.

Messer, D. J., McCarthy, M. E., McQueston, S., et al. (1986): Relation between mastery behavior in infancy and competence in early childhood. *Developmental Psychology, 22*(3), 366–372.

Meyers, C. E., & Dingman, H. F. (1960). The structure of abilities at the preschool ages: Hypothesized domains. *Psychological Bulletin, 57,* 514–532.

Moskowitz, D. S. (1986). Comparison of self-reports, reports by knowledgeable informants, and behavioral observation data. *Journal of Personality, 54*(1), 294–317.

Murphy, L. B., & Moriarty, A. E. (1976). *Vulnerability, Coping, and Growth From Infancy to Adolescence.* New Haven: Yale University Press.

Oakland, T. D., & Zimmerman, S. A. (1986). The course on individual mental assessment: A national survey of course instructors. *Professional School Psychology, 1*(1), 51–59.

Palisin, H. (1986). Preschool temperament and performance on achievement tests. *Developmental psychology, 22*(6), 766–770.

Palmer, J. O. (1983). *The psychological assessment of children.* NY: Wiley.

Ramey, C. T., Campbell, F. A., & Wasik, B. H. (1982). Use of standardized tests to evaluate early childhood special education programs. *Topics in Early Childhood Special Education, 1,* 51–60.

Richman, N., Stevenson, J., & Graham, P. J. (1982). Preschool to school: *A Behavioural Study.* NY: Academic Press.

Rolf, J. E., & Hasazi, J. E. (1977). Identification of preschool children at risk and some guidelines for primary intervention. In G. W. Albee and J. M. Joffe (Eds.). *Primary Prevention of Psychopathology, Volume I: The Issues.* Hanover, NH: University Press of New England, 122–152.

Rubin, R. A., Balow, B., Dorle, J., & Rosen, M. (1978). Preschool prediction of low achievement in basic school skills. *Journal of Learning Disabilities, 11,* 664–666.

Sigman, M., Cohen, S. E., Beckwith, L., & Parmalee, A. (1986). Infant attention in relation to intellectual abilities in childhood. *Developmental Psychology, 22,* 788–792.

Simeonsson, R. J., Huntington, G. S., & Parse, S. A. (1980). Expanding the developmental assessment of young handicapped children. In J. J. Gallagher (Ed.). *New Directions for Exceptional Children.* San Francisco: Jossey-Bass, 51–74.

Smith, B. J., & Schakel, J. A. (1986). Noncategorical

identification of preschool handicapped children: Policy issues and options. *Journal of the Division for Early Childhood, 11,* 78–86.

Stott, L. H., & Ball, R. S. (1965). Infant and preschool mental tests: Review and evaluation. *Monographs of the Society for Research in Child Development,* serial No. 101, *30*(3).

Ulrey, G., & Schnell, R. R. (1982). Introduction to assessing young children. In G. Ulrey and S. J. Rogers (Eds.): *Psychological Assessment of Handicapped Infants and Young Children.* NY: Thieme-Stratton.

Uphoff, J. K., & Gilmore, J. (1986). Pupil age at school entrance-how many are ready for success? *Young Children,* January, 11–16.

Vanderveer, B., & Scheweid, E. (1974). Infant assessment: Stability of mental functioning in young retarded children. *American Journal of Mental Deficiency, 79,* 1–4.

Wilson, R. S. (1985). Risk and resilience in early mental development. *Developmental Psychology, 21,* 795–805.

Wood, P. S., Powell, S., & Knight, R. (1984). Predicting school readiness; The validity of developmental age. *Journal of Learning Disabilities, 17,* 8–11.

3

The Individual Assessment Situation: Basic Considerations for Preschool-Age Children

KATHLEEN D. PAGET

The assessment of preschool-age children in a one-to-one situation provides an opportunity to observe a child's interactions with the examiner and materials in a particular setting. Within the spirit of Bandura's (1978) reciprocal determinism model, the examiner's own personal characteristics and behavior interact with characteristics and behaviors of the child, and these variables both influence and are influenced by the environmental conditions of the surroundings. Although necessarily limited by particular setting and temporal variables, observations and test results from individualized interaction with young children offer a useful complement to observations and interview information concerning children's functioning in other settings. The purpose of this chapter is twofold: to delineate special considerations related to the behavior of preschool-age children, the examiner's behavior, and characteristics of the surroundings; and to specify special adaptations to consider when evaluating children who have certain handicapping conditions.

The Examiner

The impression given by the examiner's appearance, demeanor, and behavior often affects the child's attitude toward the assessment. It is of paramount importance that an examiner of preschool children appreciates young children and displays great patience and ingenuity. It is important to act independently of prescribed formulas and to be a diagnostic investigator tracking down subtle difficulties that interfere with a child's ability to learn and function adequately. While remaining outwardly calm and relaxed, the examiner must be alert and adjust readily to any deviations in the child's behavior. Such adjustments involve decelerating or accelerating the tempo of the evaluation to meet the child's needs, removing materials skillfully, and presenting the next task quickly, thus creating a smooth transition between subtests and tests. The examiner must be sufficiently skilled to maintain the child's attention, present test materials, and record responses as well as observe and record the child's behavior in a relaxed fashion.

Certainly, a relaxed attitude, flexibility, and humor are requisite features of an examiner's repertoire of skills when evaluating young children (McLinden, 1987). Young children are often less able than older children to adapt to the evaluation situation, and test results are influenced by normal preschool characteristics such as distractibility, fatigue, restlessness, shyness, and dependency. Young children often do not conform to the "expected" behavioral patterns of older children, and they are less influenced than older children by extrinsic motives such as competition or a desire to measure up to a given standard. To adapt to such features of young children's behavior, examiners need to be flexible in how they format the assessment sessions. For example, tasks requiring close visual or auditory attention might need to be alternated with more play-like tasks requiring less concentration, such as those involving fine and gross motor movement.

Very young preschool children are apt to accept the requirements and demands of a testing situation with little question if they are evaluated at school or in other familiar surroundings. If questions arise about why the child must accompany the examiner, the issues should be discussed easily with the child in a matter-of-fact way. Because most young children are accustomed to accepting the requests of adult authority figures, assuming confidently that the child will come willingly to the testing room usually is enough to bring about that result. Raising the question of whether the child wants to come with the examiner only creates the opportunity for indecision and possible refusal. It is surprisingly easy for young children to adjust to a structured situation as long as specific expectations are set by the examiner and the assessment tasks are within the child's capacity. A very resistant child might need special allowances, such as to remain standing until he or she is comfortable, understands the requirements of the tasks, or is less threatened by the examining situation. Allowances of this sort greatly ease the introduction of the assessment process, facilitate the establishment of rapport, and demonstrate to the child that he or she has opportunities for input during the evaluation.

The examiner should be careful not to startle the child by talking too loudly or by being too formal and should be alert to the child's reactions to the assessment process. Although it is important to be less formal than when working with older children or adults, the examiner of the pre-

school child should avoid "baby talk" and should be aware of the tendency for one's voice to become slightly saccharine when interacting with young children. At the same time, it is important for the examiner to reduce his or her vocabulary to a preschool level without talking down to the child. Using too many "adult" words will only confuse the child, elicit puzzled looks, and interfere with the youngster's ability to comprehend the examiner's request.

The examiner should be prepared to move around during the evaluation of preschoolers. Physical contact used judiciously is an effective means of communicating with preschool children. Most young children respond well to an examiner who picks them up to comfort them when necessary, takes a playful poke at them, gets down on the floor to play, puts an arm around their shoulders, or takes their hand when entering or leaving the examining room. Physical contact particularly is effective with children experiencing hearing, visual, or language impairments, as well as children confined to wheelchairs. Because of their impairments, such children might need more assurance about the examining situation and the examiner's acceptance of them. Although physical contact can be effective, it can also be inappropriate; young children might use hugging, grabbing, and holding onto the examiner as a form of manipulation. It is important to strike a balance between formality and informality, to be friendly yet professional, and to accept warmly the child's natural physical contacts without encouraging dependency, manipulative behaviors, or silliness.

Establishing and Maintaining Rapport

Building and maintaining rapport while adhering to standardized procedures is somewhat of a juggling act for even the most experienced examiner. It is important to allow the child time to become accustomed to the examining situation before beginning the evaluation. Underdeveloped social skills, anxiety, and lack of comprehension of the purpose of testing all can result in reticence and withdrawal, even in gregarious young children. Children experiencing an assessment vary greatly in their level of preparation for the new experience. A good, positive introduction to the evaluation is to tell the child that the examiner is going to show him or her some puzzles and blocks, and ask some questions. Because of the fear it provokes in some children, the examiner should avoid the word "test." If the child asks, the examiner should not deny that the activity is a test. A response such as "Yes, it is a new and different kind, not like school tests" is appropriate (McCarthy, 1972, p. 45). Games that encourage children's imagination and draw on their desire to pretend are often good activities for breaking the ice and encouraging verbal expression. The examiner should keep in mind that no one technique or activity is suitable for all children; however, all children do need to feel assured that they are safe and that everything will be all right. Excitable children might need a combination of reassurance and a quiet, calming activity; shy children might do better with an activity that is very engaging.

The examiner should interact with children who have limited verbal skills by responding in a friendly manner and using few words to reduce the child's perceived pressure to speak. If the child is verbally expressive, the examiner should respond in kind. Attending sensitively to the child and reviewing pertinent referral information regarding the child's developmental history will provide the examiner an indication of the child's verbal capacities.

Capturing a young child's attention is one task; maintaining it is another. Providing frequent praise for a child's effort early in the evaluation often is a helpful technique for maintaining attentiveness. Similarly, evaluation tasks such as block building or drawing are inherently more childlike and interesting than others and can provide a good aid in initially gaining the child's attention. For tasks that do not appear to be intrinsically interesting, the examiner must manage to keep the child's attention long enough for the child to become interested. The examiner should be watchful for the first sign of discouragement, such as a sigh or a verbal signal (e.g., "When are we going to be finished?"). This should be a cue to the examiner to praise liberally the efforts of the child and to indicate that there still are many "fun things remaining."

Motivation also can be encouraged with an understanding smile, a spontaneous exclamation of approval, a pat on the head, or an appreciative comment. Spontaneity, enthusiasm, and the timing of feedback are important motivational factors for preschool children. Repetitive and stereo-typed comments, such as "you're working hard" soon become perfunctory and lose their reinforcement value. Likewise, if praise is given too frequently and generously, it no longer fits naturally into the conversational flow and can defeat its intended purpose. The examiner should remember that to be effective, praise should be given warmly for effort displayed by the child and not for particular successes.

When attempts to maintain a child's motivation are unsuccessful, it is sometimes helpful to establish a reward system so he or she can look forward to playing with certain toys after completing the required tasks. Many children are surprisingly skilled in their attempts to "test" and distract the examiner. The examiner must be alert to the possibility that a young child's eagerness to proceed to something more to his or her liking can result in offhand responses given with minimal effort rather than responses that represent best efforts. In such a situation, the child's behavior should be explicitly acknowledged and addressed to prevent further attempts to control the examining situation. Under no circumstances should the examiner disapprove of or show dissatisfaction with the child's earnest responses, although it might be necessary to challenge the child and redirect flippant answers or those given with only minimal effort. As with lapses in motivation, both discouragement and flippancy on the part of a preschool child necessitate that the examiner exude enthusiasm, while providing sufficient limits and structure within which the child can respond appropriately.

The motive behind a child's behaviors at times might be unclear, requiring the examiner to "read" carefully the child's intent. For example, young children can demonstrate a lack of cooperation in a variety of ways, and responses such as "I don't know" or "I can't" might really mean "I don't want to" or "I am afraid to try." Similarly, responses such as "You do it" or "You show me" might indicate emotional dependency on adults rather than real inability. A negative shake of the head accompanied by "I won't" or "I don't want to" might not be stubbornness or lack of cooperation; the child, indeed, might not know the answer. Furthermore, an admission of not knowing an answer can be very painful to a bright, sensitive, and otherwise cooperative child, requiring a supportive comment from the examiner such as "No one is expected to know all of the answers." Familiarity with the tasks to be administered and a great deal of experience with young children should enhance the examiner's skill in understanding the child's feelings and differentiating true failure from resistance.

Children who refuse to cooperate, are too frightened to respond, or are easily fatigued might require multiple assessment sessions and should be excused from the testing with a comment such as "We will do this another day." Making an additional comment regarding other activities that are "lots of fun" and continuing to exude enthusiasm might create a basis for increased cooperation on the second occasion. The examiner must possess a high degree of judgment and sensitivity, as well as knowledge of and regard for scientific methods, when deciding whether the evaluation session should be continued or rescheduled. An essential consideration in determining the length of any assessment session for a young child is not to make it too long. When the required tasks are novel and interesting and several "breaks" have been taken during the session, fatigue is not too likely to interfere significantly with a child's test performance. The duration of the evaluation depends to a large extent on the examiner's experience with preschool assessment, the child's responsiveness to the tasks presented, and the purpose of a specific evaluation.

Surroundings

Thoughtful preparation of the assessment room and materials facilitates the evaluation process. Specific adaptations must be made to optimize the functioning of children representing various handicapping conditions and degrees of severity. For mildly impaired children, the room should be large enough to accommodate a table, adjustable in height, on which the child can work comfortably. For more severely impaired children, accommodations must be made for conducting the evaluation on the floor. For all children, space should be available for both structured and unstructured interactions among the child, the examiner, the materials, and other family members or caregivers. The most desirable assessment room is one that is not too unfamiliar to the child, where he or she feels at ease, and where distracting stimuli are at a minimum. Certainly,

the examiner should not have to answer the telephone or protect papers from an extremely distractible and very active child! Likewise, the examiner who wears an excessive amount of jewelry can distract naturally curious preschoolers. Children should not be made to feel that they are solely in the adult's domain with the formality of desks, file cabinets, or the appearance a medical examining room. On the other hand, a playroom with too many toys and windows might encourage a child to avoid tasks that are presented.

Use of materials designed specifically for preschool children, such as large crayons instead of pencils, should be used and will lend an appropriately childlike atmosphere. The room should be appropriate for gross motor activities on the part of the examiner and the children. Give particular attention to ensuring that the room is brightly lit and has proper acoustics. Rooms that are completely soundproof might be necessary for some neurologically impaired and extremely distractible children. In addition, because young children's body temperatures tend to be a few degrees warmer than those of adults, set the room temperature a few degrees lower than what might normally be comfortable for an adult. Should it be necessary to conduct the assessment in a clinic, make sure the assessment room is close enough to a waiting room so the child can be reassured that a parent is nearby. Inviting significant others (e.g., parents, siblings, teachers) into the assessment room for a portion of the evaluation often yields invaluable results. Such a situation provides an opportunity to observe interaction patterns, and the examiner might discover unique strategies developed by caregivers for communicating with the child. With such observations, the examiner is in a much better position to develop intervention plans that involve significant others in functional, meaningful ways.

ADAPTATIONS FOR PRESCHOOL CHILDREN WITH SPECIFIC HANDICAPPING CONDITIONS

Although specific issues related to the evaluation of handicapped children are discussed in other chapters, a general overview of some basic considerations is provided here. Each child has unique needs that require the examiner to adapt the evaluation situation. Some preschoolers with handicapping conditions might be able to relate to the examiner and the evaluation situation, but might not be able to perform many of the assessment tasks. Such children are those with mild to moderate physical, auditory, visual, or language and speech handicaps; or children experiencing problems from brain injuries or mental retardation. Children with severe and multiple disabilities might be able to relate only minimally to the examiner or to the assessment situation. Children with problems created by different language and cultural backgrounds, or a severe yet transient emotional strain (e.g., from a recent hospitalization) also might relate minimally. Whatever behaviors and characteristics the child brings to the evaluation session, the examiner should make every attempt to adjust and optimize the assessment results. On some occasions, it might become necessary to reschedule the session and provide parents with a tentative report of the child's behavior and performance.

Although the examiner's observations of the child's behavior are important in the accurate assessment of any preschooler, such observations take on even greater importance in the assessment of a youngster with a specific handicapping condition. Children who are unaccustomed to long periods of concentrated work can fatigue easily, and attentional deficiencies related to a handicapping condition can interfere with the evaluation. Some handicaps, such as speech, language, and hearing deficits, can "mask" a child's true intellectual ability, and feelings of dependency and inadequacy can be communicated by statements such as "I can't do that." As stated earlier, such statements must be judged by the examiner and a decision made as to the child's intent. In many cases, with encouragement, a child with a handicapping condition can succeed at an activity never before attempted. The demand characteristics of the setting, the specific behaviors exhibited by the child with a particular handicap, and the conditions influencing success and failure comprise essential components of our observations.

Some general suggestions for conducting successful and complete evaluations of children with handicapping conditions have been made (Haeussermann, 1958). Children who display resistance and negativism should be given structured choices of activities rather than open-ended questions or directions that are easier to refuse. It is important to involve frightened children in the evaluation process immediately to allay anxieties raised by the assessment materials and the examiner. Similarly, shy, nonverbal children should begin the evaluation with performance-type material to avoid the frustration caused by demanding use of the less preferred verbal modality. With some excessively shy preschoolers, the examiner might need to communicate the directions for the early tasks through a nonthreatening medium such as a doll or puppet. Furthermore, to maintain the attention of very distractible and hyperactive children, it is necessary that the examiner present materials and administer subtests as quickly as possible, keeping the pace brisk. It also might help for the examiner to touch the child supportively, especially during verbal items, when touching will not interfere with the child's manipulation of test materials. For children whose physical or language handicap prevents them from responding verbally, it might be necessary to devise a nonverbal alternative response such as a smile or an upward turning of eyes for affirmation, and a frown or a sidewise turning of the eyes for negation. Some children with speech and language disorders will need more time for responding, slower paced directions, or the opportunity to lipread or attend to other visual cues presented by the examiner. Preschoolers with behavior disorders require tighter structure, more limits on their behavior, and more reminders of the consequences of their actions.

Indeed, young children with handicapping conditions, particularly those with multiple handicaps, challenge the examiner to find the children's best means of expression, to evaluate their strengths, and minimize as much as possible the interference caused by their handicapping conditions. Handicapping conditions of various types or degrees of severity present the examiner with such a variety of factors to consider that it is important to review in greater detail the various adaptations necessary for the successful assessment of children with specific handicapping conditions. The reader should bear in mind that many of the strategies discussed are appropriate across various handicapping conditions and that the following discussion is organized by handicapping condition only for purposes of clarity.

Children with Physical Handicaps

Remember that physically handicapped children might be more self-conscious than nonhandicapped children, and that their reactions to the assessment situation depend largely on their self-confidence and how they perceive their own abilities. The examiner must first determine the ability of a physically handicapped child to respond to the various demands of the evaluation. Specific abilities or inabilities can be identified through the referral information, by talking briefly with the child's parents, teachers, and other professionals who have interacted with the child, and through informal observation of the child's speech, balance, arm–hand use, and gestural abilities.

Some physically impaired children have poor head or body balance and require a special chair that has supportive "wings," or a seat belt for extra body support. Children who are unable to sit at all might need to have test items administered while they remain lying down. Other children might be limited in their eye focus, requiring the examiner to change positions and move assessment materials directly into the child's field of vision. Some physically impaired children, such as those with cerebral palsy, are at a distinct disadvantage when time limits are imposed. Large writing utensils should be given to children who have limited coordination. Tables should be adjusted to accommodate the needs of children confined to wheelchairs. Even with these modifications and adaptations, the examiner still might feel uncertain whether the child's subtest failures were the result of physical disability or limited intellectual ability.

Children with Visual Impairments

Blind and visually or perceptually impaired children often use tactile clues, with or without auditory clues, along with their memory and verbal reasoning skills to compensate for the insufficiency of their vision. Certainly, the examiner should rely more heavily, and sometimes exclusively, on the results of verbal items that assess verbal and tactile skills to estimate the true intellectual ability of such children. Furthermore, with partially sighted children it is imperative to determine whether they typically wear glasses or use other visual aids, and then make certain that the

assessment situation approximates optimal conditions as much as possible.

Children with Hearing Impairments

Deaf and hearing-impaired children are likely to seek visual clues to enhance their test performance, thus making it essential to provide adequate lighting and position the children properly to view the examiner's facial expressions and gestures. Nonverbal clues should be offered to facilitate children's understanding of test directions. Some very young children might not have acquired any compensatory skills and will be unable to comprehend either visually or auditorily, while other children might have learned to interpret lip movements. To determine the degree to which a child is able to compensate for a hearing impairment, the child's responses should be compared when the examiner speaks in a normal tone with his or her mouth covered to those responses made when the examiner merely moves his or her lips without making a sound. Be aware that deaf and hearing-impaired children often have learned socially appropriate communication behaviors such as smiling and nodding when spoken to. These otherwise appropriate behaviors can create the impression that the children understand what is being communicated when, in fact, they might not. Examiners who evaluate hearing-impaired preschoolers would be wise to learn the international hand signal language because some deaf children understand language only through that medium.

Distinguishing between deafness, aphasia, autism, and retardation sometimes presents an interesting challenge for an examiner, because indifference to or difficulty in understanding language is a common result of all four conditions. One simple clinical technique for determining hearing loss, offered by Haeussermann (1958), consists of the examiner drawing his or her fingers over the teeth of a comb held unobtrusively under the table. A child who is deaf or has a severe hearing loss will not hear the sound, while a child with aphasia, autistim, or retardation (or a child with a mild hearing loss) might search for the source of the sound. Furthermore, a child who seems unable to hear during the testing situation might reveal an ability to hear a familiar sound at a later time, such as when he or she hears a parent approaching as the evaluation draws to a close.

Further complications arise when a child has multiple involvements. A physically impaired child who also has a hearing impairment, for example, might be unable to raise his or her head and lip-read outside the restricted field of vision imposed by the handicap. This situation makes it necessary for the examiner to adjust his or her position relative to the child so as to remain in the child's field of vision at all times. A child who speaks a different language from the examiner can be approached somewhat similarly to a deaf child, through gestures, pictures, or pantomime. Under many circumstances, however, it is necessary to secure the services of a translator.

Children with Mental Retardation

Children whose cognitive functioning is well below that of their age mates occasionally exhibit negative and resistant behaviors as a means of maintaining their self-esteem in the face of difficult intellectual demands (Haeussermann, 1958). Thus, such children might become aggressive, hyperactive, or use denial as a means of covering feelings of vulnerability. Although most mentally impaired children respond favorably to standardized testing, it is important to reduce the probability of negative behaviors by beginning the evaluation with easy tasks that guarantee success and by alternating difficult tasks with easier ones. Severely impaired children might exhibit autistic-like behavior at the beginning of an evaluation because of their anxiety and fear, but are more likely than a truly autistic child to warm up gradually to the examiner and to the assessment situation.

Children with Neurological Impairments

Children with neurological impairments present a wide variety of problems (Haeussermann, 1958). Some exhibit hyperactivity, whereas others are more lethargic. Some are verbally expressive, whereas others are quiet. Some are visibly anxious, whereas others appear comfortable. These behaviors vary according to the degree and location of the neurological impairment.

In the beginning of the session, the examiner might wish to present the child with a choice of warm-up material unrelated to the assessment; or the examiner might begin to play with a toy nonchalantly, giving the impression that the child is encouraged but not pressured to join in the play. Another technique for enlisting cooperation and encouraging participation consists of nonchalantly "spilling" blocks or other toys into a corner of the examining room to pique the child's interest. Most children will become involved in an activity if they do not feel pushed. Watching carefully to assess whether the child wishes to play along with the examiner and respecting that wish can determine the course of the assessment. Humor is an effective means of "breaking the ice" with a resistant or fearful preschooler with neurological impairments, and the examiner might find that putting him- or herself in a midly ridiculous position or making a friendly joke will cause the child to laugh and feel more comfortable.

It is important to remember that children with neurological impairments might need more time than most to organize their responses and need to proceed at their own pace. They can become emotionally labile when they can no longer cope with test demands and can give aberrant responses to resist various stages of the evaluation. If a child is unusually difficult to work with and no strategy or amount of encouragement seems to work, the evaluation should be rescheduled.

Children with Behavior Disorders

The evaluation of preschoolers who exhibit behavioral disorders challenges the abilities of even the most capable examiner. Several evaluation sessions might be necessary to ensure that the children are comfortable; however, it is important to make every effort to complete the evaluation during the first session to communicate the message that the examiner is in control of the examining situation. Children who exhibit psychosis, perhaps, are the most difficult to evaluate because their preoccupations frequently interfere with their ability to comprehend and follow instructions. It is imperative when evaluating such preschoolers to avoid indicating the child's failure, to introduce new tasks and materials slowly, and to stop the evaluation if the child's emotional lability becomes too severe. When evaluating a hyperactive child, it is important to keep unused materials out of the child's reach and field of vision. To reduce distractions, the work table should face a relatively blank wall rather than a window, and the examiner should provide the child with a great deal of structure. It is often helpful to give the child the impression that both the examiner and the child will have to tackle the job together in a joint effort. The evaluation should include built-in "breaks" to provide the child opportunity to look out the window or put used test materials away. Because the evaluation is the time for identifying and not retraining deep-seated behavioral difficulties, the examiner should not be a disciplinarian. The examiner should use the child's excessive energy by presenting test items in rapid, smooth succession. It also is somewhat soothing for the child when the examiner touches his or her hands or arms in a calming way. Finally, because hyperactivity frequently is a concomitant symptom of hearing, visual, or neurological impairments, the examiner should attend to the possibility that a sensory or neurological impairment might be contributing to the child's activity level.

SUMMARY

The successful evaluation of preschooler children, especially handicapped preschoolers requires special expertise. The suggestions in this chapter are meant to serve as guidelines, certainly not rigid rules, for the individual evaluation of very young children. The ability to create flexible variations on these suggestions to meet the needs of individual preschoolers should be considered the hallmark of a competent examiner. Though some examiners have a natural ability to relate well to very young children, others can develop the necessary flexibility and relaxed manner only after many hours of observation and interaction with young children. Regardless of the examiner's experience, it is certain that evaluations of children between the ages of 2 and 6 years will always prove interesting and challenging.

REFERENCES

Bandura, A. (1978). The self-system is reciprocal determinism. *American Psychologist, 33,* 344–358.

Haeussermann, E. (1985). *Developmental potential for preschool children.* New York: Grune & Stratton.

McCarthy, D. (1972). *McCarthy Scales for Children's Abilities: Manual.* San Antonio, TX: The Psychological Corporation.

McLinden, S. (1987, November). Flexibility and humor important in the assessment of preschoolers. *Communique,* p. 6.

4

The Clinical Observation of Preschool Assessment Behavior

BRUCE A. BRACKEN

Anastasi (1988) defined a psychological test as ". . . essentially an objective and standardized measure of a sample of behavior" (p. 23). Psychoeducational assessment, on the other hand, encompasses much more than merely the administration of tests. Assessment is a multifaceted process that incorporates the use of formal and informal devices such as classroom tests and products, standardized tests, rating scales, as well as a variety of procedures, including direct test administration, interviews, and clinical observations and judgments. The focus of this chapter is on the importance and use of clinical observations during the assessment of preschool children.

Psychological tests, as objective and standardized samples of behavior, have many assets. Typically tests provide the examiner with several convenient bits of diagnostic information, including discernable profiles of performance, standard scores, percentile ranks, and age and grade equivalents. Tests also are expected to meet some minimal levels of technical adequacy (AERA, APA, NCME, 1985; Bracken, 1987). Clinical observations and judgments, in comparison, are frequently less objective and standardized than tests, and they allow for much more professional disagreement and debate. Clinically derived observations have no published norms, standard scores, percentile ranks, or age and grade equivalents, and the reliability, validity, and interpretations of assessment observations and interpretations frequently are questioned.

It is much easier for a practitioner to defend decisions made on the basis of test data than it is to defend judgments made on behavior observed and interpreted in a clinical fashion. On the other hand, some concerns with psychoeducational assessment seem to have stemmed from the practice of blindly using test scores for making programmatic and placement decisions about children without the full use of clinical observations, judgments, and common sense.

Clinical observations represent one critical aspect of the assessment process that can lead to a fuller understanding of the child and the child's test performance. Observations should be employed to describe and explain children's test and nontest behaviors, attest to the validity or invalidity of test scores, at least partially explain children's variable test performance, lend support for diagnosis and remediation strategies made on the basis of standardized test results, and provide the examiner with information needed to develop specific hypotheses concerning a child's learning style and individual strengths and weaknesses.

This focus on clinical observations and judgment does not imply that the issues related to subjectivity, reliability, and validity associated with observations should be ignored; rather, it is recognized that diagnosticians must develop objective, reliable, and valid observational skills. Clinical skill must compliment the use of standardized tests if diagnosticians are to make accurate diagnoses, prognostic statements, and recommendations for the remediation of young children's deficiencies.

NORMAL PRESCHOOL BEHAVIOR

When a child is described by parents and teachers as distractible, impulsive, easily frustrated, and emotionally labile, psychologists frequently consider such tentative diagnostic hypothesis as minimal brain dysfunction, emotional disturbance, learning disabilities, or similar conditions. Although behavioral descriptors of this sort frequently are cited as soft signs for neurological impairment or severe emotional disturbance among older children, the same behaviors often characterize many normal children between the ages of 2 and 6.

Normalcy is especially difficult to define among young children. During the preschool years social, physical, and cognitive development occurs at a rapid rate and the range of development among normal preschool children is great. As children increase in age their rate of development decreases and the range of behaviors among normal children likewise decreases. It is sometimes difficult to differentiate mildly handicapped preschool children from normal preschoolers (hence the preference for such descriptors as developmental delay rather than retardation), whereas older children with mild handicaps are more easily identified. Preschool children, for example, typically exhibit higher energy levels, less self-control, and much more physical activity than socialized school-age children; at what point does an energetic and active preschooler cease being considered normal and begin to be considered abnormal? Because there are no norms that give a clear indication of normal energy levels (or other behaviors) for children of various ages, the question is impossible to answer; experience and "internalized" norms guide most clinicians in the determination of whether the child's behavior is exhibited with more intensity, frequency, or in longer duration than is typical.

ENVIRONMENTAL EFFECTS

It is often assumed that a child's behavior during an evaluation is similar to the child's home or classroom behavior. In many cases this assumption is invalid. Test behavior should never be interpreted unconditionally as being representative of a child's typical behavior in any other setting. The dynamics of an evaluation are much different from those of a typical preschool, day care, kindergarten, or home environment. Even with older children it should not be assumed that assessment behavior is typical behavior; but preschool children especially have had little contact with schools, teachers, authority figures other than parents, and the extensive probing, questioning, and the formality that is part of a psychoeducational evaluation. Thus, the preschool child's test behavior often can be specific to the evaluation and generalize poorly to other assessment sessions or nonassessment situations.

It is not uncommon that when teachers or parents hear the diagnostician's description of the child's behavior during an evaluation, they respond that the examiner must not have seen the child's typical behavior. The evaluation setting provides enough structure and personal attention to keep some children eagerly on task, while other youngsters resist the structure and formality, and refuse to participate in the assessment process or participate only half-heartedly. The unfamiliar adult-child interactions, materials, and settings that are part of psychoeducational evaluations can frighten or intimidate some children, whereas other youngsters can respond positively to the novel situation and personal attention.

Psychoeducational evaluations are extremely structured events. Children are directed to do as the examiner instructs; test items, whether enjoyable or not, must be attempted, and the abundance of test rules and directions have an effect on the child's behavior. Although psychoeducational assessments frequently are described by examiners as "fun games," it becomes readily apparent to most preschool children that the examiner is more interested in the child's performance than "having fun." There are very few occasions in a preschooler's life when time and behavior are as structured and controlled as during psychoeducational evaluations. Because atypical behavior can be a common occurrence during an evaluation, test behavior should be noted and interpreted cautiously by diagnosticians so that inappropriate generalizations about the child's behavior are not made.

Situational structure and interpersonal interactions are but two possible environmental influences on a child's evaluation behavior. The examiner should be sensitive to the effects of a wide variety of environmental influences on the child's performance. To develop a better understanding of the child's typical behavior, the examiner should observe the child in a variety of environments and contrast the child's nonevaluation behavior with behavior observed during testing. The diagnostician should observe the child in the preschool classroom during structured and unstructured activities that require a wide range of behaviors, including quiet listening, active and passive individual and group participation, learning activities, cooperation, sharing, and interactions with peers and adults. Observations also should be made while the child is involved in free play on the playground for a more total picture of the child's typical behavior. If clinical observations are made in a variety of settings, the diagnostician will have a greater sample of behavior from which diagnostic inferences can be more reliably made.

SPECIFIC BEHAVIORS AND BEHAVIORAL TRENDS

To evaluate a child's behavior, the examiner must notice specific behaviors and integrate them into meaningful behavioral trends. Because the length of the evaluation provides a relatively small sample of behavior, the observer must look carefully for noteworthy behavioral trends. Frequently diagnosticians come away from an evaluation with a "feeling" about the child as a result of observing specific behaviors that together formed a behavioral trend. Undocumented and unsupported feelings about a child's behavior, however, are not enough. It is the task of the diagnostician to observe, note, and integrate assessment and nonassessment behavior so that when behavioral trends are reported they are sufficiently supported with specific observed behaviors. Rather than merely reporting that a child was fearful during the evaluation, for example, the examiner should support this claim with instances when the child's "fearful" behavior was exhibited. If the child withdrew from the examiner's touch, began to weep silently during an attempt to build rapport, spoke hesitantly in a shaky and quiet voice, was startled when the examiner placed test materials on the table, and avoided direct eye contact with the examiner, the behavioral trend described as "fearful" would be well documented and easily supported. Most professionals would agree that a young child who exhibited these or similar behaviors indeed appeared to be frightened.

It also is important to document support of behavioral trends for later reference. If diagnosticians are questioned months later about behavioral judgments, it is much easier to support the existence of behavioral trends if the child's specific behaviors also were observed and recorded during the evaluation. Likewise, when children are reevaluated some time after the initial evaluation, it is helpful to contrast the child's specific behaviors across time.

Specific behaviors should be noted not to identify only trends of behavior but also should be examined carefully to identify behaviors that are inconsistent with the general trends. Inconsistent specific behaviors often form subtrends that give an indication of less obvious, yet important, strengths, weaknesses, fears, likes, dislikes, and so on. A child who smiles frequently, converses freely, jokes and teases with the examiner, readily complies with the examiner's requests, and spontaneously laughs and sings during an evaluation likely would be identified as a friendly and cooperative child. The same child, however, might at times exhibit mild resistance, express a desire to terminate the evaluation, and require occasional redirection and encouragement. If the antecedent conditions for these incongruent specific behaviors are scrutinized, a diagnostically important behavioral subtrend might emerge. For instance, the child might find the verbal exchange with the examiner enjoyable but might have an aversion to tasks that require visual-motor integration. If the pattern of incongruent resistant behaviors is considered in the context of the tasks being performed, the examiner should see that this typically friendly preschooler becomes resistant only when faced with activities requiring visual-motor integration. Observations of this sort, combined with qualitative test data, might provide concomitant evidence for a diagnostic claim of relative weakness in that area.

INABILITY VERSUS UNWILLINGNESS

One distinction that should be made through the use of behavioral observations is whether a child failed individual test items because of an inability to complete the task successfully or because of an unwillingness to attempt the task. It is not uncommon for shy preschoolers to refuse to attempt assessment tasks, especially motor activities that require active physical participation and verbal tasks that require extensive vocalization. In such a case, the diminished subtest score has the effect of lowering the scale score (e.g., Verbal or Performance Scale, Simultaneous or Sequential Scale) as well as the total test score (e.g., IQ, MPC). Moreover, the skill assessed by the subtest might be identified inappropriately as an area of weakness relative to the child's other abilities because of the low score. An alternative in this instance would be to attest to the invalidity of the subtest, prorate the scale and total test scores, and suggest reevaluation of the skill at a later date.

It is imperative that the diagnostician be more than a test giver. If behavioral observations are used properly to distinguish between a child's inability and unwillingness to perform tasks, the diagnostician will avoid making foolish statements about the child's relative weaknesses and the need for unnecessary remediation.

DESCRIBING WHAT IS SEEN

Diagnosticians frequently view the purpose of the evaluation as the identification of a child's difficulties so that the child can be properly serviced by the school or agency. In many instances this is the function of a diagnostician, because most preschool referrals are made by parents or preschool teachers who perceive problems in the child's development or adjustment. However, this deficit model of evaluation often results in a biased orientation toward behavioral observations. Rather than observing actual assessment behavior, many diagnosticians observe and report on the absence of behavior; noting, for example, that a child was "neither overly active nor impulsive during the assessment process." To say that a child was not overly active nor impulsive provides the parent or teacher with little useful information. It usually is inferred from statements such as these that no problems were noted in the areas mentioned; however, when it is reported that a specific behavior was not observed, the person informed is left to imagine where on a continuum of behavior the child actually performed. If a child is "not overly active," it cannot be safely inferred that the child was moderately active or even appropriately active. Without an accurate description of the child's actual behavior, one cannot safely infer anything except that the child was "not overly active."

Preferably, the examiner should note exactly what the child does and then describe and interpret the behavior in accurate and descriptive terms. Rather than describing a child as neither overly active nor impulsive, a more clear image of the child is communicated when the examiner notes that the child eagerly performed all tasks presented, yet waited patiently for instructions to be read, materials to be readied, and the examiner's direction to begin. In this instance the diagnostician could have characterized the child as interested and patient (or used similar descriptors) and then provided sufficient support for the positively stated clinical judgment.

BEHAVIORAL INFERENCES

Too often, psychoeducational reports contain behavioral observations that are a running chronology that fail to draw any meaningful inferences. Merely reporting what a child did during an evaluation without also providing an interpretation of that behavior in the context of the evaluation environment is insufficient. It sometimes is tempting to cite only what was actually observed during an evaluation rather than interpret the behavior because interpretations and inferences are much more subject to professional disagreement than are behavioral citings; but this temptation should be resisted. The value of behavioral interpretations by far outweighs the difficulties that arise from professional disagreement.

Eye contact, for instance, is a behavior that diagnosticians are fond of reporting, but frequently do not interpret. It is fairly common that examiners will report in a psychoeducational report that the child made, or failed to make, eye contact throughout the evaluation. What is the significance of this observation? Alone, it is meaningless; yet when coupled with an inferential interpretation this observation provides relevant and meaningful information. The possible explanations for a child's continued (or absence of) eye contact are numerous, and selecting the appropriate interpretation is important. Did the child make eye contact in an effort to secure assurance from the examiner that the child's test performance was acceptable? Was the eye contact hostile in nature and used as a nonverbal, passive–aggressive message of resistance? Was eye contact made with teary eyes, suggesting fear and a desire to terminate the evaluation session? Did the child make eye contact with eyes that expressed a lack of understanding and a need for a slower pace and greater explanation? Or, did the child's continued eye contact inform the examiner that the evaluation was viewed positively by the youngster? The answers to these questions are not found solely in the observation of eye contact, but are answered through the compilation of other specific facial and nonfacial behaviors that form a meaningful behavioral trend.

MEANINGFUL COMMUNICATION OF BEHAVIORAL OBSERVATIONS

The ability to communicate the meaning of a child's behavior to the child's parents, teachers, and others is an important and necessary assessment skill. To do this, examiners must expand their repertoire of behavioral descriptors and describe children's behavior in terms that reflect accurately not only the frequency, intensity, and du-

ration of the child's behavior, but also the spirit in which the behavior was performed.

To report that a child walked around the room during the rapport-building phase of the evaluation only minimally describes the child's behavior. The reason for the child's walking and the intensity of the behavior are unclear. Was the child interested in exploring the new environment? Was the child afraid and unready to sit? Was the child angry and walking off that anger? It is unclear what the child's intentions were without more detailed information. There also are a host of terms that refer to the nuances in walking behavior that give a more clear indication of the child's state of being at the time. If it was reported that the child *darted* around the examining room, there is a suggestion of more energy being exerted by the child than if the child was described as *sauntering*. Likewise, skipping suggests a lighter mood than *trudging, pacing* connotes a higher level of anxiety than *strolling,* and *stomping* alludes to a greater degree of emotion than *tiptoing*.

Although there is a greater likelihood of disagreement among professionals over whether a child was sauntering or strolling, marching or stomping, diagnosticians should not hesitate to describe the behavior in terms that they believe accurately connote the nuance of emotion underlying the child's behavior or the energy with which the behavior was exhibited. As psychologists and educators, our task is to make diagnostic decisions based on the best data available at the time. Tests results are fairly easily defended, but clinical observations are essential for making sense of the test results and provide a clearer understanding of the child.

WHEN TO OBSERVE BEHAVIOR

Behavior is a continuous attribute that flows unendingly. Literally every moment during an evaluation the child is doing something worth noting. To make sense of the continuous behavior flow, it is necessary to study the child's behavior temporally.

Because much of the child's behavior is a reaction to the examiner or the examining situation, the child's responses to various situations should be studied meticulously to determine possible relationships between the task the child is asked to perform and the child's behavior. Identification of relationships between tasks and resulting behaviors can lead to meaningful hypotheses about the child's abilities. Why might a child kneel and lean forward in anticipation when presented with a verbal memory subtest, yet recoil and become anxious when asked to repeat numbers on a numerical memory task? The child's differential response to the two similar subtests might suggest a tentative hypothesis about the child's relative comfort with verbal as opposed to numerical stimuli.

The examiner's hypothesis should be investigated to determine whether similar responses were made to other memory and nonmemory, verbal and numerical subtests. If the child's response pattern is consistent and verbal items are continually responded to more favorably than numerical items, then information is gained, which can be used, along with obtained test scores, to explain the differences in the child's verbal and numerical abilities.

Less contiguous temporal units also should be considered when analyzing trends in a child's behavior. The examiner should compare the child's behavior at the beginning of the evaluation with that near the end of the evaluation. Did the child begin eagerly, but finished frustrated? Did the child separate from his or her parents with difficulty but gradually warm in mood so that by the end of the evaluation the examiner and child were mutually comfortable? Does the child work well once he or she gets started, but become anxious or frightened when required to cease one activity and initiate another? The child's reaction to transitions in tasks, subtests, tests, and other activities and settings also should be noted by the examiner. By considering temporal units of behavior, whether large or small, the examiner can obtain information that will not only help explain the child's test performance, but will provide parents and teachers insight into the child's variable behavior at home and in school.

WHAT TO OBSERVE

Although it would be impossible to list all behaviors that are worthy of notice during a diagnostic evaluation, behaviors that should not go unnoticed are discussed shortly. It is hoped that the reader will become more aware of preschool behavior, expand these suggestions as necessary, and learn to attend selectively to childhood behaviors that provide diagnostically useful information.

Appearance

During the course of an evaluation, the examiner should note with photographic clarity the child's actual physical appearance. This carefully recorded description will prove a useful aid to recall at a later date when the details of the evaluation are no longer vivid. A description of this sort also is useful for professionals who will be working with the child in the future because it provides a concrete referent. Photographic descriptions also humanize the assessment report and make it clear that the report concerns an actual child, not a faceless entity. It is important that future teachers, counselors, and other school personnel see the preschooler as a living, breathing, red-haired, freckle-faced youngster, for example, rather than merely a name–IQ paired association.

Height and Weight

A physical description of a child should include notes about weight and height, especially relative to the child's peers. Height and weight charts usually are available from pediatricians, but also are found in books on child development. As with most traits and characteristics, variance for normal height and weight is great during the preschool years. The examiner should take care to note the interaction between the child's size and his or her performance on the assessment tests or how it relates to his rate of development. It is more meaningful, for instance, to describe a child as being seriously overweight and discuss the ways in which the child's excess weight interfered with fine and gross motor abilities as measured on a diagnostic evaluation than to cite only that the child's weight is at the 99th percentile when compared to same-age peers.

The examiner needs to be acutely sensitive to the effects that extreme height or weight might have on a youngster's test performance, school performance, self-concept, peer relations, and so forth. The question of whether a child's deviant weight is a result of a physiological problem should be investigated by a physician. The diagnostician should be aware that deviancy in a child's physical development can have implications for the emotional, social, and educational well-being of the child and should be considered within the context of the psychoeducational evaluation. As with all areas of development, early intervention for health related problems is preferred to later interventions.

Physical Abnormalities

The diagnostician should be watchful for physical characteristics that are unusual and/or indicative of insufficient or inappropriate diet, physical or emotional abuse, lack of proper medical or dental attention, improper sleep or rest patterns, and physiological, psychological, or educational disorders.

The child should be surveyed for obvious sensory and motor abnormalities. The child should evidence fairly symmetrical motor development and functioning. While the young child's movements are typically not as smooth as an older child's, movements should be neither jerky nor spasmodic. The child should be observed for tics, tremors, excessive clumsiness, and uncontrolled body movements.

The examiner also should be observant for signs of visual and/or auditory impairments. Visually, the examiner should look for obvious signs, such as red, swollen eyelids, crusty drainage around the eyes, eyes that neither track nor align properly, squinting, excessive blinking, grimacing, or evidence of impaired perception of orientation in space, size, body image, and judgment of distance. The examiner also should watch for signs for auditory impairment such as drainage from the ears, complaints of earaches or itchy ears, repeated requests for questions to be restated, tilting of the head for better reception, and so on. The child's speech should be considered carefully for indications of auditory disfunctioning, such as frequent auditory discrimination errors, expressed confusion when there is auditory confusion or commotion, and inappropriate responses to questions, directions, and requests.

Grooming and Dress

Observations of the child's grooming frequently provide the examiner with an indication of the care afforded the child at home. If the child's hands and face are covered with an accumulation of dirt and the clothing bears traces of compounded soil, then it might be safely inferred that little attention has been given to the child's hygiene. A diagnostician should be careful, however, to discern if the child is temporarily disheveled and dirty because of recent play or whether the observed dirt is more permanent and global.

The intent of considering a preschooler's clothing is not to attend to whether the child is stylishly dressed, but rather to infer the amount of adult suprvision given to the child's daily routines. As with grooming, a child's dress reflects somewhat the attention and care given the child at home. It would be foolish to infer necessarily that a child in old clothes does not have his or her physical needs met; however, a young boy who comes to an evaluation with his shirt buttons and buttonholes misaligned, wearing socks of different colors, and has shoes on the wrong feet obviously had little attention paid to his dress! The examiner should follow up on this observation by asking the parents and preschool teacher about the child's usual dress and dressing routine. It is possible that this situation was unique because of a rushed schedule the day of the evaluation or possibly that the parents are attempting to teach the child to become more independent in his daily functioning. Although the potential explanations for disheveled dress are many, the examiner should pursue the reasons to rule out the possibility of parental neglect.

Children's dress also can be a valuable source of information about their level of dependence on adults. If a child's shoes become untied during the evaluation, does he or she immediately ask the examiner to tie them or does the child attempt to tie them himself or herself? Does the child attempt to tuck in a shirt when it comes untucked or does he or she obliviously leave it untucked? Does the child attempt to button buttons or snap snaps that have come undone or ask to have them done by an adult? The essence of the observation is whether the child evidences an attempt at independent functioning or is content and used to having others do for him. Obviously, the average 2-year-old child would be expected to be quite dependent on adults for dressing assistance, but 3 and 4 year olds should be evidencing attempts at independent functioning even if these attempts prove unsuccessful; 5 and 6 year olds should be quite independent in much of their normal daily functioning, requiring assistance much less frequently than their younger peers.

Speech

A preschooler's speech yields a great deal of information about not only the quality of the child's language skills, but also the child's overall cognitive ability and level of social–emotional development. Eisenson (1978) provides a useful guide that describes qualitative characteristics of speech in children up to 36 months of age. Also, language development and basic concept attainment for preschool children are discussed in chapters 11 and 12. Therefore, little will be added here concerning the specifics of early childhood language development; however, it is important that a child's speech be noted carefully during an evaluation for insight into the child's thought patterns, problem-solving style, tolerance to frustration, awareness and understanding of the examining situation, and ability to communicate needs and follow directions.

Although stuttering, stammering, and mild lisps caused by the loss of baby teeth and imperfect enunciation are common among young children (especially among first graders), the examiner should note the child's speech difficulties and be particularly sensitive to whether the child evidences discomfort over speech production. If the child's speech is unintelligible, is marked by severe stuttering or stammering, or causes concern to the child or parents, then the diagnostician should make a referral for a language assessment and attempt to determine in what ways and to what degree the child's imperfect speech interfered with the test results. In situations where a child's poor expressive speech results in lowered test scores the examiner should measure the youngster's receptive vocabulary and nonverbal reasoning skills with instruments such as the Peabody Picture Vocabulary Test—Revised (Dunn & Dunn, 1981) or the Columbia Mental Maturity Scale (Burgermeister et al., 1972), both of which require no verbal expression and are appropriate for preschool children.

Many preschoolers express their thoughts verbally while attempting to solve problems, which provides the diagnostician with insights into the processes used in obtaining the solution. Although intelligence tests have been criticized historically for measuring intellectual product but not process, the astute diagnostician can infer aspects of the child's cognitive processing from the resultant product and the child's steps taken while working toward producing that product.

During the test administration, when test items become increasingly difficult, the examiner should note the child's response to the increasingly difficult tasks and more frequent item failures. Frequently young children remain on task as long as the task is within their ability. When the tasks become taxing many children focus only on particular words within the test questions and respond verbally in an eluding and tangential manner. For example, the examiner who asks a young child to complete the following sentence, "A table is made of wood; a window of . . ." (Terman & Merrill, 1973, p. 85), might get a response such as "I want to look out the window." Many preschoolers use manipulative ploys in an attempt to avoid failure, while others use verbal redirection to avoid participating in the evaluation once they discover that the "games" are not as much fun as they first seemed. A clinician's reported observations about a child's redirective attempts frequently astonish parents who have been manipulated successfully by their children, though some parents might be unaware that they have been redirected so effectively by their child. An awareness of this sort of observation is all some parents need to begin setting consistent limits and better managing their young children.

A child's level of verbal spontaneity often can be an indication of the child's level of comfort in the examining situation. A verbally expressive youngster who chatters happily throughout the evaluation is visibly more comfortable than a reticent child who speaks haltingly and only when questioned. The examiner should question the validity of evaluation results when it is deemed that the child was overly inhibited during the assessment process. The examiner might contrast the child's performance on subtests that require verbal expression with subtests that require little or none for a better determination of the extent to which the child's shyness affected the test results. If the child scored consistently lower on verbal expressive measures than on verbal receptive items, the examiner should further determine whether the child is reticent because of a verbal deficiency or whether the assessed verbal deficiency was a result of reticence. If the child is observed to be verbally fluent and spontaneous in nontest situations, it might be hypothesized that the child's shyness might have been the cause of the poor verbal test performance; in such a case, interventions of an entirely different sort would be warranted.

The examiner should attend to the preschooler's speech for insights into the child's overall affect. Does the child tease, joke, or attempt to be humorous verbally? Does the child use baby talk or regressive language at times of stress or frustration? When tasks become difficult, does the child utter silly nonsense phrases or respond seriously with a relevant response, whether correct or not? Does the youngster become verbally aggressive when faced with failure and petulantly inform the examiner, "I don't like you. I want to go home!"?

The diagnostician should be watchful for how the child responds verbally and nonverbally to the multitude of situations that arise during the evaluation. It is helpful, for example, if a diagnostician notes that a particular child, like many preschoolers, becomes silent when faced with failure, disappointment, embarrassment, or frustration. Many examiners react to a young child's silent dejection with over-stimulating attention; the diagnostician should be advised that increased attention frequently exacerbates the problem and a more relaxed, soothing, and accepting approach might be most helpful in reopening the temporarily closed lines of communication.

The content of a child's verbalizations should be considered carefully, not only to determine the relative maturity of the child's speech, but also to detect emotional projections the child is making while performing tasks during the evaluation. The examiner should listen intently to the young child's interpretations of test pictures, test items, and spontaneous comments. With a verbally expressive preschooler, the examiner frequently has available a great store of additional psychological information; preschoolers typically have not acquired the sophistication to mask their feelings and have not yet developed strong defense mechanisms. Their problems often can be detected readily by a diagnostician who observes as well as tests.

Fine and Gross Motor Skills

Because many early school experiences are motoric in nature, the examiner should pay particularly close attention to the child's motor development. Tests such as the McCarthy Scales of Children's Abilities (McCarthy, 1972) and the Meeting Street School Screening Test (Harnsworth & Siqueland, 1969) have direct measures of motor ability while most other preschool tests at least indirectly measure motor skill. The Wechsler Preschool and Primary Scale of Intelligence–Revised (Wechsler, 1989) is heavily weighted in fine motor tasks on the Performance Scale, and the Stanford-Binet, IV (Thorndike, Hagen, & Sattler, 1986) also is well represented with fine motor tasks.

Formal motor assessment procedures always should be supplemented with direct behavioral observation. The examiner should discern the child who performs poorly on formal motor measures for reasons other than poor motor coordination. Children can score low on motor scales because of shyness, an unwillingness to attempt the task, fear of failure, embarrassment, or because motor tasks might lack necessary structure for some children. Also, one must question whether the child understood the test directions; even subtests that are motoric in nature frequently have long and complex verbal directions (Bracken, 1986; Cummings & Nelson, 1980; Kaufman, 1978).

Children should be watched carefully to note how well they perform nontest motor tasks as well as formal motor tasks. Children who are lacking in educational experiences can look clumsy when drawing, coloring or cutting with scissors, yet are able to button buttons, zip zippers, and manipulate small objects with obvious facility. The nature of the remediation for a child of this sort should be to engage the child in educationally relevant motor activities because their nonacademic, adaptive behavior motor skills appear to be well developed already.

When assessing preschoolers, the examiner should observe the child's gross motor abilities, including the ability to climb stairs, walk, run, skip, hop, balance on one foot, walk backward, throw, and catch. Obvious signs of gross asymmetrical development should be noted as possible indicators of neurological impairment, and referrals should be made for a neuropsychological evaluation if warranted. As with fine motor development, the examiner should discern whether the child's gross motor difficulty is because of a lack of meaningful experiences or is because of a physical or perceptual limitation. While perceptual difficulties can be the cause of poor coordination in the truly awkward and clumsy child and might require educational or physical intervention, the child lacking in experience might need only additional experience to develop better motor skills.

Activity Level

How active a child is during an evaluation has direct implications for the validity of the test results. It is likely that a child who is either lethargic or extremely active is not participating in the assessment process to an optimum degree, thus reducing the test's validity. A child who must be extrinsically motivated to attempt tasks, encouraged to continue the assessment, and prodded to complete test items is problematic. The diagnostician should qualify the report of the child's poor performance with a note about the child's diminished activity level and reluctance to participate. The examiner should contrast the child's test and nontest behaviors, search for relevant behavioral trends, and watch for instances in which the child displays isolated bursts of interest and energy before making inappropriate diagnoses based on the affected test scores. If a child actively participates in subtests of a particular nature and remains listless for others, the resultant test profile and the examiner's behavioral notes, when coupled, should lead to diagnostically useful information.

The examiner should be aware of whether a child is currently medicated and any effect such medication might have on the child's activity level. If the youngster is taking medication that has a depressant effect, the evaluation should be postponed and rescheduled when the youngster is healthier and better able to give maximum effort. In instances of prolonged medical treatment, the diagnostician should acknowledge that it is likely that the test scores are depressed because of medication, and caution the user of the results to consider judiciously the effects of the child's physical condition on the test results. Likewise, ill health itself can adversely affect the child's energy level. The examiner should note symptoms that indicate

the onset of an illness and decide whether the evaluation should continue or be rescheduled for a later date.

Similarly, fatigue and drowsiness, common among preschoolers in the early afternoon, should be an indication to the examiner that optimal results on cognitive and achievement measures will not be obtained; upon observing the child's fatigue or sleepiness, the examiner should cease testing for the time being. Fatigue frequently accentuates soft signs of neurological impairment in children and the examiner should be watchful for those signs.

Attention

Artifacts in test results caused by a child's inattentiveness can bring about inappropriate remediation recommendations unless the test results are further explained through behavioral observations. For example, if a child obtains a relatively weak score on the Memory Scale of the McCarthy Scales of Children's Abilities, a diagnostician might conclude that the child's short-term memory is deficient. However, the diagnostician should be able to explain this weakness if the child did not attend fully to the directions or the stimuli on short-term memory items. Because memory items cannot be readministered, as most other items can, the child might consistently miss the crucial element of test items because of inattentiveness rather than poor memory. The logical recommendation based on this observation would be to ensure that the child is attending carefully before teachers or parents present information they expect the child to recall.

Distractibility

Some children, although attentive during much of the evaluation, miss crucial information because they are distracted easily. These children might be attending appropriately but momentarily discontinues attending to the task and shift their attention to inappropriate stimuli. Distractibility interferes with successful completion of many test activities, but is particularly harmful on memory tests and tasks that are timed. The examiner should differentiate a child's failure because of inability and failure because of inconsistent attention. If the child's low scores are properly explained by the examiner, the subsequent recommendations should be more pertinent to the child's actual area of difficulty.

Impulsivity

As with inattentiveness and distractibility, impulsivity can severely limit the child's success on cognitive and achievement tests. If a child blurts out a response before the examiner completes the tests question, initiates a task before the directions are finished, or says, "I know how to do it—let me try" as the examiner readies the test materials, the child is likely to fail many times and do poorly on the test overall.

Examiners need to be aware that typical preschoolers are at times inattentive, distractible, and impulsive. However, the crux of the examiner's observations should be to determine the degree to which the child's test performance was adversely affected by extreme behaviors and then judge the usefulness of the test scores. Although the diagnostician might believe that the test results are seriously deflated because of the child's test behavior and might be able to support this belief with a raft of behavioral notes, he or she should be careful when making optimistic claims about the child's likelihood of success in the classroom. If the child's behavior has interfered with his performance on the test, it also can interfere with his performance in the classroom and indeed might have been the reason for the initial referral.

Affect

Emotional lability is a common characteristic among preschool children. The examiner should become aware of the ways in which a child responds differentially to various situations. It is not uncommon for a young child to be exhilarated by success at one moment and demoralized by failure the next. Unfamiliar tasks can arouse fear and anxiety in a child who had previously completed familiar tasks calmly and confidently. An otherwise compliant and cooperative child can become "testy" and difficult during the unstructured interim between tests in a battery. A youngster who enters the examining room clinging to doors and furniture in fear might leave the room striding and exuding confidence.

The examiner should attend carefully to shifts in a child's affect as a result of changes in the environment and seek answers to the following types of questions: How does the child respond to structured versus unstructured activities? What is the child's reaction to praise, rebuke, failure, success, redirection, encouragement, and so forth? What causes the child to become silent, to start crying, to withdraw, to jump up in excitement, to sing out with pleasure, or strike out in anger? To what test activity is the child most attentive and which activities arouse the least interest? How does the child react to test materials, being timed, the examiner, the examining room, the parents, verbal interaction, and nonverbal, performance-related activity?

Although the examiner might see many mild or even dramatic shifts in the child's mood, the child's general mood should be noted as well. On the whole, did the youngster seem happy? Negative? Fearful? Sullen? Confident? All of the child's affective behaviors should be drawn together diagnostically and inferences should be made about the child's overall mood, level of adjustment, areas of concern, and areas of strength.

Anxiety

Closely associated with affect is the child's level of anxiety. The diagnostician should note what causes the child to become anxious and how the child displays signs of anxiety. When asked several difficult questions near the ceiling of a test, does the youngster begin to suck his thumb while tears well in his eyes? Does the child stare at the floor in silence while sitting on her hands? Does the child giggle nervously, cry, constantly clear her throat, bite her nails, urinate, blush, block while talking, breathe unevenly, or hyperventilate?

Although a psychoeducational evaluation frequently arouses anxiety in preschoolers, some children are more affected than others. Some youngsters are aroused to an optimal level, whereas others are totally debilitated. Some are anxious throughout the evaluation, and others become anxious only in reaction to specific events or situations. By noting the child's behavior in several settings, the diagnostician is better able to determine whether the child's anxiety was specific to the evaluation or more general in nature, and the degree to which the child's anxiety interfered with the evaluation.

Comprehension and Problem Solving

The examiner should attend to the problem-solving approach used while the child seeks solutions to puzzles, mazes, block designs, and similar problems. The approach taken by a youngster yields clues regarding his or her comprehension of the tasks. Does the youngster draw directly through the maze without regard for walls? Remain between the walls yet continually enter blind alleys? Remain within the walls and attempt to avoid blind alleys but proceed too slowly and still fail the task? In each case, the child's earned raw score is zero, but the child's level of comprehension differs dramatically across examples. It is quite likely that the first child did not understand the nature of the task. The second child might have understood the nature of the task, but was not fully cognizant that blind alleys should be avoided. The third child seems to have fully understood the task, but was unable to complete the item successfully because of the speeded nature of the task.

The child's reaction to test materials at times provides the diagnostician with surprising insight into the child's level of understanding. In low functioning young children, it is fairly common for the child to sniff or suck the mallet of the McCarthy xylophone thinking that it is a lollipop. Similarly, the brightly colored chips that are part of the McCarthy Conceptual Grouping subtest are sometimes mistaken for candy. Observations of this sort, when added to other behavioral notes, yield valuable information about the child's maturity and level of comprehension.

The examiner should be watchful for such events as the following: Does the child make random attempts to solve problems in a trial-and-error fashion or appear to have a strategy? If an attempt is unsuccessful, does the child continue to try the same approach or try other approaches? When solving a puzzle and puzzle pieces do not fit, does the child try a second piece or try to force the first piece into place? Does the child understand the puzzle pieces must be right-side-up to fit properly in the puzzle? On simple two or three piece puzzles, does the child impulsively shove adjacent pieces together without regard for the total picture? Observations of this sort add a qualitative nature to the test score. Although any two children can obtain the same scores on a given subtest, no two children will exhibit exactly the same behaviors while attempting the subtest items.

Reactions to Other People and Situations

The preschool child's interactions with both parents together and each parent apart, siblings, teachers, classmates, and strangers should be noted. It should be noted whether the child interacts with others by moving forward confidently or timidly holding back? Is the youngster aggressive with classmates or bullied? Does the child seek independence from the teacher or frequently ask for help, reassurance, and support? Does the child obey one parent's commands but ignore the other parent's directions? The child's interactions with the examiner also should be noted. Overall, is the child compliant, manipulative, fearful, confident, respectful, or flippant?

In many cases children who have difficulty adjusting come from environments that contribute to their problems. Although teachers and parents mean well and attempt to do what they believe is in the child's best interest, they at times fail to see their role in the child's lack of adjustment. Consider, for example, the father who drops off his daughter at the nursery school. At the moment the father attempts to leave his daughter in her class, she begins to cry. As the daughter cries her father attempts to console her, yet every time he begins to leave she becomes more upset. This cycle repeats itself daily until the child begins crying before ever leaving her home, and school becomes a negative experience to which she reacts strongly. As any experienced preschool teacher knows, most young children stop crying almost immediately after their parents leave, and the best way to avoid unpleasant separations is to make them warm yet brief.

SUMMARY

Although the administration of psychoeducational tests alone requires a great deal of skill, concentration, and coordination, an effective diagnostician also must have the resources to observe and record the preschool child's behavior. With a carefully collected sample of behavioral observations, the examiner should be able to support or refute test findings, explain a child's variable test performance, and attest to the validity or invalidity of test results. The diagnostician also should note the child's appearance and determine whether signs or symptoms of physical, emotional, or educational difficulties are present. Behaviors that indicate a child's preferred cognitive style, language abilities, problem-solving approach, level of understanding, and reasons for individual item and subtest performance likewise must be observed and interpreted. These behaviors, along with observations of the child's affect, distractibility, dependence, reactions to others, fears, likes, and so on, need to be integrated with obtained test data to formulate accurate diagnosis, prognosis, and remedial recommendations.

REFERENCES

Anastasi, A. (1988). *Psychological testing* (6th ed.). New York: Macmillan.

AERA, APA, NCME. (1985). *Standards for educational and psychological testing*. Washington, DC: American Psychological Association.

Bracken, B. A. (1986). Incidence of basic concepts in the directions of five commonly used American tests of intelligence. *School Psychology International 7,* 1–10.

Bracken, B. A. (1987). Limitations of preschool instruments and standards for minimal levels of technical adequacy. *Journal of Psychoeducational Assessment 5,* 313–326.

Burgermeister, B., Blum, L., & Lorge, I. (1972). *Columbia Mental Maturity Scale*. New York: Harcourt Brace Jovanovich, Inc.

Cummings, J. A., & Nelson, R. B. (1980). Basic concepts in oral directions of group achievement tests. *Journal of Educational Research 73,* 259–261.

Dunn, L., & Dunn, L. (1981). *Peabody Picture Vocabulary Test—Revised*. Circle Pines, MN.: American Guidance Service.

Eisenson, J. (1978). Is my child delayed in speech? *School Psychology Digest 7,* 63–68.

Harnsworth, P., & Siqueland, M. (1969). *Meeting Street School Screening Test*. East Providence, R.I.: Easter Seal Society.

Kaufman, A. S. (1978). The importance of basic concepts in individual assessment of preschool children. *Journal of School Psychology, 16,* 207–211.

McCarthy, D. (1982). *McCarthy Scales of Children's Abilities*, San Antonio, TX: The Psychological Corporation.

Terman, L., & Merrill, M. (1973). *Stanford-Binet Intelligence Scale*. Boston: Houghton Mifflin.

Thorndike, R. L., Hagen, E. P., & Sattler, J. M. (1986). *Stanford-Binet Intelligence Scale: Fourth Edition*. Chicago: Riverside Publishing.

Wechsler, D. (1989). *Wechsler Preschool and Primary Scale of Intelligence*–Revised. San Antonio, TX: The Psychological Corporation.

5

The Assessment of Preschool Children with the McCarthy Scales of Children's Abilities

BRUCE A. BRACKEN

The McCarthy Scales of Children's Abilities (MSCA) (McCarthy, 1972) was the culmination of the clinical and developmental experiences of Dorothea McCarthy. McCarthy, who studied under another historical preschool assessment figure, Florence Goodenough, assembled a wealth of practical experience and developmental theory into the first major preschool intelligence test designed to meet the unique needs and characteristics of preschool children. Unlike the Wechsler Preschool and Primary Scale of Intelligence (WPPSI) (Wechsler, 1967), the MSCA was not a downward extension of an existing instrument designed for adults or older children; it was intentionally designed to be a full scale cognitive measure appropriate for preschool and primary grade children between the ages of 2 years, 4 months and 16 days (2½ years) and 8 years, 7 months, and 15 days (8½ years).

With her extensive clinical experience, McCarthy built many elements into the MSCA that accommodate the unique foibles of preschool children. For example, she accounted for the wide-spread response variability among preschool children by allowing examinees a second opportunity to respond on many subtests if their first response to an item was inaccurate. Similarly, given the preschool child's propensity toward reticence, the McCarthy subtests were arranged such that the initial tasks require no overt verbal response from the examinee. These initial fine motor subtests were followed by tasks that require simple single-word responses, and then later, only after the child has had an opportunity to "warm up," do the subtests require lengthier verbalizations or more active motor involvement. The decision to discontinue the table-top assessment tasks midtest was also clinically astute. Those initial table-top tasks are replaced by more physically active Motor scale items, thus providing what Kaufman and Kaufman (1977, p. 8) refer to as a built-in "intermission" midpoint in the examination. Before returning to the table-top assessment tasks, McCarthy provided a transitional subtest (Imitative Action) to facilitate the child's return to the pencil and paper assessment activities.

Additionally, Kaufman and Kaufman (1977) cite several aspects of the MSCA that make it particularly appropriate for early childhood assessment, including: attractive, manipulatable test materials (blocks, colored puzzles, toy-like xylophone, ball, beanbag, and other game-like equipment); the arrangement of subtests to facilitate building and maintaining rapport and minimizing fatigue; the opportunity for extra trials and second chances; the examiner's demonstration of the correct response in some instances, and the inclusion of developmental theory in the test development. It is just this type of clinical and developmental experience, mixed with good assessment common sense that makes the MSCA an attractive instrument for use with young children. Despite its several attractions, the MSCA is used infrequently relative to other major measures of intelligence (Chattin & Bracken, 1989).

TEST DESCRIPTION

The MSCA consists of 18 subtests; all but one are administered to every child, regardless of age. The one exceptional subtest (Right-Left Orientation) is administered to all children above 4 years, 10 months, and 16 days. The eighteen McCarthy subtests combine, and in many instances overlap, to form five major scales: Verbal, Perceptual-Performance, Quantitative, Memory and Motor (Fig. 5-1). The five McCarthy scales were based intuitively on, "...the author's extensive teaching and clinical experience in developmental psychology and her many years of training and supervising test examiners" (McCarthy, 1972, p. 2), as well as empirically on the preliminary results of factor analyses. Hence, the scales are practically and theoretically drived, and partially supported factor analytically.

The 18 McCarthy subtests produce raw scores that are weighted and combined additively to produce norm-based standard scores for each of the five MSCA scales. Scores from three of the five subscales (Verbal, Perceptual-Motor, and Quantitative) are combined to form a total test composite score termed the General Cognitive Index (GCI). The MSCA scales each produce standard scores (T scores) with means set at 50 and standard deviations of 10; the GCI is a Binet-like IQ equivalent score with a mean of 100 and standard deviation of 16. The McCarthy Manual presents percentile ranks and General Cognitive Ability Levels (GCAs) for the scales and GCI.

Following is a description of each of the McCarthy subtests and the scale or scales to which the subtest belongs. Each subtest is described according to the cognitive skills that appear to be assessed, the item format and general administration procedure, and an evaluation of floor, ceiling, and item gradient. Before describing the McCarthy subtests, points should be made regarding the skills and abilities assessed by the McCarthy subtests, the weighting procedure used for the determination of subtest scores, and issues related to subtest technical adequacy.

First, the description of abilities assessed by the MSCA subtests is not empirically based, but rather represents a conservative task analysis of abilities that are presumed necessary to successfully complete the task. Bracken and Fagan (1988) demonstrated that there frequently is disagreement between practitioners and authors regarding the skills assessed by tests of cognitive abilities. The abilities assigned to the subtests cited in this chapter are provided for the reader as general guidelines for a better understanding of the subtests' underlying skill requirements. The descriptions do not represent a definitive classification of skills assessed by the McCarthy subtests; such a definitive classification scheme does not exist for any test (Bracken & Chattin, 1990).

Second, MSCA subtest raw scores are differentially weighted, resulting in an increased or decreased effect on the various scale and total test scores. McCarthy (1972) weighted some subtests differentially, based on two factors: 1) "the author's judgement of the relative importance of the individual test," and 2) "the size of the standard deviations of the raw scores on the test for the normative groups" [p. 20]. Subtests that generated more variance than typical were adjusted through the weighting procedure to produce variance that was more typical of the remaining nonweighted subtests.

Third, the technical adequacy of the McCarthy scales and subtests is judged against criteria that Bracken (1987) proposed as minimal psychometric standards for preschool psychoeducational instrumentation. Bracken recommended that subtests and scales should have floors that differentiate among all children who are functioning as low as two standard deviations below their normative mean; subtests and scales should have ceilings that differentiate among all

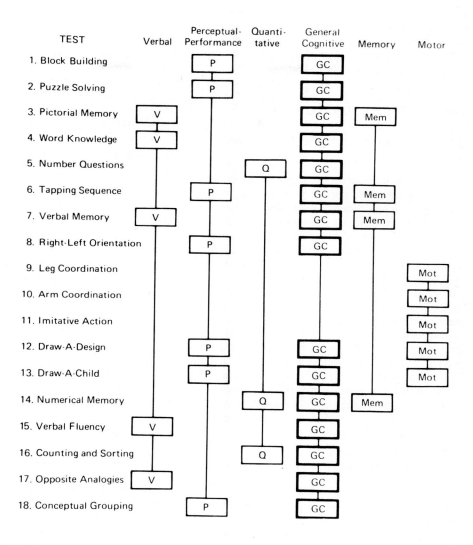

TEST	Verbal	Perceptual-Performance	Quantitative	General Cognitive	Memory	Motor
1. Block Building		P		GC		
2. Puzzle Solving		P		GC		
3. Pictorial Memory	V			GC	Mem	
4. Word Knowledge	V			GC		
5. Number Questions			Q	GC		
6. Tapping Sequence		P		GC	Mem	
7. Verbal Memory	V			GC	Mem	
8. Right-Left Orientation		P		GC		
9. Leg Coordination						Mot
10. Arm Coordination						Mot
11. Imitative Action						Mot
12. Draw-A-Design		P		GC		Mot
13. Draw-A-Child		P		GC		Mot
14. Numerical Memory			Q	GC	Mem	
15. Verbal Fluency	V			GC		
16. Counting and Sorting			Q	GC		
17. Opposite Analogies	V			GC		
18. Conceptual Grouping		P		GC		

Figure 5.1   The McCarthy's six scales and 18 subtests. Used with the permission of The Psychological Corporation, San Antonio, Texas.

children who are functioning as high as two standard deviations above their normative mean; and, items within subtests and scales should be graded such that a single raw score does not affect the respective subtest or scale standard score by more than one-third standard deviation.

Because the McCarthy subtests do not produce standard scores, the raw score means and standard deviations were used to evaluate the quality of the floors and ceilings. Likewise, the McCarthy subtest item gradients were described qualitatively. Determination of floors and ceilings for scales is predicated on the condition that at least one item is answered correctly on each of the scale's subtests. Without this condition the assessment would be a senseless activity, because the child would have been compared on subtests on which he or she had absolutely no success. Other aspects of subtest and scale technical adequacy (i.e., reliability and validity) will be considered in separate sections of this chapter.

THE MCCARTHY SUBTESTS

Block Building (Perceptual-Performance Scale)

This four-item subtest requires the examinee to copy the examiner's production of simple structures constructed from one-inch cubes, including: a six block tower; an L-shaped, three block "chair;" a "building" requiring the horizontal aignment of four blocks with a fifth block placed on top; and a "house" with a four-block foundation and a fifth block that serves as a roof covering the open space created by the foundational walls. The Block Building subtest requires a variety of cognitive abilities for successful completion, including: fine motor coordination, visual-motor integration, the imitative ability to copy a model, and spatial abilities. Each item is point scored according to the degree of completion and accuracy, with as many as two points assigned to two items and as many as three points assigned to the remaining two items. The subtest yields a total raw score of 10 points.

Technical Characteristics

Block Building has an adequate floor for young children, but a severely limited ceiling for older children. At 2½ years the "average" child obtains a raw score of 4.4 (out of a maximum of 10), with a standard deviation of 1.9; by age 4 the mean raw score is 8.6, and from age 5 through 8½ years the average child earns a raw score between 9.3 and 9.9 (Table 5-1). Thus, there is virtually no discrimination between levels of advanced ability after age 4.

Likewise, the subtest item gradient (the degree to which raw scores increase as a function of age) is poor at younger age levels and virtually nonexistent beyond age 4. Between 2½ and 4 years the mean subtest raw score increases by approximately one point per six-month interval. Beyond age 4, the total gain of 1.3 raw score points

is distributed across a four and one-half year age span.

The conclusions reached regarding the Block Building subtest is that the test is too limited in ability range and number of items. The test is too easy for most children older than 4 years, and it yields little valuable information in the assessment process *except* when an older child does poorly on the subtest.

Puzzle Solving (Perceptual-Performance Scale)

This subtest, like Block Building, requires the examinee to assemble six multicolored puzzles, each ranging from two to six puzzle pieces. When solved, each puzzle renders a picture of a common and easily recognized animal or object (i.e., *cat, cow, carrot, pear, bear,* and *parrot*). Puzzle Solving appears to require spatial abilities, visual-motor integration, attention to detail, and nonverbal reasoning. Each item is point scored based on degree of completion and accuracy. With bonus points assigned for rapid and accurate completion, maximum possible raw scores range from one point (items 1 and 2) to nine points (items 5 and 6). The total possible subtest raw score of 27 is divided by one-half as part of the overall McCarthy weighting procedure, yielding a total maximum score of 14 points (partial scores are rounded up).

Technical Characteristics

For young children, the Puzzle Solving subtest lacks sufficient floor. The average 2½ year old child earns a raw score of less than one (0.90), even after the weighting procedure is applied it is not until age 3 that the average child earns a weighted raw score of one (an unweighted raw score of 2) (See Table 5-1). Thus, this subtest lacks discrimination at the lower functioning levels and youngest ages. The subtest's ceiling is somewhat better than its floor, with the average 8½ year old child earning an unweighted raw score of 21.3 out of a possible 27 points. Items are fairly gradually graded throughout the age levels, with a slightly steeper gradient at the upper age levels.

It is concluded that, although the subtest possesses a very weak floor, its attractive materials, adequate ceiling, and fairly gradual item gradient renders the subtest a nice addition to the battery, especially when used with children above 4 years in age.

Pictorial Memory (Verbal and Memory Scales)

The stimulus for the Pictorial Memory subtest includes one item plate with six full-color artist's depictions of common objects and animals (i.e., *button, fork, paper clip, horse, padlock,* and *pencil*). The examiner presents the item plate and points to each of the six objects while naming them during a ten-second exposure. The examinee then is required to name as many of the objects as possible within 90 seconds. This subtest appears to require short-term verbal memory and the ability to attend to a combined auditory and visual presentation.

Technical Characteristics

Pictorial Memory has only six items, for a total subtest raw score of six points. Memory assessment typically does not require many items to attain a gradual gradation in discrimination; however, the gradation on the Pictorial Memory subtest is so fine that sample characteristics seem to have affected the gradient as much or more than the gradation in difficulty level. The mean raw scores across four six-month intervals, including ages 4-0, 4-6, 5-0, 5-6 are 3.3, 3.2, 3.6, and 3.8 respectively (See Table 5-1). There are just too few items in the Pictorial Memory subtest to render a reliable assessment of ability.

The subtest also lacks a sufficient floor at the youngest age level (the average 2½ year old child obtains a raw score of less than one, 0.90) and the ceiling is likewise limited in range (the average 8½ year old earns a raw score of 4.9 out of a total possible 6 points). Thus, the item gradient is not sufficiently steep to allow for discrimination across age levels, and the subtest's floor and ceiling are both limited at the extreme age levels. This subtest is not adequate for discerning anything but gross developmental differences among children and is limited in all technical aspects because of its small number of items.

Word Knowledge, Parts I & II (Verbal Scale)

This two-part subtest actually assesses three different aspects of vocabulary. Part I is subdivided such that the child first points to five consecutive objects named by the examiner, for example "Show me the clock" (receptive vocabulary). The second phase of Part I requires the child to identify (name) each of four objects presented by the examiner (labelling/naming vocabulary). Word Knowledge, Part II requires the child to define ten common vocabulary terms named by the examiner (expressive vocabulary), with each response scored as 0, 1, or 2 points. Thus, the subtest assesses three distinct and important aspects of vocabulary; however, to aid in the differential diagnosis of ability or disability there should be ideally three separate subtests to assess these distinct abilities. As the subtest is constructed, the attained scores are treated additively and provide only one total raw score and no basis for comparison across subskills.

Technical Characteristics

The Word Knowledge subtest has an ample floor, with the average 2½ year old earning a raw score of 7.6. Its ceiling is mildly restricted; the average 8½ year old earns a raw score of 23.2 (SD = 3.4) out of 29 possible points (See Table 5-1). The subtest's items are graded in difficulty such that differentiation of ability across age levels is apparent. The technical quality of this subtest rests primarily on the number of items used, 19.

Number Questions (Quantitative Scale)

This twelve-item numerical subtest assesses the child's ability to place count, make monetary change, and conduct basic addition, subtraction, multiplication, and division from information presented in story problems. The subtest assesses numerical reasoning and computation, and additionally requires verbal comprehension, knowledge of basic numerical concepts, and the ability to retain and process numerical information for successful execution. Scoring on this subtest is weighted such that obtained scores are doubled in weight.

Technical Characteristics

The unweighted performance of young children on this subtest suggests a weak floor; the average 2½ year old child earns less than one raw score point (0.80) credit (See Table 5-1). Although the mean raw score for 8½ year olds is 9.6 the standard deviation of 2.0 indicates the existence

TABLE 5.1
MEANS AND STANDARD DEVIATIONS OF RAW SCORES ON THE EIGHTEEN MSCA TESTS, BY AGE, FOR THE STANDARDIZATION SAMPLE

Test	Maximum Possible Score		Age in Years										
			2½ (N = 102)	3 (N = 104)	3½ (N = 100)	4 (N = 102)	4½ (N = 104)	5 (N = 102)	5½ (N = 104)	6½ (N = 104)	7½ (N = 104)	8½ (N = 106)
1. Block Building	10	Mean	4.4	6.0	7.1	8.6	8.9	9.3	9.7	9.9	9.9	9.9
		SD	1.9	2.5	2.2	1.6	1.7	1.2	0.8	0.1	0.4	0.3
2. Puzzle Solving	27	Mean	0.9	2.0	3.8	4.6	6.9	10.7	11.6	15.9	18.1	21.3
		SD	1.0	2.6	4.3	4.4	4.9	6.8	6.4	5.9	6.2	4.4
3. Pictorial Memory	6	Mean	0.9	1.8	2.2	3.3	3.2	3.6	3.8	4.0	4.4	4.9
		SD	1.0	1.4	1.5	1.4	1.1	1.2	1.2	1.2	1.2	0.9
4. Word Knowledge Parts I & II	29	Mean	7.6	10.0	11.0	13.0	14.5	16.1	17.2	18.9	21.4	23.2
		SD	3.0	2.8	3.3	2.9	2.9	3.0	2.9	3.3	4.0	3.4
5. Number Questions	12	Mean	0.8	2.0	2.3	3.1	3.6	4.4	4.5	6.2	8.0	9.6
		SD	1.1	1.4	1.4	1.2	1.0	1.4	1.4	1.6	1.9	2.0
6. Tapping Sequence	9	Mean	0.8	1.3	1.6	2.1	3.0	3.5	4.0	4.9	5.3	6.0
		SD	0.8	1.1	1.0	1.1	1.3	1.6	1.5	1.5	1.3	1.4
7. Verbal Memory Part I	30	Mean	4.3	8.7	12.2	17.4	20.1	22.0	23.6	25.5	26.8	28.0
		SD	3.9	5.5	7.3	7.7	6.5	6.5	4.7	4.5	2.9	2.2
Part II	11	Mean	0.2	1.0	1.8	3.1	4.6	5.2	6.1	7.5	8.1	8.3
		SD	0.7	1.9	2.6	3.1	2.9	3.0	2.8	2.5	2.2	1.8
8. Right-Left Orientation[a]	12	Mean	—	—	—	—	—	6.1	6.5	7.3	8.6	10.2
		SD	—	—	—	—	—	3.2	3.1	3.1	3.2	2.3

9. Leg Coordination	13	Mean	3.5	5.9	7.3	9.5	9.9	11.1	11.5	12.3	12.6	12.6
		SD	2.9	2.8	2.8	2.4	2.3	1.8	2.0	1.1	1.0	0.8
10. Arm Coordination Parts I, II, & III	28	Mean	1.6	2.5	4.4	5.4	6.6	8.3	9.7	13.2	16.7	19.2
		SD	1.9	2.7	3.7	3.7	4.0	4.0	4.1	4.3	3.7	3.3
11. Imitative Action	4	Mean	2.1	2.8	3.2	3.5	3.6	3.8	3.8	3.9	3.9	4.0
		SD	1.1	0.9	0.7	0.6	0.5	0.4	0.4	0.3	0.2	0.0
12. Draw-A-Design	19	Mean	1.4	2.2	2.8	4.2	5.6	6.7	8.0	10.9	13.9	14.7
		SD	1.2	1.3	1.4	1.8	2.8	3.0	2.9	2.9	2.7	2.5
13. Draw-A-Child	20	Mean	0.2	1.0	2.3	5.2	7.2	9.1	10.1	11.4	13.8	14.6
		SD	1.0	2.2	2.9	3.8	3.9	3.7	3.2	2.7	2.9	2.7
14. Numerical Memory Part I	12	Mean	1.8	2.6	3.8	4.5	5.2	5.9	5.6	7.1	7.7	8.4
		SD	1.8	1.8	1.9	1.7	1.9	1.9	1.8	1.7	1.7	1.9
Part II	10	Mean	0.0	0.1	0.1	0.1	0.4	1.1	1.5	2.8	3.6	4.3
		SD	0.0	0.2	0.4	0.6	1.0	1.6	1.6	1.8	1.7	1.9
15. Verbal Fluency	36	Mean	2.5	4.7	6.2	9.1	11.1	12.9	14.8	18.4	21.5	23.5
		SD	2.7	3.6	3.8	4.3	5.2	4.8	5.3	4.3	5.5	5.3
16. Counting and Sorting	9	Mean	0.7	1.9	2.6	4.1	5.2	6.3	7.2	8.6	8.8	8.9
		SD	1.0	1.8	2.2	2.2	1.9	1.9	1.6	0.8	0.8	0.2
17. Opposite Analogies	9	Mean	0.4	1.5	2.2	3.5	3.8	4.6	5.1	6.2	7.0	7.6
		SD	0.9	1.5	1.7	1.8	1.8	1.5	1.3	1.4	1.3	1.2
18. Conceptual Grouping	12	Mean	1.4	3.1	4.1	5.4	6.5	7.6	8.0	9.3	9.7	10.3
		SD	1.7	2.6	2.7	2.6	2.7	2.4	2.4	1.7	1.6	1.4

Note.—The means and standard deviations presented here are for unweighted totals. Parts I and II of Verbal Memory are presented separately, as are the two parts of Numerical Memory. The component parts of each of these tests are treated separately in determining composite raw scores and are not weighted the same. (See Table for weights.)

[a] Means and standard deviations for Right-Left Orientation are not presented for children between the ages of 2½ and 4½ because when this test was given to the standardization group, the means showed only chance correct responses below age 5.

This table is reprinted with permission: McCarthy, D. (1972). *McCarthy Scales of Childrens' Abilities.* San Antonio, TX: The Psychological Corporation.

of a restricted ceiling, given a total possible sub-test score of 12. Items are fairly evenly distributed across the full age span, but the somewhat limited number of items allows for only gross differentiation of ability across the ages. For example, there are only 1.4 raw score points to distinguish between the abilities of the average 4 year old and 5½ year old. With an unknown and unreported reliability coefficient and standard error of measurement, it is unknown how much of the 1.4 raw score points that separate this 1½ year age span is measurement error, rather than a reflection of "true" developmental differences.

Tapping Sequence (Perceptual-Performance and Memory Scales)

This subtest requires the examinee to replicate a sequence of taps produced by the examiner on a four key xylophone. Requiring primarily fine motor coordination and visual short-term memory, this subtest utilizes unique materials to assess the child's abilities; however, it is unfortunate that the quality of the xylophone and mallet are both poor. Rather than producing melodious tones, the poorly constructed plastic and metal xylophone frequently produces dull, off-key notes that result in unnecessary second efforts by the examinee in an attempt to attain a less cacophonous sound. These second efforts spoil the child's response, and thus conflict with the assessment process; a child's failed effort should be because of lack of ability, not poor quality assessment materials.

Technical Characteristics

The Tapping Sequence subtest is yet one more subtest on which the average 2½ year old fails to earn at least one raw score point (0.80). As such, the subtest lacks any semblance of discrimination among low functioning children below the age of 4; not until age 4 does the average child earn two raw score points. With a raw score mean of 6.0 and standard deviation of 1.4 at age 8½ the test seems to possess an adequate ceiling (See Table 5-1). With only 8 items distributed across the full age span of the test, the gradient of discrimination is minor and at some adjacent age levels is likely similar to the parameters of the standard error of measurement. Because of the subtest's limited technical adequacy and overall poor quality materials, the Tapping Sequence subtest is a poor measure of cognitive functioning for most clients.

Verbal Memory (Parts I & II) (Verbal and Memory Scales)

As with the Word Knowledge subtest, Verbal Memory, Part I combines aspects of verbal memory that would be better assessed as distinct abilities. The first four items (of six in toto) in Part I require the child to repeat unrelated multiple-word stimuli (e.g., *stove-tree-dog*). Recitation of the first four items is not aided by the meaningful imagery evoked by the eventful sentences represented in the latter two items. Both item types are scored on the basis of successful repetition of the stimuli, in the proper sequence. Part I is differentially weighted to reduce its contribution to the total test by one-half and is scored separately from Part II.

Part II of the Verbal Memory subtest requires the child to listen to a story and recount as much of the story as possible. Success on Part II is enhanced by the meaningful nature of the story and the fact that the stimuli/response sequence is not important (i.e., the child's response can be out of sequence relative to the order in which the stimuli were presented).

The two parts of the subtest assess different aspects of verbal memory, including memory for meaningful (Parts I and II) and nonmeaningful verbal stimuli (Part I only), as well as sequential (Part I) and nonsequential memory (Part II). Diagnostic interpretations of the subtest would be enhanced if the item types and underlying skills assessed by Part I were assessed by two separate subtests. Both subparts of the test would benefit from additional items.

Technical Characteristics

With 6 items and 30 attainable unweighted raw score points (15 raw score points after the application of reduced weighting), Part I of the Verbal Memory subtest evidences an adequate floor at the youngest age level, a truncated ceiling at the oldest age level, and a fairly evenly distributed and appropriately steep item gradient (See Table 5-1). Part II, with 11 possible raw score points, evidences a grossly inadequate floor (the average 2½ year old earns only 0.20 raw score points) and a minimal ceiling (average 8½ year old earns a raw score of 8.3 out of 11 possible points). Likewise, the items in Part II are adequately graded by difficulty level for appropriate age related discrimination. Verbal Memory is one more example of a subtest that is not sufficiently versatile for use with its intended population.

Right-Left Orientation (Perceptual-Performance)

This subtest has nine items and generates a total of 12 raw score points. The subtest assesses the child's ability to discriminate *right* from *left*, from both the child's perspective and the perspective of another individual. The required knowledge of body parts confounds the assessment of directionality somewhat by requiring the child to follow directions such as, "Touch Roger's (a pictured child) right *shoulder* with your left *hand*." Because this (and only this) subtest is administered exclusively to children older than 4 years, 10 months, and 16 days, the inclusion of body parts in the directions presents only a minor problem; however, the examiner should note instances in which failures are because of errors in directionality versus errors in body part discrimination. The subtest assesses the child's understanding of the spatial concepts *right* and *left*, from both the child's perspective and that of another person facing the child. Additionally, the subtest requires the knowledge of several body parts (e.g., *elbow, shoulder, chin*).

Technical Characteristics

By eliminating the younger age groupings from consideration, the Right-Left Orientation subtest evidences an adequate floor at its entry level (age 5), but a truncated ceiling at age level 8½ years (See Table 5-1). The subtest item gradient is adequate, but not robust; only four items distinguish between an average 5 year old and an average 8½ year old. Most of the items on the subtest are greatly affected by a guessing factor, with only two options available from which to choose (e.g., "Show me your *right* hand"). There are five such items, resulting in a chance score of 2.5 among those five items. Thus, with its limited technical adequacy, significant guessing factor, and potential body part confound, the subtest lacks a desired level of psychometric precision.

Leg Coordination (Motor)

This six part-subtest marks the beginning of the gross motor tasks, and constitutes half of the McCarthy's built-in "intermission." Five of the six Leg Coordination tasks are scored in a range from zero to two raw score points; the sixth task is scored zero to three points, for a total of 13 raw score points attributed to the subtest. The six tasks include: Walking Backwards, Walking on Tiptoe, Walking a Straight Line, Standing on One Foot, Standing on the Other Foot, and Skipping. Administration of these items is somewhat difficult because the examiner must demonstrate the activity, while reading the test directions. It helps for the examiner to memorize the directions for these items (although memorization of the directions is not recommended in the McCarthy Manual). Leg Coordination, as the name implies, assesses gross motor coordination and balance while using the legs and feet.

Technical Characteristics

The subtest has a moderately strong floor, with an average raw score of 3.5 for 2½ year old children, but a very restricted ceiling. With a maximum raw score of 13 for the Leg Coordination subtest, the average child above 5½ years earns scores exceeding 12.0, and average scores of 11.1 and 11.5 are earned by 5 and 5½ year old children respectively (See Table 5-1). The subtest item gradient is adequate between the ages of 2½ and 5 years, but fails to discriminate levels of ability beyond age 5 because of the subtest's limited ceiling. While this subtest provides a nice diversion for the examinee, it lacks sufficient discrimination except among younger and more disabled children.

Arm Coordination Parts I, II, & III (Motor)

The Arm Coordination subtest is a three part subtest with a total of 28 raw score points assigned it. All three parts of this subtest assess the child's ability to coordinate his or her hands and arms to catch, throw, and bounce small objects within an open visual space. Part I of the subtest (Ball Bouncing) requires the child to imitate the examiner's demonstrated dribbling of a small rubber ball. The child is given two trials, with the better of the two trials credited. The child is required to dribble the ball 15 consecutive bounces to attain the maximum raw score of 7 points.

Part II (Beanbag Catch Game) requires the child to catch a bean bag first with both hands, then (if the child manages to catch the bag at least once out of three tosses) the child attempts to catch the bean bag with his or her preferred hand, and finally with the other hand (three tosses each). The bean bag is thrown to the child from a distance of nine feet. Poorly thrown bean bags are rethrown to ensure the child has a reasonable chance to make the catch. A total of nine points is assigned to Part II.

Part III (Beanbag Target Game) is a carnival-like activity that requires the child to throw a bean bag through a small opening on a target placed six feet away. The bag is thrown three times with each hand, resulting in a total possible raw score of six points. Although this activity generally is considered to be quite fun by young children, the quality of the "target" limits the accuracy of the task as a test item. The target frequently collapses upon impact by the bean bag, or it "jumps" when struck. In either case some successful tosses are spoiled and some unsuccessful tosses must be readministered in fairness to the child.

Technical Characteristics

This subtest is difficult for young children, with the average 2½ year old child earning a mere 1.6 raw score points (See Table 5-1). Children's raw scores are inflated frequently by the truly "lucky" snares made by some young children. In reality, average 2½ year olds are frequently pummeled in their effort to catch the bean bag with two hands. If they "accidently" snare the bean bag on this first part, they are then pummeled further in Part II. The subtest has a mildly weak floor. The subtest ceiling is much better than its floor, with the average 8½ year old earning only 19.2 points out of a total possible score of 28. Likewise, the item gradient adequately discerns level of ability across the entire age span. Despite the subtest's weak floor and poor quality target, it is a fun activity for young children and is technically adequate at all but the lowest age levels.

Imitative Action (Motor)

Imitative Action is a four-item subtest that has *only* one obvious purpose: to provide a transition between the gross motor tasks administered previously and the reinitiation of the table-top tasks. The items require the child to: cross his or her feet at the ankle, fold hands in his or her lap, twiddle thumbs, and sight through a plastic tube, in response to the examiner's demonstration. Each of these tasks is completed while seated at the examining table. The tasks assess the child's ability to copy simple fine and gross motor movements.

Technical Characteristics

Psychometrically, this subtest is probably the worst example of psychoeducational assessment available. While the subtest has an adequate floor (most young children can copy all of the demonstrated movements), it has virtually no ceiling. The average 2½ year old, for example, earns a raw score of 2.1 (SD = 1.1) out of 4 possible points, and above 3 years the average child earns a score greater than 3.0 (See Table 5-1). Item discrimination is limited to tenths of a single raw score from age 4 through 8½ years, evidencing almost no discrimination across the age span. By any standard this subtest is worthless, and the inclusion of its scores into the GCI is meaningless.

Draw-A-Design (Perceptual-Motor and Motor)

The Draw-A-Design subtest is a paper and pencil geometric design copying task, similar to the Bender-Gestalt. Beginning with the examiner demonstrating a circle, vertical and horizontal lines, the examinee progresses eventually to more complex designs (e.g., interlocking circles, parallelogram) that are printed and copied in a separate test protocol. The task assesses attention to detail, visual discrimination, and fine motor, perceptual motor, and eye-hand coordination. Additionally, for young children the task is very experiential in nature, assessing the child's level of comfort and familiarity with paper and pencil activities.

The Draw-A-Design subtest is part scored, according to the degree of accuracy in the child's reproduction of the stimulus. The subtest has a total possible raw score of 19 points for the nine stimulus items. Scoring is sometimes difficult because of the nuances in scoring criteria.

Technical Characteristics

Inter-scorer reliability is one aspect of technical adequacy that should have been investigated for the Draw-A-Design subtest, though there is nothing mentioned in the *Manual* regarding the topic. With over 15 pages devoted to the subtest in the *McCarthy Manual*, (roughly 13 pages devoted to scoring criteria and procedures) some evidence of inter-scorer reliability in the *Manual* is warranted.

The subtest evidences a mildly weak floor, with the average 2½ year old earning a mere 1.4 raw score points. The subtest also demonstrates a mildly weak ceiling, with the average 8½ year old earning a raw score of 14.7 (SD = 2.7) out of 19 possible points. The Draw-A-Design item gradient distinguishes developmental differences across the age span fairly well. This subtest is highly experiential in nature and possesses minimal technical standards at both ends of the age/ability continuum.

Draw-A-Child (Perceptual-Motor & Motor)

The Draw-A-Child subtest requires the child to draw a picture of a person of his or her gender. This task is developmentally scored (maximum of 20 raw score points), much like the commonly used Human Figure Drawing or Draw-A-Man test. The subtest assesses body awareness, familiarity and comfort with paper and pencil, and perceptual-motor coordination.

Technical Characteristics

Although the subtest has a poor floor for young children, with the average 2½ year old child earning a raw score of only 0.20, it has a moderate ceiling; the average 8½ year old child earns a raw score of 14.6 (SD = 2.7) (See Table 5-1). The proven developmental nature of human figure drawings ensures ample gradation of points across the age levels served by the McCarthy.

Numerical Memory, Parts I & II (Quantitative & Memory)

As with the Wechsler Intelligence Scale for Children—Revised (Wechsler, 1974), the McCarthy Numerical Memory subtest assesses sequential short-term memory for digits, both forward and backward. Additionally, attentiveness, low anxiety, and ability to reverse stimuli facilitate successful completion. Each successively longer numerical sequence is presented to the examinee at a rate of one digit per second. Part I of the subtest has a maximum attainable score of 12 raw score points; each item on Part II is doubly weighted and the second part has a maximum raw score of 20. The additional weight assigned to Part

II is probably because of the higher level cognitive processes required to recall and mentally reverse stimuli (Jensen, 1975).

Technical Characteristics

Part I of the subtest has an adequate floor for young children and an adequate ceiling for older children (See Table 5-1). Likewise, the dispersion of raw score points across the age span indicates an adequate item gradient. These positive technical characteristics are common among measures of short-term forward memory.

Part II has a much more limited floor. It is not until 5 years that the average child can correctly reverse a single two digit sequence. By 8½ years the average child still responds correctly to only two out of ten items. Thus, the subtest lacks sufficient floor, even at the older age levels, but possesses a sufficient ceiling at all age levels. There is little item gradient across the age levels, with mere tenths of a point distinguishing between the average performance of children from age level to age level. Without a doubt, the task is too difficult for most preschool children.

Verbal Fluency (Verbal)

This subtest has four items, each of which generate from zero to nine raw score points. The child is asked to identify as many examples of a given category as possible (e.g., Name as many things to drink as possible). The task requires verbal labelling, as well as fluency and flexibility of thought.

Technical Characteristics

Given a total 36 possible raw score points, the subtest possesses an adequate floor (mean raw score of 2.5 for 2½ year olds) and adequate ceiling for older children (mean raw score of 23.5 for 8½ year olds), and an excellent item gradation. Verbal Fluency possesses the best item characteristics of all the McCarthy subtests because of the high number of raw score points assigned the subtest.

Counting and Sorting (Quantitative)

The Counting and Sorting subtest requires the child to count blocks (to five) and sort them according to equal sets. For example, given a line of 10 one-inch cubes, the child must divide the set into two equal numbered subsets of five, and then count the number of blocks in each subset. The task requires place counting, understanding of sets, and the comprehension of basic numerical concepts of the sort assessed by the Numbers/Counting and Quantity subtests of the Bracken Basic Concept Scale (BBCS; Bracken, 1984), e.g., "...the *same number*...", "...*second* from this end," and "...*fourth* from this end." The Counting and Sorting subtest has nine items and yields a maximum raw score of 9 points.

Technical Characteristics

The Counting and Sorting subtest has a very limited floor, with the average 2½ year old child earning less than one point credit (0.70) and a very limited ceiling. At ages 6½, 7½, and 8½ years, the average child earns raw scores of 8.6, 8.8, and 8.9 respectively out of 9.0 possible points (See Table 5-1). Thus, the subtest evidences little discrimination at either the lower or upper age levels. Between 2½ years and 6½ years the subtest possesses an adequate item gradient.

Opposite Analogies (Verbal)

This subtest provides the child with a verbal stem, to which the child is required to provide an opposite conceptual term to complete the analogy (e.g., father is a *man*, mother is a _____?). The subtest has nine items, each worth one raw score point. Opposite Analogies assesses the child's understanding of common conceptual terms, verbal comprehension, opposites, verbal expression, and word finding ability.

Technical Characteristics

With a mean raw score of 0.40 for 2½ year-olds, the subtest evidences a weak floor; the ceiling is only slightly better (the average 8½ year old earns a raw score of 7.6 out of a possible 9 points). The item gradient across the age span is fairly gradual despite the weak ceiling and floor. The analogy format of this subtest provides a nice reasoning component to the Verbal Scale subtest, but its limited technical adequacy limits the task's usefulness. Unfortunately, most of the subtest's items are fairly automatic, once the child grasps the analogy format (e.g., hot/cold, up/down, big/little).

Conceptual Grouping (Perceptual-Performance)

The Conceptual Grouping subtest requires the child to identify the appropriate plastic chip or chips described by the examiner (e.g., find all the *small, round, blue ones*). The nine-item subtest assesses the child's understanding of BBCS related color, shape, comparison, and size concepts. The subtest assesses verbal concept formation, and produces a total possible raw score of 12 points.

Technical Characteristics

The subtest evidences an inadequate floor at the younger age levels, with the average 2½ year old earning a raw score of 1.4 and standard deviations of 1.7; the subtest standard deviation exceeds the subtest mean at age 3 also. Likewise, the ceiling is minimal, as the average 8½ year old earns a raw score of 10.3 out of a possible 12 points. The items are fairly gradually graded between the youngest age level and the upper-most age level. The colorful materials make an attractive contribution to the assessment process; however, a few more easy and difficult items would benefit the subtest greatly.

The McCarthy Scales and GCI

Verbal

Five subtests contribute to the Verbal scale: Pictoral Memory, Verbal Memory I and II, Word Knowledge I and II, Verbal Fluency, and Opposite Analogies; the first two subtests also contribute to the Memory scale (See Fig. 5-1).

Technical Characteristics

With a mean of 50 and standard deviations of 10 for the McCarthy scales, a range of standard scores between 20 and 80 would represent the expected range of abilities for children functioning within +/− 3 standard deviations, and would include approximately 99 percent of the children in the population. Bracken (1987) recommended a minimal floor and ceiling for subtests, scales, and total test scores of +/− 2 standard deviations, to ensure discrimination among all but the most extreme 2 percent of individuals in the population.

A 2½ year old child who earns a raw score of only one on each of the five verbal subtests will obtain a Verbal scale score of 36, which is only 1.4 standard deviations below the mean score of 50. Thus, the McCarthy Verbal Scale has a limited floor for the youngest age level and fails to meet the recommended −2SD criterion; however, the scale does meet the criterion by 3½ years. The Verbal scale evidences ample (+2 SD range) ceiling at all age levels. Bracken's suggested item gradient criterion (no more than ⅓ standard deviation standard score incremental change associated with a single raw score) also is met by the Verbal Scale.

Although the Verbal Scale floor is weak at the youngest age levels, it is adequate at all ages beyond. The scale evidences ample ceiling and an adequate item gradient at all age levels.

Perceptual/Performance

The Perceptual/Performance scale consists of seven subtests: Block Building, Puzzle Solving, Tapping Sequence (also on the Memory scale), Right-Left Orientation, Draw-A-Design, Draw-A-Child (both drawing tasks are also on the Motor Scale), and Conceptual Grouping.

Technical Characteristics

Given a raw score of one on each of the Perceptual/Performance scale subtests, the average 2½ year old would earn a standard score of 48, which is only two-tenths of a standard deviation below the scale mean. By 3½ years a raw score of 7 yields a scale score of 30, which meets the desired −2 SD floor criterion. The scale possesses an acceptable ceiling at all age levels, and with the exception of rare instances of marginally or unacceptably steep item gradients at younger age levels, the scale demonstrates an acceptable item gradient throughout the remaining ages.

Quantitative Scale

This scale consists of three subtests: Number Questions, Numerical Memory I and II (which also is included on the Memory Scale), and Counting and Sorting.

Technical Characteristics

With the requirement that the examinee pass at least one item on each of the three Quantitative scale subtests, the resulting scale standard score

at 2½ years would be 48, just two-tenths of a standard deviation below the mean. Not until 4 years does the scale produce standard scores at or below 30. Throughout the age levels, the scale evidences an adequate item gradient.

Memory

There are no Memory subtests assigned *only* to the Memory scale; each of the four memory subtests also are included on one of the three following nonmemory scales: Verbal (Pictorial Memory and Verbal Memory I and II), Perceptual/Performance (Tapping Sequence), or Quantitative (Numerical Memory I and II).

Technical Characteristics

It is not until 3½ years that a raw score of one on each of the four Memory subtests yields a scale score of 30, −2SD; at the lowest age level, a raw score of 4 yields a standard score of 47, just three-tenths of a standard deviation below the mean. As with the three previous scales, the Memory scale has an adequate ceiling at all ages and an adequate item gradient at all age and ability levels, except in rare individual instances.

Motor

The Motor scale is comprised of five subtests, with two that overlap with the Perceptual/Performance Scale (i.e., the Draw-A-Child and Draw-A-Design subtests). The three independent Motor subtests include, Leg Coordination, Arm Coordination, and Imitative Action.

Technical Characteristics

With a raw score of one on each of the five Motor scale subtests, a 2½ year old child would earn a standard score of 45 (-0.5 SD). From 3½ years and beyond, such a raw score would yield a standard score below the -2 standard deviation criterion of 30. The scale evidences ample ceiling at all age levels, and an adequate item gradient in all but two instances across the age and ability levels served by the McCarthy.

General Cognitive Index

The GCI is a result of the combined scores from subtests included on the Verbal, Perceptual-

Performance, and Quantitative scales. In reality the GCI is a result of the combined scores from all subtests except Leg Coordination, Arm Coordination, and Imitative Action; all other Memory or Motor subtests are included on one of the three GCI contributing scales.

Technical Characteristics

With a raw score of 17 at the youngest age levels (i.e., one item passed on each of the appropriate subtests), a standard score of 88 would be earned at age 2½. A GCI of this magnitude is classified in the Dull Normal cognitive range, and is less than one standard deviation below the average GCI of 100. As with all of the MSCA scales, the McCarthy total test score (GCI) reflects an inadequate floor for sound evaluation at the youngest age levels. If a child earns less than one raw score point on more than two or three McCarthy subtests, it is recommended that the examiner not consider the evaluation valid. Little distinction in ability level can be made reliably when a child answers so few items correctly.

The McCarthy GCI evidences ample ceiling and floor at most age levels, producing standard scores between 50 and 150 at all age levels above 3½ years. Hence, at all age levels above 3½ years, the McCarthy produces a range of GCI's sufficiently broad to distinguish among all but the most exceptional cases. Likewise, the item gradient for the GCI meets Bracken's (1987) criterion of no more than one-third standard deviation change in standard score as a result of a change in a single raw score.

STANDARDIZATION

According to the *Manual* (McCarthy, 1972), the test is appropriate for children of both sexes and various ethnic, regional, and socioeconomic groups. The McCarthy was standardized on 1,032 children, sampled according to sex, color (white or nonwhite), geographic region, and father's occupation. Nonwhite subjects included Blacks, American Indians, Orientals, and Filipinos; Hispanics were classified according to their ethnic background as either white or nonwhite. With the McCarthy "white/nonwhite" classification, there is no way of discerning whether any particular nonwhite ethnic group was representatively sam-

pled (e.g., Hispanics, Blacks, Orientals). Examination of the *McCarthy Manual* suggests that on the basis of ethnic representation (i.e., white/nonwhite), the sample fairly closely fits the U.S. population, according to the 1970 census.

The McCarthy regional representation also appears to be a close fit with the national population, as does gender and father's occupation. The sample's "fit" to the national population is less close in combined cells, where "color" by region varies a few percentage points from the population and "color" within father's occupational group varies by as much as six percentage points.

The McCarthy standardization sample characteristics cited in the *Manual* support the contention that a conscientious effort was made to match the U.S. population on critical demographic variables. However, it would have been much better if the percent representation of each major ethnic group had been listed according to region of the country, gender, and socioeconomic status. Attempting to discern white/nonwhite status of Hispanics and combining all dark skinned individuals into the nonwhite category was an unfortunate act in the McCarthy standardization. Revision and restandardization of the McCarthy would help the instrument immeasurably in this respect.

RELIABILITY

Internal Consistency

Using the criterion of .90 internal consistency for a test of individual assessment (Bracken, 1987), the McCarthy GCI meets the criterion at each age level. The *McCarthy Manual* reports a range of internal consistency coefficients from .90 to .96 across the age span, with an average reliability of .93 for all ages combined. The McCarthy GCI appears to be adequately reliable for the individual assessment of young children.

In many instances the internal consistency coefficients for the five McCarthy Scales are somewhat less than the .90 criterion. The Verbal scale ranges from a low of .84 at age 6½ years to a high of .92 at 3½ years. Although each age level approaches or meets the desired criterion, the average Verbal scale internal consistency coefficient of .88 is less than the desired .90 criterion. The Perceptual-Performance Scale coefficients range from .75 (age 8½) to .90 (age 3½), with an average internal consistency of .84; the Perceptual-Performance scale lacks the desired level of reliability at all age levels except one. The third scale that contributes to the GCI, Quantitative, is somewhat less reliable than the previous scales. The Quantitative Scale ranges in internal consistency from .70 (age 4) to .86 (ages 5 and 5½); none of the age levels possess sufficient reliability to meet the .90 criterion.

The remaining two scales, Memory and Motor, do not contribute directly to the GCI, but are still intended to be interpreted at an individual level. Thus, these remaining scales also should meet the .90 criterion. Both scales fail to meet the minimal criterion at any age level; Memory ranges from .72 to .84 (average coefficient of .79) and the Motor Scale ranges from .60 to .84 (average coefficient of .79).

None of the McCarthy Scales is sufficiently reliable to warrant anything except cautious interpretation. Recognizing that each of the cognitive scales (i.e., Verbal, Perceptual/Performance, and Quantitative) in most instances are above the .80 level of internal consistency recommended for subtests but are less than the desired .90 level for scales and total test scores, it is recommended that the scales be interpreted with much the same emphasis as assigned to subtests. The Memory and Motor scales both have average internal consistencies of .79, which is slightly below the .80 criterion set for subtests, and considerably below the .90 desired criterion for a scale. In this respect, the McCarthy Scales should be considered and interpreted with much the same emphasis as individual subtests, combined to form a five subtest instrument.

This position is further supported by the fact that none of the 18 McCarthy subtests' reliability coefficients are reported in the *McCarthy Manual*. Without evidence of sufficient reliability for interpretation (and considerable reason to suspect poor reliability for most of the subtests), the McCarthy subtests should not be considered individually, but only collectively as they contribute to their respective scales, and those scales should only be interpreted cautiously.

STABILITY

The *McCarthy Manual* reports a 3- to 5-week stability study for children in three age groupings (i.e., 3 to 3½ years; 5 to 5½ years; 7½ to 8½ years) for each of the McCarthy scales and GCI. Using the .90 criterion proposed for short-term stability (Bracken, 1987), the McCarthy GCI barely meets the criterion at the two extreme age levels (.91 and .90), and minimally fails to meet the criterion at the middle most age level (.89). Thus it appears that the McCarthy GCI has sufficient evidence of stability at two age levels to interpret on an individual basis; however, stability of the McCarthy at ages 2½, 4, 4½, 6, and 6½ was not reported in the *Manual*. In independent studies, Bryant and Roffe (1978) report a three- to six-week GCI stability coefficient of .85 and David and Slettedahl (1976) report a one-year coefficient of .84, suggesting further that the short- and long-term instrument's stability is consistently close to but less than the .90 desired level.

In these studies, none of the McCarthy Scales, at any age level met the minimal .90 criterion; most of the scales were in the vicinity of .80. As with internal consistency, the McCarthy scales generally possess sufficient stability to be treated as individual subtests.

VALIDITY

Although the *McCarthy Manual* reports only one concurrent validity and one predictive validity study, there have been scores of studies completed and synthesized since the publication of the test (Bracken, 1981; Kaufman, 1982; Nagle, 1979). The MSCA validation evidence published in the *Manual* pales in comparison to newer cognitive instruments such as the Kaufman Assessment Battery for Children (Kaufman & Kaufman, 1983), Woodcock-Johnson Psychoeducational Battery-Revised (Woodcock & Johnson, 1977) and the Stanford-Binet, IV (Thorndike, Hagen, & Sattler, 1986). Despite the lack of validity data published in the MSCA Manual, the Bracken, Kaufman, and Nagle publications provide a review of the MSCA validity literature from its inception to 1982. In each of the sections that follow, the pre-1982 validity evidence is synthesized and then the post-1982 MSCA validation literature is reviewed.

Pre-1982 Concurrent Validity

In general, the pre-1982 literature suggests that the McCarthy GCI correlates positively and moderately with other major measures of intelligence for preschool and primary level children, regardless of exceptionality. For example, Kaufman's (1982) synthesis (which also includes studies cited in Bracken, 1981 and Nagle, 1979) reveals a weighted mean correlation of .82 among nine studies in which the MSCA and Stanford-Binet, L-M (Terman & Merrill, 1973) were compared for normal children. Kaufman cites two studies with correlation of .76 and .77 for gifted children, and a range of moderately strong correlations (.60 to .76) is reported for retarded children.

Concurrent validity correlations between the MSCA GCI and WPPSI (Wechsler, 1967) and WISC-R (Wechsler, 1974) Full Scale IQs (FSIQ) also provide ample support for shared variance between the MSCA and the Wechsler Scales. Again, using the data for "normal samples" presented in Kaufman (1982) the MSCA GCI correlates quite strongly with the FSIQ range between .71 and .86 for the WPPSI and .51 and .90 for the WISC-R. Exceptional samples also produce equally strong correlations between the MSCA and Wechsler Scales; ranging from .72 to .82 for retardates and .64 to .90 for learning disabled samples.

Differences in the interpretation of the McCarthy concurrent validity data have occurred primarily because of the sometimes quite large mean score differences that have resulted between the MSCA and other tests of intelligence. Nagle (1979) described several studies that had resulted in large mean score differences between the MSCA and other tests of intelligence and concluded,

> "Presently, the MSCA can be judged at least as reliable and stable as other preschool intelligence tests (cf. Sattler, 1974), however, several concurrent validity studies appear to suggest tentatively that GCI and IQ are not comparable among normal (Gerken et al., 1978; Phillips et al., 1978) and exceptional (DeBoer et al., Note 1; Kaufman and Kaufman, 1974) children." (p. 324)

Similarly, in his review of McCarthy studies Bracken (1981) concluded, "The MSCA appears to produce GCI's which are consistently lower than IQ's for children with lesser abilities, whether due to age or handicap" (p. 129). Further support for this claim is derived from Kaufman's (1982) review, in which the McCarthy was shown to consistently produce lower GCI's than Binet IQ's (weighted mean difference of 6.42 points) and lower GCI's than WPPSI FSIQ's when the sample was younger than six years (weighted mean difference of 5.48 points). Additionally, Kaufman reports MSCA and Stanford-Binet, L-M weighted mean differences of 10 points for gifted and 19 points for retarded, with the GCI being the lower score in every study cited. Comparisons between the MSCA and the WPPSI and WISC-R yield weighted mean differences of 5 points for retarded children and 9 points for learning disabled children, with the GCI being lower in every sample except one; that sample was for older children (ages 6–6 to 8–11) and produced no difference between the two tests.

Given the comparability of the McCarthy national norms (1972) with those of the Binet, L-M (1972) and WISC-R (1974), one would not expect such large discrepancies to exist among the exceptional and youthful samples because of the phenomenon of norm "softening" with age (Flynn, 1984). The differences between global scores obtained on the McCarthy and Binet, L-M and the MSCA and Wechsler Scales appear to be related to a quirk in the MSCA standardization sample. It was just these large mean score differences that caused Bracken (1981) to conclude, "Although the MSCA does provide promising use as a diagnostic tool for determining a child's relative strengths and weaknesses, its use for the classification of children is not recommended." (p. 129)

Post-1982 McCarthy Concurrent Validity

A more recent review of the literature revealed several studies that have compared the MSCA with more current instruments, such as the K-ABC (Kaufman & Kaufman, 1983). Table 5-2 presents a listing and summary findings of these more recent studies. A synthesis of the findings suggests, as did the earlier literature reviews, that

TABLE 5.2
POST-1982 MCCARTHY VALIDATION STUDIES

Study	Sample	Method	Results
Bickett, Reuter, & Stancin (1984)	21 moderately retarded primary age children	MSCA and Stanford-Binet were administered concurrently in a counterbalanced format	MSCA correlation with S-B = 69.
Bracken (1983) (Cited in Kaufman and Kaufman, 1983)	32 nonexceptional preschool children	MSCA and K-ABC administered concurrently in counterbalanced order	MSCA GCI = 101.8, SD = 13.5 K-ABC MPC = 101.0, SD = 11.7 KABC ACH = 104, SD = 13.6 MSCA correlations with MPC = .60 ACH = .75
Bracken (1985)	21 nonexceptional preschool children; 10 males, 11 females	Concurrent comparison of MSCA with BBCS, CMMS and K-ABC	MSCA GCI = 110.5, SD = 19.8 BBCS Total Test = 109.7, SD = 16.6 Columbia ADS = 113.6, SD = 9.7 K-ABC MPC = 109.8, SD = 16.4 MSCA correlations with: BBCS = .96 ADS = .82 MPC = .65
Bracken et al., (1988)	55 3, 4, and 5 year old, nonexceptional preschool children	Concurrent comparison in which the MSCA was administered to all children then the BBCS and K-ABC were administered in a counterbalanced format within five months of the MSCA	MSCA GCI = 119.4, SD = 10.8 BBCS Total Test = 109.3, SD = 14.2 K-ABC MPC = 113.5, SD = 14.2 MSCA correlations with the: BBCS = .69 K-ABC = .51
Funk, Sturner, & Green (1986)	117 preschool children	117 children were administered the MSCA. 110 children were later tested on the kindergarten California Achievement Test; 98 were retested on the first grade CAT; 70 were retested on second grade CAT	MSCA GCI = 92.8, SD = 18.0 MSCA correlations with: K CAT Reading = .70 1st CAT Reading = .65 1st CAT Math = .56 2nd CAT Reading = .66 2nd CAT Math = .53
Klanderman, Brown, Stranges, & Page (1983) (Cited in Kaufman & Kaufman, 1983)	40 normal preschool children	MSCA and K-ABC were compared concurrently in counterbalanced order	MSCA GCI = 110.0, SD = 15.5 K-ABC MPC = 115.5, SD = 18.4 K-ABC ACH = 113.9, SD = 17.3

TABLE 5.2 *(continued)*

Study	Sample	Method	Results
Klanderman et al. (continued)			MSCA correlations with MPC = .68 ACH = .73
Lidz & Ballester, (1986)	70 "referred" preschoolers	MSCA and Stanford-Binet administered concurrently in a counterbalanced order	MSCA = 80.4, SD = 12.5 Binet LM = 84.3, SD = 9.9 MSCA-Binet correlation = .73
Lyon & Smith, (1986)	43 "referred" preschoolers;	MSCA and K-ABC were compared concurrently in a counterbalanced format	MSCA GCI = 86.3, SD = 16.6 K-ABC MPC = 85.9, SD = 11.8 K-ABC ACH = 88.5, SD = 12.6 MSCA correlations with: MPC = .59 ACH = .59
Massoth (1985)	24 kindergarten children	MSCA 5 year prediction of performance on Comprehensive Testing Program	MSCA GCI = 108.1, SD = 14.5 MSCA correlations with CTP Verbal = .71 Quantitative = .50 Total = .68
Massoth & Levenson (1982)	33 kindergarten children	MSCA administration predicted MacMillan Reading Readiness Test (1 yr) and Metropolitan Achievement Test (1 yr, 9 mo) performance	MSCA GCI = 107.6 MSCA correlations with MRRT = .53 MAT = .39
Naglieri (1985)	51 nonexceptional first, second, and third grade students	MSCA and K-ABC administered concurrently in a counterbalanced format; PIAT administered three months later	MSCA GCI 101.3, SD = 15.0 K-ABC MPC = 102.4, SD = 14.0 K-ABC ACH = 103.6, SD = 14.8 PIAT Total Test = 106.6, SD = 11.8 MSCA GCI correlations with: MPC = .55 ACH = .79 PIAT = .74
Reilly, Drudge, Rosen, Loew, & Fischer (1985)	30 first grade students (concurrent) 26 first grade students (predictive)	MSCA, WISC-R, and Woodcock-Johnson were administered concurrently; two years later the WRAT and teacher's ratings were gathered	MSCA GCI = 110.7 WISC-R FSIQ = 108.2 W-J Full Scale = 111.0 MSCA concurrent correlation with: FSIQ = .89 W-J = .77

TABLE 5.2 (*continued*)

Study	Sample	Method	Results
Reilly et al. (continued)			MSCA predictive correlation with: WRAT reading = .72 WRAT spelling = .70 WRAT Math = .67 Reading rating = .74 Spelling rating = .76 Math rating = .79
Zucker & Copeland, (1988)	51 "at-risk" and 33 nonexceptional preschool and primary grade children	Concurrent comparison in which the MSCA and K-ABC were administered in a counterbalanced order	"At Risk" MSCA GCI = 83.3, SD = 20.0 K-ABC MPC = 90.0, SD = 14.2 K-ABC ACH = 89.5, SD = 13.3 Normal MSCA GCI = 112.9, SD = 10.6 K-ABC MPC = 110.6, SD = 10.3 K-ABC ACH = 113.7, SD = 10.6 MSCA "at risk" correlations MPC = .84 ACH (not reported) MSCA "normal" correlations MPC = .54

the McCarthy correlates moderately to strongly with tests of achievement and cognitive ability. The correlations between the MSCA and the Bracken Basic Concept Scale (Bracken, 1984) yielded correlations of .96 and .69 for two samples of preschool children. This finding makes sense when one considers the vast number of basic concepts used in the MSCA test directions (Bracken, 1986) and the wide variety of concepts assessed by items in the Number Questions, Right-Left Orientation, Counting and Sorting, Opposite Analogies, and Conceptual Grouping subtests.

In its comparison with the K-ABC, the MSCA GCI appears to correlate moderately with the MPC, with correlations ranging from .54 to .84. In the majority of the studies reported in Table 5-2, there were small (2 to 3 point) differences between the GCI and MPC, with an occasional difference of greater magnitude (e.g., 5.5 and 6.7 point difference). It appears that "normal" chil-

dren in an age range from 4 to 7½ years perform comparably on both instruments.

Of those instances in which the GCI produced lower scores than the K-ABC, one was with normal preschool children (Klanderman et al., 1983) and produced a 5.5 point discrepancy between the instruments. The second example, Zucker and Copeland (1988), reported a significantly lower GCI than MPC for at-risk preschool and primary grade children (6.7 point difference), but a *higher* GCI than MPC for nonexceptional children (+2.3 point difference). Likewise, Lidz and Ballester (1986) report significant differences between the Stanford-Binet, Form L-M and MSCA for young educable mentally retarded (EMR) children (6.8 point lower mean GCI than IQ), learning disabled (LD) children (mean GCI was 4.1 points lower than IQ), and children with speech difficulties (6 point lower mean GCI than IQ). Each exceptional sample earned mean GCI's between 86 and 64, and were thus functioning intellectually at a below average level. In contrast, Lidz and Ballester's "normal" subjects earned a mean Binet IQ that *exceeded* their mean GCI by about 1.5 points.

It appears that the post-1982 literature continues to support Bracken's (1981) and Nagle's (1979) notion that exceptional children perform poorer on the McCarthy than other measures of intelligence. Given that the GCI appears to underestimate intelligence relative to other tests for low functioning children, concern about over- and/or misidentification of low functioning children resurfaces the question of the MSCA's applicability for placement decisions.

Pre-1982 Predictive Validity

In addition to the fact that the McCarthy frequently produces noncomparable scores when contrasted with other major measures of intelligence, the test also appears to predict academic achievement only moderately well. McCarthy (1972) reports just one predictive validity study in the MSCA *Manual*; that study revealed a validity coefficient between the GCI and the Metropolitan Achievement Test total raw score of .49. While the Perceptual-Performance and Quantitative scales both correlated .51 with the MAT total raw score, the Verbal scale correlated only .18. Although verbal abilities tend to be among the best predictors of academic achievement, verbal abilities assessed by the MSCA did not predict very well in this study. In his review of the MSCA, Kaufman (1982) cites several predictive validity studies, mostly dissertations, that evidence low to moderate correlations between the McCarthy and a variety of achievement tests and teachers' ratings. In sum, the pre-1982 literature suggests that the McCarthy predicts or correlates concurrently with achievement criteria at a moderate level.

Post-1982 Predictive Validity

The MSCA also correlates concurrently with the K-ABC Achievement Scale total score moderately well, with correlations ranging from .59 to .79 (See Table 5-2). Likewise, the McCarthy predicts performance on a variety of achievement tests at a moderate level, including the California Achievement Test (r = .53 to .70), Comprehensive Testing Program (r = .50 to .71) McMillan Readiness Test (r = .53), Metropolitan Achievement Test (r = .59), Wide Range Achievement Test (r = .67 to .72) and teachers' ratings (r = .74 to .79) (See Table 5-2). It appears that the MSCA predicts achievement fairly well, even over extended periods of time (e.g., five years) and correlates concurrently with achievement tests at appropriately high levels as well. Thus, although the test performs differentially relative to other intelligence tests for below average children, and might result in the misclassification of nonexceptional children, it predicts achievement moderately well.

Construct Validity to Date

Construct validity is a reflection of the degree to which a test and its subtests assess the hypothetical and theoretical constructs that underlie the test. Construct validity frequently is tested by way of factor analysis. Instruments that combine subtests rationally or theoretically into scales should have those subtests load on the factors that represent their respective scales. The McCarthy is designed to produce five subscales and one general cognitive scale. Thus, ideally one would expect to extract five factors representing each of the five scales, plus one *g* factor. Although tests of mental ability typically produce a *g* factor, finding factor support for theoretically derived subscales is a more difficult task.

Kaufman (1975a) factor-analyzed the MSCA standardization data and reported on the factor structure across five age levels. He found that the factor structure changed somewhat as a result of developmental changes across the samples, but he reports that three to five factors (disregarding the *g* factor) emerged at each of the five age levels. For children age 2½ years, Kaufman reports only Verbal, Motor, and Memory factors, with no Quantitative or Perceptual/Performance factors to match their respective scales. Across the standardization sample age groupings additional factors emerged, including Perceptual/Performance, Drawing, Semantic Memory, Quantitative, and Reasoning. Although many of the McCarthy subtests loaded on their appropriate factors at each age level, they also frequently loaded on inappropriate factors (e.g., Arm Coordination loaded .43 on the Verbal factor at age 2½ years; Conceptual grouping, a Perceptual/Performance subtest, also loaded significantly on the Verbal factor at ages 3 to 4½ years). Although these factor loadings can be explained in terms of what the subtests measure and their respective task demands, the question of whether the MSCA scales are interpretable as measures of their umbrella abilities subsumed by their titles is clouded. When one considers that there were scales with unrepresented factors and/or additional factors present at *each* age level, interpretation of the MSCA scales is even less clear across the entire McCarthy age span.

Six McCarthy factor analyses conducted since the Kaufman (1975a) analysis are described shortly. The first study (Kaufman & Dicuio, 1975) is an analysis of the McCarthy standardization data by race (whites, study 1a; blacks, study 1b). Kaufman and Dicuio limited the analyses to 688 whites and 124 blacks from the MSCA standardization data between the ages of 3-0 to 7-6 years. The second factor analytic study (Keith & Bolen, 1980) includes 300 children referred for school related problems between the ages of 6-0 to 8-6 years. Mishra's (1981) factor analysis represents the third study reported, and it included 126 Mexican-American (study 3a) and 186 Anglo (study 3b) children between the ages of 5-6 and 7-6 years. The fourth study (Naglieri, Kaufman, & Harrison, 1981) consisted of 77 low functioning children between the ages of 6 and 8½ years. Teeter (1984) conducted the fifth analysis on 105 normal kindergarten children (ages 4-11 to 6-7). The last analysis was a study conducted by Wiebe and Watkins (1980) in which they factor analyzed the scores of 100 male (study 6a), 100 female (study 6b), and a total sample of 200 preschoolers (study 6c), ages 2-6 to 5-0. All of the above analyses include preschool and primary grade children.

Although factor analyses can be viewed from the perspective of the integrity of given scales as demonstrable factors, the analyses also can be viewed from the perspective of whether specific subtests load on their appropriate factors (i.e., the factors representing the scales to which they are theoretically assigned). It is this latter view that will be examined, across each of the 18 McCarthy subtests. Obviously, if subtests fail to load on the factors representing their respective scales, then the integrity of the scales also are in question. All subtests that load .30 or above on a given factor

are considered significant contributors to that factor.

Block Building

Block Building is a subtest that yields somewhat consistent loadings across the factor studies. It was not included in two analyses because it failed to generate enough variance across the age range. Also, it failed to load significantly on any factor in two other comparisons; however, in the remaining studies it loaded on factors identified as Visual Performance, Perceptual/Performance, Motor, Nonverbal Cognitive, and Remote Verbal Memory. Thus, in studies where there was sufficient variance for meaningful analysis, Block Building tended to load on factors related to and consistent with its perceived underlying abilities and the scale to which it is assigned (Perceptual/Performance).

Block Building	Assigned Factor	Study
	Not Cited	1a
	Not Cited	1b
	Visual Performance	2
	Perceptual/Performance & Motor	3a
	Motor	3b
	Not Cited	4
	None	5
	Nonverbal Cognitive	6a
	Remote Verbal Memory	6b
	None	6c

Puzzle Solving

Puzzle Solving loaded on the Verbal and Remote Verbal Memory factors in three contrasts. Additionally, the subtest loaded significantly on Perceptual/Performance, Nonverbal Cognitive, and Motor factors, either concurrently with its verbal loadings or alone, in six of the ten contrasts. It is apparent that Puzzle Solving assesses perceptual and motor related skills, but it also appears to assess verbal abilities to some degree.

Therefore, the subtest appears to be appropriately placed on the Perceptual-Motor scale, but also should be considered to some degree as a measure of verbal abilities.

Puzzle Solving	Assigned Factor	Study
	Perceptual/Performance	1a
	Verbal & Motor	1b
	None	2
	Verbal & Perceptual/ Performance	3a
	Verbal	3b
	Perceptual/Performance	4
	Perceptual/Performance	5
	Nonverbal Cognitive	6a
	Remote Verbal Memory	6b
	None	6c

Pictorial Memory

Pictorial Memory is assigned to both the MSCA Verbal and Memory scales. Although the subtest loaded significantly on Verbal factors in seven of the ten contrasts, it loaded only once on a Memory factor (Remote Verbal Memory). Pictorial Memory appears to be appropriately placed on the Verbal scale, but is misplaced on the Memory scale; memory does not appear to be a major underlying skill assessed by the subtest.

Pictorial Memory	Assigned Factor	Study
	Verbal	1a
	Verbal	1b
	Verbal	2
	Verbal	3a
	Verbal	3b
	none	4
	Verbal Comprehension	5
	g	6a
	Abstract Verbal Reasoning	6b
	g	6c

Word Knowledge

The Word Knowledge subtest was analyzed as one unified entity in five studies and divided into Parts I and II for separate analyses in another study. Separate analyses suggest that Part I is a measure of Visual Performance, while Part II is Verbal. These two distinct factor loadings provided partial explanation why the combined Word Knowledge comparisons (Parts I and II combined) load on Motor, Perceptual/Performance, and Nonverbal Cognitive factors in addition to loadings on Verbal factors in seven of the eight contrasts. This author's earlier recommendation of dividing the various subskills assessed by Word Knowledge appears to be supported by the differntial effects the different item types have on the factor loadings. Word Knowledge appears to be appropriately placed on the Verbal scale, but it also appears to assess an uncredited perceptual, nonverbal component.

Word Knowledge	Assigned Factor	Study
Word Knowledge I	Visual Performance	2
Word Knowledge II	Verbal	2
Word Knowledge I & II	Verbal	1a
	Verbal	1b
	Verbal & Motor	3a
	Verbal & Perceptual/Performance	3b
	Verbal	4
	Verbal Comprehension	5
	Nonverbal Cognitive	6a
	Remote Verbal Memory	6b
	g	6c

Number Questions

Number Questions fails in every analysis to support its position on the Quantitative scale. In seven of the ten contrasts the subtest has significant loadings on Verbal, Verbal Comprehension, or Remote Verbal Memory factors. Additionally, Number Questions loads on Perceptual/Performance and Motor factors in four of the ten contrasts. The subtest assesses several BBCS related mathematical concepts (e.g., *half, more, each, altogether, dozen, how many*) and requires the comprehension of story problems in addition to computation for successful completion. Therefore, the subtest's high verbal loadings make sense; however, its position on the MSCA Quantitative scale does not make interpretive sense.

Number Questions	Assigned Factor	Study
	Verbal & Perceptual/Performance	1a
	Verbal	1b
	None	2
	Verbal & Perceptual/Performance	3a
	Verbal & Perceptual/Performance	3b
	Verbal & Motor	4
	Verbal Comprehension	5
	None	6a
	Remote Verbal Memory	6b
	None	6c

Tapping Sequence

Tapping Sequence, found on both the Perceptual/Performance and Memory scales, loads quite consistently on Perceptual/Performance, Motor, and Nonverbal Cognitive factors as would be hoped. In addition, the subtest loaded on Sequential Memory and Memory factors in three of the ten factor contrasts. It appears that Tapping Sequence is primarily a perceptual-motor task, with a secondary memory component. Its position on two McCarthy scales appears warranted, but it might make more contribution to the Perceptual/Performance Scale than the Memory Scale. Given such a differential contribution to the Perceptual/Performance factor, its *equal* weighting on the two McCarthy scales might not be warranted.

Tapping Sequence	Assigned Factor	Study
	Perceptual/Performance & Motor	1a
	Perceptual/Performance & Motor	1b
	None	2
	Perceptual/Performance	3a
	Perceptual/Performance	3b
	Perceptual/Performance & Memory	4
	Perceptual/Performance	5
	Sequential Memory & Nonverbal Cognitive	6a

Tapping Sequence	Assigned Factor	Study
	None	6b
	Sequential Memory	6c

Verbal Memory I & II

Verbal Memory I and II were treated factor analytically as a single subtest in two studies and as a measure of two distinct abilites in the remaining four studies. Considered as a single entity, Verbal Memory loaded jointly on Verbal and Memory factors in two contrasts, Verbal and Motor in two contrasts, and Nonverbal Cognitive in the final contrast. It appears that Verbal Memory I and II combined, provides a somewhat confusing picture, with Verbal loadings appearing quit consistently but Memory interchanging with Motor and Nonverbal Cognitive in the remaining contrasts.

Considered separately the picture becomes somewhat clearer. Verbal Memory I is clearly a measure of verbal memory, with four of the seven contrasts loading on either a Verbal or Verbal Comprehension factor and four contrasts loading on Memory or Verbal Memory factors. Verbal Memory II, though, indicates a lone Verbal loading in three contrasts, a lone Memory loading on the fourth contrast, and no significant loadings on the remaining three contrasts. Thus, Verbal Memory I clearly appears to assess verbal memory, whereas Verbal Memory II is primarily a verbal comprehension measure.

Verbal Memory	Assigned Factor	Study
Verbal Memory I	Verbal	1a
	Verbal & Memory	1b
	Verbal	2
	Verbal Comprehension & Memory	5
	None	6a
	Remote Verbal Memory & Memory	6b
	None	6c

Verbal Memory	Assigned Factor	Study
Verbal Memory II	Verbal	1a
	Verbal	1b
	Verbal	2
	Memory	5
	None	6a
	None	6b
	None	6c
Verbal Memory I & II	Verbal & Motor	3a
	Verbal & Motor	3b
	Verbal & Memory	4

Right-Left Orientation

Right-Left Orientation was not considered in six of the contrasts, most likely because of the lack of variance generated by the subtest. Although the subtest is positioned on the Perceptual/Performance scale, it loaded significantly on both a perceptual/performance and verbal factor in two contrasts and evidenced no significant loading in the remaining two studies. Right-Left Orientation's verbal loadings make sense, because the subtest requires the child to follow oral directions containing common directionality and body part concepts (e.g., right, left, chin, elbow).

Right-Left Orientation	Assigned Factor	Study
	Not Cited	1a
	Not Cited	1b
	None	2
	Verbal & Perceptual/Performance	3a
	Verbal & Perceptual/Performance	3b
	Not Cited	4
	None	5
	Not Cited	6a
	Not Cited	6b
	Not Cited	6c

Leg Coordination

Leg Coordination evidenced significant factor loadings on several factors that are motoric in nature (e.g., Motor, Visual Performance, Perceptual/Performance, Motor Imitation), as well as more language and cognitively oriented factors (e.g., Verbal, Memory, Nonverbal Cognitive). Given the significant loadings on the motorically oriented factors, Leg Coordination appears to be appropriately placed on the Motor Scale; however, it appears that the subtest has an underlying cognitive requirement. The cognitive requirement appears to be because of the subtest's verbal directions and the child's need to understand the nuance of what is expected (e.g., to stand on one foot *for as long as possible,* rather than to merely stand on one foot).

Leg Coordination	Assigned Factor	Study
	Motor	1a
	Motor & Memory	1b
	Verbal, Visual Performance, & Motor	2
	Perceptual/Performance & Motor	3a
	Perceptual/Performance & Motor	3b
	Motor	4
	None	5
	Nonverbal Cognitive	6a
	Motor Imitation & Memory	6b
	None	6c

Arm Coordination

Arm Coordination very consistently loaded on motoric factors (e.g., Motor, Motor Imitation). In only two contrasts Arm Coordination was cited as loading significantly on Verbal factors, and it was identified once as loading on a Nonverbal Cognitive factor. It appears that Arm Coordination is primarily motoric in nature. The subtest seems to have less verbal and/or cognitive demand than its companion subtest, Leg Coordination. This finding makes intuitive sense when one examines the nature of the items in both subtests; Arm Coordination emphasizes muscular coordination and agility (e.g., bouncing, catching and throwing) more than endurance (e.g., *how many* backward steps can be made successfully or *how long* can the child do a specified activity) as is required in Leg Coordination.

Arm Coordination	Assigned Factor	Study
	Motor	1a
	Motor	1b
	Motor	2
	Verbal	3a
	Verbal & Motor	3b
	Motor	4
	Motor	5
	Nonverbal Cognitive	6a
	Motor Imitation	6b
	None	6c

Imitative Action

Imitative Action's psychometric uselessness is further evidenced in its factor loadings reported in the six studies. Two studies did not cite the Imitative Action subtest in their analyses, most likely because of miniscule variances generated by this four-item subtest with an extremely limited ceiling. Three additional contrasts show the subtest as having no significant factor loadings. The remaining contrasts cite an assortment of factor loadings, including: Visual Performance, Motor, Nonverbal Cognitive, Motor Imitation, and Memory. Collectively, these tangential loadings make sense given the task demands of the subtest (i.e., imitative motor activity); however, there is little consistent evidence that the subtest belongs on the MSCA scale to which it is assigned (Motor).

Imitative Action	Assigned Factor	Study
	Not Cited	1a
	Not Cited	1b
	Visual Performance & Motor	2
	Motor	3a
	None	3b
	Not Cited	4
	None	5
	Nonverbal Cognitive	6a
	Motor Imitation & Memory	6b
	None	6c

Draw-A-Design

Draw-A-Design is unequivocally placed appropriately on the MSCA Perceptual/Performance Scale. The six-factor analytic studies overwhelmingly list the subtest as loading on Perceptual/Performance factors in six of the ten contrasts. Additionally, the subtest loaded significantly on Motor and Nonverbal Cognitive factors, which make sense given the subtest's task demands. Draw-A-Design evidenced no significant factor loadings in three contrasts.

Draw-A-Design	Assigned Factor	Study
	Perceptual/Performance	1a
	Perceptual/Performance & Motor	1b
	None	2
	Perceptual/Performance	3a
	Perceptual/Performance	3b
	Perceptual/Performance & Motor	4
	Perceptual/Performance	5
	Nonverbal Cognitive	6a
	None	6b
	None	6c

Draw-A-Child

Draw-A-Child evidenced substantial support for its inclusion on the Perceptual/Performance scale of the McCarthy. In seven contrasts it had significant loadings on Perceptual/Performance, Motor, or Nonverbal Cognitive factors. In addition to a single significant loading on a Verbal factor, it had no significant factor loadings in three contrasts. The perfomance of Draw-A-Child was nearly identical to Draw-A-Design among the six studies.

Draw-A-Child	Assigned Factor	Study
	Perceptual/Performance	1a
	Perceptual/Performance	1b
	None	2
	Perceptual/Performance & Motor	3a

Draw-A-Child	Assigned Factor	Study
	Verbal, Percept/Perform, & Motor	3b
	Perceptual/Performance	4
	Perceptual/Performance	5
	Nonverbal Cognitive	6a
	None	6b
	None	6c

Numerical Memory I & II

Numerical Memory I and II were treated as separate measures in the majority of the studies but were collapsed for analyses in two studies. Separately, the two parts performed similarly, though not identically. Each part (I and II) had significant loadings on Memory factors (Memory, Sequential Memory, and Remote Verbal Memory) and Quantitative Reasoning, but Numerical Memory I also had a significant Verbal loading in one contrast and no significant loadings in three other contrasts. Numerical Memory II was not cited in two contrasts (minimal variance associated with its very weak floor) and had no significant loadings in two additional contrasts.

With the two subparts combined, the subtest evidenced significant loadings on Verbal and Perceptual/Performance factors in two contrasts and Memory on the remaining contrast. It appears that with the different task demands (repeating digits forward versus backward) combined, the task becomes influenced by the child's overall verbal and perceptual abilities in addition to memory.

Numerical Memory	Assigned Factor	Study
Numerical Memory I	Verbal	1a
	None	1b
	None	2
	Quantitative Reasoning	5
	Sequential Memory	6a
	Remote Verbal Memory & Memory	6b
	None	6c
Numerical Memory II	Not Cited	1a

Numerical Memory	Assigned Factor	Study
	Not Cited	1b
	None	2
	Quantitative Reasoning	5
	Sequential Memory	6a
	None	6b
	Sequential Memory	6c
Numerical Memory I & II	Verbal & Perceptual/Performance	3a
	Verbal & Perceptual/Performance	3b
	Memory	4

Verbal Fluency

Although Verbal Fluency appears to be a measure of overall verbal ability, its task demands are closely akin to those that are required in creativity. Fluency and flexibility of thought are both aspects of creativity (Torrance, 1968) that affect one's ability to generate original ideas. As a child evidences more fluency on this subtest, it is likely that the examiner will see more flexibility (i.e., more responses from diverse areas) and originality of thought (i.e., statistically infrequent or rare responses). As such, it would be expected that the subtest would load on other factors in addition to a Verbal factor. While Verbal Fluency did load significantly on the verbally oriented factors in seven contrasts, it also loaded frequently on Perceptual/Performance and Memory factors. It is apparent that the subtest requires verbal skill, but it also requires some additional nonverbal cognitive skill(s) for success.

Verbal Fluency	Assigned Factor	Study
	Verbal	1a
	Perceptual/Performance & Memory	1b
	Verbal	2
	Verbal & Perceptual/Performance	3a
	Verbal, Percept/Performance Motor	3b

Verbal Fluency	Assigned Factor	Study
	Verbal & Memory	4
	Verbal Comprehension	5
	Nonverbal Cognitive	6a
	Remote Verbal Memory & Memory	6b
	None	6c

Counting and Sorting

Counting and Sorting is another Quantitative scale subtest with no significant loadings on a Quantitative factor. In the six studies considered, Counting and Sorting tended to load on Perceptual/Performance and/or Verbal factors, with Motor, Memory, and Nonverbal Cognitive factors emerging in single contrasts. There also were three instances of no significant factor loadings. The Perceptual/Performance factor loadings were expected, because of the visual orientation and fine motor manipulation of the one-inch blocks required to complete the task. The Verbal factor loadings also make sense, because the subtest assesses knowledge of common numerical and sequential concepts such as: *all, some, same, each, more, second, fourth, end.* Nevertheless, Counting and Sorting provides additional evidence for the uselessness of the MSCA Quantitative scale for interpretive purposes.

Counting and Sorting	Assigned Factor	Study
	Perceptual/Performance	1a
	Perceptual/Performance & Verbal	1b
	None	2
	Verbal & Perceptual/Performance	3a
	Verbal & Motor	3b
	Memory	4
	None	5
	Nonverbal Cognitive	6a
	None	6b
	None	6c

Opposite Analogies

Opposite Analogies is a Verbal scale subtest that evidences consistent Verbal loadings of one sort or another. For example, it loaded on factors identified as Verbal in five contrasts, Verbal Comprehension in another, and Abstract Verbal Reasoning in two more. Its secondary loadings on Perceptual/Performance, Memory, and Nonverbal Cognitive factors appear to be related to the reasoning component of the subtest. The ability to complete analogies in some instances appears to require some visual imagery and reasoning, both of which are associated with most Perceptual/Performance related tasks.

Opposite Analogies	Assigned Factor	Study
	Verbal & Perceptual/Performance	1a
	Perceptual/Performance	1b
	Verbal	2
	Verbal	3a
	Verbal & Perceptual/Performance	3b
	Verbal & Memory	4
	Verbal Comprehension	5
	Nonverbal Cognitive	6a
	Abstract Verbal Reasoning	6b
	Abstract Verbal Reasoning	6c

Conceptual Grouping

The last McCarthy subtest, Conceptual Grouping, loaded significantly on Verbal and Perceptual/Performance related factors consistently (e.g., Verbal, Abstract Verbal Reasoning, Perceptual/Performance, Motor, Nonverbal Reasoning). Interestingly, this is the only subtest assigned by any of the researchers to a Quantitative (Reasoning) factor. As with Number Questions and Counting and Sorting, Conceptual Grouping assesses many early language concepts, hence the loadings on Verbal factors. Also, as with the previously mentioned subtests, Conceptual Grouping requires the visualization and manipulation of small test pieces, which supports the Motoric and Perceptual/Performance loadings. It appears that the additional task demands required to complete the subtest successfully resulted in loadings on Reasoning (Abstract Verbal and Quantitative) and Memory factors. Overall, Conceptual Grouping's placement on the Verbal and Perceptual/Performance scales appears to be quite appropriate.

Conceptual Grouping	Assigned Factor	Study
	Verbal & Perceptual/Performance	1a
	Perceptual Performance	1b
	None	2
	Verbal & Perceptual/Performance	3a
	Verbal, Percept/Perform, & Motor	3b
	Memory	4
	Quantitative Reasoning	5
	Nonverbal Cognitive	6a
	Abstract Verbal Reasoning	6b
	Abstract Verbal Reasoning	6c

MCCARTHY INTERPRETATION

Overview of GCI Interpretation

Strategies for the meaningful interpretation of the MSCA GCI need to take into consideration the psychometric characteristics of the test. It should be remembered that the McCarthy GCI tends to produce deflated estimates of children's ability relative to other intelligence tests for exceptional children, regardless of exceptionality. The McCarthy GCI should be interpreted very cautiously if it is used for placement or classification purposes. Recognizing the tendency for the GCI to provide low estimates of cognitive functioning among retarded, learning disabled, at-risk, gifted, and speech disordered children, the examiner should question the accuracy of the McCarthy GCI when the client is referred because of suspected exceptionality.

An examiner might expect fewer gifted children to be identified with the McCarthy than other cognitive tests that possess stronger ceilings. Additionally, because discrepancy-based formulae are used for the diagnosis of learning disabilities in many states, one might expect deflated GCI—achievement score discrepancies among low functioning primary grade children with academic difficulties. As a result, some children might in fact possess a greater intelligence—achievement discrepancy than is evident in the GCI—achievement comparison, thus denying the child services for which he or she might actually qualify. Further, in some instances slow learners might appear borderline in intelligence; borderline children

might appear retarded; and some mildly retarded children might appear to be more moderately involved than is truly the case.

The issue is not whether the McCarthy GCI can identify low functioning children; it seems to do that quite well. The real issue is whether the degree of functioning as assessed on the McCarthy is comparable to the accepted standards of the profession (e.g., Stanford-Binet, WISC-R). Without some reasonable degree of comparable standards, misclassification should be a real concern to the practitioner. Although it is not always practical for practitioners to do so, it is recommended that the McCarthy be interpreted *only* in conjunction with a second intelligence test when placement decisions or classifications are required.

Overview of Scale Interpretation

Considering the limited technical adequacy and factor support for some of the individual McCarthy Scales, the practitioner should be very cautious in the interpretation of a child's test performance. The Verbal and Perceptual/Performance scales possess the best internal consistency and factor support. The practitioner can feel fairly comfortable interpreting the MSCA Verbal scale as a fairly diverse measure of verbal abilities and the Perceptual/Performance scale as a measure of perceptual–organizational and visual–motor abilities.

The subtests assigned to the Quantitative Scale received very little support for their scale placement in the six factor analytic studies reviewed here. It appears that the Quantitative scale has virtually no support for its existence as a unique entity.

The Memory scale is not as clearly defined as the Verbal and Perceptual/Performance scales, but is much more defensible than the Quantitative Scale. The Memory Scale subtests do not all load strongly on a Memory factor. Pictorial Memory, for example, does not load well at all on a Memory factor, and Tapping Sequence appears to be primarily perceptual and motor in nature; however, Verbal Memory and Numerical Memory do load quite consistently on Memory factors. It also should be noted that several other nonmemory subtests evidence occasional significant loadings on factors identified as Memory (e.g., Conceptual Grouping, Opposite Analogies, Leg Coordination). Thus, the Memory Scale consists of some subtests that clearly involve memory, but it also includes some that are not primarily mnenestic in nature. The Memory Scale can be interpreted cautiously, especially if one considers that Dorthea McCarthy recognized the dual nature of the Memory Scale tasks and placed every Memory Scale subtest on an additional nonmemory scale.

Although the Motor Scale has more support for its existence than does the Quantitative Scale, some of its subtests load weakly on Motor factors. Leg Coordination and Arm Coordination both appear to be fairly good measures of motor abilites, but they also carry a cognitive component related to the child's ability to understand test directions. Imitative Action frequently does not generate sufficient variance to load significantly on any factor, and consequently should not be considered as a very good measure of motor ability. Draw-A-Design and Draw-A-Child are two subtests that evidence much more support for their Perceptual/Performance Scale placements than for their Motor Scale placements. Overall, the Motor Scale is at best a marginal example of motor assessment because of the confounds of language, perceptual-motor, and other cognitive related abilities. The Motor Scale should be interpreted cautiously, especially when the child is cognitively low functioning and might have difficulty understanding the task requirements.

Subtest Interpretation Overview

In many respects the McCarthy subtests represent little more than small collections of items similar to those found on the Stanford-Binet, Form L-M. Like the Binet, L-M, the MSCA subtests frequently have few items and are supported by no reliability data. Additionally, the MSCA subtests tend to possess minimal floors and ceilings at many ages and evidence poor item gradients across the age levels. The only clear benefit of the MSCA subtests is they constitute groupings of similar items for ease in administration.

Because the subtests are woefully lacking by most psychometric standards, it is recommended that the McCarthy subtests not be interpreted, except informally as they contribute to clinical impressions. The test's publisher, The Psychological Corporation, also recommends against intepretation of the MSCA subtests (Personal communication with John Noonan, 1985). In addition, the test author provides no guidance or rationale for subtest interpretation in the *Manual*. Although

Kaufman and Kaufman (1977) suggest procedures for examining MSCA subtest variation and the unique and shared contributions of each of the subtests, interpretation is simply not appropriate given the severe limitations of the subtests and the nonempirical determination of subtests' unique and shared abilities.

McCarthy Interpretation, Step-by-Step

Interpreting the McCarthy GCI is a five-step procedure, that considers systematically the various aspects of the total test score.

Step 1. Determine the GCI and its confidence interval, at a desired level of confidence (e.g., 85%, 90%, 99%). Age-based norm tables in the McCarthy *Manual* are available for GCI generation. Table 5-3 provides the SEM and confidence bands associated with three levels of confidence for each age level. These figures were computed from the Standard Errors of Measurement reported in the McCarthy *Manual*.

Step 2. Determine the Descriptive Classification for the GCI (Table 5-4).

Step 3. Determine the percentile rank associated with the GCI.

Step 4. Compare the GCI to other available measures of intelligence to determine the degree of agreement between the GCI and other estimates of intelligence. Using a one-standard deviation "rule-of-thumb," any intelligence test score that deviates >

TABLE 5.3
STANDARD ERROR OF MEASUREMENT AND CONFIDENCE INTERVALS FOR THE GENERAL COGNITIVE INDEX

Age		Percent Confidence			
	SEM	85%	90%	95%	99%
2½	4.2	6.05	6.93	8.23	10.84
3	3.8	5.47	6.27	7.45	9.80
3½	3.4	4.90	5.61	6.66	8.77
4	4.7	6.77	7.76	9.21	12.13
4½	3.8	5.47	6.27	7.45	9.80
5	3.9	5.62	6.44	7.64	10.06
5½	4.2	6.05	6.93	8.23	10.84
6½	5.0	7.20	8.25	9.80	12.90
7½	3.9	5.62	6.44	7.64	10.06
8½	4.5	6.48	7.43	8.82	11.61

TABLE 5.4
GENERAL COGNITIVE ABILITY LEVELS

GCI	Descriptive Classification	Theoretical Percent	Actual Percent (MSCA Normative Sample)
130 and above	Very Superior	3.0	3.1
120–129	Superior	7.5	8.5
110–119	Bright Normal	16.0	15.9
90–109	Average	46.8	46.7
80–89	Dull Normal	16.0	15.7
70–79	Borderline	7.5	7.3
69 and below[a]	Mentally Retarded	3.0	2.8

[a] In a symposium presented at a meeting of the Council for Exceptional Children (New York, April 1974), Dr. Dorothy DeBoer reported that some children who had been diagnosed as learning disabled obtained GCIs in the "Mentally Retarded" range, but had IQs higher than those considered indicative of mental retardation. The report was based on a study conducted by DeBoer at the Learning Disabilities Center, Mercy Hospital and Medical Center, Chicago. Additional research is needed to confirm and illuminate the finding.

This table is reprinted with permission: McCarthy, D. (1972). *McCarthy Scales of Childrens' Abilities*. San Antonio, TX: The Psychological Corporation.

+/− 1 SD is considered to be significantly different from the GCI in magnitude. Significant discrepancies should be resolved, if possible, by contrasting the characteristics of the child, the tests, and the environment on the days that the tests were administered. For a detailed explanation of common psychometric conditions that cause similar tests to produce dissimilar scores, see Bracken (1988).

Step 5. Compare the GCI with other obtained noncognitive measures, such as: achievement, language, and adaptive behavior. Discrepancies and agreement between the MSCA assessed intelligence and other abilities should be considered diagnostically (e.g., a discrepancy between low cognitive and average adaptive functioning provides increased rationale for avoiding an early label of retardation).

Scale Interpretation

Interpreting the MSCA scales also is comprised of five steps.

Step 1. Raw scores are converted to scaled scores for each of the five McCarthy scales using the appropriate age-based norm tables found in the McCarthy *Manual*.

Step 2. Compute an Average Scale Score by adding the obtained scale scores for each of the five scales, and divide that sum by 5.

Step 3. Subtract each obtained scale score from the Average Scale Score to determine the degree of discrepancy between each scale and the Average Scale Score.

Step 4. Consult Table 5-5 to determine whether the scales' deviation scores differ significantly from the Average Scale Score and determine which scales are *strengths,* are *average,* or are *weaknesses* compared to the child's average performance.

Table 5-5 is based on Davis' (1959) formula for determining whether a child's performance on a single subtest or scale deviates significantly from the child's mean subtest or scale score. Kaufman (1975b) originally determined the magnitude of difference needed for significance at both the .05 and .01 levels for MSCA scale interpretation. Kaufman recommended that, if the Verbal, Perceptual-Performance, or Quantitative scales deviated from the average scale score by 7 points or more, practitioners should consider the difference to be statistically significant. A discrepancy of 8 points from the Average Scale Score was recommended for the Memory and Motor Scales to be considered as significant deviations.

Naglieri (1982) argued that Kaufman's (1975) calculations were too liberal and did not take into consideration the increased error associated with conducting multiple contrasts. Using Silverstein's (1981) guidelines that incorporated the Bonferroni correction for multiple contrasts, Naglieri recomputed the critical significance levels (See Table 5-

TABLE 5.5

DIFFERENCES REQUIRED FOR SIGNIFICANCE WHEN COMPARING A CHILD'S INDEX ON ONE SCALE WITH THAT CHILD'S AVERAGE INDEX FOR THE FIVE SCALES

Age	Verbal		Perceptual-Performance		Quantitative		Memory		Motor	
	.01 Level	.05 Level	.01 Level	.05 Level	.01 Level	.05 Level	.01 Level	.05 Level	.01 Level	.05 Level
2½	9.7	8.1	13.0	10.8	13.2	11.0	12.5	10.5	11.3	9.4
3	9.5	7.9	10.3	8.6	11.5	9.6	13.2	11.0	11.3	9.6
3½	8.4	7.1	9.2	7.7	11.3	9.4	11.1	9.3	11.1	9.3
4	9.6	8.0	10.4	8.7	14.0	11.7	11.2	9.3	12.5	10.4
4½	10.2	8.5	9.8	8.1	12.4	10.4	13.3	11.1	11.4	9.5
5	10.3	8.6	10.5	8.8	10.5	8.8	13.0	10.9	11.7	9.8
5½	10.2	8.5	11.0	9.2	10.6	8.9	14.0	11.7	12.3	10.2
6½	11.2	9.4	12.9	10.7	12.0	10.1	11.4	9.6	14.6	12.2
7½	9.8	8.2	11.4	9.5	11.4	9.5	11.2	9.3	13.5	11.3
8½	11.0	9.2	13.7	11.4	12.0	10.0	12.3	10.2	16.2	13.6
All ages combined	10.0	8.3	11.2	9.4	11.8	9.9	12.2	10.3	12.7	10.5

5). Naglieri reports that the average difference required for significance at the $p = .05$ level is $+/- 9$ points for the Verbal and Perceptual/Performance Scales, $+/- 10$ points for the Quantitative and Memory Scales, and $+/- 11$ points for the Motor Scale.

Step 5. Determine the meaningfulness of the scales that deviate significantly from the Average Scale Score. The interpretative meaningfulness of a scale that differs significantly from the Average Scale Score must be considered in light of the scale's technical characteristics (e.g., floor, ceiling, reliability, factor support). To say, for example, that the child's Quantitative Scale (which has received very little factor support) was significantly lower than his or her Average Scale Score indicates only that the child performed poorer on whatever skills are assessed by that fairly disparate collection of subtests than is reflected in his or her overall MSCA performance. It does not mean necessarily that his quantitative knowledge is inferior to his overall cognitive abilities because the Quantitative Scale is not a very robust measure of quantitative ability.

At this juncture in the MSCA interpretation, one must rely very heavily on clinical experience, behavioral observations, teacher and parent re-

ports, past psychoeducational history, informal assessment methods, and the child's performance on other psychoeducational measures. If the child in the previous example performed poorly on the Quantitative Scale, the examiner would likely want to informally assess the child's ability to perform common arithmetic operations such as: identify specific numerals, print specific numerals on request, rote count, place count, count backward, respond to quantitative concepts (e.g., *more, less, half, dozen, pair, first, third*), and conduct simple addition and subtraction. Likewise, the examiner would want to observe the child during mathematical instruction and talk to the preschool teacher about the child's quantitative understanding. The examiner also might decide to administer specific measures of quantitative ability to corroborate his or her MSCA findings. With such additional information, the examiner would be in a much better position to support or refute the child's "quantitative weakness" as suggested by the MSCA. See Chapter 4 for a detailed coverage of the observation, interpretation, and integration of assessment behavior.

SUMMARY

Because of the McCarthy's attractive materials, innovative and fun assessment activities, wise developmental and administration considerations, and the voluminous, pertinent professional literature that exists, the McCarthy is in many respects an appropriate test to use in conjunction with another test of intelligence. If the test is used intelligently and in conjunction with other measures, in a true multidisciplinary team spirit, it can provide valuable information for preschool assessment.

With its 18 subtests, the examiner has ample opportunity to observe the child while reacting to and processing a wide variety of multisensory stimuli, using both manual and verbal expressive modes. The examiner can see first hand how the child reacts to visual–spatial problem-solving activities, verbal questions and directions, gross and fine motor activities, and a long, sometimes frustrating and very structured formal psychoeducational assessment. The McCarthy activities provide invaluable insight to the astute clinician and offer many opportunities for informal developmental or task analyzed follow-up assessment.

Despite its considerble weaknesses, the McCarthy is an excellent test in many respects. The examiner who is sufficiently familiar with its foibles and who has sufficient preschool, clinical, and developmental experience and knowledge base, can benefit greatly from what the McCarthy has to offer. True, the McCarthy has many weaknesses that limits its usefulness; but its many strengths continue to argue for its use. The McCarthy is overdue for a thorough revision and restandardization. If such a revision and restandardization were conducted adequately, the test's unfavorable characteristics could be largely eliminated.

REFERENCES

Bickett, L., Reuter, J., & Stancin, T. (1984). The use of the McCarthy Scales of Children's Abilities to assess moderately retarded children. *Psychology in the Schools, 21,* 305–312.

Bracken, B. A. (1981). McCarthy Scales as a learning disability diagnostic aid: A closer look. *Journal of Learning Disabilities, 14,* 128–130.

Bracken, B. A. (1984). *Bracken Basic Concept Scale.* San Antonio, TX: The Psychological Corporation.

Bracken, B. A. (1985). Comparison of the Bracken Basic Concept Scale with the McCarthy Scales of Children's Abilities, Kaufman Assessment Battery for Children, and the Columbia Mental Maturity Scale (Unpublished Data).

Bracken, B. A. (1986). Incidence of basic concepts in the directions of five commonly used American tests

of intelligence. *School Psychology International, 7,* 1–10.

Bracken, B. A. (1987). Limitations of preschool instruments and standards for minimal levels of technical adequacy. *Journal of Psychoeducational Assessment, 5,* 313–326.

Bracken, B. A. (1988). Ten psychometric reasons why similar tests produce dissimilar results. *Journal of School Psychology, 26,* 155–166.

Bracken, B. A., & Fagan, T. K. (1988). Abilities assessed by the K-ABC Mental Processing subtests: The perceptions of practitioners with varying degrees of experience. *Psychology in the Schools, 25,* 22–34.

Bracken, B. A., & Chattin, S. (1990). Practitioners' Perceptions of skills assessed by the WISC-R and Binet IV. Paper presented at the Annual Conference of the National Association of School Psychologists, San Franciso, CA.

Chattin, S., & Bracken, B. A. (1989). School Psychologists' evaluation of the K-ABC, McCarthy Scales, Stanford-Binet IV, and WISC-R. *Journal of Psychoeducational Assessment, 7,* 112–130.

Davis, F. B. (1959). Interpretation of differences among averages and individual tests scores. *Journal of Educational Psychology, 50,* 162–170.

DeBoer, D. L., Kaufman, A. S., McCarthy, D. (1974). The use of the McCarthy Scales in identification, assessment, and deficit remediation of preschool and primary age children. Symposium presented at the meeting of the Council for Exceptional Children. New York.

Flynn, J. R. (1984). The mean IQ of Americans: Massive gains 1932 to 1978. *Psychological Bulletin, 95,* 29–51.

Funk, S. G., Sturner, R. A., & Green, J. A. (1986). Preschool prediction of early school performance: Relationship of McCarthy Scales of Children's Abilities prior to school entry to achievement in kindergarten, first, and second grades. *Journal of School Psychology, 24,* 181–194.

Gerken, K. C., Hancock, K. A., & Wade, T. H. (1978). Comparison of the Stanford-Binet Intelligence Scale and the McCarthy Scales of Children's Abilities with preschool children. *Psychology in the Schools, 15,* 468–472.

Jensen, A. R. (1975). Forward and backward digit span interaction with race and IQ: Predictions from Jensen's theory. *Journal of Educational Psychology, 67,* 882–893.

Kaufman, A. S. (1975a). Factor structure of the McCarthy Scales at five age levels between 2½ and 8½. *Educational and Psychological Measurement, 35,* 641–656.

Kaufman, A. S. (1975b) Note on interpreting profiles of McCarthy Scale Indexes. *Perceptual and Motor Skills, 41,* 262.

Kaufman, A. S. (1982). An integrated review of almost a decade of research on the McCarthy Scales. In T. R. Kratochwill (Ed.). *Advances in School Psychology, Volume II* (pp. 119–170.) Hillsdale, NJ: Lawrence Erlbaum Associates, Publishers.

Kaufman, A. S., & Dicuio, R. F. (1975). Separate factor analyses of the McCarthy Scales for groups of Black and White children. *Journal of School Psychology, 13,* 10–17.

Kaufman, A. S., & Kaufman, N. L. (1974). Comparison of normal and minimally brain dysfunctional children on the McCarthy Scales of Children's Abilities. *Journal of Clinical Psychology, 30,* 69–72.

Kaufman, A. S., & Kaufman, N. L. (1977). *Clinical Evaluation of Young Children with the McCarthy Scales.* San Antonio, TX: The Psychological Corporation.

Kaufman, A. S., & Kaufman, N. L. (1983). *Interpretative Manual for the Kaufman Assessment Battery for Children.* Circle Pines, MN: American Guidance Service.

Keith, T. Z., & Bolen, L. M. (1980). Factor structure of the McCarthy Scales for children experiencing problems in school. *Psychology in the Schools, 17,* 320–326.

Lidz, C. S., & Ballester, L. E. (1986). Diagnostic implications of the McCarthy Scale General Cognitive Index/Binet IQ discrepancies for low-socioeconomic-status preschool children. *Journal of School Psychology, 24,* 381–385.

Lyon, M. A., & Smith, D. K. (1986). A comparison of at-risk preschool children's performance on the K-ABC, McCarthy Scales, and Stanford-Binet. *Journal of Psychoeducational Assessment, 4,* 35–44.

Massoth, N. A., & Levenson, R. L. (1982). The McCarthy Scales of Children's Abilities as a predictor of reading readiness and reading achievement. *Psychology in the Schools, 19,* 293–296.

Massoth, N. A. (1985). The McCarthy Scales of Children's Abilities as a predictor of achievement: A five-year follow-up. *Psychology in the Schools, 22,* 10–13.

McCarthy, D. (1972). *Manual for the McCarthy Scales of Children's Abilities.* San Antonio, TX: The Psychological Corporation.

Mishra, S. P. (1981). Factor analysis of the McCarthy Scales for groups of White and Mexican-American children. *Journal of School Psychology, 19,* 178–182.

Nagle, R. J. (1979). The McCarthy Scales of Children's Abilities: Research implications for the assessment of young children. *School Psychology Digest, 8,* 319–326.

Naglieri, J. A. (1982). Interpreting the profile of McCarthy Scale Indexes: A revision. *Psychology in the Schools, 19,* 49–51.

Naglieri, J. A. (1985). Normal children's performance on the McCarthy Scales, Kaufman Assessment Battery, and Peabody Individual Achievement Test. *Journal of Psychoeducational Assessment, 3,* 123–130.

Naglieri, J. A., & Harrison, P. L. (1982). McCarthy Scales, McCarthy Screening Test, and Kaufman's short form correlations with the Peabody Individual Achievement Test. *Psychology in the Schools, 19,* 149–155.

Naglieri, J. A., Kaufman, A. S., Harrison, P. L. (1981). Factor structure of the McCarthy Scales for school-age children with low GCIs. *Journal of School Psychology, 19,* 226–232.

Phillips, B. L., Pasewark, R. A., & Tindall, R. C. (1978). Relationship among McCarthy Scales of Children's Abilities, WPPSI, and Columbia Mental Maturity Scale. *Psychology in the Schools, 15,* 352–356.

Reilly, T. P., Drudge, O. W., Rosen, J. C., Loew, D. E., & Fischer, M. (1985). Concurrent and predictive validity of the WISC-R, McCarthy Scales, Woodcock-Johnson, and academic achievement. *Psychology in the Schools, 22,* 380–382.

Sattler, J. M. (1974). *Assessment of Children's Intelligence.* Philadephia: Saunders.

Silverstein, A. B. (1981). Pattern analysis on the PIAT. *Psychology in the Schools, 18,* 13–14.

Teeter, P. A. (1984). Cross-validation of the factor structure of the McCarthy Scales for kindergarten children. *Psychology in the Schools, 21,* 158–164.

Terman, L. M., & Merill, M. A. (1973). *Stanford-Binet Intelligence Scale: Manual for the Third Revision, Form L-M.* Boston: Houghton Mifflin.

Thorndike, R. L., Hagen, E. P., Sattler, J. M. (1986). *Stanford-Binet Intelligence Scale: Fourth Edition.* Chicago: Riverside Publishing.

Torrance, E. P. (1968). Examples and rationales of test tasks for assessing creative abilities. *Journal of Creative Behavior, 2,* 165–178.

Wechsler, D. (1967) *Wechsler Preschool and Primary Scale of Intelligence.* San Antonio, TX: The Psychological Corporation.

Wechsler, D. (1974). *Wechsler Intelligence Scale for Children-Revised.* San Antonio, TX: The Psychological Corporation.

Weibe, M. J., & Watkins, E. O. (1980). Factor analysis of the McCarthy Scales of Children's Abilities on preschool children. *Journal of School Psychology, 18,* 154–162.

Woodcock, R., & Johnson, M. (1977). *Woodcock-Johnson Psychoeducational Battery.* Allen, TX: DLM Teaching Resources.

Zucker, S., & Copeland, E. P. (1988). K-ABC and McCarthy Scale performance among ''at-risk'' and normal preschoolers. *Psychology in the Schools, 25,* 5–10.

6

The Assessment of Preschool Children with the Wechsler Preschool and Primary Scale of Intelligence-Revised

JAMES S. GYURKE

INTRODUCTION

The Wechsler Preschool and Primary Scale of Intelligence-Revised (WPPSI-R) (Wechsler, 1989) is the result of a four-year development effort undertaken to update the norms and extend the age range of the scale both upward and downward. The WPPSI-R, like the WPPSI (Wechsler, 1967), reflects Wechsler's view that intelligence is a global entity that is multidimensional and multifaceted with each ability being equally important.

In revising the WPPSI, a great deal of attention was focused on making the test attractive and interesting for young children. Steps such as adding color to the stimulus materials, adding an Object Assembly subtest, and maintaining the alternating verbal and performance subtest format were undertaken to make the WPPSI-R an interesting test for young children.

The WPPSI-R has retained many of the features of the WPPSI that made it a highly regarded assessment tool. Among these features are the outstanding normative sample reflecting 1986 U.S. Census data for 3 to 7 year olds, excellent reliability and validity, and standard score parameters that are consistent with the other Wechsler scales. Retaining these characteristics along with the revised stimulus materials and new tasks for the expanded age range make the WPPSI-R a useful tool for assessing preschool age children.

DESCRIPTION OF THE WSPPSI-R

The WPPSI-R is an individually administered clinical instrument for assessing the intelligence of children aged 3 years through 7 years, 3 months. It is organized much like the WPPSI, with one group of primarily perceptual-motor Performance subtests and a second group of Verbal subtests. There are a total of 12 subtests (See Table 1), of which ten are required and two (Animal Pegs and Sentences) are optional.

The 12 subtests are divided into two scales labeled Verbal and Performance. This division has both logical and empirical support. The logical basis for this division rests on the apparent nature of the child's responses to the task: motor responses to the Performance subtests and spoken responses to the Verbal subtests. The empirical rationale for this division comes from the results

TABLE 6.1
WPPSI-R SUBTESTS AND CORRESPONDING SCALE PLACEMENT

Performance	Verbal
1. Object Assembly	2. Information
3. Geometric Design	4. Comprehension
5. Block Design	6. Arithmetic
7. Mazes	8. Vocabulary
9. Picture completion	10. Similarities
*11. Animal Pegs (formerly "Animal House")	*12. Sentences

* Optional subtests.

(Wechsler Preschool and Primary Scale of Intelligence—Revised. Copyright © 1989 by The Psychological Corporation. Reproduced by permission. All rights reserved.)

of several factor analytic studies of both the WPPSI-R and WPPSI structure. (A complete review of these studies is provided in the WPPSI-R manual.) These studies have consistently found two subtest clusters within the scale (e.g., Hollenbeck & Kaufman, 1973). The two clusters or factors invariably correspond to the Verbal and Performance scales.

Each of the 12 WPPSI-R subtests produces raw scores that are converted to norm-referenced standard scores (M = 10, SD = 3). These scaled scores are then summed across the five required subtests within the Verbal scale and the five required subtests within the Performance scale to obtain sums of scaled scores. Each of the individual sum of scaled scores is transformed to an IQ (M = 100, SD = 15). These two sums of scaled scores also are summed to produce a Full Scale Score that is transformed to an IQ (M = 100, SD = 15). In addition to the raw-score-to-scaled-score and scaled-score-to-IQ conversion tables, a test-age table that can be used to estimate a child's functional age based on his or her performance also is provided in the manual.

USE OF THE SCALE

The WPPSI-R is intended for use as a measure of intellectual ability in a wide range of educational, clinical, and research settings. The primary use of the scale is in the diagnosis of exceptionality in schools and private practice settings.

Because the upper end of the age range of the WPPSI-R overlaps approximately one year with the lower end of the age range of the WISC-R, (Wechsler, 1974) examiners have a choice of which scale to use with a child in this age range. In most cases, if the child is expected to be of average or above-average intellectual ability with average communicative ability, the examiner should administer the WISC-R. However, if the child is expected to be below average in either of these areas, the examiner should administer the WPPSI-R. The WPPSI-R's difficulty level is more appropriate for lower-ability children in this age range, and the WISC-R is more appropriate for higher-ability children.

SUBTEST DESCRIPTION

The following section describes each subtest in detail. Included in this description is the skill measured by the subtest, the format of administration and scoring, and the technical evaluation of the subtest. In the context of describing the subtests, the term "age level" refers to a discrete band of age. For example, the 4 year age level refers to the band of ages from 3 years 11 months 16 days to 4 years 2 months 15 days. Also, for the purpose of describing the ceiling of the individual subtests, the 6¼ year age level will be used because, from ages 6 years 6 months through 7 years 3 months, the WPPSI-R is intended for use only with lower ability children.

WPPSI-R SUBTESTS

Performance Scale

Object Assembly. This new subtest, as with the WISC-R Object Assembly subtest, requires the child to assemble a puzzle picturing a common object. This subtest contains six full-color puzzles of common objects. The child receives credit for both the correct assembly of the puzzle and the speed of performance. This subtest yields a maximum raw score of 32. The summary skills required to successfully complete the tasks include visual-motor integration, visual perception, and fine motor coordination.

The Object Assembly subtest has adequate floor for young children. A floor or ceiling of a subtest is considered adequate if it produces scores that are two or more standard deviations above or below the mean, respectively. A raw score of 0 at the 3 year age level yields a scaled score of 1, three standard deviations below the mean. The median raw score (raw score that receives a scaled score of 10) is 10 out of a possible 32. The ceiling of this subtest also is adequate. The median raw score at the $6\frac{1}{4}$ year age level is 25 and the maximum raw score of 32 receives a scaled score of 17. Beyond this $6\frac{1}{4}$ year age level the ceiling becomes more limited. In general, this new subtest has sufficient floor and ceiling to test young children and is suitable for use with children across the entire age span of the WPPSI-R.

Information. The Information subtest requires the child to demonstrate knowledge about events or objects in the environment. This 27-item subtest includes a new set of full color pictures and requires less advanced verbal skills than its WPPSI counterpart. This set of new picture items was added to a set of items similar to those of the WPPSI Information subtest. Each item is dichotomously scored as 1 (pass) or 0 (failed) with the maximum raw score equal to 27. The skills required to perform this task include long-term memory, verbal fluency, and knowledge of the environment.

As would be expected with a subtest that is primarily verbal, Information has a somewhat weak floor at the youngest ages. At the 3 year age level a raw score of 0 yields a scale score of 5, a score slightly less than two standard directions below the mean; however, by the 4 year age level this same raw score yields a scaled score of 2, showing that the floor problem is quickly resolved. The ceiling of this subtest is more than adequate, because the median raw score at the $6\frac{1}{4}$ year age level is 22 and the maximum raw score of 27 receives a scaled score of 19.

Overall, the Information subtest has a slightly limited floor, but an adequate ceiling. Despite the limited floor there appears to be a smooth, albeit a slower, progression in the upper age levels of raw scores across the entire age span.

Geometric Design. The Geometric Design subtest includes two distinct types of tasks among its 16 items. First is a set of visual-recognition tasks that require the child to match a pictured design from an array of four designs. The second type of item requires the child to draw a copy of a geometric figure from a printed model, as in the Geometric Design subtest of the WPPSI. The primary skills required to complete these tasks include visual-perception, visual-motor organization, fine motor coordination and attention to detail. The scoring of this subtest has been significantly changed in response to criticism regarding the subjective nature of the scoring. Scoring is now based on the critical features of each figure; a child receives credit for each feature of the drawing that he or she has reproduced correctly. These points are summed within an item (drawing) to obtain the raw score for that drawing. With this change in the scoring system, the maximum raw score for the subtest is now 64. By scoring the critical features of each drawing, WPPSI-R scoring accuracy was improved over that of the WPPSI.

The floor of Geometric Design is slightly weak; a raw score of 0 at the 3 year age level yields a scaled score of 5; however, by the 4 year age level the floor is adequate because a raw score of 0 yields a scaled score of 2. This subtest has an adequate ceiling at all ages. At the $6\frac{1}{4}$ year age level a maximum raw score of 64 yields a scaled score of 17, while at age 7 this same raw score yields a scaled score of 16. At the 7 year level, there are six possible raw score points above the median suggesting that even at the upper ability levels there is some differentiation among average-to-high ability children.

In summary, the Geometric Design subtest has been changed to include more appropriate items for young children and more objective scoring rules. There is a slightly limited floor for this subtest at the youngest ages, but in general there is ample differentiation across the entire age span.

Comprehension. The Comprehension subtest is similar to the WPPSI subtest of this name, however, a majority of the items are new. This subtest requires the child to demonstrate an understanding of the reasons for actions, or of the consequences of certain common events in the environment. The child's responses are scored either 2, 1, or 0 depending on the level of understanding the child demonstrates. Comprehension has a maximum raw score of 30. The primary skills used in completing the Comprehension subtest include verbal ability, logical reasoning, and understanding of relationships.

The floor of this subtest is limited. At the 3 year level, the median raw score is 3 to 4 and a raw score of 0 yields a scaled score of 6. The floor of this subtest is sufficient at the 4 year age level where the median raw score is 11 to 13 and a raw score of 0 yields a scaled score of 4. Regarding the ceiling at the 6¼ year age level, the median raw score is 24 and the maximum raw score of 30 yields a scale score of 18 indicating that this subtest possesses a sufficient ceiling at this upper age level. In fact, comprehension has an adequate ceiling through the 7 year age level where the maximum raw score of 30 yields a scaled score of 17.

In summary, the WPPSI-R Comprehension subtest is similar to that of the WPPSI; however, a majority of the items are new. The floor of the subtest is limited, but the ceiling is adequate through the 7 year age level.

Block Design. The Block Design subtest is similar to the WPPSI version. It requires the child to analyze and reproduce, within a specified time limit, geometric patterns made from flat, two-colored blocks. The child's responses are scored as 2 (correct on first trial), 1 (correct on second trial), or 0 (no correct response in either trial). For items 8 through 14 the child can obtain up to two additional "bonus" points for quick, accurate performance on the first trial. The primary skills required by Block Design include visual-motor coordination, visual integration, and synthesis of part whole information.

The floor of the Block Design subtest is adequate. The median raw score at the 3 year age level is 5 and a raw score of 0 receives a scaled score of 4 at this age. Likewise, this subtest has an adequate ceiling because at the 6¼ year age level the median raw score is 26 to 27 and the maximum raw score of 42 receives the maximum scaled score of 19. There is an adequate ceiling through the 7 year age level where the median raw score is 29 to 30 and the maximum raw score of 42 receives a scaled score of 18.

In conclusion, the WPPSI-R Block Design subtest is much the same as the WPPSI Block Design subtest. There is an adequate floor at the youngest ages and an adequate ceiling at the older ages.

Arithmetic. The Arithmetic subtest assesses the child's understanding of basic quantitative concepts. As in the WPPSI, this subtest begins with pictured stimuli, progresses through simple counting tasks, and ends with more difficult word problems. The 23 items are scored as pass or fail, so the maximum raw score is 23.

The primary skills required for this subtest are visual discrimination, nonverbal reasoning ability, and knowledge of numerical concepts.

The floor of this subtest is more than adequate because the median raw score at age 3 is 5 and a raw score of 0 receives a scaled score of 3. The ceiling of this subtest also is more than adequate with the median raw score at the 6¼ year age level equal to 18 and the maximum raw score of 23 receiving a scaled score of 18. The ceiling remains adequate through the 7 year age level where the median raw score is 20 and the maximum raw score of 23 receives a scaled score of 16.

To summarize, the Arithmetic subtest on the WPPSI-R is very similar to its counterpart on the WPPSI. The floor and ceiling of this subtest is more than adequate through the entire age span of the scale.

Mazes. The Mazes subtest requires the child to solve pencil- and paper-mazes of increasing difficulty. Although similar to the Mazes subtest on the WPPSI, several new, easier mazes have been added for young children. The child's responses are scored according to the number of errors made on each maze, with the total possible score reduced by each error made. The maximum raw score for this 11-item subtest is 26. The primary skills required by mazes include attention to detail, planning, perceptual-organization, and fine-motor control.

Despite the inclusion of easier items, there remains a weak floor for this subtest at the 3 year age level. The 3 year median raw score is 5 and a raw score of 0 receives a scaled score of 5. This weak floor disappears by the 3¼ year age level where the median raw score is 6 to 7 and a raw score of 0 receives a scaled score of 4. The ceiling of this subtest is adequate through the 7 year age level where the median raw score is 20 and the maximum raw score of 26 receives a scaled score of 18.

In summary, the Mazes subtest on the WPPSI-R is similar to that of the WPPSI with the exception of several new, easier mazes for young children. The floor is weak at the 3 year age level, but adequate by the 3¼ year age level. The ceiling of this subtest is adequate through the 7-year age level.

Vocabulary. The Vocabulary subtest is a two-part subtest. The first part, which is completely new, contains picture identification items, while the second part consists of items on which the child is required to provide verbal definition for orally presented words. The items are scored 2, 1, or 0 depending on the quality of the child's definition. The maximum raw score for this 25-item subtest is 47. The primary skills required by Vocabulary include long-term memory, verbal fluency and, in some cases, formal education (i.e., items where the definition of the word has most likely been learned in an educational setting).

The floor of Vocabulary is adequate at the 3 year age level because the median raw score is 8 to 9 and a raw score of 0 receives a scaled score of 3. The ceiling of this subtest is also more than adequate through the 7 year age level with the median raw score being 28 to 29 and the maximum raw score of 47 receiving the maximum scaled score of 19.

In summary, this two-part subtest has both a sufficient floor and a sufficient ceiling across the entire age span of the scale.

Picture Completion. The Picture Completion subtest is similar to that of the WPPSI in that it requires the child to identify what is missing from pictures of common objects or events. The items are scored dichotomously as pass or fail, (i.e., 1 or 0) thus the maximum raw score is 28. The primary skills required by the subtest include attention to detail, visual organization, and long-term visual memory.

The floor of this subtest is weak at the 3 year age level where the median raw score is 5 to 6 and a raw score of 0 receives a scaled score of 5. The floor becomes more adequate at the $3\frac{1}{4}$ year age level where the median raw score is 6 to 7 and a raw score of 0 yields a scaled score of 4. The ceiling of this subtest is adequate through the 7 year age level where the median raw score is 22 and the maximum raw score of 28 receives a scaled score of 18.

In conclusion, the WPPSI-R Picture Completion subtest is similar to that of the WPPSI. There is a weak floor at the 3 year age level that is corrected by the $3\frac{1}{4}$ year age level. The ceiling of this subtest is adequate through the 7 year age level.

Similarities. The Similarities subtest requires the child to demonstrate an understanding of the concept of similarity in three ways. The first set

of tasks requires the child to choose which one of several objects pictured is most similar to a second group of objects. The second set of items requires the child to complete a verbally presented sentence that reflects a similarity or analogy between two things. The final set of items requires the child to explain how two verbally presented objects or events are alike. In the first two sections, the child's response is scored as pass or fail. In the third section, the child's responses are scored as 2, 1, or 0 depending on how accurately the child describes the essential nature of the similarity. This 20-item subtest has a maximum raw score of 28. The primary skills required in the first section include visual organization and attention to detail and common features. Logical reasoning, verbal fluency, and concept formation are required skills for success on the last two sections.

The Similarities subtest has a weak floor at the 3 year age level where the median raw score is 5 and raw score of 0 receives a scaled score of 6. It is not until the $3\frac{3}{4}$ year age level when the median raw score is 7 to 8 that a raw score of 0 yields a scaled score of 4. The ceiling of this subtest is more than adequate through the $6\frac{1}{4}$ year age level where the median raw score is 21 to 22 and the maximum raw score of 28 yields a scaled score of 18. In fact, the ceiling is adequate through the 7 year age level, where the median raw score is 24 and the maximum raw score of 28 receives a scaled score of 17.

In summary, the Similarities subtest requires the child to demonstrate an understanding of the concept of similarity in three different fashions. An adequate floor occurs at the $3\frac{3}{4}$ year age level, and there is sufficient ceiling through the 7 year age level.

Animal Pegs. The Animal Pegs subtest, the same subtest as Animal House in the WPPSI, requires the child to place pegs of the correct colors in holes below a series of pictured animals. The child's performance is scored for both speed and accuracy. The maximum raw score for this subtest is 70. The primary skills required include memory, attention, concentration, and fine motor coordination.

There is sufficient floor for this subtest at the 3 year age level where the median raw score is 8 to 12 and a raw score of 0 receives a scaled score of 2. The ceiling of this subtest is adequate through the 7 year age level where the median raw score is 56 to 58 and the maximum raw score of 70 receives the maximum scaled score of 19.

In summary, the Animal Pegs subtest is the same as the Animal House subtest on the WPPSI. This subtest has sufficient floor and ceiling across the entire age span.

Sentences. The Sentences subtest, similar to that of the WPPSI, requires the child to repeat verbatim a sentence read aloud by the examiner. The child's response is scored by the number of errors committed in repeating the sentence. The maximum raw score for this 12-item subtest is 37. The primary skills required include verbal facility and memory.

This subtest has a slightly weak floor at the 3 year age level, where the median raw score is 8 and a raw score of 0 receives a scaled score of 5. This is corrected by the $3\frac{1}{4}$ year age level where the median raw score is 9 to 10 and a raw score of 0 yields a scaled score of 4. The ceiling of this subtest is adequate through the 7 year age level where the median raw score is 26 to 27 and the maximum raw score of 37 receives a scaled score of 17.

In summary, the Sentences subtest is similar to that of the WPPSI. There is an adequate floor from the $3\frac{1}{4}$ year age level and the ceiling is adequate up through the 7-year age level.

Subtest Summary

The subtests of the WPPSI-R are, in general, quite similar to those of the WPPSI. The changes and additions reflect the attempt to expand the age range of the test and update the content.

The floor of a few subtests is weak at the 3 year age level; however, by the $3\frac{1}{4}$ year level almost all subtests have sufficient floor. As for the ceiling, all subtests have sufficient ceiling through the $6\frac{1}{4}$ year age level and most through the 7 year age level. This suggests that the WPPSI-R subtests provide a suitable assessment of abilities for most children through a majority of the age span of the scale.

CHARACTERISTICS OF THE SCALES

Verbal Scale

The Verbal Scale consists of six subtests: Information, Comprehension, Arithmetic, Vocab-

ulary, Similarities, and Sentences. Only five of these subtests (all but Sentences) are required to compute the Verbal sum of scaled scores. For each of the five required subtests, the raw score for each subtest is transformed into a scaled score (M = 10, SD = 3). These scaled scores are summed to obtain the verbal sum of scaled scores (VSS). The VSS is transformed into a Verbal IQ (VIQ) (M = 100, SD = 15). The distribution of VIQs ranges from 46 to 160, or approximately $3\frac{2}{3}$ standard deviations below the mean and 4 standard deviations above the mean. This range exceeds that recommended by Bracken (1987) to ensure discrimination among all but the most extreme 1 percent of the population.

In regard to the floor of the Verbal scale, the lowest possible sum of scaled scores at the 3 year age level is 28, which yields a VIQ of 74. Because this score does not exceed the two standard deviation criterion, there is a limited floor for the Verbal scale at this age level; however all subsequent age levels have floors that are at least two standard deviations below the mean. The Verbal scale has an adequate ceiling at all age levels, because the maximum obtainable sum of scaled scores at the 7 year age level is 86, which is equivalent to an IQ of 152, well above the two standard deviation criterion. Overall, the Verbal scale provides a sufficient range of scores to ensure an adequate floor and ceiling for a large majority of the population aged 3 years and 0 months to 7 years 3 months.

Performance Scale

The Performance scale consists of six subtests: Object Assembly, Geometric Design, Block Design, Mazes, Picture Completion, and Animal Pegs. Only five of these subtests (all but Animal Pegs) are required to compute the Performance sum of scaled scores.

For each of the five required subtests, the raw score for each subtest is transformed into a scaled score (M = 10, SD = 3). These scaled scores are summed to obtain the Performance sum of scaled scores (PSS). The PSS is transformed into a Performance IQ (PIQ) (M = 100, SD = 15). The distribution of PIQ range from 45 to 160, or from $3\frac{2}{3}$ standard deviations below the mean to 4 standard deviations above the mean. This range, like that of the Verbal scale, exceeds the recommended two standard deviation criterion, assuring discrimination among the most extreme portion of the population.

The Performance scale possesses an adequate floor and ceiling. At the 3 year age level, the lowest possible PSS of 20 yields a PIQ of 63, well beyond the two standard deviation criterion. At the 7 year age level, the maximum PSS of 86 translates into a PIQ of 156, well beyond the two standard deviation criterion. Therefore, the Performance Scale provides a sufficient range of scores to ensure adequate floor and ceiling for the population aged 3 years 0 months to 7 years 3 months.

Full Scale

The Full Scale Score (FSS) is the sum of scaled scores from both the Verbal and Performance scales—the sum of the 10 required subtest scaled scores. The FSS is transformed into a Full Scale IQ (FSIQ) (M = 100, SD = 15). The distribution of FSIQs ranges from 41 to 160, or approximately 4 standard deviations below and above the mean, which captures more than 99 percent of the population.

Both the floor and ceiling of the Full scale are more than adequate. For example, at the 3 year age level the lowest possible FSS is 48, which converts to a FSIQ of 65, exceeding the two standard deviation criterion. Likewise, the maximum sum of scaled scores obtainable at the 7 year age level is 172, which translates into an IQ of 160, again well beyond the two standard deviation criterion.

In summary, the Verbal Performance and Full scales of the WPPSI-R provide sufficient range for both low- and high-ability children across the entire age span.

STANDARDIZATION

The WPPSI-R is appropriate for a majority of the children ages 3 years 0 months through 7 years 3 months (See "Uses of the Scale.") The standardization sample included 1,700 children stratified by sex, race (White, Black, Hispanic, other), geographic region (Northeast, Northcentral, South, and West), parents' occupation (Table 6-2) and parent's education (Table 6-3). The quotas for all stratification variables were determined from 1986 U. S. Census Bureau data.

TABLE 6.2
OCCUPATIONAL CATEGORIES USED IN WPPSI-R STANDARDIZATION SAMPLE SELECTION

Category	Description
I.	Managerial and professional worker
II.	Technical, sales, and administrative support workers
III.	Service workers
IV.	Farming, forestry, and fishing workers
V.	Precision, production workers, craftsmen, and repairman
VI.	Operators, fabricators, and laborers
VII.	Not currently in the labor force, others

(Occupational categories were derived from 1986 Census survey of family heads. Wechsler Preschool and Primary Scsale of Intelligence—Revised. Copyright © 1989 by The Psychological Corporation. Reproduced by permission. All rights reserved.)

There were 200 children at each of the nine age groups, except the 7 year age group where there were 100 children. The sample participants were evenly divided by sex. Nineteen percent of the children came from the Northeast, 26.4 percent were from the North Central, 33 percent were from the South and 21.5 percent were from the West. Children in the sample were 70.3 percent white, 15.1 percent Black, 11 percent Hispanic and 3.5 percent "other". Of the children's parents, 24.3 percent had 16 or more years of education; 22 percent had 13–15 years; 38.2 percent had 12 years; 10.2 percent had 9–11 years, and 5.2 percent had 8 or fewer years. This sample also was stratified by parent occupation as follows: 25.1 percent were in managerial/professional positions; 26.2 percent were in farming, forestry, and

TABLE 6.3
EDUCATIONAL LEVELS USED IN WPPSI-R STANDARDIZATION SAMPLE SELECTION

Level	Description
I	8 or fewer years of education
II	9–11 years of education
III	12 years of education
IV	13–15 years of education
V	16 or more years of education

(Wechsler Preschool and Primary Scale of Intelligence—Revised. Copyright © 1989 by The Psychological Corporation. Reproduced by permission. All rights reserved.)

related fields; 10.9 percent were working in precision, production, and related jobs; 11.5 percent were operators, fabricators, and so on; and 12.5 percent were not currently in the labor force.

The match between the obtained sample and the target population is extremely close. The fit is good both for individual stratification variables (e.g., race and region) and for combinations of variables (e.g., race by region). The good fit between the obtained sample and target population indicates that a truly representative sample was used in the standardization of the WPPSI-R.

In addition to obtaining a representative sample, an oversample of approximately 400 minority children was obtained. This oversample, although not used to construct the normative tables, was used to analyze potential item bias. The results of bias analyses were used as part of the item selection procedures.

RELIABILITY

The WPPSI-R, like its predecessor, is a highly reliable instrument. Three types of reliability are provided in WPPSI-R manual, including internal consistency, stability, and interscorer.

Internal Consistency

The average Verbal, Performance, and Full scale internal consistency coefficients across the nine age groups are .95, .92, and .96, respectively. These high reliabilities exceed the recommended .90 criterion (Bracken, 1987) indicating that, at the scale level, the WPPSI-R is sufficiently reliable for the individual assessment of children aged 3 years to 7 years 3 months.

The within-age reliabilities also tend to be quite high. The only age at which the .90 criterion is not met is the 7 year age level, where the Verbal and Performance internal consistency reliabilities estimates are .86 and .85, respectively. This result was not unexpected because the WPPSI-R is appropriate only for lower ability children at age 7. Overall, the evidence lends support to interpreting the three scales individually at all age levels.

In addition to being highly reliable at the scale level, the WPPSI-R possesses good reliability at the individual subtest level. The average internal

consistency reliability of the six verbal subtests ranges from .80 for the Arithmetic subtest to .86 for the Similarities subtest. The Performance scale subtests tend to be slightly less reliable than the Verbal scale subtests. The average internal consistency reliability of the Performance subtests ranges from .63 for the Object Assembly subtest to .85 for the Block Design and Picture Completion subtests. Applying the .80 criterion suggested by Bracken (1987) as evidence for sufficient subtest reliability, eight of the 12 WPPSI-R subtests exceed this criterion and two subtests (Geometric Design and Mazes) narrowly miss this criterion. The only subtests that are clearly below the .80 criterion are the Object Assembly and Animal Pegs subtests.

In summary, the WPPSI-R is highly reliable at the scale level, and it also possesses good reliability at the subtest level. Therefore, one may feel confident in interpreting individually the three scales and a large majority of the subtests.

STABILITY

A test–retest study of 175 children in the standardization sample was conducted with an interval of 3 to 7 weeks (M = 4 weeks). The sample approximated the standardization sample for ethnicity and geographic region. Using the .90 criterion for the test–retest stability of IQs, the Verbal and Full scale stability meet or exceed this criterion (correlations of .90 and .91, respectively) and the Performance scale narrowly misses the .90 criterion (.88). These stability coefficients suggest that the WPPSI-R scales are adequately stable over a brief period and provide further evidence of the reliability of this test.

Interscorer Agreement

Most WPPSI-R subtests are objectively scored, however, some subtests are subjectively scored, and are therefore more vulnerable to scoring error. For these subtests, which include Comprehension, Vocabulary, Similarities, and Mazes, it was necessary to evaluate interscorer reliability. In addition, previous research with the WPPSI indicated a low rate of scoring agreement on the Geometric Design subtest (Sattler, 1976). A more objective set of scoring rules and procedures were created for this subtest, and its effect on scorer agreement also was evaluated.

To assess the interscorer reliability of the Comprehension, Vocabulary, Similarities, and Mazes subtests, a sample of 151 cases (83 males and 68 females) stratified by age was randomly selected from all cases collected for the standardization. For the Geometric Design subtest, a sample of 188 cases (105 males and 83 females) was randomly selected. A group of research scorers was trained and given practice in scoring the subtests. The cases were subdivided by age to control for age effects, and two scorers were selected at random to score all the cases in each age group.

To assess interscorer reliability, a type of intraclass correlation was used that takes account of differences in scorer leniency as well as random error (Shrout & Fleiss, 1979). Interscorer reliability coefficients were as follows: .96 on Comprehension, .94 on Vocabulary, .96 on Similarities, .94 on Mazes, and .88 on Geometric Design. These results indicate that the scoring rules for these subtests are objective enough for different scorers to produce similar results and provides further evidence of the reliability of the WPPSI-R.

VALIDITY

The WPPSI-R manual reports studies of both construct and concurrent validity. Given that the WPPSI-R has been published only recently, predictive validity data is not yet available; however, a good indicator of the predictive power of this instrument can be found in the research literature on the predictive validity of the WPPSI. Several studies have found that performance on the WPPSI is highly predictive of later intellectual functioning (Rasbury, McCoy, & Perry, 1977) and academic achievement (Feshback, Adelman, & Fuller, 1977). Based on this evidence of the predictive validity of the WPPSI and the strong relationship between the WPPSI-R and the WPPSI it is reasonable to expect the WPPSI-R to be predictive of later intellectual functioning and academic achievement.

Construct Validity

The construct validity of the WPPSI-R was established through two exploratory factor analytic studies. First, the data from the entire standardization sample was subjected to a principal axis factor analysis with orthogonal rotation. Using an eigenvalue greater than 1 criterion, a two-factor, (Verbal–Performance) solution was obtained (Table 6-4). The second study explored the consistency of the two-factor structure across age. A principal axis factor analysis with an orthogonal rotation and eigenvalue greater than 1 criterion was applied to three groups within the standardization sample: 3 years 0 months to 4 years 6 months; 4 years 7 months to 6 years 0 months; and 6 years 1 month to 7 years 3 months. Similar to the results from the entire standardization sample, the by-age results within age groups indicate a two-factor (Verbal–Performance) solution. The one notable exception to these results occurs in the first age group, where the Picture Completion subtest had equal loadings on both factors. Except for this split loading, all Verbal scale subtests loaded more highly on the verbal factor and all Performance scale subtests loaded more highly on the performance factor at all age levels.

The results of factor analyses for both the entire standardization sample and for three narrower age groups support the conclusion that the WPPSI-R has an underlying two-factor structure. Furthermore, these findings lend support to in-

TABLE 6.4
WPPSI-R PRINCIPAL AXIS FACTOR MATRIX WITH ORTHOGONAL ROTATION FOR STANDARDIZATION SAMPLE

Subtest	Factor I	Factor II
Comprehension	.75	.19
Information	.74	.33
Vocabulary	.73	.21
Sentences	.65	.24
Similarities	.64	.30
Arithmetic	.57	.44
Block Design	.26	.70
Geometric Design	.20	.64
Object Assembly	.17	.61
Mazes	.19	.59
Picture Completion	.39	.53
Animal Pegs	.25	.41

N = 1,700

(Wechsler Preschool and Primary Scale of Intelligence—Revised. Copyright © 1989 by The Psychological Corporation. Reproduced by permission. All rights reserved.)

terpreting the verbal and performance abilities separately at all ages.

Concurrent Validity

Several studies comparing the WPPSI-R to other intellectual assessment scales are reported in the manual. These are summarized in Table 6-5.

As would be expected, the highest correlations obtained across these five studies were between the Wechsler scales, in particular WPPSI-R with the WPPSI. The correlations between the corresponding IQ on these two instruments were all above .80. Given that the WPPSI-R contains many of the same tasks as the WPPSI, these findings were expected. The WPPSI-R also correlates very highly with the WISC-R, with correlations between corresponding IQs ranging from .75 to .85, likewise, an anticipated finding.

The lowest correlations obtained were those between the WPPSI-R and the K-ABC (Kaufman & Kaufman, 1983). The correlations between WPPSI-R IQs and K-ABC Processing Scores ranged from .31 to .49. These results are not surprising in view of the fact that the K-ABC does not resemble the WPPSI-R in terms of scope or content.

Comparing the mean WPPSI-R IQs with mean scores on other instruments, the mean WPPSI FSIQ was approximately 8 points higher than that for the WPPSI-R, and the WPPSI VIQ and PIQ were 5 and 9 points higher, respectively, than the corresponding WPPSI-R IQs. Differences of this magnitude also were found between the WPPSI-R and the WISC-R. Thus, these discrepancies in mean scores were expected given the 15- to 20-year period between the standardization of these instruments. As the between-standardization interval decreased, so too did the discrepancy between the mean scores. For example, there was a 2 to 3 point mean difference between the 3 WPPSI-R IQ scales and the corresponding area scores on the Stanford-Binet, Fourth Edition, (Thorndike, Hagen, & Sattler, 1986) a scale that was standardized within 3 years of the standardization of the WPPSI-R.

In summary, the WPPSI-R correlates highly with previous Wechsler scales and, to a somewhat lesser extent, with other measures of intelligence. These correlations provide direct evidence of the concurrent validity of the WPPSI-R. Further evidence for the concurrent validity of the WPPSI-R is found in the fact that the obtained mean differences between the WPPSI-R and the various other instruments are in the direction and of the magnitude one would expect based upon the between-standardization intervals.

INTERPRETING THE WPPSI-R

Interpreting the WPPSI-R is, to a large extent, quite similar to interpreting the WISC-R. Although much less is known about interpreting the WPPSI-R than the WISC-R, the fact that there is a large overlap in the subtests of the two instruments and that they are scaled in a similar fashion lends support to using the same interpretive method. This method is fully described in both Sattler (1988) and Kaufman (1979). The major difference in method exists when interpreting factor scores. The WISC-R yields a three factor solution including "Freedom from Distractability" which is the third factor. Unlike the WISC-R, the WPPSI-R yields only a two-factor, Verbal-Performance solution. Because the WPPSI-R's factors directly parallel the Verbal and Performance scales, there is no rationale for exploring discrepancies beyond the two factors.

As with any interpretive approach, there are certain limitations and precautions one should take to ensure that conclusions are drawn correctly. The most reliable conclusions can be made at the Full scale level. Conclusions drawn at successive lower levels (e.g., at the scale or subtest levels) have lower reliability because the accuracy of the conclusions drawn is affected by the reliability of the scales or subtests being compared.

The following procedures for interpretation should be treated as general guidelines and not as required procedures. They should serve as an aid to the examiner in generating and testing hypotheses about the child's particular strengths and weaknesses. The procedures recommended here do not include interpretation at the item level. It is believed that item interpretation is risky given the low reliability of any individual item.

Step 1. Interpretation of the Full Scale IQ

Conclusions based on the Full Scale IQ will tend to be the most reliable. Interpretation of the Full scale IQ can be approached in two ways.

TABLE 6.5
SUMMARY OF CONCURRENT VALIDITY STUDIES WITH THE WPPSI-R

Measure	Sample	Design	Results
WPPSI	144 children (73 females, 71 males) ethnic and regional proportions match standardization sample.	Tests were administered in alternating order. Between test interval ranged from 3 to 5 weeks.	Correlations between the scales were: VIQ (.85), PIQ (.82) and FIQ (.87)
WISC-R (Urbina & Clayton, in preparation)	50 children (25 males, 25 females), age 72–86 months (mean = 79) from Jacksonville, Florida metropolitan area.	Tests were administered in alternating order. Between-test interval ranged from 7 to 8 days.	Correlation between the scales: VIQ (.76), PIQ (.75), and FIQ (.85)
Stanford Binet Fourth Edition	115 children, age 48–86 months (mean = 70) from 3 of 4 geographic regions (excluding Northeast).	Tests were administered in alternating order. Between-test interval ranged from 1 to 90 days.	Correlation between the WPPSI-R FSIQ and the SB Composite was .74, between PIQ and SB Abstract/Visual Reasoning was .54, and between VIQ and SB Verbal Reasoning was .63.

Results detail for WPPSI row:

WPPSI-R

	VIQ	PIQ	FSIQ
M	104.0	102.8	103.9
SD	15.9	15.9	16.2

WPPSI

	VIQ	PSQ	FSIQ
M	109.1	112.2	111.6
SD	16.9	15.7	16.3

Results detail for WISC-R row:

WPPSI-R

	VIQ	PIQ	FSIQ
M	106.9	99.8	103.8
SD	11.3	13.1	11.6

WISC-R

	VIQ	PSQ	FSIQ
M	111.6	108.7	111.3
SD	15.3	12.3	11.7

Measure	Sample	Design	Results

McCarthy Scales of Children's Abilities

Sample: 93 children (44 males, 49 females), ages 48–72 months (mean = 62.5) from the Northeast and Northcentral regions.

Design: Tests were administered in alternating order. Between-test interval ranged from 7 to 21 days.

Results:

	WPPSI-R			SBIV		
	VIQ	PIQ	FSIQ	Verb Reas	Abst Vis	Comp
M	104.1	104.8	105.3	107.0	106.6	107.2
SD	15.1	13.2	14.0	11.7	15.2	12.8

Correlation between the WPPSI-R FSIQ and MSCA GCI was .81, between the VIQ and MSCA Verbal was .75 and between the PIQ and MSCA Perceptual/Performance was .71.

	WPPSI-R			MSCA		
	VIQ	PIQ	FSIQ	Verb	Percep Perform	GCI
M	103.3	101.2	102.4	52.1	54.7	104.8
SD	12.9	14.4	13.5	9.8	8.8	14.3

K-ABC

Sample: 59 children ages 37 to 76 months (mean = 61) from the Northeast and South regions.

Design: Tests were administered in alternating order. Between-test interval ranged from 5 to 15 days.

Results:

Correlation between the WPPSI-R FSIQ and KABC Mental Processing Score was .49, between the VIQ and Sequential Processing score was .31 and between the PIQ and the Simultaneous Processing Score was .37.

	WPPSI-R			KABC		
	VIQ	PIQ	FSIQ	Simult	Seq	Mental
M	94.4	100.4	96.8	101.3	104.4	103.1
SD	12.5	13.5	12.6	13.0	14.3	13.1

The first approach is a quantitative one. The child's Full scale IQ will can be viewed in terms of its deviation from the norm and its percentile rank (Table 6). An IQ of 100 on the Full scale defines performance of the average child of a given age. An IQ of 85 or 115 correspond to one standard deviation below and above the mean, respectively, whereas an IQ of 70 or 130 are each two standard deviations from the mean. About two thirds of all children obtain IQs between 85 and 115, about 95 percent score in the 70 to 130 range, and nearly all obtain IQs between 55 and 145 (three standard deviations on either side of the mean). In addition to determining the distance from the mean, one also can determine the approximate rank of an IQ. Using Table 6-6, which provides selected IQ to percentile rank conversions, the examiner can determine the ranking of

the child's IQ relative to the standardization sample.

The second approach is a qualitative system aimed at describing the child's performance. This method might be of most use when describing the child's test performance to someone unfamiliar with the statistical base of the IQ. Table 6-7 presents specific IQ ranges and their corresponding qualitative diagnostic categories. The range provided might not apply to all possible situations; however, if alternative limits are used, the statistical basis for determining the limits must be stated.

Step 2. Comparisons of the Verbal and Performance Scales

The second step in interpreting a child's performance on the WPPSI-R is to examine the discrepancy between the Verbal and Performance Scale IQs. Table 6-8 presents, by age, the differences required for statistical significance at both the 15 percent and 5 percent levels.

The information on significance should aid the examiner in determining which differences should be examined in greater detail and which, because they occur by chance, should not be interpreted as meaningful. However, the fact that a difference between the VIQ and the PIQ is significant does not tell the entire story. It also is useful to know how frequently a difference of a certain magnitude occurred in the standardization sample. A discrepancy might be statistically significant and still occur frequently in the population. Table 6-9 presents the frequency of VIQ–PIQ differences found in the standardization sample. The following example illustrates the use of the significant difference and frequency of difference information contained in Tables 6-8 and 6-9:

> A 5½ year old child obtains a VIQ of 105 and a PIQ of 92. A discrepancy of 13 or more points is significant at the .05 level. However, this 13-point discrepancy, according to the frequency table on page 130 of the Manual, occurred in approximately 25 percent of the standardization sample suggesting that a discrepancy of this magnitude is a fairly common occurrence.

Interpretation of differences at the scale level should incorporate information on both the significance and frequency of the discrepancy.

TABLE 6.6
RELATION OF IQS TO DEVIATION FROM THE MEAN AND PERCENTILE RANKS

Verbal Performance, or Full Scale IQ	Number of SDs from the Mean	Percentile Rank[a]
145	$+3$	99.9
140	$+2\frac{2}{3}$	99.6
135	$+2\frac{1}{3}$	99
130	$+2$	98
125	$+1\frac{2}{3}$	95
120	$+1\frac{1}{3}$	91
115	$+1$	84
110	$+\frac{2}{3}$	75
105	$+\frac{1}{3}$	63
100	0 (Mean)	50
95	$-\frac{1}{3}$	37
90	$-\frac{2}{3}$	25
85	-1	16
80	$-1\frac{1}{3}$	9
75	$-1\frac{2}{3}$	5
70	-2	2
65	$-2\frac{1}{3}$	1
60	$-2\frac{2}{3}$	0.4
55	-3	0.1

[a] The percentile ranks are theoretical values for a normal distribution.

(Wechsler Preschool and Primary Scale of Intelligence—Revised. Copyright © 1989 by The Psychological Corporation. Reproduced by permission. All rights reserved.)

TABLE 6.7
INTELLIGENCE CLASSIFICATION

IQ Range	Classification	Percent Included	
		Theoretical Normal Curve	Actual[a] Sample
130 and above	Very superior	2.2	2.7
120–129	Superior	6.7	6.5
110–119	High average	16.1	17.3
90–109	Average	50.0	49.4
80–89	Low average	16.1	15.7
70–79	Borderline	6.7	6.4
69 and below	Intellectually Deficient[b]	2.2	2.0

[a] The percentages shown are for the Full Scale IQ and are based on the total standardization sample (N = 1,700). The percentages obtained for the Verbal IQ and Performance IQ are very similar.

[b] In place of the term mentally retarded used in the WPPSI, the WPPSI-R uses the term intellectually deficient. This practice avoids the implication that a very low IQ is sufficient evidence for the classification of ''mental'' retardation. The term intellectually deficient is descriptive and refers only to low intellectual functioning. This usage is consistent with the standards recommended by the American Association of Mental Deficiency (Grossman, 1983) and the American Psychiatric Association (1980).

(Wechsler Preschool and Primary Scale of Intelligence—Revised. Copyright © 1989 by The Psychological Corporation. Reproduced by permission. All rights reserved.)

Step 3. Comparing the Mean Verbal and Performance Scaled Score to an Individual Subtest Scaled score

Comparisons of the scaled scores on individual subtests to the average scaled score of the scale to which those subtests belong provides information on specific strengths and weaknesses within a particular ability domain. Table 6-10 presents the differences between the scaled scores on any individual subtest and the average subtest score required for statistical significance at the .05 and .01 levels. The knowledge that a difference is significant is again only part of the story. It also is important to know the frequency of a discrepancy between a subtest scaled score and the average scaled score.

Table 6-9 provides differences obtained by various percentages of the standardization sample. The following is an example of how to use information on both significance of difference and frequency of this difference.

A 4-year-old child obtains a scaled score of 5 on the Object Assembly subtest. The child's average

TABLE 6.8
DIFFERENCE BETWEEN WPPSI-R PERFORMANCE IQ AND VERBAL IQ REQUIRED FOR SIGNIFICANCE AT 15 AND 5 PERCENT LEVELS

Level of Significance	Age Group									Average of Nine Groups
	3	3½	4	4½	5	5½	6	6½	7	
15%	7.30	7.27	7.39	7.56	7.90	8.50	8.34	8.91	10.06	8.13
5%	9.90	9.89	10.06	10.29	10.76	11.56	11.36	12.12	13.70	11.07

(Wechsler Preschool and Primary Scale of Intelligence—Revised. Copyright © 1989 by The Psychological Corporation. Reproduced by permission. All rights reserved.)

TABLE 6.9
FREQUENCY OF PERFORMANCE IQ—VERBAL IQ DIFFERENCE IN THE STANDARDIZATION SAMPLE BY AGE

Percentage Obtaining Given or Greater Discrepancy	VIQ-PIQ Discrepancies Age									
	3	3½	4	4½	5	5½	6	6½	7	Average[a]
50	8	9	9	8	9	9	9	8	10	9
25	13	14	16	14	16	16	16	15	16	15
20	15	16	17	17	18	18	18	16	17	17
10	19	21	23	22	24	22	23	22	21	22
5	23	28	26	26	28	25	28	28	25	26
2	28	34	31	29	33	38	33	33	32	32
1	35	35	32	35	34	46	38	38	33	36

[a] Average values have been rounded to the nearest whole number.

(Wechsler Preschool and Primary Scale of Intelligence—Revised. Copyright © 1989 by The Psychological Corporation. Reproduced by permission. All rights reserved.)

scaled score for the Performance scale (average of 5 subtests) is 11. Thus, there is a 6 point difference between the child's subtest scaled score and average scaled score. This 6-point difference exceeds the critical value of 4.88 for the Object Assembly subtest at the .01 level (See Table 6-10). A difference of this magnitude is rare, as evidenced by the fact that it occurred in less than one percent of the standardization sample (Table 6-11).

Discrepancies between subtest scaled scores and the average scaled score for the scale to which they belong are interpreted in much the same way as a discrepancy between VIQ and PIQ. Information on both the significance and frequency of the discrepancy are important when determining a child's relative strengths and weaknesses.

Step 4. Comparing Scaled Scores on Individual Subtests.

After having compared discrepancies in the VIQ and PIQ and the average subtest scaled score with individual subtest scaled scores, the examiner frequently seeks more detailed information regarding the child's particular strengths and weaknesses. By comparing the child's scores on individual subtests, the examiner can explore hypotheses about a child's particular strengths and weaknesses.

Tables 6-12 and 6-13 show differences be-

tween scaled scores on pairs of WPPSI-R subtests that are required to reach significance at the .15 and .05 levels averaged across the nine age groups. The following example illustrates the use of these tables.

A 5-year-old child obtains a scaled score of 10 on the Block Design subtest and 13 on the Mazes subtest. This three-point difference is significant at the .15 level (critical value = 2.67) but not at the .05 level (critical value = 3.64).

An important point to remember when interpreting discrepancies between subtests is that the SE_M varies from subtest to subtest and from age to age within subtests. The lower the subtest reliabilities (and hence the higher the SE_M of the difference), the greater the likelihood that the difference between scores is because of chance rather than a real difference in the child's abilities. For example, for a child aged 3, a larger difference is required for statistical significance when comparing the child's scaled scores on Object Assembly and Arithmetic (with reliability coefficients of .63 and .78, respectively) than when comparing scores on Information and Picture Completion (with reliability coefficients of .90 and .87, respectively). An additional precaution is suggested by Sattler (1988). He recommends that the values are more accurate when prior rather than post hoc comparisons are made since the use of post hoc comparisons tends to capitalize on chance.

TABLE 6.10
DIFFERENCES REQUIRED FOR SIGNIFICANCE BETWEEN SCALED SCORES ON INDIVIDUAL SUBTESTS AND THE AVERAGE SUBTEST SCORE

Subtest	Mean of 5 Performance Subtests[a]		Mean of 6 Performance Subtests		Mean of 5 Verbal Subtests[b]		Mean of 6 Verbal Subtests		Mean of 10 Subtests[c]		Mean of 11 Subtests[d]		Mean of 12 Subtests	
	.05	.01	.05	.01	.05	.01	.05	.01	.05	.01	.05	.01	.05	.01
Object Assembly	4.07	4.88	4.32	5.12	—	—	—	—	4.83	5.68	4.93	5.71	4.99	5.74
Geometric Design	3.20	3.83	3.39	4.02	—	—	—	—	3.65	4.29	3.74	4.32	3.79	4.36
Block Design	2.86	3.43	3.00	3.55	—	—	—	—	3.18	3.73	3.22	3.73	3.27	3.73
Mazes	3.30	3.96	3.47	4.11	—	—	—	—	3.79	4.46	3.85	4.46	3.90	4.49
Picture Completion	2.92	3.49	3.05	3.61	—	—	—	—	3.79	4.46	3.85	4.46	3.90	4.49
Animal Pegs[e]	—	—	4.11	4.79	—	—	—	—	3.23	3.80	3.31	3.83	3.33	3.83
Information	—	—	—	—	2.89	3.46	3.02	3.58	3.34	3.93	3.39	3.93	3.44	3.96
Comprehension	—	—	—	—	2.97	3.55	3.13	3.71	3.46	4.06	3.51	4.06	3.56	4.09
Arithmetic	—	—	—	—	3.10	3.71	3.26	3.86	3.63	4.26	3.71	4.29	3.73	4.29
Vocabulary	—	—	—	—	2.81	3.37	2.97	3.52	3.26	3.83	3.33	3.86	3.36	3.86
Similarities	—	—	—	—	2.81	3.37	2.94	3.49	3.23	3.80	3.31	3.83	3.33	3.83
Sentences	—	—	—	—	—	—	3.10	3.67	—	—	3.51	4.06	3.53	4.06

Note: To compute the deviations from average that are significant at the .05 and .01 levels, the formula provided by Davis (1959) was used. Values are corrected using Bonferroni adjustment for multiple comparisons.

[a] Animal Pegs excluded. [b] Sentences excluded. [c] Animal Pegs and Sentences excluded. [d] The differences for 11 subtests were calculated with the 10 required subtests and the Sentences subtest.

[e] The average SE_M for the Animal Pegs subtest was obtained by averaging the SE_Ms across the two age groups in the test-retest study.

(Wechsler Preschool and Primary Scale of Intelligence—Revised. Copyright © 1989 by the Psychological Corporation. Reproduced by permission. All rights reserved.)

TABLE 6.11
DIFFERENCES OBTAINED BY VARIOUS PERCENTAGES OF THE STANDARDIZATION SAMPLE WHEN EACH
SUBTEST IS COMPARED TO THE AVERAGE SUBTEST SCORE

Subtest	Performance Scale (6 Subtests)				Verbal Scale (6 Subtests)				Full Scale (12 Subtests)			
	10%	5%	2%	1%	10%	5%	2%	1%	10%	5%	2%	1%
Object Assembly	3.5	4.2	4.8	5.3	—	—	—	—	4.0	4.8	5.7	6.1
Geometric Design	3.3	4.0	4.7	5.3	—	—	—	—	3.8	4.4	5.5	6.0
Block Design	3.2	3.8	4.5	5.2	—	—	—	—	3.6	4.3	5.2	5.7
Mazes	3.5	4.2	5.0	5.7	—	—	—	—	4.0	4.8	5.9	6.7
Picture Completion	3.5	4.2	5.0	5.5	—	—	—	—	3.6	4.2	5.1	5.8
Animal Pegs	3.8	4.8	5.7	6.7	—	—	—	—	4.1	5.0	6.2	6.9
Information	—	—	—	—	2.7	3.2	3.8	4.2	3.2	3.8	4.4	4.9
Comprehension	—	—	—	—	2.8	3.7	4.5	5.2	3.6	4.3	5.3	5.9
Arithmetic	—	—	—	—	3.2	3.8	4.5	5.0	3.2	3.9	4.8	5.3
Vocabulary	—	—	—	—	3.0	3.5	4.3	4.7	3.5	4.2	5.1	5.6
Similarities	—	—	—	—	3.0	3.8	4.5	5.0	3.5	4.2	4.9	5.4
Sentences	—	—	—	—	3.2	3.8	4.8	5.3	3.7	4.4	5.2	5.8

(Wechsler Preschool and Primary Scale of Intelligence—Revised. Copyright © 1989 by The Psychological Corporation. Reproduced by permission. All rights reserved.)

HYPOTHESIS TESTING BASED ON DISCREPANCY INFORMATION

The primary purpose for interpreting discrepancies in a child's performance is to confirm or discount hypotheses about that child's abilities. Statistically significant discrepancies, whether among scales or subtests, indicate real differences in ability.

The Verbal scale measures primarily verbal ability. The questions are presented orally and the child responds orally. On the other hand, the Performance scale consists of primarily perceptual motor tasks. The tasks generally are presented in a nonverbal manner and the child's responses are primarily motoric.

A significant discrepancy between Verbal and Performance scores can be interpreted several ways, including interest patterns, cognitive style, psychopathology or specific deficiencies, or strengths in an ability (Sattler, 1988). It is left to the clinician to determine which of the possible interpretations is feasible in light of the child's performance and clinical history.

When interpreting a significant Verbal-Performance discrepancy the examiner must determine the clinical significance of the discrepancy.

For example, a significant difference exists between a Verbal IQ of 145 and a Performance IQ of 130, yet in reality this difference does not suggest the child is deficient in the Performance area. Sattler (1988) points out that hypotheses should be formulated in relationship to the child's absolute Verbal, Performance or Full Scale IQ.

Similar to discrepancies at the Verbal-Performance Scale level, discrepancies among the individual subtests from average and pairs of subtests (see section on description of subtests for specific abilities measured by each subtest) should be examined for clinical significance. For example, if a child obtains a scaled score of 8 on Information and has a Verbal Scale mean of 13, one can conclude that the child's general knowledge about the environment and long-term memory is significantly less well developed than his or her other Verbal skills. Further, if this Information scaled score is compared to the child's scaled score of 12 on both the Comprehension and Vocabulary subtests, one can further conclude that the child's logical reasoning and understanding of relationships is significantly better than his or her long-term memory skills and knowledge of the environment. In general, the examiner should interpret subtest discrepancy information in light of the

TABLE 6.12
DIFFERENCES BETWEEN SCALED SCORES REQUIRED FOR STATISTICAL SIGNIFICANCE AT THE 15 PERCENT LEVEL

Subtest	Object Assembly	Geo. Design	Block Design	Mazes	Picture Comp.	Animal Pegs	Information	Comprehension	Arithmetic	Vocabulary	Similarities
Geometric Design	3.34	—									
Block Design	3.17	2.61	—								
Mazes	3.39	2.87	2.67	—							
Picture Completion	3.20	2.64	2.42	2.70	—						
Animal Pegs[a]	3.67	3.21	3.02	3.25	3.06	—					
Information	3.23	2.68	2.47	2.74	2.49	3.10	—				
Comprehension	3.28	2.73	2.52	2.79	2.54	3.14	2.58	—			
Arithmetic	3.32	2.79	2.59	2.85	2.62	3.18	2.66	2.71	—		
Vocabulary	3.20	2.65	2.43	2.71	2.46	3.06	2.51	2.56	2.62	—	
Similarities	3.20	2.64	2.43	2.71	2.45	3.07	2.49	2.54	2.62	2.47	—
Sentences	3.26	2.71	2.51	2.77	2.53	3.12	2.58	2.63	2.70	2.55	2.54

Note: Table 11 is based on average values for 9 age groups. To determine whether the difference between two subtests is reliable, the following formula was used:

$$\text{Difference Score} = Z \sqrt{SE_{MA}2 + SE_{MB}2}.$$

Where Z is the normal curve value associated with the desired confidence level (i.e., 15 percent level = 1.44). SE_{MA} and SE_{MB} are the standard errors of measurement of the two subtests.
[a]The SE^M for Animal Pegs was determined from the test-retest study to be 1.74 for the entire retest sample (N = 175).
(Wechsler Preschool and Primary Scale of Intelligence—Revised. Copyright © 1989 by The Psychological Corporation. Reproduced by permission. All rights reserved.)

TABLE 6.13
DIFFERENCES BETWEEN SCALED SCORES REQUIRED FOR STATISTICAL SIGNIFICANCE AT THE 5 PERCENT LEVEL

Subtest	Object Assembly	Geo. Design	Block Design	Mazes	Picture Comp.	Animal Pegs	Information	Comprehension	Arithmetic	Vocabulary	Similarities
Geometric Design	4.55	—									
Block Design	4.31	3.55	—								
Mazes	4.61	3.91	3.64	—							
Picture Completion	4.36	3.59	3.30	3.68	—						
Animal Pegs[a]	4.99	4.36	4.11	4.43	4.15	—					
Information	4.40	3.64	3.36	3.73	3.39	4.21	—				
Comprehension	4.46	3.71	3.43	3.80	3.46	4.27	3.52	—			
Arithmetic	4.52	3.80	3.52	3.88	3.56	4.33	3.62	3.69	—		
Vocabulary	4.35	3.60	3.31	3.68	3.35	4.16	3.41	3.48	3.57	—	
Similarities	4.36	3.60	3.31	3.68	3.34	4.17	3.39	3.46	3.57	3.36	—
Sentences	4.44	3.70	3.41	3.78	3.45	4.25	3.51	3.58	3.67	3.46	3.46

Note: Table 12 is based on average values for 9 age groups. The difference required for statistical significance was computed using the following formula:

$$\text{Difference Score} = Z \sqrt{SE_{MA}^2 + SE_{MB}^2}.$$

where Z is the normal curve value associated with the desired confidence level (i.e., 5 percent level = 1.96), and SE_{MA} and SE_{MB} are the standard errors of measurement of the two subtests.

[a]The SE^M for Animal Pegs was determined from the test-retest study to be 1.74 for the entire retest sample (N = 175).

(Wechsler Preschool and Primary Scale of Intelligence—Revised. Copyright © 1989 by The Psychological Corporation. Reproduced by permission. All rights reserved.)

original hypotheses about the child's strengths and weaknesses. That is to say, one should compare subtests that measure those abilities that are hypothesized to be particularly strong or particularly weak. Whether one's hypotheses about the child are confirmed or discounted, examining discrepancy information will aid the examiner in more fully understanding the child's abilities and devising a set of practical and useful recommendations based on the child's performance. One also should remember that interpretations going beyond the scale level are more subjective and tend to be less reliable and valid. Thus, the wise examiner will interpret the child's performance carefully and in light of all information that is known about the child.

SUMMARY

The revision of the Wechsler Preschool and Primary scale was undertaken with two primary goals as the focus: to update the norms and extend the age range of the scale both upward and downward. The WPPSI-R has retained many of the features of the WPPSI that made it a highly regarded assessment instrument.

For the most part, the WPPSI-R subtests are similar to those of the WPPSI. A majority of the subtests have sufficient floor and ceiling to assess children from ages 3 to 6½ years. At the scale level the floor and ceiling of the Verbal, Performance, and Full scales is sufficient for both low and high ability children across the entire age span.

The standardization sample of 1,700 children closely approximates the target population from the 1986 Census Bureau data. In addition to obtaining a representative sample for the standardization, and oversample of minority children also were collected to analyze potential bias.

The reliability if the WPPSI-R is excellent at the scale level with all three scales exceeding the .90 criterion. In addition, a majority of the subtests also exceed the criterion (.80) to be considered reliable. Further evidence of the WPPSI-R's reliability is the fact that the stability estimates obtained in a test–retest study generally met the criterion of .90.

The validity of the WPPSI-R has been established through both concurrent and construct validity research. Studies of the concurrent validity indicate that the WPPSI-R correlates highly with other measures of intellectual ability, particularly other Wechsler scales. The construct validity of the WPPSI-R was established through factor analytic studies that consistently yielded a two-factor solution.

The approach to interpreting the WPPSI-R is quite similar to that of interpreting the WISC-R. The successive levels approach recommended here allows the examiner to generate and test hypotheses at the highest level of certainty first before proceeding to hypothesis testing at a lower level of certainty. In general, this approach should lead to more systematic and appropriate interpretation of the WPPSI-R.

The WPPSI-R is a well-standardized, reliable, and valid instrument for the assessment of intellectual functioning of children aged 3 through 7 years 3 months.

Future research should focus on the issues of predictive and discriminant validity. Also, further work in the area of interpreting the WPPSI-R would aid the clinician using this instrument of diagnostic purposes.

REFERENCES

Bracken, B. A. (1987). Limitations of preschool instruments and standards for minimal levels of technical adequacy. *Journal of Psychoeducational Assessment, 5,* 313–326.

Bureau of the Census. (1986). Current population survey, March 1987 [machine-readable data file]. Washington, DC.

Davis, F. (1959). Interpretation of differences among averages and individual test scores. *Journal of Educational Psychology, 50,* 69, 299–308.

Feshback, S., Adelman, H., & Fuller, W. (1977). Prediction of reading and related academic problems. *Journal of Educational Psychology, 69,* 299–308.

Hollenbeck, G. R., & Kaufman, A. S. (1973). Factor analysis of the Wechsler Preschool and Primary Scale of Intelligence (WPPSI). *Journal of Clinical Psychology, 29,* 41–45.

Kaufman, A. S. (1979). *Intelligent Testing with the WISC-R.* New York: John Wiley and Sons.

Kaufman, A. S., & Kaufman, N. L. (1983). *Kaufman Assessment Battery for Children.* Circle Pines, MN: American Guidance Service.

McCarthy, D. (1972). *Manual for the McCarthy Scales of Children's Abilities.* San Antonio, TX: The Psychological Corporation.

Rasbury, W. C., McCoy, J. G., & Perry, N. W. (1977). Relationship of scores on WPPSI and WISC-R at a one-year interval. *Perceptual and Motor Skills, 44,* 695–698.

Sattler, J. (1976). Scoring difficulty of the WPPSI Geometric Design subtest. *Journal of School Psychology, 14,* 230–234.

Sattler, J. (1988). *Assessment of Children.* San Diego, CA.

Shrout, P., & Fleiss, J. (1979). Intraclass correlations: Uses in assessing rater reliability. *Psychological Bulletin, 86,* 420–428.

Thorndike, R. L., Hagen, E. P., & Sattler, J. M. (1986). *Guide for administering and scoring the Stanford–Binet Intelligence Scale: Fourth Edition.* Chicago: Riverside Publishing.

Urbina, S., & Clayton, J. (in press). WPPSI-R/WISC-R: A comparative study.

Wechsler, D. (1967). *Manual for the Wechsler Preschool and Primary Scale of Intelligence.* San Antonio, TX: The Psychological Corporation.

Wechsler, D., (1974). *Manual for the Wechsler Intelligence Scale for Children-Revised.* San Antonio, TX: The Psychological Corporation.

Wechsler, D. (1989). *Manual for the Wechsler Preschool and Primary Scale of Intelligence-Revised.* San Antonio, TX: The Psychological Corporation.

7

The Assessment of Preschool Children with the Stanford-Binet Intelligence Scale: Fourth Edition

R. STEVE MCCALLUM

Historically, practitioners who have provided services to preschool children have been severely limited in their choice of individual, standardized tests of intelligence. That situation is rapidly changing, and the change began with the introduction of the WPPSI (Wechsler, 1967), followed by the development of the MSCA (McCarthy, 1972), the revision of the Stanford-Binet (Terman & Merrill 1973), and the K-ABC, a 1983 publication (Kaufman & Kaufman). The Psychological Corporation is currently standardizing the Differential Ability Scales (DAS) (Elliott, 1990), an Americanization of the British Ability Scales (BAS) (Elliott, 1983).

In 1986 the Stanford-Binet, Form L-M, was replaced by the Stanford-Binet Intelligence Scale: Fourth Edition (Binet IV) (Thorndike, Hagen, & Sattler, 1986); the Binet IV, like its predecessor, contains normative data for children as young as two years. Of these recent developments, the release of the new Binet has been perhaps the most eagerly anticipated. Because the Binet L-M has been the test of choice for many practitioners since its restandardization, expectations for the new Binet have been high. The primary purpose of this chapter is to aid practitioners in the intelligent use of the Binet IV, and more specifically, to aid interpretation of the instrument. Subtest descriptions and general test administration procedures of the Binet will be presented, followed by a discussion of its technical adequacy, including reliability and validity. Other technical characteristics will be considered, such as the Binet IV subtest floors, ceilings, item gradients, and so forth. Various interpretive strategies will be discussed, followed by a limited list of recommendations for use.

TEST DESCRIPTION

Test Model

The new Binet was developed according to a hierarchical model of intellectual functioning, using a three level schemata. The model posits a global to specific flow, with *g*, general intelligence, at the apex; crystallized abilities, fluid and analytic abilities, and short-term memory constructs at the second level; and verbal reasoning, quantitative reasoning, and abstract visual reasoning at the third level. As is apparent from Fig. 7-1, the constructs become more specific at each successive level. The Binet's 15 subtests were assigned logically as measures of the global constructs, yielding four global scores and a test composite. Three of the global scores are formed from subtests assigned as measures of the third-level verbal reasoning, quantitative reasoning, and abstract-visual reasoning constructs; the global scores are assigned the construct names. The fourth global score, called the Short-Term Memory score, is based on performance on short-term memory subtests. Although the model is appealing intuitively and logically, it might not provide the foundation for appropriate interpretation, at least for most children. That is, the construct validity of the model is not fully supported by the factor analytic findings from the standardization sample, as shown in the *Stanford-Binet: Fourth Edition Technical Manual (1986)*. Consequently, the "best-fit" model for the greatest number of children might not be the model described by the test authors. The best interpretive strategy for a given child can be determined only after attention

to and consideration of the available interpretative models.

Subtests for Preschool Children

The new Binet is not an omnibus test as was the third edition; that is, dissimilar items or tasks are not assigned to age blocks for administration. Rather, the new Binet follows the test format of the Wechsler scales in that the subtests are assigned to more global scales, and each subtest contains homogeneous item content. Each subtest is administered, from start to finish, according to a child's ability.

The particular items administered are determined by the chronological age of the child and the quality of his or her performance on the "router" subtest, Vocabulary. Performance on the Vocabulary subtest aids in the determination of the appropriate starting points on the other subtests, hence it functions as the router subtest. The starting item for the Vocabulary subtest is determined by chronological age. Importantly, not all 15 subtests are administered to all children. In fact, there are only six core subtests that are administered to

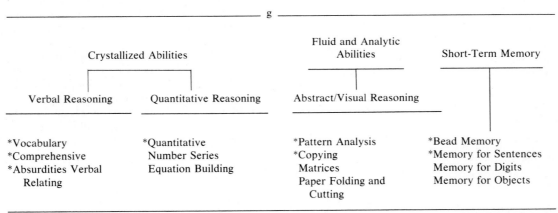

Note—The asterisked (*) subtests are appropriate for preschool children. Scores yielded by the Fourth Edition include a Composite score, four Area scores (for Verbal Reasoning, Quantitative Reasoning, Abstract Visual Reasoning, and Short-Term Memory), and 15 individual subtest scores.

Making many un*planned* comparisons capitalizes on chance differences, and results in a highly liberal procedure, one in which there is overinterpretation. (A similar phenomenon occurs commonly in research settings when too many unplanned comparisons are made; as you may remember, the Bonferoni *t* procedure provides a correction in the case of too many pairwise comparisons.)

Figure 7-1.   The Stanford-Binet: Fourth Edition structure, as defined by its authors. From Delaney, E.A. & Hopkins, T.F. (1987). *Examiners handbook: An expanded guide for fourth edition users*. Courtesy The Riverside Publishing Company.

all examinees. The other subtests are administered according to a child's chronological age and cognitive ability. Also, the examiner is free to pick and choose certain subtests according to the particular referral reason and needs of the child. For example, the test authors recommend specific subtests for children who are suspected of being intellectually gifted, primarily because of the extended ceiling of these subtests. Other subtests, those characterized by an extended floor, are recommended for children suspected of being mentally retarded.

Functioning on the subtests is impacted by a host of variables as has been suggested by Sattler (1988). Some of those influences are listed in Table 7-1. Additional information regarding technical interpretive characteristics is depicted in Tables 7-2 and 7-3. The 15 subtests include Vocabulary, Comprehension, Absurdities, Verbal Relations, Pattern Analysis, Copying, Matrices, Paper Folding and Cutting, Quantitative, Number Series, Equation Building, Bead Memory, Memory for Sentences, Memory for Digits, and Memory for Objects. Of these, only eight are administered to preschool children; items from all eight subtests are scored dichtomously, correct or incorrect. These eight include:

Vocabulary

The vocabulary subtest is divided into picture vocabulary and oral vocabulary sections. Of 46 items, the first 14 are of a picture vocabulary format. For the oral vocabulary section, the examinee is asked to define a word presented orally by the examiner. Although the authors are to be commended for addressing the needs of preschool children by including the less difficult picture vocabulary section, the combined format limits interpretability for children who respond to both types of items (i.e., receptive and expressive vocabulary). Because task demands are different, a single score representing performance on both types of items cannot be given a meaningful interpretation. However, all items probably assess verbal comprehension.

Because the subtest is amenable to administration to a wide range of ages, it is part of the core battery. Technical properties of this subtest are quite good (e.g., the range of Kuder-Richardson 20 formula reliabilities, for ages 2 through 6 are .78 to .85). Vocabulary is a good measure of

g; by squaring the g loading from the standardization sample it is shown that .64% of its variance is attributed to g (See Table 7-2 for a minimal description of technical data for all subtests). The g loading cited in the *Technical Manual* from a factor analysis of 2- through 6-year-old children is .65, yielding a 42% estimate of variance attributable to g. Table 7-2 presents g figures from Sattler (1988) and from the *Technical Manual*. They differ because of the different types of Factor analytic techniques used to determine g. Subtest specificity, the extent to which a subtest can be considered a measure of some unique attribute, is adequate for age 2 (Sattler, 1988). (If the unique variance of a subtest equals at least 25%, and is greater than the error variance, the subtest is said to possess adequate subtest specificity.) Vocabulary contributes substantially to the Verbal Comprehension factor at all ages; Verbal Comprehension is one of three "factors" that emerged for most ages from a factor analysis reported by Sattler (1988).

Comprehension

This subtest requires two somewhat different sets of skills. The first 6 of the 42 Comprehensive items require pointing responses and assess knowledge of body parts; the remaining items require oral responses to aural questions, and tap a broad range of knowledge including understanding of basic personal, economic, and social needs and practices. This subtest is part of the core battery, and is administered to all examinees. The technical properties of Comprehension are good. (See Table 7-2 for details.) According to Sattler (1988), Comprehension correlates with the Composite Score moderately highly ($r = .76$), and subtest specificity is adequate at only age 2, for the preschool ages 2 through 6. Comprehension contributes substantially to the Verbal Comprehension factor for preschool children.

Absurdities

The first 4 of a total of 32 items require a multiple choice pointing administration format; the remaining items require a verbal response. The subtest, does not as do the previous two, lend itself to clear interpretation for very young children who respond to both types of items. Even though the response mode changes, all the items require the ability to discern incongruities and absurdities

TABLE 7.1
POSSIBLE ABILITIES INFLUENCING AREA, FACTOR, AND SUBTEST SCORES FOR PRESCHOOL CHILDREN

Areas

Verbal Reasoning	Abstract/Visual Reasoning	Quantitative Reasoning	Short-Term Memory
Crystallized skills	Fluid abilities	Crystallized skills	Attention
Formal schooling	Novel problem solving	Formal schooling	Concentration
General life experiences	General life experiences	Mathematics	Visual processing and storage
Receptive/expressive language	Visual imagery	Number fluency	Verbal processing and storage
Verbal comprehension	Spatial relationships		
Verbal fluency	Nonverbal concept formation		
Verbal reasoning	Inductive reasoning		
Word knowledge	Visual/motor coordination		

Nonverbal Reasoning/Visualization
Nonverbal concept formation and reasoning
Fluid ability
Visual/spatial skills
Visual–motor coordination
Visual memory
Visual analysis/synthesis

Factors

Verbal Comprehension
Verbal skills/language facility
Receptive/expressive language
Crystallized skills
Verbal memory
Formal schooling/life experiences

Subtests

Pattern Analysis	Comprehension	Absurdities	Copying
Spatialization	Vocabulary skills	Visual perception	Visual-motor coordination
Visual–motor coordination	Verbal comprehension and expression	Long-term visual memory	Spatialization
Planning	Knowledge of culture	Knowledge of culture	Attention/concentration
Visual analysis and synthesis	Verbal fluency	Choose essential/nonessential details	Persistence
Nonverbal concept formation	Long-term verbal memory		
Resistance to time pressure			

Vocabulary	Bead Memory	Quantitative	Memory for Sentences
Expressive language	Visual memory	Number fluency	Short-term auditory memory
Verbal memory	Visual sequencing	Preschool math	Verbal fluency
Long-term memory	Chunking	Number facts	Verbal comprehension
Formal schooling	Attention		Syntax
General life experience	Visual-motor coordination		Attention
Verbal fluency			Concentration

110

TABLE 7-2
SUBTESTS FOR PRESCHOOL CHILDREN

Subtest	Median Reliability	g^2 loading (technical manual)	g^2 (Sattler, 1988)	Ages (ample, adequate) Subtest Specificity
Vocabulary	.78–.85	.42	.64	2
Comprehension	.79–.86	.45	.56	2
Absurdities	.79–.91	.48	.45	all
Pattern analysis	.80–.91	.48	.45	all
Copying	.74–.88	.38	.36	all
Quantitative	.81–.88	.48	.61	all, except 6
Bead memory	.83–.89	.34	.48	all
Memory for sentences	.85–.88	.35	.45	all

presented visually. This subtest is available for children who range in age from 2 to 14 years. The technical properties are good (See Table 7-2). According to Sattler (1988) its correlation with the composite score is 72. Absurdities is a good measure of g. The subtest loads reasonably well on the Verbal Comprehension factor for most ages, and significantly at some ages on a second factor, referred to by Sattler (1988) as Nonverbal Reasoning/Visualization, the second primary factor for preschool children.

Pattern Analysis

This subtest contains items of low difficulty for very young children. Of 42 total items, the first 6 require use of a form board. The remaining items require examinees to use blocks to build designs as seen from examiners' models and/or stimulus pictures. This subtest is part of the core battery, and is administered to children of all ages. The technical properties are good (See Table 7-2), and the subtest correlates reasonably well with the Composite Score at .74 (Sattler, 1988). Pattern Analysis is a good measure of g. The subtest contributes substantially to the Nonverbal Reasoning/Visualization factor at all age levels.

Copying

As with several other subtests that are available to examinees across the entire age range, Copying requires two somewhat different responses. Of 28 items, the first 12 require the examinee to use three or four blocks to copy a block

design constructed by the examiner. The remaining items require the examinee to copy pictured line drawings. This subtest is available for children 2 through 13 years, and the technical properties are good (See Table 7-2). The correlation coefficient with the Composite Score is .66; Copying loads moderately well on the Nonverbal Reasoning/Visualization factor for preschool children (Sattler, 1988).

Quantitative

This subtest requires prearithmetic and arithmetic skills at the preschool level. The difficulty level ranges from basic matching and counting to rather complex word problems. The Quantitative subtest is appropriate for individuals across the entire preschool age range. The technical characteristics are good (See Table 7-2). Quantitative correlates .82 with the Composite score (Sattler, 1988), and its specificity is ample/adequate at all age levels except 6 and ages 18 to 23. This subtest loads moderately to substantially on the Nonverbal Reasoning/Visualization factor, and modestly on the Verbal Comprehension factor (Sattler, 1988).

Bead Memory

Bead Memory requires the youngest and/or less able children to match beads shown by the examiner to photographs of the beads (items 1 through 10). Older children must place beads vertically onto a cylindrical rod held in place by a small base platform. The beads must be placed in

TABLE 7.3
COMPUTING FACTOR SCORES

Verbal Comprehension

Ages 2 through 7 Subtest	Standard Score
1 Vocabulary (VR)	————
6 Comprehension (VR)	————
7 Absurdities (VR)	————
4 Memory for Sentences (STM)	————

Steps

(1) Sum of standard scores on Vocabulary
+ Comprehension + Absurdities ————
(2) Verbal Reasoning Area SAS (p. 183 of
Guide for 3 subtests) ————
(3) Short-Term Memory Area SAS
(multiply the standard score by 2) ————
(4) Sum of (2) + (3) ————
(5) *Verbal Comprehension Factor Score*
(p. 187 of *Guide* for 2 area scores) ————

Nonverbal Reasoning/Visualization

Ages 2 through 11 Subtest	Standard Score
5 Pattern Analysis (A/VR)	————
9 Copying (A/VR)	————
3 Quantitative (QR)	————
2 Bead Memory (STM)	————

Steps

(1) Sum of standard scores on Pattern
Analysis + Copying ————
(2) Abstract/Visual Reasoning Area SAS
(p. 184 of *Guide* for 2 subtests) ————
(3) Quantitative Reasoning Area SAS
(multiply the standard score by 2) ————
(4) Short-Term Memory Area SAS
(multiply the standard score by 2) ————
(5) Sum of (2 + 3 + 4) ————
(6) *Nonverbal Reasoning/Visualization
Factor Score* (p. 187 or 188 of *Guide*
for 3 area scores) ————

Memory

Age 7 Subtest	Standard Score
8 Memory for Digits (STM)	————
10 Memory for Objects (STM)	————

TABLE 7.3
(*continued*)

Steps

(1) Sum of standard scores on Memory for
Digits + Memory ————
(2) Short-Term Memory Area SAS (p. 186
of *Guide* for 2 subtests) ————
(3) *Memory Factor Score* (p. 187 of *Guide*
for 1 area score) ————

the correct juxtaposition according to the stimulus shown. The stimulus is presented for 5 seconds, after which the examinee is asked to duplicate the model. The beads are of different shapes (i.e., cylindrical, cone shapes, saucer round, and round spherical) and colors (i.e., red, blue, and white), which complicates recall of the model. Item difficulty is increased by adding beads to the successive item. At a minimum the task requires visual discrimination and memory, color vision, and some visual motor coordination for all but the beginning 10 items. Bead Memory is appropriate for all preschool ages. The correlation with the Composite Score is .72 (Sattler, 1988). The subtest is a moderate estimate of *g*. For preschool children this subtest loads on the Nonverbal Reasoning/Visualization factor, and on the Memory factor at some older ages.

Memory for Sentences

This subtest requires examinees to repeat sentences, exactly as read by the examiner. The sentences range from very short two-word phrases to much longer, more convoluted sentences. Auditory short-term memory, verbal facility, and concentration are essential for success on these items. Memory for Sentences is appropriate for all ages. Its technical properties are good (See Table 7-2). The correlation coefficient with the Composite Score is .73 (Sattler, 1988). For preschool children, Memory for Sentences loads on the Verbal Comprehension factor, but loads on the Memory factor for older examinees (Sattler, 1988).

TECHNICAL ADEQUACY

According to *Standards for Educational and Psychological Testing*, published by the American Psychological Association (1985), test publishers should provide enough information for a qualified user to evaluate the appropriateness and technical adequacy of the test. Minimal information includes a discussion of item analysis procedures, revelant standardization data, and appropriate reliability and validity indices. The following discussion includes revelant information from the *Technical Manual*, as well as from other sources, as indicated.

ITEM ANALYSIS

The authors of the new Binet tried to maintain continuity with Form L-M. Consequently, they included as many of the more popular item types as possible from the old test. According to the authors, item types from the old Binet were retained if they were acceptable measures of verbal reasoning, quantitative reasoning, abstract/visual reasoning, or short-term memory; could be scored reliably; were perceived by experts as being relatively free of ethnic and gender bias; and functioned across a wide range of ages. Many of the item types were retained (e.g., Vocabulary, Comprehension, Verbal Absurdities, Picture Absurdities, Opposite Analogies, Paper Folding and Cutting, Copying, Ingenuity, Repeating Digits). However, an additional 29 new item types were generated for field testing. Initial item tryouts began in 1979, prior to standardization; items that failed to operate similarly across ethnic groups were eliminated.

STANDARDIZATION

Stratification variables for the standardization included geographic region, community size, ethnic group, age, and gender. The examinees SES also was obtained. Data from the 1980 U.S. Census were used to stratify variables. Tables in the *Technical Manual* reveal the extent to which the standardization sample conforms to the census figures. In general, the sample is quite representative. Of the four geographical regions, the largest "error" or misrepresentation occurred because the Northeast underrepresented the population by 5%. The South also was underrepresented slightly, by about 1.4%. The North Central and West were overrepresented by about 3%.

Community size representation was similarly impressive. Six "community size" categories were used, ranging from the largest cities (1,000,000 or more) to rural areas (less than 2,500). The largest misrepresentation was 4.1%; the rural areas were underrepresented by that much. Ethnic/Race representation closely approximated the population according to the census. Whites were underrepresented by about 5%, blacks were overrepresented by about 2.9%. Other groups were more closely represented. For example, Hispanic examinees comprised 6.3% of the sample; Hispanics represent 6.4% of the population. Gender representation was impressive. Males comprised 47.3% of the sample and 47.2% of the population; females comprised 51.7% of the sample and 52.8% of the population. Age categories from 2-0 to 18-0 to 23-11 were approximately equally represented, with a few planned exceptions. Extra children were selected for certain transition ages, such as 5-0 to 5-11 and 8-0 to 8-11; these are ages at which children face increased scrutiny and are at increased risk for academic failure. Although the sampling was generally carefully conducted and accurate, there is one glaring misrepresentation within the sample. The sample was grossly overrepresented for the higher SES categories, as defined by the Parental Occupation and Parental Education criteria. For example, the sample contained 45.9% examinees whose parents were described as managerial/professional, compared to 21.8% in the population. On the other hand, the sample contained 8.3% examinees whose parents were described as Operators, Fabricators, and laborers; these individuals comprise 19.5% of the population. Similarly, children of college graduates comprised 43.7% of the sample, but only 19% of the population. To compensate for these sampling errors the authors utilized a weighting procedure that overvalues the scores of the lower SES examinees and undervalues those of the higher SES examinees. However, the effects of the weighting procedure are not yet known; only further research will clarify the possible impact of the misrepresentation.

RELIABILITY

Reliability can be defined as the extent to which scores are free from errors of measurement.

Estimates presented in the *Technical Manual* are generally impressive. The authors present two types of reliability estimates—indices of internal consistency and test-retest (stability) coefficients. The bulk of the reliability data are internal consistency estimates (from the Kuder-Richardson 20); test–retest coefficients were obtained from children within two age groups. Internal consistency values are presented initially for preschool-age children, followed by test–retest values. Almost without exception, the KR-20 coefficients are higher. Another general finding, one that could be anticipated from the measurement literature, is that the reliabilities increased as a function of age. Younger children yielded lower reliability estimates.

Internal Consistency

According to the authors, the KR-20 estimates should be considered upper bound values because the assumption required by the formula—that all items above the ceiling level be failed—cannot be met. KR-20 coefficients range from .95 to .97 for ages 2 through 5 for the composite score. Typically, coefficients get larger as age increases, and the same pattern can be observed for these values; that is .95 was obtained for 2 year old children and .97 for 5 year old children. As can be seen in the *Technical Manual*, this pattern holds for all the estimates across all the various types of standard scores provided. Estimates range from .74 to .91 for the various subtests (See Table 7-2). Because the standard errors of measurement (SEM) are a function of the reliabilities, they fluctuate accordingly. For example, the SEM for a reliability coefficient of .80 is 3.6, versus a value of 2.4 for a reliability coefficient of .91.

The *Technical Manual* also contains KR-20 reliability estimates for area scores as well as for the composite and subtest scores. For preschool children, the Verbal Reasoning area score is calculated from either one, two, or three subtests; for the Abstract/Visual Reasoning area, one or two subtests is used; for the Quantitative Reasoning area, one subtest is necessary; and for Short-Term Memory, one or two subtests is required. When two subtests are used to calculate area scores for the Verbal Reasoning area scores, the KR-20 estimates range from .90 to .92 depending on age; when three subtests are used the values range from .93 to .94. When two subtests are used to calculate the Abstract/Visual Reasoning area score, the KR-20 estimates range from .85 to .93. The Quantitative Reasoning area score is calculated from only one subtest for preschool children; hence the reliabilities are the same as reported for the Quantitative subtest. However, the SEM changes. Because the standard deviation used in the formula to derive SEM increases twofold, from 8 to 16, the SEM increases proportionately. Finally, the Short Term Memory area KR-20 reliability estimates range from .90 to .92.

Test-Retest

Although some writers argue cogently that stability is really different, conceptually, from reliability (Jensen, 1980), the Stanford-Binet IV authors cite test–retest data as evidence for reliability. These "reliability" data were obtained by retesting 112 children. Fifty-seven of the children were approximately 5 years of age; 55 were approximately 8 years of age. The length of time between the two administrations varied from two to eight months, with an average test–retest interval of 16 weeks. Subtest test–retest reliability coefficients for the preschool children range from .56 (Bead Memory) to .78 (Memory for Sentences). Area coefficients range from .71 (Quantitative) to .88 (Verbal Reasoning). The composite coefficient .91 is similar, with one notable exception. The test–retest coefficient for the Quantitative subtest is only .28. The authors offer limited variability as a possible reason. However, the standard deviations (6 and 6.3) obtained for these children on the two administrations are not appreciably different from some of the other subtests with higher coefficients (e.g., Number Series yielded standard deviation values of 5.4 and 5.3, and a coefficient of .61). Apparently restriction of range is not the sole explanation for the diminished test–retest reliability.

Although both the preschool and the elementary groups showed higher mean scores on retest, the younger group improved most. The preschoolers improved by an average of 9.2 points on the Abstract/Visual Reasoning, but only 4.9 points on the Verbal Reasoning area; most of the mean subtest increases were on the order of 2 to 4 points.

The increases shown for the older group were similar, but slightly smaller.

Brief-Form Reliabilities

The authors suggest the use of abbreviated forms of the test for certain purposes, and report KR-20 reliabilities for two-, four-, and six-test composite scores. These values range from .88 for the two-test composite at the two year level to .99 for the six-test composite for the 18 to 23 level. Two caveats are offered by the test authors. First, the two- and four-test batteries should be used for screening only; second, only the composite scores should be used to make decisions from any of the abbreviated batteries.

VALIDITY

Validity is defined generally as the extent to which a test accomplishes what it purports to, and is more technically defined as the extent to which evidence is available to support inferences made from test scores. Test validity is specifically defined as content validity (the extent to which a test assess some predetermined content area), concurrent validity (the extent to which a test assess the content assessed by a second test), construct validity (the extent to which a test assesses some hypothetical construct), predictive validity (the extent to which a test predicts some future performance), and treatment validity (the extent to which test results contribute to interventions). Of course, content validity is especially revelant for academic achievement tests, but less so for constructs such as intelligence. Predictive and treatment validity are determined over time as a test is available for research over the years; consequently little evidence is available for the Stanford-Binet IV predictive validity so far. (There are some predictive validity data available in the new *Examiner's Manual* from the publishers of the Stanford-Binet IV), and cited in Table 7-4. There is no treatment validity evidence available. On the other hand, there is considerable evidence available addressing construct validity, including factor analytic data focussing on the test structure, concurrent validity studies focussing on the relationship of the new Binet to other tests that assess similar constructs, and studies of Binet per-

formance groups of individuals who are high or low on the construct presumably assessed by the Binet (i.e., intelligence). Much of the currently available evidence has been summarized by the Stanford-Binet authors and is presented in the *Technical Manual*. Evidence from other sources is beginning to surface. The available evidence from all sources is presented here.

Construct Validity

The structure of the Stanford-Binet, as determined by factor analytic results, provides some limited support for the logically derived model adopted by the authors. The model originally suggested by the authors promotes the notion of a first level *g* factor, followed by a second level of general or pervasive abilities, namely fluid and crystallized abilities, and short-term memory. The third more specific level of abilities include verbal reasoning and quantitative reasoning, both subsumed under the super-ordinate "crystallized ability". Abstract/Visual reasoning is the other third-level category and is subsumed under the superordinate "fluid analytic abilities." Figure 7-1 depicts the relationship among the various categories, levels, and subtests.

Factor Analytic Results

Evidence for construct validity can be provided by results of confirmatory factor analytic procedures using the entire standardization sample. If the subtests load as predicted, the structure is supported. The confirmatory factor analysis used by the Stanford-Binet authors for the entire standardization sample required extraction of a general factor first (using median correlations among the subtests), followed by extractions of group factors. The analysis provides limited support for the organizational scheme as shown in Fig. 7-1; however there are considerable discrepancies.

In support of the model, all subtests load significantly on *g*; the loadings range from .51 (Memory for Designs) to .79 (Number Series) for the total standardization sample. Some of the subtests load appreciably on predicted factors. All the Verbal Reasoning subtests load higher on the verbal factor than on any other factor (except the first large *g* factor). The loadings on the verbal factor by verbal subtests range from .26 to .47. Similarly,

TABLE 7.4
PREDICTIVE VALIDITY STUDIES

Study	Sample	Results
Delaney & Hopkins, 1987	46 nonexceptional children, $\overline{X}$ age = 12-9, SD = 6 months	Correlations among the WRAT-R and SB IV range from .36 to .74; WRAT-R means range from 90.8 to 96.7; SB IV, 94.2 to 100.4.
Delaney & Hopkins, 1987	40 emotionally disturbed children, $\overline{X}$ age = 13-4, SD = 33 months	Correlations among the WRAT-R and SB IV range from .36 to .60; means from 76.5 to 83.6; SB IV, 88 to 91.6.
Delaney & Hopkins, 1987	30 nonexceptional children, $\overline{X}$ age = 5-4, SD = 2 months	Correlations among scores from the Woodcock-Johnson (WJ Achievement) range from .36 to .92; means from the WJ and Binet are similar (WJ, 97.5 to 104.8; SB IV, 96.9 to 109.0).
Delaney & Hopkins, 1987	Nonexceptional children, $\overline{X}$ age = 8-3, SD = 4 months	Correlations among scores from the WJ and SB IV range from .34 to .80; means from the WJ range from 102.8 to 107.6, SB IV, 102.6 to 105.7.
Delaney & Hopkins, 1987	Nonexceptional children, $\overline{X}$ age = 12-10, SD = 5 months	Correlations among scores from the WJ and SB IV range from .65 to .80; means from the WJ range from 100.1 to 105.9; SB, 98.3 to 103.3.

all the Short-Term Memory subtests load higher on the memory factor than on any other factor, with one exception. Bead Memory loads modestly (.13) on the memory factor as well as the abstract/visual factor (.13). Memory factor loadings from other Short-Term Memory subtests range from .29 to .48. The three Quantitative Reasoning subtests load more heavily on the quantitative factor than any other, with loadings ranging from a very modest .21 to a moderate .49. With one exception, the four Abstract/Visual subtests load more heavily on the abstract/visual than on any other factor. The Matrices subtest loads most highly on the quantitative factor (.11), though it fails to load appreciably on any one of the four area factors. And, although Copying and Paper Folding and Cutting yield their highest loadings on the appropriate abstract/visual factor, both loadings are low. Only the Pattern Analysis produces a robust loading in this factor (.65).

Thorndike, Hagen, and Sattler (1986) conclude from the factor structure that there is ". . . positive support for the rationale underlying the battery." The support should be considered modest. There is a strong *g* factor loading; also the subtest variance attributable to some unique characteristic or ability, the subtest specificity, is very large for almost all the subtests. The median subtest specificity loading is .53. Consequently, there is little variance remaining to be invested in the more specific area constructs for most subtests. Of course, the type of factor analysis used can affect the solution; that is, a factor solution emphasizing the independence of factors, rather than their interdependence, can reflect more robust area loadings. However, the authors present the solution as presented in the *Technical Manual* as most appropriate, and it apparently emphasizes the interdependence of the subtests rather than their independence.

Another factor analysis is also presented in the *Technical Manual* that has implications for the construct validity, especially for preschoolers. The solution was obtained from only preschool children, those ranging in age from 2 to 6 years. As is apparent, only two factors emerged, other than the large general factor; Thorndike, Hagen, and Sattler identify these factors as Verbal and Abstract/Visual. This solution is partially a function of the eight subtests that are appropriate for the children in this age range. According to the test authors, the fact that only one quantitative subtest is included in the battery for children this age precluded the emergence of a separate quantitative factor. In addition, of the four short-term memory subtests included on the complete battery, only two are included on the battery for this age group—Bead Memory and Memory for Sentences. According to the authors, Bead Memory loaded on the Abstract/Visual factor; Memory for Sentences loaded on the verbal factor. The authors note that these loadings could be anticipated because of the content of the two tests. Consequently the emergence of a two-factor structure was not surprising. Sattler (1988) also presents a two-factor structure for young children, as shown in Table 7-3. For whatever reason, the most parsimonious explanation of what the test assesses for preschoolers should rely on an estimate of *g*, and the two other constructs defined by this two-factor structure (verbal comprehension and nonverbal reasoning/visualization). More specific explanations should follow, only if the global explanations fail to satisfy because of particular patterns of scores.

Concurrent Validity

Another source of support for claims of construct validity come from results of studies comparing the new Binet to existing measures of general intellectual ability. There are several studies that present revelant results; five of these are summarized in Table 7-5; others are available from convention papers and journal articles. Those studies are revelant for young children; those for preschool and elementary age children, are presented in Table 7-5.

Several of the concurrent studies present data comparing the new version of the Binet to the old. Thorndike, Hagan, and Sattler (1986) report that area and composite scores from the Stanford-Binet IV correlate moderately to strongly with global scores from the third edition, and means are similar, in general. Table 7-5 also presents summaries of these studies.

In summary, for older preschool and elementary age children the old and new Binet yield similar mean scores; when differences occur, and they are more apparent at the extreme ranges, the old Binet yields slightly more extreme scores. However, some of the differences appear to be because of regression to the mean effects, as well as to any standardization sample differences. Correlations between the two are moderate to strong. This relationship is less strong for populations showing restriction in range, such as gifted children. Also, on a more molecular level the Verbal Reasoning area score for the Fourth Edition seems to be more closely related to the total Form L-M IQ than any of the other three area scores, at least for the ages studied thus far. The relationship between the two tests is not well defined for very young preschool children, those ranging in age from 2 to 5. More research is needed to clarify the relationship for these children. Of course, the psychometric limitations of the tests for that age, such as a limited floor, will reduce the magnitude of the relationship between the two tests.

One of the most relevant concurrent validity studies compares the new Binet to the WPPSI. According to the Binet authors, the most meaningful mean comparisons might not be across the existing similar-named scales; for example, because the Verbal Scale of the WPPSI includes the Arithmetic Test and sometimes the Sentences Test, in addition to other verbal tests, an average of the Binet areas of Verbal Reasoning and Quantitative Reasoning *or* an average of these two plus Short-Term Memory might be more appropriate when comparing Binet performance to the WPPSI Verbal Scale. The Binet authors note that several of their predictions were supported by the data from this study. For example, the Composite score on the Fourth Edition was expected to correlate more highly with the WPPSI Verbal Scale

TABLE 7.5
CONCURRENT VALIDITY STUDIES

Study	Sample	Results
Thorndike, Hagan, & Sattler, 1986	139 Nonexceptional $\overline{X}$ age = 6-11, SD-30 months	Correlations between SB III and IV range from .56 to .76; SB III Mean, 108.1 vs. 105.8 for SB IV composite
Thorndike, Hagan, & Sattler, 1986	82 gifted children $\overline{X}$ age = 7-4, SD = 17 months	Correlating between SB III and IV range from .09 to .40; SB III Mean IQ, 135.3 vs. 121.8 for SB IV composite
Thorndike, Hagan, & Sattler, 1983	14 LD children $\overline{X}$ age = 8-4, SD = 34 months	Correlations between SB III and IV range from .54 to .86; SB III Mean is slightly lower (76.9) than all SB IV mean global scores (79.9 to 87.6)
Thorndike, Hagan, & Sattler, 1986	22 mentally retarded children $\overline{X}$ age = 11-11, SD = 68 months	Correlations between SB III and IV range from .84 to .91; SB II Mean IQ of 49.5 is slightly lower than SB IV means (50.9 to 57.9).
Livesay & Mealor, 1987	120 gifted referrals $\overline{X}$ age = 6.81, SD = 6 months	Correlations between SB III and IV range from .24 to .57; SB III Mean (130.45) is higher than SB IV means (IV composite, 122.46).
McCallum & Karnes, 1987	38 gifted children $\overline{X}$ age = 10-10, range 9-5 to 12-6	Correlations among WISC-R and SB IV range from − .02 to .49; means from the WISC-R range from 124.80 to 129.28; means from the SB IV range from 116.87 to 124.08.
Thorndike, Hagan, & Sattler, 1986	175 nonexceptional children $\overline{X}$ age = 70, SD = 29 months	Correlations among K-ABC and SB IV range from .68 to .89, means are similar (K-ABC, 107.4 to 112.3; SB IV, 110.2 to 112.7).
Thorndike, Hagan, & Sattler, 1986	Not apparent.	Correlations among K-ABC and SB IV range from .28 to .74; means from the K-ABC are from 91.1 to 97.5, and for the SB IV, 88.6 to 99.1.
Delaney & Hopkins, 1987	Preschool children $\overline{X}$ age = 5-4, SD = 2 months	Correlations among the WRAT-R and SB IV range from .33 to .58 over a 6-month interval; means from the WRAT-R range from 96 to 98.8; SB IV, 101.2 to 105.5.
Delaney & Hopkins, 1987	63 nonexceptional children $\overline{X}$ age = 7-11, SD = 5 months	Correlations among the WRAT-R and SB IV range from .41 to .61; means from the WRAT-R range from 94.4 to 99.3; SB IV, 99.6 to 104.9.

TABLE 7.5
(*continued*)

Study	Sample	Results
Thorndike, Hagan, & Sattler, 1986	75 nonexceptional children $\overline{X}$ age = 5-6, SD = 6 months	Correlations among global WPPSI and SB IV scores range from .46 to .80; WPPSI means (108.2 to 110.3) are slightly higher than SB IV (100.4 to 109.8).
Thorndike, Hagan, & Sattler, 1986	205 nonexceptional children $\overline{X}$ age = 9-5, SD = 27 months	Correlations among global WISC-R and SB IV scores range from .60 to .83; means are similar (WISC-R, 103.9 to 105.3; SB IV, 98.9 to 104.4).
Thorndike, Hagan, & Sattler, 1988	19 gifted children $\overline{X}$ age = 12-11, SD = 36 months	Correlations among global WISC-R and SB IV scores range from .21 to .71; means are similar (WISC-R, 114.5 to 117.7) SB IV, 109.6 to 117.2).
Thorndike, Hagan, & Sattler, 1986	20 LD children $\overline{X}$ age = 11-0, SD = 30 months	Correlations among global WISC-R and SB IV scores range from .55 to .87; means are similar (WISC-R, 85.2 to 92.3; SB IV, 84.8 to 88.8).
Thorndike, Hagan, & Sattler, 1986	61 mentally retarded children $\overline{X}$ age = 13-11, SD = 49 months	Correlations among WISC-R and SB IV range from .20 to .68; means were similar (WISC-R, 66.2 to 71.9; SB, 66.2 to 73.9).

IQ and Full Scale IQ than with the Performance Scale IQ. Also the Verbal Reasoning, Quantitative Reasoning, and Short-Term Memory Areas of the Fourth Edition were expected to correlate more highly with the Verbal Scale of the WPPSI than with the Performance Scale.

In general, when the relationship between WISC-R and Binet scores are depicted from studies in the *Technical Manual*, the following patterns seem to emerge: Scores from the Verbal Reasoning and Quantitative Reasoning areas correlate more highly with WISC-R Verbal IQs than do scores on the other areas of the new Binet; scores on the Abstract/Visual Reasoning Area correlate more highly with the WISC-R Performance Scale IQs than do scores from the other Binet areas; also scores from the Abstract/Visual Reasoning Area correlate more highly with the WISC-R Performance IQ than with the Verbal IQ.

Of interest, an independent study comparing the WISC-R to the new Binet for 38 gifted children ranging in age from 9-5 to 12-6 (mean age = 10-10) reported relatively low correlation coefficients (ranging from − .02 to .49). In general, the coefficients are higher for the WICS-R Full Scale IQ and the various Binet scores than for the Verbal and Performance IQs and the Binet global scores. The mean Binet scores range from 116.87 (Verbal Reasoning) to 124.08 (Quantitative Reasoning), with a composite of 125.03. Contrast these means with those from the WISC-R, which range from 124.80 to 129.28. However, according to the authors of the study, the mean differences could result partially from regression to the mean because the WISC-R was administered first to all children (McCallum & Karnes, 1987). These authors caution practitioners that the regression effect operates in daily practice, and should be considered when gifted children are reevaluated for placement after a period of service.

Two studies from the *Technical Manual* report data comparing the new Binet to the K-ABC. The first study, reported in Table 7-5, reveals high correlation coefficients depicting the interrelationships among the various global scores. According to the Binet authors the most meaningful mean difference comparisons should be between areas that purport to assess similar constructs or cognitive skills. For example, the following comparisons seem most reasonable: K-ABC Sequential Processing and Binet Short-Term Memory; K-ABC Simultaneous Processing and Binet Abstract/Visual Reasoning; K-ABC Mental Processing Composite and Binet Composite; and K-ABC Achievement and Binet Verbal Reasoning Quantitative Reasoning. All these various pairwise comparisons reveal very similar mean scores. The difference between the two Composites was only 0.4. Another study comparing the K-ABC and the new Binet reveals very similar mean scores across the two tests, but the correlation coefficients are lower in general than those from the first study. The reduced coefficients might be a function of restriction in range; standard deviations were all below the population standard deviations for both tests, typically by about 3 to 4 points.

Performance of Exceptional Groups

The performance of exceptional groups is sometimes used to provide evidence of construct validity. The reasoning is as follows. If exceptional groups perform as predicted on some new test, then the new test is said to be sensitive to the exceptionally in question. That is, if the exceptionality is defined in part by modified cognitive functioning, and the new test is sensitive to and reflects the modified cognitive functioning, then evidence is available in support of the new test for use with that exceptional group. The *Technical Manual* of the Binet reports three such studies, and all are somewhat supportive of the construct validity of the new Binet. For example, for 217 gifted students (mean age = 9-0, standard deviation = 2-10), the means were all well above average, ranging from about 1.2 to 1.5 standard deviations above the population mean of 100. On the other end of the continuum, mean scores were all well below the population mean of 100 for 223 students labeled as mentally retarded by their schools (mean age = 14-4, standard deviation =

6-1). Means ranged from 54.9 to 61.9. Finally, for a sample of 227 learning disabled children (mean age = 10-7, standard deviation = 2-10) mean scores ranged from 84.7 to 89.1.

Predictive Validity

Although the *Technical Manual* includes several studies describing construct validity, there are no predictive studies cited. As the Binet authors note, predictive validity studies are available for new instruments over time as practitioners use them. Predictive validity studies are just now beginning to appear for the Stanford-Binet IV. Several appear in the recently published *Examiner's Handbook: An Expanded Guide for Fourth Edition Users*, authored by Delaney and Hopkins (1987). Three of these report data from samples of nonexceptional children, and the first is particularly useful for those who specialize in preschool assessment—the sample is comprised of preschool children (see Table 7-4).

A second study, using a test–retest interval of about 6 months and a sample of slightly older nonexceptional children reveals means of similar magnitude and pattern, but stronger correlation coefficients. The larger coefficients reported for these older children are reasonable, given that older children obtain less error in their scores. In general, the strongest correlation coefficients were obtained from the analyses comparing the Binet Composite and Wide Range Achievement Test–Revised (WRAT-R) subtests, ranging from .55 to .61. Slightly lower values were obtained when the relationship between Verbal Reasoning Area scores and WRAT-R subtests was explored. Values of similar magnitude were obtained when the Short-Term Memory Area scores and WRAT-R subtests were analyzed. Somewhat lower values resulted from analysis of the relationship between the Abstract/Visual Reasoning area scores and the WRAT-R subtests; similar low coefficients were obtained from analysis of the relationship between the Quantitative Reasoning area and the WRAT-R subtests.

A third study exploring the relationship between the Binet and the WRAT-R included older children still (see Table 7-4). The test-retest interval was again about 6 months. In general, the results from these 46 children were consistent with expectations. That is, just as with the younger children, the means from the WRAT-R are, in general, slightly lower than those from the Binet, and the correlation coefficients are moderate.

A fourth predictive validity study to use the WRAT-R as the criterion, and reported in the *Handbook*, reveals a similar pattern of means but a pattern of correlation coefficients slightly lower than the one obtained from the 12 year old children (see Table 7-4). A possible explanation might be the nature of the sample—all the children had been designated by their schools as emotionally disturbed. There is some evidence that emotionally disturbed children are more erratic in performance, which contributes to test error and ultimately to reduced estimates of relationships. Another difference between this study and the three others reported is that the test-retest interval for this study was only 1 month. However, this reduced time interval between administration of the two tests did not reduce the magnitude of the coefficients.

Three additional predictive validity studies reported in the *Handbook* use the *Woodcock-Johnson Psycho-educational Battery/Part Two: Tests of Achievement* (WJ) (Woodcock & Johnson, 1977) as the criterion measure. Table 7-4 reveals summary data. More specifically, these children yielded coefficients ranging from .36 to .92, and most are in the .50s for the interrelationships between the area and composite Binet scores and the Reading, Mathematics, Written Language, and Knowledge subtests of the WJ. In general, the highest correlation coefficients were obtained for the relationships between the Verbal Reasoning and WJ subtests, ranging from .53 to .92. The coefficients defining the relationships between the composite Binet scores and the WJ subtests rank second in magnitude, ranging from .57 to .84. The coefficients defining the relationship between the Short-Term Memory area from the Binet and the WJ subtests rank third in magnitude; values range from .51 to .72. In general, the Quantitative Reasoning and WJ subtests relationships ranked next (ranging from .40 to .56), followed in magnitude by the coefficients describing the relationships among the Abstract/Visual Reasoning area and WJ subtests (ranging from .36 to .53). A consistent finding is that the Knowledge subtest of the WJ shares more of its test variance with the various Binet Area scores than any of the other WJ subtests. That is, the Knowledge subtest appears to have more in common with the Binet areas than the other WJ subtests. Means from the WJ and the Binet are very similar. The WJ means range from 97.5 to 104.8; means from the Binet range from 96.9 to 109.0.

Two other studies designed to explore the predictive relationship between the Binet and the WJ are reported in the *Handbook*; both report data from older nonexceptional children and are summarized in Table 7-4.

TECHNICAL ADEQUACY: ADDITIONAL CONSIDERATIONS AND SUMMARY ANALYSIS

In general, the technical adequacy of the Binet is impressive. However, the technical properties are less impressive for preschool children, relative to older children. For example, reliabilities are less impressive for young children. Because reliability values effect various other statistics, the interpretation for young examinees is subsequently impacted. Bands of error are larger, because the standard errors of measurement are increased. Differences between various global and subtest scores have to be larger to be significant. Also, validity indices are depressed. Even so, many of the Binet characteristics do meet minimum standards for preschoolers. For example, the median subtest reliabilities (internal consistency estimates) do meet the criterion recommended by Bracken (1987) as minimal (.80). In addition, the Total Test internal consistency coefficients are adequate at all preschool ages and meet Bracken's criterion of .90.

Although some of the test–retest stability estimates are low and unimpressive for subtests, the Total Test estimate is slightly better than Bracken's recommended minimum of .90. On the other hand, some of the technical properties are problematic. For example, the subtest floors are inadequate for very young examinees. The average subtest floor for the Binet is so high that it fails to differentiate among approximately the lowest 37% of the children in the normal population (Bracken, 1987). In fact, the Binet fails to produce subtest scores that are at least two standard deviations below the mean through age 3-6, and again fails to meet this criterion at age 5-0 when new subtests with weak floors are introduced.

Limited ability to discriminate is the result. For a hypothetical two-year-old examinee, a raw score of one on the subtest Bead Memory produces a standard score, of 53, which is slightly above average ($\overline{X} = 50$, SD = 8); raw scores of one on each of the Verbal Reasoning subtests leads to a Verbal Reasoning area score of 86, which is about one standard deviation below the mean ($\overline{X} = 100$, SD = 16); raw scores of one on each of the Abstract/Visual Reasoning subtests yields an area score of 91, about two-thirds of a standard deviation below average for the population; a raw score of one on the Quantitative subtest yields a Quantitative Reasoning area score of 104, slightly above the population average; raw scores of one on each of the Short-Term Memory subtests yield an Area score of 101, just about the population average. This examinee would have earned a composite score of 95, an average score, even though only one raw score point was earned per subtest.

Two related technical considerations include the item analysis quality and the item gradient levels as described in the Binet *Manual*. Much attention was paid to the item analysis procedures, but there is a lack of specific information describing item parameters. Users must depend on the wisdom of the authors in making the best selections; however, this state of affairs is fairly typical. The item gradient appears appropriate. That is, each item is worth no more than one-third standard score standard deviation. Items that are too steeply graded reduce precision, and lead to gross discriminations.

A final technical consideration to be addressed is subtest specificity. Subtest specificity is the proportion of the variance accounted for by a subtest that is unique, that is, not attributed to error or to some other construct. For example, the Vocabulary subtest of the Binet measures the Verbal Comprehension construct in common with the other subtests included in that "factor," but it measures something that is unique to it, discounting error. If this unique variance is equal to at least 25% of the total subtest variance, and is larger than error variance, the subtest is said to possess adequate subtest specificity for interpretation (of this unique ability or abilities). According to Sattler (1988), the following subtests have inadequate subtest specificity for preschoolers at the ages indicated: Vocabulary, ages 3 through 9; Comprehension, ages 3 through 6; and Quantitative at 6 years of age (see Table 7-2).

TEST INTERPRETATION

The ultimate worth of a test is determined by the wealth and quality of information it provides. Such information is obtained from knowledgeable test interpretation. Competent interpretation requires a particular plan of action, a scheme, or framework for making sense of variability from the myriad of subtest scores a test typically produces. There are several approaches for attacking subtest scatter, or subtest patterns. Three of these seem particularly reasonable and defensible and will be presented in this section; although an examiner can use any one of these, the third, as presented, appears the most reasonable for the greatest number of children. If that procedure fails to provide a satisfactory interpretive solution, one of the others can be chosen.

The three interpretative strategies will be labeled the *Pooled or g-Factor* procedure, described by Delaney and Hopkins in the *Examiner's Manual*, the *Rational-Intuitive* procedure, and the *Independent Factors* procedure. All three approaches make use of the standard scores, such as the composite score, the area scores, and subtest scores; subtest scores are referred to in the Binet manual as Standard Age Scores (SAS). Although percentile ranks and age equivalants are available, these are not amenable to scatter analysis.

The three specific interpretative procedures are addressed in detail. First, however, some general interpretive strategies are presented. After presentation of the three interpretative procedures, there is a discussion of interpretive limitations. The interpretation of choice for each child must be designed to avoid limitations or pitfalls such as overemphasis of small subtest differences when multiple comparisons are made, inattention to subtest specificity, and inattention to poor floor and ceiling effects. The final section of the chapter presents some interpretive recommendations for preschoolers.

General Interpretive Strategies

Primary goals of this section are to describe general interpretive strategies available, and to present three specific interpretive strategies, including recommendations/limitations associated with Binet use for preschool children. This focus requires consideration of the technical adequacy of the new Binet. Because the test manual presents basic administration instructions, there is little attention devoted to such matters here. Suffice it to say that the "adaptive testing" format, which uses the establishment of a starting point from the examinee's chronological age and Vocabulary score, and the use of a basal and ceiling to reduce testing time are laudatory, even though they occasionally produce administrative difficulties. It is noteworthy that the new *Handbook* devotes several pages to attempt to clarify some of the administration problems not addressed in the original manual, such as the need to present lower level task "orientation" directions when examiners must move below the original starting point to establish a basal.

The most effective test interpretation relies on a formal and an informal data base. Informal assessment requires the observation and recording of characteristic problem-solving strategies employed by the examinee, the level/number of anxiety indicators, the level of enthusiasm displayed for the different tasks, the level of support required, quality of grooming, and so on. This type of qualitative assessment can never be replaced by use of quantitative methods that rely only on the use of scores to characterized performance. The examiner must be able to provide elaboration and clarification of scores based on these kinds of observations. Consequently, a quality interpretation relies on both qualitative and quantitative data. Because qualitative assessment is described elsewhere in this text, the following discussion focuses primarily on building quantitative interpretive skills. It is noteworthy that the authors of the new Binet retain a brief checklist of test behavior to aid qualitative assessment; the examiner can use this to characterize the performance of the examinee.

Meaningful quantitative interpretation requires analysis of standard scores. The Binet IV retains the global scale properties of the old Form L-M. That is, the total or composite score for the Binet IV uses a standard score population mean of 100, and a standard deviation of 16, rather than 100 and 15, like most of the more recently developed test (e.g., K-ABC, Wechsler Scale revisions). The SAS assigned by the new Binet are somewhat atypical. That is, the subtest population is set to 50, and the standard deviation to 8, rather than the more conventional 10 and 3 or 50 and 10. Some mental adjustment is necessary for those

examiners who are familiar with the more conventional score schemes.

The first step in the quantitative interpretation process is the transformation of raw scores to standard scores. Once raw scores have been transformed to standard scores, there are some general guidelines to follow, no matter which type of subtest pattern analysis procedure an examiner chooses. Although, these strategies are appropriate for examinees of all ages, special attention is devoted to making the interpretive strategies useful for preschool children. These strategies include:

1. *The composite score must be interpreted in some context.* Typically the Composite score is related to the normative sample by describing how the score ranks relative to the population (typically by providing a percentile rank). Also, occasionally the score is interpreted relative to previous scores, other tests scores, and so on.

2. *The composite score is discussed briefly within a band of error.* This is described as a function of the SEM of the instrument for that age child. The composite score is placed within a band of scores, and the probability of the examinee's "true score" falling within that band of scores is presented. (The true score can be conceptualized as the average score an examinee would obtain upon repeated testing using the same instrument, minus the effects of practice, fatigue, and other sources of test error.) The *Handbook* presents the confidence bands by ages and confidence levels, including 99%, 95%, 90%, and 85%. An additional confidence band table is provided for a "General Purpose Abbreviated Battery" for the examiner's convenience.

3. *The global scores are compared.* The area scores or Factor scores are compared to each other. The area scores are available from straightforward raw to standard score transformations using calculations and tables, as described in the *Administration and Scoring Manual* of the Fourth Edition; the factor scores are available by following a set of instructions described by Sattler (1988), and reproduced here by permission in Table 7-3. (Table 7-3 contains steps for calculating factor scores for children ranging in age from 2 to 7; factor scores for older children can be calculated by relying on the directions provided in Sattler's textbook.)

Whether an examiner uses area scores or factor scores as a point of departure for analyzing subtest patterns is somewhat arbitrary, and depends upon the examiner's predisposition to prefer either the Rational–Intuitive or the Independent Factors subtest analysis procedures described shortly. In any case, if the global scores are not significantly different from each other, then the composite score is very likely a good estimate of the child's overall performance. That is, there is likely little variability in performance and the composite score can be considered a good reflection of overall ability. Of course a highly variable set of scores would be taken to mean highly variable underlying abilities and a composite score that is less of an overall indicator of performance. A highly variable performance would not nor could not be summarized very well by any one composite score. The level of significance required to establish clinically meaningful differences among scores is not clearly established in the literature, but differences that occur less than 1%, 5%, or 15% of the time by chance are typically interpreted as "meaningful," even though differences of this magnitude can occur fairly often in the population. Differences that occur relatively often in the normal population can still reflect real differences in abilities for a given child, and consequently might have implications for intervention. For example, a 10 point, or larger, difference between the Binet Verbal Reasoning and Composite Score occurs for about 20% of the population, yet a difference of that magnitude would not be expected *by chance* more than 5 times 100. Hence, the difference might require interpretation from a clinical standpoint even though it is a relatively common occurrence. The table describing differences required for significance among the various global scores and the "base rates" for actual differences in the population are presented in the *Handbook*. A portion of this table depicting differences between area and composite scores required for statistical significance is reproduced in Table 7-6; differences required for significances between the composite score and factor scores would be similar. Other tables depicting values required for significancé for various comparisons, by age, has been developed by Rosenthal and Kumphaus (1988) and reproduced here as Tables 7-7 and 7-8; and by Sattler (1988), and reproduced here as Table 7-9; these tables present values for preschool children, taking into consideration the varying SEMs.

One caveat is necessary at this time. Even if the composite and area/factor scores are similar, there still can be considerable variance in performance. For example, subtest scores can differ from each other significantly, but still occur in such a pattern as to render area or factor scores similar. That is, assuming more than one subtest is administered to obtain an area or factor score, subtest highs and lows can cancel, leaving a sort

TABLE 7.6
DIFFERENCES BETWEEN THE AREA AND THE COMPOSITE REQUIRED FOR STATISTICAL SIGNIFICANCE AT THE 15% AND 5% LEVELS OF CONFIDENCE FOR PRESCHOOL CHILDREN

Between Areas	Confidence Level	Ages 2	3	4	5	6
Verbal Reasoning	15%	8	7	7	8	8
and Composite	5%	11	10	10	10	11
Abstract/Visual	15%	10	10	8	8	8
Reasoning and Composite	5%	14	13	11	10	11
Quantitative	15%	11	10	9	9	11
Reasoning and Composite	5%	15	14	13	12	15
Short-term Memory	15%	9	8	8	8	9
and Composite	5%	12	11	11	10	12

Figures reproduced from *The Technical Manual*, Thorndike, Hagen, Sattler (1988).

TABLE 7.7

DIFFERENCES BETWEEN SUBTEST SCORES REQUIRED FOR STATISTICAL SIGNIFICANCE AT THE 1% AND 5% LEVELS OF CONFIDENCE FOR 2- TO 5 YEAR OLDS

	Voc	Comp	Abs	PA	Copy	Quant	B-Mem	MemS
Voc		12	11	12	12	12	11	11
Comp	9		11	11	11	11	11	11
Abs	9	8		11	11	11	10	10
PA	9	9	9		12	12	11	11
Copy	9	9	8	9		11	11	11
Quant	9	8	8	9	9		11	11
B-Mem	9	8	8	9	8	8		10
MemS	9	8	8	9	8	8	8	

Note: Values above the diagonal line are at the .01 level; values below the diagonal line are at the .05 level. Voc = Vocabulary, Comp = Comprehension, Abs = Absurdities, PA = Pattern Analysis, Copy = Copying, Quant = Quantitative, B-Mem = Bead Memory, MemS = Memory for Sentences.

DIFFERENCES BETWEEN SUBTEST SCORES REQUIRED FOR STATISTICAL SIGNIFICANCE AT THE 1% AND 5% LEVELS OF CONFIDENCE FOR 6- TO 10 YEAR OLDS

	Voc	Comp	Abs	PA	Copy	Mat	Quant	NS	B-Mem	MemS	MemD	MemO
Voc		12	13	11	12	11	12	11	12	12	12	14
Comp	9		13	11	12	11	12	11	12	12	12	14
Abs	10	10		11	12	12	13	12	12	12	13	14
PA	8	8	9		10	9	11	9	10	10	11	12
Copy	9	9	9	7		10	12	10	11	11	11	13
Mat	8	8	9	7	8		11	9	10	10	11	13
Quant	9	9	10	8	9	8		11	12	12	12	14
NS	8	8	9	7	8	7	8		10	10	11	13
B-Mem	9	9	9	8	8	8	9	8		11	12	13
MemS	9	9	9	7	8	8	9	8	8		11	13
MemD	9	9	10	8	9	8	9	8	9	9		14
MemO	11	11	11	9	10	10	11	10	10	10	10	

Note: Values above the diagonal line are at the .01 level; values below the diagonal line are at the .05 level. Voc = Vocabulary, Comp = Comprehension, Abs = Absurdities, PA = Pattern Analysis, Copy = Copying, Mat = Matrices, Quant = Quantitative, NS = Number Series, B-Mem = Bead Memory, MemS = Memory for Sentences, MemD = Memory for Digits, MemO = Memory for Objects.

of average area or factor score, relative to other such scores. So Step 3 is not complete until the possibility of subtest variability is checked even though the area or factor scores look flat. (Of course, preschool children sit for only one Quantitative subtest, and it produces the Quantitative Area score; consequently, there is no within area scatter for that area.)

A rule of thumb for determining subtest variability is simply to observe whether there is a least one significant difference between/among subtests; an eight-point difference is recommended as the criterion for significance for this purpose, which is slightly more rigorous than the 7-point difference recommended by Delaney and Hopkins (1987). The additional rigor is suggested to compensate from the greater error in scores of very young children. (Spruill, 1988, has produced a table of differences required for significance across ages; for the younger children the differ-

TABLE 7.8
DIFFERENCES BETWEEN AREA SCORES REQUIRED FOR STATISTICAL SIGNIFICANCE AT THE 1% AND 5% LEVELS OF CONFIDENCE FOR 2- TO 5 YEARS OLDS

	VR 2	VR 3	A/V 2	Q 1	STM 2
VR 2		16	18	20	17
VR 3	13		17	19	16
A/V 2	14	13		21	18
Q 1	15	15	16		20
STM 2	13	13	14	15	

Note: Values above the diagonal line are at the .01 level; values below the diagonal line are at the .05 level. VR = Verbal Reasoning, A/V = Abstract Visual Reasoning, Q = Quantitative Reasoning, STM = Short-Term Memory.

DIFFERENCES BETWEEN AREA SCORES REQUIRED FOR STATISTICAL SIGNIFICANCE AT THE 1% AND 5% LEVELS OF CONFIDENCE FOR 6- TO 10 YEAR OLDS

	VR 2	VR 3	A/V 2	A/V 3	Q 1	Q 2	STM 2	STM 3	STM 4
VR 2		18	18	17	23	19	20	19	18
VR 3	14		16	15	22	17	18	17	16
A/V 2	14	12		14	21	16	18	17	16
A/V 3	13	11	11		21	15	17	16	15
Q 1	18	17	16	16		22	23	23	22
Q 2	14	13	12	12	17		19	17	16
STM 2	15	14	14	13	18	14		19	18
STM 3	15	13	13	12	17	13	15		17
STM 4	14	12	12	11	16	12	14	13	

Note: Values above the diagonal line are at the .01 level; values below the diagonal line are at the .05 level. VR = Verbal Reasoning, A/V = Abstract Visual Reasoning, Q = Quantitative Reasoning, STM = Short-Term Memory.

ences average 8.5 at the .05 level of confidence.) If there is not at least one subtest difference that reaches statistical significance, then interpretation stops. If there is, one of the three specific interpretative strategies must be applied. A flat profile, one with no subtests that deviate significantly from their cohort mean, indicates that the composite score is a good estimate of the child's ability.

Each of the three of the scatter analysis procedures are similar in that they all represent a systematic and logical subtest scatter attack strategy. Each one describes an averaging strategy, although for preschoolers the averaging process is limited. The averaging process prevents haphazard pair-wise comparisons. With the exception of the Verbal Reasoning area, which contains three subtests designed for preschool children, the av-

eraging strategy becomes problematic for *preschool* examinees. Both the Abstract/Visual Reasoning and the Short-Term Memory area include (only) two subtests for preschoolers. For scatter analysis of these two areas, rather than averaging, determine whether the two subtests are significantly different from each other. If the two are significantly different, and again an 8-point difference seems reasonable to define significance, the area is not uniformly or homogeneously developed. (See Table 7-7 for specific differences required for significance at the .01 and .05 levels for preschool children.) Consequently, the area score is not definitive, and requires elaboration. Remember the Quantitative Reasoning area includes only one subtest for preschool examinees; consequently, this area score should be interpreted cautiously for this age group.

TABLE 7.9
DIFFERENCES REQUIRED FOR SIGNIFICANCE WHEN EACH STANFORD-BINET, FOURTH EDITION SUBTEST SCALED SCORE IS COMPARED TO THE RESPECTIVE MEAN FACTOR SCALED SCORE FOR ANY INDIVIDUAL CHILD

Verbal Comprehension

Subtest	Ages 2 through 7	
	.05	.01
Vocabulary	6.18	7.51
Comprehension	5.74	6.99
Absurdities	6.18	7.51
Memory for Sentences	5.74	6.99
Verbal Relations	—	—

Nonverbal Reasoning/Visualization

Subtest	Ages 2 through 11	
	.05	.01
Pattern Analysis	5.30	6.44
Copying	6.15	7.41
Quantitative	6.02	7.33
Bead Memory	6.15	7.41
Matrices	—	—

All three of the scatter analysis procedures are ipsative; they allow conclusions to be drawn about relative strengths and weaknesses within the individual's performance. SAS scores are compared to an individual's personal subtest average. This ipsative approach lends itself more easily to the development of interventions. The extent to which Binet scores impact intervention, referred to as treatment validity, is the topic of discussion later in this chapter.

4. *The final general step is actually a transition step.* This step leads directly into the scatter analysis and cannot be separated from that procedure; this step is necessary if there are differences among the area/factor scores, or among the subtests. Otherwise, statistically based interpretation stops. If there is no appreciable test variability, that is, there are no significant differences among the global scores, and if subtest variability is not apparent, the interpretation ends with a statement describing the composite score as a good estimate of overall ability. If there is evidence of variability among the global scores, those significant global score differences should be discussed, including some presentation of the general abilities assumed to be assessed by the areas/fac-

tors. See Table 7-1 for a presentation of the general abilities purported to be assessed by the area/factors, as described in the various Binet manuals by Sattler and others. Of course, if there is considerable variability within a given area or factor, characterized by several within area/factor significant differences, then any discussion of the abilities assessed by a given area/factor must be tempered accordingly. In such cases, specific subtest interpretation will be required; certain limitations should be kept in mind, such as whether adequate subtest specificity exists for relevant subtests, and the hazard of overinterpreting when there are several significant differences.

Three Specific Interpretive Strategies

The following three scatter analysis procedures are offered as aids to developing interpretive strategies. Any one might be appropriate, depending on the examiner's orientation and the pattern of scores obtained.

The Pooled or g-factor Procedure

The Pooled procedure is described by Delaney and Hopkins in the new *Handbook* for the Fourth Edition. Delaney and Hopkins adapted the technique from a procedure first described by Davis in 1955. The procedure as described in the *Handbook* is described as "pooled" because all the subtests from the entire test are pooled to obtain an average, rather than averaging subtest within areas or factors. After focusing on the global scores, the relationship of the composite score to global scores, and other indicators of test variability, the examiner must make a decision. If the area scores do not differ significantly among themselves, none of them is likely to differ from the composite, yet, there might be subtest scatter. In this situation, the pooled procedure can be used to determine the presence of meaningful subtest scatter.

Use of the pooled procedure to determine the existence of meaningful scatter requires an averaging of all the subtests administered; the number and choice of subtests administered depends on the child's age, ability, and whether a "brief form" is used as opposed to the full battery. After the full complement of subtests is averaged, each subtest score is compared to this average subtest score. Based on the degree of difference from the mean subtest scores, each subtest is designated as being average, a strength or a weakness. The criterion difference recommended by Delaney and Hopkins is a +7 point deviation from the average subtest score. An eight-point difference should be used as the criterion for significance for preschoolers, because the psychometric properties of the subtests are less impressive for that age examinee (Spruill, 1988). Particular abilities presumably assessed by the subtests are noted. When conflicts arise, as when some subtest assessing a given ability is deemed a strength and another subtest assessing the same ability is judged a weakness, the conflict is resolved by qualitative analysis, by evaluating the particular task demands of the subtests, and by evaluating scores and information from other sources (e.g., other tests, teacher and parent reports).

To provide aid in developing hypotheses regarding abilities assessed by the subtests, Delaney and Hopkins provide an "Inferred Abilities and Influences Chart" in the *Examiner's Handbook*. This chart lists the subtests across the top and various abilities and influences suspected of impacting performance on subtests along the left margin. The juxtaposition of a particular subtest and some ability forms a cell, which can be designated a strength or a weakness, or neither, as is appropriate. Use of the chart is helpful in making tentative hypothesis about the test performance of any examinee. Examiners should note that the particular abilities and influences listed are somewhat arbitrarily determined, that is, many of the entries are determined by logic rather than by empirical findings. Consequently, not all practitioners will agree with the rationale used to construct the existing chart. In fact, there is considerable evidence available to suggest that practitioners do not agree totally with test authors analysis of such hypothesis-generating aids (Bracken & Fagan, 1988). Practitioners can choose to construct a separate chart for themselves, using the one provided by Delaney and Hopkins as a beginning point. Table 7-1, which describes some of the abilities/influences thought to impact each of the subtests appropriate for preschoolers, should help that process. After determining the abilities that are specific strengths/weaknesses for the examinee, from whatever source, the next step is to reconcile the specific strengths and weaknesses with the more general strengths and weaknesses identified earlier from analysis of the global scores (i.e., area or factor scores).

Use of the pooled procedure rests on the assumption that the total test is designed to assess *g* and that subtests are first and foremost a measure of that underlying ability. Consequently, the extent to which any subtest measures other constructs should depend on the distance of that subtest from an estimate of whatever the total test assesses, in this case defined by the subtest average, and whether the subtest possesses adequate Subtest Specificity. Also *intra*subtest scatter might be informative in some situations (e.g., wide variability of item performance within a subtest). Because of the relatively strong reliance on *g* as the interpretive basis, this procedure is referred to as the *g-factor* procedure. As a final consideration in the interpretive process, the examiner must consider how identified strengths can be used to guide interventions for those identified weaknesses.

The interpretive steps for the pooled procedure are:

1. Average all subtest scaled scores.
2. Identify strengths by identifying subtest scaled scores that are eight or more points higher than the subtest average scaled score.
3. Identify weaknesses by identifying subtest scaled scores that are eight or more points below the subtest average scaled score.
4. Identify abilities and influences from tables and/or task analysis, which correspond to the "strong" and "weak" subtests, remembering subtest similarities ("clusters of ability") and specificity data.
5. Resolve conflicting scores, that is, task analyze and cross-reference subtest demands and review strong and weak abilities.
6. Reconcile strong and weak subtest abilities with general strong and weak abilities identified from either global scores from the Binet or from other tests.
7. Consider intrasubtest scatter by examining specific item responses and patterns of subtest responses.
8. Conceive of intervention strategies and steps to evaluate the recommended strategies. Intervention would take advantage of identified strengths to guide educational instruction.

The Rational-Intuitive Procedure

This scatter analysis procedure is referred to as the Rational-Intuitive procedure because it takes into account the theoretical model upon which the new Binet is based, which is rationally and intuitively derived. This procedure allows for analysis using the areas defined by the test model, that is, Verbal Reasoning, Quantitative Reasoning, Abstract-Visual Reasoning, and Short-Term Memory. After the general steps are completed, and assuming variability has been identified (i.e., Area scores are significantly different among themselves), the meaningfulness of area score differences are discussed. If an examiner accepts the test model of the new Binet as described by Thorndike, Hagen, and Sattler, General Step 4 requires use of area scores to describe functioning rather than factor scores. The examiner would describe abilities presumed to underlie the area scores in interpreting test performance, and specifically, significant area differences. Further subtest scatter would be defined from within each area by using area means as a point of departure. For preschool children, scatter would be defined for two of the areas by simply comparing the two subtest scores for the two relevant subtests included for examinees of that age. These two areas are Abstract/Visual Reasoning and Short-Term Memory. Because the Quantitative Reasoning area includes only one subtest for preschoolers, the issue of scatter within that area is moot. Subtests strengths and weaknesses and their corresponding "abilities" would be determined by establishing whether an eight-point (for preschoolers) difference occurred for the relevant scatter analyses. Specific subtest strengths and weaknesses and the unique and idiosyncratic abilities assessed by them become grist for scatter interpretation if significant differences are found. If differences occur, and the particular subtests have adequate subtest specificity at the particular age in question, then unique abilities as defined on the examiner's "Inferred Abilities and Influences Chart" could be meaningfully interpreted. Finally, checks and balances are required to validate the hypotheses raised by the interpretive procedure. Strengths must be verified by other subtest scores, or other sources, as must weaknesses. Finally, strengths are "wedded" to interventions in a meaningful way, and the efficacy of the resultant recommendations determined. (To determine strengths and weaknesses use Tables 7-7 and 7-8.)

The interpreted steps for the Rational-Intuitive procedure are:

1. Use the Binet model to interpret abilities that underlie area scores. Area scores become the focus, initially.
2. Average the within area subtest scores. For preschool children this required only one average, an average of the three subtests comprising Verbal Reasoning; all other areas are assessed by two or less subtests. In the case of a two-subtest area, simply check to determine if the two subtests are significantly different one from the other.
3. Interpret significant scatter, comparing unique abilities and influences to area constructs, remembering subtest specificity data.
4. Validate strengths and weaknesses, and resolve apparent conflicts by task analysis and cross-referencing scores.
5. Evaluate intrasubtest scatter, characteristics, and patterns of responses.
6. Begin to think of intervention strategies and steps to evaluate these strategies.

The Independent Factors Procedure

This procedure is referred to as the independent factors procedure because it relies on the factor analytic structure of the Binet, obtained by using a principle factors approach, varimax rotation. That is, the analysis sought to maximize the independence of the constructs that underlie the Binet, rather than maximize the commonality of the largest underlying construct, or *g*. This approach has been described by Kaufman for the WISC-R and the K-ABC, and by Sattler for use with the new Binet. Scatter analysis based on this procedure is much like the analysis described for the rational-intuitive approach, except rather than relying on area scores and the Binet model for interpretive direction, this procedure relies on the factor structure obtained empirically via the factor analysis. For preschool children, there are two basic factors that underlie Binet performance—a Verbal/Comprehension Factor and a Nonverbal/Visual Factor. For older children, there are three factors, the two just mentioned and a separate Memory factor. This Memory factor emerges for 7 year old children, and consists of the Memory for Sentences, Memory for Digits, and Memory for Objects subtests. See Table 7-3 for description of the factors, as defined by their subtests, and Table 7-1 for a list of possible abilities/influence that impact the factors. The logic for this scatter analysis procedure is similar to that defined in the rational-intuitive approach, except that the term factor should be substituted for area, and the procedure for calculating factor scores is slightly different than the procedure for calculating area scores. Factor scores are determined by a procedure described by Sattler (1988) and presented in Table 7-3. A set of criteria values of such a magnitude as to be significantly different for factor scores also are provided by Sattler, and reported in the next paragraph. Subtest scatter is facilitated by examining the values reproduced in Table 7-9, which provide the magnitudes required for a particular subtest to be significantly different from the *mean* of the particular factor. That is, the mean for each factor is determined, and each subtest score is compared to that mean to determine significant subtest strengths and weaknesses. Scatter is evaluated by hypothesis generation, as dictated by the subtest profile.

Table 7-3 described the procedures for calculating scores. Sattler (1988) provides some tentative hypotheses for greater Verbal Comprehension than Nonverbal Reasoning/Visualization factor scores, as well as for the reverse pattern. For example, for preschoolers a Verbal Comprehension/Nonverbal Reasoning/Visualization might suggest relatively stronger verbal fluency skills as compared to performance-type skills, or perhaps that the child's crystallized abilities are better than novel problem solving abilities. Factor score differences large enough to be statistically significant are 13/18, 10/14, 10/13, 9/12, 12/15, and 12/16 for the .05/.01 level of confidence levels for ages 2 through 7, respectively, for the Verbal Comprehension versus Nonverbal Reasoning/Visualization Factors. Factor score differences required for significance are 15/19 for the Verbal Comprehension versus Memory Factor Comparison for 7-year-old children, and 14/19 for the Nonverbal Reasoning/Visualization versus Memory Comparison for 7-year-old children (Sattler, 1988).

The steps for the interpretive approach for the independent-factors procedure are:

1. Use the factor structure defined by a principle factors solution, varimax rotation, to identify factors. These factors, calculated as described in Table 7-3, become the basis for interpreting Binet performance, rather than area scores.
2. Calculate the factor scores, and interpret any

differences, taking into account subtest scatter.
3. Examine significant subtest scatter using Table 7-9.
4. Interpret strengths and weaknesses, assuming adequate subtest specificity, relative to constructs identified via the factor structure.
5. Validate apparent strengths and weaknesses by task analyzing and cross-referencing strengths and weaknesses.
6. Determine relevance of intrasubtest scatter characteristics.
7. Consider appropriate intervention strategies and evaluation of those strategies.

SUMMARY

All three of the procedures just described are valuable approaches for Binet interpretation. All are systematic and offer hypothesis generating strategies. Consider all three procedures for every examinee. Any one of these procedures might be most appropriate, depending upon the particular child; use the most appropriate procedure under the circumstances. Evaluate each procedure for each examinee, and choose the one that fits your examinee best. For example, for examinees who exhibit little global score scatter, as evidenced by a lack of significant differences among the area/factor scores, the pooled procedure seems most reasonable; when there are differences, use the independent factors procedure first. If the factor scores fail to offer a satisfactory interpretation, then try the rational-intuitive procedure. Perhaps for a particular examinee, that model will provide the best fit.

Finally, there are many interpretive schemes available. The three described here seem reasonable; others can be chosen to supplement these. Subtests can be grouped according to any number of constructs or skills. Consider the following dichotomies: verbal versus nonverbal; timed versus untimed; simultaneous versus successive; left-brain versus right-brain; memory versus no memory; abstract versus concrete; motoric versus nonmotoric, and so on. As is apparent, subtests can be rearranged according to any dichotomy of interest. Of course, examiners of preschool children have less latitude because there are fewer subtests available for that age group. Remember, no matter what scheme is employed, the ultimate purpose is to aid and improve the examinee's life. For many practitioners, that translates into making test information relevant for educational program planning or for developing classroom management strategies.

Psychologists and educators have not been very successful in developing effective treatment strategies from tests of cognitive abilities, despite all the optimism generated by discussions of uncovering appropriate *Aptitude by Treatment Interactions* (Reynolds, 1981). To date, if academic program planning is the goal of evaluation, the most relevant and useful test is one designed to discover educational strengths and weaknesses, that is, a criterion-referenced test of specific academic content. The more closely the test is tied to the curriculum, the more relevant and useful the test information is, despite the psychometric problems associated with this type of assessment. Nontheless, tests of general cognitive ability can provide a wealth of useful information. Even hypothetical constructs or aptitudes might prove useful in educational program planning, assuming you carefully identify them, consider how they might impact on instruction, develop hypotheses designed to aid instruction, and then test those hypotheses with the help of classroom teachers. Perhaps the search for the aptitude treatment interaction has failed so far because of gross measurement techniques, or inappropriate research designs, rather than the inability of aptitudes to impact performance. As professionals continue to try to bridge the gap between direct assessment and cognitive assessment, and continue to improve the treatment validity of existing instruments, remember an old line—do not throw out the baby with the bathwater. But if, as practitioners, we continue to make recommendations for educational or behavioral programming—from the Binet or some similar instrument, let us be rigorous in the assessment of the abilities and constructs, let us be diligent and creative in working with teachers in devising directly applicable educationally relevant recommendations, and let us be willing to evaluate the success of the intervention strategy employed. Practitioners must be accountable; the time is long past when poorly conceptualized and irrelevant recommendations will impress teachers, parents, and other consumers.

Recommendations from testing must be academically relevant and amenable to evaluation.

RECOMMENDATIONS FOR PRACTICE

The following list of recommendations cover a range of topics but certainly is not exhaustive; rather it is offered as a beginning. Examiners are encouraged to add to this short list in an effort to build test interpretation knowledge. After all, interpretation leads to information, and information sharing is the *raison d'etre* for tests such as the Binet.

1. Some subtests can be grouped to make a battery amenable for administration to special populations. For example, the Nonverbal Reasoning/Visualization subtests can provide a rough index of ability for hearing-impaired examinees. Several of the verbal subtests can be grouped for a similar battery for the visually impaired examinees.

2. Remember the instruments' technical limitations and their effect on interpretation (e.g., limited floor for children ranging in age from 2-0 to 3-6, and for children 5-0 years).

3. Interpret the unique variance of subtests *if* the subtests have adequate subtest specificity, and if their scores differ significantly in magnitude from the average of the global constructs or from each other; patterns of scores should be combined into clusters of abilities as is possible.

4. Remember that the test does not contain the same subtests across the age range; consequently the same abilities might not be assessed to the same degree on reevaluations.

5. Check the *Technical Manual* for suggestions regarding short forms when available testing time is limited. The authors report various short forms for specific purposes (e.g., assessment of gifted children, using the subtests with the "best" ceiling).

6. Be careful of administrative error; the Binet IV administration directions are somewhat unwieldy. Check the new *Handbook* for additional clarification of administration details.

7. Consider and report bands of error for global scores.

8. Keep in mind that Binet score parameters are

somewhat atypical, especially the scores for the subtests (e.g., population means of 50 and standard deviations of 8).

9. Use the independent factors procedure first because it has better empirical support, and follow this procedure with others as needed.

10. Develop relevant recommendations from a rigorous interpretation strategy, and evaluate the succes of recommendations.

REFERENCES

Bracken, B. A. (1987). Limitations of preschool instruments and standards for minimal levels of technical adequacy. *Journal of Psychoeducational Assessment*, 5, 313–326.

Bracken, B. A. & Fagan, T. K, (1988). Abilities answered by the K-ABC Mental Processing subtests: the perceptions of practitioners with varying degrees of experience. *Psychology in the Schools*, 25, 22–34.

Delaney, E. A., & Hopkins, T. F. (1987). *Examiners handbook: An expanded guide for fourth edition users.* Chicago, IL: The Riverside Publishing Company.

Elliott, C. D. (1983). *British Ability Scales.* San Antonio, TX: The Psychological Corporation.

Kaufman, A. S., & Kaufman, N. L. (1983). *Kaufman Assessment Battery for Children.* Circle Pines, MN: American Guidance Services.

Livesay, K. K., & Mealor, D. J. (1987). *A comparison of the Stanford-Binet Intelligence Scale (3rd) to the Stanford-Binet (4th).* unpublished manuscript.

McCallum, R. S., & Karnes, F. A. (1987). Comparison of the Stanford-Binet Intelligence Scale (4th ed.), the British Ability Scales and the WISC-R. *School Psychology International*, 8, 133–139.

McCarthy, D. A. (1972). *McCarthy Scales of Children's Abilities.* San Antonio, TX: The Psychological Corporation.

Naglieri, J. A. (1987). Interpreting area score variation on the Stanford-Binet: Fourth Edition. *Journal of Psychoeducational Assessment.*

Reynolds, C. R. (1981). Neuropsychological assessment and the habilitation of learning: Considerations in the search for the aptitude X treatment interaction. *School Psychology Review, 10,* 343–349.

Rosenthal, B. L., & Kumphaus, R. W. (1988). Interpreting tables for test scatter on the Stanford-Binet Intelligence Scale: Fourth Edition. *Journal of Psychoeducational Assessment, 6,* 359–370.

Sattler, J. A. (1988). *Assessment of children* (3rd ed.). San Diego: J. M. Sattler, Author.

Spruill, J. (1988). Two types of tables for tables for use with the Stanford-Binet Intelligence Scale: Fourth Edition. *Journal of Psychoeducational Assessment, 6,* 76–86.

Thorndike, R. L., Hagen, E. P., & Sattler, J. M. (1986). The Stanford-Binet Intelligence Scale: Fourth Edition. Chicago, IL: The Riverside Publishing Company.

Terman, L. M., & Merrill, M. A. (1973). The Stanford-Binet Intelligence Scale. Boston: Houghton Mifflin.

Wechsler, D. (1974). *The Wechsler Intelligence Scale for Children-Revised.* San Antonio, TX: The Psychological Corporation.

Wechsler, D. (1972). *The Wechsler Preschool and Primary scale of Intelligence.* San Antonio, TX: The Psychological Corporation.

Woodcock, R. W., & Johnson, M. B. (1977). *Woodcock-Johnson Psycho-Educational Battery.* Allen, TX: DLM/Teaching Resources.

8

Preschool Cognitive Assessment with the *Differential Ability Scales*

COLIN D. ELLIOTT
MARK H. DANIEL
GRETCHEN W. GUITON

The *Differential Ability Scales* (DAS) (Elliott, 1990) is a new individually administered battery of cognitive and achievement tests for children and adolescents aged 2½ years through 17 years. As a revision of the *British Ability Scales* (BAS) (Elliott, Murray, & Pearson, 1979), the DAS has recently been standardized in the United States. After discussing the conceptual basis of the DAS, this chapter will focus on one section of the DAS, the preschool level of the Cognitive Battery. The purpose of this chapter is to introduce the DAS to practitioners; to examine the preschool subtests in detail with respect to their content, administration, and interpretation; to present data on the technical quality of the instrument for use with preschool children; and to describe an approach to interpreting the child's profile of scores.

The predecessor to the DAS, the *British Ability Scales* was published in England in 1979 and expanded in 1983. Work has been underway since 1984 on a substantially modified version of the battery to better suit the needs of psychologists in the United States and internationally. This revision has involved creating and trying out new subtests, deciding which BAS subtests to retain, drop, or modify, adding items to increase subtest reliability, and removing any uniquely British elements that would interfere with test use in other countries.

DESCRIPTION OF THE DAS

The DAS contains two distinct but integrated components: a Cognitive Battery with two levels, one for preschool-age children and one for school-age children, and a set of academic achievement screening tests for school-age children. Developed and normed as a single unit, these components form a wide-ranging and coordinated assessment instrument. The Cognitive Battery provides a broad composite referred to as the General Conceptual Ability (GCA) score, cluster scores for narrower ability areas, and individual subtest scores including measures of specific abilities unrelated to the GCA score. The Achievement tests provide individual scores in the areas of Basic Number Skills, Spelling, and Word Reading. Thus, the DAS permits exploration of intraindividual differences among cognitive abilities and between cognitive abilities and achievement.

Theoretical Background

The DAS and its predecessor, the BAS, were designed to measure a wide range of cognitive abilities distinctively to provide a sound basis for the analysis of strengths and weaknesses. No single cognitive theory provided the basis for their development; instead the author drew on a number of theoretical perspectives and selected abilities for inclusion that might help in understanding children's learning problems. In a general sense, Elliott adopted Thurstone's view of intelligence as multidimensional and consisting of "primary mental abilities." In this way, Elliott developed an instrument that could be interpreted from a variety of theoretical perspectives.

In particular, the preschool level of the Cognitive Battery includes separate measures of a number of the abilities that are of interest when evaluating young children. Receptive and expressive language abilities are measured separately by the Verbal Comprehension and Naming Vocabulary subtests, respectively. A third subtest, Early Number Concepts, also is verbal in nature, but focuses on the domain of prenumerical and numerical concepts.

One of the major changes in the revision from the BAS to the DAS was the addition of two new nonverbal subtests for preschoolers to provide a better balance between verbal and nonverbal abilities. These new subtests are Block Building, a perceptual matching task, and Picture Similarities, an abstract reasoning test that does not require the use of language for administration or response. Visual-perceptual abilities also are measured by the Copying and Matching Letter-Like Forms subtests. Pattern Construction, a variation on the familiar Block Design task, assesses perceptual and spatial ability. Finally, the preschool level includes three measures of short-term memory: Recall of Digits and Recall of Objects, which are verbal in content, and Recognition of Pictures, a nonverbal subtest.

Both the DAS and the BAS were designed to measure specific abilities more distinctively than has been done in other individually administered batteries. Because valid diagnostic measurement requires well-defined, differentiated, and reliable ability measures, an effort was made to design subtests that are relatively pure and interpretable measures of specific abilities. In this way the instrument provides a more psychometrically sound basis for diagnostic (profile) analysis.

At the same time, to be generally useful, a cognitive battery must provide a composite score that can serve as an index of intellectual ability for applications in classification and placement. The GCA score of the DAS is designed as a relatively homogeneous measure of the reasoning and conceptual abilities that are important for learning. Because this composite is focused rather than representing a mixture of all of the varied abilities represented in the battery, it is both efficient and easily interpreted.

Scores and Subtests

The Cognitive Battery is composed of two types of subtests: *core subtests*, which make up the GCA composite, and *diagnostic subtests*, which measure relatively independent abilities. All of these subtests can be interpreted individually. Subtest age norms are provided in the form of T scores ($M = 50$, $SD = 10$), percentiles, and age equivalents, reported for three-month age groups. Each of the two sets of subtests will be described in turn.

Core Subtests

At each age level, 4 to 6 subtests that were found in analyses of the standardization data to be the best measures of reasoning and conceptual abilities make up the core of the cognitive battery. These subtests form the starting point for most assessments. They are balanced to reflect both verbal and nonverbal content, and are administered first in a prescribed sequence.

The sum of these core subtests forms the GCA score, reported as a standard score with a mean of 100 and standard deviations of 15. The GCA score is based on 6 subtests at all ages except 2–6 through 3–5, where 4 subtests are used. Constructed according to results of factor analysis and, at school ages, correlations with academic achievement, the GCA score focuses on reasoning and conceptual abilities, and does not incorporate measures of specific, independent abilities such as short-term memory.

As age and ability increase, the general factor underlying the core subtests becomes differentiated. At the early preschool level (ages 2–6 to about 3–5) the 4 core subtests measure a single dominant factor, and no subfactors are discernable. At about ages 3–6 to 5–11, the six core subtests can be separated into two distinct factors, verbal and nonverbal. (One of the core subtests, Early Number Concepts, loads highly on both factors.) By age 6, a three-factor pattern emerges within the 6 core subtests: The verbal factor from the younger level remains, and the nonverbal factor branches into a spatial factor and a nonverbal reasoning factor.

For these reasons, in addition to providing a GCA score, at ages 3–6 and older the core subtests also provide two or three *cluster* scores representing the factors just named. Like the GCA, the cluster scores are reported as standard scores with a mean of 100 and standard deviations of 15.

Diagnostic Subtests

At each age, the DAS also includes diagnostic cognitive subtests that can be used selectively to address specific questions and to provide information that supplements that obtained from the core subtests. The diagnostic subtests can be grouped into three content areas: perceptual matching, speed of information processing, and short-term memory. Because these abilities are relatively distinct from reasoning and conceptualization, scores on these subtests do not contribute to the GCA or cluster scores. However, their relative independence makes the diagnostic subtests potentially useful for a number of applications.

The structure of the DAS allows the examiner to select the most appropriate battery for an individual child. Administration of the core subtests usually takes about 30 to 50 minutes, and because these subtests are administered by most examiners, they provide consistency and comparability across different examiners and different children. Optional selection of the diagnostic subtests permits the examiner to address specific questions of interest without administering unnecessary subtests. Table 8-1 presents the core and diagnostic subtests at each level of the Cognitive Battery and shows their relationship to the GCA and cluster scores.

Achievement Tests

In addition to the Cognitive Battery core and diagnostic subtests, children ages 6 and older (5

TABLE 8.1
COGNITIVE SUBTESTS AT EACH LEVEL OF THE COGNITIVE BATTERY

Ages	Core Subtests (Cluster*)	Diagnostic Subtests
2–6 to 3–5	Block Building Picture Similarities Naming Vocabulary Verbal Comprehension	Recall of Digits Recognition of Pictures
3–6 to 5–11	Copying (NV) Pattern Construction (NV) Picture Similarities (NV) Naming Vocabulary (V) Verbal Comprehension (V) Early Number Concepts**	Block Building Matching Letter-Like Forms Recall of Digits Recall of Objects Recognition of Pictures
6 to 17	Matrices (NVR) Sequential and Quantitative Reas. (NVR) Pattern Construction (S) Recall of Designs (S) Similarities (V) Word Definitions (V)	Recall of Digits Recall of Objects Speed of Information Processing

Note: The core subtests make up the GCA score.

* NV = Nonverbal, NVR = Nonverbal Reasoning, S = Spatial, V = Verbal

** Early Number Concepts is not included in either cluster because it correlates highly with both the verbal and nonverbal factors.

and older for Word Reading) can take three achievement tests that measure developed skill in arithmetic computation, spelling, and word recognition (decoding). Each of these screening tests can be scored using age-based standard scores that are scaled like the cognitive composites for easy comparison ($M = 100$, $SD = 15$). In addition, grade-based percentiles, Normal Curve Equivalents (NCEs), and age- and grade-equivalents are available. Administration of all three achievement tests takes about 20 to 25 minutes.

Adaptive Testing

One of the primary needs in assessment at all levels, but particularly at the preschool level, is for instruments that can be used reliably with children who are very low or high in ability. To assess children who are functioning at low ability levels, a test must have two features. First, it must have item content that is sufficiently easy to allow success for low-ability children, because accurate assessment depends on presenting tasks that are appropriate in difficulty for the child. Second, the test should be normed for the child's age. The DAS development addressed both of these requirements.

The preschool-level subtests were designed specifically for that lower age range, rather than being downward extensions of school-age tests. (More details are given in the next section.) This approach permitted very easy items to be developed for many of the subtests. Data on the floor of the preschool subtests are presented later in this chapter.

The DAS also incorporates a number of features that aid in the selection of the most appropriate subtests and items for an individual child. Although subtest selection generally involves administering the core and diagnostic subtests prescribed for general use at a particular age range, children expected to be quite low or high in ability can also (or instead) be administered subtests designated as "out of level" for their age. These out of level subtests were normed on the full sample at that child's age, but are most appropriate in difficulty for the upper or lower range of the ability distribution at the child's age.

On most subtests, items are grouped into overlapping sets across the subtest's range of difficulty. Different sets of items are recommended for children of different ages, although an easier or more difficult set can be selected by the examiner in light of the child's expected ability level. The objective of item selection is to administer a set of items that is moderately difficult for the child and, therefore, provides the most information about the child's ability. Items that are very easy or very difficult for the child give little information, are not an efficient use of testing time, and can be frustrating for the child. For this reason, the DAS does not use the traditional system of basals and ceilings. Instead, the child's ability is estimated from his or her performance on the specific set of items administered, using a procedure based on the Rasch model of item response theory.

If the set of items initially selected proves to be too easy or difficult, additional items are administered. A child must pass at least three items and fail at least three items on a subtest to ensure that the items accurately measure the child's level of ability. Starting points based on age and flexible stopping points, called *decision points*, guide the examiner in selecting items and continuing testing until a reliable measure of the child's ability has been obtained. The overall procedure is designed to balance efficiency and accuracy of measurement.

PRESCHOOL LEVEL OF THE COGNITIVE BATTERY

Eleven of the 20 DAS subtests are appropriate for most or all of the preschool age range (2–6 through 5–11). Most of these subtests are normed through age 7 and can be used for assessing low-functioning children of school age.

The preschool subtests were designed specifically for this age group. These subtests employ many manipulable objects (such as toys, blocks, wooden figures, and plastic chips) and brightly colored pictures, so that they appeal to young children and hold their attention. Boehm (1982) notes the importance of materials and tasks that are enjoyable when assessing the preschool child. Both Boehm (1982) and Ulrey and Rodgers (1982) discuss various difficulties in assessing young children, such as children's unfamiliarity with the testing situation, shyness when working with a strange adult, and short attention span. Recognizing these concerns, the DAS provides varied and attractive materials. It also employs sample items and provides for teaching following failure on any of the initial subtest items.

DESCRIPTION AND INTERPRETATION OF THE CORE SUBTESTS

The four core subtests for preschool children ages 2–6 through 3–5 are described below.

- *Block Building* measures the ability to copy two-dimensional or three-dimensional designs using wooden blocks. The first item requires the child to build as tall a tower as possible using eight blocks. The remaining 11 items require the child to build a four-block structure or a flat design exactly like a model demonstated by the examiner. The model remains intact while the child copies it. This subtest measures perceptual matching ability and motor skill. The two-dimensional items, which are more difficult than the three-dimensional ones, are sensitive to errors of reversal or rotation.
- *Verbal Comprehension* measures understanding of spoken language in a manner that requires no verbal response from the child. In response to spoken instructions, the child points to pictures or manipulates objects (toys, wooden figures, or colored chips). The easiest items require the child to point to body parts on a full-color picture of a Teddy Bear, and then to point to objects that are identified by name or by function. More difficult items require the child to point to or manipulate objects to demonstrate understanding of prepositions, other basic concepts, and complex sentence structures. The subtest contains a total of 36 items.
- *Picture Similarities* assesses nonverbal reasoning. Shown a row of four pictures, the child places a fifth picture under the one it goes with best. The first two items are based on perceptual identity, to teach the nature of the task without using words. The remaining 30 items involve conceptual similarity based on a common element, such as a feature or function.
- *Naming Vocabulary* assesses expressive vo-

cabulary. The child names an object shown in a full-color picture. Any appropriate label is scored as correct, but functions, materials, or subcomponents are incorrect reponses that are questioned. A total of 26 items constitute this subtest.

All these subtests, except Block Building, also contribute to the GCA score for children at the upper preschool level, ages 3–6 through 5–11. Three additional subtests combine with Verbal Comprehension, Picture Similarities, and Naming Vocabulary to make up the GCA score for these children, as follows:

- *Pattern Construction*, similar to the Block Design subtest of the Wechsler scales, measures spatial imagery and is scored according to accuracy and speed. The child reproduces a two-dimensional design using yellow and black flat square pieces or solid cubes. Stimulus patterns can be presented in picture form, or as a model that the examiner constructs in front of the child. Either the picture or the model remains while the child constructs the pattern. Some items also require the examiner to demonstrate how to construct the correct response. For situations where an unspeeded score is thought to be more appropriate or valid for the child, such as when evaluating a child who has a motor impairment, an alternative administration and scoring procedure is available, based on the number of items completed within liberal time limits. This subtest, which extends to age 17, has a total of 7 items using flat squares and 19 using cubes. Preschool-age children generally take 7 to 10 items.
- *Early Number Concepts* assesses the child's understanding of number, size, one-to-one correspondence, and other prenumerical and numerical concepts. The items are presented using chips or full-color pictures. The child usually responds by pointing, although a few of the 28 items require counting aloud or saying a number.
- *Copying* measures visual-motor integration. Presented with an abstract line drawing that is either drawn by the examiner or shown in a booklet, the child is asked to reproduce it. Scoring criteria address accuracy of repro-

duction, including the orientation of the figure and the angle and size relationships among the lines. This is one of the few preschool subtests on which partial credit is given: An examinee can earn zero, one, two, or three points per item. Twenty drawings are included in this subtest, of which most children take 10 to 12.

DESCRIPTION AND INTERPRETATION OF THE DIAGNOSTIC SUBTESTS

In addition to the core subtests, four diagnostic subtests at the preschool level supply information about specific abilities in the areas of memory and visual perception. Two of the four diagnostic subtests, Recall of Objects and Matching Letter-Like Forms, are appropriate for children 4 years of age and older; the other two subtests, Recognition of Pictures and Recall of Digits, are appropriate for children as young as 2 years, 6 months. These four subtests are described below.

- *Recall of Objects (Immediate and Delayed)* tests short-term verbal memory. Initially the child views a card containing pictures of 20 objects that are named aloud by the examiner. Following a one-minute exposure, the child attempts to recall as many objects as possible after the card is removed. The Immediate Recall portion of the subtest consists of this trial plus two additional trials with briefer exposure times. After about 15 minutes, during which other subtests are administered, the child again attempts to recall as many objects as possible, but without being shown the picture card. The Immediate Recall score can be interpreted for all children. The Delayed Recall score, less reliable because it is based on a single trial, is interpreted only if it is significantly higher or lower than the Immediate Recall score.
- *Recognition of Pictures* measures short-term visual memory. After viewing for 5 or 10 seconds a picture containing one or several familiar objects, the child is shown a second picture and is asked to identify the original object(s) by pointing to them among a set of distractors. To emphasize visual rather than verbal memory, the distractors usually belong to the same semantic categories as the target objects. The subtest consists of 20 items, of which children generally take 9 to 16, depending on their age.
- *Recall of Digits* measures short-term memory for sequences of from 2 to 8 digits that are presented orally at half-second intervals. The child must recall all digits in correct sequence to obtain credit for an item. The 36 items are grouped into 8 blocks, each consisting of 2 to 5 items with the same number of digits. The relatively rapid presentation is designed to emphasize auditory memory by not providing enough time for the child to mentally "elaborate" the stimulus. For the same reason, backward recall trials are not included because they tend to demand more general intellectual ability than forward recall.
- *Matching Letter-Like Forms* measures visual discrimination and perception of spatial orientation. Shown an abstract, letter-like shape, the child must point to the identical shape from among 6 answer choices that differ from the target by being rotated or reversed. This subtest is similar to Block Building and Copying in the ability being measured, but does not require the motor skill called for by those subtests.

Special Nonverbal Scale

If the examiner judges that subtests involving verbal presentation or response might not be reliable and valid measures of a particular child's ability, a briefer battery can be administered to obtain a Special Nonverbal composite score in place of the GCA score. This option is particularly useful at the preschool level because children in this age range frequently present difficulties in assessment. Shy preschoolers, those reluctant to talk to an unfamiliar adult, children with delayed language or speech problems, elective mutes, children from culturally different backgrounds, children whose primary language is not English, and children with middle ear infections or suspected hearing loss frequently are referred for assessment at a young age. Directions for the subtests of the Special Nonverbal scale can be conveyed through gestures, and the child's responses require only pointing, drawing, or manipulation of objects.

For a young preschool child (ages 2–6 to 3–

5), the Special Nonverbal battery consists of Block Building and Picture Similarities. In addition, Recognition of Pictures can be administered, but is not incorporated into the composite. For preschool children ages 3–6 through 5–11, the Special Nonverbal battery includes Pattern Construction, Copying, and Picture Similarities—the three subtests of the Nonverbal cluster. Block Building, Matching Letter-Like Forms, and Recognition of Pictures also can be administered as diagnostic subtests. At each age, norms for this Special Nonverbal scale are based on the full standardization sample. Because the reliability of the Special Nonverbal scale is somewhat lower than for the GCA (especially at ages 2–6 to 3–5) and the range of abilities measured is more limited, the Special Nonverbal scale should be used only when the full GCA is clearly inappropriate for the child.

TECHNICAL CHARACTERISTICS

The Normative Sample

The DAS is normed on a representative sample of the general population that includes children exhibiting a variety of special characteristics (such as learning disabilities, speech and language impairments, mild mental retardation, emotional disturbance, mild visual, hearing, or motor impairments, and above-average ability or special talents). The normative sample of 3,475 children, tested between 1987 and 1989, is closely matched to the March 1988 U.S. Census data. From ages 5 through 17 the sample includes 200 cases per year (100 males and 100 females). At the younger ages (2–6 to 4–11) the sample includes 175 cases per half-year or 350 cases per year, again evenly divided by sex. Within each six-month or one-year age group, the sample reflects the general population distributions of race, SES, and region. SES was measured by the average educational level of the parent(s) living with the child. Table 8-2 shows the overall demographic characteristics of the DAS sample ages 2–6 through 5–11 in comparison to the distribution of these characteristics in the general U.S. population.

The preschool-age sample was selected from a variety of sources including preschools, day care centers (both formal and in home), social welfare

TABLE 8.2

DEMOGRAPHIC CHARACTERISTICS OF THE DAS STANDARDIZATION SAMPLE, AGES 2–6 to 5–11 (N = 1,075)

Characteristic	DAS Sample	U.S. Population
Race		
White	70.6%	70.2%
Black	15.5	15.2
Hispanic	10.6	10.9
Other	3.2	3.7
Parental education		
Less than 12 years	16.1	18.4
12 years	37.9	37.1
13–15 years	26.4	25.7
16 or more years	19.5	18.8
Region		
Northeast	19.3	18.8
North Central	25.0	25.1
South	36.5	34.9
West	19.2	21.2
Enrollment in an educational program		
Age 3	30	29
Age 4	48	49
Age 5	77	87

Note: U.S. population data for race, parental education, and region are from the March 1988 *Current Population Survey* (Bureau of the Census, 1988). Data for education enrollment are from the October 1986 *Current Population Survey* (Bureau of the Census, 1986).

Data and table copyright © 1990 by The Psychological Corporation, and may not be reproduced without permission. All rights reserved.

agencies, churches, and through direct contact with parents. The proportion of children in educational programs was controlled to match census figures by age, as shown in Table 8-2. This was done on the assumption that children in educational programs would differ in important ways from those who stay at home or are in noneducational day care settings.

The sampling method used did not select students according to their special education classification, but instead sampled children randomly. After selecting the sample, information was obtained for the school-age sample regarding special education status to determine how closely the sample matched the incidence of exceptional children in the schools. The sample closely reflects 1984 percentages for special education categories in the population. Although the normative sample represents the population of noninstitutionalized children, the inclusion of small numbers of children with exceptionalities, while consistent with the goal of representativeness, does not automatically assure the appropriateness or validity of the DAS for these children. Only research involving large samples of exceptional children can lead to this determination.

New techniques for determining the demographic targets aided the construction of a representative sample. Demographic information for the general population was obtained from the March 1988 Current Population Survey tape (Bureau of the Census, 1988) rather than from published tables so that important demographic variables could be defined in an appropriate way. In particular, use of the raw-data tape made it possible to match the sample to the SES of the general population of children (rather than of adults), and to accurately reflect current social conditions.

Out-of-Level Assessment

Out-of-level testing refers to the practice of administering a test at a child's functional or skill level rather than at the child's grade or age level. Out-of-level testing can occur at both the high and low ends of the ability spectrum, although the practice is most common with low-ability and learning disabled children. Traditionally, out-of-level testing has been viewed as raising problems of score reliability and validity, because tests are standardized for specific age levels and their technical properties might be optimal only at these levels (Berk, 1984). However, this viewpoint reflects a concern with the average accuracy of a test for an age group; reliability and validity are, after all, statistics that describe the behavior of a test for a group. When one instead considers score accuracy at the level of the individual child, whose ability might be well above or below the average for his or her age, then the availability of out-of-level testing can improve a test's technical properties. A test that has high overall reliability at a particular age nevertheless might be inaccurate for children of that age who are at the extremes of the ability distribution, and vice versa.

The accuracy of an individual child's score depends on two things: administering items that are appropriate in difficulty for the child, and knowing the score distribution on that test for chil-

dren of the same age in the general population (i.e., having accurate norms). Items that are moderately challenging for a child, on which the child has about a 50% chance of responding correctly, provide the most useful information about the child's ability level. Items that are very easy or very difficult yield little information. Thus, a test that is appropriate for the average level of ability at an age might not include many items that are sufficiently easy or difficult to accurately measure the low-ability or high-ability child.

Administering a test out of level might be the best way to obtain an accurate index of a high- or low-ability child's level of functioning. This might mean giving a test that has low reliability for the child's age as a whole because the average child of that age finds the test too easy or too difficult. However, item response theory (IRT) makes it possible to evaluate a test's accuracy at different ability levels, and this approach has been used in the construction of the DAS.

Having a method for administering items that are suited to the child's ability is one condition for accurate out-of-level testing. The second is having good norms. The DAS furnishes complete norms to support out-of-level testing with many of the subtests outside their typical age range. All norms for all subtests are based on full samples at the ages for which norms are reported, even when this meant administering subtests in standardization that were too easy or difficult for many of the children at a given age. Almost all of the preschool and school-age subtests were administered to all children ages 5 to 7, because out-of-level subtest selection often is needed most at the later preschool and early elementary ages.

Two methods exist for conducting out-of-level testing on the DAS. Individual subtests not normally administered at a given age can be selected, or the entire Cognitive Battery can be shifted to a higher or lower level. Out-of-level testing at the subtest level might be done to measure an ability not covered by the usual battery for the child's age. For example, Pattern Construction could be administered to a bright child aged 3–3 because full norms exist at that age even though the subtest is not usually given until age 3–6. Conversely, Verbal Comprehension could be administered to a low-ability 6-year-old child and scored with full norms.

At the battery level, out-of-level testing

means giving the core subtests for an older or younger age. Because the lower preschool level (for ages 2–6 to 3–5) and upper preschool level (3–6 to 5–11) have three subtests in common, the decision to do out-of-level testing can be made after the first several subtests have been administered with little or no waste of testing time. As Table 8-3 shows, full norms exist for the lower preschool level (four core subtests) through age 4–11. That level also can be administered to children ages 5 or 6 who are very low in ability (GCA scores down to about 25); even though not all of the subtests are individually normed above age 4, "extended" GCA norms were developed through an equating of the different levels of the battery. Table 8-3 also shows the normed age ranges for the upper preschool level and the school-age level of the Cognitive Battery.

It should be apparent that although full norms for out-of-level testing might be available, such testing must be done selectively. To make appropriate decisions about using out-of-level subtests, the examiner needs to know for which portion of the ability range the subtest performs reliably. This information is provided in the subtest norm tables. For each age, the range at which T score accuracy is low is shaded. Thus, if the examiner sees that a certain test has relatively low reliability for T scores above 65 (i.e., the 93rd percentile and above) at the child's age, he or she would know that the subtest would not be very accurate for a child in about the top 10% of the ability range. The subtest could safely be used, however, with children expected to be functioning at an average or below average level.

In summary, out-of-level testing makes it possible for examiners to select subtests that are suited in difficulty to the individual child and the purpose of testing, and consequently to obtain more reliable scores for the child with very low or very high ability. The benefits of out-of-level testing are greatest for the assessment of children who are gifted or developmentally delayed.

Reliability and Standard Error of Measurement

Reliability addresses the issue of test score stability or dependability and of the decisions for which scores are used (Berk, 1984). Bracken (1987, p. 317), following the recommendations of Nunnally (1978) and Salvia and Ysseldyke (1985), suggests that instruments used to make diagnostic decisions about individual children should have an internal consistency reliability of at least .80 for individual subtest scores and at least .90 for composite scores. Table 8-4 presents the reliabilities of subtests and composites of the preschool level of the Cognitive Battery.

Because the DAS does not use the basal and ceiling method of scoring, it is not founded on assumptions about how a child would have performed on items that were not administered, as most tests are. Such assumptions make it difficult to estimate reliability accurately, and tend to introduce some degree of overestimation (Thorndike, Hagen, & Sattler, 1986a, p.145).

The reliabilities of the GCA score and cluster scores are at or very near the levels recommended by Bracken (1987) for making diagnostic decisions about individual children. In addition, many of the subtests are reliable enough to be interpreted individually, although others should be interpreted only as they contribute to composite scores. Two of the preschool-age diagnostic subtests—Matching Letter-Like Forms and Recall of Digits—have high reliability; the other two—Recall of Objects–Immediate and Recognition of Pictures—are less

TABLE 8.3
AGES AT WHICH EACH LEVEL OF THE COGNITIVE BATTERY IS NORMED

Level	Usual Age Range	Full Norms	Extended GCA Norms (scores of 25 to 45)
Lower Preschool	2–6 to 3–5	2–6 to 4–11	2–9 to 6–11
Upper Preschool	3–6 to 5–11	3–6 to 6–11	3–9 to 13–11
School-Age	6 to 17	5 to 17	6–3 to 17–11

Note: Some individual subtests within each level are normed over a wider age range than shown in the table.

TABLE 8.4
RELIABILITIES OF PRESCHOOL SUBTESTS AND COMPOSITES, BY AGE (Revised June 4, 1990)

Subtest	2–6 to 2–11	3–0 to 3–5	3–6 to 3–11	4–0 to 4–5	4–6 to 4–11	5–0 to 5–11	6–0 to 6–11	7–0 to 7–11	Mean
1 Block Building	68	74	80	84	76	—	—	—	77
2 Verbal Comprehension	86	83	85	85	82	83	(74)	—	84
3 Picture Similarities	84	78	76	70	73	72	(60)	(33)	76
4 Naming Vocabulary	77	74	73	79	76	84	78	77	78
5 Pattern Construction	—	(80)	84	89	82	90	90	89	88
6 Early No. Concepts	(53)	(80)	88	87	85	87	81	(57)	86
7 Copying	—	—	82	86	88	88	85	82	86
8 Matching LL Forms	—	—	—	(78)	84	87	(68)	(49)	85
9 Recall of Digits	(86)	90	87	89	85	88	88	88	88
10 Recall of Objects	—	—	—	76	66	67	77	69	71
11 Recog. of Pictures	(68)	78	78	80	74	74	66	71	73
Composite									
GCA[a]	91	89	94	94	94	95	—	—	90/94
Verbal	—	—	88	89	86	90	—	—	88
Nonverbal	—	—	88	90	88	—	—	—	89
Special Nonverbal	82	81	—[b]	—[b]	—[b]	—[b]	—	—	81/89

[a] The GCA consists of subtests 1–4 for ages 2–6 to 3–5 and subtests 2–7 for ages 3–6 to 5–11.

[b] Same as for the Nonverbal cluster.

Note: Decimals omitted. $N = 175$ per age group from 2–6 through 4–11, and 200 per age group from 5–0 through 7–11. Values in parentheses are for ages at which the subtest is out of level, that is, not appropriate for the full range of ability at the age. These values are not included in the mean.

Data and table copyright © 1990 by The Psychological Corporation, and may not be reproduced without permission. All rights reserved.

reliable and should be interpreted more cautiously. Guidelines presented in the manual for identifying individual subtests as significant strengths or weaknesses take the level of subtest reliability into account.

Item response theory makes it possible to report the standard error of measurement at each score level. This information is provided as part of the scoring procedure for each subtest, and can be used to construct confidence intervals for subtest *T* scores and percentiles. The standard error of measurement more directly indicates the accuracy of a particular examinee's test score than does reliability. The standard error of measurement describes how close an obtained score is likely to be to a person's hypothetical "true score." The standard error of measurement varies for different levels of ability, and is lowest among people whose raw scores are in the middle range of the test.

Test–Retest Reliability

A random subset of about 100 members of the standardization sample at each of three ages (3–6 to 4–5, 5–0 to 6–3, and 12–0 to 13–11) was readministered the DAS after an interval of two to six weeks. The correlations between first and second test scores for the preschool level are shown in Table 8-5. The retest reliabilities of the composite scores are high. Subtest reliabilities are similar at the two ages, and range from .54 to .89 with an average of .72. Those subtests with high retest reliabilities also tend to have high internal-consistency reliability, and are those in which the greatest confidence can be placed in interpretation at the subtest level.

Floor and Ceiling

It has already been noted that the accuracy of a test is, in large part, a function of the match between an individual's ability level and the difficulty of the items. Because a primary use of a test such as the DAS is to identify children who are functioning well above or below normal, it is important for the test to discriminate well at the extreme tails of the distribution. To accomplish this, a test must contain an adequate number of easy and difficult items.

Bracken (1987, p. 320) identifies a test's

TABLE 8.5
RETEST RELIABILITIES OF SUBTESTS AND COMPOSITES (Revised June 4, 1990)

| | | Ages 3–6 to 4–5 (*N* = 100) | | | Ages 5–0 to 6–3 (*N* = 90) | |
| | | Mean Score | | | | Mean Score | |
Variable	*r*	Time 1	Time 2	*r*	Time 1	Time 2
Subtests						
Block Building	.67	50.9	51.0	—	—	—
Verbal Comprehension	.81	48.8	50.8	.77	47.3	47.9
Picture Similarities	.56	48.9	50.7	.63	48.4	52.6
Naming Vocabulary	.80	49.2	49.8	.89	48.0	48.8
Pattern Construction	.62	49.1	51.4	.73	49.5	52.4
Early No. Concepts	.68	50.2	50.6	.83	47.6	48.9
Copying	.71	50.5	51.1	.68	50.1	49.1
Match. Let-Like Fms	—	—	—	.68	48.9	51.4
Recall of Digits	.81	50.4	52.7	.80	48.9	48.5
Recall of Objects	—	—	—	.54	48.5	54.0
Recog. of Pictures	.58	51.6	52.6	.54	51.5	52.7
Composites						
GCA	.90	98.9	101.9	.94	96.6	100.0
Verbal cluster	.84	98.2	100.3	.89	95.8	97.0
Nonverbal cluster	.79	98.4	101.7	.86	98.2	102.7

Note: The retest interval was 2 to 6 weeks.

Data and table copyright © 1990 by The Psychological Corporation, and may not be reproduced without permission. All rights reserved.

floor—that is, the degree to which a test "spreads out" examinees at the low end of the ability range—as one of the most important characteristics of a preschool instrument. For a given age level, the floor can be indicated by the standard score associated with a raw score of one. If such a subtest standard score is two standard deviations below the subtest mean, then the subtest differentiates the lowest-functioning 2½% (or fewer) of children from the remainder of the sample. Table 8-6 reports the floor of each core subtest in the preschool level of the DAS for several ages. The average floor at the lower preschool level is nearly two standard deviations below the mean at the youngest age group (2–6 to 2–8) and exceeds two standard deviations at every other age. For the upper preschool level, the average subtest floor is more than two standard deviations below the mean for every age group.

The floor of the overall composite score is of greater importance than the average subtest floor because the composite is more likely to be used in making decisions. Table 8-6 shows that a child who obtains a raw score of 1 on each subtest would have a GCA score more than two standard deviations below the mean (i.e., less than 70) at every age level.

Although Bracken is not as concerned with ceiling effects as with floor effects, similar considerations of content appropriateness are important when assessing gifted preschoolers. The ability of a subtest to differentiate among children functioning at average and above-average levels depends on having a sufficient number of difficult items. Table 8-6 also presents the distance of each preschool core subtest's ceiling (maximum raw score) from the mean, along with the maximum obtainable GCA. At both the lower and upper preschool levels of the Cognitive Battery, the average ceiling is about three standard deviations above the mean.

In summary, the DAS preschool level has a good floor and excellent ceiling when used at the usual age ranges. When out-of-level testing is considered, the floor and ceiling are extended. For example, to obtain a lower floor, a child aged 3–6 to 4–11 could be administered the lower preschool level (four core subtests) and scored on full norms. For a higher ceiling, a 5 year old child could be administered the school-age-level.

Item Gradient

The sensitivity of a test to small differences in ability is evidenced by the amount of increase (or decrease) in the standard score when an additional item is passed (or failed). Bracken (1987) refers to this as the *item gradient*, and proposes a standard of at least three items per standard deviation. Table 8-7 reports the average number of items (or score points) per standard deviation on each subtest between a raw score of zero and the median subtest score, for ages 2–6 to 3–5 (lower preschool level) and 3–6 to 4–5 (upper preschool level). The item gradients for older ages are, of course, higher than for the ages shown. Most of the subtests meet or surpass the criterion of three points per standard deviation at these young ages. The exceptions are Block Building, which has a total of only 13 score points, and Naming Vocabulary and Copying at the youngest 3 or 6 months of their age ranges.

Bias Analysis

Three approaches have been used to minimize the possibility of race or sex bias in the DAS. First, items were scrutinized by an item review panel. Next, item bias analyses were conducted. Finally, the regression lines predicting academic achievement from the GCA score were compared for Blacks, Hispanics, and Whites.

In the first, judgmental analysis, a panel of psychologists representing the perspectives of females, Blacks, Hispanics, and Native Americans reviewed the items in the standardization edition. A number of items, particularly on the Naming Vocabulary, Similarities, and Word Definitions subtests, were eliminated or modified based on the panel's review.

As part of the DAS standardization, additional cases of Black and Hispanic children were collected with the goal of administering every item to at least 100 children of each ethnic group. Item difficulties were computed for each group, and items with difficulty levels that were "out of sequence" for a particular group were identified. This notion of bias presumes that if an item is unbiased its difficulty relative to other items in the subtest should be comparable from one group to another. That is, the items that are most difficult for Blacks also should be the most difficult for

TABLE 8.6
DISTANCE OF THE FLOOR AND CEILING OF EACH PRESCHOOL CORE SUBTEST FROM THE MEAN IN STANDARD DEVIATION UNITS, BY AGE

Subtest	Floor (Raw Score of 1) 2–6 to 2–8	2–9 to 2–11	3–0 to 3–2	3–3 to 3–5	3–6 to 3–8	3–9 to 3–11	4–0 to 4–2	Ceiling Maximum Raw Score 3–3 to 3–5	5–9 to 5–11
Block Building	-1.3	-1.6	-1.9	—	—	—	—	+3.0	—
Verbal Comprehension	-2.7	-3.0	-3.0	-3.0	-3.0	-3.0	-3.0	+3.0	+2.1
Picture Similarities	-1.5	-1.8	-2.1	-2.6	-2.9	-3.0	-3.0	+3.0	+3.0
Naming Vocabulary	-1.9	-2.2	-2.5	-3.0	-3.0	-3.0	-3.0	+3.0	+3.0
Pattern Construction	—	—	—	-1.8	-1.8	-2.0	-2.3	—	+3.0
Early Number Concepts	—	—	—	-1.6	-2.0	-2.0	-2.2	—	+3.0
Copying	—	—	—	-1.5	-1.7	-1.7	-2.0	—	+2.5
Mean	-1.9	-2.2	-2.4	-2.3	-2.4	-2.4	-2.6	—	+2.8
GCA*	-2.4	-2.7	-3.0	-2.8	-3.1	-3.1	-3.2	+4.6	+4.6

* General Conceptual Ability score corresponding to a raw score of 1, or a maximum raw score, on each subtest.

TABLE 8.7
ITEM GRADIENTS OF PRESCHOOL CORE SUBTESTS, BY AGE

Subtest	Age 2–6 to 2–8	2–9 to 2–11	3–0 to 3–2	3–3 to 3–5	3–6 to 3–8	3–9 to 3–11	4–0 to 4–2	4–3 to 4–5
Block Building	1.2	1.3	1.6	1.8	—	—	—	—
Verbal Comprehension	5.2	5.5	6.0	6.6	7.3	7.7	8.2	8.7
Picture Similarities	5.0	5.2	5.6	5.9	6.0	6.3	6.8	7.0
Naming Vocabulary	2.6	3.0	3.3	3.5	3.9	4.3	4.5	4.8
Pattern Construction	—	—	—	—	4.8	5.5	6.0	5.9
Early Number Concepts	—	—	—	—	4.2	4.8	5.0	5.3
Copying	—	—	—	—	2.0	2.5	3.2	3.7
Mean	3.5	3.8	4.1	4.5	4.7	5.2	5.6	5.9

Note: The item gradient is the number of raw-score points between a raw score of zero and the median raw score for the age, divided by the number of standard deviations spanned by that raw score range.

Whites and Hispanics. An item that is one of the most difficult items for one group but is of only moderate difficulty for other groups would be considered biased. Presumably, something about such an item makes it unfairly difficult for the first group. Several items that were found to be differentially difficult for minorities, for males or females, or for children from a particular region of the country were identified and eliminated from the test.

Finally, the way in which the GCA predicts an important criterion—academic achievement—was compared across groups. This notion of freedom from bias presumes that errors in prediction are independent of group membership, so that the regression lines predicting achievement from GCA will be the same for each group. Regression lines were computed separately for Blacks, Hispanics, and Whites in grades 1 through 12, using scores on standardized group tests of reading and mathematics as criteria. (Full details of the analyses are provided in the DAS manual.) Equivalent slopes were obtained for all three groups. Blacks and Whites had the same intercept, and Hispanics had a lower intercept. These results indicate that the strength of the relationship of achievement with ability as indicated by the DAS's GCA score is the same for all groups. Use of the same regression equation for Hispanics as for Blacks and Whites would tend to overpredict Hispanics' achievement and underpredict Blacks' and Whites' performance; that is, the test would be "biased" in favor of Hispanics. There is certainly no evidence in these data to suggest that the DAS underestimates the cognitive ability of either Blacks or Hispanics.

These approaches to detect and minimize bias reflect current standards of practice, but they in no way guarantee that different groups will obtain comparable test scores. To a large degree, group differences in test performance undoubtedly reflect differences in home environments, and as long as these environmental differences exist group differences in developed cognitive abilities will persist. The intent of conducting the bias analyses is to ensure that no items contain content that is unfair to any group.

Validity

In the validation of a multifaceted instrument such as the DAS, there are several fundamental

questions that should be addressed to provide users with the information they will need for proper interpretation. One question concerns the structure of the DAS scores: What is the empirical basis for the division of the subtests into an increasing number of cluster scores as children get older, and for the selection of subtests that constitute the GCA? A second basic question relates to the constructs assessed by the subtests and composite scores: How do they relate to known measures of well-understood constructs? Third, a prospective DAS user will want to know the extent to which DAS scores function in a fashion similar to scores from other widely used batteries, to decide on the appropriateness of using DAS scores in place of these other scores. Information is presented here that addresses all three topics as they concern the preschool level of the DAS.

Additional important aspects of validation research include the evaluation of a test's ability to predict important outcomes and to identify subtypes of children. Research along these lines has been conducted with the school-age level of the DAS and is reported in the DAS test manual, but has not been carried out so far at the preschool level.

Factor Structure

Factor analyses guided the configuration of subtests into clusters and the GCA. The LISREL VI program (Jöreskog & Sörbom, 1986) was used to evaluate various "measurement models" at each of several age ranges, the ranges were determined by the ages at which the Cognitive Battery remained the same in the number and makeup of subtests. Separate investigations were conducted at ages 2–6 to 3–5, 4–0 to 5–11, 6 to 8, 9 to 12, and 13 to 17. At the youngest age level, the correlations among the six available subtests were explained almost fully by a single general factor on which all of the subtests had substantial loadings. Because this one-factor model had almost perfect fit, no significant improvement in fit was possible with two factors. Thus, at this young age there is no evidence of differentiation between verbal and nonverbal abilities. Rather, all of the subtests reflect a general ability factor as well as, to some extent, subtest-specific abilities.

At the next age level (4–0 to 5–11) 10 cognitive subtests were analyzed. Models having one, two, and three factors were examined. The two-factor model with verbal and nonverbal factors fit considerably better than the one-factor model. Adding a third factor measuring memory did not, however, improve the model's explanation of the data. What this suggests is that verbal and nonverbal dimensions of ability can be identified and separately measured at this age, but the memory subtests do not have enough in common to support a third factor. Instead, the memory subtests are relatively independent of the verbal and nonverbal factors and of one another. At this older preschool level, then, it is possible to identify children who differ in verbal and nonverbal ability.

The 6 core subtests for this age range are those that loaded highest on the general factor in the analysis of the one-factor model. Early Number Concepts, one of the highest-loading subtests, had approximately equally strong loadings on both the Verbal and Nonverbal factors in the two-factor model. Combining this subtest with either the verbal or nonverbal cluster would have made the resulting cluster less homogeneous and interpretable, and would have made the two clusters less distinct. Therefore, Early Number Concepts contributes to the GCA but is not part of either cluster.

Finally, the analyses of the school-age Cognitive Battery gave strong support for a six-subtest core battery that could be further divided into verbal, nonverbal reasoning, and spatial abilities. The three other subtests (Recall of Digits, Recall of Objects, and Speed of Information Processing) did not correlate highly with the GCA or with one another, suggesting that they are best used as diagnostic measures of specific abilities.

This progressive differentiation of ability with increasing age is consistent with research from a number of sources suggesting that people whose overall level of cognitive ability is less well developed tend to perform at a relatively consistent level on a wide range of measures, whereas when overall ability is higher independent dimensions of ability emerge (see Anastasi, 1970, for a review). When the examinee's ability is less well developed, whether because of young age or developmental delay, there is less justification for measuring and reporting specific factors of ability. The DAS construction recognized this phenomenon and incorporated it into the structure of the composite scores.

Correlations with Other Tests

Several studies in which the DAS was correlated with other cognitive instruments were carried out during standardization. Some were conducted in conjunction with the DAS norming; in these, children from numerous sites around the country were selected at random, and testing was counterbalanced with a 1 to 6 week interval between administrations. At the preschool level, data were collected in this way for the WPPSI-R (Wechsler, 1989) and the Binet IV (Thorndike, Hagen, & Sattler, 1986b). Other studies were conducted independently by researchers who collected their own samples, and the details of administration sequence and between-test interval vary among these studies. These studies examined the WPPSI-R, the K-ABC (Kaufman & Kaufman, 1983), and the MSCA (McCarthy, 1972). One study correlated the DAS with the *Woodcock-Johnson Psycho-Educational Battery Part 2, Achievement* (Woodcock & Johnson, 1977). Finally, one independent study compared several popular preschool measures of specific cognitive abilities with selected DAS subtests.

The findings of those studies involving the complete DAS battery are summarized in Table 8-8. Samples are described in the note to that table. If administration sequence was counterbalanced, correlations were computed separately for each sequence and averaged, and the between-test practice effect was estimated and subtracted from the second administration. All correlations have been corrected for differences in dispersion from the DAS standard deviation of 15.

The DAS's GCA score correlates higher with the WPPSI-R Full Scale IQ than with the overall composite from any other battery. The correlations with the McCarthy GCI and the Stanford-Binet Total Composite also are high, in the high .70s to low .80s. The two sets of McCarthy correlations reported are for the two levels of the DAS Preschool Cognitive Battery, using essentially the same sample for both. The upper-level GCA based on 6 subtests correlates slightly higher with the McCarthy GCI than does the lower-level GCA derived from four subtests. GCA correlations with the composite score from the K-ABC and with the Woodcock-Johnson Preschool Skills Cluster are moderately high at about .70.

The DAS's Verbal and Nonverbal cluster scores clearly show the expected pattern of dif-

TABLE 8.8
CORRELATIONS OF DAS COMPOSITE SCORES WITH SCORES FROM OTHER INSTRUMENTS

Sample	Instrument & Scale	DAS Composite Score			Criterion Test	
		GCA	Verbal	Nonverbal	Mean	SD
	Wechsler Preschool & Primary Scale of Intelligence—Revised					
A	Full Scale IQ	.89	.77	.72	101.0	14.7
	Verbal IQ	.76	.74	.51		
	Performance IQ	.83	.62	.75		
	DAS GCA: Mean	98.3				
	SD	12.8				
B	Full Scale IQ	.81	.70	.76	97.9	13.8
	Verbal IQ	.77	.75	.63		
	Performance IQ	.77	.57	.80		
	DAS GCA: Mean	96.5				
	SD	11.8				
C	Stanford-Binet Intelligence Scale: Fourth Edition					
	Total Composite	.77	.74	.69	106.9	13.3
	Verbal	.67	.72	.55		
	Abstract/Visual	.64	.54	.64		
	Quantitative	.48	.44	.51		
	Short-term Memory	.62	.66	.46		
	DAS GCA: Mean	104.5				
	SD	16.4				
	McCarthy Scales of Children's Abilities					
D	General Cognitive Index	.76	—	—	101.9	11.9
	Verbal	.68	—	—		
	Perceptual-Performance	.70	—	—		
	Quantitative	.42	—	—		
	Memory	.56	—	—		
	DAS GCA: Mean	94.7				
	SD	10.7				
E	General Cognitive Index	.82	.84	.55	102.5	12.1
	Verbal	.70	.79	.37		
	Perceptual-Performance	.78	.64	.66		
	Quantitative	.70	.72	.39		
	Memory	.69	.66	.50		
	DAS GCA: Mean	94.8				
	SD	11.9				
B	Kaufman Assessment Battery for Children					
	Mental Processing Composite	.68	.63	.67	101.4	13.7
	Sequential Processing	.74	.62	.75		
	Simultaneous Processing	.49	.50	.45		
	DAS GCA: Mean	96.5				
	SD	11.8				

(*continued*)

TABLE 8.8
(*continued*)

Sample	Instrument & Scale	DAS Composite Score			Criterion Test	
		GCA	Verbal	Nonverbal	Mean	*SD*
B	Woodcock-Johnson Psycho-Educational Battery Preschool Skills Cluster	.67	.56	.67	102.0	13.9
	DAS GCA: Mean	96.5				
	SD	11.8				

Note: The samples are as follows.
A. 62 children aged 4 and 5 collected with the DAS standardization. Counterbalanced administration, 1–6 week interval.
B. 23 children aged 3–6 to 5–11; all DAS cases administered about 10 weeks after the WPPSI-R, K-ABC, and WJ. Data collected as part of an independent study by Dr. Paulette Thomas.
C. 58 children aged 4 and 5 collected with the DAS standardization (no overlap with Sample A). Counterbalanced administration, 1–6 week interval.
D. 49 British children aged 3–4 to 3–7. Counterbalanced administration: median interval 2 weeks.
E. 40 children from Sample D who were aged 3–6 to 3–7.

Data and table copyright © 1990 by The Psychological Corporation, and may not be reproduced without permission. All rights reserved.

ferential correlations with the Verbal and Performance IQ's of the WPPSI-R. Interestingly, the DAS Verbal cluster score correlates about as highly as the GCA with the overall composite scores of both the Stanford–Binet and the McCarthy, suggesting that those latter composites might be more verbally oriented than is the GCA. The DAS Verbal cluster has relatively high correlations (in the .70s) with the Verbal scores from both the Stanford–Binet and the McCarthy as well as the WPPSI-R, indicating that verbal ability is consistently measured by a number of batteries. There is less uniformity, however, in the measurement of nonverbal ability: The DAS Nonverbal cluster correlates in the .70s with the WPPSI-R Performance IQ, but the correlations with the McCarthy Perceptual-Performance Index and the Stanford–Binet Abstract/Visual Reasoning Area Scores are in the .60s.

The pattern of loadings with the K-ABC mental processing scores is rather surprising because the Sequential scale correlates higher with the Nonverbal than the Verbal cluster of the DAS, and the Simultaneous scale correlates slightly higher with the Verbal than the Nonverbal cluster. Larger samples should be collected before any attempt is made to interpret the relationship between these instruments. The correlations with the Woodcock-Johnson Preschool Skills Cluster, an achievement index, likewise show an unex-

pected pattern but are again based on a small sample.

An additional study has been conducted to explore the construct validity of three of the preschool core subtests: Verbal Comprehension, Naming Vocabulary, and Picture Similarities. They were administered along with the *Peabody Picture Vocabulary Test–Revised* (PPVT-R) (Dunn & Dunn, 1981), the *Test for Auditory Comprehension of Language–Revised* (TACL-R) (Carrow-Woolfolk, 1985), and the *Columbia Mental Maturity Scale* (CMMS) (Burgemeister, Blum & Lorge, 1972), a nonverbal measure of abstract reasoning, to 39 children aged 3 to 5 years. All tests were administered on the same day, in counterbalanced order. The goal of the study was to examine the degree of differential validity of the DAS subtests as measures of language comprehension, word knowledge, and nonverbal reasoning. Results are presented in Table 8-9.

The distinction between the verbal and nonverbal measures is well supported by the data. Verbal Comprehension and Naming Vocabulary correlate higher with the PPVT-R and TACL-R than with the CMMS, and the reverse is true for Picture Similarities. Verbal Comprehension appears to be a more global measure of verbal ability than Naming Vocabulary, because it correlates higher than Naming Vocabulary with both the PPVT-R and the TACL-R.

TABLE 8.9
CORRELATIONS OF THREE DAS SUBTESTS WITH MEASURES OF VERBAL AND REASONING ABILITIES

| Test | DAS Subtest or Cluster | | | | | |
	Verbal Compre- hension	Naming Vocabulary	Verbal Cluster	Picture Similarities	*M*	*SD*
PPVT-R	.78	.76	.84	.52	100.8	15.6
TACL-R						
Word Classes	.66	.51	.64	.63		
Grammatical Morphemes	.65	.62	.68	.44		
Elaborated Sentences	.59	.50	.59	.45		
Total	.75	.65	.75	.51	109.1	13.2
CMMS	.60	.54	.61	.70	107.7	11.1

Data and table copyright © 1990 by The Psychological Corporation, and may not be reproduced without permission. All rights reserved.

Note: *N* = 39 children aged 3 to 5 years. All tests were administered on the same day.

AN APPROACH TO INTERPRETATION

Because the goal of the DAS is to measure a broad range of cognitive abilities, users will naturally want to interpret the child's pattern of strengths and weaknesses as shown by the core and diagnostic subtests. The structure of the preschool level of the Cognitive Battery, as revealed by the factor analyses discussed earlier, suggests a recommended approach to such profile analysis. Furthermore, statistical guidelines are available for judging when score differences are statistically significant and therefore interpretable. For convenience, these numerical guidelines are printed on the summary page of the record form (Fig. 8.1). The following section briefly describes this method of interpreting DAS test results.

The GCA score can be viewed as a measure of the conceptual and reasoning abilities that underlie intellectual skill. Because this index does not incorporate measures of such specific abilities as short-term memory, it is a relatively focused score. Furthermore, the correlational studies reviewed earlier suggest that the GCA reflects a good balance of verbal and nonverbal skills, and it can be interpreted as a general index rather than being primarily verbal.

For children taking the upper preschool level of the Cognitive Battery, the Verbal and Nonverbal cluster scores are differentiated measures of, on the one hand, verbal comprehension and expression, and on the other, a composite of abstract reasoning, spatial imagery, and perceptual matching. An initial step in profile analysis is to determine whether the two cluster scores differ significantly from each other, and whether either of them differs from the GCA. (These two questions are not the same, because the Early Number Concepts subtest influences the GCA but does not affect either cluster.) The standard-score differences required for statistical significance at the .05 level are printed on the record form to enable examiners to decide easily whether the child has a reliable strength or weakness in either verbal or nonverbal ability.

Subtest-level profile interpretation is not recommended for subtests that belong to clusters unless there is statistically significant variability among the subtest scores within the cluster. That is, if (for example) the Verbal Comprehension and Naming Vocabulary *T* scores do not differ significantly from each other, then the Verbal cluster score can be viewed as reliably representing the ability that the two subtests share, and the subtests probably should not be further interpreted individually. If significant within-cluster variability does exist, however, the component subtests can be evaluated usefully. The cluster score is still the best measure available of the ability that the subtests have in common, but it is not a sufficient summary of the subtests. Guidelines for detecting significant within-cluster variability are printed on the summary page of the record form as well as in the manual.

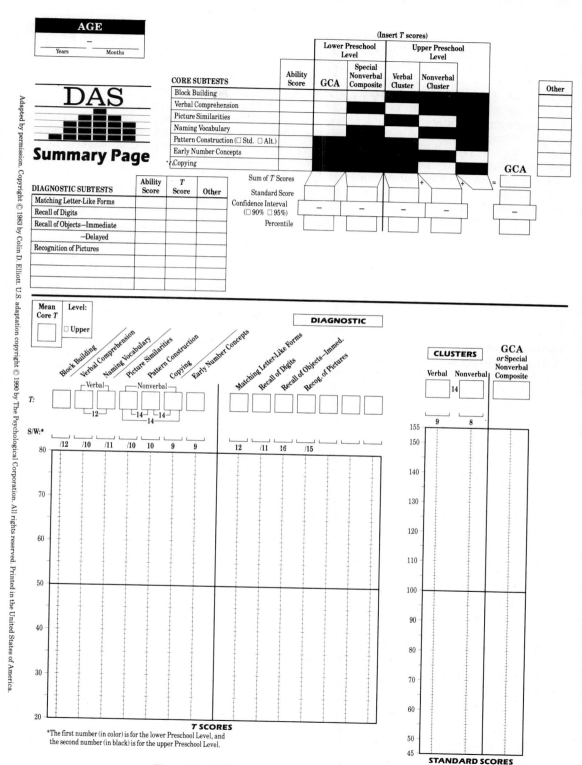

Figure 8.1 *Differential Ability Scales*, summary page.

The next step in analysis is to identify individual subtests as strengths or weakness. The recommended approach is to compare subtest *T* scores with the mean *T* score for the core subtests in the GCA. For convenience, the mean *T* score is provided in the GCA norm table, and the requirements for statistically significant differences (at the .05 level) between subtest scores and the mean *T* score are printed on the record form summary page below each subtest. Thus, the examiner can see easily which subtests are reliably higher or lower than the average level of performance on the GCA. This comparison can be made whether the subtest is a component of a cluster that has significant internal variability, or is a diagnostic subtest. The comparisons also can be made for all subtests at the lower preschool level of the Cognitive Battery.

The critical values given as guidelines for interpretation take into account the reliability of each subtest, whether or not it is a component of the GCA, and the number of simultaneous comparisons being made. Thus, a less reliable subtest must show a larger deviation from the mean than a highly reliable subtest to be interpreted as a strength or weakness, and diagnostic subtests must deviate farther than core subtests of equal reliability to be considered significantly high or low.

In many instances, when there is not significant within-cluster variability, profile analysis will focus on the scores for the clusters and the diagnostic subtests. Because the cluster scores are highly *g* loaded (being made up of core subtests), one might expect them to be similar in magnitude. A statistically significant difference between the Verbal and Nonverbal cluser scores is therefore of interest. To support appropriate interpretation of such a difference, the manual provides information on the frequency of occurence in the standardization sample of between-cluster differences of various sizes. A difference that is statistically significant but common shows that the child is stronger in one area of ability than in the other, but is unlikely to suggest clinical significance. Larger differences that are rare in the general population might warrant more detailed investigation and concern.

The approach to interpreting strengths and weaknesses among the diagnostic subtests is somewhat different. Because the diagnostic subtests do not correlate highly with the general ability factor, there is little reason to expect similarity between the scores on the diagnostic subtests and the GCA. Rather, statistically significant strengths and weaknesses frequently should be found among the diagnostic subtests. Information about the rarity of such differences is not provided because even large deviations from the mean *T* score of the GCA subtests are unlikely to have clinical significance.

CONCLUSION

The DAS development represents an attempt to bring new technical and theoretical perspectives to bear on the assessment of cognitive abilities in children from ages 2½ through adolescence. Technically, its most useful feature might prove to be the facilities it offers for tailoring content to the individual child's ability level to obtain maximum accuracy, while still providing normative interpretation even for out-of-level testing. This feature is of particular importance when working with children who are either very high or very low in ability, for whom more traditional tests might encounter floor or ceiling effects.

From a theoretical point of view, the DAS is unusual in its provision of a composite score structure that becomes more differentiated with age. The DAS overall composite score, the GCA, also is more focused and homogeneous than the total scores of most other batteries. Although much remains to be learned through research about the significance of individual scores, particularly those on the diagnostic subtests, an attempt has been made to provide differentiated components that are readily interpretable.

REFERENCES

Anastasi, A. (1970). On the formation of psychological traits. *American Psychologist, 25*, 899–910.

Berk, R. A. (1984). *Screening and Diagnosis of Children with Learning Disabilities*. Springfield, Illinois: Charles Thomas.

Boehm, A. (1982). Cognitive assessment of preschool children. In C. R. Reynolds, & T. B. Gutkin, (Eds.), *The Handbook of School Psychology*. New York: Wiley.

Bracken, B. A. (1987). Limitations of preschool instruments and standards for minimal levels of technical adequacy. *Journal of Psychoeducational Assessment, 5*, 313–326.

Bureau of the Census. (1986). *Current Population Survey, October 1986*. Washington, D.C.: Author.

Bureau of the Census. (1988). *Current Population Survey, March 1988* (machine-readable data file). Washington, D.C.: Author.

Burgemeister, B. B., Blum, L. H., & Lorge, I. (1972). *Columbia Mental Maturity Scale*. San Antonio, TX: The Psychological Corporation.

Carrow-Woolfolk, E. (1985). *Test for Auditory Comprehension of Language–Revised*. Allen, TX: DLM Teaching Resources.

Dunn, L. M., & Dunn, L. M. (1981). *Peabody Picture Vocabulary Test–Revised*. Circle Pines, MN: American Guidance Service.

Elliott, C. D. (1990). *The Differential Ability Scales*. San Antonio, TX: The Psychological Corporation.

Elliott, C. D., Murray, D. J., & Pearson, L. S. (1979). *The British Ability Scales*. Windsor, England: National Foundation for Educational Research.

Jöreskog, K. G., & Sörbom, D. (1986). *LISTREL VI: Analysis of linear structural relationships by maximum likelihood, instrumental variables, and least squares methods*. Uppsala, Sweden: University of Uppsala.

Kaufman, A. S., & Kaufman, N. L. (1983). *Kaufman Assessment Battery for Children*. Circle Pines, MN: American Guidance Service.

McCarthy, D. (1972). *McCarthy Scales of Children's Abilities*. San Antonio, TX: The Psychological Corporation.

Nunnally, J. C. (1978). *Psychometric Theory (Second Edition)*. New York: McGraw-Hill.

Salvia, J., & Ysseldyke, J. (1985). *Assessment in Special and Remedial Education*. Boston: Houghton Mifflin.

Thorndike, R. L., Hagen, E. P., & Sattler, J. M. (1986a). *The Stanford-Binet Intelligence Scale: Fourth Edition, Guide for Administering and Scoring*. Chicago: Riverside Publishing Company.

Thorndike, R. L., Hagen, E. P., & Sattler, J. M. (1986b). *The Stanford-Binet Intelligence Scale: Fourth Edition*. Chicago: Riverside Publishing Company.

Ulrey, G., & Rogers, S. J. (1982). *Psychological Assessment of Handicapped Infants and Young Children*. New York: Thieme-Stratton.

Wechsler, D. (1989). *Wechsler Preschool and Primary Scale of Intelligence-Revised*. San Antonio, TX: The Psychological Corporation.

Woodcock, R. W., & Johnson, M. B. (1977). *Woodcock-Johnson Psycho-Educational Battery*. Allen, TX: DLM Teaching Resources.

9

The Assessment of Preschool Children with the Kaufman Assessment Battery for Children

RANDY W. KAMPHAUS
ALAN S. KAUFMAN

INTRODUCTION

One of the most important test development goals for the K-ABC was to make the test especially appropriate for use with preschoolers (Kaufman & Kaufman, 1983). There are numerous opinions as to the use of the K-ABC with preschool and other populations (Kaufman, 1984). Hence, the problem for many clinicians who assess the intelligence of preschoolers is deciding whom to believe, or how to best integrate the various opinions. The K-ABC shares a great deal of overlap with existing measures (Kamphaus & Reynolds, 1987), and like many assessment instruments, it has its strengths and weaknesses. Hence, the key question is determining the assessment situation for which the K-ABC is best suited. To complicate things further, the K-ABC differs markedly from many other intelligence tests because it measures two constructs: intelligence and achievement. Fortunately, for researchers and clinicians alike, guidance as to the utility of the K-ABC for particular populations is available in the research literature. This chapter will serve as a compendium of research on the use of the K-ABC with preschoolers that can be used to guide clinical assessment practice.

For those readers who are unfamiliar with the K-ABC, there are a number of sources that provide basic information about the test. The test manuals themselves provide a wealth of pertinent psychometric information (Anastasi, 1984), and provide an excellent introduction to the test. In addition, a recent book by Kamphaus and Reynolds (1987) provides more detailed information for experienced K-ABC users, fostering comprehensive psychometric and clinical interpretation of the battery, and encouraging its intelligent application for preschool and elementary school children.

Following is a brief overview of the structure of the K-ABC, its underlying theory, and the features of the K-ABC that were included specifically for preschoolers. A number of research studies that have used the K-ABC with preschoolers will be explored. Finally, some conclusions regarding the use of the K-ABC with preschoolers will be drawn.

K-ABC STRUCTURE

The K-ABC is a battery of tests, as opposed to an intelligence test only. It is a battery in the sense that it purports to measure two constructs: intelligence and achievement. The achievement scale of the K-ABC will seem familiar to many test users because part of the scale is an analog of the Verbal scale of the WISC-R. Tests of vocabulary, oral arithmetic, and general information appear on the achievement scale in alternate forms to similar subtests on the WISC-R. The authors of the K-ABC are simply asking clinicians to think differently about these types of tasks. Kaufman and Kaufman (1983) believe that these tests are certainly influenced by intelligence, but they are similarly influenced by so-called nonintellective factors such as English language proficiency, acculturation, and quality of school experiences. The K-ABC achievement scale correlates highly with the Verbal scale of the WISC-R, and "behaves" very similarly in clinical evaluations. The K-ABC measures intelligence and achievement constructs with 16 subtests that span the age range of 2½ through 12½ years. The subtests are described here in a similar manner to the descriptions given in the *K-ABC Interpretive Manual* (Kaufman & Kaufman, 1983).

MENTAL PROCESSING SCALE

Sequential Scale Subtests

Hand Movements

Ages 2½ to 12½

The child is required to imitate a series of hand movements in the same sequence as the examiner performed them.

Number Recall

Ages 2½ to 12½

The child must repeat a series of digits in the same sequence as the examiner said them.

Word Order

Ages 4 to 12½

The examinee is required to touch a series of pictures in the same sequence as they were named by the examiner, with more difficult items using a color interference task.

Simultaneous Scale Subtests

Magic Window

Ages 2½ to 4

The child must identify a picture that the examiner exposes by moving it past a narrow slit,
making the picture only partly visible at any one time.

Face Recognition

Ages 2½ to 4

The child must select, from a group photograph, the one or two faces that were exposed briefly in the preceding photograph.

Gestalt Closure

Ages 2½ to 12½

The child must name the object or scene pictured in a partial drawing.

Triangles

Ages 4 to 12½

The child is required to assemble several identical triangles into an abstract pattern that matches a model.

Matrix Analogies

Ages 5 to 12½

The child has to select the picture or abstract design that best completes a visual analogy.

Spatial Memory

Ages 5 to 12½

The child must recall the placement of pictures on a page that was exposed briefly.

Photo Series

Ages 6 to 12½

The child is required to place photographs of an event in chronological order.

Achievement Scale Subtests

Expressive Vocabulary

Ages 2½ to 4

The child has to name the object pictured in a photograph.

Faces and Places

Ages 2½ to 12½

The child must name the well-known person, fictional character, or place pictured in a photograph or illustration.

Arithmetic

Ages 3 to 12½

The child is required to answer a question that requires knowledge of math concepts or the manipulation of numbers.

Riddles

Ages 3 to 12½

The child must name the object or concept described by a list of three characteristics.

Reading/Decoding

Ages 5 to 12½

The child has to name letters and read words.

Reading/Understanding

Ages 7 to 12½

The child has to act out commands given in written sentences.

The K-ABC subtests possess many unique characteristics in comparison to their predecessors. This is not surprising because the most popular IQ tests, such as the WISC-R, have subtests selected prior to World War II. One of the more important criteria for mental processing subtest selection was that the subtest not be too heavily influenced by so-called nonintellective factors. Hence, subtests that have been traditionally included as measures of verbal intelligence are not included on the Mental Processing (intelligence) Scale of the K-ABC. This is a dramatic departure from past practice that has led to both criticism (Sternberg, 1984) and praise (Telzrow, 1984). Even though these efforts to limit cultural influences were taken, minority group reviewers still identified some items on tests—such as Gestalt Closure—as culturally inappropriate. These items were subsequently removed (Kaufman & Kaufman, 1983). The minority group reviewers did not, however, identify any entire mental processing subtests as inappropriate.

This is not to say that the K-ABC mental processing subtests are immune to cultural or linguistic differences. Rather these subtests are *less influenced* by these variables. It is quite likely that a child's performance on tests such as Gestalt Closure and Magic Window is affected by English language proficiency. A young child's level of language development could affect his or her performance on tests such as these. K-ABC subtests also were selected on the basis of their ability to assess sequential and simultaneous processing, a topic discussed next.

K-ABC THEORY

The theory of Sequential and Simultaneous processing underlying the K-ABC represents the Kaufmans' distillation of a variety of theories and research findings. The K-ABC theory does not align itself completely with those of Luria, Das, Sperry, Gazzaniga, Neisser, or others. Rather, it reflects the convergence that has emerged regarding mental processing from numerous laboratory and clinical settings within the domains of neuropsychology, psychobiology, and experimental psychology.

Simultaneous processing refers to the mental ability of the child to integrate input to solve a problem correctly. Simultaneous processing frequently involves spatial, analogic, or organizational abilities (Kaufman & Kaufman, 1983). The Triangles subtest on the K-ABC (an analog of Wechsler's Block Design task) is a prototypical measure of simultaneous processing. To solve these items correctly, one must mentally integrate the components of the design to "see" the whole. Similarly, the Spatial Memory subtest (a novel task) requires the child to memorize the spatial locations of stimuli and then identify the correct locations of the stimuli on a blank grid, but in no particular sequence. Whether the tasks are spatial or analogic in nature, the unifying characteristic of simultaneous processing is the mental synthesis of the stimuli to solve the problem, independent of the sensory modality of the input. As Kaufman and Kamphaus (1984) found, even a verbal test, such as Riddles, can have a substantial loading on the simultaneous factor.

Sequential processing, on the other hand, emphasizes the arrangement of stimuli in serial order for successful problem solving. In every instance, each stimulus is linearly or temporally related to the previous one (Kaufman & Kaufman, 1983) creating a form of serial interdependence. An example is the Word Order subtest, a task that requires the child to point to a series of silhouettes of common objects (e.g., tree, shoe, hand) in the same sequence as the objects were named by the examiner—sometimes following a color-interference activity. In this task, and in other sequential processing subtests, the child has to place the stimuli in their proper order; it is not acceptable merely to reproduce the input without regard to the serial order. Other sequential processing tasks include Hand Movements, which involves visual input and a motor response, and Number Recall, which involves auditory input and a verbal response. As is the case with the simultaneous subtests, neither the modality of presentation nor the mode of response determines the scale placement of a task, but rather it is the mental processing demands of the task that are most salient (Kaufman & Kaufman, 1983).

Of course, no one uses only a single type of information processing to solve problems. These two methods of information processing are constantly interacting, though one approach usually will take a lead role in processing. Which method of processing takes the lead role can change according to the demands of the problem or, as is the case with some individuals, persist across problem type (i.e., forming what Das, Kirby, and Jarman (1979) refer to as habitual modes of processing). In fact, almost any problem can be solved through either method of processing. In most cases, one method is clearly superior to another and when the appropriate method is used to complete a task, superior results are obtained.

An equally important component of the K-ABC is the achievement scale. This scale measures abilities that serve to complement the intelligence scales. The achievement scale contains measures of what have been traditionally identified as verbal intelligence (verbal concept formation and vocabulary), general information, and acquired school skills (arithmetic, letter and word reading, and word and sentence comprehension). Performance on the achievement scale is viewed as an estimate of children's success in the application of their mental processing skills to the acquisition of knowledge from the environment (Kaufman, Kaufman, & Kamphaus, 1985). Knowing all the while that it is not possible to separate completely what you know (achievement) from how well you think (intelligence), the Kaufmans tried to distinguish the two variables better than in the past. For example, the Wechsler intelligence scales and the Peabody Individual Achievement Test (PIAT), although supposedly measures of different constructs, overlap on two subtests: measures of arithmetic ability and general information. Similarly, the Woodcock-Johnson Psycho-Educational Battery includes picture naming and mathematical tasks on *both* its aptitude and achievement portions.

The scale division of the K-ABC is at least partially supported by studies of the factorial validity of the K-ABC for preschoolers. Kaufman and Kamphaus (1984) evaluated the factor structure of the K-ABC using the national standardization sample. These authors concluded that the

K-ABC produces only two meaningful factors at ages 2 and 3; a third (achievement) factor does not emerge until age 4. Moreover, this achievement factor becomes even more distinct shortly after the onset of formal schooling.

For preschool children, between the ages of 2½ and 5 years, factor analysis of all K-ABC subtests (mental processing and achievement) produces readily identifiable sequential and simultaneous factors for ages 2½, 3, 4, and 5 years. The subtests that have their highest loadings on these factors, almost without exception, are the subtests that are included on the Sequential and Simultaneous Processing Scales, respectively (Kaufman & Kamphaus, 1984). Even when a third (achievement) factor is extracted for ages 4 and 5, the sequential and simultaneous dimensions remain robust. Not one mental processing task for children in the 4- to 5-year age range has a factor loading on the achievement factor that is .40 or above. However, the subtests that comprise the K-ABC Achievement Scale all have an average loading above .50 at ages 4 and 5 on the achievement factor. Thus, even though the third factor is only partially supported for preschool children, and is not as robust for 4 and 5 year olds as it is for school-age children, the factor analyses of all K-ABC tasks for preschool children does provide good support for the validity of the sequential-simultaneous dichotomy for all age groups, and the validity of the three-scale structure of the K-ABC for children who have reached their fourth birthday. For children below age 4, the Expressive Vocabulary, Faces & Places, and Riddles subtests are best interpreted as measures of simultaneous processing; in contrast, Arithmetic is primarily a sequential subtest.

The most important finding from factor analyses of the K-ABC is the consistent emergence of sequential and simultaneous factors for preschool children, both normal and exceptional, from a variety of cultures; this result had been well established for elementary school children prior to the development of the K-ABC (Das, Kirby, & Jarman, 1979). Yet, evidence of this processing distinction for preschool youngsters was scarce prior to the research leading up to the construction of the K-ABC (Kaufman et al., 1982). Therefore, support for the theoretical constructs underlying the K-ABC was essential, because of the theoretical underpinnings claimed for the battery, and it was especially invaluable for ages 2½ through

5 years because of the unavailability of previous construct validity data for that age group.

Probably the most effective way to evaluate the validity of the sequential and simultaneous theory-based constructs for preschool children is to explore factor analyses of just the mental processing tasks, a procedure followed by Kaufman and Kamphaus (1984). Their results are presented in Table 9-1 for the preschool age groups. As is evident from this table, the separate processing dimensions emerged for each of the four homogeneous age groups. The subtests labeled sequential processing by Kaufman and Kaufman (1983) loaded much higher on the sequential than the simultaneous factor with only one exception— Hand Movements at age 5. The simultaneous tasks consistently aligned themselves with the factor of the same name, again with only one mild exception—Face Recognition at age 2½. The mean loadings shown in Table 9-1 emphasize the decisive construct validation support for the sequential-simultaneous theoretical dichotomy at the preschool ages. Because Hand Movements is about equally associated with the sequential and simultaneous factors for school-age children (Kaufman & Kamphaus, 1984), the support for the

theoretical structure is actually more impressive for preschool children than it is for youngsters in elementary school.

Table 9-2 reveals that the construct validation support applies equally for preschool boys and girls. This table, constructed from data analyzed by Kamphaus and Kaufman (1986), includes preschoolers in the 2½ to 4 year, 11 month age range; data for 5 year olds was merged with data for elementary school children by Kamphaus and Kaufman (1986). As shown, the sequential and simultaneous subtests behaved exactly as predicted, except for Triangles for the sample of males.

The data for preschool children in Tables 9-1 and 9-2 attest to the robust nature of the processing constructs defining the K-ABC intelligence subtests for preschool children. The fact that Face Recognition (a memory test) loads decisively on the simultaneous factor for boys and girls and for each age group, except 2½, discourages interpretation of the factor pattern from a Jensen (1973) memory-reasoning hierarchy. Similarly, Keith and Dunbar's (1984) alternative interpretation of the K-ABC two-factor solution as verbal memory and nonverbal reasoning seems far less defensible than a mental processing orienta-

TABLE 9.1
VARIMAX-ROTATED FACTOR LOADINGS OF THE K-ABC MENTAL PROCESSING SUBTESTS ON THE SEQUENTIAL AND SIMULTANEOUS FACTORS FOR PRESCHOOL CHILDREN (AGES 2½ TO 5 YEARS)

Subtest	Age in Years									
	2½ (N = 100)		3 (N = 200)		4 (N = 200)		5 (N = 200)		Mean	
	SEQ	SIM	SEQ	SIM	SEQ	SIM	SEQ	SIM	SEQ	SIM
Sequential										
Hand Movements	**60**	12	**57**	19	**62**	25	26	**51**	**51**	27
Number Recall	**59**	**38**	**74**	31	**58**	16	**62**	24	**63**	27
Word Order	—	—	—	—	**69**	32	**89**	34	**79**	33
Simultaneous										
Magic Window	17	**80**	17	**62**	30	**47**	—	—	21	**63**
Face Recognition	**36**	34	23	**37**	24	**50**	—	—	28	**40**
Gestalt Closure	**36**	**48**	20	**50**	14	**79**	22	**63**	23	**60**
Triangles	—	—	—	—	**36**	**47**	21	**74**	28	**60**
Matrix Analogies	—	—	—	—	—	—	32	**54**	32	**54**
Spatial Memory	—	—	—	—	—	—	30	**68**	30	**68**

SEQ = Sequential, SIM = Simultaneous. Decimal points are omitted. Loadings of 35 and above are printed in **bold**.
Data are from Kaufman and Kamphaus (1984).

TABLE 9.2
MEAN VARIMAX-ROTATED FACTOR LOADINGS OF THE K-ABC MENTAL PROCESSING SUBTESTS ON THE SEQUENTIAL AND SIMULTANEOUS FACTORS FOR SEPARATE GROUPS OF MALE AND FEMALE PRESCHOOLERS (AGES 2–6 TO 4–11 YEARS)

Subtest	Girls (N = 250)		Boys (N = 250)	
	Sequential	*Simultaneous*	*Sequential*	*Simultaneous*
Sequential				
Hand Movements	**.69**	.24	**.59**	.29
Number Recall	**.63**	.28	**.63**	.22
Word Order	**.62**	**.35**	**.68**	.33
Simultaneous				
Magic Window	.22	**.55**	.30	**.59**
Face Recognition	.24	**.50**	.24	**.56**
Gestalt Closure	.24	**.68**	.28	**.64**
Triangles	**.37**	**.66**	**.39**	.27

Loadings of .35 and above are printed in **bold**. Data are from Kamphaus and Kaufman (1986).

tion. Keith and Dunbar's approach is arguable for school-age children, but pales in comparison to the sequential-simultaneous model for preschool youngsters. The nonverbal Hand Movements task loads so well on the sequential factor for preschoolers (it is the *best* measure for girls), that the label verbal memory for that factor seems unwarranted. Similarly, the perceptual, nonreasoning Gestalt Closure subtest (a paradigm of simultaneous processing) is the best measure of the simultaneous factor for boys *and* girls, making Keith and Dunbar's (1984) nonverbal reasoning label seem unjustified.

Goldstein and coworkers (1986) factor analyzed data on the K-ABC Mental Processing Composite, along with other instruments, for a small group of 40 three year olds. The two sequential subtests at age 3 loaded together, as did two of the three simultaneous tasks (Magic Window, Gestalt Closure); Face Recognition loaded by itself on a third factor. Magic Window and Gestalt Closure, which both require verbal responses, loaded on a factor that the authors interpreted as verbal ability. Indeed, for a sample as young as age 3 (all subjects were between 35 and 38 months), it is quite possible that vocabulary will be a crucial determinant of performance on Magic Window and Gestalt Closure, as Goldstein and coworkers (1986) suggest.

Kaufman and Kaufman (1983) also state that some mental processing subtest scores might be depressed by poor language development. In the case study of 4-year-old Jack (pp. 214–215), they say "His great deficiency in basic labeling vocabulary is conceivably the cause of his below normal performance on Magic Window, Gestalt Closure, and Word Order. For Jack, these subtests functioned more as vocabulary and achievement tests than as measures of his mental processing skills. Consequently, his standard scores on the Mental Processing scales are likely to be underestimates, perhaps even gross underestimates, of his true intellectual functioning" (p. 215).

Kaufman and Kaufman (1983) suggest that examiners can gain insight into the nature of a young child's language problem by studying his or her responses to Magic Window, Gestalt Closure, Expressive Vocabulary, Riddles, and Faces & Places. Many of the suggestions made by German (1983) concerning the identification of possible word finding disorders are especially helpful, for example, noting a child's tendency to describe words instead of naming them ("that monkey thing" for "banana" on Expressive Vocabulary) or to substitute a wrong card for the correct word ("caw" for "saw" on Magic Window, or "ring" for "key" on Riddles).

Goldstein and coworker's (1986) study is a

good reminder that some K-ABC mental processing subtests might be measuring vocabulary for very young or language disabled children. Their factor analysis does not at all establish that fact, although their results make it clear that verbal ability is certainly involved in the 3 year old's performance in Magic Window and Gestalt Closure. Unfortunately, those researchers excluded the K-ABC Achievement scale from their study, preventing follow-up of Goldstein and coworkers' specific hypotheses about the two simultaneous processing subtests. Also, they (Goldstein, et al.) analyzed 12 variables with only 40 subjects, a ratio of subjects to variables of only about 3 : 1; the desired ratio is 10 : 1 to reduce the influence of chance factors on the obtained factor structure.

FEATURES OF THE K-ABC FOR PRESCHOOLERS

Childlike Materials

The K-ABC differs greatly in its appearance from widely used tests such as the WPPSI. The K-ABC was designed to attract the interest of preschoolers by using colorful and true-to-life materials, not unlike the McCarthy Scales. Tests such as Magic Window, Face Recognition, Expressive Vocabulary, and Arithmetic use either full color artwork or photographs. As Telzrow (1984) notes, "Unlike other measures of preschool intelligence . . . the K-ABC utilizes marvelous color photographs in place of static (and too often unfamiliar) line drawings" (p. 312). On the other hand a number of clinicians feel that although the K-ABC is very attractive to young children, it could benefit from having more manipulatives to pique the interest of young children. Some clinicians bemoan the fact, for example, that the Triangles subtest is not administered until age 4.

Sensitivity to Attention Span

The K-ABC also shows an awareness of increases in attention span with age. Instead of requiring all preschoolers to take the same number of subtests, the number of K-ABC subtests that a child must take begins with 7 at age 2½ and pro-

gresses to 9 at age 3, and 11 at ages 4 and 5. While even 7 subtests can be interminable for a 2½ year old (or for the examiner!), the K-ABC still makes more reasonable requirements of the attention of young children than do other similar tests; even the child-oriented McCarthy Scales includes 17 subtests for 2½ year olds. Additionally, Telzrow (1984) remarks, "The easel format facilitates the direction of attention where it should be—on the child—instead of on myriad boxes, manuals, and test materials. And the child's attention is easy to maintain, given the attractiveness of the materials and their appeal to children" (pp. 311–312).

Clear Instructions

The K-ABC authors took great care to ensure that young children are able to understand the test instructions. This was accomplished by removing potentially difficult verbal concepts from the examiner instructions. Such concepts as "middle" and "after," which Boehm (1971) has found to be difficult for young disadvantaged children, appear commonly in the directions spoken by the examiner when administering various standardized preschool instruments (Kaufman, 1978). Many examiners have asked why, for example, the Photo Series instructions do not use the words *sequence* or *order*. These words were not used because it was felt that they would be difficult for some 6 year olds to understand. In the K-ABC, however, there is an additional "fall back" position if a young child does not understand even these simplified directions.

Sample and Teaching Items

Every Mental Processing Scale subtest begins with an unscored sample item where, if the child fails the item, the examiner can use his or her own words to explain the nature of the task. The examiner then can give the child a second trial and, if necessary, explain the demands of the task to the child again. This same procedure is applied to the teaching items (the first two items administered to the child after the sample item) with the exception that the first trial of each teaching item is scored. Examiners should consult the K-ABC test manuals for more information on the use of sample and teaching items. Some practitioners have expressed concern that the introduction of flexibility into the use of test instructions can adversely affect the reliability of the obtained scores. Although this seems to be a logical conclusion, it does not have any support to date. If this were a problem of significant magnitude the K-ABC would not show such strong evidence of concurrent validity. For the time being it appears that examiners should not be concerned about this as a problem unless they have some difficulties of this nature in their everyday practice with the K-ABC.

Adequate Floor

Kamphaus and Reynolds (1987) note that the K-ABC has a number of easy items for preschoolers that mitigate against the problem of having a number of zero raw scores. They note further that the MCSA is one of the few tests that includes data in the manual to gauge the amount of floor that the test has available. Kamphaus and Reynolds (1987) cite data showing that the K-ABC has more easy subtests at age 2½ than the McCarthy Scales. Nonetheless, there are not enough easy items on the K-ABC to permit evaluation of the profiles of preschool children with abilities that are well below average (Bracken, 1987). Unfortunately, this problem affects virtually all preschool multiscore intelligence batteries.

Telzrow (1984) described several potential uses of the K-ABC with preschoolers. She proposed that the Nonverbal Scale is a needed addition for preschoolers. She noted the deficiencies in other measures, such as the Leiter International Performance Scale and the Hiskey-Nebraska Test of Learning Aptitude. The Nonverbal Scale should be given a trial by those charged with the evaluation of hearing-impaired and severely speech-impaired preschoolers. Telzrow cautioned that some severely language disordered children might be misidentified, possibly as mentally retarded, by many existing measures of intelligence that depend heavily on the assessment of verbal skills and knowledge.

Telzrow also argued that the K-ABC offers two advantages in the identification of preschool gifted children. One of these advantages is the availability of an achievement scale that is normed down to age 2½. She noted that academic achievement has been proposed as an important measure of early academic potential and that the K-ABC is unusual in that it possesses one of the few achievement scales that is appropriate for this age group. Furthermore, the K-ABC out-of-level norms allow the examiner to administer tests designed for school-age children (such as Reading/Decoding) to 4 year olds. The interested reader can find other advice regarding the use of the K-ABC with preschoolers in the Telzrow article.

INTERPRETATION

Practical Aspects

The K-ABC adopts and expands on the interpretive system first introduced in Kaufman's (1979) text, *Intelligent Testing with the WISC-R*. This system has proven to be well received by the assessment community. Aspects of the approach have even been incorporated into other types of tests, such as the *Vineland Adaptive Behavior Scales*. Anastasi (1982) writes of Kaufman's book

> [T]he most important feature of [Kaufman's] approach is that it calls for individualized interpretation of test performance, in contrast to the uniform application of any one type of pattern analysis. . . . The basic approach described by Kaufman undoubtedly represents a major contribution to the clinical use of intelligence tests. (p. 466)

Initially, the K-ABC interpretive system departs from others by changing the interpretive labels given different levels of performance. These labels are shown in Table 9-3. They differ considerably from older scales by doing away with descriptions of performance that sound like diagnoses. The description "mentally deficient," for instance, that is used by some other tests sounds similar to the diagnosis of mental retardation. Using this label places too much emphasis on the IQ as a determinant in the diagnosis of mental retardation, when in fact intelligence deficits are only one aspect of the diagnosis, not the least of which is the determination of adaptive behavior deficits.

After describing the level of performance of the child on the K-ABC scales the examiner then follows the various steps given in the K-ABC in-

TABLE 9.3
K-ABC DESCRIPTIVE CATEGORIES

Standard Score Range	Descriptive Category
69 and below	Lower Extreme
70 to 79	Well Below Average
80 to 89	Below Average
90 to 109	Average
110 to 119	Above Average
120 to 129	Well Above Average
130 and above	Upper Extreme

terpretive manual, which are presented in adapted form as the following:

Step 1. Try to interpret the significant strengths and weaknesses from the vantage point of the sequential-simultaneous model.

Step 2. Select a significant strength or weakness. Write down all shared abilities and influences affecting performance on this subtest.

Step 3. Evaluate, one by one, the merits of each ability and influence that was written down.

Step 4. Repeat steps 3 and 4 for every other significant strength and weakness, taking each in turn.

Step 5. Identify the most appropriate hypotheses about strengths and weaknesses by integrating K-ABC data with background information, test behaviors, and scores on other tests.

The various tables for using the steps are given in the K-ABC interpretive manual (Kaufman & Kaufman, 1983). Essentially these are virtually the same steps to interpretation that many psychologists have been taught to use through the Kaufman's (1979) book on the WISC-R. Consequently, there is considerable transfer of training from WISC-R to K-ABC interpretation for many practitioners.

Probably the greatest nuance of the K-ABC interpretive model is the theory itself. The simultaneous-sequential model might seem a little forboding to new users. Fortunately, the K-ABC manuals provide extensive explanations of these two constructs. In addition, because of the multisubtest format of the K-ABC, it is possible that a number of clinicians are able to apply their existing theoretical knowledge to interpretation of

the K-ABC through profile analysis and recategorizations of K-ABC subtests. This notion of applying alternate theories also is entirely consistent with Kaufman's (1979) popular approach to intelligence test interpretation.

RELIABILITY AND VALIDITY OF THE K-ABC FOR PRESCHOOLERS

Reliability

Although internal consistency coefficients are reported in many test manuals, including the K-ABC, the primary purpose for computing these coefficients is that they serve as good estimates of stability coefficients, which are the coefficients of most interest to practitioners. Test–retest or stability coefficients are also reported in the K-ABC interpretive manual (Kaufman & Kaufman, 1983). These coefficients generally are in the middle–80s for the Mental Processing scales for preschool children. The stability coefficients generally are higher (in the middle–90s) for the Achievement scale. This is an interesting finding in that the K-ABC Achievement scale is very similar to traditional measures of verbal intelligence (Kamphaus & Reynolds, 1987). Furthermore, the K-ABC Achievement scale is the best predictor of future achievement on the battery. Because prediction of future achievement is one of the central purposes of preschool intelligence testing, it is fortuitous for practitioners that the best predictor on the K-ABC clearly possesses the best reliability.

In fact, the Achievement scale of the K-ABC yields comparable or higher stability coefficients at the preschool level than tests such as the Binet IV, WPPSI, and MSCA (see Bracken, 1987, for a review of the stability of these other scales and the Mental Processing scales of the K-ABC).

Relationship of the K-ABC to Other Tests

The K-ABC is predictably a little tougher than measures possessing older normative samples. The term "predictably" is used because of the wealth of data to show that norms for intelligence tests get tougher (yield lower standard scores for the same raw scores) with every new norming. In an exhaustive study, Flynn (1984) analyzed changes in the difficulty of norms from 1932 to 1978, and concluded that, on the average, intelligence test norms get about 3 standard score points tougher with each decade. These findings are remarkably consistent with those of Doppelt and Kaufman (1977) and Kaufman (1979) who found the WISC-R IQ's to be about 6 points lower than WISC IQ's. Similar results were obtained when comparing the Wechsler Adult Intelligence Scale (WAIS) to the WAIS-R (Wechsler, 1981).

It is striking to observe how aptly Flynn's (1984) rule of thumb applies to the relationship between the K-ABC norms and norms for the WISC-R, the Binet L-M, and Binet IV (Kamphaus & Reynolds, 1987). Kamphaus and Reynolds (1987) found the K-ABC norms to be about two points lower than those for the WISC-R and 1972 Binet. This is consistent with Flynn's prediction because these two measures were normed about a decade prior to the K-ABC. The Binet IV norms, however, are strikingly similar to those for the K-ABC. This too is predictable from Flynn's data because these two measures were normed in the same era.

One of the few studies comparing the K-ABC with another test for a normal sample of preschoolers was conducted by Lampley and Rust (1986). They administered the K-ABC and Slosson Intelligence Test to a group of 50 preschoolers between the ages of 2½ and 4. In this study, the K-ABC Mental Processing Composite (MPC) (M = 108.7) was predictably lower than the Slosson (M = 123.2). Although the Slosson Intelligence Test lacks the more sophisticated psychometric properties of the K-ABC, it does appear to produce lawful differences (i.e., higher scores) in at least this one investigation.

This trend for the K-ABC to produce lower scores than older measures is, however, moderated by ethnic and linguistic differences. One of the few studies comparing different ethnic groups of preschoolers that sheds some light on this issue was conducted by Valencia (1984). In this study a group of 42 Mexican-American children from a Head Start program was administered the K-ABC and WPPSI in counterbalanced fashion. The K-ABC mean (104.1) was slightly higher than the WPPSI mean (102.4). Although for most children administered these two tests it would be expected that the K-ABC would give lower scores than the WPPSI by almost 5 points (the WPPSI was

normed about 15 years before the K-ABC) this trend is reversed for a sample of Mexican-American children. On the other hand, this finding is consistent with research showing that the K-ABC produces smaller ethnic group differences (Kaufman & Kaufman, 1983). It is reasonable to expect a linguistically different population such as the one used in the Valencia (1984) investigation to score higher on the K-ABC than on the WPPSI because the WPPSI requires more English language proficiency. It appears that the tendency for more modern tests, such as the K-ABC, to produce lower scores holds—except when cultural variables such as dominant primary language exert an influence.

Predictive Validity

The K-ABC Achievement scale, like the Verbal scale of the WISC-R, is the best predictor of subsequent school achievement (Kamphaus & Reynolds, 1987). This finding is an important reminder to psychologists that measures of achievement, basic concepts, readiness skills, and related measures are likely to be better predictors of future school achievement than intelligence measures. This conclusion implies that using only an intelligence test to assess a preschooler portrays an inadequate picture of a child. Preschool assessment batteries should include measures such as the K-ABC Achievement scale and related measures to better understand the child's ''at-risk'' status. Because of the strong predictive validity of the Achievement scale it is recommended that it be administered routinely when assessing preschoolers. This is consistent with the recommendations of Kaufman and Kaufman (1983) that the Achievement scale always be administered in conjunction with the Mental Processing scales of the K-ABC.

USE OF THE K-ABC WITH ''AT-RISK'' PRESCHOOLERS

Lyon and Smith (1986) assessed the long-term stability of the K-ABC with at-risk preschoolers. The K-ABC was administered at a 9-month interval to 53 children between the ages of 49 and 73 months. The stability coefficients ranged from .83 for the MPC to .73 for the Sequential scale.

The coefficient was .76 for the Simultaneous scale and .82 for the Achievement scale. Although these results support the overall accuracy of the K-ABC, an equally useful finding for practitioners was the level of gain over this time period. The Simultaneous scale was the big gainer (87.9 on test 1 to 97.2 on test 2) which is highly consistent with the test–retest data presented in the K-ABC *Interpretive Manual* (Kaufman & Kaufman, 1983). The Sequential and Achievement scales each improved by about 3 points. The MPC improved by about 8 points over the 9-month time period.

Other research with at-risk preschoolers compares the K-ABC to other popular tests. Lyon and Smith (1986) compared the K-ABC, Stanford-Binet, Form L-M, and MSCA for a group of 72 children referred for early intervention. The children ranged in age from 49 to 73 months. The correlation between the K-ABC and the other tests was moderate: .59 with the GCI and .45 with the Binet IQ. The correlation between the K-ABC Achievement scale and the GCI was also .59. The correlation between the Achievement scale and the Binet IQ, however, was considerably higher (.71). This strong relationship between achievement and the Binet Form L-M is consistent with early research on the K-ABC (Kaufman & Kaufman, 1983). In this study the K-ABC MPC (M = 85.9) and McCarthy GCI were highly consistent (M = 86.3). The Binet mean IQ of 82.4 was somewhat lower.

Bing and Bing (1985) compared the K-ABC and PPVT-R for a group of predominantly Black children enrolled in a Head Start program. Given our current knowledge of the K-ABC regarding reduced differences in the scores earned by Blacks and Whites, we would expect the PPVT-R scores to be lower than the K-ABC scores. This discrepancy would be expected despite the fact that these two tests were normed within five years of each other. These predictions were in fact realized. The PPVT-R means of 75.0 for Form L and 73.5 for Form M were significantly lower than the K-ABC MPC mean of 90.2 and the Achievement scale mean of 86.8. The correlations between the MPC and PPVT-R Forms L and M were .50 and .58, respectively. The correlations between the Achievement scale and PPVT-R were considerably higher: .76 and .70, respectively. A similar coefficient between the K-ABC Achievement Scale and PPVT-R (r = .66) was reported by

Mcloughlin and Ellison (1984) for 32 nonreferred, White, middle class 3 and 4 year olds.

Lyon, Smith, and Klass (1986) used the K-ABC to differentiate normal from high-risk preschoolers. They compared the performance of 49 normal and 44 high-risk children between the ages of 45 and 70 months. They found all of the K-ABC Global scales to be excellent discriminators between the normal and high-risk groups. On every scale the high-risk group mean was below average. The mean scores for this group ranged from a low of 89.3 on the MPC to a high of 92.5 on the Achievement scale. The means for the normal group were considerably higher, ranging from 107.0 on the Simultaneous scale to 111.8 on the Achievement scale. The mean scores for the normal group raise the question as to how "normal" this group is. Whether or not the normal sample is well matched to the high-risk sample does not detract, however, from the ability of the K-ABC to discriminate the high-risk group; their means were still well below the national norm.

In a similar fashion, Smith and Lyon (1987) compared the McCarthy and K-ABC performance of groups of repeating and nonrepeating preschoolers. One group had been recommended for kindergarten (N = 27) and a second group of children had been recommended for retention in the preschool program (N = 13). Both the K-ABC and the McCarthy scores discriminated between the two groups. The mean GCI for the repeaters was 67.0, whereas for the nonrepeaters the mean GCI was 86.5. In parallel fashion the MPC for the repeaters was 76.2 as opposed to 91.4 for the nonrepeaters. All of the K-ABC scales discriminated between the two groups. The mean scores for the repeaters were uniformly lower (Sequential M = 80.3, Simultaneous M = 77.5, Achievement M = 80.5) than for the nonrepeaters (Sequential M = 91.3, Simultaneous M = 93.4, and Achievement M = 94.7). In this study the McCarthy scores are lower for both the repeater and nonrepeater groups. This finding is consistent with other research showing that the McCarthy tends to produce lower scores than other tests (Sattler, 1982).

Ricciardi and Voelker (1987) conducted a thorough study of the K-ABC with four groups of preschoolers: normals (N = 15), language impaired (N = 14), behavior problems (N = 17), and language impaired-behavior problems

(N = 13). As was the case in the Smith and Lyon (1987) investigation the K-ABC Global scales clearly differentiated between the handicapped and normal samples. On the MPC the normal group had a mean of 104.0, which was substantially higher than the means for the language impaired group (83.1), the behavior problem group (95.3), and the language impairment plus behavior problem group (77.0). Among other interesting trends in this study was the finding that the children with behavior problems consistently performed better than the other two handicapped samples. Next in line was the language impaired sample. Apparently, language impairment has a more detrimental impact on intelligence than does the presence of behavior problems. The most devastating impact, however, was caused by the presence of the dual handicaps of both language and behavior problems; this group scored lower than both samples with singular handicapping conditions.

All of these early studies reinforce our opinion that the K-ABC is a useful tool for diagnostic evaluations of preschoolers. All K-ABC scales appear capable of differentiating normal children from handicapped and high-risk groups of preschoolers.

IMPLICATIONS FOR PRACTITIONERS

This chapter has presented a number of findings regarding the use of the K-ABC with preschoolers. To ensure that the implications of these findings are clear, the numerous practical implications of K-ABC research will be outlined in this section.

Generally speaking the K-ABC produces lower than average scores for preschool children who are at risk for learning problems in school. In this regard the K-ABC serves the same identification purpose as other intelligence tests.

The K-ABC has some floor problems that are, in large part, because of having new subtests introduced at a variety of ages. This problem is shared with a number of preschool intelligence tests. As a result, K-ABC users have to be wary of obtaining too many zero raw scores when assessing handicapped children. Because populations vary so greatly, it is recommended that examiners try the K-ABC with their population and see if this is a frequent or infrequent problem. The

K-ABC has plenty of difficulty to challenge precocious preschoolers, especially beginning at age $4\frac{1}{2}$ where tests such as Reading/Decoding can be administered via the out-of-level norms procedure.

Many people (Kaufman & Kaufman, 1983; Bracken, 1985; Kamphaus & Reynolds, 1987) have concluded that the K-ABC measures verbal expression to a lesser extent than tests such as the Wechsler scales or the Binet. In fact, none of the K-ABC subtests, including those on the Achievement scale, require a multiple word response. Nevertheless, there is an increasing body of data that challenges this conclusion. Data from recent studies reported in the *Stanford-Binet Fourth Edition Technical Manual* (Thorndike, Hagen, & Sattler, 1986), for example, show a great deal of overlap in variance between the Verbal scale of the WISC-R, the Verbal Reasoning scale of the Binet IV, and the *Achievement* scale of the K-ABC. All of the intercorrelations of these "verbal" scales are well above .70 with some being in the high 80s. These correlations are very high, in some cases as high as the reliabilities of the tests allow, and suggest that appearances might be illusory. Despite the fact that K-ABC Achievement subtests require only one-word or a few word responses, the wealth of data (including data on non-English speakers as reported by Kamphaus & Reynolds, 1987) imply that the Achievement scale might—like other verbal scales of intelligence— serve as a screener for language abilities. Based on this screening, further evaluation with a language assessment battery might be advised. A local trial of the test would help determine if these data apply.

The K-ABC norms (as well as the Binet IV norms) might provide a more modern and accurate norming standard than intelligence tests normed in the 1970s or earlier. It should be expected that, on the average, K-ABC scores should be a few standard score points lower than scores yielded by tests normed in the 1970s.

The K-ABC Nonverbal scale has proven quite useful with school-age populations of hearing impaired children (Kamphaus & Reynolds, 1987). To date, no studies have been reported on the use of this scale with preschoolers at age 4. This scale might be of use to individuals who are working with children with limited English proficiency, or hearing-impaired, or language-impaired children.

Although some factorial validity has been established for the applicability of the K-ABC Sequential and Simultaneous processing model with preschoolers, there is a need for further research to determine the utility of this model for the understanding of preschool children's cognitive performance. Much research remains to be done with preschoolers.

CONCLUSIONS

Although on the face of it the K-ABC is very different from its predecessors regarding its theoretical underpinnings, its typical results are quite similar to those found on other popular intelligence tests. In other words, in diagnostic evaluations there usually is not going to be dramatic differences between K-ABC scores and those found on other intelligence tests.

This similarity between the K-ABC and other tests does, however, depend on certain child characteristics. If a child is linguistically different, there are some data to suggest that the Mental Processing scales of the K-ABC will yield higher scores than many other intelligence measures. The K-ABC tends to assess intelligence in a manner that is less dependent on English language capability.

The K-ABC has a number of characteristics to recommend its use with preschoolers. If additional research data are as promising as the early results, then the K-ABC will continue to be a widely accepted measure of preschool intelligence. At present, the K-ABC is among the most frequently used tests in handicapped children's early education programs (HCEEP) (Lehr, Ysseldyke, & Thurlow, 1987), and in programs for preschool children with learning disabilities (Esterly & Griffin, 1987). Of the instruments used by five or more HCEEP demonstration projects, the K-ABC was one of only three instruments (the McCarthy and Vineland were the others) to be rated by Lehr and coworkers as possessing technical adequacy in all five selected areas pertaining to norms, reliability, and validity. Interestingly, the K-ABC was one of 12 tests used in various preschool programs for children with learning disabilities (Easterly & Griffin, 1987), but it was the only multisubtest intelligence test on the list (the WPPSI and McCarthy were excluded).

As is the case with other tests, whether or not the K-ABC will be useful in a particular setting depends on a variety of factors, in addition to its relative strengths and weaknesses noted in this chapter. One factor that looms large is the training of the test users. Even if the K-ABC is technically superior to another test, if the clinician knows a great deal about the other test and virtually nothing about the K-ABC then there is considerable opportunity to do the child being evaluated a disservice by misinterpreting the K-ABC. A number of clinicians have approached the problem of a lack of experience with the K-ABC by using the K-ABC in conjunction with other measures, such as the WPPSI or WISC-R, that they typically use. This is an excellent practice because it allows the user adequate time to learn about the K-ABC using the WPPSI or WISC-R. This seems to be particularly appropriate given the data that showed that the K-ABC and WISC-R possess substantial overlap. Fortunately, enough is now known about the K-ABC that chapters such as this one and works such as that by Kamphaus and Reynolds (1987) can supplement practical experience with research findings for a variety of special populations. This clinical trial approach to using the K-ABC has served many professionals well and should prove to be a valuable strategy for other diagnosticians.

REFERENCES

Anastasi, A. (1982). *Psychological Testing* (5th ed.). New York: Macmillan.

Anastasi, A. (1984). The K-ABC in historical and contemporary perspective. *Journal of Special Education*, *18*, 357–366.

Bing, S. B., & Bing, J. R. (1985). Comparison of the K-ABC and PPVT-R with head start children. *Psychology in the Schools*, *22*, 245–249.

Boehm, A. E. (1971). *Manual for the Boehm Test of Basic Concepts*. San Antonio, TX: The Psychological Corporation.

Bracken, B. A. (1985). A critical review of the Kaufman Assessment Battery for Children. *School Psychology Review*, *14*, 21–36.

Bracken, B. A. (1987). Limitations of preschool instruments and standards for minimal levels of technical adequacy. *Journal of Psychoeducational Assessment*, *5*, 313–326.

Das, J. P., Kirby, J. R., & Jarman, R. F. (1979). Simultaneous and successive processes, language and mental abilities. *Canadian Psychological Review*, *20*, 1–11.

Doppelt, J. E., & Kaufman, A. S. (1977). Estimation of

the differences between WISC-R and WISC IQ's. *Educational and Psychological Measurement, 37,* 417–424.

Esterly, D. L., & Griffin, H. C. (1987). Preschool programs for children with learning disabilities. *Journal of Learning Disabilities, 20,* 571–573.

Flynn, J. R. (1984). The mean IQ of Americans: Massive gains 1932 to 1978. *Psychologidal Bulletin, 95,* 29–51.

German, D. (1983). Analysis of word finding disorders on the Kaufman Assessment Battery for Children (K-ABC). *Journal of Psychoeducational Assessment, 1,* 121–133.

Goldstein, D. J., Smith, K. B., & Waldrep, E. E. (1986). Factor analytic study of the Kaufman Assessment Battery for Children. *Journal of Clinical Psychology, 42,* 890–894.

Jensen, A. R. (1973). Level I and level II abilities in three ethnic groups. *American Educational Research Journal, 10,* 263–276.

Kamphaus, R. W., & Kaufman, A. S. (1986). Factor analysis of the Kaufman Assessment Battery for Children (K-ABC) for separate groups of boys and girls. *Journal of Clinical Child Psychology, 3,* 210–213.

Kamphaus, R. W., & Reynolds, C. R. (1987). *Clinical and research applications of the K-ABC.* Circle Pines, MN: American Guidance Service.

Kaufman, A. S. (1984). K-ABC and controversy. *The Journal of Special Education, 18,* 409–444.

Kaufman, A. S. (1979). *Intelligent testing with the WISC-R.* New York: John Wiley & Sons.

Kaufman, A. S. (1978). The importance of basic concepts in the individual assessment of preschool children. *Journal of School Psychology, 16,* 207–211.

Kaufman, A. S., & Kamphaus, R. W. (1984). Factor analysis of the Kaufman Assessment Battery for Children (K-ABC) for ages 2½ through 12½ years. *Journal of Educational Psychology, 76,* 623–637.

Kaufman, A. S., & Kaufman, N. L. (1983). *Interpretive manual for the Kaufman Assessment Battery for Children.* Circle Pines, MN: American Guidance Service.

Kaufman, A. S., Kaufman, N. L., & Kamphaus, R. W. (1985). The Kaufman Assessment Battery for Children (K-ABC). In C. S. Newmark (Ed.), *Major Psychological Assessment Instruments.* Newton, MA: Allyn & Bacon.

Kaufman, A. S., Kaufman, N. L., Kamphaus, R. W., & Naglieri, J. A. (1982). Sequential and simultaneous factors at ages 3–12½: Developmental changes in neuropsychological dimensions. *Clinical Neuropsychology, 4,* 74–81.

Keith, T. Z., & Dunbar, S. B. (1984). Hierarchical factor analysis of the K-ABC: Testing alternate models. *The Journal of Special Education, 18,* 367–375.

Lampley, D. A., & Rust, J. O. (1986). Validation of the Kaufman Assessment Battery for Children with a sample of preschool children. *Psychology in the Schools, 23,* 131–137.

Lehr, C. A., Ysseldyke, J. E., & Thurlow, M. L. (1987). Assessment practices in model early childhood special education programs. *Psychology in the Schools, 24,* 390–399.

Lyon, M. A., & Smith, D. K. (1986). A comparison of at-risk preschool children's performance on the K-ABC, McCarthy Scales, and Stanford-Binet. *Journal of Psychoeducational Assessment, 4,* 35–43.

Lyon, M. A., Smith, D. K., & Klass, P. D. (1986, April). A comparison of K-ABC performance between at-risk and normal preschoolers. Paper presented at the meeting of the National Association of School Psychologists, Hollywood, FL.

Mcloughlin, C. S., & Ellison, C. L. (1984). Comparison of scores for normal preschool children on the Peabody Picture Vocabulary Test—Revised and the Achievement Scales of the Kaufman Assessment Battery for Children. *Psychological Reports, 55,* 107–114.

Reynolds, C. R. (1982). Neuropsychological assessment in education: A caution. *Journal of Research and Development in Education, 15,* 76–79.

Ricciardi, P. W. R., & Voelker, S. L. (1987). Measuring cognitive skills of language impaired preschoolers. Paper presented at the meeting of the American Psychological Association, New York, NY.

Sattler, J. M. (1982). *Assessment of Children's Intelligence and Special Abilities* (2nd ed.). Boston: Allyn & Bacon.

Smith, D. K., & Lyon, M. A. (1987, March). K-ABC/McCarthy performance for repeating and nonrepeating preschoolers. Paper presented at the meeting of the National Association of School Psychologists, New Orleans, LA.

Starr, D. (1983). Split-brain I.Q. test. *Omni, 5,* 35.

Sternberg, R. J. (1984). The Kaufman Assessment Battery for Children: An information processing analysis and critique. *The Journal of Special Education, 18(3),* 269–279.

Telzrow, C. F. (1984). Practical applications of the K-ABC in the identification of handicapped preschoolers. *The Journal of Special Education, 18,* 311–324.

Thorndike, R. L., Hagen, E. C., & Sattler, J. M. (1986). *Technical manual for the Stanford-Binet Intelligence Scale: Fourth Edition.* Chicago: Riverside.

Valencia, R. R. (1984). Concurrent validity of the Kaufman Assessment Battery for children in a sample of Mexican-American children. *Educational and Psychological Measurement, 44,* 365–371.

Wechsler, D. (1981). *Manual for the Wechsler Adult Intelligence Scale-Revised.* San Antonio: The Psychological Corporation.

10

Assessment of Adaptive Behavior

PATTI L. HARRISON

Does Jessie eat with a spoon? Is Mickey toilet trained? Does Jonathan open a door on his own? Does Betsy play games with her friends? Does Antonia speak in full sentences? These questions represent concerns about adaptive behavior, or children's ability to take care of themselves and get along with others. Assessment of adaptive behavior is an extremely important aspect of multidimensional assessment and development of interventions for preschool children. The purpose of this chapter is to explore the uses of adaptive behavior assessment for diagnosing possible handicaps and developmental problems of preschoolers and planning effective home, family, and school programs. Major adaptive behavior scales, as well as informal assessment techniques, are reviewed. Because adaptive behavior assessment traditionally has been problematic and controversial, some of the issues facing professionals who assess adaptive behavior are discussed.

THE DEFINITION OF ADAPTIVE BEHAVIOR

According to the American Association on Mental Deficiency (AAMD), adaptive behavior is defined as "the effectiveness or degree with which individuals meet the standards of personal independence and social responsibility expected for age and cultural group" (Grossman, 1983, p. 1). The AAMD indicates that deficits in adaptive behavior, in addition to subaverage intellectual functioning, are essential requirements for a classification of mental retardation. Deficits in adaptive behavior are not limited to mentally retarded individuals (to be discussed later in this chapter). The assessment of adaptive behavior for individuals with other handicapping conditions, such as emotional disturbance and learning disabilities, is necessary to determine the effects of the handicaps on daily functioning (Harrison, 1984, 1985; Holman & Bruininks, 1985; Sparrow et al., 1984a, 1984b).

Adaptive behavior has been incorporated into the broader concept of *social competence*. Greenspan (1979, 1981), for instance, outlined a model of social competence consisting of the components of physical competence, adaptive intelligence, and socioemotional adaptation. The component of adaptive intelligence includes conceptual, practical, and social intelligence. Greenspan's descriptions of practical and social intelligence are similar to the AAMD definition of adaptive behavior. In a somewhat simpler model of social competence, Gresham and Elliot (1987) suggested that social competence includes two interrelated dimensions, adaptive behavior and social skills.

Many have argued that adaptive behavior is not as clearly defined as other constructs assessed for children, for instance, intelligence and achievement (Clausen, 1972; Gresham & Elliot, 1987; Zigler et al., 1984). Others have pointed out the many *consistencies* in definitions of adaptive behavior and the close correspondence among the structures of different adaptive behavior scales (Holman & Bruininks, 1985; Kamphaus, 1987; Meyers et al., 1979; Reschly, 1982). Kamphaus (1987) argued that definitions of adaptive behavior have the homogenizing influence of the AAMD definition of adaptive behavior. Other constructs, such as intelligence, do not have the support of a broad unifying definition such as the AAMD's definition of adaptive behavior. Common elements in definitions and measures of adaptive behavior include the developmental nature of the construct, the basic dimensions of adaptive behavior, and emphasis on cultural influences, situational specificity, and performance rather than ability (Bruininks, Thurlow, & Gilman, 1987; Holman & Bruininks, 1985; Kamphaus, 1987; Meyers et al., 1979; Reschly, 1982; Witt & Martens, 1984).

Developmental Nature

Most definitions indicate that adaptive behavior is developmental in nature, increasing in complexity as children grow older. According to Grossman (1983), the infancy and early childhood periods emphasize sensorimotor, communication, self-help, and socialization skills. Later childhood and adolescence are characterized by the acquisition of basic academic skills necessary for daily life activities, judgement and reasoning in the mastery of the environment, and social skills. Vocational and social skills are required for late adolescents and adults.

Basic Dimensions

Definitions and measures of adaptive behavior typically include two major components: in-

dependent or personal functioning and social responsibility. Furthermore, analysis of adaptive behavior scales indicates that the items typically assess similar domains of adaptive behavior (Holman & Bruininks, 1985; Kamphaus, 1987; Reschly, 1982). For preschool children, the following domains are routinely assessed:

Self-help skills (e.g., eating, toileting, dressing, hygiene)
Interpersonal skills (e.g., interacting with others, cooperating, playing)
Cognitive/communication skills (e.g., expressive and receptive language skills, basic reading and writing)
Motor skills (e.g., fine and gross motor)

For older children, adolescents, and adults, several new domains are added:

Vocational responsibility (e.g., job-related skills)
Domestic skills (e.g., food preparation, housekeeping)
Community skills (e.g., telephone, money, safety skills)

Cultural Influences

In various conceptualizations of adaptive behavior, the construct is recognized as being dependent on the expectations of the culture to which a person belongs. Undoubtedly, different cultures have different expectations for the behavior of children. As indicated by Leland (1983), it is perfectly acceptable for children to urinate in public in some countries. In other countries, this practice is unacceptable. There also are different expectations for children within the different subcultures of the same country. For example, different subcultures within the United States place different amounts of emphasis on dress, hygiene, and other variables related to adaptive behavior.

Situational Specificity

Children's adaptive behavior is very much influenced by the demands of settings in which they are expected to exhibit the behavior. Adaptation occurs through interactions with significant people in children's environments (Horn & Fuchs, 1987; Leland, 1983). Children's development of adaptive behavior is influenced by the expectations of the significant others and the situations in which they must interact with others. For example, the child in a one-child family might not have acquired the adaptive behavior of taking turns. When this child enters a preschool program, he or she might be expected to acquire this behavior.

Performance Versus Ability

Adaptive behavior is defined as the *performance* of daily activities required for personal and social self-sufficiency. An implicit assumption is that children must have the *ability* to perform daily activities. However, the concept of adaptive behavior stresses the observable performance of these activities and places less emphasis on the ability necessary to perform them. Adaptive behavior measures typically focus on what children *usually* do, rather than what they are capable of doing, and adaptive behavior is considered to be deficient if children have a skill but do not routinely perform it. For example, a child might be able to tie his or her shoes, but does not routinely do so, perhaps because he or she does not want to or prefers a parent to do it. This emphasis on performance, not ability, implies that the concept of adaptive behavior includes the *motivation* for performing activities. This emphasis also requires a method of assessment that measures what children do daily, rather than what they can do. Most adaptive behavior scales utilize a *third-party informant* approach and individuals familiar with children's daily activities are questioned about the performance.

THE IMPORTANCE OF ADAPTIVE BEHAVIOR ASSESSMENT FOR PRESCHOOL CHILDREN

The ability to take care of oneself and get along with others represents important goals for everyone, regardless of age or handicapping condition. Traditionally, adaptive behavior assessment was emphasized because of the needs for nonbiased assessment and training of mentally retarded individuals. Nonbiased assessment and training obviously have implications for preschool children, but typically have been focused on

school-age children and adults. The developmental characteristics and needs of preschool children are quite different from those of older individuals and the assessment of adaptive behavior takes on new and increased importance during the preschool years. In this section of the chapter, the traditional importance for adaptive behavior assessment and the specific importance of adaptive behavior assessment for preschool children are discussed.

Traditional Importance

Adaptive behavior assessment has its roots in the field of mental retardation. In the past 20 years, adaptive behavior assessment has played an increasingly important role in the definition and treatment of mental retardation for two primary reasons (Meyers et al., 1979; Witt & Martens, 1984). The first reason is the need for nonbiased assessment of mentally retarded individuals. Several lawsuits in the 1970s focused on the use of intelligence test scores as the sole criterion for placing children into programs for the mentally retarded, and the disproportionate placement of minority children into these programs. Because many of the minority children had adequate adaptive behavior outside of school, the appropriateness of using intelligence tests to classify minority children as mentally retarded was questioned. These lawsuits resulted in an emphasis on adaptive behavior assessment for promoting nonbiased assessment of minority children.

The second reason for increased interest in assessment of adaptive behavior was the need to train mentally retarded individuals and enable them to live more independently. Training of adaptive behavior for mentally retarded people in institutions is seen as a vehicle for placement into community settings. In public school settings, training is seen as a way to mainstream mentally retarded children into regular education programs.

Importance for Preschool Assessment

The recent passage of Public Law 99-457, as described by Ballard and colleagues (1987), provides early educational services for handicapped preschool children. Major requirements of the law include assessment and intervention in all developmental areas (cognitive, speeach/language, psychosocial, motor, and self-help). Public Law 99-457 focuses on the needs of both preschool age children *and* their families, unlike other similar laws. The law recognizes adaptive behavior as an integral part of preschool children's development and indicates that remediation of deficits in adaptive behavior represents an important goal for early intervention programs. Thus, adaptive behavior assessment is an important component of the flexible, multidimensional assessment process recommended for evaluating the development of preschool children. Characteristics of this process include assessment of multiple domains, assessment from multiple sources, the involvement of parents in the assessment, ecologically valid assessment, and assessment that leads to early intervention (Ballard et al., 1987; Barnett, 1984; Paget, 1987; Paget & Nagle, 1986; NASP Position Statement, 1987).

Multiple Domains

The first requirement of preschool assessment is that information should be obtained about multiple domains of development. Adaptive behavior measures typically assess activities in several areas. Definitions and measures of adaptive behavior include the domains of self-help, interpersonal, cognitive/communication, and motor skills for preschool children. The assessment of these domains allows a sampling of behavior from the five developmental areas (cognitive, speech/language, psychosocial, motor, and self-help) required by Public Law 99-457. Although adaptive behavior assessment should not, of course, be the only type of measure used with a preschool child, it does offer information about several important areas of functioning.

Multiple Sources

The second requirement of the preschool assessment process is that information should be obtained from multiple sources. Most adaptive behavior scales utilize a third-party informant (e.g., parent, teacher, caregiver) to describe children's adaptive behavior instead of structured, individual testing of children. This format provides a source of information other than structured test-

ing of children, as well as a way of gathering information from several informants.

Parental Involvement

The third requirement of preschool assessment is that parents should be involved in every phase. Again, the third-party method of administration used in adaptive behavior assessment provides an excellent opportunity to tap the rich store of information that parents have about their children. It also allows parents to express their concerns about their children and discuss issues about parenting, schooling, and other important factors.

Ecologically Valid Assessment

Preschool assessment must be ecologically valid, or sample behavior appropriate to the various environments (e.g., home, school, community) in which preschool children must function (Barnett, 1984; Paget, 1987). Third-party adaptive behavior assessment is based on informants' observations of children's activities in natural settings, rather than being based on observation of children in an artificial, structured testing situation. In addition, informants can provide information about behavior in a variety of different environments and specific situations.

The administration of a structured test to a preschool child, especially one who is handicapped, often presents problems not typically encountered with a school-age child and is impossible in some cases (Paget, 1983). Third-party adaptive behavior assessment provides a unique solution to this problem. Developmental assessment is possible without the administration of a structured test to children because informants, rather than children, are used as the sources of information.

Assessment That Leads to Early Intervention

Adaptive behavior influences not only the ability to succeed in school, but the ability to succeed in the environment (Weller & Strawser, 1987). This basic assumption is seen in Public Law 99-457's inclusion of adaptive behavior skills in early intervention programs for handicapped preschoolers. Adaptive behavior, unlike intelligence, is considered to be modifiable and direct training of children can result in increases in adaptive behavior (Keith et al., 1987; Meyers et al., 1979). Furthermore, deficits in adaptive behavior can be related to home, family, and school factors that are amenable to change. Interventions to promote changes in children's environments might result in increased adaptive functioning.

Until recently, early intervention programs attempted to measure outcomes by determining increases in intelligence test scores. Zigler (Zigler & Seitz, 1980; Zigler & Trickett, 1978) suggested that intelligence was emphasized because intelligence test scores are typically the best predictors of school performance. However, he criticized the use of intelligence for training and measuring outcomes because intelligence test scores provide little information about how people function in everyday life. He supported the inclusion of adaptive behavior in early intervention programs when he indicated that social competence might be a viable alternative to intelligence. The concept of social competence, although not equivalent to adaptive behavior, includes both the components of adaptive behavior and intelligence.

SELECTED ADAPTIVE BEHAVIOR SCALES FOR USE WITH PRESCHOOL CHILDREN

There are many adaptive behavior scales in use, with some sources reporting more than 100 adaptive behavior scales (Meyers et al., 1979). In this section, adaptive behavior scales that can be used with preschool children are described. The scales to be discussed are those that are standardized and readily available. There are many other scales that are not standardized or were developed for in-house use by specific organizations. The more well-known scales are described in detail and, at the end of this section, a brief summary of scales that are less well known or have limited use with preschoolers is provided.

Scales of Independent Behavior (SIB)

The SIB (Bruininks et al., 1984, 1985) provides a norm-referenced assessment of adaptive behavior for infants through mature adults. It consists of four adaptive behavior skill clusters encompassing 14 subscales, as seen in Table 10-1.

TABLE 10.1
CONTENT OF THE SCALES OF INDEPENDENT BEHAVIOR (SIB)

Clusters	Subscales
Motor skills	Gross motor
	Fine motor
Social interaction and communication skills	Social interaction
	Language comprehension
	Language expression
Personal living skills	Eating and meal preparation
Toileting	
Dressing, personal	
Self-care	
Domestic skills	
Community living skills	Time and punctuality
	Money and value
	Work skills
	Home/community orientation
Broad independence (full scale)	
Internalized maladaptive behavior	Hurtful to self
	Unusual or repetitive habits
	Withdrawal or inattentive behavior
Asocial maladaptive behavior	Socially offensive behavior or uncooperative behavior
Externalized maladaptive behavior	Hurtful to others
	Destructive to property
	Disruptive behavior
General maladaptive behavior (full scale)	

(The domestic skills, time and punctuality, money and values, work skills, and community orientation subscales are not comprehensively assessed for preschoolers). The four adaptive behavior clusters are combined to form the Broad Independence Scale. The SIB also contains a problem behavior scale that measures eight areas and yields four maladaptive indexes. The SIB is administered to a third party who knows the examinee well, such as a parent or teacher. It also can be administered to the examinee. An easel is used during administration and the informant is shown possible responses to items on the easel pages.

The SIB yields a wide variety of derived scores, including age equivalents, percentile ranks, standard scores with a mean of 100 and standard deviation of 15, and normal curve equivalents. A sample of 1,764 individuals was used for standardization; the sample was stratified according to sex, community size, geographic location, socioeconomic status, and race. Internal consistency estimates range from .64 to .95, test–retest reliability estimates from .78 to .91, and interrater reliability estimates from .74 to .86. The SIB technical manual reports a respectable amount of validity evidence including developmental progression of scores, differences between scores of handicapped and nonhandicapped individuals, and correlations with other adaptive behavior scales and intelligence tests.

A particularly useful feature of the SIB for preschool assessment is the Early Development scale. This scale includes a sample of items from 12 of the 14 subscales and is intended for use with subjects whose developmental level is below 2½ years of age.

Vineland Adaptive Behavior Scales

The Vineland (Harrison, 1985; Sparrow et al., 1984a, 1984b), a revision of the Vineland Social Maturity Scale (Doll, 1935, 1965), consists of three versions. The *Survey Form* is administered to parents and caregivers of infants, children through 18 years of age, and low functioning adults and provides a norm-referenced assessment of adaptive behavior. The *Expanded Form* also is administered to parents and caregivers of infants through adults and provides a norm-referenced assessment. However, the primary purpose of the Expanded Form is to provide detailed information about specific deficits in adaptive behavior and a sequential guide for planning intervention programs. The *Classroom Edition* is administered to teachers of children aged 3 through 12 and provides a norm-referenced assessment of adaptive behavior in the classroom.

All three versions of the Vineland measure adaptive behavior in four domains and 11 subdomains of adaptive behavior, as seen in Table 10-2. (The written and domestic subdomains typically will be assessed briefly for preschool age children.) The four domains are combined to form a general measure of adaptive behavior, the adaptive behavior composite. The Survey Form and Expanded Form include a maladaptive behavior domain. This domain is only administered for children ages 5 and older because many of the behaviors assessed by this domain (e.g., thumb

TABLE 10.2
CONTENT OF THE VINELAND ADAPTIVE BEHAVIOR SCALES

Domain	Subdomains
Communication	Receptive Expressive Written
Daily living skills	Personal Domestic Community
Socialization	Interpersonal relationships Play and leisure time Coping skills
Motor skills	Gross Fine
Adaptive behavior composite	
Maladaptive behavior	

sucking, bed wetting) usually are not considered maladaptive for preschool age children.

The Survey Form and Expanded Form are administered to parents and caregivers during a semistructured interview. Although this type of interview requires a trained professional, its flexible nature allows clinicians to make valuable observations about parental concerns. The Classroom Edition is administered with a questionnaire completed by teachers.

The Survey Form was standardized on a stratified sample of 3,000 individuals selected on the basis of sex, race, socioeconomic status, geographic region, and community size. The Expanded Form was not standardized, but an equating study allowed the generation of norms using Survey Form standardization data. The Classroom Edition was standardized with a sample of 2,984 children, also stratified according to sex, race, socioeconomic status, geographic region, and community size. Standard scores with a mean of 100 and standard deviations of 15, percentile ranks, stanines, and age equivalents are yielded by all three versions of the Vineland.

Internal consistency estimates range from .83 to .94 for the Survey Form, .86 to .97 for the Expanded Form, and .80 to .98 for the Classroom Edition. Test–retest reliability coefficients for the Survey Form range from .81 to .88 and interrater reliability coefficients for the Survey Form range from .62 to .75. The manuals for the three Vineland versions report an impressive array of validity data including factor analyses, developmental progression of scores, differences between scores of handicapped and nonhandicapped individuals, and correlations with other adaptive behavior scales and intelligence tests.

Normative Adaptive Behavior Checklist (NABC) and Comprehensive Test of Adaptive Behavior (CTAB)

The NABC and CTAB (Adams, 1984a, 1984b, 1986) are two related measures of adaptive behavior for individuals from birth to 21 years of age. The NABC includes a sample of CTAB items and provides a brief norm-referenced assessment. The longer CTAB is designed to provide both a norm- and criterion-referenced assessment. Each instrument measures six categories of adaptive behavior: self-help, home living, independent living, sensory-motor, social skills, and language and academic concepts. The CTAB also includes several subcategories, listed in Table 10-3. A total, general adaptive score also is possible. The NABC consists of a questionnaire completed by an informant, such as a parent or teacher. The CTAB assesses adaptive behavior through observations conducted by an examiner, by direct testing of the subject, or reports by informants can be used when a behavior cannot be observed.

The NABC was standardized with 6,130 subjects from all regions of the country. Gender was the only stratification variable used in the standardization. The CTAB was not standardized with normal subjects, but an equating study allowed the development of CTAB scores for normal subjects based on the NABC standardization. The CTAB also was standardized with two groups of mentally retarded subjects: a group of 4,525 non-school retarded subjects from three regions of the country and a group of 2,094 in-school retarded subjects from Florida. Derived scores available for the NABC and CTAB include standard scores with a mean of 100 and standard deviation of 15, percentile ranks, performance rankings, and age equivalents. Norm-referenced scores for the CTAB are available for children aged 15 years and older only.

Internal consistency coefficients range from .21 to .99 for the NABC and .78 to .99 for the

TABLE 10.3
CONTENT OF THE COMPREHENSIVE TEST OF ADAPTIVE BEHAVIOR (CTAB)

Categories	Subcategories
Self-help skills	Toileting
	Grooming
	Dressing
	Eating
Home living skills	Living room
	Kitchen—utensil use and cooking
	Kitchen—cleaning
	Bedroom
	Bath and utility room
	Yard care
Independent living skills	Health skills
	Telephone skills
	Travel skills
	Time-telling skills
	Economic skills
	Vocational skills
Social skills	Self-awareness
	Interaction skills
	Leisure skills
Sensory and motor skills	Sensory awareness and discrimination
	Motor skills
Language concepts and academic skills	Language concepts
	Math skills
	Reading and writing skills

CTAB. Test–retest reliability estimates for the CTAB range from .81 to .99. Limited validity information, consisting primarily of correlations wtih the WISC-R and Vineland Social Maturity Scale, is reported in the technical manual.

Developmental Profile II

The Developmental Profile II (Alpern, Boll, & Shearer, 1980) is designed to estimate development of children birth to 9 years of age. It includes five scales (Physical Skill, Self-Help, Social, Academic, Communication) and can be administered either through direct observations of the child or from caregiver reports. The norms for the Developmental Profile II are based on the standardization conducted with the 1972 version of the scale. The standardization subjects were from Indiana and Washington and no stratification variables were used to select subjects. Age equivalents are available for the five scales, and a ratio IQ can be computed for the academic scale. There are limited reliability and validity data reported in the manual; the data consist primarily of agreement rates between parents and teachers and an indication of a high correlation between the academic scale and the Stanford-Binet.

Adaptive Behavior Scale-School Edition (ABS-SE)

The ABS-SE (Lambert, 1981; Lambert & Windmiller, 1981) is a norm-referenced instrument designed for children 3 to 17 years of age. The ABS-SE also includes criterion-referenced techniques for determining detailed information about deficits in adaptive behavior and for program planning. The instrument measures five factors representing 21 subdomains, as seen in Table 10-4, and a comparison score from the first three factors can be computed. The ABS-SE can be ad-

TABLE 10.4
CONTENT OF THE AAMD ADAPTIVE BEHAVIOR SCALE-SCHOOL EDITION (ABS-SE)

Factors	Domains
Personal self-sufficiency	Independent functioning Physical development
Community self-sufficiency	Economic activity Language development Numbers and time
Personal-social responsibility	Withdrawal Self-direction Responsibility
Comparison score (Total)	
Social adjustment	Aggressiveness Antisocial versus social behavior Rebelliousness Trustworthiness Habits Activity level Symptomatic behavior
Personal adjustment	Mannerisms Appropriateness of interpersonal manners Vocal habits

ministered by asking a parent, teacher, or other informant to complete a questionnaire booklet or by conducting an interview with the informant.

The ABS-SE was standardized with 6,523 children from California and Florida who were classified as normal, educable mentally retarded, or trainable mentally retarded. No stratification variables were used to select the sample. Percentile ranks can be obtained using any of the three reference groups and factor scores are reported as scaled scores with a mean of 10 and standard deviations of 3. Internal consistency reliability estimates range from .27 to .97 and validity data consist of correlations with intelligence and achievement tests, comparison of handicapped and nonhandicapped children, and factor analyses.

An older version of the ABS (Nihira, Foster, Shellhaas, & Leland, 1975) is available for use with children 3 years of age and older and adults. This instrument is very similar in content to the ABS-SE, but norms are based on samples of individuals in institutional settings.

Battelle Developmental Inventory

The Battelle (Newborg et al., 1984), although not called an adaptive behavior scale, is included in this chapter because it measures several areas typically associated with adaptive behavior assessment. The Battelle is used with children from birth to age 8 and assesses five domains of development (Personal-Social, Adaptive, Motor, Communication, and Cognitive). Each domain consists of 2 to 6 subdomains, listed in Table 10-5. The five domains are combined to yield a total measure of development. The Battelle can be administered in one of three ways: structured testing, observation, or parent/teacher interview. Some of the items in the battery can be administered with another procedure if the suggested procedure is not possible.

The Battelle was standardized using a stratified sample of 800 subjects selected according to region of the country, race, and sex. No information about the socioeconomic status of the sample is reported. Percentiles ranks, age equivalents, and several standard scores (*z* scores, *T* scores, deviation quotients, and normal curve equivalents) can be determined. Test–retest reliability coefficients range from .84 to .99 and interrater reliability coefficients range from .85 to .99. Limited validity data, primarily factor analysis, and

TABLE 10.5
CONTENT OF THE BATTELLE DEVELOPMENTAL INVENTORY

Domains	Components
Personal-social Expression of Feelings/ Affect Self-Concept Peer Interaction Coping Social Role	Adult interaction
Adaptive Eating Dressing, Personal Responsibility, toileting	Attention
Motor	Muscle control Body coordination Locomotion Fine muscle
Communication	Receptive Expressive
Cognitive	Perceptual discrimination Memory Reasoning and Academic Skills Conceptual Development

TABLE 10.6
CONTENT OF THE PYRAMID SCALES

Zone	Area
Sensory zone	Tactile responsiveness Auditory responsiveness Visual responsiveness
Primary zone	Gross motor Eating Fine motor Toileting Dressing Social interaction washing/grooming Receptive language Expressive language
Secondary zone	Recreation/leisure Writing Domestic behavior Reading Vocational Time Numbers Money

differences between handicapped and nonhandicapped children, are reported.

Pyramid Scales

The Pyramid Scales (Cone, 1984), for infants to adults, are quite different from the previously discussed adaptive behavior scales. It consists of 20 scales, listed in Table 10-6, tied to three sensory areas. No norm-referenced scores are provided; instead, the percentage of items usually performed on each of the scales is computed for a criterion-referenced assessment. The Pyramid Scales are linked to 5,000 specific objectives and a complete curriculum for training adaptive behavior (Cone, 1986). The scales can be administered either through a structured interview with an informant or questionnaire.

Others

Several scales might provide useful information with specific preschool children. The Adap-

tive Behavior Inventory for Children (ABIC) (Mercer & Lewis, 1978) is administered through a structured interview with parents of children age 5 to 11 years. The ABIC consists of six scales (Family, Community, Peer Relations, Nonacademic School Roles, Earner/Consumer, and Self-Maintenance) and a total score was normed with a sample of children from California. The Children's Adaptive Behavior Scale (CABS) (Richmond & Kicklighter, 1980), for children age 5 to 10 years, consists of a structured administration of tasks to children. Six areas (Language Development, Independent Functioning, Family Role Performance, Economic-Vocational Activity, Socialization, and Total) are assessed. Norms for the CABS are based on a small sample of children from Georgia and South Carolina. The Learning Accomplishment Profile (LAP) (LeMay et al., 1983), like the CABS, requires the direct administrations of tasks to children. Physical, psychomotor, cognitive, linguistic, and self-management skills are assessed for children ages 2½ to 6 years. Standardization of the LAP was conducted with a small sample of Head Start children.

INFORMAL ADAPTIVE BEHAVIOR ASSESSMENT

The scales discussed in the previous section can provide only a limited amount of information about preschool children's adaptive behavior. Standardized procedures are an integral part of the assessment of preschoolers, but fail to take into account a variety of factors necessary to obtain a complete picture of adaptive functioning (Leland, 1983). The informants used in a third-party assessment of adaptive behavior might present biased information or might not have the knowledge of a child's activities necessary for a valid assessment of adaptive behavior (Harrison & Sparrow, 1981; Holman & Bruininks, 1985). If, on the other hand, a direct assessment such as the CABS or LAP is used, children's performance might indicate what they can do in a structured testing situation, but might not generalize to other situations. Although adaptive behavior scales contribute to the ecologically valid assessment described by Barnett (1984) and Paget (1987), they cannot sample children's adaptive activities in every possible situation encountered in daily life. Finally, standardized adaptive behavior scales measure behavior only to a given point in time. As with instruments that measure other constructs, such as intelligence and achievement, adaptive behavior measures neglect the rapid behavioral and developmental changes that characterize preschool children (Mcmann & Barnett, 1984; Paget, 1987).

Given these limitations of standardized adaptive behavior scales, informal assessment of adaptive behavior always should be conducted to supplement and expand the information obtained from the scales. As is true with any type of assessment with preschooler children, adaptive behavior assessment must depend as much on non-test-based assessment as it does on test-based assessment (Barnett, 1984; Paget, 1987). Informal observation techniques, informal assessment with parents and teachers, assessment in a variety of settings, and dynamic assessment are described in this section.

Informal Observation Techniques

Informal observations of adaptive behavior provide opportunities for assessing behaviors in a variety of settings and situations. Although adaptive behavior scales yield a fund of information about children's activities, they usually are limited to behaviors that can be reliably and validly measured in an interview, questionnaire, or direct testing format. When the third-party informant method of assessment is used, there is a great reliance on respondents' memory of a wide variety of activities. Informal observations of children's adaptive behavior by a psychologist, counselor, teacher, or other professional allows them to see, first hand, children's responses to the environment.

A prerequisite for informal observation is knowledge of what behaviors to observe. Table 10-7 presents a list of typical adaptive behaviors

---

TABLE 10.7

SELECTED BEHAVIORS FOR INFORMAL ASSESSMENTS OF ADAPTIVE BEHAVIOR

Ages 0 to 1 Year

Shows understanding of 10 words
Imitates sounds of adults
Opens mouth for food
Chews on crackers
Eats solid food
Responds to voice of caregiver
Distinguishes caregiver from other people
Shows interest in objects and people
Shows affection to caregiver
Reaches for caregiver
Plays with toy or household object
Plays peek-a-boo and other games

Shows interest in other people's activities
Imitates waving good-bye and other movements
Sits
Picks up objects
Transfer objects between hands
Crawls
Opens doors by pushing or pulling
Rolls ball

Ages 1 to 2 years

Gestures to indicate yes and no
Listens to and follows simple instructions
Uses first names of family and friends
Says at least 50 words

(*continued*)

TABLE 10.7
(continued)

Listens to a story for five minutes
Shows a preference when offered a choice
Talks about experiences in simple terms
Delivers simple messages
Drinks from glass
Feeds self with spoon or fork
Shows understanding of hot
Indicates when wet or soiled
Allows nose to be wiped
Removes front-opening garments
Laughs in response to others' statements
Tries to please others
Plays with others
Imitates sweeping, cooking, hammering, etc.
Walks
Gets in and out of bed or chair
Marks with crayon
Walks up and down stairs, putting both feet on each step
Runs
Opens doors by turning doorknobs

Ages 2 to 3 Years

Speaks in sentences
Says at least 100 words
Follows fairly complex instructions
Says own first and last name
Asks questions
Uses toilet
Bathes self with assistance
Asks to use toilet
Puts on garments with elastic waistbands
Shows simple understanding of money
Puts toys away
Imitates adult phrases
Plays make-believe
Shows preference for friends
Says please
Jumps over small objects
Unscrews lids of jars
Pedals tricycle
Hops on one foot while holding on to something
Builds objects with blocks
Opens and closes scissors

Ages 3 to 4 Years

Talks about experiences in detail
Is toilet-trained at night
Gets own drink of water
Brushes teeth
Shows understanding of the function of a clock

Helps with chores
Washes and dries face
Puts shoes on correct feet
Answers the telephone
Dresses self, except for shoes
Tells others about emotions
Describes people other than by name
Shares toys
Walks up and down stairs with alternating feet
Climbs on high play equipment
Cuts on paper with scissors
Completes simple, noninset puzzles

Ages 4 to 5 Years

Articulates fairly clearly
Tells simple stories or jokes
Recites alphabet
Helps others set table
Takes care of all toileting needs
Looks both ways when crossing streets
Puts clean clothes away
Cares for nose by self
Dries self with towel
Fastens buttons, zippers, etc.
Helps in food preparation
Demonstrates need to be wary of strangers
Names favorite television programs
Follows rules in games
Has a preferred friend
Follows school rules
Apologizes for unintentional mistakes
Draws people and animals
Cuts lines on paper with scissors
Uses eraser without tearing paper
Hops with ease

Ages 5 to 6 Years

Reads a few common signs
Says date of birthday
Prints name
Says telephone number and address
Ties shoelaces
Bathes on own
Crosses street alone
Covers mouth when coughing and sneezing
Follows rules of community
Has a group of friends
Plays fairly complex card and board games
Unlocks doors with keys

Adapted from Harrison et al. (1986).

for children in the preschool age range. Table 10-7 also includes, as a guideline for observation, age periods, in years, by which most normally developing children exhibit the target behavior. The information in Table 10-7 can serve as a basis for informal observation. The age periods in the table should be used with caution, however, because they only indicate the age period at which most children exhibit the behavior; they do not indicate that children who do not exhibit the behavior by that age are delayed. Many reasons can explain why a particular child is not exhibiting a given behavior by a certain age and the variability in children's functioning results in some skills being acquired before others. The age periods in Table 10-7 are provided only to give the reader some guidelines of the behaviors to observe at given ages.

The data in Table 10-7 is adapted from item data on the Vineland Adaptive Behavior Scales (Harrison et al., 1986). The data reported by Harrison and coworkers includes Vineland Survey Form item ages, or ages at which 50% and 70% of children that age in the Vineland standardization sample were performing the activity described by the item. A total of 100 children in each half-year age interval was used to develop the item ages. The information presented in Table 10-7 includes a list of activities which, according to their item ages, are in the preschool age range. All items in the preschool age range are not reported in Table 10-7; some similar items were combined to form one general activity.

Informal Assessment with Parents and Teachers

The third-party interview used with many adaptive behavior scales also presents a means of discussing, on an informal basis, issues that are related to adaptive behavior. The information in Table 10-7 can be used as a guide in informal discussions. One important issue to discuss with parents and teacher after the administration of an adaptive behavior scale is the activities or behaviors of the child that parents and teacher find worrisome (Leland, 1983). Parents often have limited knowledge of normal child development and they might expect more of their children than a child of that age is capable of doing. For example, a parent of a 3 year old child might be concerned that the child continues to wet the bed occasionally and will be relieved to know that this is typical of many 3 year old children. In other cases, the worries of parents and teachers might be well founded and informal discussion of the issue with them might yield information that is important for planning interventions.

An informal discussion with parents and teachers can provide details about parenting and teaching techniques that are being used with children. Deficits in children's adaptive behavior might be more a function of teaching, parenting, or other environmental factors than delayed development. Informal discussions can often serve as a foundation for parent and teacher education and changing parenting and teaching strategies to meet the needs of a particular child.

Assessment in a Variety of Settings

Several topics discussed earlier are relevant to the need for informally assessing adaptive behavior in a variety of situations. First, one characteristic of the construct of adaptive behavior is its situational specificity; children's adaptive behavior changes to meet the demands of different situations. Second, adaptive behavior scales, when used with parents, teachers, and other informants, can provide information about children's behavior in different settings, such as home and school. However, the response to an adaptive behavior scale by parents or teachers is often a generalized response; the informants are required to indicate what children usually do across *all* situations in that environment. Informal assessment of children's behavior in response to different situations is needed to allow a more comprehensive assessment of adaptive behavior.

There are many specific situations where children's adaptive behavior can be observed. For example, children can be observed on the playground interacting with younger versus older peers. They can be observed meeting new people and going to places they have never been before. Their interactions with parents and teachers can be compared. Table 10-7 can, again, serve as a guide for informal observations of children in different situations, but an astute observer should also assess the *situation*, in addition to assessing the child. For instance, what are the characteristics of a situation that might prevent a child from exhibiting an adaptive behavior in one situation but not another? What interactions seem to motivate the child and promote adaptive behavior? What interactions appear to threaten the child and impede the adaptive behavior? How does adaptive behavior change as the child gains more experience with the situation?

Most children are evaluated with an adaptive behavior scale as a prerequisite for entering a preschool program. An important area to informally assess is children's reaction to the new program and changes in adaptive behavior that occur as a result of the program. School or daycare might result in increases in adaptive behavior or, with some children, might extinguish previously acquired skills.

Dynamic Assessment and On-Going Evaluation of Training

Feuerstein's (1979) concept of *dynamic assessment*, although typically applied to cognition, provides a model for the ongoing evaluation of adaptive behavior. His model, using a test–teach–retest approach, determines children's level of functioning, provides training, and evaluates children's responses to training. Although Feuerstein's dynamic assessment of cognition is conducted in a structured testing situation, the model easily can be applied to the informal assessment of adaptive behavior. Children's current performance of an activity can be determined, either through informal assessment, direct testing, or with a third-party informant. If the activity is not performed, training can be given and response to training can be determined. In addition, generalization of the training to other situations can be assessed and the training can be evaluated to determine the techniques that seem to be most influential on changing children's behavior.

USES OF ADAPTIVE BEHAVIOR ASSESSMENT

There are two major uses of adaptive behavior assessment (Coulter, 1980; Holman & Bruininks, 1985; Meyers et al., 1979; Witt & Marteins, 1984). The first is to provide information that leads to

decisions about the nature, diagnosis, and classification of handicaps and placement of children into special programs based on the diagnosis. The second use of adaptive behavior assessment is to acquire information that can serve as the basis for planning intervention programs.

Diagnosis/Classification

Historically, adaptive behavior assessment has been used to diagnose and classify individuals as mentally retarded. The AAMD definition of mental retardation requires that deficits in adaptive behavior, as well as in intellectual functioning, must be substantiated before a person can be classified as mentally retarded. Most states use the concept of adaptive behavior in their definitions of mental retardation and require assessment of adaptive behavior to determine eligibility for special services for the mentally retarded (Patrick & Reschly, 1982).

Adaptive behavior assessment also can be used for the identification of handicaps or problems other than mental retardation, because it is reasonable to expect that many handicaps will be related to deficits in personal and social functioning. It has been suggested that emotionally and behaviorally disturbed children are characterized by average intelligence and deficits in adaptive behavior (Coulter, 1980; Mercer, 1973) and research supports that emotionally disturbed children can be distinguished from normal children by their deficits in adaptive behavior (Mealor, 1984; Sparrow & Cicchetti, 1987). Although adaptive behavior assessment might not be necessary for the identification of sensory and physical handicaps, it is important for determining the effects these handicaps have on daily functioning (Meacham et al., 1987; Pollingue, 1987; Sparrow et al., 1984a, 1984b). There is evidence to support that different subtypes of learning disabled children have characteristic patterns of adaptive behavior and that learning disabled children exhibit adaptive behavior that is lower than that of normal children, but higher than that of mentally retarded children (Bruininks et al., 1985; Rainwater-Bryant, 1985; Weller & Strawser, 1987).

Diagnostic categories such as mental retardation, emotional disturbance, and so on might not be used with preschool children, depending on the guidelines of the state in which they reside.

Instead of using categories, Public Law 99-457, as described by Ballard and coworkers (1987), defines children who are *developmentally delayed*, with conditions that might *result* in developmental delay, or *at-risk* of developmental delay. These children are eligible for early intervention services under this legislation.

Adaptive behavior assessment can be used for identifying children who might be classified into any of the three groups defined by Public Law 99-457. Deficits in adaptive behavior, along with deficits in other developmental areas, can supply evidence of delay or possible delay. However, children who do not have deficits in adaptive behavior might have deficits in other developmental areas. School-age children with these characteristics face the risk of *declassification*, or the denial of special services because they cannot be classified as mentally retarded (Reschly, 1985). Early intervention services for preschoolers with deficits in intellectual functioning, but average adaptive behavior, might be justified because these children might be at risk of developing deficits in adaptive behavior without early home and school intervention (Leland, 1983).

Intervention Planning

All assessment of preschoolers must lead to appropriate intervention plans. Verhaaren and Conner (1981) indicated that the results of assessment have three major purposes. Assessment should lead to *education*, or the teaching of skills to children that enable them to achieve their potential. Assessment should lead to *prevention*, or keeping any further problems or handicaps from occurring. Finally, assessment should lead to *correction*, or the reduction of any handicaps or disabilities.

Adaptive behavior scales have several features that are useful for planning intervention programs for preschool children. Most adaptive behavior scales yield scores for several domains of adaptive behavior, indicating children's strengths and weaknesses. Intervention programs can be planned to enhance strengths and remediate weaknesses. Items on adaptive behavior scales can be reviewed to determine specific adaptive activities and these activities can become goals in intervention programs (Witt & Martens, 1984). Informal assessment of adaptive behavior also can

be used to determine strengths and weaknesses and evaluate the effectiveness of intervention programs.

Langone and Burton (1987) suggested that adaptive behavior training requires carefully designed task sequences. These task sequences should be hierarchically arranged, from the simplest component of an activity to the most difficult. Three adaptive behavior scales, the ABS-SE, Vineland Expanded Form, and Pyramid Scales, list activities in hierarchical sequences. The Pyramid Scales also have the advantage of a well-designed, comprehensive curriculum as its base.

Adaptive behavior training programs will be more effective when they occur in the environments where the children are expected to exhibit the skills (Langone & Burton, 1987). Thus, interventions for preschool children must involve parents as well as teachers because many activities, such as dressing and hygiene, occur more often at home than at school. Other adaptive activities, such as eating and interpersonal skills, occur both at home and school. Doll (1953) reported that parental education was one of the primary uses of assessment with the Vineland Social Maturity Scale, the first major measure of adaptive behavior.

Training of adaptive behavior should be an ongoing process and not limited to structured training situations. Certain skills can be learned by children through direct teaching, but efforts should be made to foster generalization of the skills to daily activities. For example, using dolls or other toys to teach dressing skills should be accompanied by teaching what occurs when children are actually dressing themselves.

Cone (1987) listed a series of steps to be used for planning adaptive behavior intervention programs. The first step is to determine a long-range goal for the child, which, according to Cone, should be the behavior that is required for a specific situation, such as entry into the next less restrictive program. The second step is to determine the child's performance of that activity. The third step is to determine the skills needed by the child to achieve the long range goal. The fourth step is to estimate the amount of time it will take for the child to achieve the long-range goal. The final steps are to establish annual goals, monthly goals, short-term goals, and immediate instructional objectives. Cone's steps easily can be incorporated into the components of the individual family service plan required by Public Law 99-457 (Ballard et al., 1987).

ISSUES IN ADAPTIVE BEHAVIOR ASSESSMENT

Adaptive behavior assessment, like any other area of assessment, is not without its inherent problems. These problems are of both a conceptual and methodological nature. Three major issues in adaptive behavior assessment are reviewed: differences in adaptive behavior and cognitive functioning, the limitations of the third-party assessment technique, and psychometric problems with many adaptive behavior scales.

Adaptive Behavior Versus Cognitive Functioning

A common misconception about adaptive behavior is that adaptive behavior and cognitive funcioning are equivalent (Coulter, 1980). Although the two constructs are obviously related, Meyers and coworkers (1979) indicated that the measurement and conceptualization of adaptive behavior and intelligence differ in many respects, including the following: (1) intelligence is conceptualized as a thought process while adaptive behavior emphasizes everyday behavior, (2) intelligence scales measure maximum performance (potential) while adaptive behavior scales measure typical performance, and (3) intelligence scales assume a stability in scores while adaptive behavior scales assume that performance can be modified. Keith and colleagues (1987) provided support for the suggestions of Meyers and coworkers (1979) by investigating three hypotheses: intelligence and adaptive behavior are components of the same underlying construct, intelligence and adaptive behavior are two separate but related constructs, and intelligence and adaptive behavior are two unrelated constructs. The results of their investigation supported the hypotheses that intelligence and adaptive behavior are two separate but related constructs.

The correlations between scores from intelligence tests and adaptive behavior scales tend to be low to moderate. Harrison (1987) reviewed a number of studies investigating the relationship between intelligence and adaptive behavior and found that the majority of correlations were in the low-to-moderate-range. For example, Arffa and coworkers (1984) reported correlations of .25 to .49 between intelligence and adaptive behavior scores of Head Start students and Harrison and Ingram (1984) found a correlation of .41 between intelligence and adaptive behavior scores of developmentally delayed preschoolers. There also is some evidence to support that adaptive behavior scales directly administered to children through structured tasks have higher correlations with intelligence tests than do third-party adaptive behavior scales (Barnett et al., 1987; Poth & Barnett, 1987).

The obvious implication of the low-to-moderate correlations between adaptive behavior and intelligence scales is that children's adaptive behavior scores, in many cases, will not be equivalent to their intelligence test scores. Practitioners might find that one child has a below average adaptive behavior score and average intelligence test score, while another child has an average adaptive behavior score and below average intelligence test score. It is the latter example that results in declassification of mental retardation, according to AAMD guidelines. As stated earlier, declassification might not be as much an issue under Public Law 99-457, where developmental delay is used instead of categories such as mental retardation.

Adaptive behavior scales usually have low-to-moderate correlations with achievement test scores, as well. In a review of research with adaptive behavior scales, Harrison (1987) reported correlations with achievement tests that ranged from −.18 to .57. Harrison (1981) and Oakland (1983), using multiple regression analyses, found that although adaptive behavior exhibited a significant, but moderate, correlation with school achievement, it did not significantly improve the prediction of achievement beyond that accounted for by intelligence. Keith and coworkers (1987), in a study using path analysis instead of regression analysis, reported that adaptive behavior had a small, but significant, effect on achievement beyond that accounted for by intelligence. Adaptive behavior scales appear to have a very modest effect on school achievement, but as suggested by Kamphaus (1987), perhaps a more important criterion for adaptive behavior is *life* achievement. Several studies support the positive relationship between adaptive behavior and measures of life achievement (Malgady et al., 1980; Irvin et al., 1977).

Third-Party Assessment

Throughout this chapter, the third-party assessment used with many adaptive behavior scales has been described. This method of assessment is deemed the most appropriate and efficient way of assessing adaptive behavior because it measures what children do daily to take care of themselves and get along with others (Adams, 1986; Harrison, 1985; Holman & Bruininks, 1985). Less efficient alternatives to third-party assessment include direct assessment of children, which determines what they *can* do instead of what they *usually do*, and observation of children day after day in home and school by a trained observer. Although the third-party method is attractive, it presents several problems for professionals who assess adaptive behavior.

Parents and teachers are the two primary informants for third-party adaptive behavior scales. Parents might lack objectivity and overestimate their children's adaptive behavior, while teachers may not have enough knowledge about adaptive behavior to give valid information (Harrison & Sparrow, 1981; Holman & Bruininks, 1985). Harrison (1985) reported that preschool teachers usually have more information about adaptive behavior than teachers of school-age children. Furthermore, many studies report alarmingly low correlations between adaptive behavior scores obtained from parent and teacher reports (Harrison, 1987). For example, Ronka and Barnett (1986) reported correlations as low as .06 between parents and teachers of educable mentally retarded children and Arffa and colleagues (1984) reported a correlation of − .05 between parents and teachers of Head Start children. Such findings led Bracken and Barnett (1987) to suggest that adaptive behavior scales lack interrater reliability and convergent validity.

Bracken and Barnett's (1987) suggestion is certainly warranted but another alternative should be considered when interpreting low correlations between parents and teachers on adaptive behavior scales. The issue of low correlations between parents and teachers might be a conceptual, rather than psychometric, issue. Bracken and Barnett's conclusion assumes that parents and teacher's scores *should* correlate highly, but the definition of adaptive behavior suggests that it is feasible to assume that they should not. Adaptive behavior is situationally specific and influenced by cultural expectations; parents and teachers observe children in different situations and might have different expectations.

It is suggested that research reporting low correlations between parents and teachers might support the necessity of using *both* parents and teachers as informants in adaptive behavior assessment. If parents and teachers disagree in their estimates of a child's adaptive behavior, important information can be gained. Informal assessment should be conducted to answer questions such as the following: Do the parents and teachers have different expectations? What implications do the different expectations have for the development of the child? Is the child behaving differently at home and school? How do parents and teachers affect the child's behavior at home and school?

Psychometric Standards

Many adaptive behavior scales fail to meet basic psychometric standards. A large number of scales were normed on nonrepresentative samples and the manuals for the scales often report limited reliability and validity data. Earlier in this chapter, several adaptive behavior scales were described but a complete evaluation of their psychometric properties is beyond the scope of this chapter. The brief descriptions provided in this chapter contain enough details about psychometric properties to observe that, for several of the scales, standardization was conducted with samples from one or two states, important stratification variables such as socioeconomic status were not used, and basic reliability and validity data are not reported. These scales are often used for placement decisions, but as indicated by Kamphaus (1987), it is difficult to imagine using an intelligence test with such poor psychometric properties. Kamphaus specifically discussed the problem of inadequate norms for adaptive behavior scales and cautioned practitioners against using poorly standardized scales for placement of children. He did, however, suggest that poorly normed instruments such as the ABS-SE and ABIC might be useful for criterion-referenced assessment. Kamphaus cited the Vineland and SIB as scales with adequate samples. Review of the psychometric properties of these two scales clearly shows that their manuals also report more detailed information about reliability and validity scales than do manuals for other scales.

CONCLUSION

Adaptive behavior assessment has finally attained its deserved status in the psychoeducational assessment of children. If this book had been written 10 or 15 years ago, it might not have included a chapter on adaptive behavior or, if it had, it would have been limited to a discussion of two or three adaptive behavior scales and a small number of research studies. Now, practitioners have a number of scales to use and the newer scales are meeting psychometric standards much better than scales used in the 1970s. There is a wealth of research on adaptive behavior assessment (Harrison, 1987; Heath, 1986) and more research is being conducted every day.

Perhaps more importantly, adaptive behavior assessment has become an integral part of early childhood intervention programs. Public Law 99-457, with its emphasis on assessment and intervention of all developmental areas and the needs of children and families, delineates more clearly than any past legislation the need to consider adaptive behavior. Public Law 99-457 widens the scope of adaptive behavior beyond the field of mental retardation and supports the use of the construct with children who have any handicaps or problems.

The knowledge we have about adaptive behavior is not complete by any means. One of the greatest needs is research investigating the effectiveness of adaptive behavior training programs for preschool children. Holman and Bruininks (1985) reviewed the research in the area and, although they found numerous studies supporting the positive effects of training, few of these studied dealt with children below the age of 4 years. In the future, more research will pave the way for increased understanding of adaptive behavior and for better interventions to enhance the development of children.

REFERENCES

Adams, G. L. (1984a). *Comprehensive Test of Adaptive Behavior Examiner's Manual*. Columbus, OH: Charles E. Merrill.

Adams, G. L. (1984b). *Normative Adaptive Behavior Checklist Examiner's Manual*. Columbus, OH: Charles E. Merrill.

Adams, G. L. (1986). *Comprehensive Test of Adaptive Behavior and Normative Adaptive Behavior Checklist Technical Manual*. Columbus, OH: Charles E. Merrill.

Alpern, G. D., Boll, T. J., & Shearer, M. S. (1980). *Development Profile II*. Aspen, CO: Psychological Development Publications.

Arffa, S., Rider, L., & Cummings, J. (1984). *An investigation of cognitive and adaptive functioning of Head Start children*. Unpublished manuscript, Indiana University, Bloomington.

Ballard, J., Ramirez, B., & Zantal-Weiner, K. (1987). *Public Law 94-142, Section 504, and Public Law 99-457: Understanding what they are and are not*. Reston, VI: Council for Exceptional Children.

Barnett, D. W. (1984). An organizational approach to preschool services: Psychological screening, assessment, and intervention. In C. Maher, R. Illback, & J. Zins (Eds.), *Organizational psychology in the schools: A handbook for practitioners* (pp. 53–82). Springfield, IL: Thomas.

Barnett, D. W., Faust, F., & Sarmir, M.A. (1987). *A validity study of two preschool screening instruments: the LAP-D and DIAL-R*. Manuscript submitted for publication.

Bracken, B. A., & Barnett, D. W. (1987, June). The technical side of preschool assessment: A primer of critical issues. *Preschool Interests*, pp. 6–7, 9.

Bruininks, R. H., Thurlow, M., & Gilman, C. J. (1987). Adaptive behavior and mental retardation. *Journal of Special Education*, *21*, 69–88.

Bruininks, R. H., Woodcock, R. W., Hill, B. K., & Weatherman, R. (1984). *Scales of Independent Behavior Examiner's Manual*. Allen, TX: DLM Teaching Resources.

Bruininks, R. H., Woodcock, R. W., & Hill, B. K. Development and standardization of the Scales of Independent Behavior. Allen, TX: DLM Teaching Resources.

Clausen, J. (1972). The continuing problem of defining mental deficiency. *Journal of Special Education*, *6*, 97–106.

Cone, J. D. (1984). *The pyramid scales*. Austin, TX: PRO-ED.

Cone, J. D. (Ed.). (1986). *The pyramid system: Comprehensive assessment and programming for handicapped persons*. Morgantown, WV: Pyramid Press.

Cone, J. D. (1987). Intervention planning using adaptive

behavior instruments. *Journal of Special Education, 21,* 127–148.

Coulter, W. A. (1980). Adaptive behavior and professional disfavor: Controversies and trends for school psychologists. *School Psychology Review, 9,* 74.

Doll, E. A. (1935). A generic scale of social maturity. *American Journal of Orthopsychiatry, 5,* 180–188.

Doll, E. A. (1953). *Measurement of social competence.* Circle Pines, MN: American Guidance Service.

Doll, E. A. (1965). *Vineland Social Maturity Scale.* Circle Pines, MN: American Guidance Service.

Feuerstein, R. (1979). *Dynamic Assessment of Retarded Performers.* Baltimore: University Park Press.

Greenspan, S. (1979). Social intelligence in the retarded. In N. R. Ellis (Ed.), *Handbook of Mental Deficiency: Psychological Theory and Research,* (2nd ed., pp. 483–531). Hillsdale, NJ: Lawrence Erlbaum.

Greenspan, S. (1981). Social competence and handicapped individuals: Practical implications and a proposed model. *Advances in Special Education, 3,* 41–82.

Gresham, F. M., & Elliot, S. N. (1987). The relationship between adaptive behavior and social skills: Issues in definition and assessment. *Journal of Special Education, 21,* 167–182.

Grossman, H. J. (1983). *Classification in Mental Retardation.* Washington, DC: American Association on Mental Deficiency.

Harrison, P. L. (1981). Mercer's adaptive behavior inventory, the McCarthy scales, and dental development as predictors of first grade achievement. *Journal of Educational Psychology, 73,* 78–82.

Harrison, P. L. (1984). The application of the Vineland Adaptive Behavior Scales in educational settings. *Techniques: A Journal for Remedial Education and Counseling, 7,* 101–112.

Harrison, P. L. (1985). *Vineland Adaptive Behavior Scales, Classroom Edition Manual.* Circle Pines, MN: American Guidance Service.

Harrison, P. L. (1987). Research with adaptive behavior scales. *Journal of Special Education, 21,* 37–68.

Harrison, P. L., & Ingram, R. P. (1984, May). Performance of developmentally delayed preschoolers on the Vineland Adaptive Behavior Scales. In S. S. Sparrow (Chair), *The Vineland Adaptive Behavior Scales: Results of National Standardization and Clinical and Research Applications.* Symposium conducted at the meeting of the American Association on Mental Deficiency, Minneapolis, MN.

Harrison, P. L., Robertson, G. J., Cicchetti, D. V., & Sparrow, S. S. (1986). *Vineland Technical Supplement.* Unpublished Manuscript Circle Pines, MN: American Guidance Service.

Harrison, P. L., & Sparrow, S. S. (1981, April). *Adaptive behavior: What teachers know.* Paper presented at the meeting of the National Association of School Psychologists, Houston, TX.

Heath, C. P. (1986, April). *Trends in adaptive behavior research over the decade.* Paper presented at the meeting of the National Association of School Psychologists, Hollywood, FL.

Holman, J., & Bruininks, R. (1985). Assessing and training adaptive behaviors. In K. C. Lakin & R. H. Bruininks (Eds.), *Strategies for Achieving Community Integration of Developmentally Disabled Citizens* (pp. 73–104). Baltimore, MD: Paul H. Brookes.

Horn, E., & Fuchs, D. (1987). Using adaptive behavior assessment and intervention: An overview. *Journal of Special Education, 21,* 11–26.

Irvin, L. K., Halpern, A. A., & Reynolds, W. M. (1977). Assessing social and prevocational awareness in mildly and moderately retarded individuals. *American Journal of Mental Deficiency, 82,* 266–272.

Kamphaus, R. W. (1987). Conceptual and psychometric issues in the assessment of adaptive behavior. *Journal of Special Education, 21,* 27–36.

Keith, T. A., Fehrmann, P. G., Harrison, P. L., & Pottebaum, S. M. (1987). The relationship between adaptive behavior and intelligence: Testing alternative explanations. *Journal of School Psychology, 25,* 31–43.

Keith, T. Z., Harrison, P. L., & Ehly. S. W. (1987). Effects of adaptive behavior on achievement: Path analysis of a national sample. *Professional School Psychology, 2,* 205–216.

Lambert, N. M. (1981). *AAMD Adaptive Behavior Scale, School Edition: Diagnostic and Technical Manual.* Monterey, CA: Publishers Test Service.

Lambert, N., & Windmiller, M. (1981). *AAMD Adaptive Behavior Scale, School Edition.* Monterey, CA: Publishers Test Service.

Langone, J., & Burton, T. A. (1987). Teaching adaptive behavior skills to moderately and severely handicapped individuals: Best practices for facilitating independent living. *Journal of Special Education, 21,* 149–166.

Leland, H. (1983). Assessment of adaptive behavior. In K. D. Paget & B. A. Bracken (Eds.), *The Psychoeducational Assessment of Preschool Children* (pp. 191–206). New York: Grune & Stratton.

LeMay, D. W., Griffin, P. M., & Sanford, A. R. (1983). *Learning Accomplishment Profile-Diagnostic Edition.* Winston-Salem, NC: Kaplan Press.

Malgady, R. G., Barcher, P. R., Davis, J., & Towner, G. (1980). Validity of the Vocational Adaptation Rating Scale: Prediction of mentally retarded workers' placement in sheltered workshops. *American Journal of Mental Deficiency, 84,* 633–640.

Mcmann, G. M., & Barnett, D. W. (1984). An analysis of the construct validity of two measures of adaptive behavior. *Journal of Psychoeducational Assessment, 2,* 239–247.

Meacham, F. R., Kline, M.M., Stovall, J. A., & Sands, D. I. (1987). Adaptive behavior and low incidence handicaps: Hearing and visual impairments. *Journal of Special Education, 21,* 183–196.

Mealor, D. J. (1984). *An analysis of intellectual functioning and adaptive behavior of behaviorally disordered students.* Unpublished manuscript, University of Central Florida, Orlando.

Mercer, J. R. (1973). *Labeling the mentally retarded.* Berkeley, CA: University of California Press.

Mercer, J. R., & Lewis, J. F. (1978). *Adaptive Behavior Inventory for Children Interview's Manual.* New York: Psychological Corp.

Meyers, C. E., Nihira, K., & Zetlin, A. (1979). The measurement of adaptive behavior. In N. R. Ellis (Ed.), *Handbook of Mental Deficiency: Psychological Theory and Research* (2nd ed., pp. 215–253). Hillsdale, NJ: Lawrence Erlbaum.

NASP position statement and supporting paper on early intervention services in the schools (1987). *Communique,* pp. 4–5.

Newborg, J., Stock, J. R., Wnek, L., Guidubaldi, J., & Svinicki, J. (1984). *Battelle Developmental Inventory Examiner's Manual.* Allen, TX: DLM Teaching Resources.

Nihira, K., Foster, R., Shellhaas, M., & Leland, H. (1975). *AAMD Adaptive Behavior Scale,* Monterey, CA: Publishers Test Service.

Oakland, T. (1983). Joint use of adaptive behavior and IQ to predict achievement. *Journal of Consulting and Clinical Psychology, 51,* 298–301.

Paget, K. D. (1983). The individual examining situation: Basic considerations for preschool children. In K. D. Paget & B. A. Bracken (Eds.), *The Psychoeducational Assessment of Preschool Children* (pp. 51–62). New York: Grune & Stratton.

Paget, K. D. (1987). Preschool assessment. In C. R. Reynolds & L. Mann (Eds.), *Encyclopedia of Special Education* (pp. 1237–1239). New York: John Wiley.

Paget, K. D., & Nagle, R. J. (1986). A conceptual model of preschool assessment. *School Psychology Review, 15,* 154–165.

Patrick, J. L., & Reschly, D. J. (1982). Relationship of state educational criteria and demographic variables to school system prevalence of mental retardation. *American Journal of Mental Deficiency, 86,* 351–360.

Pollingue, A. (1987). Adaptive behavior and low incidence handicaps: Use of adaptive behavior instruments for persons with physical handicaps. *Journal of Special Education, 21,* 117–126.

Poth, R. L., & Barnett, D. W. (1987). *A validity study of two preschool developmental scales: Establish-*

ing the limits of interpretive confidence. Manuscript submitted for publication.

Rainwater-Bryant, B. J. (1985). *Comparisons of parent obtained and teacher obtained adaptive behavior scores for handicapped children.* Unpublished doctoral dissertation, Memphis State University, Memphis, TN.

Reschly, D. J. (1982). Assessing mild mental retardation: The influence of adaptive behavior, sociocultural status, and prospects for nonbiased assessment. In C. R. Reynolds & T. B. Gutkin (Eds.), *The Handbook of School Psychology* (pp. 209–242). New York: John Wiley.

Reschly, D. J. (1985). Best practices: Adaptive behavior. In A. Thomas & J. Grimes (Eds.), *Best Practices in School Psychology* (pp. 353–368). Stratford, CT: National Associaton of School Psychologists.

Richmond, B. O., & Kicklighter, R. H. (1980). *Manual for the Children's Adaptive Behavior Scale.* Atlanta, GA: Humanics Ltd.

Ronka, C. S., & Barnett, D. (1986). A comparison of adaptive behavior ratings: Revised Vineland and AAMD ABS-SE. *Special Services in the Schools, 2,* 87–96.

Sparrow, S. S., Balla, D. A., & Cicchetti, D. V. (1984a). *Vineland Adaptive Behavior Scales, Expanded Form Manual.* Circle Pines, MN: American Guidance Service.

Sparrow, S. S., Balla, D. A., & Cicchetti, D. V. (1984b). *Vineland Adaptive Behavior Scales, Survey Form Manual.* Circle Pines, MN: American Guidance Service.

Sparrow, S. S., & Cicchetti, D. V. (1987)). Adaptive behavior and the psychologically disturbed child. *Journal of Special Education, 21,* 89–100.

Verhaaren, P., & Conner, F. P. (1981). Physical disabilities. In J. M. Kauffman & D. P. Hallahan (Eds.), *Handbook of Special Education.* Englewood Cliffs, NJ: Prentice-Hall.

Weller, C., & Strawser, S. (1987). Adaptive behavior of subtypes of learning disabled individuals. *Journal of Special Education, 21,* 101–116.

Witt, J. C., & Martens, B. K. (1984). Adaptive behavior: Tests and assessment issues. *School Psychology Review, 13,* 478–484.

Zigler, E., Balla, D., & Hodapp, R. (1984). On the definition and classification of mental retardation. *American Journal of Mental Deficiency, 89,* 215–230.

Zigler, E., & Seitz, V. (1980). Early childhood intervention programs: A reanalysis. *School Psychology Review, 9,* 354–368.

Zigler, E., & Trickett, P. K. (1978). IQ, social competence, and evaluation of early childhood intervention programs. *American Psychologist, 33,* 789–798.

11

Assessment of Language and Communication

DIANE N. BRYEN
DIANNE GALLAGHER

If you were to enter a preschool or kindergarten class, one of your first reactions might be an awareness of the unusually high noise level. Sounds of physical movement of the children, block structures being built and knocked down, vocalizations accompanying actions, and the chatter, chatter, chatter of children's voices are all a part of this social and educational environment. Interaction between children and both the physical and social environment during the preschool years is generally accompanied, supplemented, or mediated by language, and as children progress through the school years, language plays an increasingly critical role. Language is the common "coin of exchange" among peers and with teachers. It is through language that children have access to most social encounters in school as well as to the world of academic experiences. Generally, children come to their early school experiences prepared to use language for a variety of social, informational, and regulatory functions. However, there are many young children who enter school unready to use language to meet the social, cognitive, and linguistic demands of formal education.

Who are these unready children? DeHirsch (1981) describes them as somehow unfinished—unfinished physically, perceptually, motorically, emotionally, or linguistically. Although each of these variables is important to current and subsequent school functioning, language difficulties—"even subtle ones—are red flags in terms of subsequent learning difficulties" (p. 63). These unready children are at risk in terms of learning to read, write, and do mathematics, as well as following classroom rules and procedures, especially when communicated linguistically. They are at risk for becoming inattentive and distractible because they are poor processors of linguistic information. They are also at risk of not being able to effectively obtain their share of peer, teacher, informational, and material resources in the classroom (Garnica, 1981). For all of these reasons, the assessment of language development and use should be a major focus of early educational evaluations.

Before the practice of language assessment is discussed, it is necessary that the reader have an understanding of the nature and development of language. Without this background, data obtained from various language assessments are virtually uninterpretable. As Siegel and Broen (1976) stated, "The most useful and dependable language assessment device is an informed clinician (or educator) [parenthesis added] who feels compelled to keep up with developments in psycholinguistics . . . and related fields." (p. 75). An overview of current knowledge about language development and disorders is presented in the next two sections. (For more detailed discussions see Bloom & Lahey, 1978; Bryen, 1982; Gerber & Bryen, 1981; Lindfors, 1987.)

NATURE AND SCOPE OF DEVELOPMENT

It is from the broader perspective of communication that questions about the nature, development, and disorders of language derive meaning. Communication is the act of "making one's thoughts, feelings, experiences, needs, desires . . . known to one or more other people" (Stelle, 1978, p. 1). It involves the following components: a sender and receiver(s)—the *who*; an intended message—the *what*; a desire to influence the physical and social world—the *why*; and a means of transmitting the message—the *how*. The dimensions of communication are illustrated in Fig. 11-1. Furthermore, as illustrated in Fig. 11-1, communication is embedded in a social and physical context. The *social context* can be most simply described as knowledge that is shared by both sender and receiver. Given a variety of sender-receiver episodes, shared knowledge can range from minimal (e.g., in the case of a person meeting an unknown foreign visitor), to quite extensive (e.g., a mother interacting with her young child). The *physical context* of objects might also directly affect the *why*, *what*, and *how* of communication. Each of these dimensions affects the child's competence when communicating in different social contexts (e.g., home versus school) and for different purposes (e.g., social-interpersonal versus instructional).

THE DEVELOPMENT OF COMMUNICATION—BIRTH TO 6 YEARS

This brief exploration of the developmental trends in communication is intended to serve several purposes. It illustrates the qualitative and quantitative differences in children's abilities across the age range of birth to 6 years—the most critical age range for development of communication. As the various stages of development are considered, the continuous interrelationship among the *how*, *what*, and *why* of communication becomes apparent. The sequence in which various communication abilities emerge should yield a criterion-referenced approach to viewing any child as a developing communicator—that is, a view of what a child has accomplished and where the child is heading in the process of further development. By adding approximate age intervals, there is a tentative view of how a child's development conforms to the development of age mates (a norm-referenced approach). Finally, a comprehensive developmental perspective is fundamental to planning and implementing sound assessment and intervention strategies (Harrison et al., 1986–87). Without this general knowledge, the particulars of any assessment or intervention plan are meaningless.

An overview of the major milestones in the development of cognition, communication, language, and speech is presented in Appendix 11-1. Age ranges are presented in roughly 6-month to 1-year intervals, but these intervals can be misleading. The typical rate of development might be more variable than is indicated in Appendix 11-1, for most developmental data have been traditionally obtained from children of middle class, professional families and may not generalize well to children from different socioeconomic backgrounds. Furthermore, even though developmental abilities are presented as typically "appearing" at a particular age, in reality development is a continuous process of new abilities building on or transforming earlier ones.

Developmental changes in communication are illustrated in the following vignettes from Bryen (1982, pp. 65–66):

Vignette I

(12 mos.)

Child: (*Looks at and reaches for a squeak toy*)
Adult: Ya gonna squeak it?
Child: (*Tries to squeak the toy, then looks at adult*)
Adult: (*Reaches and squeaks the toy*) Uh, there it goes. (*Looks at child*)

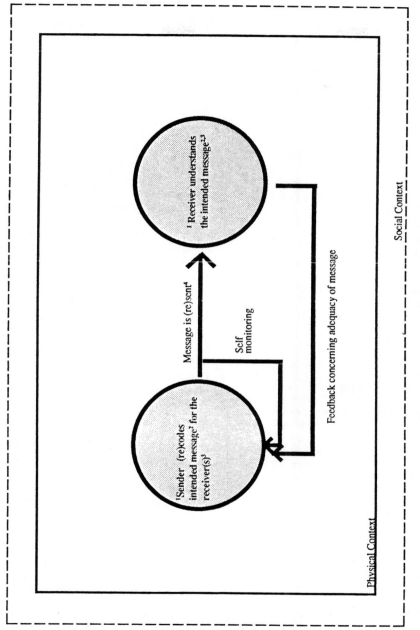

Figure 11.1   Communication model.
Note. Based on *Project: Communication,* by D. N. Bryen et al., 1980, Temple University, Philadelphia.   Used with permission of the author.

Child: (Watches adult's actions)
Adult: Squeak, squeak *(while squeaking the toy).*
Child: (After watching adult's actions, leans over and squeaks the toy)
Adult: Oh! You made it squeak.

Vignette II

(16 mos.)

Child: Dat. *(Points to a stuffed dog in a truck)*
Dat. *(Points to pick-up sticks)*
(Reaches for the sticks and all but two fall on the floor)
All gone. *(Looks at mother)*
Tick. *(Looks at mother and then at the sticks on the floor)*

Vignette III

(3 yrs.)

Child: Where my ice ceam is?
I want dat samich.
It good.
Mommy, want some?
It good ice cream.

Vignette IV

(5 yrs.)

Child 1: Le's make sumin else.
Le's make de airplane.
Child 2: I know, le's make da jet.
Le's make da jet.
Child 1: (Pointing to the cover of the Lego box)
Wanna make dis *(point)* an dis *(point)* and dat *(point)*?
Child 2: Yeah, le's make dese *(pointing to one of the demonstration pictures on the lid of the box).*
Child 3: Yeah, an le's make dose *(pointing to lid).*
Child 1: Okay, le's go. Come on, get ta work.

Vignette V

(7 yrs.)

Child 1: I watch Marine Boy, I watch Star Track.
Child 2: (Smiling and moving hands in acknowledgement) That's great?
Child 1: My cousin, that's his favorite guy, and I can even do this *(makes a peace sign with two fingers).* It's some kind of peace sign for the Vikings. You know Spock, that guy who's a Viking?
Child 2: Do you like Spock? I do. Except that

Spock is not a Viking.
Child 1: Yes he is! He's half Viking and half human.

In all five vignettes, communication occurs in a physical and social context. This context includes senders and receivers who apparently have as a goal the desire to interact with each other (the *why* of communication). Even when the sender dominates the conversational episode (as in Vignettes II and III), the goal of influencing the social or physical environment is present. Similarly, in all five vignettes communicative signals exist as a means for sending messages (the *how* of communication). These signals include eye contact, vocalization, pointing, facial expression, and spoken language. Finally, even though the nature of the communicative message or content (the *what* of communication) varies, unintentional and intentional messages are continually being sent.

In what ways do communications differ as children develop cognitively, socially, and linguistically? Developmental differences in communication include the following factors:

1. Nature and variety of signals used
2. Nature and content of the message itself
3. Spatial and temporal orientation of the message
4. Function(s) of communication
5. Presuppositional quality of the message
6. Precision and elaborateness of the linguistic message

One of the most obvious differences in Vignettes I through V is the nature and variety of *communicative signals* used. In Vignette I, looking, body posture, and actions are the only signals used. Although these signals continue to be used in subsequent vignettes, others also emerge (for example, smiling, pointing, vocalization, and spoken language). By Vignette V, spoken language is the primary vehicle for communicating the content of the message, although smiling, gestures, and eye contact accompany the interaction. Not evident in these vignettes is a whole array of nonverbal communicative signals that have a compelling effect on the communicative exchange. These include facial expressions and visual interaction, body movements and gestures, paralinguistic features of tone and pitch, and proximity.

As children develop, the quality of their speech and language changes in complexity, accuracy, and explicitness. Contrast the cryptic language and immature speech patterns in Vignette II (16-month-old child) with the relatively complex language and well-developed speech patterns in Vignette V (7 year olds). Even when language becomes more fully developed (for example, in Vignettes III and IV, ages 3 and 5, respectively), speech patterns are not completely mastered.

Along with an expansion in the types of signals used, there is an expansion in the *content* of the communicative message. Interest in objects, states, and actions (as evidenced in Vignettes I to IV) expands to include events, attitudes, and attributes (Vignette V). The content of the message evolves from a preoccupation in communicating about (and understanding) the present, palpable physical environment to discussing (and trying to understand) the somewhat subjective, hypothetical social world.

In Vignettes I to IV, communication is oriented to the *ongoing temporal* and *spatial* context. There is little distancing between *I* and *it* (the present, palpable environment). At first, objects and people that are present are indexed by eye contact, gestures, or pointing. Even when children begin to develop language (Vignettes II to IV), the primary function continues to be one of communicating about the "here-and-now" world of objects, people, actions, and events. This present orientation (contextualization) continues into the early school years, only gradually giving way to communication that is distanced in time and space (decontextualization). This gradual decontextualization of *I* and *it* is evidenced in Vignette V. Here, the children communicate about events that occurred in the past and, although not evident, there is the cognitive and linguistic freedom and desire to communicate about future occurrences.

The intent or *functions* of communicative episodes also expand as children develop. At first, communication is largely instrumental in obtaining desired material and social objects (Vignettes I to III). By the early preschool years, communication expands to include regulatory, informational-sharing, and informational-seeking functions (Vignette IV). By the early school years, added to these functions are those of criticism and the rudiments of persuasion (Vignette V).

Presupposition—the "use of an utterance (or any communicative signal) to comment upon information assumed to be shared by speaker and listener" (Bates, 1976, p. 97)—is an ability that is refined as children develop and can coordinate the *I* and *thou*. In Vignettes I to III, there is little separation of the *I* and *thou*. Here the youngsters are quite egocentric in their communication. The children presume that their interests are automatically shared by their conversational partner. In Vignette II, for example, the content relates exclusively to objects and actions that are an extension of the child's object interests. The adult is primarily an agent for the child. Perhaps the primary communicative paradigm is the following: If the child does (says) X, the adult will do Y. In Vignette IV, although there is a continuation of ego interest, there is also some awareness of the perspective of the conversational partner ("Le's make dese"). Even the choice of pronouns—*my* and *I* in Vignette III in contrast to *us* (*le's* = *let us*) in Vignette IV—differs. Finally, in Vignette V, there is a further decentration of *I* and *thou* and the conversation takes on a more cooperative quality. The topic introduced by Child 1 is continued by Child 2. Questions are used to acknowledge that the listener has indeed understood the speaker's intended message. In contrast, in Vignette IV, the partners, while maintaining a joint topic (building with Legos), pursue the topic from their own perspectives (Child 1: "Le's make da airplane." Child 2: "I know, le's make da jet.")

As children expand their cognitive, social, and linguistic abilities, their *communicative messages* become *more precise and explicit*. In contrast, the developmentally young child's communications are quite cryptic, relying heavily on the physical context and shared knowledge to disambiguate the message. The nonverbal signals in Vignette I (e.g., looking and reaching) and the one-word utterances accompanied by pointing and looking in Vignette II are examples of the potentially imprecise and cryptic quality of the young communicator. Although the precision and explicitness of the messages increase during the preschool years (Vignettes III and IV), because of the continued presuppositional nature of children, communication continues to rely heavily on context clues. This is illustrated in Vignette IV ("Yeah, le's make dese," pointing to the lid of the box). Pragmatically, one can argue validly that given the presence of shared visual information, the use of the pronoun *dese* (*these*) was a sufficient indexer. However, even in the absence of shared visual information, the preschoolers' communication continues to be characteristically presuppositional in quality and somewhat imprecise in form.

By the early school years, communication becomes more elaborate in form and more explicit in communicating the child's intended message. This is illustrated in Vignette V (e.g., "It's some kind of peace sign for the Vikings," making a peace sign with two fingers). The form of the message is primarily linguistic, and extralinguistic features, such as the peace sign, are used merely to add emphasis or affect to the message.

With this overview of development through the early school years as a background, let us now return to the unready child. The unready child is discussed in the context of classroom demands because (except for the small minority of children with severe communication problems) entrance into school is generally the occasion when mild problems become significant educational concerns. The following section is based partly on Bryen (1982).

THE LANGUAGE OF INSTRUCTION AND THE LINGUISTICALLY UNREADY CHILD

During the preschool and early school years, teachers might be faced with children who are unready for the linguistic code found in the typical classroom. These preschool and early elementary school children may be quite normal, but somewhat slower in the acquisition of language; they might suffer from mild to moderate hearing losses that have not been previously detected (Griffith et al., 1985); or they might be mildly mentally retarded or learning disabled (Calculator, 1985; Donahue, 1985). They might be youngsters who, because of emotional problems, are preoccupied with fantasies and consequently have problems attending to the ongoing flow of speech. They might be children who are not motivated to use their linguistic knowledge for purposes of communication. Some youngsters might be members of cultural or linguistic minorities whose communication codes and rules of discourse are dif-

ferent from those required in the classroom (Heath, 1983; Iglesias, 1985; Phillips, 1983).

The problems of unready children are as diverse as the causes for their unreadiness. First, unready children might not be motivated to engage actively in the cooperative process of communication. Having inadequately received the message that their communicative attempts can powerfully affect their social and physical environment, these children might not initiate communication. Consequently, they fail to say to the teacher, "I don't understand this," to solicit help. Instead, they struggle independently to resolve the lack of understanding, and frustration and failure can result—reinforcing their belief in their own powerlessness.

Unready children also might be delayed in the acquisition of the syntactic and semantic (meaning) components of language. As a result, communication attempts frequently can be cryptic, omitting necessary grammatical and semantic elements. Receptively, these children might fail to process complex sentences, and consequently lose needed information or instructions.

Limited vocabulary also can affect these children's access to the language of instruction. All children are constrained by limits in vocabulary, but parents engage in several discourse strategies to aid children in the comprehension and acquisition of unfamiliar words. For example, by repeating and emphasizing particular words, and utilizing the physical context as a communicative supplement, parents can help children learn new words. In the classroom, however, where the teacher is interacting with the group, not the individual child, repetition and context clues might not be employed and the child might not comprehend the unfamiliar vocabulary (Gruenewald & Pollak, 1984).

The instructional code generally is more abstract than those to which children have been exposed previously. Language used in the classroom is frequently displaced from the here and now and from the child's ongoing actions, and therefore cannot be supplemented by gestures and contextual clues. Most children entering the elementary school grades no longer require language that is context and action based, but many preschool and developmentally immature youngsters continue to require the aid of the physical context or their own actions in the comprehension and production of language. This psychological factor has been recognized as important in learning basic arithmetic concepts and has been incorporated in the teaching of arithmetic. However, it has not been applied as readily in other areas in which language plays a key role. Children who are unready to deal with language that is completely abstracted from a physical context are likely to miss much of the information communicated in the classroom.

Any child who spends time in a classroom typically must process complex language that coordinates more than one proposition. The preschool child will continually hear requests such as "Get your coat and form a line at the door." The school-aged child will be told, "Take out your pencil, turn to page 42 of your arithmetic book, and complete all of the addition problems there." To follow these directions, the child must be able to comprehend all propositions of these complex linguistic messages. For some children who are cognitively or linguistically immature, following directions like these will be problematic. In some cases, only the first proposition of the message will be processed, so that the preschool child will get his or her coat but not join the other children in forming a line at the door. In other cases, the child will only process part of the message and wait for a nonlinguistic cue from other children (e.g., children walking to the door) to compensate for the unprocessed linguistic message. The child might randomly process one proposition of the sentence and ignore others, and thus attempt to begin the arithmetic work without having processed the page number of the assigned task. Children who have these difficulties not only find classroom interactions and assignments confusing and frustrating, but also are frustrating to their teachers who do not understand the nature of their problem.

The majority of children enrolled in regular classes might have subtle language problems not based on specific linguistic structural delays. If assessed on their ability to produce and comprehend single sentences that measure different syntactic and semantic structures, these youngsters do fine; however, they might inadequately comprehend expanded discourse when it occurs in the classroom. An increase in background noise might interfere with their ability to accurately process ongoing target discourse, or the natural rate of speech might be frustratingly fast. They might need pauses between complex sentences to have adequate processing time. They also might need exaggerated stress and heightened pitch when critical information is embedded in ongoing speech, so that this information is made more perceptually salient.

Some youngsters have difficulty comprehending ongoing language when there are rapid changes in speaker–listener roles. In a dyadic context, the child is either the speaker or the person spoken to; therefore, dyad-based pronouns such as *you*, *me*, *I*, *we*, and *us* are somewhat more stable. When the size of a group increases beyond two, however, the listener–speaker roles vary. The child also can be referred to as *he/she*, *him/her*, *they*, or *them*. To complicate the situation further, other children in the group also will be referred to as *you*, *I*, *they*, *we*, *me*, and so on, depending on shifts in listener–speaker roles.

Pronouns other than those relating to the speaker–listener relationship also can cause problems in comprehension. Pronouns that refer to previously specified information either within the sentence or in other sentences might not be accurately coordinated. For example, in the sentence "The boy had a car and he gave it to me," the child might not recognize that the pronoun *he* refers back to the noun phrase *the boy* and the pronoun *it* refers to the noun *car* in the verb phrase. Pronouns also can refer to information specified in a previous sentence, such as "Your arithmetic work begins on page 14. When you finish it, you can have free time." Some youngsters might not understand that the pronoun *it* in the second sentence refers to the phrase *your arithmetic work* specified in the first sentence.

Not only might language-based classroom problems affect access to instructional information, but also access to other classroom resources might be limited. Some children might not have adequately learned the rules for effective speaking, which include being direct, relevant, and informative, designating a particular listener to whom a request is addressed, and revising one's initial request when it is ineffective (Garnica, 1981; Grice, 1976; Wilkinson & Calculator, 1982). An example of an ineffective speaker follows:

> A kindergarten boy sits in the doorway to his classroom, head down, ineffectively repeating, "I have a shoe problem. . . . I have a shoe problem. . . . I have a shoe problem. . . ." No one comes because

he has failed to (1) designate a particular listener, (2) be informative, and (3) revise his initial request when it was ineffective. (Feskanin, 1987)

Other school discourse problems include trouble maintaining a topic (or sticking to the subject), and not learning the implicit communicative rules for soliciting and maintaining attention.

There also are youngsters who apparently have adequate language abilities but are not ready for language-related processes such as reading and writing. A strong case can be made for assessing metalinguistic abilities that extend beyond the tacit knowledge of language (Bryen, 1987; Bryen & Gerber, 1987). Learning to read, spell, and write requires more than the *use* of language; in traditional instruction, the child must think about speech and language themselves in addition to thinking about their use. For example, when the phonics approach to reading is employed or when spelling is taught, the child must think about how words are segmented into phonemes and how these segmented phonemes are more or less represented by graphic symbols. Similarly, when writing, the child must analytically segment the natural flow of language so that each word can be accurately and precisely represented graphically.

For many youngsters, the transition from natural language to the more formal, deliberately arrived at written form is very difficult. The reasons for this difficulty are not clear. Some authors have suggested that the difficulty is based more on differences in how oral and written language are *taught* than on how they are *learned* (Goodman & Goodman, 1977; Smith, 1971). Others have used direct and indirect evidence to demonstrate the relationship between literacy problems and dysfunction in the semantic, syntactic, or phonological aspects of language (Vellutino, 1977). Still others have maintained that poor writing is connected to certain inherent cognitive and social demands of the writing process itself and to the cognitive and social readiness of the writer (Elasser & John-Steiner, 1977).

The problems discussed in this section are only representative of the variety of language and communication problems likely to be encountered in the classroom. This topic is discussed in greater depth elsewhere (Berry, 1976; Berry, 1980; Bloom & Lahey, 1978; Gerber & Bryen, 1981; Gruenewald & Pollak, 1984; Morehead & Morehead,

1976; Muma, 1978; Ripich & Spinelli, 1985; Wilkinson, 1982; Yaden & Templeton, 1986).

It is time to return to the primary focus—the assessment of language and the educational implications of such assessment. Both formal assessment techniques and informal strategies that can be adapted from current research in socio- and psycholinguistics are discussed, and the use of results from informal strategies to generate meaningful diagnosis is considered. In the final section, implications for language intervention are discussed briefly.

FORMAL, STANDARDIZED ASSESSMENT OF LANGUAGE

In the late 1970s and early 1980s there was a trend away from heavy reliance on formal, standardized testing of language and toward the use of descriptive, informal assessment strategies. Muma (1973, 1978), Leonard and coworkers (1978), and Miller (1981) are prominent among the writers who have built a strong case against undue use of formal tests. Muma (1973), for example, argued that developmental scales and other normative measures of language are of questionable value. He maintained that these measures provide little information about the nature of the problems in language and its use. The highly specific, structured tasks characteristic of many standardized tests are only remotely related to the pragmatic demands of language that vary with differences in context and function. If standardized tests must be administered to determine normative deviation, Muma urged that information beyond the numerical score be gleaned from that formal observation "It is more important to learn *how* an individual functions in obtaining a score than *what* the score is" (Muma, 1978, p. 265).

Teachers, clinicians, and diagnosticians should, however, be aware of the most common standardized tests of language, because they continue to be in widespread use in language evaluations of young children. A number of the tests used with children from birth to 6 years are described in Appendix 11-2. That list is by no means exhaustive; other sources contain additional catalogues, descriptions, and critiques of standardized tests of language (Bloom & Lahey, 1978; Lloyd, 1976; McCauley & Swisher, 1984; Minife

& Lloyd, 1978; Muma, 1978; Wiig & Semel, 1976, 1980).

Considerations in Testing Language

Strategies for the formal assessment of the young child's language development should reflect current research, which is moving in divergent directions as speech and language come to be seen as part of a much more inclusive system of communication. Historically, the emphasis in testing has evolved from articulation and phonology, through language structure and content, to a current awareness of the pragmatics or uses of language. Although all of these skills are necessary elements of the language system, it is from the successful integration of these dimensions of form, content, and use that meaningful language abilities develop (Bloom, 1980).

With a growing awareness of the complexity of child language acquisition, there has been increasing evidence of considerable variation among children in the ways in which linguistic competence develops and is demonstrated. Young children are in a period of such rapid development that their behavior differs measurably from one time to another; thus assessment is at best an approximation of true abilities at any given point in time. Other factors also can influence intrasubject variability: inherent attributes, such as the child's personality, sex, intelligence, social background (e.g., family structure), cultural affiliation, and style of interaction (linguistic and behavioral); and characteristics of the situation, such as setting, activities, and the number, status, and familiarity of other participants (Wells, 1979).

There also are methodological concerns of data collection and analysis. One major issue is the representativeness of the language behavior observed. Controversy abounds as to the relative advantages of assessment based on spontaneous language samples, elicited language samples, or structured tasks. Clearly, the language sample to be scrutinized should be as complete and representative of the child's linguistic competence as possible. In many test situations, however, the language behavior is either so artificially separated from a meaningful context that it is distorted, or represents such a small portion of the child's repertoire of linguistic competence that it is grossly inaccurate.

Another methodological consideration is the question of what to quantify. What linguistic structures, communicative strategies, and behaviors demonstrating receptive and/or expressive abilities should be counted? How can these competencies be inferred from behavior? The question of how to quantify these entities is an equally perplexing problem. Is it sufficient to note the presence of a structure or an appropriate response, or is frequency a more accurate parameter? No one theorist, researcher, or assessment technique proposes a remedy to all of these obstacles to successful child language assessment; rather, each addresses some portion of the overall task.

In this review, the formal testing paradigms are classified according to the performance tasks required of the child. Generally, the responses solicited by the examiner fall into one of these categories: (a) elicited imitation; (b) manipulation of objects (demonstration of a nonverbal response); (c) picture identification; (d) language completion, in which the child supplies a missing word or otherwise finishes an incomplete linguistic structure; and (e) sample of spontaneous language used by the child. The examiner also can use inventories of language development that rely on either observation of the child or on interviews with the child's primary caregiver.

Elicited Imitation

Elicited imitation tasks require the child to repeat lists of phrases or sentences spoken by the examiner. Sentences presented typically vary in grammatical construction and complexity. The control the examiner has over the type of grammatical structure used provides this strategy with an advantage over the analysis of spontaneous language samples by ensuring that specific constructions will be attempted by the child. The theory behind the use of elicited imitation derives primarily from the early work of Menyuk (1964) and Fraser and colleagues (1963), which addressed the interrelationship among imitation, comprehension, and production of language. Testing the hypothesis that comprehension precedes production of language, Fraser and colleagues determined that, for their sample of 3-year-old children, production at the imitative level was indeed an easier task than comprehension of the same grammatical structure. Furthermore, they found that spontaneous production of that structure followed developmentally its comprehension by the children. Hence, the Imitation Comprehension Production (ICP) hypothesis established that imitative ability is a separate linguistic skill that precedes comprehension and production.

More recent research has shown that imitation of sentences that exceed the child's short-term memory span reveals a great deal about the comprehension and expression of language. Children, it is believed, reproduce sentences using the grammatical rules they know. According to this position, one can deduce the extent to which the message is understood (comprehension) and the linguistic rules that govern the child's production of language.

Some difficulties with the primary assumption underlying the imitation paradigm are worth noting, especially as they affect interpretation of the child's ability to repeat grammatical structures. The major challenge to the universality of children's imitative ability in spontaneous speech came from Bloom and coworkers (1974). Their research with children whose linguistic development ranged from 1.0 to 2.0 mean length of utterance (MLU) showed that the extent of imitation in normal interactive speech varied from child to child; indeed, some children do not spontaneously imitate language. Bloom and coworkers suggested that when imitation did occur, only moderately new semantic-syntactic structures were imitated; those that were entirely new or had already been mastered were not repeated in normal discourse.

Moreover, a large body of research has shown that children might not imitate structures that have previously appeared in their spontaneous speech. The following example taken from the data as reported by Bloom (1974, p. 299) illustrates this point:

Peter (32 months of age playing "Simple Simon Says")
Examiner says: "This is a big balloon."
Peter says: "This is a big balloon."
Examiner says: "This is broken."
Peter says: "What's broken?"
Examiner says: "This is broken."
Peter says: "That's broken."
Examiner says: "I'm trying to get this in there."
Peter says: "Cow in here."
Examiner says: "I'm gonna get the cow to drink milk."

Peter says: "Get the cow to drink milk."
Examiner says: "You made him stand up over there."
Peter says: "Stand up there."

As Bloom (1974) points out, it might be assumed from this exercise that Peter does not yet know the productive rules governing use of the uncontracted copula *is*. However, each of these stimulus sentences had been spoken spontaneously by Peter the preceding day while he was playing with a variety of toys and explaining his activity to the same examiner. Bloom's explanation of this apparent dichotomy of linguistic ability is that Peter was able to generate the more complex sentences within the natural situation because of the support given by the contextual events themselves and his own behavior as part of that event. When asked to repeat sentences that were unrelated to his immediate context and behavior, he was unable to do so.

Some child language research findings contradict this predominant view of imitation as an imprecise underestimate of productive ability. Moerk (1977), in comparing the speech of 2 year olds under both conditions, concluded that imitative utterances surpassed those produced in spontaneous speech. However, the critical distinction is that the usefulness of children's imitative ability is not to analyze how the child comes to know and use adult speech but rather to analyze how adults as teachers and clinicians can better understand child language. As a clinical tool, elicited imitation does allow for a rather fine-grained analysis of the child's production strategies (Slobin & Welsh, 1971).

Formal assessments presented in Appendix 11-2 that depend upon the child's imitation of stimulus sentences include the expressive portion of the *Patterned Elicited Syntax Test* (Young & Perachio, 1983), *Oral Language Sentence Imitation Screening Test* (Zachman et al., 1978), the *Measurement of Language Development* (Melnick, 1975), *Northwestern Syntax Screening Test* (Lee, 1971), and the *Carrow Elicited Language Inventory* (Carrow, 1974). Elicited imitation also is a paradigm used in other formal tests that require a variety of response behaviors from the child (e.g., *Porch Index of Communicative Ability in Children*, Porch, 1979; *Sequenced Inventory of Communication Development*, Hedrick, et al., 1984).

There is a final caveat in the administration and interpretation of tests of elicited imitation. Children might respond to items in the testing situation as though they were related to normal discourse exchange (Prutting & Rees as cited in Kretschmer & Kretschmer, 1978; Rose & Blank, 1974). It would be reasonable for the child to respond with an answer to the question "Where are the dolls?" (Carrow, *Elicited Language Inventory,* Item 38) rather than imitate the sentence. The recommendation of Slobin and Welsh (1971) seems sound: elicited imitation is a valuable tool for use in child language analysis, but information obtained in this fashion should be supplemented by data from spontaneous language samples.

Comprehension Tasks

The assessment of language comprehension in young children seems at first to be a relatively straightforward process of providing a spoken message and requesting that the child respond in some way that illustrates his or her understanding of the linguistic content of the message. It can be difficult, however, to distinguish between comprehension based on the child's decoding of linguistic stimuli and that which is based on the nonlinguistic features of the situation itself.

Research findings have demonstrated the existence of several nonlinguistic strategies that young children use at different developmental stages to assist them in their comprehension of language. The probability of events occurring in the natural environment, and an understanding of some semantic relationships (especially related to animateness and temporal order of event), are contextual cues that play an important role in the child's demonstration of comprehension (Clark, 1973b, 1980; Koff et al., 1980; Strohner & Nelson, 1974; Wallach, 1984). Indeed, Shatz (1978) and Chapman (1978) described comprehension strategies as short cuts or heuristics that children use to determine sentence meaning when they do not have the linguistic sophistication to comprehend, based on syntactic knowledge. Chapman's taxonomy summarized comprehension strategies from sensorimotor Stage IV infants (8 to 12 months), whose nonlinguistic response patterns are entirely context related, to late preoperational and concrete operational children (4 to 11 years), whose lexical and syntactic comprehension provide understanding of simple structures, but whose past experience (probable relation of events) determines complex sentence meaning.

Knowledge of events in the world plus familiarity with lexical terms allow children who might not yet have mastered the linguistic rules of word order to respond as if they did to sentences such as "The cat chases the mouse" or "The boy eats the apples." However, the child's inability to use word order as the basis of comprehension can be inferred from tasks that ask the child, for example, to demonstrate with toys or select the pictures illustrating the reversible phrases "Mommy kissing Daddy" and "Daddy kissing Mommy" (Miller & Yoder, 1972). Although children 2 to 3 years of age use appropriate subject–verb–object ordering in their own speech production, their correct responses to questions and commands in which word order is distorted (Wetstone & Friedlander, 1973) and their inability to demonstrate correctly reversible active and passive sentences (Chapman & Miller, 1975; deVilliers & deVilliers, 1973) provide support for early reliance upon nonlinguistic cues for comprehension.

The developmental shift from children's dependence on context to their increasing facility with word order as a comprehension strategy was documented by Bever (1970), Lempert and Kinsbourne (1978, 1980) and Strohner and Nelson (1974). These researchers traced the comprehension strategies used by children from approximately 2 to 6 years of age and provided analyses similar to that of Chapman (1978), mentioned earlier. Their findings corroborate the notion that there is a developmental progression in which maximum use of probable event strategy occurs at about 3 years of age (Strohner & Nelson, 1974). Between 3½ and 5 years of age, simple noun–verbal–noun word order strategy causes the child to assign the agent role to the first noun and object role to the second noun. Simple active sentences such as "The car bumps the train" and "The train bumps the car" can be acted out correctly; however, application of this strategy to passive sentences ("The car is bumped by the train") results in consistently incorrect comprehension (Bever, 1970; Chapman, 1978). Lempert and Kinsbourne (1978) found that this noun–verb–noun strategy served as the basis of comprehension with this age group provided the implied relation was consistent with probable event theory.

At about 4½ or 5 years of age, a systematic change occurs in the child's ability to process passive sentences according to syntactic information (Bever, 1970; Lempert & Kinsbourne, 1978, 1980; Strohner & Nelson, 1974; Wallach, 1984). The few inconsistencies in performance at this level result from sentence interpretation of improbable content. Although there is a decrease in dependence on an agent/action approach to comprehension, there are more complex sentence constructions to which the preschool-age child might again apply this strategy. For example, 5 and 6 year olds use surface structure clues of noun as agent to interpret sentences such as "The duck is happy to bite" or "The wolf is easy to bite" and thus indicate the named animal as doing the biting (Cromer, 1972, 1974). Similarly, responses of 3, 4, and 5 year old children to sentences containing relative embedded clauses (e.g., "The boy who is talking to the girl is wearing a hat") provide evidence of the difficulty of this construction for children (Brown, 1971).

Lempert and Kinsbourne (1980) addressed the issue of the child's development of increased flexibility in sentence processing. A variety of comprehension strategies was observed in those children who demonstrated correct interpretation of the passive voice, but could not master the interpretation of inverted cleft sentences (e.g., "It's the horse that the cow kisses"). Such adaptive problem-solving skill in 5 to 7 year-old children is viewed as a reflection of their increased awareness of the syntactic elements of sentence construction.

Some methodological constraints in the evaluation of children's comprehension of spoken language relate to the form of the adult's examiner's linguistic message. The research of Shipley and coworkers (1969) suggested that young children who are at a telegraphic stage of language development demonstrate more correct responses when the adult directive is given in a form similar to the child's speech. Petretic and Tweney (1977) found, however, that all children in the 1 year 9 months to 3 year 6 months group responded more accurately to the more fully developed adult forms than to the telegraphic speech characteristic of their own ability. Interpretation of five *wh-* questions (i.e., *who, where, what, why, how*) by 3 to 5½ year old children reveals a sequence of acquisition of these forms that is parallel in the child's production and comprehension. Facility with *yes/no, what,* and *where* questions appears first; these forms are closely related to the child's immediate context, whereas *how* and *when* are dependent on more abstract concepts of cause, manner, and time (Tyack & Ingram, 1977).

Other important factors are the speech rate and the use of pauses in the messages given by adults to young children. Speech slightly slower than the normal adult rate has been found to improve comprehension of children at the kindergarten to second grade level (Berry & Erickson, 1973). Moreover, the comprehension of adult messages by 3 to 4 year-old children was improved when pauses occurred at major phrase boundaries in the sentence. Comprehension by 5 to 6 year olds was not dependent on the suprasegmental feature of pausing (LaBelle, 1973). The importance of these findings to the administration and interpretation of language tests of comprehension should be clear.

As indicated earlier, formal assessment of comprehension can be categorized according to the response required by the child. The preferred response modalities in young children are presented in Table 11-1.

In so far as Miller (1978) found that the picture-pointing tasks require recognitive ability and object manipulation tasks require reconstructive ability, he predicted that the latter would be more

TABLE 11.1
DEVELOPMENTAL NATURE OF COMPREHENSION TASKS

Task	Lower Limit of Age Appropriateness
Behavioral compliance with commands	12 months (Huttenlocher, 1974)
Question answering	24 months (Chapman, cited in Miller, 1978
Picture pointing	Single words: 18 months Sentences: 24 to 30 months
Object manipulation	20 months (Chapman & Miller, 1975)

Note: From "Assessing children's language behavior: A developmental process approach," by J. F. Miller, in *Bases of Language Intervention* (p. 300), R. L. Schiefelbusch, Ed., 1978, Baltimore: University Park Press. Copyright 1978 by University Park Press. Reprinted by permission.

difficult for children to complete than the former. Considerations of recognition and reconstruction will be discussed later. Miller and Yoder (cited in Miller, 1978) reported that preliminary data suggested that for mildly and moderately retarded children, the tasks of picture identification and object manipulation are of equal difficulty and equal reliability across syntactic structures sampled.

Object Manipulation

Object manipulation frequently is used as an indicator of comprehension in research, but few formalized tests of language comprehension make use of the child's active manipulation of objects in response to the examiner's questions. The only assessment procedure that relies exclusively on the format of manipulation of objects is the *Bellugi-Klima Comprehension Tests for Syntactic Constructions* (Bellugi-Klima, 1971), which is not standardized with normative data. The assessment procedures described by Bellugi-Klima, however, include carefully controlled situations that have significant value in determining the child's understanding of syntactic structures. Some standardized tests that include object manipulation or identification as opposed to picture identification are the *Reynell Developmental Language Scales* (Reynell, 1977) and the *Sequenced Inventory of Communication Development* (Hedrick et al., 1984). Specific comprehension items in the *Preschool Language Scale* (Zimmerman et al., 1969), the *Environmental Prelanguage Battery* (Horstmeier & MacDonald, 1978), and the *Porch Index of Communicative Ability in Children* (Porch, 1979) require object identification.

Some investigators view the manipulation of objects in response to instructions given by the examiner as the preferred method of assessing comprehension (Bellugi-Klima, 1971; Huttenlocher, 1974). The child is asked to manipulate objects according to the directions provided; accurate demonstration indicates whether comprehension was based on an understanding of syntactic elements. In the *Bellugi-Klima Language Comprehension Tests* (Bellugi-Klima, 1971), for example, the child is given small toys representing the lexicons of the statements and is asked to demonstrate the sentences "The boy feeds the girl" and "The girl feeds the boy" (p. 161). Similarly, the child can be asked to "Give me the marbles"

(p. 162) or "Show me the truck's driver" and "Show me the driver's truck" (p. 163) to assess the child's understanding of syntactic structures. Receptive items of the *Reynell Developmental Language Scales* (Reynell, 1977) use object manipulation in conjunction with object identification to assess increasingly difficult abilities of verbal comprehension. The questions proceed from the earliest stages of identity ("Where is the dog?"), to understanding the functions ("Which one do we sleep in?"), to integrating attributes and sequence of directions relative to the materials ("Pick up the biggest pink pig and show me his eyes").

Beyond the situational cues that affect all comprehension tasks, specific cautions need to be taken with object manipulation. Children's behavioral preferences of play with objects might give the impression that they have comprehended the examiner's message when, in fact, their natural predisposition to perform according to that pattern might be responsible (Chapman, 1978; Shatz, 1978). Clark found that certain nonlinguistic strategies of young children can give the appearance of semantic understanding of *in*, *on*, and *under* (Clark, 1973b) and *top/bottom*, *front/back* (Clark, 1980). For example, at the earliest stage (1½ to 2 years), children follow a nonlinguistic strategy involving two rules: if *X* is a container, put the object *in* it; if *X* has a surface, put the object *on* it. Between 2 and 3 years of age, children generally correctly express *in* during their own productions and provide semantically correct answers for *on*, but can do the same only half the time for *under* (Clark, 1973b, p. 177). Not until children are about 3 years old do they demonstrate full semantic knowledge of these words.

Another consideration, pointed out by Bellugi-Klima (1971), is that if the intent of the investigation is to determine syntactic competence, then the vocabulary must be familiar to the children; otherwise, it is not possible to determine whether incorrect performance is attributable to a lack of syntactic understanding or a lack of familiarity with the vocabulary items.

Huttenlocher (1974) is one of the few investigators interested in comprehension as it is influenced by the ways in which materials are presented. In collaboration with other psycholinguists (Huttenlocher et al., 1968; Huttenlocher & Strauss, 1968; Huttenlocher & Weiner, 1971), she systematically varied the contextual arrangements of objects, observed children's abilities to carry out tasks under various arrangements, and inferred the interrelationship between context and linguistic comprehension. In fact, Huttenlocher posited that elements of the context predispose specific responses; to the extent that the verbal message is redundant in relation to the context, it need not be understood. Given a ladder with tiers, one block fixed on one tier and another to be placed, the interpretation of the sentence "The red block is on top of the green block" differs in difficulty depending on other aspects of the context. If the ladder has only two tiers and there is only a red block to place, no comprehension of linguistic information is necessary. On the other hand, if two ladders having three tiers each are presented and an assortment of blocks of different colors are available to be moved, the listener must understand relational terms and subject and object terms to perform correctly (Huttenlocher & Weiner, 1971).

Huttenlocher and Strauss (1968) found that among 5, 7, and 9 year old children, the extra-linguistic context, not the stimulus sentence, was likely to determine the logical actor. More errors in a demonstration of comprehension were made when children were asked to place a block that was the object of the sentence than a block that was the subject. Huttenlocher and Weiner (1971) also demonstrated that the movement of one object relative to a second, fixed object was easier for grade school children than the placement of two movable objects relative to each other. Presumably, the former context provided a conceptual, if not grammatical, subject or point of reference.

Huttenlocher (1974) enumerated some specific suggestions that might be helpful in evaluating receptive language. If one is assessing the listener's knowledge of object names, she recommends that a wide range of possible choices be offered and the examiner be aware that children might choose an object, not because they understand the name, but because it is a favorite toy. Knowledge of the word *ball*, for example, should not be assumed until the child *does not* select a ball when asked for a different object, or does not select any object when *ball* is asked for and *ball* is not presented.

McCabe and coworkers (1974) examined the effects of overt manipulation of objects on simultaneous sentence production by 4- to 5-year-old children. Their major prediction—that sentence production would be improved when children were simultaneously engaged in manipulating objects—was not supported; rather, the number of sentences produced was depressed when children were both demonstrating and telling about the actions involved, presumably because they had difficulty coordinating the motor acts of speaking and manipulating objects, both acts being controlled by the left hemisphere (Witelson, 1987). Although this mixing of response requirements is not an element in the demonstration formats of the tests presented in Appendix 11-2, these findings are presented to caution teachers and clinicians as to the potential intereference of one motor act with another in tests for young children.

Picture Identification

In picture identification tasks, the child is presented with an array of pictures and asked to point to the picture that shows the stimulus object or situation given by the examiner. This strategy is widely used in standardized tests of young children's comprehension. It provides the basis for the *Comprehension of Oral Language* (Manuel, 1973), the *Assessment of Children's Language Comprehension* (Foster, Giddan, & Stark, 1973), the *Bracken Basic Concept Scale* (Bracken, 1984), Carrow's (1973) *Test for Auditory Comprehension of Language*, the *Miller-Yoder Test for Grammatical Comprehension* (Miller & Yoder, 1972), and the receptive portions of the *Northwestern Syntax Screening Test* (Lee, 1971), the *Measurement of Language Development* (Melnick, 1975), the *Peabody Picture Vocabulary Test* (Dunn & Dunn, 1981), and the *Preschool Language Scale* (Zimmerman, Steiner, & Evatt, 1969).

In addition to the issues addressed previously regarding the assessment of comprehension, the picture identification paradigm involves several concerns unique to this manner of presentation. Briefly, they are factors associated with guessing and the consideration of recognition versus reconstruction as they relate to comprehension.

Factors of chance, such as the number of foils and the use of contrastive or nonconstrastive stimulus sentences, can bias test results. Fraser and colleagues (1963), in constructing their experimental test of comprehension, attempted to correct for chance effects by requiring the child to identify both pictures of contrasting sentence pairs before being credited with comprehension of the specific structure being tested. Among the group of 3 year old subjects evaluated, the response to each contrastive test sentence was independent of the other. Children who could not make the necessary lexical distinctions required by the sentences either pointed to the same picture in response to both sentences, pointed to two pictures simultaneously, or provided an unscorable response. This observation is in keeping with that made by Clark (1973b, 1980): Children at an early stage in acquisition of the relational concepts *top*, *bottom*, *in*, and *on* responded to demonstration tasks by indicating the same position for each lexicon of the opposing concept pair.

Although these data suggest the importance of the child's ability to differentiate between contrasting sentences, formal test construction rarely addresses this issue. Unless children are asked to identify pictures for contrastive sentences, there might not be the opportunity to observe their response ambivalence. Clark (1980), Huttenlocher (1974), and Miller and Yoder (1978) suggested that the assumption of mastery of lexical comprehension be made only after it has been demonstrated under situations of contrast. Although most test designers have not included this criterion, it is advisable to bear this distinction in mind when interpreting test results and planning an intervention program.

At later stages of cognitive and linguistic mastery, young children appear to be relatively skillful at understanding the implicit contextual cues of the testing paradigm (Rose & Blank, 1974). If the asking of two different questions requires that children respond with dissimilar answers, then knowledge of one of the contrastive members ensures a correct response to the other when just two alternatives are presented. Similarly, children's ability to eliminate known incorrect choices within a noncontrastive task might enable them to make a correct selection even when the stimulus item is not understood. In both instances, the number and plausibility of foils presented within the array of options can alter the probability of success by chance alone. For example, if a child chooses from among four alternative pictures, and each has an equal probability of being chosen, then the likelihood of chance success is 25%; however, if by process of elimination or other response strategy the child reduces the number of viable options to two, then the probability of chance success increases to 50%.

Finally, consideration of the different processing requirements imposed might provide an additional basis for the selection and use of formal comprehension tests or test items. Tasks might demand the recognition, recall, or reconstruction of information. According to Huttenlocher (1974), the child's association between an event and/or object and its corresponding word sound underlies early linguistic knowledge; comprehension implies the retrieval of these stored associations of meaning and sound. In the case of recall, the word sound is used as the stimulus to transfer information regarding the object properties to active memory. Recognition, however, depends only upon remembering the familiar word sound, then searching among available percepts for the object or event previously linked with the sound. That recognition ability is acquired before the more complex, more abstract ability to recall information is accepted widely among professionals (Brown, 1973; Oviatt, 1980; Piaget, 1952/1963). Moreover, Miller (1978) defined another dimension of the child's processing strategy as it relates to language assessments: the tasks required by the object manipulation paradigm involve reconstruction of the stimulus sentence. In this sense, reconstruction is more closely related to the definition of recall offered by Huttenlocher than to the easier task of recognition. Thus object manipulation is more difficult than picture identification despite the fact that three-dimensional, concrete objects were used. Object identification items (e.g., "Where is the shoe?") in which options are real objects rather than pictorial representations do not fall, of course, within the reconstruction definition; they require recall of information.

Language Completion

Language completion tasks require children to complete an incomplete phrase or sentence. Verbal conceptual skills are often assessed by asking children to complete verbal analogies. Similarly, children's ability to apply syntactic rules of grammatical inflection is frequently tested by the language completion paradigm. Both of these assessment items are found in the *Illinois Test of Psycholinguistic Abilities* (ITPA) (Kirk et al., 1968). The Auditory Association subtest taps children's ability to provide the correct analogous term after listening to an incomplete verbal stimulus (e.g., "Bread is to eat, milk is to _____"). As representational level tasks, these items require an understanding of complex symbolic associations and an ability to organize and manipulate linguistic symbols (Paraskevopoulos & Kirk, 1969). For purposes of the present analysis, the more controversial application of the language completion format is in the assessment of morphological development. This assessment occurs in the Grammatic Closure subtest of the ITPA, in which tasks depend less upon conceptual abilities than upon children's facility with grammatic forms that, once acquired, are used automatically (e.g., "This dog likes to bark; here he is _____" [barking]).

The major concern in the adoption of this test format using real lexical items is the influence of dialect on test results. Grill and Bartel (1977) identified this phenomenon in the Grammatic Closure subtest of the ITPA. Children who speak a dialect other than standard English tend to do less well on this subtest than those who speak the standard dialect. As a measure of general language development, then, this approach underestimates the abilities of children who might have acquired the rules of inflection in their own dialect but not those of standard English.

The same assessment paradigm is used with Berko's (1958) *Test of Morphology*, except that this test requires inflection of nonsense words as a measure of the child's knowledge of linguistic rules. As in the ITPA subtest, children are first presented with both a picture and a referential sentence frame; then the picture is modified so that the stimulus word must be inflected (e.g., "Here is a wug. Now there is another one; there are two of them. There are two _____"). Criticism regarding this assessment procedure relates to the lack of correspondence between children's ability with inflected nonsense words and their use of the same inflected structures in spontaneous speech. Dever (1971, 1972) demonstrated that performance on Berko's test with nonsense words did not predict errors or lack of errors in the free speech of mildly retarded children, with mental ages between 6 to 10 years. Dever (1971, p. 7) also proposes that because inflections "do not carry much of the burden of the grammar of English," the value of such tests to an overall picture of language development is slight.

Developmental Inventories

Developmental inventories of young children's language competence provide information about their accomplishments of specific language milestones. Interviews with parents or caregivers and observation of the child's vocal/verbal behaviors provide the basis for completion of these scales. Tests of this nature include the *Clinical Linguistic and Auditory Milestone Scale* (Capute et al., 1987), *Developmental Assessment for the Severely Handicapped* (Dykes, 1980), *Developmental Communication Inventory* (Hanna et al., 1982), *Environmental Language Inventory* (MacDonald, 1978), *Home Observation for Measurement of the Environment* (Caldwell & Bradley, 1978–1979), *Inventory of Language Abilities* (Minskoff et al., 1972), *Kent Infant Development Scale* (Reuter et al., 1981), the *Receptive-Expressive Emergent Language Scale* (Bzoch & League, 1971) and Part I of the *Houston Test of Language Development* (Crabtree, 1963). As a measure of spontaneous language facility, the *Developmental Sentence Analysis* (Lee, 1974) provides a system of evaluation of language development in nonstructured situations. (The analysis of free speech is discussed later.)

Having identified the major language assessment paradigms and some considerations regarding their usefulness, it is the task of the teacher or language clinician to decide which test or parts of tests are to be employed to meet specific asessment objectives. The purpose of the assessment (i.e., identification, diagnosis, or prescriptive treatment) and the individual child's overall cognitive, social, and physical development will influence the choice. This decision also must be based on a thorough understanding of the nature of communication. According to Miller (1978), this approach "depends primarily on a knowledgeable clinician rather than on a test, procedure, or set of methodologies. Language tests are available as aids to the teacher or clinician, but they cannot substitute for informed judgement" (p. 272).

INFORMAL ASSESSMENT APPROACHES

Leonard and coworkers (1978) presented a strong case (supported by many teachers and clinicians) for the use of informal, nonstandardized clinician- or teacher-constructed tasks for assessing language and communication: Clinician-constructed tasks have the potential for studying in greater detail features that might have seemed suspect during formal, standardized testing; through the use of informal testing an examiner is able to assess a linguistic "feature that is not assessed at all in a standardized test" (p. 374); and follow-up testing with informal tasks might help to determine the "cause of a child's difficulty with a particular feature of language" (p. 374). In addition to those benefits mentioned by Leonard and coworkers, informal testing has other important benefits. It permits an examiner to probe further to determine the strategies children presently use in comprehending and producing language. Finally, and perhaps of greatest value, informal tasks can broaden the examiner's assessment perspective to include the larger phenomenon of communication. This broader view can include valuable information about a child as a sender or receiver of information in a variety of contexts and for a variety of functions. Not only is the child assessed, but so are his conversational partners (e.g., parents, peers, teachers). Important communicative factors such as conversational turn taking and topical initiation also can be studied. All of this added information gained through informal assessments is essential to diagnosing the nature, extent, and perhaps reason(s) for the language difficulty.

Approaches to informal assessment can be divided into two general categories—structured tasks and spontaneous samples of language. In the former case, examiners generally sacrifice information concerning how children use language in the natural process of communication so that examiners might investigate more closely structural aspects of children's language, as well as the strategies they employ in their solutions to various tasks. Linguistic features of concern (e.g., comprehension of adverbs of time—*before, after*—in complex sentences) that might not occur in a spontaneous sample can be studied. Structured assesment tasks also are used to determine what the child knows about language. The real test of children's language abilities, however, is how

they use language for a variety of communicative purposes, with a variety of conversational partners, in a variety of contexts.

Spontaneous Samples of Language

The analysis of spontaneous samples of language has two primary advantages over more formalized, structured assessment approaches; as summarized by Kretschmer and Kretschmer (1978):

> Research on normal language development has focused primarily on spontaneous speech production, resulting in a sizeable body of normative data. Second, (more) formal testing situations are generally artificial estimates of performance whereas a conversational format should yield more natural behavior from the child. (p. 172, parenthesis added)

After obtaining and transcribing an episode of communication, the assessor must decide what aspect(s) of the interaction to analyze (See Bryen, 1982, and Miller, 1981, for suggestions on obtaining and transcribing spontaneous language samples). The possibilities of areas to analyze include: phonological, syntactic, semantic, conversational turn taking, initiation of conversational topics, egocentric speaking and listening, communicative function and signal analyses. *Who* to assess (e.g., child with parent, sibling, peer, or teacher) and *where* to assess (e.g., informal, familiar context of home, or a more formal and less familiar context of the classroom), also must be decided. Selected examples of these choices are presented here.

Several formats for analyzing spontaneous language samples are worth noting. *The Linguistic Analysis of Speech Samples* (Engler et al., 1973) provides a procedure for analyzing patterns of language used by the child to determine linguistic constructions that are deviant and/or conspicuously absent. Results of this analysis can be used to generate specific intervention strategies either for correction of deviant constructions or for expansion of the complexity of specific constructions. Similarly, in the *Language Analysis System* (Tyack & Gottsleben, 1974), a child's utterances are syntactically analyzed, taking into account the communicative intent of the utterance. The corpus of utterances then is compared to complete adult forms so that expected forms and syntactic constructions that have not been mastered can provide the basis for intervention goals and strategies.

Bloom and Lahey (1978) proposed a semantically based, rather than a syntactic, system for analyzing language. Utterances (ranging from single words to complex sentences) are analyzed to secure information about the child's use of various semantic categories, grammatical morphemes (*-ing*, *to be*, *have*, *has*, *in*, and *on*, possessives and plural *-s*, and *-ed*), and complex forms of connectives and relative clauses. This information provides the basis for establishing language goals.

The following sample and analysis from Bryen (1982, pp. 267-278) illustrates how one can derive syntactic information from a spontaneous sample:

Sample 1: 5-year old language-delayed child
What that? (*referring to the recorder*)
No! No help.
No big book. (*rejecting*)
Where . . . what . . . where the police car?
What they call those things?
What that guy?

Analysis:

$$\text{Negative sentences} \rightarrow No + \begin{Bmatrix} \text{Verb (V)} \\ \text{or} \\ \text{noun phrase (NP)} \end{Bmatrix}$$

$$\text{Wh- questions} \rightarrow Wh + \begin{Bmatrix} \text{NP} \\ \text{or} \\ \text{V + NP} \\ \text{or} \\ \text{NP + V + NP} \end{Bmatrix}$$

$$\text{where: } Wh \rightarrow \begin{Bmatrix} What \\ \text{or} \\ Where \end{Bmatrix}$$

Here is an illustration for the same negative and question constructions in the linguistically mature form (linguistic features that are absent from the child's utterances appear in boldface).

Sample 2: Mature form
What **is** that? (*with proper nonlinguistic indexing*)
No. **I don't want** help.
No, **I don't want the** big book.
Where . . . **is** the police car?
What **do** they call those things?
What **is** that guy?

Analysis:

$$\text{Negative sentences} \rightarrow \text{NP + auxiliary V + not + (NP)}[1]$$

$$\text{Wh- questions} \rightarrow Wh + \begin{Bmatrix} \text{auxiliary V + NP} \\ \text{or} \\ \text{auxiliary V + NP} \\ \text{+ V + NP} \end{Bmatrix}$$

$$\text{where: } Wh \rightarrow \begin{Bmatrix} What \\ \text{or} \\ Where \end{Bmatrix}$$

A comparison of the two samples and their respective analyses reveals that the youngster has not fully developed the transformational rules for generating either a negative or question sentence type (usually accomplished before the age of 5). In the case of negation, this child is simply attaching the negative morpheme *no* to either the verb or noun phrase. It should be noted that this strategy is the earliest and most economical way of marking negation. The mature form requires several additional operations: (a) embedding the appropriate auxiliary verb between the noun phrase and the main verb while tense marking the auxiliary; and (b) embedding the negative marker *not* between the auxiliary verb and the main verb. Note the complete absence of any auxiliary verbs in either negative or question sentence types. In the case of the question sentence type, two factors emerge. First, *wh-* words are limited to *what* and *where*. Notice the difficulty this youngster had in determining which *wh-* word was appropriate for asking about location. Second, note the absence of obligatory transformation rules. The child used the very economical strategy of prefixing the *wh-* word to the declarative sentence and used the sentence final rise in intonational contour to index the intent of a question. Auxiliary verbs were neither present nor inverted, as required by the transformational rules of questions.

The information derived from this and similar analyses, used in conjunction with available developmental data (e.g., Appendix 11-1; Brown, 1968, 1973; Ervin-Tripp, 1970; Hsu et al., 1987), can be invaluable in identifying both the linguistic content of intervention and the sequencing of intervention targets.

Analyses of spontaneous samples of language

---

[1] ( ) means optional.

can be expanded to include the following linguistic aspects: (a) semantic categories used; (b) the use of propositionally complex and coordinated sentences; and (c) the appropriate use of pronouns (*it, that one, those*) to index previously specified nouns and noun phrases within or between sentences. Both the presence or absence of a feature and its frequency can be significant. Leonard and coworkers (1976), in analyzing the spontaneous samples of 20 normal and 20 language delayed 3 and 5 year olds, found that one of the major differences was the infrequent use of complex semantic relations by the language delayed group. Leonard (1979) later reported further confirmatory evidence. Examples of how one might use spontaneous samples of language to obtain this type of information can be found in Bloom and Lahey (1978), Bryen (1982), and Miller (1981). The information obtained from procedures just described can be used to establish language goals. These analyses fail, however, to focus on the broader phenomenon of communication, which includes not just language but conversational turn taking, the comprehension and use of nonverbal communicative signals, and a variety of communicative functions. Because pragmatic analyses focusing on the social organization of discourse are described elsewhere (Bryen, 1982; Roth & Spekman, 1984a, 1984b), only brief mention is made here of how such information can be used to determine intervention goals.

Conversational Turn-Taking

The ability to shift the roles of sender and receiver is an essential factor in the cooperative and reciprocal nature of communication. If conversational analyses reveal that children spend much of their time either as receivers of communicative messages or as responders to other's topical initiations, then they might not have learned that their communication can *actively* affect their physical and social environments in addition to being used to *react* to other's communicative message and demands. Empirical support for this position has been reported by Morgenstern (1975) and Bryen and colleagues (1980). Implications for intervention are twofold: first, intervention must focus on more than just the children if we accept the position that communication is a social process involving at least two people reciprocally af-

fecting each other. Second, children must receive the message that their communicative signals (linguistic and otherwise) can affect their environment. Therefore, goals must focus on the children, their physical and social environments, and the interaction among the three.

Communicative Signals

Vocal and nonvocal signals that serve to convey a message between sender and receiver also require assessment. Eye contact, actions, facial expression, gestures, proximity, and vocal intonation all serve informational or affective communicative functions. Assessment of a child's ability to accurately and efficiently comprehend and produce a variety of communicative signals is even more critical when that child has limited language abilities. The competent conversational partner (e.g., parent, teacher, or care worker) also must be able to interpret the intended meaning of the nonverbal communicative signals sent by the language handicapped individual if the foundation for communication is to be established. Finally, because the handicapped child might not have adequate access to the complexities of linguistic symbols, other signals must be used by the adult conversational partner to supplement language. Analysis of communicative interactions focusing on the variety of signals used and interpreted by sender and receiver can yield valuable information related to the establishment of communication goals (Bryen, 1982; Bryen et al., 1980). This includes goals for the child (e.g., increased use of pointing to index a desired object) and for the parent or teacher as well (e.g., increased interpretation of the child's vocalizations and eye contact as indicators of desired objects or actions).

Communicative Functions

Assessing the underlying intent or purposes of the interaction is just as important as assessing the explicit content and vehicles of communication. Communicative functions establish the sociopsychological context between conversational partners. Because communication is characterized by reciprocity, both communicators need to be assessed. Several researchers have assessed the development of communicative functions used by children (Dore, 1975; Garvey, 1975;

Halliday, 1975). Others have done similar assessments with parents and other adult caretakers (Bryen et al., 1980; Garrad, 1986; Mazur et al., 1976; Morgenstern, 1975; Prior et al., 1979).

These assessment results can yield information about the balance and variety of functions used by the conversational partners in a variety of contexts. A balance of communicative functions (e.g., social–interpersonal, tutorial, regulatory, information giving and seeking) is the ideal. If assessment findings portray consistent imbalances in the use of certain communicative functions—such as a disproportionately high frequency of tutorial and regulatory functions (demands) by the adult—then conversation goals can be established to increase the frequency of less demanding functions, such as social–interpersonal and information giving and seeking.

Linguistic Modifications

Analyzing spontaneous interactions between adults and children permits the examiner to assess if and how the adults adjust their language to the linguistic level of the child. Attention to the parental linguistic modifications is important in the assessment of both normal (Gleason, 1977; Schaffer, 1978; Snow, 1972, 1977), and handicapped language learners (Buckhalt et al., 1978; Buim et al., 1974; Cheseldine & McConkey, 1979; Cramblit & Siegel, 1977; Frankel et al., 1987; Marshall et al., 1973; Seitz & Marcus, 1976). Although somewhat scant, research efforts exploring linguistic modifications in other environments, such as schools and institutions, underscore the importance of assessing this factor (Blindert, 1975; Bryen et al., 1980; Circourel et al., 1974; George, 1986; Granowsky & Krossner, 1970; Prior et al., 1979; Ray, 1980).

Linguistic modifications of adult input include, among others, the following structural and pragmatic features:

1. Reduced semantic and syntactic complexity
2. Types of questions asked
3. Complexity and diversity of vocabulary used
4. Differential use of repetition and expansion
5. Sentence types used (e.g., declarative, imperative, interrogative)
6. Differential use of intonational pattern (e.g., stress, pitch, juncture)
7. Rate of speech flow

Linguistic modificadtions serve several purposes. They maximize children's access to the stream of speech and its meaning. Certain linguistic input features serve to indirectly teach new grammatical structures and words by making them more salient to children. Finally, adjusting communicative functions and sentence types teaches children indirectly about their role as conversational partners.

Several procedures can be used to analyze spontaneous language samples of the child and the adult conversational partner. Calculating the MLU (Brown, 1973) of child and adult is probably the most heuristic approach. If the adult's linguistic complexity is adjusted to that of the child, the adult's MLU should be only slightly higher than the child's. The frequency with which the adult uses linguistic aids (e.g., repetition, a slow rate of speech, pauses) and extralinguistic aids to clarify communication can indicate whether the child is receiving adequate assistance.

Special attention also should be given to assessing the nature and frequency of sentence types used by the adult. The optimal balance of various sentence types has yet to be determined. Logic would suggest, however, that a disproportionately high frequency of declarative sentences might offer much information to the child, but might not engage the child as an active conversational partner; conversely, a disproportionately high frequency of questions might lend a threatening, intimidating, or demanding tone to the interaction.

The nature of questions the adult poses to the child also should be assessed. In general, as children increase their linguistic abilities, adults ask increasingly complex questions that stimulate and demand higher levels of linguistic and cognitive formulations (Blank et al., 1978a; Ray, 1980). When interacting with children possessing more limited language skills, adults generally ask less complex questions. A general developmental hierarchy of question forms, from least to most complex, was described by Brown (1968); Ervin-Tripp (1970) Hsu and coworkers (1987):

yes/no questions	*whose* (possession)
what (object)	*which* (selection)
what (action)	*when* (time)
where (location)	*how* (manner)
what (attributes)	*why* (cause-effect).
who (persons)	

In assessing the quality of *wh-* questions, Blank and colleagues (1978b) focused on the distance between perception of the here-and-now environment and language. Their assessment scheme reflects a hierarchy of abstraction containing four main levels:

I. Matching perception ("What is this? What do you see?")

II. Selective analysis of perception ("What can we use here for drawing?")

III. Recording perceptions ("What do we see that cannot be used for drawing?")

IV. Reasoning about ("What do you think would happen if the crayons were left in the sun?")

When analyzing the types of questions asked of children one should consider the following points. Is the complexity of questions commensurate with the child's current linguistic and cognitive abilities? Do questions only tap yes/no and convergent right/wrong answers or do they also call for divergent responses? Feedback from the child is probably the key answer to these questions.

Analysis of spontaneous interactions can be a valuable assessment tool. However, because of technical and practical problems frequently encountered in obtaining, recording, transcribing, and analyzing them, structured nonstandardized approaches often are more practical.

STRUCTURED/NONSTANDARDIZED APPROACHES

Recent linguistic and psycholinguistic research has provided teachers and clinicians with a conceptual base from which to study normal, delayed, and deviant child language. A wide range of structured nonstandardized assessment approaches also has grown out of this research. Specific strategies for constructing informal language tasks have been covered elsewhere (Leonard et al., 1978). Some of the nonstandardized tasks that are helpful in going beyond or supplementing information obtained from standardized tests and spontaneous language samples are described here,

and additional examples are summarized in Appendix 11-3. A detailed listing of various research studies that can aid in the development of additional assessment tasks can be found in Leonard and coworkers (1978); further examples are in Bryen and Gerber (1981) and Bryen (1982). Because the range of tasks available to the evaluator is so great, the assessment tasks presented are meant to be illustrative rather than prescriptive or exhaustive.

When selecting, developing, or adapting these nonstandardized tests, examiners should consider those factors described earlier (e.g., the test paradigm, expressive versus receptive test demands, and the evaluator's language) that might affect the type of information obtainable and the child's performance.

Means-End Relationships: Prelinguistic Communication

Means-end relations is a precondition for the emergence of intentional communication and its subsequent symbolic form of language. This sociocognitive structure, originally described by Piaget, emerges when the child begins to see that objects and people can be *means* (instruments) for obtaining desired *ends* (e.g., desired objects, actions, or interactions). This coordinated relationship is evidenced in both the physical and social sense when two conditions exist:

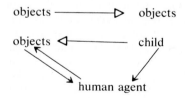

This assessment approach is based on the research of Bates (1976, 1979), Greenwald and Leonard (1979), and Sugarman-Bell (1978).

Objective. Determine whether the child can use objects (and human agents) to obtain desired objects or actions.

Materials. Wind-up toys such as Fisher Price carousel or music box, a ball, a ruler or stick, a cloth, and a plastic bowl full of cookies.

Procedure. To assess the child's instrumental use of objects, the following procedures can be used:

1. Play ball with the child for a short time. Then have the ball roll out of the child's physical reach (e.g., under a bed or couch). Placing a ruler near the child, observe and note what strategies the child uses to retrieve the ball. For example, does the child lose interest in the ball, cry, use his or her arms to attempt to retrieve it, or spontaneously use the ruler as a tool for retrieval? Hand the child the ruler and observe.

2. Place a plastic bowl with two small cookies within easy reach of the child and say, "Here's some cookies for you. Want the cookies? Here." After the child has eaten the cookies, place more cookies in the bowl, placing the bowl out of the child's reach but on a movable cloth. Say to the child, "Here's more cookies. Want the cookies? Here." Again observe and note what the child does. Does the child cry, give up, flail with his or her arms, attempt to use you as an agent for obtaining the cookies, or pull the cloth to move the bowl within reach? If the child fails to instrumentally use the cloth, demonstrate its use, return the bowl to its original position and observe.

3. Present one of the wind-up toys to the child. Demonstrate how it is wound up and then let the child play with it. Once the toy has wound down, observe and note what the child does. Does the child try to reactivate the toy? If failing, does the child hand it to you as if to say, "More. You do it"? Repeat with the carousel.

Results. From your noted observations, determine whether the child (a) uses objects as a means to obtain desired ends (another object) and (b) uses people as agents or means for obtaining desired ends (objects, actions). If the child fails to use objects, the goal would be continued use of objects exploratorily, functionally, *and* instrumentally. If the child has not established people as agents, game-like routines where the teacher is both agent and recipient of objects and actions would encourage the attainment of this goal. If, however, the child successfully accomplished the tasks, then one goal could be to expand the child's repertoire of instrumental use of objects as well as the variety of intentional communicative signals used.

Sentence Imitation

Menyuk (1964) and Miller and Isard (1963) are among several researchers who have investigated the value of using the sentence repetition paradigm as a method of studying a child's linguistic capacity. In this method, sentences of various lengths and syntactic complexities are presented to the child to imitate. Findings, especially those of McNeill (1970) and Miller and Chomsky (1963), support the idea that a child will not imitate a particular linguistic feature within a sentence unless that feature is already part of the child's linguistic competence. Therefore, this method is useful for diagnosing the acquisition of various grammatical rules.

Objective. Determine the child's acquisition of particular grammatical rules.

Materials. The only material necessary for this task is a series of sentences that tap a wide range of grammatical features or focus on a particular set of features. These sentences can be developed by referring to any source that provides a thorough analysis of semantic/syntactic structures and stages of acquisition. For example, sentences that involve subordinate clauses of a temporal nature could be developed as follows:

"After he went to the store, he came home to take a nap."

"He went to the store, and then he came home to take a nap."

"Before he came home to take a nap, he went to the store."

Procedure. Present each sentence to the child and ask the child to imitate it. The examiner might want to follow Menyuk's (1964) procedure, saying, "We are going to play the game *Follow the leader.* I'm going to say some sentences for you. I want you to say just what I say. If I say, 'The boy runs,' I want you to say _____." Tape record both your reading of the sentences and the child's responses for later analysis.

Analysis and Results. Transcribe the child's imitation of the stimulus sentences. Several levels of analysis can be undertaken. First, determine whether the child provides an exact repetition of the stimulus sentence. If this did occur, evidence exists for the child's competence (i.e., knowledge) regarding this particular structure. For example, if the child accurately imitates sentences (1) through (4) following, one can at least tentatively conclude that the structure is within the child's linguistic capacity.

Sentence → NP + VP

NP → Pronoun; or Det + N; or N

$$VP \rightarrow be + V + ing + PP$$
$$PP \rightarrow prep + det + N; \text{ or } prep + N$$

1. "He is going to the store."
2. "The men are walking down the street."
3. "Sally is running to school."
4. "I am sitting on the chair."

If, however, deviations occur in the child's attempts to imitate the stimulus sentences, further analysis is made. The following deviations from the above sentences provide some examples of error analysis:

1a. "He going to the store."
2a. "They are walking down the street."
3a. "Sally running school."
4a. "Me sitting."

In sentence 1a, the child, although maintaining the basic semantic relation of agent, action, and location, is not yet incorporating the auxiliary verb *be* in the present progressive verb phrase. Therefore, his knowledge of the syntactic rule $VP \rightarrow be + V + ing$ might be inadequate. This verb phrase structure then could be analyzed in other sentence types, such as:

$$VP \rightarrow be + V + ing; \text{ or }$$
$$be + V + ing + adverb; \text{ or }$$
$$be + V + ing + and + V + ing$$

In contrast, sentence 2a maintains both the semantic and syntactic structures of the stimulus sentence 2. Even the lexical substitution of *they* for *the men* represents an accurate knowledge of pronominal usage. Sentence 3a, although maintaining the basic semantic content of the stimulus sentence 3, reflects a rather unelaborated set of syntactic rules:

$$VP \rightarrow V + ing + PP$$
$$PP \rightarrow N$$

Finally, in sentence 4a, both semantic and syntactic aspects are limited.

Here is one last note about the use of sentence imitation as a diagnostic tool: Sentence imitation provides the examiner with information concerning the child's *knowledge* of linguistic rules; it does *not* assess the use of this linguistic knowledge in the spontaneous use of language. Analysis should be conducted at both levels (i.e., sponta-

neous use of language and sentence repetition). Berry-Luterman and Bar (1971) provided a helpful strategy whereby the child's performance can be assessed under the following conditions: "(1) The repetition of grammatically incorrect sentences taken from the child's own spontaneous productions; (2) the repetition of grammatically correct versions of these sentences; and (3) the repetition of the reversed word order of these grammatically correct versions" (p. 31).

The results obtained from using the sentence imitation paradigm in conjunction with a spontaneous sample of language are helpful in answering the following questions: (a) What is the difference, if any, between what the child *knows* about language and how he *uses* this linguistic knowledge? (b) What is the child's competence to deal with syntactic/semantic structures such as interrogation, possession, infinitival complement, and the like? (c) At the morphological level, what is the child's competence in relation to verb forms, pluralization, pronoun substitution, and so on? All of this information can be used to determine the need for, starting point, and sequential steps in language intervention.

Egocentric Listening

Much attention has been given to the construct of egocentric thought and its effects on the ability to communicate accurately. Most research has centered on egocentricity as it relates to the role of the speaker (e.g., Bearison & Levey, 1977; Glucksburg & Krauss, 1967; Meissner, 1975); however, egocentric communication also can critically affect the listener's ability to process ongoing language. Youngsters, especially during the preschool and early school years, might confirm messages that either are ambiguous or lack critical information. They might fail to ask questions of the speaker that might aid the speaker in reformulating the message so that it provides more accurate and adequate information; they might give no feedback at all. Karabenck and Miller (1977) reported that 7 year old listeners still had not completely developed the ability to accurately offer or utilize listener feedback. When one considers that youngsters with language delays have a disproportionately high incidence of linguistic processing problems *and* that much time in school is spent listening to information, directions, and so on, it is clear that the effects of egocentric listening are crucial.

Objective. Assess the child's ability to function as a listener in a communication task.

Materials. Two identical sets of blocks (6 to 10) are provided that vary in shape, size, color, and configuration (optional). A child-sized table is set up with two chairs that face each other. A visual barrier is erected so that the two children engaged in the block-building task cannot see each other's blocks, but can see each other.

Procedure. Build a configuration of one child's blocks in two stages: arrange three or four blocks first, and then another three or four blocks after the speaker has given the first set of directions. Have the child whose blocks are being used for the examiner's construction give directions to the other child (i.e., the listener being evaluated) with the objective that the listener will construct an identical configuration without seeing the original. Tape record both the speaker's directions and the listener's verbal feedback; also observe and note all listener feedback.

Results. Analyze, from your observations and tape recording, the nature of the feedback that the listener provided to the speaker. Did the listener confirm the adequacy of the message? If so, how? When the speaker's message was either inadequate or inaccurate, what did the listener do? Did the listener simply proceed with the task, apparently thinking (egocentrically) that the information was sufficient for task completion, or did the child provide feedback to the speaker concerning the inadequacy of the message? The results of this and similar tasks can yield valuable information concerning how the child might function as a listener at home or in school. This information then can be used to suggest compensatory classroom strategies as well as therapeutic developmental listening strategies.

The three assessment tasks just described illustrate how research findings in the areas of prelinguistic communication, expressive language competence (via imitation tasks), and listening can be transformed into valuable nonstandardized approaches to language assessment. They serve to underscore the position that language assessors are required to have a sound and current knowledge of language and its acquisition as well as a sensitive and analytic style of interaction; these are the examiner's most important resources.

Refer to Appendix 11-3 for additional research-based assessment tasks.

IMPLICATIONS: ASSESSMENT AND RESULTS

The purpose of language assessment is to compare a child's behavior with that of a "normal" peer group and, where significant deficiencies are identified, to determine goals for intervention. Screening for identification purposes utilizes formal, standardized tests or procedures to examine preselected aspects of language comprehension, production, and use. Goal selection is then derived from results of informal tests (e.g., spontaneous samples of language) that are compared with the sequence of normal language development. Is this two-step process really needed or is it actually duplicative? Comparison of the results of a standardized test (such as the *Carrow Elicited Language Inventory* (CELI) and a language sample was evaluated (Blau et al., 1984). Findings indicated that although the standardized test was effective in *identifying* language impairment in children, the language responses were *not* useful in determining what goals would be appropriate. Information obtained from the language sample led to more specific goals, including the content and context of appropriate interventions. Thus, different assessment approaches should continue to be used for different assessment purposes.

Once assessment results have been obtained, decisions concerning their use must be made. Additional information gathering and further assessment might be required. Some of the factors that influence these decisions are dialect variation, situational effects, and the approach to intervention.

Dialect Variation

Because a child's language diverges from expected responses, one should not automatically infer that the child has a language problem. Dialects within a given language vary with respect to vocabulary, pronunciation, grammar, and conversational styles, as well as nonverbal aspects of the communication process. All of these factors can affect the child's performance. Therefore, one must look beyond the data from the assessment to determine whether divergent language patterns reflect a deficiency in learning or simply a variant dialect. This generally can be accomplished by familiarizing oneself with members of the child's immediate speech community (generally the child's parents) and learning about how dialects typically vary in English (Bryen, et al., 1979).

Situational Effects

A reliable assessment of the child's language ability must include a careful examination of the effects of various situational characteristics, such as the topics, the task, the examiner or listener, and the nature of the interaction.

Cazden (1977) argued "contextual influences . . . will limit the inferences that can be made from any test response, and thereby limit the validity and reliability of the information the teacher (or examiner) seeks" (p. 44, parenthesis added). According to Cazden's (1971) summary of relevant research, the assessment situation can influence the fluency and spontaneity, length and complexity, content, style, and standard English usage of the young child's language performance.

Approach to Intervention

The approach to language intervention goes well beyond the results of any given assessment. It is tacitly or explicitly influenced by one's view of the following issues: The nature of the language problem as delay or deviance (see Leonard, 1979, for an analysis of relevant findings); the nature of language and how it is mastered—whether it is acquired, learned, or taught (see Bryen, 1982, 1986, for a discussion of differential implications); and primacy of function and structure in language learning and remediation (see Bryen, 1986).

Concerns about the particulars of language assessment, such as those discussed in this chapter, are just a preface to more general and basic questions about language. Resolution of these general considerations will be the real guide to effectively understanding young children's language.

REFERENCES

Adler, S. (1979). *Poverty Children and Their Language: Implications for Teaching and Treating.* New York: Grune & Stratton.

Anastasiow, N. (1972). Review of *Language Facility Test.* In O. K. Buros (Ed.), *The Seventh Mental Measurements Yearbook* (Vol. 2). Highland Park, NJ: Gryphon Press.

Arlt, P. B. (1977). *Illinois Children's Language Assessment Test.* Danville, IL: Interstate Printers & Publishers.

Arndt, W. B. (1977). A psychometric evaluation of the Northwestern Syntax Screening Test. *Journal of Speech and Hearing Disorders, 42*(3), 316–319.

Baker, H. J., & Leland, B. (1959). *Detroit Tests of Learning Aptitude.* Indianapolis, IN: Bobbs-Merrill.

Bannatyne, M. (1975). Review of the Northwestern Syntax Screening Test. *Journal of Learning Disabilities, 8*(4), 196–197.

Barrie-Blackey, S. (1973). Six-year-old children's understanding of sentences adjoined with time adverbs. *Journal of Psycholinguistic Research, 2,* 153–165.

Bartel, N., Bryen, D., & Keehn, S. (1973). Language comprehension in the moderately retarded child. *Exceptional Children, 39,* 375–382.

Bates, E. (1976). *Language and Context: The Acquisition of Pragmatics.* New York: Academic Press.

Bates, E. (1979). *The Emergence of Symbols: Cognition and Communication in Infancy.* New York: Academic Press.

Bearison, D. J., & Levey, L. M. (1977). Children's comprehension of referential communication: Decoding ambiguous sentences. *Child Development, 48,* 716–720.

Belugi-Klima, U. (1971). Some language comprehension tests. In C. S. Lavatelli (Ed.), *Language Training in Early Childhood Education.* Champaign-Urbana: University of Illinois Press.

Berko, J. (1958). The child's learning of English morphology. *Word, 14,* 150–177.

Berndt, R. S. (1985). Review of Inventory and Language Abilities. In J. V. Mitchell, Jr. (Ed.), *Ninth Mental Measurements Yearbook* (Vol. 1). Lincoln: University of Nebraska, Buros Institute of Mental Measurements.

Berry, M. F. (1980). *Language Disorders of Children.* Englewood Cliffs, NJ: Prentice-Hall.

Berry, M. D., & Erickson, R. L. (1973). Speaking rate: Effects on children's comprehension of normal speech. *Journal of Speech and Hearing Research, 16*(3), 367–374.

Berry, P. (Ed.) (1976). *Language and Communication in the Mentally Handicapped.* Baltimore: University Park Press.

Berry-Luterman, L., & Bar, A. (1971). The diagnostic significance of sentence repetition for language impaired children. *Journal of Speech and Hearing Disorders, 36,* 29–39.

Bever, T. G. (1970). The cognitive basis for linguistic structures. In J. R. Hayes (Ed.), *Cognition and the Development of Language*. New York: Wiley.

Blank, M., Rose, S., & Berlin, L. (1978a). *The Language of Learning: The Preschool Years*. New York: Grune & Stratton.

Blank, M., Rose, S. A., & Berlin, L. J. (1978b). *Preschool Language Assessment Instrument: Experimental Edition*. New York: Grune & Stratton.

Blau, A., Lahey, M., & Oleksuik-Velez, A. (1984). Planning goals for intervention: Can a language test serve as an alternative to a language sample? *Journal of Childhood Communication Disorders, 7*(2), 27–37.

Blindert, H. D. (1975). Interactions between residents and staff: A qualitative investigation of an institutional setting for retarded children. *Mental Retardation, 13*, 38–40.

Bliss, L. S., Allen, D. V., & Wrasse, K. W. (1977). A story completion approach as a measure of language development in children. *Journal of Speech and Hearing Research, 20*, 358–372.

Bloom, L. (1973). *One Word at a Time*. The Hague: Mouton.

Bloom, L. (1974). Talking, understanding, and thinking. In R. L. Schiefelbusch & L. L. Lloyd (Eds.), *Language Perspectives: Acquisition, Retardation, and Intervention*. Baltimore: University Park Press.

Bloom, L. (1980). Language development, language disorders, and learning disabilities: L. D.[3] *Bulletin of the Orton Society, 30*, 115–133.

Bloom, L., Hood, L., & Lightbown, P. (1974). Imitation in language development: If, when, and why. *Cognitive Psychology, 6*, 380–420.

Bloom, L., & Lahey, M. (1978). *Language Development and Language Disorders*. New York: Wiley.

Boehm, A. E. (1971). *Boehm Test of Basic Concepts*. New York: The Psychological Corporation.

Boehm, A. E. (1986a). *Boehm Test of Basic Concepts-Revised*. San Antonio, TX: The Psychological Corporation.

Boehm, A. E. (1986b). *Boehm Test of Basic Concepts-Preschool Version*. San Antonio, TX: The Psychological Corporation.

Bracken, B. (1984). *Bracken Basic Concept Scale*. San Antonio, TX: The Psychological Corporation.

Brody, J. (1987, May 5). Child development: Language takes on new significance. *The New York Times*, pp. C1, C11.

Brown, H. D. (1971). Children's comprehension of relativized English sentences. *Child Development, 32*, 1923–1936.

Brown, R. (1968). The development of questions in child speech. *Journal of Verbal Learning and Verbal Behavior, 7*, 279–290.

Brown, R. (1973). *A First Language: The Early Stages*. Cambridge, MA: Harvard University Press.

Bryen, D. N. (1982). *Inquiries into Child Language*. Boston: Allyn & Bacon.

Bryen, D. N. (1985). Review of Reynell Developmental Language Scales (Revised). In J. V. Mitchell, Jr. (Ed.), *Ninth Mental Measurements Yearbook* (Vol. 2). Lincoln: University of Nebraska, Buros Institute of Mental Measurements.

Bryen, D. N. (1986). Early language intervention: A conceptual and clinical critique. *Special Education and Rehabilitation, 1*, 51–66.

Bryen, D. N. (1987). Do the meta's matter? *Information/Edge: Language and Language Disorders, 3*(2), 1 & 4.

Bryen, D. N., & Gerber, A. (1981). Assessing language and its use. In A. Gerber & D. Bryen, *Language and Learning Disabilities*. Baltimore: University Park Press.

Bryen, D. N., & Gerber, A. (1987). Metalinguistic abilities and reading: A focus on phonological awareness. *Journal of Reading, Writing, and Learning Disabilities, 3*(4), 357–367.

Bryen, D. N., Hartman, C., & Tait, P. (1979). *Variant English: An Introduction to Language Variation*. Columbus, OH: Charles E. Merrill.

Bryen, D. N., Hutchinson, D., Joyce, D., Liebowitz, A., Kurtz, A., Poag, L., & Rossi, A. (1980). *Project: Communication*. Unpublished manuscript, Temple University, Philadelphia.

Buckhalt, J. A., Rutherford, R. G., & Goldberg, K. E. (1978). Verbal and nonverbal interactions of mothers with their Down's Syndrome and nonretarded infants. *American Journal of Mental Deficiency, 82*, 337–343.

Buim, N., Rynders, J., & Turnure, J. (1974). Early maternal linguistic environment of normal and Down's syndrome language learning children. *American Journal of Mental Deficiency, 79*, 52–58.

Bzoch, K. R., & League, R. (1971). *The Bzoch-League Receptive Expressive Emergent Language Scale*. Gainesville, FL: Tree of Life Press.

Cairns, H. S., & Hsu, J. R. (1978). Who, why, when, and how: A developmental study. *Journal of Child Language, 5*, 477–488.

Calculator, S. N. (1985). Describing and treating discourse problems in mentally retarded children: The myth of mental retardese. In D. N. Ripich & F. M. Spinelli (Eds.), *School Discourse Problems*. San Diego: College-Hill Press.

Caldwell, B. M., & Bradley, R. H. (1978–1979). *Home Observation for Measurement of the Environment*. Little Rock: University of Arkansas.

Capute, A. J., Shapiro, B. K., & Palmer, F. B. (1987). *Clinical Linguistic and Auditory Milestone Scale*.

Baltimore: Kennedy Institute for Handicapped Children.

Carrow, E. (1973). *Test for Auditory Comprehension of Language*. Austin, TX: Learning Concepts.

Carrow, E. (1974). *Carrow Elicited Language Inventory*. Austin, TX: Learning Concepts.

Cazden, C. B. (1971). Language Programs for Young Children: Notes from England and Wales. In C. B. Lavatelli (Ed.), *Preschool Language Training*. Urbana, IL: University of Illinois Press.

Cazden, C. B. (1977). Concentrated versus contrived encounters: Suggestions for language assessment in early childhood education. In A. Davies (Ed.), *Language and Learning in Early Childhood*. London: Heinemann.

Chapman, R. S. (1978). Comprehension strategies in children. In J. R. Kavanagh & W. Strange (Eds.), *Speech and Language in the Laboratory, School and Clinic*. Cambridge, MA: MIT Press.

Chapman, R. S., & Miller, J. E. (1975). Word order in early two and three word utterances: Does production precede comprehension? *Journal of Speech and Hearing Research, 18*, 355–371.

Chappell, G. E., & Johnson, G. A. (1976). Evaluation of cognitive behavior in the young nonverbal child. *Language, Speech and Hearing Services in Schools, 1*, 17–24.

Cheseldine, S., & McConkey, R. (1979). Parental speech to young Down's syndrome children: An intervention study. *American Journal of Mental Deficiency, 83*, 612–620.

Chipman, H., & de Dardel, C. (1974). Developmental study of comprehension and production of the pronoun *It. Journal of Psycholinguistic Research, 3*, 91–99.

Cicciarelli, A., Broen, P. A., & Siegel, G. M. (1976). Language assessment procedures. In L. L. Lloyd (Ed.), *Communication Assessment and Intervention Strategies*. Baltimore: University Park Press.

Circourel, A., Jennings, K., Jennings, S., et al. (1974). *Language Use and School Performance*. New York: Academic Press.

Clark, E. (1973a). What's in a word? In T. E. Moore (Ed.), *Cognitive Development and the Acquisition of Language*. New York: Academic Press.

Clark, E. V. (1973b). Non-linguistic strategies and the acquisition of word meanings. *Cognition 2*(2), 161–182.

Clark, E. V. (1980). Here's the top: Non-linguistic strategies in the acquisition of orientational terms. *Child Development, 51*, 329–338.

Crabtree, M. (1963). *Houston Test of Language Development*. Houston, TX: Houston Press.

Cramblit, N., & Siegel, G. (1977). The verbal environment of a language impaired child. *Journal of Speech and Hearing Disorders, 42*, 474–482.

Cromer, R. (1972). The learning of surface structure clues to deep structure by a puppet show technique. *Quarterly Journal of Experimental Psychology, 24*, 66–76.

Cromer, R. (1974). Child and adult learning of surface structure clues to deep structure using a picture card technique. *Journal of Psychological Research, 3*, 1–14.

Dailey, J. T. (1968). *Language Facility Test*. Arlington, Va: Arlington Corp.

Dailey, K., & Boxx, J. R. (1979). A comparison of three imitative tests of expressive language and a spontaneous language sample. *Language, Speech and Hearing Services in Schools, 10*, 6–13.

de Hirsch, K. (1981). Unready children. In A. Gerber & D. Bryen (Eds.), *Language and Learning Disabilities*. Baltimore: University Park Press.

Dever, D. (1972). A comparison of the results of a revised version of Berko's test of morphology with the free speech of mentally retarded children. *Journal of Speech and Hearing Disorders, 15*, 169–178.

Dever, R. B. (1971). *The use of language by mentally retarded children: A review of the literature* (Technical Report No. 1.24). Bloomington: Indiana University, Center for Research and Development on the Improvement of Handicapped Children.

deVilliers, J. G., & deVilliers, P. A. (1973). Development of the use of word order in comprehension. *Journal of Psycholinguistic Research, 2*(4), 331–341.

DiSimoni, F. (1978). *The Token Test for Children*. Boston: Teaching Resources Corp.

Donahue, M. (1985). Communicative style in learning disabled children: Some implications for classroom discourse. In D. N. Ripich & F. M. Spinelli (Eds.), *School Discourse Problems*. San Diego: College-Hill Press.

Dore, J. (1975). Holophrases, speech acts, and language universals. *Journal of Child Language, 2*, 21–40.

Dunn, L. M., & Dunn, L. M. (1981). *Peabody Picture Vocabulary Test—Revised*. Circle Pines, MN: American Guidance Services.

Duran, R. P. (1985). Review of Comprehension of Oral Language. In J. V. Mitchell, Jr. (Ed.), *Ninth Mental Measurement Yearbook* (Vol. 1). Lincoln: University of Nebraska, Buros Institute of Mental Measurements.

Dykes, M. K. (1980). *Developmental Assessment for the Severely Handicapped*. Austin, TX: Exceptional Resources.

Elasser, N., & John-Steiner, V. P. (1977). An interactionist approach to advancing literacy. *Harvard Educational Review, 47*, 355–369.

Engler, L., Hannah, E., & Longhurst, T. (1973). Linguistic analysis of speech samples: A practical guide for clinicians. *Journal of Speech and Hearing Disorders, 38,* 192–204.

Ervin-Tripp, S. (1970). Discourse agreement: How children answer questions. In Hayes (Ed.), *Cognition and the development of language.* New York: Wiley.

Feiring, C. (1985). Review of Kent Infant Development Scale. In J. V. Mitchell, Jr. (Ed.), *Ninth Mental Measurements Yearbook* (Vol. 1). Lincoln: University of Nebraska, Buros Institute of Mental Measurements.

Feskanin, C. (1987). Pragmatics goes to school. *Information/Edge: Language and Language Disorders, 3*(4), 1&4.

Fewell, R. R., & Rich, J. S. (1987). Play assessment as a procedure for examining cognitive, communication, and social skills in multihandicapped children. *Journal of the Association for Persons with Severe Handicaps, 12,* 2–10.

Foster, R., Giddan, J. J., & Stark, J. (1973). *Assessment of Children's Language Comprehension Test.* Palo Alto, CA: Consulting Psychologists Press.

Frankel, F., Simmons, J. Q., III, & Richey, V. E. (1987). Reward value of prosodic features of language for autistic, mentally retarded, and normal children. *Journal of Autism and Developmental Disabilities, 17*(1), 103–114.

Fraser, C., Bellulgi, U., & Brown, R. (1963). Control of grammar in imitation, comprehension, and production. *Journal of Verbal Learning and Verbal Behavior, 2,* 121–135.

Garnica, O. K. (1981). Social dominance and conversational interaction—The omega child in the classroom. In J. L. Green & C. Wallat (Eds.), *Ethnography and language in educational settings.* NJ: Ablex.

Garrad, K. R. (1986). Mothers' questions to delayed and nondelayed children. *Journal of Childhood Communication Disorders, 9*(2), 95–106.

Garvey, C. (1975). Requests and responses in children's speech. *Journal of Child Language, 2,* 41–63.

George, P. (1986). Teaching handicapped children with attention problems: Teacher verbal strategies make a difference. *Teaching Exceptional Children, 18*(3), 172–175.

Gerber, A., & Bryen, D. N. (1981). *Language and Learning Disabilities.* Baltimore: University Park Press.

Gleason, J. (1977). Talking to children: Some notes on feedback. In C. Snow & C. Ferguson (Eds.), *Talking to Children.* Cambridge, England: Cambridge University Press.

Glucksberg, S., & Krauss, R. M. (1967). What do people say after they have learned how to talk? Studies of the development of referential communication. *Merrill-Palmer Quarterly, 13,* 309–316.

Goodman, K. S., & Goodman, Y. M. (1977). Learning about psycholinguistic processes by analyzing oral reading. *Harvard Educational Review, 47,* 317–333.

Granowsky, S., & Krossner, W. (1970). Kindergarten teachers as models for children's speech. *Journal of Experimental Education, 38,* 23–28.

Greenwald, C. A., & Leonard, L. B. (1979). Communicative and sensorimotor development of Doen's syndrome children. *American Journal of Mental Deficiency, 84,* 296–303.

Grice, H. P. (1976). Logic and Conversation. In P. Cole & J. K. Morgan (Eds.), *Syntax and Semantics III: Speech Acts.* New York: Academic Press.

Griffith, P. L., Johnson, H. A., & Dastoli, S. L. (1985). If teaching is conversation, can converation be taught? Discourse abilities in hearing impaired children. In D. N. Ripich & F. M. Spinelli (Eds.), *School Discourse Problems.* San Diego: College-Hill Press.

Grill, J., & Bartel, N. (1977). Language bias in tests: ITPA grammatical closure. *Journal of Learning Disabilities, 10,* 229–235.

Gruenewald, L. J., & Pollak, S. A. (1984). *Language Interaction in Teaching and Learning.* Baltimore: University Park Press.

Haber, L. (1985). Review of Oral Language Imitation Screening Test. In J. V. Mitchell, Jr. (Ed.), *Ninth Mental Measurements Yearbook* (Vol. 1). Lincoln: University of Nebraska, Buros Institute of Mental Measurements.

Halliday, M. A. K. (1975). *Learning How to Mean—Exploration in the Development of Language.* London: Edward Arnold.

Hanna, R. P., Lippert, E. A., & Harris, A. B. (1982). *Developmental Communication Inventory.* Columbus, OH: Charles E. Merrill.

Harrison, J., Lombardino, L., & Stepell, J. B. (1986–1987). The development of early communication: Using developmental literature for selecting communication goals. *Journal of Special Education, 20*(4), 463–473.

Heath, S. B. (1983). *Ways with Words.* Cambridge, England: Cambridge University Press.

Hedrick, D. L., Prather, E. M., & Tobin, A. R. (1984). *Sequenced Inventory of Language.* London: Edward Arnold.

Horstmeier, D. S., & MacDonald, J. D. (1978). *Environmental Prelanguage Battery* (rev. ed.). Columbus, OH: Charles E. Merrill.

Hresko, W. P., Reid, D. K., & Hammill, D. D. (1981). *The Test of Early Language Development.* Austin, TX: PRO-ED.

Hsu, J. R., Cairns, H. S., & Bialo, N. (1987). When-questions: A study of how children linguistically encode temporal information. *Journal of Psycholinguistic Research, 16*(3), 241–256.

Huer, M. B. (1983). *The Nonspeech Test for Receptive/Expressive Language.* Lake Zurich, IL: Don Johnson Developmental Equipment.

Huttenlocher, J. (1974). The origins of language comprehension. In R. L. Solso (Ed.), *Theories in Cognitive Psychology.* Potomac, MD: Erlbaum.

Huttenlocher, J., Eisenberg, K., & Strauss, S. (1968). Comprehension: Relation between perceived actor and logical subject. *Journal of Verbal Learning and Verbal Behavior, 7,* 527–530.

Huttenlocher, J., & Strauss, S. (1968). Comprehension and a statement's relation to the situation it describes. *Journal of Verbal Learning and Verbal Behavior, 7,* 300–304.

Huttenlocher, J., & Weiner, S. L. (1971). Comprehension of instructions in varying contexts. *Cognitive Psychology, 2,* 369–385.

Iglesias, A. (1985). Cultural conflict in the classroom: The communicatively different child. In D. N. Ripich & F. M. Spinelli (Eds.), *School Discourse Problems.* San Diego: College-Hill Press.

Johnson, D. L. (1973). Review of Bzoch-League *Receptive-Expressive Emergent Language Scale. Journal of Personality Assessment, 37*(6), 581–582.

Johnson, M. R., & Tomblin, J. B. (1975). The reliability of Developmental Sentence Scoring as a function of sample size. *Journal of Speech and Hearing Research, 18,* 372–380.

Karabenck, J. D., & Miller, S. A. (1977). The effects of age, sex and listener feedback on grade school children's referential communication. *Child Development, 48,* 678–683.

Katz, J. J., & Fodor, J. A. (1963). The structure of a semantic theory. *Language, 39,* 170–210.

Kirk, S. A., McCarthy, J. J., & Kirk, W. D. (1968). *Illinois Test of Psycholinguistic Abilities.* Urbana: University of Illinois Press.

Koff, E., Kramer, P. E., & Fowles, B. (1980). Effects of event probability and animatedness of children's comprehension of active and passive sentences. *The Journal of Psychology, 104,* 157–163.

Kretschmer, R. R., Jr., & Kretschmer, L. W. (1978). *Language Development and Intervention with the Hearing Impaired.* Baltimore: University Park Press.

LaBelle, J. L. (1973). Sentence comprehension in two age groups of children as related to pause position or the absence of pause. *Journal of Speech and Hearing Research, 16,* 231–237.

Lee, L. (1971). *Northwestern Syntax Screening Test.* Evanston: Northwestern University Press.

Lee, L. L. (1974). *Developmental Sentence Analysis.* Evanston: Northwestern University Press.

Lempert, H. & Kinsbourne, M. (1978). Children's com-

prehension of word order: A developmental investigation. *Child Development, 49,* 1235–1238.

Lempert, H., & Kinsbourne, M. (1980). Preschool children's sentence comprehension: Strategies with respect to word order. *Journal of Child Language, 7,* 371–379.

Leonard, L. B. (1979). Language impairment in children. *Merrill-Palmer Quarterly, 25,* 205–232.

Leonard, L. B., Bolders, J. G., & Miller, J. A. (1976). An examination of the semantic relations reflected in the language usage of normal and language-disordered children. *Journal of Speech and Hearing Research, 19,* 371–392.

Leonard, L. B., Perozzi, J. A., Prutting, C. A., & Berkley, R. K. (1978). Nonstandardized approaches to the assessment of language behaviors. *ASHA,* 371–379.

Lindfors, J. (1987). *Children's Language-Learning* (2nd ed.). Englewood Cliffs, NJ: Prentice-Hall.

Lloyd, L. L. (Ed.) (1976). *Communication Assessment and Intervention Strategies.* Baltimore: University Park Press.

Lombardino, L. J., Stein, J. E., Kricos, P. B., & Wolf, M. A. (1976). Play diversity and structural relationships in the play and language of language-normal preschoolers: Preliminary data. *Journal of Communication Disorders, 19*(6), 475–489.

Longhurst, T. M., & File, J. J. (1977). A comparison of developmental sentence scores from Head Start children collected in four conditions. *Language, Speech, and Hearing Services in Schools, 8*(1), 54–64.

MacDonald, J. D. (1978). *Environmental Language Inventory* (rev. ed.). Columbus, OH: Charles E. Merrill.

McCabe, A. E., Levin, J. R., & Wolff, P. (1974). The role of overt activity in children's sentence production. *Journal of Experimental Child Psychology, 17,* 107–144.

McCarthy, D. (1972). *McCarthy Scales of Children's Abilities.* New York: Psychological Corporation.

McCauley, R. J., & Swisher, L. (1984). Psychometric review of language and articulation tests for preschool children. *Journal of Speech and Hearing Disorders, 49,* 34–42.

McNeill, D. (1970). *Acquisition of Language.* Evanston, IL: Harper & Row.

Manuel, H. (1973). *Comprehension of Oral Language.* Wilma Dolezal.

Marshall, N. R., Hegrenes, J. R., & Goldstein, S. (1973). Verbal interactions: Mothers and their retarded children vs. mothers and their nonretarded children. *American Journal of Mental Deficiency, 77,* 415–419.

Mazur, E. F., Holzman, M., & Ferrier, L. (1976). A pragmatic analysis of mother's speech to prelinguistic infants. Paper presented at the First Annual Boston University Conference on Language Development, Boston.

Mecham, M. J., & Jones, J. D. (1978). *Utah Test of Language Development* (rev. ed.). Salt Lake City: Communication Research Associates.

Meissner, J. A. (1975). Use of relational concepts by inner-city children. *Journal of Educational Psychology, 67,* 22–29.

Melnick, C. R. (1975). *The Measurement of Language Development.* Chicago: Stoelting.

Menyuk, P. (1964). A comparison of grammar of children with functionally deviant and normal speech. *Journal of Speech and Hearing Research, 7,* 109–122.

Menyuk, P. (1969). *Sentences Children Use.* Cambridge, MA: MIT Press.

Miller, G. A., & Chomsky, N. (1963). Binary models of language users. In D. Luce, R. Bush, & G. Gallanter (Eds.), *Handbook of Mathematical Psychology* (Vol. 2, pp. 419–492). New York: Wiley.

Miller, G. A., & Isard, S. (1963). Some perceptual consequences of linguistic rules. *Journal of Verbal Learning and Verbal Behavior, 2,* 217–228.

Miller, J. F. (1978). Assessing children's language behavior: A developmental process approach. In R. L. Schiefelbusch (Ed.), *Bases of Language Intervention.* Baltimore: University Park Press.

Miller, J. (1981). *Assessing Language Production in Children: Experimental Procedures.* Baltimore: University Park Press.

Miller, J. & Yoder, D. (1972). *Miller-Yoder Test of Grammatical Competence, Experimental Edition.* Madison: University of Wisconsin Bookstore.

Miller, L. J. (1982). *Miller Assessment for Preschoolers.* Denver, CO: Foundation for Knowledge in Development.

Minife, F. D., & Lloyd, L. L. (Eds.) (1978). *Communicative and Cognitive Abilities—Early Behavioral Assessment.* Baltimore: University Park Press.

Minskoff, E. H., Wiseman, D. E., & Minskoff, J. G. (1972). *Inventory of Language Abilities.* Ridgefield, NJ: Educational Performance Associates.

Moerk, E. L. (1977). Processes and products of imitation: Additional evidence that imitation is progressive. *Journal of Psycholinguistic Research, 6*(3), 187–202.

Morehead, D. M., & Morehead, A. E. (1976). *Normal and Deficient Child Language.* Baltimore: University Park Press.

Morgenstern, G. R. (1975). An attendant training program for increasing verbal responding in institutionalized severely retarded adolescents. Paper presented at the convention of the American Speech and Hearing Association, Washington, DC.

Muma, J. (1973). Language assessment: Some underlying assumptions. *ASHA, 15,* 331–338.

Muma, J. R. (1978). *Language Handbook: Concepts, Assessment, Intervention.* Englewood Cliffs, NJ: Prentice-Hall.

Newcomer, P. L., & Hammill, D. D. (1976). *Psycholinguistics in the Schools.* Columbus, OH: Charles E. Merrill.

Newcomer, P. L., & Hammill, D. D. (1977). *The Test of Language Development.* Austin, TX: Empiric Press.

Oviatt, S. L. (1980). The emerging ability to comprehend language: An experimental approach. *Child Development, 51,* 97–106.

Paraskevopoulos, J. N., & Kirk, S. A. (1969). *The Development and Psychometric Characteristics of the Revised Illinois Test of Psycholinguistic Abilities.* Urbana: University of Illinois Press.

Paris, S. (1973). Comprehension of language connectives and propositional logical relationships. *Journal of Experimental Child Psychology, 16,* 278–291.

Petretic, P. A., & Tweney, R. D. (1977). Does comprehension precede production? The development of children's responses to telegraphic sentences of varying grammatical adequacy. *Journal of Child Language, 4*(2), 201–209.

Phillips, S. U. (1983). *The Invisible Culture: Communication in Classroom and Community on the Warm Springs Indian Reservation.* New York: Longman.

Piaget, J. (1953/1963). *The Origins of Intelligence in Children.* New York: International Universities Press.

Porch, B. E. (1979). *Porch Index of Communicative Ability in Children* (rev. ed.). Palo Alto, CA: Consulting Psychologists Press.

Potts, M., Carlson, P. Cocking, R., & Copple, C. (1979). *Structure and Development in Child Language.* Ithaca, NY: Cornell University Press.

Prather, E. M. (1985). Review of the Test of Early Language Development. In J. V. Mitchell, Jr. (Ed.), *Ninth Mental Measurements Yearbook* (Vol. 2). Lincoln: University of Nebraska, Buros Institute of Mental Measurements.

Prior, M., Minnes, P., Coyne, T., et al. (1979). Verbal interactions between staff and residents in an institution for the young mentally retarded. *Mental Retardation, 17,* 65–69.

Prutting, C. A., Gallagher, T. M., & Mulac, A. (1975). The expressive portion of the NSST compared to a spontaneous language sample. *Journal of Speech and Hearing Disorders, 40*(1), 40–48.

Ratusnik, D. L., & Koenigsknecht, R. (1975). Internal consistency of the Northwestern Syntax Screening Test. *Journal of Speech and Hearing Disorders, 40*(1), 59–68.

Ray, V. (1980). Modifications of language input by preschool teachers as a function of young children's language competencies. Unpublished dissertation, Temple University, Philadelphia.

Reuter, J., Katoff, L., & Dunn, V. (1981). *Kent Infant Development Scale* (rev. ed.). Kent, OH: Kent Developmental Metrics.

Reynell, J. K. (1977). *Reynell Developmental Language Scales* (rev. ed.). Windsor, England: N.F.E.R. Publishing.

Ripich, D. N., & Spinelli, F. M. (Eds.) (1985). *School Discourse Problems*. San Diego: College-Hill Press.

Rose, S. A., & Blank, M. (1974). The potency of context in children's cognition: An illustration through conversation. *Child Development, 45,* 499–502.

Roth, F. P., & Spekman, N. J. (1984a). Assessing the pragmatic abilities of children: Part 1. Organization, framework and assessment parameters. *Journal of Speech and Hearing Disorders, 49,* 2–11.

Roth, F. P., & Spekman, N. J. (1984b). Assessing the pragmatic abilities of children: Part 2. Guidelines, considerations, and specific procedures. *Journal of Speech and Hearing Disorders, 49,* 12–17.

Ryckman, D. B., & Wiegerink, R. (1969). The factors of the Illinois Test of Psycholinguistic Abilities: A comparison of 18 factor analyses. *Exceptional Children, 36*(2), 107–113.

Sanger, D. D. (1985). Review of the Measurement of Language Development. In J. V. Mitchell, Jr. (Ed.), *Ninth Mental Measurements Yearbook* (Vol. 1). Lincoln: University of Nebraska, Buros Institute of Mental Measurements.

Schaffer, M. R. (Ed.) (1978). *Studies in Mother-Infant Interaction*. New York: Academic Press.

Schery, R., & Grover, A. (1982). *Initial Communication Processes*. Monterey, CA: Publishers Test Service.

Seitz, S., & Marcus, S. (1976). Mother-child interactions: A foundation for language development. *Exceptional Children, 42,* 445–449.

Semel, E. M., & Wiig, E. H. (1975). Comprehension of syntactic structures and critical verbal elements by children with learning disabilities. *Journal of Learning Disabilities, 8*(1), 46–51.

Semel, E. M., & Wiig, E. H. (1980). *Clinical Evaluation of Language Functions*. In E. H. Wiig & E. M. Semel, *Language Assessment and Intervention for the Learning Disabled*. Columbus, OH: Charles E. Merrill.

Shatz, M. (1978). On the development of communicative understandings: An early strategy for interpreting and responding to messages. *Cognitive Psychology, 10,* 271–301.

Shipley, E. F., Smith, C. S., & Gleitman, L. R. (1969). A study in the acquisition of language: Free responses to commands. *Language, 45,* 322–342.

Shipley, K. G. (1985). Review of Illinois Children's Language Test. In J. V. Mitchell, Jr. (Ed.), *Ninth Mental Measurements Yearbook* (Vol. 1). Lincoln: University of Nebraska, Buros Institute of Mental Measurements.

Shoyer, C., & Zentall, S. S. (1986). Effects of rate, nonrelevant information, and repetition on the listening comprehension of hyperactive children. *Journal of Special Education, 20*(2), 231–239.

Siegel, G. M., & Broen, P. A. (1976). Language assessment. In L. L. Lloyd (Ed.), *Communication Assessment and Intervention Strategies*. Baltimore: University Park Press.

Sinclair, H. (1970). The transition from sensorimotor behavior to symbolic activity. *Interchange, 1,* 119–126.

Slobin, D. I., & Welsh, C. A. (1971). Elicited imitation as a research tool in developmental psycholinguistics. In C. S. Lavatelli (Ed.), *Language Training in Early Childhood Education*. Champaign-Urbana: University of Illinois Press.

Smith, F. (1971). *Understanding reading: A Psycholinguistic Analysis of Reading and Learning to Read*. New York: Holt, Rinehart & Winston.

Snow, C. E. (1972). Mother's speech to children learning language. *Child Development, 43,* 549–565.

Snow, C. (1977). Mother's speech research: From input to interaction. In C. Snow & C. Ferguson (Eds.), *Talking to Children*. Cambridge, England: Cambridge University Press.

Spraldin, J. E. (1963). Assessment of speech and language of retarded children: The Parsons Language Scales. *Journal of Speech and Hearing Disorders*. Monograph Supplement 10, 8–31.

Stelle, T. W. (1978). *Language: An introduction for parents of deaf children*. Washington, DC: Gallaudet College.

Striffler, N., & Willig, S. (1981). *The Communication Screen*. Tucson, AZ: Communication Skill Builders.

Strohner, H., & Nelson, K. E. (1974). The young child's development of sentence comprehension: Influence of event probability, nonverbal context, syntactic form, and strategies. *Child Development, 45,* 567–576.

Sugarman-Bell, S. (1978). Some organizational aspects of preverbal communication. In I. Markova (Ed.), *The Social Context of Language*. New York: Wiley.

Turton, L. J. (1972). Review of the Houston Test for Language Development. In O. K. Buros (Ed.), *The Seventh Mental Measurements Yearbook* (Vol. 2). Highland Park, NJ: Gryphon Press.

Tyack, D., & Gottsleben, R. (1974). *Language Sampling, Analysis and Training: A Handbook for Teachers and Clinicians*. Palo Alto, CA: Consulting Psychologists Press.

Tyack, D., & Ingram, D. (1977). Children's production and comprehension of questions. *Journal of Child Language, 4*(2), 211–224.

Uzgiris, I., & Hunt, J. McV. (1975). *Assessment in Infancy*. Urbana: University of Illinois Press.

Vellutino, F. R. (1977). Alternative conceptualizations of dyslexia: Evidence in support of a verbal-deficit hypothesis. *Harvard Educational Review, 47,* 334–354.

Wacker, D. P. (1985). Review of the Developmental Assessment for the Severely Handicapped. In J. V. Mitchell, Jr. (Ed.), *Ninth Mental Measurements Yearbook* (Vol. 1). Lincoln: University of Nebraska, Buros Institute of Mental Measurements.

Wallach, G. P. (1984). Later language learning: Syntactic structures and strategies. In G. P. Wallach & K. G. Butler (Eds.), *Language and Learning Disabilities in School-age Children.* Baltimore: Williams & Wilkins.

Weiss, C. E., & Lillywhite, H. S. (1976). *Communication Disorders: A Handbook for Prevention and Early Intervention.* St. Louis: C. V. Mosby.

Wells, G. (1979). Variation in child language. In V. Lee (Ed.), *Language Development.* New York: Wiley.

Wetstone, H. S., & Friedlander, B. Z. (1973). The effects of word order on young children's responses to simple questions and commands. *Child Development, 44,* 734–740.

Wiig, E. H., & Semel, E. (1976). *Language Disabilities in Children and Adolescents.* Columbus, OH: Charles E. Merrill.

Wiig, E., & Semel, E. (1980). *Language Assessment and Intervention for the Learning Disabled.* Columbus, OH: Charles E. Merrill.

Wilkinson, L. C. (Ed.) (1982). *Communicating in the Classroom.* New York: Academic Press.

Wilkinson, L. C., & Calculator, S. N. (1982). Effective speakers: Student's use of language to request and obtain information and action in the classroom. In L. C. Wilkinson (Ed.), *Communicating in the Classroom.* New York: Academic Press.

Wilson, M. S. (1981). *Prescriptive Analysis of Language Disorders—Expressive Syntax Assessment.* Cambridge, MA: Educators Publishing Service.

Witelson, S. F. (1987). Neurobiological aspects of language in children. *Child Development, 58*(3), 653–688.

Wodrich, D. L. (1985). Review of Initial Communication Processes. In J. V. Mitchell, Jr. (Ed.), *Ninth Mental Measurements Yearbook* (Vol. 1). Lincoln: University of Nebraska, Buros Institute of Mental Measurements.

Yaden, D. B., & Templeton, S. (Eds.) (1986). *Metalinguistic Awareness and Beginning Literacy: Conceptualizing What It Means to Read and Write.* Portsmouth, NH: Heinemann.

Young, E. C., & Perachio, J. J. (1983). *The Patterned Elicitation Syntax Test* (rev. ed.). Tucson, AZ: Communication Skill Builders.

Zachman, L., Huisingh, R., Jorgensen, C., & Barrett, M. (1978). *Oral Language Sentence Imitation Screening Test.* Moline, IL: LinguiSystems.

Zimmerman, I. L., Steiner, V. G., & Evatt, R. L. (1969). *Preschool Language Scale.* Columbus, OH: Charles E. Merrill.

APPENDIX 11.1
DEVELOPMENTAL OVERVIEW OF COGNITION, COMMUNICATION, LANGUAGE, AND SPEECH

Age	Cognition	Communication	Language	Speech
0–3 months	• Child is fused with environment • Lacks coordination • Imitation not present • Sucking (reflexive-S-R behavior; some differentiation of sucking reflexes)	• While unintentional, signals are interpreted by others as meaningful • Caretaker imitates child's cooing sounds	None	• Crying (undifferentiated and reflexive) • Crying becomes differentiated • Cooing • Reacts to sound • Begins to discriminate speech and intonational patterns of others • Unaware of own vocalizations
3–6 months	• Begins to coordinate actions (e.g., hearing and seeing) • Attempts to repeat an action over and over again • Imitation is sporadic—constrained to familiar actions, mostly self-initiated	• Nonverbal turn-taking with caretaker • Caretaker imitates child's vocalizations • Unintentional signals are interpreted by others as meaningful	None	• Increased vocalization (greater variety of sounds) • Discrimination of speech sounds • Becoming aware of own vocalizations
6–9 months	• Separates self from environment • Further coordination of action schemes (e.g., vision/prehension) • Repetitive actions directed toward an object without a clear attempt to manipulate the environment • Differentiated actions directed toward an object • Beginning of object concept	• Repetitive and differentiated actions directed toward a person with no clear intent to manipulate the environment • Use of greater variety of communicative signals • Turn-taking continues • Caretaker imitation continues • Interpretation of signals continues	None	• Babbling—increase in phonetic repetoire • Use of suprasegmental features such as pitch, intonation • Aware of own vocalizations • Early development of imitation

Age	Cognition	Communication	Language	Speech
9–12 months	• Actions can be coordinated in novel ways • Purposeful and anticipatory actions • Tool use (one object used to obtain another) • Further development of object concept • Imitation of actions that are unfamiliar yet perceptually visible	• Beginning of intentional communication (sounds, gestures, pointing are used as intentional signaling devices) • Uses physical contact to attract adult attention and to get adult to return the touch • Elaborate play rituals appear with a specific bid for a specific response rather than for social contact in general • Coordination of object and people schemes	• Appears to comprehend some language (which is contextually oriented; may in reality be comprehending extralinguistic features, such as phsyical context, routines and gestures)	• New speech sounds emerge • Increase in dysyllabic chaining • Melody of speech in accord with that of the language community • Greater coordination of vocal and hearing schemes • Imitation of novel sounds
12–18 months	• Emphasis on the novel • Further differentiation of means and ends • Imitation of unfamiliar and invisible actions • Differentiates self and others as recipients of actions • Complex coordination of person/object schemes	• Advanced realization of communicative value of behavior • Requesting behavior • Language symbols emerge as one communicative device • Gestures, pointing and vocalizations continue as intentional communicative signals • Little differentiation of *I–it* and *I–you*	• One-word utterances reflecting various semantic categories (e.g., action, agent, location, object, possession, negation, recurrence) • Over-inclusion and under-inclusion of semantic boundaries • Language is part of action procedures	• Speech sounds now take on meaning (linguistic speech) • New consonants emerging • Perception of phonemes greater than production
18–24 months	• Thought freed from action—symbolic function • Object permanence completed • Symbolic play • Deferred imitation	• Increased functions of communication (e.g., instrumental, social, cognitive) • Separation of *I* and *it* (e.g., can talk about absent objects and people) • Little differentiation of *I* and *you* (egocentricity)	• Combinational language of up to four semantic relations (e.g., agent and action and object and location) • New semantic categories are added • Sentences are propositionally simple • Linguistic symbol and object or action are differentiated	• Phonetic inventory increasing • Rare use of medial and final consonants • Perception over production

Age				
24–36 months	• Elaboration and translation of actions into symbolic form • Egocentricity of thought • Does not coordinate several attributes or dimensions of objects (e.g., length and width)	• Increased functions • Lacks understanding of polite forms and indirect speech acts • Communicates primarily about the "here and now," although separation of *I* and *it* continues • Communication is still primarily egocentric—lacks perspective of others	• Combinational language continues • Sentences still propositionally simple • Emergence of grammatical morphemes (e.g., *-ing*, *in* and *on*, plural and possessive *-s*) • Various sentence types used (declarative, negative, questions) but not syntactically complete	• Mastery of many single phonemes but not in all positions of the word • Begins to master some consonant blends • Phonological processes used for simplication e.g.: banana⟶ nana soup ⟶ doup thanks ⟶ tanks
36–48 months	• Preoperational thought continues, characterized by —egocentricity of thought —perceptual dominance —lack of decentration —lack of reversibility • New concepts emerging	• Continuation of egocentricity (both as speaker and listener) • Continued interest in talking about ongoing actions • Frequent occurrence of monologues and collective monologues • Correctly judges appropriateness of simple polite forms but does not always use them • Begins to learn social conventions of cummunication (development continues through adulthood)	• Complex sentences are generally used including grammatical morphemes (e.g., regular past tense markers—*has, have*) • Expanded use of various sentence types • Begins to use propositionally complex sentences by (a) coordinating two propositions and (b) embedding one proposition within another	• Phonological processes for simplication continues • Continued mastery of phonetic repetoire but not in all positions of the word • Additional consonant blends are mastered
48–60 months	• Preoperational thought continues • Addition of new concepts	• Continued separation of *I—it* and *I—you* • Understands and uses different forms of requests for action	• Syntax is quite elaborate and complex • Passive transformation is not yet mastered • Semantic/syntactic development continues	• Decline in the use of phonological processes to simplify speech • Continued mastery of single phonemes and consonant blends • Certain speech dysfluencies continue (e.g., certain consonant blends and single consonants)

APPENDIX 11.1
(continued)

Age	Cognition	Communication	Language	Speech
60–72 months	• Transition from preoperational to concrete operational thought as characterized by —decentration —awareness of another perspective —emergence of reversible thought	• Begins to use listener feedback to reformulate communicative messages • Can judge and use complex polite forms • Understands indirect speech acts (e.g., "Its's cold outside" meaning close the window) • Aware of another's perceptions but not always able to represent it when communicating • Emergence of stylistic variation	• Talks about and coordinates more than one attributional dimension (e.g., "This glass is taller and thinner") • New semantic features are added (e.g., ± speaker's reference point) • Growing comprehension and use of anaphoric pronouns within and between sentences • Mastery of passive transformation • Lacks metalinguistic ability to think about language	• Mastery of most of the phonetic repertoire in most positions of the word • Contrasting features of stress, pitch and intonation continue to develop • Not yet able to think about one's speech as a critical factor in learning to spell

Note: From *Project: Communication,* by D. N. Bryen et al., 1980, Temple University, Philadelphia. Used with permission of the author.

STANDARDIZED TESTS OF LANGUAGE FOR YOUNG CHILDREN

Test Name	Aspect of Language Measured	Target Population	Test Format	Scoring	Use with Special Populations
Assessment of Children's Language Comprehension Revised Edition (Foster, Giddan, & Stark, 1973)	Ability of child to identify pictorial representations of single words, then of statements having 2, 3, and 4 "critical elements"; elements are tested individually, then in combination; they consist of common count nouns, adjectives, present progressive verb forms, and prepositions.	3 yr. to 6 yr. 11 mo.	Picture Identification: black and white drawings of four or five possible representations are presented horizontally on each plate. Part A—single item vocabulary test in which items correctly identified become core vocabulary for multielement statements. Part B—two elements ("horse standing") Part C—three elements ("ball under the table") Part D—four elements ("broken boat on table").	Number of correct responses is converted to percentage score for each of the four parts.	Normative group was "mixed" socio-economic and ethnic backgrounds, including black, Asian-American, and Mexican American children; however, children were from restricted geographical area; preliminary mean scores are given for neurologically or educationally handicapped children for age groups at 6-month intervals; verbal responses are not required; adequate vision, hearing, and pointing skills are needed.
Berko Exploratory Test of Children's Grammar (Berko, 1958)	Nonstandardized test of children's ability to to apply morphological rules regarding plurals, possessives, verb tenses, derivations, and compound words to actual and nonsense words.	4 to 7 years	Sentence completion: pictures of the stimulus word and its modified representation are presented; the original picture is labeled by the examiner; the modified picture requires the child to apply a morphological rule to complete the examiner's sentence.	No requirement is made as to current adult pronunciation of inflected words, only that adult morphological form be used.	Abilities of educable mentally retarded children to use morphological forms in spontaneous speech is not reflected by their performance on this test of morphology.
Boehm Test of Basic Concepts Revised (1986a)	Comprehension of basic vocabulary; relational concepts of size, distance, position in space, and time are included. An Applications Booklet has been developed to use with the Boehm-R. This 26 item booklet assesses mastery of concepts used in combination, used in sequences, and used to make comparisons.	Grades K–2	Picture Identification: child indicates the picture from a set of three which best illustrates the examiner's statement; two alternate forms are available; 50 items; one item is included in form C or form D for each of the 50 concepts, which are arranged in approximate order of increasing difficulty. Group or individual administration	Binary scoring of correct or incorrect; normative data available for comparison with raw scores; focus individual items and concepts scores; an optional error analysis system is included.	National norms are available for both forms C and D, tapping a wide socioeconomic range. A Spanish translation is available. Norming is in process.

Test Name	Aspect of Language Measured	Target Population	Test Format	Scoring	Use with Special Populations
Boehm Test of Basic Concepts Preschool version (1986b)	Comprehension of basic vocabulary: relational concepts of size, distance, position in space, and time are included. Downward extension of the BTBC-R	3 to 5 years	Picture Identification: child indicates the picture from a set of three which best illustrates the examiner's statement; 52 items are included, two items for each of 26 concepts, arranged in order of increasing difficulty. Individual administration	Binary scoring of correct or incorrect; normative data available for comparison with raw scores; focus individual items and concepts scores; system of error analysis suggested.	Standardization is large and geographically representative, tapping a wide socioeconomic range.
Bracken Basic Concept Scale (Bracken, 1984)	Comprehension of basic receptive vocabulary terms in eleven areas, including: Color, Letter Identification, Numbers/Counting, Comparisons, Shape, Direction/Position, Social/Emotional, Size, Texture/Material, Quantity, and Time/Sequence	2½ to 8 years	Picture identification: Child indicates one of four pictures that best illustrates the basic concept assessed in the examiners statement; 258 items arranged hierarchically by difficulty level, across eleven distinct subgroupings.	Binary scoring of correct or incorrect; normative data available for comparisons (e.g., subtest and total test standard scores, percentile ranks, normal curve equivalents, stanines, Concept Age Equivalents); interchild determination of conceptual strengths and weaknesses can be done, as well as error pattern analysis.	Normed on a large sample, representative of the 1980 U.S. Census data. The BBCS total test score provides sufficient ceiling and floor to assess 98.88 percent of the population or more at all age levels, leaving only the most extreme 1.12 percent of the population insufficiently served.
Carrow Elicited Language Inventory (Carrow, 1974)	Expressive language in elicited situation; emphasis on productive control of grammatical features (i.e., articles, adjectives, singular and plural nouns, pronouns, verbs, negatives, prepositions, adverbs, contractions, demonstratives, and conjunctions).	3 to 8 years.	Elicited imitation test sentences are read to the child, who is asked to repeat each sentence; 51 sentences and 1 phrase range in length from 2 to 10 words; sentences are either active or passive voice and are framed as declarative statements, negatives, imperatives, yes/no questions or wh-questions.	Child's responses are tape recorded so that scoring can identify errors as substitutions, omissions, additions, transpositions, or reversals; percentile ranks can be determined for total error score and for the 12 grammatical subcategories; highly correlated with a measure of the same grammatical categories taken from spontaneous samples (Dailey & Boxx, 1979).	Useful in distinguishing between a group of children developing language normally and a group diagnosed as language delayed (Cornelius, cited in Cicciarelli et al., 1976). Standardized on white, middle class children, so that its usefulness with speakers of a dialect other than standard English is questionable; may not be appropriate for testing children having problems such as severe misarticulation, severe jargon speech, or echolalia.
Clinical Evaluation of Language Functions (Semel & Wiig, 1980)	Series of subtests measuring a wide variety of language functions, including both the production and processing of language (i.e., forming sentences, understanding words and word relation-	Grades K–10	Response requirements are varied: include picture identification, imitation, sentence formulation, answering questions, and timed associations.		Msany aspects of language which present problems for learning disabled children are addressed.

ships, memory of spoken discourse and word retrieval and fluency).

Test	Description	Age Range	Administration	Scoring	Comments
Clinical Linguistic and Auditory Milestone Scale (Capute, Shapiro, & Palmer, 1987)	Screen for delay in prelinguistic and early linguistic communicative behavior; both expressive (sounds and behaviors produced by infant) and receptive (how the infant responds to auditory signals) are evaluated.	Birth to 3 years.	Parent interview and/or clinical observation of naturally occurring infant behaviors (e.g., turns toward voice, says third word, responds to one-step command without gesture).	Average age of first appearance of prelinguistic or linguistic milestones is provided for each developmental task.	Standardization sample is small with only English speaking families of varied socioeconomic levels; concern regarding accuracy of parental observation especially in low SES families; normally developing children can vary widely in language development which this norm-referenced assessment does not recognize (Brody, 1987).
The Communication Screen (Striffler & Willig, 1981)	Screening instrument for general language development (i.e., verbal expression and language comprehension skills); not meant to be used for diagnostic purposes.	2 years, 10 months to 5 years, 9 months	Individually administered in about 5 minutes; Language Comprehension subtest requires responses to tasks such as naming objects, following directions, digit memory, sentence repetition, and understanding action in pictures; Verbal Expression subtest examines child's conversation for average sentence length, intelligibility and fluency.	One-sheet form is used for each of three age groups (i.e., 3-, 4-, and 5-year-olds); criteria are provided for determining final outcome—pass/fail/suspect; lack of clear directions for scoring Verbal Expression subtest.	Standardization based on administration by speech/language clinicians to a limited number of children; severely lacking in evidence of test validity and reliability, therefore, not recommended for administration by other than trained clinician until these data are provided.
Comprehension of Oral Language (Manuel, 1973)	Receptive understanding of spoken English and Spanish by children familiar with life in the United States.	K through early grade school	Picture identification: 35 items are read aloud and child is asked to identify the correct drawing from a strip of five line drawings; administered orally in either group or individual session.	Total number of correct picture identification equals test score; pre- and posttest forms available in both English and Spanish versions.	Spanish forms are direct translations of English without regard for cultural differences and without justification for doing so in the test instructions. No data provided on normative sample, test reliability nor validity. ''Not to be used in an isolated fashion to make educational decisions involving placement of children in monolingual or bilingual programs'' (Duran, 1985, p. 374). Ability in other areas (e.g., discrimination, counting) are also required by this test and may confound interpretation of receptive language skill especially for very young children.

Test Name	Aspect of Language Measured	Target Population	Test Format	Scoring	Use with Special Populations
Detroit Tests of Learning Aptitude (Baker & Leland, 1959)	Reasoning and comprehension; verbal and auditory attention abilities.	Preschool through high school	Response requirements are varied: 19 subtests, including verbal and pictorial absurdities (e.g., adult in child's carriage; child pushing adult), oral commission, auditory attention span for related syllables, likenesses and differences, verbal and pictorial opposites.	Responses are scored for correctness according to four point scale; examples of each response category are provided in the manual.	Standardization population is restricted; norms are dated.
Development Assessment for the Severely Handicapped (Dykes, 1980)	Diagnostic or screening instrument for general language abilities; language as one of five developmental areas; others include sensory-motor, social-emotional, activities of daily living, preacademic.	Individuals functioning within 0–6 year development range; intended as a comprehensive assessment and programming guide for severely and multiply handicapped children who function at or below 96 months.	Evaluation by direct observation or interview of individuals knowledgeable of child's usual activities; multiple examples of behavior at each identified age range are meant to lead into curriculum goals for program intervention.	Each scale is divided into three or four 24-month age ranges; criterion-referenced; each item is to be scored on a 7-point scale; 7 = child accomplishes tasks without assistance, 1 = child cannot accomplish task and resists assistance by the examiner. Validity of test items for use with severely handicapped individuals is questioned (Wacker, 1985, p. 465); reliability of 7-point scale has yet to be established.	Intended for use with severely retarded individuals; no recommendations given for test adaptation in assessing children with sensory and/or motor impairment.
Developmental Communication Inventory (Hanna, Lippert, & Harris, 1982)	General communication development; focuses on development in 5 areas: response to task, attention span, response to teacher, reactions to play experience, and planning and structuring of play; intended primarily to determine child's eligibility and placement in the *Developmental Communication Curriculum.*	Severely communication handicapped, speech/language delayed or nonhandicapped children birth to 5 years.	Part I: Observation of child on developmentally sequenced tasks. Part II: Behavior checklist to use in interviewing adult informants.	Criterion-referenced; no norms provided.	Designed to be used in conjunction with specific intervention via the *Developmental Communication Curriculum.*
Developmental Sentence Analysis (Lee, 1974)	Expressive syntax in spontaneous speech.	2 to 7 years	Spontaneous speech sample; 100 different intelligible, and spontaneous utterances taken from a child's conversation with an adult; elicited language	Sentence scores are determined by analysis of length and complexity of the sentence; the score is weighted according to the presence of indefi-	Effects of various elicitation conditions and varying stimulus materials found to result in language samples that were statistically different in

Instrument	Population	Description	Method	Yields	Comments
(continued)			guage may be in response to presentation of pictures and toys as stimulus materials, to social play, or to questions posed by the adult.	nite pronoun or noun modifiers, personal pronouns, main verbs, secondary verbs, negatives, conjunctions, interrogative reversals, and wh-questions; elements that normally occur later in development are assigned greater weight.	complexity (Longhurst & File, 1977); normative data are based on performance of middle-class speakers of standard English, having normal intelligence; therefore, of uncertain validity with other populations; strength is not in distinguishing the child with deviant language from the child with normal language patterns, but in its potential for identifying the specific area(s) in which the child is having difficulty (Johnson & Tomblin, 1975).
Environmental Language Inventory (ELI) (MacDonald, 1978)	Individuals with severe expressive language delays; ages 2 through adult.	Expressive language at level of one- and two-word utterances; measures use of two-element semantic-grammatical rules, mean length of utterance and intelligibility.	Observation and evaluation in four structured communication situations: conversation I, imitation, conversation II, and free play.	Yields frequency, proportion and rank order scores for eight basic two-element semantic-grammatical rules (e.g., agent + action, agent + object), mean length of utterance (MLU) of all utterances, MLU for intelligible utterances only, proportion of intelligible words, and frequency of unintelligible multiple-word utterances.	Clinical usefulness is greater with children whose expressive language is limited to one- and two-word utterances; reliability data obtained with mentally retarded children so that generalization to those with other disabilities is questionable.
Environmental Prelanguage Battery (Horstmeier & MacDonald, 1978)	Young, developmentally delayed children who are difficult to test using standardized measures; mentally retarded, language delayed children functioning at or below single word level.	Preverbal and early verbal language skills in tasks related to foundations of communication, early receptive language, following directions, nonverbal abilities, sound imitation, beginning social conversation, and verbal abilities.	Structured observation of child's verbal abilities often with parents or other supportive adults participating; child's receptiveness to training is assessed when an item is failed, then attempted again after training by the examiner.	Performance score reflects current functioning level of child as well as child's ability to profit from training on tasks not initially demonstrated; general age equivalents provided but no standard score; score is most useful in determining pre- and post-intervention effects since it has no normative reference.	Designed to be used with young developmentally delayed preverbal child who is difficult to test using standard measures; no reliability or validity data are provided; meant to assess individual eligibility and placement in a companion language training program.
Home Observation for Measurement of the Environment (HOME) (Caldwell & Bradley, 1978–1979)	Level 1: Birth to 3 years Level 2: Preschool	Level 1: Overall measure of stimulation in the child's home environment includes emotional and verbal responsivity of mother Level 2: Overall measure as with Level 1 and includes language stimulation.	Focus on parent report and observations of parent-child interaction; administered during a home visit while child is awake; Level 1 has six subscales; Level 2 has eight subscales.	Items are scored "yes" or "no" with no judgment as to quality required.	Nonstandard interview intends to put caregiver at ease and elicit required information; construct validity was supported in that HOME discriminated among homes in terms of child's developmental delay and/or language disability.

Test Name	Aspect of Language Measured	Target Population	Test Format	Scoring	Use with Special Populations
Houston Test of Language Development, Revised (Crabtree, 1963)	Variety of expressive and receptive language and language-related tasks intended to evaluate the "language functioning" of children.	Part I: 6 months to 3 years Part II: 3 to 6 years	Part I: Observation of social, motor and vocal behavior, receptive and expressive indices (e.g., "will play pat-a-cake"; "vocalization of back vowels"). Part II: Varied response requirements—object manipulation, picture identification, geometric drawing, identification of body parts and gestures, counting, and a language sample of 10 responses; 5 subtests require only 1-word responses, 5 are nonverbal items, and 3 are serial or imitative behavior.	Scoring is binary, behavior as present or absent, response as correct or incorrect; credit is allowed for appearance of one correct response during test session; examiner makes judgments about how to score some items because scoring criteria are at times unclear; adequate performance is considered to be a score within 1 year of the norm for that age.	Test norms were established on very small sample of white, middle-class children of a single urban area; "Results must be used with extreme caution and interpreted conservatively (Turton, 1972, p. 1343); age levels of full-year intervals are not sensitive enough to differentiate language-disordered child from child with normal language competence (Turton, 1972, p. 1343); motor impairment or visual difficulties can lower scores.
Illinois Children's Language Assessment Test (Arit, 1977)	General language abilities in the context of performance in areas of expressive, receptive, auditory, visual, symbolic, and motor function.	3- to 6-year-olds who exhibit delay in speech/language acquisition; derives from assessment of adults with aphasia.	Individually administered; some of the subtests require special training of examiner in order to assess performance (i.e., articulation test, oral musculature section).	Binary + or − scoring: score compared to test means and standard deviations of normative sample of 3- to 6-year olds at 6-month intervals.	Certain subtests may be culturally biased (Shipley, 1985, p. 676); standardization data based on normally developing children; therefore, generalization to handicapped children has not been supported.
Illinois Test of Psycholinguistic Abilities (Kirk, McCarthy, & Kirk, 1968)	Correlates of language, such as duplicating a sequence of geometric designs, also vocabulary and expression; based on a model of language that separates various skills into expressive, receptive, and organizing aspects, and into representation and automatic levels.	2 to 7 years	Response requirements vary according to subtest: Tests at representational level—ability to comprehend, to express, and to organize visual and auditory symbols (e.g., "yes/ no" response to "Do dials yawn?"; picture association of stimulus pictures with one of four optional pictures, "What goes with this?"). Tests at automatic level— ability to perform nonsymbolic tasks, as with auditory and visual short-term sequential memory (e.g., sentence completion, "Here is a dog; here are two _____."); digit repetition.	Scoring procedures differ with each of 10 basic subtests and 2 optional tests; raw scores for each subtest may be converted to psycholinguistic age, to scaled (standard) scores, and to estimated mental age.	Differentiation of separate linguistic functions is not supported with children less than 6 years of age (Ryckman & Wiegerink, 1969); dialect bias with speakers of nonstandard English affects scores on grammatical closure subtest (Grill & Bartel, 1977; see Newcomer & Hammill, 1976, pp. 40–43, for additional information on diagnostic validity research).

Test	Purpose	Population	Administration/Format	Scoring	Comments
Initial Communication Processes (Schery & Grover, 1982)	Component 1: Assessment of basic skills (i.e., visual, motor, cognitive, affective, and comunication) which are precursors of later language abilities. Component 2: Instructional objectives to identify possible language learning disabilities.	Severely handicapped children, birth through developmental age of 3 years.	Individually administered; observation and structured tasks; no test kit materials provided nor are extensive guidelines for administration provided.	Norm-referenced profile of quartile scores in each of 10 skill areas is determined.	Developed for use with severely handicapped young children; the attempt to provide standardization lacks statistical and philosophical justification (Wodrich, 1985, p. 690).
Inventory of Language Abilities (Minskoff, Wiseman, & Minskoff, 1972)	Screening instrument intended to identify possible language learning disabilities.	Grades K through 2 and handicapped children in special classes.	Checklists in each of the following areas: auditory reception, visual reception, auditory association, visual association, verbal expression, manual expression, auditory memory, visual memory, grammatic closure, visual closure, auditory closure and sound blending.	Teacher observation using 12 examples of possible child behaviors in each of the check-lists of the test's identified areas.	No documentation that this instrument is related to identification of learning disabilities; "without value as an informal screening for learning disabilities" (Berndt, 1985, p. 710).
Kent Infant Development Scale (Reuter, Katoff, & Dunn, 1981)	Assesses developmental status of children in specific areas: cognitive, motor, social, language, and self-help.	Ages 13 months to 2 years; normal, at-risk, and handicapped children.	Parent or caregiver report of child behavior on each item in 5 developmental areas.	Full scale scores yields overall estimate of developmental age; use of individual domain score as separate indicator of skill in a particular area is not recommended (Feiring, 1985, p. 786).	Reliable, valid instrument for use with handicapped and nonhandicapped young children.
Language Comprehension Tests (Bellugi-Klima, 1971)	Comprehension of selected syntactic constructions.	Preschool	Object manipulation: child is asked to demonstrate comprehension by actively relating toy objects to each other (e.g., "The boy is washed by the girl").	Test items arranged in order of increasing difficulty; no standardized scoring presented.	No normative data are given for the test items; test lends itself well to diagnostic teaching.
Language Facility Test (Dailey, 1968)	Expressive use of language.	3 years and over	Language sample elicited by presentation of 3 pictures from a collection of 12 test pictures; child is shown each picture and asked to tell a story about what s/he sees (i.e., "What are they doing in this picture?").	Scoring is based on either a recording or transcription of each story; the entire story is scored on a 9-point scale; 9 = a well-organized story reflecting imagination and creativity; 4 = use of two or more sentences describing people or objects, but with no verb of action or indication of interaction; 1 = single noun response (Adler, 1979, p. 150).	Intends to assess language facility without regard for its deviation from standard English or factors of vocabulary, pronunciation, an example presented in the manual provides a lowered score for the nonstandard phrase "She sitting" (Anastasiow, 1972, p. 1344); standardization is disproportionately from Southern urban areas with no data on socioeconomic levels.

Test Name	Aspect of Language Measured	Target Population	Test Format	Scoring	Use with Special Populations
McCarthy Scales of Children's Abilities (McCarthy, 1972)	Measures general intellectual functioning by evaluating factors of word knowledge, verbal memory, verbal fluency, and analogies.	2½ to 8½ years	Response requirements are varied: 6 scales include verbal, perceptual quantitative, general cognitive, memory, and motor performance.	Normative data are available for each scale.	Useful for assessing mentally retarded children; standardization data, while restricted in age, are representative.
The Measurement of Language Development (Melnick, 1975)	Intended as an indicator of clinical progress rather than a screening or diagnostic tool; receptive and expressive linguistic structures are assessed based on 5 scales' scores: receptive scale, expressive scale, MLU, word order, and semantic relations.	Children with language impairments who are between 3 years and 7 years 11 months	Expressive scale: uses elicited imitation paradigm accompanied by line drawing representations for each item. Receptive scale: requires a pointing response to one of 4 line drawings.	Binary scoring (correct/incorrect) of the expressive and receptive performance scale which can be converted into percentile rank. Word order retention, semantic relations, and MLU scales do not have accompanying normative data, but instructions for scoring are provided. Subtest scores not recommended to be used as independent measures.	Standardization of expressive and receptive scales on large group of nonhandicapped speakers of standard American English; extension to children who do not use standard English is questionable; reliability and validity studies demonstrate adequacy for use with language delayed and moderately mentally retarded youngsters; care recommended in assessing deaf children using sign language interpretation (Sanger, 1985, p. 941).
Miller Assessment for Preschoolers (Miller, 1982)	Assessment of overall development in an attempt to identify children with moderate preacademic learning problems.	Ages 2 yr., 9 mo. to 5 yr., 8 mo.: not recommended for children with known physical, mental, or emotional disabilities	27 performance items make up assessment core that is given individually; includes variations of widely used items (e.g., draw-a-person) as well as neurologically based items; supplemental observations are in addition to structured tasks that clinically trained examiners may complete.	Separate scoring sheets are used for each of 6 age groupings so that correct/incorrect response is immediately compared with normative performance; by color coding, examiner knows if response is typical of others at or below the 5th percentile, in the 6th to 25th percentile, or above the 25th percentile.	Normative sample included nonwhite children from a variety of ethnic groups and all regions of the country; test author recommends against use with non-English speaking children or those who are known to have physical, emotional, or mental disabilities.
Miller-Yoder Test of Grammatical Comprehension, Experimental Edition (Miller & Yoder, 1972)	Diagnostic assessment of receptive understanding of the following grammatical forms: active, prepositions, possessive, negative/affirmative statements, pronouns, singular/plural noun and verb, verbal inflections, adjective modifiers, passive reversables, and reflexivizations.	3 to 6 years	Picture identification: 42 sentence pairs which are controlled for length (4 or 5 words) are used; plates contain 4 black-and-white drawings; child's task is to point to the picture that represents the stimulus sentence.	Experimental edition: standardization and normative information are not provided.	Suggested as being applicable to evaluation of mentally retarded and/or language impaired children because no oral response is required.

Nonspeech Test for Receptive/Expressive Language (Huer, 1983)	Diagnostic tool which requires systematic observation, recording, and summarization of an individual's skill as a communicator, whether speech or nonspeech (e.g., sign language, communciation boards) is used for communication.	Developmental age equivalents ranging from 0 months to approximately 48 months.	Test materials consist of a picture book containing 52 photographs, 8 line drawings, and 4 numerals, and a set of objects easily recognized by young children (doll, toy telephone, bell); Receptive language tasks include changes in behavior as examiner approaches, identification of one of three objects named, demonstration of understanding of 5 to 7 adjectives; Expressive language tasks include vocalizes playfully, imitates new behaviors (signals), spontaneously asks wh-questions.	Binary scoring: correct/incorrect response demonstrated with notation of individual's type of communicative signals; Receptive and expressive age equivalents can be determined using tables for preschool child or multihandicapped child; response summaries categorize skills in terms of general levels of development which is useful in planning intervention goals.	Standardization data based on limited sample of normally developing infants and young children (ages 1 to 63 mos.) and severely multihandicapped students (ages 5.6 to 21.4 yrs.) from an urban area and from varied socioeconomic levels; extension of preliminary test reliability and validity as well as standardization data is in progress. Intended to be used with children in infant stimulation or preschool programs, those with learning disabilities, aphasia or apraxia, mental retardation, physical disabilities or multiple handicaps.
Northwest Syntax Screening Test (NSST) (Lee, 1971)	Syntactic expression and comprehension; intends to screen those children delayed in syntactic development.	3 to 8 years	Expressive portion: elicited imitation sentences which contain syntactic structures that often are problematic for children (with accompanying pictures); Receptive portion: picture identification—child is required to point to the one representation among four line drawings which matches each of the contrasting sentence pairs spoken by the examiner. 20 items are presented for each of the receptive and expressive portions.	Expressive portion: only identical repetitions are scored as correct, even though child's production may be grammatically correct. Receptive portion: binary scoring (correct/incorrect).	Expressive portion may underestimate syntactic ability when compared with spontaneous speech of language delayed children (Prutting, Gallagher, & Mulac, 1975); discriminative ability of expressive portion to differentiate between those developing language normally and those who are not may be strongest with 4- and 5-year-olds (Ratusnik & Koenigsknecht, 1975); for 5½ to 6½ years, receptive and expressive portions lack sensitivity to syntactic development (Arndt, 1977); normative data are based on samples of children from middle-class families in a single geographical area, all of whom were speakers of standard English; therefore, "it is an inappropriate test of language development for other dialect groups [unless it is intended] to ascertain how well speakers of other dialects use standard American dialect" (Bannatyne, 1975, p. 196).

APPENDIX 11.2
(continued)

Test Name	Aspect of Language Measured	Target Population	Test Format	Scoring	Use with Special Populations
Oral Language Sentence Imitation Screening Test (Zachman, Huisingh, Jorgensen, & Barrett, 1976)	Expressive language screening instrument.	3 yr. to 1st grade	Sentence imitation administered individually in approximately 3 minutes.	Imitations are scored for syntactic correctness; criteria for analysis of overall performance are vague: pass, fail ("numerous errors"), or borderline ("several test errors") (Haber, 1985, p. 1097).	Test has no normative data; questionable reliability; does not accommodate to dialect variations common among speakers of Spanish or Black English.
Ordinal Scales of Psychological Development in Infancy (Uzgiris & Hunt, 1975)	Cognitive correlates/precursors of language and communication; specifically, six aspects of sensorimotor intelligence—object permanence, imitation, means for achieving desired ends, causality, object relations in space, schemata for relating to objects. Based on Piaget's theory of early cognitive development.	Mental age of 2 weeks to 2 years	Response requirements are varied: include child's action on objects and interactions with examiner; within each scale, eliciting situations are arranged in hierarchical order—simplest to most complex.	Criterion for scoring each item is clearly defined; data for each scale yield information regarding the developmental stage of cognitive functioning the child has reached.	Used widely with normal and handicapped infants, children, and severely retarded adolescents and adults.
Parsons Language Sample (Spraldin, 1963)	Expressive aspects of language, vocal and nonvocal; comprehension.	Children with severe mental handicaps.	Response requirements are varied: object and picture naming, elicited imitation, sentence completing, verbal analogies, gestural imitation, use of gestures, hand behavior, following directions for motor performance.	Binary scoring, correct or incorrect; percentile rank may be determined for each of 7 subtests.	Standardization based on response of ambulatory, mentally retarded children between ages of 7 and 15 years; does not measure syntax; assumes Skinnerian model of language learning and behavior.
Patterned Elicitation Syntax (Screening) Test (Young & Perachio, 1983)	Assesses morphosyntactic structures in expressive language for possible deficiencies.	3 to 7½ years.	Delayed sentence imitation tasks wherein three sentences are spoken to the child as s/he looks at corresponding pictures, then repeats the sentences as originally presented.	Unusual imitation paradigm in that only the third of the three sentences presented is counted toward the raw score on the assumption that the first sentences will be modeled but the third will represent typical language structures; response sheet provides for analysis of errors by structure; percentile rank and mean for age data derive from raw score.	May also be administered to older children who demonstrate errors in expressive language; age norms provided are not appropriate for those who use a dialect other than standard English; originally developed as a criterion-referenced test in 1981 with age norms developed in 1983.

Test	Purpose	Age Range	Response/Tasks	Scoring	Comments
Peabody Picture Vocabulary Test (Revised) (Dunn & Dunn, 1981)	Receptive vocabulary of standard English	Mental ages 2.5 years to adult	Picture identification: child points to appropriate picture in response to stimulus word spoken by examiner; four options are presented on each plate.	Binary scoring, correct or incorrect: test items are arranged in order of increasing difficulty; raw score may be converted to percentile rank, age equivalent score or to a standard score equivalent; PPVT-R no longer converts to mental age or IQ as possible with PPVT.	Because responses are not oral and choices may be indicated by modified system of pointing (e.g., eye gaze, encoding correct picture number), it is appropriate for use with speech impaired and/or physically handicapped children; PPVT-R is normed on representative nationwide sample unlike PPVT which used localized sample of predominantly white males.
Porch Index of Communicative Ability in Children (Porch, 1979)	General communication ability involving verbal, gestural, and graphic skills; does not attempt to measure psycholinguistic considerations, syntactic, or pragmatic elements of communicative ability.	Basic Battery: 3 to 6 years Advanced Battery: 6 to 12 yr.	Response requirements are varied: includes verbal, gestural, and graphic communicative tasks related to 10 common objects that serve as stimuli (e.g., verbal description of object properties and functions, picture-object matching, verbal imitation, object identification, sentence completion; for Advanced Battery, reading and writing skills are assessed.	Each item is scored on a 16-category rating scale which reflects assessment on 5 dimensions of the response (completeness, promptness, and efficiency); mean scores for each of the 15 Basic Battery and 20 Advanced Battery subtests for each modality (gestural, verbal and graphic) may be converted to percentile.	Norms based on uneven numbers of children at varying age groups; no reliability or validity data are reported; both batteries begin testing with the most difficult tasks; impact of initial failure on subsequent performance may affect results.
Preschool Language Assessment Instrument, Experimental Edition (Blank, Rose & Berlin, 1978b)	Pragmatic, conceptual, and linguistic components of communication in school; designed to assess young child's skills and ability to cope with language demands of the teaching/learning situation in preschool.	3 to 6 years, or children up to 10 years whose language skills and poor school performance warrant further assessment.	Verbal response to pictorial and auditory stimuli: four main levels of abstraction provide the basis on which items are developed (e.g., "The girl wants to pet the dog, but the boy is in the way. What should she say to the boy?" "What would happen if, ——? Why?").	Each item based on 3–0 scoring system: 3 = fully adequate, 2 = acceptable, 1 = ambiguous, 0 = inadequate; several sample responses serve as guide to scoring according to these criteria; norms consist of means, standard deviations, and score ranges for children according to age and socioeconomic background.	Adequate validity and reliability reported; standardized with small number of children from middle and lower socioeconomic classes; some visual stimuli present many items together which may be difficult for children who are visually impaired or highly distractible.
Preschool Language Scale (Zimmerman, Steiner, & Evatt, 1969)	Diagnostic test of auditory comprehension, verbal ability, and articulation.	1 year, 6 months to 6 years, 11 months	Picture identification, block manipulation, and identification of body parts; Auditory Comprehension scale (e.g., "Show me the one which is heavier . . . a bird or a cow?; a bed or a cow?"); varied formats; Verbal Ability scale (e.g., repeats three digits, elicited imitation, "What do you do when you are sleepy?").	Developmental ages for groups of test items are given at 1½ month intervals within 6-month categories; not to be considered same as statistical norms.	Minimal use of motor skills in auditory comprehension scale make this scale suitable for administration with physically handicapped children; manual states that scale may be translated for use with speakers of another language.

APPENDIX 11.2
(continued)

Test Name	Aspect of Language Measured	Target Population	Test Format	Scoring	Use with Special Populations
Prescriptive Analysis of Language Disorders—Expressive Language Syntax Assessment (Wilson, 1981)	General syntactic ability in expressive language.	2 years to 4 years, 11 months	Imitation followed by elicitation; verbal responses required to elicitation tasks (e.g., "This cat has a tail. What about this one?"); individually administered in approximately 20 to 25 minutes.	Overall scores in: imitation, elicitation and mastery; criteria for mastery are correct imitation of a syntactic construction and correct response to all three elicitation tasks within that construction section.	Designed to place language impaired students for treatment; normative sample is too small and not geographically representative, therefore, more useful as criterion-referenced scale based on developmental model of intervention; no reliability or validity data presented.
Receptive-Expressive Emergent Language Scale (Bzoch & League, 1971)	Language-related behaviors; expressive language and receptive language.	Birth to 36 months	Structured interview of parents or primary caregivers; (e.g., "Begins some 2-syllable babbling; upon verbal request selects an item from a group of five or more varied items").	Three scoring weights are applied to specific test items; behavior is fully established (+), behavior is partially established (±), behavior is absent (−).	Purports to be capable of early identification of deafness, infantile autism, and mental retardation; yet no data are reported to support this contention (Johnson, 1973); very small standardization sample.
Reynell Developmental Language Scales (Revised) (Reynell, 1977)	Expressive language ability (i.e., language structure, vocabulary, content or creative use of language) and verbal comprehension.	1 to 7 years	Expressive language scale: observation of early vocal behavior; naming and describing; use of toys and pictures; use of language to describe a concept (e.g., "What does 'sleeping' mean?"); verbally describing pictures using connected ideas. Verbal Comprehension scales: object identification and object manipulation and object manipulation (e.g., "Put the doll on the chair." "Which one do we sleep in?" "This little boy has spilled his dinner; What must he do?").	Binary scoring except for content section of Expressive Language scale, which defines sentence scoring procedure; scores can be transformed into equivalent age levels and standard scores.	Verbal Comprehension Scale A requires no speech; Verbal Comprehension Scale B requires neither speech nor hand functioning and is intended for use with hearing impaired and severely handicapped children who may need to respond by eye pointing; however, limited validity and reliability with handicapped populations; norms established with non-handicapped children in England; some items reflect linguistic differences between British and American usage (e.g., "laying the table"); caution urged in interpreting results at lower ages (Bryen, 1985, p. 1287).
Sequenced Inventory of Communication Development (Revised) (Hedrick, Prather, & Tobin, 1984)	Screens broad spectrum of early communication skills including semantic, syntactic, and pragmatic aspects of expressive and receptive language; receptive behaviors include awareness of	4 months to 4 years	Varied response requirements: object manipulation (e.g., "Put one spoon in the box. Put in all of them."); following commands involving objects; picture identification according to function (e.g.,	Binary scoring, yes/no, following criteria in manual; parent report of some typical communicative behaviors not observed in testing situation; provides expressive and receptive communication ages.	Norms for earlier 1975 edition established on mixed social class level of white children within one geographical area; For 1984 Revision, field study results included in the test manual present findings

Test	Age Range	Description	Administration	Scoring	Comments
		sounds and/or speech, discrimination by differential responses to sounds/speech, and comprehension of verbally directed tasks; expressive behaviors include imitation, initiation and response to communication, and a 50-response language sample for children over 2 years.	"Show me what you read?"); naming pictures; elicited imitation: sentence completion with pictures (e.g., "Here is a car. Here are two _____.").		with black and white children of middle and lower social classes; manual also presents suggestions for use with difficult-to-test children (autistic, hearing impaired, and Yup'ik speaking Eskimo): Spanish translation is included in test manual for use with Spanish-speaking children.
Tests for Auditory Comprehension of Language (Carrow, 1973)	3 years to 6 years, 11 months	Auditory comprehension of vocabulary, morphology, syntax; English and Spanish versions available.	Picture identification: child identifies by pointing to one of three pictures which describes the test item presented verbally by the examiner; items evaluate comprehension of form classes and function words (adjectives, nouns, verbs, and adverbs), morphology, grammar, and syntax (e.g., "pair/par"; "The lion has eaten.")	Binary scoring, correct/incorrect; test items grouped by grammatical category, not by level of difficulty; ages at which 75% and 90% of children respond correctly are given with each item.	Spanish version direct translation of English version; experimental version of this test proved to be useful with moderately retarded children; when equated for mental age with nonretarded children, retarded children's use of lexical items was similar, but use of grammatical categories was inferior to that of nonretarded children (Bartel, Bryen, & Keehn, 1973); children with learning disabilities demonstrated reduced scores in comprehension of syntactic structures; useful in identification of language deficits of learning disabled children (Semel & Wiig, 1975).
Test of Early Language Development (Hresko, Reid, & Hammill, 1981)	3 years to 7 years, 11 months	Designed to screen children with significantly delayed language skills by evaluating the form (syntax, phonology, and morphology) and content (word and concept knowledge and interpretation of meaning) of receptive and expressive language.	38-item test is administered individually; child is required to repeat words and sentences, answer questions, and respond appropriately to a set of printed stimulus cards presented by the examiner.	Samples of acceptable responses are given after each item; raw scores may be converted into percentiles, age equivalents, language quotients (LQ); caution is expressed by the test authors regarding the use of age equivalents or misrepresentation of LQ's as IQ's.	Normative data based on national sample of children varying in race, geographical distribution and urban/rural residence; reliability is adequate with weaker support for test validity: "Most effective for children at 4, 5, 6 years of age but has value in identifying 3- or 7-year-olds with delay in spoken language" (Prather, 1985. p. 1559).
Test of Language Development (Newcomer & Hammill, 1977)	4 to 8 years	Semantics, syntax, and phonology tested by five principal and two supplemental subtests.	Varied response requirements: picture identification of vocabulary and grammatical understanding; sentence imitation; sentence completion; oral vocabulary (e.g., "What does 'true' mean?").	Binary scoring, correct/incorrect; subtest scores may be converted to age equivalents.	Geographically and racially mixed standardization sample; purportedly useful in identifying linguistically impaired children.

APPENDIX 11.2
(continued)

Test Name	Aspect of Language Measured	Target Population	Test Format	Scoring	Use with Special Populations
Token Test for Children (DiSimoni, 1978)	Ability to process and recall verbal directions of increasing length and complexity; five parts of the test increase the demands to comprehend and process conjunctions, coordination of clauses, and compound and complex sentences.	3 to 12½ years	Object manipulation: tokens of five colors, two shapes, and two sizes are placed according to directions of the examiner (e.g., "Touch the small, yellow circle and the large green square." "Except for the green one, touch the circles.").	Binary scoring, correct/incorrect; if multiple-step command, each step must be formed accurately to receive credit.	Standardized with group of children of mixed socioeconomic levels, all speakers of American dialect; youngest (3- to 4-year-olds) and oldest 12- to 12½-year-olds) group norms are based on smaller numbers of children, therefore interpret scores at these levels cautiously.
Utah Test of Language Development (Revised) (Mecham & Jones, 1978)	Intended to screen language development of children by providing a broad overview of production and comprehension skills.	1 year, 6 months to 14 years, 5 months	Varied response requirements: repeating digits and sentences; reproducing geometric forms; picture identification (e.g., "Point to eating."); object manipulation (e.g., with five objects on the table, "Put the pencil by the gun.").	Binary scoring, correct/incorrect; language age, percentile score, and stanine score for each level may be derived.	Revised edition was meant to provide improved standardization over the 1967 edition by including more children of greater geographical and socioeconomic diversity, but revised norms still lack appropriate standardization information; validity is seriously questioned because most items are taken from existing tests of general intelligence; does not adequately discriminate between problems in language development and problems in cognitive or motor processes.

APPENDIX 11.3
STRUCTURED, NONSTANDARDIZED ASSESSMENT PROCEDURES

Target Language Aspect to be Assessed	Materials Needed	Response Paradigm[a]	Procedures
Object/use and play (Chappell & Johnson, 1976; Sinclair, 1970; Lombardino, Stein, Kricos & Wolf, 1986; Fewell & Rich, 1987)	Familiar objects (e.g., cup, doll, ball, pillow, hair brush, spoon, plastic spoon)	OM	1. Place objects in groups of three in front of the child. Observe interaction. Does child interact with the object (1) exploratively, (2) functionally, or (3) symbolically? 2. If child does not spontaneously interact with objects, hand the child one object at a time. Observe and note quality of interaction, as in (1) above. 3. Follow up with verbal directives at a symbolic level (e.g., "Make dollie sleep on the pillow.").
Early Language Comprehension (Bloom, 1973; Brown, 1973; Weiss & Lillywhite, 1976)	Contexts of familiar, naturally occurring activities.	NC	1. Using commonly occurring activities, present simple sentences or words that relate to the context (at the door say, "Want to go bye-bye?"). Observe and note child's response. 2. Use same procedures as in (1) above, but not in context in which that activity typically occurs (e.g., at a table say, "want to go bye-bye?"). Observe and note the influence of context on language comprehension.
Early Language Production (Bloom, 1973; Brown, 1973)	Familiar objects/toys	S, A	1. Place familiar toys/objects in front of child, one at a time. Engage child in play. Record any utterances child makes and the context. Analyze the semantic categories used by the child (e.g., agent, action, object, location, recurrence). 2. If no spontaneous utterances, try eliciting utterances by asking early wh-questions, such as: "What's this?" "What's the ball doing?" "Where's the ball?"

Target Language Aspect to be Assessed	Response Paradigm[a]	Materials Needed	Procedures
Referent Description/ Semantic Features (Katz & Fodor, 1963; Clark, 1973a)	D	Common objects (e.g., nail, envelope, ball) and a list of words without a specific referent (e.g., "toy," "animal," "hungry," "arithmetic")	1. Ask the child to tell you all about the object presented. Probe, saying, "Tell me more." 2. After using the referent-words, ask child to tell you about the words without referents. Probe. 3. Record responses and analyze semantic features used to describe each word (function, name, attributes, class membership).
Semantic Features at the Sentence Level (Katz & Fodor, 1963; Clark, 1973a)	J, A, D	List of sentences, some of which are anomalous (violate semantic rules). 1. *"She is my brother."* 2. *"My mother has no children."* 3. *"The candy ate the card."* 4. *"My dog writes nice stories."* 5. *"The liquid became an odorless audience."* 6. *"The sun danced lightly through the clouds."*	1. After reading each sentence, ask whether the sentence is a "good" (makes sense) or "bad" sentence. After judging the sentence, ask why it is a good or bad sentence. Have the child correct bad sentences. Record all responses. 2. Note what factors influenced child's judgments. Note child's explanations and ability to correct anomalous sentences. Note differences, if any, between tacit and explicit language knowledge.
Specific Grammatical Structures (Menyuk, 1969; Bliss, Allen, & Wrasse, 1977; Potts, Carlson, Cocking, & Copple, 1979)	SC	Short stories with or without accompanying pictures which focus on particular grammatical structures. Example 1: Copula and deletion of past tense marker in main verb: "Carol got a rag, and what she did next _____" ("wipe it up" versus "wiped it up"). Example 2: Count or mass nouns: "Look at this sandbox. There's so many _____ (toys, things). And there's so much _____ (sand, junk)." (Potts, et al., 1979, p. 69).	Construct or obtain short stories that tap structures of interest. Where appropriate, have pictures that provide needed content clues. Read each story, having the child complete it. Note the child's response for semantic relevance, correctness of syntactic structures, and awareness of the rules of discourse.
Comprehension of Anaphoric Pronoun it (Chipman & deDardel, 1974)	OM	Flattened cake of clay, one box containing five marbles, one box with 20 marbles, and one clear empty box; one tray on which are displayed one bar of plasticine chocolate divided into demarcated squares.	Present appropriate materials saying: 1. "There is the clay. Give it to me." 2. "There is a box with 5 marbles. Give it to me." 3. "The chocolate is there. Give it to me." Note the child's comprehension of the pronoun "it".

Measure	Description	Code	Procedure
Comprehension of Temporal Connectives—before, after, until (Barrie-Blackey, 1973)	Dolls and dollhouse; Sentences containing various subordinate clauses beginning with *before, after, until* (e.g., "Daddy stands up until Mommy sits down.")	OM	Sentences are said to the child who acts them out using the toys.
Comprehension of Connectives and Propositional Logical Relations (Paris, 1973)	Paired pictures (e.g., DLM Sequential Picture Cards) related to accompanying sentences in four different truth forms: true-true, true-false, false-true, false-false. Compound sentences containing the following connectives: "and"—conjunction, "but"—conjunction, "both"-"and"—conjunction, "neither"-"nor" disjunction, "either"-"or" disjunction, "if"-"then" conditionality, "if"-"and only if then" biconditionality	A	Picture pairs are displayed and the descriptive sentence is read. Child must decide if the description was true or false (e.g., "The boy is riding the bicycle and the dog is lying down.").
Comprehension of wh-questions—who, why, when, how (Cairns & Hsu, 1978; Hsu et al., 1987)	Brief videotapes, films or pictures of family life with a father, mother, a teenage sister, a six-year-old brother and a dog. Questions of the following six types: Who-subject ("who bugged the boy?") Who-object ("Who was the Daddy feeding?") Who-object using *do* support ("Who did the boy feed?") Why-("Why did the dog eat the sandwich?") When-("When did the girl feed the dog?") How-("How did the girl feed the dog?")	A	After being introduced to each character by a photograph which remains on display, the child watches a taped segment and then is asked the six types of questions listed.
Comprehension Ongoing Discourse (Glucksberg & Krauss, 1967)	Crayons and drawing paper or paste and construction paper of different sizes, colors, and shapes. A pretend script about a fantasy story which the child will draw following your dictation of the script, or directions about the cut-out shapes that the child will follow to	OM	Administer directions or read pretend scripts to the child in two or three sentences at a time. Encourage the child to make his or her picture story (or design) exactly like the story you tell. If possible, have the child retell the story to you or direct you to make the design.

Target Language Aspect to be Assessed	Materials Needed	Response Paradigm[a]	Procedures
	construct a design, mask, or scene. Script sentences should vary in complexity, have an ongoing coherent theme, and utilize, where appropriate, anaphoric pronouns. **Example:** *Hi, I'm Mary Martian from Mars. I'm a little purple Martian with red, round eyes; a square head, and green pointed ears.* *Through the window of my spaceship I can see your planet earth. It has a big round yellow sun and blue clouds. It has trees, flowers and birds.*		Analyze child's picture to determine if s/he was able to accurately and completely process elaborate ongoing language. This includes expanded NP's, anaphoric pronouns, etc.
Effective Speaking (Garnica, 1981)	Small group of children seated around a table; 1 or 2 sets of crayons or markers to share; drawing paper.	NC, S	Seat the small group of children around a table with their own drawing paper and 1 or 2 sets of crayons or markers to share. Have them draw an agreed-upon picture. Observe the target child to determine if and how s/he obtains the use of a desired marker. Note use of Grice's rules of effective speaking: · Designates the listener to whom request is made. · Is direct and clear. · Is informative. · Is relevant. · Revises strategy if request is unsuccessful.

Note. Derived, in part, from *Inquiries into Child Language* (pp. 297–299) by D. N. Bryen. 1982. Boston: Allyn & Bacon. Copyright 1982 by Allyn & Bacon. Adapted by permission.

[a] **Response paradigms:** A = Answers to stimulus questions; D = descriptions; J = judgments about grammaticality; NC = natural context; OM = object manipulation: S = spontaneous language; SC = story completion.

12

Assessment of Basic Relational Concepts

ANN E. BOEHM

An understanding of basic concepts is necessary for the young child to deal with the demands of everyday living and to build upon in later learning. Basic concepts, as the term is used here, involve the child's ability to make relational judgments, either among objects, persons, or situations, or in reference to a standard. Basic concepts help the child understand and later describe relationships between and among objects, locations of objects and persons, characteristics of objects (dimensions, positions, movements, quantity, and presence), and sequences of events. Basic concepts are called upon early in the child's life as interactions take place in situations, such as the child pointing to a table and saying: "Cookie *on* table" or with the mother responding to the child and saying "Look *under* the bed for the ball." As the child develops, basic concepts are used to order, to make comparisons, to classify, and to conserve. All these abilities are applied in a wide variety of situations (Boehm, 1976). As deVilliers and deVilliers (1979) pointed out when describing the development of word meaning, "Still more complex are the meanings of relational words, such as the dimensional adjectives big and little, tall and short or thick and thin. Their correct use depends on reference to some standard that varies with the object described and with the context in which it is placed" (p. 123).

As Flavell (1970) noted, there is no one universally accepted definition of a concept. Contributing to the diversity of definitions is the fact that concepts vary in their inclusiveness, generalizability, preciseness, and importance. Consistent with this observation, there is no one definition of what constitutes a basic concept. A writer's definition thus determines the scope and range of possible concepts included on a particular assessment instrument. This definition can be more delimited such as that used by Boehm (1969, 1971, 1976, 1986a,b) to include the relational concepts of size, distance, position in space, time, and quantity. Or, it can be used more generally to include al receptive concept areas likely to be encountered by young children including color, shape, letter identification, numbers and counting, social and emotional concepts, and textural material, along with relational concepts, such as that used by Bracken (1984). Many preschool assessment tasks encompass such a broad definition. Some examples will be presented later in this chapter.

The term basic concepts, as used in this chapter, refers only to relational concepts of size, distance, position in space, time, and quantity. These basic concepts differ from other concepts the young child is called upon to use. For example, when the child has developed a concept of an object such as a table, the internal image of a table—that of an object with a flat surface on four legs—soon becomes fairly stable. As the child encounters new objects that are tables, he or she can make a match between the new object and the internal image (concept) of a table. In contrast, consider the basic concept pairs *first–last* and *near–far*. The child will not easily form a stable image of these concepts, for they are shifting in nature and must be applied to new and different situations. In addition, they can be applied at different levels of complexity. *First* and *last* can be used to designate positions in space and in time. The car *first* in line on one occasion can be *last* on another. The *last* thing a child worked on yesterday might be the *first* thing he or she worked on today. Likewise with *near* and *far*, which help describe distance in space or time and illustrate other levels of complexity. We can speak of the animal *near* or *far* away from a tree that we can see, a friend who lives *far* away who we cannot see, and a planet so *far* away we may never be able to see it.

The child's ability to make such relational decisions is necessary at the preschool level to do the following: follow instructions ("Justin, go to the *front* of the *line*"); comprehend stories ("When the dog was frightened, she hid *under* the bed"); describe situations or events to other ("I went to bed *early* because I was tired"); facilitate communication with others ("I want the long jump rope"); and describe thoughts and feelings ("My friend moved *far* away").

As children engage in readiness activities and later in the formal learning of reading and arithmetic, they increasingly need to draw upon their fund of basic concepts to follow directions and understand instructions such as "Mark all the words that *begin* with the letter b," or "Which is *more*, 5 + 2 or 3 + 7?" Given these examples, it readily becomes apparent that the assessment of basic concepts among preschool children, age 2 to 6 years, is of importance and interest. This assessment needs to focus on at least two dimensions of basic concept use: The child's under-

standing of these terms as demonstrated through action, manipulation of objects, or in response to pictured situations; and the child's use of these concepts in his or her everyday language.

The set of basic concepts of concern in this chapter includes relational terms such as *top–bottom*, *same–different*, in *front of–behind*, *near–far*, and *right–left*, many of which have been identified in the Boehm Test of Basic Concepts-Revised (Boehm-R) (1986) and Boehm Test of Basic Concepts-Preschool Version (1986) which measure 50 and 26 basic relational terms, respectively. Bracken (1984) also includes relational concepts in The Bracken Basic Concept Scale. Other tests include a small sample of basic relational concepts and will be detailed later.

IMPORTANCE OF BASIC RELATIONAL CONCEPTS

Instruction

The importance of understanding basic concepts can be documented in a number of ways. Studying the complexity of verbal directions used by teachers in grades K through 5, Kaplan (1978) recorded the verbal interactions of three teachers at each of these grade levels while engaged in different areas of instruction; each teacher was recorded for a total of 1 hour. The level of complexity of teacher directions (number of behavior steps to be followed and qualifying statements such as "put the big ball on the small box") was found to be similar across the grade levels studied, with 82% of all teacher directions containing no more than two behaviors and two qualifiers. Kaplan then developed "the directions game," a task designed to assess the extent to which children understood teacher directions. Of the qualifiers contained in "the directions game," at least 41% were basic concepts as defined in this chapter. The better the performance on the Boehm-R, the better the performance was on "the directions game" ($r = .71$).

Reanalysis of Kaplan's transcripts of teacher verbal directions (Boehm et al., 1980) revealed that 33 of the 50 Boehm-R terms (plus 18 antonyms, synonyms, or other comparative forms of these terms) were used by grade K through 2 teachers. Of the teacher directions recorded,

34.7% contained at least one Boehm-R term, its synonym, antonym, or comparative form. This count did not include the use of other basic concepts or ''easier'' basic concepts such as *in* and *on*, which occurred frequently.* These findings highlight the importance of basic concepts in following teachers' direction, and are now included on the Boehm-Preschool Version. Using a similar approach, Boehm and coworkers (1986) recorded the basic concepts used by prekindergarten teachers in their verbal directions. One hour samples of two teachers of three year old children and of four teachers of four year old children were included. These teachers used 47 of the relational concepts assessed by the BTBC-PV or BTBC-R, plus 10 synonyms of these terms: (e.g., *apart* for *separated*). These findings help highlight the importance of basic concepts in following teacher directions, both during a child's preschool and early school experiences.

The frequency with which basic concepts appeared in current reading and mathematics curricula was also studied by Boehm and coworkers (1980). Counting all words (on a 20-page sample from 5 reading series and 5 arithmetic series) read by teachers to children or by the children themselves in workbooks at each grade level, K through 2, revealed that all Boehm-R words were used; they accounted for 9.5% and 8.8% of all words presented in the reading and arithmetic workbooks sampled, respectively. Antonyms, synonyms, and comparative forms of the Boehm-R terms accounted for another 9.7% and 6.8% of the words used, and easier basic concepts (especially *in* and *on*) for a further 11.1% and 8.1%.

This review helps underscore the importance of basic concepts in understanding early instruction. At the time of school entrance, however, many school children have not yet learned the meaning of these concepts (Boehm, 1966, 1969, 1971, 1986a,b), which might handicap them in their early school experience. Therefore, assessment of children's understanding of basic concepts during the preschool years is an important consideration.

Test Taking

The importance of basic concepts in following directions on standardized tests was reported by Kaufman (1978), who reviewed the directions on four individual tests of ability: the ITPA, McCarthy Scales (Cognitive Scale), Binet L-M (years 2 through 7), and WPPSI. Kaufman found that these tests often ''assumed'' children's understanding of basic concepts as measured by the Boehm-R. On the four tests, respectively, 0, 7, 5, and 14 basic concepts were required to comply with the directions. In addition, easier concepts that could be troublesome for preschoolers (3, 10, 10, and 10 easier concepts for the four tests, respectively) were included.

Kaufman concluded that it is important for the assessor to review what the child is *required to do to comply with test directions*. Kaufman's findings relative to tests of ability were confirmed by Bracken (1986a), who studied the incidence of 258 concepts from the Bracken Scale in 11 categorized areas (color, shape, letter identification, number, and counting, social/emotional and textural material along with comparison, direction/position, size, quantity, and time) in the directions of five intelligence tests commonly used in the U.S. Many of these concepts appeared frequently in the verbal directions.

Cummings & Nelson (1980) extended Kaufman's conclusions regarding the understanding of basic concepts to verbal directions of achievement tests. These researchers analyzed the incidence of the Boehm-R concepts in the oral directions of four commonly used achivement measures: The California Achievement Tests, Iowa Tests of Basic Skills, Metropolitan Achievement Tests, and the Stanford Diagnostic Reading Test. Each of these tests assumed children's understanding of basic concepts (11, 8, 15, and 8, respectively) in addition to easier relational concepts assessed on the BTBC-PV (1986). Across tests, a child needs to understand basic concepts, however they are defined, to comply with test demands. This finding clearly needs to be a concern for professionals who work with preschool children. Kaufman (1978) recommended that assessors working with preschool children need to determine their knowledge of basic concepts, teach those concepts needed to comply with the administrative aspects of test directions, and question results from individual tests already administered that contain many basic concepts in the test directions, a concern underscored by Cummings and Nelson (1980) and Bracken (1986a). Some tests, such as the Gates-MacGinitie Reading Tests

(MacGinitie, 1978) and the K-ABC (Kaufman & Kaufman, 1983), alert test users to basic concepts needed to comply with directions.

Kennedy (1970) pointed out other problems children encounter in following language used in test instructions and items: The use of the passive voice, the order of presentation in directions not following the order of actions called for, long sentences placing severe demands on memory, and functional words, which include relational terms, not being stressed despite their importance.

In addition, to assess children's understanding of individual basic concepts, assessors need to consider children's ability to use the concepts in combination with other concepts. In samples of first grade teachers, verbal statements collected by Kaplan (1978), 29.9% included two or more relational concepts. Thus, an application's booklet was introduced with the Boehm-R to assess concepts in combination and as tools of thinking in making higher order relational decisions.

DEVELOPMENT OF BASIC CONCEPTS

Developmental Framework

The ways in which children learn the use of basic concepts and the developmental order of their acquisition have important implications both for assessment and instruction. Our understanding about concept acquisition comes from the fields of cognitive development and language acquisition. The typical stages children pass through as they acquire individual concepts, the types of errors they make, and some of the reasons that have been offered to explain the stages of acquisition are considered next.

The work of Piaget and his associates has given us important insight into how the young child's thinking develops (Flavell, 1970; Piaget, 1967). These researchers emphasized that the young child does not perceive the world in the same way as does the adult, but progresses through a sequential order of developmental stages in solving problems. Of the four stages detailed, the first two have particular relevance to assessing concept understanding in the two- to six-year-old child (Table 12-1).

Another avenue for understanding basic concept development is the child's development of

language. Among the earliest words used by the child, according to deVilliers and deVilliers (1979), are those used "to regulate his interaction with his parents—In, more, no, up, out, open, and the like" (p. 31). Relational words are used by 18- to 24-month-old children, and their correct and incorrect usage has been traced in many studies (Bloom & Lahey, 1978; deVilliers & deVilliers, 1978, 1979). For example, the young child might over-extend a word beyond its appropriate application by calling any moving vehicle a "car." The earliest uses of words made by the child refer to a variety of objects or situations, and the very young child probably understands more than he or she is able to communicate.

Going beyond single words to two-word utterances and phrases, the two-year-old child is able to communicate relationships that express location (e.g., "ball *in* box"), recurrence (e.g., "*more* cookie"), and negation (e.g., "no more cookie"), all of which are related to basic concepts. Examples cited by deVilliers and deVilliers (1979) included the relational terms *all*, *again*, *outside*, *more*, *some*, *in*, *off*, *another*, and *on*.

From the ages 2 to 4, children's ability to express themselves expands greatly as they learn to respond to different types of questions and relational terms. Some relational terms can have the same meaning for the child of 2½ or 3 as for the adult (E. Clark, 1978). E. Clark (1973) traced a number of stages in the development of the easiest relational terms, in, on, and under. These stages, along with those noted in other studies, apply to the acquisition of basic concepts in general:

1. The child does not know the concept of its term.
2. The child knows something about the object, attribute, or event the concept designates; this understanding is gained through general experience.
3. The child has partial knowledge of a specific concept or concept pair.
4. The child might have certain preferences (nonlinguistic strategies) by which he or she responds to a task, for example, liking to put things in other things or choosing things with more, irrespective of the concepts. [Clark (1973, 1980) clarified this issue by noting that the child's response preferences might make it appear that the child understands or knows

TABLE 12.1
ASSESSMENT FEATURES AT EARLY DEVELOPMENTAL STAGES

Behaviors	Implications for Assessment
Sensorimotor stage (0 to 2 years)	
Child reacts to the world through motor behavior	Observation of child's manipulation of objects
Child observes the world around and develops rudimentary concepts	Imitation of assessor's behaviors
Child learns that objects have permanence (object concept)	Response to assessor's verbal requests, including concept labels
Child engages in trial-and-error play and looks for hidden objects	
Preoperational stage (2 to 7 years)	
Language plays an increasingly important role	Observation of child's manipulative and verbal response to questions
Child's perspective continues to be egocentric observation of child's ability to take the perspective of another	
Child focuses on visual appearance of objects	
Child begins to be able to group on the basis of one characteristic	Grouping of objects together based on one common characteristic assessed
Child follows sequence of events	Child's ability to sequence events assessed
Child begins to reverse	Observation of child's ability to reverse a procedure
One-to-one correspondence is developed	Observation of child's ability to engage in one-to-one correspondence

what he or she really does not. For example, the tendency to put things on other things conforms to the correct position of top and might make it appear that the child knows top versus bottom when given a task tapping this concept pair. It also might facilitate learning the concept top. When this response tendency does not conform, however, it might appear that the child does not understand the concept, whereas the child might actually have some partial understanding.]

5. The child uses the positive or most extended member of a concept pair before the negative or least extended member so that it is likely the child will learn top before learning bottom.
6. The child might overextend the concept term to include other similar concepts (big is used to refer to things that are tall).
7. The child confuses the positive member of a concept pair with its opposite (much also is used to refer to less).
8. The child understands and can use the concept in the same way as an adult would, but not at all levels of complexity.

9. The child might know a concept in some contexts and not be able to apply it in others.

In addition to basic concepts that denote location, deVilliers and deVilliers (1978) reviewed the development of many spatial concepts from the more general *big–little* to the more specific *tall–short, long–short, high–low, wide–narrow,* and *thick–thin.* As terms become more specific, they become more difficult because more components of meaning are associated with them. A number of other researchers have explored the acquisition of relational concepts and have contributed to the understanding of their development; among these are Blewitt (1982), Clark (1983), French and Nelson (1985), Richards and Haupe (1981), and Richards (1982).

Individual Basic Concepts

In relation to concept attainment in general (see D. Clark, 1971, for a helpful review), it is known that children's understanding increases with age and progresses from general application to specific, precise application, and from concrete to abstract levels of application. This developmental progression at different age levels and rates for different concepts. The concepts learned can be applied more accurately in some contexts or situations than others. Children might have partial rather than complete mastery of more complex concepts by the time they enter school. Furthermore, children might have some understanding of the concepts, but not have the words for them, even by 8 or 9 years (deVilliers & deVilliers, 1978; Meisner, 1973).

The types of errors children make on concept tasks provide us with insights into how they think: a review of studies exploring the acquisition of some relational terms uncovers a number of rather systematic errors. Most studies have focused on preschool children who attend university-based nursery schools or who come from middle-class backgrounds (the assessment of concepts among children from many backgrounds is discussed later). Implications for the assessor based on these studies include the following:

- By the age of five or six years, children have a fairly complete mastery of most basic concept terms.
- There are systematic, sequential stages of acquisition of meaning of a concept.
- Different basic concepts are the sources of different types of errors.
- Acquisition of one member of a concept pair usually precedes acquisition of the other.

Different studies have assessed the acquisition of the same concepts in different ways (pantomime, imitation, spontaneous speech, acting out, elicitation, teaching comprehension, reaction time, opposite games). In addition, basic concepts have been assessed in different contexts from study to study and at different levels of complexity. These comparative studies have revealed the following:

- The nature of the task affects the ease of the concept.
- Words that have both spatial and temporal meanings are not learned at the same time to apply to both senses.
- Some tasks present a greater demand on the child's memory load.

- Some concepts are more difficult than others and require the child to learn more components of meaning.

Most basic concepts develop gradually in stages, and learning is not an all-or-none process. Some of the major findings are highlighted next to provide a focus for the assessor of the preschool child. The examples given typify problems children encounter as they acquire different basic concepts.

Before–After (*First–Last*)

Many studies (Amidon & Carey, 1972; Beilin, 1974; Carni & French, 1984; E. Clark, 1970, 1971; Coker, 1978; French & Brown, 1977; French & Nelson, 1985; Friedman & Seely, 1976; Johnson, 1975; Richards & Haupe, 1981) have revealed the following patterns among children 2 years 11 months to 8 years of age: *Before* and *after* are easier for the child to respond to when the order of mention corresponds to the order of their occurrence. For example, "drink your milk *before* you eat the cake" is easier to follow than "*before* you eat the cake, drink your milk." Although omissions and/or reversals can occur, acquisition seems to proceed in the following order: understanding neither *before* nor *after*; understanding the concept term *before*; possibly overgeneralizing the concept term *before* to refer to *after*; and understanding both *before* and *after*. Moreover, some words are understood in the spatial sense first, while others are understood in their temporal sense first. The complexity of modifiers and subordinate clauses can increase the difficulty of a task involving these concepts (e.g., "Put the blue box on the line *after* you put the red car on the line").

In Front of–Behind (*Ahead of, Front, Back of, Beside, Side*)

In addition to the problems common to the acquisition of other relational terms, *in front of* and *behind* present additional problems (Harris & Strommen, 1971; Kuczaj & Maratos, 1975; Levine & Carey, 1982). Objects with defined front and back features are easier to respond to than non-featured objects for which the child has to use himself or herself as the point of reference. Therefore, it is easier to respond to the back and front of a car than the back and front of a block. *Front* and *back* are acquired at about the same time, but *side* is more difficult, probably because *side* lacks specificity. The child needs to be able to take the perspective of another to understand how that person sees the *back* and *front* of objects.

More–Less

The considerable interest in the concepts *more–less* (Donaldson & Balfour, 1968; Donaldson & Wales, 1970; Gathercole, 1985; Kavanaugh, 1976; Palermo, 1973, 1974; Trehub & Abramovitch, 1978; Weiner, 1974) has been an important stimulus to our present understanding of basic concept acquisition. More specifically, these studies have shown that a response preference for *more* might make this concept appear easier than *less*, when in fact this might not be the case, and the frequently observed confusion of *less* or *more* might be related to the number of response options presented in the task (often only two).

Same–Different

Fewer studies have focused on the concepts *same–different* than on some others (Blake & Beilin, 1975; Fein & Eshleman, 1974; Glucksberg, 1975; Josephs, 1975), but their findings provide insight into the problems confronting the learner. They have shown that the context of the task, as well as singular and plural referents, are related to complexity. When attributes such as size and color are named, the child is better able to respond, so that the direction "Point to the boxes that are the *same* size is easier than "Point to the boxes that are the *same*."

The correct application of basic concepts takes place gradually and is dependent on the nature and complexity of the task and the context in which it is presented, as well as the developmental level of the child.

Assessment Procedures

Procedures currently available for the assessment of basic concepts, from informal observation to formal standardized tests, typically are not intended to and do not assess the breadth and scope of the preschool child's concept understanding; instead, they serve as guideposts for assessing general understanding of individual basic concepts. The tasks and tests presented here are designed to assess the level of a child's basic concept knowledge for the purpose of curriculum planning. All can be followed up by more intense observations of child behavior as demonstrated in sequentially ordered series of tasks that break down concepts into their different components and levels of complexity.

Informal Measures

Observation is the essential beginning point for understanding children's thinking. Kamii (1971) stressed the need for observation of child behavior, with teachers probing to get at a child's meaning. This exploratory method can be used to record the child's spontaneous and elicited use of basic concepts. Cazden (1971) also stressed that assessment must relate to teaching goals, and pointed to the importance of enriching the child's receptive and productive use of words. Children's understanding can be observed, according to Cazden, as they repeat sentences or phrases, describe and explain activities and events, retell stories, engage in classification activities, play games that involve following directions of increasing length, and so forth. Cazden presented a unit on relational words and exemplified a formative evaluation for each unit objective; this perspective might be useful to the assessor interested in observing the child's basic concept understanding. The assessor should take into account the child's comprehension and production of both positive and negative applications of the concept in relation to objects and pictures, simple uses as well as uses in multiple part directions, viewing objects from different vantage points, and understanding opposites.

Systematic observation is the only practical way currently available to assess the breadth and scope of concept understanding and development over time. Many behaviors associated with basic concept acquisition can be viewed through observation (Boehm, 1976). Although simpler applications of concepts can be developed during the preschool years, the child's ability to apply these concepts to situations and events that represent increasing levels of complexity continue to develop during the elementary grades. Therefore, assessment of basic concepts should take place from different perspectives over time and should take into account both the receptive and expressive use of these concepts. A sample checklist for the development of basic concept is presented in Table 12-2.

Lidz (1983) urged that observation be used to observe the process and/or style children use to solve problems in addition to the adequacy of their responses. Such observation focused on process has important implications for basic concept assessment.

Other informal measures are available that ask the assessor to observe the presence or absence of a broad range of specified behaviors on the part of the child; a number of basic concepts can be among the behaviors covered. Although the assessor's attention might be directed to individual basic concepts, more frequently concepts are used in combination with other concepts, such as "Point to the star in the *top left-hand corner*." Two examples of informal measures are listed below:

1. Preschool Attainment Record (Doll, 1966): This extension of the Vineland Social Maturity Scale is used with children to seven years old. The presence or absence of several basic concepts such as *right* and *left* are assessed through interviewing the parent or other child care workers along with other concepts children need to deal with their environment.
2. Meeting Street School Screening Test (Hain-

TABLE 12.2
BASIC CONCEPT DEVELOPMENT CHECKLIST

Name of child _____

Concept pair _____

I. Levels of development/concept differentiation
   A. No understanding of the concept pair
   B. Responds correctly to one number of the concept pair (indicate which)
   C. Confuses one member of the concept pair with its opposite (indicate which is confused)
   D. Can respond correctly when order of mention corresponds to order of presentation (for terms such as before and after)
   E. Omits parts of longer concept directions (give example)
   F. Reverses parts of concept directions (give example)
   G. Responds correctly when features or attributes of objects are named
   H. Responds correctly when nonfeatured objects or without attributes being named
   I. Responds correctly to both members of a concept pair
   J. Can produce the opposite of a concept pair when asked to
II. Use of verbal label for concept
   A. No spontaneous use of concept term
   B. Concept term used by child in natural communications with others to
     1. Describe events or objects
     2. Respond to general questions
     3. Express desires or needs
     4. Gain information
   C. Concept term used to respond to specific questions that are asked to elicit term
III. Response through actions in situations structured to elicit such response
   A. Can respond appropriately using concept in relation to self, objects, and pictures
   B. Can respond when the concept is used in combination with other concepts
   C. Can respond to the concept used in its comparative forms
   D. Can use the concept to order
   E. Can use the concept to classify
   F. Can perceive the concept relation from another person's perspective
   G. Can respond to the moral as well as spatial use of the concept term

sworth & Siqueland, 1969): On this test children are requested to act out concepts, such as *right* and *left* or *above* and *below*, by following multiple-part directions such as "Put (body part/object) above your head and *in front of* you."

In addition, the Meeting Street School Screening Test assesses children's motor patterning abilities; visual, perceptual and motor skills; language memory of words and sentences; counting of numbers forward, backward and by twos; and, ability to tell a story from a picture. Each of these areas is assessed to identify children in kindergarten and first grade who do not possess adequate language, visual, and motor skills to deal adequately with the symbolic information of traditional school curriculum and who might be at risk for learning disability. The test, which is the individually administered, was developed for use with children 5–0 to 7–5 years.

Other informal measures are tied to teaching activities, some of which center around basic concepts. Two examples follow:

1. Brigance Diagnostic Inventory of Basic Skills (Brigance, 1976/1977): This inventory assesses readiness and entry skills related to the subjects covered in grades kindergarten through sixth. The outcomes of informal assessment lead to instructional objectives and guides to instruction. At the readiness level, directional and positional concepts are assessed in relationship to the children's own bodies (e.g., children identify their own *right* and *left* hands or place their hand *behind* or *next to* another body part).
2. Portage Guide to Early Education, Revised (Bluma et al., 1976): This guide includes a checklist of 580 behaviors in six areas that are organized sequentially and are tied to activities. It was developed to be used by home-based teachers working with parents of very young children (birth to six years of age identified as handicapped in one or more areas). Its purpose is to assess children's behavior and plan learning programs. Among the activities included are those involving cognitive and thinking skills, and seeing relationships. Some basic concepts are included.

Formal Assessment

Although numerous tests are available to assess the child at the preschool level, few of these have as their major focus specific assessment of basic concepts. Basic concepts are incorporated within some subtest items, but the intent of these subtests is to get at functions other than basic relational concept understanding. For example, the Detroit Tests of Learning Aptitude (DTLA-2) (Hammill, 1985) are used to assess children age six through high school. Basic relational concepts are included on a Word Opposites subtest that requires children to give words that mean the opposite of the stimulus words. In another subtest, Oral Directions, children need to respond to complex multiple-part directions, many of which contain basic concepts such as *right, under, first,* and *last.* Thus, although basic concepts are involved both in the items and instructions of this test, the child's specific strengths or difficulties in dealing with basic concept terms are not assessed.

Tests of reading readiness include some assessment of basic concepts. It is important to note, however, that it is the total readiness score that is the focus of these tests and individual items are infrequently reviewed. In addition, the small size of the items and the child's familiarity with the object or situations depicted in the pictures present a further problem in assessing concept understanding (see, for example, the Lee Clark Readiness Test, Lee & Clark, 1962); the Metropolitan Readiness Test, Nurss & McGauvran, 1976; and the Murphy-Durrell Reading Readiness Analysis, Murphy & Durrell, 1964).

Other tests focus on the preschool and early school years, and either specifically or along with other skills and objectives, include the assessment of some basic concepts measured individually or in combination with other concepts. The following are some examples:

1. The Basic Concept Inventory, Field Research Edition (Engelmann, 1967): This informal inventory assesses preschool and kindergarten children's familiarity with a wide range of concepts involved in learning in grade 1. It is intended to be used with disadvantaged and LD children to provide guidelines for teaching. Multiple trials are possible and directions can be expanded to get at children's understanding. The inventory is made up of three parts: Basic Concepts, Sentence Repetition and Comprehension, and Pattern Awareness. The directions in part 1 assess children's understanding of concepts in combination with other concepts, such as *big, little, in, on, next to, how many, tallest,* and *between.*

2. *The Boehm Test of Basic Concepts-Revised (Boehm-R, 1986):* This test surveys the kindergarten through second grade child's understanding of 50 basic relational concepts of position in space, direction, quantity, sequence, time, and size for the purpose of instructional planning. A total score can be obtained, and norms are provided for both Form C and D of the test. However, the child's performance on each item serves as the major basis for interpretation, with information presented on items by grade, socioeconomic status, and time of year used. The items, in which pictures are named, focuses on the child's understanding of the basic concepts being tapped. The Boehm-R, was normed on children in kindergarten through second grade. An *Applications* booklet that assesses mastery of concepts used in combination, used in sequences, and used to make comparisons is available.

The Boehm Test of Basic Concepts-Preschool Version (Boehm-PV, 1986): This test extends downward the Boehm-R and surveys the 3 to 5 year old child's understanding of 26 easier basic relational concepts that help children understand and describe the world around them. The test is individually administered. The results are intended to be used by teachers to plan instruction and as indicators of school readiness.

3. *The Bracken Basic Concept Scale (Bracken, 1984):* This scale assesses 258 concepts in 11 categorical areas (color, letter identification, numbers/counting, comparison, shapes, direction/position, social emotional, size, textural/material, quantity, and time/sequence. The test was developed to be used with children 2–6 to 8–0 years. Bracken divides his scale into two instruments, a diagnostic full-scale instrument and a alternate form screening test. The Diagnostic Scale is administered individually and assesses the full range of concepts included. The screening test, which can be administered individually or in small groups, consists of 30 items to identify children who might benefit from more intensive assessment. The primary use of the screening test is with kindergarten and first grade children. Thus relational concepts, along with concepts in other skill areas such as color knowledge and letter identification, are included. An instructional program also has been developed to accompany the test, *The Bracken Concept Development Program* (Bracken, 1986b).

4. *Circus (Anderson et al., 1974, 1976, 1979):* Circus was developed to provide prekindergarten and kindergarten teachers with comprehensive assessment information to help them diagnose children's instructional needs and evaluation programs. Level A covers the preprimary level; Level B, grade 1; Levels C and D extend the test through grades 3 through 5. Circus consists of 17 instruments. Six of these assess basic concepts along with other concepts and areas of understanding. What Words Mean assesses understanding of nouns, verbs, and modifiers. How Much and How Many assesses counting skills, number concepts, and relational terms. How Words Work includes verbs, prepositions, and conjunctions. Listen to the Story assesses story comprehension and includes the terms first and last. Do You Know . . .? assesses picture recognition and comprehension that includes concept understanding, such as most (in relationship to money). Think It Through assesses understanding of group membership, sequences, and classification. The assessor can choose to use all or several of the 17 measures and a total score is obtained for each subtest. Teachers are encouraged to examine errors made by items and by children. A set of instructional activities, After the Circus, also has been developed.

5. *The Cognitive Skills Assessment Battery, Second Edition (CSAB) (Boehm & Slater, 1981):* The CSAB was developed to provide a profile of strengths and weaknesses of the prekindergarten and kindergarten child in the cognitive skills area and simultaneously a profile for the class as a whole. The skills areas included cover orientation to one's environment; large muscle and visual motor coordination; discrimination of similarities and differences; auditory, visual, picture and story memory; comprehension; and concept formation. Each task areas is divided by levels of difficulty, providing teachers important information for program planning. Some relational concepts are included in the multiple directions task.

6. *The Preschool Inventory, Revised (Caldwell, 1968/1970):* This inventory was developed as a screening device for Head Start children 3

through 6 years of age. The inventory consists of 64 items and covers a broad range of skills considered necessary for success in school. As such, it is a readiness instrument for kindergarten. In addition to toal scores, the percentage of children who pass each item at each age level is presented. Several basic concepts are assessed individually; others in combination with other concepts. Other items draw upon the child's overall concept comprehension. For example, an item assessing concepts in combination might ask the child to put two objects *behind* a box; an item that ask the child to compare the size of two objects assesses overall comprehension.

7. *Stanford Early School Achievement Test (Madden & Gardner, 1967/1970):* This group-administered test was developed to be used in kindergarten and beginning first grade and includes among its items the basic concepts *longest* and *beginning*. Concepts assessed when used in combination with other concepts include basic concepts such as *after, of, most, same, farthest,* and *third.*

8. *Tests of Basic Experiences (TOBE; Moss, 1978):* The purpose of this group-administered test is to assess the child's conceptual understanding to plan cirricular experiences. It has two overlapping levels, one appropriate for preschool and kindergarten, and the other for kindergarten or grade 1. Each level consists of a battery of four tests: Mathematics, Language, Science, and Social Studies. Each of the four area tests include a breakdown of concepts and skills. Throughout, the focus is on a child's conceptual understanding gained through experience rather than on facts. Some basic relational concepts are assessed individually or in combination with other concepts, along with other areas of understanding, on each test. Different tests can assess the same concept from different perspectives. In many cases the child needs to be familiar with the function of the picture depicted to respond to the concept terms. Mathematics assesses fundamental quantitative operations and terms, including basic concepts of size and quantity. Language assesses vocabulary and sentence structure, including position terms and identification of ''same'' sounds. Science assesses understandings gained through observation. It includes concepts that denote quality, such as hardest, and comprehension of objects and their functions, such as determining which

ship is heaviest by its level in the water. Social Science assesses children's understanding of social groups and roles, safety facts, and emotions and includes the relational concepts such as slow and fast. The Test of Basic Experiences yields scores for each test in the battery and item scores can be obtained if desired.

Prepositions and adjectives, some of which are basic relational concepts, can be tapped to some extent on these measures. For example, the ability of the child to note similarities and differences and to produce opposites among the items presented often is assessed. In addition, understanding of basic concepts might be required to comply with task directions.

In this section a sample of preschool assessment tasks has been presented to illustrate how basic relational concepts are measured and the extent with which they are covered among commonly used tests.

IMPLICATIONS FOR DIAGNOSIS AND REMEDIATION

Because the author is most familiar with the BTBC, this section focuses on results that have been evidenced through the use of that test. The issues raised, however, can be addressed to other formal and informal measures of concepts as well.

Basic concept assessment is used to determine the extent to which children understand those relational terms that are essential for complying with teacher directions and meeting the demands of early reading and mathematics tasks. The preschool child 3 to 6 years of age is in the process of acquiring these basic concepts. Although the child understands and is able to use few relational words at age 3, most children of normal ability acquire the majority of these concepts by the time they enter grade 1. The child's understanding, however, probably does not encompass the many levels of concept application that will be called upon in reasoning tasks that involve ordering, classifying, talking, and, later, inductive reasoning.

Norms for both Forms C and D of the Boehm-R and the Boehm-PV increase with increasing grade level, and from the beginning to midyear within grade levels. Children from lower socioeconomic levels perform on the test in grades 1 and 2; as do children from more advantaged backgrounds at the end of kindergarten. The same concepts, however, are relatively easy or difficult across socioeconomic levels. The concepts *top, through, away from, next to,* and *first* are among the easiest, while the concepts *pair, fewest, left,* and *right* are among the most difficult. The major focus is on identifying concepts with which children are familiar and those in which they need instruction. Increased concept understanding by age was also evidenced on the BBCS (Bracken, 1984).

Special Needs Children

The results of studies of basic concept understanding and development in special needs populations help us understand how these children develop relational concepts and have important implications for remediation.

Blind Children

A tactile analogue to the BTBC, called the Tactile Test of Basic Concepts, was developed by Caton (1976, 1977) using raised geometric forms that paralleled all BTBC (1971) items. Using it with a sample of 25 blind children, at each grade level from kindergarten through grade 2 attending residential and public schools in 1974, Caton found that the blind children performed in a manner generally similar to lower socioeconomic level children in the normative sample; those enrolled in public schools performed somewhat better than those in residential schools. When the understanding of individual concepts of blind children was compared to that of sighted children in the normative population, a moderately similar concept difficulty was seen in kindergarten, but 11 and 12 concepts were more difficult in grades 1 and 2, respectively. The easiest concepts were those that required the child to use himself or herself as the reference, such as behind and next to. The most difficult concepts were those that required comparative judgments, such as third and in order. Caton pointed to the need for continued emphasis on basic relational concepts in instruction after kindergarten.

Educable Mentally Retarded Children

BTBC performance of 100 EMR children from middle-class backgrounds was studied by Chin (1976). All attended public schools in a large urban setting. Four age groups were studied, with mental age equivalents generally comparable to those of children in kindergarten through third grade (mean mental ages of 4–6, 6–6, 7–3, and 8–6 corresponding to chronological ages of 6–7, 9–7, 11–5, and 13–2, respectively). The mean BTBC scores for each of these groups was 20.0, 34.2, 38.1, and 43.0, respectively. The 9- and 11-year-old EMR children responded like normal kindergarten children, and 13-year-old EMR children like normal first graders. Although a four- to seven-year lag was demonstrated when chronological age was used as the basis for comparison, the difference was less pronounced when mental age was used as the basis of comparison. EMR children do acquire basic concepts, although the rate of development is slower than among normal children, suggesting the importance of early instruction. The order of concept difficulty largely paralleled that found in the normative population.

Nelson and Cummings (1981) also demonstrated a significant developmental trend in basic concept understanding among 45 EMR black and white children in a semirural area of Northeastern Georgia. The children studied range in age from 7–0 to 10–7. While significant gains were demonstrated, the oldest group continued to demonstrate a gap in their concept repertoire, incorrectly responding to a mean of 10.2 concepts. The four most difficult concepts for this group were *in order, least, pair,* and *third.* These authors also underscored the importance of systematic instruction of basic concepts.

Hearing-impaired Children

When the BTBC was used with hearing-impaired children, Davis (1974) found that those of normal intelligence fell increasingly behind their normal age mates; more than two-thirds of the 24 children age 6–0 to 8–11 studied fell below the first percentile. The greater their hearing loss, the poorer their performance was on the BTBC. Although there was no overall pattern of errors over the concept types, the most difficult concepts were generally the same for these children as for those in the normal-hearing group studied by Davis, and included *between, always, medium-sized, separated, left, pair, skip, equal, third,* and *last.* Davis stressed the need for specific instruction of basic relational concepts with these children.

Brown (1976), who studied 30 hearing-impaired children aged 7–1 to 11–11, found that deaf children who are taught signed English acquired basic relational concepts at an earlier age than those taught speech reading only. Brown also documented error patterns exhibited by hearing impaired as contrasted with normally hearing children. Results of Dickie's (1980) study supported a total communication approach over the aural/oral approach in instruction of basic concepts with 30 severely and profoundly hearing impaired children.

Bracken and Cato (1986) compared the rate of concept development across two samples of children, those diagnosed as deaf and those with normal hearing abilities. The sample of 34 subjects was matched on the basis of age, sex, race, and geographic region. It was found that the deaf children performed consistently poorer than the hearing children on each of the BBCS (Bracken, 1984) subtests and Total Test. In fact, the deaf children scored approximately two standard deviations below the nonimpaired children on each of the subscales and the total scale and were consistently retarded in their conceptual development, though none was intellectually retarded and none was diagnosed as exceptional in any way other than hearing ability.

Syntactically Deviant Children

Spector (1977) studied the BTBC performance of syntactically deviant kindergarten children with normal intelligence. Generalized weakness was noted when they were compared to their normal age-mates, and 16 of the concepts assessed were much more difficult for these children. Spector's findings with kindergarten children were consistent with the work of Wiig and Semel (1976), who also reviewed the research relevant to language-processing problems among LD school-age children. These authors stressed that although LD children can have adequate vocabulary, the task of processing spoken language is a complex one involving auditory memory, understanding of syntax, and comprehension of concepts. Each of these areas can present problems for the LD child and decrease the rate at which spoken language is processed. Adjectives and prepositions that designate location, space, time, quantity, and quality (many of which are basic relational concepts) present special problems. Therefore, concepts that are conveyed in verbal

teacher directions would be poorly processed by these children. Spector (1979) speculated on possible difficulties syntactically deviant children might encounter when responding to directions containing relational concepts. She elaborated strategies and the cognitive abilities language therapists needed to consider during instruction with basic concepts.

Learning Disabled Children

There is consistent evidence that young children who have been classified as learning disabled also have difficulty with many basic relational concepts. When compared with their peers who do not demonstrate problems, LD children demonstrated both lower mean scores and greater score variability on the BTBC (Di Napoli et al., 1980; Kavale, 1982). In both of these studies LD children lagged behind their peers in their understanding of basic concepts.

Children from Non-English Speaking Backgrounds

A Spanish version of the BTBC (Form A, 1971; Form B, 1973) was normed on 1,292, 1,280, and 1,279 pupils at the beginning of the year, mid-year, and end of year, respectively, in Puerto Rico (Preddy, Boehm & Shepherd, 1984). Achievement data were collected one year later. The results, which largely paralleled the mainland U.S. norms, demonstrated both increasing mastery with age and a similar relative order of concept difficulty. The BTBC results showed a strong predictive relationship one year later with language and mathematics as measured by two Spanish-Language achievement tests. Translated versions of the BTBC used with other cultural groups repeatedly have pointed to the need for basic concept instruction in bilingual programs (Mickelson & Galloway, 1973; Patterson, 1981).

The procedures for translation of the BTBC into Spanish were repeated with the Spanish translation of the Boehm-R (1987). These included: (a) an initial translation from English to Spanish, (b) a blind back-translation, (c) repetitions of steps a and b until the back-translation resembled the original English version, (d) a review by a national bilingual committee of teachers, and (e) field testing with bilingual children from Texas, California, and Missouri. The validation of the Spanish translation of the Boehm-R (1987) is currently in progress.

BBCS also has been translated into Spanish, and has been partially validated in the United States, Puerto Rico, and Venezuela (Bracken et al., in press). Bracken and Fouad (1987) conducted a comprehensive multistep translation and validation process that included: (a) an initial translation from English to Spanish, (b) a blind back-translation, (c) repetitions of steps a and b until the back-translation was very similar to the original English version, (d) review by a multinational bilingual committee, (e) pilot field testing, and (f) a more extensive pilot testing and item analysis.

After this initial translation and validation project, the BBCS was further validated through a large scale administration (approximately 300 subjects) of the instrument in Puerto Rico, Venezuela, and Southwestern United States (Bracken et al., in press). The results of this large scale validation evidenced high age–score subtest developmental corelations across the three samples (median correlations, Puerto Rican = .76, Venezuelan = .55, and Mexican-American = .71); subtest intercorrelations across the three samples that were consistently as high or higher than the U.S. Anglo standardization sample intercorrelations by age; and item rank–order correlations between the three samples and the U.S. Anglo standardization sample that were fairly uniformly moderate to high (with a few low and negative correlations); and coefficient alpha reliabilities for the Total Test that exceeded .90 for all samples and all age levels.

The study by Bracken and coworkers (1987) demonstrated that across cultural samples, the basic concept construct is quite similar in its sequence of acquisition and age-related progression. The comparability of the intercorrelations across the three Latin samples and the U.S. Anglo standardization sample demonstrates a similar construct structure across the samples. Cross cultural equivalence of the BBCS for the three distinct Latin samples and the U.S. Anglo sample was supported.

The studies cited all indicate that within a broad range of special populations there is delayed acquisition of basic concepts. For many children, their lack of concept mastery becomes more pronounced with time in school. While the relative ease of difficulty of individual concepts tends to follow the same overall pattern as for the normative population, specific concepts can present special problems for different groups of children.

The poorer performance among these groups suggests that children with special learning needs are likely to have difficulty processing teacher directions and learning materials that involve basic concepts. Furthermore, because the complexity of concept use increases with time in school to include multiple-part directions and more abstract applications, the assessor can anticipate that the difficulty these children encounter will be compounded.

Although the need for remedial instruction is clear, it is necessary to question whether specific instruction in basic concepts is effective. Studies have suggested two benefits of such training. Blai (1973) reported that nursery school children who participated in a concept-learning program made significant improvement on the BTBC from pre- to posttesting. Concept instruction was also reported to result in significant improvement with Head Start children (Levin et al., 1975). Instruction, then, seems to benefit preschool children's understanding of basic concepts.

Moers and Harris (1978) reported a study of two groups of children from low-middle to middle-class backgrounds. The experimental group participated in an organized sequence of concept instruction that lasted for 15 weeks, while the control group was engaged in placebo activities. Both the experimental and control groups were then tested and received increased scores on the BTBC. After a semester of no specific training, however, the experimental group performed better on both the reading and mathematics sections of the Stanford Achievement Test. The authors concluded that the concept-training program resulted in a generalized improvement in academic functioning. First grade, low- to middle-class children at the Central Arkansas Education Center (1972) who received enrichment experienced based on the BTBC also achieved higher BTBC scores and reading scores than children taught by traditional methods. These results were corroborated by Nason (1986) who studied the effects of systematic instruction of basic concepts using a translated version of the Boehm Resource Guide for Basic Concept Teaching (Boehm, 1976) on achievement of first grade children from low income families in Puerto Rico. Not only did systematic instruction improve children's understanding of basic concepts, but children receiving such instruction also demonstrated significantly higher scores on tests of achievement in language and mathematics.

A number of major reviews suggest considerations to be taken into account when planning concept instruction (See, for example, D. C. Clark, 1971; Klausmeir, 1976; Tennyson & Park, 1980; Tennyson & Cocchiarella, 1986).

SUMMARY

Assessment of the preschool child's understanding of basic relational concepts can supply the classroom teacher and specialist with important information about the child. From a developmental perspective, a child's ability to identify basic concepts and/or produce their labels provides cues as to their concept and language acquisition. Formal testing can serve only as the beginning point for understanding concept development; it can be followed up by tasks devised to determine specific levels of responding, which can be compared with those levels noted in the literature. Ongoing, systematic observation can help us understand the breadth and scope with which specific concepts are applied.

Because basic concepts occur frequently in teachers' verbal directions and in directed learning experiences in reading and mathematics, assessment of basic concepts can help in planning instruction. Instruction and remediation are the primary uses of assessment procedures that measure basic concepts. Children who have special learning needs also have more pronounced gaps in their basic concept repertoire. Special attention needs to be given to basic concepts when teaching or testing these children.

Finally, the use of basic concepts in the administrative sections of other tests underscores the need to determine which of these terms children need to know to comply with the demands of the tests. Because it is difficult to present verbal directions without using basic concepts, their assessment should be an integral component of assessment procedures used with young children.

REFERENCES

Amidon, A., & Carey, P. (1972). Why five year-olds cannot understand before and after. *Journal of Verbal Learning, Verbal Behavior, 11*, 417–423.

Anderson, S. B., et al. (1974, 1979). Circus. Princeton, NJ: Educational Testing Service.

Anderson, S. B., et al. (1976). Teacher's edition of the Manual and Technical Report. Circus. Levels A and B. Menlo Park, CA: Addison-Wesley.

Ault, R. L., Cromer, C. C., & Mitchell, C. (1977). The Boehm test of basic concepts. A three-dimensional version. *Journal of Educational Research, 70*(4), 186–188.

Beilin, H. (1975). *Studies in the Cognitive Basis of Language Development*. New York: Academic Press.

Blai, B. (1973). Concept learning-mastery in Harcum Junior College Laboratory Nursery School/Kindergarten. *Psychology, 10*(2), 35–36.

Blake, J., & Beilin, H. (1975). The development of "same" and "different" judgments. *Journal of Experimental Child Psychology, 19*, 177–194.

Blewitt, P. (1982). Word meaning acquisition in young children: A review of theory and research. In H. W. Reese & L. P. Lipsitt (Eds.), *Advances in Child Development and Behavior* (Vol. 17, pp. 139–195). NY: Academic Press.

Bloom, L., & Lahey, M. (1978). *Language Development and Language Disorders*. New York: Wiley.

Bluma, S., et al. (1976). *Portage Guide to Early Education* (Rev. ed.). Portage, WI: Portage Project.

Boehm, A. E. (1966). The development of comparative concepts in primary school children. Unpublished doctoral dissertation. Columbia University, New York.

Boehm, A. E. (1969, 1971). *Boehm Test of Basic Concepts*. New York: Psychological Corporation.

Boehm, A. E. (1970, 1973). *Prueba Boehm de Conceptos Basicos*. New York: The Psychological Corporation.

Boehm, A. E. (1976). *Boehm Resource Guide for Basic Concept Teaching*. New York: The Psychological Corporation.

Boehm, A. E. (1986a, Rev. Ed.). *Boehm Test of Basic Concepts-Revised*. San Antonio, TX: The Psychological Corporation.

Boehm, A. E. (1986b). *Boehm Test of Basic Concepts-Preschool Version*. San Antonio, TX: The Psychological Corporation.

Boehm, A. E. (1987, Ed. Rev.). *Prueba Boehm de Conceptos Basicos*. New York: The Psychological Corporation.

Boehm, A. E., Classon, B., & Kelly, M. (1986). *Preschool teachers' spoken use of basic concepts*. Unpublished manuscript, Teachers College, Columbia University, New York.

Boehm, A. E., Kaplan, C., & Preddy, D. (1980). How important are basic concepts to instruction: Validation of the Boehm test of basic concepts. Unpublished paper, Teacher College, Columbia University.

Boehm, A. E., & Slater, B. R. (1981). *The Cognitive Skills Assessment Battery,* (2nd ed.). New York: Teachers College, Columbia University.

Bracken, B. A. (1984). *Bracken Basic Concept Scale.* San Antonio, TX: The Psychological Corporation.

Bracken, B. A. (1986a). Incidence of basic concepts in the directions of five commonly used American tests of intelligence. *School Psychology International, 7,* 1–10.

Bracken, B. A. (1986b). *The Bracken Concept Development Program.* San Antonio, TX: The Psychological Corporation.

Bracken, B. A., & Fouad, N. (1987). Spanish translation and validation of the Bracken Basic Concept Scale. *School Psychology Review, 16,* 94–102.

Bracken, B. A., Barona, A., Bauermeister, J. J., Howell, K. K., Poggioli, L., & Puente, A. (in press). Multinational validation of the Spanish Bracken Basic Concept Scale for cross-cultural assessments. *Journal of School Psychology.*

Bracken, B. A., & Cato, L. A. (1986). Rate of conceptual development among deaf preschool and primary children as compared to a matched group of non-hearing impaired children. *Psychology in the Schools, 23,* 95–99.

Brigance, A. (1976, 1977). *Brigance Diagnostic Inventory of Basic Skills.* Woburn, MA: Curriculum Associates.

Brown, D. (1976). Validation of the Boehm Test of Basic Concepts. (Doctoral Dissertation, University of Wisconsin). *Dissertation Abstracts International, 36,* 4338A.

Caldwell, B. (1968, 1970). *The Preschool Inventory.* Menlo Park, CA: Addison-Wesley.

Carni, E., & French, L. A. (1984). The acquisition of *before* and *after* reconsidered: What develops? *Journal of Experimental Child Psychology, 37,* 394–403.

Caton, H. (1976). *The Tactile Test of Basic Concepts.* Louisville, KY: American Printing House for the Blind.

Caton, H. (1977). The development and evaluation of a tactile analogue to the Boehm Test of Basic Concepts, Form A. *Journal of Visual Impairment and Blindness, 71,* 382–386.

Cazden, D. (1971). Evaluation of learning in preschool education: Early language development. In B. Bloom, J. Hastings, & G. Madaus (Eds.) *Handbook on Formative and Summative Evaluation of Student Learning.* New York: McGraw-Hill. pp. 345–398.

Central Arkansas Education Center (1972). The detection and remediation of deficiencies in verbal understanding of first grade students. Little Rock, AR: Central Arkansas Education Center, (ERIC Document Reproduction Service No. ED 080 967, EC 000 705).

Chin, J. (1976). The development of basic relational concepts in educable mentally retarded children (Doctoral dissertation. Teachers College. Columbia University. 1976). *Dissertation Abstracts International, 36,* 4338.

Clark, D. C. (1971). Teaching of concepts in the classroom: A set of teaching prescriptions derived from experimental research. *Journal of Educational Psychology Monograph, 63*(3), 253–278.

Clark, E. (1970). How young children describe events in time. In G. Flores D'Arcais & W. J. Levelt (Eds.), *Advances in Psycholinguistics.* New York: American Elsevier.

Clark, E. (1971). On the acquisition of the meaning of before and after. *Journal of Verbal Learning. Verbal Behavior, 10,* 266–275.

Clark, E. (1973). Non-linguistic strategies and the acquisition of word meanings. *Cognition, 2,* 161–182.

Clark, E. (1978). In, on, and under revisited again. Papers and Reports in Child Language Development from Stanford University, Palo Alto, *15,* 38–45.

Clark, E. (1980). Here's the top: Nonlinguistic strategies in the acquisition of orientation terms. *Child Development, 51,* 329–338.

Clark, E. (1983). Meanings and concepts. In P. H. Mussen (Ed.), *Handbook of Child Psychology.* P. H. Flavell & E. M. Markman (Eds.), Vol. 3: *Cognitive development,* (pp. 787–840). New York: Wiley.

Coker, P. I. (1978). Syntactic & semantic factors in the acquisition of *before* and *after. Journal of Child Language, 5,* 261–277.

Cummings, J. A., & Nelson, R. B. (1980). Basic concepts in oral directions of group achievement tests. *Journal of Educational Research, 73,* 259–261.

Davis, J. (1974). Performance of young learning-impaired children on a test of basic concepts. *Journal of Speech and Hearing Research, 17,* 342–351.

deVilliers, J. G., & deVilliers, P. A. (1978). *Language Acquisition.* Cambridge, MA: Harvard University Press.

deVilliers, J. G., & deVilliers, P. A., (1979). *Early Language.* Cambridge, MA: Harvard University Press.

Dickie, D. C. (1980). Performance of severely and profoundly hearing impaired children on aural/oral and total communication presentations of the Boehm Test of Basic Concepts. (Doctoral dissertation, Michigan State University). *Dissertation Abstracts International, 49,* 6227–6228A.

DiNapoli, N., Kagedan-Kage, S. M., & Boehm, A. E. (1980). Basic concept acquisition in learning-disabled children. (*ERIC Document Reproduction Service No. ED 240 718*).

Doll, E. (1966a). *Preschool Attainment Record*. Circle Pines, MN: American Guidance Service.

Donaldson, M., & Balfour, G. (1968). Less is more: A study of language comprehension in children. *British Journal of Psychology, 59*, 461–472.

Donaldson, M., & Wales, R. (1970). On the acquisition of some relational terms. In J. Hayes (Ed.). *Cognition and the Development of Language*. New York: Wiley pp. 235–268.

Engelmann, S. (1967). *The Basic Concept Inventory (Field Research Edition)*. Chicago: Follett.

Fein, G., & Eshleman, S. (1976). Individuals and dimensions in children's judgment of "same" and "different." *Developmental Psychology, 10*, 793–796.

Flavell, J. (1970). Concept development. In P. H. Mussen (Ed.). *Carmichael's Manual of Child Psychology*. New York: Wiley.

French, L., & Brown, A. (1977). Comprehension of before and after in logical and arbitrary sequences. *Journal of Child Language, 4*(2), 247–256.

French, L. A., & Nelson, K. (1985). *Young Children's Knowledge of Relational Terms: Some Ifs, Ors, or Buts*. New York: Springer-Verlag.

Friedman, W., & Seely, P. (1976). The child's acquisition of patial and temporal word meanings. *Child Development, 47*, 1103–1108.

Gahtercole, V. C. (1985). More and more and more about more. *Journal of Experimental Child Psychology, 40*, 73–104.

Glucksberg, S. (1975). Word versus sentence interpretation: Do adults overextend the meaning of "different"? Paper presented at the meeting of the Society for Research and Development. Denver.

Hainsworth, P., & Siqueland, E. (1969). *Meeting Street School Screening Test*. East Providence, RI: Crippled Children and Adults of Rhode Island.

Hammill, D. D. (1985). *Detroit Tests of Learning Aptitude (DTLA-2)*. Austin, TX: Pro-Ed.

Harris, L., & Strommen, E. (1971). The role of front-back features in children's "front, back, and beside" placement of objects. *Merrill-Palmer Quarterly, 18*, 259–271.

Johnson, H. (1975). The meaning of before and after for preschool children. *Journal of Experimental Child Psychology, 19*, 88–99.

Josephs, J. (1975). Children's comprehension of same and different in varying contexts. Unpublished doctoral dissertation. Columbia University.

Kamii, C. (1971). Evaluation of learning in preschool education: Socio-emotional, perceptual-motor, and cognitive development. In B. Bloom, J. Hastings,

& G. Madaus (Eds.). *Handbook on Formative and Summative Evaluation of Student Learning*. New York: McGraw-Hill, 281–344.

Kaplan, C. (1978). A developmental analysis of children's direction following behavior in grades K-5. Unpublished doctoral dissertation. Columbia University.

Kaufman, A. (1978). The importance of basic concepts in individual assessment of preschool children. *Journal of School Psychology, 16*, 207–211.

Kaufman, A. S., & Kaufman, N. L. (1983). *Kaufman Assessment Battery for Children*. Circle Pines, MN: American Guidance Service.

Kavale, K. A. (1982). A comparison of learning disabled and normal children on the Boehm Test of Basic Concepts. *Journal of Learning Disabilities, 15*, 160–161.

Kavanaugh, R. (1976). Developmental changes in preschool children's comprehension of comparative sentences. *Merrill-Palmer Quarterly, 22*, 309–318.

Kennedy, G. (1970). *The Language of Tests for Young Children* (CSE Working Paper 7). Los Angeles: Center for the Study of Evaluation. UCLA Graduate School of Education.

Klausmeier, H. J. (1976). Instructional design and the teaching of concepts. In J. R. Levin & V. I. Allen (Eds.), *Cognitive Learning in Children*. New York: Academic Press.

Kuczaj, S., & Maratos, M. (1975). On the acquisition of front, back, and side. *Child Development, 46*, 202–210.

Lee, J., & Clark, W. (1962). *Lee-Clark Reading Readiness Test*. Monterey, CA: California Testing Bureau.

Levin, J., Henderson, B., Levin, A. M., et al. (1975). Measuring knowledge of basic concepts in disadvantaged preschoolers. *Psychology in the Schools, 12*, 132–139.

Levine, S., & Carey, S. (1982). Up front: the acquisition of a concept and a word. *Journal of Child Language, 9*, 645–657.

Lidz, C. S. (1983). Issues in assessing preschool children. In K. D. Paget & B. A. Bracken (Eds.). *The Psychoeducational Assessment of Preschool Children*. NY: Grune & Stratton.

MacGinitie, W. H. (1978). *Gates-MacGinitie Reading Tests (2nd ed., Basic R)*. Boston: Houghton Mifflin.

Madden, R., & Gardner, E. (1967, 1970). *Stanford Early School Achievement Test*. New York: Harcourt Brace Jovanovich.

Meisner, J. (1973). Use of relational concepts by inner city children. *Journal of Educational Psychology, 46*, 22–29.

Mickelson, N. I., & Galloway, C. G. (1973). Verbal concepts of Indian and non-Indian school beginners. *Journal of Educational Research, 67*, 55–56.

Moers, F., & Harris, J. (1978). Instruction in basic concepts and first grade achievement. *Psychology in the Schools, 15,* 84–86.

Moss, M. (1978). *Test of Basic Experiences.* CA:CTB/McGraw-Hill.

Murphy, H., & Durrell, D. (1964). *Murphy-Durrell Reading Readiness Analysis.* New York: Psychological Corporation.

Nason, F. O. (1986). Systematic instruction of basic relational concepts: Effects on the acquisition of concept knowledge and of language and mathematics achievement of Puerto Rican first graders from low income families (Doctoral dissertation, Teachers College, Columbia University).

Nelson, R. B., & Cummings, J. A. (1981). Basic concept attainment of educably mentally handicapped children: Implications for teaching concepts. *Education and Training of the Mentally Retarded, 16,* 303, 306.

Nurss, J. R., & McGauvran, M. (1976). *Metropolitan Readiness Tests.* New York: Psychological Corporation.

Palermo, D. S. (1973). More about less: A study of language comprehension. *Journal of Verbal Learning and Verbal Behavior, 13,* 211–221.

Palermo, D. S. (1974). Still more about the comprehension of "less." *Developmental Psychology, 10,* 827–829.

Patterson, M. C. (1981). Performance of Hutter children in English and Hutterish versions of the Boehm Test of Basic Concepts. *Dissertation Abstracts International, 41,* 2987.

Piaget, J. (1967). *Six Psychological Studies.* New York: Random House.

Preddy, D., Boehm, A. E., & Shepherd, M. J. (1984). PBCB: A norming of the Spanish translation of the Boehm Test of Basic Concepts. *Journal of School Psychology, 22,* 407–413.

Richards, M. M. (1982). Empiricism and learning to mean. In S. Kuczaj (Ed.), *Language Development, Vol. 1: Syntax and Semantics.* Hillside, NJ: Lawrence Erlbaum Associates.

Richards, M. M., & Haupe, L. S. (1981). Contrasting patterns in the acquisition of spatial/temporal terms. *Journal of Experimental Child Psychology, 32,* 485–512.

Silverstein, A. B., Mouh, D. N., & Belger, K. (1983). Sex differences and sex bias on the Boehm Test of Basic Concepts: Do they exist? *Psychology in the Schools, 20,* 269–270.

Spector, C. C. (1977). Concepts comprehension of normal kindergarten children with deviant syntactic development. Unpublished doctoral dissertation. New York University.

Spector, C. C. (1979). The Boehm Test of Basic Concepts: Exploring the test results for cognitive deficits. *Journal of Learning Disabilities, 12,* 564–567.

Tennyson, R. D., & Park, D. (1980). The teaching of concepts: A review of instructional design research literature. *Review of Educational Research, 50,* 55–70.

Tennyson, R. D., & Cocchiarella, M. J. (1986). An empirically based instructional design theory for teaching concepts. *Review of Educational Research, 86,* 40–71.

Trehub, S., & Abramovitch, R. (1978). Less is not more: Further observations on nonlinguistic strategies. *Journal of Experimental Child Psychology, 25,* 160–167.

Weiner, S. (1974). On the development of more and less. *Journal of Experimental Child Psychology, 17,* 271–287.

Wiig, E., & Semel, E. (1976). *Learning Disabilities in Children and Adolescents.* Columbus, OH: Merrill.

13

Assessment of Perceptual–Motor and Fine Motor Functioning

ZONA R. WEEKS
BARBARA EWER-JONES

This chapter focuses on perceptual and fine motor development and assessment. The areas of perceptual–motor/sensory integrative assessment for a preschool child can include: cognitive functioning with an underlying perceptual or perceptual–motor base; reflex and voluntary motor functioning; sense receptor deficiencies that affect motor performance (e.g., vision, hearing, touch); sensory integration deficits, perceptual and perceptual–motor deficiencies; speech and language disorders; activity level; and social and emotional functioning. Some of these assessment areas are covered in depth, while others are touched upon only briefly.

Assessment of perceptual–motor abilities is essential in the total evaluation of preschool children, because failure to identify and remediate deficiencies can present social, emotional, academic, and physical consequences. Problems in the percentual–motor area can influence a child's performance on commonly used tests of intelligence and render the results inaccurate as measures of cognitive ability.

Perceptual–motor skills involve the ability to perceive and attach meaning to sensory input and the use of that information in carrying out gross and fine motor acts. Accurate perceptions are necessary not only for adequate motor responses, but also for such cognitive abilities as forming concepts. For example, accurate perceptions of the physical world lead to the formation of concepts of size, shape, depth, temperature, motion, sound, and so forth.

Bergan (1969) defines perception as having four components: the stimulus characteristic observed, the perceptions of the person observing, the content classification of the stimulus observed, and the sensory modality through which the stimulus is observed. Bergan (1969) identifies three distinct aspects of a perceptual task: the components and properties of the stimulus, the instructions, and the behavior required for completion. Each sensory stimulus has components that can be perceived only through a specific sensory system (e.g., loudness and depth affect different sensory systems). Other characteristics, such as texture, can be perceived through more than one sensory mode (i.e., texture can be seen and felt).

Individuals must be able to attend selectively and be ready to respond to those sensory stimuli that are important to their functioning at the moment. The ability to attend to a stimulus or to concurrent stimuli depends upon the condition of the individual's sensory receptors, effective sensory transmission, and appropriate internal sensory processing. In addition, the nature of the stimulus has an effect on attention. For example, such stimulus features as size, motion, color intensity or contrast, loudness and repetition affect one's ability to attend.

PERCEPTUAL–MOTOR DEVELOPMENT

Infants are born with some inherent reflexes and perceptual modes of action that help them gain consistent sensory input from their repetitive actions. Sensations are perceived repeatedly until the child forms useful concepts about his body and the environment. Concepts of space, size, shape, time, sound, direction, and so forth develop from increasingly meaningful perceptions of environmental stimuli in tactual, proprioceptive, vestibular, visual, auditory, olfactory, and gustatory modes. Intersensory integration and comparison of bi- or multisensory input expand the environmental picture as a child ages (Bartley, 1969; Weeks, 1982). Concepts develop more completely with age and experience, giving the child a cognitive framework on which to build. The child must either determine that current perceptual experiences are consistent with old concepts or develop new concepts that help explain the perceptions.

Gradually, the child learns that perceptual illusions can occur and that vision, touch, hearing and other senses cannot always be trusted as reality. Misperceptions can occur because of factors such as weak stimulus intensity, overintensity, competing stimuli from the same or other sensory avenues, and incomplete or conflicting information (Gibson, 1966; Weeks, 1982).

Enriching the environment of infants and children to promote development is a practice espoused by many professionals. Information from some experts indicates that perceptual growth is virtually complete by approximately 12 years of age in the normal individual (Wilentz, 1968). Although some remediation is possible in older children and adults, perceptual enhancement at younger ages appears to be most effective.

Early learning involves motor and tactile learning in which the haptic system is used to touch and explore the environment. The more the child manipulates the environment, the more enriched will be his or her perceptual experience and comprehension (Ayres, 1969, 1972a). The child's understanding of the environment is dependent on what can be received through the senses. Memory becomes a representation of a child's experience involving one or more of the perceptual modalities, because memory is necessary for meaningful perceptions.

Many of the properties of objects are learned through touch. Until the child has shape, color, or form constancy, he or she will not be ready to differentiate or discriminate letters or numbers. Larson (1968) describes these constancy concepts as including form, size, and context. Figure-ground properties are needed for the child to discriminate what is to be the center of attention in a visual field before he or she is able to transfer that ability to the written page.

Larson (1968) describes a child who lacks good development of figure-ground skill as being inattentive and disorganized, easily distracted, unable to stay on task, prone to skip lines when trying to read, unable to pick out the relevant details from the irrelevant, and unable to find his or her place on a written page.

According to McGee (1979), spatial ability is made up of two components—spatial visualization and spatial orientation. He describes the spatial visualization as the ability to mentally rotate an object, and spatial orientation as the ability to determine the orientation of an object in relation to one's self and the ability to maintain orientation when an object is perceived from a different position. Ayres (in Siev & Freishtat, 1976) believes that spatial perception and visual form are dependent on the development and integration of visual, tactile, proprioceptive, and vestibular systems and information. Spatial skills are essential in many areas of the child's play, as well as in reading, writing, math, science, and later in high school and specialized college curricula such as drafting, dress design, and dentistry. McKim (1980) perceives spatial and visual skill development as essential for computation and solution of verbal math problems.

Sensory deprivation studies on animals demonstrate the influence of experience and learning on perceptual development and performance. Also, visual deprivation has been shown to retard normal eye movements and pattern vision, and tactual deprivation leads to tactual discrimination problems (Dember & Warm, 1979).

During the preschool years, children develop their early perceptual–motor skills and refine both gross and fine motor abilities. They become able to perform more complex motor skills, partly as a result of increased perceptual development. Central nervous system (CNS) maturation progresses throughout infancy, allowing the typical gross and fine motor milestones (e.g., creeping, walking, prehension) to evolve sequentially, and providing the basis for future skills. Reflexes play an essential part in motor development, with voluntary movements superimposed on the underlying reflexive base. As lower CNS level reflexes are inhibited and higher level reflexes appear, the child becomes able to do more complex motor tasks, including those involving balance. Fine motor ability is not possible unless there is body stability and balance. Accurate tactile, kinesthetic, and visual perceptions require motor control to stabilize or move the body as needed while sensory information is being obtained.

By age 19 months the basic postural reflexes have evolved, and the child now relies on maturation and experience to strengthen useful responses and build a voluntary movement repertoire that both incorporates and inhibits reflexes, as necssary. In children whose lower level reflexes persist longer than normally expected, and whose higher level reflexes do not evolve as expected, clumsiness, poor balance, ineptness in sports, poor handwriting, and numerous other inadequacies might be apparent. Such factors as strength, range of motion, and coordination also are dependent upon neurophysiological intactness and maturation.

In any discussion of perceptual and fine motor problems, it is necessary to reiterate that perception and motor behavior (gross or fine) are inextricably linked. Motor behavior occurs in response to sensory input. One cannot perform a motor task without sensory input and its integration and perception by the CNS. Guidance and correction of initiated movement come about through sensory input created during the movement (feedback). Sensory input of various kinds (e.g., tactile, proprioceptive, vestibular, visual,

auditory) must be integrated appropriately to make possible adaptive responses to environmental situations. As development progresses, greater CNS organization is expected to occur normally, allowing for increasingly complex responses to environmental demands—including those of an academic nature. In some children these developmental changes do not occur in the expected sequence.

The role of sensation in perception in gross and fine motor skills development is readily apparent. Without proper sensory input and the ability to interpret sensations, motor skills cannot develop normally. As movements occur at large and small joints of the body, and cutaneous inputs occur, proprioceptive and tactile sensations aid perception of position and movement.

In perceptual development, children become more discriminative with age and experience, make perceptual distinctions more rapidly, and improve their attentional mechanisms; they also become more efficient in gathering perceptual data and relating them to other incoming and stored sensory and perceptual information (Bartley, 1969; Epstein, 1967; Gibson, 1969). As children age they develop strategies of information seeking; they also become able to organize distinctive attributes of perceptual occurrences into mental structures, making it easier to make sense of partial information (Mussen et al., 1974). Language helps children label and define these concepts (Gibson, 1966) and gives them the means to validate their early percept-based concepts with other persons. Coding information verbally also helps children retain perceptual data about objects (Swanson, 1977).

In a study of free classification based on size and brightness with 5-, 8-, and 11-year-old children, Smith and Kemler (1977) found evidence that young children process perceptual stimuli differently from older children. Young children seem to process information integrally, whereas older children process information in a dimensional structure by which they perceive multidimensional stimuli (such as size and brightness) in a separable manner. Young children's difficulty with selective attention might be in part a result of problems in determining the relevant and irrelevant features of input.

Familiarity of visual stimuli appears to be of major developmental importance in visual memory (Mandler & Robinson, 1978). With organized scenes, patterns of performance were similar in first-, third-, and fifth-grade children, although accuracy increased with age. With unorganized pictures, children not only were less accurate than adults, but they also showed different patterns of response. Children, at least to 11 years of age, apparently have difficulty organizing visual material that is unfamiliar in structure.

Martin and coworkers (1969) studied developmental patterns of perceptual functioning in 160 children ages 3 through 10 years. They assessed visual, tactile, kinesthetic, haptic, and auditory perception, as well as motor performance. They found that 70% of perceptual growth occurs by 3 to 4 years of age; 20% more occurs between ages 4 and 7; and another 10% between ages 7 and 10. In this research, perceptual performance was related to socioeconomic status until age 6, suggesting that school and other experiences help the delayed child to advance to age-appropriate levels. No differences were noted between right and left hands in tactile, kinesthetic, or haptic abilities. Interestingly, no performance differences between males and females were found at any age.

Goodgold-Edwards (1984) reviewed literature pertinent to development of motor learning; her conclusions follow. *Speed of movement* improves with age; influencing factors can include strength, acceleration, and braking abilities, faster processing of information, and ability to plan future movements, among other abilities. Increase in speed, however, causes a decrease in accuracy. *Anticipatory timing behavior* (or coincidence-anticipation), the ability to respond coincident with environmental events (e.g., catch a ball), can require accurate event visualization and performance memory, experience, movement initiation decisions, or control. This behavior improves from early childhood until about 14 or 15 years of age. The relationship between anticipatory timing behavior and reaction time is not yet clear. *Knowledge of results of performance* is believed to be an important variable in motor skill learning, as is knowledge of response proficiency; thus knowledge of results might be useful not only for informing but also for motivation and reinforcement.

The importance of proprioceptive and exteroceptive cues in motor learning was investigated by Fleishman and Rich (1963), who found that ex-

troceptive (spatial-visual) cues were important later in the learning.

Conrad and colleagues (1983) compared LD and normal children's performance on praxis tests. LD children scored lower than normal controls on the tests as a whole, and significantly lower on the optic-spatial and dynamic tests. There was no significant difference on the kinesthesia or symbolic tests. Preadolescent children with cerebral dysfunction or learning disabilities have difficulty maintaining preparation in reaction-time tasks, a characteristic shared by younger children without evident learning or neurological deficits (Adams & Lambos, 1986).

Smothergill (1973), determined that 6 and 7 year olds localized spatial targets as well as older children and adults. Laszlo and Bairstow (1980) found that 7-year-old children discriminate position and movement as well as adults, but that ability to memorize kinesthetic information is incomplete and improves beyond that age. Henderson and Duncombe (1982) found that kinesthetic judgment of distance improves in accuracy before judgment of angle, but that older children (9, 12, and 15 year olds) scored significantly better than 7 year olds on both measures.

The difficulties in identifying and classifying clumsy children are pointed out by Henderson and Hall (1982). Children identified as clumsy scored significantly lower in both motor and intellectual tests and had a higher incidence of social problems. Gubbay (1978) advocates early diagnosis and referral of apraxic children to specialist teachers, occupational therapists, and physical educators. He believes that early therapy leads to an excellent prognosis in children whose clumsiness results from maturational lag and a relatively poor prognosis if there is organic structural etiology. Four tests that Gubbay has found effective in identifying apraxic children use common objects (throwing a tennis ball up and clapping before catching it, rolling a tennis ball underfoot, threading beads, and inserting different-shaped objects into the proper slots).

Cermak and Ayres (1984) evaluated crossing the body midline as a discriminating factor in 120 normal and 179 LD children. Results indicated that this measure was useful in discriminating between normal and learning disabled children at ages 5, 6, and 7, but not at age 8.

Rourke and Telegdy (1971) determined that

LD children with high verbal and low performance scores on the WISC did not perform better on complex motor tasks with the right hand, lending no support to the idea that their right hand skills might be better than their left. Similarly, the high performance, low verbal children did not demonstrate higher left hands scores. A number of researchers have found a significant advantage of left brain-damaged individuals over right in, for example, imitating gestures or movement (De-Renzi et al., 1980; Kimura & Archibald, 1974; Naas, 1983). In tests of motor sequencing skills, LD boys were poorer than nonlearning disabled on alternating-hand tapping trials, especially with the left hand. In single hand tapping they found learning disabled boys performed as well as normal boys (Badian & Wolff, 1977).

DYSFUNCTION

Causes of perceptual–motor problems remain obscure, but some associations with other conditions have been found. For example, low birth weight children in some studies have shown deficient perceptual–motor performances (Lee, 1977), presumably because of neurological damage. Autistic children and many children with emotional disturbances of other types also have been found to have perceptual disturbances that interfere with motor functioning (DeMyer, 1975; Goldfarb, 1964; Llorens, 1968; Rider, 1973; Silberzahn, 1975; Weeks, 1979). Children diagnosed as having minimal brain dysfunction from numerous known and unknown causes frequently have been found to show defective perceptual and motor abilities (Clements, 1973). Frequency of physical anomalies, indicating embryological maldevelopment, has been associated with poor coordination, hyperactivity, and other motor disorders (Halverson & Victor, 1976; Waldrop et al., 1968).

QUALITATIVE AND QUANTITATIVE ASPECTS

Disturbances in the quality of perceptual–motor functioning can range from mild to severe, and be in only one perceptual–motor area or many. Some of these disturbances can be quantitatively defined by degree of dysfunction, while others defy attempts at quantification and can be communicated only through descriptions of performance or general behaviors.

Qualitative disturbances of fine motor function relate to the preciseness or degree of skill with which fine motor tasks are accomplished. Factors interfering with quality of fine motor performance are neurological or musculoskeletal in nature. In the view of Noller and Ingrisano (1984), many gross and fine motor developmental assessments currently available omit or only vaguely describe performance criteria, and quality of movement is often not addressed.

A brief listing of some representative perceptual fine-motor abilities by age of performance is shown in Table 13-1 and some skills are described in Table 13-2. (Note that the age range of normal performance might be wider than the tables indicate.)

Delays in auditory development and anomalies in auditory-feature processing can contribute to the learning problems of LD children, according to Watson and Rastatter (1985). They found that LD children exhibited auditory processing abilities similar to younger normal children.

A disordered nervous system could lead to perceptual and motor problems and to learning or emotional problems. Learning disabilities and emotional disturbances are not always associated, of course, but there appears to be a strong link. Psychiatrists sometimes find that children referred to learning disabilities clinics have emotional disturbances, and they might conclude that the emotional problem is primary and the learning problem a secondary result (Westman et al., 1987). Educators might believe that learning problems and school failure lead to emotional problems more often than the reverse. Children with school problems also might be having trouble in areas of physical life functioning. Because children with actual disordered nervous systems might have difficulties in many aspects of life, it might be simplistic to say that one problem area ''causes'' difficulties in another area, although frustration can certainly carry over to other areas.

Children with motor problems have varying neurological deficits. Some might have abnormally high or low muscle tone, others might have coordination difficulties, and still others might have difficulty planning motor actions (dyspraxia)

TABLE 13.1
PERCEPTUAL-FINE MOTOR DEVELOPMENT

2 years
Rotates forearm (supinates), turns knobs
Turns pages singly
Strings several beads
Unwraps piece of candy
Imitates vertical stroke
Crudely imitates circular stroke
Imitates a V stroke
Aligns 2 or more blocks for a train
Makes 6–7 block tower
Can match 2 or more simple shapes
Places blocks on form board separately with demon-
  stration

2½ years
Grasps too strongly with overextension
Places blocks in formboard with no demonstration
Might imitate H in drawing
Imitates horizontal line
Holds crayon with fingers
Builds 8-block tower
Adds 1-block chimney to block train
Matches 1 color form
Dries own hands

3 years
Good rotation of wrist
Builds 9–10 block tower
Imitates cross
Copies circle from a model
Cuts with scissors
Matches 3 color forms
Puts on socks and shoes
Unbuttons medium shirt buttons
Places 10 pellets in bottle in 30 sec (1 at a time)

3½ years
Traces a diamond
Builds 3-block bridge from model
Washes and dries hands and face
Feeds self well
Matches simple colors

4 years
Throws overhand
Cuts with scissors
Copies cross from a model
Draws crude pictures of familiar things

Builds with large blocks
Copies a diagonal line
Buttons large buttons
Knows front from back on clothes
Brushes teeth
Places 10 pellets into bottle in 25 sec
Performs serial opposition of thumb to fingers

4½ years
Copies a square
Draws a person with several body parts
Draws pictures of familiar objects
Identifies simple objects by feeling, such as ball,
  block, or crayon
Catches a bounced ball
Can name several colors

5 years
Prehends precisely and releases well
Tries to color within lines
Can copy an X
Can copy a triangle
Enjoys coloring, cutting, and pasting
Laces shoes without tying
Can dress and undress alone except for small buttons
  and bows
Draws a house with windows and doors
Draws a man with arms, legs, feet, and facial features

6 years
Ties shoelaces loosely in a bow
Throws ball with with follow-through
Can print some letters and numbers (might be
  reversed)
Draws person with detailed body parts and some
  clothing
Imitates inverted triangle
Can imitate horizontal diamond
Buttons small buttons on shirt or blouse
Might know right and left on self
Might have stable hand preference

7 years
Copies a Maltese cross
Cuts with knife
No longer has b-d confusion
Draws human figure with clearly represented clothing

Compiled from Gesell and Amatruda (1947), Gesell and Ilg (1946), Hartlage and Lucas (1973), Kaufman (1978), and Werner (1980).

or difficulty comprehending visual, auditory, tactile, or other sensations (agnosia) needed for motor performance. In severe deficiencies motor problems are obvious and therapy often is initiated; in less obvious cases, the motor problems might be undetected or only some recognition given to clumsiness and poor handwriting, but no serious remediation attempted. Ridicule from other children might accompany these problems.

Handwriting requires fine motor skill with

TABLE 13.2

SKILL CHART OF MOTOR INTEGRATION, TACTILE, AND VISUAL-MOTOR DISCRIMINATION

Motor Integration	Tactile Discrimination	Visual-Motor Discrimination
4 years		
Buttons own shirt and coat, laces shoes	Should be able to find without using eyes; nail, spoon, penny, bolt (gives insight to handedness or preference)	Can reproduce:
Throws a ball overhand		1, 0, +, /
Skips		Which is different?
Climbs well	Can name by feeling: block, ball, scissors, penny, crayon	b d b b
Can cut on a line		0 0 x 0
Holds brush in adult manner		+ + 0 +
Touches fingers to thumb in succession		Copies a square (four clearly defined sides)
Balances on one foot for up to 10 sec (if child cannot, might indicate a short attention span)		Draws a person (head, arms, legs, mouth, nose, hair, no trunk)
Catches a bounced ball		Can fix blocks to a certain design
Walking board: walks forward, alternating feet; walks backward, sliding feet; walks sideward, sliding feet (preferred foot leading)		Can identify shapes by comparison (not by name)
		Builds tower of 10 or more blocks
		Traces triangle, diamond
5 years		
Skips	Can find out of a bag without using eyes: crayon, pencil, stick, nail, string, rubber band, ribbon, belt	Draws a picture (any kind)
Can tie a simple bow		Draws a square by an example
Stands on tiptoe (balance 10 sec)		Can put triangles together to form a rectangle
Walks on tiptoe for 10 ft		Can draw a picture like this:
Marches		
Hops well on 1 foot		
Uses alternating feet on stairs or ladder		
Jumps		Can make a block design
Puts together a circle or rectangle that has been cut in two		Can copy XXXX, △
Rides tricycle, backing and turning		Draws a person (all facial details)
Uses hands more than arms when catching ball		Draws a house (windows, door, roof, chimney)
Washes self without getting clothes wet		Puts matches neatly in box
		Builds three-dimensional block structures
Laces shoes		Copies rectangle, diamond, by tracing
Completely dresses self		Uses scissors skillfully
6 years		
Large muscles are better developed than small; eyes are not mature (tendency toward farsightedness); permanent teeth appear; heart is in period of rapid growth	Can find blindfolded in a bag: bolt, nail, tack, crayon, cloth, leather, sponge, paper	Copies diamond
		Copies more complex block design
		Can draw a more complex picture
Knows right from left		After first 3 of 5 circles are placed in ascending order, can tell which comes next
Stands on one foot longer than 10 sec		Can answer: Find one just like mine
Walks backward heel to toe		＿＿ 2 ＿＿ tac
		＿＿ home ＿＿ 4
		＿＿ cat ＿＿ sat

TABLE 13.2 *(continued)*

Motor Integration	Tactile Discrimination	Visual-Motor Discrimination

Copies
Keeps time to music by walking
   or skipping
Ties a bow
Combs or brushes hair
Blows and cleans nose
Spreads with knife
Can aim when bouncing ball
Jumps rope
Can ride a scooter, wagon,
   tricycle, sled, skates
Can imitate body movements of
   another
Begins to try a bicycle
		Can answer: Now watch carefully,
		   I'm going to show and hide my
		   card, then you find one like it
		   (cards same as above)

Items taken from Gesell Developmental Evaluation (1947), the Valett Developmental Survey of Basic Learning Abilities (1969), Mental Development Evaluation of the Pediatric Patient (Hartlage & Lucas, 1973) and the Guide to Early Developmental Training (Indiana State Department of Public Instruction, 1972).

gross motor stability, as well as many other abilities. Taylor (1985) discusses processes children need for handwriting. Gross and fine motor abilities, and visual–perceptual skills must be sufficient to allow sitting, positioning the paper, holding a writing instrument, and forming letters joined into cursive script. Directionality must be adequate to allow correct production of letters, words, and numbers. To be independent, the child must be able to recall and reproduce these symbols and critique his or her own performance. However, because researchers have been unable to find consistently common neurological test results in children with learning and/or behavioral problems (Black, 1976; Kenny & Clemmens, 1971), educational test results might be more useful for educational remediation planning. Occupational and physical therapists and speech clinicians, who attempt to correct certain neurological dysfunctions, might find neurological or neuropsychological test results are of greater usefulness to them.

Vestibular dysfunction as a possible factor in learning disabilities has been studied by Ayres (1978), deQuiros (1976), and others (Ottenbacher 1978, 1979, 1980; Keating, 1979). These researchers believe that a relationship might exist between vestibular dysfunction and learning disabilities, as evidenced by decreased responsiveness to vestibular stimulation in many LD children. Polatajko (1987), however, reports that although eye movement problems during reading can lead to learning difficulties, her methods of testing show no difference between normal and LD children in vestibular or optokinetic nystagmus. Polatajko (1985) questions hypotheses of singular vestibular of visual oculomotor dysfunction, but she does not rule out the possibility that the LD child might have poor interaction of the two (that is, poor opto-vestibular function). Brown and coworkers (1985) found no differences in static postural stability between normal control children and dyslexic children who had been screened to rule out neurological problems. The authors state that a vestibular-cerebellar defect is not supported as a necessary accompaniment to dyslexia, but it might be a factor in some dyslexic subgroups. Other aspects of their study demonstrated that dyslexics experience more dysequilibrium in complex situations, such as those involving whole body movement and in performing unpracticed tasks with demanding conditions. The authors believe that higher integrative mechanisms should be of more focus in evaluation and education, because they found no evidence for elementary vestibular or visual–motor system problems.

Kavale and Andreassen (1984) found that the most important factor in diagnosing children as learning disabled was academic underachievement. The next most important indicator to educational personnel was the presence of behavior problems. Intelligence, socioeconomic status, and possible neurological involvement as a basis for learning disabilities were considered of little importance in educators' judgement.

Children with Attention Deficit Disorders (ADD) were found by Chelune and coworkers (1986) to show a pattern of deficits on tests that purport to measure frontal lobe inhibitory control. The age trends they noted suggested a possible maturational lag in frontal lobe functioning in these children. Current definitions identify two types of ADD, either with or without hyperactivity.

Several theories have been proposed regarding causes of developmental dyslexia, including poor hemispheric specialization, impaired hemispheric processing, and poor interhemispheric interaction. Broman and coworkers (1986) present the possibility that dyslexia results from a left hemispheric linguistic processing deficit, combined with a generalized slowing of cortical and/or subcortical information processing (rather than from an abnormality of interhemispheric transfer). Broman and colleagues (1986) further suggest that linguistic information processing is poor in the left hemispheres of dyslexics, and that cortical and/or subcortical information processing is slow; however, the rate and accuracy of interhemispheral transfer of information does not appear to be abnormal.

Some researchers have proposed that many learning disabled children have trouble learning at their grade levels because their development is immature and they are functioning in ways similar to younger children in learning. Dyslexic children might develop visual selective attention in a slower manner than nonreading disabled children (Tarver, et al., 1977). Boone (1986) observes that children who reverse letters might not be maturationally ready for reading and reports research that appears to support a "critical period" approach to reading. Greater success was experienced in readiness training for directional orientation and sentence tracking by 5 or 6 year olds than in 8 or 9 year olds. Boone (1986) also notes that visual reversals in preschool children are common, but that they decline over grades K through 3 and should have disappeared in most children by age 9.

According to Scarpati and Swanson (1980), some LD readers cannot integrate visual information spontaneously while using linguistic coding. In their study, forced naming of individual shapes (verbal encoding) caused an improvement in visual recall.

Sadlick and Ginsburg (1978) provide reviews and support for the view that a lag in language lateralization in children age 8 years and above, as well as advanced lateralization in younger children (5, 6, and 7 years old) could be factors in reading problems. In their view, the gradual attainment of cerebral lateralization is an important developmental step in the process of acquiring language skills and in learning to read. Young children in the learning-to-read stages need both sides of the brain for processing the large amount of visual-spatial and linguistic information. Older, more fluent readers benefit from asymmetry favoring hemispheric specialization for language.

The relationship of poorly established eye, hand, and foot dominance to abnormal hemispheric specialization for language has been studied (Gordon, 1986; Obrzut & Boliek, 1986); however, research results related to abnormal lateralization and learning disabilities are inconclusive. Crossed dominance (hand and foot of different preference) is reportedly common and thus not atypical; and rather than mixed handedness being a result of immature cerebral lateralization, some believe that it is more likely to be a result of immature motor or cognitive development (Gordon, 1986).

ASSESSMENT PROCEDURES

Informal Assessment

Informal assessment for children with perceptual motor problems can include interviews with parents and nursery school teachers. Information on fine and gross motor abilities during development, as well as clues to visual and auditory perception and other sensory perceptual abilities can be obtained. Family history and hand dominance, motor problems, reading difficulties, and so on can alert the examiner to possible problems.

Some assessment procedures, although not truly informal, are placed in that category because they are not standardized in the technical sense, and complete norms are not available. An example would be the clinical observations frequently done by occupational therapists, primarily with developmentally delayed or LD children. These include eye movements and preference, muscle tone and contraction, reflexes, and other items. Dunn (1981) described these measures and provided some insight into the performance expected from typical kindergarten children.

Another type of informal evaluation can be completed while the child is at play. The types of free play activities chosen or avoided, preferred hand used predominantly by the child in play, tilt of the head when playing, amount and type of communication with self or others when playing, and problem-solving approaches attempted when thwarted by an unknown obstacle all can be part of an informal evaluation. Does the child revise the purpose of the play objects or play within the usual confines of the materials? Are paper and pencil or other fine motor tools preferred and what is the level of the results if used? When working with fine motor materials, does the child shift the paper or his body when there is a directional change? What is the level of frustration reached, and how long can the individual stay with an activity without moving on or becoming distracted by something else? Does the child look toward the source of sound? Is there ultrasensitivity to sound or ability to concentrate despite environmental noise? Does the child choose to play where there is a great amount of light, or is dimness preferred? At what distance from the body are books and pictures held? How does the child react to music? Is he or she able to carry or match a tune, and how does the body move when there is music? Is there muscle overflow, in that the opposite limb performs along with the functioning limb? Is there awareness of the body in space or are falls common? Does the child break things when playing? When looking at pictures, can essential visual details be discriminated and described? Does the child see and comprehend a visual story line, and is there the beginning development of cause and effect relationships and predicting ability? Can the child imitate the body movement of another? Travers (1985) believes that perceptual training needs to begin soon after birth because the child has much to learn and the perceptual skills become the tool by which the child learns to understand the world.

Teachers who observe children in comparison with their peers often see differences in ability. In informal assessment, tasks are presented by which performance can be rated somewhat objectively according to approximate age-appropriate behaviors. DeGenaro (1975) described a number of informal perceptual and other assessment procedures for use by teachers.

Behavioral observations and informal assessment results must be carefully studied for patterns of dysfunction. Strengths also should be noted because they might be avenues of approach to the remediation of learning or other problems as well as a means to increase the child's self-confidence. Weeks (1982) further describes perceptual and sensorimotor integrative assessment.

Evaluation of Fine Motor Skills

A number of factors enter into the evaluation of fine motor abilities because many underlying sensory, motor, and perceptual functions must be adequate to ensure that fine motor performance will be coordinated. Anatomical structure must permit freedom of movement; muscle tone and control must be appropriate to support the body structure and allow smooth, unhindered movement; proximal joint stability is necessary before distal fine motor control is possible; postural reflexes must be age appropriate to allow the expected motor developmental tasks and skills to be performed adequately; and sensory abilities must allow the child to distinguish and discriminate among touch, pain, temperature, proprioceptive, visual, and auditory stimuli. Attitudes and emotions also can positively or negatively affect motor performance. Thus, the assessment of perceptual–motor problems, with an emphasis on fine motor skills, must be extremely broad if all factors are to be considered.

The area of fine motor functioning that is most commonly assessed is hand function. Proximodistal and ulnoradial directional development occurs in arm and hand control. In addition, such skeletal factors as length of fingers have an effect on grasp and manipulation. Some fine motor abilities are impossible until vision perception and numerous cognitive abilities develop appropriately. The child must be able to see, perceive, and comprehend the nature of the task.

Hand function can be analyzed in terms of grasp and pinch strength, joint range of motion, coordination (dexterity), and patterns of gross grasp and fine prehension. Tools are available to assess grasp and pinch strength (dynamometers and pinch meters), and persons trained to perform manual muscle testing also can use that modality. Joint range of motion can be assessed by means of a goniometer, as well as by informal tests of functional movement. Coordination or dexterity can be tested through the use of pegboards, manipulative items, handwriting, eye–hand coordination tests, finger movements (such as thumb-to-finger serial opposition), and so forth. Gross grasp and fine prehension patterns are assessed in terms of developmental levels and ranges of ability by means of charts or tests describing or showing the patterns. All of these areas are commonly tested by occupational and physical therapists. Some are assessed by physical educators, classroom teachers, and psychologists.

Several works have built upon previous developmental studies of hand function. Tests have been designed according to age-related abilities. Cliff (1979) divided prehension into the following components: regard, approach, grasp, manipulation, and release. Her evaluation chart for the development of reach and grasp extends only through the first year of life, but her descriptions and analyses of these components are helpful for a developmental understanding of hand use skills. Kamakura and coworkers (1980) describe static prehension patterns in hands.

The study of prehension by many researchers has resulted in a variety of terms for the same or similar patterns, making comparison of patterns confusing at times. Examiners should be aware of this when using different sources. In 1981 Erhardt and coworkers reviewed numerous hand function studies and compiled normative data. They also explained the process involved in the development of the Erhardt Developmental Prehension Assessment and presented a representative segment of the test, along with an example of its use in individualized educational planning. Lundberg (1979) presented the Drawing Test as a tool for assessing arm-hand function in 1- to 3-year-old children. This test takes less than 10 minutes to perform and is said to be useful in studying developmental level and fine motor performance. Although both of these tests will require further work to develop complete norms for various age levels, they provide a consistent framework for the assessment of young children's fine motor hand function.

FORMAL ASSESSMENT TESTS

Early childhood tests that have been developed formally and standardized are available in many perceptual areas. Tests included in this chapter are examined in terms of the interrelationship of perceptual and perceptual–motor factors with language, cognition, and other school-related abilities.

There is a complex integration of many skills and factors involved in any single response given by an individual. The recorded test behaviors and response for each child will give clues to possible deficit learning areas and contributing factors that inerfere with learning. Results also will determine programming for that child, guide teaching techniques, aid in the development of coping skills, and help set realistic expectations for that child's abilities and skill development.

The process of learning takes place in integrated states that cannot be specifically broken down chronologically. Piaget stated that stages can vary according to the individual's experience and inherited possibilities (Wadsworth, 1971). Learning is not a simple process and is continuous throughout life.

Selected specialized and general assessment tests are discussed and tasks are analyzed here to demonstrate how the examiner can determine perceptual, language, and learning problems that might delay reading readiness skills and interfere with cognitive development. All the tests analyzed are to be used with regular test procedures and language requirements and are administered in a one-on-one evaluation session.

Intelligence Tests
WPPSI and WISC-R

The WPPSI (Wechsler, 1967), for children ages 3 to 7 years 3 months, is similar to the WISC-R (Wechsler, 1974), approrpriate for ages 6 years to 16 years 11 months, in form and content. Both tests are useful for planning special school programs and pinpointing weak skill areas that might reflect lack of school readiness for the preschool- or school-age child (see Table 13-3). Visual and visual–motor perceptual development is necessary for successful completion of the many of the Wechsler subtests; consequently, when these skills are poorly developed they can be identified as areas in need of remediation and curriculum programming (Sattler, 1974).

McCarthy Scales of Children's Abilities

The MSCA (McCarthy, 1972) comprise verbal, perceptual, quantitative, memory, and gross

TABLE 13.3
PERCEPTUAL-MOTOR SKILLS ASSESSED BY THE WPPSI and WISC-R[b]

Subtest	Skills Tapped	Related Observation
Animal Pegs[a] Child matches symbolic house with color code by manipulating colored pegs	Shape constancy; color constancy; receptive language for understanding directions: auditory discrimination; fine motor coordination; visual memory; motor recall	Hand dominance; crossing of midline; speed of response; endurance; distractibility reaction to stress
Picture Completion[a,b] Child identified missing portion of stimulus pictures	Language (names of items); visual closure; visual discrimination	Visual problem (head tilting, covering one eye, eye rubbing); attentiveness
Picture Arrangement[b] Child sequences visual stories into logical order of events	Organization; planning; visualization of stories; cause and effect relationships	Knowledge of left and right; stress level; revealing perceptual deficits
Mazes[a,b] Child draws line within the confines of a maze	Visual–conceptual symbolization; language development to follow directions; fine motor coordination; auditory sequential memory	Hand dominance, lack of previous experience with a pencil; attention span; low critical listening skills
Geometric Designs[a] Child draws specific shapes	Fine motor coordination; shape constancy; visual sequential memory; position in space; directionality	Hand preference; method pencil held; use of space awareness of Gestalt relationship of design types of developmental errors (for clues to perceptual problems)
Block Design[a,b] Child copies a stimulus design with colored blocks	Fine motor coordination; spatial orientation; figure ground; directionality	Type of problem in reproduction (Gestalt, color, direction, number of blocks); awareness of mistakes but unable to correct; method of problem solving
Object Assembly[a,b] Child assembles related puzzle pieces	Fine motor dexterity; spatial organization; comprehend directions	Awareness of visual clues; method of organization and problem solving; reaction to stress
Coding[b] Child reproduces abstract symbols	Fine motor dexterity; figure ground; spatial orientation; numbers/symbol matching; short-term visual memory	Speed of reproduction; visual problems (previously noted); tolerance for pressure; activity level; automatic number sequencing

[a] WPPSI (Wechsler, 1989)
[b] WISC-R (Wechsler, 1974)

and fine motor tasks for children 2½ to 8½ years of age. To respond to the various subtests the child must first understand the instruction and comprehend the intent of the questions. Also, to solve the Block Building subtest, the child must be able to balance and stack blocks, be visually aware of spatial relations, and use fine motor skills to copy the model structure correctly.

The Puzzle Solving subtest is a timed test that requires the child to assemble simple puzzles of commonly known objects. The child must comprehend the directions, understand the terms for the object presented in the puzzle, visually perceive the relationship of the colors and lines of each segment, and use fine motor coordination and dexterity to assemble the segments.

The Tapping Sequence test uses a four-key xylophone on which notes are played in a given sequence to be copied by the child. The child's response is affected by his or her coordination and ability to attend to the correct stimuli. Some children are so intent upon making their responses sound right that they tap a key repeatedly, thereby producing a different and incorrect sequence of sounds. The perceptual skills of position in space and spatial relations, auditory sequential memory, and visual sequential memory skills are involved on this test.

The Right-Left Orientation subtest requires laterality and directionality development in relation to one's own body and the picture of another child. This test, presented only to children 5 years and older, measures whether the child knows the various parts of his or her body and is able to follow simple directions involving left and right orientation. The child must be able to reverse the left-right body orientation when relating these concepts across from him- or herself, as in a mirror image.

In the Arm Coordination subtest a small rubber ball is bounced like a basketball and a bean bag is caught and thrown, and thrown at a small target. To perform these tasks, near and far vision, tracking, and convergence visual skills are needed. The child must have knowledge of where his or her body is in relation to space and to the ball or bean bag to catch successfully. The child must be able to aim and project an object into space at an intended location, hitting the target six feet away.

The child draws simple designs in the first three items of the Draw-A-Design subtest and copies complex designs in the later items. Many visual skills and visual–motor coordination skills are assessed, such as figure-ground perception, visual discrimination, shape constancy, visual sequential memory, and fine motor coordination skills. The child's method of organizing material should be observed. The examiner also should note the child's method of holding the pencil, because a poor technique can inhibit the results, and if not corrected can later cause problems in speed, slant, and so on, of writing. The examiner should watch for left to right progression of the written material as the child performs. How aware is the child of the details and Gestalt of the design? Does the child make corrections if the results do not match the stimulus design? Is the child satisfied with the results, or are the child's expectations less than his or her ability level indicates? Which hand is preferred for writing? The throwing and catching arm and hand might be different from the writing hand. How does the child hold his or her head in relation to the paper?

The child is requested to draw a person of the same gender in the Draw-A-Child subtest. It is graded for fine motor, perceptual, and general cognition scores. To perform adequately, the youngster must have some awareness of his or her body and the interrelationship of the parts to each other. A child who lacks previous experience with drawing and working with a pencil will have a lower score on this fine motor coordination test.

The child works with blocks of different colors, sizes, and shapes on the Conceptual Grouping subtest. The child must attend, critically listen and recall directions to perform this task successfully. There are many perceptual terms, such as color, size, and shape concepts, that the child must understand and use to generalize and classify the blocks.

Because of the involvement of perception in many of the McCarthy subtests, this test is an effective tool for identifying possible perceptual delays or problems.

Stanford-Binet Intelligence Scale: Fourth Edition

The Binet IV discontinued the age-scale organization but kept the variety of tasks. Each subtest appraises a specific cognitive ability in a developing hierarchy from easy to more difficult. The subtests for Cognitive Ability, Verbal Reasoning, Quantitation Reasoning, Abstract/Visual

Reasoning, and Short-Term Memory are divided into a three-level hierarchical cognitive model. The first level of that model is an assessment of general ability. Level two appraises abilities that are influenced by experiences gained in and out of school. For example, the Verbal Reasoning subtests include pictorial identification of common objects, definition of common vocabulary words, verbal comprehension, pictorial absurdities, and verbal relations. The abstract/visual reasoning sections include subtests that involve pattern analysis, copying, matrices, paper folding, and cutting. The last level involves short-term memory with bead memory, memory for sentences, memory for digits, and memory for objects as the various subtest divisions.

To identify the objects depicted on the pictorial vocabulary task, the child must have adequate visual acuity to focus on specific details, and visual discrimination to form generalizations and classification skills. Visual discrimination skill requirements include visual closure, objects constancy, and figure–ground abilities. Vocabulary definition requires auditory skill analysis and the ability to form a visual imagery of the object to cognitively generalize the object's use, meaning, or interpretation. The Absurdities subtest require a host of perceptual skills, including: visual closure, cognitive awareness, visual discrimination, figure-ground, visual association, and visual recall. As the visual content progresses in difficulty, more and more logical associations and previous practical experience are needed for a correct response.

Two sections of the Abstract/Visual Reasoning subtest are normed for young children. The first subtest, Pattern Analysis, assesses shape and directional constancy of the original configuration, fine motor dexterity, visual memory, and position in space.

The Copying subtest begins with blocks laid flat on the desk in a design that is to be produced by the child and copied by the examinee. Visual memory for the recall of the design, figure-ground and position in space in relation to the design parts, mirror image or reversals, as well as the stimulus design skills, become more of influencing factors as the distance between the examiner's copy and the child's version increase. Some children will have difficulty seeing the total Gestalt of the design, instead, perceiving the design as separate unrelated blocks.

The more advanced copying section involves a developmental sequence of stimulus forms or designs to be reproduced in the record booklet. Fine motor coordination to hold a pencil and reproduce the design, visual discrimination, shape, constancy, position in space, laterality and directionality for the correct angles, and short-term visual recall of the design to be reproduced are necessary skills for success.

To succeed on the Binet Quantitative subtests the child needs visual skills including acuity, discrimination, figure–ground, and the ability to associate what is received through the auditory channel with the visual stimulus before the quantitative problem is solved by a verbal response.

The last two subtests involve short-term memory analysis in the form of bead visual memory and auditory sequential memory for sentences. The test begins with a visual representation of all the colors and various shapes of beads to be used in the solution. A child who has not learned that a pictorial form symbolizes the object will have difficulty with this test. The plastic beads laid out in front of the child might elicit more accurate visual memory than representation in a picture. Visual discrimination, form constancy, color constancy, spatial relationship, visual sequential memory, laterality, and figure–ground problems can interfere with the child's ability to recall correctly what he sees. The more advanced segment of the visual sequential memory task involves placing the appropriate beads onto a stick in their proper order after the visual stimulus has been removed. If a child has not internalized the directional concepts of *top* and *bottom*, the beads might be reversed.

The child is shown a single pictorial representation of a common object in the Memory for Objects task. The sequence begins with two singletons. Afterwards, a group picture with other nonessential items is shown, the child is to identify, in order of presentation, the objects seen. Shape and color constancy, figure–ground skills, visual discrimination, and visual sequential recall for the correct order of the presented objects are some of the visual perceptual skills that are prerequisite for success.

Test of Nonverbal Intelligence

The Test of Nonverbal Intelligence-2 (TONI-2) (Brown, Sherbenou, & Johnsen, 1990) was developed to evaluate intelligence when the traditional methods, procedures, or tools are not successful. The test was designed to be used with persons who do not speak English, aphasics, retarded, learning disabled, deaf, or culturally different persons. To solve problems on the TONI, the subject must identify the correct geometric figure that completes a stimulus set. The child must study the differences or similarities of the figures, identify the problem solving rule, and identify the correct figure from among the distractors. All of the stimulus symbols include one or more of the properties of shape: position, rotation, contiguity, shading, size or length, movement, and patterns within the figure (Brown, Sherbenou, & Johnsen, 1990).

Visual perceptual skills are required to solve the various TONI-2 items. Visual reception, visual discrimination, identification of directional differences, and the ability to differentiate central and background figures are requisite skills for success.

Southern California Sensory Integration Tests

The Southern California tests (Ayres, 1972b) are designed for children 4 to 8 years of age, with some subtests applicable to children up to 10 years, 11 months. The tests are divided into visual–spatial, perceptual–motor, and tactile-kinesthetic areas. As standardized neuropsychological tests, they are useful in evaluating children for sensory integrative dysfunction; but because of low reliability, they are not generally recommended for reevaluation during treatment. These tests are difficult to administer; the examiner must skillfully perform the required demonstrations and must be alert to many behaviors to score the subtests. See Table 13-4 for a description of the subtests.

Slingerland Screening Tests for Identifying Children with Specific Language Disability

The primary purpose for the Slingerland tests (Slingerland, 1975) is to identify children with language related perceptual–motor problems, such as abnormal or delayed development, and to pinpoint the type of perceptual difficulty (visual, auditory, or kinesthetic) that underlies the language problem. The test can be used to demonstrate strengths and weaknesses in the learning modalities and help classroom teachers choose appropriate methods and materials for each child. The

battery helps identify children who, because of superior intelligence, are able to compensate for perceptual–motor inadequacy at levels required in lower grades but not at higher levels of complexity.

Three forms of the test are designed for different grade levels. Form A, for grades 1 and 2, is discussed here. The perceptual motor tasks are the same for all grades, differing in vocabulary only; therefore, the various forms can be used in subsequent grades for assessing gains from remediation.

Tests 1 and 2 require copying at near and far points and require visual perception along with a kinesthetic response. Visual discrimination of shape, shape constancy, sequence of symbols, eye–hand coordination, spatial orientation, laterality and directionality, visual sequencing of letters, and organization of material with only momentary memory are other perceptual factors required for solution.

Test 3 requires short-term visual perception, memory of words, letters, and numbers seen briefly in the task of matching the recalled item to the correct one in a group of items. Rotations and similarity of configuration require visual discrimination with a fine motor response.

Test 4 eliminates memory in a visual–motor matching task that requires a motor response with a word, symbol, and sequence discrimination and perception. Rotations and similar word configurations are possible problems. The skills involve fine eye–hand coordination, position in space, laterality, directionality, and spatial orientation.

Auditory memory, visual perception, and kinesthetic-motor performance are skills tapped on Test 5. The child listens to a brief description and marks the appropriate picture. Figure–ground problems, low language understanding, and poor visual discrimination skills can interfere with the child's performance.

Test 6 links visual–kinesthetic motor association with auditory perception and memory by requiring production of dictated letters after a brief period of distraction and delay. Letter constancy, visual memory, figure–ground perception, visual discrimination, and aural–visual letter association are skills needed for solution.

Test 7 assesses the auditory–visual–kinesthetic linkage by requiring discrimination of various shapes and designs. Visual discrimination is not a required skill, but auditory perception–dis-

TABLE 13.4
SUBTESTS OF THE SOUTHERN CALIFORNIA SENSORY INTEGRATION TESTS

VISUAL—SPATIAL SUBTESTS
Space Visualization: Child manipulates and places forms. Requires visual perception of form and space and mental manipulation of objects in space.
Figure—Ground Perception: Child selects superimposed foreground figures from competing backgrounds.
Position in Space: Child is required to recognize simple geometric forms presented in different directional orientations or different sequences.
Design Copying: Child copies geometric dot-to-dot designs, a visual-motor task.
Motor Accuracy: Child attempts to keep a pencil moving directly along a printed line. Right and left hands are used separately.

TACTILE—KINESTHETIC SUBTESTS
Kinesthesia: Child must replicate a movement after the examiner has moved the child's finger to successive points and returned each time to the starting point. (Vision is occluded during this subtest.)
Manual Form Perception: Child matches successive geometric forms held in his or her hand to the same shape among a group pictured on a card. The task requires matching visual perceptions with tactile and kinesthetic perceptions.
Finger Identification: Child is required to touch the finger on one of his or her hands that was just touched by the examiner. Vision is occluded while the child is touched, but not when the child touches his or her own finger.
Graphesthesia: Child attempts to reproduce a design that has been drawn on the back of the child's hand by the examiner while the child's vision was occluded.
Localization of Tactile Stimuli: With the child's vision occluded, the examiner touches the child on one of his or her arms or hands, after which the child attempts to touch the same spot with his or her finger. Distance between the child's fingertip and the stimulus spot is measured.
Double Tactile Stimuli Perception: Child attempts to point to two places touched simultaneously by the examiner on the cheeks, the hands, or one cheek and one hand. The examiner notes whether the child is aware of both stimuli.

PERCEPTUAL—MOTOR SUBTESTS
Imitation of Postures: Child is required to reproduce body positions assumed quickly by the examiner, necessitating motor planning.
Crossing the Midline of the Body: Child attempts to mirror motions on his or her own body as the examiner points to the eyes or ears on his or her own body. Motor planning and midline crossing abilities are required for ease of performance.
Bilateral Motor Coordination: Child attempts to accurately and rhythmically reproduce the examiner's hand movements, which requires smooth use of arms working together as well as motor planning ability.
Right-Left Discrimination: Child must make right-left discriminations in relationship to himself, the examiner, and a pencil held in front of him or her on either side. Few children under the age of six can successfully accomplish these items.
Standing Balance—Eyes Open: Child balances on one foot with eyes open.
Standing Balance—Eyes Closed: With eyes closed optical righting information is eliminated, forcing the child to rely primarily on labyrinthine (inner ear) righting mechanisms.

crimination/sequencing–memory must be associated with the inner visual–kinesthetic memory.

Test 8 involves aural comprehension of a short story. The child is to mark the correct picture. To respond successfully, visual memory, language comprehension, auditory memory, figure–ground discrimination, and visual and auditory discrimination skills are necessary.

Test 9 requires kinesthetic responses to visual perceptual stimuli as the child copies a chart of shapes and letters from a distance. Near and far vision, figure–ground perception, visual discrimination, shape constancy of the complete Gestalt of the figure, visual memory, and motor memory with a fine motor reproduction are necessary skills.

The results of the Slingerland tests provide valuable information on the youngster's specific style of learning and problem-solving approach as well as indications of nonfunctioning pathways of learning.

Grassi Basic Cognitive Evaluation

A perceptual test, the Grassi (Grassi, 1973) resulted from 15 years of experience and studies of young children who did not achieve as expected. This test can be used as a screening device for early childhood programs. All of the exercises involve left-to-right orientation, laterality, and directionality. Grassi did not standardize the verbal directions for each subtest, and it is left to the examiner to explain the subtests, which consist of five sections: color, form, size, color-form, and color-size.

The Visual Discrimination section evaluates visual discrimination and color constancy. The child must be able to focus on the various circles of color and match each with another circle of the same color. If a youngster has a figure–ground problem, the colors seem to "pop" off the page, blur, or move around. Children who have any type of color blindness have difficulty with this test. If color blindness is suspected, further responses should be elicited using other values and intensities of the hue. Color constancy and awareness of colors are concepts needed for success.

In the Geometric Figures subtest, the child matches geometric figures with the one correct response for each shape. Visual discrimination problems, shape constancy problems, and figure–ground problems will interfere with the child's response.

The child matches shapes in different sizes in the Size subtest. Visual discrimination, shape constancy, figure–ground problems, and size constancy problems will interfere with the child's correct motor response.

Three colors and six shapes are used on the Color–Form subtest. The child is to match the correct color and shape of a geometric figure. Visual discrimination, figure–ground, shape constancy, and color constancy problems will interfere with the results. Color, shape, and size awareness help a child organize and categorize objects; all of these concepts involve vocabulary and some understanding of these terms.

On the Color–Size subtest the child must match two concepts—the size and color of the circle; this requires size and color constancy. Figure–ground and visual discrimination problems could interfere with the child's responses.

The Concepts section has subtests that evaluate premath and spatial concepts. On the first subtest, Positions, the child matches boxes and the position of a ball in relation to each box. The exercise involves the vocabulary concerning the position of the ball in space on the two-dimensional paper. The concepts include body image and the child's experience with the words *on top of, inside of,* and *below.* Critical listening skills, short–term auditory memory, visual discrimination, and figure–ground perception are needed to follow the directions and perform the task.

The Quantity subtest requires the child to identify and match circles containing a given number of dots. The concepts *same, fewer,* and *more* are assessed, and previous experience with visual discrimination, figure–ground perception, and position in space are skills needed to perform the exercise. Form constancy, and generalization of the original circle and its dots might interfere with the child's response, because the child might respond to the dot design instead of counting the dots.

In the Length subtest the child visually discriminates the length of a line. The terms involved include *same size, longer,* and *shorter.* Figure–ground skills, size constancy, position in space, and spatial relations are requisite for success.

The child uses the terms *thicker, thinner,* and the *same* to compare lines that vary in thickness on the Density subtest. In addition to understanding the vocabulary, visual discrimination, size constancy, figure–ground perception, and position in space skills are needed.

In the Spatial subtest, a black ball is placed either in front of or behind a white box. The child needs the perceptual skills involved in the visual discrimination of the position of the ball in relation to the box and body awareness skills. Previous experience with the directional terms as well as awareness of the ball on the *left* or *right* side of the box will increase the child's score. If the child attends to the directionality of the ball, rather than the position of the ball in relation to the box, the score will be depressed.

Basic Identification (of colors, numbers, and letters) is the third section of the test: The child names three primary colors, two secondary colors, and one neutral color; color constancy and recall of the names is necessary to do this successfully. The child identifies numerals to 12, out of sequence; long-term visual memory, visual association of the numeral and its name, shape constancy, and recall of numbers in and out of sequence (visual and auditory sequential memory) are the necessary skills; laterality and directionality problems will be a hindrance. Recognition of the capital/lowercase letters of the alphabet out of sequence involves many perceptual skills. The child must be able visually to focus on and discriminate the letter, use visual memory and shape constancy, and associate the name with the visual image, to identify each letter correctly.

Orientation of numbers, letters, and words is the fourth section. On the Numbers subtest the child matches various number combinations in which there are possible reversals. Laterality and directionality skills are the main concern.

The child matches lowercase letters of the alphabet in which there are possible reversals on the Letters subtest. Laterality and directionality skills are the target of task analysis.

On the last subtest of this section the child matches 12 words that are often transposed by readers. Laterality, directionality, position of space, figure–ground, and word closure problems will interfere with the child's performance.

In the Visualization section the child matches partially completed forms with the finished image presented below the examples. Closure, shape constancy, position in space, figure–ground, and directionality problems will interfere with the child's results. A child might draw in the rest of the form with his or her finger, thereby giving some visual clue to that child's method of learning and concrete visualization level.

Quantity understanding is evaluated as the child matches figure units to figure units (i.e., : :), symbol to figure units, and figure units to symbol (is a simple math operation). The child must have number value awareness and sequential memory of the number in both the auditory and visual channels, one-to-one correspondence for the number match, and general configuration value of the figural unit to solve the tasks.

The Kinesthetic section involves the fine motor reproduction of five drawn geometric shapes; the child copies each in a box from left to right. This exercise requires short-term visual memory, shape constancy, laterality and directionality, position in space, and fine motor coordination skills.

The next fine motor exercise rqeuires the child to write his or her name. Fine motor coordination and the previously listed perceptual skills are needed for success, as well as long-term memory of the letters to be written and recall of correct sequential order. The examiner observes the manner in which the child holds the pencil, the amount of pressure exerted, possible reversals, words or letters erased, and so forth.

The Visual Sequencing section requires the child to match (one line at a time) three lines of sequences of shapes, one line of number sequence, and two lines of letter sequences. The necessary skills include shape constancy, laterality, directionality, line progression, number constancy, and letter constancy. The figure–ground problem is eliminated by covering up all the lines except the one being solved by the child.

The Revisualization subtest consists of a card of geometric shapes in a sequence, which is observed and remembered by the child. The child views a card with a series of three different sequences of shapes and identifies the sequence on the original card. Short-term visual sequential memory, shape constancy, laterality, and directionality are necessary perceptual skills.

Purdue Perceptual–Motor Survey

The Purdue (Kephart & Roach, 1966) is difficult to interpret unless the examiner has had previous experience with children of various ages with or without perceptual problems. The Purdue is a survey, not a test. It can identify perceptual–motor areas that are in need of training or experiences for development. The survey is divided into five basic perceptual motor areas.

In the Balance of Posture section the child performs various activities on a $2'' \times 4''$ walking board placed on brackets. This subsection evaluates the integration of locomotion skills. The child's confidence on the board, resistance or relaxed movement, body posture, and general balance are observed. Jumping exercises are included in this area to detect problems in laterality, body image, rhythm, and neuromuscular control.

The second section of the Purdue involves body parts. Body awareness, identification, and control are encompassed by the term body image. The child is requested to touch various parts of his or her body as named by the examiner in the Body Identification subtest. On the Imitation of Movements subtest, the child copies unilateral, bilateral, and contralateral movements. The examiner observes the child's ability to control his or her limbs, isolate a movement without involvement on the opposite side of the body, and so on.

In the Obstacle Course subtest, the child must prejudge where his or her body is in space in relation to an object in the environment. This task requires balance, preplanning, motor control, position in space, and awareness of the body in relation to objects in the environment.

The Kraus-Weber section was standardized by Kraus and Hirshland (1954) to assess physical control and muscular fitness. This section is used as an indicator of attention span. Muscle tone and reflex integration also are factors in performance.

The Angels-in-the-Snow section requires the child to complete lateral and bilateral as well as combinations of body movements with the limbs while lying on his or her back. The child's response to verbal versus tactile directions, ability to identify and move the correct limb, awareness of internal and external laterality, motor movement overflow or perseveration, and muscle resistance are some of the important observations made.

The third section, called Perceptual/Motor Match, involves fine motor reproduction and rhythmic writing on a chalkboard. While the child reproduces circles and lines with one and then both hands, the examiner observes for example, whether the child is able to match what he or she sees with a motor response or attend to the task for a length of time.

The child reproduces eight "motifs" in the Rhythmic Writing subtest. This task provides a visual and auditory example of the child's fine motor coordination and inner rhythm. The type of reproduction and the manner in which the child's body and its various parts respond are observed.

The Ocular Pursuit section allows the examiner to observe the child's eyes tracking an object in near vision. The smoothness of the pursuit, the ability to keep on target and regain the target once lost, and the activity of each eye and both together are observed in detail. Referral for further in-depth examination might be appropriate if the findings seem to be unusual.

Children with serious visual problems typically will experience learning problems as vision is one of the basic processes for gathering information (Greenstein, 1976; Sherman, 1973). Some examples of visual problems are an inability to fixate on an object without turning or moving the head, problems with transfer of fixation or steady fixation (Allen, 1977), or imbalance of the eye muscles (Ludlam, 1976).

The Visual Achievement Forms section requires the child to copy seven designs originated by Gesell (1949, 1947) and adapted to the Purdue Survey by Kephart (Ilg & Ames, 1972; Knoblock & Pasamanic, 1974). Lowder (1956) found a significant correlation between a child's ability to copy designs and school achievement.

Developmental Test of Visual–Motor Integration

A whole program has been developed for the assessment and remediation of fine motor skills based upon this developmental test (Beery & Buktenica, 1967). The child must focus on each design and copy it. Figure–ground perception, position in space, spatial relations, and fine visual motor integration and coordination are skills required to complete the test successfully.

Developmental Test of Visual Perception

Frostig's and coworkers' (1966) developmental test is designed to assess visual perception problems in five basic areas: Position in Space, Spatial Relations, Perceptual Constancy, Visual–Motor Coordination, and Figure–Ground Perception.

In the Visual–Motor section the child must focus between the lines and coordinate a fine motor line drawing between the lines. The Figure–Ground section requires the child to draw an outline of the shapes requested by the examiner. In the Form Constancy section the child needs shape constancy and eye–hand coordination to outline the specific shape given in the directions. In the Position in Space section the child must understand the terms *same* and *different*, comprehend the intent of the directions, visually discriminate the object's directionality, and mark the differing object on the first page and the same object on the second page. The Spatial Relations subtest requires the child to copy lines of various lengths and angles, using dots as guide points. Awareness of the object as an "integrated whole" is an important requisite for this task (Pitcher-Baker, 1975).

Motor Free Visual Perceptual Test

The motor-free test by Colarusso and Hammill (1972) is used to identify children with visual perceptual deficits. It is designed to evaluate visual memory and visual closure, but not the various other perceptual skills that can become involved in many perceptual assessment tests. Visual perceptual skills not assessed are visual discrimination, figure–ground perception, and visual association. The test is objectively and simply scored (Donovan & Mitchell, 1978).

Assessment Implications

Early childhood is the best time to identify perceptual–motor problems so that remediation can begin at once. According to the critical periods theory, when a child begins performing later skills over earlier skill performance deficiencies, there might be gaps in ability and slow progress. The child who has no severe problems, but is merely slightly delayed, also will benefit from preschool training that enhances school readiness.

Those responsible for the curriculum in early childhood education programs should develop specific goals for each child's developmental level. Perceptual considerations should be integrated into the child's overall general experiences and should not be taught in isolation.

Because P.L. 94-142 has strict requirements for the diagnosis of learning disabilities, few children in kindergarten or first grade receive remedial help. Those critical years might be wasted for children who could benefit from the unique, multidisciplinary instructional approach often used by resource specialists. The learning problems resulting from inadequate perceptual development in early childhood can inhibit conceptual and academic growth, possibly throughout a youngster's school years. Perceptual–motor development, as one of the foundations for cognitive development, can be enhanced by proper training. As more is learned about the CNS, its sensory processing, and the effects of various sensorimotor and academic treatment procedures, more specific and effective remediation methods will be developed.

Although assessment procedures can detect perceptual–motor dysfunction, they often cannot determine causes; simply labeling the problem does not ensure that remediation is possible. In some cases, identification of the problem makes remediation probable and provides clues for strategies that might help the child function better. A more intangible benefit to assessment is that the child, the parents, and the teachers can know the nature of the problem and deal with it with greater understanding. Children themselves might feel less inadequate if they have some comprehension of the nature of their difficulties and are shown how to use other sensory or perceptual avenues to compensate for their deficits.

There is insufficient research into the various perceptual–motor remediation methods to state with certainty which procedures are the most effective for specific problems. Some logical, but tentative, general conclusions can be drawn, however, from examination of current research and treatment reports. Because perception is based on sensation, as is motor functioning, methods that improve sensory abilities should be considered. Knowledge of developmental progression of sensory abilities helps in planning treatment or remediation. Although such developmental information is incomplete, thoughtful study of the available material is extremely helpful. In addition, by keeping abreast of educational research, such as in the area of aptitude–treatment interaction, one can pursue possible fruitful avenues of remediation (Cronbach & Snow, 1977).

Occupational therapists and physical therapists are being trained to provide services to developmentally delayed and LD children through complete sensorimotor treatment programs. At present, sensory integrative therapy, as it is commonly called, appears to be reaching beyond the pioneering stage, with effective techniques being developed to enhance a child's total sensorimotor integrative functioning (Weeks, 1982). Therapists providing sensory integrative therapy introduce sensory stimuli, usually through activities of a motoric nature, and work toward eliciting adaptive response behaviors in the child. As the CNS becomes better organized, and sensory stimuli are more effectively integrated, perceptual and motor behaviors improve. In some cases, this leads to improved academic performance and social behavioral changes, and self-concept also improves in many individuals. The interested reader can find numerous books and articles detailing sensory integrative treatment methods and results (Ayres, 1972a, 1979; Knickerbocker, 1980).

Remediation of perceptual–motor problems often has taken the form of physical education programs and visual–motor training. Some researchers have found academic benefits after such programs, but often the child improves only in the areas in which training occurred, with little or no carry-over to academic performance (Rosen, 1966). Some teachers and other specialists have tried multidisciplinary approaches in the teaching of reading, with varying success. The perceptual skills needed for reading are being studied, but confusion remains as to the relative importance of visual and auditory abilities, and in regard to intersensory aspects of reading. Berry (1969), in discussing speech and language learning, supported successive training by unisensory, bisensory, and multisensory stimuli, suggesting that some children might be able to process input from only one sensory modality at a time, while others might benefit from stimulus presentation through more than one sensory avenue.

Despite conflicting results regarding the relationship of perceptual–motor abilities or remediation to academic skills, it is apparent that perceptual–motor abilities form a foundation for the learning in many academic areas. The task at hand is to define clearly the skills that are important to specific academic learning and successful academic remedial programs must be designed. Given the different learning styles of children and the varying responses to treatment interventions, these are not easy tasks. It is not known to what degree basic sensorimotor or sensory integrative treatment programs improve performance in various academic skill areas, or which children might benefit from a sensorimotor program in addition to cognitive-style interventions, but continuing research should help provide answers.

REFERENCES

Abrams, D. I., & Meeker, M. (1980). Learning disabilities: A diagnostic and educational challenge. *Journal of Learning Disabilities, 13,* 492–495.

Adams, R. J., & Lambos, W. A. (1986). Developmental changes in response preparation to visual stimuli. *Perceptual and Motor Skill, 62,* 519–522.

Allen, M. J. (1977). Role of vision in learning disabilities. *Journal of Learning Disabilities, 10,* 411–415.

Ayres, A. J. (1972). An Interpretation of the Role of the Brain Stem in Intersensory Integration. In A. Henderson and J. Coryell, *The Body Senses and Perceptual Deficit,* symposium on somatosensory aspects of perceptual deficit. Boston.

Ayes, A. J. (1969). Relation between Gesell developmental quotients and later perceptual-motor performance. *American Journal of Occupational Therapy, 23,* 11–17.

Ayres, A. (1972a). *Sensory integration and learning disorders.* Los Angeles: Western Psychological Services.

Ayres, A. J. (1972b). *Southern California Sensory Integration Tests.* Los Angeles: Western Psychological Services.

Ayres, A. J. (1978). Learning disabilities and the vestibular system. *Journal of Learning Disabilities, 11* (1), 30–41.

Ayres, A. J. (1979). *Sensory integration and the child.* Los Angeles: Western Psychological Services.

Badian, N. A., & Wolff, P. H. (1977). Manual Asymmetries of Motor Sequencing in Boys with Reading Disability. *Cortex, 13,* 343–349.

Barbe, W. B., Swassing, R. H., & Milone, M. N., Jr. (1980). *Teaching Through Modality Strengths: Concepts and Practices.* Columbus, OH: Zaner-Bloser, Inc.

Bartley, S. H. (1969). *Principles of Perception* (2nd ed.). New York: Harper & Row.

Bauer, B. A. (1977). Tactile-sensitive behavior in hyperactive and non-hyperactive children. *American Journal of Occupational Therapy, 31,* 447–453.

Beery, K. K., & Buktenica, N. A. (1967). *Developmental test of visual-motor integration.* Chicago: Follett Educational Corporation.

Bergan, J. R. (1969). The Structure of Perception. Paper presented at the Spring Conference of Association of Study of Perception, Peoria, IL.

Berry, M. F. (1969). *Language disorder of children: The bases and diagnoses.* Englewood Cliffs, NJ: Prentice-Hall.

Birch, H. G., & Belmont, L. (1964). Auditory-visual integration in normal and retarded readers. *American Journal of Orthopsychiatry, 34,* 852–861.

Bishop, D. V. M., & Edmundson, S. (1987). Specific language impairment as a maturation language: Evidence from longitudinal data on language and motor development. *Developmental Medicine and Child Neurology, 29,* 442–459.

Black, F. (1976). Cognitive, academic, and behavioral findings in children with suspected neurological dysfunction. *Journal of Learning Disabilities, 9,* 182–187.

Boder, E. (1973a). Developmental dyslexia: A diagnostic

approach based on three atypical reading-spelling patterns. *Developmental Medicine and Child Neurology, 15,* 663–687.

Boder, E. (1973b). Developmental dyslexia: Prevailing concepts and a new diagnostic approach. *Bulletin of the Orton Society, 23,* 106–118.

Boder, E. (1971a). Developmental dyslexia: A diagnostic screening reading and spelling. In B. Bateman (Ed.). *Learning Disorders* (Vol. 4). Seattle: Special Child Publications.

Boder, E. (1971b). Developmental dyslexia: Prevailing diagnostic concepts and a new diagnostic approach. In H. R. Myklebust (Ed.). *Progress in Learning Disabilities* (Vol. II). New York: Grune & Stratton.

Broman, M., Rudel, R. G., Helgfott, E., & Krieger, J. (1986). Inter and intrahemispheric processing of letter stimuli by dyslexic children and normal readers. *Cortex, 22,* 447–459.

Boone, H. C. (1986). Relationship of left-right reversals to academic achievement. *Perceptual Motor Skills, 62,* 27–33.

Brown, B., Haegerstrom-Portnoy, O. D., Herron, J., et al. (1985). Static postural stability is normal in dyslexic children. *Journal of Learning Disabilities, 18,* 31–34.

Brown, L., Sherbenou, R. J., & Johnsen, S. K. (1990). Manual for the Test of Nonverbal Intelligence-2. Austin, TX: Pro-ed.

Brown, R. (1986). Teacher ratings and assessment of attention deficit disordered children. *Journal of Learning Disabilities, 19,* 95–100.

Bundy, A. C., & Fisher, A. G. (1980). The relationship of prone extension to other vestibular functions. *The American Journal of Occupation Therapy, 35,* 782–787.

Carbo, M. (1980). An analysis of the relationships between the modality preferences of kindergartners and selected reading treatments as they affect the learning of a basic sight-word vocabulary (Doctoral dissertation, St. John's University, New York, 1980)/Dissertation Abstracts International, 41-04A, 1389. (University Microfilms No. 80-21790).

Cermak, S. A., & Ayres, A. J. (1984). Crossing the body midline in learning-disabled and normal children. *The American Journal of Occupational Therapy, 38,* 35–39.

Chelune, G. J., Feguson, W., Koon, R., & Dickey, T. O. (1986). Frontal lobe disinhibition in attention deficit disorders. *Child Psychiatry and Human Development, 16*(4).

Clements, S. D. (1973). Minimal brain dysfunction in children. In S. Sapir & A. Nitzburg (Eds.). *Children with Learning Problems.* New York: Brunner/Mazel.

Cliff, S. (1979). *The development of reach and grasp.* El Paso, TX: Guynes.

Colarusso, R. P., & Gill, S. (1975). Selecting a test of visual perception. *Academic Therapy, XI* (Winter), 157–167.

Colarusso, R. P., & Hammill, D. D. (1972). *Motor-Free Visual Perception Test.* San Antonio, TX: The Psychological Corporation.

Conners, C. K. (1969). A teacher rating scale for use in drug studies with children. *American Journal of Psychiatry, 126,* 884–888.

Conrad, K. E., Cermak, S. A., & Drake, C. (1983). Differentiation of praxis among children. *The American Journal of Occupational Therapy, 37,* 466–473.

Cronbach, L. J., & Snow, R. E. (1977). *Aptitudes and Instructional Methods.* New York: Irvington.

DeGenaro, J. J. (1975). Informal diagnostic procedures: "What can I do before the psychometrist arrives?" *Journal of Learning Disabilities, 8,* 24–30.

DeHirsch, K., Jansky, J., & Langford, W. S. (1966). *Predicting Reading Failure.* New York: Harper & Row.

DeRenzi, E., Matti, F., & Nichelli, P. (1980). Imitating gestures: A quantitative approach to ideomotor apraxia. *Archives of Neurology, 37,* 6–10.

Dember, W. N., & Warm, J. S. (1979). *Psychology of Perception* (2nd Ed.). New York: Holt, Rinehart & Winston.

DeMyer, M. (1975). The nature of the neuropsychological disability in autistic children. *Journal of Autism and Childhood Schizophrenia, 5,* 109–127.

de Quiros, J. B. (1976). Diagnosis of vestibular disorders in the learning disabled. *Journal of Learning Disabilities, 9,* 39–47.

de Quiros, B., & Schrager, L. (1978). *Visual and Auditory Foundations of Learning: Neuropsychological Fundamentals in Learning Disabilities.* San Rafael, CA: Academic Publishers.

Donovan, G. L., & Mitchell, M. M. (1978). Analysis of the developmental test of visual perception and the motor-free visual perception test. *Perceptual and Motor Skills, 46,* 1248–1286.

Dunn, W. (1981). *A Guide to Testing Clinical Observations in Kindergartners.* Rockville, MD: American Occupational Therapy Association.

Dunn, R., & Dunn, K. (1968). *Teaching Students Through Their Individual Learning Styles.* Reston, VA: Reston Publishing Co.

Epstein, W. (1967). *Varieties of Perceptual Learning.* New York: McGraw-Hill.

Erhardt, R. P., Beaty, P. A., & Hertsgaard, D. M. (1981). A developmental prehension assessment for handicapped children. *American Journal of Occupational Therapy, 35,* 237–242.

Fishers, A. G., & Bundy, A. C. (1982). Equilibrium reactions in normal children and in boys with sensory integrative dysfunction. *The American Journal of Occupational Therapy, 2,* 171–183.

Fleishman, E. A., & Rich, S. (1963). Role of kinesthetic and spatial-visual abilities in perceptual motor learning. *Journal of Experimental Psychology, 66*, 6–11.

Flitcher, M. C., & Brandon, S. (1955). Myopia of prematurity. *American Journal of Ophthalmology, 40*, 4.

Friedrich, D., Fuller, G. B., & Davis, D. (1984). Learning disability: Fact & fiction. *Journal of Learning Disabilities, 17*, (4), 205–209.

Frostig, M., Lefever, W., & Whittlesey, J. R. B. (1966). *Developmental Test of Visual Perception.* Palo Alto: Consulting Psychologists Press.

Gensemer, I. B., Walker, J. C., & Gadman, T. E. (1976). Using the Peabody Picture Vocabulary Test with children having difficulty learning. *Journal of Learning Disabilities, 9*, 179–181.

Gesell, A., & Amatruda, C. (1947). *Developmental Diagnosis.* New York: Harper & Row.

Gesell, A., & Ilg, F. (1946). *The Child From Five to Ten.* New York: Harper & Row.

Gesell, A., Ilg, F. L., & Brellis, G. E. (1941). *Vision: Its Development in Infant and Child.* New York: Paul B. Hoeber, Inc.

Gibson, E. J. (1969). *Principles of Perceptual Learning and Development.* New York: Appleton-Century-Crofts.

Gibson, J. J. (1966). *The Senses Considered as Perceptual Systems.* Boston: Houghton Mifflin.

Goldfarb, W. (1964). An investigation of childhood schizophrenia. *Archives of General Psychiatry, 11*, 620–631.

Goodgold-Edwards, S. A. (1984). Motor learning as it relates to the development of skilled motor behavior: A review of the literature. *Physical and Occupational Therapy in Pediatrics, 4* (4), 5–18.

Gordon, N. (1986). Left-handedness and learning. *Developmental Medicine and Child Neurology, 28*, 656–661.

Grassi, J. R. (1973). *Grassi Basic Cognition Evaluation.* Miami, FL: University of Miami.

Greenstein, T. (1976). *Vision and Learning.* St. Louis: American Optometric Association.

Gubbay, S. S. (1978). The management of development apraxia. *Developmental Medicine & Child Neurology, 20*, 643–646.

Gubbay, S. S., Ellis, E., Walton, N. J., & Court, S. D. M. (1965). *Clumsy children: A study of apraxic and agnosic defects in 21 children. Brain, 88*, 295–312.

Halverson, C., & Victor, J. (1976). Minor physical anomalies and problem behavior in elementary school children. *Child Development, 47*, 281–285.

Hartlage, L. C., & Lucas, D. G. (1973). *Mental development evaluation of the pediatric patient.* Springfield, IL: Charles C. Thomas.

Henderson, A., & Duncombe, L. (1982). Development of kinesthetic judgments of angle and distance. *The Occupational Therapy Journal of Research, 2*, 131–144.

Henderson, S. E., & Hall, D. (1982). Concomitants of clumsiness in young school children. *Developmental Medicine and Child Neurology, 24*, 448–460.

Herscher, L. (1985). The effectiveness of behavior modification on hyperkinesis. *Child Psychiatry & Human Development, 16*(2), 87–96.

Hessler, G. L., & Kitchen, D. W. (1980). Language characteristics of a purposeful sample of early elementary learning disabled students. *Learning Disability Quarterly, 3*, 36–41.

Hessler, G. L. (1982). Use and Interpretation of the Woodcock-Johnson Psycho-Educational Battery. Hingham, MA.

Ilg, F. L., & Ames, L. B. (1972). *School readiness: Behavior tests used at the Gesell Institute.* New York: Harper & Row.

Indiana State Department of Public Instruction. (1972). *Guide to early developmental training.* Lafayette, IN: Wabash Center for the Mentally Retarded.

Johnson, D. L., & Myklebust, H. R. (1967). *Learning Disabilities: Educational Principles and Practices.* Orlando, FL: Grune & Stratton.

Kamakura, N., Matsuo, M., & Ishii, H. (1980). Patterns of static prehension in normal hands. *American Journal of Occupational Therapy, 34*, 437–445.

Kaufman, N. A. (1978). Occupational therapy theory, assessment, and treatment in educational settings. In H. L. Hopkins & H. D. Smith (Eds.). *Willard and Spackman's Occupational Therapy.* New York: Lippincott.

Kavale, K., & Andreassen, E. (1984). Factors in diagnosing the learning disabled: Analysis of judgmental policies, *Journal of Learning Disabilities, 17*, 273–278.

Keating, N. R. (1979). A comparison of duration of nystagmus as measured by the Southern California Postrotary Nystagmus Test and electronystagmography. *American Journal of Occupational Therapy, 33*, 92–97.

Kenny, T. J., & Clemons, R. L. (1971). Medical and psychological correlates in children with learning disabilities. *Journal of Pediatrics, 78*, 273–277.

Keough, B. K. (1971). A compensatory model for psychoeducational evaluation of children with learning disorders. *Journal of Learning Disabilities, 4*, 544–548.

Kephart, N. C., & Roach, E. G. (1966). *Purdue Perceptual-Motor Survey.* Columbia, OH: Charles E. Merrill.

Kimura, D., & Archibald, Y. (1974). Motor function of the left hemisphere. *Brain, 97*, 337–350.

Kirk, S. A. (1972). *Educating exceptional children.* Boston: Houghton Mifflin.

Knickerbocker, B. M. (1980). A holistic approach to the

treatment of learning disorders. Thorofare, NJ: SLACK.

Knoblock, H., & Pasamanick, B. (Eds.) (1974). *Gesell and Amatruda's Developmental Diagnosis* (3rd ed.). New York: Harper & Row.

Kolb, D. (1983). *Experiential Learning: Experience as the Source of Learning and Development.* Englewood Cliffs, NJ: Prentice-Hall.

Koppitz, E. M. (1977). *The Visual Aural Digit Span Test.* Orlando, FL: Grune & Stratton.

Kraus, H., & Hirschland, R. P. (1954). Minimum muscular fitness tests in school children. *Research Quarterly, 25*(1), 178–188.

Larson, C. E. (1968). Perceptual Development in Young Children. *Journal of Association of Study of Perception, 3,* 11–18.

Laszlo, J. I., & Balrstow, P. J. (1980). The measurement of kinaestetic sensitivity in children and adults. *Developmental Medicine and Child Neurology, 22,* 454–464.

Lee, A. M. (1977). Relationship between birth weight and perceptual motor performance in children. *Perceptual and Motor Skills, 45,* 119–122.

Llorens, L. (1968). Identification of the Ayres' syndromes in emotionally disturbed children: An exploratory study. *American Journal of Occupational Therapy, 22,* 286–288.

Lowder, R. B. (1956). *Perceptual abilities and school achievement: An exploratory study.* Winter Haven, FL: Winter Haven Lion's Club.

Ludlam, W. (1976). Review of the psychophysiological factors in visual information processes as they relate to learning. In T. Greenstein (Ed.). *Vision and Learning.* St. Louis: Americfan Optometric Association.

Lundberg, A. (1979). The drawing test: A tool for assessment of arm-hand function in children 1-3 years of age. *Neuropaediatrie, 10,* 29–34.

Mandler, J. M., & Robinson, C. A. (1978). Developmental changes in picture recognition. *Journal of Experimental Child Psychology, 26,* 122–236.

Martin, H. P., Gilfoyle, E. M., Fischer, H. L., & Greuter, B. B. (1969). Assessment of perceptual development. *American Journal of Occupation Therapy, 23,* 387–396.

McCarthy, D. O. (1972). McCarthy Scales of Children's Abilities. San Antonio, TX: The Psychological Corporation.

McGee, M. G. (1979). "Human Spatial Abilities: Psychometric Studies and Environmental Genetic, Hormonal and Neurological Influences." *Psychological Bulletin, 86,* 889–918.

McKim, R. H. (1980). *Experiences in Visual Thinking.* (2nd ed.). Monterey, CA: Brooks/Cole.

McNutt, G. (1986). The status of learning disabilities in the states: Concensus or controversy? *Journal of Learning Disabilities, 19,* 12–16.

Meeker, M. (1980). *Developmental visions: Assessing its implications for learning and school achievement.* El Segundo, CA: SOI Institute.

Merrill, D. W., & Reid, R. H. (1981). *Personal Styles and Effective Performance.* Rador, PA: Chilton Book Co.

Moffitt, M. W. R. (1972). Play as a medium for learning. *Journal of Health, Physical Education, and Recreation, 43*(6), 45–47.

Mussen, P. H., Conger, J. S., & Kagan, J. (1974). *Child Development and Personality* (4th ed.). New York: Harper & Row.

Nass, R. (1983). Ontogenesis of hemispheric specialization: Apraxia associated with congenital left hemisphere lesions. *Perceptual and Motor Skills, 57,* 775–782.

Newcomer, PL. L., & Magee, P. A. (1977). The performance of learning (reading) disabled children on a test of spoken language. *The Reading Teacher, 30,* 896–900.

Noller, K., & Ingrisano, D. (1984). Cross-sectional study of gross and fine motor development: Birth to six years of age. *Physical Therapy, 64*(3), 308–316.

Obrzut, J. E., Boliek, C. A. (1986). Lateralization characteristics in disabled children. *Journal of Learning Disabilities, 19*(5), 308–314.

Ottenbacher, K. (1978). Identifying vestibular processing dysfunction in learning disabled children. *American Journal of Occupational Therapy, 32,* 217–221.

Ottenbacher, K., Watson, P. J., & Short, M. A (1979). Association between nystagmus hyporesponsivity and behavioral problems in learning disabled children. *American Journal of Occupational Therapy,* 317–322.

Ottenbacher, K. (1980). Excessive postrotary nystagmus duration in learning disabled children. *American Journal of Occupational Therapy, 34,* 40–44.

Ottenbacher, K. (1983). Developmental implications of clinically applied vestibular simulation. *Physical Therapy, 63,* 338–342.

Piaget, J., & Inhelder, B. (1976). *The Child's Conception of Space.* New York: Norton.

Pitcher-Baker, G. (1975). *Clinical and Psychometric Merits of the Frostig Developmental Test of Visual Perception.* Lafayette, In: St. Elizabeth Hospital Medical Center.

Polatajko, H. J. (1985). A critical look at vestibular dysfunction in learning-disabled children. *Developmental Medicine and Child Neurology, 27,* 283–292.

Polatajko, H. J. (1987). Visual-ocular control of normal and learning-disabled children. *Development Medicine and Child Neurology, 29,* 477–485.

Richman, L. C. (1979). Language variables related to reading ability of children with verbal deficits. *Psychology in the Schools, 16,* 299–305.

Rider, B. (1973). Perceptual-motor dysfunction in emotionally disturbed children. *American Journal of Occupational Therapy, 26,* 316–320.

Rosen, C. L. (1966). An experimental study of visual perceptual training and reading achievement in first grade. *Perceptual and Motor Skills, 22,* 979–986.

Ross, A. O. (1980). Psychological Disorders of Children. New York: McGraw-Hill.

Rourke, B. P. (1978). Reading, spelling, arithmetic disabilities. A Neuro-psychologic perspective. In H. R. Mykleburst (Ed.). *Progress in Learning Disabilities* (Vol. 4). Orlando, FL: Grune & Stratton.

Rourke, B. P., & Telegdy, G. A. (1971). Lateralization significance of WISC verbal-performance discrepancies for older children with learning disabilities. *Perceptual and Motor Skills, 33,* 875–883.

Sadick, T. L., & Ginsburg, B. E. (1978). The development of the lateral functions and reading ability. *Cortex, 14,* 3–11.

Sapir, S. G., & Wilson, B. A. (1973). A developmental scale to assist in the prevention of learning disability. In S. G. Sapir & A. C. Nitzburg (Eds.). *Children with Learning Problems.* New York: Brunner/Mazel.

Sattler, J. M. (1974). *Assessment of Children's Intelligence.* Philadelphia: Saunders.

Scarpati, S., & Swanson, L. (1980). Implicit verbal coding of visual information from normal and learning disabled readers. *Perceptual and Motor Skills, 51,* 1158.

Schaaf, R. C. (1985). The frequency of vestibular disorders in developmentally delayed preschoolers with otitis media. *The American Journal of Occupational Therapy, 34,* 247–242.

Sherman, A. (1973). Relating vision disorders to learning disability. *Journal of the American Optometric Association, 44,* 140–141.

Siev, E., & Freishtat, B. (1976). *Perceptual Dysfunction in the Adult Stroke Patient.* Charles B. Slack.

Silberzahn, M. (1975). Sensory integrative function in a child guidance clinic population. *American Journal of Occupation Therapy, 29,* 29–34.

Slingerland, B. H. (1975). *A Multi-sensory Approach to Language Arts for Specific Language Disability Children: A Guide for Primary Teachers.* Cambridge, MA: Educators Publishing Service.

Smith, L. B., & Kemler, D. G. (1977). Development trends in free classification: Evidence for a new conceptualization of perceptual development. *Journal of Experimental Child Psychology, 24,* 279–298.

Smothergill, D. W. (1973). Accuracy and variability in the localization of spatial targets at three age levels. *Developmental Psychology, 7,* 62–66.

Swanson, L. (1977). Effect of verbal and nonverbal short-term memory coding with normal and retarded children. *Perceptual and Motor Skills, 44,* 917–918.

Tarnopol, L. (1971). *Learning Disabilities.* Springfield, IL: Charles C Thomas.

Tarver, S. G., Hallahan, D. P., Cohen, S. B., & Kauffman, J. M. (1977). The development of visual selective attention and verbal rehearsal in learning disabled boys. *Journal of Learning Disabilities.*

Taylor, J. (1985). The sequence and structure of handwriting competence: Where are the breakdown points in the mastery of handwriting? *British Journal of Occupational Therapy, 48*(7), 205–207.

Terman, L. W., & Merrill, M. A. (1972). The Stanford-Binet Intelligence Scale, Form L-M. Boston: Houghton Mifflin.

Thorndike, R. L., Hagen, E. P., Sattler, J. M. (1987). *Stanford-Binet Intelligence Scale: Fourth Edition Technical Manual.* Chicago, IL: The Riverside Publishing Co.

Travers, R. M. W. (1985). *Training Human Intelligence, Developing Exploratory and Aesthetic Skills.* Holmes Beach, FL: Learning Publications.

Valett, R. E. (1966). *Developmental Survey of Basic Learning Abilities.* Palo Alto, CA: Consulting Psychologists Press.

Vellutino, F. R. (1980). Dyslexia: Perceptual deficiency or perceptual inefficiency. In J. F. Kavanaugh & R. I. Venzky (Ed.). *Ortography Reading, Dyslexia.* Baltimore: University Park Press.

Wadsworth, B. J. (1971). *Piaget's theory of cognitive development.* New York: McKay.

Waldrop, M. F., Pedersen, F. A., & Bell, R. Q. (1968). Minor physical anomalies and behavior in preschool children. *Child Development, 39,* 391–400.

Watson, M. M., & Rastatter, M. P. (1985). The effects of time compression on the auditory processing abilities of learning disabled children. *Journal of Auditory Research, 25*(3), 167–173.

Wechsler, D. (1989). *The Wechsler Preschool and Primary Scale of Intelligence-Revised.* San Antonio, TX: The Psychological Corporation.

Wechsler, D. (1967). *The Wechsler Intelligence Scale for Children.* San Antonio, TX: The Psychological Corporation.

Weeks, Z. R. (1979). *An investigation of the relationship between sensory integrative dysfunction and emotional disturbance.* Unpublished manuscript, Indiana University Medical Center, Indianapolis, IN.

Weeks, Z. R. (1982). Sensorimotor integration theory and the multisensory approach. In S. D. Farber (Ed.). *Neurorehabilitation: A Multisensory Approach.* Philadelphia: Saunders.

Werner, J. K. (1980). *Neuroscience: A Clinical Perspective.* Philadelphia: Saunders.

Westman, J. C., Dunby, R. L., & Smith, S. (1987). An analysis of 190 children referred to a university hospital learning disabilities service. *Child Psychiatry and Human Development, 17*(4).

Wilentz, J. S. (1988). *The Senses of Man.* New York: Crowell.

14

Assessment of Gross Motor Functioning

HARRIET G. WILLIAMS

Motor development has been considered an important part of child development and is a universally recognized means for assessing the overall rate and level of development of the child during the early months and years after birth (Egan et al., 1969; Gesell, 1973; Illingworth, 1975). Motor development can be defined as the gradual acquisition of control and/or use of the large and small muscle masses of the body (neuromuscular coordination). The development and assessment of the young child's use of the large muscle masses of the body is the primary focus of this chapter.

The years from 2 to 6 are considered the "golden years" for motor development (Flinchum, 1975; Gesell & Amatruda, 1947; Williams & DeOreo, 1980). During this period, most children acquire their basic repertoire of manipulative and locomotor skills, develop goal-directed motor behaviors, and learn to put together two or three movement sequences to help them accomplish specific end goals (Bruininks, 1978; Cratty, 1970; Piaget, 1963). All of these behavioral achievements are forerunners of important aspects of adult functioning and are contingent upon the child's acquiring an adequate base of motor development. The early years of motor development set the foundation of neuromuscular coordination that will be used by the individual throughout life to deal with a variety of social, emotional, mental, and recreational dimensions of living.

Learning in the early years centers around play and physical activity (Flinchum, 1975; Riggs, 1980). Most children have a natural tendency to seek stimulation and to learn about themselves and their environment. They spend many hours actively exploring and examining both their bodies and the physical environment that surrounds them. Such activities necessarily involve and rely upon the use of fundamental motor skills. Adequate motor development is important in optimizing this early concrete and sensorimotor-based learning. A process instrumental in the child's development from early primitive levels of thinking to those of higher abstraction is that of the symbolization of objects and events and the relationship between the two (Cratty, 1972; Piaget, 1963). Physical activity provides the basis for such important symbolic activities as imitation (use of the body to represent objects and events), symbolic play (use of objects to represent other objects), and modeling, drawing, and cutting (construction of objects in two and three dimensions). Motor development and the physical activity associated with it thus are integral to promoting selected aspects of the early, active learning process.

Motor development also is linked during the early years to general health, to social and emotional adjustment, and to some degree to integrity of neurological functioning (Fowler, 1975; Illingworth, 1975; McGraw, 1963; Zaichowsky et al., 1980). Motor development delays frequently accompany a number of serious health conditions (e.g., mental subnormality, emotional disturbances, cerebral palsy, etc.) that might require medical or other special professional attention and needs to be identified early. A child whose motor development is considerably below that typically observed in children of similar chronological age is more likely than others to exhibit soft and/or hard neurological signs—an indication that systems that provide support for the growth and refinement of neuromuscular coordination are not functioning appropriately (McGraw, 1963; Paine & Oppe, 1966; Prechtl, 1977; Prechtl & Beintema, 1964). Pediatric neurologists often use, as a part of their assessment of the neurological status of the young child, items that directly involve neuromuscular coordination (e.g., evaluation of posture, gait, balance, alternating movements of the limbs, etc.). Most tests of mental development in infants and young children include a large number of items that essentially are neuromuscular coordination or motor development tasks (Bayley, 1965; Cratty, 1972; Stott & Ball, 1965). Gesell (1973) grouped such items into a separate "motor category" in his development schedules. In addition, there is a greater incidence of difficulty in making appropriate social and emotional adjustments to both play and learning situations in children whose motor development is below that of other children their age. For these reasons, assessment of gross motor development in the preschool-age child is an essential component in the planning for and providing of optimal conditions for development and learning during one of the most significant periods of growth in the life of the child.

GROSS MOTOR DEVELOPMENT IN THE PRESCHOOL CHILD

Gross motor development in the preschool years is charcterized by the appearance and mastery of a number of fundamental motor skills.

These gross motor skills include body projection (locomotor movements), body manipulation (non-locomotor movements), and object manipulation (ball handling) skills. Body projection or locomotor skills include running, jumping, hopping, skipping, galloping, leaping, and sliding (DeOreo, 1980). These skills all focus on the use of the large muscle masses of the body in moving the total body horizontally through space. Body manipulation skills, on the other hand, are concerned with moving the body and/or body parts within a well-defined, but small area of space and include stretching, curling, twisting, rolling, bending, and balancing skills. Universally recognized object manipulation skills include throwing, catching, striking, kicking, and ball bouncing (DeOreo, 1980). Not all of the skills included under the heading of fundamental motor skills can be addressed here. This discussion focuses primarily on the locomotor skills of running, jumping, hopping, and skipping, the object projection skills of throwing, catching, and striking, and that dimension of body manipulation concerned with balance.

Some general parameters that describe the development of selected locomotor and ball-handling skills are given in Table 14.1. More specific developmental changes typically observed in gross motor skills during the preschool years are given in Table 14.2. The list of steps in the developmental sequence of skill mastery describes the qualitative changes that occur in children's gross motor development during this period. Quantitative changes are listed as general accomplishments. There is a striking lack of convergent information about developmental changes that occur in gross motor control in the preschool child.

It is important to note that although the steps that are described for each skill can be loosely associated with chronological age, the relationship between the steps and chronological age per se is at best a tenuous one. One of the most dramatic characteristics of gross motor development in the preschool child is its great variability (Garfield, 1964; Keogh, 1969, 1975). Some children fall nicely into a rather traditional age-step association, but most do not. It is for this reason that ages have intentionally been deemphasized in the discussion of developmental changes in gross motor skills in the preschool child. The steps described in Table 14.2 are typically achieved by children during the period from 2 to 6 years.

TABLE 14.1
GENERAL PARAMETERS OF GOOD MOTOR DEVELOPMENT

Locomotor Skills

Walking, Running, and Jumping

Children accurately walk or run a straight path before a circular or curved one

Children progress from a stage of aided jumping to jumping alone with one foot in front of the other to jumping alone with a two-foot propulsion

Children pass through the same progression as noted above at each height from which a jump is attempted

Children execute jumps from lower heights before attempting jumps from greater heights

Children jump down from something before they jump up onto something

Hopping, Skipping, and Galloping

Children hop on both feet prior to the development of a true hopping movement on one foot

Skipping progresses from a shuffle, to a skip on one foot, to skipping on alternate feet

Climbing

Marking time (both feet placed on rung or step before next step is attempted) precedes alternation of feet in climbing

Use of alternating feet appears first in ascending skills, later in descending skills

Children will ascend an object before they will descend it

Children acquire proficiency in climbing a short flight of stairs or a ladder with the rungs close together before they gain proficiency in climbing a long flight of stairs or a ladder with the rungs farther apart

Children use alternate feet in climbing short flights of stairs although they still mark time when climbing a longer flight of stairs

Ball-handling Skills

Throwing

Children progress from dominant anteroposterior plane movement to movements primarily in the horizontal plane

There is a progression from an unchanging base of support (body fixed in space) to a changing base of support (an exactly timed transference of weight)

There is a progression toward shorter periods of acceleration; that is, the necessary joint actions occur in shorter periods of time, thus aiding in increased force development

At a given age, children can throw a smaller ball farther than a large one

Catching

Attempts to intercept a ball rolling on the ground usually precede attempts to intercept an aerial ball

There is a progression from the use of hands and arms as a single unit to "corral" the ball against the body to definite attempts to judge the speed and direction of the moving ball and consequently to adjust the movements of the arms to meet the oncoming ball and the hands to make contact with it

Children successfully intercept a large ball before successfully intercepting a small ball

Children revert to using the hands and arms as a single unit when first attempting to intercept a small ball, although they might skillfully coordinate their movements in catching a large ball.

Striking

Observations concerning striking skills in the preschool child are sparse

Children begin by using a one-arm strike and gradually develop a two-arm striking pattern

Children are successful in hitting a stationary ball before they are successful in hitting a moving ball

Children project a stationary ball with more force initially than they do a moving ball

Ball Bouncing

Children attempt a two-hand bounce before a one-hand bounce

Children skillfully bounce a small ball before a large ball

Children perform a series of "bounce-and-catches" before they perform a continuous bounce

Children successfully bounce a ball from a stationary position before they successfully bounce a ball while moving

TABLE 14.2
DEVELOPMENTAL CHANGES IN GROSS MOTOR SKILLS

Steps in Developmental Sequence	General Accomplishments
Running: Moving the body through space via alternate shifting of weight from one foot to the other with a period of nonsupport	

Step 1

Rudimentary run resembles fast walk Series of hurried steps is taken without a nonsupport phase Knees move up and down quickly Force of movement is directed vertically Arms swing randomly at sides; gait is uneven and jarring	Takes walking/running steps on toes Walks a straight line Walks backward Walks 10-ft pathway (1-in wide) without stepping-off Has difficulty walking circular path

Step 2

True run has definite nonsupport phase Elbows are slightly flexed and at low-guard position (hands about waist height) Forward/backward arm swing is limited There is occasional arm-foot opposition Stride is stiff and uneven in length and timing Knees swing out, around, and forward Base of support is wide (feet about shoulder width) Feet tend to toe out Child has difficulty stopping, starting, and turning Weight shifts onto flat foot	Walks 2.25-in board partway before stepping off Walks circle (1-ft wide, 4-in circumference) Run improves in form and power

Step 3

Running speed increases Elbows are flexed at high-guard position (hands at shoulder level) Arms swing through larger arc Arms tend to swing across body Arms-leg opposition is evident Some twisting of the trunk might be present Length of stride increases Feet still land flat Support leg extends more fully Child has better control in stopping, starting, and turning	Runs forward effectively Runs backward with hesitancy Runs 25 ft in 2.8 sec Runs 30-yd dash in 6–7 sec Completes 40-yd agility run in approximately 15 sec

Step 4

Running speed is increased Running pattern is more automatic Elbows are flexed at right angles Arms are used to aid forward motion rather than for balance Foot is placed on the ground in a heel-to-toe fashion (slow run) Knee of swing leg is raised high Run is even (little vertical motion)	Runs 25 ft in 2.5 sec Changes directions easily Uses running skills well in games Performs 10-ft shuttle run (5 trips in 17.5 sec) Runs 30-yd dash in 5–6 sec Completes 40-yd agility run in approximately 14 sec

(continued)

TABLE 14.2 (*continued*)

Steps in Developmental Sequence	General Accomplishments

Jumping: Projection of the body into the air from a two-foot take-off with the landing of two feet[a]

Step 1

Jump is in form of step down from a low object or up and down vertically in place (feet parallel or in stride position)

Flexion is primarily at knees

Leg extension (knees) is uneven (first one leg and then the other extends)

Arms are at sides and are used in limited ways

Steps down aided onto one foot
Steps down unaided onto one foot
Steps down aided onto two feet
Steps down unaided onto two feet

Step 2

Two-foot take-off and landing is used

Arms are not used in a coordinated way with the legs

Arms swing back and forth before take-off but are not used at take-off

Knee and hip flexion increase to add to force of take-off

Legs are not fully extended at take-off

Thighs are perpendicular to the ground during flight

Knee and hip flexion increase to absorb momentum of landing

Balance might be lost on landing

Jumps down from 8-in height alone
Jumps over an 8-in piece of paper
Jumps distance of 14–24 in
Steps over rope approximately 7 in high
Jumps down from 28-in height with help

Step 3

Distance and height of jump increase

Arms are used to initiate take-off

Knee and hip flexion are increased (deeper crouch)

Legs extend fully at take-off

Thighs are more parallel to ground during flight

Arms are brought down and forward to maintain balance on landing

Jumps distance of 23–36 in
Attempts jumps over low barriers (1–3 in)
Jumps down from 12–18 in height without help
Performs vertical jump of 17 in

Step 4

Preparatory crouch is deeper

Arms are used in coordinated fashion with legs

Hips, knees, and ankles are in full extension at take-off

Hips and knees are flexed during flight (thighs are now parallel to ground)

Legs reach out, arms are brought down, and knees flex to aid in landing

Balance is maintained on landing

True broad jump is present

Jumps distance of 28–35 in
Performs vertical jump of 19 in
Jumps down from 28-in height without help

Hopping: Projection of the body into the air from one foot with the landing on the same (one) foot[b]

Step 1

Arms are raised sideways and nonsupport leg is lifted in attempt to hop

Trunk is bent slightly forward

Support leg flexes slightly

No true hopping present

TABLE 14.2 *(continued)*

Steps in Developmental Sequence	General Accomplishments
Might be momentary retraction of support foot from ground	

Step 2

Arms are held in high-guard position, elbows flexed Nonsupport leg (hip and knee) is held high and flexed at right angle Body weight is suspended momentarily; little or no elevation occurs in hop	Performs 1–3 consecutive hops Hops forward but not backward

Step 3

Child leans forward and shifts weight to balls on feet Arms are held at middle-guard position for balance Nonsupport leg is less flexed Body weight is suspended for longer time Hops are more horizontal	Hops slowly and deliberately Hops forward and backward Hops 4–6 times consecutively Hops 2–16 ft with variable skill Hops better on preferred side

Step 4

Arms are used to assist in projection of body Nonsupport leg swings to aid in take-off Support leg is more fully extended at knee and ankle Weight is received on ball of foot	Performs up to 10 consecutive hops Hops arrhythmically Hops 25 ft in approximately 17 sec Speed of hopping is increased Has difficulty but can occasionally alternate on right and left feet

Step 5

Arms are used to assist in force production Range of motion of arms and legs is increased Nonsupport leg flexes and extends to aid in force production Trunk is inclined forward Support leg flexes on landing to absorb body weight Weight is received on ball of foot	Hops smoothly and rhythmically Hops 25 ft in 5 sec Hops 50 ft in 8 sec Can alternate hops on right and left feet

Skipping: Projection of the body through space by a combination of a step and hop on one side followed by a step-hop on the opposite side[b]

Step 1

Skip is a shuffle on one of both feet No hop is present Arms are not used	Performs shuffle step No true skip present

Step 2

Skip is a step-hop on one side and a walk on the other Arms are held extended to side and slightly flexed Hands are held at chest level Movement is arrhythmical	Performs one-sided skip Performs 4 one-sided skips in sequence No true skip present

Step 3

Skip is a step-hop on alternate sides Running or walking steps might be interspersed into skipping pattern	Performs alternate skipping pattern (true skip) Skips 25 ft in approximately 4 sec

(continued)

TABLE 14.2 (*continued*)

Steps in Developmental Sequence	General Accomplishments
Length of skips in short; elevation of body is minimal Arms not used in opposition and may swing randomly Some toeing out of feet might occur Movements are still arrhythmical and slow	

Step 4

Support leg quickly flexes to receive weight and extends to produce take-off Nonsupport leg is flexed and swings forward to aid in momentum of skip Body might be turned from side to side Arms are used in opposition Arms are flexed at elbows and held at middle-guard position Feet follow a path approximately shoulder width Skipping movements are smoother, more rhythmical	Skips 25 ft in approx. 3.5 sec.

Throwing (overarm): Ability to project an object through space with some degree of speed and accuracy

Step 1

Body faces direction of throw Feet are stationary No body or shoulder rotation is present Movement is primarily in the vertical plane Arm movement is largely elbow flexion and extension Trunk moves backward and forward in vertical plane Ball is released before elbow is extended	Simply drops/tosses objects Often throws underhand

Step 2

Feet are stationary (either together or spread) No weight shift is present Some passive body rotation is present Trunk rotates backward toward throwing side and then forward Arm initiates throwing action, which is in a flat or oblique plane	Is fascinated with throwing Throws ball 4–5 ft using one or two hands Throws without losing balance

Step 3

Weight shift is present Step-out is on foot on side of throwing arm Body rotation decreases Range of arm-trunk movement is limited by forward position of throwing foot Trunk flexion/extension increases Arm follows through across body	Successfully tosses ring at a peg 4 feet away Throws a distance of over 10 ft

Step 4

Step-out is on foot opposite throwing arm Body rotation increases Trunk rotates as unit Shoulder rotation is present	Throws a distance of over 17 ft at velocity of 27 ft/sec

TABLE 14.2 (*continued*)

Steps in Developmental Sequence	General Accomplishments
Elbow lags behind as trunk rotates forward	
Wrist snap is present	
Arm follows through across body	

Step 5

Differentiated trunk rotation appears (pelvic followed by spinal rotation)	Throws a distance of over 20 ft at velocity of 35 ft/sec
Ball is released from fingertips	

Catching: Ability to stop and control aerial objects[d]

Step 1

Rolling ball is stopped or trapped
Aerial ball is not responded to

Step 2

Arms are held out straight in front of body in response to aerial ball (stiff elbows, arms supinated)
Timing is off—ball often rebounds off arms, trunk, or face
Fear reaction is present: child turns head, closes eyes, leans back, tenses fingers
Catching is passive and by "chance"

Step 3

Arms are held in front of body with elbows slightly flexed
Active attempt is made to catch ball
Ball is scooped or trapped between arms and chest or between arms
Attempt is made to trap ball with clapping motion
Timing is still awkward but improved

Step 4

Arms are held at sides, hands are cupped, and fingers are pointed at oncoming ball	Might catch large ball thrown from 5 feet 1 of 3 times
Arms and hands are used to stop catch the ball	
Arms and hands adjust to meet oncoming ball	
Arms and hands give to absorb momentum of ball	
Child watches ball as it approaches	

Step 5

Fingers and hands adjust skillfully to close around ball at contact	Catches large ball 50% of time
	Catches 8-in ball bounced from 15 feet 3 of 5 times
	Catches small balls with varying degrees of skill
	Attempts one-hand catch
	Catches ball bounced from 10 ft 4 of 10 times

Step 6

Entire body adjusts to receive balls thrown at various speeds and from different directions	Catches balls of various sizes skillfully
	Catches balls bounced from 10 ft 7 of 10 times

(*continued*)

TABLE 14.2 (*continued*)

Steps in Developmental Sequence	General Accomplishments

Two-Arm Striking: Ability to make contact with a stationary or moving object using the hands and/or other implement[e]

Step 1

Child faces oncoming ball
Implement is held and swung in vertical plane
Attempt is made to contact stationary object using one-
arm pattern

Step 2

Child experiments with using two hands and swings in
vertical plane
Trunk flexion is present
"Chopping" motion is made

Step 3

Child stands with side to oncoming ball
Bat is held on or near back shoulder
Weight is shifted in a kind of rocking motion
Two hands are used and swing is made with sidearm
motion in flat arc
Arms, hands, and wrists are held stiffly
Swing is adjusted to height of ball by flexion at waist

Step 4

Child stands with side to oncoming ball   Projects ball with two-arm strike at velocity of 3 ft/sec
Bat is on or near back shoulder
Definite shift of weight to forward foot occurs prior to
arm swinging forward
Trunk rotates as unit (backward and forward)
Range of arm motion is increased

Step 5

Child stands with side to oncoming ball   Hits stationary ball 17 of 20 times
Definite shift of weight to forward foot occurs   Hits moving ball 27 of 40 times
Differentiated trunk rotation appears   Projects tennis ball with two-arm strike at velocity of
Bat is swung with greater force   26–31 ft/sec
Bat is swing in horizontal plane   Projects whiffle ball with two-arm strike at velocity of
17–20 ft/sec

Balance: Ability to maintain the body in state of equilibrium whether stationary or moving[f]

Step 1

Balances on all fours
Balances on knees
Maintains standing position

Step 2

Attempts to stand on objects (e.g., balance beam)
Attempts to walk beam (2¼ in wide), one foot on, one
foot off
Flails arms and tenses hands and face

TABLE 14.2 (*continued*)

Steps in Developmental Sequence	General Accomplishments

Step 3

Attempts to walk beam (2¼ in wide), alternating feet
Walks 1-in line for 10-ft distance

Step 4

Stands heel to toe, eyes closed, hands on hips (on floor)
Walks 1-in circular line
Slowly walks entire length of beam (2¼ in)
Diminishes tension and flailing of arms

Step 5

Balances on preferred foot minimum of 3–5 sec
Walks standard-length beam using natural gait with
   relative ease
Walks 12 ft on 4 in beam before stepping off
Walks 10–11 ft on 3-in beam before stepping off
Walks 5–8 ft on 2-in beam before stepping off
Balances on unstable platform 8–9 sec

Step 6

Balances on preferred foot, eyes open, 54 sec (average)
Balances on nonpreferred foot, eyes open, 41 sec (average)
Balances on preferred foot, eyes closed, 7 sec (average)
Balances on one foot on 1-in stick, 3 sec (average)
Walks balance beam in heel-to-toe controlled manner,
   23 sec (average)

[a] Cratty, 1970; DeOreo & Keogh, 1980; Espenschade & Eckert, 1980; McClenaghan & Gallahue, 1978; Milne et al., 1975; Seefeldt et al., 1972; Wickstrom, 1977; Williams & Breihan, 1979; Williams & DeOreo, 1980.
[b] Cratty, 1970; DeOreo & Keogh, 1980; Espenschade & Eckert, 1980; McClenaghan & Gallahue, 1978; Williams & Breihan, 1979; Williams & DeOreo.
[c] Cratty, 1970; Deoreo & Keogh, 1980; Espenschade & Eckert, 1980; McClenaghan & Gallahue, 1978; Seefeldt et al., 1972; Wickstrom, 1977; Wild, 1938; Williams & Breihan, 1979; Williams et al., 1970.
[d] Cashin, 1975; Cratty, 1970; DeOreo & Keogh, 1980; Espenschade & Eckert, 1980; McClenaghan & Gallahue, 1978; Wickstrom, 1977; Williams & Breihan, 1979; Williams & DeOreo, 1980; Williams et al., 1970.
[e] Cratty, 1970; DeOreo & Keogh, 1980; Espenschade & Eckert, 1980; McClenaghan & Gallahue, 1978; Shope, 1976; Skovran, 1977; Wickstrom, 1977; Williams & Breihan, 1979; Williams & DeOreo, 1980; Williams et al., 1970.
[f] Cratty, 1970; DeOreo 1971; DeOreo & Keogh, 1980; Espenschade & Eckert, 1980; Williams & Breihan, 1979; Williams et al., 1970.

The reader also should be aware that the steps identified in individual skills sequences are not mutually exclusive; it is not unusual for children to display characteristics from more than one step at any given time in their development (Roberton, 1978; Roberton & Langendorfer, 1980). Children typically display characteristics from steps that are adjacent to one another; although they also might exhibit characteristics of performance that are from nonadjacent steps. This is uncommon and is usually a reflection of special developmental difficulties.

• Running. (Cratty, 1970; DeOreo & Keogh, 1980; Espenschade & Eckert, 1980; McClenaghan & Gallahue, 1978; Milne et al., 1975; Seefeldt et al., 1972; Wickstrom 1977; Williams & Breihan, 1979; Williams & DeOreo, 1980.) In general the early running pattern resembles a fast walk. The base of support is wide (feet are shoulder-width apart), and little or no use is made of the arms. The feet toe out and the child run flat-footed. With increasing skill, the base of support narrows (feet are placed one in front of the other), rhythmical arm/foot opposition is integrated into the run, and the foot is placed on the ground in a heel-to-toe fashion (slow running). Quantitively, the length of stride steadily increases as does the speed and versatility of the running pattern (the child starts, stops, turns, and runs at a variety of speeds and in a variety of directions skillfully).

- Jumping. (Cratty, 1970; DeOreo & Keogh, 1980; Espenschade & Eckert, 1980; McClenaghan & Gallahue, 1978; Milne et al., 1975; Seefeldt et al., 1972; Wickstrom, 1977; Williams & Breihan, 1979; Williams & DeOreo, 1970) Jumping proceeds developmentally from a one-foot step down from a low object to a skillful execution of a standing broad (long) jump that covers a distance of about 44 inches. In the beginning, the arms are used very little and when they are used, they are used ineffectively (the arms are moved but not in conjunction with the legs). Skillful jumping is manifested most clearly in the smooth coordination of arm and leg movements. In early jumping patterns leg movements are charcterized by incomplete flexion and extension. That is, the young or inexperienced jumper fails to assume a semi-crouched position in jumping and at take-off fails to fully extend the body. The skillful 6 year old jumper assumes a flexed semi-crouched position prior to jumping and fully extends the ankle, knee, and hip at take-off. In actuality the body of the mature jumper at take-off forms a straight line that extends from the ankle to the fingertips. Last but not least, young jumpers tend to lose their balance upon landing and often fall backward or in general lose control. The skillful jumper flexes (most obviously at the knees) to absorb the momentum of the body upon landing and rarely loses balance. Quantitatively, the distance of the jump (vertical, running broad, or standing broad) increases from step to step in a nonlinear fashion.
- Hopping. (Cratty, 1970; DeOreo & Keogh, 1980; Espenschade & Eckert, 1980; Mc-

Clenaghan & Gallalue, 1978; Williams & Breihan, 1979; Williams & DeOreo, 1980) Early hopping patterns involve little or no elevation of the body (the child doesn't get very high off the ground), little or no arm usage, and limited use of the nonsupport leg. Early hopping patterns are jerky, staccato, and arrhythmic. Gradually the arms and nonsupport leg are used to add to the elevation of the body, and the nonsupport leg actually 'pumps' (flexes and extends rapidly) to add in the forward momentum of the hopping action. The hop becomes smoother with practice and the child advances from being unable to execute a series of coordinated hopping movements to hopping a 25-foot distance skillfully in 5 seconds. In addition, the versatily of the hopping pattern increases; the child develops the ability to hop backward and sidward and to alternate hops between the right and left feet.

- Skipping. (Cratty, 1970; DeOreo & Keogh, 1980; Espenschade & Eckert, 1980; McClenghan & Gallahue, 1978; Williams & Breihan, 1979; Williams & DeOreo, 1980) The early skip is a shuffle step; the shuffle step is followed by a one-sided skip; the final step in development is the true skip-a-step-hop on alternate sides of the body. Early skipping patterns are characterized by a lack of use of the arms, a toeing out of the feet, and a lack of ability to maintain a continuous skipping sequence. Skillful skipping involves smooth arm/leg opposition (the arms swing smoothly and in opposition to the legs). The toes are pointed forward. Mastery of a continuous skipping action is seen in the growing capacity of the child to skip long distances in less time. The more skillful 6-year-old skipper can cover a distance of 25 feet in under 4 seconds.
- Throwing. (Cratty, 1970; DeOreo & Keogh, 1980; Espenschade & Eckert, 1980; McClenaghan & Gallahue, 1978; Seefeldt et al., 1972; Wickstrom, 1977; Wild, 1938; Williams & Breihan, 1979; Williams et al., 1970) The early overarm throwing pattern consists largely of flexion and extension of the trunk and arm (elbow). Little or no weight shift or trunk rotation is present. Gradually a shift of weight and trunk rotation appear and help to increase the force or velocity of the throw. The weight shift is first seen as a shift of

weight forward onto the foot on the same side as the throwing arm; later the skillful thrower steps onto the foot opposite the throwing arm. Trunk rotation first occurs in block form (the lower and upper trunk—pelvis and spine—rotate together as a unit). Later trunk rotation is differentiated (the lower trunk or pelvis rotates first; this is followed by upper trunk or spinal rotation). Quantitatively, developmental changes are seen primarily in increases in the distance and velocity of the throw. Increases in both distance and velocity from one step in the developmental sequence to the next are nonlinear in nature. There are dramatic quantitative changes in throwing in Steps 4 and 5.

- Catching. (Cashin, 1975; Cratty, 1970; DeOreo & Keogh, 1980; Espenschade & Eckert, 1980; McClenaghan & Gallahue, 1978; Wickstrom, 1977; Williams & Breihan, 1979; Williams & DeOreo, 1980; Williams et al., 1970) Early and/or immature catching patterns are characterized by lack of skillful use of the arms, hands, and fingers. Initially the arms and hands are held stiffly in front of the body and the ball often rebounds off of them. Later the arms are held at the sides with the hands relaxed and cupped. The arms/hands/fingers of skillful catchers are positioned according to the flight of the oncoming object. The fingers and hands are pointed toward the ball. For balls above the waist, the finger/hands point upward; for balls below the waist, the fingers/hands point downward. When ball contact is made, the fingers close around the ball. Young or inefficient catchers rarely display this fingertip control in making contact with the ball. A part of the child's early catching response is a 'fear reaction' in which the child turns the head, closes the eyes, and really doesn't track the ball at all. This reaction disappears in skillful catching and the child watches the ball intently as it approaches. The major characteristic of the highly proficient catcher is his/her ability to adjust the total movement of the body to receive balls thrown at different speeds and from varying distances and directions. Young catchers are unable to do this. Quantitatively, the number of successful catches (ball skillfully caught) increases slowly. Changes in

catching skills have not been quantified to any great extent.

- Striking. (Cratty, 1970; DeOreo & Keogh, 1980; Espenschade & Eckert, 1980; McClenaghan & Gallahue, 1978; Shope, 1976; Shovran, 1977; Wickstrom, 1977; Williams & Breihan, 1979; Williams & DeOreo, 1980; Williams et al., 1970) The development of striking skills is an important part of early gross motor development. Although not a lot of normative or descriptive data are available on the nature of developmental changes in striking skill in young children, the little that is available suggests that striking patterns proceed from one-arm attempts at contacting stationary objects to skillful two-arm striking patterns made in an effort to contact objects moving at different speeds and in different directions. Initially, the striking movement is a vertical chopping motion; later it becomes a sidearm motion executed in the horizontal plane (the swing is flat). Early in the development of the striking pattern (as in throwing), the trunk rotates as a single unit; later, differentiated or two-part trunk rotation occurs. Another important developmental change in striking behavior is the appearance of a definite shift of weight onto the forward (opposite) foot prior to the beginning of the arm swing. The child will also gradually change from assuming a position facing the oncoming ball to one in which the side of the body is placed toward the ball. Quantitatively, with advancing development, the bat is swung with greater force (the range and timing of the movement of the body are improved) and the ball is projected with increasingly greater velocity.

- Balance. (Cratty, 1970; DeOreo, 1971; DeOreo & Keogh, 1980; Espenschade & Eckert, 1980; Williams & Breihan, 1979; Williams et al., 1970) Early balance development is manifested in the child's ability to maintain equilibrium in a variety of positions (e.g., on all fours, on the knees, in a standing position). This is followed by attempts to stand and to walk on objects. Once some success is achieved in these skills, the child will attempt to walk narrow objects (e.g., balance beams, rails, lines.) and shows some beginning ability to maintain balance on one foot. By 6 years, most children can balance for fairly long periods of time on the preferred foot with the eyes open (M = 54 sec.). Balancing on the nonpreferred foot is more difficult (M = 41 sec.) and balancing with the eyes closed is just beginning to be mastered (M = 7 sec.). Most children can, at this age, walk a balance beam (2½ in. wide) in a controlled heel-to-toe manner in 23 seconds.

ASSESSMENT OF GROSS MOTOR DEVELOPMENT

Gross motor development is most often and effectively evaluated by considering both process and product characteristics of children's movement behaviors (Stewart & DeOreo, 1980; Williams & DeOreo, 1980). Process characteristics of

movement have to do with how a child moves the body in performing a motor task. Thus, evaluation of process characteristics is concerned with assessing the form or quality of the movement itself (e.g., by observing how the body is positioned, which limbs or joints are moved or moving, and how movements are sequenced). Product characteristics of movement, in contrast, have to do with the end product or outcome of the movement and usually are move quantitative in nature. Evaluation of product characteristics of movement answer such questions as the following: How far did the child run? How high did he jump? How fast did she move? Techniques used for assessing gross motor development often incorporate measures of both process and product aspects of movement performance. Most motor development scales or tests available for use with younger children tend to emphasize process characteris-

TABLE 14.3
CRATTY'S PERCEPTUAL-MOTOR BEHAVIORS CHECKLIST

2–3 Years

Displays a variety of scribbling behaviors
Can walk rhythmically at an even pace (*process*)[a]
Can step off low object, one foot ahead of other (*process*)[a]
Can name hands, feet, head, and some face parts
Opposes thumb to fingers when grasping objects and releases objects smoothly from finger thumb grasp (*process*)
Can walk a 2-in wide line placed on ground for 10 ft (*product*)[a]

4–4½ Years

Can forward broad jump both feet together and clear of ground at the same time[a]
Can hop two or three times on one foot without precision or rhythm (*process and product*)[a]
Walks and runs with arm action coordinated with leg action (*process*)[a]
Can walk a circular line a short distance (*product*)[a]
Can draw a crude circle
Can immitate a simple line cross using a vertical and horizontal line

5–5½ Years

Runs 30 yd in just over 8 sec or less (*product*)[a]
Balances on one foot (girls 6–8 sec. boys 4–6 sec) (*product*)[a]
Catches large playground ball bounced to him or her chest high from 15 ft away, 4–5 of 5 times (*product*)[a]
Draws rectangle and square differently (one side at a time)
Can high jump 8 in or higher over bar with simultaneous two-foot take-off (*product*)[a]
Bounces playground ball using one or two hands a distance of 3–4 ft (*product*)[a]

6–6½ Years

Can block print first name in letters 1½–2 in high
Can gallop, if it is demonstrated (*product*)[a]
Can exert 6 lb or more of pressure in grip strength measure (*product*)[a]
Can walk balance beam 2 in wide, 6 in high, and 10–12 ft long (*product*)[a]
Can run 50 ft in about 5 sec (*product*)[a]
Can arise from ground from backlying position in 2 sec or less (*product*)[a]

Adapted from Catty, B. J. (1970) *Perceptual and Motor Development in Infants and Young Children.* New York: Macmillan.
Note: The above tasks are reasonable to expect in 75% to 80% of the children of the indicated ages. The data upon which this has been based have been collected from children in white middle-class neighborhoods. A child failing to master 4 to 6 of the tasks for his or her age probably needs a more thorough evaluation and possibly remedial help.
[a] Gross motor items.

tics, while tests for older children tend to emphasize product-related measures. Both types of information are needed at all ages if a complete and comprehensive assessment of motor development of the child is to be made. A good example of a simple checklist that contains both process and product characteristic items is Cratty's Perceptual-Motor Behaviors Checklist (Cratty, 1970). Examples of items that emphasize process characteristics are "can walk rhythmically at an even pace" (2 to 3 years), "can step off low object, one foot-ahead of the other" (2 to 3 years), and "walks and runs with arm action coordinated with leg action" (4 to 4½ years). Items that are more product-oriented include "can walk a two-inch wide line for 10 feet" (2 to 3 years), "can jump 8 inches or higher" (5 to 5½ years) and "can run 50 feet in 5 seconds" (6 to 6½ years) (Table 14–3).

Product Measures

The most common approach to the evaluation of motor development is that of product assessment. Normative data for such test batteries usually are give in standard score, percentile, or some other quantitative form derived from means, standard deviations, and/or standard errors. The normative data provided are used for comparing individual children to standards typical for children of comparable chronological ages. There are no test batteries of this type for very young children (2 to 3 year olds); several have been developed for 4-, 5-, and 6-year-old children. Four of the more recent and widely used product-oriented motor performance test batteries are reviewed here; all are formal, standardized measures of motor development. Brief mention is made of informal measures of product characteristics because few are available.

Denver Developmental Screening Test

The Denver test (Frankenburg & Dodds, 1967; Frankenburg et al., 1970; Frankenburg et al., 1971) is one of the most universally recognized and widely used standardized procedures for assessing gross motor development in young children. It uses simple tasks that are essentially product characteristic measures that test the child at minimal skill levels. The items in this battery are helpful to the educator and clinician in that they provide information about whether certain common gross motor skills are within the behavioral repertoire of a child at a given age. They do not, however, provide information about why a given motor skill is not a part of a child's set of behavioral skills. Thus, this test is most properly used as a screening device (for which it was designed) and not for detailed diagnosis of motor development difficulties.

The Denver Developmental Screening Test (DDST) can be used to outline the general nature and/or level of motor skill development in children from birth to 6 years. Standards for passing items on the test are described in simple language and are based on normative date gathered on 1,036 children. The major gross motor items included in the test and the age at which 90% of the children pass these items are given in Table 14.4.

Peabody Developmental Motor Scales and Activity Cards

A very widely used tool for assessing motor development in young children is the Peabody Developmental Motor Scales (1983). The scales were designed to evaluate gross and fine motor skills in both handicapped and nonhandicapped children ages birth to 6 years. The Gross Motor Scale

TABLE 14.4
SELECTED GROSS MOTOR ITEMS FROM THE DENVER DEVELOPMENTAL SCREENING TEST

Item	Age[a]
Walks backward	21 mo
Walks up steps	22 mo
Kicks ball forward	2 yr
Throws ball overhand	2½ yr
Jumps in place	3 yr
Pedals tricycle	3 yr
Performs broad jump	3¼ yr
Balances on 1 foot for 1 sec	3¼ yr
Balances on 1 foot for 5 sec 2 of 3 times	4¼ yr
Hops on 1 foot	4¾ yr
Performs heel-to-toe walk 2 of 3 times	5 yr
Catches bounced ball 2 of 3 times	5½ yr
Balances on 1 foot for 10 sec 2 of 3 times	5¾ yr
Performs backward heel-to-toe walk 2 of 3 times	6 yr

Adapted from Frankenburg, W. K., Dodds, J. B. (1967). The Denver Developmental Screening Test. *Journal of Pediatrics, 71,* 181.

[a] Age at which 90% of children pass.

consists of a total of 170 items, 10 items at each of 17 age levels. From age 2 years, items are grouped at 6-month intervals. The areas of gross motor development that are considered include: reflexes (in children up to 1 year of age), balance, nonlocomotor behaviors, locomotor skills and receipt and propulsion of objects skills. Examples of each of these skill areas and the criterion for passing (for 4 year olds) are provided in Table 14.5. The gross motor development scale requires approximately 30 minutes to administer and is straightforward in administration, scoring, and interpretation. All items are scored 0 (the child cannot/does not perform the task), 1 or 2 (the child performs the task according to the differential criteria listed). Basal and ceiling ages are determined, and raw scores can be converted into percentile ranks, standard scores, and a developmental motor quotient. Normative data exist for 617 children (85.1% Caucasian) from a wide variety of geographical locations (northeastern, north central, southern, and western United States). Of the total number of children in the standardization sample, there were 92 2 year olds, 103 3 year olds, 50 4 year olds, and 55 5 year olds.

Cashin Test of Motor Development

The Cashin test (Cashin, 1975) was designed for use with 4 and 5 year olds and its data base is approximately 1,000 children. This test assesses five different gross motor skills: static balance, dynamic balance, agility, throwing (over arm), and catching. General task descriptions, testing procedures, and some normative data are give in Table 14.6.

The Cashin test was developed with facility of administration in mind. Space requirements are

TABLE 14.5
EXAMPLES OF ITEMS FROM THE PEABODY GROSS MOTOR SCALE (4 YEAR OLDS)

Skill Area	Item	Criterion for Passing
Balance	Walks a 4″ balance beam	Completes 4 steps without support Stands on tiptoes with hands over head Maintains position for 8 seconds with good stability
Nonlocomotor	Jumps up with hands overhead as high as possible	Jumps 3″ beyond normal reach
Performs sit-ups	Performs 3–4 situps in 30 seconds	
Locomotor	Jumps down from 32″	Jumps without support, leading with one foot Jumps forward as far as possible Jumps forward 16″ on one foot Jumps forward on opposite foot Jumps forward 12″ on opposite foot
	Rolls forward (somersault)	Rolls forward over head without turning head 15° to either side
Receipt & Propulsion	Throws ball	Throws ball 10″ on 1 of 2 trials

minimal and, on the average, a child can complete the entire test in 20 minutes. Some minimal training or experience in observing throwing and catching patterns in young children is necessary to use the battery successfully. Young children often have difficulty understanding exactly what to do on the agility task, and several practice tries might be needed if an accurate assessment of the child's agility is to be made. The normative data provided supply a rough standard for assessing the level of motor development in individual children. Three categories of development are identified; *average, accelerated,* and *developmental lag.* The score(s) corresponding with these three levels of motor development are based on group means and standard deviations (average level of development is within +/- 1 SD; accelerated development is at least + 2SD; developmental lag is at least -2SD). Important male-female differences are also noted in Table 14.6.

Williams-Breihan Motor Performance Test Battery

The Williams-Breihan test (Williams & Breihan, 1979) was developed for use in assessing product characteristics of motor performance in 4-, 6-, and 8-year-old children. Although the tasks in this battery were designed to assess both fine and gross motor skills, only selected gross motor skills are discussed here. Ten of these skills are illustrated in Table 14.7. Normative data are presented in the form of percentile ranks for each age group.

Once the child's raw score on a given task is obtained, it can be compared to an average percentile score, and a determination can be made of how the child's level of skill mastery compares to other 4-, 6-, or 8-year-old children. By using percentile rank information for the 10 gross motor skills described here, simple but informative profiles of motor development can be outlined for the young child. An example of a locomotor skill profile is provided in Figure 14.1. The graph provides a general visual profile of the child's level of achievement for a particular set of gross motor skills.

One of the difficulties with normative data-based tests lies in its interpretation. What exactly does it mean to have a score above or below the 50th percentile? Even the experts cannot say for

certain. In addition, norms established on one population of children might not be applicable to other groups of children. Caution always must be exerted in using normative data for comparative purposes.

Bruininks-Oseretsky Test of Motor Proficiency

The Bruininks-Oseretsky test (Bruininks, 1978) is designed for use with chilren 4½ through 14½ years of age. It consists of 8 subtests (46 separate items) that provide a broad index of the child's proficiency in both gross and fine motor skills. A short form of the test (14 items) provides a brief overview of the child's general motor proficiency. Four of the subtests measure gross motor skills: Running Speed and Agility, Balance, Bilateral Coordination, and Upper Limb Coordination. Selected items used to assess these four aspects of gross motor development are described in Table 14.8.

Raw scores on gross motor items are converted to point scores, which are then converted to standard scores. The standard scores are summed to give a gross motor composite, which is converted into a composite standard score. This score is used to determine a corresponding percentile rank for the individual child. Some age-equivalent data are provided, and norms are established for 6-month intervals. The standardization sample was based on 68 children for the 4-year 6-month to 5-year 5-month range and 82 children for the 5-year 6-month to 6-year 5-month range.

McCarthy Scales of Children's Abilities

Another example of a product approach to the evaluation of young children's motor development is the McCarthy scales—a test battery designed to help fulfill the need for a single instrument to evaluate strengths and weaknesses of young children's abilities (McCarthy, 1972). The McCarthy scales involve systematic observaton of a variety of cognitive and motor behaviors that are subdivided into 6 scales. The Motor Development Scale assesses gross and fine motor skills through the following subtests: Leg Coordination, Arm Coordination, Imitative Action, Draw-A-Design, and Draw-A-Child. The latter two tasks are

TABLE 14.6
CASHIN TEST OF MOTOR DEVELOPMENT

Task	Scoring	Age/Sex	Average	Accelerated	Developmental Lag
Agility (obstacle course)					
On the signal "Go" the child follows this path.[a]	One practice and 3 test trials are given: time to nearest .1 sec is recorded; score is average of 3 trials (in seconds)	4/M	9.5–1.02	Below 9.0	Above 11.0
		4/F	9.5–10.2	Below 9.0	Above 11.0
		5/M	8.1–8.6	Below 7.9	Above 9.0
		5/F	9.0–10.2	Below 8.5	Above 11.0
Static balance (stork stand)					
Child places hands on hips and foot of choice against inside part of supporting leg just below the knee	One practice and 3 test trials are given; time to nearest .1 sec is recorded; score is average of 3 trials (in seconds, 30-sec maximum)	4/M	13.7–16.9	Below 19.0	Above 12.0
		4/F	17.6–21.1	Below 23.0	Above 15.0
		5/M	20.3–22.5	Above 24.0	Below 19.0
		5/M	20.3–22.5	Above 24.0	Below 19.0

over

under

Dynamic balance (plank walk)

Child places hands on hips; steps on 2-in beam and walks 10 steps (heel to toe), stops, returns to end of beam and repeats task

Three trials are given; each trial is 2 trips of 10 steps; the child is allowed 2 errors on each trip; score is average number of steps for 3 trials (in steps)

4/M	7.9–5.8	Above 9.0	Below 4.7
4/F	14.2–11.9	Above 15.0	Below 10.7
5/M	14.8–13.2	Above 16.0	Below 12.0
5/F	14.8–13.2	Above 16.0	Below 12.0

Throwing

Child stands behind a line 20 ft from a wall and throws the ball, overarm, as hard as he or she can against the wall

Two trials of 12 throws each given; score is total number of points for two trials; and overarm rating scale is used to determine points (in points, maximum of 50 points per trial, 5 per throw)

4/M	55–55	Above 59	Below 53
4/F	45–48	Above 49	Below 43
5/M	56–58	Above 49	Below 55
5/F	46–49	Above 51	Below 45

Catching (spot controlled)

Child stands on an "x" 13 ft from the ball tosser and attempts to catch an 8½" playground ball; 4 tosses 2 ft to the child's right, and 4 tosses 2ft to the child's left in random order in each trial.

Two trials of 12 tosses each are given; score is average points accumulated in two trials; a catching rating scale is used to determine points (in points, maximum of 50 points per trial, 5 per toss)

4/M	30–32	Above 33	Below 29
4/F	30–32	Above 33	Below 29
5/M	34–36	Above 38	
5/F	34–35	Above 38	

From Cashing, G. The Cashin Test of Motor Development. (1975). Unpublished master's thesis, Bowling Green State University.

[a] Path is 10 ft long; total width is 6 ft; each line represents 2. The under obstacle is 12 ft-high and the over obstacle is 8 in high; both are placed at 5 ft from the end line.

TABLE 14.7
GROSS MOTOR ITEMS ON THE WILLIAMS-BREIHAN MOTOR PERFORMANCE TEST BATTERY

Task	Scoring	Age	Percentile			Mean ± SD	r*
			25th	50th	75th		
Locomotor							
Running							
On signal, "Ready, Begin," child runs a 25-ft distance as quickly as he or she can	Average time for 2 trials to nearest .6 sec (in seconds)	4	3.12	2.80	2.47	2.80 ± .48	.85
		6	2.68	2.46	2.24	2.46 ± .32	.95
		8	2.42	2.24	2.07	2.24 ± .26	.94
Hopping							
On signal, "Ready, Begin," child hops a 25-ft distance as quickly as he or she can	Average time for 4 trials to nearest .11 sec (in seconds)	4	8.33	7.11	5.90	7.11 ± 1.80	.92
		6	5.94	5.12	4.30	5.12 ± 1.21	.88
		8	4.17	3.77	3.37	3.77 ± .59	.98
Galloping							
On signal, "Ready, Begin," child gallops a 25-ft distance as quickly as he or she can	Average time for 3 trials to nearest .1 sec (in seconds)	4	4.70	4.24	3.77	4.24 ± .69	.75
		6	4.40	3.82	3.23	3.82 ± .41	.84
		8	3.36	3.07	2.78	3.07 ± .43	.92
Skipping							
Child skips a 25-ft distance as quickly as he or she can	Average time for 3 trials to nearest .1 sec (in seconds)	4	4.35	3.89	3.44	3.89 ± .67	.75
		6	4.21	3.65	3.09	3.65 ± .83	.84
		8	3.15	2.94	2.73	2.94 ± .31	.92
Balance Beam							
Child walks length of 2-in beam heel-to-toe fashion	Average time for 4 trials to nearest .1 sec (in seconds)	4	26.49	21.12	15.75	21.12 ± 7.96	.84
		6	23.31	19.30	15.29	19.30 ± 5.95	.77
		8	16.92	14.11	11.30	14.11 ± 4.16	.99

Ball Handling

Thowing

		Age				Mean ± SD	
Child throws ball against wall 20 ft away as hard as he or she can	Average ball velocity for 5 trials (in ft/sec)	4	21.03	27.45	33.87	27.45 ± 9.52	.98
		6	26.65	34.91	43.17	34.91 ± 12.25	.88
		8	33.48	44.83	56.17	44.83 ± 16.82	.94

Catching

Child stands 10 ft from tester and catches 12-in playground ball tossed chest height or below waist	Total number of catches in 10 trials	4	3.24	4.00	4.76	4.00 ± 1.13	.99
		6	4.32	4.65	4.98	4.65 ± .49	.98
		8	4.57	4.82	5.07	4.82 ± .38	.94

Two-Arm Strike

Child strikes suspended moving tennis ball against wall 20 ft away	Average ball velocity for 5 trials (in 4 ft/sec)	4	4.84	12.95	21.07	12.95 ± 12.03	.57
		6	14.87	26.28	37.69	26.28 ± 16.91	.89
		8	26.19	38.35	50.51	38.35 ± 18.02	.98

Ball Bounce

Child bounces 8-in playground ball in a 1-ft square	Average number of bounces in 4 trials	4	—	1.88	4.39	.88 ± 3.73	.82
		6	1.22	4.07	6.91	4.07 ± 4.21	.87
		8	3.50	10.15	16.79	10.15 ± 9.86	.94

Kicking

Child kicks 12-in ball against wall 20 ft away as hard as he or she can	Average ball velocity for 5 trials (in ft/sec)	4	13.60	22.07	30.53	22.07 ± 12.55	.52
		6	25.01	29.99	34.96	29.99 ± 7.37	.99
		8	30.61	35.25	39.88	35.25 ± 6.87	.99

Name: Peter Z   Age: 4 years

75th					
50th	×———————I	×			×
25th			×		
			×		
	RUN	BEAM	HOP	SKIP	GALLOP

Raw Scores   2.68 sec   17.50 sec   7.55 sec   4.20 sec   4.00 sec

Figure 14.1

TABLE 14.8
GROSS MOTOR SKILLS SUBTEST ON THE BRUININKS-OSERETSKY TEST OF MOTOR PROFICIENCY

Running Speed Agility

Child runs from a start line to an end line 15 yd away, picks up a block, runs back across the start line (timed to nearest .2 sec)

Balance

Child stands on preferred leg on floor and holds position for 10 sec

Child stands on preferred leg on balance beam and holds position for 10 sec

Child stands on preferred leg on balance beam with eyes closed (timed to nearest second)

Child walks line on floor in normal stride for 6 steps

Child walks forward on balance beam in normal stride for 6 steps

Child walks forward in heel-to-toe fashion on line on floor for 6 steps

Child walks forward in heel-to-toe fashion on balance beam for 6 steps

Child walks forward on balance beam (normal gait) and steps over a stick held at knee height; hands are on hips

Bilateral Coordination

Child taps feet alternately while making circles with index fingers (must complete 10 consecutive foot taps in 90 sec)

Child simultaneously taps foot and index finger on one side of body and then on the other (must complete 10 consecutive taps in 90 sec)

Child simultaneously taps right foot and left index finger and then taps left foot and right index finger on opposite side of body

Child jumps in place with leg and arm on opposite sides of body—right leg, left arm together, then left leg right arm together (must complete 10 consecutive jumps in 90 sec)

Child jumps as high as possible and touches heels (pass or fail)

Upper Limb Coordination

Child bounces tennis ball on floor and catches it using both hands (number of correct catches in 5)

Child uses preferred hand and bounces tennis ball on floor and catches it (number of correct catches in 5)

Child catches tennis ball tossed from 10 ft in two hands (number of correct catches in 5)

Child catches tennis ball tossed from 10 ft in preferred hand (number of correct catches in 5)

Child throws ball overarm at target 4 ft away (number of points in 5 trials)

Child attempts to touch with the index finger a ball swung horizontally in front of him or her (number of points in 5 trials)

Adapted from Bruininks, R. H. (1978) Bruininks-Oseretsky Test of Motor Proficency. Examiner's Manual. Circle Pines, MN.: American Guidance Service.

fine motor tasks and are included in the Perceptual-Performance and General Cognitive Scales.

Leg Coordination is evaluated by having the child walk backward, walk on tiptoe, walk on straight line, stand on one foot, and skip. Arm coordination involves three tasks: bouncing a ball, catching a bean bag, and throwing a bean bag at a target. Four tasks are included in the imitative action sequence: crossing feet at the ankles, folding hands, twiddling thumbs, and sighting through a tube. In the Draw-A-Design task, the child is asked to reproduce various geometric designs including a circle, vertical and horizontal lines, a parallelogram and so on. In the Draw-A-Child task, the child is asked to draw a picture of boy or girl, according to the gender of the child. During the performance of the motor items, observations concerning hand usage and eye preferences also are made.

For each of the scales, including the Motor Scale, the child's raw scores are converted into T scores, based on the child's chronological age. Percentile ranks are also presented for purposes of interpretation. The scales are based on normative data gathered on 1,032 children ages 2½ through 8½ years.

The Vulpé Assessment Battery

The Vulpé Assessment Battery (1982) was developed by physical and occupational therapists to assess a wide variey of behaviors using a clinical approach. Among the areas of behavior that are evaluated are basic sensory functions, expressive and receptive language, object, body, size, space, time, and number concepts as well as gross and fine motor skills. The test, which is a product-oriented assessment tool, also includes tests of muscle strength, motor planning, reflex development and balance which are useful tools for conducting a comprehensive analysis of the young child's gross motor development. With regard to specific gross motor skill development, significant individual motor development achievements are identified for different ages beginning at 1 month and extending to 6 years of age. These skills are organized in an age-based sequence and criteria for assessing mastery of each skill at each age is provided. The gross motor skills assessed by the Vulpé include: sitting, kneeling, standing, walking, stair climbing, running, jumping, kicking, throwing, and balancing. A number of different tasks (usually 1 to 3) are used to assess each motor skill; performance is judged on a number of dimensions ranging from whether the child requires physical or verbal assistance to perform the tasks to whether the child can perform the skill alone and/or can transfer the skill to a different task or environmental context. Overall the test is most useful as a source of information about age-related motor skill and other behavioral achievements in young children. An important limitation is that there has been no formal standardization of the test.

DeOreo Fundamental Motor Skill Inventory (DFMSI)

The DFMSI (DeOreo, 1974) is an informal measure of the product characteristics of motor performance in young children. It was designed to provide simple information about the level of motor skill achievement in children 3, 4, and 5 years of age. Three skill examples are given in Table 14.9. Such an inventory should be used primarily for making decisions about whether more formal assessment of the child's motor development is needed.

Illingworth's Simple Product Checklist

Another informal measure of product characteristics of gross motor development is the checklist provided by Illingworth (1975). The observer simply checks whether the child can perform certain motor skills, such as, jumps with both feet, walks on tiptoes (2½ years), jumps off bottom steps, stands on one foot (3 years), skips on one foot (4 years), and skips on both feet (5 years). It is equally as important to know how long the child has been able to perform the skill and the degree of maturity that he or she has achieved in mastering such skills.

Other Tests

Other product-oriented assessment tools that include gross motor items as a part of a more comprehensive evaluation of the preschool child are the Cooperative Preschool Inventory (Caldwell, 1970; French, 1972), the School Readiness Survey (Egeland, 1972; Jordan & Massey, 1967), the

TABLE 14.9
SELECTED PRODUCT ITEMS FROM THE DEOREO FUNDAMENTAL MOTOR SKILL INVENTORY

Skill	Achievements by Age		
	3 years	4 years	5 years
Striking			
Hits a softly tossed aerial ball (5–8 in) with one-handed sidearm swing	5 of 5 tries		
Using batter's stance and large plastic bat, hits rubber ball on tee (two-arm swing)	2 of 6 tries	3 of 6 tries	5 of 6 tries
Using batter's stance and large plastic bat, hits softly tossed aerial ball (two-arm swing)	1 of 7 tries	2 of 7 tries	3 of 7 tries
Kicking			
Kicks soccer ball	contact 50% of time	Boys 12 ft Girls 8 ft	Boys 18 feet Girls 10 ft
Galloping			
Gallops 20 ft with right foot in lead	Yes	Yes	Yes
Gallops 20 ft with left foot in lead	No	No	Yes

From DeOreo, K. (1974). The DeOreo Fundamental Motor Skill Inventory. Unpublished paper, Kent State University.

Thorpe Developmental Inventory (Thorpe, 1972), and the Head Start Developmental Screening Test and Behavior Rating Scale (Dodds, 1967). These inventories are critically and objectively reviewed by Thorpe and Werner (1974). The Stott Test of Motor Impairment (Henderson & Stott, 1977; Stott, 1966, 1972) also has potential for use in the evaluation of motor skill difficulties in the young child.

PROCESS MEASURES

A more recent approach to the assessment of gross motor development in young children is that of observing and evaluating process characteristics of movement performance (i.e., motor control), that is, the quality, form, or action sequence involved. These techniques focus on how the child moves his or her body to perform a given motor skill. Process evaluation instruments usually are informal in nature; they are subjective in procedure and are rarely based on large standardization. The process approach to the assessment of gross motor skill in young children often is used in clinical settings to provide initial screening of children's movement problems as well as insight into possible contributing factors to movement problems that already have been diagnosed. Most of these instruments require some understanding of the developmental steps involved in the acquisition of motor skills in young children as well as some experience in observing children's movement behavior in play or other naturalistic environments. Most process assessment techniques are organized in a checklist format that contains a series of descriptive statements designed to identify important aspects of movement performance. The interpretation of the information from the checklists is usually simple and varies from one instrument to another.

Williams' Preschool Motor Development Checklist

Williams' checklist (Williams, 1974) is an informal measure of process characteristics of motor development in children ages 3 to 6 years. This checklist deals with basic motor development "immaturities" in 6 of the most common gross motor skills. It includes 4 locomotor skills (running, jumping, hopping, skipping) and 2 ball-handling or object projection skills (throwing and catching). Williams' checklist uses a "question" format and presents some simple guidelines for determining the presence or absence of developmental lags in each skill area. This checklist is best used for outlining the nature of potential movement control problems in young children. Information provided by this checklist can indicate whether the child has isolated motor control problems (e.g., difficulty executing the movements involved in hopping but not in skipping, jumping, or running), general locomotor control difficulties (e.g., immaturities in the movements involved in three or more of the four locomotor skills), or ball-handling problems (e.g., poor control in throwing and catching movements). Data from the checklist can provide subjective insight into the nature of the gross motor control profile of the young child. Information about the nature of the movement control difficulty is detailed enough such that beginning enrichment programs can be planned.

This checklist was developed from published research as well as observational data on characterstic motor development of young children. It is used in both clinical and educational settings. The checklist items and score sheet are given in Table 14.10, and guidelines for interpreting the information gathered are given in Table 14.11.

Motor Control Process Checklists

In these checklists, Williams and Breihan (1979) attempted to create a standardized approach to the assessment of process characteristics of movement control in young children. There are 16 checklists in the battery; they describe movement characteristics of selected gross and fine motor skills and are based on data from 150 children 4, 6, and 8 years of age. The statements in each checklist are descriptions of the movements required for mastery of each skill. Typi-

cally, full mastery of most of the tasks included in this test is not expected until after 6 years of age.

Ten of the gross motor skill checklists are presented in Table 14.12. Each checklist consists of four to six statements about process characteristics to look for in the movement behavior of the child as he or she performs the skill. Percentages of 4-, 6-, and 8-year old children who show various process characteristics in their skill performances are given to the right of each statement. The statements in these checklists are more detailed than those discussed earlier and allow the evaluator to assess more precisely the quality of the child's movement as well as to identify the nature of the motor control problem if one is present. The child performs the skill at least four times, preferably in a naturalistic setting. While the child moves, the evaluator checks those statement that typify or characterize the movement behavior of the child. The general rule of thumb is that the child must display a given process characteristic in at least 75% of the performances if that characteristic is to be considered typical of his or her movement behavior. In addition, if the child does not exhibit two or more of the process characteristics that 70% of same-age children display, he or she might be experiencing some motor control difficulties. Such a child should receive further assessment of motor skills and enrichment activities in the area of delayed motor development.

Test of Gross Motor Development

Ulrich (1985) has recently developed and published the Test of Gross Motor Development. This test is an excellent example of a battery that emphasizes process characteristics of movement and is both norm referenced and criterion refernced. It is one of the few standarized tests that uses a quantitative approach to evaluating process aspects of gross motor skill development in young children (data are provided on children between the ages of 3 and 10 years). The battery is designed to, among other things, identify children who are significantly behind age-expected levels of motor development. It also has the potential, because of its quantitative approach, to an excellent research tool for individuals interested in the scientific study of motor skill acquisition in young children.

TABLE 14.10
WILLIAMS PRESCHOOL MOTOR DEVELOPMENT CHECKLIST

Directions: Carefully observe the child perform each skill several times in different settings. Ask yourself the following questions about the way the young child performs the individual motor skills.

Questions	Yes	No	Questions	Yes	No

Running

1. Does the child experience difficulty in starting, stopping, or making sudden turns?
2. Does the child run with a flat-footed pattern, that is, does he or she receive the weight of the body on the whole foot?
3. Does the child run with toes pointed outward?
4. Do the arms move back and forth in a sideways motion across the body?

Jumping

1. Does the child fail to flex hips, knees, and ankles in the preparatory phase of the jump?
2. Does the child fail to execute a two-footed take-off?
3. Does the child fail to swing the arms back in the preparatory phase and then forward and upward on the executory phase?
4. Does the child land with the hips and knees straight (in extention)?
5. Does the child lose balance on landing?

Skipping

1. Does the child fail to skip a 20-ft distance maintaining smooth, sequential, rhythmical movement?
2. Does the child skip on one foot while the other foot executes a walking or running step?
3. Does the child skip using a flat-footed pattern?
4. Does the child skip with the toes turned outward in duck-walk fashion?
5. Does the child fail to use arm-foot opposition?

Hopping

1. Does the child hop two or three steps and lose control?
2. Are the hopping movements staccato and/or arrhythmical?
3. Do the hands and fingers show tension?
4. Is the nonsupport foot kept in contact with the floor?

Throwing

1. Does the child's body move primarily in the anteroposterior plane?
2. Does the child's body move primarily in the horizontal plane?
3. Does the child hold the ball in the palm of the hand?
4. Does the child show no evidence of weight transfer?
5. Does the child throw by stepping on the same foot as the throwing arm?
6. Does the child fail to follow through?

Catching

1. Does the child catch the ball with arms outstretched and straight?
2. Does the child use the arms, hands, and body as a single unit to trap the ball?
3. Does the child turn his or her head from the ball as he or she catches it?
4. Does the child seem to let the ball bounce off the outstretched arms?
5. Does the child receive the ball with no weight transfer?
6. Does the child fail to watch the flight of the ball?

From Williams, H. Williams' Preschool Motor Development Checklist. (1974) Unpublished paper, University of Toledo.

TABLE 14.11
INTERPRETATION OF WILLIAMS' PRESCHOOL MOTOR DEVELOPMENT CHECKLIST

Running: If 3 of the 4 questions are answered yes, there might be a developmental lag in running

Jumping: If 4 of the 5 questions are answered yes, there might be a development lag in jumping

Skipping: If the child is 4 or 5 years old and the answer to all 5 questions is yes, there might be a developmental lag in skipping

Hopping: If 3 of the 4 questions are answered yes, there might be a developmental lag in hopping

Throwing: If a child is 4 or 5 years old and the answer to 5 of the 6 questions is yes, there might be a developmental lag in throwing

Catching: If the child is 3 years old, and the answer to questions 3, 4, and 6 is yes, keep a watchful eye on this aspect of motor develpmental lag in catching; if the child is 5 years, and the answer to any question is yes, there might be a developmental lag in catching

From Williams, H. Williams' Preschool Motor Development Checklist. (1974). Unpublished paper, University of Toledo.

Two areas of gross motor development are evaluated: locomotion (body projection) and object control (ball handling). Locomotor skills evaluated include running, hopping, leaping, jumping, skipping, and sliding. Object control skills include two-hand striking, bouncing, catching, kicking, and throwing. Each skill is scored according to the presence or absence of selected movement process characteristics. An example of the specific locomotor and object control skill process characteristics that are evaluated, are reported in Table 14.13. If the process characteristic is present, a score of 1 is given; if it is absent, a score of 0 is given. Scores are summed for each skill and can be converted into percentile ranks (recommended for parental use) or standard scores (recommended for educational or clinical program planning). A scale is provided for arranging individual skill standard scores into seven steps ranging from Very Poor to Very Superior. Standard scores for each of the areas of locomotion and object control are summed to arrive at a Gross Motor Development Quotient. This quotient provides an estimate of the child's overall gross motor development and is interpreted in the same way (Very Poor to Very Superior) as individual standard scores. Normative data for the battery are based on 909 children from many racial backgrounds from eight states; a careful analysis of reliability and validity issues also is provided.

McClenaghan-Gallahue Checklists

McClenaghan and Gallahue (1978) provided a set of checklists for observing process characteristics of five gross motor skills. Excerpts from the checklists on throwing behaviors are given in Table 14.14. Information on the checklist includes the position from which the child's movement should be observed, suggested directions for the task, special considerations to be aware of when observing the skill performance, and the actual descriptive statements themselves. The statements focus independently on arm, trunk, and leg actions at three different developmental levels: initial (early), elementary (middle) and mature (advanced and/or adult). The evaluator observes the child perform the desired motor skill several times and checks the statements that typify the child's movement behavior. The information provided by use of the checklists can be used to develop either group or individual profiles of motor development.

USE OF ASSESSMENT RESULTS

Because we know that children who experience lags in motor develoment are more likely than their age mates to display difficulties in adapting to both school and play environments, information about their level of motor skill development is of major importance to the teacher, the school psychologist, and the physician. A scientifically sound and useful diagnosis of gross motor development must be based on information from formal and informal product and process assessments of the child's gross motor behavior. Formal measures of gross motor development are needed to support, clarify, and extend observations of motor behavior made with informal instruments. Formal product measures of motor development are valuable because they provide a frame of reference for interpreting the current status of the child's motor development. It is important to note, however, that it is imprudent and unfair to act as though figures in a table or on a

TABLE 14.12
MOTOR CONTROL PROCESS CHECKLISTS

Skill	Percentage* at Age		
	4	6	8

Object Projection Skills

Throwing

1. Trunk is rotated backward and the weight is shifted to the back foot	44	52	70
2. Throwing arm is moved backward with rotation occurring at the shoulder joint	66	66	84
3. A step is taken toward the intended target	52	74	74
4. The step is in opposition to the throwing arm	44	54	64
5. Body width is shifted forward; the arms lag behind and begins moving forward in the horizontal plane, with the elbow leading	40	56	74
6. Medial rotation of the shoulder and elbow extension occur; the elbow is nearing complete extension at the time of release	56	82	76
7. Wrist is flexed rapidly just before ball is released	32	62	88
8. On the follow through the body and arm continue to rotate forward	18	48	72

Stationary Catching

1. Arms move to a position in front of the body, hands juxtaposed, with the palms of the hands facing each other	72	90	92
2. Hands are turned to accommodate the high or low trajectory of the ball	8	42	84
3. Hands and fingers are "loose" but slightly cupped and pointed in the direction of the oncoming ball	26	62	82
4. Eyes pick up and follow the flight of the ball until ball contact is made	62	88	90
5. Initially, the ball contact is made with both hands simultaneously	34	68	94
6. Adjustments in the elbow and shoulder joint positions are made to accommodate "changes" in the flight of the ball	12	48	80
7. Fingers close immediately around the ball and the arms "give" to absorb the momentum of the ball	14	36	78

Two-Arm Striking

1. Feet are positioned approximately shoulder width apart; the body position is perpendicular to the line of flight of the oncoming ball	56	62	82
2. Trunk is rotated backward and the weight is shifted onto the back foot	32	36	58
3. Lead elbow is held up and out from the body with the bat off the shoulder	50	48	56
4. Eyes follow the flight of the ball until just before contact is made	44	72	88
5. Body weight is shifted forward (onto the opposite foot) in the direction of the intended hit	38	48	58
6. Hips and trunk rotate in the direction of the intended hit, with the hips leading	14	34	74
7. Arms move forward independent of hip action	42	76	74

Ball-Bouncing

1. Body is flexed at the knees, hips, and waist	28	28	48
2. Child uses fingertip control, does not slap at ball	6	40	88
3. Eyes track the ball	24	84	96
4. Height of ball is kept at waist level	12	44	50

Kicking

1. A preliminary step is taken on the support leg toward the ball	30	54	74
2. The kicking leg swings backward	56	74	88
3. The kicking leg swings forward with flexion occurring in the lower leg	88	92	98
4. Body is inclined slightly backward	22	44	60

TABLE 14.12
(*continued*)

Skill	Percentage* at Age		
	4	6	8
5. As the upper leg becomes perpendicular to the floor, extension of the lower leg (at knee) in the direction of the ball	30	74	74
6. The opposite arm swings forward	22	44	60
7. The kicking leg extends and makes contact with the ball	62	90	96
8. The contact is made with the toes; the ankle is in a slightly flexed position	40	64	96
9. Some extension of the lower leg (at the knees) and flexion at the hip occurs	36	48	72
10. The opposite arm continues to swing forward and upward in the follow through	10	20	32
11. Trunk becomes slightly more vertical	12	42	54

Locomotor Skills

Running

1. Arms and legs used in opposition	74	84	98
2. Extension and flexion evident in both legs during running cycle	86	90	98
3. Arms swing freely, close to body	54	68	96
4. Arms are bent at the elbow	64	82	100
5. Support foot hits floor heel first	56	48	66
6. Trunk is inclined slightly forward	56	70	98
7. Head is held erect, facing forward	66	88	100

Hopping

1. Weight is balanced easily on one foot	68	84	100
2. Nonsupport foot is flexed at the knees and does not touch the floor	58	88	98
3. Arms are either held out to the sides to assist with balance or moved up and down to help lift the body	56	74	98
4. In landing, body weight is received on ball of foot and is immediately shifted to entire foot	42	62	62
5. Hips and knees flex on landing to absorb the momentum of body movement	54	74	98
6. Head and trunk are held erect	48	84	98

Galloping

1. Lead foot absorbs body's weight on the heel; weight is transferred to the toes; there is heel-to-toe action in lead foot	68	66	82
2. Trailing foot moves toward lead foot but does not pass lead foot	34	48	74
3. Extension and flexion are evident in both legs during complete galloping cycle	56	66	92
4. Trunk is extended and inclined slightly forward·	52	76	98
5. Arms swing freely from shoulder	34	60	84
6. Body is momentarily suspended in air	58	72	100
7. Child continually leads with same foot	66	80	98

Skipping

1. A normal walking step is combined with a hop; a forward step-hop on one foot is followed by a forward step-hop on the opposite foot	34	86	96
2. There is a continuous sequential and alternating step-hop action	32	80	94
3. Arms swing freely in opposition to leg movements	8	48	42
4. Knee and hip of the nonsupport leg are flexed to aid in the speed of the skip	40	84	96
5. The body is suspended in the air momentarily	42	86	92
6. There is obvious smoothness and rhythm in the total movement sequence	12	50	52

TABLE 14.12
(*continued*)

Skill	Percentage* at Age		
	4	6	8
Balance Beam Walk			
1. Child alternates feet and can execute a simple walking pattern	84	96	98
2. Child can maintain a heel-to-toe walking sequence	24	60	72
3. Arms are held below shoulder height; there is no flailing	24	54	74
4. Movement is smooth; there is no exaggerated body sway	26	50	74
5. Feet are placed straight (pointing forward) on the beam	42	62	82
6. Head is errect, facing forward	0	2	0

From Williams, H., & Breihan, S. (1979) Motor Control Tasks for Young Children. Unpublished paper, University of Toledo.
* Percentage of children at specified age who show the process characteristic in their skill performance.

chart are an irrefutable indication of whether or not a child is "normal."

Process information is used to elaborate on the product frame of reference. Process information is especially important because it considers directly body movement to determine what is missing from or contributing to the child's lack of adequate motor control. Informal process assessment techniques are particularly important for gaining insight into how the child goes about solving the problem of performing a task. These techniques often provide information about the child's level of understanding of the task to be performed. This type of information is integral to an accurate diagnosis because lags in motor development can be as much a function of the young child's un-

TABLE 14.13
A LOCOMOTOR AND OBJECT CONTROL EXAMPLE FROM THE GROSS MOTOR DEVELOPMENT TEST

Skill	Description	Process Characteristics (PC)	Age at Which 60% of Children Achieve PC
Hop	Child hops 3 times on each foot	Foot of nonsupport bent and carried in back of body	5 years
		Nonsupport legs swings in pendular fashion	7 years
		Arms bent at elbows/swing forward on take-off	7 years
		Able to hop on right & left feet	4 years
Bounce	Child bounces 8–10″ ball 3 times; 3 trials	Contacts ball with 1 hand at hip height	7 years
		Pushes ball with fingers	6 years
		Ball contacts floor in front of foot on side of hand used for bouncing	7 years

TABLE 14.14
EXCERPTS FROM THE MCCLENAGHAN-GALLAHUE CHECKLIST ON THROWING

Body Part	Level of Development		
	Initial	*Elementary*	*Mature*
Arm	Motion is mainly from elbow Fingers spread at release	Ball is held behind head Arm is swung forward high over the shoulder	Arm is swung backward in preparation Throwing elbow moves forward horizontally as it extends
Trunk	Trunk remains perpendicular to target Little rotary action occurs during throw	Trunk rotates forward throwing side during preparatory action Definite shift of body weight occurs	Trunk markedly rotates to throwing side during preparatory action Throwing shoulder drops slightly
Leg	Feet remain stationary	Leg on same side as throwing arm steps forward	Weight during preparatory movement is on rear foot As weight is shifted, there is a step with the opposite foot

From McClenaghan, B., & Gallahue, D. (1978). Fundamental Movement: A Development and Remedial Approach, Philadelphia: Saunders.

derstanding of the *what* and *how* of a task as they are of the child's ability to do the task.

The most significant, direct, and immediate uses that can be made of information from gross motor development screening and evaluation are the following:

1. *Planning and evaluating effective gross motor curricula for young children.* To individualize early sensory and motor learning experiences for young children, professionals need to be able to group or to identify children according to motor skill development levels. When specific aspects of the gross motor behavior of the child are know, basic tasks can be modified in a variety of ways to encourage individual refinement of and success in motor skill performance at the child's present level of development as well as to promote growth toward higher levels of skill mastery.

2. *Early identification of motor dysfunctions.* Motor dysfunctions can impede the child's physical, mental, social, and emotional development. Information about gross motor skill development can be valuable to the teacher of the young child for early learning and educational counseling. Such information is vital when making decisions about whether the child possesses the basic skills needed to succeed in simple classroom activities. The child who devotes a major share of his or her energy to assuming and maintaining basic postures or to controlling movements of the body will have much less energy to devote to other important activities that are part of early development. Data about the child's level of gross motor development are important determinants as to when a child should enter school or whether he or she should be placed in a developmental enrichment environment.

3. *Design of individual programs of enrichment activities.* Motor skill deficiencies often accompany and contribute to other learning, behavior, and attention problems of the young child. When this is the case, some attention almost always is required to improve the motor capacities of the child before other learning and behavior problems can be effec-

tively remediated. If, on the other hand, the young child has learning, memory, and attentional problems but no accompanying motor development difficulties, gross motor tasks might be used in creative ways to help stimulate improvement in these other dimensions of development.

Results of gross motor skill screening and evaluation in the preschool child are most useful in a comprehensive, multidimensional assessment of the young child. Motor development data are best interpreted for prognosis and remediation purposes in association with information from other educational, psychological, and medical measures. At a minimum, information about the child's fine motor control or eye-hand coordination (e.g., cutting, peg manipulation, and pencil or crayon usage), simple perceptual skills (e.g., identification of colors, color matching, visual, verbal, and tactile kinesthetic discrimination of shapes and sizes, and figure–ground perception) and general characteristics of eye movement control ought to accompany the child's motor development record. It is only when information from gross motor development testing is used or viewed in conjunction with information about these other aspects of sensory and motor development that appropriate prognostic statements and remediation techniques for gross motor development can be established or prescribed.

If the child has only gross motor deficiencies (e.g., no accompanying deficits in other sensory and motor behaviors), it is more likely that the motor development problems observed are temporary and simply reflect an uneven growth process that will self-correct with time. If, on the other hand, gross motor deficits are accompanied by fine motor and/or other sensory–perceptual difficulties, there might be underlying neurological problem(s). In this case, referral to a pediatric neurologist and/or other appropriate medical personnel for futher evaluation might be appropriate. The motor system (including the control of eye muscles) is more likely than other systems to show deficits when something has gone awry with basic central and/or periphereal neurophysiological processes.

At a behavioral level, information-gathering behaviors (e.g., the way children use their eyes to pick-up information from the environment) and information interpretation skills (e.g., figure–ground perception) can contribute significantly to the lack of refined fine and gross motor skills. Gross motor deficits are often, at least in part, a reflection of inadequate support skills in visual perception. Therefore, remediation and enrichment programs for children with both gross motor and simple perceptual deficits need to focus on improving the supporting perceptual behaviors as well as the movement behaviors themselves.

Professionals working in educational settings with preschool children should use the following guide to gross motor development:

1. Screen all children in gross motor development prior to or early in their entry into the preschool program.
2. For initial screening, use a simple motor development checklist such as those developed by Cratty (1970) or Williams (1974).
3. Observe the children in naturalistic play settings.
4. Use this information to determine which children might need closer observation.
5. Use a formal instrument to screen more carefully the identified children for gross motor process and product deficiencies.
6. Examiners who must choose one measure over another, should be sure to include some evaluation of the process characteristics of the child's motor behavior.
7. Children with questionable abilities should be referred to a motor development specialist, physical education teacher, or school psychologist for a more formal and comprehensive evaluation.
8. When in doubt about the child's motor development difficulties, talk to or refer the child to the appropriate personnel within or outside the school setting.

REFERENCES

Bayley, N. (1965). Comparisons of mental and motor test scores for ages 1–15 months by sex, birth order, race, geographical location and education of parents. *Child Development, 36,* 379–411.

Bruiniks, R. H. (1978). *Bruininks-Oseretsky Test of Motor Proficiency. Examiner's Manual.* Circle Pines, MN: American Guidance Service.

Caldwell, B. M. (1970). *Cooperative Preschool Inven-*

tory (Revised). Berkely, CA: Educational Testing Services.

Cashin, G. (1975) *The Cashin Test of Motor Development*. Unpublished master's thesis, Bowling Green State University.

Cratty, B. J. (1970). *Perceptual and Motor Development in Infants and Young Children*. New York: Macmillan.

Cratty, B. J. (1972). *Physical Expressions of Intelligence*. Englewood Cliffs, N.J.; Prentice-Hall.

DeOreo, K. L. (1971). *Dynamic and Static Balance in Preschool Children*. Unpublished doctoral dissertation, University of Illinois.

DeOreo, K., & Keogh, J. (1980). Performance of fundamental motor tasks. In C. Corbin (Ed.), *A Textbook of Motor Development*. Dubuque, IA: W. C. Brown, 1980, pp. 76–91.

DeOreo, K. Refining locomotor skills. (1980). In C. Corbin (Ed.), *A Textbook of Motor development*. Dubuque, Iowa: W. C. Brown, pp. 59–67.

DeOreo, K. (1974). *The DeOreo Fundamental Motor Skill Inventory*. Unpublished paper, Kent State University.

Dodds, J. (1967). *The Head Start developmental screening test and behavior rating scale* CAP-HS Form 56, July, GSA-DC.

Egan, D., Illingworth, R. S., & MacKeith, R. C. (1969). Developmental screening 0 to 5 years. In *Clinics in Developmental Medicine*, (30). London: Heinemann.

Egeland, B. Review of School Readiness Survey. (1972). In O. Boros (Ed.), *The Seventh Mental Measurement Yearbook*. Highland Park, N. J.: Gryphon Press, p. 763.

Espenschade, A. S., & Eckert, H. M. (1980). *Motor development*. Columbus, OH: Merril.

Flinchum, B. F. (1975). *Motor Development in Early Childhood: A Guide for Movement Education with Ages 2 to 6*. St. Louis: Mosby, pp. 10–51.

Folio, M. R. & Fewell, R. R. (1983). *Peabody Developmental Motor Scales and Activity Cards*. Allen, Tx: Developmental Learning Materials Teaching Resources.

Fowler, W. (1975). The role of cognitive learning in motor development. In *Final Report of the State of the Art Research Review and Conference, Psycho-Motor Development in Preschool Handicaped Children*. Milwaukee: Vasquez Associates, 1975.

Frankenburg, W. K., & Dodds, J. B. (1967). The Denver Developmental Screening Test. *Journal of Pediatrics, 71*, 181.

Frankenburg. W. K., & Dodds, J. B., Fandal, A. (1970) *The Revised Denver Developmental Screening Test Manual*. Denver: University of Colorado Press.

Frankenburg, W., Goldstein, A., & Camp, B. W. (1971). The Revised Denver Developmental Screening

Test: Its accuracy as a screening instrument. *Journal of Pediatrics, 71*, 988.

French, J. L. (1972). Review of cooperative preschool inventory, revised edition. In O. Buros (Ed.). *The Seventh Mental Measurement Yearbook*. Highland Park, N.J.: Gryphon Press, p. 730–731.

Garfield, J. C. (1964) Motor impersistence in normal and brain damaged children. *Neurology, 14*, 623.

Gesell, A. (1973) *The First Five Years of Life: A Guide to the Study of the Preschool Child*. New York: Harper & Row.

Gesell, A., & Amatruda, C. (1947). *Developmental Diagnosis*. New York: Heever.

Henderson, S. E., & Stott, D. H. (1977). Finding the clumsy child: Genesis of a test of motor impairment. *Journal of Human Movement Studies, 3*, 38–48.

Illingworth, R. S. (1975). *The Development of the Infant and Young Child: Normal and Abnormal*. Edinburgh: Livingstone.

Jordan, F. L., & Massey, J. (1967). *School Readiness Survey ages 4–6*. Palo Alto, CA: Consulting Psychologists Press.

Keogh, J. F. (1969). Change in motor performance during early school years (Tech. Rep. 2–69). Los Angeles: University of California at Los Angeles, Department of Physical Education.

Keogh, J. F. (1975). Consistency and constancy in preschool motor development. In H. J. Muller, R. Decker & F. Schilling (Eds.). *Motor Behavior of Preschool Children*. Schorndorff: Hofman, 1975.

McCarthy, D. (1972). *McCarthy Scales of Children's Abilities*. New York: Psychological Corporation.

McClenaghan, B., & Gallahue, D. (1978). *Fundamental movement: A Developmental and Remedial Approach*. Philadelphia: Saunders.

McGraw, M. (1963) *The Neuromuscular Maturation of the Human Infant*. (Reprint Ed.) New York: Hafner.

Milne, C., Seefeldt, V., & Reuschlen, P. (1975). Relationship between grade, sex, race and motor performance in young children. *Research Quarterly, 47*, 726.

Paine, R. S., & Oppe, T. E. (1966). *Neurological Examination of Children*. Philadelphia: Lippincott, pp. 150–195.

Piaget, J. (1963) *The origins of intelligence in children*. New York: Norton.

Prechtl, H. F. R. Assessment and significance of behavioral states. In S. R. Berenberg (Ed.) (1977). *Brain—fetal and infant—current research on normal and abnormal development*. The Hague: Nijoff, pp. 79–90.

Prechtl, H. F. R. & Beintema, D. J. (1964). *The neurological examination of the full term newborn infant*. London: Heinemann.

Riggs, M. L. (Ed.). (1980). *Movement Education for Pre-*

school Children. Reston, Va.: Association of the American Alliance for Health, Physical Education, Recreation and Dance.

Roberton, M. A. (1978). Longitudinal evidence for developmental stages in the forceful overarm throw. *Journal of Human Movement Studies*, 167–175.

Roberton, M. A. & Langendorfer, S. (1980). Testing motor development sequences across 9—14 years. In C. Nadeau, et al. (Eds.). *Psychology of Motor Behavior and Sport*, Urbana, Ill.: Human Kinetic Press, pp. 269–279.

Seefeldt, V., Reuschlein, S., & Vogel, P. (1972). *Sequencing Motor Skills Within the Physical Education Curriculum*. Paper presented at the American Association of Health, Physical Education, and Recreation National Convention, Houston, Texas.

Shope, G. N. (1976). *Relationships Between Striking Skills and Various Perceptual Components in 5 year olds*. Unpublished master's thesis, Kent State University.

Skovran, S. K. (1977). *The Relationship Between Usual Information Processing and Motor Proficiency in 5 year old Children*. Unpublished master's thesis, Kent State University.

Stewart, M., & DeOreo, K. (1980). Motor skill developmental analysis: An introduction In C. Corbin (Ed.), *A Textbook of Motor Development*. Dubuque, IA: W. C. Brown, pp. 42–43.

Stott, D. H. (1966). A general test of motor impairment for children. *Developmental Medicine and Child Neurology, 8*, 523.

Stott, L. H., & Ball, R. S. (1965) Infant and preschool mental tests: Review and evaluation. *Monographs of the Society for Research in Child Development, 101*, 30.

Stott, D. H., Moyes, F. A.., & Henderson, S. E. (1972). *A Test of Motor Impairment*. Guelph, Ont.: Brook Educational Publishing Ltd.

Thorpe, H. S. (1972). *The Thorpe Developmental Inventory: Ages three to six years: Instructional manual*. Davis, CA: Office of Medical Education, The University of California at Davis, School of Medicine.

Thorpe, H. S., & Werner, E. E. (1974) Developmental screening of preschool children: A critical review of inventories used in health and educational programs. *Pediatrics 53*, 362–370.

Ulrich, D. A. (1985). *Test of Gross Motor Development*. Austin, TX: Pro-Ed, Inc.

Vulpe, S. G. (1982). *Vulpe' Assessment Battery*. Toronto, Ontario, Canada: National Institute on Mental Retardation.

Wickstrom, R. (1977). *Fundamental Motor Patterns*. Philadelphia: Lea & Febiger.

Wild, M. (1938). The behavior pattern of throwing and some observations concerning the course of development in children. *Research Quarterly, 9*, 20–24.

Williams, H. (1974). *Williams' Preschool Motor Development Checklist*. Unpublished paper, University of Toledo.

Williams, H., & Breihan, S. (1979). *Motor Control Tasks for Young Children*. Unpublished paper, University of Toledo.

Williams, H., Clement, A., Logsdon, B., Scott, S., & Temple, I. (1970). *A Study of Perceptual Motor Charcteristics of Children in Kindergarten Through Sixth Grade*. Unpublished paper, University of Toledo.

Williams, H. G., & DeOreo, K. (1980). Perceptual-motor development in children. In C. Corbin (Ed.), *A textbook of motor development*. Dubuque, IA: W. C. Brown.

Zaichkowsky, L. D., Zaichkowsky, L. B., & Martinek, T. J. (1980). *Growth and development: The child and physical activity*. St. Louis: Mosby.

15

Assessment of Visual Functioning

REBECCA R. FEWELL

The world and how it is experienced is significantly different for blind individuals than it is for the sighted. Unquestionably, blindness affects not only those who are blinded, but also those around them. Gowman (1957) considered blindness the most severe of all handicaps and noted the negative stereotype blindness evokes by arousing feelings of pity, threat, and fundamental impotence. Scott (1969) pointed out that blindness can have a variety of effects on social behavior. The severity of difficulty experienced by a person with visual loss is influenced by the cause of the impairment, degree of visual loss, age at the time of loss, eye care or degree of correction, reactions of others to the loss, and the individual's strengths, weaknesses, and attitudes. The assessment of visual impairment must be broad based. It would include the physical attributes as well as the needs, resources, and expectations of the visually impaired person and his or her family. Especially because of the compounding detrimental effects of limited visual ability, it is particularly important that visual assessment occur during the early years when the child is most receptive to correction and intervention.

This chapter will review the developmental characteristics of vision, visual impairments in young children, and the impact visual impairments can have on other aspects of human development. The chapter concludes with a review of informal and formal procedures for the assessment of vision and practical suggestions are made to facilitate the assessment of young children with visual impairments.

DEVELOPMENTAL ASPECTS OF VISION

The normal newborn has a well-developed visual system that is immediately used to gain information about the environment and how to interact with the environment. In the early months immediately following birth visual acuity, accommodation, and ocular control improve rapidly, giving the normal child a visual acuity of approximately 20/100 (Fantz et al., 1962). Many vision specialists maintain there is little change in visual abilities during the first month of life, but a steady increase in spatial abilities occurs between one and six months of age (Atkinson & Braddick, 1979; Dobson & Teller, 1978; Morse & Trief, 1985;

Sokol, 1978). Different measurement techniques used to assess vision can influence visual acuity estimates. According to Hoyt and colleagues (1982), the following acuities have been recorded at birth, 6, and 12 months respectively: optokinetic nystagmus: 20/300, 20/100, 20/60; forced preferential looking: 20/400, 20/100, 20/50; visually evoked potential: 20/100, 20/20, 20/20.

Early functional behaviors require the use of vision in hand–mouth, mouth–eye, and hand–eye skills. These skills enable infants to visually locate and suck their fingers, bottles, rattles, and so forth and prepare them to act on their environment by using their hands to grasp spoons and feed themselves, bat mobiles, and eventually direct their own play activities. Increased precision in reaching, placing, and tracking objects leads to developing visual competence. By two years, many of the tasks used to determine cognitive competence depend on vision as the major source of stimulus input (for example, block building, puzzles, etc.). The assessment of visual acuity can provide some understanding of central vision and the loss of visual efficiency. Table 15.1 provides comparisons of Snellen Equivalents to visual efficiency ratings.

VISUAL IMPAIRMENTS IN YOUNG CHILDREN

Fortunately, very few people are totally blind; however, the number of individuals requiring

TABLE 15.1
COMPARISON OF VISUAL ACUITY RATINGS IN SNELLEN EQUIVALENTS WITH VISUAL EFFICIENCY EXPRESSED IN PERCENTAGES

Snellen Rating of Visual Acuity	Central Visual Acuity (%)	Loss of Visual Efficiency (%)
20/20	100	0
20/40	85	15
20/50	75	25
20/80	60	40
20/100	50	50
20/200	20	80

From Farrell, G. (1958) Snellen and the E Chart. *The Sight-Saving Review, 28,* 96–99. Reprinted with permission of The National Society to Prevent Blindness. (The primary source of these ratings is from the Section on Ophthalmology of the American Medical Association, 1955.)

some level of eye care is quite large. Of the 83.8 million youth 0 to 26 years old in the United States in 1970, almost one-fourth had eye problems; approximately 21 million required eye care, 180,000 were partially sighted (measurable acuity in the better eye 20/80 or less with correction); 32,000 of these were legally but not totally blind, and about 13,000 were totally blind (Kakalik et al., 1974).

The American Printing House for the Blind (author, 1986) provides a registry of visually impaired students based on federal figures from four major data sources. According to the 1986 registry, there were 2,519 visually impaired children enrolled in infant programs, 2,993 enrolled in preschool programs, and 1,027 enrolled in kindergarten programs. It is interesting to note that the totals for all elementary grades are consistent, within 200 pupils, with the enrollment in kindergarten programs. These figures indicate that 1,000 to 2,000 visually impaired children are being provided special education services each year. These figures represent actual counts and provide accurate information regarding the number of children with serious visual problems. The consistency of these data across age levels might be a result of the existence of a central agency that tracks visually impaired children from the age at which initial diagnosis is made and service is provided. Reliable databases enable states and community agencies to project service needs and allocate funding and services in a careful and consistent manner.

It is widely accepted that the earlier visual defects are recognized and treated, the more favorable the prognosis, both in terms of the child's vision, as well as development in other areas closely related to vision (Ellingham et al. 1976; Morse & Trief, 1985; Odom et al., 1982; Sokol, 1978).

Ellingham and coworkers (1976) reported four possible factors that identify a child as being at risk for developing a visual impairment:

1. Prematurity
2. Family history of a visual defect
3. Infection during pregnancy
4. Difficult or assisted labor

Correctable visual impairments can become

permanent if early problems are not diagnosed and treated before the child is six years of age (Spellman et al., 1979). For example, amblyopia, the loss of function of one eye because of excessive use of the stronger eye, cannot be corrected once the damage occurs. In many amblyopia cases, the child appears visually alert, with no obvious difficulty and the unequal usage of the eyes goes unnoticed. The only indicator of this disorder might be an obvious incoordination of binocular vision, which might be noticed if the child has strabismus or a turning in or out of either eye. Difficulty in muscular control, focusing, or tracking a moving object also might indicate visual problem, but these impaired functions often go unnoticed and untreated until too late.

In young children, eye muscles develop, cranial nerve pathways form, and the brain learns to decode messages relayed to it, all in an interdependent and simultaneous fashion. It is important that in these formative years development proceeds optimally. If a visual problem is noted during this developmental period, it is important that an eye specialist be seen and corrective measures be taken to ameliorate the problem early, before concommitant difficulties develop.

Significant visual impairment, particularly blindness, severely affects the child's skill development in all areas. Early identification of visual impairment can lead to careful monitoring of developing skills in all areas, specialized assessment, and remedial instruction that has proven effective with children with sensory problems.

A young child's visual impairment can seriously affect the lives of family members. The family can and should learn ways to help the child acquire the necessary skills to lead as normal a life as possible. Professional support services are available to families of the visually impaired to help them adjust and cope with related problems. The attitudes of parents greatly influence the child's social and emotional adjustment (Lowenfeld, 1964); by accepting the child and his or her impairment, the parents are better able to help the child develop a positive self-concept that will eventually affect how others view the child. Early identification and successful treatment of visual impairment can lead to the amelioration of the deleterious long-term effects associated with the disability.

IMPACT OF VISUAL IMPAIRMENTS ON DEVELOPMENT

Visual impairments have very serious interactive effects on a child's skill development in all areas. This section briefly describes the major developmental problems associated with visual impairment that are cited in the literature.

Motor Development

Children who are blind, or have light perception only, experience the world differently than those with normal vision; as a consequence, selected motor behaviors develop slower than normal, are less efficient, or, in some cases, never develop fully (DuBose, 1979). Unfortunately, although the progression of motor development among sighted children is well known, there is very little information on the progressive development of motor skills in young visually impaired children. Warren (1977) traced this lack of knowledge to two sources: school-age populations are much more accessible to study than preschool-age children, and the methodology available for assessing motor skills is more appropriate for the older group. Thus, the focus of research with visually impaired children has been mostly on the older child. There have been many studies of motor skill achievement in blind children over five years of age, but very few before age five. The importance of mobility training and its relationship to motor skill achievement accounts for many of these studies (Buell, 1950; Cratty et al., 1968; Graham, 1965; Harley et al., 1980). However, few researchers have provided systematic data on the hierarchial progression of motor skill development in the younger child. In general, researchers agree that blind children do not meet sighted norms; Buell (1950) attributed these developmental lags to insufficient physical activity before the child enters school, while Burlingham (1965), DuBose (1976), and Eichorn and Vigaroso (1967) stressed the critical role parents play in failing to effectively encourage independent movement among their young blind children.

Primarily because of the efforts of two research groups, some information on motor skill development among blind infants is available (Adelson & Fraiberg 1974; Fraiberg, 1977; Norris et al., 1957). Norris and coworkers (1957) found evidence for developmental delay in certain areas, most notably, unilateral reaching, persistent reaching, scissors grasp, manipulation of pegs into holes, and scribbling. Adelson and Fraiberg (1974) found that blind babies lagged behind controls on the following gross motor skills included in the psychomotor developmental subscale of the Bayley Scales of Infant Development: elevating one's self by one's arms, in prone position (6.65 month delay); pulls up to standing position (4.40 month delay); walks alone for three steps (3.55 month delay); and walks across a room alone (7.15 month delay). Motor skills that require relatively stable, in-place movement, such as sitting, rolling, and standing were delayed only slightly, while skills that require movement in space such as holding up head, crawling, creeping, and walking were more severely delayed. There is more to visual development delay than just achieving the motor milestone more slowly than normally sighted age peers. It is also the quality of the movement that is significantly less efficient among visually impaired children. When walking, the blind child will not only be delayed in initiation, but also is likely to retain a wide lateral gait, walk with toes outward, evidence less cross lateral rotation, and walk with his or her head held in a downward position.

Selected motor skills among preschool blind and partially sighted children appear to be delayed when compared to the development of their sighted peers. The delay might be caused by the interaction of impaired vision and the lack of early motor activity. In the assessment of motor skill achievement in children with visual impairments, it is important to examine the ways in which these factors contribute to or detract from the child's performance. It is important to train young blind children to acquire efficient and effective motor patterns because later skills build on earlier foundational skills, and the continued use of poor skills at lower stages contribute to poor skills at higher levels. This is illustrated in the examination of how wide gait, shuffle step walking contributes to a slow and motorically inefficient, thus tiring and awkward, running pattern. With early walking and running patterns of this sort, the blind child is less likely to be a successful active play partner with sighted peers and will, in many cases, elicit glances of pity.

Although little research has been conducted on visually impaired young preschool children, even fewer studies have focused on the motor skill development among older preschool children with visual impairments. Folio (1974) examined a population of multiply handicapped visually impaired children and found them to be delayed in the advanced projectile skills of running, hopping, jumping, and skipping. While considerable motor delay is expected because of severe visual impairment, cognitive, hearing, and even social deficits each contribute to motor delays. Such multiply handicapped children frequently fail to understand how complex movements are made and how movement sequences are linked in smooth routines. They frequently also have balance problems in conjunction with some hearing problems and fail to participate in coactive movements and learn movements in tandem with peers and adults.

Language Development

Although very few researchers have investigated language development among blind or visually impaired children, a number of investigators have made extensive studies into the ways in which blind children use language in what is called ''verbalism'' or ''parroting'' (Burlingham, 1961; Cutsforth, 1932; DeMott, 1972; Dokecki, 1966; Harley, 1963; Nagera & Colonna, 1965). Blind children appear to use words that describe things seen, but the words frequently convey a feeling or reaction rather than a visual perspective. After reviewing numerous studies on the language abilities of blind children, Warren (1977) concluded that the language development of blind and sighted children is essentially similar by the age of four to five years, but prior to that time some differences are noted. First words spoken can differ in these two populations, reflecting the difference in their early experiences. For example, the word *ball* appears very early in the vocabulary of sighted infants as it is a favorite first toy and is associated with pleasant exchanges with a parent as a play partner. When a ball escapes the clutches of a blind infant the child might be unable to relocate it or track its trajectory. Without object permanence and no visual presence, the ball is dropped from the child's thoughts and is pursued no further. Thus a *ball* is not a favorite first toy for a blind child and the word *ball* does not become a high priority word for the blind child. Parents of blind children recognize that a ball has distinct disadvantages as a toy for their baby and make other toy selections. For all these reasons, the word *ball* is less familiar and learned later by blind babies than sighted babies.

Blind children tend to be slower to demonstrate the surge of vocabulary growth seen in very active and mobile sighted children between 16 and 18 months of age (Burlingham, 1961). The early expressions of blind children are dominated by agent–action–object constructions, that focus on what is currently happening or on an immediate need. For example, they state, "Mommy cook dinner," or "Sissy kiss me," to comment on present happenings rather than future projections of what is about to transpire. These expressions contain fewer questions and adjectives than do language samples of sighted children because visually impaired children are slower in acquiring labels that can be generalized across multiple conditions. They have not had as many opportunities as sighted children to associate shapes, colors, and sizes, with objects in their environment, thus inhibiting the attachment of visual connections to verbal labels. Often, blind children demonstrate higher receptive than expressive language skills when assessed. Although they have frequently stored many concepts in their receptive memories, they cannot always retrieve the visually related expressions to use the terms appropiately. Blind children, however, equal or exceed sighted children's norms for sentence length (Wilson & Halverson, 1947). Expressive language among blind children is often characterized by repetitions of stored facts or of statements previously heard or made with less active extemporaneous expressions.

Verbal comprehension problems can be seen in the difficulty some blind children have in following two and three stage commands and in making sequenced discriminations among objects (e.g., "*Before* you touch the *little circle,* give me the *large triangle.*"). The use of personal pronouns illustrates further difficulties for blind children. Sighted children begin to use the personal pronouns *me* and *I* at about 2½ years of age, whereas blind children do not use them until 3 to 4½ years. This might be related to the blind child's identity of himself or herself as others refer to him

or her rather than as an individual capable of acting on the environment. If differences in the rate of language development between sighted and visually impaired children continue after the children are 4 to 5 years old, the differences might be related to delayed cognitive or emotional development.

Cognitive Development

Warren (1977) indicated that blind and sighted children differ in several areas of cognitive development. Fortunately, many of the blind child's deficiencies can be remediated through intervention. Many sensorimotor schemas are delayed in young blind children (DuBose, 1979; Piaget & Inhelder, 1969; Stephens, 1972). For example, there is delayed understanding of object concept because objects must be brought to the blind child for tactile exploration. Object permanence typically is delayed by one to three years in blind children because the children are unable to readily follow and note the appearance or disappearance of objects. The sighted child can construct and visually compare structures, thus learning about spatial constructions, such simultaneous comparisons are not a part of the young blind child's experiences. Therefore, concepts related to such sensorimotor schemata are delayed among blind children relative to their sighted peers. Cause–effect relations also are less likely to be perceived by the young blind child because he cannot view the consequences of his actions. Using objects and strategies to obtain desired outcomes is a means–ends scheme and blind children are deprived of opportunities to observe events, and their antecedents and less able to acquire methods to reach desired ends. As a result, they have fewer and somewhat fractionated experiences in developing a repertoire of problem-solving skills.

Higgins (1973) examined classification skills among blind children between the ages of 5 and 11 years, and found no evidence of a general developmental classificatory lag. However, the blind children did not perform as well on abstract concepts as they did on concrete concepts. Blindness can result in a delay in the acquisition of relational concepts, such as *in front of, behind, beside, between,* and so forth. Additionally, as concepts are used to describe different settings and conditions, they can become increasingly difficult to generalize. Likewise, concepts involving conservation are frequently delayed in the blind child. Educators might facilitate the development of conservation in the blind child by availing information to the child's nonimpaired senses so that adequate information is available from which to perceive relationships, draw inferences, and make conclusions.

Because most intelligence tests require vision of the examinee, it is difficult to make comparisons between the measured intelligence of blind and sighted children. Smits and Mommers (1976) and Tillman and Bashaw (1968) examined subscale performance on the WISC (Wechsler, 1949, 1974) and found superior numerical memory performance by the blind on the Digit Span subtest, while sighted children performed significantly higher on the abstract verbal subtest Similarities. Crucial to the education and general functioning of the blind child is his ability to adapt to new and novel situations. Until ability tests are developed to assess the blind child's performance on variables crucial to adaptation in a sighted world, we continue to fall far short in the assessment of intelligence among blind children.

Perceptual Development

The tactile discrimination abilities of blind and sighted children have been compared in several studies. Cutaneous localization (Jones, 1972), form discrimination (Schwartz, 1972), and weight discrimination (Block, 1972) were all found to be developed to a slightly better degree among the blind subjects. Although significant, the differences were small. More extensive studies are needed to determine why these differences favor blind children. When more complex or cross-modal perceptual skills (e.g., form identification, spatial relations, perceptual motor integration) were examined, blind children tended to lag behind their sighted peers. However, most of these perceptual studies used subjects over 6 years of age, and the age of onset of blindness appeared to be a crucial variable. To determine the nature of the development of complex and cross-modal perceptual skills in blind children, it is necessary for researchers to undertake studies with younger

subjects and to follow these subjects longitudinally. It is likewise essential that the studied population be limited to totally blind students. Given the small numbers of subjects available at most research sites, it is understandable why the field continues to have many unanswered questions.

Social Development

Considerable evidence suggests delayed and aberrant social skills among the blind. Vision plays a major role in facilitating the process of human bonding that enables the human infant and his or her parents to develop a special attachment for one another. Without vision, the process is more difficult and complex. The attachment between the blind infant and his or her parent emerges at a slower pace and expresses itself through interactional patterns that involve touching and vocal play. For example, the author observed a mother and her blind infant engage in repeated dyadic exchanges during a series of tactile games involving the child's and the mother's arms and hands. The infant was seated in front of the mother with his back to her and the dyadic exchanges were made through touching one another.

The play of blind children is characterized by delayed expressions of symbolic representation and of the self in play. With fewer opportunities to observe naturally occurring environmental events, it is understandable why play using deferred imitations is both delayed and impoverished among blind children.

Play enables children to practice social behaviors that they are expected to demonstrate proficiency with at later ages. The inability to observe and interpret the context or situation in which interactions occur makes the learning of nonverbal social skills particularly difficult, resulting in delayed social maturity and interpersonal behavior.

Hallenbeck (1954) studied blind residential students and found that a crucial correlate of emotional adjustment was whether the child had had a positive relationship with another person before entering school. Other studies have demonstrated the importance of supportive early emotional relationships to the healthy development of visually impaired children. The ways in which parents relate to their young blind child invariably affects the child's developing self concept.

Blindisms or abberant stereotypic mannerisms such as rocking, hand flicking, eye poking, and echolalia are common problems with some blind children. If these behavioral peculiarities persist, they call increased negative attention to the child and serve to distance others from the child.

Self-care Development

Independence and self-maintenance are essential for the healthy development of visually impaired and blind students. Without visual models to imitate, blind children must learn eating, dressing, bathing, toileting, and grooming skills through more concrete activities and through verbal instruction with physical prompting; easier nonconventional routes to the terminal behavior might be more appropriate than the conventional approach in some situations (e.g., the blind child can learn to apply toothpaste to teeth instead of to a brush). Toileting problems are reported more frequently with blind children than sighted children; however, this appears to be related to the lack of visual images and unclear expectations rather than to physical delay. In all areas of self-care, training can be modified for easier task completion. The blind child might be slower in achieving independence, but the same degree of proficiency experienced by sighted individuals can be achieved eventually.

General Observation of Visual Problems

Observations of children performing routine classroom, home, or play activities provide important information concerning the children's functional vision. A parent might wonder why a child sits so close to the television, a playmate might observe that a friend always reaches too far to the left when trying to catch a ball, or a teacher might notice that a child tilts his or her head to one side when reading. If these behaviors are observed in conjunction with other signs of visual impairment, the child should be seen by an eye

specialist. Common indications of eye problems are listed in Table 15.2.

ASSESSMENT OF VISION

A crucial first step in the assessment of children is to determine the efficiency of their sensory receptors. When visual impairments are suspected, children should be referred to an eye care specialist for assessment, diagnosis, and physical management. Psychologists and diagnostic personnel who suspect visual impairment should select tests that are less likely to be influenced negatively by the child's visual problem, unless the effects the child's visual impairment on various developing skills is to be assessed. Teachers and other caregivers should use vision screening information to influence their selection of curriculum materials and plan effective instruction. In the section that follows a number of tests for screening vision and assessing skill domains most af-

TABLE 15.2
OBSERVABLE SIGNS OF VISUAL PROBLEMS

Eyes turning in or out at any time
Red or watery eyes
Encrusted eyelids
Frequent styes
Swollen eyes
Frequent head adjustment when looking at distant objects
Focusing difficulties
Tracking difficulties
Rubbing eyes frequently
Complaints of itchy, scratchy, or stinging eyes
Avoidance of close work
Frequent blinking, frowing, or scowling
Tilting of turning of head to focus on objects
Tiring after visual tasks
Movement of head rather than eyes while looking at a page
Frequent confusion of similarly shaped letters, numbers, and words
Covering of one eye to sight with other eye
Unusual clumsiness or awkwardness
Poor eye–hand coordination
Headaches or nausea after close visual tasks

Reprinted from *Educating Young Handicapped Children* by S. Gray Garwood by permission of Aspen Systems Corporation, copyright 1979.

fected by visual problems during the preschool years are described.

Screening Tests

Vision screening tests focus on the identification of visual disorders that might be caused by refractive errors and/or extraocular muscle imbalances. Stangler and coworkers (1980, p. 221) listed five factors that place children at risk for visual impairment:

1. Prenatal infectious processes such as maternal rubella, in utero toxoplasmosis, or cytomegalic inclusion disease
2. Congenital conditions such as cyanotic heart disease or glaucoma
3. Structural abnormalities such as opacity of the lens or hypoplasia of the optic nerve
4. Family history of vision problems
5. The supplemental oxygen therapy often necessary for premature infants, which can cause retrolental fibroplasia

Screening tests for high-risk children can begin at birth; the test are performed by medical personnel and call attention to immediate medical needs. For many more children, screening is assessed by one of several tests of visual acuity administered during the preschool or early elementary school years.

Vision screening is a very inexpensive procedure that requires minimal time and in some cases minimal examiner training. Once characteristics that indicate the presence of refractive errors or physical anomalies have been identified, diagnostic and treatment services can be initiated. If vision screening reveals a possible problem, no further assessment of the child's remaining skills should occur until the vision problem has been corrected. A number of screening tests have been developed to assist examiners in assessing the vision of difficult-to-test children.

Project APT Vision Screening Test

Formal assessment of severely impaired and developmentally disabled children requires a comprehensive assessment of the child's functional use of vision. Jose and coworkers (1980) suggested that evaluation of visual functioning should include sensation, visual–motor and visual–perceptual skills. Jose and coworkers (1980), Langley (1980a, 1980b), and Langley and DuBose (1976) described batteries of collected activities that can be used to evaluate each of the three areas. The tests include pupillary reactions to light, muscle balance or binocular coordination, blink reflex, eye preferences, use of central and peripheral visual fields, tracking and scanning skills, reaching for lights or for visually presented objects, and shifting attention between visual targets. Many of these visual behaviors are included in a very practical vision screening procedure prepared by Project APT (1980) (Fig. 15.1).

Formal Picture and Symbol Tests

Several formal tests of vision screening rely on the child's ability to recognize familiar pictures, and are based on the premise that young children are inherently more interested in pictures than letters. In other tests, children are required to name or match simply shaped letters or symbols.

Assessment of Visual Functioning

Preschool Vision Test

In this test (Allen, 1957), familiar pictures printed on individual cards are used instead of the row of symbols used when testing older children. The pictures include a birthday cake, a telephone, a man driving a jeep, a bear, a house, a man on a horse, and a Christmas tree. A distance of 15 feet is used for testing, because young children have been shown not to attempt deciphering tasks at the usual distance of 20 feet. The test has been used successfully to screen acuity in each eye separately to detect amblyopia. For children three years of age, the Preschool Vision Test makes testing easier than the Snellen Illiterate E Test or other symbol tests.

Lighthouse Flashcard Test for Children

Three symbols, an apple, an umbrella, and a house are used in this test (Project APT, 1980). In children as young as 27 months, this test is usually performed at a distance of ten feet and verbal, manual, or matching skills can be measured. The form for recording the responses and the admin-

Pupil _____   Homeroom Teacher _____
D.O.B. _____   Date _____
Center _____   Screened by _____   _____
                                           _____   _____

Vision Screening

Physical Observation

_____ Size or shape difference in pupils   _____ Squinting
_____ Excessive tearing   _____ Blinking
_____ Cloudiness   _____ Inflammation or redness
_____ Eyes not aligned properly (describe)   _____ Other (describe)

Materials and Screening Team Needed

1. two penlights
2. lollipop, coke or favorite food (if pupil fails to respond to the penlight any of these stimuli may be used)
3. whiffle ball with string attached
4. spinning toy
5. eye patch and/or cloth drape or adapted glasses
6. three chairs of appropriate size for pupil
7. screening forms
8. pencils
9. N.Y. Lighthouse Vision Screening (as appropriate)
10. screener
11. recorder
12. assistant (if possible)

Administration and Scoring

Place a + in appropriate column for correct response, a − for poor response. If the pupil fails to respond or responds inappropriately, record what you have observed. Items may be repeated three or four times to elicit an observable response.

	Both	Right	Left	Comments
1. Pupillary Reaction (12″)				
2. Muscle Balance (12″)		/////	/////	
3. Convergence (12″)		/////	/////	
4. Can Track at 12″: a) Horizontally ⟶				
b) Vertically ↓				
c) Left Oblique ↘				
d) Right Oblique ↙				
5. Peripheral Field (12″)	/////			
6. Blink Reflex		/////	/////	
7. Distance Vision: Can localize familiar people at 10′ ☐ Yes ☐ No Can track familiar people at 10′ ☐ Yes ☐ No or Can fixate on a spinning object at 10′ ☐ Yes ☐ No				

Figure 15.1   Vision screening procedure developed by the Project APT. (From the Screening Manual of the Project APT, pp. 21, 22, and 24. Reproduced with permission of the Project APT, Department of Special Services, Fairfax County Public Schools, Fairfax, Virginia, 1980.)

Instructions for Vision Screening

This screening tool is designed to assist in identifying those pupils who may need referral for additional evaluation. It is not intended as a diagnostic instrument or a test for visual acuity. The screening attemps to assess the pupil's ability to use the small muscles of the eyes in a smooth, coordinated manner.

Occluding vision to test eyes individually may produce irritable behavior or even acute anxiety. If this occurs, do not force the pupil to accept an eye patch, but plan to rescreen later. In the interim, the classroom teacher can help the pupil become accustomed to having one eye occluded as well as improving tolerance to touch around the face.

Materials
1. two penlights
2. lollipop, coke, or favorite food (if pupil fails to respond to the penlight any of these stimuli may be used)
3. whiffle ball with string attached
4. spinning toy
5. eye patch and/or cloth drape or adapted glasses
6. three chairs of appropriate size for pupil
7. screening forms
8. pencils
9. N.Y. Lighthouse Vision Screening (as appropriate)

Screening Team
The screening team includes a screener, a recorder, and an assistant when needed (if possible).
1. The *screener:*
   a) presents the stimuli
   b) maintains pupil's level of interest
   c) observes pupil's responses

2. The *recorder:*
   records data and pupil's behaviors

3. The *assistant:* (if possible)
   produces stimuli for peripheral vision and blink reflex

Setup

| Pupil | Screener | Recorder | Assistant (if possible) |

Administration
Administer the screening in a quiet room that can be darkened. If necessary, a screen may be used to eliminate distractions within the room. (The very young severely involved pupil may be adequately screened while positioned on a mat.)

Scoring
Place + in appropriate column for correct response, − for poor response. If the pupil fails to respond or responds inappropriately, record what you have observed. Items may be repeated three or four times to elicit an observable response.

Figure 15.1 *(continued)*

istration procedures used by Project APT are presented in Figure 15.2.

The Letter Chart for Twenty Feet—Snellen Scale

This chart (National Society to Prevent Blindness, 1974a) is commonly used to measure acuity in older children and adults who are able to read letters. For individuals lacking these skills, an adaptation of the letter chart can be used that displays the arms of the letter E and is known as the Symbol Chart for Twenty Feet—Snellen Scale (National Society to Prevent Blindness, 1974b). The letter chart displays the arms of the letter E

Procedure

As the pupil enters, he or she is told to "sit down in the chair and look". The screener begins by checking the following:

1. <u>Pupillary Reaction:</u> The penlight is held 12″ in front of the pupil's eyes. The light is flashed directly into the eyes, then away. Pupil dilation and contraction are noted.

Light causes pupil to contract: Darkness causes pupil to dilate:

The screener checks both eyes together by flashing the light in front of the bridge of the nose, then right, then left. If the student's pupils dilate and contract, score a plus in the proper box. If you have a question, score a minus. The screener conveys data to the recorder by saying "positive" for plus and "negative" for minus.

2. <u>Muscle Balance:</u> Again the screener holds the penlight 12″ from the pupil's eyes at midline. The light should reflect on the student's pupils if there are no muscle problems. If it is possible to see the light reflected in the center of one pupil and not in the center of the other, this indicates an imbalance and is scored as such.

3. <u>Convergence:</u> Check convergence by moving the penlight from the 12″ point toward the bridge of the pupil's nose. The eyes should follow the light to approximately 2″ from the bridge of the nose.

4. <u>Tracking:</u> Check horizontal, vertical, right and left oblique on both eyes simultaneously before obscuring the vision of one eye with a patch or drape. Covering one eye can elicit interfering behaviors in some pupils. Left oblique is to the pupil's left; right oblique is to the pupil's right.

5. <u>Peripheral Vision:</u> The recorder or assistant stands behind pupil, turns on the penlight, and brings the light around the side of the pupil's head at a distance of 12″. The recorder brings the light forward until the pupil responds by looking at the light. The pupil has adequate peripheral vision if he or she responds by looking at the stimulus as it appears alongside the face.

6. <u>Blink Reflex:</u> The screener says, "Sheila, look at me" and the recorder or assistant produces the blink stimulus. (Whiffle ball on a string is dropped from behind, without pupil's prior knowledge, to within 2″ of face.) For the young involved pupil lying on a mat, a quick movement of the screener's hand toward the pupil's face will elicit a blink.

7. <u>Distance Vision</u>:
   a) The screener walks away 10′ and calls, "Sheila, look at me." The next direction is "watch me." The screener walks across the field of vision at 10′.
   b) For those pupils whose fixation is questionable, the examiner should activate a spinning toy 10′ away from pupil. The pupil should visually fixate on the object while it spins.

If the response to any given item is questionable, you may go back and retest.

Under "Comments", you may include any behavioral descriptions as well as any difficulties with the individual items.

Figure 15.1 *(continued)*

---

pointing in different directions. The child is taught to point in the same direction as the arms of the E. The child is tested on several rows, each decreasing in size, while standing at a distance of 20 feet. The symbol and letter charts also are available for 10 feet. The Snellen Scale has been used successfully for testing children as young as three years. However, in some studies, young children experienced difficulty copying the arms of the E. Sheridan (1960) found that children below the age of four frequently made letter reversal errors; an incorrect response to letter positions might rep-

resent a problem with directionality rather than vision problems. Furthermore, the letter E itself might not be a sufficiently interesting stimulus to encourage full participation in the young child.

Stycar (Screening Test for Young Children and Retarded)

This test battery was developed for screening vision in young children (Sheridan, 1960, 1970). The only skill required by the child is the ability to match a series of letters that are among the first

Pupil _____   Homeroom Teacher _____

D.O.B. _____   Date _____

Center _____   Screened by _____

N.Y. Lighthouse Vision Screening

Distance from Pupil	Size & Type of Card	"200" House	"200" Apple	"200" Umbrella	"100" House	"100" Apple	"100" Umbrella	"50" House	"50" Apple	"50" Umbrella	"40" House	"40" Apple	"40" Umbrella	"20" House	"20" Apple	"20" Umbrella	"10" House	"10" Apple	"10" Umbrella
5'																			
10'																			
20'																			

If response is correct, place a + in the appropriate column on scoring sheet.
If response is incorrect, place a − in the appropriate column on scoring sheet.

Comments:

Visual Acuity _____

Administration

Present the "200" cards at 5'. If responses are correct, present the "200" cards at 10'. At this distance, present the "100," "50," "40," and "20" cards. The test may be completed at 10' by showing the "10" card. This produces the same result as showing the "20" card at 20'.

The test may also be done at the conventional 20' range. However, interest and participation may be higher when both the examiner and the cards are at 10'.

Scoring

If the response is correct, place a + in the appropriate column on scoring sheet. If response is incorrect, place a − .

To determine visual acuity, divide the distance at which all three symbols have been identified by the smallest size of card that was correctly identified, e.g., at 10', the "100" cards were correctly identified. The acuity would then be 10/100 or converted to standard symbols, 20/200.

Figure 15.2   Administration procedure and response record for the Lighthouse Flashcard Test for Children developed by the Project APT for use with the N.Y. Lighthouse Vision Screening. (From the Screening Manual of the Project APT, pp. 23 and 25. Reproduced with permission of the Project APT, Department of Special Services, Fairfax County Public Schools, Fairfax, Virginia, 1980.)

learned by children (H, L, T, C, O, X, A, V, U). Children at the youngest ages are shown only those shapes that they are able to copy; older children are taught to copy letters in mid-air with their fingers. A more easily interpretable response, used successfully to test children under 5 years of age, is for children to view a letter on the wall chart then point to the letter on a table in front of them. Testing is most easily performed at a distance of 10 feet, because rapport with young children frequently is lost at greater distances. The examiner stands near the chart, points to each of the stimulus letters, and asks the child to point to the same letter on the response board. Each eye can be tested separately by using eye patches alternately. The young child is presented individually blocked letters, one at a time, instead of being presented with the entire chart. Several letters can be effectively used with 4 year olds, whereas 3 year olds use only five simple shapes (T, H, O, V, X). The Stycar test has been used successfully with children as young as 2 years 2 months and with young handicapped children. This test format also can be used to assess near vision.

An adaptation of the Stycar is suitable for children 21 months to 3 years of age who are unable to match either single letters or colored pictures. In this adapted format, miniature models of toys are displayed on a table at a specified distance from the child (initial training involves ensuring that the child can identify the toys). The examiner, ten feet from the child, holds the toy up and asks, "What is this?" Verbal children might give a verbal response, whereas shy and nonverbal children can hold up a similar toy to demonstrate recognition. A precaution is made to vary the color of the object, because color matching is a more primitive form of visual discrimination and it is not dependent on visual acuity to the same degree as object recognition. Near vision is assessed by asking the child to pick up small crumbs of bread or pieces of thread presented at close range; each eye can be tested separately.

Parsons Visual Acuity Test

Spellman and colleagues (1979) worked with retarded and seriously impaired children to design a visual acuity assessment procedure based on the theory of errorless learning. This test requires children to discriminate among pictures of a bird, a hand, and a cake, all presented together in a series of mixed cards. Children can respond by pointing, blinking their eyes, or verbalizing a yes/no response to indicate the correct picture. In addition, special training using an intensity-fading program can be used with children who have difficulty discriminating forms. This additional training makes the test particularly useful for moderately to severely handicapped students. Both far- and near-point testing have been accomplished using these procedures.

As noted, this test was developed specifically for children with handicapping conditions, and has been used effectively with a large number of children with developmental ages below 2 years (Cibis, et al., 1985; Cress, 1987; Cress et al., 1982).

Preferential Looking Models

Some time ago, Fantz and coworkers (1962) found that infants consistently preferred to look at patterned targets over plain targets. Researchers in Fantz's lab began using preferential looking to test visual acuity using black and white gratings or striped targets of various sizes. The task requires the use of resolution acuity as opposed to the typical test of recognition acuity. In the resolution task, a far less sophisticated response is needed, thus younger or more severely limited children are able to be assessed using this technique (Cress, 1987).

A number of researchers have used preferential looking acuity test procedures with handicapped persons (Duckman & Selenow, 1983; Fagan & Singer, 1983; Lennerstrand et al., 1982; Mayer et al., 1983; McDonald et al., 1985). These researchers report successful testing of children with Down syndrome, cerebral palsy, and multiple impairments. Cress (1987) studied 500 children, of whom 80% were developmentally disabled, using a simplified five-minute preferential looking test developed by McDonald and coworkers. The procedure involved presenting acuity cards in front of the child at distances of 38 cm, 35 cm, or 84 cm (depending on the child's age), and having an observer, blind to the placement of the card, determine whether the target is seen by the child. Cress reported on the testing of binocular and monocular acuities in 59 children ranging in age from 10 days to 6 years. The procedure yielded useful threshold on all developmentally disabled children in the study and demonstrated the procedure's usefulness for the early detection of visual impairment.

Stereoscopic Vision Testing

Children with normal visual functioning fuse input from both eyes to achieve stereopsis. When stereopsis is not present, problems such as amblyopia, strabismus, and severe refractive error differences between the two eyes can occur. Stereoscopic testing has been conducted successfully in large-scale visual screening programs (Ehrlich et al. 1983). Four stereotests (Frisby, Random-Dot E, TNO, and Randot Circles) have been compared by Simons (1981a, 1981b) and norms for 3 to 5 year old children have been provided. The Frisby test missed cases of binocular dysfunction. The TNO under-referred cases relative to the RDE. The Randot circles test produced better-indicated stereoacuities than the RDS tests and reliably graded stereoacuity in patients with poor stereopsis.

Visually Evoked Potential

Visually Evoked Potential (VEP) is an objective, noninvasive technique to assess visual functioning through the electrical activity of the occipital cortex produced in response to a visual stimulus (Cress, 1987; Morse & Trief, 1985).

CONSIDERATIONS OF VISUAL ABILITIES IN COGNITIVE ASSESSMENT

It is sometimes impossible to separate a child's response to a visual stimulus from the cognitive or attitudinal component of the response. Awareness that vision and cognition are related is important in determining why a child performs as he or she does and what, if anything, should be done to intervene. The examiner must be aware that limited visual development and responses to formal and informal assessment might be in part because of the child's cognitive level and attitudes (Jose et al., 1980; Langley, 1980b).

Informally, examiners might find it useful to observe a child's performance on cognitive assessment tasks that require visual skills. Table 15.3 lists several visual-oriented tasks found on typical developmental schedules. If it appears a child's difficulties are visual in nature, it might be

**TABLE 15.3
DEVELOPMENTAL SEQUENCE OF SKILLS
INVOLVING VISION**

2 to 2½ year
  Copies two vertical strokes in imitation; identifies objects in a group pictured; might look at pictures upside down
2½ to 3 years
  Copies circle; matches colored blocks; engages in domestic make-believe play
3 to 3½ years
  Copies cross; points to forms that are like a model; discriminates between three- and four-object arrays
3½ to 4 year
  Traces around diamond; writes letters of first name; identifies colors correctly
4 to 4½ years
  Copies letter O; traces cross; identifies ten letters of alphabet on sight
4½ to 5 years
  Copies rectangle; copies star; reads five sight words
5 to 5½ year
  Reads eight words, draws line from dot to dot inches apart; identifies numerals through ten
5½ to 6 years
  Copies rectangle with intersecting lines diagonal; reads at a preprimer level; identifies 12 of 26 upper case letters

helpful to assess downward to determine the developmental age at which the child is successful at using vision to complete fine motor and cognitive tasks.

Listed here are some cognitive skills that can be affected by visual impairments and clues as to whether a visual problem might be interfering with the child's cognitive responses.

1. *Accuracy of approach to objects.* When the child works with nesting toys, pegboards, or pounding benches, note whether the child's approach to the object is on target. Note the direction of the child's movement when it is off-center (i.e., is it consistently in one direction or is it random in nature). Also, note whether the child relies on tactual cues to perform the activity.
2. *Matching.* It is important to note if the child matches objects by shape or color and which attribute is preferred. It also is useful to note

the distance at which the child matches common object of varying sizes.

3. *Following moving objects.* Observe whether the child follows the trajectory of objects spilling from a container or moving through an arc.

4. *Imitation.* Observe the child's ability to imitate both gross and fine motor activities. Determine whether the child can perform the skill without a model.

5. *Recognition.* Observe the child's response to pictures or printed material. Some pictures might elicit attention and recognition although others do not; note the picture characteristics that distinguish these behaviors.

6. *Object permanence.* Visual memory can be observed in simple situations in which objects are viewed, then removed; note whether the child demonstrates awareness of the unseen object and where it is located.

7. *Reactivation.* Activate an object as the child observes. Give the object to the child to reactivate. Observe visual memory and the child's ability to sequence the operation task.

In addition to testing how clearly a child perceives objects at specified distances, it also is important to determine whether both eyes operate in tandem. Patching one eye and observing the child's activities is one way to determine eye preference and assess the strength of each eye separately. A child's negative reaction to being patched might indicate that the covered eye is the child's better one; however, the child might be reacting negatively to the presence of the patch itself and the examiner must discern the difference.

ASSESSMENT OF COGNITION

If informal or formal screening results suggest the presence of a visual problem, it is important that steps be taken to attend to the problem immediately, because uncorrected visual problems will obviously affect all other unrelated assessments that rely on vision. PL 94–142 requires that a child's handicap be taken into consideration when a test battery is assembled and an assessment scheduled. The impact of blindness and visual impairment on many areas of a child's development should be kept in mind when selecting

tests of motor, language, social, and self-care development. Assessment measures for blind and visually impaired preschool children can be found in DuBose (1979), Silberman (1981), and Genshaft and coworkers (1980), and for a more detailed explanation of assessment of totally blind children see Bauman (1973).

Through careful selection of tests and subtests of cognition and visual perception, examiners can compile a battery of tests that can be given to young blind children with slight modifications in administration procedures. A list of such tests (to which many others can be added) is provided in Appendix 15.1. Many of these subtests can be administered to children whose records indicate limited visual problems.

ASSESSMENT OF VISUAL PERCEPTION

Visual perception is the detection of a form from an image. If the form is labeled or described, the perception becomes a concept as some degree of cognition and memory are used. In very young infants, visual perception is observed through the duration of the child's attention to stimuli. However, by the time a child is able to label forms or recognize similarities and differences, visual perception usually implies interpretation of what is seen.

Although many educators have developed programs to teach visual perception, this skill obviously cannot be taught to the totally blind child. However, as Barraga (1964) demonstrated, it can be taught to many children with some degree of usable sight. The visual skills described in this section should be assessed whenever visual competence is questioned.

Buktenica (1968) separated visual perception into five somewhat arbitrary skills that overlap, but nonetheless provide guidelines for assessment and training.

1. *Visual discrimination.* Visual discrimination is the recognition of similarities and differences. It begins in the very young child when responses to one stimulus differ from responses to other stimuli. For example, newborns discriminate different levels of brightness and prefer to look at a patterned stimuli more than no pattern at all (Appleton et al.,

1975). Visual discrimination can be examined through the presentation of very similar pictures that differ in only a small way. The child can be asked if the pictures are different or the same. Once the child correctly indicates that the pictures are different, the examiner can expand questioning to include the nature of the differences. It is important to determine first whether the child understands the concepts *same* and *different*.

2. *Visual–motor development.* An early form of visual–motor development is tracking or scanning, in which the child follows the movement of an object across his or her field of vision. The integration of visual and motor skills is the basis for many other skills (e.g., caring for self, playing, reaching, aiming, positioning), and it is difficult to identify many tasks that are completely free of this important behavior.

3. *Figure–ground perception.* The ability to see a figure separate from its background is a crucial visual skill. It can be assessed informally with picture books by asking the child to locate objects among groups of objects or by asking the child to select a key element from a visual array.

4. *Spatial relationships.* This aspect of vision includes the ability to orient oneself in space. It can be evaluated by observing the child's ability to orient to *left, right, up,* or *down,* and to arrange and space objects on a page.

5. *Perceptual constancy.* Visual imagery and visual memory are involved in perceptual constancy. The child must recognize an image even though it might vary slightly when seen in a different context. Variations can include changes in size, shape, color, position, design, or placement. Perceptual constancy requires the four previously described skills of perception (i.e., visual discrimination, . . .) and can be assessed through tasks that require children to recognize slight variations in objects or identify whole objects when only a portion is viewed.

The five forms of visual perception overlap, and performance and training in one area affects performance and training in another. These visual skills are a part of everyday life; they enable one to receive, process, integrate, and synthesize more information. However, one cannot assume that by training a child to use these visual skills more effectively the child will necessarily perform better on academic tasks such as reading and spelling. The best way to improve reading and spelling performance is to teach reading and spelling. Visual training does, however, encourage the child to be more visually sensitive to what is present. For some children, heightened sensitivity can open the way to changes in the use of vision as it is applied in reading, writing, and other academic skills.

Informal tests of visual perception can be developed by the preschool teacher or examiner by gathering materials traditionally encountered in the classroom and observing the child's interactions with the stimulus materials. Several sources are particularly rich in suggesting these informal tasks (Buktenica, 1968; Cohen & Gross, 1979, Vol. I, pp. 45–65, Vol. II, pp. 47–49; Cratty, 1970, Chapter 4, pp. 67–94; Hohmann et al., 1979, pp. 191–265; Langley, 1980a; Wallace & Kaufman, 1973, Chapter 7, pp. 146–163).

Formal assessments of visual perception are useful to assess the rate of development over time. A few tests that measure aspects of visual perception are the Developmental Test of Visual-Motor Integration (Beery & Buktenica, 1967), Illinois Test of Psycholinguistic Abilities (Kirk et al., 1968), Developmental Test of Visual Perception (Frosig et al., 1964), and the Visual Efficiency Scale (Barraga, 1970).

CONSIDERATIONS AND ADAPTIONS OF PHYSICAL REQUIREMENTS

Factors Influencing the Test Performance of Visually Impaired Children

The visual environment can have a significant impact on the child's performance. For example, if the materials are placed outside of the child's visual field, or the contrasts between the stimulus and the background are not apparent to the child, responses might be recorded as errors when in fact the child did not have sufficient information to make an informed response. For this reason, informal assessment should include observations of the child's responses to stimuli similar to those used in the test and to those under modified environments. Once optimal testing conditions have been determined, formal assessment using the desired measures can begin under those conditions. Harley and Lawrence (1977) described five elements affecting visual performance: brightness, contrast, time, distance, and image size. Regardless of the particular assessment setting, these factors always need to be considered when one selects the materials and conditions to be used when assessing visually impaired children.

Brightness

Most visually impaired children benefit from high illumination; however, children should be positioned so that they do not face the glare of a window or work in the darkness of their own shadow. Optimally, the light source should come from behind the opposite shoulder of the writing hand. Protection from glare can be controlled through blinds and shades and by redirecting the light source, the visual task, or the child, so that reflections are not directed into the child's line of vision. Optimum uniform lighting is produced indirectly through luminous ceilings or walls, and fluorescent lighting that distributes light in equal amounts from all angles is preferred.

Contrast

Visual efficiency is improved when contrast is heightened. Harley and Lawrence (1977) reported that black on white or white print on black paper offers the needed contrast for visually impaired children, but black print on buff-colored paper is preferred because buff paper reduces glare. Color combinations that are best for displaying pictures or objects include, yellow on black, blue, green, or purple, and black-ink felt-tipped pens are best for writing on light-colored papers.

Time

Visually impaired children might have a difficult time identifying and attending to events. Informal testing permits the examiner to determine how quickly and efficiently visually impaired children respond to timed, visually demanding test items. It might be deemed necessary to eliminate or substantially adapt tests with timed items if they create an unfair disadvantage.

Distance

If assessment involves viewing material from a distance, the older preschool child can determine and suggest to the examiner the best viewing distance. For young children, the examiner should experiment with the materials and systematically change the distances until an optimal distance is found. Some children with particularly low-vision might need to be as close as one to two inches from the material, and in such cases easels, bookstands, or adjustable desk tops can facilitate visibility.

Size of image

The size of pictures, letters, and forms is an important factor to consider in the assessment of the visually impaired. Although many low-vision children can read small print at very close distances, this is very tiring and slow. Some tests are available in large print and others might need to be retyped in large print to facilitate testing low-vision children. Relettering or retyping is more likely to be needed with school-age children than with preschoolers, because few preschool tests require the child to examine materials with small print.

Setting

Whenever possible, the setting for assessing visually impaired children should be the same as that for other children. The importance of the assessment milieu has been documented by several investigators (Barker, 1968; Bortner & Birch, 1970; Brooks & Baumeister, 1977; Bruner, 1973; DuBose et al., 1977; Sroufe et al., 1974), and they stress the impact environmental circumstances have on test performance. The appropriateness of the environment for the skills being assessed can be determined by observing the child in various settings. For example, if expressive language is to be examined through a language sample procedure, the spontaneous language gathered by taking the sample on the playground might be far richer than that taken in the traditional sterile testing room. When children are free to be themselves, select the activities they wish to pursue, and interact with their favorite peers, they are more motivated to communicate than when they are with a strange adult and surrounded by a few selected toys.

Observation of the child in the environment in which assessment is to take place can provide valuable information on how the child uses the surroundings. By observing how the child positions himself or herself relative to the lighting, or observing if the child uses his or her fingers to produce changes in the light, one can learn much about the meaning of light for the child. The child's movement in the environment indicates how responsive he or she is to objects and their spatial relationships. These observations can be used to identify the way to position the child for testing and optimal positions for material placement.

Materials

Informal visual assessment using a variety of materials can yield crucial data for both the examiners who will formally assess the child and teachers who will plan instructional programs. Many commercially available tests are inadequate for the assessment of visually impaired children because many of the items lack optimal visual stimulus value. Appealing and stimulating materials attract and motivate the child more (Kiernan & DuBose, 1974).

The testing materials should be as appropriate for the tasks as possible. Increasing item size, heightening contrast, substituting three-dimensional materials for standard materials, projecting items onto a television or movie screen, increasing space between items by decreasing the number of items on a page, and outlining items with a heavy black line or a raised line are just a few of the material changes that can increase visual reception without changing the nature of the concept being assessed.

To determine the effects various materials have on a particular visual behavior, observe the child's performance using a number of different items. For example, to examine visual pursuit, the following brightly colored objects serve well:

- Very bright lemon yellow, hot pink, or chartreuse yarn ball
- Two-tone slinky toy
- Flashlights with colored disks
- Halloween toys that sparkle, spin, or move in some way
- Lollipops
- Spinning toys

- Pinwheels
- Weebles
- Brightly colored pop beads
- Rolling toys (trucks, balls, etc.) in bright colors

Special Aids

Optical aids such as magnifying lenses and large print material are available to render assessment and instruction easier for both the child and the examiner or teacher. The child's instructors probably will be able to suggest a number of useful aids to the examiner. In some cases, formal tests can be presented through the use of these aids, thus expanding the range of tests that can be used with the impaired child. These facilitative aids become even more valuable when the child enters elementary school and receives assisted instruction. Informal assessment can include observations of the child's reaction to auditory aids such as audio cassette recorders, talking books, talking calculators, Cramner Abacus, closed-circuit television, reading machines, and special low-vision activities.

ROLE OF VARIOUS PROFESSIONALS IN ASSESSMENT AND REMEDIATION

The knowledge that a visual problem is interfering with a child's normal skill acquisition is extremely important to everyone responsible for the child's education, growth, and development. The visual problem can become a focus of immediate medical attention or educational planning; it can suggest a long-term treatment procedure or crucial changes in the child's program during the school years. It can lead to the use of visual aids or even to the introduction of braille in preparation for anticipated loss of vision. Decisions about major needs and possible strategies are made in consultation with a number of professionals, each with specific skills that are needed in decision making.

Medical Service Providers

Medical service providers include the following: oculists or ophthalmologists, who specialize in disease or defects of the eye; optometrists, who measure visual acuity and refraction for the prescription of glasses; and opticians who produce glasses according to prescriptions.

Diagnosis

The determination of a visual problem and its cause requires immediate medical services. Refractive errors are treated with corrective ophthalmic lenses. Strabismus frequently is treated with vision therapy in addition to lenses. Treatment can consist of procedures as simple as placing a patch over one eye; however, in more severe cases, eye surgery might be required.

Prognosis

Visual maturity is not reached until the child is 5 to 6 years of age; therefore, early treatment can be very effective in ameliorating the impact of a visual deficit. Some indication for the immediate functional use of vision can be based on the Snellen measures of visual acuity (See Table 15.1).

Remediation

Corrective procedures used by eye care specialists include prescriptive lenses and in some cases vision therapy. In either case, trained specialists prescribe treatment that is carried out by other care providers. After therapy, vision is assessed for improvement, and the prescription can be modified according to the assessment results. Remediation can also take a number of other forms. For example, an eye specialist might recommend a change in room lighting, size of print, and so on; however, these recommendations are best made in consultation with other care providers who observe the child's use of vision in more natural environments.

Psychologists

Few psychologists gain experience testing blind and visually impaired preschool children during their training. This training deficit leaves examiners with a lack of understanding about the appropriateness of assessment procedures and/or instrumentation.

Diagnosis

A clear diagnosis of visual impairment by a medical care provider indicates that the psychol-ogist must plan carefully to administer a psychoeducational test battery that will produce results that will be minimally affected by the child's visual loss or deficit. The examiner must determine whether a particular response failure was related to poor vision or because of other unrelated reasons (e.g., limited intellectual functioning). Differentiation of this sort might require presenting a task in several different formats to separate visual from cognitive variance.

Prognosis

Psychologists must examine a child's performance on tests that require vision and determine the long-term impact of a visual deficit on the child's behavior in all domains. The age of onset of blindness can be a major factor influencing a child's comprehension of concepts such as size, distance, and understanding of environmental events. Prognostic statements must be based on information from many sources in addition to test results; particularly important is information on the child's adaptive and social-interactive skills. The adjustment young children make to their impairments is highly predictive of their future success in adjusting to environmental demands.

Remediation

If consistent patterns of response occur and apparently result from the child's visual deficits, the psychologist should note these patterns, convey their impact, and suggest procedures to remediate the child's difficulties. The solutions to visual perceptual problems can be elusive; the proper remedial techniques can be ascertained only after several strategies have been tried. A test–teach–test approach might be needed to gather sufficient data to suggest remedial strategies that are likely to prove successful.

Educators

In contrast to medical service providers and psychologists, educators have a direct and continuous involvement in the implementation of assessment findings and recommendations. They must translate test findings into daily educational strategies and then determine the effect program alterations have on the child's behavior. This task is not easy because the implications of assessment results are not always clear, and many medical and psychological reports do not offer concrete remediation suggestions for the teacher.

Diagnosis

A teacher's first task is to understand thoroughly a diagnosis and its impact on the child and his or her learning environment. The teacher needs to know which functional visual skills the child possesses, which conditions will increase or decrease the child's visual performance, and which tests can be used to evaluate the effectiveness of a recommended remedial strategy. Fortunately, most visual impairments (e.g., hyperopia, myopia, astigmatism) can be corrected through the use of lenses; however, eye conditions such as albinism, asthenopia, and retinitis pigmentosa have definite implications for the conditions under which the child can learn.

Prognosis

The teacher is less likely than other team members to project long-term outcomes of visual impairment and more likely to provide the daily accounts that indicate whether remedial measures are affecting the child's behavior. Physicians frequently ask parents and teachers to try certain therapies and then make a report on the results before making a prognosis about the future.

Remediation

The 5 or 6 year old child who cannot visually attend, scan, discriminate, remember, or use visual closure skills quickly enough to produce comprehension is not ready for reading training. Visual perceptual training might prepare some children for reading, whereas other children might require reading instructional programs that are more dependent on auditory strengths. At some point however, all children will need training in visual analysis to identify the visual code used in reading.

For the developmentally young or severely delayed child, assessment results might suggest more attention to the training of vision as an end in itself rather than to the training of a skill that is accomplished through vision. Barraga (1964) demonstrated that visually impaired students can improve the efficiency of their vision through training, although they might not change their visual acuity. This finding suggests that any child who responds to light and consequently reacts to the stimulus can benefit from visual training activities.

Training programs should be conducted throughout the day and not just at a specified time set aside for visual training. The use of visual skills must be integrated into daily routines and made a continuous part of the child's life to become incorporated into the child's behavioral repertoire. Practice in using one's visual skills should take place in a variety of settings. Langley (1980a) suggested the use of multisensory materials for added cues when working with more severely impaired children. Initially, when a specific visual skill is being trained, the visual response should be paired with a different sensory stimulus. For example, to train a child to focus on an object, a bell could be attached to the visual stimulus (if the child uses the sense of hearing consistently). Initially, the auditory and visual stimuli are paired; then the auditory stimulus is gradually faded until the child responds to the visual stimulus alone.

Other suggestions for training include the use of simple and manipulative materials. Color is an important attribute to consider when choosing objects with which to work. Red, yellow, and orange are considered the most visually stimulating colors, and black and yellow provide the greatest color contrast (Zaporazhets & Elkonin, 1971). It is necessary to have a high contrast between the visual materials and the working surface at all times.

Proper illumination of materials is essential, as is the use of nonglare materials. When the children are working on discrimination tasks, teachers should begin by emphasizing the greatest differences (e.g., size, color, brightness), then reduce the differences until the child can perform the task without cues.

Illumination can be altered if the angle of the material is changed. Some students use their vision more efficiently if classwork is placed on a table easel rather than flat on a table or desk. When the teacher observes a child cocking his or her head to one side, it suggests visual field preferences that might influence the placement of materials for optimum visibility.

It is important to remember that visual training on such tasks as tracking, closure, discrimination, and memory might not affect academic performance. Such training might indeed improve visual perception, but will probably have little if

any direct effect on reading. A far more conse-
quential plan involves task analysis, in which the
content or tasks to be learned form the basis for
the assessment; analysis of errors indicates what
the child knows and does not know and identifies
misconceptions and strategy errors.

SUMMARY

This chapter has provided examiners with
some basic information on visual development in
children and how assessment procedures and tests
might be selected that are less likely to penalize
children with impaired vision. Initially reviewed
were developmental aspects of vision and the impact of visual impairments on motor, language,
cognitive, perceptual, social, and self-care development. Readers were provided a list of observable signs of possible visual problems that might
be noted during a testing experience. Several visual screening tests and tests of functional vision
were described with procedures included for two
tests should readers want to use these with children. Special attention was given to the role of
vision in cognitive and perceptual assessment as
it is important to examiners to separate, to the
extent possible, a child's cognitive competence
from competence that is dependent on intact and
highly functioning visual abilities. Suggestions
and considerations are provided for testing visually impaired children. The chapter closes with
descriptions of the roles of the major service providers who will need to be involved in educational
and medical decision making regarding visually
impaired children. An appendix is provided that
lists tests appropriate for preschool children with
varying degrees of visual impairment.

REFERENCES

Adelson, E., & Fraiberg, S. (1974). Gross motor development in infants blind from birth. *Child Development, 45*, 114–126.

Allen, H. F. (1957). A new picture series for preschool
vision testing. *American Journal of Ophthalmology,
44*, 38–41.

American Printing House for the Blind, Inc. (1986). *Distribution of federal quota based on the January 6,
1986, registration of eligible students*. Louisville,
KY: Author.

Appleton, J., Clifton, R., & Goldberg, S. (1975). The
development of behavioral competence in infancy.
In F. D. Horowitz (Ed.). *Review of Child Development research*, Vol. 4. Chicago: University of
Chicago Press.

Atkinson, J., & Braddick, O. (1979). Assessment of vision in infants: Applications to amblyopia. *Transactions of the Ophthalmological Societies of the
United Kingdom: Cambridge Ophthalmological
Symposium, 49*, 338–343.

Barker, R. (1968). *Ecological Psychology: Concepts and
Methods for Studying the Environment of Human
Development*. Stanford, CA: Stanford University
Press.

Barraga, N. (1964). *Increased Visual Behavior in Low
Vision Children*. Research Series, American Foundation for the Blind, No. 13.

Barraga, N. (1970). *Visual Efficiency Scale*. Louisville,
American Printing House for the Blind.

Bauman, M. (1973). Psychological and educational assessment. In B. Lowenfeld (Ed.). *The Visually
Handicapped Child in School*. New York: Day.

Beery, K., & Buktenica, N. A. (1967). *Developmental
Test of Visual-Motor Integration*. Chicago: Follett.

Block, C. (1972). *Developmental Study of Tactile-Kinesthetic Discrimination in Blind, Deaf, and Normal
Children*. Unpublished doctoral dissertation, Boston University.

Bortner, J., & Birch, H. (1970). Cognitive capacity and
cognitive competency. *American Journal of Mental
Deficiency, 74*, 735–744.

Brooks, P., & Baumeister, A. (1977). A plea for consideration of ecological validity in the experimental
psychology of mental retardtion: A guest editorial.
American Journal of Mental Deficiency 81, 407–
416.

Bruner, J. (1973). Organization of early skills action.
Child Development, 44, 1–11.

Buell, C. (1950). Motor performance of visually handicapped children. *Exceptional Children, 17*, 69–72.

Buktenica, N. (1968). *Visual Learning*. San Rafael, CA:
Dimensions.

Burlingham, D. (1961). Some notes on the development
of the blind. *Psychoanalytic Study of the Child, 16*,
121–145.

Burlingham, D. (1965). Some problems of ego development in blind children. *Psychoanalytic Study of
the Child, 20*, 194–208.

Caton, H. (1976). *The Tactile Test of Basic Concepts*.
Louisville, KY: American Printing House for the
Blind.

Cibis, G. W., Maino, J. H., Crandall, M. A., Cress, P.,
Spellman, C. R., & Shores, R. E. (1985). The Parsons visual acuity test for screening children 18 to
48 months old. *Annals of Ophthalmology, 17*, 471–
478.

Cohen, M. A., & Gross, P. J. (1979). *The Developmental Resource*, Vols. I and II. New York: Grune & Stratton.

Colarusso, R. P., & Hammill, D. D. (1972). *Motor-Free Visual Perception Test*. San Rafael, CA: Academic Therapy Publications.

Cratty, B. J. (1970). *Perceptual and Motor Development in Infants and Children*. London: Macmillan.

Cratty, B. J., Peterson, C., Harris, J., et al. (1968). The development of perceptual-motor abilities in blind children and adolescents. *New Outlook for the Blind, 62,* 111–117.

Cress, P. J. (1987). Visual assessment. In M. Bullis (Ed.), *Communication Development in Young Children with Deaf-blindness: Literature Review III.* Monmouth, OR: Teaching Research Division of Oregon State System of Higher Education.

Cress, P., Johnson, J. L., Spellman, L. R., Sizemore, A. C. & Shores, R. E. (1982). The development of a visual acuity test for persons with severe handicaps. *Journal of Special Education Technology, V*(3), 11–19.

Cutsforth, T. D. (1932). The unreality of words to the blind. *Teachers Forum, 4,* 86–89.

DeMott, R (1972). Verbalism and affective meaning for blind, severely visually impaired, and normally sighted children. *New Outlook for the Blind, 66,* 1–8.

Dobson, V., & Teller, D. (1978). Visual acuity in human infants: A view and comparison of behavioral and electrophysiological studies. *Vision Research, 18*(11), 1469–1403.

Dokecki, P. C. (1966). Verbalism and the blind: A critical review of the concept and the literature. *Exceptional Children, 32,* 525–530.

DuBose, R. F. (1976). Developmental needs in blind infants. *New Outlook for the Blind, 2,* 49–52.

DuBose, R. F. (1979). Working with sensorily impaired children (Part I): Visual Impairments In S. G. Garwood (Ed.) *Educating Young Handicapped Children.* Germantown: Aspen Systems.

DuBose, R. F., & Langley, M. B. (1977). *Developmental Activities Screening Inventory.* Hingham, MA: Teaching Resources Corporation.

DuBose, R., Langley, M. B., & Stagg, V. (1977). Assessing severely handicapped children. *Focus on Exceptional Children, 9,* 1–13.

Duckman, R. H., & Selenow, A. (1983). Use of forced preferential looking for measurement of visual acuity in a population of neurologically impaired children. *American Journal of Optometry & Physiological Optics, 60*(10), 817–821.

Ehrlich, M. I., Reinecke, R. D., & Simons, K. (1983). Preschool vision screening for amblyopia and strabismus programs, methods, guidelines. *Survey of Ophthalmology, 28*(3), 149–163.

Eichorn, J. R., & Vigaroso, H. R. (1967). Orientation and mobility for preschool blind children. *International Journal for the Education of the Blind, 17,* 48–50.

Ellingham, T. R., Silva, P. A., Buckfield, P. M., & Clarkson, J. E. (1976). Neonatal at-risk factors, visual defects and the preschool child: A report from the Queen Mary Hospital multidisciplinary child development study. *New Zealand Medical Journal, 83,* 74–77.

Fagan, J. F. III, & Singer, L. T. (1983). Infant recognition memory as a measure of intelligence. *Advances in Infancy Research, II,* 31–78.

Fantz, R., Ordy, J., & Udelf, M. (1962). Maturation of pattern vision in infants during the first six months. *Journal of Comparative and Physiological Psychology, 55,* 907–917.

Folio, M. R. (1974). *Assessing Motor Development in Multiply Handicapped Children.* Paper presented at the annual meeting of the Council on Exceptional Children, New York.

Fraiberg, S. (1977). *Insights from the Blind.* New York: Basic Books.

Frostig, M., Maslow, P., Lefever, D. W., & Whittlesey, J. R. B. (1964). *The Marianne Frostig Developmental Test of Visual Perception.* Palo Alto, CA: Consulting Psychologists Press.

Genshaft, J. L., Dare, N. L., & O'Malley, P. L. (1980). Assessing the visually impaired child: A school psychology view. *Journal of visual impairment and blindness, 9*(74), 344–350.

Gowman, A (1957). *The War Blind in American Social Structure.* New York:. American Foundation for the Blind.

Graham, M. (1965). Wanted: A readiness test for mobility training. *New Outlook for the Blind, 59,* 157–162.

Hallenbeck, J. (1954). Two essential factors in the development of young blind children. *New Outlook for the Blind, 48,* 308–315.

Harley, R. K. (1963). *Verbalism Among Blind Childre.* Research Series, American Foundation for the Blind, No. 10.

Harley, R., & Lawrence, A. (1977). *Visual Impairments in the Schools.* Springfield, IL: Thomas.

Harley, R., Wood, T., & Merbler, J. (1980). *The Peabody Mobility Kits.* Chicago: Stoelting.

Higgins, L. C. (1973). *Classification in Congenitally Blind Children.* Research Series, American Foundation for the Blind, No. 25.

Hohmann, M., Banet, B., & Weikart, D. (1979). *Young Children in Action.* Ypsilanti, MI: High/Scope Educational Research Foundation.

Hoyt, C., Nickel, B., & Billson, F. (1982). Ophthalmological examination of the infant development aspects *Society of Ophthalmology 26*(4) 177–185.

Jones, B. (1972). Development of cutaneous and kinesthetic localization by blind and sighted children. *Developmental Psychology, 6,* 349–352.

Jose, R. T., Smith, A. J., & Shane, K. G. (1980). Evaluating and stimulating vision in the multiply impaired. *Journal of Visual Impairment and Blindness, 74,* 2–8.

Kakalik, J. S., Brewer, G. D., Dougharty, L. A., Fleischauer, P. D., Genensky, S. M., & Wallen, L. M. (1974). *Improving Services to Handicapped Children.* Santa Monica, CA: Rand Corporation.

Kaufman, A. S., & Kaufman, N. L. (1983). *Kaufman Assessment Battery for Children.* Circle Pines, MN: American Guidance Service.

Kiernan, D. W., & DuBose, R. F. (1974). Assessing the cognitive development of preschool deaf-blind children. *Education of the Visually Handicapped, 6*(4), 103–105.

Kirk, S. A., McCarthy, J. J., & Kirk, W. D. (1968). *Examiner's Manual: Illinois Test of Psycholinguistic Abilities* (Rev. ed.) Urbana, IL: University of Illinois Press.

Langley, M. B. (1980a). *Assessment of Multihandicapped, Visually Impaired Children.* Chicago: Stoelting.

Langley, M. B. (1980b). *Functional Vision Inventory for the Multiply Severely Handicapped.* Chicago: Stoelting.

Langley, M., & DuBose, R. (1976). Functional vision screening for the severely handicapped children. *New Outlook for the Blind, 70,* 346–350.

Lennerstrand, G, Anderson, G, & Axelsson, A (1982) Clinical assessment of visual functions in infants and young children. *Acta Ophthalmologica,* Suppl., 157, 63–67.

Lowenfeld, B. (1964). *Our Blind Children.* Springfield, IL: Thomas. Maxfield, K. E., & Buchholz, S. B. (1957). *A Social Maturity Scale for Blind Preschool Children.* New York: American Foundation for the Blind.

Mayer, D. L., Fulton, A. B., & Sossen, P. L. (1983). Preferential looking acuity of pediatric patients with developmental disabilities. *Behavioral Brain Research, 10,* 189–198.

McCarthy, D. (1972). *Manual for the McCarthy Scales of Children's Abilities.* New York: The Psychological Corporation.

McDonald, M., Dobson, V., Sebris, L., Baitch, L., Varner, D., & Teller, D. Y. (1985). The acuity card procedure: A rapid test of infant acuity. *Investigative Ophthalmology and Visual Science, 26,* 1158–1162.

Morse, A. R., & Trief, E. (1985). Diagnosis and evaluation of visual dysfunction in premature infants with low birth weight. *Journal of Visual Impairment and Blindness, 79*(6), 248–251.

Nagera, H., & Colonna, A. B. (1965). Aspects of the contributions of sight to ego and drive development. *Psychoanalytic Study of the Child, 20,* 267–287.

National Society to Prevent Blindness. (1974a). *The Letter Chart for Twenty Feet-Snellen Scale.* New York.

National Society to Prevent Blindness. (1974b). *The Symbol Chart for Twenty Feet-Snellen Scale.* New York.

Norris, M., Spaulding, P. J., & Brodie, F. H. (1957). *Blindness in Children.* Chicago: University of Chicago Press.

Odom, V., Hoyt, C., & Marg, E. (1982). Eye patching and visually evoked potential acuity in children four months to eight years old. *American Journal of Optometry and Physiological Optics, 59*(9), 706–717.

Piaget, J., & Inhelder, B. (1969). *The Psychology of the Child.* New York: Basic Books.

Project APT. (1980). *Screening Manual.* Fairfax, VA: Fairfax County Public Schools, Department of Special Services.

Project APT. (1980). *Lighthouse Flashcard Test for Children.* Fairfax, VA: Fairfax County Public Schools, Department of Special Services.

Schwartz, A. (1972). *A Comparison of Congenitally Blind and Sighted Elementary School Children on Intelligence, Tactile, Discrimination, Abstract Reasoning, Perceived Physical Health, Perceived Personality Adjustment and Parent-Teacher Perceptions of Intellectual Performance.* Unpublished doctoral dissertation, University of Maryland.

Scott, R. A. (1969). The socialization of blind children. In D. S. Goslin (Ed.), *Handbook of Socialization Theory and Research.* Chicago: Rand McNally.

Sheridan, M. (1970). *Stycar Vision Test Manual* (2nd Ed.), Berks, England: NFER Publishing Co.

Sheridan, M. D. (1960). Vision screening of very young or handicapped children. *British Medical Journal, 5196,* 453–456.

Silberman, R. K. (1981). Assessment and evaluation of visually handicapped students. *Journal of Visual Impairment and Blindness, 3*(75), 109–114.

Simons, K. (1981a). A comparison of the Frisby, random-dot E, TNO, and randot circles stereotests in screening and office use. *Archives of Ophthalmology, 99,* 446–452.

Simons, K. (1981b) Stereoacuity norms in young children. *Archives of Ophthalmology, 99,* 439–445.

Smits, B., & Mommers, M. J. C. (1976). Differences between blind and sighted children on WISC verbal subtests. *New Outlook for the Blind, 70,* 240–246.

Sokol, S. (1978). Measurement of infant visual acuity from pattern reversal evoked potentials. *Vision Research, 18*(1), 33–39.

Spellman, C. R., DeBriere, T. J., & Cress, P. J. (1979). *Final Report from the Project for Research and Development of Subjective Visual Acuity Assessment*

Procedures for SeverelS Handicapped Persons. Bureau of Education for the Handicapped Grant No. G00–76–02592.

Sroufe, A., Walters, E., & Matas, L. (1974). Continual determinants of infant affective response. In M. Lewis, & L. A. Rosenblum (Eds.), *The Origins of Fear.* New York: Wiley.

Stangler, S., Huber, C., & Routh, D. (1980). *Screening Growth and Development of Preschool Children: A Guide for Test Selection.* New York: McGraw-Hill.

Stephens, B. (1972). Cognitive processes in the visually impaired. *Education of the Visually Handicapped, 4,* 106–111.

Stutsman, R. (1948). *Merrill-Palmer Scale of Mental Tests.* Chicago: Stoelting.

Terman, L. M., & Merrill, M. A. (1973). *Stanford-Binet Intelligence Scale.: Manual for the Third Revision Form L-M.* Boston: Houghton Mifflin.

Thorndike, R. L., Hagen, E. P., & Sattler, J. M. (1986). *The Stanford-Binet Intelligence Scale: Fourth Edition.* Chicago: Riverside Publishing Co.

Tillman, M. H., & Bashaw, W. L. (1968). Multivariate analysis of the WISC scales for blind and sighted children. *Psychological Reports, 23,* 523–526.

Wallace, G., & Kauffman, J. M. (1973). *Teaching Children with Learning Problems.* Columbus, OH: Merrill.

Warren, D. H. (1977). *Blindness and Early Childhood Development.* New York: American Foundation for the Blind.

Wechsler, D. (1949). Wechsler Intelligence Scale for Children. New York: The Psychological Corporation.

Wechsler, D. (1974). Wechsler Intelligence Scale for Children—revised. New York: The Psychological Corporation.

Wechsler, D. (1967). *Manual for the Wechsler Preschool and Primary Scale of Intelligence.* New York: The Psychological Corporation.

Wilson, J., & Halverson, H. M. (1947). Development of a young blind child. *Journal of Genetic Psychology, 71,* 155–175.

Woodcock, R., & Johnson, B. (1977). *Woodcock-Johnson Psycho-educational Battery.* Hingham, MA: Teaching Resources Corporation.

Zaporazhets, A. V., & Elkonin, D. B. (1971). *The Psychology of Preschool Children.* Cambridge, MA: M.I.T. Press.

16

Assessment of Auditory Functioning

CHANDRAKANT P. SHAH
MARILYN F. H. BOYDEN

There is increasing evidence that hearing impairment in infancy and early childhood adversely affects the acquisition of speech and language as well as mental, emotional, and social development. Although profound hearing impairment in preschool children always has been relatively easily recognized, lesser degrees of hearing impairment have not been as readily detected and the child's difficulties frequently have been attributed to behavioral disorders, hyperactivity, autism, or mental retardation. As a result of recent advances in assessment techniques, however, remarkably accurate diagnoses of hearing impairment can now be made during the first few months of life and appropriate habilitation procedures can be started early.

IMPORTANCE OF EARLY ASSESSMENT

Language Acquisition

One of the most important aspects of children's development is their acquisition of language, which enables them to communicate and relate to the environment. The satisfactory development of two-way communcation depends on an intact auditory system. The ear provides the primary sensory input for the montoring and feedback that are necessary while children are learning to talk (McConnell & Liff, 1975). Today many theorists believe that language is innate and all that is needed to trigger language development is an appropriate environment. It also is postulated that the brain is in an optimal condition for acquiring language between the ages of 2 and 10 years; if speech has not developed by the late teens acquisition of language is virtually impossible (McConnell & Liff, 1975). Superficially, hearing-impaired children appear similar to children with normal hearing up to 6 months of age. By 3 years of age, however, when the onset of connected speech occurs normally, the differences marking children as hearing impaired had developed exponentially.

Mental and Social Development

Hearing impairment can adversely affect children's mental and social development. They might have to deal with denial, rejection, or overprotective parental attitudes. Depending on the degree of impairment, they might be unable to communicate with or relate to their parents and peers during the early years that are so important for the development of a healthy personality. The frustrations encountered in the educational system by children with fluctuating hearing loss might be even greater than those experienced by profoundly hearing impaired children because the latter have had the problem diagnosed and have been placed in specialized educational settings. Mild to moderate hearing impairment often is mistaken for mental retardation even though there is no direct causal relationship between intelligence and hearing impairment. The range of intelligence is the same in hearing-impaired children as in those with normal hearing. Only when a potentially brain-damaging condition (e.g., maternal rubella during pregnancy or prematurity) is present does a relationship appear between deafness and lowered intelligence appear (Vernon & Mindel, 1978).

CLASSIFICATION AND EPIDEMIOLOGY OF HEARING LOSS

Classification

Hearing impairment is a general term that is applied to all degrees of hearing loss and includes the previously used terms deaf and hard of hearing. Deaf was used to describe the person in whom the auditory sense is nonfunctional, even with a hearing aid, for use in communication. Hard of hearing, on the other hand, describes a person in whom the auditory sense remains the primary method of language acquisition and communication even though a hearing aid usually is required.

Categories of hearing impairment in the literature vary depending on the author but can be generally defined by levels of decibels (dB) as follows: mild, 20–40 dB; moderate, 41–65 dB; severe, 66–90 dB; and profound, over 90 dB. In addition, hearing losses can be classified as conductive, sensorineural, mixed, or central.

Conductive losses result from a breakdown in the normal physical transmission of sound from the external ear to the cochlea because of such factors as congenital abnormalities of the external

canal (e.g., atresia), middle ear disease, particularly chronic otitis media, or otosclerosis. Conductive losses cannot exceed approximately 70 dB because at this level sound is conducted to the cochlea via the cranial bones. Pure conductive losses are characterized by normal bone conduction thresholds and reduced air conduction thresholds, which produce an air-bone gap. Many conductive losses can be medically or surgically corrected.

Sensorineural hearing losses occur because of cochlea or auditory nerve damage and often are the result of genetic factors, viral infections, ototoxic drugs, or overexposure to noise. Bone and air conduction thresholds are similar but reduced and the loss is irreversible. An additional problem is that, because the sensory end organ is damaged, the child has difficulty distinguishing speech sounds even in the presence of amplification.

Mixed hearing losses occur when both conductive and sensorineural components are present. The air-bone gap is equivalent to the conductive portion of the loss, but both air and bone threshold levels are lower than normal. English and coworkers (1973) studied the charts of 404 adult patients with a history of chronic otitis media and found that a significant proportion had had sensorineural deficits in addition to their conductive hearing losses, the degree of sensorineural impairment being directly proportional to the duration of and complications resulting from the otitis media. Middle ear disease can be superimposed on sensorineural loss and it is particularly important to watch for this in children to avoid compromising the residual hearing in a child with a sensorineural impairment.

Central deafness is the result of a problem arising between the auditory end organ and the interpretive or cortical areas of the brain. A delay in speech or language development or difficulty in interpreting speech can occur in the presence of normal auditory sensitivity threshold levels.

It is assumed that all readers of this chapter are familiar with details of the pure-tone audiogram available in any standard audiology text, and therefore they are not discussed here. Unless otherwise indicated, levels are reported in this chapter in tems of either the 1964 International Organzation for Standardization (ISO) or the 1969 American National Standards Institute (ANSI)

Specifications for Audiometers which, for all practical purposes, are equivalent.

Epidemiology

Clearly, the definition of hearing impairment determines its apparent incidence and prevalence. The National Association of the Deaf defined the prevocationally deaf as those members of the population who cannot hear and understand speech and who have lost, or never had, that ability before 19 years of age (Schein & El, 1974). This population formed the basis of the 1971 National Census of the Deaf Population. In this census, the prevalence of prevocational deafness (in a non-institutionalized population) was estimated at 2/1000 in the general population. Of the prevocationally deaf sample, more than 50% had lost their hearing before one year of age and about 75% had lost their hearing before three years (Schein & Elk, 1974). If congenital deafness is defined as deafness "present at or existing from the time of birth," its incidence in Canada is approximately 1/1500 in the general population (Stewart, 1977).

What constitutes significant hearing impairment? Northern and Downs (1978) cited a Health Examination Survey completed by the U.S. Department of Health, Education and Welfare from 1963 to 1965 that studied children 6 to 11 years of age. The survey showed that 4% were judged by their parents as having "trouble hearing" while less than 1% were objectively considered to be hearing impaired according to the criterion that hearing begins with an average 26-dB loss in the frequencies 500–2000 Hz. Kessner and colleagues (1974) examined 1,639 children 4 to 11 years of age utilizing a failure criterion of only 15 dB in the speech and high frequencies. They found that 2.2% of these children had a bilateral loss and 4.5% had a unilaterial loss in the speech frequencies. Among 4 to 5 year olds, 4.1% had significant bilateral loss in the speech frequencies and the vast majority of these losses were conductive (Kessner et al., 1974). The similarity between this figure and that obtained from parents' questionnaires in the Health Examination Survey is obvious. Hearing loss was found to be greatest for serous otitis media; the difference in threshold values in the speech frequencies between normal ears and those with clinical serous otitis media

was only 7.4 dB. The prevalence of ear pathology reached a peak at 2 years of age, when 30% of the ears studied were abnormal (Kessner et al., 1974). Of concern was the residual hearing loss found in the speech frequencies of children 8 to 11 years old in whom the prevalence of ear pathology had significantly declined.

Northern and Downs (1978) proposed that the criteria for significant hearing loss in a child under 18 months include a hearing loss of at least 15 dB, indications of serous otitis media present for more than one-half the time during a six month period, and hearing levels fluctuating between zero and 15 dB or more for more than one-half the time for one year. In light of these criteria, they estimate that in children 2 to 6 years old the average prevalence of bilateral hearing loss of at least 15 dB is 4.1% and that of unilateral hearing loss is 7.2%. The prevalence of unilateral loss, however, falls steadily from a high of 10.8% for children between 12 months and 2 years to 3.7% for children between 8 to 9 years of age.

ETIOLOGY OF HEARING IMPAIRMENT

The causes of hearing impairment in childhood are classified as prenatal, perinatal, and postnatal factors to avoid the sometimes misleading terms of congenital versus acquired. Congenital refers to a condition existing at or before birth and can include both genetic and nongenetic factors. Some genetic syndromes might not be manifested until after birth and therefore are not congenital. Most prenatal and perinatal hearing impairment becomes evident in early infancy; however, a review of the literature by Wong and Shah (1979) revealed that one-fifth to one-third of cases are not discovered until the age of 2 years.

Prenatal Factors

Genetic

Hereditary deafness is estimated to account for about 35% to 50% of profound childhood deafness (Konigsmark & Gorlin, 1976). The mechanisms of genetic transmission can be derived from any standard genetics text and are not discussed here. Konigsmark and Gorlin (1976) identified approximately 150 types of hereditary deafness syndromes, which they classified into eight groups depending on the nature of the associated anomalies. In the following syndromes deafness characteristically develops during the age period under consideration:

- *Cockayne syndrome (autosomal recessive).* This syndrome is characterized by dwarfism senile appearance, mental retardation, and retinal degeneration. Hearing usually is normal at birth, but progresses to a moderate to severe sensorineural loss during childhood.
- *Crouzon's disease (autosomal dominant).* Crouzon's disease is associated with a conductive hearing loss in approximately one-third of patients. It is characterized by craniofacial dysostosis.
- *Waardenburg syndrome (autosomal dominant with varying expressivity).* Widely spaced medial canthi, flat nasal root, and confluent eyebrows characterize this syndrome. Approximately 20% of patients have sensorineural deafness ranging from mild to severe unilateral or bilateral deafness. This syndrome is estimated to account for 2% of cases of congental deafness.
- *Lemieux-Neemeh syndrome.* This syndrome is characterized by progressive distal muscular atrophy, nephropathy, and progressive sensorineural hearing loss beginning in childhood.
- *Macrothrombocytopathlia, nephritis, and sensorineural deafness.* Moderate to severe deafness begins between the ages of 3 to 10 years.
- *Richards-Rundle syndrome (autosomal dominant).* This syndrome is characterized by ataxia, hypogonadism, mental retardation, and progressive sensorineural hearing loss first noted at about age 2.
- *Pendred syndrome (autosomal recessive).* This syndrome involves goiter and profound sensorineural hearing loss in more than 50% of cases. The deafness usually is diagnosed about age 2 and progresses slightly through childhood. This syndrome accounts for about 10% of cases of congenital deafness.
- *Turner syndrome.* This syndrome is characterized by short stature, sexual infantilsm, various other physical stigmata, and abnormalities of the sex chromatin pattern. This syndrome is associated with an increased incidence of otitis media and sensorineural loss with recruitment in about 65% of cases. Severe deafness, however, is noted in only about 10% of cases.

Nongenetic

- *Maternal viral infections.* Rubella was recognized as a common prenatal cause of childhood hearing impairment as well as eye defects, congenital heart defects, congenital heart disease, and mental retardation during the mid-1960s. Infection by rubella virus can lead to the inhibition of mitosis, death of infected cell populations, ischemic damage, and chromosomal abnormalities. The probability of a fetus having congenital defects as a result of maternal infection is directly related to the time of onset of the disease; about 50% are affected if the disease occurs during the first month of pregnancy and the incidence falls steadily thereafter (Bergstrom, 1977). As the immunization of susceptible children increases, rubella should become a less frequent etiological factor.
- *Cytomegalovirus* Cytomegalovirus has been reported to infect ten times as many infants as rubella (Bergstrom, 1977). It produces clinical syndromes in the infant ranging from no symptoms to a picture similar to rubella. Dahle and coworkers (1979) reported progressive hearing loss in four of twelve children with sensorineural hearing impairment. Children with known congental cytomegalovirus require close monitoring to ensure prompt detection of delayed or progressive hearing loss.

    It has not been conclusively demonstrated that other viruses acquired during pregnancy are associated with an increased incidence of congenital defects.
- *Ototoxic drugs.* Many drugs can cause hearing impairment if ingested during pregnancy. Those most commonly implicated in prenatal deafness are streptomycin, quinine, and chloroquine phosphate. The most severe damage to the fetus occurs when the drugs are ingested during the first trimester of pregnancy, particularly in the sixth and seventh weeks.

Potential auditory apparatus injury includes damage to the hair cells, middle ear anomalies, absence of the seventh and eighth nerves, and dysplasia of the organ of Corti (Northern & Downs, 1978).

Perinatal Factors

Prematurity

Prematurity is a commonly mentioned perinatal cause of hearing impairment. The incidence of hearing loss because of prematurity ranges from 3.3% to about 10% (Catlin, 1978). The pathogenesis has been attributed to intrapartum hemorrhage into the inner ear.

Hypoxia

Some degree of hypoxia is reported to be present in 5% to 10% of all births and produces hearing loss in 0.9% to 10% of infants (Catin, 1978). Hypoxia can have a toxic effect on the cochlear nuclei and can result in other neurological damage, such as cerebral palsy or mental retardation.

Birth Trauma

As with prematurity, the hearing impairment because of birth trauma is thought to result from hemorrhage into the inner ear that produces irreversible damage to the organ of Corti from the toxic effects of extravasated blood.

Kernicterus

Kernicterus usually is caused by maternal isoimmunization (because of Rh incompatibility) but also can result from such diverse causes as congenital hemolytic anemia, certain drugs (e.g., vitaimin K, sulfonaimides), and hypoxia (Catlin, 1978). Hearing loss ranges from mild to profound, is usually sensorineural, and is commonly bilateral. It is thought to be the result of toxic damage to the cochlear nuclei and/or central auditory pathways. Kernicterus is a good example of how prenatal, perinatal, and postnatal causes of deafness can be related. It has been shown, for example, that the incidence of kernicterus can be increased by such factors as low birth weight, prematurity, birth asphyxia, and certain drugs. Because it is not always possible to separate the contribution made by the various factors to the development of hearing impairment, a high-risk register for neonates that includes the following criteria (Gerber & Mencher, 1978) has been developed:

- Family history of severe hearing loss in early childhood
- Signficant viral illness during the mothers' pregnancy
- Congenital anomaly of the skull, face, ear, nose, or throat
- Prematurity with a birth weight of less than 1500 g
- Neonatal icterus with a serum bilirubin of 20 mg/dl or greater in an infant of normal weight, or a lower value in a smaller infant
- Hypoxia at birth with persistent neurological abnomalities

Postnatal Factors

Otitis Media

Otitis media usually is divided into acute, chronic, and secretory types. The last is not a distinct entity but a phase preceding or following the acute phase and possibly giving rise to chronc middle ear disease. Secretory otitis media is the most common cause of conductive hearing impairment among preschool children; it is particulary common among children with allergies and cleft palate (Eliachar, 1978).

Klein (1977) reported that 25.3% of the children ages 4 to 6 months who were brought to the ambulatory clinic of the Boston City Hospital had otitis media. This percentage fell steadily to 10.3% for children 3 to 5 years of age and rose to 41% for children over 5 years of age. Recurrence of otitis media tended to be related to the child's age at the first attack; 17% of the children had had three or more episodes by the age of 12 months.

The prevalence of otitis media is higher among North American Indians and Inuit, although the reasons for this have not been determined. In a survey of 1,109 native Indian children in British Columbia, Roberts (1976) found that 22.5% of those under two years of age and 17.5% of those 2 to 4 years of age had middle ear disease requiring treatment. Baxter and Ling (1974) examined 3,770 Inuit in the Baffin Zone and found acute otitis media in 6% and serous otitis media in about 12% of children under 3 years of age. About 20% of the population under 20 years of age had scarring of the tympanic membrane, indicating a history of either suppurative or serous otitis media. The authors found no evidence that Inuit had any unique characteristics of the external canal that could contribute to the high prevalence of middle ear disease; however, the authors did suggest that socioeconomic conditions, specifically lower hygiene standards, might have contributed to the increased prevalence.

In a study of children in Washington, D.C., who were between 6 months and 11 years of age, Kessner and coworkers (1974) found a prevalence of middle ear pathology in 35.6% of whites and only 19% of blacks.

Otitis media is common among children with cleft palate. Bess and colleagues (1986) examined 34 children with cleft palates and found the incidence of hearing loss and associated middle ear disease varied from 57% to 68% depending on the detection procedure used. Bluestone (1978) reviewed the pertinent literature and confirmed that about 50% of children with cleft palate have associated impairment. The hearing impairment is generally conductive and usually bilateral. The pathogenesis of middle ear disease in children with cleft palate usually is attributed to eustachian tube dysfunction.

Meningitis

Meningitis is the most common cause of severe postnatal sensorineural hearing impairment (Wong & Shah, 1979). In a review of 547 cases of meningitis at the Massachusetts General Hospital, Nado (1978) found that 21% of the 236 children over 2½ years of age who had bacterial meningitis (*Neisseria meningitidis*) and 5% of those under that age suffered partial or complete sensorineural hearing loss. The loss was bilateral in 77% of patients. In all cases of partial hearing losses, the chochlea was the site of the lesion, as evidenced by high speech discrimination scores and negative tone decay testing. Three of seven patients with fungal meningitis suffered hearing impairment,

whereas none of the 304 patients with aseptic or viral meningitis was found to have hearing loss. The low incidence of hearing loss in children under 2½ years of age might be partly attributed to difficulties in obtaining accurate sensitivity thresholds at that age. Nevertheless, a diagnosis of bacterial meningitis should always alert the physician to the need for careful follow-up so that any hearing impairment is detected as quickly as possible.

Viral Infections

Common viral diseases that have beem implicated in the etiology of childhood hearing impairment include measles, mumps, chicken pox, influenza, and infectious mononucleosis. The measles virus can enter the inner ear directly via the bloodstream or the CNS, or it can result in purulent otitis media with subsequent suppurative labyrinthitis and inner ear destruction. Mumps is one of the leading causes of unilateral sensorineural hearing loss in children. Deafness associated with viral diseases usually results from inner ear damage because of direct infiltration of the virus through the internal auditory meatus and generally is of the mild to profound sensorineural type (Northern & Downs, 1978).

Ototoxic Drugs

A number of drugs can injure or destroy the cochlear hair cells in children, thereby causing profound sensorineural deafness. Kanamycin and neomycin are the worst offenders; other drugs include certain antibiotics (particularly dihydrostreptomycin) and antimalarial medication. The hearing loss is usually bilateral and can be of varying degree because of individual susceptibility to the toxic effects of the drug.

Noise

Noise-induced hearing loss usually is considered an occupational health hazard of the older patient; however, children also can be exposed to noise of sufficient intensity to produce the characteristic sensorineural dip at 4000 Hz. Sources of noise include model aircraft engines, firecrackers, toy caps, toy firearms, and rock music. The incubator with its ambient noise level of 66 to 75 dB has been suspected but not conclusively proven to contribute to hearing impairment in premature infants.

SPEECH AND LANGUAGE DEVELOPMENT

Normal Skills

Knowledge of the landmarks of normal speech and language development is important in conducting an audiological assessment. The material presented in this section is derived from various sources (Berry, 1969; Lillywhite, 1958; Sheridan, 1968).

Ages 2–3

Children 2 to 3 years old use all vowels and the consonants *m, b, p, f, k, g, w, h, n, t,* and *d.* They tend to omit most final consonants, and their articulation lags behind their vocabulary. The intelligibility of their words when heard in context improves from about 65% at 2 years of age to about 70% to 80% by age 3. This is the period of most rapid vocabulary growth; it has been estimated that children's vocabularies double between 2½ and 3 years of age, from approximately 450 to 900 words. Throughout the stages of language development, children's ability to understand words exceeds their actual, expressive vocabulary. They experiment grammatically, putting two or more words together. They enjoy talking to themselves continually while playing, and echolalia is common. They are able to join in nursery rhymes and enjoy listening to simple stories read from picture books. They ask questions beginning with *what* and *where* and use the pronouns *I, me,* and *you.*

Ages 3–4

Children's use of the consonants *b, t, d, k,* and *g* improves and they attempt *v, th, s,* and *z* as well as such combinations as *tr, bl, pr, gr,* and *dr.* They might, however, have difficulty with *r* and *l,* and might substitute *w* for these letters or omit them. Speech is approximately 90% to 100% intelligible provided it is heard in context. Children's vocabulary comprehension increases to about 1,500 words at age 4 and they regularly use 600 to 1,000 words. Their sentences consist of

three to four words and they ask questions beginning with *who* and *why.* They are able to use plurals and personal pronouns, carry on simple conversations, and enjoy listening to their favorite stories. They develop standard subject–predicate sentences and attempt to form the past tense. They can understand the concept of *two* but count objects by repeating *one* the appropriate number of times. Their rate of speech increases and they often respond in a loud voice or yell.

Ages 4–5

Children 4 to 5 years of age consistently use *f* and *v* together with a number of consonant combinations. They might still have problems with *r, l, s, z, sh, ch, j,* and *th,* but there is little or no omission of intial and final consonants. Their speech usually is intelligible in context. They can comprehend 1,500 to 2,000 words and use 1,100 to 1,600 words. The complexity of their words has increased to three to four syllables and their sentences can be up to six words long. They ask questions beginning with *when* and *how* and use more adjectives, adverbs, prepositions, and conjunctions. Their use of pronoun in place of proper nouns has increased and they are able to carry out commands necessitating two to three actions. At this age, children enjoy both listening to and telling long stories. Their voices are better modulated and they tend to copy their mother's intonation and rhythmic patterns.

Ages 5–6

Children who are 5 to 6 years old have mastered the use of *r, l,* and *th* as well as such combinations as *tl, gr, bl, br,* and *pr.* They might still have difficulty with *thr, sk, st,* and *shr* and might continue to distort *s, z, sh, ch,* and *j.* Their general intelligibility is good. Their usable vocabularies have increased to 1,500 to 2,100 words and they understand 2,500 to 2,800 words. Their syntax is almost normal and they use five- to six-word compound or complex sentences. They experiment orally with various verb forms representing tense, number, or person; they can distinguish among types of nouns and use negation freely in their sentences. They ask the meaning of abstract words, enjoy listening to all types of stories, and might act them out in detail. By the age of 6, they might be able to read simple stories aloud.

It goes without saying that there is wide individual variation and considerable overlap among the various stages described here, which are, after all, only arbitrary divisions. Children's progress depends not only on the quality of their auditory system and mental capacity, but also on the stimulation they receive from the environment.

Hearing-impaired Children

Language development can be impeded whether or not hearing loss is profound. Holm and Kunze (1969) compared two groups of children 5 to 9 years of age who were matched for age, sex, and socioeconomic background to determine what effect fluctuating hearing loss associated with chronic otitis media had on speech and language development. The selection criteria for the study included the onset of middle ear disease before the age of 2 years with hearing fluctuations continuing until the time of the study, bilateral normal bone conduction, and at least one record of bilateral air conduction thresholds of 25 dB or greater. Using a standard battery of language performance tests, Holm and Kunze demonstrated that the experimental group was significantly delayed in all language skills requiring the reception or processing of auditory stimuli or the production of verbal responses. In contrast, the tests that measure primarily visual and motor skills showed no significant differences. Kaplan and coworkers (1973), in a study of 489 Inuit children, found that those with a history of otitis media before 2 years of age and a hearing loss of 26 dB greater had a statistically significant loss of verbal ability and were behind normal children in reading, mathematics, and language.

In a study of 40 children between the ages of 6 and 11, Zinkus and colleagues (1978) found that those with a history of chronic and severe otitis media during the first three years of life had significantly delayed speech and language development, deficits in specific verbal tasks involving auditory processing, difficulty performing tasks requiring the integration of visual and auditory processing skills, reading disorders, and poor spelling.

The impact of hearing impairment on speech development ranges from significant delay in language acquisition and faulty articulation, inflec-

tion, and pitch patterns in profoundly hearing-impaired children, to articulation problems (particulary with respect to high-frequency sounds, word endings, and some inital consonants) in those with less severe hearing impairment. Speech sounds vary in their frequency distribution and the ability of a hearing-impaired child to detect them varies similarly. For example, the frequencies of vowels range from 250 to 3300 Hz and their sound is relatively longer (≥ 100 ms) and more intense than that of consonants. Fricative consonants such as *z* and *s* (zoo, sun) have higher frequencies (3500 to 8000 Hz), whereas, *zh* and *sh* (measure, shop) have frequencies of 2500 to 4500 Hz; these consonants are more intense and longer than other fricatives such as *h, f,* and the unvoiced *th* (thin), which are especially difficult for children with hearing losses to identify (Skinner, 1978).

As stated earlier, hearing impairment is categorized as mild (20 to 40 dB loss), moderate (41 to 65 dB), severe (66 to 90 dB), or profound (>90 dB). Average sound pressure levels (SPL) for speech range from 45 to 60 dB (Skinner, 1978). For children with the mild hearing loss depicted in Fig. 16.1, many speech cues below 500 Hz are inaudible and consonants are more easily heard than vowels. With a moderate hearing loss, on the other hand, vowels are heard more easily than consonants. Short words without auditory cues such as *if, it,* or *the,* which are unstressed and therefore of low intensity, are especially difficult to hear, as are unvoiced stops (*p, t, k*) and fricative consonants (*f, h, s, th*).

Children with a severe loss can hear speech only if it is spoken at close range, whereas children with a profound loss cannot hear speech at all, even their own vocalizations, except with suitable amplification. Obviously, particular problems depend not only on the magnitude of hearing loss but also on the threshold configuration. For example, children with a predominantly high-frequency loss might successfully detect most speech sounds, and consequently their hearing can be assessed initially as grossly normal. The precise nature of the hearing deficit might not be suspected until the children are brought to the speech pathologist for continued distortion or lack of discrimination of such high-frequency sounds as *f, s,* and *th.*

A child with a conductive hearing loss can still discriminate between two sounds of different fre-

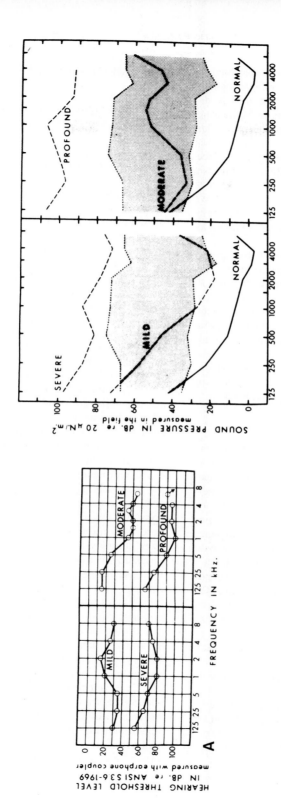

Figure 16.1(A). Pure-tone air conduction thresholds representing mild, moderate, severe and profound hearing losses for the right ear. (B). Monaural thresholds measured in the field for the audiograms shown in part A. Gray area: intensity range of speech. Solid curve: normal hearing threshold. (From Skinner, M. W. (1978) The hearing of speech during language acquisition. *Otolaryngologic Clinics of North America, 11,* 631–650. With permission)

quencies, whereas a child with a sensorineural loss cannot unless the frequencies are widely separated; the extent of separation required is directly proportional to the magnitude of hearing loss. A child with sensorineural loss has particular difficulty distinguishing sounds such as *t/k, r/w,* and *ch/sh,* and a hearing aid is of no assistance (Skinner, 1978). Children with either conductive or sensorineural loss cannot hear sounds below threshold levels. Sounds above threshold, however, seem abnormally loud to a child with cochlear hearing loss because of the process known as recruitmemt.

In conclusion, it should be noted that speech is rarely heard against a silent background; it has been estimated that background noise averages 35 to 68 dB (Skinner, 1978), only 10 to 15 dB below speech level. For normal adults, this situation presents no problem because their knowledge of the language allows them to deduce the sounds from the message context. Because children who are still learning the language lack the knowledge needed to supply missing acoustic clues, a hearing loss of only 15 dB can be highly significant.

Presenting Problems

Delay in identification of hearing impairment in preschool children is quite common (Shah, et al., 1977, Wallace 1973) Shah and his colleages identified stages of delay after parents or others suspected hearing loss and before the child received proper help. The average age of suspicion in young children is 16 months. From suspicion of hearing loss to receiving appropriate diagnostic tests takes from 3 months to 66 months. Hence it is imperative for individuals working with preschool children to be knowledgeable of manifestations of hearing impairment in young children. Table 16.1 shows manifestations of deafness reported by parents of affected children (Shah et al., 1977). A hearing loss of any degree will cause speech and language delay. How well a child develops communication skills depends on the degree of hearing loss and early intervention. A mild hearing loss is educationally significant. Whether a hearing impaired child will need speech and language therapy or a complete auditory training program will depend upon the degree of hearing loss (Table 16.2)

ASSESSMENT PROCEDURES

Clinical indications of hearing loss in infants and young children can include the following: lack of response to ordinary speech, startling noises, or persons or noises outside the visual field; no startle response to loud sound; slow speech development or poor articulation; behavioral disorders; hyperactivity; and chronic ear infections. Children can be referred for hearing assessment for any of these reasons, because they have been placed on the high-risk register, or as part of routine follow-up after a viral or bacterial infection such as meningitis or encephalitis. The audiological problem might be only one aspect of other disorders, such as cerebral palsy, autism, and mental retardation.

Because deafness might be only one part of a larger disease entity and can significantly influence other aspects of the child's development, audiological evaluation should involve a team approach. At The Hospital for Sick Children in Toronto a complete assessment for newly identified hearing impaired infants and young children can take up to four days. The primary team includes an otologist, audiologist, speech pathologist, pediatrician, neurologist, psychologist, opthalmologist, public health nurse, social worker, teacher of the hearing impaired, and a representative from the local school authority. In addition, a geneticist, neuroradiologist, and psychiatrist can be consulted (Wong & Shah, 1979). The specific tests described in this section do not constitute a complete audiological assessment because the results obtained must be viewed within the framework of the case history, otological and general medical findings, related educational, social, and psychological information, and receptive and expressive communication data (Lloyd & Cox, 1975).

During the intial period of establishing rapport with the mother and child and obtaining a clinical history, the audiologist can, through simple observation, obtain valuable information about the child's developmental level, voice quality, articulation, extent of vocabulary, and the presence or absence of other physical handicaps or congenital abnormalities. The information gained at this time will assist the audiologist in selecting the appropriate test protocol. A brief inspection of the

TABLE 16.1
MANIFESTATIONS OF DEAFNESS REPORTED BY THE PARENTS OF 200 AFFECTED CHILDREN

Mentioned by Parents (% of Cases)	Area of Difficulty Manifestations
	Hearing
43%	No response to ordinary speech/soft sounds/calling name
37%	No response to startling noises/loud sounds/ringing and honking
30%	No response to noises or persons outside visual field
27%	My child is deaf/has a hearing problem
11%	Wants to see your face when you talk/watches mouths
6%	Listens for and responds to vibration (by placing ear against the stereo or washing machine
5%	Doesn't play with noisemaking or musical toys
	Talking
39%	Slow to talk/poor speech/no speech
8%	No babbling/doesn't babble like he or she used to
8%	A quiet baby/slept well (through noise)
	Behavior
14%	Doesn't pay attention/doesn't understand/irregular disobedience/hard to handle/have to raise voice often and repeat things
9%	Hyperactive/pulls and points a lot (excessive use of gestures)/frequently bites/won't play some games with others
7%	Frequent and unusually loud screaming and crying
	Other Ear Problems
23%	Chronic ear infections
6%	Balance problems (slow to sit up and walk)
2%	Fingering the ears frequently (at age 6 to 12 months)

Reprinted from Shah, C. P., Dale, M. A. & Chandler, D., The Challenge of Hearing Impairments in Children, *Canadian Family Physicians 23:* 175–183, with permission of the authors & the Journal.

child's external ear canal can be done at this time to rule out the presence of congenital abnormalities (e.g., atresia), foreign bodies, or impacted cerumen. Audiological evaluation of the 3 to 6 year old child normally consists of measuring pure-tone air and bone conduction thresholds, the speech reception threshold, speech discrimination and impedance/immittance audiometry. Where indicated, electrophysiological response audiometry also can be employed. Lloyd and Cox (1975) outlined various factors contributing to audiometric reliability, such as background noise level, calibration of equipment, type and level of instructions provided to the child, response criteria, and method of response.

Selecting the appropriate test battery to obtain the most information about the child's hearing is considered the hallmark of pediatric audiology. There is no "right" order in which to conduct the tests; for example, impedance audiometry can be used to verify behavioral results or the evaluation can begin with impedance audiometry to rule out gross middle ear dysfunction. Much depends on the child's developmental level, which changes rapidly during the age range under consideration, the presence of medical or psychological problems, and willingness of the child to cooperate on the day of the hearing assessment. Success in audiological assessment of the preschool child depends, in no small way, on the enthusiasm, ingenuity, and experience of the audiologist.

Audiological evaluation of the infant to 2 year old is not as sensitive in obtaining hearing threshold information as in older children. Routine as-

TABLE 16.2
DEGREES OF HEARING IMPAIRMENT

Category	Handicap	Special Needs
Normal (0–15 dB)	None	None
Mild/slight (16–40 dB)	Educationally significant. Faint or distant speech might be difficult to understand, especially in the presence of background noise.	Monitor condition. Preferential classroom seating is needed. Mild gain amplification might help this child.
Moderate (41–55 dB)	Vocabulary might be limited. Articulation problems can occur; language, reading and writing skills can be affected.	Might need speech and language intervention. Amplification usually will help. Preferential seating in the classroom is desirable.
Moderate/severe (56–70 dB)	Speech and language are delayed. Group discussion will be very difficult to follow.	Might need special assistance in regular classroom. Might require tutor, and speech and language help. Amplification is a must.
Severe (71–90 dB)	Speech and language will be distorted, and might not develop spontaneously	Amplification necessary. Needs speech and language remediation and auditory training. Might need special education.
Profound (90+ dB)	Might be more aware of vibrations than tonal sounds. Speech and language are defective and will not develop spontaneously. Hearing does not serve as the primary means for the acquisition of spoken language or for the monitoring of speech.	Usually requires special classes. Might benefit from amplification to monitor own voice and for gross discrimination of sounds.

sessment techniques for this population include behavioral observation audiometry (BOA) and visual response audiometry. These procedures are performed in a sound field test site. The test stimuli are presented through speakers rather than headphones. Results obtained reflect the better hearing ear. The definition of an age-appropriate response falls within a broad category of acceptable responses because the developmental criteria in this age group is not as well defined as are the developmental norms in the 3 to 6 year olds.

Early detection of hearing loss is especially important in the birth to 2-year-old age group because of its potentially adverse effects on language acquisition. The first months of an infant's life are crucial for developing language. Normal language development is rapid. Before a child expresses language, that child has experienced more than a year of receptive language with complex intellectual events occurring. Mild and moderate hearing loss, whether conductive or sensorineural, can delay language development. In measuring the auditory function of infants and young children, it is therefore necessary to have quantitative audiometry. Electrophysiological measures, especially brainstem electric response audiometry (BERA) have gained an important role in assessing infants hearing. The BERA provides a precise measure of the peripheral auditory system (from the ear to the upper auditory brainstem) and does not provide information about the child's receptive and expressive language.

The audiometric procedures used to assess the hearing of infants and children are classified as subjective (observation of the infant's or young child's responses to controlled auditory signals) and objective (physiological) assessments. Behavioral assessments, such as behavioral observation audiometry, visual response audiometry, and play audiometry are subjective in nature. The most quantitative of these procedures is play audiometry, which cannot be used successfully until the child is 2½ or 3 years of age. Objective measurements include impedance audiometry and electrophysiological measurements of the auditory system.

Subjective Audiometry

Subjective audiometry is useful in children because it allows the audiologist to evaluate the overall development of the child as well as the functional relationship between the child and his or her environment. This information is essential in selecting the most appropriate test protocol and interpreting the results obtained. Appropriate test selection will be determined by the functional capabilities of the child as a child's responses are contingent upon his level of mental development. Northern and Downs (1978) developed an Auditory Behavioral Index that correlates an infant's developmental level to his or her ability to respond to auditory stimuli. Normal development is as follows:

- *0 to 4 months:* the responses are reflexive consisting of eye widening, cessation of activity and limb movement. The auditory stimuli are presented at levels of 70 to 80 dBnHL to initiate change in behavior.
- *4 to 7 months:* turning of the head toward the the auditory stimuli. Intensity of the auditory stimuli to elicit a head turn range from 50 to 60 dBnHL at four to five months to 30 to 40 dBnHL at six to seven months. As the infant matures, his minimum level of response (MLR) decreases.
- *7 to 9 months:* direct localization of sound to the side and indirectly below ear level Hrs MLR ranges from 40 (seven months) to 30 dBnHL (nine months).
- *9 to 13 months:* direct localization of sound to

the side, below and indirectly above ear level. The MLR ranges from 20 to 30 dBnHL.
- 13 to 16 months: direct location of sound to the side, above, and below ear level MLR ranges from 20 to 30 dBnHL.

The meaningfulness of sound to the child also is significant in obtaining a response. Speech is most likely to elicit the lowest minimal response level because it is the most familiar auditory stimulus to the infant and it is a broad frequency (acoustic energy from 500 to 3000 Hz stimulus) (Lloyd & Cox, 1975). However, normal hearing should not be assumed only on the basis of a response to such broad-frequency stimuli as speech; neither should a failure to respond to warbled pure tones at speech threshold levels be assumed to indicate hearing loss. In the sound field environment, the recorded response to all stimuli reflects the sensitivity threshold for the better hearing ear. The behavioral assessment of an infant's auditory threshold can be differentiated by whether reinforcement is used. Behavioral observation audiometry (BOA), when no reinforcement is used, is a passive approach to assessing an infant's auditory threshold. The use of reinforcement is a form of operant conditioning—the desired response to an auditory signal is reinforced. Among conditioning procedures for infants, visual reinforcement audiometry (VRA) has emerged as a successful assessment tool for infants 6 months through 2 years of age (Wilson & Thompson, 1984).

Behavioral Observation Audiometry

BOA involves observing the newborn's or infant's response to a variety of sound stimuli such as voice, warbled pure-tones, and narrow band noise. The infant should be tested in a sound-treated room with two trained observers, preferably pediatric audiologists, observing the infant's responses to selected stimuli. One audiologist is in the sound room with the infant, the other is located at the audiometer. The examiner observes the infant's reaction to the stimuli presented through a two-way mirror. The use of the audiometer allows for control of the stimuli, both in frequency (pitch) and intensity (loudness). The most common stimuli used are narrow band noise at 500, 2000, and 4000 Hz. and a speech signal (the infant's name, for example or the repetition of ba,ba,ba). The narrow band noise (NBN) is preferable to the warbled pure-tone because it contains the most acoustic energy, while remaining frequency specific, which is necessary to elicit a repeatable response from a very young infant. A warbled pure-tone is effective as the infant nears 4 months of age. A speech signal is included because it is familiar to the infant and comprises the largest amount of acoustic energy, resulting in a better response than the NBN. The three frequencies presented are selected for their appropriateness in eliciting frequency specific information within the are of speech. As well, information from the high frequency area contribute knowledge about the possibility of a sensorineural hearing loss while the low frequency response provides information regarding the possibility of a conductive hearing loss. Sensorineural hearing loss results from damage to the sensory organ (the cochlea). The damage initially develops in the basal end of the cochlea where the high frequencies are heard and will be more severe in the high frequencies (above 2000 Hz). A conductive hearing loss is caused by a stiffness in the mechanical portion of the hearing organism, the eardrum and the ossicular chain, that results in improper conduction of sound. Conductive hearing losses have a greater effect on the lower frequency range of hearing (below 500 Hz).

Bone conduction results are not reliably obtained from infants. To determine the type of hearing loss in this population, it is important to note the configuration of the infant's response to the various frequencies. If the child responds age appropriately for the low frequency stimulus but not in the high frequency range, a sensorineural hearing loss is suspected. Conversely, a poorer response to the low frequency stimulation improving in the high frequency range might be indicative of a conductive hearing loss. Responses that are not age appropriate throughout the frequency range with the greatest abnormality in the low frequency range might indicate a mixed hearing loss. Results obtained using impedance audiometric measurements play a major role in defining the type of hearing loss in infants.

The intensity of the auditory signal that will result in an obvious change in the less than 4 month old infant's behavior is signficant, in the range of 70 to 80 dBnHL. Therefore it is difficult to determine a hearing loss of less than a severe to profound degree. Whether the infant being tested is sleeping, crying, or awake and happy will determine how successful the test will be. An infant's responses are reflexive in nature and can include increasing or decreasing activity, change in breathing, eye widening, or cessation of babbling. It is difficult to observe these subtle responses to the auditory stimuli unless the infant is quiet.

A typical response recorded in a normal hearing 6 week old is recorded in Fig 16.2. The speech awareness threshold of 60 dBnHL hearing level is better than the results obtained with the NBN at the three frequencies tested. As the infant matures, his or her minimal response level improves (Fig. 16.3).

Behavioral observation audiometry is, at best, a method to screen severe-to-profound hearing loss in very young infants. It is the least precise indicator of an infant's hearing. It will not result in information discrete enough to adequately describe auditory function and the need for habilitation in the very young infant. Nevertheless, valuable information about the child's general development and his ability to interact with his environment will assist in interpreting more objective test results that are influenced in their interpretation by the neurophysiological state of the infant. Although BOA is generally used for testing infants under 4 months of age, it also might be necessary to use this method of assessment in the mentally retarded child.

Visual Reinforcement Audiometry

VRA is successful in determining the auditory response of infants and children from 6 months to 2 years of age. As the infant begins to localize to "interesting" or "unusual" sounds, he or she can be reinforced with a visual stimulus the most popular being a lighted, animated toy. This procedure is geared to the developmental level of the young infant. Visual stimuli are used because they are

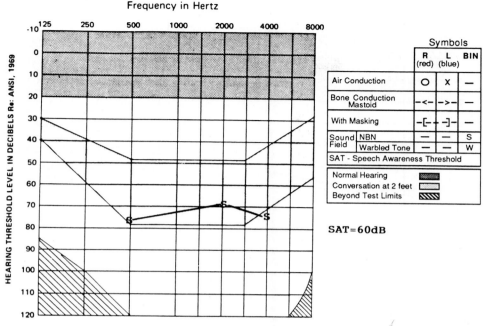

Figure 16.2 Behavioral Observation Audiometry responses of a 6-week-old infant. (The Hospital for Sick Children, Toronto.)

particularly interesting to this age group. Babies are interested in the myriad of toys presented to them in their natural environments. It is not surprising that a visual stimulus will provide an excellent reinforcing function for auditory responses obtained in a formal testing situation (Wilson & Thompson, 1984). This type of audiometry can be performed either in a sound field environment (6 to 12 months of age) or with the use of earphones. It progresses from simple sound localization techniques to threshold definition (Murphy & Shallop, 1978). Two examiners are necessary to complete the assessment; one to occupy the child and one to operate the audiometer. As in BOA, the frequencies tested are 500, 2000, and 4000 Hzn. The stimuli can consist of warbled pure-tones or NBN, and speech. The more frequency specific warbled pure-tones are the stimulus of choice if the developmental level of the infant and his cooperative ability will result in a response to stimuli with less acoustic energy. If the child is old enough (1 to 2

years of age) to allow the use of headphones, pure-tone stimuli are used. Whenever any type of alerting response occurs, such as turning in the direction of the auditory signal, visual reinforcement in the form of a lighted, animated toy is presented. In a sound field environment, this technque tests the better hearing ear. As the infant matures, distractive toys, such as bright colored pegs, are added to the test protocol. The child's attention is drawn to the colored pegs by the observer in the sound room, distracting him from continued observation of the animated toys between presentations of the stimuli. If the child's attention is not distracted from the visual reinforcer, false positive responses will result. If the distractive toys are too interesting or complex for the child he will become so involved in the task before him that he will fail to respond when the stimuli are presented.

Visual reinforcement audiometry can produce responses at sound levels 10 to 15 dBnHL less

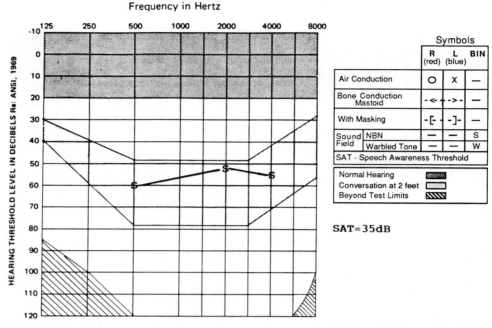

Figure 16.3   Behavioral Observational Audiometry response of a 4-month-old infant. (The Hospital for Sick Children, Toronto.)

than those obtained through behavioral observation audiometry (Fig. 16.4) resulting in more definitive information about the infant's hearing. However, this method is not definitive enough to identify a mild hearing loss, especially in the 6 to 8 month old child (Figs. 16.4 and Fig 16.5). As with other forms of testing, minimal response levels improve as the child gets older (Figs. 16.5 and 16.6).

Tangibly Reinforced Audiometry

Tangible reinforcement operant conditioning audiometry (TROCA) is similar to VRA because threshold measurements are the objective; however, reinforcements are tangible (e.g., candy, dry cereal, small toys, trinkets) instead of visual. The technique was first described by Lloyd and colleagues (1968) for use with mentally retarded children. The children tested had no usable speech and had difficulty following verbal commands. The first and most important step was to deter-

mine an effective reinforcer for the particular child; this was followed by training, sound field screening, and finally threshold testing. When food was used as the reinforcer, the researchers had little difficulty persuading the child to wear earphones. Once again, social reinforcement enhances the procedure's effectiveness. This technique is of limited use in the normally developed child in this age group, but it is valuable for testing severely disabled or retarded children, because it requires no verbal skills.

Play Audiometry

In play audiometry children are taught a play response to a stimulus (e.g., stacking rings on a peg, stacking blocks or dropping them into a box) (Hodgson, 1978a). This procedure has been advocated for use with children as young as 2 years; however, the probability of successful evaluation increases as the child approaches 3 years of age.

The audiologist can utilize the initial moments

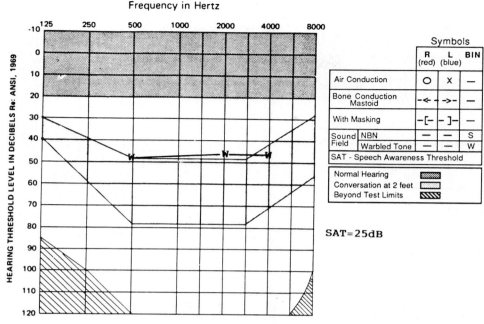

Figure 16.4 Visual Reinforcement Audiometry responses of a 6-month-old infant. (The Hospital for Sick Children, Toronto.)

of the testing session to establish rapport with the child, observing the child's reaction to gross sounds to form some idea of the response threshold, introduce the idea of responding to sound in a play setting, and, most importantly, select procedures and responses suited to the child's interest and abilities (Hodgson, 1978b). A major hurdle to overcome is persuading the child to accept the earphones. This can be facilitated if the examiner wears the headset for a few moments or provides the child with the opportunity to watch another cooperative child being tested. If the child still refuses, nothing will be lost by trying to sneak the set onto the child's head, and the audiologist might have to settle for sound field testing. If the child has a marked hearing loss, verbal instructions might be inappropriate and the audiologist might have to utilize pantomime and demonstration to convey the expected response to the child.

Once the child has accepted the earphones, the audiologist must work quickly to complete the testing of essential frequencies before the child becomes tired of the game. Rather than attempting to complete an entire audiogram in one ear, test 500, 2000, and 4000 Hz in each ear, followed, if possible, by testing at 1000 and 250 Hz. The audiologist always must be alert to signs of boredom or restlessness; changing the method of response might be sufficient to get the child to complete the testing session. The game should not be so interesting that the child becomes absorbed in it to the exclusion of responding to the stimuli. Other distractions must be avoided and the child kept ready to respond as soon as the auditory signal is presented.

Play audiometry is a well proven and popular method of testing the preschool child's auditory sensitivity. If a 3-year-old child cannot respond to play audiometry, some problems other than simple hearing impairment should be suspected. Although play audiometry might be useful to the age of 6, children 5 to 6 years of age are capable of responding to conventional hand-raising techniques. The method that is appropriate to the

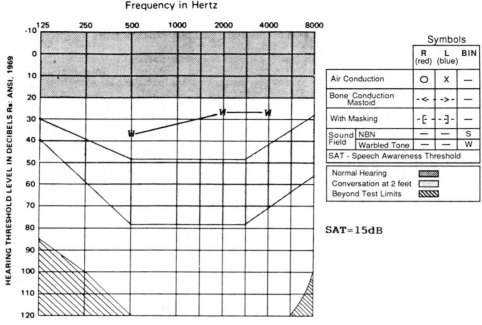

Figure 16.5   Visual Reinforcement Audiometry responses for an 8-month-old infant. (The Hospital for Sick Children, Toronto.)

child's level of maturation and cooperation should be utilized.

Conventional Audiometry

Children 4 years of age and older with no developmental delay can be expected to particpate in the test procedures used to test adults. Children are taught either to raise a hand or push a button whenever they hear a sound through earphones. They should be encouraged to respond to the smallest sound they think they hear. For clinical purposes, the threshold is defined as the faintest puretone that can be heard 50% of the time and can be approached by a descending-ascending technique. Thresholds are obtained in the ascending mode (i.e., progressing from silence to sound).

Northern and Downs (1978) recommended that the first frequency to be tested should be 2000 Hz because it is the most important indicator of sensorineural hearing loss, followed by 500 Hz, which is significant in determining conductive hearing loss. If children continue to cooperate,

these two frequencies can be followed by testing at 1000, 4000, 250, and 8000 Hz in that order. At the conclusion of the air conduction tests, the puretone procedure should be repeated, using the bone conduction oscillator. Because the skull is a good conductor of sound it is possible to by-pass the middle ear process and obtain a response directly from the inner ear (Cochlea) by placing the bone conduction reciever on the mastoid process. The inner ear responds to the vibration of the bone oscillator. A conductive hearing loss is present if the bone conduction results are within the normal range of hearing and the air conduction results are elevated (Fig. 16.7). A sensorineural hearing loss is recorded when the air conduction and bone conduction test results are within five db of each other and both are abnormal (Fig. 16.8). A mixed hearing loss occurs when both air conduction and bone conduction test results are abnormal, but the bone conduction results are better than the air conduction results (Fig. 16.9).

Masking should be used in bone conduction test whenever the bone conduction threshold is better than the air conduction threshold in the ear

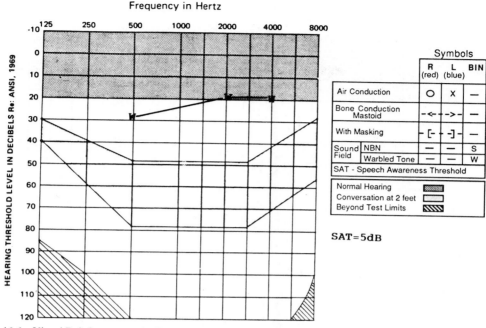

Figure 16.6 Visual Reinforcement Audiometry responses of a 10-month-old infant. (The Hospital for Sick Children, Toronto.)

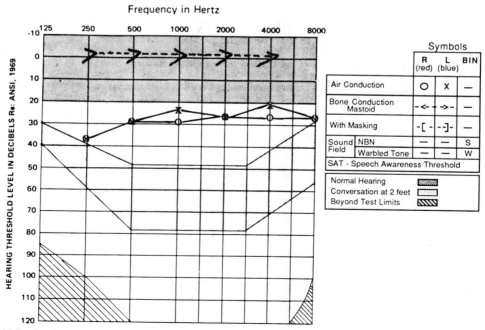

Figure 16.7 Conductive Hearing Loss. (The Hospital for Sick Children, Toronto.)

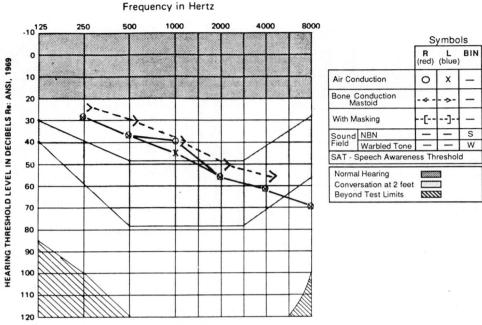

Figure 16.8   Sensorineural Hearing Loss. (The Hospital for Sick Children, Toronto.)

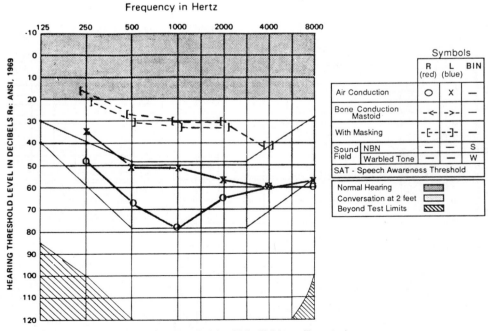

Figure 16.9   Mixed Hearing Loss. (The Hospital for Sick Children, Toronto.)

being tested. In air conduction tests, masking is recommended when the air conduction threshold in the ear being tested exceeds the bone conduction threshold in the other ear by 40 dBnHL or more (Price, 1978). The puretone signal presented to the poorer hearing ear cannot be heard through the broad band masking signal that is being presented simultaneously to the better hearing ear.

Middle ear pathology, producing conductive losses can result in fluctuating audiograins from one test period to another. Impedance audiometry plays an important role in clarifying these situations.

Speech Audiometry

The use of pure-tones provides an accurate description of a child's auditory sensitivity threshold. Equally important, however, is the use of speech stimuli to determine a child's recognition and use of speech for verbal communication. In speech audiometry, the *extent* of hearing loss is measured by the speech detection threshold and/or the speech reception threshold. The *nature* of the hearing loss determines the child's ability to understand speech at a comfortable loudness level and is measured using speech discrmination tests. The audiologist must use words that are within the child's language experience and must not provide visual cues to the child during the test procedures.

Speech Awareness Threshold

The speech awareness (or detection) threshold (SAT) is the most basic measurement of speech recognition or speech awareness. It can be used effectively with children who have delayed speech or language development in whom it is impossible to elicit verbal responses to speech. This threshold is the decibel level at which the child identifies the presence of a speech stimulus approximately 50% of the time. Any behavioral response is acceptable and various reinforcements might be required. The normal SAT is nine dBnHL SPL, and, at this level, speech stimuli are unintelligible even to adults with normal hearing (Shepherd, 1978). The speech stimulus can be "running speech," calling the child's name, nonsense syllables, or familiar words. The stimulus might affect the value of the response; it also in-

dicates the child's language level and should be noted in the report (Lloyd & Cox, 1975).

In younger or retarded children, SATs can be obtained when pure-tone stimuli cannot. The pure-tone audiogram can predict the SAT reasonably well but the reverse is not true. The broad band range of the speech signal will elicit a response, although the more frequency specific pure-tone signal indicates a hearing loss. Considerable variability in the SAT can be expected when testing children. For example, normal SATs might be obtained in children who have a total loss of hearing above 1000 Hz (Shepherd, 1978). The SAT is a measure only of the child's ability to detect the presence or absence of sound, the child can do so effectively when two of these major speech frequencies (500 and 1000 Hz) are within normal hearing ranges. It is omitted when speech reception thresholds can be obtained.

Speech Reception Threshold

The speech reception threshold (SRT) has been defined as the decibel level at which a child can either correctly repeat or otherwise identify 50% of a group of test words (Lloyd & Cox, 1975). It has been shown to agree closely with the pure-tone average for the speech frequencies (i.e., 500, 1000, and 2000 Hz) and provides a useful check on the consistency of test results and a baseline value for determining the level for speech discrimination testing (Epstein, 1978).

The speech reception threshold is obtained using spondaic (two syllable) words that are familiar to the child. Words especially applicable for children include *airplane, baseball, birthday, cowboy, and hot dog.* Children first should be familiarized with the test words and encouraged to respond to all words, even if they must "guess." The use of earphones is preferable; however, a sound field environment is acceptable if a child will not wear the earphones. When live voice is used, care must be taken to ensure that each syllable of the test word is given equal emphasis. If no significant hearing problem is apparent, a starting level of 40 dBnHL hearing level is recommended; this can be increased by 15 to 20 dBnHL increments if the child is not responding appropriately. The SRT threshold is reached by decreasing the intensity of presentation in 10 db steps until the child is unable to recognize the words, increasing the intensity in 5 db increments until three of six words are correctly identified, the speech reception threshold.

The relationship between SRT and pure tone averages of 500, 1000, and 2000 Hz obtained with children 4 years of age and older is as strong as that with adults (Shepherd, 1978). However, certain test modifications might be required, especially with younger children. If the child refuses to talk, the child can be asked to point to the appropriate picture, toy, object, or body part. Similarly, pictures or objects representing the various spondaic words can be used. Martin and Coombes (1976) described a method of tangibly reinforced speech audiometry that utilized words describing parts of a large, colorful clown. Each time the correct part was pressed, the device immediately rewarded the child with a small piece of candy. By this method, SRTs were successfully obtained in children as young as 2½ years of age. However, the fewer the words used in the test, the easier the child's task becomes; as a result, the threshold obtained might more closely approximate an SAT than a true SRT (Hodgson, 1978b). When there is a marked discrepancy between the SRT and pure-tone thresholds, particularly in the direction of better SRTs, the possibility of a functional (exaggerated) hearing loss must be considered (Epstein, 1978).

Speech Discrimination

The purpose of speech discrimination tests is to discover how well children can understand a speech signal once it has been made loud enough that they can hear it comfortably (Epstein, 1978). It must be preceded by determination of the SRT. Speech discrimination is determined by repetition of monosyllabic (one syllable) words presented at a quiet conversational level; usually 30 db above the child's SRT. Each word list is phonetically balanced with each phoneme occurring in the word list in accordance with its use in the English language. The word lists are presented with no visual or contextual cues to assist in identification of the individual words. Interpreting speech discrimination tests can be difficult because children with hearing loss are likely to have retarded speech and language development. Even if the child hears the word correctly, the examiner might have trouble understanding the response. A writ-

ten response cannot be expected in this age group. Consequently, a number of picture identification tests have been developed, the most popular being the Word Intelligibility by Picture Identification (WIPI) test developed by Ross and Lerman (1970). The child is required to select the correct picture from a group of six pictures displayed, thereby decreasing the likelihood of selecting the correct picture through chance alone. This test is suitable for 4 to 6 year olds.

The exact intensity at which the words are presented to the child is relatively unimportant provided it is at a loudness level at which the child can comfortably hear the word list. This is usually 30 to 50 dBnHL above the SRT. The maximal speech discrimination score for the W-22 test normally is obtained at a level of 30 dBnHL above the threshold for spondaic words (Epstein, 1978). Discrimination is reported in terms of percentage of correct responses at a given level. Children with conductive hearing loss usually have a raised SRT but normal speech discrimination. Children with sensorineural hearing loss can have a elevated SRT and poor speech discrimination. Care must be taken in interpreting results of discrimination tests, particularly in children with retarded language development. A poor discrimination score will reflect the language delay and, unless some pure-tone threshold information is obtained, can lead to the assumption of hearing loss in the child rather than language delay. In a person of any age, there might be little or no correlation between speech discrimination scores and ability to function in ordinary conversation with the additional cues of context and vision available. A discrimination score of less than 50%, for example, does not necessarily mean the person understands less than one-half of a contextual message (Epstein, 1978). There are problems in accurately assessing speech discrimination, especially in children, and there is a need for the development of standardized speech discrimination tests for use with this age group.

Objective Audiometry

Impedance/Immittance Audiometry

Otitis media is the most common cause of hearing impairment in preschool and school-age children. Chronic middle ear disease can be painless but nevertheless can adversely affect the child's hearing and his language development, especially during the crucial first three years. Otitis media often results in a conductive hearing loss ranging from 15 to 35 dBnHL, although it also can contribute to or be superimposed on a sensorineural hearing loss. Unfortunately, it is during the early years when detection of a mild or fluctuating hearing loss is most crucial, that the behavioral audiometry is most unreliable; consequently, the mild hearing loss often escapes detection.

The development of impedance audiometry by Metz in 1946 and its use in North America since 1970 has significantly advanced the assessment of conductive hearing loss in all age groups, but especially in infants and small children (Northern & Downs, 1978). It is objective, relatively acceptable to young children, and quick and easy to administer. Many children have been tested by this means and, although reservations still exist about its use in screening programs, its value in diagnosing hearing impairment in young children has been firmly established.

The use of impedance audiometry in the pediatric population can provide objective information on the status of the middle ear (Hayes & Jerger, 1978). Figure 16.10 indicates the principal components of the impedance bridge. The headset consists of an earphone and a probe tip that is inserted in the test ear, forming an airtight seal. The probe tip contains three tubes; one delivers a 220 Hz probe tone; the second, a microphone, monitors the SPL of the 220-Hz probe tone in the closed cavity between the probe tip and the tympanic membrane; and the third, which is connected to an air pump, varies the air pressure in the same closed cavity between + 200 and − 400 mm H20 (Jerger, 1970).

The proper placement of the probe tip will determine if the assessment of the infant's middle ear function is accurate. The infant's ear canal is cartilaginous and curved rather than bony and straight as in older children and adults. If the probe tube is not placed corectly, the measurement from the middle ear system might be sound reflected from the infant's ear canal wall rather than the eardrum.

An impedance measurement is based on the ability of the middle ear to act as a mechanical transducer by posing a certain resistance to vi-

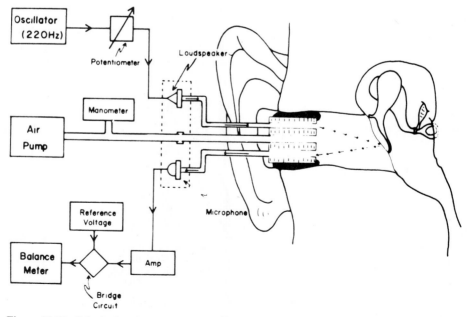

Figure 16.10 Principal components of the electroacoustic impedance bridge. (From Jerger, J. Clinical experience with impedance audiometry. (1970) *Archives of Otolaryngology, 92,* 311–324. Copyright 1970, American Medical Association. Reprinted with permission.)

bratory motion in response to acoustic stimuli. The resistance is the algebraic sum of the mass, friction, and elasticity of the system (Sanders, 1975). When sound is presented at the tympanic membrane, some of it is absorbed, but some is reflected back into the external ear canal. The ratio of acceptance to rejection of sound depends upon the total resistance of the middle ear. If the middle ear system is stiff, as in the case of otitis media or ossicular fixation, an increased amount of sound will be reflected back into the canal, indicating increased impedance, or, conversely, decreased compliance. Classically, the impedance audiometry battery consists of three tests: tympanometry, static compliance, and acoustic reflex.

Tympanometry

Tymanometry is a measurement of the relative change in the compliance (mobility) of the middle ear system as air pressure is varied in the external ear canal. The typanogram is the graphic display of the tympanometric measurements and generally is classified in terms of depth, shape, and point of middle ear pressure. It is assumed that compliance is maximal when the air pressure in the external canal equals that in the middle ear. To obtain a tympanogram, the tympanic membrane is put into a position of know poor mobility, with an air pressure of + 200 mm H20 being pumped into the external canal. As the positive air pressure is reduced gradually, changes in the compliance of the tympanic membrane are measured. More sound energy is transmitted into the middle ear as the compliance increases, resulting in a fall in the SPL of the external ear canal cavity. It is this fall in SPL that actually is measured by the electracoustic meter (Northern & Downs, 1978).

Jerger (1970) originally described three basic tympanogram types (Fig. 16.11). Type A curves show a relatively sharp maximum at or near a mid-

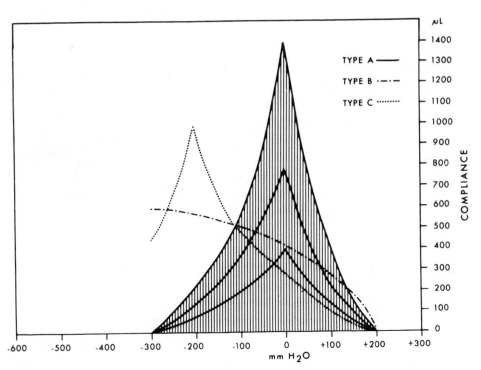

Figure 16.11   Classification of tympanograms.

dle ear pressure of 0 mm H20 and are found in normal ears. There is still some controversy about the range of normal middle ear pressures, but a value of + 100 mm H20 usually is considered within normal limits (Cooper et al., 1975; Hopkinson & Schramm, 1979; Sanders, 1975. Brooks (1978b) found that 95% of children with normal acoustic reflexes had pressures between 0 and 170 mnm H20, with no evidence of any other abnormality. Deciding the limits of normal depends largely on the actual clinical presentation and whether the test is being used for screening purposes, when lower values might be acceptable to avoid unnecessary medical referrals.

Two subtypes of Type A tympanogram have been identified (Northern & Downs, 1978). The first, Type A_S, is characterized by limited compliance with normal middle ear pressures. This type of tympanogram is seen routinely in infants and might be seen in otosclerosis, thickened or scarred tympanic membranes, and tympanosclerosis. The other extreme, Type A_D, demonstrates large changes in compliance with relatively small changes in middle ear pressure. This indicates an unusually flaccid tympanic membrane and can be associated with disarticulation of the ossicular chain.

A Type B tympanogram is a relatively flat curve showing little change in compliance with changes in air pressure. Usually no point of maximum compliance can be demonstrated. Type B curves are seen in children with serous and adhesive otitis media as well as those with perforations of the tympanic membrane, ventilation tubes, or ear canals occluded with cerumen.

In Type C tympanograms, a relatively normal compliance is demonstrated but at a middle ear pressure of -200 mm H20 or lower. The tympanic membrane is still mobile and there might or might not be fluid in the middle ear. A Type C tympanogram typically is seen with poor eustachian tube function. The pathological significance of the Type C tympanogram, particularly in children, and its relation to the presence or absence of fluid in the middle ear have been questioned.

Static compliance (acoustic impedance)

Static compliance, measured in cubic centimeters, represents a measurement of the compliance of the middle ear system in its resting state. It is the difference between the volume of the ex-

ternal canal space with the eardrum clamped at + 200 mn H20 pressure and that with the eardrum in its most compliant air pressure condition (Northern & Downs, 1978). The measurement of volume is based on the inverse relation of SPL to cavity volume size.

The static compliance is the least useful impedance test for children under 6 years of age because of extensive overlap between those with normal hearing and those with conductive or sensorineural hearing losses. Although the test has limited diagnostic value when viewed in isolation, it can contribute to the diagnostic picture when considered in conjunction with the other impedance tests. An offshoot of the static compliance is the physical volume test, which measures the volume from the probe tip to the eardrum. This is especially important in assessing whether surgically inserted ventilating tubes are patent (open) or if the eardrum is perforated. A small volume in the presence of ventilating tubes would indicate blockage resulting in ineffective use of the ventilating tubes. A large volume in the presence of ventilating tubes indicates the tubes are patent and effective. A large volume in the absence of ventilating tubes can indicate a perforated eardrum.

Acoustic reflex

Loud sound results in a contraction of the stapedius muscle, thereby tightening the ossicular chain and temporarily increasing the impedance of the middle ear (Sanders, 1975). This is a bilateral reflex and is thought to be protective in that the stiffening of the occicular chain impedes the sound transmmission resulting in the attenuation of loud sounds. The acoustic reflex threshold is the lowest signal level capable of eliciting the reflex in the stimulated ear and ranges from 70 to 100 dBnHL for pure-tone signals (measured at 500, 1000, 2000, and 4000 Hz) and approximately 65 dBnHL for white noise (Northern & Downs, 1978). In a study in which impedance audiometry was performed immediately before myringotomy for suspected serous otitis media, a single reflex measurement at 500, 1000, or 2000 Hz appeared to be as accurate an indicator of middle ear effusion as measurements at all test frequencies (Orchik et al., 1978). The reflex can be absent at 4000 Hz even when there is no objective evidence of any abnormality. Because the acoustic reflex is bilateral, both ipsilateral and contralateral re-flexes can be recorded. Typically, the ipsilateral reflex is elicited and recorded in the same ear by the impedance probe. For measurement of the contralateral reflex, on the other hand, the ear-phone delivers the signal while the reflex is mea-sured in the other ear by the probe (Hayes & Jer-ger, 1978). The recording of this reflex can lead to confusion in terminology, and Jerger (1972) sug-gested that the test ear be defined as the ear to which sound is being delivered.

The stapedial reflex threshold has two major contributions to the assessment of hearing status in the pediatric population: the identification of a conductive hearing loss and the evaluation of a sensorineural hearing loss. The acoustic reflex is absent bilaterally in all conductive hearing losses greater than 30 dBnHL (Northern & Downs, 1978). For example, with a left-sided conductive loss greater than 30 dBnHL, when sound is intro-duced to the left ear, the conductive loss atten-uates the signal loudness to such a degree that the ipsilateral reflex cannot be triggered. When the sound is presented contralaterally to the normal right ear, the probe tip in the left ear will not detect the contraction due to the inherent middle ear pa-thology (Jerger, 1970). A unilateral hearing loss coupled with bilaterally absent contralateral re-flexes indicates a unilateral middle ear disorder. Ipsilateral reflexes will be present in the normal ear. Jerger and coworkers (1972) showed that the minimum sound level necessary to produce an acoustic reflex was approximately 25 dBnHL sen-sation level. Acoustic reflex testing is important for children who cannot be tested behaviorally be-cause it tells the clinician the maximum hearing loss a child can have if the reflex is present. There is no sharp dividing line between a present and absent reflex, but rather a zone of uncertainty be-tween approximately 60 and 100 dBnHL. Never-theless, a general rule is that the presence of a reflex response normally means a hearing level of 80 dBnHL or better (Jerger, 1970). The absence of the stapedial reflex does not confirm the pres-ence of a sensorineural hearing loss and must be considered in relation to all information obtained. For example, the excess activity of an infant dur-ing testing can mask the stapedial muscle con-traction.

Impedance audiometry is a simple procedure that normally can be completed in a few minutes.

It is difficult to complete impedance audiometry while the child is talking, or vocalizing in any man-ner because of changes these actions produce in eustachian tube function. The swallowing that oc-curs with crying or talking will result in opening and closing of a patent eustachian tube, changing the air pressure in the middle ear cavity. With the young child, the test can be performed best by two people; one operates the impedance audiometer while the other stabilizes the child's head and ma-nipulates the probe tip. Various distractions such as animated toys might be used to advantage with children under 3 years old; children over this age usually can be handled with a pleasant, positive approach accompanied by simple instructions. Depending on the individual situation, however, a complete impedance battery might not be pos-sible and a typanogram and single acoustic reflex measurement in each ear might have to suffic (Northern & Downs, 1978). The proper placement of the probe in the child's ear is curcial in obtain-ing correct information regarding the status of the middle ear. A skilled examiner will significantly decrease the chance of incorrect information being obtained.

Each of the three tests in the impedance bat-tery has its limitations, but when they are consid-ered together various diagnostic information is ob-tained (Table 16.3). It should be remembered that impedance audiometry cannot evaluate sensori-neural deficits in the presence of conductive hear-ing losses and must be used in combination with subjective hearing tests that are appropriate for the age of the child. Despite its limtations, imped-ance audiometry is now firmly established as an essential tool in assessing hearing impairment in infants and children.

Electrophysiological Response Audiometry

In the cooperative child, behavioral audiom-etry and impedance audiometry provide the most accurate assessment of hearing sensitivity, type of hearing impairment, and ability to understand speech. Unfortunately, in the younger child (birth to 2 years of age), behavioral and even impedance audiometry can be difficult or impossible to per-form and results can be confusing or inconclusive. This particularly is true for multiply handicapped, mentally retarded, or autistic children. Conse-quently, the development of objective physiolog-ical measures to assess auditory function in other-

TABLE 16.3
IMPEDANCE AUTIOMETRY IN CLINICAL EVALUATION

Tympanometry	Impedance	Acoustic Reflex	Confirms Behavioral Audiometric Impression of
A in both ears	Normal in both ears	Normal bilaterally	Bilateral normal hearing, bilateral mild to moderate. Sensorineural loss, or unilateral mild to moderate sensorineural loss
A in both ears	Normal in both ears	Absent bilaterally	Severe bilateral sensorineural loss
A in one ear; B or C in other ear	Normal in A ear; high in B or C ear	Absent bilaterally	Unilateral conductive loss
B or C in both ears	High in both ears	Absent bilaterally	Bilateral conductive loss

wise difficult-to-test patients has filled an important diagnostic need (Riko et al., 1985). Auditory evoked potentials were identified in the human electroencephalogram by Davis in 1939 (Glasscock, et al., 1981). The development of averaging computer technology has enabled this procedure to be adapted for clinical use. Responses generally are grouped, based on their individual latencies, into three groups: slow cortical responses (50 to 60 msec.), middle responses (12 to 50 msec.), and early responses (occurring within the first 10 msec.). The early responses from the cochlea and brainstem pathways are most appropriate in the clinical assessment of infants and difficult-to-test children. These early responses, measured through electrocochleagraphy and brainstem evoked response audiometry, are the most reliable in the pediatric population because they are the least affected by sedation (Jacobson, 1985).

Electrocochleography

Electrocochleography (Ecog.) is the measurement of the compound action potential from the auditory nerve. The best recordings are measured from the promontory in the middle ear using a small-gauge needle passed through the patient's eardrum. General anesthesia is necessary to complete this assessment in a pediatric population. Recordings can be obtained with the electrode attached to the wall of the external auditory canal but the results are not as easy to determine. Elec-

trode placement is crucial and can be disturbed easily if the stimulator (headphone) is not carefully placed.

Test stimuli consist of clicks, bursts of noise, or filtered pure-tone. The threshold of detectability usually approaches the behavioral threshold at or above 2000 Hz, while at 1000 Hz the threshold is 10 to 15 dBnHL above the behavioral threshold (Fig. 16.12). A conductive hearing loss will result in elevation of the cochlear response, but not alter shape of the electrocochleagram. Sensorineural hearing loss will elicit changes in the electrocochleagram depending upon severity of the hearing loss. Sensorineural hearing loss affects the latecy and amplitude of the action potential from the auditory nerve. The more severe the hearing loss the later the latency and the smaller the amplitude of the response. The advantages of electrocochleography are: (1) information is obtained from each ear; (2) it is not affected by abnormalities in the auditory brainstem of the patient because the response is recorded from the auditory nerve; and (3) it is not affected by sedation or anesthesia. Disadvantages of electrocochleography, which have limited its use as a clinical procedure, are: (1) the invasive nature of this procedure (needle placement through the eardrum); (2) the need for general anesthesia in the pediatric population; and (3) the lack of information provided in frequencies below 1000 Hz. The advances in the BERA procedure have ad-

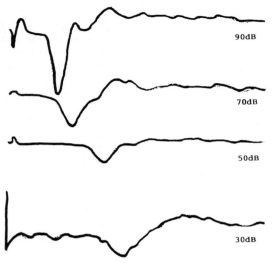

Figure 16.12   Electocochleography response at 90dB to threshold in a 6-month-old infant. (The Hospital for Sick Children, Toronto.)

dressed the disadvantages of electrocochleography.

Brainstem Evoked Response Audiometry

BERA assessment is the most useful electrophysiological response assessment for infants and young children. (Alberti et al., 1983) It can be detected noninvasively (electrodes are attached to the patient's vertex and mastoids, or ear lobes) and it is not affected by sedation or anesthesia. This is particularly important in assessing the difficult-to-test child who must be sedated to obtain information regarding his hearing. In 3 month olds, BERA can be obtained while the infant is sleeping, eliminating the need for sedation or anesthesia.

The auditory brainstem response (ABR) is the early evoked response with a latency between one and ten msec. An infant's brainstem electric response differs from the adult recording in morphology. Three major waves are represented, rather than the six or seven recorded in the adult population (Fig. 16.13). Wave I has been accepted as representing the eighth nerve action potential. The subsequent waves are assumed to represent the combined electrical input of many centers along the auditory pathway, although each is believed to be the product of specific neural generators (Wave III, at the midauditory brainstem, Wave V from the upper auditory brainstem, the inferior colliculus). The infant ABR varies from the adult recording in latency as well. The latency is prolonged in children under 18 months, occurring between two and ten msec.; but approximates adult values in children over this age. The latency of each of the three major waves and the interpeak latency differences (I-II, I-V, III-V) in the brainstem evoked response are used to determine the threshold. At loud intensities (70 to 90 dBnHL) the three waves are clearly recorded in the normal hearing infant. Wave V usually occurs 6 to 9 msec. following stimulus presentation and is the most consistent and reproducible response, remaining visible as the stimulus intensity is decreased to threshold (Fig. 16.14).

The type of hearing loss, whether conductive or sensorineural, can be defined using BERA. A conductive hearing loss will delay the latencies of waves I, III, and V equally across the tracing. The interpeak latencies (I-III, I-V, III-V) will not change. A sensorineural hearing loss can delay all three waves, waves III and V, or only wave V depending upon the severity of the hearing loss. As well, the interpeak latencies will increase, especially the I-V and III-V latencies. The waveform recorded from an infant with a severe to profound sensorineural hearing loss might have wave I at a very high intensity (95 dBnHL) with absent waves III and V. Neurological disorders affecting the brainstem might result in an abnorinal BERA recording in the presence of a norinal hearing ear.

Normal hearing infants produce a brainstem evoked response to clicks 10 to 15 dBnHL above their behavioral threshold at or about 2000 Hz. Early clincal use of the BERA in assessing hearing utilized a click stimulus for threshold definition. Click BERA thresholds correlate to the pure-tone thresholds in the 1000 to 4000 Hz and are 10 to 20 dBnHL higher than the average pure-tone threshold in that frequency range. Hearing impaired infants can have hearing in the low frequency range that will be undetected if only the mid to high frequency region is tested. The development of frequency specific stimuli (filtered clicks and tone pips) has resulted in BERA information that can more closely quantify the puretone audiometric contour (Hyde et al. 1984). An objective neurophysiological test cannot replace information ob-

Figure 16.13 Brainstem Evoked Response Audiometry response at 70 dBnHl in a 12-month-old infant. (The Hospital for Sick Children, Toronto).

70 dB

tained from standard pure-tone and speech tests. These subjective measures are the most reliable determinators of what the child "hears." The BERA monitors the functional intensity of the peripheral auditory system, from the ear up to and including the brain-stem auditory centers. How well the child is able to understand the auditory information, his cortical integrative function, is not evaluated. BERA is a precise index of the efficiency with which the peripheral auditory system receives and transmits information to the auditory cortex but does not provide information about the child's ability to integrate auditory information in developing receptive and expressive language.

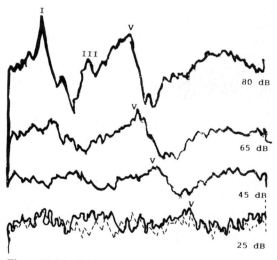

80 dB

65 dB

45 dB

25 dB

Figure 16.14 Brainstem Evoked Response Audiometry response at 80dB to threshold in a 7-month-old infant. (The Hospital for Sick Children, Toronto).

Central Auditory Dysfunction

The authors have been concerned, to this point, with assessing the integrity of the peripheral auditory apparatus, that is, from the outer ear to the termination of the acoustic nerve in the cochlear nucleus of the brain stem (Northern & Downs, 1978). For auditory stimuli to be meaningful, however, a complex auditory perceptual system to transmit, process, store, and retrieve the information provided by the peripheral mechanism is required. This perceptual system involves auditory discrimination (the ability to recognize similarities or differences in sound), auditory association (the ability to relate meaning to environinental sounds or spoken words), auditory closure (the ability to complete the missing parts of a message), auditory memory (the ability to recall a sequence of auditory information, both long term and short term), auditory localization (the ability to localize sound), and auditory figure–ground perception (the ability to discriminate relevant signals from background noise) (Mencher & Stick, 1974). The child with an auditory perceptual problem cannot organize the auditory events in the environment so that they are meaningful.

Initially, it might be difficult to distinguish the child with central dysfunction who presents with delayed language acquisition, poor oral expression, difficulty in responding to or remembering the sequence of oral instructions, or difficulty with sound localization, from the child with a peripheral hearing deficit. All too often, the problems are attributed to immaturity, hyperactivity, behavioral disorders, or mental retardation. One should suspect central dysfunction in the child who demonstrates an abnormally slow or fast reaction time, particularly to speech tests, unusual errors on speech tests, slight discrepancies between tests, especially between pure-tone and speech thresholds, exaggeratedly poor thresholds, mild high-frequency losses, abnormal physical activity or lethargy during testing, or, total absence of abnormal peripheral findings in the presence of auditory complaints (Demsey, 1978).

A detailed discussion of the tests currently available to assess central auditory dysfunction is beyond the scope of this chapter; however, the tests that apply to preschool children 5 years of age and older are listed here:

1. *Binaural resynthesis:* The patient is provided with low-frequency information from a stimulus word in one ear and high-frequency information in the other ear. When these stimuli are played simultaneously, the intact central auditory system can combine them into an intelligible message. This subtest assesses the ability to combine different but complementary pieces of information and has been related to phonics/reading where the sound/letter information must be fused to read.

2. *Competing sentences:* This task assesses the cortical ability to attend to a message presented to a designated ear and ignore a competing message presented to the other ear at a level 15 dBnHL higher than the stimulus message (Demsey, 1978). This subtest assesses selective attention skills similar to those required in the classroom when the child must selectively listen to the teacher's voice while ignoring the other noise in the background.

3. *Filtered speech:* This tests the cortical abilty to perceive frequency-distorted speech in which much of the high-frequency energy has been removed. Even after filtering, the selected words remain intelligible to adults with normal hearing (Willeford, 1977). This subtest assesses the resistance to distortion and auditory closure—the ability to complete an incomplete auditory signal. This can be related to the classroom situation in which the teacher's instructions might not be heard clearly by the child because of interferring noise, yet the message must be completed by the child.

4. *Alternating sentences:* These evaluate the ability of the brain stem to integrate temporal information presented to both ears alternately in 300-sec. segments (Demsey, 1978).

5. *Staggered spondaic word lists:* These test the ability of the cortex to separate competing bisyllabic words separated in time (Demsey, 1978). This test has a strong neurological basis and relates to a number of difficult listening situations found in a normal classroom setting such as selective attention, binaural separation, and auditory memory.

Allowances are made for the child's level of development in these tests in that younger children are not asked to repeat back sentences verbatim but only to provide the concept in their own language. Every effort is made to interpret articulation errors (Willeford, 1977). Although these five tests can all be clinically useful with children over the age of 5 years, they are heavily language dependent and their success is related to the extent of the child's vocabulary and comprehension. Any delay in language acquisition secondary to peripheral hearing loss (or any other reason) can adversely affect the test results.

A test of central auditory dysfunction designed especially for young children is the Flowers-Costello test of central auditory abilities (Costello, 1977). This consists of a low-pass filtered-speech test and a competing message test that can be administered to 4 to 6 year old children. The test is not designed to find specific lesions in the auditory system but to identify children who have unusual difficulty with these stimuli that cannot be explained simply as a peripheral hearing loss. The task consists of sentence completion: the child is given a choice of three pictures and is asked to point to the most appropriate one. Thus, word-finding difficulties and lack of intelligibility of speech responses are avoided. As with the other tests mentioned, performance improves with age; however, 4 to 6 year olds obtained almost perfect scores when the tests were administered with the competing message or frequency distrotion. Although the test is easy to administer to young children and has been found useful in identifying central auditory dysfunction, it is dependent on adequate aural comprehension.

Central auditory dysfunction in the school-age child might be seen first as a learning disability or behavioral disorder. Its early detection and differentiation from a peripheral hearing loss are essential for appropriate habilitation and suitable placement in the classroom. Accurate diagnosis presents a considerable challenge in such a multifaceted condition; nonverbal tests are needed for very young children and normative values in the tests already developed require confirmation.

DIFFICULT-TO-TEST CHILDREN

The type of test used and the level of response expected depend on the child's mental development and the presence of other physical problems; nowhere is this more true than in evaluating the difficult-to-test child. With recent advances in audiological assessment, the definition of "difficult-to-test" has changed; what was difficult 30 years ago (i.e., any child under the age of 5 years) is now, as we have seen, routine.

Deafness usually is suspected when speech is absent, delayed, or impaired. Myklebust (1954) found that of 228 children 6 months to 7 years of age in whom hearing loss was suspected, 45% actually had disorder of the peripheral auditory apparatus; the auditory disorders of the others were the result of emotional distrubances, aphasia, or mental deficiency.

Blindness also can affect language acquisition, even in the presence of normal hearing. Blind children have difficulty associating sounds with their source, a process that normally gives meaning to sounds. Consequently, they might react abnormally to sounds and seem to have impaired hearing (Brooks, 1978a). Uncomplicated peripheral hearing losses might be detected readily within the first few months of life; however, accurate diagnosis of hearing impairment in the child with multiple handicaps might be significantly delayed because it is difficult to assess the contribution of each factor of the handicap to the communication disorder.

Mental Retardation

Between 7% and 9% of the children referred to clinics have been reported to be mentally retarded (IQ lower than 70) (Brooks, 1978a). Mental retardation in itself does not decrease auditory acuity but children might seem to be hearing impaired because of their general level of retardation. The most important principle to remember in dealing with this group of children is that if general retardation is their only problem, they will behave consistently at the level of their mental age not that of their chronological age. The retarded 5-year-old child can be tested by methods appropriate to a $3\frac{1}{2}$ year old; the 2 year old can show the localizing responses of a 17 month old. A response to pure tones of 45 to 55 dB is not considered abnormal if the child is functioning at a mental level of 8 months (Northern & Downs, 1978). If results from intelligence tests are not available the audiologist must use clinical judgment to estimate the child's development level.

Children with severe mental retardation can show a complete lack of response to their environment. With these children, a good startle response to 65 dB might be all that can be hoped for. If the child is hyperactive, mild sedation can be used to facilitate behavioral observation and impedance audiometry. The value of the latter test in these children should be emphasized because of its simplicity and objectivity in detecting middle ear disorders. Schwartz and Schwartz (1978) used impedance audiometry and pneumo-otoscopy to assess 38 children (mean age 3.1 years) with Down's syndrome and found evidence of middle ear effusion in 60%; a similar incidence has been reported in older children and adults with Down's syndrome. In addition, they found that of 29 ears with normal tympanograms, 14 had an absent contralateral, and 11 an absent ipsilateral acoustic reflex, indicating that this particular measurement might not be a reliable parameter for confirming the presence of middle ear effusion in these children.

Greenberg and coworkers (1978) investigated the use of visual reinforcement audiometry with 41 Down's syndrome subjects between the ages of 6 months and 6 years. They found that less than 50% of the infants 13 to 24 months of age initially demonstrated a localization response to sound, and it was not until 5 to 6 years of age that all subjects localized sound. Reliable audiometric thresholds were obtained through visually reinforced audiometry for 81% of the children who initially oriented to sound. They concluded that this was useful testing technique provided the child had attained a mental age equivalent of at least 10 months. Their results were confirmed by Thompson and colleagues (1979). It also might be remembered that tangibly reinforced audiometry was originally developed for use with the mentally retarded who have few or no verbal activities.

Cerebral Palsy

The difficulty of audiological testing in children with cerebral palsy is largely related to the extent of their physical impairment. Varying degrees of spasticity might prevent the child from performing the physical responses commonly associated with behavioral audiometry, and this can lead to frustration and anger. Furthermore, the involuntary movements associated with athetosis can increase the difficulty of judging an actual response, and these movements can be aggravated by the stress of the testing situation.

Children with severe hypertonia or hypotonia might have difficulty in turning to locate acoustic stimuli, thereby complicating assessment of the orientation reflex. In addition, they can be distracted easily by other environmental stimuli (Brooks, 1978a); consequently, the number of visual and tactile stimuli present in the testing area should be reduced as much as possible. Clinical assessment also can be complicated by visual abnormalities and/or mental retardation. The audiologist must take time at the beginning of the test period to determine the best way for the child to respond and then condition the response. Physical stress can be directly proportional to the hearing threshold; when the stress is decreased (e.g., lying rather than sitting), hearing thresholds might improve. Ample time for response must be allowed in the testing procedure. Various forms of behavioral audiometry can be adapted for use with these children, and impedance and possibly electrophysiological response audiometry also can be used.

CNS Disorders

Pre- or postnatal brain damage can result in disorders of auditory function that are necessarily accompanied by decreased threshold sensitivity. Northern and Downs (1978) made two basic assumptions in testing brain-damaged children: first, any reduction in auditory acuity is because of lesions peripheral to the cochlear nuclei, and, second, only in the child with the most severe CNS damage will all four basic auditory reflexes (startle, head-turn, eye-blink, and arousal from sleep) be completely absent. The child's level of behavior must be determined before attempting any formal testing. Tests of central auditory dysfunction already have been discussed; the concern here is with sensitivity thresholds in the presence of CNS damage.

Inconsistency of response within one type of stimulus and between stimuli is common in children with CNS damage. In dealing with these children, the audiologist must be adaptable and constantly ready to change the approach or test. If formal testing techniques cannot be used, the examiner must start at the lowest level of response for the infant under 4 months. Even the demonstration of an unequivocal startle response to 65 dB provides useful clinical information. With severely brain-damaged children, cortical and brain stem evoked response audiometry might help to localize the site of the lesion; however, the results must be viewed with caution because the primary disorder can produce such aberrant electroencephalograph responses that accurate interpretation of the auditory status is impossible.

Blind–Deaf Children

Blind children attempt to localize sound normally at first; however, because of the lack of association and reinforecement, they might eventually stop turning toward the source of sounds and give the appearance of deafness. If they do, in fact, have significant auditory impairment, they might never develop natural orientation responses. Nevertheless, their remaining auditory reflexes can be utilized to advantage. When there is no language development, testing as recommended for infants should be completed. Even if a hearing loss appears unilateral, Northern and Downs (1978) firmly recommended a trial of binaural amplification to provide the blind child with every possible binaural clue.

Emotionally Disturbed/Functionally Hearing Impaired

Deafness can coexist with psychiatric conditions such as childhood schizophrenia and autism. On the other hand, it is not uncommon for deafness itself to result in behavioral problems such as aggressiveness or, conversely, a withdrawal from reality, simulating autism. Functional hearing loss has been reported in 1% to 5% of children examined in audiology clinics, depending on the examiner's expectations (Brooks, 1978a). Functional hearing loss in children is not malingering; it is an unconscious cry for help and therefore it is important to diagnose it as early as possible.

Autistic children are completely withdrawn and often lack communication. Conventional behavioral audiometry usually is nonproductive with them. However, auditory reflexes cannot be suppressed and will be elicited in the presence of peripheral auditory function. In addition, observation of children while at "play" might provide some clue about their hearing; they might show an interest in some quiet sound while ignoring louder stimuli. Impedance and evoked response audiometry, as objective measurements, can provide invaluable information about the hearing mechanism.

The child with a functional hearing loss can show a variety of symptoms such as exaggerated behavior, inconsistent intratest results, variable interest results, and speech reception thresholds that are normal or signficantly better than puretone responses (Northern & Downs, 1978). Northern and Downs recommended a test procedure to be followed in suspected functional losses using a pure-tone ascending technique. Usually the functional nature of the complaints can be determined through behavioral audiometry, particularly speech audiometry. If necessary, impedance or evoked response audiometry can be utilized to verify clinical impressions.

IMPLICATIONS OF HEARING IMPAIRMENT

An accurate, timely diagnosis of hearing impairment in the preschool child is essential so that medical or surgical treatment and/or genetic counseling can be provided when indicated. It also is extremely important to provide a training program for both child and parents to ensure that the child develops adequate communication skills. Because detailed discussion of treatment and habilitation of the hearing-impaired child is beyond the scope

of this chapter, only the general philosophy of management is presented. Clearly, medical or surgical management must first be employed to reduce any conductive losses that might exist alone or in conjunction with a sensorineural impairment.

Educational Considerations

Hearing impairment already has been classified in various degrees from mild to profound based on the pure-tone threshold average of 500, 1000, and 2000 Hz. This classification is related to the child's ability to hear and comprehend speech and therefore has signficant educational implications.

Children with a mild loss (20 to 40 dB) can expect to encounter difficulty hearing distant sounds or hearing in a noisy classroom situation; however, their speech discrimination usually is normal. If the hearing loss is prelingual, there can be some delay in speech development. Preferential classroom seating might be required, and, as the loss approaches 40 dB, the use of a hearing aid might be helpfal.

A hearing loss of 40 to 65 dB can be classified as moderate. If the loss is prelingual, there are significant delays in speech and language development, usually in association with articulation problems. Special preschool training is necessary and the child might need to start school in special classes for the hearing impaired. A hearing aid is most beneficial to children in this category because their speech discrimination usually is good.

A severe congenital loss (65 to 90 dB) results in only rudimentary speech and language development unless special training is provided. A speech and language training program should be instituted as soon as the loss is identified and a hearing aid fitted. However, because there is always a sensorineural component with any loss over 70 dB, poor auditory discrimination can be expected, which can limit the effectiveness of the hearing aid. Children with profound loss (>90 dB) do not develop speech and language without extensive special training. Hearing aids should be used but their value is often very limited, particularly in the child with no hearing above 1000 Hz, because of the extremely poor auditory discrimination (Hodgson, 1978a; Kemker, 1975). An important consideration is that the hearing aids will provide awareness to acoustic signals in the child's environment.

Northern and Downs (1978) list four goals for educating the deaf child: adequate language skills, sound mental health, intelligible speech, and the ability to communicate easily with peers. The main methods used to teach communication to hearing-impaired children are auditory, auditory/oral, visual/oral, and total communication.

The auditory method forces the child to use only auditory clues. Intensive training by specialized teachers and parental cooperation are essential. This method can produce the most natural development of speech and language but is clearly dependent upon the child's functional residual hearing as well as the benefit received from use of a hearing aid.

The auditory/oral method relies on a combination of lip reading and residual hearing. McConnell and Liff (1975) advocated establishing the acoustic channel as the primary input when possible, followed by the visual clues as required. Although this method facilitates the child's itegration into a normally hearing society, lip reading does have a number of disadvantages, not least of which is the variation in people's styles of speaking, the similarity in appearance of many sounds or words, and the invisibility of such sounds as *k* or *ng*. From a practical viewpoint, lip reading is virtually useless in groups of people, in dimly lit environiments, or when the person speaking is any distance from the deaf person.

The visual/oral method utilizes sign language and/or finger spelling in conjunction with lip reading. Total communication is not, in fact, a separate method of training, but utilizes all available means of communication—residual hearing, sign language, finger spelling, lip reading, facial expressions, and body language.

Each method has advantages and disadvantages and slavish adherence to any one to the exclusion of the others is not recommended. The total communication approach is becoming increasingly popular in North America and reflects the shift in emphasis from using one particular method to developing comunication by whatever means best suit the individual.

It must be remembered that the presence of a deaf child in the home can arouse feelings of rejection, guilt, or denial in the parents and places a significant strain on parents and siblings. Con-

sequently, the parents should receive counseling, guidance, and teaching that is designed to increase their ability to provide their child with the necessary auditory and linguistic stimulation in the environment (Northcott, 1975).

Hearing-impaired children can receive their education in a normal classroom setting, in part- or full-time special classes for the hearing impaired in normal schools, or in a residential school for the deaf. The choice of educational facility depends upon such obvious factors as the degree of deafness, the age of onset, the language skills already developed, the type of previous communication training, the presence of other physical or mental handicaps, and the available resources. The educational goals of hearing-impaired children are not necessarily met by integrating them into a normal educational setting for which they are ill equipped or ill prepared. Every effort must be made to individualize their training programs according to their unique abilities.

Screening and Registration Programs

The establishment of a screening program for a given disease or disorder must be based on the following criteria (Paradise & Smith, 1979): the disease produces significant morbidity or mortality; the disease is prevalent; there are accepted criteria for diagnosis; the disease can be treated or controlled; early treatment is beneficial and there is enough time to initiate treatment; diagnostic and treatment facilities are available; and the test used in the screening program is acceptable, reliable, and valid.

There is no single acceptable method for routine screening of neonates. However, in recent years great emphasis has been placed on early identification of children at risk who might develop hearing impairment, and screening programs for high-risk groups.

In 1978, the Saskatoon Conference on Early Diagnosis of Hearing Loss recommended that neonates to whom any of the following criteria applied by registered as being at high risk for hearing impairment (Gerber & Mencher, 1978):

1. A family history of onset of severe hearing loss in early childhood
2. A significant illness during the mother's preg-

nancy (e.g., rubella, cytomegalovirus, or herpes infections

3. A congenital anomaly of the skull, face, ear, nose, or throat, including absent, malformed or low-set pinna, cleft lip, cleft palate, and submucous cleft of the palate
4. Prematurity, with a birth weight of less than 1500 g
5. Neonatal icterus, with a serum bilirubin value of 20 mg/dl (342 umoles/liter) or greater in a baby of normal weight, or lower value in a smaller baby
6. Hypoxia at birth, with persisting neurological abnormalities (e.g., neonatal convulsions)

The Saskatoon conference passed a resolution requesting provincial and local governments to make registration mandatory (Gerber & Mencher, 1978). A register would increase the probability of the early identification of hearing-impaired infants and would lead to supervision, including periodic screening, of hearing losses not apparent in the first months of a child's life. Registered infants should be referred for detailed audiological evaluation before they are 2 months old; evaluation would include an arousal test, crib-o-grain screening, and brain stem evoked responses audiometry; there also are sensitive nonbehavioral procedures for obtaining supplemental evidence. Even if hearing appears to be normal, it must be evaluated periodically by the family doctor, pediatrician, or well-baby clinic staff, because some of the hearing loss might not develop until later. Use of the first five criteria can lead to the identification of two-thirds of the congenitally deaf (Northern & Downs, 1978). The addition of two more criteria (hypoxia with an Apgar score less than 4 and neonatal sepsis) increases the proportion to 75% and application of the arousal test increases it to 80% (Mencher, 1976).

Play audiometric screening of children 4 years of age and over has been well established. These children are tested using a pure-tone audiometer at frequencies of 1000, 2000, amd 4000 Hz. There are no generally accepted screening programs; however, for relatively healthy 2 to 4 year olds in whom mild to moderate degrees of hearing impairment secondary to otitis media might develop.

Acoustic impedance audiometry provides an apparently ideal tool by which to assess middle ear function. However, questions have been raised about the significance and natural history of middle ear effusion in the presence of normal hearing thresholds. Hence, the Task Force on the Use of Acoustic Impedance Measurement in Screening for Middle Ear Disease in Children (Harford et al., 1978) did not recommend the use of impedance measurements for routine mass screening at any age. However, where screening programs already have been instituted using impedance audiometry, they recommended that positive test results include an absent acoustic reflex to a stimulus of 105 dB or an abnormal tympanogram (i.e., flat or rounded or with a peak at or more negative than -200 mm H20.

SUMMARY

Childhood hearing impairment can cause delayed speech and language acquisition as well as problems in emotional and social adjustment. With improved health care and reduced infant mortality, the proportion of cases of congenital (and therefore prelinnual) hearing impairment can be expected to increase. Hearing thresholds can be assessed through behavioral audiometry in children as young as 2 years of age. Acoustic impedance and electrophysiological-evoked response audiometry provide objective means of diagnosing hearing impairment in children within the first few months of life. Screening programs should be undertaken for high-risk infants and children as well as for children in certain ethnic groups or those with certain congenital abnormalities. Physicians and parents must remain alert to problems that suggest hearing impairment. A delay in diagnosis until the child enters school can no longer be justified and can have profound adverse effects on the child's intellectual and social development.

REFERENCES

Alberti, P. A., Hyde, M. L., Riko, K. Corbin, H., & Abramovich, S. (1983). An evaluation of BERA for hearing screening in high-risk neonates. *Laryngoscope 93,* 1115–1121.

Baxter, J. D., & Ling, D. (1974). Ear disease and hearing loss among the Eskimo population of the Baffin Zone. *Canadian Journal of Otolaryngologia 3,* 110–122.

Bess, F. H., Schwartz, D. M., & Redfield, N. P. (1986). Audiometric impedance, and otoscopic findings in children with cleft palates. *Archives of Otolaryngology 102,* 465–469.

Bergstrom, L. (1977). Viruses that deafen. In F. H. Bess (Ed.). *Childhood Deafness: Causation, Assessment and Management.* New York: Grune & Stratton, 53–68.

Berry, M. F. (1969). *Language Disorders of Children: The Bases and Diaos.* New York: Appleton-Century-Crofts.

Bluestone, C. D. (1978). Prevalence and pathogenesis of the ear disease and hearing loss. In M. D. Graham (Ed.). *Cleft Palate Middle Disease and Hearing Loss.* Springfield, IL: Thomas, 27–55.

Brooks, D. N. (1978). Evaluation of "Hard-to-Test" children and adults. In S. Singh & J. Lynch (Eds). *Diagnostic Procedures in Hearing, Language and Speech.* Baltimore: University Park Press, 105–137(a).

Brooks, D. N. (1977). Impedance screening for school children: state of the art. In E. R. Harford, F. H. Bess, C. D. Bluestone (Eds.). Impedance Screening for Middle Ear Disease in Children, Proceedings of a Symposium held in Nashville, Tennessee, June 20–22. New York: Grune & Stratton, 172–180(b).

Catlin, F. I. (1978). Etiology and pathology of hearing loss in children. In F. N. Martin (Ed.). *Pediatric Audiology.* Englewood Cliffs, N.J.: Prentice-Hall, 3–34.

Cooper, J. C., Jr., Gates, G. A., Owen, J. H., & Dickson, H. D. (1975). An abbreviated impedance bridge technique for school screening. *Journal of Speech and Hearing Disorder, 40,* 260–269.

Costello, M. R. (1977). Evaluation of auditory behavior of children using the Flowers-Costello test of central auditory abilites. In R. Keith (Ed.). *Central Auditory Dysfunction.* New York: Grune & Stratton, 257–276.

Dahle, A. J., McCollister, F. P., Stagno, S., Reynolds, D. W., & Hoffman, H. E. (1979). Progressive hearing impairment in children with congenital cytomegalovirus infection. *Journal of Speech and Hearing Disorders, 44,* 220–229.

Demsey, C. (1978), A Guide to tests of central auditory function. *Otolaryngologic Clinics of North America, 11,* 677–700.

Eliachar, I. (1978). Audiologic manifestations in otitis media. *Otolaryngologic Clinics of North America, 11,* 769–776.

English, G. M., Northern, J. L., & Fria, T. J. (1973). Chronic otitis media as a cause of sensorineural hearing loss. *Archives of Otolaryngology, 98,* 18–22.

Epstein, A. (1978). Speech audiometry. *Otolaryngologic Clinics of North America, 11,* 667–676.

Glasscock, M., Jackson, C. G., & Josey, A. (1981). Brainstem Electric Response Audiometry. New York: Thieme-Stratton, Inc.

Gerber, S. E., & Mencher, G. T. (Eds.) (1978). Early Diagnosis of Hearing Loss. New York: Grune & Stratton.

Greenberg, D. B., Wilson, W. R., Moore, J. M., & Thompson, G. (1978). Visual reinforcement audiometry (VRA) with young Down's Syndrome children. *Journal of Speech and Hearing Disorders, 43,* 448–458.

Harford, E. R., Bess, F. H., Bluestone, C. D., Harrington, D. A., & Klein, J. O. (1978). Use of acoustic impedance measurement in screening for middle ear disease in children. *Annals of Otology, Rhinology and Laryngology, 87,* 288–292.

Hayes, D., & Jerger, J. (1978). Impedance audiometry in otologic diagnosis. *Otolaryngologic Clinics of North America, 11,* 759–767.

Hodgson, W. R. (1978a). Disorders of hearing. In P. H. Skinner & R. L. Shelton (Eds.). *Speech, Language, and Hearing: Normal Processes and Disorders.* Reading, MA: Addison-Wesley, 316–349.

Hodgson, W. R. (1978b). Testing infants and young children. In J. Katz (Ed.). *Handbook of Clinical Audiology* (2nd ed.). Baltimore: Williams & Wilkins, 397–409.

Holm, V. A., & Kunze, L. H. (1969). Effect of chronic otitis media on language and speech development. *Pediatrics, 43* 833–839.

Hopkinson, N. T., & Schramm, V. L. (1979). Preschool otolagic and audiologic screening. *Otolaryngology and Head and Neck Surgery, 87,* 246–257.

Hyde, M. L., Riko, K., Corbin, H., Moroso, M., & Alberti, P. W. (1984). A neonatal hearing screening research program using brainstem electric response audiometry. *Otolaryngology, 13,* 49–54.

Jacobson, J. T. (1985). An overview of the auditory brainstem response. In J. T. Jacobson (Ed.). *The Auditory Brainstem Response.* San Diego: College-Hill Press.

Jerger, J. (1970). Clinical experience with impedance audiometry. *Archives of Otolaryngology, 92* 311–324.

Jerger, J. F. (1972). Suggested nomenclature for impedance audiometry. *Archives of Otolaryngology, 96,* 1–3.

Jerger, J., Jerger, S., & Mauldin, L. (1972). Studies in impedance audiometry: I. normal and sensorineural ears. *Archives of Otolaryngology, 96,* 512–523.

Jerger, S., Jerger, J., Mauldin, L., & Segal, P. (1974). Studies in impedance audiometry: II. children less than 6 years old. *Archives of Otolaryngology, 99,* 1–9.

Kaplan, G. J., Fleshman, J. K., Bender, T. R., Baum, C., & Clark, P. S. (1973). Long-term effects of otitis media: a ten-year cohort study of Alaskan Eskimo childen. *Pediatrics, 62,* 577–585.

Kemker, F. J. (1975). Classifications of auditory impairment. *Otolaryngologic Clinics of North America, 8,* 3–17.

Kessner, D. M., Snow, C. K., & Singer, J. (1974). Assessment of medical care for children: Contrasts in health status. Vol. 3. Washington, D.C.: Institute of Medicine, National Academy of Sciences.

Klein, J. O. (1977). Epidemiology of otitis media. In E. R. Harford, F. H., Bess, C. D. Bluestone, et al. (Eds.). Impedance Screening for Middle Ear Disease in Children. Proceedings of a Symposium held in Nashville, Tennessee, June 20–22. New York: Grune & Stratton, 11–16.

Konigsmark, B. W., & Gorlin, R. J. (1976). *Genetic and Metabolic Deafness.* Philadelphia: Saunders.

Lillywhite, H. (1958). Doctor's manual of speech disorders. *Journal of the American Medical Association, 167,* 850–858.

Lloyd, L. L., & Cox, B. P. (1975). Behavioral audiometry with children. *Otolaryngologic Clinics of North America, 8,* 89–107.

Lloyd, L. L., Spradin, J. E., & Reid, M. J. (1968). An operant audiometric procedure for difficult-to-test patients. *Journal of Speech and Hearing Disorders, 3,* 236–245.

Martin, F. N., & Coombes, S. (1976). A tangibly reinforced speech reception threshold procedure for use with small children. *Journal of Speech and Hearing Disorders, 41,* 333–338.

McConnel, F., & Liff, S. (1975). The rationale for early identification and intervention. *Otolaryngologic Clinics of North America, 8,* 77–87.

Mencher, G. T. (1974). Proceedings of the Nova Scotia Conference, on Early Diagnosis of Hearing Loss. Halifax, Nova Scotia, September 9–11.

Mencher, G. T., & Stick, S. L. (1974). Auditory perceptual disorders: "He won't outgrow them." *Clinical Pediatrics,* (Philadelphia), *13,* 977–982.

Murphy, K. P., & Shallop, J. K. (1978). Identification of hearing loss in young children: prenatal to age six. In S. Singh & J. Lynch (Eds.). *Diagnostic Procedures in Hearing, Language and Speech*: Baltimore: University Park Press, 29–55.

Nadol, J. B., Jr. (1978). Hearing Loss as a sequela of meningitis. *Laryngoscope, 88,* 739–755.

Northcott, W. H. (1975). Normalization of the preschool child with hearing impairment. *Otolaryngologic Clinics of North America. 8,* 159–186.

Northern, J. L., & Downs, M. P. (1978). *Hearing in Children* (2nd ed.) Baltimore: Williams & Wilkins.

Orchik, D. J., Morff, R., & Dunn, J. W. (1978). Impedance audiometry in serius otitis media. *Archives of Otolaryngology, 104,* 409–412.

Paradise, J. L., & Smith, C.G. (1979). Impedance screening for preschool children: State of the art. *Annals of Otology, Rhinology and Laryngology, 88,* 56–65.

Price, L. L. (1978). Pure tone audiometry. In D. E. Rose (Ed.). *Audiological Assessment (2nd ed.).* Englewood Cliffs, N.J.: Prentice-Hall, 189–226.

Riko, K., Hyde, M. L., & Alberti, P. W. (1985). Hearing assessment in early infancy: incidence, detection and assessment. *Laryngoscope, 95,* 135–144.

Roberts, M. E. (1976). Comparative study of pure-tone, impedance, and otoscopic hearing screening methods: A survey of native Indian children in British Columbia. *Archives of Otolaryngology, 102,* 690–694.

Ross, M., & Lerman, J. (1970). A picture identification test for hearing-impaired children. *Journal of Speech and Hearing Research, 13,* 44–53.

Sanders, J. W. (1975). Impedance measurement. *Otolaryngologic Clinics of North America, 8,* 109–124.

Sanders, R. A., Duncan, P. G., & McCullough, D. W. (179). Clinical experience with brain stem auditometry performed under general anesthesia. *Journal of Otolaryngology, 8,* 24–32.

Schein, J. D., & Elk, M. T., Jr., (1974). *The Deaf Population of the United States.* Silver Spring, MD.: National Association of the Deaf.

Schwartz, D. M., & Schwartz, R. H. (1978). Acoustic impedance and otoscopic findings in young children with Down's Syndrome. *Archives of Otolaryngology, 104,* 652–656.

Shepherd, D. C. (1978). Pediatric audiology. In D. E. Rose (Ed.). *Audiological assessment (2nd ed.).* Englewood Cliffs, N.J.: Prentice-Hall, 261–300.

Sheridan, M. D. (1968). *The Developmental Process of Infants and Young Children* (2nd ed.). London: Her Majesty's Stationery Office.

Skinner, M. W. (1978). The hearing of speech during language acquisition. *Otolaryngologic Clinics of North America, 11,* 631–650.

Skinner, P., & Glattke, T. J. (1977). Electrophysiologic response audiometry: state of the art. *Journal of Speech and Hearing Disorders, 42,* 179–198.

Stewart, I. F. (1977). Newborn infant hearing screening - a five year pilot project. *Journal of Otolaryngology, 6,* 477–481.

Thompson, G., Wilson, W. R., & Moore, J. M. (1979). Application of visual reinforcement audiometry (VRA) to low-functioning children. *Journal of Speech and Hearing Disorders, 44,* 80–90.

Vernon, M., & Mindel, E. (1978). Psychological and psychiatric aspects of profound hearing loss. In D. E. Rose (Ed.). *Audiological Assessment (2nd ed.).* Englewood Cliff, N.J.: Prentice-Hall, 99–145.

Willeford, J. A. (1977). Assessing central auditory behavior in children: A test battery approach. In R. Keith (Ed.). *Central Auditory Dysfunction*. New York: Grune & Stratton, 43–72.

Wilson, W. R., & Thompson, G. (1984). Behavior audiometry. In J. Jerger (Ed.). *Pediatric Audiology*. San Diego College-Hill Press, 1–44.

Wong, D., & Shah, C. P. (1979). Identification of impaired hearing in early childhood. *Canadian Medical Association Journal, 121,* 529–546.

Zinkus, P. W., Gottlief, M. I., & Schapiro, M. (1978). Development and psychoeducational sequelae of chronic otitis media. *American Journal of Diseases of Children, 132,* 1100–1104.

17

Assessment of Multicultural Preschool Children

ANDRÉS BARONA

The need for appropriate evaluation of culturally different preschoolers is increasing. This need results from two major developments in the United States. The first development was because of federal involvement in education in the 1960s and 1970s that resulted in legislation affecting preschool and school-age children. The 1964 Maternal, Child Health and Mental Retardation Act and the 1964 Educational Opportunity Act required that educational and social opportunities be provided for all children, while public Law 94–142 mandated that a free and appropriate education be provided to handicapped children from the age of 3 (Kelley & Surbeck, 1983). Educational programs receiving federal funding designed to implement the terms of these acts were required to have a performance-based evaluation demonstrating that participating children had made strides in the areas of achievement, intelligence, or some other measurable dimension (Kelley & Surbeck, 1983). Appropriate preschool assessment instruments therefore became necessary to measure and demonstrate such gains.

The second development creating an increased need for assessment of culturally different preschoolers is the population shift occurring in the United States. Currently, approximately 80% of the United States can be considered to be White and non-Hispanic. It is projected that this percentage will be reduced to 72% by the year 2000 and to 59% by the year 2040 (Fradd, 1987a). Thus, it can be seen that the number of persons from minority cultures in this country is sizeable and growing. This increase in the minority population is perhaps most evident when studying school-age and younger children; whereas only about 7.5% of the total U.S. population is under 5 years of age, for Hispanics the percentage is 11.1 (Fradd, 1987a).

By definition, a culturally different child is one who comes "from an ethnic group having sociocultural patterns that differ from those of the predominant society. These groups include blacks, Hispanic-Americans, American Indians, and Asian-Americans" (Sattler, 1988, p. 592). A child of preschool age who is a member of a culturally different family might share few common experiences with age peers of the dominant American culture. For this young age group, it is expected that the family will be the primary socializing influence because preschool programs reach only about 37% of the total population and less than 25% of minority 3 and 4 year olds (Fradd, 1987a).

The values, behaviors, experiences, and attitudes of these culturally different families vary significantly from those of the typical middle-class family. These differences can be demonstrated by contrasting two cultures' perceptions of giftedness. In mainstream America, a gifted middle-class child is commonly thought to demonstrate high achievement or potential in general intellectual ability, or academic, creative, or psychomotor aptitude (Marland, 1972). In American subcultures, this perspective can vary dramatically. The results of at least one study (Bernal, 1974) indicate that the traits of obedience, common sense, responsibility, respectfulness, independence, self-reliance, and the ability to influence others were emphasized as much as the trait of intelligence when Mexican-Americans identified gifted children. From this example, it can be seen that not only do experiences differ for preschool children of different cultures but that certain abilities and characteristics are likely to be selectively reinforced.

Similarly, cultural differences can affect the way learning occurs as well as what information is learned. Some evidence exists to suggest that individuals of different cultures will recall and understand those aspects of a lesson that are most relevant to their own culture. In a cross-cultural study of reading comprehension (Steffensen et al., 1979), American and Indian students read passages describing weddings in both cultures. Members of each culture recalled more information related to the wedding within their own culture. In addition, each culture focused on different aspects of the passages: Americans emphasized the romantic while Indians highlighted the monetary exchange between families. Results of these studies suggest that culturally different students might need assistance in learning information with which they have had little or no experience (Fradd, 1987b).

Many of the individuals from culturally different groups will be from linguistically different backgrounds, more specifically, non-English language backgrounds: It has been estimated that the number of limited English proficient persons living in the United States will near 40 million by the year 2000 (National Advisory Council for Bilingual Education, 1980–81). Although the great majority will speak Spanish as their primary language, many other languages also will be represented.

Young children who are non-English speakers or who have as their primary language a language other than English have the potential to develop school learning problems if placed in monolingual English classes upon school entry. Their lack of exposure to the English language creates a high probability that they will not understand much of the information that is communicated. Unable to process information provided in English and unaware of what is being said to them, they can become inattentive and distractible. These children not only can be considered to be at risk for learning content areas such as reading, writing, and arithmetic, but also for knowing what behaviors are expected in their new, unfamiliar, and structured environment (Bryen & Gallagher, 1983).

It also is suggested that preschool children with limited English proficiency might have additional difficulties with the way in which information is conveyed in group situations. Whereas parents of young children often use repetition, emphasis, and the physical environment to assist the child in learning new words, classroom teachers often interact with the entire group and are unable to use repetitions and context clues (Bryen & Gallagher, 1983). Information also can be conveyed in more abstract forms. Unfortunately, preschoolers of limited English proficiency are largely unable to benefit fully from these approaches until their English skills are better developed. Instead, they often must rely on the aid of the physical context or their own actions to understand and produce language. Without these aids, learning and possibly behavior problems will occur.

As one might imagine, defining normal development and behavior as well as being able to identify mild learning problems in young children is a difficult task given the rapid and variable rate of development among preschoolers. For some children, the acquisition rate of cognitive and motor skills is sudden: one moment the skill is not observable while the next it is clearly present. For other children, skill acquisition is a gradual process. Definition of normal development and behavior is even more difficult when a culturally different or limited-English-proficient preschool child is involved because it is necessary to be aware of critical individual differences.

THE PURPOSES OF ASSESSMENT

Assessment of the preschool child serves several purposes. First, assessment can screen children for potential learning problems by comparison to same-age peers. This technique quantifies differences between individuals by describing the child's performance in light of the average performance of a relevant comparison group. Second, it can be diagnostically useful to determine if deficiences exist in any number of areas. Preschool assessment can measure competencies in either developmental areas or readiness skills (McLoughlin & Lewis, 1986). Criterion-referenced measures can be included here; scores on such measures would be interpreted relative to an established standard of performance. Finally, assessment can be used to monitor progress that is a result of intervention (Garber & Slater, 1983). Generally, assessment can be viewed as a means of confirming or denying the presence of a problem for an individual. During the assessment process, information is obtained that specifies the individual's level of functioning and identifies areas of strength and weakness. This information is used to make decisions to facilitate the development of that individual.

THE PROBLEMS OF ASSESSMENT

Problems Related to the Preschool Child

Obtaining the appropriate information with which to make decisions to assist in further development is likely to be a challenge when preschool children are to be tested. Generally preschoolers' social behavior is not conducive to psychoeducational assessments; preschool children can follow their own impulses and be unaccepting of the constraints of the testing situation (Gelman, 1979; Ulrey, 1981). Young children often express their feelings easily and can be quite uninterested in their own performance. In addition, test performance can be affected by biological drives such as the need to eat or sleep, and behavior can vary

significantly over short periods of time. Thus, the examiner needs special skills and understanding to work with the preschooler. Patience and creativity are essential and it is necessary to be both positive and confident in interactions with the child. Finally, the examiner must be able to modify the assessment to work with or around any changes in a child's behavior. These requirements generally represent a departure from the more traditional methods followed for school-age children (Paget, 1983).

Problems Related to Differences in Culture

In the most ideal circumstances, assessment is a complicated process. It is made even more complex when the individual to be evaluated is from a culturally diverse or limited English speaking background (Barona & Santos de Barona, 1987). When the unique age-related problems inherent to testing preschool children are added, it becomes crucial to conduct an assessment with even greater care given to both accuracy and an awareness of those social, cultural, and linguistic factors that can influence test performance.

The culturally different preschooler can differ from a mainstream American peer on a number of important dimensions. If from a disadvantaged environment, the minority child might be less attentive (Garber & Slater, 1983) and therefore less likely to do well on tasks with an academic orientation. Solutions to social intervention problems can be both more limited in variety and more aggressive (Spivack & Shure, 1976). It should be noted, however, that when provided with learning environments that reinforced more appropriate learning styles, improvement in reflection and in problem-solving approaches were noted (Garber, 1977; Slater & Heber, 1979; Spivack & Shure, 1976).

Expressive skills and style of interaction with an adult also can differ among culturally different preschoolers. Vocabulary for preschoolers revolves around their experiences. To the extent that a culturally different child has experienced significantly different events from either the mainstream American child or from what the assessment materials cover, that child might be unable to respond in the same manner as his or her peers who have had more exposure with the general subject matter.

Even more significant is the differences in styles of interaction that can be demonstrated among children of varying cultures. In some cultures, for example, it is considered impolite and even challenging for eye contact to be maintained between a child and an adult; for a child to contradict an adult or to express an opinion that might differ; or to speak to an adult unless spoken to directly. A well-mannered Vietnamese child, for instance, will speak only when spoken to. As a result, voluntary responses in a classroom might be interpreted as showing off or even as rude. Respect is shown by sitting quietly and listening attentively. Much can be communicated nonverbally: thankfulness or apology can be conveyed with silence or a smile. Indeed, within the Vietnamese culture, a verbal expression of thanks would reflect a lack of modesty (Huynh, 1987). In a similar vein, preschool Chinese children frequently are passive participants in a classroom setting and do not compete with other children (Garber & Slater, 1983). After completing a task, they rarely proceed automatically to other work (Tikunoff, 1987). A teacher or evaluator unfamiliar with such cultural characteristics might, unfortunately, conclude that a child who demonstrates any of the above characteristics is dull, sullen, unmotivated, or even developmentally delayed.

In still another culture, eye contact has very different connotations than in American society. Unlike American parents and teachers, who when scolding might tell a child to "Look at me when I speak to you," Hispanic adults would interpret maintained direct eye contact as an act of defiance. This cultural characteristic holds throughout life. Prolonged eye contact between adolescent or even adult males in the Hispanic culture can lead to fighting because it is read as a challenge. An often-used phrase among adolescent Mexican males is "soy o me paresco?" or "Is it me or do I look like him?", the implication being is it me that you are looking for (to fight) or do I just look like him?

Related to this issue is the point that individuals must not be lumped together because of apparent physical similarities. For example, it must be recognized that great diversity in cultural patterns and values exists among Asian cultures. Whereas the parameters of social situations are carefully defined within Cambodian society

(Chhim, 1987), Lao adults avoid overt guidance. Rather, Lao children learn through observation and modeling (Khamchong, 1987). A lack of awareness of such variations between cultures that to many Americans appear strikingly similar again can result in erroneous conclusions about the culturally different child.

In the preschool assessment situation in particular, these differences can require special intervention to maximize the information that is obtained. It has been suggested that when a culturally different child is involved, the examiner might need to initiate conversation or even prod the child to respond (Cummins, 1980). Strategies such as the alternation of test items (Zigler & Butterfield, 1968) or the location of the assessment (Silverman, 1971) have had significant and positive effects on test performance. It also is possible that the style and tempo of the examination might need to be modified. The examiner might need to adopt a more facilitative style. As the situation demands, the examiner might need to become more nurturing, affectionate, soft-spoken, directive, "laid-back," or reserved. Thus, it is extremely important that the examiner be both aware of basic styles of interaction considered appropriate to the child's background and be equipped with a variety of strategies to get the child to demonstrate skill and knowledge levels.

Knowledge of social and cultural differences is vital for the appropriate interpretation of test results. Knowledge of sociocultural differences alone, however, will not ensure a valid assessment. It is necessary to be aware of the limitation of many of the commonly used assessment instruments as well as the issues and controversy surrounding assessment (Bracken, 1987).

Problems Related to Traditional Assessment Methods and Instruments

As is widely known, much criticism has been levelled at the area of cross-cultural assessment. One criticism has been that traditional methods of assessment have made little allowance for cultural differences. Methods that incorporate standardized administration procedures limit the amount and nature of interaction between child and examiner. These methods also permit only a narrow repertoire of acceptable responses, many of which can be completely unknown to a child of an American subculture. Because such a child might respond to an examiner or to the testing situation in a nontraditional way, information related to the child's knowledge base and/or ability level might not be adequately demonstrated. Much of the material in traditional standardized tests are geared primarily toward white, middle-class homes and values (Reynolds & Clark, 1983). Indeed, it is quite likely that an examiner in a nontraditional standardized assessment situation would make erroneous conclusions about a culturally different child's level of functioning and cognitive or educational strengths and weaknesses when in reality a lack of exposure to pertinent stimuli might be the reason for poor performance.

Additional problems noted with traditional assessment methods include the fact that many culturally different groups are underrepresented in test standardization samples. The lack of sufficient numbers of minority children in the standardization samples makes it extremely difficult to obtain a representative sample of performance and to interpret test results for the culturally different child with much degree of confidence.

Traditional assessment methods also have been plagued with an inability to uniformly predict outcomes for children from diverse backgrounds. Traditional measures typically are most accurate in prediction when white middle-class children are involved but are generally unacceptable in their level of predictive ability for minority children (Reynolds & Clark, 1983). Thus, diagnosis and long-range planning are hampered when children from American sub-cultures are involved.

The tests might not measure the same underlying constructs for all children (Bracken et al., in press). As an example, the factor structure of one popular test of intelligence for school-age children was found to differ for white, black, and Hispanic children (Santos de Barona, 1981) and it has been hypothesized that using intelligence tests with minorities might measure only the degree of acculturation (Mercer, 1979) rather than level of ability. Similarly, constructs can be measured differently at different ages within the same instrument (Bracken, 1985), thus further limiting the ability to validly interpret test results.

One of the major criticisms aimed at the assessment of all preschool children involves limitations in the reliability and validity of the available assessment instruments (Ulrey, 1981). Many measures lack adequate predictive ability for clinical appliation (Sattler, 1988) and uncertainty exists surrounding their accuracy (Nagle, 1979). Some differences have been noted, however, by the targeted ages of the instruments and by the level of ability of the young child. Infant assessment instruments such as the Bayley Scales of Infant Development (Bayley, 1969) or the Apgar Scale (Apgar, 1953) are poor predictors of intelligence and neurological dysfunction, respectively (Thurman & Widerstrom, 1985). Such infant scales are considered to be limited in their ability to estimate future levels of functioning. An exception to this, however, is when low functioning children are assessed for intelligence in this case, measured IQs tend-to remain relatively stable (Goodman & Cameron, 1978; Keogh, 1970; Lewis, 1976; McCall et al., 1973; Sattler, 1988; Share et al., 1964).

Preschool tests appear to fare better in their ability to predict future outcomes than do infant tests. The increased predictiveness of the preschool tests appears in part to be a function of item content; whereas infant tests are limited largely to perceptual-motor tasks, preschool measures contain items better able to tap the cognitive domain (Sattler, 1988). However, stability of test scores and prediction of future academic performance also appear related to the age at which the initial assessment occurs (Bayley, 1969; McCall et al., 1972; Sattler, 1988). IQs obtained before age 5 must be interpreted cautiously (McCall et al., 1973) because "many of the indicators of later learning difficulties and behavior problems simply are not measurable before the age of 6" (Ulrey, 1981, p. 486).

Although numerous screening, diagnostic, and prescriptive measures that target the preschool population exist, most are unacceptable because of their poor psychometric characteristics (Arffa et al., 1984; Bracken, 1987; Rubin et al., 1978). Test results might lack usefulness for numerous reasons. First, instruments that utilize norms for comparison purposes might be unacceptable because standardization samples are inadequate in overall size or are unrepresentative of the population for which it is used. For example, many developmental scales were normed on white, middle-class populations (Garber & Slater, 1983) and therefore provide little valid data for interpretation of diverse populations. At the very least, the standardization sample should include a sampling of variables such as age, sex, ethnicity, SES, and geographic region in adequate numbers so that interpretation of test results can occur along these dimensions.

Second, the test might not be able to predict equally well for individuals of all ethnic, socioeconomic, or ability groups. The content of test items might favor a particular group or groups through disproportionate representation of a group, stereotyping, or the use of concepts or materials that are more familiar to some groups than others (Wiersma & Jurs, 1985).

Third, insufficient technical information might be provided, making it difficult to make decisions about a test's usefulness and soundness; reliability and validity studies might not have been conducted or might be limited in scope. Reliability refers to consistency of measurement and might take several forms. Test–retest reliability studies, which examine the consistency of measurement across time (Wiersma & Jurs, 1985), might be difficult to conduct given the rapid rate of development that occurs at the preschool level; such studies would need to determine a retest period that would reduce the probability of practice effects as well as the likelihood that any change in scores really is because of the child's acquisition of knowledge and skills (Goldman et al., 1983). Equivalence reliability, which involves the consistency of measurement across parallel test forms and can involve a measure of internal consistency (Wiersma & Jurs, 1985), can be obtained in an easier manner (See Bracken, 1987 for suggested technical standards).

A fourth criticism relates to the fact that many assessment measures fail to provide enough specificity to enable useful decision making regarding service delivery or educational programming and as a result areas of deficit might not receive adequate precriptive attention. These limitations have resulted in some reluctance to refer for formal evaluation to avoid problems caused by premature labelling or possible misclassification. Because labelling or classification can create a negative and lasting stigma, many professionals avoid assessment at early ages to avoid the negative consequences that occur as a result of this process.

A PROCESS FOR THE ASSESSMENT OF CULTURALLY DIFFERENT PRESCHOOL CHILDREN

The complexity involved in evaluating the culturally different child makes it necessary to devote a great deal of time to the process of assessment. Traditionally, evaluation has taken a client-centered approach where data is collected through the use of standardized instruments and observations in the testing situation. Although the rationale for this approach is valid and ample evidence supports this notion of testing, the approach has a number of shortcomings when a culturally different child is involved. A number of areas require close attention and monitoring to ensure that a clear understanding of the child emerges and these areas might extend beyond the limits of the traditional assessment.

When traditional standardized instruments are used in isolation for culturally different preschoolers, the possibility for confounding test results is great. The unique characteristics of the preschool period, which often is marked by uneven development and growth spurts, combined with the effects of cultural variations in style of interaction, language issues, and problems associated with the assessment instruments creates significant difficulties in interpreting test results. This development-culture-instrument interaction in preschool assessment makes it difficult to determine if test findings are attributable to cultural, language, environmental, developmental, or measurement factors.

What is needed, therefore, are additional methods to obtain valid information about the culturally different preschooler. These methods should provide the opportunity to systematically assess areas of strength and deficit without fear of immediate classification. Thus, the assessment of the culturally different preschooler must allow for sufficient interaction with the child so that conclusions regarding the child's capacity to learn are arrived at with confidence. This strategy should allow for adequate time to identify the relevant factors in the child's learning style as well as effective teaching strategies for that child.

What follows is a suggested process for the assessment of culturally different preschool children. This method uses a number of strategies to obtain comprehensive information about the child.

Preassessment Data

Information obtained prior to the actual assessment is extremely important. This information can be obtained through written questionnaires but should include interviews with parents where the reasons for referring the child for evaluation are explored in depth. Parental concerns about the child, the evaluation process, and its potential consequences regarding further education should be discussed and clarified. Other referral agents, if applicable, also should be contacted for information. Information gathered in this phase should be comprehensive and include language, motor, and social developmental histories. Medical information and data from day care or preschool settings, if available, also are important. In addition, information related to the family composition, status within the community, and level of acculturation can add significantly to a more complete understanding of the culturally different child.

Language Assessment

Language assessment must be a major focus in evaluating culturally different children. Potential or ongoing problems related to limited English proficiency must be separated from either language disorders or slow development so that appropriate planning and intervention occur. This can be difficult unless the evaluator is both skilled in the assessment of language and a proficient speaker of the relevant language.

The purpose of this language assessment "is not merely to determine whether the child can communicate well enough to be tested in English but rather to determine the actual levels of skill and fluency in each language spoken and the role that language may play in potential learning problems" (Barona & Santos de Barona, 1987, p. 194). In addition to determining home language and the degree, if any, to which the child has been exposed to English, it is necessary to assess language structure and the child's ability to make functional use of language (Barona & Santos de Barona, 1987). Vocabulary, comprehension, and syntax should be examined within both receptive and expressive aspects of language. This language assessment should enable a decision regarding the language or languages with which to conduct the remainder of the assessment. Generally, clear dominance in one language would lead to assessment in that language. Frequently dominance is not clearly established and in these instances evaluation in both English and the home language is recommended to ensure that an adequate sampling of abilities is obtained (Barona & Santos de Barona, 1987).

In the event that a child cannot be evaluated in English, a number of important questions must be addressed. First, a decision must be made as to whether the child should be evaluated only in the home language or if a combination of English and the home language should be used. Often, a monolingual evaluation, even if it is in the home language, is not appropriate because the language familiar to the child is actually a combination of the home language and English. Second, it must be determined if a translated version of the test is available in the child's language. If so, technical information related to the translation should be examined and a determination of the adequacy of its psychometric properties should be made. In particular, attention should be paid to whether norms exist for the translated version as well as to the specific composition of the standardization sample. In addition, some attention should be paid to whether the test is a direct translation of English and if it allows for dialectical differences. Exact equivalents of English concepts might not exist and the difficulty level of both concepts and test items can change in the translation. Also, within the same language, it is possible that multiple acceptable answers can exist depending on the child's region of origin (Barona & Santos de Barona, 1987; Bracken et al., in press; Bracken & Fouad, 1987; Wilen & Sweeting, 1986).

If a formal translation of the desired test is not available, it might be necessary to create one for the local area. Such a translation should be developed carefully prior to the actual testing session. Standardized procedures should be established for use by all evaluation personnel; both the translation and the procedures should be reviewed by several proficient speakers of the language to ensure the most accurate translation possible (Bracken & Fouad, 1987; Wilen & Sweeting, 1986).

In the event that a bilingual evaluator is not available, it might be necessary to use an interpreter not related to the child who is fluent in standard English and the home language, and who has had some formal education. This interpreter should receive training in such general aspects of the assessment process as establishing rapport, using standardized test administration procedures, objective observation, and the precise recording of verbal and nonverbal behaviors during the assessment process (Wilen & Sweeting, 1986).

The Traditional Assessment

A number of reviews of various standardized instruments already have been written (Bracken, 1985; McLoughlin & Lewis, 1986; Schakel, 1986) and that information will not be reiterated here. Rather, the purpose of this section is to provide some guidelines for use of information derived from such instruments.

Although to this point only the problems associated with standardized assessment instruments have been dealt with as they pertain to culturally different individuals, it must be recognized that standardized instruments do have a useful function. Standardized instruments provide a systematic way to collect data about the child in various domains. Even though the value of specific test items might not be equivalent because of the problems of representation and exposure that have been discussed earlier, the fact that the test was administered under relatively uniform conditions creates some basis for comparison as well as a means with which to judge interactive styles.

When a culturally different child is involved, results of standardized intelligence tests should not be used as an absolute index of cognitive functioning. Rather, such results should be viewed as a general estimate of the child's *current level of measurable functioning* where information has been obtained about the level and types of skills and knowledge that the child has demonstrated relative to other children. As such, it should serve as a marker from which to begin to build for further assessment, if needed, or for making educational recommendations.

The results of assessment with standardized instruments should provide crucial information re-

garding the culturally different preschooler. Based on the assessment, the examiner should determine the *relative* level of functioning and whether either overall test performance or specific responses might be related to factors other than ability or achievement. The examiner should have a sense of the validity of test results by evaluating the degree to which the child invested energy and effort in the evaluation tasks. The examiner also should determine how well the child appeared to understand the language in which the assessment was conducted and whether language appeared to affect test results as well as the ability to perform specific tasks.

During this phase, the examiner must bring together all data gathered in earlier stages and evaluate test findings with that data in mind. For example, if the child appeared to attend more when test items were communicated in the home language than in English, the examiner might conclude that the distractibility was primarily because of a language factor. Similarly, a newly immigrated Vietnamese child would not be expected to engage in elaborate or animated verbal interactions in any language. An examiner who encountered such a child would need to conduct additional investigation to determine why the child was not behaving in the manner expected. Thus, the traditional assessment phase should serve as a forum where information about the child is integrated, hypotheses are generated and explored, and strategies for either educational recommendation or further assessment are developed.

Diagnostic Placement

Following assessment with traditional standardized instruments, a decision might be made that insufficient information exists with which to make recommendations about the child. There might be several possible reasons for this realization. First, language, developmental, or cultural factors can appear to have influenced the standardized test results. As noted earlier, normal preschool behavior, such as distractibility, easy fatigue, shyness, and difficulties in separating from mother; lack of familiarity with or inability to successfully work with a specific cultural interaction style; or concern over language involvement can raise questions as to the reliability of test findings. Second, the examiner might feel that the standardized instruments just did not provide an adequate arena in which to sample the child's repertoire of skills and knowledge. It also is possible that more information is needed concerning the way in which the child learns to get clearer ideas regarding future planning for the child.

To avoid the constraints and pitfalls of both cultural and developmental variables and yet obtain useful information, it is necessary that the culturally different child be sufficiently acclimated to and comfortable within the assessment setting. To accomplish this, it is suggested that the child first undergo a diagnostic placement. This consists of an already established preschool enrichment program where children of various ethnic and cultural backgrounds are cared for on a daily basis and where bilingual/bicultural personnel are available to assist the child with communication needs. This setting ideally should serve a high proportion of children with apparently normal development toward facilitating socialization and appropriate modeling behavior, as well as provide an informal means of comparison. Such a program can provide, within a nurturing atmosphere, age-appropriate activities geared toward facilitating the child's growth in motor, social, and cognitive areas. As part of its curriculum, mediated learning experiences (Feuerstein, 1979) can be incorporated where emphasis is on encouraging children to explore a variety of ways to obtain information and solve problems in all dimensions of development and where the child's progress in accomplishing these tasks can be monitored and measured.

It is expected that the child's involvement in a diagnostic placement setting will last for an extended period, ranging from 3 to 6 months. During this time, the child should be encouraged to participate in activities and opportunities for appropriate social interactions should be provided

This diagnostic placement can serve several purposes. For those children who demonstrated difficulty in separation from a significant adult, the routine of daily attendance will accustom the child to interaction with a number of adults. Assessments, when performed, will be less emotionally charged and will occur in an environment with which the child is familiar, resulting in increased responsiveness and attention to task.

While in attendance, the child will come to view learning activities and the presentation of new information as a regular part of the daily routine. The actual measurement of skills, learning styles, and progress often can be accomplished either unobtrusively or with minimal fanfare.

Participation in an ongoing diagnostic setting has a number of advantages. It provides personnel with the opportunity to observe the child in group situations and to assess preferential language and learning styles as well as effective teaching strategies over time. In addition, social adjustment can be monitored because preschool teacher-pupil ratios are relatively small and it is possible to have a greater awareness of the child's overall personality and needs.

Diagnostic placement also permits an assessment of the effects of culture because in many cases an enrichment facility will have children in attendance of both same and different cultures as well as some personnel with similar language skills. The rate with which the child acquires new skills and concepts can be measured and monitored throughout the child's attendance and personnel can identify effective reinforcing conditions to provide the child. Diagnostic placement assessment also will permit a judgment as to the amount of effort that will be needed to work successfully with one child, relative to other children in the center.

Several methods of assessment can be used in this setting to gather useful information. These include observations, criterion-referenced tests, and dynamic assessment techniques. *Observations* of the child can assist in assessing social skills and in describing patterns of behavior and styles of interaction in both individual and group settings. Knowledge of information that can facilitate the culturally different child's attending to tasks and responding is extremely useful in the design of effective teaching strategies. For example, if an examiner in the traditional phase of assessment had difficulty getting a culturally different child to invest in the evaluation, one goal of observation might be to determine if the preschooler interacts differently with the adults in the diagnostic setting. If interaction is limited only to adults of similar culture, or if the child has established rapport with some other subset of adults then goals can be set to broaden the child's interaction patterns. Similarly, it also would be useful to observe the child's interactions with other children and to determine those conditions under which such interactions occur: information related to whether the child interacts only with a particular child or group of children, whether most interactions occur in free play or in structured activities, how the child communicates with others in the diagnostic placement setting, and the nature of the interactions that do occur are all helpful in identifying relevant factors in instructional programming.

Criterion-referenced testing measures "the performance levels of examinees in relation to a set of well-defined objective competencies" (Hambleton, 1982, p. 352). Whereas norm-referenced measures generally allow comparisons among examinees, criterion-referenced measures do not make comparison among examinees or groups as a primary purpose. Rather, criterion-referenced tests describe what a child specifically knows or can do, and therefore are useful in planning additional instructional activities.

For example, an examiner might have noted in the standardized assessment that a preschooler had difficulty following directions communicated in either the home language or in English and as a result performed poorly on a number of tasks. During the diagnostic placement, a criterion-referenced measure focusing on basic readiness skills indicated that the child was deficient in demonstrating knowledge of directional concepts such as *through, beside, beneath, right, left*, and so on, and in addition had difficulty remembering and executing directions consisting of more than two parts. Remedial planning for this child therefore would involve two components. First, the child would receive direct training in directional concepts. Second, a number of strategies could be interspersed throughout the day in a variety of formal and informal situations to facilitate the child's memory, ability to follow directions, and use the newly acquired directional concepts.

Dynamic assessment (Feuerstein, 1979) modifies traditional assessment practice in three ways. First, the nature of the interaction between examiner and examinee is shifted from one where the examiner is neutral and adheres to a standardized script to one where the examiner assumes the role of teacher and provides mediated learning experiences. In this role, the examiner-turned-teacher intervenes, provides advance organizers and explanations for problems and activities, summarizes experiences, and interjects

insightful and clarifying remarks whenever and wherever necessary. Second, training is considered an important part of the assessment and the child is provided not only the principles, skills, and techniques to accomplish a task but also the opportunity to apply these functions to novel tasks. Finally, dynamic assessment results are not interpreted within a product modality where emphasis is on *what* is known, but rather the results are viewed from a process orientation in which *how* learning occurs is considered important. In this final phase, both unique responses and strategies toward learning are examined to provide direction for both remediation and further education.

Using a test-train-retest paradigm (Sattler, 1988), the child's ability to perform specific tasks and/or solve particular problems first is measured with unfamiliar stimuli. After the initial testing is conducted, the child is taught to solve the task through a variety of methods aimed at helping the child develop appropriate problem-solving strategies. Upon completion of the training phase, the child is again tested on either the original task or on one of its alternate forms.

Contrary to traditional assessment where the goal is to determine how much and what is known, the dynamic assessment or process-oriented approach seeks to determine the degree to which cognitive structures can be modified, the amount and type of teaching effort that is needed to bring about such modification, the areas of functioning that require intervention to produce the desired effects, as well as identify the child's preferential learning strategies. Thus, in the course of the total assessment, data related to the rate of acquisition of strategies, skills, and concepts, as well as the generalizability of these strategies is obtained through interaction with the child and systematic observation (Feuerstein, 1979; Feuerstein et al., undated; Sattler, 1988).

Although process-oriented techniques for preschool children are in a relatively early stage of development, they "offer the potential of more accurate and less discriminatory diagnostic information, more relevant to an educational or treatment setting than norm-referenced assessment" (Lidz, 1983, p. 60). Although there does not yet exist a well-developed or widely accepted standardized dynamic preschool measure (Lidz, 1983), at least one technique (Brown & Ferrara,

1985) has been suggested to be useful for children from a variety of cultures. This technique involves giving children "a set of increasingly explicit hints toward solution of a problem until they are able to solve it" (Schakel, 1986, p. 209).

Diagnostic assessment placement should continue until assessment and program personnel conclude that sufficient information has been obtained with which to make a set of educational recommendations about the child. At that time, a meeting should be covened of all programmatic personnel who have been involved in aspects of assessment, including the parents and appropriate school and/or agency representatives. During this meeting, all data obtained throughout the assessment process should be thoroughly reviewed and recommendations for the most appropriate way to meet the child's educational needs should be generated. For those children for whom an ongoing education placement is suggested, an individualized education plan specifying those areas requiring remediation should be developed. In addition, the placement setting should be specified. It should be noted that it is entirely possible that a placement recommendation would be to continue participation in the preschool enrichment program in which the diagnostic placement occurred. In such cases, emphasis would shift from assessment to teaching.

SUMMARY

The process of assessing culturally different preschool children is complex. The problems associated with working with young children, with relatively little exposure to American culture, vastly different ways of interacting with adults, and measurement instruments with a limited degree of psychometric soundness causes considerable concern regarding the degree of confidence with which test results can be interpreted, as well as the implications for instructional planning. Assessment of the culturally different preschooler therefore must be approached with a great deal of care and with sufficient opportunity to obtain accurate and relevant information.

A suggested procedure for assessment expands the standard assessment process. First, *preassessment data* should go beyond the typical social, medical, and developmental data generally obtained and should include relevant information from all significant individuals involved with the child. Information regarding the family's assimilation into American society is crucial. Second, in-depth investigation of the child's communicative competence must occur. This should include determining the language or combination of languages that the child uses as well as the level of skill and fluency demonstrated in each. *Traditional assessment* with standardized measures should take place to enable a general estimate of current level of measurable functioning and to determine a relative level of performance compared to age-equivalent peers. During this phase of the assessment, the examiner should develop a sense for the potential effects of cultural factors in the testing process and should determine the degree of validity of test results. *Diagnostic placement* in an established preschool enrichment program should be conducted if questions arise concerning the validity of test results or if it is believed that additional information is needed to make educational decisions. A variety of techniques are appropriate for this phase of assessment. Finally, parents, assessment personnel, and appropriate school and agency representatives review all assessment data in a *review meeting* and together develop educational recommendations for the child.

REFERENCES

Apgar V. (1953). A proposal for a new method of evaluation of the newborn infant. *Anesthesia and Analgesia, 32,* 260–267.

Arffa, S., Rider, L. H., & Cummings, J. A. (1984). A validity study of the Woodcock-Johnson Psychoeducational Battery and the Stanford-Binet with black preschool children. *Journal of Psychoeducational Assessment, 2,* 73–77.

Barona, A., & Santos de Barona, M. (1987). A model for the assessment of limited English proficient students referred for special education services. In S. H. Fradd & W. J. Tikunoff (Eds.). *Bilingual Education and Bilingual Special Education; a Guide for Administrators* (pp. 183–210). Boston: College Hill Press.

Bayley N. (1969). *Bayley Scales of Infant Development.* New York: The Psychological Corporation.

Bernal, E. M. (1974). Gifted Mexican-American children: An ethnoscientific perspective. *California Journal of Educational Research, 25,* 261–273.

Bracken, B. A. (1985). A critical review of the Kaufman Assessment Battery for Children (K-ABC). *School Psychology Review, 14,* 21–36.

Bracken B. A. (1987). Limitations of preschool instruments and standards for minimal levels of technical adequacy. *Journal of Psychoeducational Assessment, 5,* 313–326.

Bracken, B. A., Barona, A., Bavermeister J., Howell, K. K., Poggioli, L., & Puente, A. (in press). Multinational validation of the Spanish Bracken Basic Concept Scale for Cross-*Cultural Assessments*. *Journal of School Psychology*.

Bracken, B. A., & Fouad, N. A. (1987). Spanish translation and Validation of the Bracken Basic Concept Scale. *School Psychology Review, 16,* 94–102.

Brown, A. L., & Ferrara, R. A. (1985). Diagnosing zones of proximal development. In J. Wertsch (Ed.). *Culture, Communication, and Cognition* - Vygotskian Perspectives. London: Cambridge University Press.

Bryen, D. N., & Gallagher, D. (1983). Assessment of language and communication. In K. D. Paget & B. A. Bracken (Eds.). *The Psychoeducational Assessment of Preschool Children* (pp. 81–144). New York: Grune & Stratton.

Cummins, J. (1980). Psychological assessment of minority language students. Unpublished manuscript of Ontario Institute for Studies in Education, Toronto, pp. 1–91.

Feuerstein, R. (1979). *The Dynamic Assessment of Retarded Performers: The Learning Potential Assessment Device Theory Instruments and Techniques*. Baltimore: University Park Press.

Feuerstein, R., Rand, Y., Haywood, H. C., Hoffman, M. B., & Jensen, M. R. (undated). *L.P.A.D. Learning Potential Assessment Device manual experimental version*. Jerusalem: Hadassah-Wizo-Canada Research Institute.

Fradd, S. H. (1987a). The changing focus of bilingual education. In S. H. Fradd & W. J. Tikunoff (Eds.). *Bilingual Education and Bilingual Special Education - A guide for Administrators* (pp. 1–44). Boston: College Hill Press.

Fradd, S. H. (1987b). Accommodating the needs of limited English proficient students in regular classrooms. In S. H. Fradd & W. J. Tikunoff (Eds.). *Bilingual Education and Bilingual Special Education, a Guide for Administrators* (pp. 133–182). Boston: College Hill Press.

Garber, H. (1977). Preventing mental retardation through family rehabilitation. In B. Caldwell & J. Stedman (Eds.). *Infant Education: A Guide for Helping Handicapped Children in the First Three Years*. New York: Walker and Company.

Garber, H. L., & Slater, M. (1983). Assessment of the culturally different preschooler. In K. D. Paget & B. A. Bracken (Eds.). *The Psychoeducational Assessment of Preschool Children* (pp. 443–471). New York: Grune & Stratton.

Gelman, R. (1979). Preschool thought. *American Psychologist, 34,* 900–905.

Goldman, J., L'Engle Stein, C., & Guerry, S. (1983). *Psychological Methods of Child Assessment*. New York: Bruner/Mazel.

Goodman, J. F., & Cameron, J. (1978). The meaning of IQ constancy in young retarded children. *The Journal of Genetic Psychology 132,* 109–119.

Hambleton, R. K. (1982). Advances in criterion-referenced testing technology. In C. R. Reynolds & T. B. Gutkin (Eds.). *The Handbook of School Psychology* (pp. 351–379). New York: John Wiley & Sons.

Huynh, D. T. (1987). *Introduction to Vietnamese culture*. San Diego: Multifunctional Resource Center, San Diego State University.

Kelley, M. F., & Surbeck, E. (1983). History of preschool assessment. In K. D. Paget & B. A. Bracken (Eds.). *The Psychoeducational Assessment of Preschool Children* (pp. 1–16). New York: Grune & Stratton.

Keogh, B. V. (Ed.) (1970). Early identification of children with potential learning problems. *Journal of Special Education, 4,* 307–363.

Khamchong, L. (1987). *Laos Culturally Speaking: Introduction to the Lao Culture*. San Diego: Multifunctional Resource Center, San Diego State University.

Lewis, M. (1976). Infant intelligence tests: Their use and misuse. *Human Development 16,* 108.

Lidz, C. S. (1983). Dynamic assessment and the preschool child. *Journal of Psychoeducational Assessment, 1,* 59–72.

Marland, S. (1972). *Education of the gifted and talented: Report to the Congress of the United States by the U.S. Commissioner of Education*. Washington, D.C.: U.S. Government Printing Office.

McCall, R. B., Appelbaum, M., & Hogarty, P. S. (1973). Developmental changes in mental performance. *Monographs of the society for research in child development, 38* (3, Serial No. 150).

McCall, R. B., Hogarty, P. S., & Hurlburt, N. (1972). Transitions in infant sensorimotor development and the prediction of childhood IQ. *American Psychologist, 27,* 728–748.

McLoughlin, J. A., & Lewis, R. B. (1986). *Assessing special students* (2nd ed). Columbus, OH: Merrill.

Mercer, J. (1979). *Technical manual; SOMPA: System of Multicultural Pluralistic Assessment*. New York: The Psychological Corporation.

Nagle, R. J. (1979). The McCarthy scales of children's

abilities: Research implications for the assessment of young children. *School Psychology Digest, 8,* 319–326.

National Advisory Council for Bilingual Education (1980–81). *The Prospects for Bilingual Education in the Nation.* Washington, DC: Office of Bilingual Education and Minority Language Affairs, U.S. Department of Education (ERIC Reproduction No. ED 203 664).

Paget, K. D. (1983). The individual examining situation: Basic considerations for preschool children. In K. D. Paget & B. A. Bracken (Eds.). *The Psychoeducational Assessment of Preschool Children* (pp. 51–62). New York: Grune & Stratton.

Reynolds, C. R., & Clark, J. (1983). Assessment of cognitive abilities. In K. D. Paget & B. A. Bracken (Eds.). *The Psychoeducational Assessment of Preschool Children* (pp. 163–190). New York: Grune & Stratton.

Rubin, R. A., Balow, B., Dorle, J., & Rosen, M. (1978). Preschool prediction of low achievement in basic school skills. *Journal of Learning Disabilities, 11,* 62–64.

Santos de Barona, M. (1981). A study of distractibility utilizing the WISC-R factors of intelligence and Bender error categories in a referred population. *Dissertation Abstracts International, 42,* 4775a.

Sattler, J. M. (1988). *Assessment of Children* (3rd ed.). San Diego: author.

Schakel, J. (1986). Cognitive assessment of preschool children. *School Psychology Review 15,* 200–215.

Share, J., Koch, R., Webb, A., & Graliker, B. (1964). The longitudinal development of infants and young children with Down's syndrome. *American Journal of Mental Deficiency, 68,* 689–692.

Silverman, E. (1971). Situational variability of pre-

schoolers' dysfluency: Preliminary study. *Perceptual and Motor Skills, 33,* 4021–4022.

Slater, M. A., & Heber, F. R. (1979). *Final Performance Report Modification of Mother–Child Interaction Processes in Families at Risk for Mental Retardation.* Bureau of Education for the Handicapped, Grant 780012, Washington, D.C., November.

Spivack, G., & Shure, M. B. (1976). *Social Adjustment of Young Children.* San Francisco: Jossey-Bass.

Steffensen, M. S., Joag-Dev, C., & Anderson, R. C. (1979). A cross-cultural perspective on reading comprehension. *Reading Research Quarterly, 15,* 10–29.

Chhim, S. (1987). *Introduction to Cambodian culture.* San Diego: Multifunctional Resource Center, San Diego State University.

Thurman, S. K., & Widerstrom A. H. (1985). *Young Children with Special Needs.* Boston: Allyn & Bacon.

Tikunoff, W. J. (1987) Mediation of instruction to obtain equality of effectiveness. In S. H. Fradd & W. J. Tikunoff (Eds.). *Bilingual Education and Bilingual Special Education: a Guide for Administrators* (pp. 99–132). Boston: College Hill Press.

Ulrey, G. (1981). The challenge of providing psychological services for young handicapped children. *Professional Psychology, 12,* 483–491.

Wiersma W., & Jurs, S. G. (1985). *Educational Measurement and Testing.* Boston: Allyn & Bacon.

Wilen, D. K., & Sweeting, C. M. (1986). Assessment of limited English proficient Hispanic students. *School Psychology Review, 15*(1), 59–75.

Zigler, E., & Butterfield, E. (1968). Motivational aspects of changes in IQ test performance and culturally deprived nursery school children. *Child Development, 39,* 1–14.

18

Assessment of Preschool Children with Severe Handicaps

KATHRYN C. GERKEN

In 1968 Congress passed P.L. 90–538 authorizing the Handicapped Children's Early Education Program (HCEEP), and by the 1985–86 school year, 56 states and territories of the United States were participating in State Plan Grant funding for HCEEP. As of October 1, 1986, the United States of America and insular areas were providing services to 260,931 3- to 5-year-old handicapped children and in the 1984–85 school year, states and insular areas reported providing services to 36,533 handicapped birth to 2-year-old children (U.S. Department of Education, 1987). The overall increase in number of handicapped children recciving special services has been smaller each year since the 1980–81 school year, yet services to birth to 5 year olds have increased during the 1980s. This increase might be because of several factors such as improvement in identification procedures and instruments, but a major reason for the increase has been because of increased incentives and mandates to provide services to this population. The amendments that have followed P.L. 94–142 have emphasized early identification and intervention. The primary focus of P.L. 98–199 in 1983 was the expansion and improvement of services to handicapped preschoolers (Paget & Nagle, 1986). P.L. 98–199 amended Section 623 of the Education of Handicapped Children's Act to require in the annual report to Congress a description of the status of special education and related services for children birth to 5 years old. This description is to include those children receiving services in Head Start and Developmental Disability Programs, Crippled Children Services, the Mental Health/Mental Retardation Agency, state child development centers, and private agencies under contract with local schools.

In 1984–85, P.L. 98–199 also instituted a new HCEEP State Grant program that is awarded to state agencies to plan, develop, and implement a comprehensive service delivery system for special education and related services to handicapped children from birth to 5 years.

The most recent legal mandate affecting services to preschoolers is P.L. 99–457, the Education of the Handicapped Amendments of 1986. The provisions of these amendments require states to provide education and related services for handicapped children between the ages of 3 and 5 years by 1991. In addition, the amendments include new discretionary programs to provide early intervention services to handicapped children, birth to 2 years, and their families. The basis for these amendments appears to be the testimony and research that was presented to Congress indicating the economic and educational benefits of programs for young handicapped children. To receive funding, the early intervention services must meet seven criteria. The fifth and sixth criteria are especially relevant for psychologists and others who provide assessment services. The fifth criterion indicates the kinds of services that must be included and the sixth criterion indicates the qualifications of personel who will provide the services. It is clear that quality assessment services will be needed. The United States Department of Education's proposal for implementation of P.L. 99–457 addresses the standards for personnel who will provide services to these infants and todlers (Section 303.72). However, these standards use such terms as "highest requirements in the state" thus focusing on quantity of training and not necessarily quality of training. Advanced degrees and licensure do not ensure that "assessors" have had appropriate training and experience with handicapped children from birth to 5 years or with the families of these children.

There should be increased attention nationwide on child find activities, screening, diagnosis and intervention for handicapped infants/preschoolers during the 1990s. Does that mean there should simply be more of the same kinds of services provided now? For the 1984-85 school year, the states and insular areas indicated that improved services were needed for 32,741 of the 3- to 5-year-old handicapped children already identified. Ysseldyke's and coworkers' (1986) review of the preschool screening process in a midwestern state that has a comprehensive and widespread screening network, indicated there were problems with the screening for 3 to 5 year olds, as well as birth to 3 year olds. There appeared to be no differentiation among those individuals selected as the best people to administer instruments. There was little empirical support for the technical adequacy of the instruments selected and, in many instances, the same instruments were used for screening and diagnosis. There also were problems with coordination and cooperation among agencies. The *Ninth Annual Report to Congress* (U.S. Department of Education, 1987)

cited a need for improved services to handicapped preschoolers and to handicapped 18 to 21 year olds. The Report also listed programs and services that a majority of the states indicated needed improvement. Physical therapy and occupational therapy services were cited most often as needing improvement; however, 34 states cited a need for improvement in assessment and 33 states cited a need for improvement in psychological services.

Assessment and other psychological services provided to handicapped infants/preschoolers must improve in the 1990s if it is our desire as a nation to do the following:

> (1) to enhance the development of handicapped infants and toddlers and to minimize their potential for developmental delay,
> (2) to reduce the educational costs to our society, including our Nation's schools, by minimizing the need for special education and related services after handicapped infants and toddlers reach school age,
> (3) to minimize the likelihood of institutionalism of handicapped individuals and maximize the potential for their independent living in society, and
> (4) to enhance the capacity of families to meet the special needs of their infants and toddlers with handicaps.
>
> Section 671 of P.L. 99–457, 1986

There have been improved services to handicapped preschoolers during the 1980s, yet problems persist, especially in the area of assessment and intervention (Browder, 1987; Rogers, 1986; Simeonsson, 1986; Simeonsson et al., 1979; Ulrey & Rogers, 1982).

Gerken (1983) stated that few trained personnel, inadequate identification procedures and instruments, and a lack of precise definitions, along with limited funds and facilities, have kept services at a minimal level. Lessen and Rose (1980) surveyed the states to determine whether they had specific definitions for preschool handicapping conditions and guidelines for identification and placement of the preschool handicapped population. Of the 44 states that responded, 25 indicated that they had delineated a specific definition or had provisions for identifying this population; only 5 states indicated that they had a definition that is unique for this population.

Action must be taken to improve and increase assessment practices and services to handicapped infants/preschoolers and their families. The purpose of this chapter is to provide guidelines for the assessment of handicapped preschoolers, specifically severely handicapped preschoolers from birth to 5 years.

Alter and coworkers (1986) believe the major limitations in assessment of severly/profoundly handicapped children center on the tests; overuse of norm-referenced tests, or tests not sufficiently sensitive to detect educational or behavioral gains, tests that have little, if any, educational relevance. Bagnato (1984) states that the major dilemma when assessing handicapped infants/preschoolers is finding scales that are technically adequate, yet appropriate for the child's functional disabilities, practical for planning intervention, and sensitive for monitoring developmental progress. He states that these elements are rarely complimentary when assessing young developmentally disabled children. The psychometric limitations of preschool instruments have been detailed extensively by Bracken (1987).

In 1979, Simeonsson and coworkers stated that the major problems in assessing severely handicapped children were: definitional issues; limitations of the child; limitations of the instrument; and limitations of the examiner. Simeonsson (1986) expounded upon these assessment problems and provided guidelines to improve assessment. Table 18.1 lists the important assessment issues and Simeonsson's suggestions to improve assessment.

Simeonsson (1986) also provides an excellent Inventory of Assessment Variables that should help an examiner eliminate or at least recognize some of the problems in assessment. The inventory asks for the usual demographic information about a child, but also asks the examiner to report the child's current medications, functional status for vision, hearing, health, limbs, and body tone, and the child's state/responsivity. The examiner also is asked to describe the assessment context and indicate the assessment procedure in terms of modifications needed and judgment of adequacy of assessment.

ASSESSMENT ISSUES

Definitions

Who are the severely handicapped? Geiger and Justen (1983) reported that 35 states had definitions for the severely handicapped. Nineteen definitions focused on categories while 16 definitions focused on educational needs. There is considerable overlap in definitions, specifically the definitions for developmental disabilities and severely and profoundly handicapped. There also is considerable discussion as to whether definitions should reflect categories, behavioral descriptions, or service needs (Browder, 1987; Powers & Handleman, 1984; Sailor & Guess, 1983; Snell, 1987).

Categorical

Relative to categorical definitions, terms such as severely developmentally disabled or severely handicapped usually include children diagnosed as autistic, severely and profoundly mentally retarded, or severely and profoundly emotionally handicapped (Blacher, 1984; Powers & Handleman, 1984; Van Etten et al., 1980).

In 1974, Paul Thompson, the director of Programs for Severely Handicapped Children and Youth, U. S. Office of Education, defined the severely handicapped child as:

> one who, because of the intensity of his physical, mental or emotional problems, needs educational, social, psychological, and medical services beyond those which have been offered by traditional, regular, and special educational programs, in order to maximize his full potential for useful and meaningful participation in society and for self-fulfillment.

The target population would include:

> . . . those classified as seriously emotionally disturbed, schizophrenic and autistic, profoundly and severely mentally retarded, and those with two or more serious handicapping conditions, such as the mentally retarded-deaf and mentally retarded-blind (p. 73).

A combination of the Developmental Disabilities Act of 1970, P.L. 91–517, and the Developmental Disabled Assistance and Bill of Rights Act of 1975, P.L. 94–103 defined developmental disability as follows:

> A disability attributable to mental retardation, cerebral palsy, epilepsy, autism or any other conditions closely related to mental retardation. The disability must originate before age 18, must be expected to continue indefinitely, and must constitute a substantial handicap in order to be classifed as a developmental disability. (McGovern, 1978, p. 4)

TABLE 18.1
PROBLEMS AND SOLUTIONS IN THE ASSESSMENT OF SPECIAL CHILDREN

Problems	Solutions
Definitional issues	
a. Lack of agreement on definitions of basic terms	Reduce inconsistency. Consider alternative ways in which to define children and designate severity of their handicap (functional or educational needs).
b. Need designations that will reflect both presence of handicap and degree of impairment	
Child	
a. Impaired functioning in more than one area	Consider other limitations. Assess the child's state. Determine child's modality preference (how can child best receive information and how can child best respond).
b. Performance and functioning affected by medication and state	
c. Presence of idiosyncratic behaviors	
d. Variability in rate of development across areas	
Examiner	
a. Lack of knowledge/experience with special children	Provide appropriate traiining at preservice and inservice levels.
b. Personal biases and expectations	Training will require knowledge and skill acquisition, awareness of one's own biases and expectations, and supervised field experiences
c. Invalid assumptions concerning effects of the handicap	
d. Difficulty interpreting a child's response	
e. Lack of special communication skills (i.e., signing skills)	
Measurement	
a. Standardization populations exclude handicapped	Modify assessment materials. Modify assessment procedures. Expand or vary content of assessment materials.
b. Extreme normative values cannot be derived	
c. Test assumptions violated when used with handicapped	
d. Difficult to compare results from different tests	
e. Insufficient data base for the various handicapping conditions	
Setting	
a. Inadequate or inappropriate setting in terms of light, sound, other physical features	Consider physical and psychological aspects of situations and settings
b. Artificial nature of setting	
c. Failure to consider positioning needs of a child	
d. Failure to consider the presence or absence of reinforcement in the environment	

Note. Adapted from Simeonsson, 1986, p. 27, and Browder, 1987.

Whereas P.L. 95–602, the Developmental Disabled Assistance and Bill of Rights of 1978, enacted a new functional definition of developmental disability:

> severe chronic disabilities attributable to mental or physical impairments which are manifested before age 22; are likely to continue indefinitely; result in substantial limitations in three or more of the following areas of major life activity: self-care, receptive and expressive language, learning, mobility, self direction, capacity for independent living, and economic self sufficiency; and result in the need for services over an extended period.
>
> Section 102(7) of P.L. 98–527

This definition of developmental disabilities eliminated all categorical references thus emphasizing the commonality of service needs and the importance of varying combinations and sequences of services over time.

Categorical definitions are present in P.L. 94–142 and in the Revised Diagnostic and Statistical Manual (DSM-III-R) (American Psychiatric Association, 1987). DSM-III-R (1987) contains separate definitions for levels of mental retardation and for pervasive developmental disorders.

The classifications of severe and profound mental retardation describe the skills typically acquired by individuals in each category and their physical and instructional needs.

The most widely recognized definitin of mental retardation is that by Grossman (*Federal Register*, 1977; Grossman, 1983). Mentally retarded means significantly subaverage general intellectual functioning existing concurrently with deficits in adaptive behavior and manifested during the developmental period, which adversely affects a child's educational performance. (*Federal Register*, 1977, p. 42478).

The severely/profoundly mentally retarded usually function four or more standard deviations below the mean on a standardized intelligence test (Robinson & Robinson, 1976) and usually have some type of physical abnormality or neurological involvement.

In DSM-III-R (1987) the pervasive developmental disorders are those that are characterized by qualitative impairments in the development of reciprocal social interaction, verbal and nonverbal communication skills, and imaginative activity that frequently is associated with a variety of other conditions such as distortions or delays in intellectual skills, comprehension of language, production of speech, posture and movements, patterns of eating, drinking, or sleeping, and responses to sensory input. Terms, such as atypical development, symbiotic psychosis, childhood schizophrenia and others have been used to describe these disorders in the past. However, DSM-III recognized only one subgroup of this general category: autistic disorder. Specific criteria are listed for a diagnosis of autistic disorder.

The following is the DSM-III-R diagnostic criteria for Autistic Disorder:

At least 8 of the following 16 items are present, these to include at least two items from A, one from B, and one from C. Note: Consider a criterion to be met only if the behavior is abnormal for the person's developmental level.

A. Qualitative impairment in reciprocal social interaction as manifested by the following: (The examples within parentheses are arranged so that those first mentioned are more likely to apply to younger or more handicapped, and the later ones, to older or less handicapped persons with this disorder.)

(1) marked lack of awareness of the existence or feelings of others (e.g., treats a person as if he or she were a piece of furniture; does not notice another person's distress; apparently has no concept of the need of others for privacy)

(2) no or abnormal seeking of comfort at times of distress (e.g., does not come for comfort even when ill, hurt, or tired; seeks comfort in a stereotyped way, e.g., says "cheese, cheese, cheese" whenever hurt)

(3) no or impaired imitation (e.g., does not wave bye-bye; does not copy mother's domestic activities; mechanical imitation of others' actions out of context)

(4) no or abnormal social play (e.g., does not actively participate in simple games; prefers solitary play activities; involves other children in play only as "mechanical aids")

(5) gross impairment in ability to make peer friendships (e.g., no interest in making peer friendships; despite interest in making friends, demonstrates lack of understand-

ing of conventions of social interaction, for example, reads phone book to uninterested peer)

B. Qualitative impairment in verbal and nonverbal communication, and in imaginative activity, as manifested by the following: (The numbered items are arranged so that those first listed are more likely to apply to younger or more handicapped, and the later ones, to older or less handicapped persons with this disorder.)

(1) no mode of communication, such as communicative babbling, facial expression, gesture, mime, or spoken language

(2) markedly abnormal nonverbal communication, as in the use of eye-to-eye gaze, facial expression, body posture, or gestures to initiate or modulate social interaction (e.g., does not anticipate being held, stiffens when held, does not look at the person or smile when making a social approach, does not greet parents or visitors, has a fixed stare in social situations)

(3) absence of imaginative activity, such as play-acting of adult roles, fantasy characters, or animals; lack of interest in stories about imaginary events

(4) marked abnormalities in the production of speech, including volume, pitch, stress, rate, rhythm, and intonation (e.g., monotonous tone, question-like melody, or high pitch)

(5) marked abnormalities in the form of content of speech, including sterotyped and repetitive use of speech (e.g., immediate echolalia or mechanical repetition of television commercial); use of "you" when "I" is meant (e.g., using "You want cookie?" to mean "I want a cookie"); idiosyncratic use of words or phrases (e.g., "Go on green riding" to mean "I want to go on the swing"); or frequent irrelevant remarks (e.g., starts talking about train schedules during a conversation about sports)

(6) marked impairment in the ability to initiate or sustain a conversation with others, despite adequate speech (e.g., indulging in lengthy monologues on one subject regardless of interjections from others)

C. Markedly restricted repertoire of activities and interests, as manifested by the following:

(1) stereotyped body movements, e.g., hand flicking or hand twisting, spinning, head banging, complex whole-body movements

(2) persistent preoccupation with parts of objects (e.g., sniffing or smelling objects, repetitive feeling of texture of material, spinning wheels of toy cars) or attachment to unusual objects (e.g., insists on carrying around a piece of string)

(3) marked distress over changes in trivial aspects of environment, e.g., when a vase is moved from usual position

(4) unreasonable insistence on following routines in precise detail, e.g., insisting that exactly the same route always be followed when shopping

(5) markedly restricted range of interests and a preoccupation with one narrow interest, e.g., interested only in lining up objects, in amassing facts about meteorology, or in pretending to be a fantasy character.

D. Onset during infancy or childhood. Specify if childhood onset (after 36 months of age). (American Psychiatric Association, 1987, pp. 38–39)

Both the DSM-III-R (1987) diagnostic criteria/ definition of autism and the National Society for Autistic Children's Criteria describe the children as those who exhibit language deficiencies, disturbed interpersonal relationships, inconsistent responses to sensory stimulation, and developmental delays and associated cognitive disorders.

Autism is a serious handicapping condition that occurs in preschoolers, and converges with other developmental disabilities. It can occur by itself or in association with other disorders that affect the function of the brain, such as viral infections, metabolic disturbance, and epilepsy. Autistic children show wide variations in performance on different tests and at different times. Only 20% of the children identified as autistic obtain standard scores above 70 on intelligence tests, 20% obtain standard scores between 50 and 70, and 60% have scores below 50 (Ritvo & Freeman, 1978, pp. 162–167).

Prior (1979) found evidence to support abnormal hemisphere function in this group of children, while Rutter (1979) found evidence of a basic cognitive deficit in autism involving impaired language, sequencing, abstraction, and coding function generally, as well as specific abnormalities in language function and usage that appear to be characteristic of the autistic syndrome. He suggested that the extent and severity of the cognitive deficit are powerful indicators of outcome and that intervention reduces social and behavioral problems but does little to alter cognitive development. Even with optimal testing conditions and techniques, the majority of autistic children are found to be functioning within the retarded range, with a significant number in the severely retarded range (DeMeyer et al., 1974; Ornitz & Ritvo, 1976).

McGovern (1978) defined a multiple handicap as the existence of two or more handicapping conditions of equal severity in one person. Multihandicapped is defined in the *Federal Register* (1977) as

concomitant impairments . . . the combination of which causes such severe educational problems that they cannot be accommodated in special education programs solely for one of the impairments. The definition does not include deaf-blind children. (p. 42478)

The *Federal Register* (1977) defines deaf-blind as concomitant hearing and visual impairments, the combination of which causes such severe communication and other developmental and educational problems that they cannot be accommodated in special education programs solely for deaf or blind children. (p. 42478)

Functional

Those who support functional definitions believe that the primary basis for a diagnosis of exceptionality varies as a function of the nature of the condition and there is no uniform criterion or dimension suitable to define all conditions (Simeonsson, 1986). Simeonsson suggests that the use of diagnostic criteria and labeling leads to focusing on negative deviations and simplistic reductionism. She suggests that categorization be restricted as a general principle, its limitations recognized, and wherever possible, one should use alternative conceptualizations that are better suited to assessing, evaluating, and planning.

The following is Sailor's and Guess' (1983) functional definition of severely handicapped:

Children who are severely handicapped are significantly delayed in their development relative to their non-handicapped peers. They learn, under the most ideal conditions, at a significantly slower rate than non-handicapped students or students in remedial special education programs. Their learning impairment is usually associated with significant delay in several critical aspects of development (p. 12).

These children exhibit retardation in living skills development, social development, physical development, and sensory development.

Although Bellamy (1985) was describing severely handicapped adults, his functional definition is applicable to severely handicapped individuals of any age. He describes individuals who need ongoing support in several major life areas to participate in the mainstream. These individuals are expected to require such support throughout life. The emphasis in this chapter is on those preschoolers who, because of the intensity of their physical, mental, or emotional problems, or the combination of two or more serious handicapping conditions, need services beyond those offered by regular and special education programs (DuBose, 1978). There are three major groups within the severely handicapped preschool population: mentally retarded, autistic, and multihandicapped children.

Incidence/Prevalence

How many severely handicapped preschoolers are there? Snell (1987) estimates that .05% of the United States' population has a severe handicap. However, it has not been possible to determine accurately how many severely handicapped children 5 years old and younger there are in the United States and its territories because of problems with definitions, and confusion in discussing incidence and prevalence figures. Gabel and Erickson (1980) and Hogg and Sebba (1986) point out the distinction between incidence and prevalence. Incidence is the measure of frequency with which a condition (severe disability) occurs anew in a population whereas prevalence is the measure of how many people in the population have the condition (severe disability) at a particular time. Thus the variance may be because of differences in definitions and/or differences in when the presence of a condition is measured.

A generally accepted prevalence figure was 1

severely or profoundly retarded student per 1,000 school-age children and youth (Gerken, 1983). Yet Magrab and Johnston (1980) estimate that there are 3 to 4 severely or profoundly handicapped individuals for every 1,000 persons. The prevalence of severe retardation has increased in recent years because of reduced infant mortality, but trends in incidence rates are not yet clear (Hogg & Sebba, 1986).

Autism was estimated to occur in approximately 5 of every 10,000 births and to be 4 times more common in boys than girls. Yet Short and Marcus (1986) estimate that the prevalence figure is 15 in every 10,000 children. The broader classification of pervasive developmental disorder also has estimated prevalence figures of 15 in every 10,000 children (American Psychiatric Association, 1987). It is estimated that only .5% to 7% of the school-age population is multihandicapped. Danielson (1980) found that .09% of the 3- to 5-year-old population in 1979–1980 were classified as multihandicapped and received services. Yet 4.4% of the 3 to 5 year olds receiving special education services in 1985–86 were diagnosed as multiply handicapped (U.S. Department of Education, 1987). The number of multihandicapped children served has grown 76.8% since information was first gathered in the 1978–79 school year. Very few children are diagnosed as deaf-blind. A percentage was not even calculated for 3- to 5-year-old deaf-blind children being served in 1979–80 (Danielson, 1980); however, .05% of the 3 to 5 year olds receiving services in 1985–86 were diagnosed as deaf-blind (U.S. Department of Education, 1987).

Approach

It is clear that severely handicapped preschoolers are a diverse group in terms of their learning potential and behavioral characteristics, yet they share many commonalities. Until recently, the seriously handicapped were regarded as untestable and untreatable (Sabatino, 1979a) and appropriate services for them were generally nonexistent (Snell, 1987). They most often were given medical labels and viewed as the problems of the medical professionals rather than educators. Robinson and Robinson (1976) reported some of the most common causes of severe handicaps: chromosomal abnormality; genetic disorders; disorders of metabolism, maternal infection; neural tube closure defects; gestational factors; hazards at birth; postnatal hazards; psychiatric disorders; and environmental influences.

Although many of the profoundly handicapped children are identified at birth or shortly thereafter, identification alone is not sufficient to provide services for the children. Initial medical intervention does not provide a sufficient basis for educational programming, and even definitions based on measured intelligence do not describe children adequately. The intellectual functioning of many children in this group cannot be measured in the traditional way. An instructional definition is needed, and it cannot be formulated without appropriate assessment.

Although controversy abounds regarding how services should be delivered to these children, most of the professionals who work with severely handicapped preschoolers would agree to the following: early identification and intervention is vital to maximize these children's potential.

More than routine health care is needed by most of the children because as a group they have a high incidence of health-related problems. There has been a scarcity of skilled and knowledgeable professionals to provide services to these children; their assessment requires ingenuity as the examiner might have to learn a new communication system or teach the child one before proceeding. There are technical limitations to the screening and diagnostic procedures, and there are problems in linking these procedures to intervention services. These children have combined response deficits and it is necessary to discover unsuspected disability-producing conditions. The examiner must be aware of how much information and what type is being received by the child's central nervous system and must recognize the limitations imposed by disabling conditions. A thorough differential diagnosis is needed to rule out what is or is not contributing to the handicapping conditions. Research with animals and with normal infants and children must be reviewed to understand the capabilities of the severely handicapped preschooler. A much closer look at early biological development concerning activity levels, perceptual responsiveness, sleep-wake cycles, and so forth, is necessary.

All children can make progress with appropriate assessment and intervention—a continuous process that requires an interdisciplinary team approach, with the family involved in all aspects of the process. Parent/professional interactions have not been as positive as they could have been during the 1970s (Snell, 1987). The 1990s call for family-centered assessment and the study of families who have ''succeeded'' rather than focusing on the families with pathology (Blacher, 1984; Simeonsson, 1986).

Two basic approaches to assessment have been used with the severely handicapped—the developmental approach and the behavioral approach. In the developmental approach, norm-referenced devices are used, such as scales developed for young normal children, scales designed for assessing subnormal children based on normal development, and scales comparing the child with other handicapped children. In the behavioral approach, criterion-referenced devices are used that focus on observable behaviors, frequency measures, environmental factors, and the relationship of measures to intervention goals (Haring, 1977). A combined developmental-behavioral model appears to be the most appropriate orientation in working with these children. During the 1980s new perspectives and new labels have been given to these assessment approaches. Bagnato and Neisworth (1981) have labeled their approach a developmental task approach, whereas under the behavioral approach, there are models such as the strict behavioral assessment model, the task analytic model, ecological inventory model, massed trial assessment, individualized curriculum sequencing model, and precision teaching model. Browder (1987) provides a thorough review of these behavioral models and advocates using some features from each model to conduct applied behavior analysis and life skills curriculum planning. Table 18–2 provides a brief overview of developmental and behavioral models. No matter which model is used, the current emphasis is on frequent and direct assessment that is linked to curriculum objectives.

Professional Preparation

Prior to the passage of P.L. 94–142 in 1975, psychologists had limited experience with preschoolers (Bagnato & Neisworth, 1981) and also limited experience with severely handicapped children of any age. Considerable progress has been made in training personnel to work with preschoolers, but Lidz (1986) questioned even in the 1980s whether those who are currently assessing preschoolers are qualified to do so. Irons and co-workers (1984) conducted a survey of assessment personnel in Texas; 77.5% of 200 respondents had been asked to assess children with severe handicaps as part of their employment. The majority of the respondents did not perceive themselves as competent to assess children with severe handicaps, as 83.4% wanted more training. Less than 50% of the respondents perceived themselves to be competent on at least 13 of the 20 competencies listed. The assessors had little or no training in activities such as positioning a child for testing, adjusting adaptive equipment, finding a way to communicate with a nonverbal child, and coping with seizures. Olley and Rosenthal (1985) believe that school psychologists could contribute to better services for children with autism. Yet they report that there is no evidence that either knowledge or skills related to autism are emphasized in school psychology training programs.

Paget and Nagle (1986) expressed concern about improving services to handicapped preschoolers and state that training is needed across many content and practice areas. The preservice and inservice training needed to be effective service providers for severely handicapped preschoolers must deal with problems of reduced age and level of functioning. Assessing mildly handicapped preschoolers is different from assessing severely handicapped preschoolers, and thus requires a more extensive knowledge base and additional supervised field work. Paget and Nagle (1986), Ulrey and Rogers (1982), and Rogers (1986) all discuss professional training needs, but only Simeonsson (1986) discusses specific examiner requirements for specific types of severely handicapped children.

A thorough knowledge of typical and atypical infants and children is mandatory for the professionals who will work with severely handicapped infants/preschoolers. It is not sufficient to know about typical or normative development. It soon becomes apparent that there are not only quantitative differences in children's abilities from birth to 5 years of age, but also many qualitative differences. New efforts are being made by educators and medical professionals to learn about these children. Guralnick and Richardson (1980), for example, wrote a book that focuses on improving the education of pediatricians so that they might better serve exceptional children. The professional should have both introductory and advanced coursework in child development, as well as specific courses in atypical child development.

Excellent resources containing research results and tables of normal and abnormal development are available: Egan and coworkers (1971); Harel (1980); Hartlage and Lucas (1973); Horowitz (1978); Illingworth (1975); Johnston and Magrab (1976); Knobloch and Pasamanick (1974); and Stangler and colleagues (1980). Mussen (1983) provides one of the best overviews of research in child psychology and Osofsky (1987) provides an excellent review of research in infant development.

Besides having knowledge of development, the assessor must acquire the skills to evaluate critically any measurement or assessment instrument, be trained in formal and informal assessment procedures, be aware of the reliability and validity of results, understand how the preschooler's behavior influences test performance and outcome, and be aware of medical management issues that could interfere with assessment results. It also is important for the assessor to have knowledge and skills in family systems assessment.

Supervised practicum experiences must take place at a preservice level, and continuous supervised inservice experiences must be provided. Preservice training can begin via simulation activities. Then, through direct observation and gradual participation, the professional can learn how to interact with the severely handicapped preschooler. No trainees, whether from the medical or educational professions, should be allowed to work directly with severely handicapped preschoolers until they have demonstrated, via simulated activities, that they have sufficient knowledge and skill to interact appropriately with the children. To do this they must be aware of the child's medical and environmental needs, and be able to communicate with the child, at least to the extent of recognizing if the child is in pain or in need of assistance.

ASSESSMENT PROCESS

Severely handicapped preschoolers present special problems in assessment because of their age and handicaps. Yet, the same comprehensive sequence of assessment procedures should be used for these children as is used for others: casefinding/identification, screening, diagnosis, educational assessment, performance monitoring, and program evaluation (Brown, 1987; Harrington, 1984; Peterson, 1987). For the severely handicapped population, casefinding/identification and screening are often collapsed because screening is not needed (Brown, 1987; Harrington, 1984). Table 18.3 briefly describes the purpose of this sequence of procedures.

Browder (1987) states that assessment of individuals with severe handicaps has, as its primary purpose, the identification of skills that will increase opportunities for normalized living in community settings. Professionals and lay persons would agree on the basic purpose, but differences emerge when determining which methodology is the best foundation for conducting such assessment. Browder (1987, p. 16–17) describes eight criteria that should be used to plan assessment that will lead to skill selection and ongoing evaluation of student progress:

1. Skills must be selected that will enhance student's integration in their community environments with nonhandicapped peers, and lead to the opportunities available to nonhandicapped people (e.g., employment).
2. Reliable, valid assessment strategies must be developed for skill selection and ongoing assessment.
3. Ongoing assessment must be frequent (e.g., daily or semiweekly) and direct.
4. Data must be collected during ongoing assessment.
5. The data must be summarized on a graph or chart.
6. The graph must be periodically reviewed to make and record data-based instructional decision.
7. These instructional decisions must be implemented.
8. Skills selected should be reviewed annually, and comprehensive assessment should be

TABLE 18.2
ASSESSMENT MODELS FOR SEVERELY HANDICAPPED PRESCHOOLERS

Name	Description	Advantages	Disadvantages	Example of Instruments	References
Develop-mental mile-stones/Psychometric	Judgment is based on performance on a norm-referenced device assessing basic developmental skills.	Know how a child compares to others in a normative group relative to basic developmental skills.	Do not know what functional skills a child has or needs. There is not a link between assessment and intervention.	Bayley Scales of Infant Development	Bailey & Wolery, 1984; Browder, 1987; Bagnato & Neisworth. 1981; Peterson, 1987; Simeonsson, 1986.
Theory-Based Developmental	Judgment is based on performance of the cognitive stages of development (such as Piagetian stages)	Enhances understanding of observed behavior. Compare progress of child with developmental age rather than chronological age peer.	Performance dependent on motor skills and cooperation of infant. Do not know what functional skills a child needs. Do not know if skills of severely handicapped follow same sequence. Intervention program based on this might waste instructional time.	Ordinal Scales of Psychological Development	Bailey & Wolery, 1984; Peterson, 1987; Seibert, 1987; Simeonsson. 1986; Ulrey & Rogers. 1982.
Developmental Diagnostic-Prescriptive Model	Judgment is based on performance on norm-referenced and criterion referenced devices.	Separates child from the norm plus provides a detailed profile of skills and deficit	Comprehensive assessment, but episodic. No systematic review of learners' progress and adaptations based on this review.	Perceptions of Developmental Skills	Bagnato & Neisworth. 1981; Neisworth & Bagnato, 1986.
Ecological	Judgment is based on natural unobtrusive observation of child.	Can observe influence of environment on behavior and development of child. Comprehensive.	Might have problems with objectivity, reliability of observers. Does not consider developmental level, or make peer comparisons.	Specimen Records, Chronology of Events	Simeonsson, 1986.
*Behavioral Models/*Functional	Judgment is based on systematic observation in the natural environment and analysis of behavior and situational variables influencing behavior.	Age-irrelevant assessment strategies, criterion-referenced, pinpoints behaviors of concern.	Does not document progress compared to peers, does not consider developmental level.	Checklists, rating scales	Bailey & Wolery, 1984; Browder, 1987; Peterson, 1987; Powers & Handleman. 1984; Powers, 1985; Simeonsson, 1986.

Task Analysis	Judgment based on observation of a child completing a task.	Specifies the subcomponents necessary to complete a task; identifies specific steps for assessment and instruction.	Different steps or behaviors might have different levels of difficulty, often there is no timebased measure, thus an accomplished task might have limited functional utility if performed slowly.	Checklists	Bagnato, 1984; Browder, 1987; Van Etten, Arkell, & Van Etten, 1980.
Ecological Inventory	Environment (not infant/child) is assessed; judgment is based on the characteristics of the infant/child's current and future environment. The infant/child is then assessed to see if he/she has the skills needed in the environment.	Helps generate or adapt individualized curriculum.	Can lead to an unmanageable list of skill needs. Setting priorities can be difficult. Must use other procedures to assess infant/child's performance of selected skills.	Checklists, Inventories	Browder, 1987; Brown, 1987; Snell & Grigg, 1987.
Precision Teaching	Judgment is based on observation of a child's performing a response repetitiously or performing a chain of responses without teacher interruption.	Assessment is direct and frequent. Provides systematic data.	Model does not specify how skills should be selected. Age relevance and environmental relevance may be ignored.		Browder, 1987 White, Edgar, & Haring, 1978.
Adaptive-transactive Perspective	Judgment is based on interactions and transactions between a child and external stimuli.	Evaluates child behavior in context of environment in which it occurs or in relationship to the interactions surrounding its occurrence.	Does not document progress compared to peers, does not consider developmental level.	Home, Infant Questionnaire.	Peterson, 1987; Sameroff & Cavanaugh, 1979.

TABLE 18.3
SEQUENCE OF ASSESSMENT PROCEDURES

Sequence	Purpose	Target Population
Casefinding/Identification	To increase public awareness of services available for handicapped preschoolers To find infants/preschoolers likely to have a handicap	General Public Parents Medical Personnel Infants/Preschoolers
Screening	To identify children who are not within the normal range of development and need further evaluation	At risk or handicapped infants/preschoolers Parents/guardians
Diagnoses	Pinpointing the nature and degree of a problem	Handicapped infants/preschoolers
Educational Assessment	Pinpoint specific skills and learning needs of infant/preschooler	Handicapped infants/preschoolers
Performance Monitoring	Continuous and ongoing evaluation of child's performance	Handicapped infants/preschoolers
Program Evaluation	Evaluate overall effectiveness of intervention program	Handicapped infants/preschoolers Parent/guardians Teachers/therapists

Note. Sources: Brown, 1987; Harrington, 1984; Peterson, 1987.

conducted at least every 3 to 5 years to prioritize skills for instruction.

She has also developed a flow chart for the development of a comprehensive education plan for students with severe handicaps. This chart can be used as a model for initial placement, update, or for assessing specific areas such as motor skills, or communication skills. The assessment process should result in an in-depth understanding of the child's functional abilities and degree of independence in many spheres. There should be a slow and evolving picture of the child's developmental status that reveals what the child can do currently and leads to specific intervention or remediation efforts.

Identification/Screening

Since the passage of P.L. 94–142 in 1975, the majority of screening programs for 3 to 5 year olds have typically been carried out by public school personnel. The purpose of that screening is to determine if a child is sufficiently delayed to be considered at risk in one or more domains and in need of further diagnosis. Chapter 5 contains important information and resources regarding the screening of 3 to 5 year olds, thus this chapter will focus on the identification/screening of the severely handicapped, which usually takes place during infancy or no later than 1 year of age.

Developmental research during the past two decades has been directed toward studying the effects of various high-risk factors on the developing organism. Attention has focused on the socio-economically disadvantaged child and the infant with high potential for organic damage.

At-risk registers are in operation in many areas of the United Kingdom as well as in other parts of the world (Woods, 1975). Infants who are considered at risk are placed on the list for immediate assessment as well as for short- and long-term follow up. Many of the people who have written about developmental risk factors have listed all the possible prenatal, perinatal, and postnatal factors that might be related to a child's mental and physical development and indicated the possible effects on the child. Objections to at-risk registers focus on their cost and the possibility of false labeling or over screening. Many checklists, interview forms, and health history inventories have been developed to gather such information at a later point; however, with the latter approach conditions can develop that might have been prevented by earlier detection.

It is now possible to determine early risk status through procedures that go beyond the at-risk registers. Francis and coworkers (1987) provide an excellent review of instruments available to assess risk factors and to assess the neonate.

Several scales that summarize prenatal and perinatal risk factors have been developed. One of the most commonly used scales is the Obstetric Optimality Measures developed by Prechtl (1968). The original scale had 42 items, but Prechtl (1982) has developed a 62-item scale and Touwen and colleagues (1980) have elaborated the scale to include 74 items. Information on standardization and reliability is available and these scales appear to be valid for identifying clusters of difficulties that might lead to less than optimal development. Another promising approach is that of Parmelee and his colleagues (Littman & Parmelee, 1978; Parmelee & Michaelis, 1971; Parmelee et al., 1975, 1976).

The Obstetric Complications Scale (OCS) and the Postnatal Complication Scale (PCS) were both proposed by Parmelee and derived generally from Prechtl's work on optimality. In addition, Parmelee and his colleagues have described the Pediatrics Complication Scale (PdCS) to be used at 4 to 9 months of age. They have developed a rank scoring system to define the infant at risk and to lead to more accurate prediction of developmental outcome. Based on prior research, they decided to consider multiple factors as additive in determining degree of risk; thus they use a strategy of multiple short-term predictions.

This system scores pregnancy, perinatal, and neonatal biological events and behavioral performances in an additive fashion, reassesses the infant in the first months of life (3 and 4 months) to sort out those infants with transient brain insult, and reassesses the infant later in the first year of life (8 and 9 months), primarily on a behavioral basis (Parmelee & Michaelis, 1971, p. 290).

Another systematic approach is that of Scurletis and coworkers (1976). They developed a system for providing Comprehensive Developmental Health Services (CDHS). The system provides for preventive services, early detection and screening, diagnosis and evaluation, individualized planning, and access to necessary services.

Ross and Leavitt (1976) suggested a process-oriented approach to identify children who might be at risk. Attention, habituation, and the processing of speech samples were investigated as examples of cognitive functioning that can be assessed during infancy as well as later in life. Meier (1973, 1976a, 1976b) provided a table that indicates risk factors from preconception through early childhood and provides suggestions for evaluation, observation, diagnosis, and intervention. Also, Hobel (1980) developed a maternal risk factor scale, the Problem Oriented Risk Assessment System.

Malone (1980) reported the efforts of a High Risk Committee to screen, identify, and intervene with high-risk infants. If infants receive a score greater than 10 on the UCLA Risk Factor Index, the Brazelton Neonatal Behavioral Assessment (Brazelton, 1973, 1984) is used. The committee reviews the infant's risk factors status, the assessment on the Brazelton, and the nature of the mother–child interaction. A recommendation for referral is made and periodic reviews take place.

Zelazo (1979) and Lipsitt (1979) agreed that the behavior of the newborn can provide the best indices of its condition that can be obtained; however, specific infant responses upon which intellect is inferred have not been systematically researched. Furthermore, Zelazo stated that brain damage can be severe to extensive without impairing cognitive capacity. It is doubtful that very many of our current screening procedures would be able to detect cognitive capacity. In the 1990s the newborn infant is available for evaluation in many areas of development and immense progress has been made in infant screening. Yet still lacking are multivariate investigations of the interrelationships that exist between infants' abilities, their social nature, and transactions with their environment. Francis and coworkers (1987) believe such investigations are essential if neonatal assessment is to continue to keep pace with the ever-increasing awareness of the human infants vast complexity.

Relative to the direct assessment of infants, the Apgar scoring system (Apgar, 1953) is used extensively by medical personnel to rate newborns' heart rate, respiratory effort, reflex irritability, muscle tone, and color at 1 and 5 minutes after birth. The Brazelton Neonatal Behavioral Assessment Scale (NBAS) (Brazelton, 1973, 1984) is the most widely used neonatal behavioral assessment instrument. The NBAS and the Neonatal Behavioral Assessment Scale with Kansas supplements (NBAS-K) (Horowitz et al., 1978; Sullivan & Horowitz, 1978) assess a broad range of neonatal behaviors, both reflexive/elicited and behavioral. The Brazelton has not been formally standardized but Horowitz and her colleagues are preparing a normative report. High interobserver reliability appears attainable but not test–retest stability. Content and concurrent validity appear sufficient, but predictive validity depends on the use of repeated tests. The NBAS has been used extensively in neonatal research and in assessing at risk and atypical infants.

Coons and Frankenburg (1980) contended that traditional developmental screening procedures only assess a child's biological integration and range of past experience. They developed the Home Screening Questionnaire to evaluate the efficiency of a combined developmental/environmental screening procedure. Preliminary results indicated that the questionnaire might not be appropriate for environmental assessment of children under 1 year; however, additional research is in progress.

The screening of all children by physicians would be an example of secondary prevention; however, such mass screening does not take place because of a lack of money, time, and/or provider skills. Frankenburg and coworkers (1980) suggested that a modified version of such screening might be possible. They developed two new screening tests based on the DDST. The Short-Full DDST is to be administered by a trained examiner when the parents have less than a high school education. The Pre-screening Developmental Questionnaire (PDQ) is to be completed by parents who have a high school education or above. Both instruments are part of a two-stage screening procedure in which "suspect" children require further screening. Both the DDST and the PDQ have been revised: DDST-R (Frankenburg, Fandal, Sciarillo, & Burgess, 1981) and R-DPDQ (Frankenburg, 1986). Frankenburg and coworkers (1987) found the R-DPDQ to have a high level of agreement with the DDST-R in a large sample of children (N = 1,434). According to the developers, research to date has shown that these instruments identify all children with significant developmental delays and a large number of those with borderline delays. However, Sattler (1988) reports that little is known about the validity or reliability of the R-DPDQ because there is no manual.

The overview of identification/screening provides some maxims to guide the research and work in this area: there should be continued effort to identify those variables that result in neurological or developmental disabilities; there should be continued research regarding the responses of typical and atypical infants; there is a need to proceed on the basis of identified risks and needs, and not defer services for a final diagnosis; identification and screening require a unified effort involving parents, the medical profession, educators, the community, and soon early identification/screening might prevent a compounding of problems that occur when the environment cannot adjust appropriately to the infant at risk.

Diagnosis/Educational Planning

To pinpoint the strengths and weaknesses of a severely handicapped infant/preschooler, one must decide what model or combination of models will be used to assess the severely handicapped preschooler, what type of team approach will be used, and whether assessment at this point should be in and for the home, in and for the community, or both. For the preschooler, one is most concerned about the skills in the home and in the community. A multidisciplinary team approach is mandated, but Garwood and Fewell (1983) point out some distinctions in team approaches:

> multidisciplinary, each member does his or her separate job; interdisciplinary, each member does his or her separate job but there is communication among all members; transdisciplinary, assessment is a joint effort by team members, "role release" occurs, jobs may vary for each child.

One also must attempt to evaluate the plethora of assessment instruments and techniques that are available before using them. Some instruments assess one specific area or skill, whereas others cover many. A few instruments have been developed specifically for handicapped children, but the majority have not. The content of the instruments for ages up to 2 years generally consists of simple, readily observable motor actions, whereas the instruments for ages 3 to 6 years usually measure communication, motor, cognitive, self-help, and preacademic skills. Other assessment techniques include curriculum-based assessment, environmental assessment, observation, task analysis, and error pattern analysis.

Informal Assessment

During the 1980s the terms curriculum-based assessment (CBA) and curriculum-based measurement (CBM) have been used to talk about the process of determining a student's instructional needs within a curriculum by assessing specific curriculum skills (Fuchs & Fuchs, 1986; Tucker, 1985). This is one more form of informal assessment and although CBA and CBM are new "catchwords" there is nothing new about the necessity of linking assessment to instruction.

A term used during the 1980s to describe one aspect of environmental assessment is ecological inventory (Browder, 1987; Brown, 1987). An ecological inventory is viewed as a top-down approach that focuses on the natural environment as a source for curriculum content and as a location for training identified needs. This is a time-consuming approach because one is assessing for the discrepancies between the child's present skills and what is needed to function in various current and subsequent environments. If this approach becomes more widely accepted, formalized and structured inventories will likely be produced and

published. An ecological inventory consists of observing the environment (home, school, etc.) to determine what skills are needed to operate in that environment. However, it will become necessary to identify those behaviors that are needed only on an intermittent or episodic basis.

Environmental assessment should assess the child and family characteristics, emotional climate in the family, the social network supports, and the effects of cultural influences. Brown (1987) provides an example of a parent questionnaire that elicits information about a child's present environment and potential future environments.

Appropriate assessment for the severely handicapped infant/preschooler requires the assessment of six initial learning behaviors and these can best be assessed via observation. Rotatori and coworkers (1985) provide guidelines for assessing these behaviors: visual fixation; auditory localization skills, visual tracking, eye contact, attending behavior, and following verbal directions.

Hogg and Sebba (1986) review excellent checklists on feeding, preverbal communication, and visual skills that should be part of the assessment process for severely handicapped infants/preschoolers. The Early Feeding Checklist (Werner, 1981) asks for very specific observations from parents/guardians regarding the control of tongue and lips for feeding and drinking. See Bell's (1983) Guidelines for observing visual behavior and Sebba's (1978) Visual Assessment Checklist for other examples of observation techniques. These visual assessments are not to be used in place of an examination by an eye specialist, but to assist staff in working daily with a child. Preassessment checklists are especially helpful when assessing severely handicapped preschoolers because one must determine what is already known about the infant/preschooler to determine the most appropriate assessment strategy. Wilhelm and coworkers' (1986) "Pre-assessment of Physical Handicap" form requests information regarding seizure disorders, medications, communication, optimal positioning, ambulation, and type of motivator needed. This is an excellent example of necessary preassessment.

Application

When one is choosing informal assessment or analysis techniques, it is important to remember that each of these techniques can be useful in gaining information about students. However, each is just one part of the assessment process and is not valid alone. They need to be used in conjunction with other techniques. One of the major weaknesses of the informal techniques is lack of specificity whether pinpointing behaviors to be observed, writing behavioral objectives or performing task analyses. Intra- and interrater reliability and/or test retest reliability data need to be gathered for these techniques.

FORMAL ASSESSMENT

General Considerations

Formal assessment serves an important purpose when used judiciously and in conjunction with other techniques. It is important that both quantitative and qualitative analyses of the results take place and that the data are put to use in decision making. One of the ways to ensure that the data will be useful is to use informal techniques to analyze the results of formal techniques; error pattern analysis should be a routine procedure in all types of assessment.

Important changes are taking place in the search for appropriate assessment instruments. In the past, attempts were made to modify the tests developed for normal children to fit the needs of handicapped children. In the 1980s, however, instruments were revised and/or developed that are much more appropriate for children with severe handicaps and adaptations necessary for specific children have been specified. It must be kept in mind, however, that there is no one instrument that can adequately assess severely handicapped children and the instruments that are used are not interchangeable.

Modifications

The assessment of severely handicapped preschoolers with formal or standardized tests has been viewed as inappropriate because it was often impossible to find an instrument designed specifically for the child; it was necessary to modify the existing tests thus altering the reliability and validity of the test, or it was necessary to use indirect assessment via third party informants. Few studies have indicated how modifications of standard-

ized tests affect resulting IQs (Harrington, 1979; Sattler, 1972a, 1972b, 1974; Sattler & Theye, 1967; Sattler & Tozier, 1970).

Chase (1985) recommends using tools that allow normed comparisons even if the sole purpose is to observe responses under standard conditions along with informal assessment techniques. Her adaptive approach would be to administer an instrument with standard procedures, then "test the limits" to see what means are necessary to have the child perform. There appears to be conflict regarding test modification versus adaptive testing. Newland (1980) differentiates adapting testing procedures and devising modifications as follows: adapting testing procedures leaves the content of the instrument intact, but alters the procedures of administration to fit the child, such as reading items to a blind child or allowing a motorically impaired child to use a head pointer to respond; modifying instruments consists of omitting certain item types, or only using parts of a test.

Strichart and Lazarus (1986) describe adaptive testing as the us of *response fair* tests, test modifications, nonstandardized administration, and alternate response requirements. Response fair tests are instruments in which assessment takes place via the child's intact modalities. All modifications must be described and justified and interpreted as estimates of functioning.

Suggestions for adaptations and modifications are contained throughout Ulrey's and Rogers' (1982) book on assessing handicapped infants/preschoolers. They vary from selecting "response-fair" tests to deviating from standardized procedures, changing the interpersonal process between the child and examiner to fit the child's needs (e.g., frequent breaks, physically holding the child, using reinforcement for attending and responding), and allowing alternative methods of task presentation and task response.

Simeonsson (1986) provides general guidelines for adaptation and modification. She emphasizes flexibility in test administration and establishing an appropriate structure for assessment by allowing alternative modes of communication, increasing motivation, handling attentional problems and atypical behaviors, altering the sequence of items, modifying instructions, simplifying tasks for success, and providing frequent breaks. Simeonsson's text provides information on specific modifications needed for hearing impaired, visually impaired, motor impaired, autistic, and chronically ill children.

Neisworth and Bagnato (1986) define their assessment approach as a developmental diagnostic prescriptive model. They stress an adaptive skill assessment method and describe adaptive modification such as detailing special stimulus and response alterations and excluding sequences of skills and tasks that a particular child is unable to demonstrate because of a specific impairment (e.g., asking a motor-impaired child to draw). They also describe the few commercial instruments that allow for an adaptive skills assessment.

Rotatori and coworkers (1985) discuss the types of adaptations that might be needed when assessing severely and profoundly handicapped individuals. General adaptations include changing or deleting items from the test, changing the manner of administering the test, and changing the materials or equipment used in the test. Specifically, it might be necessary to test a child in nonconventional positions (e.g., sitting on the examiner's lap, strapped in a particular sitting position), allow alternative presentation and response modes, and increase time limits. Alternative communication aids are frequently needed and an examiner must determine what mode is best for presentation and response. Specific training is needed for the examiner to use and understand these modes. The three responding modes described by Rotatori and colleagues (1985) are direct selection, scanning, and encoding. Direct selection requires some direct movement of hand, fingers, foot, fist, head, or mouth. Manual response or a mechanical replacement can be utilized. Scanning requires the individual to survey a visual array and give a signal when to stop. The signal can be a vocal or motor response. Encoding requires that the individual indicate the desired character according to a pattern/code that is memorized or referred to on a chart. This requires less refined motor skills as choices are widely spaced.

Table 18.4 provides some of the common adaptations needed for assessing the severely handicapped. Emphasis needs to be placed on the fact that adaptations and modifications can alter the reliability and validity of standardized instruments. Neisworth and Bagnato (1986) state that to ensure validity, the assessment process for severely handicapped infants/preschoolers must be multipurpose, contain multimeasures of multidomains from multisources.

Instruments

Excellent and extensive resources are available that list, describe, and evaluate the existing assessment instruments and specific guidelines are available for specific groups of children. Thus, only a few instruments are described here; they are not necessarily the best instruments, but they either represent a certain type of instrument, a new or revised instrument, or are instruments that are not widely known.

Screening

During the 1980s several screening instruments were revised (DDST-R, Frankenburg et al., 1981; DIAL-R, Mardell-Czudnaiski & Goldenberg, 1983; DASI-II, Fewell & Langley, 1984; Developmental Profile II, Alpern et al., 1986), but their usefulness for screening severely handicapped preschoolers varies considerably. Ysseldyke and coworkers (1986) found in surveying the screening and diagnostic practices of a midwestern state that there was an overwhelming preference for using the Developmental Indicators for the Assessment of Learning (DIAL) and DDST for speech/language, motor, social/emotional, and cognitive screening. The authors expressed concern about the technical adequacy of both instruments.

The DDST is an individually administered instrument designed for the early identification of children with developmental and behavioral problems (Frankenburg et al., 1975). The various skills assessed by the test are clustered into four general developmental areas: personal–social adjustment, fine motor development, language development, and gross motor development. The DDST has been widely used since its development in 1967 because it is quick and easy to administer, score, and interpret (Frankenburg & Dodds, 1967). Nonprofessional examiners often administer it and spend no more than 20 minutes from start to finish.

The DDST was standardized on 1,036 boys and girls from 2 weeks to 6 years of age. Children who were adopted, premature, or known to be handicapped in any way were excluded from the standardization population. Although the authors

TABLE 18.4
STRATEGIES/ADAPTATIONS NEEDED FOR ASSESSING THE SEVERELY HANDICAPPED

Handicapping Condition	Examiner Requirements	Test Selection	Strategies/ Adaptations
Severe Communication Deficit	Awareness of child's limitations. Knowledge and experience with alternative communication systems.	Use tests with limited or no language demands Select tests designed for communication-disabled children.	Modify verbal instruction, alternate verbal and nonverbal instructions. Use gestures, pictures, visual cues to present tasks and allow the same techniques for responses. Provide language boards, rigid head pointers, bliss symbols, electronic voice synthesizers.
Motor Impairment	Awareness of child's limitations, medical management issues, positioning. Consultation with appropriate medical personnel; knowledge and experience with motor-impaired children. Be able to informally evaluate the child's vision, hearing, speech, sitting balance, arm-hand use, ability to indicate yes or no verbally or nonverbally.	Use tests requiring limited or no motor demands. Select tests designed for motor-impaired population.	Modify instructions and allow modification of response, such as choice-pointing, multiple choice format, stabilizing the child's hand, enlarging objects (blocks, beads, etc.) Allow enough time for child to respond. Provide rest periods.
Deficits in Social Interactions	Awareness of child's limitations. Experience with children with such deficits.	Use tests requiring minimal social interaction.	Keep social interactions simple, low demands for child.
Deficits in Attention, Organization	Awareness of child's limitations. Experience with children with such deficits.	Choose simple tests with clear guidelines.	Simple presentations of materials, short work periods.
Deficits in Motivation	Awareness of child's sources of motivation.		Use wide variety of reinforcers. Provide success experiences.

Note. Sources: Powers & Handleman, 1984; Short & Marcus, 1986; Sattler, 1988; and Wilhelm, Johnson, & Eisert, 1986.

of the test (Frankenburg et al., 1975) and some reviewers (Buros, 1972; Cross & Goin, 1977; Meier, 1976a; Salvia & Ysseldyke, 1981, 1988) reported adequate reliability and validity for its use as a screening device, Werner (1972) questioned the data reported in the 1968 manual because of the small samples of children included in the reliability and validity studies. Later studies seemed to confirm that the test has adequate tester–observer agreement, test–retest stability, and face and concurrent validity (Meier, 1976a; Salvia & Ysseldyke, 1981).

Several reviewers questioned the appropriateness of the norms because the standardization population contained a significantly higher proportion of white children and children whose fathers were white collar workers than warranted by the census distribution (Buros, 1972; Meier, 1976a; Salvia & Ysseldyke, 1981, 1988).

The DDST appears to be especially inappropriate for predicting future development and/or behavior for low socioeconomic status children and minority children who reside outside the Denver area. Werner (1972) also questioned the method for retaining items in the standardization of the test; the items were chosen on the basis of a pretest by four medical students.

Moriarity (1972) and Werner (1972) reported that the DDST is most useful at the intermediate age range (4 to 4½ years); it has questionable reliability in the first 2 years of life and a limited number of items in the age range below 3 months. It underidentified at-risk children under 30 months of age (identified by superior tests) and overidentified some older children. Thus, it seems to have limited value for identifying severely handicapped preschoolers. Harper and Wacker (1983) found that for a sample of 555 rural, lower SES preschool children, the DDST failed to identify 66% of the children who obtained scores in the mentally retarded range on the Stanford-Binet, Form L-M or the WPPSI. Werner (1972) emphasized that a screening tool is only as good as the sensitivity of its user to the behavior of young children, and she expressed doubt in the author's claim that after a few hours of training almost any adult could administer the test competently. The DDST-R (Frankenburg et al., 1981) is an abbreviated version of the DDST that provides a more graphic portrayal of a child's rate of development. However, the reports of underreferrals and ov-

erreferrals do not justify its use beyond a very gross screening instrument (Francis et al., 1987).

The Developmental Indicators for the Assessment of Learning-Revised (DIAL-R) (Mardell-Czudnaiski & Goldenberg, 1983) is an individually administered screening test designed to identify children with potential learning problems. It is intended to assess the motor, conceptual, and language skills for 2 to 6 year olds. Salvia and Ysseldyke's (1988) review of this instrument states that the norms are questionable, reliability is poor, and validity is not clearly established.

The Developmental Profile II (Alpern et al., 1986) is identical with the original Developmental Profile except for the deletion of items for ages 10 to 12, and changes in the manual such as clarification and rewording of directions using nonsexist language, including suggestions for assessment and the inclusion of a Profile Sheet. It is intended to be used with birth to 9 year olds to assess their physical, self-help, social, academic, and communication skills. Reviews by Harper (1985), Powers and Handleman (1984), White (1985), and Salvia and Ysseldyke (1988) are somewhat incongruent in that Harper states that the instruments can provide a reasonably accurate and brief review of developmental strengths and weaknesses, and Powers and Handleman view it as a useful screening device for children with severe developmental disabilities, whereas Salvia and Ysseldyke and White express concern about the representativeness of the norms and the use of IQ equivalency and age scores. Salvia and Ysseldyke also state that the degree of reliability is unknown and the evidence for validity scant.

The Developmental Activities Screening Inventory-II (DASI-II) (Fewell & Langley, 1984) is a revision of the DASI (Dubose & Langley, 1977) and is one of the few screening instruments designed for the severely handicapped infant/preschooler (Birth to 60 months of age). The DASI essentially is an informally administered, nonverbal screening instrument that has no data on norms, reliability, and validity (Dunst, 1985). However, it does have adaptive administration procedures for the examiner. The DASI-II (Fewell & Langley, 1984) remains an informal screening instrument that allows adaptation and can serve as an excellent prescriptive tool for classroom planning (Stahlecker, 1986). The authors reported reliability and validity data on the DASI (Rotatori et al., 1985) and concurrent validity data, but no information on reliability.

Cognition/Development

The Bayley Scales of Infant Development are individually administered scales that assess the developmental status of infants from birth to 30 months of age (Bayley, 1949;, 1969). There are Mental and Motor Scales as well as Infant Behavior record. Average testing time is 45 minutes for the Mental and Motor Scales. The examiner needs specific training and practice to administer and interpret the scales competently. There have been several reviews of the Bayley Scales (e.g., Buros, 1972, 1978; Francis et al., 1987). Damarin (1979) stated that "the standardization of the mental and motor scales is as good as or better than that of any other individual test, whether for infants, children, or adults" (p. 292). This opinion is shared by most reviewers. Damarin (1979) expressed concern because there are less complete data available for the Infant Behavior Record. His major concerns, however, were the paucity of interpretive information in the manual and the questionable retest reliability of the scales; both of these should be considered when using the scales with severely handicapped preschoolers. The predictive validity of the scales is dependent on the population of children being assessed; the scales have fairly high predictive validity for certain groups of medically subnormal children. The reliability data available on the scales suggest that over longer periods of time, the abilities assessed by the scales might change qualitatively with age. Therefore, one would need to be very careful about using the scales to measure a child's progress.

The Bayley scales are very valuable in assessing the current developmental functioning level of preschoolers. They can be used to determine developmental levels of severely handicapped young children over 30 months of age as long as one remembers that the normative tables should not be used to determine scores and that interpretation should be done cautiously. The test is widely used by occupational and physical therapists, nurses, psychologists, and educators for assessing severely handicapped preschoolers. It is imperative that those who use the instrument remember that the examiner must be well trained to administer the test and also must understand the principles underlying normal and abnormal development.

A modified version of the Bayley is available (Cross & Goin, 1977; Hoffman, 1974). It is designed to be used as a second-level test. After an initial score is obtained via standard procedures, the procedure is modified by changing the positioning of the child, having additional adults participate in the testing, or using alternative equipment. This version is useful as an informal way of using the Bayley scales.

Francis and colleagues (1987) report that the Bayley scales are the most frequently utilized measure of infant cognition, there has been extensive use of the scales in research, and although the scales might not predict later IQs, they probably are unrivaled in determining a child's developmental status relative to its age mates.

The Ordinal Scales of Infant Development/Infant Psychological Development Scale (IPDS) (Uzgiris & Hunt, 1975; 1987) consists of six ordinal scales developed to delineate the specific cognitive domains of sensorimotor development (based on Piaget's sensorimotor model) (Ulrey & Rogers, 1982). Uzgiris and Hunt (1975) developed these scales because of the shortcomings they perceived in traditional psychometric tests and to provide an instrument that could enable research to be conducted on theoretical issues in child development (Hogg & Sebba, 1986). Although Uzgiris and Hunt (1975) relied heavily on Piaget's observations for the development of the ordinal scales, they were most concerned about the sequential nature of development in various sensorimotor domains rather than the specific stages. The Uzgiris Hunt scales were to be independent of both chronological age and Piagetian stage placements. The Scales include: The Development of Visual Pursuit and the Permanence of Objects, The Development of Means for Obtaining Desired Environmental Events, the Development of Imitation (Vocal and Gestural), The Development of Operational Causality, The Construction of Object Relations in Space, and The Development of Schemes for Relating to Objects. These scales cover the developmental period from birth to 24 months. Uzgiris and Hunt describe the materials and the instructions needed for administering the scales and provide record forms for the scales. The actual materials must be gathered by the examiner. This is not a norm-referenced test and there are no scores obtained that would be analogous to an intellectual or developmental quotient.

However, Dunst (1980) published a manual for use with the scales that provides record forms and guidelines for intervention activities as well as age norms for scale items based on a survey of infant tests and developmental literature. His retrospective validation data for these age norms revealed significant positive correlations between scores on the Griffiths Mental Developmental Scales and the Uzgiris Hunt Scales for 36 handicapped and at-risk infants. Hefferman and Black (1984) report highly significant correlations (r = .92) between the Uzgiris and Hunt Scales and the Mental Scale of the Bayley Scales of Infant development for a population of 39 handicapped infants/toddlers. Ulrey and Rogers (1982), Gorrell (1985) Hogg and Sebba (1986), Francis and coworkers (1987), and Kahn (1987) report satisfactory test–retest and interobserver reliabilities for most of the items on the scales. A new text edited by Uzgiris and Hunt (1987) presents a review of theoretical and applied issues regarding the use of the scales since 1975.

Both of these issues are of import in judging the usefulness of these scales with severely handicapped infants. The book also provides a "select" bibliography on the scales. Uzgiris and Hunt (1975) did not foresee the use of the scales with other than normal infants, but the chapters by Kahn (1987), Cichetti and Mans-Wagener (1987), and Robinson and Rosenberg (1987) describe the use of the scales with populations other than normal infants. Siebert's chapter reviews the use of the scales both in planning programs for intervention and in assessing the effectiveness of different intervention strategies. Uzgiris and Hunt (1987) believe that the research described in the text demonstrates the validity of the scales for assessing the intellectual functioning of different types of populations.

However, Robinson and Rosenberg (1987) provide some cautionary notes regarding the use of the scales with children who have handicaps. An especially cogent consideration is that many severely handicapped infants/preschoolers have physical handicaps and sensory handicaps as well. Robinson and Rosenberg (1987) state that the sensory impairments can be integrally related to the child's primary condition or can be a consequence of problems created by that condition. They point out that in either case consideration must be given to the possibilities that the infant's sensory mechanisms or perception of input might be atypical and the effects the impairments have on opportunities for learning and organization of experience might be synergistic rather than just additive. They stress that the knowledge of multiple disabilities is essential to meaningful assessment and intervention with infants. Hefferman and Black (1984) state that even with the greater flexibility in administration and scoring of the scales, the cognitive level of children with motor impairments will be underestimated to a degree dependent on the child's ability to make adaptive, compensatory movements. Kahn's (1987) review of research indicates the scales can be considered reliable with severely and profoundly retarded persons, but that validity is not firmly established with this population.

Seibert (1987) provides a thorough review of the use of the scales in early intervention programs for children between birth and three years of age. He found three different intervention-related uses of the scales: documenting developmental level and monitoring child progress; evaluating the effectiveness of intervention; and guiding curriculum development. He also found that some researchers have adapted the scales to increase their utility by either modifying the administration procedures, reorganizing the results and scoring format, or reorganizing the content of the scales into different branches or domains. His review indicates that the use of the scales is not widespread in intervention settings and suggests that the degree of conceptual sophistication required to use the scales along with practical problems related to administration procedures, scoring, summarizing and interpreting results might have restricted the use of the scales. However, some writers believes that in Seibert's (1987) explanation of the role of assessment in intervention, he might be explaining the most important reason there is not widespread use of the scales. He describes three general functions of assessment in intervention: expanding one's categories for looking at children, providing the objectives for intervention, and suggesting how intervention can be conducted. The scales simply might not provide the functional objectives needed for assessing severely handicapped infants/preschoolers.

The Kent Infant Development Scale has 220 items that are considered appropriate for assessing children during the first year of life (Katoff, 1978; Katoff & Reuter, 1980). It takes approximately 30 minutes for a parent to administer, and the results are reported via one global score and five developmental domains. A manual is available that contains norms appropriate for use with at-risk populations and reports high reliability and concurrent validity. Clearly, this is an instrument worth investigating.

The Carolina Record of Infant Behavior (CRIB, 1979; Simeonsson, Huntington, Short, & Ware, 1982) is an experimental scale developed at the Carolina Institute for Research on Early Education of the Handicapped. It is designed to assess basic areas of development in children and is divided into three sections that assess a total of 39 behaviors. A unique feature of the CRIB is that it considers the variability that might be present in states of arousal or responsivity (Simeonsson, 1986). Simeonsson also reports that a multiyear research study with several hundred young handicapped children has demonstrated the CRIB's utility in documenting developmental and behavioral characteristics. Experimental use of the instrument is encouraged by the developers.

Shuster (1980) described a 300-item scale, the Indiana Preschool Developmental Assessment Scale, that assesses the developmental progress of children from birth to 6 years of age in six areas: gross and fine motor skills, receptive and expressive language, social skills, preacademic skill, personal autonomy, and reflex behavior (optional). Adaptation grids provide information on possible ways to adapt either the testing procedures and/or level and type of the child's responses.

Two other examples of prescriptive instruments that might be used with severely handicapped preschoolers are the Koontz Child Development Program (Koontz, 1974) and the Brigance Diagnostic Inventory of Early Development (Brigance, 1978). In the Koontz, four functional areas of development are assessed: gross motor, fine motor, social, and language abilities. Activities are suggested to teach or improve performance on the items. This program covers the developmental levels from 1 to 48 months. Although the reliability and validity data reported in the manual are limited, the interrater reliability for 23

children was .95 and validity was reported in terms of change in children after the Koontz program was initiated. The Brigance Inventory of Early Development was designed to be used with children below the developmental level of 7 years. It contains 98 skill sequences and lists objectives for the skills. It is both criterion- and norm-referenced; however, the normative information is based on age norms already published by other authors.

Bagnato and his colleagues (Bagnato et al., 1977; Bagnato et al., 1978) developed a screening instrument for standardizing and profiling the perceptions of significant adults who interact with a handicapped preschooler.

The Perception of Developmental Skills Profile is a rating scale of functional skills in communication, social/emotional adjustment, physical development, and cognitive development. It can be used to assess entry skills, estimate curriculum entry points, monitor progress, facilitate communication, compare the subjective measures of various adults, and work on eliminating discrepancies. The preliminary research findings indicated that it is a reliable method for assessing perceptions and that it appears to be promising as a means of monitoring progress. However, the authors emphasized that it should be used as an adjunct to other assessment procedures.

The Uniform Performance Assessment System (UPAS) (Haring, et al., 1981; White et al., 1978) was designed to monitor the progress of individuals who are learning skills normally acquired between birth and 6 years of age. Although the instrument resembles other developmental measures, relative to the areas/ domains that are assessed (Preacademic, Communication, Social/ Self-Help, Gross Motor, Inappropriate Behaviors), it is different because it is curriculum referenced and allows for adaptations to fairly assess a handicapped child's ability to accomplish certain types of activities. Reviewers of the instrument (Gresham, 1985; Harrington, 1984; Roszkowski, 1985) are uniformly positive in their praise of the instrument's adaptability and content validity but express concern about the lack of or unclear information regarding reliability and validity.

One of the most promising new instruments for handicapped infants/preschoolers is the Batelle Developmental Inventory (BDI) (Newborg et al., 1984). This is an individually administered inventory designed to assess the developmental strengths and weaknesses of children from birth to 8 years old. Numerous reviewers (Harrington, 1984, 1985; Neisworth & Bagnato, 1986; Sattler, 1988) point out the unique features of the instrument such as providing adaptive administration and scoring procedures for handicapped children, both norm-referenced and criterion-referenced data, and a multidemensional structure that allows for comprehensive analyses of functional capabilities based on input from multiple people and settings. The organization of the instrument into five domains (Personal-Social, Adaptive, Motor, Communication, and Cognitive) makes it easy for interdisciplinary team members to assess children independently so that both formative and summative evaluations can be done efficiently. All reviewers felt that standardization was adequate even though the sample size was small (N = 800) and most reviewers reported information on reliability and validity that support the use of the BDI (Harrington, 1984, 1985; Neisworth & Bagnato, 1986; Sattler, 1988). The usefulness of the BDI should be assessed with futher research but its usefulness also will depend on the examiner's ability to administer, score, and interpret it and the informant's ability to provide accurate information. A recent study (Bailey et al., 1987) investigated teachers' perceptions of the BDI when it was implemented statewide with handicapped preschoolers.

Overall, the teachers stated the usefulness of the BDI in a "moderately positive" direction. However, it was clear that it was not viewed as useful with severely/profoundly handicapped preschoolers as with mildly/moderately handicapped. Also of interest is the fact that the teachers reported that most of the items had clear administration procedures (90%), specified materials to be used (87%), and clearly indicated the criteria by which the item was to be scored (86%). Yet only 11 out of 76 teachers (14.5%) and 50 out of 247 protocols (20.2%) had no scoring errors. The errors ranged from simple math errors to correctly establishing a basal on one or more subtests. Relative to adaptations, teachers used adaptations with 86 of the 247 children (36%) and generally the teacher reported that about half of the adap-

tations were appropriate. Another area of concern was the calculation of extreme scores as the norm tables do not provide deviation quotients below 65. A formula is provided to calculate extreme scores, and in this sample, it was necessary to do this for 174 of the 247 children (75%). For 49 children, this resulted in a negative developmental quotient. Obviously, such a negative quotient is of no value. Although the findings of this particular study cannot be generalized across all professions, the findings do point out difficulties with even this well developed, well standardized instrument. The difficulties are especially apparent in its use with the severely handicapped.

An instrument created specifically for assessing the severely handicapped is the Developmental Assessment for the Severely Handicapped (DASH) (Dykes, 1980). The DASH is a criterion-referenced instrument that can be used either for screening or diagnosis of individual functioning within the birth to 6-year-old developmental range. The instrument covers five developmental areas: language, sensory–motor, social emotional, activities of daily living, and preacademic. Reviews of the DASH (Rotatori et al., 1985; Switzky, 1985; Wacker, 1985) vary considerably as Rotatori and colleagues simply report what is stated in the manual, including a concurrent validity study of the DASH and the Bayley Scales, resulting in a correlation coefficient of .97. Switzky (1985) describes the DASH assessment system as the best assessment/curricular system commercially available for the severely handicapped. Wacker (1985) evaluates both the assessment and programming components of the DASH and reports that the major difficulties with both components is the insufficient data regarding the reliability and validity of the system. He states that the use of the system in applied settings appears premature.

Adaptive Behavior

Technical adequacy and comprehensiveness were major shortcomings in the adaptive behavior measures of the 1970s. During the 1980s, new adaptive behavior instruments and revisions of old instruments were introduced. Two instruments that appear most appropriate for assessing the adaptive behavior of severely handicapped preschoolers are the SIB (Bruininks et al., 1984) and the Wisconsin Behavior Rating Scales (WBRS) (Song & Jones, 1980).

The SIB is an individually administered norm-referenced measure of skills needed to function independently in home, school and community settings. It was designed to be used with individuals ranging in age from infancy through adulthood. The SIB contains 14 subscales that are organized into four clusters: Motor Skills, Social Interaction and Communication Skills, Personal Living Skills, and Community Living Skills. These clusters can be combined into a total score called *Broad Independence*. There are also eight problem behavior areas grouped into three maladaptive behavior clusters plus a General Maladaptive Index. Reviews by Sattler (1988) and Salvia and Ysseldyke (1988) indicate adequate standardization and mixed opinions regarding the reliability and validity of the SIB. As usual, individual subscales have poor reliability, whereas Broad Independence is highly reliable. Salvia and Ysseldyke (1988) state that the evidence for the validity of the scale is excellent wheras Sattler (1988) states that additional research is needed with regard to the validity of the specialized scores. There is no doubt that research needs to be conducted with a severely handicapped preschool population to determine the usefulness of the SIB with this population.

The WBRS (Song & Jones, 1980; Song et al., 1984) is an adaptive behavior rating scale designed specifically for profoundly retarded individuals who function developmentally below the three-year-old level. The WBRS combines norm, criterion, and adaptive features to assess skills in 11 domains: Gross Motor, Fine Motor, Expressive Communication, Play Skills, Socialization, Domestic Activities, Eating, Toileting, Dressing, and Grooming. Reviews of the WBRS (Mace, 1985; Neisworth & Bagnato, 1986; Powers & Handleman, 1984; Rotatori et al., 1985; Sattler, 1988) indicate that it is one of the best adaptive behavior scales available for the severely and profoundly handicapped because it combines norm, criterion, and adaptive features in analyzing skills, it appears to have high interrater reliability, and good content and concurrent validity, and nearly all items have been operationalized and are directly observable.

Concerns center on the need to establish non-institutionalized norms. Mace (1985) also is concerned about the use of Age Equivalent scores and the present Percentile Ranks.

Motor Skills

The Peabody Developmental Motor Scales and Activity Cards (PDMS) (Folio & Fewell, 1983) are an assessment instrument and program guide in the area of developmental motor skills. There are two major scales: Gross Motor and Fine Motor. This is a standardized version of an original criterion-referenced instrument. According to Venn (1986) the 1982 version of the test offers important improvements over earlier versions. The program is intended for use with handicapped and nonhandicapped children from birth to 7 years of age and for handicapped children over 7 years of age whose motor development is within the birth to 7 developmental age range. The instrument was standardized on 617 infants and children in 20 states. Venn (1986) reports limited studies showing adequate test–retest and interrater reliability coefficients for both scales and criterion-related validity. He emphasizes the need for additional reliability and validity studies.

Both Venn (1986) and Neisworth and Bagnato (1986) view the package as unique and useful because it is a comprehensive system that can be used to develop a diagnostic-prescriptive program for children with neuromotor problems.

Diagnosing Autism

The assessment procedures that are being used with autistic children range from structured interview schedules to more formal standardized instruments. Churchill and colleagues (1971) developed a Standard Subject Description Checklist that can be useful in gathering information about other handicapped preschoolers as well. A structured psychiatric interview (DeMeyer et al., 1971) also has been developed that demonstrates that behavior traits can be coded, reliably rated, and profiled. Through use of the interview, the researchers were able to differentiate groups of children who ordinarily would be called autistic without further differentiation. Wing (1976b) provided a list of characteristic impairments, special skills, and behavior problems upon which a descriptive diagnosis can be based. She also developed a Standardized Scheme for Assessment (Wing,

1976a), which describes what the autistic child actually does. Wing and Gould (1978, 1979) developed the Children's Handicaps, Behaviour and Skills structured schedule; it is used "to obtain clinical information concerning a child's level of development in different areas of function, practical or school work skills require, and abnormalities of behavior present during the preceding month" (1979, p. 14).

Freeman and her colleagues (1979) developed the Behavior Observation Scale for Autism, which was designed to differentiate 30- to 60-month-old autistic, normal, and mentally retarded children along objective symptom axes. They found that merely recording frequency of behaviors was not sufficient to differentiate the children. All of the 67 objectively defined behaviors occurred in all groups except toe walking and finger wiggling, which did not appear in the normal group. The authors stated that percentages and frequencies must be reported and that the measures need to be applied developmentally.

Flaharty (1976a, 1976b) described the Evaluation and Prescription for Exceptional Children, which assesses a child's level of functioning from birth to 6 years of age in 15 skill areas. The items in each skill area were taken from published developmental and standardized tests. Patterns of strengths and weaknesses are indicated along with prescriptive goals to be met. It is a comprehensive procedure that can be administered by a teacher.

Schopler and Reichler (1979) developed a comprehensive inventory of behaviors and skills that is used to assess autistic and psychotic children as well as those with related developmental disabilities. The Psychoeducation Profile (PEP) is designed to identify uneven and idiosyncratic learning patterns in children who are functioning at a preschool level but are chronologically 1 to 12 years of age. Developmental functioning is assessed in seven areas: imitation, perception, fine motor skills, gross motor skills, eye-hand integration, cognitive performance, and cognitive verbal. A Pathology Scale identifies degrees of behavioral pathology. This is considered a prescriptive assessment instrument that will lead to an individualized education plan. A separate volume contains teaching strategies (Schopler et al., 1980). The age equivalents obtained on this test can be compared to the mental ages from other tests, but the test was designed primarily for planning in-

dividualized curricula rather than for arriving at a global score.

During the 1980s there were some improvements in the assessment of autistic individuals. Lerea (1987), Morgan (1988), Parks (1983), Powers and Handleman, (1984), and Short and Marcus (1986) review some of the assessment instruments available. The Childhood Autism Rating Scale (CARS) (Schopler et al., 1980) consists of directly observing a child in 15 different areas considered significant for autism. Parks (1983) reports adequate interrater reliability for the CARS but a need for additional validity data. Powers and Handleman (1984) report good reliability and validity for the ages studied. In Morgan's (1988) review of five objective instruments used for diagnosing autism, he states that the CARS is the strongest scale in terms of demonstrated psychometric properties. He believes additional discriminant validity and cross-validation studies are needed.

The Autism Screening Instrument for Educational Planning (ASIEP) (Knug et al., 1979, 1980) has been reviewed by Lerea (1987), Morgan (1988), Parks (1983), Short and Marcus (1986), Turton (1985), and Wikoff (1985) and the conclusions regarding its usefulness are inconsistent. The ASIEP consists of five separate scales: Autism Behavior Checklist (ABC), Sample of Vocal Behavior, Interaction Assessment, Educational Assessment of Functional Skills, and Prognosis of Learning Rate. The ASIEP was intended to be used with preschool and school-aged severely handicapped and autistic children. Each scale is a standardized checklist but the sample size and characteristics vary for each scale. The ABC is both the most widely used and most widely studied scale. The initial study of the ABC included 1,049 children (normal and handicapped). Much smaller samples were obtained for the other scales. Turton (1985) views the ASIEP as a "remarkable instrument" that can reliably and validly assess severely handicapped children in a school setting. Parks (1983) and Short and Marcus (1986) review only the ABC and indicate that the information on reliability and validity is limited. Wikoff (1985) reports that the ABC is the best subscale of the ASIEP relative to standardization, reliability, and validity, but he is concerned with its interpretation, as neither percentile ranks nor standard scores are provided. Raw scores are used for profile comparisons. He states that the

ASIEP might be used cautiously by trained professionals, but further reliability and validity studies are needed. Lerea (1987) states that the ASIEP and its ABC component require further validation.

There are numerous assessment instruments available, but each must be evaluated individually to determine its usefulness for severely handicapped preschoolers. Assessment instruments can be useful components of the assessment process, but the criteria suggested by Simeonsson and colleagues (1979) should be met. The instruments must have a theoretical or conceptual base, meet acceptable measurement standards, and be practical.

Brown (1987) developed an assessment rating scale for systematically examining an instrument on dimensions that are relevant for meaningful assessment. The rating scale asks the assessor to indicate the domains covered in the instrument, who administers the instrument, administration time, and data collection strategy. Then the assessor is asked to rate the clarity of administration and scoring methods, the relevance of the instrument (in terms of meaningfulness of items, for instruction, and as outcome indicators, whether data collection reflects the natural environment, and whether items cover an adequate range of behaviors) and how the instrument was individualized (by chronological age, physical abilities, student preference, parent input, and/or current environmental requirements/resources. Brown (1987) believes that on the basis of the information on the rating scale, an assessor can choose to reject a particular instrument, or adapt items, or include input that is missing. Thus, the rating scale is a reminder to the experienced assessor of what to include in meaningful assessment and provides guidelines for the novice assessor.

INTERVENTION

Two major purposes of assessment are the determination of eligibility for special services and the development of an individualized intervention plan. The mandatory components of the individualized education program (IEP) described in the *Federal Register* (1977) are a vital part of the as-

sessment process, not activities that are completed after assessment.

For the severely handicapped preschooler, the IEP should be called an individualized intervention program, because thorough assessment should have resulted in a statement of the child's present level of performance in many areas. Education is only one aspect of the services these children will need. In addition, Section 677(a) of P.L. 99–457 states that each handicapped infant or toddler's family must receive a multidisciplinary assessment of unique needs and services appropriate to meet such needs and a written individualized family service plan.

To translate data into an intervention program, the interdisciplinary team must do the following: record all data gathered for each area (environment, health, cognition, etc.); determine the present level of performance by describing the child's strengths and weaknesses; summarize what the child can do; establish priorities; write goal statements; make decisions regarding what types of intervention will lead to those goals; develop evaluation procedures for determining whether the intervention is working; and schedule follow-up meetings to ensure that the process continues. This process is not an exercise in listing test scores, it is the integration of quantitative and qualitative data from a variety of sources into a description of present level of functioning; that description then is analyzed to determine the priorities for the areas of concern. Obviously, one would try to modify on a behavior that is dangerous or potentially dangerous to the child or others before targeting an "annoying" mannerism. Once priorities are established and goals and specific objectives are determined, intervention should begin.

Brown and coworkers (1976) used the criterion of ultimate function as a standard for educational activities and established priorities on that basis. DuBose (1978) asserted that it is very important to establish priorities for activities and not focus on isolated units of behavior that do not lead to important changes in the child.

Hupp and Donofio (1983) stress the importance of conducting assessments that will enable the development of functional objectives that encompass learning needs from several related areas of instruction. They refer to these objectives as cross-referenced objectives because they are based on assessments that provide information regarding specific disabilities, general curriculum needs, and environmental demands.

Noonan and Reese (1984) make it clear that there are no curriculum models for the severely handicapped that are satisfactory in all regards. The following texts are a sample of those that provide guidelines and/or specific information for intervention: Bagnato and Neisworth (1981); Hogg and Sebba (1986, Vol. II.); Popovich (1981); Popovich and Laham (1981); Sailor and Guess (1983); Snell (1987); Van Etten and coworkers (1980); and Wambold and colleagues (1981).

The conflict over an operant, developmental, or functional approach to assessment and intervention has not ceased. Table 18.2 lists the advantages and disadvantages that are of concern in both intervention as well assessment models. Switzky (1979) contended that the normative developmental model has the greatest promise for a comprehensive approach, while Hogg (1975) questioned the relevance of normative development for programming objectives. There seems to be general agreement that developmental assessment should provide a description of developmental sequences along which a child would be expected to demonstrate developmental progress. Just how directly the developmental sequence of behaviors should translate into actual intervention targets is where disagreements arise. Specific behavioral items from the motor domain, such as maintaining head control, crawling, and soon appear to be legitimate objectives in themselves, whereas the behavior described in a cognitive item only might be the typical way a particular concept is manifested; alternative behaviors could conceivably be appropriate. Thus the concept, rather than the behavior, is more appropriately the target. Seibert (1987) states that an interventionist should ask why an objective has been chosen and what the child's mastery of the concept should enable him or her to do in an adaptive sense.

Cognitive objectives should be defined in terms of adaptive strategies rather than specific behaviors in a specific context. The focus must be on the adaptive performance of the child across a variety of contexts.

It must be emphasized that many of the behaviors included in developmental assessments might be physically impossible for severely handicapped infants/preschoolers, yet that does not mean there is nothing the child can master. Instead the goal becomes one of determining how the handicapped child might provide evidence of the concept through whatever behavioral or sensory systems that are intact. Another concern one must address relative to developmentally based intervention models is, should the intervention consist of general or prescriptive enrichment? The nonintrusive enrichment approach is not likely to work with the severely handicapped infant/preschooler, and the prescriptive approach might not lead to improvement beyond the specific "test behavior." A combination of strategies that allows the infant/preschooler opportunities to use the behavior across settings is most appropriate. When establishing an intervention program for severely handicapped infant/preschoolers, one should not only ask what is possible but what is reasonable and practical. What must this infant/preschooler learn to reach his or her potential?

The dominant instructional model is based on the behavioral approach. Haring and Bricker (1976) maintained that there is a developmental hierarchy in growth or changes in behavior—that behavior moves from simple to more complex responses and complex responses are the result of coordinating or modifying simpler component response forms. Bricker and her colleagues (Bricker et al., 1976; Bricker et al., 1976; Haring & Bricker, 1976; Robinson, 1972) indicated that the most positive intervention is a constructive interaction adaptation that consists of both the operant and developmental approaches because sequences of the preschooler's behavior depend on both biological and environmental influences. They provided developmental lattices and subsequent training routines. Their approach relies heavily upon carefully delineated sequences of developmental behavioral schemes that are for the most part unknown; years of research will be needed to verify the validity of these maps for severely handicapped preschoolers.

Bagnato and Neisworth (1979, 1981) suggested one way to ensure that data are translated into an appropriate intervention plan for handicapped preschoolers. They described a system for linking developmental diagnoses and curricula. Their process consists of selecting assessment devices in accordance with curriculum content, determining developmental levels within separate developmental areas, identifying developmental ceilings in each area, and matching the ceiling to appropriate curriculum objectives. The importance of the assessment-curriculum match is recognized by many authors; however, some authors believes that an existing curriculum should not dictate which areas of development are assessed. The child might have needs that are not included in the existing curriculum. A very specific curriculum will need to be developed to serve severely handicapped preschoolers.

DuBose (1978) stated that severely handicapped children need a functional, flexible, and qualitative assessment system that identifies current needs and appropiate strategies for meeting those needs. The outcome of such a system is individualization. She also reported that precise systematic instruction is most effective for directing the learning of severely impaired individuals.

Whatever the intervention model, the final plan must optimize the match between the learning characteristics of the child and the learning environment. It is crucial that the intervention also involve the child's family; intervention has the most positive and long-lasting effects when the family's needs are considered (Bricker & Casuso, 1979; DeMeyer, 1979; Garber, 1975, 1979; Heber, 1978; Heber & Garber, 1975; Kass et al., 1976; Los Angeles County Superintendent of Schools, 1972; Steele, 1971; Tjossem, 1976; Vincent & Broome, 1977; Wiegerink, 1980). Kaiser and Hayden (1984) state that special educators must appreciate that parenting can be every bit as important and helpful as teaching or therapy. Baker (1984) reviewed case studies and group studies of training with parents of developmentally disabled children and presents both parent and child outcome information. The results were generally positive for both groups.

Noonan and Reese (1984) believe that the educational validity of intervention for the severely handicapped child must be measured by addressing these questions: Has behavior change occurred as a function of the educational intervention (internal validity)? Did the educational intervention occur as specified in the treatment plan (educational integrity)? and Will the resultant behavior change be meaningful/beneficial to the child now and in the future, and is it considered to be valuable by those in the natural environment of that child (empirical and social validity)?

SUMMARY

Sailor and Haring (1977) defined three types of functional developmental assessment systems: screening; less systematic assessment that aids in the formulation of an IEP; and the most complex and time-consuming scheme, which proceeds from the initial screening to detailed instructional objectives. The latter is the system that is appropriate when assessing severely handicapped preschoolers.

Most tests do not "reach low enough" to pinpoint specific deficits in severely handicapped children (Webster et al., 1975). General and special assessments are needed, resulting in one continuous dynamic process in which repeated multicomponent assessment occur. A description of the child's developmental characteristics, the nature of the child's interactions with family members and others, and the environmental resources and limitations is needed (Kass et al., 1976). Minimal assessment of severely handicapped preschoolers should include medical, environmental, and behavioral evaluations as well as assessments of intellectual, perceptual, motor, language, and social/emotional development. Intervention will not "cure" these children, because most will remain severely handicapped, but intervention can lead to an improved quality of life and the prevention of deterioration.

A study by Maisto and German (1979), consistent with earlier findings reported by Brassell (1977) and Ramey and Smith (1977), showed substantial language and cognitive gains for a group of high-risk infants over a 1-year span. In this study the largest gains on the cognitive measure occurred in the sample of the youngest and most severely impaired infants. Brown and Royce (1980) reported that high-quality infant and preschool programs can have a long-term, positive impact on children's lives. Castro and Mastropieri's (1986) meta-analysis on intervention supports the importance of early identification and intervention.

Individuals who provide services to severely handicapped preschoolers have a responsibility to ensure that appropriate assessments occur so that judicious decisions are made and effective individualized interventions are developed.

REFERENCES

Alpern, G. D., Boll, T. J., & Shearer, M. (1986). *The Developmental Profile - II* (DP-II). Los Angeles: Western Psychological Services.

Alter, M., Gottlieb, B. W., & Gottlieb, J. (1986). Dimensions of assessment of severely and profoundly mentally retarded persons. In P. J. Lazarus & S. S. Strichart (Eds.). *Psychoeducational evaluation of children and adolescents with low-incidence* (pp. 123–153). Orlando: Grune & Stratton.

American Psychiatric Association. (1987). *Diagnostic and statistical manual of mental disorders*, 3rd ed. (rev.). Washington, DC: Author.

American Psychological Association. (1985). *Standards for educational and psychological tests*. Washington, DC: American Psychological Foundation.

Apgar, V. (1953). A proposal for the new method of evaluation of the newborn infant. *Current Research in Anesthesiology, 32*, 260–270.

Bagnato, S. J. (1984). Team congruence in developmental diagnosis and intervention: Comparing clinical judgment and child performance measures. *School Psychology Review, 13*(1), 7–16.

Bagnato, S. J., Eaves, R. C., & Neisworth, J. T. (1977). *Perceptions of developmental skills (PODS): A multi-source rating profile of functional capabilites for the preschool child*. University Park, PA: HI-COMP Preschool Project, Pennsylvania State University.

Bagnato, S. J., & Neisworth, J. T. (1979). Between assessment and intervention: Forging an assessment/curriculum linkage for the handicapped preschooler. *Child Care Quarterly, 8*, 179–194.

Bagnato, S. J., & Neisworth, J. T. (1981). *Linking Developmental Assessment and Curriculum*. Rockville, MD: Aspen.

Bagnato, S. J., Neisworth, J. T., & Eaves, R. C. (1978). A profile of perceived capabilities for the pre-school child. *Child Care Quarterly, 7*, 327–335.

Bailey, D. B., Vandiviere, P., Dellinger, J., & Munn, D. (1987). The Battelle Developmental Inventory: Teachers' perceptions and implementation data. *Journal of Psychoeducational Assessment, 5*(3), 217–226.

Bailey, D. B., & Wolery, M. (1984). *Teaching Infants and Preschoolers with Handicaps*. Columbus: Charles E. Merrill.

Baker, B. L. (1984). Intervention with families with young severely handicapped children. In J. Blacher (Ed.). *Severely Handicapped Young Children and Their Families* (pp. 319–376). Orlando: Academic Press.

Bayley, N. (1949). Consistency and variablity in the growth of intelligence from birth to 18 years. *Journal of Genetic Psychology, 75*, 165–196.

Bayley, N. (1969). *Bayley Scales of Infant Development*. Atlanta: Psychological Corporation.

Bell, J. (1983). Assessment of visual ability in the profoundly handicapped. *National Association of Deaf Blind Rubella Handicapped Newsletter, 29*, 16–17.

Bellamy, T. (1985). Severe disability in adulthood. *Newsletter of the Association for Persons with Severe Handicaps, 11*, 1, 6.

Bellugi, U. (1972). Development of language in the normal child. In J. E. McClean, D. E. Yoder, & R. L. Schiefelbusch (Eds.). *Language Intervention with the Retarded*. Baltimore: University Park Press.

Blacher, J. (Ed.). (1984). *Severely Handicapped Young Children and Their Families. Research in review*. Orlando: Academic Press.

Bracken, B. A. (1987). Limitations of preschool instruments and standards for minimal levels of technical adequacy. *Journal of Psychoeducational Assessment, 5*, 313–326.

Brassell, W. R. (1977). Intervention with handicapped infants: Correlates of progress. *Mental Retardation, 15*(4), 18–22.

Brazelton, T. B. (1973). *Neonatal Behavioral Assessment Scale*. Philadelphia: Lipincott.

Brazelton, T. B. (1984). *Neonatal Behavioral Assessment Scale*. Philadelphia: Lippincott.

Brazelton, T. B., Alstronic, E., & Lester, B. M. (1987). Specific neonatal behaviors: The Brazelton Behavior Assessment Scale. In J. D. Osofsky (Ed.). *Handbook of Infant Development* (2nd ed.). New York: John Wiley & Sons.

Bricker, D., & Casuso, V. (1979). Family involvement: A critical component of early intervention. *Exceptional Children, 46*(2), 108–116.

Bricker, D. D., Davis, J., Wahlin, L., & Evans, J. (1976). A motor training program for the developmentally young. *Mailman Center for Child Development Monograph Series*, No. 2.

Bricker, D. D., Dennison, L., & Bricker, W. A. (1976). A language intervention program for developmentally young children. *Mailman Center for Child Development Monograph Series*, No. 1.

Brigance, A. H. (1978). *Brigance Diagnostic Inventory of Early Development*. Woburn, MA: Curriculum Associates.

Browder, D. M. (1987). *Assessment of Individuals with Severe Handicaps*. Baltimore: Paul H. Brookes.

Brown, F. (1987). Meaningful assessment of people with severe and profound handicaps. In M. E. Snell (Ed.). *Systematic Instruction of Persons with Severe Handicaps* (3rd ed.) (pp. 39–63). Columbus: Merrill.

Brown, B., & Royce, J. (1980). Persistence of preschool effects. In S. Harel (Ed.). *The At Risk Infant.* Amsterdam: Excerpta Medica.

Brown, L., Nietupski, J., & Hamre-Nietupski, S. (1976). Criterion of ultimate functioning. In M. A. Thomas (Ed.). *Hey Don't Forget About Me.* Reston, VA: Council for Exceptional Children.

Bruininks, R., Woodcock, R., Weatherman, R., & Hill, B. (1984). *Scales of Independent Behavior.* Allen, TX: Teaching Resources/DLM.

Buros, O. K. (Ed.). (1972). *The Seventh Mental Measurements Yearbook* (2 vols.). Highland Park, NJ: Gryphon Press.

Buros, O. K. (Ed.). (1978). *The Eighth Mental Measurements Yearbook.* Highland Park, NJ: Gryphon Press.

Carolina Record of Infant Behavior. (1979). University of North Carolina, Carolina Institute for Research on Early Education of the Handicapped.

Castro, G., & Mastropieri, M. A. (1986). The efficacy of early intervention programs for handicapped children: A meta-analysis. *Exceptional Children, 52*(5), 417–424.

Chase, J. B. (1985). Assessment of developmentally disabled children. *School Psychology Review, 14*(2), 150–154.

Churchill, D. W., Alpern, G. D., & DeMeyer, M. K. (1971). *Infantile Autism.* Springfield, IL: Thomas.

Cicchetti, D., & Mans-Wagener, L. (1987). Sequences, stages, and structures in the organization of cognitive development in infants with Down Syndrome. In I. C. Uzgiris & J. M. Hunt (Eds.). *Infant Performance and Experience: New Findings with the Ordinal Scales* (pp. 281–310). Urbana, IL: University of Illinois Press.

Coons, C. E., & Frankenburg, W. I. (1980). A combined developmental and environmental screening procedure: A preliminary report. In S. Harel (Ed.). *The At Risk Infant.* Amsterdam: Excerpta Medica.

Cross, L., & Goin, K. W. (1977). *Indentifying Handicapped Children: A Guide to Casefinding, Screening, Diagnosis, Assessment, and Evaluation.* New York: Walker.

Damarin, F. (1979). Bayley Scales of Infant Development. In O. K. Buros (Ed.). *Eighth Mental Measurements Yearbook,* Vol. 1. Highland Park, NJ: Gryphon Press.

Danielson, L. (1980). *Percent of children ages 3–5 years served under P.L. 94–142 by handicapping condition. School year 1979–80.* Washington, DC: Division of Special Education of State Department of Education.

DeMeyer, M. K. (1979). *Parents and Children in Autism.* New York: Wiley.

DeMeyer, M. K., Barton, S., Alpern, G. D., et al. (1974). The measured intelligence of autistic children. *Journal of Autism and Childhood Schizophrenia, 4,* 42–60.

DeMeyer, M. K., Norton, J. A., & Barton, S. (1971). Social and adaptive behaviors of autistic children as measured in a structured psychiatric interview. In D. W. Churchill, G. D. Alpern, & M. K. DeMeyer (Eds.). *Infantile Autism.* Springfield, IL: Thomas.

DuBose, R. F. (1978). Identification. In M. E. Snell (Ed.). *Systematic Instruction of the Moderately and Severely handicapped.* Columbus, OH: Merrill.

Dubose, R. F., & Langley, M. B. (1977). *The Developmental Activities Screening Inventory.* Boston: Teaching Resources.

Dunst, C. J. (1980). *A Clinical and Educational Manual for Use with the Uzgiris and Hunt Scales of Infant Psychological Development.* Baltimore: University Park Press.

Dust, C. J. (1985). Review of Developmental Activities Screening Inventory. In J. V. Mitchell (Ed.). *The Ninth Mental Measurements Yearbook,* Vol. 1. Lincoln, NE: The Buros Institute for Mental Measurement.

Dykes, M. K. (1980). *Developmental Assessment for Severely Handicapped.* Austin, TX: Exceptional Resources.

Egan, D. F., Illingworth, R. S., & MacKeith, R. C. (1971). *Developmental Screening 0–5 years.* London: Spastice International Medical Publications.

Federal Register. (1977). *42,*(163), 42474–42517.

Fewell, R. R. (1983). New directions in the assessment of young handicapped children. In C. R. Reynolds & J. H. Clark (Eds.). *Assessment and Programming for Young Children with Low-incidence Handicaps.* New York: Plenum Press.

Fewell, R. R., & Langley, M. B. (1984). *Developmental Activities Screening Inventory* (DASI-II). Austin, TX: Pro-Ed.

Flaharty, R. (1976a). EPEC: Evaluation and prescription for exceptional children. In E. R. Ritvo, B. J. Freeman, E. M. Ornitz, & P. E. Tanguay (Eds.). *Autism Diagnosis, Current Research and Management.* New York: Spectrum.

Flaharty, R. (1976b). Preschool assessment. In E. R. Ritvo, B. J. Freeman, E. M. Ornitz, & P. E. Tanguay (Eds.). *Autism Diagnosis, Current Research and Management.* New York: Spectrum.

Folio, M. R., & Fewell, R. R. (1983). *Peabody Developmental Motor Scales and Activity Cards manual.* Allen, TX: DLM.

Francis, P. L., Self, P. A., & Horowitz, F. D. (1987). The behavioral assessment of the neonate: An overview. In J. D. Osofsky (Ed.). *Handbook of Infant Development* (2nd ed.) (pp. 723–779). New York: Wiley.

Frankenburg, W. K. (1986). *Revised Denver Prescreening Devlopmental Questionnaire*. Denver: Denver Developmental Materials.

Frankenburg, W. K., & Dodds, J. B. (1967). Denver Developmental Screening Test. *Journal of Pediatrics, 71*, 181–191.

Frankenburg, W., Dodds, J., Fandal, A., Kazuk, E., & Cohrs, M. (1975). *Denver Developmental Screening Test. Reference Manual* (rev. ed.). Denver: LADOCA Project and Publishing Foundation.

Frankenburg, W. K., Fandal, A. W., Kemper, M. B., & Thornton, S. M. (1980). A practical approach to routine and periodic developmental screening of all children. In S. Harel (Ed.). *The At Risk Infant*. Amsterdam: Excerpta Medica.

Frankenburg, W. K., Fandal, A. W., Sciarillo, W. D., & Burgess, D. (1981). The newly abbreviated and revised Denver Developmental Screening Test. *Journal of Pediatrics, 99*, 995–999.

Frankenburg, W. K., Fandal, A. W., & Thornton, S. M. (1987). Revision of Denver Prescreening Developmental Questionnaire. *Journal of Pediatrics, 110*, 653–657.

Freeman, B. J., Tonick, L., Ritvo, E. R., Guthrie, D., & Schroth, P. (1979, September). *The Behavior Observation Scale for Autism: Frequency Analysis*. Paper presented at the meeting of the American Psychological Association, New York. (ERIC Document Reporduction Service No. ED 181 702)

Fuchs, L. S., & Fuchs, D. (1986). Linking assessment to instructional interventions: An overview. *School Psychology Review, 15*(3), 318–323.

Gabel, S., & Erickson, M. T. (Eds.). (1980). *Child Development and Developmental Disabilities*. Boston: Little Brown.

Garber, H. (1975). Intervention in infancy: A developmental approach. In M. Begab, & S. Richardson (Eds.). *The mentally Retarded and Society*. Baltimore: University Park Press.

Garber, H. L. (1979). Bridging the gap from preschool to school for the disadvantaged child. *School Psychology Digest, 8*(3), 303–310.

Garwood, S. G., & Fewell, R. R. (1983). *Educating Handicapped Infants: Issues in Development and Intervention*. Rockville, MD: Aspen.

Geiger, W. L., & Justen, J. E. (1983). Definitions of severely handicapped and requirements for teacher certification: A survey of state departments of education. *Journal of the Association for the Severely Handicapped, 8*(1), 25–29.

Gerken, K. C. (1983). Assessment of severely handicapped preschoolers. In K. D. Paget & B. A. Bracken (Eds.). *The Psychoeducational Assessment of Preschool Children*. New York: Grune & Stratton.

Gorrell, J. (1985). Ordinal Scales of Psychological Development. In D. J. Keyser & R. C. Sweetland (Eds.). *Test Critiques*, Vol. II. Kansas City: Test Corporation of America.

Greenberg, N. H., & Hurley, J. (1971). The maternal personality inventory. In J. Hellmuth (Ed.). *Exceptional Infant, Vol. 2: Studies in Abnormatlities*. New York: Brunner/Masel.

Gresham, F. M. (1985). Review of Uniform Performance Assessment System. In J. V. Mitchell (Ed.). *The Ninth Mental Measurements Yearbook*, Vol. 2. Lincoln, NE: The Buros Institute for Mental Measurement.

Grossman, H. J. (Ed.). (1983). *Classification in Mental Retardation*. Washington, DC: American Association on Mental Deficiency.

Guralnick, M., & Richardson, H. (Eds.). (1980). *Pediatric Education and the Needs of Exceptional Children*. Baltimore: University Park Press.

Harel, S. (Ed.). (1980). *The At Risk Infant*. Amsterdam: Excerpta Medica.

Haring, N. G. (1977). Measurement and evaluation procedures for programming with the severely and profoundly handicapped. In E. Sontag, J. Smith, & N. Certo (Eds.). *Educational Programming for the Severely and Profoundly Handicapped*. Reston, VA: Division on Mental Retardation, The Council for Exceptional Children.

Haring, N. G., & Bricker, D. (1976). Overview of comprehensive services for the severely/profoundly handicapped. In N. G. Haring and L. J. Brown (Eds.). *Teaching the Severely Handicapped*. New York: Grune & Stratton.

Haring, N. G., White, O. R., Edgar, E. B., Affleck, J. Q., & Hayden, A. H. (1981). *The Uniform Performance Assessment System*. Toronto: Charles E. Merrill.

Harper, D. C. (1985). Review of Developmental Profile II. In J. V. Mitchell (Ed.). *The Ninth Mental Measurements Yearbook*, Vol. I. Lincoln, NE: The Buros Institute for Mental Measurement.

Harper, D. C., & Wacker, D. P. (1983). The efficiency of the Denver Developmental Screening Test with rural disadvantaged preschool children. *Journal of Pediatric Psychology, 8*, 273–283.

Harrington, R. G. (1979). A review of Sattler's modifications of standard intelligence tests for use with handicapped children. *The School Psychology Digest, 8*, 296–302.

Harrington, R. G. (1984). Preschool screening: The

school psychologist perspective. *School Psychology Review, 13*(3), 363–374.

Harrington, R. G. (1985). Battelle Developmental Inventory. In D. J. Keyser, & R. C. Sweetland (Eds.). *Test Critiques,* Vol. II. Kansas City: Test Corporation of America.

Hartlage, L. C., & Lucas, D. G. (1973). *Mental Development Evaluation of the Pediatric Patient.* Springfield, IL: Thomas.

Heber, R. (1978). Sociocultural mental retardtion—A longitudinal study. In D. Forgays (Ed.). *Primary Prevention of Psychopathology, Vol. II: Environmental Influences.* Hanover, NH: University Press of New England.

Heber, R., & Garber, H. (1975). The Milwaukee project: A study of the use of family intervention to prevent cultural-familial mental retardation. In B. Friedlander, G. Sterritt, & G. Kirk (Eds.). *Exceptional Infant, Vol. 3: Assessment and Intervention.* New York: Brunner/Mazel.

Hefferman, L., & Black, F. W. (1984). Use of the Uzgiris and Hunt Scales with handicapped infants: Concurrent validity of the Dunst age norms. *Journal of Psychoeducational Assessment, 2,* 159–168.

Hobel, C. J. (1980). A dynamic maternal risk factor scale. In S. Harel (Ed.). *The At Risk Infant.* Amsterdam: Excerpta Medica.

Hoffman, H. (1974). *The Bayley Scales of Infant Development: Modifications for Youngsters with Handicapped Conditions.* Commack, NY: Suffolk Rehabilitation Center.

Hogg, J. (1975). Normative development and educational program planning for severely educationally subnormal children. In C. C. Kiernan & F. P. Woodford (Eds.). *Behavioral Modification with the Severely Retarded.* Amsterdam: Associated Scientific.

Hogg, J., & Sebba, J. (1986). *Profound Retardation and Multiple Impairment* (Vols. 1–2). London: Croom Helm.

Horwitz, F. D. (1978). Normal and abnormal child development. In K. E. Allen, V. A. Holm, & R. L. Schiefelbusch (Eds.). *Early Intervention—A Team Approach.* Baltimore: University Park Press.

Horowitz, F. D., Sullivan, J., & Linn, P. (1978). Stability and instability in the newborn infant: The quest for illusive threads. In A. J. Sameroff (Ed.). Organization and stability of newborn behavior: A commentary on the Brazleton Neonatal Behavioral Assessment Scale. *Monographs of the Society for Research in Child Development, 43*(5–6, Serial No. 177).

Hupp, S. C., Donofio, M. N. (1983). Assessment of multiply and severely handicapped learners for the development of cross-referenced objectives. *JASH, 8*(3), 17–28.

Illingworth, R. S. (1975). *The Development of the Infant and Young Child, Normal and Abnormal* (6th ed.). Edinburgh: Churchill.

Irons, D., Irons, T., & Maddux, C. D. (1984). A survey of perceived competence among psychologists who evaluate students with severe handicaps. *JASH, 9*(1), 55–60.

Johnston, R. B., & Magrab, P. R. (1976). *Developmental Disorders: Assessment Treatment and Education.* Baltimore University Park Press.

Kahn, J. V. (1987). Uses of the scales with mentally retarded populations. In I. C. Uzgiris & J. M. Hunt (Eds.). *Infant Performance and Experience: New Findings with the Ordinal Scales.* Urbana: University of Illinois Press.

Kaiser, C. E., & Hayden, A. H. (1984). Clinical research and policy issues in parenting severely handicapped infants. In J. Blacher (Ed.). *Severely Handicapped Young Children and Their Families* (pp. 275–318). Orlando: Academic Press.

Kass, E. R., Sigman, M., Bromwich, R. R., & Parmelee, A. H. (1976). Educational intervention with high risk infants. In T. D. Tjossem (Ed.). *Intervention Strategies for High Risk Infants and Young Children.* Baltimore: University Park Press.

Katoff, L. (1978). The development and evaluation of the KID scale. (Doctoral dissertation, Kent State University) *Dissertation Abstracts International, 39,* Section B, Issue No. 2, 98.

Katoff, L., & Reuter, J. (1980). Review of developmental screening tests for infants. *Journal of Clinical Child Psychology, 9,* 30–34.

Keyser, D. J., & Sweetland, R. C. (Eds.). (1984–86). *Test critiques,* Volumes I-V. Kansas City: Test Corporation of America.

Knobloch, H., & Pasamanick, B. (1974). *Gesell and Amatruda's Developmental Diagnosis* (3rd ed.). New York: Harper and Row.

Knug, D. A., Arick, J. R., & Almond, P. J. (1979). Autism Screening Instrument for Education Planning: Background and development. In J. Gilliam (Ed.). *Autism: Diagnosis, Instruction, Management, and Research.* Austin: University of Texas at Austin Press.

Knug, D. A., Arick, J. R., & Almond, P. J. (1980). Behavior checklist for identifying severely handicapped individuals with high levels of autistic behavior. *Journal of Child Psychiatry, 21,* 221–229.

Koontz, C. W. (1974). *Koontz Child Development Program: Training activities for the first 48 months.* Los Angeles: Western Psychological Services.

Kopp, C. B. (1987). Developmental risk: historical reflections. In J. D. Osofsky (Ed.). *Handbook of Infant Development* (2nd ed.). New York: Wiley.

Korones, S. B. (1976). *High-risk Newborn Infants* (2nd ed.). St. Louis: Mosby.

Krajicek, M. J., & Tearney, A. I. (Eds.). (1977). *Detec-*

tion of Developmental Problems in Children. Baltimore: University Park Press.

Lazarus, P. J., & Strichart, S. S. (Eds.). (1986). *Psychoeducational Evaluation of Children and Adolescents with Low-incidence Handicaps.* Orlando: Grune & Stratton.

Lerea, L. E. (1987). The behavioral assessment of autistic children. In D. J. Cohen & A. M. Donellan (Eds.). *Handbook of Autism and Developmental Disorders.* Silver Spring, MD: V. H. Winston & sons.

Lessen, E., & Rose, T. L. (1980). State definitions of preschool handicapped populations. *Exceptional Children, 46*(6), 467–469.

Lidz, C. S. (1986). Preschool assessment: Where have we been and where are we going? *Special Services in the Schools, 2*(23), 141–159.

Lipsitt, L. P. (1979). The newborn as informant. In R. R. Kearsley & I. E. Sigel (Eds.). *Infants at Risk: Assessment of Cognitive Functioning.* Hillsdale, NJ: Erlbaum.

Littman, G., & Parmelee, A. H. (1978). Medical correlates of infant development. *Pediatrics, 61,* 470–474.

Lord, L. (1977). Normal motor development in the infant. In M. J. Krajicek & A. I. Tearney (Eds.). *Detection of Developmental Problems in Children.* Baltimore: University Park Press.

Los Angeles County Superintendent of Schools. (1972). *An education program for multihandicapped children.* Washington, DC: Office of Education. (ERIC Document Reproduction Service No. ED 065 951)

Mace, C. F. (1985). Review of Wisconsin Behavior Rating Scale. In J. V. Mitchell (Ed.). *The Ninth Mental Measurements Yearbook,* Vol. 2. Lincoln, NE: The Buros Institute for Mental Measurements.

Maisto, A. A., & German, M. L. (1979). Variables related to progress in a parent infant training program for high risk infants. *Journal of Pediatric Psychology, 4,* 409–419.

Magrab, P. R., & Johnston, R. B. (1980). Mental retardation. In S. Gabel & M. T. Erickson (Eds.). *Child Development and Developmental Disabilities.* Boston: Little Brown.

Malone, P. J. (1980). Program to reduce emergent exceptionalities in development. In S. Harel (Ed.). *The At Risk Infant.* Amsterdam: Excerpta Medica.

Marcus, L., & Baker, A. (1986). Assessment of autistic children. In R. J. Simeonsson (Ed.). *Psychological and Developmental Assessment of Special Children.* Boston: Allyn & Bacon.

Mardell-Czudnaiski, C., & Goldenberg, D. (1983). *Developmental Indicators for the Assessment of Learning - Revised.* Edison, NJ: Childcraft Education.

McGovern, J. E. (1978). Introduction. In N. H. Fallen & J. E. McGovern (Eds.), *Young Children with Special Needs.* Columbus, OH: Merrill.

Meier, J. (1973). *Screening and Assessment of Young Children at Developmental Risk* (DHEW Publ. No. [OS] 73–90). Washington, DC: Department of Education and Welfare.

Meier, J. H. (1976a). *Developmental and Learning Disabilities.* Baltimore: University Park Press.

Meier, J. H. (1976b). Screening, assessment, and intervention for young children at developmental risk. In T. D. Tjossem (Ed.). *Intervention Strategies for High Risk Infants and Young Children.* Baltimore: University Park Press.

Mitchell, J. V. (Ed.). (1985). *The Ninth Mental Measurements Yearbook* (2 vols.). Lincoln: The Buros Institute of Mental Measurements.

Morgan, S. (1988). Diagnostic assessment of autism: A review of objective scales. *Journal of Psychoeducational Assessment, 6,* 139–151.

Moriarity, A. E. (1972). Denver Developmental Screening Test. In O. K. Buros (Ed.), *Seventh mental measurements yearbook,* Vol. 1. Highland, NJ: Gryphon Press.

Mussen, P. H. (Ed.). (1983). *Handbook of child psychology* (4th ed.; 4 vols). New York: Wiley.

Neisworth, J. T., & Bagnato, S. J. (1986). Curriculum-based developmental assessment: Congruence of testing and teaching. *School Psychology Review, 15*(2), 180–199.

Newborg, J., Stock, J. R., Wnek, L., Guiduboldi, J., & Svinicki, J. (1984). *The Battelle Developmental Inventory.* Allen, TX: DLM Teaching Resources.

Newland, T. E. (1971). Psychological assessment of exceptional children and youth. In W. M. Cruickshank (Ed.), *Psychology of exceptional children and youth* (3rd ed.). Englewood Cliffs, NJ: Prentice-Hall.

Newland, T. E. (1980). Psychological assessment of exceptional children and youth. In W. M. Cruickshank (Ed.), *Psychology of Exceptional Children and Youth* (4th ed.). Englewood Cliffs, NJ: Prentice-Hall.

Noonan, M. J., & Reese, R. M. (1984). Educability: Public policy and the role of research. *Journal of the Association for the Severely Handicapped, 9*(1), 8–15.

Olley, J. G., & Rosenthal, S. L. (1985). Current issues in school services for students with autism. *School Psychology Review, 14*(2), 166–170.

Ornitz, E. M., & Ritvo, E. R. (1976). Medical assessment. In E. R. Ritvo, B. J. Freeman, E. M. Ornitz, & P. E. Tanguay (Eds.). *Autism Diagnosis. Current Research and Management.* New York: Spectrum.

Osofsky, J. D. (Ed.). (1987). *Handbook of Infant Development* (2nd ed.). New York: John Wiley & Sons.

Paget, K. D., & Nagle, R. J. (1986). A conceptual model

of preschool assessment. *School Psychology Review, 15*(2), 154–165.

Parks, S. L. (1983). The assessment of autistic children: A selective review of available instruments,. *Journal of Autism and Developmental Disorders, 13,* 255–267.

Parmelee, A. H., & Michaelis, R. (1971). Neurological examination of the newborn. In J. Hellmuth (Ed.). *Exceptional Infant, Vol. 2: Studies in Abnormalities.* New York: Brunner/Mazel.

Parmelee, A. H., Sigman, M., Kopp, C. B., & Haber, A. (1975). The concept of a cumulative risk score for infants. In N. Ellis (Ed.). *Aberrant Development in Infancy: Human and Animal Studies.* Hillsdale, NJ: Erlbaum.

Parmelee, A. H., Sigman, M., Kopp, C. B., & Haber, A. (1976). Diagnosis of the infant at high risk for mental, motor, and sensory hadicaps. In T. D. Tjossem (Ed.). *Intervention Strategies for High Risk Infants and Young Children.* Baltimore: University Park Press.

Peterson, N. L. (1987). *Early Intervention for Handicapped and At-Risk Children.* Denver: Love.

Popovich, D. (1981). *Effective Educational and Behavioral Programming for Severely and Profoundly Handicapped Students.* Baltimore: Paul H. Brookes.

Popovich, D., & Laham, S. L. (Eds.). (1981). *The Adaptive Behavior Curriculum,* Volume 2. Baltimore: Paul H. Brookes.

Powers, M. D. (1985). Behavioral assessment and the planning and evaluation of interventions for developmentally disabled children. *School Psychology Review, 15*(2), 155–161.

Powers, M. D., & Handleman, J. S. (1984). *Behavioral Assessment of Severe Developmental Disabilities.* Rockville, MD: Aspen.

Prechtl, H. F. R. (1968). Neurological findings in newborn infants after pre- and paranatal complications. In J. H. P. Jonxis, H. K. A. Visser, & J. A. Troelstra (Eds.). *Aspects of Prematurity and Dysmaturity.* Springfield, MA: C. C. Thomas.

Prechtl, H. F. R. (1982). Assessment methods for the newborn infant: A critical evaluation. In P. Stratton (Ed.). *Psychobiology of the Human Newborn.* New York: Wiley.

Prior, M. R. (1979). Cognitive abilities and disabilities in infantile autism: A review. *Journal of Abnormal Child Psychology, 7,* 357–380.

Public Law 98–527. (1984). *Section 102(7).* Washington, DC: 99th Congress.

Public Law 99–457. (1986). *Education of the Handicapped Act Amendments of 1986.* Washington, DC: 99th Congress.

Ramey, C. T., & Smith, B. J. (1977). Assessing the in-tellectual consequences of early intervention with high-risk infants. *American Journal of Mental Deficiency, 81,* 318–324.

Reynolds, C. R., & Clark, J. H. (Eds.). (1983). *Assessment and Programming for Young Children with Low-incidence Handicaps.* New York: Plenum Press.

Ritvo, E. R., & Freeman, B. J. (1978). National Society for Autistic Children's definition of syndrome of autism. *Journal of Autism and Developmental Disorders, 8,* 162–167.

Robinson, C. C. (1972). *Analysis of Stage Four and Five Object Permanence Concepts as a Discriminated Operant.* Unpublished doctoral dissertation. George Peabody College.

Robinson, C. C., & Rosenberg, S. (1987). A strategy for assessing infants with motor impairments. In I. C. Uzgiris & J. M. Hunt (Eds.). *Infant Performance and Experience: New Findings with the Ordinal Scales* (pp. 311–339). Urbana, IL: University of Illinois Press.

Robinson, N. M., & Robinson, H. B. (1976). *The Mentally Retarded Child* (2nd ed.). New York: McGraw-Hill.

Rogers, S. J. (1986). Assessment of infants and preschoolers with low-incidence handicaps. In P. J. Lazarus & S. S. Strichart (Eds.). *Psychoeducational Evaluation of Children and Adolescents with Low-incidence Handicaps* (pp. 17–39). Orlando: Grune & Stratton.

Ross, L. E., & Leavitt, L. A. (1976). Process research: Use in prevention and intervention with high risk children. In T. D. Tjossm (Ed.). *Intervention Strategies for High risk Infants and Young Children.* Baltimore: University Park Press.

Roszkowski, M. J. (1985). Review of Uniform Performance Assessment System. In J. V. Mitchell (Ed.). *The Ninth Mental Measurements Yearbook,* Vol. 2. Lincoln, NE: The Buros Institute for Mental Measurements.

Rotatori, A. F., Schwenn, J. O., & Fox, R. A. (1985). *Assessing Severely and Profoundly Handicapped Individuals.* Springfield, IL: Charles C. Thomas.

Rutter, M. (1979). Language cognition and autism. In R. Katzman (Ed.). *Congenital and Acquired Cognitive Disorders.* New York: Raven Press.

Sabatino, D. A. (1979a). Systematic procedure for ascertaining learner characteristics. In D. A. Sabatino & T. L. Miller (Eds.). *Describing Learner Characteristics of Handicapped Children and Youth.* New York: Grune & Stratton.

Sabatino, D. A. (1979b). The seriously handicapped. In D. A. Sabatino & T. L. Miller (Eds.). *Describing Learner Characteristics of Handicapped Children and Youth.* New York: Grune & Stratton.

Sailor, W., & Guess, D. (1983). *Severely Handicapped Students - An Instrumental Design.* Boston: Houghton Mifflin.

Sailor, W., & Haring, N. G. (1977). Some current directions in education of the severely/multiply impaired. *AAESPH Review, 2,* 3–23.

Salvia, J., & Ysseldyke, J. (1981). *Assessment in Special and Remedial Education* (2nd ed.). Boston: Houghton Mifflin.

Salvia, J., & Ysseldyke, J. E. (1988). *Assessment in Special and Remedial Education* (4th ed.). Boston: Houghton Mifflin.

Sameroff, A. J., & Cavanaugh, P. J. (1979). Learning in infancy: A developmental perspective. In J. D. Osofsky (Ed.). *Handbook of Infant Development.* New York: John Wiley & sons.

Sattler, J. (1972a). *Final Report: Intelligence Test Modificatons on Handicapped and Nonhandicapped Children.* San Diego: San Diego State University Foundation.

Sattler, J. (1972b). *Supplement to Final report: Intelligence Test modifications on Handicapped and Nonhandicapped Children.* San Diego: San Diego State University Foundation.

Sattler, J. (1974). *Assessment of Children's Intelligence* (Rev. reprint). Philadelphia: Saunders.

Sattler, J. M. (1988). *Assessment of Children* (3rd ed). San Diego: Author.

Sattler, J., & Theye, F. (1967). Procedural, situational and interpersonal variables in individual intelligence testing. *Psychological Bulletin, 68,* 347–360.

Sattler, J. J., & Tozier, L. L. (1970). A review of intelligence test modifications used with cerebral palsied and other handicapped groups. *Journal of Special Education, 4,* 391–398.

Schopler, E., & Reichler, R. J. (1979). *Individualized Assessment and Treatment for Autistic and Developmentally Disabled Children, Vol. 1: Psychoeducational Profile.* Baltimore: University Park Press.

Schopler, E., Reichler, R. J., DeVellis, R. F., & Daly, K. (1980). *Toward Objective Classification of Childhood Autism: Childhood Autism Rating Scale (CARS).* Unpublished manuscript, University of North Carolina.

Scurletis, T. D., Headrick-Hynes, M., Turnbull, C. D., & Fallon R. (1976). Comprehensive devlopmental health services: A concept and a plan. In T. D. Tjossem (Ed.). *Intervention Strategies for High Risk Infants and Young Children.* Baltimore: University Park Press.

Sebba, J. (1978). *A system for Assessment and Intervention for Preschool Profoundly Retarded Multiply Handicapped Children.* Unpublished M.Ed. thesis. University of Manchester, Manchester, England.

Seibert, J. M. (1987). Uses of the scales in early intervention. In I. C. Uzgiris and J. M. Hunt (Eds.). *Infant Performance and Experience: New Findings with the Ordinal Scales* (pp. 340–370). Urbana, IL: University of Illinois Press.

Short, A. B., & Marcus, L. M. (1986). Psychoeducational evaluation of autistic children and adolescents. In P. J. Lazarus & S. S. Strichart (Eds.). *Psychoeducational Evaluation of Chidren and Adolescents with Low-incidence Handicaps* (pp. 155–180). Orlando: Grune & Stratton.

Shuster, S. K. (1980). Programming for parents of young handicapped children. In S. Harel (Ed.). *The At Risk Infant.* Amsterdam: Excerpta Medica.

Simeonsson, R. J. (1986). *Psychological and Developmental Assessment of Special Children.* Boston: Allyn & Bacon.

Simeonsson, R. J., Huntington, G. S., & Parse, S. A. (1979). *Assessment of Children with Severe Handicaps: Multiple Problems, Multivariate Goals.* Chapel Hill, NC: Carolina Institute for Research on Early Education of the Handicapped, Frank Porter Graham Child Development Center, University of North Carolina.

Simeonsson, R. J., Huntington, G. S., Short, R. J., & Ware, W. (1982). The Carolina Record of Individual Behavior: Characteristics of handicapped infants and children. *Topics in Early Childhood Special Education, 2,* 43–55.

Snell, M. E. (Ed.). (1987). *Systematic Instruction of Persons with Severe Handicaps,* 3rd ed. Columbus: Charles E. Merrill.

Snell, M. E., & Grigg, N. C. (1987). Instructional assessment and curriculum development. In M. E. Snell (Ed.). *Systematic Instruction of Persons with Severe Handicaps,* 3rd ed. (pp. 64–109). Columbus, OH: Charles E. Merrill.

Song, A., & Jones, S. E. 1980). *The Wisconsin Behavior Rating Scale.* Madison: Center for Developmentally Disabled.

Song, A., Jones, S., Lippert, J., Metzger, K., Miller, J., & Borreca, C. (1984). Wisconsin Behavior Rating Scale: Measure of adaptive behavior for the developmental levels of 0 to 3. *American Journal of Mental Deficiency, 88,* 401–410.

Stahlecker, J. E. (1986). Developmental Activities Screening Inventory-II. In D. J. Keyser & R. C. Sweetland (Eds.). *Test Critiques,* Vol. V (pp. 100–103). Kansas City: Test Corporation of America.

Stangler, S. R., Huber, C. J., & Routh, D. K. (1980). *Screening Growth and Development of Preschool Children: A Guide for Test Selection.* New York: McGraw-Hill.

Steele, N. W. (1971). *The Special Purpose Preschool for Children with Multiple Disabilities* (Vol. 1, No. 10). Austin, TX: Department of Special Education, University of Texas. (ERIC Document Reproduction Service No. Ed 055 391)

Strichart, S. S., & Lazarus, P. J. (1986). Low-incident assessment: Influences and issues. In P. J. Lazarus & S. S. Strichart (Eds.). *Psychoeducational Evaluation of Children and Adolescents with Low-incidence Handicaps.* Orlando: Grune & Stratton.

Sullivan, J. W., & Horowitz, F. D. (1978). *Kansas Supplements to the Neonatl Behavioral Assesment Scale: A First Look.* Paper presented at the International Conference on Infant Studies, Providence, RI.

Switzky, H. N. (1979). Assessment of the severely and profoundly handicapped. In D. A. Sabatino & T. L. Miller (Eds.). *Describing Learner Characteristics of Handicapped Children and Youth.* New York: Grune & Stratton.

Switzky, H. N. (1985). Review of developmental assessment for the severely handicapped. In J. V. Mitchell (Ed.). *The Ninth Mental Measurements Yearbook,* Vol 1. Lincoln, NE: The Buros Institute of Mental Measurements.

Thompson, P. R. (1974). Wednesday morning keynote address. In J. Moore & V. Engelman (Eds.). The severely multiply handicapped. What are the issues? Proceedings from the Regional Topical Conference, University of Utah, Salt Lake City, UT. 70–76.

Tjossem, T. D. (Ed.). (1976). *Intervention Strategies for High Risk Infants and Young Children.* Baltimore: University Park Press.

Touwen, B., Huisjes, H. J., Jurgens, V. D., et al., (1980). Obstetrical condition and neonatal neurological morbidity: An analysis with the help of the optimality concept. *Early Human Development, 4,* 207–228.

Tucker, J. A. (Ed.). (1985). Curriculum based assessment. Special Issue. *Exceptional Children, 52,* 192–304.

Turton, L. J. (1985). Review of Autism Screening Instrument for Education Planning. In J. V. Mitchell (Ed.). *The Ninth Mental Measurements Yearbook,* Vol. 1. Lincoln, NE: The Buros Institute for Mental Measurements.

Ulrey, G., & Rogers, S. J. (1982). *Psychological Assessment of Handicapped Infants and Young Children.* New York: Theime-Stratton.

U.S. Department of Education. (1987). *Ninth Annual Report to Congress on the Implementation of the Education of Handicapped Act.* Washington, DC: U.S. Dept. of Education.

Uzgiris, I. C., & Hunt, J. M. (1975). *Assessment in infancy.* Urbana, IL: University of Illinois.

Uzgiris, J. C., & Hunt, J. M. (Eds.). (1987). *Infant Performance and Experience: New Findings with the*

Ordinal Scales. Urbana, IL: University of Illinois Press.

Van Etten, G., Arkell, C., & Van Etten, C. (1980). *The Severely and Profoundly Handicapped: Programs, Methods, and Materials.* St. Louis: C. V. Mosby.

Venn, J. J. (1986). Peabody Developmental Motor Scales and Activity Cards. *Test Critiques,* Vol. 5 (pp. 310–313). Kansas City: Test Corporation of America.

Vincent, L. J., & Broome, K. (1977). A public school service delivery model for handicapped children between birth and five years of age. In E. Sontag, J. Smith, & N. Certo (Eds.). *Educational Programming for the Severely and Profoundly Handicapped.* Reston, VA: Division on Mental Retardation, Council for Exceptional Children.

Wacker, D. P. (1985). Review of Developmental Assessment for the Severely Handicapped. In J. B. Mitchell (Ed.). *The Ninth Mental Measurements Yearbook,* Vol. 1. Lincoln, NE: The Buros Institute of Mental Measurements.

Wambold, C., Bailey, R., & Nicholson, D. (1981). *Instructional Programs and Activities for the Severely Handicapped.* Springfield, IL: Charles C. Thomas.

Webster, C. D., Konstantareas, M. M., & Li, J. (1975, April). *Assessing Autistic Children: Discrimination Training and Simultaneous Communication Procedures.* Presented at the biennial meeting fo the Society for Research in Child Development, Denver. (ERIC Document Reproduction Service No. ED 119–402)

Werner, E. E. (1972). Denver Developmental Screening Test. In O. K. Buros (Eds.). *Seventh Mental Measurements Yearbook,* Vol. I. Highland Park, NJ: Gryphon Press.

Werner, J. (1981). *Helping the Handicapped Child with Early Feeding.* Buckingham: Winslow.

White, O., Edgar, E., & Haring, N. G. (1978). *Uniform Performance Assessment System, Birth-6 Year Level.* Seattle: Child Development and Mental Retardation Center, University of Washington.

White, S. (1985). Review of Developmental Profile II. In J. V. Mitchell (Ed.). *The Ninth Mental Measurements Yearbook,* Vol. 1. Lincoln, NE: The Buros Insitute for Mental Measurements.

Wiegerink, R. (1980). Parental involvement in early intervention programs for high risk infants. In S. Harel (Ed.). *The At Risk Infant.* Amsterdam: Excerpta Medica.

Wikoff, R. L. (1985). Review of Autism Screening Instrument for Educational Planning. In J. V. Mitchell (Eds.). *The Ninth Mental Measurements Yearbook,* Vol. 1. Lincoln, NE: The Buros Institute for Mental Measurements.

Wilhelm, C., Johnson, M., & Eisert, D. (1986). Assessment of motor-impaired children. In R. J. Simeonsson (Ed.). *Psychological and Developmental Assessment of Special Children*. Boston: Allyn & Bacon.

Wilson, C. C. (1986). Family assessment in preschool evaluation. *School Psychology Review, 15*(2), 166–179.

Wing, L. (1976a). Assessment: The role of the teacher. In M. P. Everard (Ed.). *An Approach to Teaching Autistic Children*. Oxford: Pergamon Press.

Wing, L. (1976b). Problems of diagnosis and classification. In M. P. Everard (Ed.). *An Approach to Teaching Autistic Children*. Oxford: Pergamon Press.

Wing, L., & Gould, J. (1978). Systematic recording of behaviors and skills of retarded and psychotic children. *Journal of Autism and Childhood Schizophrenia, 8*, 769–97.

Wing, L., & Gould, J. (1979). Severe impairments of social interaction and associated abnormalities in children: Epidemiology and classification. *Journal of Autism and Developmental Disorders, 9*, 11–29.

Woods, G. (1975). *The Handicapped Child*. Oxford: Blackwell Scientific.

Ysseldyke, J. E., Thurlow, M. L., O'Sullivan, P., & Bursaw, R. A. (1986). Current screening and diagnostic practices in a state offering free preschool screening since 1977: Implications for the field. *Journal of Psychoeducational Assesment*.

Zelazo, P. R. (1979). Reactivity to perceptual-cognitive events: Application for infant assessment. In R. R. Kearsley & I. E. Sigel (Eds.). *Infants At Risk: Assessment of Cognitive Functioning*. Hillsdale, NJ: Erlbaum.

APPENDIX 18.1
RESOURCES FOR ASSESSMENT

1. Assessment Guidelines for Infants/Preschoolers with Handicaps
   Bagnato, 1984; Bagnato & Neisworth, 1981; Fewell, 1983; Gabel & Erickson, 1980; Harrington, 1984; Neisworth & Bagnato, 1986; Lidz, 1986; Paget & Nagle, 1986; Reynolds & Clark, 1983; Rogers, 1986; Ulrey & Rogers, 1982.

2. Assessment Guidelines for Individuals with Severe Handicaps
   Browder, 1987; Brown, 1987; Chase, 1985; Hogg & Sebba, 1986; Lazarus & Strichart, 1986; Powers, 1985; Powers & Handleman, 1984; Rotatori, Schwenn, & Fox, 1985; Sailor & Guess, 1983; Snell, 1987; Van Etten, Arkell, & Van Etten, 1980.

3. General Evaluations of Assessment Instruments
   Keyser & Sweetland, 1984–86; Mitchell, 1985; Salvia & Ysseldyke, 1988; Sattler, 1988.

4. Descriptions/Evaluations of Instruments for Infants/Preschoolers with Handicaps.
   Bagnato & Neisworth, 1981; Bailey & Wolery, 1984; Brazleton, Alstronic, & Lester, 1987; Fewell, 1983; Francis, Self, & Horowitz, 1987; Harrington, 1984; Neisworth & Bagnato, 1986; Peterson, 1987; Rogers, 1986; Ulrey & Rogers, 1982; Uzgiris & Hunt, 1987.

5. Descriptions/Evaluations of Instruments for Individuals with Severe Handicaps
   Alter, Gottlieb, & Gottlieb, 1986; Brown, 1987; Hogg & Sebba, 1986; Hupp & Donofio, 1983; Powers & Handleman, 1984; Sailor & Guess, 1983; Rotatori, Schwenn, & Fox, 1985; Simeonsson, 1986.

6. Evaluation of Instruments for Individuals with Autism
   Lerea, 1987; Marcus & Baker, 1986; Morgan, 1988; Parks, 1983; Powers & Handleman, 1984; Short & Marcus, 1986.

7. Evaluation of Instruments for Families of Handicapped Individuals
   Simeonsson, 1986; Wilson, 1986.

19

Assessment of Preschool Giftedness: Intelligence and Creativity

E. PAUL TORRANCE
EDWARD J. CAROPRESO

INTRODUCTION

Before entering into a discussion of preschool giftedness and the methods and techniques available for its assessment, several relevant issues need to be considered and clarified. The first of these issues, the relationship between identification and assessment, initially might seem to be merely a semantic concern or at least a moot point because of its apparent circularity. In fact, an investigation of the literature on preschool gifted assessment reveals that these terms frequently are used interchangeably. A problem arises because they often seem to refer to different processes.

The first issue is therefore a dual issue: Are identification and assessment the same process or different processes; if different, do they necessarily accompany one another, and if so, why and how; What is their relationship to preschool giftedness? The literature in this area suggests that these terms seem to be used with slightly different intentions or purposes. Identification appears to be related to the accomplishment of four general goals: uncovering gifted ability or potential; differentiating gifted from nongifted individuals within heterogeneous groupings; establishing lists of traits, features, and/or characteristics; and the specification of particular domains of giftedness, talent, or special ability. Assessment seems to be related to the evaluation or determination of relative levels of potential or functional giftedness within individuals (or groups) given specific domains of giftedness (i.e., academic/intellectual, verbal, spatial, creative, leadership, etc.) after an initial identification or screening has occurred. Paradoxically, though, assessment seems to be the more inclusive term; identification can be viewed as the initial step in a broader, more comprehensive assessment procedure. This might be an artificial division or an unnecessary semantic distinction, but it can have clarifying effects on the entire issue of conceptualizing and setting parameters for the notions underlying giftedness. This becomes especially salient in terms of the follow through involved in appropriate programming for particular individuals or subgroups. Both terms (concepts) have been associated with ensuing educational programming, but assessment seems to more directly and specifically tied to educational programming. Assessment implies specifications relevant to established program goals, that is, to determine and target potential attendants of a particular program or set of programs according to the established program structures and availability.

Individual assessment and identification appear to be considered as separate, distinct processes that are nonetheless closely, if not inextricably, interrelated. This is especially true in the case of their application to a preschool population. The process of identification of giftedness within this age group has no clearly established structure or routine. There has been a great deal of speculation and anecdotal evidence as to what constitutes giftedness within this population, but little conclusive research-based data have been developed in support of these notions, nor has there been much agreement on conceptions of preschool giftedness. There have been several attempts to develop model preschool identification/assessment/educational programs (specified later in this chapter), but no standardized or even generally accepted approach has been established. Given the needs and constraints of individual systems or program locations combined with the developmental variability evidenced within this age group, a specific and widely applicable structured identification/assessment approach might not be an attainable goal. The net result is that the assessment of preschool giftedness should include both a method of initially identifying young gifted children from within a larger, heterogenous group followed by individual assessment of exceptional ability within specific ability domains.

This point leads directly to the second issue of concern: The need for clear and concise program specifications and appropriate preparations for the handling of children directed to the program. Assessment procedures are pointless unless the system is prepared to accomodate students identified as gifted according to the assessment outcomes. Any assessment program must be affiliated and compatible with available educational programs. Assessment procedures cannot be allowed to lead to the uncovering of types and levels of giftedness for which no educational network exists. This possibility could and probably would lead to more personal and educational damage to the identified individual than nonrecognition of their abilities. These children need to be appropriately served, supported, and directed once their particular special abilities have been recog-

nized, not left with empty labels, meaningless information, and no educational outlets through which they can actualize their potential.

There are notable exceptions, of course; when special abilities are identified and parents are informed, they can arrange valuable programming. For example, early in his career the senior author administered the Seashore Test of Musical Abilities (Mitchell, 1983) to a class of fourth graders and identified a boy who achieved almost perfect scores on all of the Seashore abilities. This was reported to his parents, who had not suspected their son of having music talents. Once they had been informed of the test results, they recalled many observations of his talents. They then arranged for him to have music lessons. He loved music, excelled in music, and went ahead to a highly successful music career.

The development of assessment plans and educational programming should and can proceed simultaneously and interactively. Each component informs and responds to the development of the other. This is particularly relevant for school situations or systems in which neither assessment nor educational programs currently exist. Where some type of educational programming for gifted students does exist, the development or enhancement of an assessment program should and can lead to a reconsideration of the available educational services so that both programs remain parallel and consistent in their services and goals. Just as an assessment plan should not proceed without appropriate supporting educational programming, the educational services ought not exist in a vacuum minus the input and benefit of an appropriate and applied assessment methodology.

CONCEPTIONS OF GIFTEDNESS

First Things First

Before either an assessment or educational program can be delineated and applied, the target population must be specifically identified. Also, the precise definition of terms and description of giftedness to be used must be determined. The range and particular contents of the assessment and educational programs to be implemented will be directed by this definition and description in association with the characteristics of the target population. The range and number of characteristics of giftedness considered and applied in any given situation will in turn be limited by the specific interests, goals, abilities, and material and potential support of the system implementing the assessment/educational plan. To summarize, the applied definition of the types and range of giftedness will be limited by what the educational system has or chooses to offer, which will be specifically constrained or focused by the construct that is eventually developed and adopted by the system.

Though the target population in this discussion has been limited to preschool children, this population contains a broad range of ages and potential abilities. Generally, preschool groups range in age from 2½ to 6 or 7 years of age; the typically accepted age range is 3 to 6 years. During these years, development across cognitive, social, emotional, and motor domains is typically apparent and occasionally extreme. In part because there is no generally acknowledged stage-like level of development for this age group, especially for gifted children, there is no direct, single, simple or comprehensive form of assessment. This group of children is undergoing enormous developmental changes that can enhance or more likely interfere with or obscure assessment efforts. Because of the potential for developmental variability at this age, differential levels of social, affective, cognitive and personal development can be expected. Assessment plans should acknowledge and reflect this diversity by being multifaceted and flexible. The lack of uniformity within this group should not be allowed to preclude the possibility of discovering potential giftedness, even in narrow or specific ability areas.

One approach to the problem of identifying gifted preschoolers, despite the influences of developmental differences and the rapid changes in cognitive, affective, social, and motoric abilities, relates to training adults involved in the assessment procedures. By integrating the concepts of early childhood and developmental psychology with the study of giftedness in the training of future teachers and other related professionals, a better understanding of the characteristics and behaviors of gifted preschool children can be developed. This increased awareness would serve to maximize the accuracy and the impact of assessment procedures for the preschool population.

What Is Meant by Giftedness?

Some insight into the problems of assessing preschool giftedness can be gained from a brief review of the historical development of the concept of giftedness in the twentieth century and some of the currently held views of giftedness in older populations. From this vantage, a model of preschool giftedness can be developed based on both a downward extrapolation and observation of young children's exceptional behavior in a variety of skill areas.

Among the original contributions to the identification of exceptional ability was the psychometric view of individual differences in intellectual ability. With the advent of instruments designed to measure intelligence, giftedness quickly became associated with large numbers: the higher the rating or score on an intelligence test, the more gifted was the individual. Early conceptions of giftedness were frequently limited to this definition; giftedness typically meant exceptional intellectual ability as measured by some psychometric device. In fact, this definition has persisted and can be often noted as either the sole criterion for identification or at least the pivotal component in multidimensional identification plans currently used by many school systems.

The psychometric conception of giftedness was strongly supported by the work of Lewis Terman and later Terman and Oden in their immense longitudinal study of the growth and development of intellectually superior individuals. Their criterion was high IQ (140 or greater) as measured by the Stanford-Binet (Terman, 1925; Terman & Oden, 1947). This work greatly contributed to the belief in the long-term stability of measured intelligence, and therefore to the psychometric view of giftedness. This led to the corner stone definitional trait for identification of giftedness as being superior measured intelligence.

Though the influence of the psychometric view of giftedness is still evident, this quality or trait is not directly relevant to preschool populations. Measured IQ has been demonstrated to be highly unstable and variable, especially with very young children (Hutchins et al., 1988; Maccoby & Jacklin, 1974). An alternative view of gift-edness for this population is required, one that will accomodate both the potential for developmental variability likely to occur within this age range as well as the variety of potential manifestations of exceptional ability that can be exhibited by young children. A conception of preschool giftedness must be both developmentally appropriate and flexible in terms of the assessment indicators that are considered and evaluated.

It has been recognized for several decades that giftedness is not restricted to a single dimension, such as IQ, but can be manifested in a variety of domains. One of the most influential recent statements was a report to Congress from the U. S. Office of Education (Marland, 1972). The following definition of giftedness was presented:

> Gifted and talented children are defined as those, who, by virtue of their outstanding abilities, are capable of high performance. Their potential ability may be seen in any one or more of the following areas:
>
> • general intellectual ability,
> • specific academic aptitude,
> • creative or productive thinking,
> • leadership ability,
> • visual and performing arts,
> • psychomotor ability.

This definition expresses the breadth and richness of the potential manifestations of giftedness. But there have been critcisms of this conception, most notably that of Renzulli (1979). Renzulli's main concern is that the Office of Education definition blurs the distinction between what he considers processes (e.g., intellectual, creative) with performance (e.g., artistic, academic). Renzulli's own three-ring view of giftedness asserts that the major determinants of gifted behavior are above average abilities or talents, creative capacities, and task commitment. The addition of task commitment, or a motivational influence, to Renzulli's conception adds needed and practical flexibility. It helps convey the idea that performance of gifted children, generally, or in specific domains, can be inconsistent and related to the particular task at hand, not necessarily exhibited on demand, especially for the purposes of assessment. This issue is particularly relevant to preschoolers who might

be highly susceptible to motivationally influenced fluctuations in performance and whose performance has been shown to be affected by task and situational demands (Brown, & De Loche, 1978; Gelman, 1978; Gentner, 1977) and can result in motivational variations.

Sternberg and Davidson (1986), in an elaboration of their conception of giftedness, acknowledge and support Renzulli's three-part definition with the caveat that they doubt the meaning of these three terms remains constant across domains. They do not specify what they mean by meaning nor do they suggest ways that meaning might vary for specific domains. Sternberg and Davidson proposed a taxonomy of giftedness, and they noted several significant issues toward establishing such a proposal. First, they recognize that there has not been perfect consensus regarding the specific skills and behaviors to which the term giftedness should be applied, but a moderate consensus does exist in terms of the kinds of things that should not be considered. Second, Sternberg and Davidson indicate that, in their view, giftedness is societally defined. Given this view, they conclude that a consensus definition is appropriate in that a consensus taxonomy would reflect a prototypical representation of the societal view. Sternberg and Davidson then present the following four level taxonomy of giftedness: intellectual skills of all kinds i.e., verbal, quantitative, spatial, memorial, etc.); artistic skills of all kinds (i.e., painting, musicianship, drama, dance, etc.); niche-fitting skills of all kinds, including adaptation to, selection of, and shaping of those physical and interpersonal environments that compose one's domain of experience (i.e., lawyers, doctors, etc. who must either make or find an appropriate environment in which they can be successful); physical skills of all kinds (i.e., those skills related to various athletics as well as to survival in hostile terrains and physical circumstances). Sternberg and Davidson note that their conception intermeshes to some degree with many previous classifications. It can be viewed as a generalized attempt at establishing a rich, broad, and inclusive statement of the range of potential and functional giftedness.

A number of other conceptions or models of giftedness and a variety of trait/characteristic checklists have been proposed in recent years.

This information can be effectively used as guides for assessment plans for preschoolers. Much of this information has been derived from older populations, though, and requires some extrapolation and adjustment for the developmental differences between younger and older children. Heller and Feldhusen (1985) note Tannenbaum's (1983) psychosocial definition of giftedness, commenting that he is one of the few theorists who intentionally includes chance factors as a component of his theory. Tannenbaum's theory includes general ability, special abilities, nonintellective factors, and environmental factors, the latter suggesting that gifted achievement is potentially influenced by the social, intellectual, and physical environments impinging on the individual. The effects of the environment are particularly relevant to the performance, and therefore the assessment, of potentially gifted young children.

Heller and Feldhusen (1985) outline a general model of giftedness that draws on the work of a variety of theorists and researchers in the area of giftedness including Sternberg, Gardner, Sosniak and Bloom. These authors state that their views of giftedness typically would include superior general abilities, such as Sternberg's componential and metacognitive skills and Gardner's multiple intelligences, special focused talents that might predispose individuals to exceptional achievement in a particular ability domain, a self-concept that allows for high levels of creative or productive achievement, and the motivation necessary to sustain learning and achievement. Heller and Feldhusen (1985) expand on their meaning of general abilities, including as parts of that "complex bundle" effective thinking skills and information processing abilities, the development of insights needed for problem solutions, and efficient metacognitive processing skills. In terms of identification, Heller and Feldhusen (1985) note that self-concept and motivation factors should not be included as assessment factors. Rather, they are appropriate goals for educational programming. Gifted children should be allowed to explore and develop their own unique skills and abilities leading to a clear self-image involving a sense of the potential for a high level of achievement in any chosen field of accomplishment. This self-image will be merged, it is hoped, with the motivation to set high goals, put forth maximum effort and achieve at optimal performance levels.

A variety of checklists cataloging the characteristics or traits of gifted individuals have been elaborated and made available through many sources in recent years. These checklists often combine several different ability and behavior areas into a single list. These lists can be effective initial screening devices; they also can be useful cues as to the types of abilities and kinds of behaviors that signal potential giftedness. Checklist users should always bear in mind that rarely, if ever, will any one individual exhibit all or even many of the traits or behaviors appearing on these lists; they are typically compilations of observations of many individuals in many situations. Several representational checklists will be presented.

Tuttle and Becker (1980) present one brief list reflecting gifted ability in three areas: personal items (1–3); interpersonal items (4–7); information processing items (8–12).

A gifted individual:

1. Is curious
2. Is persistent
3. Is perceptive
4. Is critical
5. Has a highly developed sense of humor, often a verbal orientation
6. Is sensitive to injustices on personal and worldwide levels
7. Is a leader in various areas
8. Is not willing to accept superificial statements, responses, or evaluations
9. Understands general principles easily
10. Often responds to the environment through media and means other than print and writing
11. Sees relationships between seemingly diverse ideas
12. Generates many ideas for a specific stimulus

Martin (1986) presents a 20-item list of behavioral indicators of potentially talented children. A potentially talented child:

1. Shows a high level of concentration and is able to be absorbed in something for a long period of time
2. Is intensely curious, sometimes about one certain thing
3. Has keen powers of observation when pursuing interests

4. Is mentally lively and energetic; thinks very quickly; alert to all that goes on around; tuned in to the adult world
5. Is extremely well coordinated in movement and control
6. Daydreams; can't be bothered with routine tasks
7. Doesn't like limits placed on what he can do or what he is allowed to do; gets very exasperated and impatient
8. Shows a highly imaginative use of language
9. Always asks questions that might not be easy to answer
10. Doesn't like to be proved wrong or inadequate; invents excuses or reasons for failing at something
11. Is critical of own efforts
12. Likes to take charge and get others to do things
13. Likes to spend time and work with older children
14. Is eager to make collections of things
15. Talked much earlier than expected; engages in lively conversation
16. Has a good memory, but not necessarily for facts or routine matters
17. Seeks to satisfy needs and will be aggressive to get the attention needed
18. Is dependable in carrying things out
19. Doesn't seem to need to listen to a full explanation or complete something to understand the whole idea
20. Shows ability to think deeply; reasons, analyzes, comes up with new ideas and solutions to solve a problem

1. Possess superior powers of reasoning, of dealing with abstractions, of generalizing from specific facts, of understanding meanings, and of seeing into relationship;
2. Have great intellectual curiosity
3. Learn easily and readily
4. Have a wide range of interests
5. Have a broad attention span that enables them to concentrate on and persevere in solving problems and pursuing interests
6. Are superior in the quantity and quality of vocabulary as compared with children of their own age
7. Have ability to do effective work independently
8. Have learned to read early (often well before school age);
9. Exhibit keen powers of observation
10. Show initiative and originality in intellectual work
11. Show alertness and quick response to new ideas
12. Are able to memorize quickly
13. Have great interest in the nature of man and the universe (problems of origins and destiny, etc.)
14. Possess unusual imagination
15. Follow complex directions easily
16. Are rapid readers
17. Have several hobbies
18. Have reading interests that cover a wide range of subjects;
19. Make frequent and effective use of the library
20. Are superior in mathematics, particularly in problem solving

This list clearly indicates a variety of areas of potential giftedness, including personal, interpersonal, cognitive, affective, and physical, which can be observed in various combinations in different individuals.

Denton and Postwaithe (1985) present a checklist of pupil characteristics first devised by Laycock in 1957 and quoted as recently as 1980 in a pamphlet designed for the guidance of teachers. The age range is not indicated, but the parallels to the previously stated lists are obvious. The Laycock 20-item list specifies the following characteristics that might be observed in gifted pupils. Gifted pupils:

Appendix 19–1 includes Denton and Postwaithe's extensive listings of potential characteristics that might be exhibited by gifted pupils in various specific ability areas.

Denton and Postwaithe follow the Laylock list with several cautions about the development and application of such checklists. First, they note that many of these checklists were developed based on pupils identified as being highly intelligent and might, therefore, not be appropriate to use in assessing children of high specific abilities other than high global intelligence. Also, they note Freeman's warning that the use of checklists has become so pervasive and all-embracing so as to include characteristics of almost any child; in addition, little examination into validity or predictive value has apparently been done. In reference to observable classroom behavior, Denton and Postwaithe note that many of the list items were derived from nonclassroom-based research. Though they might be correlated with high general ability, the listed characteristics might not be observable in classroom contexts. Extrapolating to the relatively recent advent of the preschool classroom, this might be an especially significant problem when applying such lists of so-called gifted pupil characteristics in an attempt to identify high ability young children.

Having established a general framework for conceptualizing giftedness and its manifestations in older populations, a model or framework of preschool giftedness, including creative ability, will be presented.

A FRAMEWORK FOR PRESCHOOL GIFTEDNESS

In developing a model or framework for preschool giftedness, a distinction between potential and actual or functional giftedness must be considered. Instances, expressions, or products revealing actual, functioning gifted behavior or abilities rarely will occur. Inferences about future performance or ability must be made based on observations of naturally occurring situations and/or specially constructed situations designed to elicit particular types of behaviors. Various characteristics of individuals, even preschoolers, can be used as indicators of potential high level achievement of gifted performance. Hagen (1980) notes that the best indicator of future achievement is the present level of achievement. For preschoolers, the range of indicators and areas of achievement are restricted, at least in an academic sense. The areas of language development can be informative, though. Specific types of achievement would include the following: range of vocabulary, complexity of typically used language, the range or extent of a child's information, and early reading ability, especially self-taught (Hagen, 1980). This last ability seems to be an excellent predictor of academic achievement (Fatouros, 1986, based on Hagen, 1980).

Generally, early acquisition and display of various abilities/skills/compentencies/behaviors can be used as indicators of potential giftedness. The focus in this approach would be on an "early" display of the particular abilities, such as math or motor skills, and to consider their use as indicators, especially if little or no direct instruction was involved in the child's development of the abilities.

The issue of identification and assessment of preschool giftedness is multifaceted. This issue concerns not only the range and levels of indicators of giftedness that should be considered, but, more fundamentally, what characteristics accurately and reliably indicate a potential for high levels of future performance.

Tuttle and Becker (1980) suggest that when preschoolers' behaviors are observed, one can question whether these behaviors are different from those expected of other age peers. This can be elaborated on by adding expected behaviors in similar circumstances. Environmental factors ought to be considered in terms of their potential effects on any child's display of behavior at any given time. Implicitly, this suggestion presupposes some knowledge of development and of developmental differences, that is, some knowledge of an age-behavior baseline, without which there can be no expectation.

Tuttle and Becker (1980) present a set of six areas of characteristics and behaviors that seem to be indicative of preschool giftedness derived from the experiences of one parent of three highly and differently gifted children. Margaret Parrot's list (Tuttle & Becker, 1980) is based on her personal experiences and extensive background in literary research on giftedness. The traits she notes include the following:

1. Early language acquisition: uses a large vocabulary; speaks in long, complex sentences; talks early and often; Many gifted children, however, do not speak early but wait until they are older and then display a remarkable facility with language.
2. Fine and gross motor skills: walks, climbs, runs easily and well; controls small objects such as scissors, pencils, crayons, etc. easily; copies pictures and words; handles tools well.
3. Intellectual areas: reads signs or even books; does mathematical problems; draws associations among diverse ideas; remembers facts

and events; is interested in social and moral issues; has a long attention span; asks why.

4. Social areas: has empathy for others; is self-confident and independent; organizes and leads group activities; very active mentally and physically.

5. Creative areas: has vivid imagination; enjoys playing with words and ideas; shows a highly developed, often verbal sense of humor; uses objects, toys, colors in imaginative ways.

6. Specific areas: plays musical instrument; plays sports well; in general, shows remarkable ability in specific area.

Parrot further notes that identification by traits deals mostly with differences in degree or intensity.

This list reveals that a richer source of information about potential giftedness than perhaps is typically thought to exist can be found in the behaviors of even young children through attentive and informed observation. There is an obvious overlap or interplay between these different areas; no one area will necessarily develop independently of one or more of the other areas. This does not suggest that any child will necessarily display special abilities in all areas or in particular combinations of areas, but that giftedness might not be narrow or restricted to just a singlebehavioral manifestation.

PRESCHOOL CREATIVITY

Creative ability stands as a unique and distinctive aspect within the realm of giftedness. Perhaps the most important aspect about creativity is the fact that creative behavior is potentialy available to everyone (Guilford, 1968, 1986; Parnes, 1981; Taylor, 1964; Torrance (1962, 1972a, 1972b) and often some degree is evident at some point in almost everyone's experiences. Elements of creative behavior can be elicited, supported, trained, through a variety of methods and procedures (Amabile, 1987; Parnes, 1987). This fact has been clearly demonstrated for more than three decades (Binet, 1909; Guilford, 1956; 1960; Parnes & Meadow, 1959).

In view of current evidence concerning human functioning, it would seem unthinkable for psychologists and educators to continue ignoring children's creative functioning in the assessment of preschool children (Torrance, 1962, 1963, 1965, 1972, 1981; Torrance & Wu, 1981).

Definition

Some degree of creativity is required whenever a person is faced with a problem for which he or she has no learned or practiced response. Because preschool children are constantly facing such situations, they are constantly using and practicing their creative thinking abilities.

Torrance has offered a more formal, process definition of creativity (1969, p. vii):

> Creative behavior occurs in the process of becoming sensitive to or aware of problems, deficiencies, gaps in knowledge, missing elements, disharmonies, and so on: bringing together in new relationships available information: defining the difficulty of identifying the missing elements: searching for solutions, making guesses, or formulating hypotheses about the problems or deficiencies, testing and retesting them: perfecting them: and finally communicating the results.

This is a natural, healthy human process common among almost all children. Strong human motivations are at work at each stage.

The degree of creativity will depend upon the extent to which the result (1) shows novelty and value (either for the child or the culture), (2) is unconventional in the sense that it diverges from previously accepted solutions, (3) is true, generalizable, and surprising in the light of what the child knew at the time, and (4) required persistence in going beyond previous performances.

The creative behavior of preschool children is characterized by wonder and magic. Most healthy young children have the spirit unless they have been victims of neglect, harshness, lack of love, or severe deprivation. Because of the sense of wonder and magic, children learn through experimenting, manipulating objects, rearranging things and combining them in different ways, singing, dancing, storytelling, and the like.

Creative Ways of Learning

Preschool children are experts in creative ways of learning because by the age of 2 to 3 years they have acquired considerable experience in learning by questioning, inquiring, searching, manipulating, experimenting, and playing to find out in their own way the truth about things. If they sense that something is wrong or missing, that something is out of place, they are uncomfortable until they do something to find out about it; they start exploring, testing, questioning, and searching through whatever modalities are available to them. Whenever they discover something new, they want to tell or show it to somebody. At times, creative thinking is lightning quick. At other times, we must wait patiently and then it may come lightning quick. The following characteristics of young children help them learn creatively. (Torrance, 1969):

1. Long attention span
2. Capacity for organization
3. Seeing things in a different perspective
4. Exploring before formal instruction
5. Using silence and hesitation
6. Taking a "closer look" at things
7. Using fantasy to solve developmental problems
8. Storytelling and song making

Tentative Hierarchy of Creative Thinking Skills

There has been little serious attempt to identify the hierarchy of creative thinking skills and establish a development time table for preschool children. The expression of creative thinking skills is dependent upon the modalities accessible to the children. There are enormous individual differences among young children in the development of speech. Until a child develops speech skills, we cannot expect much verbal creativity. However, most preschool children seem to develop the following skills by the time they are ready for school. (Torrance, 1970):

1. The child will be able to produce new combinations through manipulation.
2. The child will be able to see and produce many possible combinations or new relationships.
3. The child will be able to identify missing elements in pictures and shapes, letters, etc. at a very gross level.

4. The child will be able to produce increasingly more complex combinations through manipulation and move to deliberate experimentation.
5. The child will be able to see and produce increasingly larger numbers of possibilities in combining symbols, objects, numerals, people, places, etc.
6. The child will increase verbal fluency by naming new combinations of shapes, sounds, animals, etc. at a simple level.
7. The child will be able to make syntheses by giving titles or labels to pictures, stories, songs, and poems.
8. The child will have improved skills in asking questions about missing elements in objects, pictures, stories, situations, etc.

It is not possible to specify the precise ages at which each of these characteristics and skills will emerge. Much depends upon the development of various sensory skills and verbal development.

SOURCES OF INFORMATION ABOUT POTENTIAL GIFTEDNESS

Information about potential giftedness can be derived from a rich assortment of sources. All ar potentially applicable to a preschool population, though several particular sources are more appropriate and informative for this age group than the others. The combined effects of a child's age and prior experiences support the use of different sets of indicators for specific children at different times.

Ehrlich (1980) lists eleven different techniques useful in the identification of giftedness among the very young (3 to 7 years of age). This list includes the following possibilities:

1. Biographical data
2. Checklists and rating scales
3. Objective testing: achievement in specific areas
4. Objective testing: group intelligence
5. Objective testing: individual intelligence
6. Observations: Formal and informal
7. Parent nominations
8. Peer nominations

9. Performance tests (work and behavior samples)
10. Personal interview
11. Professional nominations/judgments

This group of information sources can be categorized in several ways: formal/informal; available/unavailable; cost effective/ineffective; and so on. Fatouros (1986) suggests one method that can be used to both organize this list and contrast and evaluate different types of assessments. She suggests that these sources can be divided into two general approaches to assessment: The "traditional method" and "the case study method."

The traditional method includes what are often considered to be the "formal" sources of information, group objective screens, possibly followed by individual screening. Typically, this means the use of objective intelligence testing and/or achievement testing for specific areas of achievement. The "traditional method" has been so named because of its consistent and often exclusive use in identification of gifted individuals despite the fact that this process can be both time consuming and costly (Renzulli & Smith, 1977). Much of the attraction and use of this method stems from the history of psychological and psychoeducational assessment, from its relative origins with Binet and Simon (1916) in the early part of the nineteenth century through the longitudinal work of Terman and his associates (1925) and Terman and Oden (1947) with highly intellectually gifted individuals.

The twentieth century trend in objective testing has been built on a belief that important information can be gained through the application of these instruments. In fact, many objective intelligence tests have been demonstrated to be both valid and reliable for their particular purposes across a broad range of age groups. These basic requirements of reliability do not always extend down to the level of the very young, though (Bracker 1987). Test development with the very young is extraordinarily expensive and requires skilled administrators. Young children are quite variable in their performance and are not always motivated to perform at their best. Here lies one of the difficulties in using the traditional method, especially to the exclusion of any other source of information, with preschoolers. This point leads to another concern over the use of objective tests; objective testing alone does not adequately address the range of potential giftedness. Multiple indicators are needed, especially with the very young children. A third point of concern over objective measures is that typically only individually adminstered tests can be used with the very young. Though this has been demonstrated frequently to enhance a child's total score (i.e., they test as more "intelligent" than in group administration), it also accounts for a higher cost in time and money.

Table 19.1 lists what appears to be the most researched and most useful intelligence tests available at the present time (Mitchell, ed., 1983, 1985) for use with preschoolers. Because of the large amount of detailed literature already available on many of the widely used standardized tests, the tests will not be discussed further here, with one exception. The K-ABC, a recently developed instrument, will be discussed briefly.

The WPPSI (ages 4 to 6–6) and the Stanford-Binet IV (ages 2 and above) continue to be the most popular instruments for use with young children. The MSCA have been increasing in popularity. The K-ABC (Kaufman & Kaufman, 1983) is a recently development standardized intelligence that has been normed with very young children. Since its publication in 1983, the literature on its validity, reliability, and applicability has rapidly grown.

Instrument selection should be the result of informed consideration and thorough investigation of the available measurement tools, not a random process or a "forced" choice, if possible. To aid in this often difficult and confusing process, Ehrlich (1980) suggests a set of 10 criteria for the evaluation and selection of prospective instruments or measurement techniques that could potentially be adopted into an assessment program. These criteria are:

1. Objectivity
2. Reliability
3. Validity
4. Historical record of success
5. Appropriateness of language
6. Cultural appropriateness
7. Cost of administration
8. Time to administer

TABLE 19.1
STANDARDIZED TESTS AVAILABLE FOR THE
ASSESSMENT OF PRE-SCHOOLERS' INTELLIGENCE
AND VARIOUS TALENT AREAS

Individual Ability Tests

Bracken Basic Concept Scale (1984). The Psychological Corporation.

Cognitive Skills Assessment Battery, 2nd Edition (1981). Teachers College Press

Columbia Mental Maturity Scale, 3rd Edition (1972). The Psychological Corporation.

Concept Assessment Kit (1968). Edits/Education and Industrial Testing Service.

Cooperative Pre-school Inventory, Revised Edition (1970). Addison-Wesley.

Full-range Picture Vocabulary Test. Psychological Testing Service.

Gesell Development Schedules, 1940 Series. Programs for Education, Inc.

Gesell Preschool Test (1980). Programs for Education, Inc.

Gesell School Readiness Test (1980). Programs for Education, Inc.

Goodenough-Harris Drawing Test (1963). The Psychological Corporation.

Kaufman Assessment Battery for Children (1983). American Guidance Service.

Leiter International Performance Scale, Arthur adaptation. C. H. Stoelting.

McCarthy Scales of Childrens Abilities (1972). The Psychological Corporation.

Peabody Picture Vocabulary Test (1981). American Guidance Service.

Pictorial Test of Intelligence (1964). Riverside Publishing Co.

Porteus Maze Test, Vineland revision, new series (1965). The Psychological Corporation.

Slosson Intelligence Test (1981). Slosson Educational Publications.

Stanford-Binet Intelligence Scale, 4th Edition (4E) (1987). Riverside Publishing Co.

Vane Evaluation of Language Scale (1975). Clinical Psychology Publishing Co.

Vane Kindergarten Test (1968). Clinical Psychological Publishing Co.

Wechsler Intelligence Scale for Children—Revised (1974). The Psychological Corporation.

Wechsler Pre-school and Primary Scale of Intelligence (1967). The Psychological Corporation.

TABLE 19.1 (*continued*)

Group Ability Tests

Boehm Test of Basic Concepts—Revised (1986). The Psychological Corporation.

Bracken Basic Concept Scale (1984). The Psychological Corporation.

Cognitive Abilities Test (1974). Riverside Publishing Co.

Draw-A-Person (1963). Western Psychological Services.

Otis-Lennon Mental Ability Tests (1977). The Psychological Corporation.

Otis-Lennon School Abilities Test (1982). Revised version on OLMAT. The Psychological Corporation.

Test of Early Learning Skills (1979). Scholastic Testing Service.

Tests of General Ability: Inter-American Series (1973). Guidance Testing Associates.

Achievement/Readiness Tests

California Achievement Tests, Forms C & D (1978). McGraw-Hill.

Metropolitan Readiness Test, Level 1 (1976). The Psychological Corporation.

Peabody Individual Achievement Test (1970). American Guidance Service.

Stanford Early School Achievement Test, Level 1 (1969). McGraw-Hill.

Test of Basic Experiences, 2 (1971). McGraw-Hill.

Perceptual-Motor Development

Development Test of Visual-Motor Integration (1967). Follett Publishing Co.

Purdue Perceptual-Motor Survey (1966). Merrill Publishing Co.

Wechsler Preschool and Primary Scale of Intelligence: Performance Scale (1967). American Guidance Service.

Social Development

California Preschool Social Competency Scale (1969). Consulting Psychologist Press.

Vineland Social Maturity Scale (1965). American Guidance Service.

Creative and Productive Thinking

Thinking Creatively in Action and Movement, Research Edition (1976). Scholastic Testing Service.

Self-Concept and Achievement Motivation

Self-Concept Adjective Checklist (1971). Psychologists & Educators, Inc.

The Self-Concept and Motivation Inventory (1977). Person-O-Metrics.

TABLE 19.1 (*continued*)

Musical Ability
Seashore Measure of Musical Talents (1960). The Psychological Corporation.

Alternatives to Commonly Used Assessment

Instruments

Ability Tests
Baldwin Identification Matrix Inservice Kit for Identification of Gifted and Talented Students (1977). D.O.K. Publishers.

Conceptual Behavior Battery: Conservation of Number, Numerical Operations, Seriation A and B (1974). Office of Child Research, Arizona Center for Educational Research and Development, College of Education, University of Arizona.

Silver Test of Cognitive Skills (1979). Dr. R. A. Silver, 5 Woodland Dr., Rye, NY 10580

SOI Learning Abilities Test (SOI-LA) & SOI Learning Abilities Test Special Edition (1974). SOI Institute.

Swassing-Barbe Modality Index (1979). Zaner-Bloser, Inc.

SOMPA: System of Multicultural Pluralistic Assessment (1978). The Psychological Corporation.

Performing Arts
Four Music Conservation Tasks (1968). Dr. M. P. Zimmerman, 11 Carriage Place, Champaign, IL.

Simons Measurements of Musical Listening Skills (1978). G. Simons, 1350 S. Kostner Ave., Chicago, IL.

The Creative Dramatics Test (1973). Dr. N. Hansel, Department of Early Childhood Education, University of California at Riverside, Riverside, CA.

Creative Writing/Storytelling
Children's Apperception Test (1974). The Psychological Corporation.

Psychomotor Skills
Annotated Bibliography on Perceptual-Motor Development (1973). Washington, DC: American Association of Health, Physical Education, and Recreation. (This is an excellent reference for psychomotor measures, assessments of abilities that the authors believe to be important to identify and cultivate despite the removal of this domain from the federal definition of giftedness.)

Frostig Movement Skills Test Battery (1972). Consulting Psychologists Press.

Test information and availability according to The Ninth Mental Measurements Yearbook and Tests in Print, 1983 Edition.

9. Standardization sample
10. Pupil behaviors sampled

The remaining data sources (biographical data; checklists or rating scales; observation schedules; parent, peer, and professional judgments; performance tests or samples; and personal interviews) can be considered as various aspects of the case study approach to gifted assessment. This approach has been shown to be effective, accurate, and more cost effective than the traditional method (Renzulli & Smith, 1977). Each of these case-study techniques will be briefly discussed.

Biographical Data

For young children, a well-developed biographical record and subsequent analysis can provide a variety of valuable clues about the child's potential giftedness, despite the child's relatively brief life span. Generally, this source can provide important developmental information about a specific child in relation to his or her age peers of the same culture. Items worthy of notice includes early psychomotor, language and numerical development, early reading (especially self-taught and special interest and hobbies (especially if self-initiated and persued with dedication, enthusiam and for long or consistent periods of time). This information is highly dependent on parents' observations which form an important component of an early identification process.

Checklists and Rating Scales

These instruments often have strong intuitive appeal but frequently lack the appropriate psychometric properties of validity and reliability. For this reason, in part, they cannot be used as exclusive means of identification. This is not meant to imply that the process of appropriate psychometric development could not be undertaken; this typically involves much time and money that could be spent otherwise. Because checklists and rating scales typically are based on the observations of gifted individuals' behaviors, they often have high content validity. They do, therefore, offer a quick-screeing method of identification of gifted individuals from within a heterogeneous group. These instruments also are usually econmical in terms of time and money. With proper training and care, the use of these instruments can provide an accurate and inexpensive prescreening component of a broader and more thorough assessment program.

Observations

Observation is the general category under which the various nomination techniques, interviews, questionnaires, and the like all fall. When formally undertaken, with well-designed schedules and trained observers, children's behaviors can be observed and assessed in naturally occurring situations at home or school, during play or work, while they are alone or interacting with peers or others. Observational techniques can be developed and statistically validated, but the results most likely will not reach the level of objective validity and reliability of standardized instruments. Though these methods can provide a wealth of infomation, the less formal the process, the less reliable are the results. Informal observations are very subjective and open to observer bias or lack of appropriate observer training leading to both false-positive and false-negative misidentifications of gifted children. Observations also are costly in time and staff needs, if not in material costs.

Parent Nominations

Parents' observations offer one of the richest sources of information about children's abilities and behaviors. Other relatives also should be considered as data sources; often grandparents, aunts and uncles, and siblings can provide detailed and additional information beyond the parents' knowledge that can be used as a confirmation of a child's interests and abilities.

Parents tend to underestimate their children's abilities. Careful questioning can elicit appropriate information to be used as the basis of an informed judgment by trained professionals. Interviews and nomination forms must be prepared in such a way, as to elicit spontaneous responses, unprompted by the interviewer or nomination format. The goal should be objective reporting of the child's behaviors and abilities, not responses prompted by or intended to please the interviewer. As with other identification methods, parent nominations can provide one source of infor-

mation in a broader assessment plan, but should not be used as a single identification criterion.

Peer Nominations

Peer nominations are perhaps the least useful and reliable of the suggested methods for early identification. Young children's judgments are often subject to a variety of irrelevent factors such as clothing or attractiveness. Often, they reflect their teacher's attitudes in school settings. When a group of children have been together over a period of time, their nominations can be a significant indication of a child's abilities in specific domains such as leadership, movement or art.

Professional Judgments

Professional judgments would include those from teachers and other school personnel, health care professionals, and any other individuals with whom the child has had extensive and frequent interactions. Professionals' judgments often are useful as supportive, confirmatory information after initial screening and more objective identifications have been made. These judgments can be used in later assessments for specific program placements. This information must be considered carefully, including the circumstances of the relationship and the context, to be alert to potential biases in either direction. For example, teachers have been shown to be relatively poor identifiers of gifted children, even with in depth and appropriate training (Ehrlich, 1980). Teachers often seem to be subject to affective biases in their judgments and selections of gifted children. They mistakenly associate socially appropriate behavior as an indicator of giftedness (e.g., maturity) while discounting a variety of accurate indicators that frequently are viewed merely as disruptive and apparent challenges. Teacher judgments can be guided and might provide useful input, as can any professional judge, but clearly this information cannot be used as a primary determinant in the assessment process.

Performance Tests and Behavior Samples

Performance abilities typically refer to talent in the visual and/or performing arts. Identification in these domains should be based on observation and behavior sampling. Few, if any standardized instruments appear to be available for performance measurements of children's abilities below the age of 8 (Ehrlich, 1980).

The expression of unusual talent or ability will be evidenced by varying and different behaviors specific to the different talent areas. Talent in visual art will be manifested by a different type of behavior and product from talent in movement or athletics. These manifestations also might express creative ability, but talent in a specific performance or visual art should not be equated with creativity itself, especially in the very young. Many of their behaviors can be expressive of creative abilities, but very specific types of behaviors, which can form sets relative to a particular talent area, are what should be considered as appropriate talent indicators. Knowledgeable individuals or groups should be consulted as judges of behavior or work samples; people whose expertise in a given area can be relied upon as the criterion of evaluation.

In all situations, physical maturation probably will influence expressed behavior; this must be considered during any evaluation. Another point of concern relates to specific training: Trained behaviors should not be confused with talent because trained behavior expresses prior knowledge and experience as well as possible talent.

Personal Interviews

Interviews are another unreliable technique of assessing a child's level and range of giftedness, especially when used by itself. Many factors can influence the course and outcome of an interview, including the child's motivation level, language skills, shyness, difficulties in establishing an open, facilitating rapport between the child and interviewer, other situational factors (e.g., removal from preferred activities leading to a lack of respoisiveness of hesitancy), health and temporary dispositional affects. Interviews rarely have the needed objectivity and lack of bias needed for a valid assessment of ability.

Interviews can be useful as a vehicle for demonstrating a child's language ability and range of information. They also can serve as supplements to information gathered through other techniques, to probe issues or ideas suggested by testing or one of the other data sources. Information from interviews will best serve assessment needs if they follow some type of consistent framework or guidelines and reflect critical points of interest and particular program structures and goals.

Future Possibilities

The potential future of preschool gifted assessment and identification can be represented by two techniques, not yet widely available, which tap two very different avenues of information. Fatouros (1986) cites the work of Malone and Moonan in the mid 1970s with "behavioral identification" of gifted children. They have developed a technique that combines the Behavioral Identification of Giftedness Questionnaire (BIG) by Malone & Moonan, (1975) and, computer analysis called CHAROUSEL, which reveals the number and types of behavioral indicators that are useful identification predictors. Research on this method has indicated promising results for highly accurate identification via behavioral predictors for elementary age children. Malone and Moonan hope to develop an abbreviated form of BIG suitable for preschool identification.

Another assessment method not specifically designed for identification of giftedness seems to have potential applications in that area. The Task of Analogical Reasoning in Children (TARC) (Alexander, Wilson, White, & Fuqua, 1987) was developed specifically to assess analogical reasoning abilities in preschool children 4 through 6 years of age, though it also has been used successfully with 3 year olds. Analogical reasoning is a frequently assessed cognitive ability, represented on virtually all currently available intelligence tests. Reasoning by analogy traditionally has been considered to be a sophisticated process beyond the cognitive capacities of preschoolers. Yet, the research using the TARC has revealed that given appropriate task demands and motivational circumstances, some degree of analogical reasoning can be demonstrated in many young children. It might be that intellectually gifted young children manifest this ability earlier, more frequently or spontaneously, or with less direct instruction and more flexible transfer than nongifted children. The research in this area is just beginning, but the TARC appears to be a promising indicator of high level cognitive ability (White & Caropreso, 1987).

Both of these techniques are tests with structured formats and assessment methods. Both are currently under development and have not yet been standardized or published, though either or both soon might be available.

SUMMARY OF GENERAL INDICATORS OF GIFTEDNESS

Despite the lack of sophisticated assessment techniques, a substantial variety of sources of information about preschool giftedness clearly exists. These sources used in combinations that are appropriate for meeting specific assessment program goals can successfully identify gifted young children who can then receive the type of educational support that will enhance and promote their particular abilities.

There appear to be five general areas of exceptional ability that can be used as indications of preschool level giftedness, including:

- Language Abilities: language development, vocabulary, range of knowledge/information and early reading
- Math ability: early math interest and ability beyond developmental expectations, especially self-taught math skills
- Psychomotor skills: early and well-developed fine and gross motoric skills
- Talent areas: visual and performing arts abilities
- Creative and/or productive thinking and learning skills.

Assessment of preschool creativity will be treated separately in the following section.

ASSESSING CREATIVE GIFTEDNESS

Informal Assessment Techniques

Two types of informal techniques are useful in assessing the creativity of preschool children: indications of precocity (performance of tasks well beyond age expectations), and behavioral indicators of specific creative strengths. Information concerning these informal indicators of creative talent can be reported by parents, teachers, or others who are in a position to observe children in action.

Indications of Precocity

Among the most widely used informal procedures are the Renzulli-Hartman scales. They are based on a survey of the research concerning characteristics of gifted children (Renzulli & Hartman. 1971). Their validity is supported by at least one experimental study with preschool children (Malone & Moonan. 1975). The following are examples that appear to be particularly well suited for assessing the creativity of preschool children:

1. *The child has unusually advanced vocabulary for age level.* Creatively gifted children are particularly characterized by their use of descriptive, feeling, and action words and the way they combine these creatively to express feelings, observations, and problem solutions.
2. *The child possesses a large storehouse of information about a variety of topics.* Intellectually gifted children also possess a large storehouse of information, but creatively gifted children possess a great deal of information learned incidentally, information not deliberately taught to them by anyone. Creatively gifted children also combine their information in creative ways and use it to solve developmental and other problems.
3. *The child has rapid insight into cause-effect relationships.* It is unusual for preschool children to formulate cause-and-effect relationships: thus, the ability to do so is itself an indicator of giftedness. Creatively gifted children also express alternative cause-and-effect relationships.
4. *The child is a keen and alert observer: usually "sees more" or "gets more" out of a story, picture, film, sightseeing trip, etc.* A mark of creatively gifted children is the ability to imagine objects from different visual perspectives.
5. *The child becomes absorbed and truly involved in certain topics or problems.* A common sign of creativity is "falling in love" with something and persisting in trying to find out more about it and solve new problems regarding it.
6. *The child strives toward perfection or excellence: is self-critical.* Most children are satisfied if they are just able to complete or per-

form tasks satifactorily. This is not enough for creative children. They have an image of excellence of performance and strive for such an attainment.

7. *The child is interested in many "adult" problems such as religion, politics, sex, race, etc.* Ordinarily, preschool children cannot imagine themselves into the problems of others, especially adults.

8. *The child likes to organize and bring structure to things, people, and situations.* Intellectually gifted children tend to organize things sequentially, where creatively gifted children are likely to organize them in such ways as to show new or unusual relationships among them.

9. *The child displays a great deal of curiosity about many things and an intense curiosity about something.* Creative children are interested in almost everything, but when attending to something of intense interest they might ignore other things and resist efforts to interest them in something else.

10. *The child displays a keen sense of humor and sees humor in situations that might not appear to be humorous to others.* Creative children specialize in seeing and producing perceptual and conceptual incongruities which at first might appear to be "silly" or "nonsense" to the adult.

Behavioral Indicators of Creative Strengths

Torrance (1977) suggested detailed checklists of behavioral indicators of creative strengths. Table 19–2 is an abbreviated list of the indicators that are at least fairly common among preschool children. Most of these behavioral indicators generally are regarded as being beyond the developmental level of preschool children. Thus, children not displaying these behaviors should not be regarded as "normal" or even as "not gifted." However, if these behaviors are displayed with any degree of consistency, such behaviors can be regarded as possible indicators of creative talent.

Formal Assessment Techniques

Although there are a variety of procedures for assessing creative thinking abilities, only a few such instruments are suitable for use with pre-

school children. Most tests call for oral, verbal, or drawing responses, and most preschool children are handicapped in expressing their creativity in these modalities because the requisite skills are not adequately developed.

Starkweather (1964, 1971) pioneered the development of creativity tests for preschool children. Her test tasks required neither verbal skills nor drawing ability and were quite promising, but they required considerable equipment for their ad-

TABLE 19.2
CHECKLIST OF BEHAVIORAL INDICATORS OF CREATIVE STRENGTH

Improvisation with commonplace materials
> Makes toys from commonplace materials and junk
> Makes games from common materials, natural settings, etc.
> Uses common objects for unintended uses in the home, school, and on the playground
> Makes "inventions" from common objects
> Uses common objects to solve problems in creative dramatics, art, etc.

Role playing and storytelling
> Becomes deeply absorbed in role playing, creative dramatics, or storytelling
> Produces many fresh ideas in the process of role playing and storytelling
> Makes up unusual, surprising solutions in stories and role playing
> Produces solutions to collision conflicts for which there seem to be no logical solutions

Visual arts
> Just loves to draw, paint, sculpt, etc.
> Experiences deep absorption and great joy in drawing, painting, sculpting, etc.
> Understands (comprehends) subject matter by "drawing it"
> Communicates skillfully and powerfully through drawings, paintings, and other visual media

Creative movement and dance
> Just loves creative movement and dance
> Becomes intensely absorbed in creative movement and dance
> Persists for long periods in creative movement and dance
> Can interpret songs, poems, stories, etc. through creative movement and dance
> Can elaborate ideas through creative movement and dane
> Movement and dance facilitate learning and understanding of events, concepts, and reading/literary materials

TABLE 19.2 (*continued*)

Music and rhythm
    Writes, draws, works, moves with rhythm
    Interprets ideas, events, feelings, and subject matter through music and/or rhythm
    Becomes deeply involved and works perseveringly at musical and rhythmic activities
    Is exceptionally responsive to sound stimuli and uses music and rhythm to facilitate the learning of subject matter
Expressive speech
    Speech is colorful and picturesque
    Speech includes analogies and metaphors
    Speech is vivid (i.e., lively, intense, exciting, etc.)
    Invents words and combinations of words to express concepts and feelings for which vocabulary is inadequate
    Tells stories and recounts happenings as though the thing is happening
Fluency and flexibility in nonverbal modes
    Produces many ideas through drawings, manipulation, movement, etc.
    Arranges blocks and other play materials in many combinations
    Assembles and reassembles complex machines with ease
    Produces images in response to music, sounds, movement
    Is good at "making things go"
Group skills
    Influences other children to engage in projects he or she initiates
    Organizes the group and group tasks with skill
    Working in groups sparks imagination and facilitates problem solving
    Becomes more alive in small groups
    Is intensely aware of feelings and skills of others in small groups
    Supports other members of group and helps just at the right time
    Initiates activities in small groups
Responsiveness to the concrete
    Produces a large flow of ideas and alternative solutions when concrete objects are involved
    Conceptualizes problems in terms of concrete objects
    Uses concrete objects to generate new ideas
    Works intensely for long periods on concrete puzzles, mechanical problems, etc.
Responsiveness of the kinesthetic
    Skillfully communicates ideas through movement
    Skillfully interprets the movements of others
    Movement is effective as a warm-up for creative activities
    Displays skillful manipulative movement

TABLE 19.2 (*continued*)

    Makes quick, precise movements in mime, creative dramatics
    Shows movement in drawings and other visual products
    Displays total bodily involvement in interpreting a story, song, etc.
Humor
    (Whenever production of humor occurs among preschool children it should be regarded as a possible indicator of creative giftedness)
    Makes people laugh a lot in games
    Makes up humorous jokes and stories
    Describes personal experiences with humor
Persistence and problem-centeredness
    Does not give up easily in solving a problem
    Persists in asking questions about a problem or event
    Is stimulated by challenging problems
    Is hard to distract when absorbed in a problem
    Returns to a problem or unfinished task time after time

(From Torrance, E. P. (1977) *Discovery and Nurturance of Giftedness in the Culturally Different.* Reston, Va.: Council on Exceptional Children.)

ministration and were never widely used. Her untimely death apparently halted further development of these instruments. However, they have been described carefully in the literature and provide possible clues for others wishing to extend the development of assessment procedures in this area.

At present, the most widely used formal procedures for assessing creative thinking abilities are those developed by Torrance (1974, 1975, 1981a, 1981b). The long-range predictive validity of these tests taken during the elementary and high school years has been reported (Torrance, 1972a, 1972b, 1974, 1975, 1981b) but thus far there have been no studies reporting a relationship between the test performances of preschool children and creative achievements in adulthood. Until such information is available, it seems desirable to be guided by the recommendation of Chambers and Barron (1978) that identification procedures be concerned with all relevant traits that have been found to characterize persons who have achieved at high creative levels, as evidenced by their scholarly, artistic, and scientific contributions. Chambers and Barron recommended further that we identify at as early an age as possible those children who show intellectual, motivational, and personality potential most similar to that of highly creative adult scientists, artists, writers, and so on.

The major instruments for use with young children are described below.

Torrance Tests of Creative Thinking

The Torrance Tests of Creative Thinking (Torrance, 1974) consist of alternate forms of two batteries: Thinking Creatively with Words (Verbal Forms A and B) and Thinking Creatively with Pictures (Figural Forms A and B). The figural forms can be administered from age 5 years upward in groups and require 30 minutes of testing time. Standard scoring provides measures of fluency, flexibility, originality and elaboration. A new alternative scoring system provides norm-referenced measures of fluency, originality, elaboration, resistance to premature closure, and abstract thinking and criterion-referenced measures or indicators of unusual visual perspective, richness and colorfulness of imagery, synthesis, humor, putting things in context, and other indicators of creative thinking in the visual modality.

The verbal forms can be administered to children from kindergarten through grade 3 as an individual test and require 45 minutes for administration. They provide scores for fluency, flexibility, and orginality. Some of the verbal tasks are difficult for most preschool children but can identify highly gifted children in the verbal creative modality.

This test was originally developed in 1958 and has been used in 1,000 published research studies. Scores on these tests show little or no racial or socioeconomic bias when used with preschool children. The figural tests have been used quite successfully with deaf children, and the verbal tests have proved quite successful with both vision-impaired and hearing-impaired children.

Thinking Creatively in Action and Movement

Thinking Creatively in Action and Movement (Torrance, 1981a) permits children to respond in movement, in words, or in a combination of both: however, the kinesthetic modality is favored by this test. It is designed for use with children ranging in age from 3 to 7 years and requires 15 to 30 minutes for administration. It is especially useful with children who are unwilling or unable to talk to an examiner. It provides a total score and subscores on fluency, originality, and imagination.

Developmental work on this test began in 1974 and it was published in 1981 following considerable pretesting and 15 research studies. This test seems to have no more than racial or socioeconomic bias. Economically disadvantaged children give more kinesthetic responses than affluent children, and affluent children give more verbal responses than their economically disadvantaged counterparts. It also has been used successfully with emotionally handicapped and deaf children. This test is more appropriate for use with preschool children than the older Torrance Tests of Creative Thinking: children are encouraged to express their thinking in the kinesthetic modality, which is more compatible with the developmental status of preschool children than the verbal and visual modalities required by the latter.

Starkweather and Moran's Work

Elizabeth K. Starkweather (1964, 1971) at Oklahoma State University initiated some very promising work in the early 1960s. She believed that the preschool creative child was original, neither conforming nor nonconforming, but held onto his or her own ideas, and was willing to try the difficult. Some of her work has been taken over by Moran, Sawyers, Fu, Milgram, and their associates (Moran, et al., 1983a, 1983b; Fu, Kelso & Moran, 1984). Moran is now at the University of Tennessee but is still collaborating with Sawyers, Fu, and others. Their emphasis has been with the validation of some of the Starkweather tests and some of their own measures and with some very basic characteristics of the tests.

IMPLICATIONS OF ASSESSMENT

The results of both the informal and formal assessment procedures described in this chapter primarily should be used to make parents, teachers, school psychologists, and others aware of the creative strengths of preschool children. The recognition and acknowledgment of these strengths can lead to programs to increase the children's success and satisfaction in learning and problem solving. Creative strengths also can be interpreted as indicators of talents which, if given practice and opportunity, will result in creative behavior in meeting developmental problems and in childhood and adult creative achievement. However, caution must be used in prediction at the preschool level; many societal conditions influence creative development and opportunities for creative expression and achievement.

It is important that parents, teachers, and school psychologists recognize that creative thinking is a skill that has to be developed by direct attention (De Bono, 1975), and the best type of attention is practice. This practice must take place in the right environment and with the right tools. Some people believe that creative thinking is so natural a skill that there is no need to make any deliberate effort to develop it; however, without deliberate effort the degree of skill developed is likely to fall far below the child's potential.

REFERENCES

Alexander, P. A., Willson, V. L., White, C. S., & Fuqua, J. D. (1987). Analogical reasoning in young children. *Journal of Educational Psychology, 79,* 401–408.

Amabile, T. M. (1987). The motivation to be creative. In S. G. Isaksen (Ed.). *Frontiers of Creativity Research,* pp. 223–254.

Binet, A. (1909). *Les Idees Modernes sur les Enfants.* Paris, France: E. Flamarion.

Binet, A., & Simon, T. (1916). *The Development of Intelligence in Children.* (E. S. Kite, Trans.). Baltimore, Williams & Wilkins.

Bracken, B. A. (1987). Limitations of preschool instruments and standards for minimal levels of technical adequacy. *Journal of Psychoeducational Assessment, 5,* 313–326.

Brown, A. L., & DeLoche, J. S. (1978). Skills, plans, and self-regulation. In R. S. Siegler (Ed.). *Children's Thinking: What Develops?,* pp. 3–35. Hillsdale, NJ: Erlbaum.

Chambers, J. A., & Barron, F. (1978). The culturally different gifted student: Identifying the ablest. *Journal of Creative Behavior, 12,* 72–74.

DeBono, E. (1975). *Think Links.* Blandford, Dorset, United Kingdom: Direct Educational Services, 1975.

Denton, C., & Postwaithe, K. (1985). *Able Children: Identifying Them in the Classroom.* Philadelphia, PA: Nfer-Nelson.

Ehrlich, V. Z. (1980). Identifying giftedness in the early

years: From 3 through 7. In Ventura County Superintendent of Schools (Ed.). *Educating the Preschool/Primary Gifted and Talented,* pp. 3–22. Los Angeles, CA: N/S LTI on the Gifted and Talented.

Fatouros, C. (1986). Early identification of gifted children is crucial . . . but how should we go about it?, *Gifted Education International, 4*(1), 24–28.

Fu, V. R., Kelso, G. B., & Moran, J. D. III. (1984). *Educational and Psychological Measurement, 44,* 431–440.

Gelman, R. (1978) Cognitive development. *Annual Review of Psychology, 29,* 297–332.

Gentner, D. (1977). Children's performance on a spatial analogies task. *Child Development, 48,* 1034–1039.

Guilford, J. P. (1956). The structure of intellect. *Psychological Bulletin, 53,* 267–293.

Guilford, J. P. (1968) *Intelligence, Creativity and Their Educational Implications.* San Diego, CA: Robert R. Knapp.

Guilford, J. P. (1986). *Creative Talents: Their Nature, Use, and Development.* Buffalo, NY: Bearly Limited.

Hagen, E. (1980). *Identification of the Gifted.* New York: Teachers College, Columbia University.

Heller, K. A., & Feldhusen, J. F. (1985). *Identifying and Nurturing the Gifted: An International Perspective.* Lewiston, NY: Hans Huber.

Hutchins, T. A., Hamilton, S. E., Town, P. A., Gaddis, L. R., & Presley, R. (1988) *The Stability of IQ in the Preschool Population: A Review.* (Unpublished manuscript.)

Kaufman, A. S. (1983). Some questions and answers about the K-ABC. *Journal of Psychoeducational Assessment, 1,* 205–218.

Kaufman, A. S., & Kaufman, N. L. (1983) *Kaufman Assessment Battery for Children Interpretation Manual.* Circle Pines, MN: American Guidance Service.

Maccoby, E. E., & Jacklin, C. N. (1974). *The Psychology of Sex Differences.* Stanford, CA: Stanford University Press.

Malone, C., & Moonan, W. J. (1975). Behavioral identificational of gifted children. *Gifted Child Quarterly, 19,* 301–306.

Marland, S. (1972). *Education of the gifted and Talented, I. Report to Congress of the United States by the Commissioner of education.* Washington, DC: U. S. Office of Education.

Martin, D. (1986). *Is My Child Gifted?: A Guide for Caring Parents.* Springfield, IL: Thomas.

Mitchell, J. V. (ed.) (1983). *Tests in Print. III.* Lincoln, NE: University of Nebraska Press.

Mitchell, J. V. (1985). *The Ninth Mental Measurements Yearbook.* Vols. I and II. Lincoln, NE: University of Nebraska Press.

Moran, J. D. III, Milgram, R. M., Sawyers, J. K., & Fu, V. R. (1983a). Original thinking in preschool children. *Child Development, 54,* 921–926.

Moran, J. D. III, Milgram, R. M., Sawyers, J. K., & Fu, V. R. (1983b). Stimulus specificity in the measurement of original thinking in preschool children, *Journal of Psychology, 114,* 99–105.

Naglieri, J. A., & Anderson, D. F. (1985). Comparison of the WISC-R and the K-ABC with gifted students. *Journal of Psychoeducational Assessment, 3,* 175–179.

Parnes, S. J. (1981). *The Magic of Your Mind.* Buffalo, NY: Bearly Limited.

Parnes, S. J. (1987). The creative studies project. In S. G. Isakson (Ed.). *Frontiers of Creativity Research,* pp. 156–188.

Parnes, S. J., & Meadow, A. (1960). Evaluation of persistence of effects produced by a creative problem-solving course. *Psychological Reports, 7,* 357–361.

Renzulli, J. S. (1979). What makes giftedness?: Reexamining a definition. *Phi Delta Kappan, 60,* 180–184, 261.

Renzulli, J. S., & Hartman, R. K. (1971). Scale for rating behavioral characteristics of superior students. *Exceptional Children, 38,* 243–248.

Renzulli, J. S., & Smith, L. H. (1977). Two approaches to identification of gifted students. *Exceptional Children, 43,* 512–518.

Starkweather, E. K. (1964). Problems in the measurement of creativity in preschool children. *Journal of Educational Measurement, 1,* 109–114.

Starkweather, E. K. (1971). Creativity research instrument designed for use with preschool children. *Journal of Creative Behavior, 5,* 245–255.

Sternberg, R. S., & Davidson, J. (Eds.). (1986). *Conceptions of Giftedness.* New York: Cambridge University Press.

Tannenbaum, A. J. (1983). *Gifted Children: Psychological and Educational Perspectives.* New York: Macmillan.

Taylor, C. W. (Ed.). (1964) *Widening Horizons in Creativity.* New York: John Wiley.

Terman, L. M. (1925). *Genetic Studies of Genius: Vol. 1. Mental and Physical Traits of a Thousand Gifted Children.* Stanford, CA: Stanford University Press.

Terman, L. M., & Oden, M. H. (1947). *Genetic studies of genius: Vol. IV. The gifted child grows up: Twenty-five years' follow-up of a superior group.* Stanford, CA: Stanford University Press.

Torrance, E. P. (1962). *Guiding Creative Talent.* Englewood Cliffs, NJ: Prentice-Hall.

Torrance, E. P. (1963) *Education and the Creative Potential.* Minneapolis, MN: University of Minnesota Press.

Torrance, E. P. (1965). *Rewarding Creative Behavior.* Englewood Cliffs, NJ: Prentice-Hall.

Torrance, E. P. (1969). *Dimensions of Early Learning Series: Creativity.* Sioux Falls, SD: Adapt Press.

Torrance, E. P. (1970). *Encouraging Creativity in the Classroom.* Dubuque, IA: William Brown.

Torrance, E. P. (1972a). Career patterns and peak creative achievements of creative high school students twelve years later. *Gifted Child Quarterly, 16,* 75–88.

Torrance, E. P. (1972b). The predictive validity of the Torrance Tests of Creative Thinking. *Journal of Creative Behavior, 6,* 236–252.

Torrance, E. P. (1974). *Norms-technical manual: The Torrance Tests of Creative Thinking.* Bensenville, IL: Scholastic Testing Service. (Original research edition published in 1966 by Personnel Press, at Princeton, NJ.)

Torrance, E. P. (1975). Creativity research in education: Still alive. In I. A. Taylor & J. W. Getzels (ed.) *Perspectives in Creativity.* Chicago: Aldine.

Torrance, E. P. (1977). *Discovery and Nurturance of Giftedness in the Culturally Different.* Reston, VA: Council on Exceptional Children.

Torrance, E. P. (1981a). *Thinking Creatively with Action and Movement.* Bensenville, IL: Scholastic Testing Service.

Torrance, E. P. (1981b). Predicting the creativity of elementary school children (1958–80)—And the teachers who made a difference. *Gifted Child Quarterly, 25,* 55–62.

Torrance, E. P., & Wu, T. H. (1981). A comparative longitudinal of the adult creative achievements of elementary school children identified as highly intelligent and as highly creative. *Creative Child and Adult Quarterly, 6,* 71–76.

Tuttle, F. B., & Becker, L. A. (1980). *Characteristics and Identification of Gifted and Talented Students.* Washington, DC: National Educational Association.

White, C. S., & Caropreso, E. S. (November 1987). Analogical reasoning in young gifted children. Paper presented at the annual meeting of the National Association for Gifted Children, New Orleans, LA.

20

Assessment of Social and Emotional Behavior

ROY P. MARTIN

Until recently, parents and child care workers were not very concerned with the assessment of the social and emotional functioning of preschool children. There were many reasons for this lack of concern. Among the most important was the idea that the development of the preschool child was the concern of the family, and it was the right and obligation of the parents to monitor the social growth and development of the child. Parents had come to understand that medical evaluations of young children were desirable and necessary, and some parents even sought assessment for school readiness (thought of in cognitive terms). The need for special assistance from professionals to obtain information about a young child's behavior or personality has not been recognized until recently.

The social and emotional life of the preschool child was considered residing in the domain of the family because the social and emotional behavior of the child was thought of as a direct reflection of the values of the parents, and parents should have a right to perpetuate their values; the social and emotional life of the preschool child is fairly simple so the vast majority of parents can handle this aspect of their child's life without professional assessment or consultation; social and emotional problems among this group are very rare, and if the child is having social and emotional problems it is because the parents are grossly neglectful of their socialization duties or are extremely punitive; public and professional concern should be applied only in these extreme cases. Many parents who raised children in the 1940s and '50s would clearly have held these views, and many parents in the '90s still probably share them. Unfortunately, these views have been demonstrated in the past decade or two to be based on an incomplete understanding of the development of the preschool child and the effects the child's behavior has on parents and teachers.

Perhaps the most important single factor fostering increased professional interest in social and emotional assessment of very young children is the downward extension of schooling and out-of-home child care arrangements for children in this age group. In 1985, 2.5 million children (39%) were enrolled in prekindergarten programs compared to 700,000 (11%) in 1965 (Elkind, 1987). For 5-year-old-children, in particular, formal public schooling is nearly universal. In 1985, 82% of 5 year olds attended kindergarten (Elkind, 1987). By 1987, only New Hampshire, New Mexico, and Mississippi did not require kindergarten, but in these states local districts could require kindergarten attendance. This means that the name applied to children in this age group (i.e., Preschoolers) is a misnomer, because most have had some schooling experience (Scarr & Weinberg, 1986).

Thus, most preschool-age children are coming into contact with socializing institutions or individuals other than the family. They are being held accountable to a set of behavioral and developmental expectations held by people who have contact with a variety of children, and who, because of their training or simply through contact with numerous preschool children, have a better understanding of developmental norms than many parents. This means that children who were developing in a manner that is outside normative expectations are being recognized much earlier now than in the past. When children do not meet normative expectations, there is a need to document the nature of the problem, to form hypotheses about the probable causes of the problem, and perhaps to begin an intervention. Out of this identification-intervention need has come the press for more formal and sophisticated assessment of preschool children.

Another important factor has created the social press for assessment of younger children, and that is the rapid growth in scientific knowledge about the psychological development of preschool children. In the last 15 years, there has been an explosion of work in the area of developmental psychopathology, development of social skills, and emotional development. This body of knowledge has begun to percolate through the culture from researchers to applied practitioners, educators, and parents. Pediatricians, preschool teachers, and the national lay media (e.g., *Parents* magazine) are particularly important disseminators of this kind of information to parents. As parents come into contact with information about learning disabilities, attention deficit disorders, and temperamental predispositions for psychopathology, (to list only a few examples), they want to know how their children are doing now, what kinds of behavior might be expected in the future, and what school programs best fit the individual needs of their children.

The economically developed countries of the world are entering an age in which information is the commodity most valued. As agriculture was the basis of the economy of our grandparents, and industrial production was the basis of the economy of our parents, information production and exchange will be the basis of the economy of our children. The world of an information economy fosters the development of experts simply because there are vast amounts of information in each area of life that must be understood, synthesized, and disseminated. It also fosters dependence on specialists for this same reason. Our grandmothers were generalists, cooking, cleaning, raising children, and perhaps plowing the fields. They were generalists because the tasks were thought to be relatively simple, and could be mastered by one person. Many mothers and fathers in the 1990s must work outside the home at tasks that are more complex, and require extensive training. They have become specialists. Thus in many families, more and more meals are eaten outside the home because food preparation can be done more efficiently by specialists. Child care is likewise more and more the province of specialists outside the home. The preschool psychologist is one facet of this specialized care. Preschool psychologists provide information derived through knowledge of relevant research and practice, but also knowledge derived through specialized procedures (i.e., tests and other assessment procedures). Thus, preschool assessment can be viewed as one manifestation of an ever increasing press toward an information economy.

SPECIAL PROBLEMS

Because many of the readers of this chapter have specialized knowledge in the area of personality and behavioral assessment of children and adolescents, it seems important to state why specific skills and training are needed to conduct a personality or behavioral assessment of a preschool child. In brief, the rationale for specialized skills for preschool children is based on the fact that children in this age group have restricted cognitive abilities, and restricted abilities to express themselves. These limitations eliminate or greatly diminish the usefulness of most assessment techniques used with older children and adults.

For example, self-report methods used so

often with adults and older children are eliminated from consideration with preschool children because most children in this age group cannot read. Thus, they cannot respond to written stimuli, understand written directions, and often cannot understand the response format. Self-report instruments require additional cognitive skills that are outside the capabilities of most preschool children. For example, Harter (1985) has reported that many children below the age of 7 have difficulty comparing their skills and behavior to those of other children. Thus when asked, "Can you run faster than your friends in class?", most children have not made or cannot make these comparisons, and their responses to such a question have little validity.

Meaningful interviews with preschool children require different techniques and different expectations on the part of the interviewer than those with older children. For example, many aspects of the relationship between the child and family members are subtle, and the child is unaware of these aspects, or cannot express them appropriately. For example, the preschool child might be able to say that mother and daddy yell at them but they will have difficulty discriminating between legitimate socialization attempts, and psychological abuse.

In addition, much of the projective technology used with older children is of limited usefulness because of these same verbal and cognitive limitations. Drawing projectives are most often not useable because of the child's limited response capabilities in this fine motor domain. The child of 3 and 4 is typically capable of drawing only vertical and horizontal lines, circles, squares, oblique lines, and crosses (Beery, 1982). For this reason, drawing productions frequently have too little detail to allow for meaningful interpretation.

One of the most difficult problems in preschool assessment is that children in this age group do not universally understand the demand characteristics of the assessment situation. They do not understand, for example, why such assessments are done, and the importance placed on their responses. Further, preschool children often do not have the ability to control their behavior to meet the expectation of the assessment situation, even if they understand them.

All these limitations restrict the psychologist to the use of parent and teacher ratings scales as the primary assessments tools. Data from such instruments are augmented by interview data from caretakers and the child, and direct observation of the child in natural settings, or in settings contrived specifically for the purposes of assessment (e.g., use of doll play for purposes of assessment). Perhaps 90% of the data reported by psychologists about the social and emotional behavior of the preschool child are taken from rating scales and observations made by psychologists in psychological or educational assessment situations, such as observations of behavior in response to measures of cognitive ability. For that reason, the discussion of instrumentation and techniques in this chapter will focus on rating scales, one of which is designed to record observations during a psychoeducational assessment. (For discussions of other techniques such as sociometry see Martin, 1986, 1988a.)

DESIGNING THE ASSESSMENT

For the assessment of the preschool child, as well as older children, five sets of decisions must be made to maximize the usefulness of an assessment. These include:

1. Determining the scope of the assessment (e.g., the number of behaviors to be sampled)
2. Determining the purpose of the assessment
3. Developing a plan that can be carried out with available resources
4. Selecting the appropriate instruments to meet the considerations listed above
5. Maximizing the reliability of the assessment information

Because of the space limitations of this chapter, only two of these considerations will be discussed, determining the purpose of the assessment and maximizing the reliability of the assessment. (For a more extensive discussion, see Martin, 1988a.)

Determining the Purpose of the Assessment

There are two broad purposes for assessment of social and emotional behavior: for prediction or classification, and for behavior change.

When the goal of assessment is prediction of future behavior, the psychologist must deal with broad behavioral tendencies (clusters of behavior) usually thought of as traits. These tendencies or traits are hypothesized to have some temporal stability and to be somewhat stable across situations. Such characteristics as anxiety, sociability, or emotionality are examples of traits that are often measured during the preschool years.

The reason that broad constructs are necessary for purposes of prediction can be made clear through considering a few simple examples. In attempting to predict emotional disturbance in the early elementary school years from a measure taken in preschool, it seems unlikely that the number of times the child cries during a two-day visit with her grandmother would be a useful measure. It would not be useful because it is an unreliable measure (Would the child cry during visits to other relatives?). The measure might be more useful if a total count was obtained for crying episodes on visits with grandmother, aunts, uncles, and babysitters over a period of six months. In augmenting the measure in this way both reliability and situational generalizability have been enhanced. If the measure were enhanced further to include withdrawing behavior on initial contact with strangers, and speed of adaptation to new surroundings, in addition to crying, the ability to predict would be even better, because psychopathology is a broad construct encompassing many kinds of behaviors, not just crying or expressions of emotional distress.

If the goal of the assessment is to change the behavior of a child in a given setting, assessment of broad traits or large clusters of behavior is inappropriate and wasteful. If, for example, the psychologist wished to help parents control the crying behavior of their 3-year-old-child at grandmother's house, then crying behavior at grandmother's house must be assessed. Reliability of the data is important so an appropriate sample of behavior would be required. However, cross-situation stability and long-range temporal stability are irrelevant concerns in that the problem is defined in a situational manner.

If the psychologist has decided that the purpose of assessment is one of managing behavior in a specific setting, techniques that include observation, coding behavior, and sampling behavior during intervention become paramount. This chapter will not deal in any detail with these issues or other issues of design of this kind of assessment because there are a number of excellent sources available on this subject (e.g., Bellack & Hersen, 1988; Boehm & Weinberg, 1987; Kent & Foster, 1977; Sackett 1978; Simeonsson, 1986).

With regard to the general category of predictive/classification assessment, it is useful to differentiate four more specific purposes of assessment. These are screening, classification within the normal range of behavior, differentiating normal from abnormal behavior, and differential diagnosis of abnormal behavior (Martin, 1988). Persons engaged in preschool assessment can engage in each of these types of assessment and must be able to differentiate among them to design an appropriate assessment.

Screening is used as a procedure to isolate those who are to assessed further from a larger group (Anastasi, 1988), and also can be useful in identifying persons at risk of some unwanted condition (Salvia & Ysseldyke, 1988). Both purposes are among the most frequent reasons for a preschool assessment. Because most preschoolers referred for an assessment have not developed a diagnosable pathology, the dominant purpose of the assessment is to determine whether the child is at risk for later school failure or psychopathology.

Because screening is applied to a large group of children, screening assessments must be brief. Further, most screenings are designed to cover a wide range of behaviors. Thus screening assessments sacrifice depth of coverage for breadth of coverage. Because no single cluster of behaviors is assessed with many items, the dominant characteristic of screening data from a psychometric point of view is that it tends to be less reliable than data from intensive assessments.

In a small percentage of preschool evaluations the primary purpose is to determine whether a significant clinical problem exists, and if so, what the nature of the problem is. As has been pointed out elsewhere (Martin, 1988a), the purpose of determining *if* a problem exists can be differentiated from determining *what* problem exists. The first purpose can be thought of as a type of screening in which a broad spectrum pathology measure is administered with a total score above a specified cut-off being indicative of a problem without specifying the problem. Such measures are routine in medicine (e.g., the thermometer), but are rare in psychology. The Behavior Rating Profile (Brown & Hammill, 1983) is one of the few measures that is designed to accomplish this specific task in the social-emotional realm for children, but unfortunately for those interested in the preschool population, it is not designed or normed for children below the age of 6½ years.

Differential diagnosis is the most complex type of assessment. In addition to requiring an empirically sound classification system and measures of different types of psychopathology that are relevant to this system, it requires the ability to determine whether a significant problem exists, and if so, which one of several types of pathology is present. For the preschool child, it is fair to say that the classification system of pathology is poorly developed (Achenbach et al. 1987). Further, the instruments that are now used with preschoolers are few in number, rarely designed for this population, and in the initial stages of development. This makes the diagnosis of a specific type of social/emotional disturbance among preschool children extremely difficult.

To summarize, the purpose of this section has been to sensitize those who do assessments of preschool children to think carefully about what they are attempting to accomplish before they begin to see the child. The psychologist who uses the same battery of instruments for all assessments is giving no consideration to purpose, and is reducing himself/herself to the role of a technician. This discussion also should leave the psychologist with the message that rigid theory-based adherence to principles of personality assessment (assessment of broad traits) or behavioral assessment (assessment of specific behaviors manifested in limited environments) as the sole approach is unjustified and inappropriate. The purpose of the assessment is to determine whether further assessment of traits or behaviors is necessary.

Maximizing the Reliability of the Assessment Information

It is more difficult to describe the social and emotional characteristics of children (particularly young children) in an objective manner than it is to describe many other characteristics of children. Physical characteristics, gender, perceptual–motor skill, cognitive ability, and educational achievement level can all be described with greater reliability than social or emotional behavior.

There are many reasons why social and emotional behaviors are difficult to describe. First, other characteristics of children are more stable over time (Brim & Kagan, 1980). Second, social and emotional behavior is more sensitive to environmental factors than many other characteristics (Mischel, 1968). For example, color naming skill can be assessed on the play ground, in the classroom, or at home. If questions about color are presented in the same way in all settings, the child who can name red and black in one setting should be able to do it in all settings. However, the social behavior of the child might change significantly across these settings. For example the child might be an isolate at play with peers, but interact a great deal with teachers and parents.

Third, characteristics such as stature, cognitive skills performance, and perceptual–motor skills performance also can be directly observed and measured with current technology. However, assessors who are interested in generalized social tendencies often cannot afford to observe the behavior for several weeks or months to obtain the measure. Thus, the behavior must be measured through the perceptual apparatus and memories of another human being, usually the parent or preschool teacher for young children. When events are measured in this way, distortion is an inevitable byproduct (Brody & Forehand, 1986).

Because the social and emotional behavior of young children is temporally and situationally unstable, and because the problem of rater bias exists, the assessor of preschool children, must design the assessment in such a way that these problems are controlled or measured. Because these factors create variance in data that detracts from the reliable measurement of characteristics, it is referred to as error variance. Four types of error variance must be considered: temporal variance, setting variance, source variance, and instrument variance (Martin, 1988a).

The primary method for controlling error variance in an assessment is through the principle of aggregation (Epstein, 1979; Ghiselli et al., 1981). Thus, to control for temporal variance, data are collected at different times and then is averaged to eliminate this variation. To control setting variance, data are obtained across settings and averaged to obtain a generalized index of the behavior. To control for source variance in rating measures, the ratings of multiple persons are averaged. The principle in operation in these examples is the same principle that dictates a test of more than one item, or a jury of more than one person.

Obviously, to make aggregation possible, data must be collected on multiple occasions, from multiple sources, in multiple settings. The best assessment design also collects data using multiple measures in each setting, for each rater, at each time, because different instruments produce somewhat different results even if they were designed to assess the same characteristic. Such a design is a goal to be aimed for, but one that is often impractical. However, to the extent that this type of assessment is not used, a source of error variance is introduced into the assessment, and the assessor becomes less confident in the outcome.

For example, if a 4-year-old child had been referred because of aggressive behavior toward peers (e.g., unprovoked biting, hitting,) and general impulsivity, the psychologist might obtain ratings reflecting the extent of these behaviors from the mother, the teacher, and a teaching aide. In this design, two settings are sampled, using one measure, and the assessment is carried out on one occasion. This design will provide some useful information, but falls far short of the ideal described previously. The shortcomings of the design will become clear if the mother provides ratings that are quite different from those of the teacher and aide. In this case it will be impossible to determine if the child behaves differently at home than at school, or that the mother is biased in her observations of the child in the home. If the father's ratings were available, and agreed with the teacher and aide, we would have a better idea that the problem was the mother's defensiveness or some other such biasing factor. Following this example through to issues of instrument and temporal variance, it can be seen that the assessor must be careful in generalizing about the nature of the child.

To summarize, methods of controlling error variance are important considerations in designing an assessment. Not only should the assessor design the assessment to control for temporal, source, instrument, and setting variance, but if cost factors ultimately limit the comprehensiveness of design, the assessor should be keenly aware of how the design limitations might have

effected the reliability and thus the meaningfulness of the resulting data.

DEVELOPMENTAL TASKS FOR PRESCHOOLERS

Assessment typically involves procedures designed to determine if a child can perform some class of behaviors that typical children of that age group can perform. To understand which social and emotional behaviors of preschool children are most frequently assessed, it is important to understand the major developmental tasks of children in this age group.

As has been pointed out by Lamb and Baumrind (1978), the preschool years are noted for their beginning. They mark the beginning of socialization attempts by the parents (or at least the beginning of serious disciplinary attempts), the beginning of extra-familial child care, the beginning of peer relations and peer influence on behavior, and the beginning of the media as socialization agents. Consistent with this theme of beginnings, most theorists do not posit many significant milestones or major attainments of this period; rather it is a period in which progress toward recognized milestones is noted.

Despite a general familial and societal tolerance for progress toward goals as opposed to attainment, there remain some behaviors that socialization agents, at least in the U.S.A. and similar cultures, believe most preschoolers should be able to perform. For example, children should be able to control bowel and bladder well enough by age five so that they can use a toilet for purposes of elimination. They should be able to sleep by themselves through the night most of the time. Also, they should be willing and able to eat many of the foods served by the family for other family members. Thus, there is a cluster of functions dealing with control of biological function that the child is expected to have made major progress on attaining.

A second group of behaviors involves the control of activity and attention. Three year old children are active and tend to have short attention spans. However, by age 5 there is a general expectation that activity level will have come under some control, and that attention span will have increased.

A third cluster of behaviors has to do with

dependency on adults. Toddlers are extremely dependent, demanding the proximity and attention of the caretaker a good deal of the time. However, by the preschool years children are expected to be able to exercise some independence, and there is strong socialization pressure toward this end in most families.

The preschool child is expected to be happy some of the time, if not most of the time, and to have overcome some of the fears that were in evidence during infancy and the toddler years. Further, the frequency of temper tantrums that probably reached a peak during the second and third year, should be beginning to reduce in frequency during the subsequent years. These behaviors related to the emotions of the preschooler constitute a fourth cluster of expectations.

As children begin to interact with others, they are expected to begin to do so without the presence of aggression and hostility. The 5 year old is not expected to be a facile social problem solver, but he or she is expected to interact with other children at least some of the time in a manner that enhances the enjoyment of both parties, and does not demand constant refereeing by the caretaker. Thus there is a cluster of social expectations for preschoolers.

Finally, the preschool child is expected to respond to the socialization attempts made by the caretaker in an appropriate way. If repeated attempts to change a behavior of the child are unsuccessful, or the child resists most socialization attempts in an intense and emotional manner, the parents might begin to think of their child as difficult, developmentally slow, or stubborn. This cluster of expectations can be thought of as a more general or higher-order set of expectations that are reflected in the ease with which the child responds to socialization demands toward more specific self-help and adaptive expectations (e.g., toileting expectations).

THE BASE RATE OF PROBLEM BEHAVIORS AMONG PRESCHOOLERS

When behavior expectations are not met, the parent might seek the help of a psychologist or some other mental health professional. To determine whether a problem exists (in the sense of statistical rarity of the behavior), the assessor

must have some idea about the base rate of problems in the areas mentioned. Unfortunately, there is a serious lack of simple descriptions of problem behaviors of preschool children.

One of the best sources of such data come from a study by Richman, and associates (1982). (While the data were obtained in England and thus might have been open to criticisms of limited relevance to U.S.A. children, the researchers compared the data to that obtained by MacFarlane, and coworkers (1954) and found a good deal of similarity.) Table 20.1 presents the percentage of the population studied (all 3-year-old children) that exhibited each of the problem behaviors. For purposes of clarity, the problem behaviors have been organized into the clusters similar to those described above.

Table 20.1 reveals that the parents of these children found eating, elimination, sleep, activity control, and general difficulty in management problematic in 10% or more of this sample.

Previous unpublished data obtained from a preschool clinic sample on children 3 through 6 years of age provides a slightly different view of the problematic behavior of this age group (Table 20.2). The data were obtained on an experimental preschool form of the Behavior Problem Checklist (Quay & Peterson, 1983). The children seen in the clinic tended to be above average intellectually, and from middle- and upper-middle-class homes.

Table 20.2 reveals that approximately 10% to 30% of the parents in the sample reported that each behavior listed was a mild problem, but only 1% to 5% reported that each item was a severe problem.

Although these two data sets are not comparable because different questions were used and different age groups were studied, they do provide a framework for the development of expectations about the frequency of problematic behaviors among preschool children. Primarily, they both indicate that many preschool children are viewed by their mothers as exhibiting problematic behavior.

INSTRUMENT SELECTION

Instrument selection in the social–emotional realm is a difficult task for assessments of preschool child because there are few instruments

TABLE 20.1
PERENTAGE OF THREE-YEAR-OLD CHILDREN RATED BY MOTHERS HAS HAVING EACH PROBLEM BEHAVIOR

Problem Behavior	3 years old (N = 705)
Eating Problems	
Poor appetite	16.3
Faddy eating	11.8
Elimination Control	
Soiling (once a week or more)	12.8*
Night wetting (at least 3 nights per week)	37.4*
Day wetting (once a week or more)	16.9*
Sleep Problems	
Difficulty settling at night	12.1
Waking at night (at least 3 times per week)	14.5
Sleeping in parents' bed	11.2
Activity Control Problems	
Overactive, restless	12.9*
Attentional Control Problems	
Poor concentration	5.7
Dependency	
Dependency	5.4
Attention Seeking	9.2
Emotional Problems	
Tempers	5.1
Unhappy mood	3.8
Worries	2.3
Fears	9.2
Social Relationship Problems	
Relations with siblings	8.5
Relations with peers	5.8
Difficult to Manage	

Based on data from Richman, Stevenson, and Graham (1982).

* Items that are followed by an asterisk indicate that there was a gender difference in which males exhibited more of the problem than females. There were no problems exhibited more by females than males.

TABLE 20.2
PERCENTAGE OF CHILDREN THREE THROUGH SIX YEARS OF AGE RATED BY THEIR MOTHERS AS HAVING A MILD OR SEVERE PROBLEM ON EACH ITEM OF THE EXPERIMENTAL PRESCHOOL REVISION OF THE BEHAVIOR PROBLEM CHECKLIST

Problem Behavior	Mild	Severe
Eating Problems		
Chews on inedible things	12.6	2.8
Sleep Problems		
Has trouble getting to sleep; wakes easily during the night	14.6	3.7
Talks or cries out during sleep	16.3	1.6
Activity Control Problem		
Restless, unable to sit still	33.3	4.1
Hyperactive; always on the go	24.0	4.9
Attentional Control Problems		
Short-attention span; poor concentration	20.3	2.8
Distractible; is easily diverted from task at hand	24.0	3.7
Dependency		
Resists leaving mother's side	9.8	1.6
Seeks attention; shows off	33.3	5.7
Emotional Problems		
Has temper tantrums	35.3	5.3
Generally fearful and anxious	14.2	2.4
Self-conscious; easily embarrassed	21.1	2.0
Social Relationship Problems		
Uncooperative in group situations	11.0	.8
Disruptive; annoys and bothers others	23.2	4.5
Aloof, socially reserved	11.0	.8
Disobedient; difficult to control	22.8	4.9
Refuses to take direction; won't be told	23.2	2.8
Punishment doesn't affect his or her behavior	16.7	3.3
Other		
Tells imaginary things as though they were true; unable to tell real from imaginary	12.6	.4
Repeats what is said to him or her; "parrots" others speech	9.3	1.2
Repetitive speech; says some things over and over	9.3	1.2
Gets into everything; shows no fear of getting hurt	17.5	2.4
Destructive in terms of own or others property	12.2	.4

n = 245

that meet standard psychometric criteria for reliability and validity, some of the instruments that are used are not available through commercial publishing houses so even obtaining materials can be difficult, some instruments have been used extensively in research but do not have a manual that brings together all the pertinent data on the instrument, and some instruments can be used for multiple purposes. All these problems are related to the fact, discussed earlier, that social and emotional assessment of preschool children is a new professional endeavor, practiced by a small though growing number of psychologists. Thus, there are few researchers or developers of instruments for this age group, and fewer commercial publishers who want to take a risk on what is perceived to be a small market.

Table 20.3 lists a sampling of rating scales that can be used with this age group. The list contains some research instruments that can be useful to the practitioner, as well as commercially available instruments designed for practitioners. Parent, teacher, and clinician rating instruments are sampled. The instruments are grouped into three categories: instruments designed to measure traits with emphasis place on behaviors within the normal range; instruments designed to measure social and emotional behaviors that are highly relevant to preschool instruction and classroom settings; and instruments designed to aid in the discrimination between normal and abnormal behavior, as well as to be helpful in differential diagnosis.

All of these instruments could be considered screening devices, although they vary a great deal in the depth in which they assess the behaviors in question. They are screening devices because none could stand alone as a definitive measure of a trait, cluster of behaviors, or as a diagnostic instrument. Each will provide some data that might raise issues that would require further assessment.

Measures of Normal Characteristics in Trait Form

One of the most active areas of research and of practitioner interest in child development during the 1980s was the area of temperament. The greatest impetus to research and general interest in this area was the New York Longitudinal Study of Thomas, Chess and their colleagues. These researchers (Thomas & Chess, 1977; Thomas, Chess, & Birch, 1968; Thomas et al., 1963) analyzed data obtained from interviews of parents conducted in the first year of each target child's life, as well as from those conducted periodically thereafter. Evidence of individual variation in activity level, biological rhythmicity, speed of adaptability to environmental change, strength of initial approach tendency in new social situations,

emotional intensity, mood, distractibility, and persistence/attention span emerged. They found, in addition, that individual differences in such characteristics predicted rates of clinical referrals for problem behavior during the late preschool years and beyond (Terestman, 1980).

Both the Martin Temperament Assessment Battery for Children (TABC) (Martin, 1988b) and the McDevitt Behavioral Style Questionnaire (BSQ) (McDevitt & Carey, 1978) are second generation instruments built on the instruments *used by* Thomas, Chess, and colleagues. The Martin TABC is a three-instrument battery (one for use by parents, one for teachers, and one for the examiner to record observations made during a psychoeducational assessment), and it measures six of the original Thomas and Chess dimensions. The McDevitt and Carey BSQ is a parent form that measures all nine of the original dimensions. Both are designed for children 3 through 7 years of age.

Both instruments have been used in a sizeable number of studies. A subset of these studies has focused on the ability of the instruments to predict later psychopathology and educational outcomes. (For a recent review see Martin, 1988c). With regard to educational outcomes, it has been found that activity level, distractibility, and persistence measured in kindergarten and first grade is predictive of latter reading and mathematics achievement over periods of of one to five years in the range of .40 to .65 (Martin et al., in press).

Given the concurrent validation of both the TABC and the BSQ, either could be used as a first step in a screening process for children whose social and emotional characteristics put them at risk of later psychoeducational difficulties. Another important use of these instruments is to have parents of preschool children complete the instruments, then to provide parents feedback with regard to how the results compare to their perceptions (assessed through interview) of the child, and how their child compares to other preschool children. This kind of information can go a long way in improving parental understanding of the individual differences of their children. It also provides a very useful piece of background information for instruction in parenting. Used as a feedback tool in teacher groups, this information provides foundation for discussions of individualized instruction methods among preschool teachers.

Measures of Preschool Classroom Behavior

The two instruments summarized in Table 20.3 under the head of "measures of preschool classroom behavior" are designed to measure the social and behavioral competence of the preschool child as he or she interacts with peers, teachers, and learning materials in the preschool classroom. The California Preschool Social Competence Scale (Levine et al., 1969) is a relatively brief teacher rating scale that has much in common with the adaptive behavior scales, that is, it taps social skills as well as behaviors that are not in the social and emotional realm. One of the strongest aspects of the scale is that the normative data that are reported in the manual are among the best of any measure for children this age.

The McDermott Study of Children's Styles Questionniare was designed by McDermott and Beitman (1984) to assess the manner in which children approach the learning skills that are presented to them in kindergarten. It is a very brief teacher rating scale (16 items) that includes items such as: Is willing to try on his own; Acts without taking time to look or to think things out. McDermott and Beitman report data showing that scores on this scale predict first grade achievement in the .30 to .60 range.

These instruments tap a more restricted sample of behaviors than the temperament instruments. However, the behaviors that are reported on these questionnaires are behaviors that are highly salient to schooling, such as attention, impulsivity, motivation, and social skills. These instruments are clearly brief screening instruments designed to provide a summary impression of a child. Before programming changes or even teacher consultation is implemented for an individual child, additional assessment would be required.

Measures of Problem Behaviors

A larger set of instruments are available for the assessment of problem behaviors than for assessment of normal traits (e.g., temperament) or preschool classroom behavior. This results from the fact that most referrals to psychologists are initiated because problem behaviors are perceived to be present by the referring agent. Further, a number of the instruments that are available in this group are downward extensions of measures designed to assess problem behaviors in school-age children and adolescents.

Table 20.3 summarizes the characteristics of six measures that might be used by a psychologist if the purpose of the assessment was to determine whether significant abnormal behavior was present, and to aid in making a differential diagnosis if abnormality is seen. Because the Achenbach Child Behavior Checklist (Achenbach & Edelbrock, 1983) the Louisville Behavior Checklist (Miller, 1984) Personality Inventory for Children (Wirt, et al., 1984) are well known by many child psychologists, have strong manuals that review the research on the instruments, and have been reviewed extensively elsewhere (e.g., Knoff, 1986; Martin, 1988a), they will not be reviewed here. (A downward extension of the Achenbach Child Behavior Checklist for children 2 through 4 years of age that will be of interest to preschool psychologists will soon be available. Little research has been reported on this instrument to date (Achenbach, et al., 1987).

The Behar Preschool Behavior Questionnaire (Behar & Stringfield, 1974) is a screening instrument designed to assess symptoms of emergent emotional problems. It is a modification of the Children's Behavior Questionnaire developed by Michael Rutter in 1967. It is a brief 30-item teacher rating scale listing troublesome behaviors. Three factor analytically derived scales are scored and labeled *Hostile-Aggressive Dimension, Anxious-Fearful Dimension,* and *Poor Attention Span and Restlessness Dimension.* One of the nice aspects of the scale is that it is designed expecially for children 3 through 6 years of age, and the behaviors sampled are stated in terms that preschool teachers to respond to with ease. The manual is relatively poor in that there is incomplete discussion of the psychometric characteristics of the instrment and there is little discussion of clinical interpretation of outcome, but there has been some provocative research done with the instrument (Martin, 1988a).

The Burks Behavior Rating Scales—Preschool Version (Burks, 1977) is a downward extension of the original instrument designed for children and adolescents. It is a behavior problem scale useful for teachers or parents. It is rather lengthy (105 items) and scoring is somewhat burdensome. Scores can be obtained for 18 scales.

TABLE 20.3
DESCRIPTIONS OF PRESCHOOL RATING SCALES

Name of Scale	Age Range	Rater	Subscales	Administration Scoring	Manual
Measures of Normal Characteristics in Trait Form					
Martin Temperament Assessment Battery (Martin, 1988)	3–7	Parent Teacher Clinician three separate norms	Activity; Adaptability; Approach–Withdrawal; Emotional intensity; Distractibility; Persistence	Moderate	Good
McDevitt Behavior Style Questionnaire (McDevitt & Carey, 1978)	3–7	Parent	Activity; Rhymicity; Mood: Emotional intensity; Distractivility; Persistence; Adaptability; Approach–withdrawal; Threshold	Moderate	None
Measures of Preschool Classroom Behavior					
California Preschool Social Competence Scale (Levine, Elzey, & Lewis, 1969)	3–5	Teacher	Total score on social competence	Easy	Poor
McDermott Learning Styles Questionnaire (McDermott & Beitman, 1984)	K	Teacher	Avoidance behavior; Inattentive behavior; Overly independent	Easy	None
Measures Designed to Discriminate between Normal and Abnormal Behavior, and to be Helpful in Differential Diagnosis					
Achenbach Child Behavior Checklist (Achenbach & Edelbrock, 1983)	4–16	Parent	Social withdrawal[a]; Depressed; Immature; Somatic complaints; Sex problems; Schizoid; Aggressive; Delinquent	Difficult	Excellent
Behar Preschool Behavior Questionnaire (Behar & Stringfield, 1974)	3–6	Teacher	Hostile-Aggressive; Anxious–fearful; Poor attention–restless; Total score	Easy	Poor

Name	Age	Respondent	Scales	Ease of use	Quality
Burks Behavior Rating Scale-Preschool Kindergarten Edition (Burks, 1977)	3–6	Teacher or Parent	Excessive self-blame; Excessive anxiety; Excessive withdrawal; Excessive dependency; Poor ego strength; Poor physical strength; Poor coordination; Poor intellectually; Poor attention; Poor impulse control; Poor reality control; Poor sense of identity; Excessive suffering; Poor anger control; Excessive sense of persecution; Excessive aggressiveness; Excessive resistence; Poor social conformity	Moderate	Very Poor
Eyberg Child Behavior Inventory (Robinson, Eyberg, & Ross, 1980)	2–16	Parent	Conduct problems; Intensity of parent feelings about problem	Easy	None
Louisville Behavior Checklist (Miller, 1984)	4–17	Parent	Infantile aggression; Hyperactivity; Anti-social behavior; Aggression; Social withdrawal; Sensitivity; Fear; Inhibition; Intellectual deficit; Immaturity; Cognitive disability; Severity level; Normal irritability; Prosocial deficit; Rare deviance; neurotic behavior; Psychotic behavior; Somatic behavior; Sexual behavior; School disturbance predictor	Difficult	Average
Personality Inventory for Children (Wirt, Lachar, Klinedinst, & Seat, 1984)	3–16	Parent	Undisciplined/poor self-control[b]; Social incompetence; Internalization/ somatic symptom; Cognitive development; General adjustment; Achievement screening: Intellectual screening; Developmental rate; Somatic concern; Depression; Family relations; Delinquency; Withdrawal; Anxiety; Psychosis; Hyperactivity; Social skills	Difficult	Excellent

This table is a modification of Table 1, Martin, 1986.

[a] The scales listed are for boys. Slightly different scales are scored for girls.

[b] Three scales are also scored as a check on respondent response styles and truthfulness.

The manual is written explicitly for clinicians and helpful interpretative hints are discussed. However, the technical details on which these interpretative guidelines are based are so poorly done that it casts a negative shadow over the guidelines. A further shortcoming is that downward extension has not replaced items that are of very limited utility for preschool children, or at least are stated in a manner that is less than sensitive to the developmental level of the children being rated. The strength of the scale is that it does sample a wide range of troublesome behaviors.

The Eyberg Child Behavior Inventory (Robinson et al., 1980) is one of the most interesting instruments of this group. It was exclusively designed to assess behaviors related to conduct disorder (e.g., hostility, aggression, impulsivity, hyperactivity). Because the scale is designed to measure only one cluster of behaviors, (there are no subscales to measure hyperactivity or aggression, for example), the reliability and validity are enhanced, because all of the 30 items contribute to this one conduct problem score. The Eyberg inventory is a parent rating scale that has two responses for each problem behavior; first the parent indicates whether the behavior is a problem, and then the parent is asked about his or her tolerance for such behaviors. This latter data provide a great advantage in assessment because the measurement of individual differences among parents regarding how much a given behavior bothers them is assessed. The scale was not designed exclusively as a preschool scale, but a good deal of the research using the instrument has been with preschool samples (Eyberg & Robinson, 1982; Eyberg & Ross, 1978).

A final note about the problem behavior measures just reviewed seems in order. There is reason to be skeptical of all instruments that utilize the same items (or lists of problems) for children ranging in age from adolescence to preschoolers. First, many items that are relevant to 14-year-old children (issues around sexuality, substance abuse, etc) are obviously not relevant to the 4 year old. Second, even if an item is general enough to apply to all ages (e.g., is aggressive with peers), the meaning of the problem can change drastically from one age to another (e.g., fighting for the 14 year old has different psychological and social meaning than for the 4 year old). It is better to have a problem checklist that deals with problems as parents and day care personnel experience them. That is, such a scale should contain items about "picky eaters," children who have difficulty with toilet training, children who are slow to learn to share toys, and soon. These items then could be aggregrated through factor analysis or some other technique into large dimensions to increase the predictive value of the scale. Unfortunately, most of the problem-oriented instruments that are available were designed by general child psychopathologists, who have an interest in the dimensions of pathology over large age ranges. This means that items are generally stated, or apply in varying degrees to children at different ages. For the consumer of diagnostic rating scales, this problem should engender an extra degree of caution in interpreting the Achenbach Child Behavior Checklist, Burks Behavior Rating Scale-Preschool and Kindergarten Edition, Eyberg Child Behavior Inventory, Louisville Behavior Checklist, and the Personality Inventory for Children when applied to preschool children, particularly the youngest children in this age group.

SUMMARY

This chapter has been designed to aid the general child psychologist design and implement a personality (social–emotional) assessment of a preschool child: There is a clear trend toward earlier assessment of children, an although the assessment of social and emotional behavior has developed more slowly than the assessment of intellectual behavior, the practical press for more and better assessments in this area also is being widely felt.

Assessment design and instrument selection have been the areas of primary focus of this chapter. Assessments of social and emotional behavior are designed and planned even if poorly, and the discussion has touched on a few of the factors that must be controlled or measured to improve assessment design. Finally, the assessor must choose an instrument or set of instruments to help quantify the behaviors of the young child. A sampling of rating instruments has been discussed, with some evaluative data presented on each.

Several limitations of this chapter deserve mention. First, the chapter has focused on rating scales. The interview and sociometry could not be discussed because both require substantial space to provide even a brief overview. A second area that has not been discussed is the emerging area of social skills assessment (e.g., Gresham & Elliot, 1990). It is hoped that as preschool assessment becomes a more developed area of professional practice, these specialized techniques will be subjected to detailed scrutiny in the professional writing of the field.

REFERENCES

Achenbach, T. M., & Edelbrock, C. (1983). *Manual for the Child Behavior Checklist and Revised Child Behavior Profile.* Burlington, VT: Department of Psychiatry, University of Vermont.

Achenbach, T. M., Edelbrock, C., & Howell, C. T: (1987). Empirically based assessment of the behavioral/emotional problems of 2- and 3-year-old children. *Journal of Abnormal Child Psychology, 15,* 629–650.

American Psychiatric Association. (1987). *Diagnostic and Statistical Manual of Mental Disorders* (3rd ed., revised). Washington, D.C.: American Psychiatric Association.

Anastasi, A. (1988). *Psychological Testing* (5th ed.). New York: Macmillan.

Beery, K. E. (1982). *Administration, Scoring, and Teaching Manual for the Developmental Test of Visual-Motor Integration*: Cleveland, Ohio: Modern Curriculum Press:

Behar, L., & Stringfield, S. (1974). *Manual for the Preschool Behavior Questionnaire.* Learning Institute of North Carolina, Durham, N.C.

Bellack, A. S., & Hersen, M. (1988). *Behavioral Assessment: A Practical Handbook* (3rd ed.). Elmsford, N.Y. Pergamon.

Boehm, A., & Weinberg R. A. (1987). *The Classroom Observer: Developing Observation Skills in Early Education* (2nd ed.). New York: Teacher's College Press.

Brim, O. G., Jr., & Kagan, J. (Eds.) (1980). *Constancy and Change in Human Development.* Cambridge, MA: Harvard University Press.

Brody, G. H., & Forehand, R. (1986). Maternal perception of child maladjustment as a function of the combined influence of child behavior and maternal depression. *Journal of Consulting and Clinical Psychology, 54,* 237–240.

Brown, L. L., & Hammill, D. D. (1983). *Manual for the Behavior Rating Profile.* Austin, TX: Pro-Ed.

Burks, H. F. (1977). *Burks' Behavior Rating Scales: Preschool and Kindergarten Version.* Los Angeles: Western Psychological Services.

Elkind, D. (1987). *Miseducation: Preschoolers at Risk:* New York: Knopf.

Epstein, S. (1979). The stability of behavior I: On predicting most of the people much of the time. *Journal of Personality and Social Psychology, 37,* 1097–1126.

Eyberg S. M., & Robinson, E. A. (1982). Parent-child interaction training: Effects on family functioning. *Journal of Clinical Child Psychology, 11,* 130–137.

Ghiselli, E. E., Campbell, J. P., & Zedeck, S. (1981). *Measurement Theory for the Behavioral Sciences.* New York: Freeman.

Gresham, F. M., & Elliot, S. N. (1990), *Social Skills Rating Systems.* Circle Pines, MN: American Guidance Services.

Harter, S. (1985). Processes underlying the construction, maintenance, and enhancement of self-concept in children. In J. Suls & A. Greenwald (Ed.), *Psychological Perspectives on the Self* (Vol 3, pp. 127–143). New York: Erlbaum.

Kent, R. N., & Foster, S. L. (1977). Direct observation procedures: Methodological issues in naturalistic settings. In A. R. Ciminero, K. S. Calhoun, & H. E. Adams (Eds.), *Handbook of Behavioral Assessment* (pp. 279–328). New York: Wiley.

Knoff, H. (1986). *Psychological Assessment of Child and Adolescent Personality.* New York: Guilford.

Lamb, M. E., & Baumrind, D. (1978). Socialization and personality development in the preschool years. In M. E. Lamb (Ed.). *Social and Personality Development* (pp. 50–69). New York: Holt, Rinehart, & Winston.

Levine, S., Elsey, F. F., & Lewis M. (1969). *The California Preschool Social Competence Scale—Manual.* Palo Alto, CA: Consulting Psychologists Press.

MacFarlane, J. W., Allen, L., & Honzik, P. (1954). *A developmental study of behavior problems of normal children between 21 months and 14 years.* Berkeley & Los Angeles: University of California Press.

Martin, R. P. (1986). Assessment of the social and emotional functioning of preschool children. *School Psychology Review, 15,* 216–232.

Martin, R. P. (1988a). *The Assessment of Personality and Temperament: Infancy through Adolescence:* New York: Guilford.

Martin, R. P. (1988b). *The Temperament Assessment Battery for Children—Manual.* Brandon, VT: Clinical Psychology Publishing Company.

Martin, R. P., Drew, D., & Gaddis, L. (in press). Prediction of elementary school achievement from preschool temperament: Three studies. *School Psychology Review.*

McDermott, P. A., & Beitman, B. S. (1984). Standardization of a scale for the study of children's learning styles: Structures, stability, and criterion validity. *Psychology in the Schools, 21,* 5–14.

McDevitt S. & Carey W. (1978). The measurement of temperament in 3–7 year-old children. *Journal of Child Psychology and Psychiatry, 19,* 245–253.

Miller, L. C. (1984). *Louisville Behavior Checklist: Manual.* Los Angeles: Western Psychological Services.

Mischel, W. (1968). *Personality and Assessment.* New York: Wiley.

Quay, H. C., & Peterson, D. R. (1983). *Interim Manual for the Revised Behavior Problem Checklist.* Privately printed.

Richman, N., Stevenson, J., & Graham, P. J. (1982). *Pre-School to School: A Behavioral Study.* London: Academic Press.

Robinson, E. A., Eyberg, S. M., & Ross, A. W. (1980). The standardization of an inventory of child conduct problem behavior. *Journal of Clinical Child Psychology, 9,* 22–29.

Sackett, G. P. (Ed.) (1978). *Observing Behavior (Vol.II): Data Collecting and Analysis Methods.* Baltimore: University Park Press.

Salvia, J., & Ysseldyke, J. E. (1988). *Assessment in Special and Remedial Education* (2nd ed.). Boston: Houghton-Mifflin.

Scarr, S., & Weinber, R. A. (1986). The early childhood enterprise. *American Psychologist, 41,* 1140–1146.

Simeonsson R. J. (1986). *Psychological and Developmental Assessment of Special Children.* Boston: Allyn & Bacon.

Terestman, N. (1980). Mood quality and intensity in nursery school children as predictors of behavior disorders. *American Journal of Orthopsychiatry, 50,* 125–138.

Thomas, A., & Chess, S. (1977). *Temperament and Development.* New York: Brunner/Mazel.

Thomas, A., Chess, S., & Birch, H. G. (1968). *Temperament and Behavioral Disorders in Children.* New York: New York University Press.

Thomas, A., Chess, S., Birch, H. G., Hertzig, M. E., & Korn, S. (1963). *Behavioral Individuality in Early Childhood.* New York: New York University.

Wirt, R. D., Lachar, D., Klinedinst, J. K., & Seat, P. D. (1984). *Multidimensional Description of Child Personality: A Manual for the Personality Inventory for Children* (rev.ed.). Los Angeles: Western Psychological Services.

21

Neuropsychological Assessment of the Preschool Child: Issues and Procedures

STEPHEN R. HOOPER

INTRODUCTION

Child neuropsychology is the study of brain–behavior relationships in the developing human organism (Rourke, 1983). As a discipline, child neuropsychology has seen unprecedented growth over the past decade. This growth is illustrated by the proliferation of texts devoted exclusively to issues and procedures in child neuropsychology (Hynd & Obrzut, 1981; Obrzut & Hynd, 1986a, 1986b; Rourke et al., 1983; Rourke et al., 1986; Tramontana & Hooper, 1988a). This growth also is because, in part, of the notion that children are not scaled down adults but, rather, are qualitatively and quantitatively different from their adult counterparts. Despite the rapid development of child neuropsychology as a discipline, this subspecialty of clinical neuropsychology has been estimated as being about 25 years behind adult neuropsychology (Wilson, 1986). This difference undoubtedly is increased further when the neuropsychology of the preschool child is considered.

Although the examination of brain–behavior relationships in the preschool child is a fledgling area, some work already has begun to emerge that has set the stage for future efforts with this population (Aylward, 1988; Blackman et al., 1983; Deysach, 1986; Hartlage & Telzrow, 1982, 1986; Levine, & Schneider, 1982; Wilson, 1986), especially with respect to proposed preschool neuropsychological assessment strategies. Further, these efforts have been fueled by recent legislative mandates directed to address the needs of the handicapped preschooler.

For example, The Education for All Handicapped Children's Act (i.e., P. L. 94–142) requires that a free and appropriate education be provided to all handicapped children from birth to 21 years age. Although this act included the preschool handicapped child, it only has been recently that services for infants and preschoolers have received explicit attention. More directly related to the preschooler, P. L. 99–457 (i.e., The Education of the Handicapped Act Amendments of 1986) is concerned with the accurate identification of the handicapped preschool child and the development of appropriate treatment plans based on assessment findings.

In addition, The National Joint Committee on Learning Disabilities (NJCLD, 1986) has put forth a position statement regarding the needs of the LD preschool population. The NJCLD position statement included a list of recommendations for training professionals to work effectively with the preschool child, improve assessment procedures, and increase family involvement. The NJCLD also noted the need for the development of systematic identification programs and increased early intervention efforts.

Given the rapid growth of interest in this area, this chapter will discuss the current status of the neuropsychological assessment of the preschool child. For purposes of this discussion the preschool years largely will be defined as the ages 3 through 5, although occasional references will be made to infants (birth through 2 years) and toddlers (ages 2 through 3 years). The utility of neuropsychological testing for this population will be elucidated and, subsequently, will be followed by specific neurodevelopmental issues. The various preschool neuropsychological assessment models proposed to date will be presented along with an attempt to extract relevant neuropsychological constructs for assessment of children in this age range. The chapter will conclude with a brief discussion of some broader issues associated with neuropsychological testing of preschool children.

UTILITY OF A NEUROPSYCHOLOGICAL APPROACH

There are numerous complexities related to the neuropsychological assessment of children (Rourke et al., 1983). Some of these complexities include test selection, interpretation issues, assessment–treatment linkages, and crucial developmental factors. These concerns are magnified further when a neuropsychological perspective is applied to children below the age of 6 years. Aylward (1988) has described this latter area as a "no man's land" with respect to its current level of development.

Despite these concerns, several investigators have asserted the utility of employing a neuropsychological approach with preschoolers (Aylward, 1988; Deysach, 1986; Hartlage & Telzrow, 1982, 1986; Hooper, 1988; Wilson, 1986). Consistent with the use of neuropsychological methods with school-age children and adults, such an approach holds promise for clinicians and research-

ers working with a preschool population. A comprehensive neuropsychological approach for the preschool child can yield a wealth of information pertaining to detailed diagnostic profile descriptions, prognosis, and various treatment factors. Its potential utility is underscored by emergent data describing prevalence rates of suspected or known brain-based disorders in preschoolers and the subsequent need for neuropsychological assessment of these children. More generally, a neuropsychological perspective will serve to advance the understanding of brain–behavior relationships in the preschool population.

Diagnostic Profile Description

Historically, the primary role of a neuropsychological approach in diagnosis was to determine the presence of neurological deficits or dysfunction. Assessment procedures were designed to detect and localize brain lesions that would contribute to the discrimination between normal children and those with brain impairment. Prior to the mid-1970s neuropsychological assessment strategies were appealing because of their noninvasive nature. However, a review of various attempts at lesion localization in children concluded that this has received minimal support to date (Chadwick & Rutter, 1983). Further, given the recent advances of other neurodiagnostic methods, such as Magnetic Resonance Imaging and Brain Electrical Activity Mapping, the utility of diagnosing brain damage solely with neuropsychological methods has been lessened. Difficulties with neuropsychological diagnosis have been compounded by the lack of an adequate nosology for various kinds of neurologically based disorders.

Despite these difficulties, neuropsychological diagnosis has not been abandoned completely, but it has shifted roles with respect to its emphasis. In this regard, Behr and Gallagher (1981) have proposed that a more flexible definition of what constitutes a handicap is needed for preschool children with special needs. They suggested that the definition should describe not only the *extent* of developmental variation, but the *type* of variation. Consistent with this, neuropsychological diagnosis currently is concerned with the accurate and comprehensive description of a child's profile of strengths and weaknesses, particularly because the profile might reflect the effects of a brain lesion or neurodevelopmental anomaly. This shift in focus has contributed to possible syndrome definition (e.g., learning disability subtypes), the potential for improved assessment–treatment connections, and increased understanding of brain–behavior relationships. The emphasis on profile description also has forced clinicians to address the ecological validity of a set of neuropsychological findings. In this regard, clinicians have begun to apply their findings to the actual day-to-day functioning of the child (e.g., classroom performance, adaptive behaviors) and, consequently, to show greater interest in treatment planning for neuropsychologically impaired children.

Neuropsychological testing also offers a unique diagnostic complement to other neurological procedures by providing specific descriptions of the behavioral manifestations of brain impairment (Tramontana & Hooper, 1988b). This will apply to preschool children with acquired brain injury and related neurological disorders, systemic illness, psychiatric disorders, or neurodevelopmental disorders, and requires a keen understanding of the particular environmental demands on a child over time (e.g., shifting school requirements for learning).

For example, one of the most common neurosurgical interventions in childhood involves the insertion of a shunt for the treatment of hydrocephalus. Children who have been treated successfully for hydrocephalus by shunt insertion have been shown to demonstrate cognitive deficits ranging from attention and impulse problems (Fennell et al., 1987; Hurley et al., 1983) to more specific problems with memory (Cull & Wyke, 1984) and visual–motor skills (Raimondi & Soare, 1977). The neuropsychological assessment of a preschool child with a shunt requires not only a comprehensive appraisal of a wide range of abilities, but careful and systematic monitoring of the child's developing skills, particularly as the child moves from the demands of preschool to those of more formal schooling.

The diagnostic utility of preschool neuropsychological assessment also is relevant to children in the nonclinical domain in that approximately 10% of preschool children are estimated to experience learning and behavioral difficulties secondary to minor neurological disorders (Kal-

verboer, 1971). Similar prevalence estimates (i.e., 8.3%) have been provided for preschool learning disabilities (U. S. Department of Education, 1984). Neurobehavioral connections also might be more clear with preschoolers because of the relatively minimal influences of factors such as feelings of failure, labelling, expectancy artifacts, and social–emotional concerns (Ellison, 1983). In older children these psychosocial variables can play a larger role in a child's overall functioning, thus blurring possible neurobehavioral linkages. Generally, a comprehensive neuropsychological evaluation will contribute to obtaining a detailed description of a child's specific strengths and weakness and, consequently, to the early identification and treatment of neurocognitive difficulties. It also might begin to elucidate risk factors associated with certain developmental outcomes.

Prognosis

Obtaining a detailed description of a child's neurocognitive functioning is only part of the process for understanding a preschooler's difficulties. Unless the child is inflicted with a degenerative neurological process that is progressing rapidly, it is extremely difficult to predict a particular behavioral outcome. Although some longitudinal efforts have been initiated in areas concerning learning disability (Satz et al., 1978; Spreen & Haaf, 1986; Stevenson & Newman, 1986) and infant hemispherectomy (Dennis, 1985a, 1985b; Dennis & Whitaker, 1977;), little is known about preschool prognosis.

An important role for preschool neuropsychological assessment is the monitoring of a child's acquisition and/or reacquisition of function after brain injury. There is a complex array of factors that interact to influence the recovery patterns and developmental progress of children who experience early brain insults (Chelune & Edwards, 1981). Knowledge with respect to the impact of specific neuropathological processes on a child's prognosis is only beginning to surface (Dennis, 1985a, 1985b). Further, deficits involving "silent" brain regions might not become apparent until challenged during later developmental stages (Hooper, 1988; Rourke et al., 1983), thus making the need for detailed, comprehensive, and ongoing systematic neuropsychological assessment crucial to issues of prognosis.

To illustrate these concerns, in the Florida Longitudinal Project Satz and associates (1978) demonstrated an overall correct classification rate of 84% in predicting second grade reading skills. Although the prediction rate was lowered to about 76% of fifth grade outcomes, Satz and associates were able to identify a different set of predictors that proved useful in the early prediction of learning disabilities. However, when these data were examined more closely, a high rate of false negatives (i.e., children initially estimated to be functioning at a satisfactory level in kindergarten) was noted. In fact, more than a quarter of the "normal" functioning kindergarten children later showed significant reading problems during the fifth grade. It should be noted that these findings occurred with one of the most validated set of screening procedures currently available.

The neuropsychological screening procedures employed by Satz and associates did prove useful in accurately predicting the extreme ends of the reading continuum and the model did suggest possible neurobehavioral prognostic indicators of future learning problems (e.g., sensory–perceptual delays). Since that time other prognostic indicators of learning problems have been asserted. For example, using meta-analysis Horn and Packard (1985) found behavioral measures, language tasks, and IQ to be the best single predictors of reading achievement in grades 1 and 3. In a more recent review, Tramontana and coworkers (1988) found effective predictors to span cognitive, verbal, and perceptual/perceptual–motor areas of functioning. These reviewers noted the complexities involved in accurately identifying specific predictor-criterion relationships. They also called for more detailed questions in describing prognostic relationships in the learning patterns of preschool children.

Although more research is needed with respect to preschool prognosis, particularly with special populations at risk for central nervous system dysfunction (e.g., hydrocephalus, closed head injury, spina bifida, birth anoxia), the evidence generated to date would show promise for using a comprehensive neuropsychological approach with preschoolers. In particular, as brain–behavior relationships in the preschool-age child become elucidated, the prognostic implications relative to particular syndromes and profiles will become more clear.

Treatment Issues

The neuropsychological assessment of the preschool child perhaps has its greatest potential impact in contributing to the development of treatment programs, the monitoring of the intervention process and suggesting adjustments based on follow-up findings, and the minimizing of educational and emotional difficulties associated with brain impairment. These concerns are particularly relevant for the preschooler who has the benefit of participating in early intervention programs. Neuropsychological assessment can play a formative role in developing a treatment program for a brain-impaired youngster. This becomes even more important when the efficacy of early intervention programs is considered. By providing a detailed profile of a child's neuropsychological strengths and weaknesses, the foundation for an aggressive treatment program can be established. Although little is known about actual assessment-treatment linkages, particularly for the preschool-age child, treatment options tend to be guided by theoretical orientation (Luria, 1966), clinical experiences, and availability of therapeutic resources (Tramontana & Hooper, 1988b).

In an attempt to provide a structured model for integrating neuropsychological data into the treatment regimen, Rourke and coworkers (1983) described a general rehabilitation framework designed to include prognostic issues, specific deficits, and the utilization of spared abilities. All basic functional areas can be incorporated into this model and consideration is given to the availability of appropriate resources. This model is compatible with the work of Luria (1963) who suggested that the rehabilitation of brain involvement should be aimed at restoring or rerouting the neurological functional system that primarily mediated the affected behavior (e.g., by providing verbal mediation strategies to children with attentional deficits and disinhibitory behavioral features). A neuropsychological approach can address these concerns dynamically by testing specific hypotheses during the assessment process.

Once an individualized intervention program is established, it becomes important for the progress of the child to be closely monitored. This is important not only from charting progress rates, but also from the standpoint of providing needed adjustments in the treatment regimen. The monitoring of a child's progress is crucial to determining the effectiveness of neurosurgical, pharmacological, or cognitive-educational interventions.

Craft and coworkers (1972) have shown the importance of monitoring developmental progress with respect to treatment planning by documenting that even mildly brain injured infants who were described as "fully recovered" continued to manifest cognitive, behavioral, and sensorimotor deficits several years following their injuries. Similarly, Aylward and colleagues (1987) noted that diagnoses of motor functioning in infants were most stable over time whereas cognitive functioning status was more likely to change. Bagnato and Dickerson-Mayes (1986) also demonstrated the importance of monitoring developmental progress with respect to treatment planning in brain-injured infants and preschoolers following approximately a 3.5 month inpatient rehabilitation. These gains were noted to occur across all developmental domains with gains ranging from 77% in gross motor functions to 93% in cognitive functions.

Several other important concerns need to be mentioned with respect to treatment. First, a comprehensive neuropsychological evaluation has tremendous potential for initiating early intervention and, consequently, minimizing educational failure and lessening secondary social–emotional difficulties. The assumption is that the earlier that a neurologically impaired child can be identified, and the more detailed the neuropsychological profile description, the greater the possibility that an intensive intervention program will be able to address a child's specific developmental needs in an adequate, yet aggressive manner (Tramontana et al., 1988). Evidence from the early intervention literature has supported this general contention (Casto & Mastropieri, 1986; White, 1986).

Second, there are some data that indicate that a child's neurological development can be susceptible to positive environmental stimulation, further supporting the early intervention philosophy for the handicapped preschooler (Kolb & Whishaw, 1985). Neurologically, a child will develop independent of environmental influences, but sustained neurological growth can be dependent upon environmental challenges and demands, particularly for the brain impaired child. The actual process(es) by which this occurs is not fully understood, but it is believed to involve either a mechanism of neural reorganization or the susceptibility of less integrated brain systems to environmental influence (Bakker et al., 1981; Zihl, 1981). Nonetheless, the implication that optimal learning periods exist for the brain-impaired preschooler provides support for the implementation of aggressive cognitive and behavioral interventions based on accurate and detailed assessment findings.

Lastly, given their knowledge of brain–behavior relationships, child neuropsychologists have become more involved in the actual treatment components of adults and school-age children. Particular involvement has spanned the cognitive, educational, behavioral, and affective rehabilitation domains (Boll & Barth, 1981; Incagnoli & Newman, 1985). As brain-behavior relationships with the preschool population are understood to a greater degree, the direct involvement of the neuropsychologist undoubtedly will extend downward to the preschool child.

Summary

This section highlighted some relevant issues regarding the utility of a neuropsychological assessment approach with preschool children. In particular, the neuropsychological assessment has the potential to contribute effectively to diagnostic descriptions, treatment, and treatment monitoring of neurologically impaired preschool children. Although little is known about the prognosis of many preschool disorders, particularly with respect to the interrelationships between neural organization and recovery patterns at this age level, an assessment model based on neuropsychological principles appears to hold promise for further describing brain–behavior relationships for this population.

NEURODEVELOPMENTAL ISSUES

The intent of this section is to provide a brief discussion of selected areas of neurodevelopment important to the neuropsychological assessment of the preschool child. It is not intended to provide a detailed overview of brain development because more comprehensive discussions of this can be obtained elsewhere (Hynd & Willis, 1988; Willis

& Widerstrom, 1986). Specifically, this section will address a general theory of neurodevelopment (Luria, 1966) and issues regarding cerebral dominance.

Neurodevelopmental Theory

From an historical perspective, localization theory and equipotential theory were the prevailing lines of inquiry that attempted to describe the functional organization of the brain. *Localization theory* described the cerebral cortex as having highly differentiated structures corresponding to specific functions. Proponents of this theoretical orientation proposed that discrete functions could be localized to specific regions of the brain. *Equipotential theory* offered a contrary perspective, proposing that all complex cognitive functions were dependent on the equal participation of all areas of the brain. This thinking precluded the need to understand potential differences between specific brain regions. Consequently, the degree of brain damage was believed to be directly proportional to the amount of tissue destruction.

Despite arguments on both sides, neither of these orientations could account for the various clinical observations that could be manifested. For example, localization theory was not able to account for the observation that highly localized brain damage could contribute to involvement of several major cognitive functions. The same observational contradiction was noted for equipotential theory in that a larger lesion did not necessarily produce generalized disruption of a broader array of cognitive abilities (Golden, 1981a). Consequently, neither theoretical orientation appeared adequate to account for the various clinical presentations that might be manifested.

Luria (1966) proposed a third theory of brain organization and function. Luria's theory allowed for an integration of the equipotential and localization perspectives, and it has accounted for specific clinical phenomena in a more satisfactory manner. Luria's theory is founded upon several major concepts including functional systems, functional units, and cortical zones. According to Luria (1966) a *functional system* involves the integrated participation of a number of cortical regions. Consequently, a complex cognitive function, such as reading, could be impaired second-

ary to damage to any one of a variety of neuroanatomical substrates comprising this functional system. Disruption of this functional system implicated that other cognitive processes could be partially involved as well. This conceptualization of functional systems allowed for the use of syndrome analysis in systematically reviewing clinical case materials.

Luria's theory proposed that three *functional units* of the brain encompassed all functional systems. These units are hierarchically organized and functionally integrated in the planning and execution of cognitive functions. The *first unit* is located in subcortical brain regions (i.e., upper and lower parts of the brain stem) and is concerned largely with arousal, wakefulness, and alertness. Impairment in this functional unit can disrupt various components of attention and, subsequently, interfere with learning and adaptive functioning. Figure 21.1 shows the first functional unit containing the brain stem and associated structures.

The *second and third units* generally comprise the cortex, with the former encompassing the temporal, parietal, and occipital lobes, and the latter

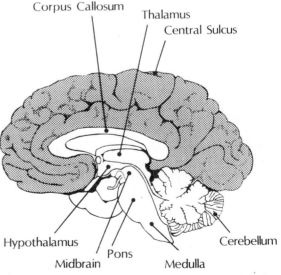

Figure 21.1 The first functional unit containing the brain stem and associated structures. [Adapted from Hynd, G. W. & Cohen, M. (1983). *Dyslexia: Neuropsychological Theory, Research, and Clinical Differentiation*. New York. Grune & Stratton. With permission.]

the frontal lobes. The second functional unit is responsible for receiving, analyzing, and storing information. Luria (1966) noted that the third unit contributed to the programming, regulation, and verification of activity. The second and third units are intimately connected to the subcortical structures and are hierarchical in their organization. Each of the cortical units contains primary, secondary, and tertiary zones. The second and third units of the brain and their accompanying cortical regions are illustrated in Fig. 21.2.

Within the second unit, *primary zones* are modality specific in their functioning. Specific regions within the temporal, parietal, and occipital lobes correspond to auditory, somatosensory, and visual stimuli, respectively. The primary zones are capable of receiving information from, and sending information to, the periphery. The *secondary zones* of this functional unit, or association regions, process incoming sensory information and relay it to the tertiary regions. Involvement of primary and/or secondary regions produce behavioral manifestations that are unimodal in appearance. The *tertiary zones* are responsible for the integration of multimodal information and, subsequently, higher-order, more complex cognitive processes (e.g., reading). Lesions involving tertiary regions can contribute to difficulties synthesizing information in an efficient manner (Luria, 1966).

Primary and secondary zones of the third functional unit are responsible for motor movement and organized motor activity, respectively. The tertiary zones have been associated with the planning and execution of goal-directed behaviors. Dysfunction in these regions can result in motor planning and execution deficits. Given their intimate afferent connections with subcortical structures, and their involvement in attentional and behavioral modulation, Luria (1966) considered the tertiary, or prefrontal, regions to contribute to the most complex human processes (e.g., speech, motor functioning).

Ontogenetically, there is an implicit theory of sequential neurological development that embraces Luria's thinking. This sequence of cortical maturation is shown in Fig. 21.2. This sequence of development is dependent upon the physiological and accompanying functional changes that occur with the maturation of various neural substrates. The arousal unit, largely involving the reticular activating system, generally is operative at birth and is believed to be fully functional by approximately one year of age. Similarly, the three primary sensory areas and the primary motor area of the cerebral cortex are intact at birth, with motor development maturing slightly earlier than sensory functions (Rhawn, 1982).

The secondary cortical regions are the next to develop and, although beginning to evolve from birth, are felt to be dominant by about age two. The development of skills associated with sec-

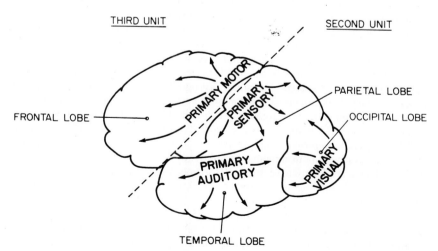

Figure 21.2 The second and third units of the brain showing the four lobes, primary cortical zones, and the sequence of cortical maturation.

ondary regions occurs through about age five. During this time, the secondary cortical areas are the major sites of learning. Thus, for the preschool child, learning is believed to occur largely within single modalities rather than among them (Golden, 1981b).

Development of these regions is followed by maturity of the tertiary areas of the second functional unit. The integrative, polymodal functions associated with the tertiary parietal region form the basic foundation for the acquisition of most formal academic skills, such as reading and mathematics (Shurtleff, Abbott, Townes, & Berninger, 1990). Anomalies in these regions have been linked to higher-order cognitive deficits of either a specific (e.g., learning disability) or global nature (e.g., mental retardation) (Golden, 1981b).

The final area to develop is the tertiary region of the frontal lobe. Injuries to the prefrontal regions have been associated with deficits in attention, abstraction, cognitive flexibility, planning, sequential processing, self-evaluation and monitoring of performance, and visuoconstructive abilities (Stuss & Benson, 1984). In fact, lesions to these areas can remain "silent" until later age-appropriate social, behavioral, and cognitive demands are required of the child (Rourke et al., 1983).

Despite this hypothesized neurodevelopmental sequence, few studies have attempted to incorporate this perspective into neuropsychological assessment methodology. However, several studies that provide limited support for use of this neurodevelopmental sequence have emerged. Luria (1959), and more recently Tinsley and Waters (1982), provided evidence that 3-year-old children typically are unable to inhibit their behaviors using overt verbal mediation. By age 4, however, these children could invoke overt verbal control over their behavior. Relatedly, using multitrait-multimethod analysis, Gnys and Willis (1990) provided empirical support for the construct of executive functioning in a preschool population. These data provided support for behaviors associated with normal frontal lobe development.

Similarly, Passler and associates (1985) and Becker and coworkers (1987) found evidence suggesting a developmental progression of behaviors associated with frontal lobe development in children from about ages 5 to 12. Using a similar population, Heverly and colleagues (1986) found a developmental progression with respect to tactile–visual discrimination functions and associated parietal lobe development. These kinds of neurodevelopmental behavioral tasks appear promising from a neuropsychological assessment perspective, but the actual validity of their application to the preschool child remains to be seen.

Cerebral Lateralization

Cerebral lateralization is the relative specialization of one cerebral hemisphere for the processing of particular material. Although neuropsychological assessment of the preschool child requires the incorporation of neurodevelopmental theory into assessment strategies to a greater extent, current views regarding cerebral lateralization suggest that it does not "develop." There is a wealth of literature that has accumulated indicating that the cerebral hemispheres are functionally specialized, at least for some processes, by birth. These data are robust in that they cut across the structure–function continuum.

Neuroanatomical findings indicate a remarkable similarity between adult and infant cerebral asymmetries. In the adult, the planum temporale region has been found to be slightly larger in the left hemisphere than in the right (Geschwind & Levitsky, 1968). This structural difference in the hemispheres also has been identified prenatally by 29 weeks gestation suggesting that there might be an inborn capacity for processing speech sounds (Witelson & Pallie, 1973). This structural asymmetry has received support from electrophysiological and behavioral studies.

Electrophysiological examinations of the infant brain indicate differential hemispheric responses depending on the stimulus used. Molfese (1977) found that responses to speech stimuli tended to be greater in the left hemisphere as opposed to the right. However, a reverse pattern was observed for nonspeech auditory stimuli (e.g., music). More recently, Molfese and Molfese (1986) reported that speech sounds can elicit auditory evoked responses from both hemispheres, but voice-related stimuli (e.g., vocal tone) showed a greater right hemispheric response and speech-related aspects (e.g., articulation) evidenced additional activity in the left hemisphere. More importantly, these investigators found these differential evoked potential patterns obtained at birth to discriminate between children with different levels of language functioning at three years of age.

Functionally, behavioral data also have provided support for the presence of early cerebral specialization. A preference for use of the right hand has been demonstrated in three month old infants (Caplan & Kinsbourne, 1976), and this finding has been replicated in infants as young as 17 days old (Petrie & Peters, 1980). Auditory perceptual asymmetries, in favor of the left hemisphere (i.e., right ear advantage), using the dichotic listening paradigm also have been demonstrated in the infant (Moffit, 1971), toddler, (Marcotte & LaBarba, 1985), and preschool-age child (Hiscock & Kinsbourne, 1977, 1980a). Similar findings have been shown with visual half-field studies (Carter & Kinsbourne, 1979) and time-sharing tasks (Hiscock & Kinsbourne, 1980b; Kinsbourne & McMurray, 1975).

It is clear that cerebral specialization does not develop but, rather, that it is present from birth. In a review of the behavioral literature, Bryden and Saxby (1986) concluded that observed cerebral asymmetries do not change significantly beyond age 3 years. This does not imply that lateralization is developing prior to that time, but probably reflects the emergence of functional mechanisms that help the child to perform a selected, lateralized task (e.g., processing speech stimuli) more efficiently (Kinsbourne & Hiscock, 1981). Generally, despite the neurodevelopmental implications in preschool neuropsychological assessment, cerebral laterlization seems to be remarkably independent of these ontogenetic factors, and this lays the foundation for giving interpretive significance to neuropsychological assessment findings.

Summary

Child neuropsychological assessment, particularly as applied to the preschool years, currently is in need of greater utilization of a neurodevelopmental perspective. Specific assessment strategies and interpretive principles should be based upon neurodevelopmental theory and current knowledge in attempting to understand preschool brain–behavior relationships in a more detailed fashion.

At present, Luria's model offers a comprehensive framework for developmental neuropsychological assessment. Further, it contributes to interpretive conceptualizations and provides the foundation for prognostic and prescriptive endeavors. However, the direct application of Luria's neurodevelopmental theory to the preschool-age child requires further validation. It should be remembered that neurological development and other biological factors account for only part of the variance of a child's overall functioning. Although it is speculated that the relationship between neuropsychological impairment and behavioral deficits might be reflected more directly during early childhood (Tramontana & Hooper, 1989), other variables, such as socioeconomic status, family intactness, and nursery school/day care experiences, can exert an influence over a preschooler's behavior and should be assessed as well.

NEUROPSYCHOLOGICAL ASSESSMENT PROCEDURES FOR THE PRESCHOOL-AGE CHILD

Despite its fledgling status, preschool neuropsychological assessment procedures are beginning to emerge. Most of the procedures parallel assessment models utilized with adults and school-age children and, generally, tend to cover a broad array of cognitive and motor functions. This section will discuss the neuropsychological assessment models proposed for the preschool-age child. The only formal battery applicable to the preschool child, along with a discussion of batteries measuring complex cognitive functions, will be presented first. This is followed by a presentation of informal approaches and their accompanying neuropsychological constructs that have been derived from clinical and empirical models. Finally, neuropsychological screening models that can be used with the preschool-age child are described.

Formal Batteries

At present there is only one recognized formal neuropsychological battery that is applicable to the preschool-age child. The Reitan-Indiana Neuropsychological Battery (Reitan, 1969) is a downward extension of the Halstead-Reitan Battery for children ages 5 years through 8 years. The tasks and accompanying directions were simplifed and shortened in an effort to adjust for the developmental differences suspected between the older and younger children. As with the version of the battery used for older children, these tasks typically are administered in conjunction with intellectual, academic/preacademic, lateral dominance, and personality measures. Traditional components of the Reitan-Indiana Battery include modified versions of the Category Test, Tactual Performance Test, and Finger Tapping Test (Electric). The allied procedures of Strength of Grip, Sensory-Perceptual Examination, Tactile Form Recognition, and Tactile Finger Localization also typically are administered. The Aphasia Screening Test and Finger-Tip Number Writing were modified slightly for the younger population. In addition, several new tests were developed for inclusion in the battery. These included the Marching Test, Color Form Test, Progressive Figures Test, Matching Pictures Test, Target Test, and the Individual Performance Tests (i.e., Matching Figures, Matching V's, Concentric Square, and Star). Collectively, these newer tasks attempt to assess gross motor coordination, selective attention, cognitive flexibility, visual perception, visual memory, motor speed, and abstract reasoning.

Taken together, the Reitan-Indiana tasks purport to assess a broad range of functions including gross and fine-motor skills, sensory–perceptual abilities, abstract thinking and problem solving, language, cognitive flexibility, and memory. Findings are interpreted in terms of four methods of inference that include level of performance, pattern of performance, pathognomonic signs, and right–left performance differences on the two sides of the body (Selz & Reitan, 1979). These four levels of inference are important in that they contribute to distinguishing neuropsychological procedures from more traditional psychological and developmental assessment approaches.

Level of performance refers to the comparison of a child's scores to an appropriate reference group. Findings from this method will indicate whether a child's performance is normal or abnormal. *Pattern of performance* provides insights into the child's relative strengths and weaknesses across various functions. This method of inference also might provide clues with respect to in-

tervention strategies for a particular child. The investigation of neuropsychological data for *pathognomonic signs* is especially relevant to the preschool child because their significance is dependent upon the developmental appropriateness of a particular behavior for a given age. For example, mild visual–spatial reversals in a 3 or 4 year old child's written output would not be pathognomonic, but their appearance in an 11 or 12 year old suggests pathology. Obviously, knowledge of normal developmental parameters is necessary for employing this method of inference with preschool children. The final method of data analysis, *left–right differences*, contributes to understanding performance differentials in the sensory and motor domains on the two sides of the body. Although slight left–right differences are expected, with the dominant side typically being stronger, more efficient, better coordinated, and accurate, lateralized sensory and/or motor deficits are considered to be among the most significant indicators of brain involvement in adults and children (Rourke, 1981).

Despite the relative popularity of the Reitan procedures, the Reitan-Indiana was designed only to address the latter stages of the preschool years. Although the applicability of the tasks has been shown to be useful with kindergarten children (Satz et al., 1978; Teeter, 1985; Townes et al., 1980), with some normative data being generated for preschoolers as young as age 2, 3, and 4 (Reitan & Davison, 1974), the application of the assessment procedures and the four methods of inference to children younger than age 5 years will require further study.

Given the dearth of appropriate neuropsychological assessment batteries for the preschool child, neuropsychologists have had to depend upon their general knowledge of brain–behavior relationships and neurodevelopmental theory in constructing assessment methodologies. In conjunction with this, a second neuropsychological assessment battery has been proposed by Korkman (1987), but limited reliability or validity data have been presented to date. The Neuropsychological Test Battery for Children (NEPSY) is based on Luria's Neuropsychological Investigation and was designed to be used for children ages 4 to 8. The battery consists of 37 homogeneous subtests scattered across five general areas. These functional areas include Control and Organization of Behavior, Verbal Processes, Sensory–Motor Processes, Visual–Spatial Perception, and Memory. Normative data reportedly are being collected for Swedish and Finnish children, and an English translation is planned.

Pending the availability and ultimate usefulness of formally developed preschool neuropsychological batteries, child neuropsychologists have employed many of the more traditional cognitive/intellectual test batteries as the core of an assessment strategy. The WPPSI-R, for example, is useful for preschoolers down to about age 3 years. As with the older age versions of the Wechsler scales, the WPPSI-R provides measures of verbal and nonverbal abilities. Specific subtests purportedly assess the retrieval and application of previously learned material as well as the acquisition of new information. Generally, the tasks provided by the WPPSI-R provide a solid foundation from which to organize additional neuropsychological assessment methods. However, whereas the Wechsler Intelligence Scale for Children-Revised (WISC-R) has been shown to be quite sensitive to brain impairment in children (Reitan, 1974), neither the WPPSI nor the WPPSI-R has been explored as extensively in this respect.

The MSCA (Kaufman & Kaufman, 1977; Teeter, 1985) and the K-ABC (Majovski, 1984) also have been discussed as having relevance to preschool neuropsychological assessment. Kaufman and Kaufman (1977) noted that the MSCA can be employed to generate a cognitive profile of a child's specific strengths and weaknesses. It can be used with children as young as 30 months and provides an adequate sampling of language, perceptual, motor, and memory abilities. In fact, Teeter (1985) found the MSCA to be roughly equivalent to the Reitan-Indiana in predicting later academic achievement in kindergarten children.

The K-ABC is an instrument that also can be used with preschoolers down to about 30 months. The K-ABC is unique in its attempt to separate problem solving or fluid abilities, as defined by simultaneous and sequential processing, from learned or crystallized functions (i.e., achievement). Although the K-ABC was not designed to serve as a single neuropsychological assessment battery, its theoretical underpinnings and its distinction between problem solving abilities and learned skills provide the foundation for developing a neuropsychological assessment strategy for the preschool-age child.

Informal Batteries

Given the relative unavailability of an appropriately validated set of neuropsychological assessment procedures for the preschool-age child, the greatest amount of work devoted to the preschool years to date has focused on the development of informal batteries. Lezak (1983) offered recommendations for the construction of informal test batteries. Lezak suggested that the construction of a battery should provide for the examination of a broad range of input and output functions. The actual procedures selected for inclusion should be developmentally appropriate, satisfactorily normed, and serve to provide for a certain degree of redundancy. The battery also should be practical in relation to the fundamental purpose(s) of the examination.

Informal batteries can address the qualitative (i.e., how a child performs a task) and/or quantitative (i.e., level and pattern of performance) aspects of a child's functioning, depending on the specific referral questions or general orientation of the examiner. Although based on neuropsychological constructs derived from work with adults and older children, several clinical and empirical preschool neuropsychological assessment models have emerged over the past several years. These models are listed in Table 21.1.

As can be seen from the models presented in Table 21.1, there is considerable overlap between the clinical models with respect to the neuropsychological constructs tested. Generally, these models attempt to assess language, motor skills, sensory-perceptual abilities, memory, higher-order problem solving, and preacademic skills, thus providing a comprehensive examination of a broad array of functions. The clinical models presented by Deysach (1986) and Wilson (1986) are noteworthy in their attempts to provide a systematic examination of a broad range of functions in an hierarchical fashion. Deysach (1986) stated that it is useful to assess simple as well as more complex functions across both input and output modalities. Similarly, Wilson (1986) presented an hypothesis testing model utilizing a branching technique. Using her model, an initial assessment strategy is employed to assess higher-order, more complex cognitive processes. Depending on how the child performs on this initial testing procedure, additional assessment strategies are selected

TABLE 21.1
INFORMAL NEUROPSYCHOLOGICAL ASSESSMENT MODELS FOR THE
PRESCHOOL CHILD AND THEIR ASSOCIATED CONSTRUCTS

Models	Neuropsychological Constructs
Clinical Models	
Aylward (1988)	Basic neurological functions
	Receptive functions
	Expressive functions
	Processing
	Mental activity
Deysach (1986)	Gross motor
	Fine motor
	Sensory-perceptual
	Verbal
	Short-term memory
	Abstraction/concept formation
Hartlage & Telzrow (1986)	Cognitive ability
	Basic language
	Preacademics
	Motor
	Sensory
	Social
	Adaptive
Wilson (1986)	Language
	Auditory integration
	Auditory cognition
	Auditory short-term memory
	Retrieval
	Visual
	Visual-spatial
	Visual cognition
	Visual short-term memory
	Motor
	Fine-motor
	Graphomotor
Empirical Models	
Jansky (1970)	Visual-motor
	Oral language (A and B)
	Pattern matching
	Pattern memory
Silver & Hagin (1972)	Auditory association
	Visual-neurological
	Psychiatric impairment
	Chronological age
	General intelligence
Satz et al. (1978)	Socioeconomic status
	Conceptual-verbal
	Sensorimotor-perceptual

based on identified areas of weakness in an effort to examine the child's difficulties in a more comprehensive manner.

The empirical models represent major contributions to the delineation of specific neuropsychological constructs relevant to the preschool child. Utilizing a battery of neurocognitive tasks Jansky (1970) provided one of the first studies uncovering specific underlying neuropsychological constructs of the preschooler. In her factor analysis of these tasks, Jansky found factors encompassing oral language, memory, visual–motor abilities, and abstract thinking. All of these factors, particularly oral language, were found to be significantly predictive of second grade reading skills.

Silver and Hagin (1972) found five factors in their preschool assessment battery. These factors were slightly different than those obtained by Jansky (1970) and included factors measuring auditory association, visual–neurological functioning, higher-order problem solving, and interestingly, chronological age and psychiatric impairment. These factors accounted for approximately 61% of their entire battery, with the auditory association and visual–neurological factors being most predictive of later reading problems.

The final empirical study generating neuropsychological assessment constructs relevant to the preschool child was conducted by Satz and associates (1978). Satz and associates conducted a factor analysis of 16 variables that resulted in three factors accounting for approximately 68% of the variance. These factors spanned sensorimotor–perceptual skills, verbal conceptual abilities, and verbal–cultural variables. These investigators found their factors, especially the sensorimotor–perceptual factor, to be predictive of later reading problems. They also found the predictive relationship to vary according to developmental parameters, thus placing differential importance upon different factors for particular developmental periods.

It should be noted that the development of the neuropsychological constructs associated with the empirical models eminated from examination of a specific population of children (i.e., children at risk for learning disabilities). Consequently, their generalizability to neuropsychological assessment of other neurologically impaired populations remains to be seen. Nonetheless, the clinical and empirical models provide the conceptual foundation for developing an informal neuropsychological assessment battery for the preschool child.

Given the clinical and empirical neuropsychological constructs generated to date, a sample of selected procedures that could be used in forming an informal preschool neuropsychological battery is illustrated in Table 21.2. In general, it is suggested that one of the major intellectual batteries be employed as the core of the assessment battery (e.g., WPPSI-R, K-ABC, MSCA). Additional procedures should be selected according to the needs of the child and in conjunction with the specific referral questions. In constructing an informal neuropsychological assessment battery, it will be important for the investigator to focus on obtaining the quantitative and qualitative aspects of a child's spared and impaired abilities, and to obtain assessment data in accordance with Reitan's four levels of inference. It also will be important for the instruments selected to have adequate normative data for the preschool child so that all scores can be converted into a common metric for comparative purposes (e.g., T-scores). The models proposed by Wilson (1986) and Deysach (1986) incorporate these strategies and, in addition, utilize hierarchical procedures in their test selection (i.e., assessment of complex to simple functions).

Informal batteries will require the child neuropsychologist to have an extensive knowledge of relevant tools to use in conjunction with a particular construct. However, preschool neuropsychologists employing an informal assessment model should be keenly aware of the potential psychometric and interpretive difficulties posed by using multiple instruments having different normative bases. Further, although other specific factors, such as attention, have not been identified in the clinical or empirical models, child neuropsychologists would be wise to evaluate the integrity of the components of a child's attention across modalities because deficits in this functional domain can have a pervasive influence on a child's cognitive functioning and behavior.

Screening Approaches

Neuropsychological screening approaches attempt to identify those children with suspected CNS involvement and differentiate them from

TABLE 21.2.
A SAMPLE OF SELECTED PROCEDURES FOR CONSTRUCTING AN INFORMAL
PRESCHOOL NEUROPSYCHOLOGICAL ASSESSMENT BATTERY

Neuropsychological Construct	Instrument
Lateral Dominance	Dichotic Listening Test
	Harris Lateral Dominance Test
	Miles Ocular Dominance Test
Motor	Bruininks-Oseretsky Test of Motor Proficiency
	Developmental Test of Visual–Motor Integration
	Finger Oscillation (Electric)
	Motor Scale of MSCA
	Purdue Pegboard
	Reitan-Indiana Subtests and Allied procedures
	Grip Strength
	Marching Test
	Color Form Test
	Progressive Figures Test
	WPPSI-R Subtests
	Animal Pegs
	Geometric Design
	Mazes
Attention	G-F-W Auditory Selective Attention Test
	Hiskey-Nebraska Visual Attention Subtest
	Matching Familiar Figures
	Gordon Diagnostic System
Sensory-Perceptual	FKSB Recognition-Discrimination
	K-ABC Subtests
	Magic Window
	Gestalt Closure
	Triangles
	Matrix Analogies Test
	Motor-Free Visual Perception Test
	MSCA Perceptual-Performance Subtests
	Reitan-Indiana Subtests and Allied procedures
	Sensory-Peceptual Exam
	Tactile Form Recognition
	Finger Localization
	Finger-Tip Symbol Writing
	Tactual Performance Test
	WPPSI-R Performance Subtests
Language	Boehm Test of Basic Concepts
	Bracken Basic Concept Scale
	Expressive One Word Picture Vocabulary Test
	G-F-W Auditory Skills Battery
	ITPA-R
	K-ABC Subtests
	Riddles
	Expressive Vocabulary
	MSCA Verbal Subtests
	Peabody Picture Vocabulary Test
	Test of Auditory Comprehension of Language-Revised
	Test of Early Language Development
	Token Test for Children
	WPPSI-R Verbal Subtests

TABLE 21.2. (*continued*)

Neuropsychological Construct	Instrument

Memory	G-F-W Auditory Memory Tests
	Hiskey-Nebraska Memory for Color Subtest
	ITPA-R Visual and Verbal Memory Subtests
	K-ABC Subtests
	    Face Recognition
	    Spatial Memory
	    Word Order
	    Hand Movement
	    Number Recall
	MSCA Memory Scale
	Reitan-Indiana Subtests and Allied Procedures
	    Target Test
	    Tactual Performance Test
	Sentences Subtest (WPPSI-R)
	Stanford-Binet (4th ed.) Memory Factor
	Woodcock-Johnson Revised Memory Subtests

Problem Solving	Columbia Mental Maturity Scale French Pictorial Test of Intelligence K-ABC Simultaneous and Sequential Scales Leiter International Performance Scale Matrix Analogies Test MSCA General Cognitive Index Stanford-Binet Intelligence Scale, 4th Edition WPPSI-R Verbal, Performance, and Full Scale IQs WPPSI-R Mazes Subtest Woodcock-Johnson Tests of Cognitive Abilities-Revised
Preacademic Skills	Alphabet Recitation Basic School Skills Inventory Bracken Basic Concept Scale Brigance Inventory of Early Development Cognitive Skills Assessment Battery K-ABC Faces-and-Places Subtest Peabody Individual Achievement Test-Revised Wide Range Achievement Test-Revised Woodcock-Johnson Tests of Achievement-Revised
Behavior	Achenbach Child Behavior Checklist Personality Inventory for Children Preschool Behavior Questionnaire Temperament Assessment Battery Vineland Adaptive Behavior Scale

their normal functioning peers. Screening procedures should not be designed to be definitive with respect to their diagnostic capabilities, but they should have significant sensitivity to the problem in question. It is unlikely that a single test could serve as an adequate neuropsychological screening tool. In fact, Lezak (1983) recommended the use of a multiple-test approach in structuring a screening battery. Lezak suggested that some tests should be sensitive to generalized neurological dysfunction and others should be selected because of their sensitivity to specific functional domains. It also might prove fruitful to include instruments that encompass Reitan's four methods of inference so as to broaden the interpretive base of a screening battery. Tupper (1986) stated that a good neuropsychological screening examination should be age/developmentally appropriate, be acceptable to the professionals who will be following the child, be easy to administer and interpret, have satisfactory reliability and validity, demonstrate acceptable sensitivity (i.e., identify true abnormals) and specificity (i.e., identify true normals), and be cost effective.

Currently, there are numerous neuropsychological screening procedures available for preschool children (Lichenstein & Ireton, 1984), most of which have been designed to identify children who are at risk for later learning impediments. Some of the more prominent preschool screening batteries include the Florida Kindergarten Screening Battery (FKSB) (Satz & Fletcher, 1982), the McCarthy Screening Test (MST) (McCarthy, 1978), the Quick Neurological Screening Test (QNST) (Mutti et al., 1978), The Neurological Dysfunctions of Children (NDOC) (Kuhns, 1979), and the Pediatric Extended Examination at Three (PEET) (Blackman et al., 1986).

The FKSB and MST were both designed to predict later academic difficulties when given during the preschool years. In particular, the FKSB was developed from a larger battery of neuropsychological measure with the final tasks being selected based on their combined predictive accuracy. It requires approximately one hour for administration and includes four tasks: Recognition-Discrimination, Finger Localization, the Peabody Picture Vocabulary Test-Revised, and the Developmental Test of Visual–Motor Integration. Alphabet Recitation is an optional fifth test. Although the FKSB has been criticized (Gates, 1984), it still represents one of the first screening batteries developed from a neuropsychological perspective.

The MST was designed as an abbreviated version of the MSCA for children ages 4½ to 6. It contains 6 of the 18 parent scale's subtests and classifies children as "at risk" or "not at risk." Specific subtests were included because of their simplicity in administration, ease of scoring, and their minimal time requirements. These included Right–Left Orientation, Verbal Memory, Draw-A-Design, Numerical Memory, Conceptual Grouping, and Leg Coordination. The MST requires about 20 to 30 minutes to administer.

The NDOC and QNST are somewhat different in their conceptualization and largely attempt to assess soft signs in neurobehavioral functioning. Neither of these procedures provided much data to support their screening capabilities, but Tupper (1986) noted that these procedures do seem to have face validity. The NDOC is an 18-item examination that is scored in a dichotomous "yes-no" fashion. It can be used for children as young as age 3 years and interpretation is aided by 13 different clusterings of the items. The QNST similarly contains 15 items measuring a variety of soft sign functions (e.g., repetitive hand movements, tandem walking). Although a numerical score is obtained for each item, a large portion of the interpretation is qualitative in nature and focuses on *how* a child performs a particular task. Based on the scores obtained, the QNST classifies children into High, Suspicious, and Normal categories, with the first two classifications suggesting possible CNS dysfunction.

A final screening instrument to be discussed is the PEET (Blackman et al., 1986). The PEET is a neurodevelopmental assessment system constructed to contribute to the early identification and understanding of learning, attentional, and behavioral problems in children ages 3 to 4. The PEET provides tasks assessing gross and fine-motor skills, language, visual–motor, memory, and intersensory integration. These tasks are structured around three major input–output channels including Auditory–Verbal Communication, Visually Directed Manipulation, and Spatial–Somatic Integration. Within each channel a hierarchy of increasingly complex functions is represented that provides a unique interpretive asset for individuals using this screening tool. A child's behavior during the examination also can be rated in a systematic fashion. Preliminary validity information has begun to surface for the PEET (Blackman et al., 1983), but other psychometric aspects (e.g., predictive validity) of this tool will require further substantiation for the preschool population. Nonetheless, in its current form it represents an advancement in screening technology when compared to most other screening batteries.

Summary

Neuropsychological assessment procedures include few formal batteries for the preschool child, although some appear on the horizon (Korkman, 1987). However, this is just as well as it is unlikely that one, all-encompassing battery would be appropriate for all preschool children. The informal assessment models represent current "state of the art" assessment technology for this population, with a particular emphasis being directed to those models providing hierarchical assessment strategies (Deysach, 1986; Wilson, 1986). Although comprehensive by design, the informal approaches also allow for the flexibility needed to examine specific areas of strength and weakness in greater detail. However, the potential problems of using multiple normative groups in the process of instrument comparison will require further study.

Neuropsychological screening approaches also are evolving for the preschool child, particularly with respect to predicting later learning difficulties and identifying children as candidates for more complete neuropsychological evaluation of general or more selective functions. Despite these advances, few of the assessment models have been founded on neurodevelopmental theory, perhaps with the exception of those models employing hierarchical assessment strategies, and it will be important for future preschool neuropsychological assessment models to incorporate neurodevelopmental factors into the assessment design in a more comprehensive fashion.

ISSUES IN PRESCHOOL NEUROPSYCHOLOGICAL ASSESSMENT

Unlike assessment with adults and older children, testing with preschool children tends to present a unique set of potential problems that can influence neuropsychological results. First and foremost is the young age of the preschooler. Preschooler's have precious little stamina for sitting still and concentrating for prolonged periods of time and, in fact, these "problems" likely will be exacerbated in a neurologically impaired child. Consequently, subjecting a preschooler to a long testing regimen actually can prove counterproductive. The clinician should attempt to modify the assessment battery to address the referral questions thoroughly, but efficiently, and to fit the needs of the child (e.g., employing multiple sessions).

Partially related to this issue are concerns regarding the reliability of a preschooler's responses. A certain amount of redundancy and task repetition should be built into a neuropsychological battery in an effort to account for these "normal" response inconsistencies. This becomes particularly important in profile interpretation and in the planning of intervention strategies. These response inconsistencies of the preschool child also possibly contribute to lowering the magnitude of predictor-criterion relationships in this population which, in turn, will interfere with prognostic implications.

Finally, the brain–behavior relationships in this population need to continue to receive investigation. Little is known about these relationships at present, although the interjection of a neurodevelopmental framework will provide a vehicle for increasing the understanding of these relationships. The interaction and possible synergistic effects between biological and psychosocial factors in a child's development might be understood further with dynamic neurodevelopmental model guiding preschool neuropsychological assessment strategies.

CONCLUSIONS

This chapter has attempted to provide an overview of issues and procedures in the neuropsychological assessment of the preschool child. The potential value of a neuropsychological perspective in the assessment of a preschool-age child not withstanding, it appears that the field is in need of strong neurodevelopmental underpinnings to direct neuropsychological assessment efforts. Although a formal battery applicable for all preschool children is not currently available, the technology is present to provide a comprehensive assessment of a child's cognitive, sensory, motor, and personality functioning in a systematic fashion. Such an assessment goes beyond what might be obtained from more traditional psychological assessments at this age level and has the potential to provide for a handicapped preschooler's needs in a highly specific and dynamic manner. With the development of neuropsychological tasks sensitive to the various aspects of brain development, and the increased understanding of the impact of various neuropathological processes during these years, the development of preschool neuropsychological assessment also will be witnessed.

REFERENCES

Aylward, G. P. (1988). Infant and early childhood assessment. In M. G. Tramontana & S. R. Hooper (Eds.). *Assessment Issues in Child Neuropsychology* (pp. 225–248). New York: Plenum Publishing Company.

Aylward, G. P., Gustafson, N., Verhulst, S. J., & Colliver, J. A. (1987). Consistency in the diagnosis of cognitive, motor, and neurologic function over the first three years. *Journal of Pediatric Psychology, 12,* 77–98.

Bagnato, S. J., & Dickerson-Mayes, S. (1986). Patterns of developmental and behavioral progress for young brain-injured children during interdisciplinary intervention. *Developmental Neuropsychology, 2,* 213–240.

Bakker, D. J., Moerland, R., & Goekoop-Hoefkens, M. (1981). Effects of hemisphere-specific stimulation on the reading performance of dyslexic boys. A pilot study. *Journal of Clinical Neuropsychology, 3,* 155–159.

Becker, M. G., Isaac, W., & Hynd, G. W. (1987). Neuropsychological development of nonverbal behaviors attributed to frontal-lobe functioning. *Developmental Neuropsychology, 3,* 279–298.

Behr, S., & Gallagher, J. J. (1981). Alternative administrative strategies for young handicapped children. A policy analysis. *Journal of the Division for Early Childhood, 2,* 113–122.

Blackman, J. A., Levine, M. D., & Markowitz, M. (1986). *Pediatric Extended Examination at Three.* Cambridge, MA: Educators Publishing Service, Inc.

Blackman, J. A., Levine, M. D., Markowitz, M. T., &

Aufseeser, C. L. (1983). The pediatric extended examination at three. A system for diagnostic clarification of problematic three-year-olds. *Developmental and Behavioral Pediatrics, 4,* 143–150.

Boll, T. J., & Barth, J. T. (1981). Neuropsychology of brain damage in children. In S. B. Filskov & T. J. Boll (Eds.). *Handbook of Clinical Neuropsychology* (pp. 418–452). New York: John Wiley and Sons.

Bryden, M. P., & Saxby, L. (1986). Developmental aspects of cerebral lateralization. In J. E. Obrzut & G. W. Hynd (Eds.). *Child Neuropsychology, Volume 1: Theory and Research* (pp. 73–94). Orlando, FL: Academic Press.

Caplan, P. J., & Kinsbourne, M. (1976). Baby drops the rattle. Asymmetry of duration of grasp by infants. *Child Development, 47,* 532–534.

Carter, G. L., & Kinsbourne, M. (1979). The ontogeny of right lateralization of spatial mental set. *Developmental Psychology, 15,* 241–245.

Casto, G., & Mastropieri, M. A. (1986). The efficacy of early intervention programs. A meta-analysis. *Exceptional Children, 52,* 417–424.

Chadwick, O., & Rutter, M. (1983). Neuropsychological assessment. In M. Rutter (Ed.). *Developmental Neuropsychiatry* (pp. 181–212). New York: The Guilford Press.

Chelune, G. J., & Edwards, P. (1981). Early brain lesions. Ontogenetic-environmental considerations. *Journal of Consulting and Clinical Psychology, 49,* 777–790.

Craft, A., Shaw, D., & Cartlidge, N. (1972). Head injuries in children. *British Medical Journal, 4,* 200–203.

Cull, C., & Wyke, M. A. (1984). Memory function of children with spina bifida and shunted hydrocephalus. *Developmental Medicine and Child Neurology, 26,* 177–183.

Dennis, M. (1985a). Intelligence after early brain injury. I. Predicting IQ scores from medical variables. *Journal of Clinical and Experimental Neuropsychology, 7,* 526–554.

Dennis, M. (1985b). Intelligence after early brain injury. II. IQ scores of subjects classified on the basis of medical history variables. *Journal of Clinical and Experimental Neuropsychology, 7,* 555–576.

Dennis, M., & Whitaker, H. A. (1977). Hemisphere equipotentiality and language acquisition. In S. J. Segalowitz & F. A. Gruber (Eds.), *Language Development and Neurological Theory* (pp. 93–106). New York: Academic Press.

Deysach, R. E. (1986). The role of neuropsychological assessment in the comprehensive evaluation of preschool-age children. *School Psychology Review, 15,* 233–244.

Ellison, P. H. (1983). The relationship of motor and cognitive function in infancy, pre-school and early school years. *Journal of Clinical Child Psychology, 12,* 81–90.

Fennell, E. B., Eisenstadt, T., Bodiford, C., Rediess, S., de Bijl, M., & Mickle, J. P. (1987). *The Assessment of Neuropsychological Dysfunction in Children Shunted for Hydrocephalus.* Paper presented at the Fifteenth Annual Meeting of the International Neuropsychological Society, Washington, D. C.

Gates, R. D. (1984). Florida Kindergarten Screening Battery (Test Review). *Journal of Clinical Neuropsychology, 6,* 459–465.

Geschwind, N., & Levitsky, W. (1968). Human brain. Left-right asymmetries in temporal speech region. *Science, 161,* 186–187.

Gnys, J. A., & Willis, W. G. (1990). *Executive functioning in preschoolers: A multitrait-multimethod analysis.* Paper presented at the Annual Meeting of the American Psychological Association, Boston, MA.

Golden, C. J. (1981a). *Diagnosis and rehabilitation in clinical neuropsychology.* Springfield, IL: Charles C. Thomas.

Golden, C. J. (1981b). The Luria-Nebraska Children's Battery. Theory and formulation. In G. W. Hynd & J. E. Obrzut (Eds.). *Neuropsychological Assessment and the School-age Child: Issues and Procedures* (pp. 277–302). New York: Grune & Stratton.

Hartlage, L. C., & Telzrow, C. F. (1982). Neuropsychological assessment. In K. Paget & B. Bracken (Eds.). *Psychoeducational Assessment of Preschool Children* (pp. 295–320). New York: Grune and Stratton.

Hartlage, L. C., & Telzrow, C. F. (1986). *Neuropsychological assessment and intervention with children and adolescents.* Sarasota, FL: Professional Resource Exchange, Inc.

Heverly, L. L., Isaac, W., & Hynd, G. W. (1986). Neurodevelopmental and racial differences in tactual-visual (cross modal) discrimination in normal black and white children. *Archives of Clinical Neuropsychology, 1,* 139–145.

Hiscock, M., & Kinsbourne, M. (1977). Selective listening asymmetry in preschool children. *Developmental Psychology, 13,* 217–224.

Hiscock, M., & Kinsbourne, M. (1980a). Asymmetry of verbal-manual time sharing in children. A follow-up study. *Neuropsychologia, 18,* 151–162.

Hiscock, M., & Kinsbourne, M. (1980b). Asymmetries of selective listening and attention switching in children. *Developmental Psychology, 16,* 70–82.

Hooper, S. R. (1988). The prediction of learning disabilities in the preschool child. A neuropsychological perspective. In M. G. Tramontana & S. R. Hooper (Eds.). *Assessment Issues in Child Neuropsychol-*
ogy (pp. 313–335). New York: Plenum Publishing Company.

Horn, W. G., & Packard, T. (1985). Early identification of learning problems. A meta-analysis. *Journal of Educational Psychology, 77,* 597–607.

Hurley, A. D., Laatsch, L. K., & Dorman, C. (1983). Comparison of spina bifida, hydrocephalic patients, and matched controls on neuropsychological tests. *Z Kinderchir, 17,* 65–70.

Hynd, G. W., & Cohen, C. (1983). *Dyslexia. Neuropsychological Theory, Research, and Clinical Differentiation.* New York: Grune & Stratton.

Hynd, G. W., & Obrzut, J. E. (Eds.) (1981). *Neuropsychological Assessment and the School-age Child. Issue and Procedures.* New York: Grune and Stratton.

Hynd, G. W., & Willis, W. G. (1988). *Pediatric Neuropsychology.* Orlando, FL: Grune and Stratton.

Incagnoli, T., & Newman, B. (1985). Cognitive and behavioral interventions. *International Journal of Clinical Neuropsychology, 7,* 173–182.

Jansky, J. J. (1970). *The Contribution of Certain Kindergarten Abilities to Second Grade Reading and Spelling Achievement.* Unpublished doctoral dissertation, Columbia University, New York.

Kalverboer, A. F. (1971). Free-field behavior in preschool boys and girls. In G. B. Stoelinga & J. J. Van der Werff Tem Bosch (Eds.). *Normal and Abnormal Development of Brain and Behavior* (pp. 187–203). The Netherlands: Leiden U. Press.

Kaufman, A. S., & Kaufman, N. L. (1977). *Clinical Evaluation of Young Children with the McCarthy Scales.* New York: Grune and Stratton.

Kinsbourne, M., & Hiscock, M. (1981). Cerebral lateralization and cognitive development. Conceptual and methodological issues. In G. W. Hynd & J. E. Obrzut (Eds.). *Neuropsychological Assessment and the School-age Child: Issues and Procedures* (pp. 125–166). New York: Grune and Stratton.

Kinsbourne, M., & McMurray, J. (1975). The effect of cerebral dominance on time sharing between speaking and tapping by preschool children. *Child Development, 46,* 240–242.

Kolb, B., & Whishaw, I. (1985). *Fundamentals of human neuropsychology.* New York: Freeman and Company.

Korkman, M. E. (1987). *NEPSY - A Neuropsychological Test Battery for Children, Based on Luria's Investigation.* Paper presented at the Fifteenth Annual Meeting of the International Neuropsychological Society, Washington, D. C.

Kuhns, J. W. (1979). *Neurological Dysfunctions of Children.* Monterey, CA: Publishers Test Service.

Levine, M. D., & Schneider, E. A. (1982). *Pediatric Examination of Educational Readiness. Examiner's*

Manual. Cambridge, MA: Educators Publishing Service, Inc.

Lezak, M. D. (1983). *Neuropsychological Assessment* (2nd Ed.). New York: Oxford University Press.

Lichenstein, R., & Ireton, H. (1984). *Preschool Screening. Early Identification of School Problems.* Orlando, FL: Grune and Stratton.

Luria, A. R. (1959). The directive function of speech in development and dissolution. *Word, 15,* 341–352.

Luria, A. R. (1963). *Restoration of Function after Brain Injury.* New York: MacMillan.

Luria, A. R. (1966). *The Working Brain.* New York: Basic Books.

Majovski, L. V. (1984). The K-ABC. Theory and applications for child neuropsychological assessment and research. *The Journal of Special Education, 18,* 257–268.

Marcotte, A. C., & LaBarba, R. C. (1985). Cerebral lateralization for speech in deaf and normal children. *Brain and Language, 26,* 244–258.

McCarthy, D. (1978). *Manual for the McCarthy Screening Test.* New York: Psychological Corporation.

Moffit, A. R. (1971). Consonant cue perception by twenty to twenty-four week old infants. *Child Development, 42,* 717–731.

Molfese, D. L. (1977). Infant cerebral asymmetry. In S. J. Segalowitz & F. A. Gruber (Eds.), *Language Development and Neurological Theory* (pp. 21–35). New York: Academic Press.

Molfese, D. L., & Molfese, V. J. (1986). Psychophysiological indices of early cognitive processes and their relationship to language. In J. E. Obrzut & G. W. Hynd (Eds.), *Child Neuropsychology, Volume 1. Theory and Research* (pp. 95–115). New York: Academic Press.

Mutti, M., Sterling, H. M., & Spalding, N. V. (1978). *QNST: Quick Neurological Screening Test* (rev. ed.). Novato, CA: Academic Therapy Publications.

National Joint Committee on Learning Disabilities (1986). *A Position Paper of the National Joint Committee on Learning Disabilities.* Baltimore: The Orton Dyslexia Society.

Obrzut, J. E., & Hynd, G. W. (Eds.) (1986a). *Child Neuropsychology, Volume 1: Theory and Research.* New York: Academic Press.

Obrzut, J. E., & Hynd, G. W. (Eds.) (1986b). *Child Neuropsychology, Volume 2: Clinical Practice.* New York: Academic Press.

Passler, M., Isaac, W., & Hynd, G. W. (1985). Neuropsychological development of behavior attributed to frontal lobe functioning in children. *Developmental Neuropsychology, 1,* 349–370.

Petrie, B. F., & Peters, M. (1980). Handedness. Left/right differences in intensity of grasp response and duration of rattle holding in infants. *Infant Behavior and Development, 3,* 215–221.

Raimondi, A., & Soare, P. (1977). Intellectual development in shunted hydrocephalic children. *American Journal of Disorders of Childhood, 127,* 142–144.

Reitan, R. M. (1969). *Manual for Administration of Neuropsychological Test Batteries for Adults and Children.* Indianapolis, IN. Author.

Reitan, R. M. (1974). Psychological effects of cerebral lesions in children of early school age. In R. M. Reitan & L. A. Davison (Eds.), *Clinical Neuropsychology: Current Status and Applications* (pp. 53–90). New York. John Wiley and Sons.

Reitan, R. M., & Davison, L. A. (Eds.) (1974). *Clinical Neuropsychology: Current Status and Applications.* New York: John Wiley and Sons.

Rhawn, J. (1982). The neuropsychology of development. Hemispheric laterality, limbic language, and the origin of thought. *Journal of Clinical Psychology, 38,* 4–33.

Rourke, B. P. (1981). Neuropsychological assessment of children with learning disabilities. In S. B. Filskov & T. J. Boll (Eds.), *Handbook of Clinical Neuropsychology* (pp. 453–478). New York: Wiley Interscience.

Rourke, B. P. (1983). Outstanding issues in research on learning disabilities. In M. Rutter (Ed.), *Developmental Neuropsychiatry* (pp. 564–574). New York: The Guilford Press.

Rourke, B. P., Bakker, D. J., Fisk, J. L., & Strang, J. D. (1983). *Child Neuropsychology.* New York: The Guilford Press.

Rourke, B. P., Fisk, J. L., & Strang, J. D. (1986). *Neuropsychological Assessment of Children: A Treatment-oriented Approach.* New York: The Guilford Press.

Satz, P., & Fletcher, J. M. (1982). *Florida Kindergarten Screening Battery.* Odessa, FL: Psychological Assessment Resources, Inc.

Satz, P., Taylor, H. G., Friel, J., & Fletcher, J. M. (1978). Some developmental and predictive precursors of reading disabilities. A six year follow-up. In A. L. Benton & D. Pearl (Eds.), *Dyslexia: An Appraisal of Current Knowledge* (pp. 315–347). New York: Oxford University Press.

Selz, M., & Reitan, R. M. (1979). Rules for neuropsychological diagnosis and classification of brain function in older children. *Journal of Consulting and Clinical Psychology, 47,* 258–264.

Shurtleff, H., Abbott, R., Townes, B., & Berninger, V. (1990). *Structural equation modeling of neurodevelopmental, intellectual, and academic factors.*

Paper presented at the Annual Meeting of the American Psychological Association, Boston, MA.

Silver, A. A., & Hagin, R. A. (1972). Profile of a first grade. A basis for preventive psychiatry. *Journal of the American Academy of Child Psychiatry, 11,* 645–674.

Spreen, O., & Haaf, R. G. (1986). Empirically derived learning disability subtypes. A replication attempt and longitudinal patterns over 15 years. *Journal of Learning Disabilities, 19,* 170–180.

Stevenson, H. W., & Newman, R. S. (1986). Long-term prediction of achievement and attitudes in mathematics and reading. *Child Development, 57,* 646–659.

Stuss, D. T., & Benson, D. F. (1984). Neuropsychological studies of the frontal lobes. *Psychological Bulletin, 95,* 3–28.

Teeter, P. A. (1985). Neurodevelopmental investigation of academic achievement. A report of years 1 and 2 of a longitudinal study. *Journal of Consulting and Clinical Psychology, 53,* 709–717.

Tinsley, V. S., & Waters, H. S. (1982). The development of verbal control over motor behavior. A replication and extension of Luria's findings. *Child Development, 53,* 746–753.

Townes, B. D., Turpin, E. W., Martin, D. C., & Goldstein, D. (1980). Neuropsychological correlates of academic success among elementary school children. *Journal of Consulting and Clinical Psychology, 6,* 675–684.

Tramontana, M. G., & Hooper, S. R. (Eds.) (1988a). *Assessment Issues in Child Neuropsychology.* New York: Plenum Publishing Company.

Tramontana, M. G., & Hooper, S. R. (1988b). Child neuropsychological assessment. Overview of current status. In M. G. Tramontana & S. R. Hooper (Eds.), *Assessment Issues in Child Neuropsychology* (pp. 1–38) New York. Plenum Publishing Company.

Tramontana, M. G., & Hooper, S. R. (1989). Neuropsychology of child psychopathology. In C. R. Reynolds & E. Fletcher-Janzen (Eds.), *Handbook of Clinical Child Neuropsychology.*(pp. 87–106). New York: Plenum Publishing Company.

Tramontana, M. G., Hooper, S. R., & Selzer, S. C. (1988). Research on the preschool prediction of later academic achievement. *Developmental Review, 8,* 89–147.

Tupper, D. E. (1986). Neuropsychological screening and soft signs. In J. E. Obrzut & G. W. Hynd (Eds.), *Child Neuropsychology, Volume 2: Clinical Practice* (pp. 139–186). New York: Academic Press.

U. S. Department of Education, Division of Educational Services (1984). *Sixth Annual Report to Congress on the Implementation of Public Law 94–142: The Education for All Handicapped Children Act.* Washington, D. C.. Author.

White, K. R. (1986). Efficacy of early intervention. *The Journal of Special Education, 19,* 401–416.

Willis, W. G., & Widerstrom, A. H. (1986). Structure and function in prenatal and postnatal neuropsychological development. A dynamic interaction. In J. E. Obrzut & G. W. Hynd (Eds.), *Child Neuropsychology, Volume 1. Theory and Research* (pp. 13–53). Orlando, FL: Academic Press.

Wilson, B. C. (1986). An approach to the neuropsychological assessment of the preschool child with developmental deficits. In S. B. Filskov & T. J. Boll (Eds.), *Handbook of Clinical Neuropsychology, Volume 2* (pp. 121–171). New York: Wiley.

Witelson, S. F., & Pallie, W. (1973). Left hemisphere specialization for language in the newborn. Neuroanatomical evidence of asymmetry. *Brain, 96,* 671–696.

Zihl, J. (1981). Recovery of visual functions in patients with cerebral blindness. *Experimental Brain Research, 44,* 159–169.

22

Preschool Screening for Developmental and Educational Problems

ROBERT LICHTENSTEIN
HARRY IRETON

PRESCHOOL SCREENING: PERSPECTIVES AND APPROACHES

The impetus behind preschool screening is that a great number of children are struggling or failing in school. Children with handicapping conditions such as physical and sensory impairment, developmental and learning disabilities, and emotional disturbance who are not receiving an appropriate education constitute a substantial population of school "casualties." This chapter addresses the issues and options involved in using screening procedures to identify young children who are at risk for school failure. Its focus is the needs of schools and other agencies to create cost-effective systems for reviewing the development and learning of preschool children.

The strongest image that preschool screening evokes is that of administering brief tests of development, vision, and hearing to young children prior to school entry. A larger view of preschool screening, however, recognizes that testing is only one element of an identification and intervention process.

The most common context for preschool screening is the early identification of children who are or might be educationally handicapped. Preschool screening is a process with a purpose—the purpose being to identify children with developmental and potential educational problems prior to school entry to provide them with special services. It is this definition of preschool screening that is the focus of this chapter. Early identification and intervention of young children with special needs was clearly established as a national priority in this country by the Education for All Handicapped Children Act of 1975 (Public Law 94–142). This federal mandate requires that states establish guidelines for providing services and that individual school districts implement, or make arrangements for, direct services at the local level.

Historically, screening of young children for the purpose of preventing school failure also has been approached in a somewhat different manner through kindergarten screening programs. In kindergarten screening, children who are chronologically supposed to enter school are evaluated to determine whether they are developmentally ready to participate in a standard kindergarten program.

In preschool screening, a brief evaluation is used to tentatively identify children whose developmental or related functioning is delayed or at risk for learning problems or school failure. These at-risk children are then formally assessed at greater length. Once identified, children who are determined to have problems can be provided with special services early on so that their disabilities can be addressed and their school performance maximized.

Developmental screening programs vary greatly with respect to comprehensiveness of screening, assessment of particular skills and abilities, the degree of disability required for intervention, and the nature and extent of available assessment and intervention services. Thurlow and associates (1986) report extreme variability in the screening practices among school districts in the state of Minnesota, with referral rates ranging from 0 to 86%. Furthermore, they report great inconsistencies in referral rates by screening areas: ". . . in some districts almost all referrals were for hearing problems, while in others almost all were for motor development difficulties" (p. 94). This is a particularly noteworthy finding given that Minnesota was among the first states to institute preschool screening on a programmatic, statewide basis.

A critical feature of screening programs is the availability of follow-up evaluation and intervention services for children who are identified. Theoretical approach and policy preferences might take a back seat to matters of finances and resources in the case of a school system that is required to identify children with special needs and provide special services while lacking the resources to do so. A system with insufficient resources or with a very needy target population might opt to respond only to fairly extreme problems or might emphasize those types of problems to which the system is most capable of responding. In such instances, a screening program might document service needs and promote efforts to respond to these needs, although this might be considered inappropriate as a primary, rather than incidental, purpose.

A number of issues and questions are introduced by the use of preschool screening programs: How accurate are the tentative decisions made through preschool screening? To what extent do we miss children who will have problems?

Might we refer so many children that we overburden an early identification system? What are the benefits and limitations of preschool screening? These questions are addressed at the theoretical, empirical, and practical levels in the remainder of this chapter. Featured topics include screening program implementation, types and sources of screening information, characteristics of screening instruments, and technical considerations in making and evaluating screening decisions. Critical analysis of the objectives of, and optimal approaches to, early identification—a theme that runs throughout the chapter—is the focus of the final section. For more in-depth coverage of these topics, the reader is referred to *Preschool screening: Identifying Young Children with Developmental and Educational Problems* (Lichtenstein & Ireton, 1984).

Approaches to Preschool Screening

The initial step of early identification is *outreach*, where children who are to be screened are located (i.e., parents are contacted and informed about the program). The next step in the early identification process is *screening*, in which brief, relatively inexpensive, easily administered measures are used to determine which individuals should be referred for further assessment. Final determination of a person's status, however, is reserved for a subsequent *assessment* phase where the individual receives a more in-depth evaluation. Hence, the term at risk is applied to individuals who are tentatively identified through screening. The term *screening* technically refers to the process of selecting out for further study those high risk individuals whose apparent problems might require special attention or intervention.

The measures used in preschool screening could involve any number of screening procedures including standardized developmental tests, reports from parents, and reviews of previous evaluations. The entire screening process might involve two or more "passes" at which the target group is narrowed down, using more accurate, time consuming, and costly measures, at each successive pass.

Implementation of P.L. 94–142 has focused much attention upon large-scale early identification efforts using a mass screening approach.

Mass screening refers to a program that is designed to screen every child in a given target population. Rather than rely upon parents' or health professionals' initiatives to make referrals (a process which, although inconsistent, constitutes an initial screen), every child is subjected to some uniform screening process. The approach offers distinct advantages and disadvantages. The potential for identifying those in need is increased and there is relatively little stigma associated with participation in a screening program designed for all. On the other hand, the total cost and effort required is great, and many children must be subjected to the process—for better or worse. Whether a mass screening project is cost-effective can hinge upon the skills it assesses and how it is conducted.

A *selective screening* approach might focus upon a particular high-risk subgroup (e.g., children in low socioeconomic areas), which offers advantages of cost effectiveness and of addressing particular sociopolitical priorities. Or, parent input can be used initially to narrow down the target population, either through self-selection (i.e., parents are given guidelines for deciding whether to have their children screened) or by having parents provide reports about their children to screening program professionals. Or, all children in a locale might be screened at a single convenient point in time (e.g., when they register for or first enter school).

Some school systems employ the practice of *kindergarten screening* to assess children's developmental status at the time of school entry. Kindergarten screening may serve such purposes as obtaining essential health and background information, determining children's classroom assignments, and identifying children with marked educational or developmental problems. Some school systems, however, conduct kindergarten screening for school readiness in an effort to identify "developmentally immature" children, who are then considered for placement in "extra year" programs—a practice that has been the subject of much attention and controversy in recent years (Lichtenstein, 1990; Meisels, 1987; Shepherd & Smith, 1986).

The age range addressed by preschool screening, as defined in this chapter, is fairly narrow. Preschool screening carries the connotation of occurring at or near the time of school entry. To screen children much in advance of age 4 offers limited prospects of assessing *educational* needs (although factors relating to later achievement, e.g., hearing and environmental exposure, might be noted). However, children must be identified sufficiently in advance of school entry if the intention of providing early intervention is to be realized. (Note that, following this logic, if services are not available prior to school age, children are best identified without the benefit of a preschool screening program after they enter school.) The 3 to 5 age range is generally regarded as the primary age focus for preschool screening.

P.L. 94–142, in mandating that children with special needs must be actively identified and served, expanded school age to encompass ages 3 to 21 for children with specified special needs. Still, delivery of services for preschoolers has been inconsistent, particularly because of the clause in P.L. 94–142 that allows individual states to establish policies regarding services for preschool children that supersede the federal law. Although funds are available for preschool services, compliance is not universally required. Many states have addressed this issue by providing services for certain conditions only, for example, those with severe vision or hearing problems.

Comprehensiveness of special services for preschool children was augmented by the enactment in 1987 of Public Law 99–457, which amends P.L. 94–142 through funding of programs that serve developmentally delayed infants and toddlers and their families. Consequently, the establishment of screening programs for children in the 0 to 3 age range, and possibly even the prenatal period, is likely. Identification in this age range can be expected to focus upon organically based handicapping conditions and physical impairments, for example, autism, moderate to severe mental retardation, cerebral palsy, and vision and hearing defects, in contrast to the more educational focus of preschool screening. As such early identification efforts can be combined administratively with preschool screening, reference to "early childhood screening" is likely to come into common use.

Assumptions in Early Identification

Early identification and early intervention for children with developmental or educational problems have been widely promoted as a valuable, responsible approach to serving children with special needs. Resources are devoted to intervention before problems become more serious and difficult to remediate. This approach, however, is predicated upon three critical assumptions, each of which merits careful consideration:

1. Early educational intervention produces a significant positive effect.

Evidence to support the efficacy of early intervention has accumulated at a modest and uneven rate. Research to date on the effects of early intervention programs for disadvantaged children suggest positive, but limited, benefits. Previously emphasized gains in cognitive development have proven to be largely limited to short-lived "bursts" upon initial exposure to an educationally oriented curriculum. Subsequent research, however, suggests that early intervention programs impact favorably upon children's subsequent needs for special services (Lazar & Darlington, 1982) and that long-term benefits could outweigh the cost of intervention programs (Weber et al., 1978). A major factor influencing this phenomenon appears to be the shaping of parental expectations and attitudes toward education (Lazar, 1981).

Although evidence has accumulated in support of the efficacy of early intervention for children with handicapping conditions (see reviews by Edmiaston & Mowder, 1985; McNulty et al., 1984), definitive research is constricted by the ethical dilemma in pursuing a "pure" research design comparing children receiving early intervention with a randomly assigned control group receiving no special services. In this case, the assumption that early intervention is of positive value interferes with empirical documentation of the claim.

2. Developmental problems in young children can be accurately identified at an early stage by means of brief screening followed by in-depth assessment.

The practice of early intervention presumes that current problems or developmental delays will persist over time. Not all children who show signs of early difficulties, however, will prove to have later problems. Predictions about future developmental and learning problems are particularly tenuous for young children, who differ considerably in their rate of maturation. Measurement difficulties pose particular limitations for

early identification. Definitions of conditions to be identified (e.g., "developmental delay," learning disabilities") elude precise definition. Direct measurement of developmental progress is subject to variability as a function of the screening instrument used, the screener, and the specific occasion when the child is evaluated. One can also question the reliability and validity of brief developmental tests, as well as the predictive accuracy of follow-up comprehensive assessments. The question is not *whether* erroneous early identification decision are made, but *how often* and *with what effect?*

3. Early identification and intervention can be accomplished in a realistically affordable manner.

Limitations of the funds and resources available for early childhood and special education programs necessitate the setting of priorities. This is particularly important for the preschool population, which is not as readily available for identification efforts as the "captive" in-school population. There is valid cause for concern that the costs of early identification are unjustifiable given competing demands for funding of educational services. In fact, cost effectiveness is central to the rationale for preschool screening. Although it is considered prohibitively expensive to conduct periodic, comprehensive developmental evaluations for each preschool child, screening offers the possibility of enabling delivery of special services to young children in a manageable and cost-effective manner. Notably, identification of children with special needs carries with it the obligation to provide appropriate services to meet these needs, which is an even more expensive proposition. The affordability of early identification and early intervention must be weighed in the context of potential benefits relative to competing priorities.

ESTABLISHING A PRESCHOOL SCREENING PROGRAM

Certain practical issues and specific questions need to be addressed to establish and operate a preschool screening program. What is the school system's (or agency's) commitment to preschool screening and early intervention? Does the system have the organizational skills and personnel to carry it out? Is the screening program part of an overall service network? Is there an adequate tracking and follow-up system?

The most effective preschool screening programs are products of cooperation among professionals (and often, volunteers) within a school system, collaboration among various agencies, and involvement of parents. Clear goals, careful planning, and commitment by the professionals involved are prerequisites for a successful screening program.

Steps in Implementation

Developing an effective preschool screening program requires thoughtful and systematic planning. The necessary steps involved in implementing a preschool screening program are outlined in Table 22.1.

The first step to be taken is the appointment of a coordinator. The first prerequisite is that the coordinator should have considerable knowledge about, and understanding of, young children and their parents. A second key qualification is the ability to function effectively within a system: to coordinate a new program that might not be initially understood or accepted by others in the program; to work effectively with colleagues, with parents, and with other agencies, and to welcome

TABLE 22.1
STEPS IN IMPLEMENTATION

Appointing a coordinator
Creating a planning group
General planning
    Purpose
    Population
Specific planning
    Outreach
    Coordination with other agencies, programs,
      profesionals
    Content
    Screening procedures
    Time and place
    Personnel/training
Screening
    Collecting data
    Interpretation: making screening decisions
    Reporting results
    Follow-up
Evaluating screening program and procedures

their input; and to be able to effect changes in the screening process while at the same time maintain a stable and supportive structure.

The diversity of expertise required to implement a screening program calls for the formation of a planning group. Ideally, the planning group as a whole should have special knowledge in the areas of program administration, community resources and public communication, child development and developmental problems, early childhood education and special education, psychoeducational measurement and evaluation, and communication with parents.

The next step involves clarification of the purposes of screening and definition of the population to be served. These issues are closely related; the purpose defines the population. School systems differ considerably in their response to federal and state mandates to identify preschool children with handicapping conditions, with some attempting to fulfill legal requirements and others choosing to provide services well beyond the minimum required. Consequently, the screening program might be directed at parents who suspect their children have serious problems, or at parents in particular neighborhoods, or at all parents of children in a given age range.

Once the overall orientation of the program is established, specific elements of the screening process must be planned. The first such element, outreach, is an essential prerequisite to successful screening. Outreach communication makes parents and professionals in the community aware of the screening program, its purpose and content, and children's eligibility for services.

Kurtz and colleagues (1977), in their review of the research, noted that outreach efforts involving direct and personal contact with parents are far more effective than mass media announcements.

Planning might require coordination with other agencies or service providers. Intervention services must be as comprehensive as the screening program. Other agencies or service providers might be in the best position to assess some select areas (e.g., vision, hearing, medical) or deliver the services required by children identified as having special needs. Collaborative arrangements should be established early in the planning process.

Other matters to be worked out by the planning group include the focus and content of screening procedures, sources of screening information, time and place of screening, personnel selection and training, and the nature and extent of parent involvement.

Parent Involvement

Information from parents about their children provides a valuable complement to information obtained through brief testing and observation. Parents' observations and reports can be valuable indicators of the child's functioning and possible problems, offering insights that might not be revealed through testing alone. Parents are a source of critical information in areas such as health status and medical history, current behavior and developmental history, and family problems or other stress factors. In fact, the screening process should be keyed to include the parents' concerns and questions regarding their children's development and functioning.

Parent involvement also should be viewed in a broader context than simply for screening and diagnostic purposes. Parents are essential participants in the planning and implementation of interventions for children. As Walker and Wiske (1981) point out:

> The assessment process should offer parents a means through which they can communicate and collaborate with other persons and community agencies to understand their child's potential and difficulties and to obtain the best set of services for their child. (p.32)

Ideally, this kind of cooperation will begin with screening, be sustained throughout the assessment process, and have its payoff with parental involvement and support at the intervention stage. The intent of parent involvement is to develop an active working collaboration with the parents. Through this process, it is hoped that parents will be empowered as "enablers" of their children.

WHAT SCREENING INFORMATION SHOULD BE OBTAINED?

Three general types of information are relevant in screening: physical and sensory functioning, environmental influences, and developmental functioning.

Physically handicapping conditions that place children at an educational disadvantage need to be identified. Screening for vision and hearing is necessary because intact sensory perception is essential to a child's capacity to learn and because it is a prerequisite to ensure that developmental testing is valid. Although a medical history also is an important part of a comprehensive developmental review, its value for preschool screening is not so clear. The time spent obtaining medical history might be better spent on a determination of the child's *current* physical and sensory status.

Environmental influences upon the young child, particularly the care, attention, stimulation, and discipline provided in the home, exert a significant ongoing impact upon a child's functioning (Werner et al., 1971).

Collecting information about the developmental functioning of the young child is central to the process of preschool screening. We must consider different dimensions, or domains, of development because development is multidimensional.

Measurement of development needs to have a different focus for infants and toddlers than it does for children age 3 and older. The functions that can be assessed before age 2 primarily involve sensorimotor development and responsivity to the environment. Although these dimensions might help to identify infants with substantial developmental delays (Ireton et al., 1970; Vander Veer & Schweid, 1974), developmental functioning during the first two years has a low correlation with later cognitive development and school achievement, and has less predictive power than environmental factors in predicting learning-related outcomes (Bayley, 1949; McCall, 1979; McCall et al., 1972; Rubin & Balow, 1979).

The predictive significance of mental measures increases dramatically during the period from 2 to 4 years of age as children begin to display skills, abilities, and behavior that relate to school functioning (Bayley, 1949; Bloom, 1964; Hozik, 1938). By age 4, developmental gains in language, symbolic/representational thinking, and fine motor and perceptual skills allow standardized measures of development to correlate substantially with subsequent measures of cognitive ability and educational progress.

Developmental Areas

Developmental areas to be considered in screening include cognitive, language, speech, motor skills, self-help, and social-emotional.

Cognitive

This area encompasses a wide range of mental abilities that are often subsumed under the rubric of "general intelligence." The cognitive area is best represented by mental activities that involve reasoning (e.g., association, classification, seriation), judgment, memory, and understanding of concepts. Frequently used tasks for the assessment of cognitive development at preschool age include sorting or matching by shape, color, and size; identifying letters, numbers, and colors; repeating digits, words, or phrases from memory; naming pictured objects and defining words; and completing analogies (e.g., brother is a boy; sister is a ----"). The substantial verbal component to many cognitive measures should be noted.

Language

Language is difficult to distinguish from the cognitive area. Certain tasks place greater emphasis upon language relative to other cognitive factors, for example, sentence repetition, defining words, following instructions. Language functioning can be divided into two general components: *receptive* language, which involves decoding and comprehension of verbal materials, and *expressive* language, the formulation and expression of thoughts in verbal form.

Speech

Speech is rather distinct from language, because it involves the mechanics of spoken language and not the underlying processes. The primary component of speech is articulation—the accurate formation of sounds. Two other components of speech are voice (i.e., quality, pitch, and intensity of vocal production) and rhythm, which when highly irregular is known as stuttering.

Fine Motor

Fine motor development primarily refers to a child's eye–hand coordination and control of fine muscles. The preschool child uses these skills in tasks such as drawing, coloring, and building with blocks. Fine motor as it is commonly used is something of a misnomer, because the term is sometimes applied to tasks (e.g., copying shapes) that involve complex cognitive and perceptual processes and adaptation to the environment in addition to motor output. A more appropriate term in these cases, perhaps, is "adaptive/fine motor."

Gross Motor

In the course of actively exploring the environment and exercising new-found physical capabilities, children develop their large muscles and gain increasing control over the coordination of their bodies. At the preschool age level, a variety of tasks can be used as indicators of gross motor control and coordination: walking backward, heel-to-toe, and up and down steps; hopping and balancing on one foot; and catching and throwing a ball.

Self-help

Adaptive behaviors related to self-care and survival (e.g., feeding, toilet training, washing, dressing and undressing, crossing the street, handling money, avoiding safety hazards) come increasingly under the child's control with gains in motoric and cognitive development. An additional factor that affects self-help skills is that of attitude: the child must not only have the capacity, but also the striving toward independence.

Social–Emotional

Behaviors that are suggestive of social–emotional problems at the preschool level include frequent temper tantrums, excessively high activity level, passivity, withdrawal from interpersonal contact, extreme aggressiveness or disobedience, bizarre verbalization, excessive worrying or crying, and persistent sad affect. The difficulties in identifying problematic social–emotional functioning should be apparent given that the behaviors just mentioned are displayed by all young children at one time or another. These behaviors are cause for concern when observed too frequently, or "to a marked degree over a period of time" (Bower, 1981), but such subjective judgements might be difficult both for professionals and parents to agree upon.

Two general categories also deserving of special attention are *neuropsychological functioning* and *school readiness*. These categories are not separate and unique, but cut across the areas of development already noted.

Neuropsychological Functioning

Higher-order mental operations such as reading and writing are a complex product of neurological maturation and learning. A child develops the capacity for increasingly complex perceptual and integrative processing over time. Although increased attention to and understanding of these processes have emanated from the burgeoning field of developmental neuropsychology, they are difficult to distinguish from other areas because they are essential elements of, or prerequisites for, other developmental functions. In the overview of development areas presented here, these processes are subsumed under other areas with which they are associated, for example, auditory processing is a part of receptive language, and visual-motor integration is an element of fine motor skills.

Distinct neuropsychological dimensions are likely to emerge in years to come as components of mental processes become better defined and measured. Thus, cognitive functions such as attention, mental organization and control, activation level, and cognitive processing might someday be standard components in the assessment of young children's learning capabilities.

School Readiness

Another category that is often distinguished in the assessment of preschool children is that of school readiness. School readiness subsumes various skills and behaviors that are presumed to be related to the demands of a school setting. More specifically, what is measured by school readiness tests is presumed to be predictive of school success or failure in the near future.

Typically, school readiness tests include cognitive, language, and adaptive/fine motor components using tasks such as copying of shapes or figures; arranging blocks to match a model; applying basic concepts of same-different, size differentiation, and numeration; naming and recognizing letters, numbers, body parts, colors; and so on. Tasks involving perceptual processing (e.g., left–right orientation, auditory and visual discrimination) and gross motor skills also are fea-

tured in some readiness tests. Others include attentional, attitudinal, and interpersonal characteristics that influence how a child adapts to classroom demands such as complying with directions, working independently, paying attention, and cooperating in groups.

It is difficult to make clear content distinctions between developmental and school readiness measures. One distinguishing characteristic is that school readiness measures are designed for a fairly specific skill and difficulty range, that is, that which corresponds to kindergarten or first grade level classroom demands. Thus, school readiness measures generally focus on a range of functioning that is more advanced than much of the content of preschool developmental screening instruments.

Perhaps the most important distinction between school readiness measures and developmental instruments is the way they are used, which is largely a function of the theoretical orientation of the user. Proponents of the school readiness model use readiness measures to assess whether a child has reached a level of functioning that is adequate for entering school or beginning formal instructions (Ilg & Ames, 1965). These proponents might conclude that a low-scoring child needs more time to mature, and recommend delaying kindergarten entry. Another professional might administer a developmental measure—with very similar content—but interpret the results to indicate that the child has developmental deficits that require special educational programming (e.g., Bracken, 1984, 1987). These differences are central to current controversies among professionals regarding school entry age, grade retention/promotion, and early childhood educational practices, all of which merit considerable research attention.

Focus of Preschool Screening

Given the areas of development described, what information should be collected and what domains should be emphasized? The first guideline is that primary importance should be given to those areas that are most relevant to a child's success or failure in school. A preponderance of research clearly reveals that the areas that are most closely related to educational status at the preschool level are cognitive, language, and adaptive/

fine motor development. Speech, self-help, social-emotional, and gross motor functioning are
relevant, but not as predictive, unless problems
are severe.

A second guideline is that the focus of screening content should relate directly to the intervention services that are available. Early identification and intervention programs usually emphasize
preacademic functioning and concentrate on cognitive, language, speech, and adaptive/fine motor
development. An intervention program also
should include a social–emotional component
(e.g., via school psychological services or through
referral to outside agencies). Similarly, screening
would include the gross motor area if occupational
therapy or adaptive physical education services
were to be provided; and speech would be
screened if speech therapy was available.

A third guideline follows from the basic rationale for early identification. An area should be
included in screening when early identification results in a benefit for the child. This is subject to
differences in opinion, however. Because resources are limited, the setting of priorities is continually debated, resolved, and revised in the public policy arena.

Notably, P.L. 94–142 has to some degree resolved the dilemma of what to identify by specifying which conditions are to be identified and
what services are to be provided. According to
regulations, those children to be identified include
"mentally retarded, hard of hearing, deaf, speech
impaired, visually handicapped, seriously emotionally disturbed, orthopedically impaired, or
other health impaired children, or children with
specific learning disabilities." This might be interpreted as indicating that identification programs should assess multiple areas of development, plus vision, hearing, and general health.
Reference to "handicapping conditions" might
allow one to interpret that problems must be fairly
severe to warrant identification. But this still begs
the question, "What degree of dysfunction constitutes a "handicapping condition"? While reference to "conditions" implies that developmental problems can be clearly distinguished from
the normal or acceptable, in actuality developmental functioning within the population tends to
be distributed along a continuum. There is no logical, measurable, or universally accepted point

along the continuum that clearly distinguishes
problematic from nonproblematic functioning.

SELECTING SCREENING MEASURES

Information about a child's functioning can be
obtained from a number of different sources. Although screening program planners usually devote
most attention to the use of screening tests, tests
alone are insufficient to screen for the full range
of physical, sensory, developmental, and environmental factors relevant to early identification.

There are two primary sources of information
available in preschool screening: direct evaluation
of the child and the teacher's or parent's report
about the child. Direct evaluation using developmental screening tests provides a sample of the
child's behavior through quantifiable responses to
test items and also through the examiner's observations of the child. There is a tendency for
professionals to minimize the value of parent information and to overemphasize the data that they
generate directly (Gradel et al., Sheehan, 1981).
However, caretakers who have extensive opportunity to observe a child's behavior across multiple contexts add important information to the assessment process. Together, parent information,
test results, and examiner observations can provide a comprehensive and meaningful array of information for making screening decisions.

Desirable Characteristics of Preschool Screening Measures

Selection of screening measures requires both
a solid understanding of how psychometric standards are best applied to screening and a clear
sense of the particular needs of the specific
screening program. Thus, an initial focus upon
questions such as "What are we screening for?"
and "Who are we screening?" is essential. The
value, or utility, of a screening procedure must be
judged on the basis of how well it fits with the goal
(i.e., accurately referring a specified target population) and requirements (e.g., age, range, cost,
etc.) of the screening program.

The following discussion presumes that the
reader is familiar with the basic psychometric concepts of reliability, validity, and test standardiza-

tion. These concepts are addressed here specifically with reference to their application to screening. In addition to traditional psychometric considerations, practical considerations relevant to screening are also addressed.

Validity and Reliability for Screening Purposes

Validity data for psychological tests are usually expressed in the degree of relationship between the test and some criterion measure. For screening tests that are intended to assign individuals to discrete categories (i.e., to refer or not to refer for further assessment), this is not sufficient. In screening, the appropriate method is to compare the classifications yielded by the screening test results with a corresponding set of classificational outcomes generated by criterion measured results. Thus, the classification of "at risk" and "not at risk" assigned by a screening measure might be validated against the classifications "delayed" and "normal range" generated by a more comprehensive assessment. Assignment to corresponding categories by the screening measure and criterion measure constitute "hits," and discrepancies constitute "errors." This concordance, or "hit rate" method of analysis, is discussed at length in the following section.

Similarly, reliability of a screening procedure is best demonstrated by test-retest results demonstrating consistency in assigning individuals to categories. The effect of this approach is to focus upon a measure's capacity to discriminate among individuals whose functioning falls near borderline range (i.e., between "normal" and "delayed" development), where the critical distinctions are to be made. Applying this logic, however it should be noted that correlational approaches to generating estimates of measurement error at key points along the continuum of test scores offer a satisfactory alternative.

Standardization

There are two essential aspects of standardization. The first aspect is that of "quality control" through uniformity of test materials and presentation and of the testing environment. Such uniformity is ensured by using instruments that provide precise instructions as to how an instrument is to be administered, scored, and inter-

preted and by rigorous training and monitoring of screening personnel to ensure that these instructions are followed.

The second essential aspect of standardization involves the establishment of norms to which an individual's performance can be compared. This does not imply that the local screening population must be comparable to the normative sample—in fact, this is quite unlikely. The important thing is that there is sufficient similarity to permit comparison between the local population and the normative sample.

The importance of psychometric considerations should be stressed to the screening user who considers the creation of a "homemade" instrument. Although it is tempting for experienced professionals to construct a new instrument by "picking and choosing" preferred items or to adapt existing measured with strategic additions or deletions, the demands and complications of undertaking a test development project and supporting psychometric studies are enormous, and the investment is rarely warranted by the product.

Cost Considerations

Because the rationale for screening hinges upon cost effectiveness for large scale identification, economic factors are of crucial importance in assessing the value of screening measures. Several factors impact upon a screening measure's cost: the cost of materials, administration time, and the amount of training or level of experience required to administer, score, and interpret a test. For this reason, a test that is suitable for use by nonprofessional examiners might offer substantial cost advantages.

Acceptability

The acceptability of screening measures to professionals and to parents and children—an aspect often described by the term "face validity"—can be a factor in whether a screening program is successfully implemented and received. For the professional who must base decisions upon screening instrument results, the content of the instrument must be suited to its purpose. Inspecting the *actual* content of a measure as opposed to relying upon the publisher's description or the names assigned to subtests or scales is the best means of ensuring adequate coverage of the desired developmental dimensions.

For participants (i.e., parents and children), screening procedures should be of such a nature as to provide a generally positive experience. Acceptability to children is determined by such factors as the interest level of measures, appropriateness of time and performance demands, and the nature of interactions with screening personnel who are involved. Providing a clear, thorough explanation of the nature and purpose of the screening process is a prerequisite to ensuring acceptability to parents. Inclusion of measures that involve direct participation of parents also can contribute to acceptance.

Fairness to children of all sociocultural, racial, and language backgrounds is another critical aspect of acceptability. It is a complex and challenging matter to ensure that a screening measure is psychometrically adequate for children of diverse backgrounds. Regardless, the measures used must meet the basic criterion of being perceived by the public as being fair and nondiscriminatory. Content and language of materials must be reviewed with sensitivity, and screening personnel must be alert to the reactions they elicit. Screening procedures will need to be adapted or developed for children and parents who are not primarily English-speaking, or for children with significant physical or sensory handicaps.

Of the many published developmental screening instruments, few adequately address the desired characteristics just described. Meisels (1985) similarly concluded that the great majority of early childhood screening instruments fail to meet the following selection criteria:

> . . . a brief procedure that identifies children at risk for learning problems or handicapping condition; a focus on developmental, rather than academic readiness, tasks; a multidimensional sampling of a wide range of developmental areas; and, availability of classificational data concerning the reliability and validity of the instrument. (p. 31)

More recently, Meisels (in press) applied the additional criterion of a quantitative standard for validity rates (i.e., sensitivity and specificity at or above .80), and found only three preschool screening instruments that met this standard: the Minnesota Child Development Inventory (Ireton & Thwing, 1974), the Early Screening Inventory (Meisels & Wiske, 1983), and the Minneapolis Preschool Screening Instrument (Lichtenstein, 1980).

Direct Evaluation: Screening Tests and Behavioral Observations

Developmental Screening Tests

Multidimensional developmental screening tests are those that cover a wide range of educationally relevant developmental functions and generate separate scores for individual areas. Some generate separate subscores for multiple areas. For example, the MST (McCarthy, 1978) yields scores for each of six subtests: Right-Left Orientation, Verbal Memory, Draw-A-Design, Numerical Memory, Conceptual Grouping, and Leg Coordination. Scores for each area are categorized as pass or fail based upon the cutoff level selected by the user, who can choose 10th, 20th, or 30th percentile. The user then selects from among alternative decision rules (e.g., 2 failures at the 10th percentile cutoff) to obtain an overall screening recommendation.

Although administration of a multidimensional screening test by a single examiner is the norm, an alternate procedure is to have a separate examiner administer each area. This is the recommended administration procedure for the widely used DIAL-R (Mardell-Czudnowski & Goldenberg, 1983). The DIAL-R consists of three broad areas—Language, Concepts, and Motor—which, like the MST, are each subjected to cutoff scores. A referral decision is determined from the pattern of passing and failing areas.

Some multidimensional tests generate a single overall score. For example, the Minneapolis Preschool Screening Instrument (MPSI) (Lichtenstein, 1980) consists of 50 items distributed over 11 subtests: Building, Copying Shapes, Information, Matching, Sentence Completion, Hopping and Balancing, Naming Colors, Counting, Preposition, Identifying Body Parts, and Repeating Sentences. The items are totaled to yield an overall score to which age-based cutoff scores are applied. The Early Screening Inventory (ESI) (Meisels & Wiske, 1983) groups its 13 subtests into four general categories: Initial Screening Items, Visual-Motor/Adaptive, Language and Cognitive, and Gross Motor/Body Awareness. The test is scored and referral decisions based on the overall score, thus the contribution of the area groupings is that they describe general test content and determine the order in which subtests are administered.

Practitioners tend to be partial to tests with separate scales that yield a "diagnostic profile," even though this is not the objective of preschool screening. Although separate scores across dimensions can provide a more fine-grained description of current functioning, there is no evidence to indicate that this improves identification of children with special needs.

Multidimensional tests often include supplementary components that are clinically interpreted. For example, the DIAL-R includes a behavioral observation checklist, the MSPI is accompanied by a speech intelligibility scale, and the ESI includes an extensive parent questionnaire.

A multidimensional test or screening battery can be supplemented by screening tests covering a single specific area to augment coverage of an underrepresented area or to emphasize an area of particular concern. Speech, language, and social–emotional functioning are areas in which supplementary measures are most commonly employed. The Denver Articulation Screening Exam (Drumwright, 1971), consisting of 30 picture-stimulus items that require 5 minutes to administer, is an example of a specific area test that can be practically integrated into a multidimensional screening battery.

Behavioral Observations During Testing

Tests generally are presumed to yield more reliable and valid information than observations of incidental behavior (that is, as distinct from directly elicited behavior). However, behavioral observation measures might be well constructed and validated in a manner similar to developmental tests. Furthermore, they might yield information that is not readily available through other means, for example, information regarding the child's disposition, attentional pattern, personal–social skills, and emotional adjustment.

Methods of observation can vary in the degree of structure they employ. At the unstructured end, observations can be recorded in open-ended narrative form, with examiners relying upon personal experience and judgement to determine which be-

haviors they find noteworthy or atypical. To enhance objectivity, observers should be instructed to record observations in concrete behavioral terms. At the structured end, the dimensions to be measured can be clearly defined, and behavioral benchmarks can be specified to help differentiate between alternative responses to items. The observational method of choice can depend in part upon the examiner's training and experience. A combination of open-ended and structured observational techniques might prove optimal.

A formal checklist or rating scale might provide a systematic guide to evaluating a preschool child's behavior, addressing such considerations as attention span, cooperation, impulsivity, anxiety level, persistence, ability to separate from parent, sociability, activity level, persistence, speech intelligibility, and language complexity. A checklist of such behaviors is often provided as a supplement to a screening or assessment measure, but without norms or other psychometric data, thereby enabling interpretation only on a clinical level.

Observation of behavior by professionals during a single brief occasion has the distinct limitation that an atypical sample of the child's behavior might be observed. This is a particular concern given that screening can be a totally novel situation for the young child, since it involves exposure to atypical demands and interactions with unfamiliar adults. An alternative approach is to observe the child in a classroom-like environment that provides opportunities for the child to interact with peers and adults, and work with developmentally appropriate materials. Classroom teachers and other educational professionals (e.g., school psychologist, early childhood specialist) then can observe a number of children at once. The diagnostic placement approach might be most feasible for small-scale screening programs, especially those dealing with a selectively referred sample consisting of a high proportion of children in the "questionable" or "refer" range. For mass screening programs, the diagnostic placement approach might be more practical as an intermediate assessment stage, that is, for children classified as "questionable" in initial screening or as an accompaniment to comprehensive follow-up assessments for referred children.

Parent Report Measures

As part of screening, it is common to ask the parent to complete a comprehensive questionnaire that provides background information about the child and family. Such questionnaires often include identifying information, family information, medical history, current physical or sensory symptoms, developmental milestones, current developmental behavior, and indicators of social–emotional adjustment. As a rule, these questionnaires are not supported by normative data or even guidelines for the interpretation of results.

Background information regarding a child's health, developmental, and family status also can be obtained through an interview. A screening interview designed to provide a brief overview of a child's functioning and to identify a parent's concerns can be useful for obtaining information and establishing rapport.

When interviewing parents it is generally best to begin by asking them to describe the child briefly in their own words (e.g., "Tell me what your child has been doing and learning lately"). Depending upon the parent's reply, more specific information can be asked about the child's motor skills, language, and so forth.

An interview can be structured by specifying exact questions for the interviewer. Taking this a step further, a structured interview can be standardized, much like a test, with accompanying guidelines for administration and scoring, and interpretation of parent responses with reference to norms. The Developmental Profile II (Alpern et al. 1980), for example, consists of specific interview questions about a child's physical, self-help, social, academic, and communication skills at age levels ranging from birth to 9 years, and responses are quantitatively scored and interpreted on a normative basis.

The parent's report of the child's current behavior also can be obtained by having the parent complete a developmental inventory. The inventory format includes specific behavioral statements (e.g., prints first name) with yes or no rating scale response options. Items can be grouped to form scales measuring areas of development or adjustment. Results can be quantitatively scored and objectively interpreted with reference to norms. Inventories are cost effective because they are self-administered and easily scored, and re-sults can be summarized in a systematic manner that facilitates interpretation.

The Preschool Development Inventory (Ireton, 1984) is a brief parent report screening inventory designed to obtain information from the parent about the child's present development and possible problems. Parents answer 60 yes–no items about the child's general developmental status, with particular emphasis upon language and comprehension, and complete a "symptoms and behavior problems" list that identifies possible problems with behavior and emotional functioning, somatic signs (eating, sleeping, toileting, physical complaints), motor coordination, speech and language, and vision and hearing. Parents also are asked to describe the child, report special problems or handicaps, and convey questions or concerns. Norms and frequency data are provided as a basis for interpreting responses.

Screening Systems

Some screening methods are in fact complete packages or comprehensive systems for conducting screening and obtaining an array of information from a variety of sources. These "already assembled" systems offer a convenient shortcut to screening program planners, who can make use of a previously developed screening program. Examples are the Comprehensive Identification Process (Zehrbach, 1975) and the Preschool Screening System (Hainsworth & Hainsworth, 1980).

The Comprehensive Identification Process consists of a comprehensive set of screening materials and manuals that cover a broad range of content (i.e., medical history, vision and hearing, developmental milestones and current behavior, social–emotional adjustment) from multiple information sources (parent interviews, direct testing, examiner observations). It does not, however, provide psychometric data to guide interpretation of results. The Preschool Screening System includes a screening test and parent questionnaire, and its lengthy manual/handbook provides a step-by-step guide to screening program development and implementation. The system does advocate some questionable practices, such as diagnostic use of screening test results and group administration of certain subtests.

Although such systems encourage a comprehensive approach to screening, the inherent drawbacks are that one accepts the entire package, even though preferable alternatives might be substituted for individual components of the system, and that the system is "generic" rather than designed to meet the specific needs of the local screening program and population.

MAKING SCREENING DECISIONS

The basic task involved in preschool screening is to make a decision about whether to refer each child for further assessment. Screening decisions can depend entirely upon scores from standardized measures, or scores can be considered in the context of other information available about the child. Information from various sources can be translated into screening decisions using professional judgment, or can be based upon empirically derived decision rules. The logic, process, and issues associated with establishing decision rules and evaluating the adequacy of these decision rules should be throughly understood by those involved in screening.

The Hit Rate Model

The rather ambitious goal of preschool screening is to identify children with certain de-velopmental and potential educational problems with the greatest possible accuracy, using relatively brief and inexpensive measures.

The correspondence between screening decisions and a subsequent determination of a child's "actual" status is best conceptualized using a concordance, or *hit rate*, model. As shown in Figure 22–1., the accuracy of screening decisions relative to some criterion measure can be characterized for a given sample, yielding one of four outcomes. Cells A and D represent the two types of accurate screening decisions: children in need of special services appropriately referred through screening, and children who do not require special services and who are not referred.

Screening errors of two distinct types inevitably occur. A child who tests "negative" (signifying "no referral") on the screening test but who subsequently evidences a problem or condition targeted by screening is called a *false negative*, signifying an underreferral error (cell B in Fig. 22.1). The opposite case, when a child tests "positive" and then if found not to need services, is a *false positive,* or overreferral error (cell C in Fig. 22.1).

A valid screening procedure is one that is effective in making accurate decisions to refer children who need help while minimizing false posi-

		FOLLOW-UP STATUS	
		Child needs special services	Does not need special services
SCREENING DECISION	REFER (+) High risk	A valid positive accurate referral	C false positive overreferral
	DO NOT REFER (−) Low risk	B false negative underreferral	D valid negative accurate nonreferral

SENSITIVITY: $A / A + B$

SPECIFICITY: $D / C + D$

PREDICTIVE UTILITY OF SCREENING POSITIVE: $A / A + C$

Figure 22.1 The hit rate model for evaluating screening decisions.

FOLLOW-UP STATUS

Example #1.		Has Problem	No Problem	
SCREENING DECISION	Refer	0	0	0
	Do not refer	5	95	100
		5	95	100

SENSITIVITY: 0 / 5   =   0

SPECIFICITY: 95 / 95   =   1.0

PREDICTIVE UTILITY OF
   SCREENING POSITIVE: 0 / 0   —

Example #2.		Has Problem	No Problem	
SCREENING DECISION	Refer	5	5	10
	Do not refer	0	90	90
		5	95	100

SENSITIVITY: 5 / 5   =   1.0

SPECIFICITY: 90 / 95   =   .947

PREDICTIVE UTILITY OF
   SCREENING POSITIVE: 5 / 10   =   .50

Figure 22.2   Hit rate illustration: identical overall hit rates.

tive errors. Thus, it is useful to make comparisons between the frequency of correct decisions (i.e., cells A and D) and of errors (cell B and C). However, simply reporting overall hit rate (i.e., the total percentage of correct decisions) can be misleading because of the interrelationship between the *hit rate, problem base rate, and referral rate*. This is most evident in the case where the rate of occurrence of the problem, called the *base rate*, is low. This usually results in numerous overreferral errors. Because the screening procedure that makes the most referrals generally makes the most errors, overall hit rate can be a misleading indicator of a screening procedure's accuracy. This is illustrated in Fig. 22.2 by a hypothetical situation in which screening is used to identify a condition with a base rate of 5% (that is, the target group comprises 5% of the population).

Consider first a screening procedure that refers no children at all. Although it made *no* ap-propriate referrals and is, therefore, practically useless, the procedure would have attained a 95% hit rate for correctly not referring the nontargeted 95% of the population. In contrast, a screening measure that correctly refers the entire target group while referring a total of 10% of the population would be extremely useful, but yield the same overall hit rate of 95%. In this second case, half of the referrals, 5% of the sample, are overreferral errors.

Statistics that retain the specific information in a hit rate table are preferable for characterizing the validity of a screening procedure. This can be accomplished using a corresponding pair of ratios termed *sensitivity* and *specificity*. *Sensitivity* is defined as the proportion of those children needing special services who are referred by the screening procedure. In Fig. 22.1, this is the ratio A / A + B. Thus, it is the proportion of target children who are correctly referred. The examples in Fig. 22.2

illustrate the opposite ends of the sensitivity range: 0/5, or 0 in the first case, and 5/5, or 1.0 (or 100%) in the second case.

Specificity is defined as the proportion of children in the nontarget group (i.e., those who do not require special services) who are correctly classified as not needing referral. This is represented by the ratio D / C + D in Fig. 22.1. Although it is also based on a scale from 0 to 1.0, specificity figures are typically .70 and above. In the examples in Fig. 22.2, specificity is 95/95, or 1.0 (100%) for the first instance in which no referrals are made, and 90/95, or .947 (94.7%), in the second instance. Although specificity is intended to serve as an indicator of overreferral errors, it is not easily translated into conceptually meaningful terms. A more interpretable index of overreferral errors is the "predictive utility of a screening positive:" the proportion, or percentage, of screening referrals that prove to be accurate (A / A + C in Fig. 22.1). In the second example in Fig. 22.2, the predictive utility of a screening positive is 5/10 or .50, signifying that there is 50% probability that a screening referral will prove accurate. (Note how much more descriptive this is of overreferral errors than the specificity rate of .95).

What might be considered an acceptable hit rate pattern?

There is no simple answer to this question for several reasons. First, population characteristics must be considered. For example, decision-making errors will be relatively high for a population in which easily classified individuals (that is, children who are obviously handicapped or who are obviously within normal range) already have been identified, leaving a high percentage of children who fall around the borderline area where risk status is difficult to determine.

The nature of the problem or condition to be identified is another factor that impacts upon hit rates. Those conditions, which are difficult to precisely define or measure and that might be situation-dependent, cannot be identified with high accuracy. Thus, we expect higher hit rates in screening for vision problems than for social–emotional difficulties.

The validity of the criterion measure used to establish a child's follow-up status is another factor affecting hit rates. Determining hit rates for developmental or educational problems is always something of an approximation because there is no definitive standard by which a child can be judged to have a "handicapping condition" or to be in need of special services. For purposes of evaluating the validity of a screening procedure, children's status is typically judged using criterion measures such as the outcome of a comprehensive diagnostic evaluation, teacher ratings, or achievement test scores as indicators of whether they appear to be in need of special services.

For these reasons, there is no standard rule of thumb to indicate whether the hit rates obtained by a given screening procedure are acceptable. Basically, any given estimate of a screening procedure's hit rate is situation specific, reflecting the outcome when a given decision rule (e.g., cutoff score) is used to predict a given outcome for a particular population and situation. Nevertheless, classificational hit rate information is essential in determining the validity of a screening procedure. It is the soundest basis for comparing the effectiveness of alternative screening procedures, or for determining what decision rules most appropriately translate screening information into screening decisions.

The task of establishing cutoff points or decision rules for specific screening measures is of particular significance. Hit rates vary with the cutoff score or decision rule used to interpret screening results—a factor that is under the control of the screening instrument user.

Referral Rates and the Hit Rate Dilemma

Referral rates vary with alternative decision rules. Raising cutoff scores will increase the referral rate and will likely increase the sensitivity of a screening measure. However, the invariable result of this is a corresponding increase in the number of overreferrals, thus lowering the predictive utility of a screening positive. Conversely, cutoff scores can be lowered and fewer children referred, which will reduce overreferral errors but result in lower sensitivity, that is, more children with problems will be missed.

It helps to know the prevalence of educationally handicapping conditions in the local population, because these prevalence rates can serve as estimates of the percentage of children in the screening population who might be expected to evidence similar problems. Whatever this problem base rate is, the screening referral rate must be somewhat higher, because more children must be referred at the initial screening stage than eventually will be identified by a more comprehensive follow-up evaluation.

There is no standard formula to determine what is a safe margin between the base rate and referral rate. The options involve a troublesome dilemma because of the ''costs'' that must be paid. The referral rate can be set far above the base rate to ensure that most children with problems will be identified. In doing so, however, a large number of children will be referred unnecessarily, sometimes at great expense. Setting the screening rate closer to the base rate reduces overreferral errors, but at the cost of failing to identify some children who need help (i.e., underreferral errors). It is possible to set referral rates to minimize underreferral errors, or to minimize overreferral errors, but not both at once. A reduction in one type of error results in an increase in the other.

Figure 22.3 illustrates how the hit rate dilemma operates even in the situation where the screening procedure produces a distinct separation between criterion groups. (It is presumed that membership in the ''problem'' and ''normal'' groups has been established through follow-up evaluation). The distributions of scores for the criterion groups still overlap in the critical range at the low end of the distribution where cutoff scores will be set. Using a cutoff score of 65 (Cutoff A), which divides the two distributions fairly well, still leaves some target group children above the cutoff point (area y represents these underreferral errors) and some normal group children below the cutoff (area x represents overreferral errors). If assessors are determined to avoid missing children with developmental problems, the cutoff score could be raised and more children referred. Setting a cutoff point as high as 70 (Cutoff B) so as to refer most of the target group, however, would result in a substantial portion of the normal group being referred. Similarly, any cutoff point in the 55 to 70 range results in a tradeoff between underreferral and overreferral errors.

Any course of action that increases referral rates produces the same effect as raising a cutoff score. For example, an effort to improve screening accuracy might involve taking into account all of the many possible ''risk factors'' (perinatal medical problems, delayed developmental milestones, family problems, etc.) that might signal subsequent problems. If one were to incorporate all possible risk factors into the decision rule, the total number of referrals would swell enormously and many overreferral errors would result.

Just how well can screening procedures predict whether young children will experience educational or developmental problems? The findings are humbling—so humbling, in fact, that they

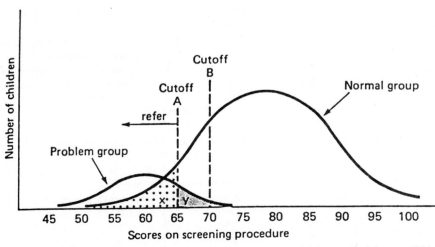

Figure 22.3   Screening errors at different cutoff scores. (From Lichtenstein & Ireton, 1984. Reprinted with permission.)

raise the question of whether preschool screening, as currently practiced, is justifiable.

A review of the early identification literature reveals that the "limits of prediction" are rather severe (Lichtenstein & Ireton, 1984). Evidence to date shows that the accuracy of predictions about future educational status falls short of the levels that might be anticipated or intended for systematic early identification. Based on 10 published studies that met the criteria established for assessing early identification rates (i.e., predictors obtained at preschool or kindergarten level, sample size of 50 or more, follow-up interval of at least one year, and results presented in hit rate form), the limits of prediction can be expressed by a general rule of thumb: when sensitivity exceeds .50 the predictive utility of the positive sign will not exceed .50 as well. In other words, when screening referral accuracy does surpass 50%, it is rarely the case that more than 50% of target group children are identified. This "50/50 standard" has been achieved in only two early identification validity studies (Kaufman & Kaufman, 1972; Lichtenstein, 1982). Interestingly, although the early identification procedures considered in this review included various types of measures and even batteries consisting of multiple measures, the 50/50 standard was achieved in these two studies by single tests that require less than 30 minutes to administer.

It should be noted that certain studies that have reported very high prediction rates did not qualify for inclusion because they relied on *post hoc* decision rules: that is, prediction rates were optimized by "tailoring" the decision rules to fit the data from the particular sample studied. Perhaps the best known example of this is the de Hirsch and associates (1966) study of early prediction of reading failure, which yielded exceptionally high hit rates that "shrunk" to a level far below the 50/50 standard when cross-validated.

It should be emphasized that the limits of prediction as described here apply to the relationship between developmental–educational assessment and future development, learning, and school performance. By comparison, a stronger relationship can be expected between screening results and in-depth developmental assessment. Reasonably high correspondence with a concurrent developmental assessment is perhaps all that can be realistically sought in preschool screening.

Several factors contribute to the lack of success in making predictions about the future status of preschool children. Much uncertainty in prediction is because of the varying nature of the interaction between child attributes and environmental demands. Problems or "deficits" in an educational setting are relative to what is being demanded of the child, and problems can develop or be exacerbated because a child is exposed to an unresponsive, discouraging, or overly demanding environment. Thus, a child's status can vary over time as a function of environmental changes. It is also the case, especially for young children, that uneven rates of development can account for changes in their level of functioning relative to age expectations.

Measurement procedures, particularly those based on a small sample of behavior, have intrinsic limitations. Direct testing is subject to situational variables that affect performance, for example, attention span, motivation, anxiety, and fatigue. Parent reports of behavior might or might not be objective; their reported concerns might be based on personal norms or expectations that are unrealistic.

Clearly, predicting the future educational and developmental status of preschool children, particularly those who are only mildly at risk, is a rather hazardous undertaking. Rather than operate upon unrealistic assumtions, early identification programs should incorporate safeguards that take the limits of prediction into account (as discussed later in this chapter). Recognizing these limitations also highlights the importance of ensuring that screening programs make use of the best available measurement instruments and procedures. This chapter will now focus on how decision rules might be established for a given screening program to ensure the most advantageous use of screening information.

Decision Rules and Local Norms

To begin with the simplest case, a screening decision can be derived from a child's performance on a published developmental screening test. One course of action is to simply apply the screening recommendation resulting from the cut-off scores specified by the screening instrument. The user makes no decisions regarding an appropriate referral rate, but simply applies whatever decision rule is provided. The obvious drawback to using this option is that a given cutoff score will not be optimal for all situations and settings, and the user might or might not find the results acceptable. Depending upon the circumstances, very few children might be identified, or an excessive number of referrals might be generated.

When using a preestablished decision rule, it is essential that the user study the information provided about the normative sample and the percentage of that sample referred by using the decision rule. For example, cutoff scores might have been established to refer 15% of a nationally representative sample. The user then can consider how the normative sample compares with the population that is to be screened. Differences between the two might lead the instrument user to expect relatively lower or higher referral rates for the local screening program.

Although some screening instruments just provide recommended decisions rules, others supply norms from which the user can determine what percentage of the normative sample falls below any given cutoff score. From this, the user might be able to adjust for differences between groups. For example, the user might guess that a cutoff score at the 12th percentile for the normative sample will refer at least 15% of the relatively less advantaged local population.

With actual use of a screening instrument, the data obtained can be used to establish local norms. More meaningful cutoff scores for the local population can then be established. It might not be feasible to institute local norms immediately, however, particularly when the numbers are low. Normative groups of less than 100 can yield unstable norms, so that the long-term referral rate obtained with a given cutoff might vary by several percentage points from the figure initially anticipated. Because it is often desirable to devise a norm group for narrow age intervals (e.g., for three-month to six-month age ranges), it might be some time before satisfactory local norms with 100 or more children in each range can be compiled.

Establishing decision rules for a screening instrument is often more complicated than simply applying a cutoff to a single score. Certain screening instruments (e.g., DIAL-R) yield separate scores in several areas of development. If the decision rules prove to be unsatisfactory, the user

has a difficult decision. Although adjustments in scoring might be attempted, this is always somewhat precarious because there is no basis upon which to estimate the resulting referral rate—and this is especially true if the separate scales lack norms so that each scale can be similarly adjusted. Trial and error using the data obtained from local screening is perhaps the best way to establish new decision rules to produce a target referral rate.

Local norms can be established in time for virtually any kind of systematically obtained screening data, even subjective judgments of observed behavior. For example, a screening examiner's rating of a child's speech articulation could be recorded on a numerical scale, (e.g., on a scale of 1 to 5). The meanings of different ratings can be standardized to some degree by "anchoring" the scores with descriptors, e.g., 1 = completely unintelligible, 3 = difficult to understand, 5 = clearly intelligible. By quantifying the ratings and compiling the results, the percentages assigned to each rating can be established. Furthermore, an examiner's "personal norms" can be evaluated by compiling a frequency distribution of the rating that he or she assigns, and this feedback can help increase consistency between different examiners.

The examples to this point, based on relatively simple decision rules (that is, as applied to individual screening measures), highlight the necessity to obtain screening information that can be subjected to consistent, meaningful interpretation. Typically, however, individual screening measures are not the sole basis for making referral decisions. A screening *battery* consisting of several sources of information might need to be interpreted using some systematic decision *process*.

It should be noted that the discussion thus far has followed from the assumption that it is meaningful to establish referral rates on a statistical basis to refer some target percentage of the population. This approach is known as *norm-referenced measurement*. An alternative is to assume that some particular level of functioning, or degree of disability, can be identified that signifies that a child needs special services. This approach is known as *criterion-referenced measurement,* because the child is assessed relative to some performance criterion or standard. An example of criterion-referenced measurement is in screening for visual acuity. Regardless of the total number of children referred, all individuals with eyesight below the level suggesting need are referred for optical examinations.

In actual practice, it is very difficult to apply absolute standards of expected functional behavior in the identification of developmental problems. Basically, there are no absolute standards for the existence of a "problem" or "disability." A child's status can vary as a function of environmental circumstances; the problem might not lie within the child. Characteristics of the educational setting, the teacher, and the peer group all influence whether a child will experience problems in school. Within a given setting, criteria for determining whether a child qualifies for special services are a function of population characteristics, assessment procedures, and policies of the particular school district. The criterion-referenced approach is impractical for screening because it assumes the reliable assessment of a preschool child's capabilities in all relevant developmental areas, rather than estimating a child's functioning from a sample of representative tasks.

Given that there is no "ideal" referral rate, what might be a desirable referral rate for a typical developmental screening program? To some degree, the choice is a subjective matter of weighing one type of screening error against the other. One guideline in setting referral rates is to regard underreferral as the more serious error. Overreferral can be corrected at the stage of further assessment but an underreferral error cannot. However, this might overburden the follow-up assessment component of an early identification program, and can have the net effect of diverting crucial resources away from direct service. Also, there is no assurance that children who are erroneously referred will be eliminated during the follow-up assessment stage. Referring a chld from screening can create a "self-fulfilling prophecy" that biases subsequent evaluations. This phenomenon was documented in a study by Algozzline and Ysseldyke (1981) in which professional educators were asked to make placement recommendations for hypothetical cases. The files included a referral statement that made reference to the child's apparent needs, but test results placed the children within normal limits. The raters recommended special education placement in 57% of the reviewed cases. There is a tendency for professionals to presume that referrals have validity.

Given these many cautions and considerations, the practitioner might feel more in need of guidance than ever. And so, with some reservations, here are some guidelines. Typically, base rates for developmental and educational problems at the preschool and primary levels fall in the 5% to 10% range. This figure will be higher for a disadvantaged population, or if relatively mild problems also are to be identified. As a general rule, referral rates might reasonably be set at a level in the range of $1\frac{1}{2}$ to $2\frac{1}{2}$ times the estimated base rate. The lower the base rate the higher this ratio will need to be. For base rates as low as 1% to 3%, perhaps three times the base rate will need to be referred.

Multiple Inputs into Screening Decisions

It is time to consider the common, yet complex situation in which multiple sources of information are integrated to arrive at a screening decision. To complicate matters, the available screening information can encompass diverse content areas (e.g., cognitive, motor, and social/behavior functioning) and might be in different forms (e.g., quantitative and qualitative) and from different sources (e.g., teachers, tests, parents).

One way to deal with this complexity is to formulate an overall composite screening score that combines various data inputs. Each element can be weighted according to its presumed importance and validity. This approach, which might be described as an additive model, is based upon the assumption that the screening decision is unidimensional in nature and that differentiation between various areas of concern can be addressed at the level of follow-up evaluation.

The opposite approach is to consider each source of screening information independently. A child who evidences possible problems in a single area of functioning (e.g., language development), or is rated as at risk from a single source of information (e.g., parental concern) might then constitute the basis for referral. In such a multiple cutoffs model, an important consideration is that referral rates can easily accelerate. Four different screening inputs each referring 10% of the population might well refer over 25% of the total population with the exact figure depending upon the degree of overlap between the referred group on each measure.

The desirability of one versus the other of these two approaches depends upon several factors. First is the extent to which the areas assessed are interrelated. The additive model is best suited to related types of information. For example, the intercorrelated cognitive, language, and fine motor areas can be meaningfully combined into a single composite index of developmental functioning, an approach that is supported by results of factor analytic studies. If, on the other hand, an extremely poor performance or rating on a single dimension is regarded as sufficient cause to regard a child as being at risk, the multiple cutoffs model enables a significant deficit in a single area to be the basis for a decision to refer. A second factor is the importance associated with a given developmental area or source of information. To further consider the case in which a child scores very low in one area, this might be considered sufficient basis for a screening referral in one area (e.g., language), but not another area (e.g., gross motor). A third factor is the degree of measurement error associated with different sources of information. A single scale of a screening instrument might have such low reliability that it is inappropriate for that scale to determine a screening decision by itself, as might result with the multiple cutoffs approach. The additive approach allows a composite scale of greater reliability to be constructed from related scales with low reliability.

An ideal solution might be to "mix and match" elements of the two models. For example, screening information from multiple measures might be combined into composite scores for a limited number of distinct dimensions (e.g., developmental, speech, and social/behavioral functioning) and each of these dimensions might serve as a basis for screening referrals, with cutoffs applied separately to refer children on any of these three dimensions. Furthermore, as local norms are established for the different composite scales, referral rates could be set to reflect the degree of emphasis to be placed upon each dimension, or the severity of the problems to be identified in each area. For example, the decision rule might involve a 15% referral rate in the developmental area and 5% referral rates for speech and social/behavioral functioning. (Further elaboration is provided in the illustration of a hypothetical multidimensional screening process at the end of this section.)

Regardless of the nature of the screening program, there are three key elements that should guide the development of the decision process. First and foremost, the process for arriving at screening decisions should be made explicit. It is not sufficient to say "decisions are based upon the outcome of Screening Test X" if the test result is not the sole basis for the final screening decision. Consider, for example, the case in which a parent's concern about the child's development is inconsistent with screening test results. If parental concern is occasionally cause to refer a child for further evaluation, this should be acknowledged as an aspect of the decision process, and all parents might be offered the same opportunity to "overrule" a nonreferral outcome.

Formally defining the decision process not only allows it to be systematically applied, but systematically investigated. As the second key element, efforts should be made to determine the referral rates that can result from implementing particular decision procedures. Referral rates can be estimated initially, and determined later as data are obtained about the local screening program. Overall program planning is greatly facilitated by making accurate estimates of referral rates. This enables arrangements to be made for timely and appropriate follow-up evaluation services. Program planners should also consider whether anticipated referral rates are consistent with the presumed prevalence of target problems or conditions, or with the extent of intervention services that are to be provided.

The third key element is that screening decisions should be evaluated using the hit rate model. A number of questions and concerns thus can be formally addressed: Which screening procedures are most accurate? Where should cutoff scores be set so as to yield an acceptable balance between underreferral and overreferral errors? How might different sources of information best be weighted or integrated to arrive at screening decisions?

A number of alternative decision-making procedures can be evaluated if the screening process has been well documented and pertinent information about each child recorded. For purposes of subsequent evaluation, such information might include screening date, location, and examiner; sex and age of the child; and relevant demographic data. This enables analysis of key population variables (e.g., sex, age, SES) to determine whether adjustments should be made in the decision process if certain subgroups are being systematically overreferred or underreferred. Quantification of various elements of the screening procedure (e.g., clinical judgment of observed behavior, or strategic weighting of several information sources) can allow seemingly elusive aspects of the screening process to be examined, and modified or deemphasized as called for by evaluation results. The merits of each alternative procedure can be gauged by comparing the hit rates obtained by each in predicting the same criterion of children's subsequent status.

In doing so, some cautions should be mentioned. First, slight differences between hit rates might be of little significance if they are of a magnitude that could be accounted for by chance. (Statistical tests enable us to judge when this is indeed the case). Second, highly specific or complex decision rules can yield optimal results for a research sample but fail to cross validate. This is most likely to result when conducting trial-and-error comparisons between many different decision rules (e.g., in searching for the "ideal" cutoff score) rather than testing predetermined alternatives of primary interest. A third consideration, which can be noted only in passing here, is that "criterion contamination" can obscure evaluation study results in that screening can lead to intervention services that mediate the course of a child's development, and possibly alter the course of a potentially problematic condition.

PRESCHOOL SCREENING AND BEYOND

To review, preschool screening is an attempt to identify children with current developmental and other problems under the assumption that these problems will subsequently interfere with school performance if they are not remediated. For children with substantial problems or major handicaps, identification can occur at an early point in time; and persistence of developmental problems, learning difficulties, and the need for special educational assistance predictably follow. But for young children with lesser degrees of "deviation" from normal developmental expectations, none of these assumptions is secure. The capacity to make accurate predictions for these

children with apparently mild development problems is severely limited.

Given the state of the art, how might the question "Does preschool screening work?" be answered? When asked, "Does psychotherapy work?" one psychologist replied (answering a question with a question, of course), "Does a hammer work?" The implication is that is depends on who is swinging the hammer, on what it is being used for, and on the properties of the particular hammer. To assess the effectiveness of preschool screening, the questions to ask are "who is doing what, with whom, for what purpose, and with what results?" Many public school system are now engaged in large scale screening of young children, usually ages 3 to 5, for the purpose of identifying and serving those children with developmental and educational problems. Do the results match the intention? Are accurate referrals made that lead to appropriate interventions that benefit significant numbers of children? The answer: it depends.

Aspects and Issues

The variables and considerations that impact upon the effectiveness of a preschool screening program are many. First of all, preschool screening is not an end in itself. The purpose of screening is to provide early intervention. Without the availability of early intervention resources, there is no point in beginning. Second, the goals of screening and the population to be screened should be clearly defined. Third, a clear system for organization and implementation of screening is essential. This overall system, or process, is more important than any single element or test within it. Fourth, a comprehensive screening program requires the expertise of professionals from a number of disciplines. Fifth, parent involvement in the process of preschool screening is critical to the development of working relationships between parents and school personnel. Sixth, cost-effectiveness is an essential part of the logic of screening. The screening process must be thorough enough to produce valid results, yet brief enough not to be prohibitive in cost. Seventh, there are three critical elements—defining the decision process, determining the referral rate, and evaluating the outcome—that are essential for ensuring that screening decisions are made on a systematic and

TABLE 22.2
DEVELOPMENTAL MAP OF THE FIRST FIVE YEARS

Age	Gross Motor	Fine Motor	Language	Self-Help	Social–Emotional
0	Lifts head and chest high Supports head (no lag) Rolls over back to front	Clasps hands together Reaches toward objects Picks up toy with one hand	Vocalizes, coos, chuckles Vocalizes spontaneously, social	Comforts self with thumb or pacifier	Social smile Distinguishes mother from others Initiates social contact
6	Sits alone-erect, steady without support	Transfers toy from one hand to other Picks up objects with thumb and finger grasp	Wide range of vocalizations (vowel sounds consonant-vowel combinations) Says mama, dada	Feeds self cracker	Pushes things away he/she doesn't want
9	Crawls on hands & knees Stands alone well Walks with support	Picks up small objects—precise thumb & finger grasp	Says mama, dada as names for parents Understands "no," "stop," etc.	Holds own bottle or drinks from a cup	Plays social games—peek-a-boo, pat-a-cake, bye-bye Expresses several emotions clearly Objects to separation
12	Walks alone "Dances" to music	Stacks two or more blocks Scribbles	Uses one or two words as names of things or actions Points to familiar things Points to parts of body	Cooperates in dressing Feeds self with spoon	Plays simple ball games Hugs parent
18	Runs well, rarely falls Kicks ball forward	Builds tower of four or more blocks Makes imitative strokes (vertical, circular)	Uses words to express wants Uses 2–3 word phrases or sentences Names pictures of familiar objects Follows simple directions	Eats with spoon, spilling little	Kisses with pucker Imitates adult activities "Helps" with simple household tasks

Age					
2-0	Rides tricycle, using pedals; Walks up and down stairs-one foot per step	Holds crayon with fingers; Handles small toys skillfully; Draws complete circle	Uses pronouns for self and others; Talks in sentences; Speech understandable 1/2 of time; Tells use of familiar objects	Puts on simple garment; Washes and dries hands; Toilet trained	Refers to self as I or me; Tells first & last name; Plays with children; Shows sympathy
3-0	Hops on one foot, without support	Draws a person that has at least three parts; Draws a cross (+)	Tells stories about daily experiences; Knows three colors; Understands concepts—big & little, etc.; Understands 2–3 prepositions; Counts 4 objects, answers "how many"	Washes & dries hands & face; Combs or brushes hair	Knows sex (own and opposite); Plays cooperatively with self
4-0	Hops—one foot, repeatedly; Skips; Dances-skillfully; Good balance & coordination	Draws a person that has at least six parts; Draws a square with good corners; Prints a few letters	Talkes in sentences; Completely understandable; Defines familiar words	Dresses & undresses without help, except for tying shoes	Plays role in "make-believe" play; Follows simple game rules
5-0					

INTERPRETATION STEPS

1. Calculate child's age by subtracting his birthdate from the date the Developmental Review was completed.

2. Draw a horizontal line across the Developmental Map at the child's age level.

3. For each area of development, mark the individual items reported by the mother or observed in the clinic. It might be necessary to mark only the more mature items in each area rather than all items.

4. For each area of development, compare the child's behavioral age level to his actual age level. In this way, it is possible to appreciate whether the child's behavior is above, within, or below age expectations.

5. Use the following developmental status categories to determine whether the child, in each area, is:

   A = **Advanced**—Displays behavior characteristic of children significantly older than himself—behavior above age interval.

   WA = **Within age expectations**—displays behavior at age interval or within age range (one interval below).

   (?) = **Questionable development**—Fails to demonstrate behaviors within his age interval and fails to demonstrate behaviors at the next younger age interval; for example, a 13-month old who is not walking (12–18 months) and not crawling (9–12 months).

   DD = **Definitely delayed**—Over 50% delayed, for example, a 2 year old who is not displaying the behavior of a 1 year old; for example, a 2 year old who is not walking, a 4 year old who is not using word combinations, etc.

6. Record the classification in the space at the bottom of the Developmental Map. When in doubt, record two categories, for example: A/WA; WA/(?); (?)/DD. Underline ratings for those areas of development where the rating is either (?) or DD.

valid basis. As a final point, it is critical to have an appreciation of the validity, limitations, and possible abuses of the measures used in developmental screening.

Alternatives to Early Identification

The "range of normal" is not easy for professionals to define, which presents a dilemma for early identification. Development is not like a disease entity, to be judged as present or absent. Development does not proceed at a consistent rate over time, nor does rate of development in one area necessarily parallel the rate of development in another area.

Regardless of how development is characterized in the course of screening, a division made at any point along the continuum of functioning in an effort to distinguish between "normal" and "problematic" status is going to be imprecise. A given child can fall on one or the other side of this point, and be classified differently, as a function of various factors: the relative emphasis upon the various areas of development, the instruments and decision rules used in screening and identification, the demands imposed by the particular educational system, environmental supports and stressors, changes in developmental functioning over time, and so on. Furthermore, the difficulties in making clear distinctions (and, hence, in making accurate predictions) increase when we choose to identify and provide special services for children with less severe developmental and educational problems.

Efforts to address the hazards of making predictions about children who fall near the imaginary borderline between normal and problematic must take account of the fact that such predictions cannot be expected to hold up well with the passing of time. Rather, a system that involves continuing consideration of a child's status over time, for example, using periodic screening or ongoing monitoring, offers a flexible alternative that is sensitive to developmental changes and consistent with measurement uncertainties.

Note that corresponding concerns can be raised regarding the arbitrary nature of eligibility decisions that are necessitated by special education regulations—and a comparable solution might be considered. Restructuring of service delivery systems to routinely offer a diverse range of service options, incorporating services currently identified with both regular and special education, would alleviate the necessity of making significant distinctions between children whose developmental functioning is fairly similar, labelling some and denying service to others. This approach would dispense special services in a manner that is consistent with the continous distribution of school-related problems among school children. If a wide range of service options were available, the press to make classificational distinctions in early identification would be reduced.

One way to significantly expand service options on an ambitious scale would be to offer preschool programs for all 3 to 5 year olds. If children were enrolled in such programs, it would then be possible to review their developmental progress and adaptation to a school-like environment in a valid and efficient manner, incorporating both the teacher's observations and the parent's knowledge of the child. Children with relatively minor special needs could be served through individualized programming within the context of such a classroom. This also would help to alleviate concerns about labelling young children. Preschool screening as an isolated approach possibly could be abandoned altogether if quality preschool programs, as well as medical care, were universally available.

Developmental Review

Another approach to identification that is oriented toward an appreciation of normal development as well as cooperative interaction with parents is developmental review. Parents often ask, "How is my child doing?" and might wonder "Is my child normal?" Developmental review is a procedure for reviewing each child's developmental progress with parents, responding to their questions and concerns in a way that enables them to become better parents.

Developmental review emerged from a series of conferences on developmental screening sponsored by the American Association of Psychiatric Services for Children under the auspices of the Department of Health, Education, and Welfare (Huntington, 1977). It is conceived as an enabling process for both parents and children because it offers affirmation of children's developmental achievements, information about child care and child development, and the opportunity for parents to raise questions and express concerns about their children.

Developmental review assumes a positive orientation that goes beyond "screening for defects." A child's progress is reviewed with the parent (usually the mother) in a way that is beneficial for parents of normally functioning children as well as developmentaly disabled children. Using information derived from parent input and direct professional observation, a child's current development is reviewed in five areas of development: gross motor, fine motor, language, self-help, and social–emotional. In conducting the parent interview and the child observation, the evaluator refers to the Developmental Map, shown in Table 22.2. The Developmental Map, designed to encourage parents to appreciate and learn about child development, displays typically expected behaviors of children from birth to age 5.

A developmental review session usually concludes with a discussion of results with parents, and provision of appropriate information and guidance. For those children with possible developmental problems, the discussion is oriented toward the parents' questions or concerns about the child. Referral for follow-up evaluation is made when needed.

CONCLUSION

Preschool screening has been presented as a means to an end, rather than as an end in itself. It is part of an overall early identification decision-making process, the ultimate objective of which is to assist children who have developmental, sensory, or physical problems that can interfere with school performance. In effect, we make the prediction that certain children will have problems in school, then attempt to thwart the prediction by providing special services early on, when they will ostensibly do the greatest good. We operate under the assumptions that early intervention is of significant value, that incipient problems of preschool can be accurately identified, and that the overall benefits of early identification and intervention justify the costs.

In examining preschool screening as it is typically approached, we outlined the essential elements of the process, noted its limitations, and proposed ways to improve the process. In doing

so, we accepted that the primary goal of preschool screening is to improve the delivery of special services to children with educationally handicapping conditions. But, we have also attempted to step outside the system for a broader perspective to weigh the value of alternatives. For example, it could be argued that preschool screening is a poor substitute for developmentally appropriate programs being available for all preschool children, or that developmental review is more likely to have the kind of impact that justifies the expenditure of resources and extensive outreach required by a preschool mass screening program. As we strive to better meet the needs of children with developmental and educational problems, we also could opt for promoting the healthy development of all children, as well as the development of their parents.

REFERENCES

Algozzine, B., & Ysseldyke, J. E. (1981). Special education services for normal children: Better safe than sorry. *Exceptional Children, 48,* 238–243.

Alpern, G. D., Boll, T. J., & Shearer, M. (1980). *Developmental Profile II.* Aspen: Psychological Development Publications.

American Psychological Association, American Educational Research Association & National Council on Measurement in Education (1985). *Standards for Educational and Psychological Tests.* Washington, DC: American Psychological Association.

Bayley, N. (1949). Consistency and variability in the growth of intelligence from birth to eighteen years. *Journal of Genetic Psychology, 75,* 156–168.

Bloom, B. S. (1964). Stability and change in human characteristics. New York: Wiley.

Bower, E. M. (1981). *Early Identification of Emotionally Handicapped Children in School* (3rd ed.). Springfield, IL: Charles C. Thomas.

Bracken, B. A. (1984). *The Bracken Basic Concept Scale.* San Antonio, TX: The Psychological Corporation.

Bracken, B. A. (1987). *The Bracken Concept Development Program.* San Antonio, TX: The Psychological Corporation.

de Hirsch, K., Jansky, J., & Langford, W. (1966). *Predicting Reading Failure.* New York: Harper & Row.

Drumwright, A. (1971). *Denver Articulation Screening Exam.* Denver: Ladoca Publishing Foundation.

Edmiaston, R. K., & Mowder, B. A. (1985). Early intervention for handicapped children: Efficacy issues and data for school psychologists. *Journal of School Psychology, 22,* 171–178.

Frankenburg, W. K., & Dodds, J. B. (1967). The Denver Developmental Screening Test. *Journal of Pediatrics, 71,* 181–191.

Gradel, K., Thompson, M. S., & Sheehan, R. (1981). Parental and professional agreement in early childhood assessment. *Topics in Early Childhood Special Education, 1,* 31–39.

Hainsworth, P. K., & Hainsworth, M. L. (1980). *Preschool Screening System.* Pawtucket, RI: Early Recognition Intervention Systems.

Honzik, M. P. (1938). The constancy of mental test performance during the preschool period. *Journal of Genetic Psychology, 42,* 285–302.

Huntington, D. (1977). *Development Review in the EPSDT program.* (DHSS Publication No. 77–24537). Washington, DC: The Medicaid Bureau.

Ilg, F. L., & Ames, L. B. (1965). *School Readiness.* New York: Harper & Row.

Ireton, H. (1984). *Preschool Development Inventory.* Minneapolis: Behavior Science Systems.

Ireton, H., & Thwing, E. (1974). *Minnesota Child Development Inventory.* Minneapolis: Behavior Science Systems.

Ireton, H., Thwing, E., & Gravem, H. (1970). Infant mental development and neurological status, family socioeconomic status, and intelligence at age four. *Child Development, 41,* 937–945.

Kaufman, A. S., & Kaufman, N. L. (1972). Tests built from Piaget's and Gesell's tasks as predictors of first-grade achievement. *Child Development, 43,* 521–535.

Kurtz, P., Neisworth, J., & Laub, K. (1977). Issues concerning the early identification of handicapped children. *Journal of School Psychology, 15,* 136–139.

Lazar, I. (1981). Early intervention is effective. *Educational Leadership, 40,* 303–309.

Lazar, I., & Darlington, R. (1982). Lasting effects of early education: A report from the Consortium for Longitudinal Studies. *Monographs of the Society for Research in Child Development, 47* (2–3, Series No. 195).

Lichtenstein, R. (1980). *Minneapolis Preschool Screening Instrument.* Minneapolis Public Schools.

Lichtenstein, R. (1982). New instrument, old problem for early identification. *Exceptional Children, 49,* 70–72.

Lichtenstein, R. (1990). Psychometric characteristics and appropriate use of the Gesell School Readiness Screening Test. *Early Childhood Research Quarterly, 5,* 359–378.

Lichtenstein, R., & Ireton, H. (1984). *Preschool Screening: Identifying Young Children with Developmental and Educational Problems.* Orlando: Grune & Stratton.

Mardell-Czudnowski, C. D., & Goldenberg, D. S. (1983). *Developmental Indicators for the Assessment of Learning - Revised.* Edison, NJ: Childcraft Educational Corporation.

McCall, R. B., Hogarty, P. S., & Hurlburt, N. (1972). Transitions in infant sensorimotor development and the prediction of childhood IQ. *American Psychologist, 27,* 728–748.

McCarthy, D. (1978). *McCarthy Screening Test.* New York: Psychological Corporation.

McNulty, B., Smith, D., & Soper, E. (1984). *Effectiveness of Early Special Education for Handicapped Children.* Denver: Colorado Department of Education.

Meisels, S. J. (1987). Uses and abuses of developmental screening and school readiness testing. *Young Children, 42,* 68–73.

Meisels, S. J. (1989). Can developmental screening tests identify children who are developmentally at-risk? *Pediatrics, 83,* 578–585.

Meisels, S. J., & Wiske, M. S. (1983). *Early Screening Inventory.* New York: Teachers College Press.

Mitchell, J. V. Jr. (Ed.) (1985). *The Ninth Mental Measurements Yearbook.* Lincoln, NE: Buros Institute of Mental Measurements.

Rubin, R. A., & Balow, B. (1979). Measures of infant development and socioeconomic status as predictors of later intelligence and school achievement. *Developmental Psychology, 15,* 225–227.

Shepard, L. A., & Smith, M. L. (1986). Synthesis of research on school readiness and kindergarten retention. *Educational Leadership, 44,* 78–86.

Thurlow, M. L., O'Sullivan, P. J., & Ysseldyke, J. (1986). Early screening for special education: How accurate? *Educational Leadership, 44,* 93–95.

Vander Veer, B., & Shweid, E. (1974). Infant assessment: Stability of mental functioning in young retarded children. *American Journal of Mental Deficiency, 79,* 1–4.

Walker, D. K., & Wiske, M. S. (1981). *A Guide to Developmental Assessments for Young Children (2nd ed.).* Massachusetts Department of Education, Early Childhood Project.

Weber, C. U., Foster, P. W., & Weikart, D. P. (1978). *An Economic Analysis of the Ypsilanti Perry Preschool Project.* Monographs of the High/Scope Educational Research Foundation, (No. 5).

Werner, E. E., Bierman, J. M., & French, F. E. (1971). *The Child of Kauai: A Longitudinal Study from the Prenatal Period.* Honolulu: University of Hawaii Press.

Zehrbach, R. R. (1975). *Comprehensive Identification Process.* Bensenville, IL: Scholastic Testing Services.

23

Fundamentals of Family Assessment

KATHLEEN D. PAGET

A multitude of reasons exists to underscore the necessity of incorporating family assessment strategies into evaluations of young children's functioning. Research investigations have systematically uncovered the potent influences of family life on young children's development (Belsky, 1981; Crnic et al., 1983), conceptual models have provided clear frameworks for understanding the importance of person-environment interactions (Bandura, 1978; Bronfenbrenner, 1979), and demographic changes have revealed the diversity of American families (Vincent & Salisbury, 1988). Collectively, the results of research, the implications of theory, and changes in demographic trends have created an appropriate platform for passage of the Education of the Handicapped Act Amendments of 1986 (Public Law 99–457).

Within the Preschool Grant Program of the law, parent involvement and all due process rights therein are an "allowable cost" as opposed to services that target the child only. Within the Early Intervention Program for handicapped infants and toddlers, Individualized Family Service Plans (IFSPs) are mandated. Among the required components of these plans are an assessment of family strengths and needs relating to enhancing the development of the child; major outcomes expected to be achieved for the child *and* family; and the specific early intervention services necessary to meet the unique needs of the child and family. With these occurrences, the stage is set for professionals who evaluate young children to acquire skills in family assessment. The purpose of this chapter is essentially twofold: to discuss conceptual issues related to family assessment; and to present specific strategies for conducting assessments of family interactions, needs, strengths, and resources. The strategies are conceptualized from the vantage point of best practices appropriate for families of all young children from birth through 5 years of age. Also, the term "assessment" is used synonymously with *intervention planning,* because every assessment strategy sets the occasion for intervention with family, and, reciprocally, every form of intervention implemented is a form of assessment.

CONCEPTUAL ISSUES

The roles played by families in early intervention programs are changing dramatically with the passage of Public Law 99–457. Concomitantly, the roles played by professionals are shifting toward more emphasis on the assessment of family needs and strengths. Because these roles are new for many professionals, it is useful to discuss limitations of traditional practice, and detail guidelines and procedures for assessing family needs.

The common practice of addressing only child needs has been the focus of recent criticism in the early childhood literature (Bristol & Gallagher, 1982; Dunst, 1985; Schultz, 1982) even prior to passage of the law and the mandate to complete Individualized Family Service Plans. Unfortunately, the major goal of early intervention programs has been to effect change in some aspect of the child's behavior or functioning level, with family concerns seldom being addressed prior to or during intervention (Dunst et al., 1988; Turnbull & Winton, 1984). Nevertheless, a handicapping condition creates unique needs for families, and their perceptions must play a key role in any assessment and intervention activities. This broader-based perspective of intervention encourages professionals to view the child as part of a family unit and not in isolation. This perspective also has led to the recognition that the child and the family, rather than the child alone, are clients. Programs adopting this view have tended to be child *and* family focused, addressing family strengths and needs in addition to child strengths and needs. Nevertheless, professionals still face challenges associated with involvement of the family as a whole system, expanding behind the "parent" mandates of Public Law 94–142.

Criticism also has focused on the practice of treating all parents or families as if they were homogeneous. Much of this criticism has been raised by family systems and ecobehavioral researchers (Crnic et al., 1983; Tertinger et al., 1984; Turnbull et al., 1987) who recognize that families often differ in fundamental ways and consequently have different strengths and needs. Families vary in their structure, ethnic and cultural backgrounds, economic status, educational resources, ideologies, person and mental health problems, and coping styles for dealing with programs (Bristol, 1987; Kaiser & Fox, 1986; Turnbull et al., 1987). Although the concept of family differences is generally *acknowledged,* it seldom has been *incorporated* into the design of early intervention programs. As a result, professionals run the risk of treating all families similarly, perhaps often failing to modify treatment programs to respond to individual family differences. The failure to recognize and respond to individual family differences can result in programs that neglect crucial areas of child and family need, fail to gain family support, and increase family stress of guilt (Dunst et al., 1988; Winton & Turnbull, 1981). Thus, realistic intervention goals must be developed that take into account the family's beliefs regarding intervention, the extent of family time and resources available for home- or center-based therapy, the family's interest in the development of certain child skills, and the family's ability to be involved in the therapy program.

The term family *needs assessment* has been used to describe a variety of assessments that: assess parents' desire for information, assess the types of stress and reactions to stress that families encounter, evaluate program effectiveness, collect information regarding the family or child, assess parent strengths and family relationships, and assess parent-child interactions and the home environment (Chandler et al., 1986). Frequently, assessment of families has focused on demographic and other descriptive information and fails to identify needs from the family's perspective. Parents often are asked about marital status, employment, family constellation, daily schedule, and the child's current level of functioning. Professionals use this information to define the parents' level of participation and select goals for intervention. However, professional expectations might not match the family's desired level of participation or the family's priorities for intervention. For example, knowing that a mother works or that she is a single parent does not indicate the mother's concern or interest level with regard to involvement in an intervention plan. Thus, parent perspectives cannot be derived or assumed from traditional demographic and descriptive information, and such assessments, when used alone, are not useful in helping professionals understand what families want or need from an intervention program.

Despite how needs assessments are applied to specific situations, the operative issue is that we must develop family-focused intervention programs that are *responsive* to family needs and concerns. Assessing family needs, if only on an informal basis, can assist families in identifying problems and understanding one another's perspectives. This type of assessment also can facilitate negotiation between families and professionals with respect to decision making and responsibility sharing. Ideally, an adequate assessment of family needs should lead to interventions that "best fit" or reflect the needs and desires of the family, the child, and professionals.

The operative conceptual issue is that all professionals must begin to examine critically the types of assessments they conduct and how they interpret the results. Questions professionals must ask themselves include: Do the assessments evaluate needs from the family's perspective? Do they help professionals and families understand each other's perspectives? Are they helpful in developing family-focused interventions? The answers to these questions will lead to the selection or development of needs assessment procedures that are likely to be most useful. Guidelines and suggestions for the design of needs assessments have been developed by Bell and colleagues (1983), Black and associates (1981), Dunst and coworkers (1988), and Fawcett and associates (1982). Specific descriptions of measures that assess varied aspects of family needs and resources are provided in Dunst and Trivette (1985a) and Dunst and colleagues (1988).

Paget and Barnett (1989) address issues related to the scope and purpose of family assessment. Because a presentation of such issues establishes an appropriate context for understanding the fundamentals of family assessment in the present chapter, portions of their earlier discussion are extracted and appear in the following sections.

The Purpose of Family Assessments

An assessment of family needs can be used in many ways to provide different types of information. Specifying the purpose of the assessment will aid in the development or selection of a particular assessment process. According to Chandler and coworkers (1986), the following questions should be asked when determining the purpose of the assessment: Will it be used to obtain descriptive information?; document the need for services?; identify family functioning?; help identify

goals for intervention?; or evaluate program effectiveness?

When determining the purpose of the assessment, consideration also should be given to the impact the assessment process will have on the family's beliefs regarding intervention. The administration of a needs assessment implies a promise to help, and professionals should consider the implications of this promise prior to obtaining information about family needs. Cautions also have been raised regarding the importance of assessing only those areas in which intervention is possible (Bailey et al., 1986) and deemed necessary by the family (Dunst, et al. 1988).

The Scope of Family Assessments

In addition to the needs expressed by families, their strengths and resources for meeting needs should be measured. Dunst and associates (1988) suggest that professionals assess family strengths (e.g., parenting skills; family/child interactions) prior to selecting intervention tasks and the resources available to the family for accomplishing the tasks. These authors suggest further that professionals identify "personal projects," where strengths within the family system as well as strengths of individual family members are recognized and used as a foundation for meeting needs. Fawcett and coworkers (1982) use the term *improvement agenda* to suggest the same process. This process helps to maintain a balanced perspective of the family system (its strengths and needs) and can be used as a preventive process, assuring that strengths are maintained during intervention. Other types of information that professionals and families will find useful include measures of the child's developmental or behavioral functioning level, the family's goals for intervention, parental expectations for the child and the program, identification of stressful events, coping strategies, well being, types of social support available to the family, parent/child interaction, and various aspects of the home environment. Bristol and Gallagher (1986) have developed assessment procedures related to mother and father perceptions of family needs, and Dunst and coworkers (1988) delineate a detailed family support model of assessment and intervention.

Participants and Level of Involvement

In programs where parents or family members are expected to participate in intervention, it is important to assess their ability or desire to do so. Too often, professionals tend to assume that all families want to be equally involved with their child's program and that all parents have the time, skills, and enthusiasm required to be involved in their child's treatment program (Winton & Turnbull, 1981). Without family input, expectations regarding involvement can be unrealistic or unreasonable. Persons responsible for the parent or family components of early intervention programs should strive to involve parents and other family members according to family needs and abilities. This might require looking beyond the immediate family to the extended family. In this respect, Vadasy and associates (1984) have identified assessment and intervention procedures appropriate for use with grandparents.

Developing Family-Focused Intervention Plans

The development of family-focused interventions can be approached by having families rank needs in order of importance, select several needs as highest priority, or indicate satisfaction or dissatisfaction with how the needs are currently being met. It is important when developing interventions that the family and professionals consider the impact of interventions on the family in terms of time, finances, and skills. For example, if a parent agrees to work on physical therapy exercises at home, the amount of time required to conduct therapy should be addressed, as well as the extent to which the therapy might compete with other tasks or family interactions. The number of goals selected for intervention also should be considered. Professionals might need to limit the number of goals simultaneously addressed during intervention, because when multiple goals are addressed, the amount of effort allocated to any one activity decreases (Ford & Heaton, 1980). The relative impact of meeting needs also should be considered. Will achievement of this goal increase the child's or the family's quality of life or affect more than one person? Will it make child care easier, reduce or increase family stress, enhance family interactions, and so forth. The an-

swers to these questions, determined with the family, will help set priorities for the needs and goal selection. Certainly it is likely that professionals and families will disagree on the choice of goals or on the importance of different goals. Chandler and colleagues (1986) describe a situation where professionals recommend that a parent work on speech training, but the parents indicate a strong desire to work on toilet training. Although speech training might have been an important intervention goal, it was decided that training the child to toilet independently would reduce the time previously spent by the family on diapering, laundering, and so on, thus resulting in increased time for the family to work on speech needs and to engage in other family activities.

Assessing needs from the family's perspective and considering the family system will help professionals understand why families select certain plans and levels of involvement. Thus, if parents do not have time to conduct intervention at home or feel uncomfortable in the role of teacher, center-based classroom treatment might be selected. If there are problems in a parent/child relationship that interfere with the delivery of intervention plans, an initial approach might be to effect changes in parent/child interactions if the family sees this as important. The process of negotiation, with professionals and families working as a team to determine intervention goals, should enhance our sensitivity to factors influencing the family.

When incorporating the results of family assessments into goals on IFSPs, we must be careful to retain the spirit of the new law. According to Dunst and coworkers (1988), the potentially most damaging aspect of the IFSP has to do with the role the "case manager" is expected to play in implementing the plan. The Congressional Record (1986) states that the IFSP must contain "the name of the case manager . . . who will be responsible for implementation of the plan and coordination with other agencies and persons" (p. 7895). This requirement implies that the case manager (a professional) and not the family will play an active role in securing resources to meet family needs. If this is done, it directly threatens a family's ability to become self-sufficient and will usurp rather than empower the family. This particular requirement of the IFSP violates many of the principles of helping relationships that are known to be both enabling and empowering (Dunst & Trivette, 1987). Rather than being responsible for implementing the plan, Dunst and associates assert that professionals should engage in roles that enable and empower the family in a manner that makes them better able to mobilize resources to meet their needs more self-sufficiently. In addition, they propose that fluid rather than static approaches must be taken wherein frequent modifications in the IFSP occur as a result of the many changes that occur within families. The six-month review of family needs called for in the legislation is not likely to be responsive to the many changes that occur in family life.

Family-Level Outcome Measures

When family needs are considered and when parent participation is expected, outcome measures will differ from those traditionally employed for assessing program efficacy. Obviously, benefits to family members from program participation cannot be assessed adequately by measuring child change on developmental assessments (Chandler et al., 1986; Sheehan, 1982). Benefits to families must be measured in terms of impact on families in areas such as satisfaction, decreased time required in child care tasks, parent and family member interactions with the child, stress, and change in parenting abilities and practices. This process must be viewed as a continuous process, with changes made over time as reflected by family needs.

In summary, the implementation of assessment and intervention practices that are responsive to the needs of the families as well as children requires changes in the ways professionals and practitioners view families (Chandler et al., 1986; Dunst et al., 1985). Many of these changes reflect a number of considerations that professionals have begun to acknowledge and address, but are typically overlooked or neglected in designing family-focused interventions. This oversight can result in programs that lack social validity and receive little or no "consumer" support. (Wolf, 1978). Thus, professionals in early education programs must assess and use families' perceptions of satisfaction as the primary guide to program development and individual educational program planning. Thus, in our movement toward "best practices" with families, information from profes-

sionals should supplement what is provided by families rather than family information supplementing professionals' perspectives.

SPECIFIC STRATEGIES OF FAMILY ASSESSMENT

The model of family assessment and intervention developed by Dunst and associates (1988) warrants particular attention in this chapter because of its comprehensiveness, practicality, and applicability toward meeting the mandates of Public Law 99–457. The essential steps in the model are described by the authors in the following way (p. 51).

1. Identify family aspirations and projects using needs-based assessment procedures and strategies so as to determine what the family considers important enough to devote time and energy to.
2. Identify family strengths and capabilities in order to (a) proactively emphasize what the family already does well and (b) determine the particular strengths that increase the likelihood of a family mobilizing resources to meet needs.
3. "Map" the family's personal social network so as to identify both existing sources of support and resources, and untapped but potential sources of aid and assistance.
4. Function in a number of different roles in order to enable and empower the family to become more competent at being able to mobilize resources to meet its needs and achieve desired goals.

The authors describe specific interviewing strategies and the use of self-report measures for implementing these steps in a manner that is responsive to family needs and concerns. Although the details of interview procedures are beyond the scope of this chapter, issues related to the use of self-report measures within the first three steps in the model are described in the following sections. The reader is advised to use interviewing strategies and self-report measures together to identify with family members their needs, functioning style, and sources of support. Dunst and associates (1988) illustrate with an item on an assessment tool that assesses the adequacy of food and shelter. A family who completes the scale might indicate food and shelter as needs rather than base an intervention on this response, the response should be used to further identify the factors that make this a need, and base the intervention on these factors and not the need itself (e.g., "You indicated that you feel you do not have adequate food to feed your family. Can you tell me more about this so I can get a better idea about this concern?") (p. 67).

IDENTIFYING NEEDS

Needs can be identified either in an interview format or through completion of any number of needs-based assessment scales. Either approach is designed to engage family members in an exercise of identifying what they *and not others* perceive to be concerns, aspirations, wants, desires, projects, and so forth. Stoneman (1985) stated this in the following way: "To be effective (in work with families, service providers must want to hear what parents have to say and must be truly interested in "understanding the family's concerns and needs" (p. 463).

The following steps and considerations are described by Dunst and his associates (1988) (pp. 70–71) and should be taken into account when self-report scales are used as a basis for assessing needs. First, explicitly state why the family is asked to complete the scale. Second, be very clear about how the results will be used. Third, use the responses in a way of helping the family clarify and define when they perceive something is a concern or need. Fourth, restate the needs as they are clarified to be sure the family agrees that your perceptions are accurate. This process should be repeated for those scale items on which the family indicates they have needs. The interviewer should be as informal as possible while at the same time structuring the interpretation of the scale results so that a clear picture of the family's needs and aspirations, emerge as one progresses through the family's responses.

Family Needs Scales

There are a number of measurement scales available for assessing family needs (see espe-

cially Dunst & Trivette, 1985b; and Fewell, 1986, for listings of needs-based assessment scales). Of all the scales that are available, those having the greatest utility for identifying family-level needs include the Family Needs Survey (Goldfarb et al., 1986; Summers et al., 1985), Parent Needs Inventory (Fewell et al., 1981; Robinson & DeRosa, 1980), Personal Projects Scale (Little, 1983), and selected subscales of the Survey for Parents of Children with Handicaps (Moore et al., 1982). Hartman and Laird (1983) describe a needs-based approach to assessment that permits identification of the types of human and physical resources necessary to meet needs as well as propose a series of assessment questions that are designed to assist the help giver in structuring the problem and need identification process. Other scales include the Family Resource Scale (Dunst & Leet, 1987), Resource Scale for Teenage Mothers (Dunst et al., 1986), Support Functions Scale (Dunst & Trivette, 1985a) and Family Needs Scale (Dunst et al., 1985). Several needs assessment scales are briefly described here to illustrate ways in which needs can be identified. The instrument descriptions on pages 519–524 are adapted with permission from Dunst, Trivette, and Deal (1988).

Personal Projects Matrix

With this instrument, a respondent is asked to list up to ten personal projects that occupy his or her time and energy, and then rate each of the projects in terms of their importance, enjoyment, difficulty, stress, impact (both positive and negative), and "progress" toward meeting the goals (needs, achieving an aspiration), etc. On the one hand, this assessment system provides a direct way of determining the activities a person considers important enough to devote time and energy. On the other hand, it provides a way of assessing a number of qualitative aspects of the projects with respect to the respondent's perceptions of how the activities impinge upon his or her life. The latter can be especially useful for determining the extent to which efforts to complete projects will occur.

Family Resource Scale

The Family Resource Scale (FRS) is an instrument that is useful to the needs identification process. The FRS measures the extent to which different types of resources are adequate in households with young children. The scale includes 30 items that assess the adequacy of both physical and human resources, including food, shelter, transportation, time to be with family and friends, health care, money to pay bills, child care, and so on. (A modified version of the FRS is available specifically for use with teen-age mothers—see Dunst et al., 1986). The individual items are roughly ordered from the most to least basic, and the respondent is asked to indicate the extent to which each resource is adequate in his or her family. Each item is rated on a five-point scale ranging from "Not At All Adequate" to "Almost Always Adequate."

Family Needs Scale

The Family Needs Scale (FNS) is similar in format to the FRS but specifically asks family members to indicate the extent to which they have a need for 41 types of resources. The items are organized into nine major categories (financial, food and shelter, employment, communication, etc.), with the items within categories roughly ordered on a continuum from the most to least basic (e.g., the financial resources items range from "Have enough money to buy necessities" to "Have enough money to save for the future." Each item is rated on a 5-point scale ranging from "Almost Never a Need" to "Almost Always a Need." Items rated "Sometimes," "Often," or "Almost Always a Need" might be taken as an indication that those needs are generally unmet, and thus provide a basis for further discussion to pinpoint and define the exact nature of the need.

Support Functions Scale

The Support Functions Scale (SFS) assesses the extent to which a person has a need for various types of help and assistance. The scale includes 20 items that assess the need for financial (e.g., loans money), emotional (e.g., someone to talk to), instrumental (e.g., child care), and informational (e.g., material describing a handicapping condition) support. Each item is rated on a 5-point scale ranging from "Never Have a Need" to "Have a Need Quite Often." The SFS items and manner in which needs are assessed are based on the results of extensive in-home interviews with more than 200 parents of preschool handicapped children in which a taxonomy of needs was generated and subsequently categorized and vali-

dated in a series of studies (Dunst & Trivette, 1985a). The scale items that are rated as "Sometimes," and "Often," or "Quite Often" a need can be taken as an indication that further interviewing (assessment) is necessary to "pinpoint" the specific type of help and assistance that is needed but lacking.

IDENTIFYING FAMILY FUNCTIONING STYLE

The purpose of this component of the Dunst and associates (1988) model is to identify a family's individual functioning style both in terms of existing intrafamily resources and strengths and capabilities that can be used to secure additional resources. In the words of Stoneman (1985), "Every family has strengths, and, if the emphasis is on supporting strengths rather than rectifying weaknesses, chances for making a difference in the lives of children and families are vastly increased" (p. 462).

Family strengths include the various qualities of strong families including the skills employed in response to demands placed upon the family, the competencies used to mobilize resources, and any other abilities that "make the family work well." Family functioning style includes both the strengths and capabilities that constitute resources for meeting needs and the ways in which a family employs strengths and capabilities as a basis for securing or creating additional resources (Dunst et al., 1988).

Family Strengths Scale

The Family Strengths Scale includes 12 items that assess two dimensions of family functioning: *family price* (loyalty, optimism, trust in the family) and *family accord* (ability to accomplish tasks, deal with programs, get along together). For each item, the respondent indicates the extent to which the quality is present in his or her family. The items assess strengths such as trust and confidence, ability to express feelings, congruence in values and beliefs, respect, and so on. Responses on individual items as well as subscale scores can be used as a way of asking families to describe the basis for why they consider particular characteristics family strengths.

Family Functioning Style Scale

The Family Functioning Style Scale assesses qualities of strong families. The scale was specifically designed as a way of assessing the extent to which a person believes his or her family is characterized by the presence of different strengths and capabilities. The individual scale items are rated on a 5-point scale in terms of the extent to which different statements are true for the respondent's household. The scale items are organized into three major categories of the family strengths: family identity, information sharing, and coping/resource mobilization. As was the case for the other family strengths scale, the responses to individual items are used as a way of probing the family with respect to the types of things they do to communicate, cope, and so on.

IDENTIFYING SOURCES OF SUPPORT AND RESOURCES

The purpose of this component of the model presented by Dunst and associates (1988), is to identify existing sources of intrafamily and extrafamily support and untapped but potential sources of aid and assistance that match a family's identified needs.

Support refers to emotional, physical, informational, and instrumental resources and includes such varied things as someone to talk to about the difficulties of rearing a young child, medical care, information about a particular handicapping condition, transportation provided by a friend, day care, and the like. Dunst and coworkers (1988) indicate that sources of support can be thought of as varying along a continuum beginning with the family unit and moving outward and progressively more distant from individual family members (Bronfenbrenner, 1979). These include the nuclear or immediate family (children, parents, other household members), relatives and kin (blood and marriage relatives), informal network members (friends, neighbors, coworkers, etc.), social organizations (church, clubs, etc.), generic professionals and agencies (family/child's physician, health department, public schools, day care centers, etc.), specialized professional services (early intervention program, specialized clinics, therapists, clinicians, etc.), and policy-making groups

and individuals (agency directors, school boards, county and state governments, etc.).

Dunst and associates also emphasize the qualitative features of support that have been found to be important factors influencing the likelihood of mobilization of resources for meeting needs. These include the extent to which the "costs" of seeking and accepting help do not outweigh the benefits (response costs), the extent to which the family can depend upon network members in times of need, how willing network members are in terms of providing aid and assistance (dependability), the extent to which help giving by network members creates a personal or psychological sense of obligation (indebtedness), the extent to which "exchange of favors" is sanctioned and approved but not expected (reciprocity), and the extent to which one is satisfied with help that is provided by network members (satisfaction). Which features tend to be most important from the family's perspective vary from family to family and from need to need because of situation-specific considerations.

The Family System and Family Functioning Style

Dunst and associates (1988) assert that the process of identifying and mobilizing resources is most beneficial when a family is conceptualized as a system comprised of unique strengths and capabilities. In the use of self-report scales and interviewing strategies to assess family strengths, assors should remain cognizant of the fact that family functioning style includes both the presence of strengths and capabilities and the manner in which these competencies are used as a basis for securing or creating resources. Dunst and coworkers (1988) state further that we should answer the following three questions with respect to family functioning style: Which qualities of a strong family are displayed by the family? How are the strengths used as intrafamily resources for meeting needs? In which ways does the family use these as well as any other capabilities for mobilizing or creating extrafamily resources for meeting needs?

Family Strength Scales

The Family Strengths Scale (Olson et al., 1983), Family Strengths Inventory (Stinnett &

DeFarin, 1985), Family Strength Questionnaire (Otto, 1975), and the Family Functioning Style Scale (Trivette et al., 1987) assess many of the qualities that have been identified as family strengths and capabilities. Each of these scales provides a basis for assessing the degree to which a family is characterized by different qualities and capabilities.

As is true with respect to the use of needs-based assessment tools, Dunst and associates (1988) emphasize that the responses on self-report, family strength measures should not be taken as the goal, but rather as a basis for further discussion with the family about the meaning of the responses. A family member might indicate that the ability to communicate is a strength in his or her household, thus providing a basis for pinpointing how a family communicates, the ways in which communication occurs, and so forth, as the means for discerning the specific behaviors that make this strength an intrafamily resource (Dunst et al., 1988).

Family Strengths Inventory

The Family Strengths inventory includes 13 items that measure six major qualities of strong families and a number of aspects of interpersonal and interpersonal relationships. Each item is rated on a 5-point scale varying in the degree to which the quality of characteristic is present in the respondent's family. Although the scale yields a total scale score that provides a basis for determining overall family strengths, it is the individual responses to the 13 scale items that are most useful for determining family functioning style. For example, a respondent might indicate that in his or her family it is very characteristic for them to deal with crises in a positive manner. This would be used as a way of querying the respondent about the manner in which this occurs. The response to the query is what gives the interviewer a better idea about how this quality contributes to overall family functioning style.

Social Support Scales

There are numerous scales available specifically designed to assess one or more components of the social support domain (Cohen & Syme, 1985; Dunst & Trivette, 1985b, Fewell, 1986). The use of these scales can aid in the identification of a family's existing support network as well as provide a basis for exploring the characteristics of help-seeking and help-giving exchanges that promote or impede mobilization of resources.

The use of self-report or clinically administered social support scales can provide information that can be used as a basis for further discussion with the family about which sources of support are most and least helpful, which sources are options for meeting needs, how the family feels about asking for help, how the family thinks persons will respond to being asked for help, and soon. A network mapping process, together with queries about the family's qualitative assessment of their social network, is a simple yet highly efficient process for matching resources with needs. According to Dunst and associates (1988), the process of identifying and evaluating the usefulness of different sources of support requires that professionals be sensitive to the verbal and non-verbal behavior of the family when matching resources to needs. This is especially true in terms of willingness to seek and ask for help; and willingness of different network members to provide aid and assistance. Therefore, one should be sensitive to how the family responds to different options for meeting needs and use the responses as a basis for prompting clarification. Follow-up probes provide a way of helping the family members clarify their reasons for not wanting to ask for assistance as well as providing a basis for exploring ways of making the particular source of support a viable option or exploring alternative options. Concerns about helpfulness, dependability, willingness, reciprocity, indebtedness, and response costs, need to be explored and examined if there is any reservation about the use of any particular sources of support as a way of meeting needs (Dunst et al., 1988).

A number of scales have been developed that measure different aspects of social support and thus have utility for identifying existing and potential sources of support for meeting family needs. These include the Family Support Scale (Dunst et al., 1984), Inventory of Social Support (Trivette & Dunst, 1986), and Personal Network Matrix (Trivette & Dunst, 1987). In addition, both the Psychosocial Kinship Inventory (Pattison et al., 1975) and Perceived Support Network Inventory (Oritt et al., 1985) are of particular clinical value because of the format they use for identifying different aspects of a family's personal social network.

Psychosocial Kinship Inventory

The Psychosocial Kinship Inventory can be particularly helpful in terms of assessing various aspects of a person's social network. The scale includes procedures for both identifying the members of the person's personal network and for assessing 11 separate dimensions of support for each network member. The dimensions include: *kind* of feelings and thoughts toward the respondent's social support members, *strength* of these feelings and thoughts, *help* provided by these network members, degree of *emotional support* they provide, frequency of *contact* with them, degree of *stability* of the relationships, physical *proximity* to the network members, *kind* of feelings and thoughts believed held toward the respondent by the network members, *strength* of feelings believed held toward the respondents, *help* provided to kinship members, and *emotional support* provided to these kinship members. Each of these dimensions is rated on a 5-point scale for each person listed by the respondent. The results generate a picture of the person's social network and provide a basis for exploring which network members are used for meeting needs and which network members represent potential but untapped sources of aid and assistance.

Perceived Support Network Inventory

The Perceived Support Network Inventory (SNI) is a particularly useful instrument because of its multidimensionality format. It provides an objective way of determining the members of a family's personal network, the relationships with these people, the types of support they provide, and the manner in which support is provided, as well as the extent to which the family is satisfied with support. The respondent is first asked to list all the people she or he would ordinarily go to if he or she needed help or assistance. Second, the respondent indicates what types of support he or she would generally seek from these people. Third, the person then rates a number of qualitative aspects of support exchanges. The SNI, although developed for research purposes, does have utility as part of many of the aspects of a family's social support network found to influence decisions about seeking and accepting help.

Family Support Scale

The Family Support Scale (FSS) is an 18-item self-report measure that assesses the degree to which different support sources are helpful to families rearing a young child. The sources of support include the respondent's own parents, spouse or partner, friends, neighbors, coworkers, the church or synagogue, professionals, and social groups and organizations. Each item is rated on a 5-point scale ranging from Not At All Helpful to Extremely Helpful. The results from the FSS can be used to query persons about members of their social network, including who is helpful and why, who is not helpful and why, which sources of support are used and not used and why, and so forth.

Inventory of Social Support

The Inventory of Social Support (IS) provides a basis for both mapping a person's social network and assessing the extent to which identified needs are being met by members of the individual's support network. The IS is used in conjunction with the SFS described in the *Identifying Family Need* section. The scale is divided into two parts: identification of family needs and support sources to meet those needs. The taxonomy of needs is identical to those on the SFS; however, the respondents indicate who in their network provides the particular types of support rather than indicating if they need the various types of aid and assistance. Nineteen potential sources of support are included on the scale, ranging from intrafamily (husband/partner, children, etc.) to informal (friends, relatives, church, etc.) to formal (day care, physicians, human service agencies, etc.) support sources. The scale is organized in a matrix format with the needs listed down the left-hand column and the sources of support displayed across the top portion of the scale. The respondent is asked to read each needs-based question (e.g., Who encourages you or keeps you going when things seem hard?) and then indicate who in the support network provides help or assistance with this type of need. A completed matrix provides a visual display of who functions as a source of support to the respondent and what types of support he or she provides. The information can be used as a basis for exploring the manner in which a family can mobilize their support network to meet identified needs.

Personal Network Matrix.

The Personal Network Matrix (PNM) is modeled after the IS and is designed to map a person's social network in terms of those network members who are currently providing aid and assistance to meet individually identified needs. The PNM includes the same sources of support included on the IS (as well as space to add other network members). Instead of preselected categories of needs, the PNM provides space to list those needs identified as part of the needs identification component of the assessment and intervention process. The person completing the scale indicates, for all of the support sources listed, the ones currently being used for meeting needs as well as marks potential but untapped sources of support. Additionally, the respondent indicates the extent to which she or he perceives network members as willing to provide aid and assistance and the extent to which she or he perceives it to be worth the time and effort to ask or seek help from those identified as potential sources of aid and assistance. A completed matrix together with the qualitative ratings provide a basis for both understanding the dynamics of the person's social network and exploring ways of mobilizing resources for meeting needs.

HELP GIVER ROLES AND HELP GIVING BEHAVIOR

In contrast to aforementioned strategies that emphasize assessment of different aspects of the family, the focus of help giver roles and behavior is the ways in which help givers work with families so that the latter can become more competent and self-sustaining with respect to their ability to mobilize resources for meeting needs (Dunst, et al., 1988). The roles are empathetic listener, teacher/therapist, consultant, resource, enabler, mobilizer, mediator, and advocate. Because a thorough description of each role is beyond the scope of this chapter, the reader is referred to Dunst and associates (1988) for more information.

OTHER MODELS

In addition to the model described by Dunst et al. (1988), other models of family-focused as-

sessment and intervention have been developed by Bailey and associates (1986) and Affleck and coworkers (1982). The Bailey and colleagues (1986) model draws on the "goodness-of-fit" concept of Thomas & Chess, 1977 to shift the goal of assessment and intervention from a focus on children or families along to an emphasis on the consonance or "fit" between characteristics of children and families and the coping demands they experience. The task is one of individualizing services to families to optimize fit. The model has four goals (Bailey & Simeonsson, 1988, p. 211).

1. To help family members cope with special needs related to caring for and raising a child with a handicap.
2. To help family members grow in the understanding of the development of their child both as an individual and as a member of the family.
3. To promote warm, enjoyable, and stimulating parent-child interactions.
4. To preserve and reinforce the dignity of families by respecting and responding to their desire for services and by incorporating them as partners in the assessment, planning, and evaluation process.

These goals are accomplished through a sequence of acitivities similar to those used in planning, implementing, and evaluating family services. The steps include functional assessment of family needs, planning, and conducting a focused interview; specifying objectives for families; planning and implementing services for families; and evaluating program effectiveness. The interested reader is referred to Bailey and associates (1986) for description of these steps.

The model developed by Affleck and his associates (1982) emphasizes relationship-focused assessment and intervention. The goals of relationship-focused programs are "(a) encouragement of warm parent-child reciprocal interactions; and (b) promotion of generalized parental competence and problem-solving skills" (Affleck et al., 1982, p. 416). The approach draws on the work of Bromwich (1981), Fraiberg (1975), and Goldberg (1977) to promote these goals through home visits whose content is largely determined by parents. The role of the professional is to support constructive ideas suggested by parents, to identify and reinforce positive parent-child interactions, to help parents develop their own goals and problem-solving skills, and to encourage the use of family and community support networks.

ASSESSMENT OF PARENT-CHILD INTERACTIONS

It is useful to use measures of parent-child interaction to structure observations during assessment. Systems for classifying behavioral observations vary in the size of the units of behavior recorded. *Molar* units are broad classes of behaviors such as responsivity or directiveness. Molar categories have the least information about specific behavioral exchanges and the highest level of summarization of what was seen. *Molecular* categories are more narrowly defined. These categories record specific behavioral events such as smiles, hugs, or vocalizations, and offer little condensation of information. The molar systems for recording behaviors use global rating scales to evaluate behavior after a period of observation. Molecular systems use predetermined categories to record the occurrence of behaviors during a period of observation. Other systems use checklists to record the presence or absence of behaviors either during or after a period of observation. Checklists can contain either molar or molecular categories.

Rosenberg and Robinson (1988) present useful information on various parent-child interaction measures. Issues related to administration, scoring, interpretation, and psychometric soundness are discussed. Molar rating scales described in their review include the Maternal Behavior Rating Scale (Mahoney, et al., 1986), the Teaching Skills Inventory (Rosenberg & Robinson, 1985). Interaction Rating Scales (Clark & Seifer, 1985), and the Parent-Child Interaction Scale (Farran et al., 1984). Selected molecular coding systems comprise the Social Interaction Assessment/Intervention (SIAI) model (McCollum & Stayton, 1985), the Interpersonal Behavior Constructs System (Kogan, 1980; Kogan & Gordon, 1975), and Kelly's (1982) system. In addition, Rosenberg and Robinson (1988) describe several checklists including the Home Inventory (Caldwell & Bradley, 1979; 1984), the Parent Behavior Progression

(Bromwich, 1978), and the Nursing Child Assessment Teaching Scales (Barnard et al. 1982).

Although parent-child interaction measures can yield useful information regarding family functioning, two caveats must be offered regarding their use. First, strengths uncovered during observations must be communicated to the family. Second, parent-child interaction measures must be administered and sensitively interpreted in conjunction with family members' self-reports of interaction patterns. Without addressing both of these caveats, professionals run the risk of adhering to a deficit model of family functioning and imposing their perceptions on the family, thus interfering with family involvement in the assessment process.

SUMMARY AND CONCLUSIONS

In this chapter, conceptual issues and related assessment strategies for families of young children have been discussed. Within the context of Public Law 99–457, emphasis was placed on assessment of family needs, strengths, and resources; and the use of parent-child interaction measures. A multi-step model of assessment was described in detail, as were specific self-report measures for operationalizing the model. A brief overview of other models also was presented. It is hoped that the concepts and strategies presented will assist professionals in the acquisition of assessment skills that appropriately complement child-focused assessment methods when conducting evaluations of young children.

REFERENCES

Affleck, G., McGrade, B., McQueeney, M., & Allen, D. (1982). Promise of relationship-focused early intervention in developmental disabilities. *Journal of Special Education, 16,* 413–430.

Bailey, D. B., & Simeonsson, R. J. (1988). Home-based early interventions. In S. L. Odom & M. B. Karnes (Eds.). *Early Intervention for Infants and Children with Handicaps: An Empirical Base.* Baltimore: Paul Brooks.

Bailey, D. B., Simeonsson, R. J., Winton, P. J., et al., (1986). Family-focused intervention: A functional model for planning, implementing, and evaluating individualized family services in early intervention.

Journal of the Division for Early Childhood, 10, 156–171.

Bandura, A. (1978). The self system in reciprocal determinism. *American Psychologist, 33,* 344–358.

Barnard, K. Booth, C., Mitchell, S., & Telzrow, R. (1982). *Newborn Nursing Models.* Seattle: Department of Parent and Child Nursing, School of Nursing, University of Washington.

Bell, R. A., Sundel, M., Aponte, J. F., Murrel, S. A., & Lin, E. (Eds.) (1983). *Assessing Health and Human Service Needs: Concepts, Methods, and Applications* (Vol. 8). New York: Human Sciences Press.

Belsky, J. (1981). Early human experience: A family perspective. *Developmental Psychology, 17,* 3–23.

Black, T., Prestridge, S., & Anderson, J. (1981). *The Development of a Needs Assessment Process.* Chapel Hill, NC: Technical Assistance Development System.

Bristol, M. M. (1987). Methodological caveats in the assessment of single-parent families of handicapped children. *Journal of the Division of Early Childhood, 11,* 135–142.

Bristol, M. M., & Gallagher, J. J. (1982). A family focus for intervention. In C. T. Tamey & P. Trohanis (Eds.). *Finding and Educating the High Risk and Handicapped Infant* (pp. 137–161). Baltimore: University Park Press.

Bristol, M. M., & Gallagher, J. J. (1986). Research on fathers of young handicapped children: Evolution, review, and future directions. In J. J. Gallagher & P. M. Vietze (Eds.), *Families of Handicapped-Persons* (pp. 81–100). Baltimore: Paul Brooks.

Bromwich, R. (1981). *Working with Parents and Infants: An Interactional Approach.* Baltimore: University Park Press.

Bronfenbrenner, V. (1979). *The Ecology of Human Development: Experiments by Nature and Design.* Cambridge, MA: Harvard University Press.

Caldwell, B., & Bradley, R. (1979). Manual for the *Home Observation for Measurement of the Environment.* Little Rock: University of Arkansas.

Caldwell, B., & Bradley, R. (1984). *Home Observation for Measurement of the Environment.* Little Rock:. University of Arkansas.

Chandler, L. K., Fowler, S. A., & Lubeck, R. C. (1986). Assessing family needs: The first step in providing family-focused intervention. *Diagnostigue, 11,* 233–245.

Clark, G., & Seifer, R. (1985). Assessment of parents' interactions with their developmentally delayed infants. *Infant Mental Health Journal, 6,* 214–225.

Cohen, S., & Syme, S. L. (1985). *Social Support and Health.* New York: Academic Press.

Crnic, K. A., Friedrich, W. N., & Greenberg, M. T. (1983). Adaptation of families with mentally retarded children: A model of stress, coping, and family ecology. *American Journal of Mental Deficiency, 88,* 125–138.

Crnic, K. A., Greenberg, M., Ragozin, A., Robinson, N., & Basham, R. (1983). Effects of stress and social support on mothers of premature and full-term infants. *Child Development, 54,* 209–217.

Dunst, C. J., (1985). Rethinking early intervention. *Analysis and Intervention in Developmental Disabilities, 5,* 165–201.

Dunst, C. J., Cooper, C. S., Weeldreyer, J. C., Snyder, K. D., & Chase, J. H. (1985). *Family Needs Scale.* Unpublished scale. Family, Infant, and Preschool Program, Western Carolina Center, Morganton, NC.

Dunst, C. J., Jenkins, V., & Trivette, C. (1984). Family support scale: Reliability and validity. *Journal of Individual, Family, and Community Wellness, 1,* 45–52

Dunst, C. J. & Leet, H. E. (1987). Measuring the adequacy of resources in households with young children. *Child: Care, Health, and Development, 13,* 11–I25.

Dunst, C. J. & Leet, H. E., Vance, S. D., & Cooper, C. S. (1986). *Resource Scale for Teenage Mothers.* Unpublished scale. Family, Infant, and Preschool Program, Western Carolina Center, Morganton, NC.

Dunst, C. J., & Trivette, C. M. (1985a). *A Guide to Measures of Social Support and Family Behaviors.* Chapel Hill, NC: Technical Assistance Development System.

Dunst, C. J., & Trivette, C. M. (1985b). *Support Functions Scale: Reliability and Validity.* Unpublished scale. Family, Infant, and Preschool Program, Western Carolina Center, Morganton, N.C.

Dunst, C. J., & Trivette, C. M. (1987). Enabling and empowering families: Conceptual and intervention issues. *School Psychology Review, 16,* 443–456.

Dunst, C. J., Trivette, C. M., & Deal, A. G. (1988). *Enabling and Empowering Families: Principles and Guidelines for Practice.* Cambridge, MA: Brookline.

Farran, D., Kasari, C., & Jay, S. (August, 1984). *Parent-child Interaction Scale: Training Manual.* Chapel Hill, NC: Frank Porter Graham Child Development Center.

Fawcett, S. B., Seekins, T., Whang, P. L., Muiu, C., & Suarez de Balcazar, Y. (1982). Involving consumers in decision-making. *Social Policy, 12,* 36–41.

Fewell, R. R. (1986). The measurement of family functioning. In L. Bickman & D L. Weatherford (Eds.). *Evaluating Early Intervention Programs for Severely Handicapped Children and Their Families* (pp. 263–307). Austin, TX: PRO-ED.

Fewell, R., Meyer, D. J., & Schell, G. (1981). *Parent*

Needs Inventory. Unpublished scale. University of Washington, Seattle, WA.

Ford, R., & Heaton, C. (1980). *Principles of Management: A Decision Making Approach*. Reston, VA: Reston Publishing.

Fraiberg, S. (1970). The development of human attachments in infants blind from birth. *Merrill-Palmer Quarterly, 23,* 315–334.

Goldberg, S. (1977). Social competence in infancy: A model of parent-infant interaction. *Merrill-Palmer Quarterly, 23,* 163–177.

Goldfarb, L. A., Brotherson, M. J., Summers,.J. A., & Turnbull, A. P. (1984). Family needs survey. In L. A. Goldfarb, M. J. Brotherson, J. A. Summers, & A. P. Turnbull (Eds.). *Meeting the Challenge of Disability of Chronic Illness: A Family Guide* (pp. 77–78). Baltimore: Paul Brookes.

Hartman, A., & Laird, J. (1983). *Family-Centered Social Work Practice*. New York: Free Press.

Kaiser, A. P., & Fox, J. J. (1986). Behavioral parent training research: Contributions to an ecological analysis of families of handicapped children. In J. J. Gallagher & P. M. Vietze (Eds.). *Families of Handicapped Persons: Research Programs and Policy Issues* (pp. 219–235). Baltimore: Paul H. Brookes.

Kelly, J. (1982). Effects of intervention on caregiver-infant interaction when the infant is handicapped. *Journal of the Division of Early Childhood, 5,* 53–63.

Kogan, K. (1980). Interaction systems between preschool handicapped or developmentally-delayed children and their parents. In T. Field (Ed.). *High-risk Infants and Children:. Adult and Peer Interactions* (pp. 227–247). New York: Academic Press.

Kogan, K. & Gordon, B. (1975). Interpersonal behavior constructs: A revised approach to defining dyadic interaction styles. *Psychological Reports, 36,* 835–846.

Little, B. R. (1983). Personal projects: A rationale and method for investigation. *Environment and Behavior, 19,* 273–309.

Mahoney, G., Powell, A., & Finger, I. (1986). The maternal behavior rating scale. *Topics in Early Childhood Special Education, 6,* 44–56.

McCollum, J., & Stayton, V. (1985). Infant/parent interaction: Studies and intervention guidelines based on the SIAI model. *Journal of the Division for Early Childhood, 9,* 125–135.

Moore, J. A., Hamerlynck, L. A., Barsh, E. T., Spicker, S., & Jones, R. R. (1982). *Extending Family Resources*. Unpublished scale. Children's Clinic & Preschool, Seattle, WA.

Olson, D. J., Larsen, A. S., & McCubbin, H. I. (1983). Family strengths. In D. A. Olson, H. I. McCubbin,

H. L. Barnes, et al., (Eds.). *Families:. What Makes them Work* (pp. 261–262). Beverly Hills, CA: Sage.

Oritt, E. C., Paul, S. C., & Behrman, J. A. (1985). The perceived support network inventory. *American Journal of Community Psychology, 13,* 565–582.

Otto, H. A. (1975). *The use of Family Strength Concepts and Methods in Family Life Education:. A Handbook*. Beverly Hills, CA: The Holistic Press.

Paget, K. D., & Barnett, D. W. (1989). Assessment of infants, toddlers, preschool children, and families. In T. B. Gutkin & C. R. Reynolds (Eds.), *The handbook of school psychology* (Rev. ed.) (pp. 458–486). New York: Wiley.

Pattison, E. M., Defrancisco, D., Word, P., Frazier, H., & Crowder (1975). A psychosocial kinship model for family therapy. *American Journal of Psychiatry, 132,* 1246–1251.

Robinson, L. E., & DeRosa, S. M. (1980). *Parent Needs Inventory*. Austin, TX: Parent Consultants.

Rosenberg, S., & Robinson, C. (1985). Enhancement of mothers' interactional skills in an infant educational program. *Education and Training of the Mentally Retarded, 20,* 163–169.

Rosenberg, S. A., & Robinson, C. C. (1988). Interaction of parents with their young handicapped children. In S. L. Odom & M. B. Karnes (Eds.). *Early Intervention for Infants and Children with Handicaps: An Empirical Base*. Baltimore: Paul Brookes.

Schultz, J. (1982). A parent views parent participation. *Exceptional Education Quarterly, 3,* 17–24.

Sheehan, R. (1982). Issues in documenting early intervention with infants and parents. *Topics in Early Childhood Special Education, 1,* 67–75.

Stinnett, N., & DeFarin, J. (Eds.). (1985). *Secrets of strong families*. New York: Berkley Books.

Stoneman, Z. (1985). Family involvement in early childhood special education programs. In N. H. Fallen & W. Umansky (Eds.). *Young Children with Special Needs* (2nd ed.) (pp. 442–469). Columbus, OH: Charles E. Merrill.

Summers, J. A., Turnbull, A. P., & Brotherson, M. J. (1985). *Coping Strategies for Families with Disabled Children*. Unpublished manuscript. University of Kansas, Kansas University Affiliated Facility at Lawrence.

Tertinger, D. A., Greene, B., F., Lutzker, J. R. (1984). Home safety: Development and validation of one component of an ecobehavioral treatment program for abused and neglected children. *Journal of Applied Behavior Analysis, 11,* 159–174.

Thomas, A., & Chess, S. (1977). *Temperament and Development*. New York: Brunner/Mazel.

Trivette, C. M., Deal, A. G., & Dunst, C. J. (1987). *Styles of Family Functioning Scale*. Unpublished scale. Family, Infant, and Preschool Program, Western Carolina Center, Morganton, NC.

Trivette, C. M., & Dunst, C. J. (1986). *Inventory Social Support:. Reliability and Validity.* Unpublished scale. Family, Infant, and Preschool Program, Western Carolina Center, Morganton, NC.

Trivette, C. M., & Dunst, C. J. (1987). *Personal Network Matrix.* Unpublished scale. Family, Infant, and Preschool Program, Western Carolina Center, Morganton, NC.

Turnbull, A. P., Summers, J. A., & Brotherson, M. J. (1987). From parent involvement to family support. In S. M. Pueschel, C. Tingey, J. E. Pynders, A. C. Crocker, & D. M. Crutcher (Eds.). *New Perspectives on Down Syndrome.* Baltimore: Paul Brookes.

Turnbull, A. P., & Winton, P. J. (1984). Parent involvement policy and practice: Current research and implications for families of young severely handicapped children. In J. Blacher (Ed.). *Severely Handicapped Children and their Families: Research in Review* (pp. 337–397). New York: Academic Press.

Vadasy, P. F., Fewell, R. R., Meyer, D. J., & Schnell, G. (1984). Siblings of handicapped children: A developmental perspective on family interactions. *Family Relations, 33,* 155–167.

Vincent, L. J., & Salisbury, C. L. (1988). Changing economic and social influences on family involvement. *Topics in Early Childhood Special Education, 8,* 48–59.

Winton, P., & Turnbull, A. P. (1981). Parent involvement as viewed by parents of preschool handicapped children. *Topics in Early Childhood Special Education, 1,* 11–19.

Wolf, M. (1978). Social validity: A case for subjective measurement or how applied behavior analysis is finding its heart. *Journal of Applied Behavior Analysis, 11,* 203–214.

24

Intervention Design for Young Children: Assessment Concepts and Procedures

DAVID W. BARNETT
KAREN T. CAREY

The recent and expected growth of mental health and educational services to preschool handicapped and at-risk children is unprecedented because of recent legislation. Further, early education has begun to achieve top priority by many concerned with education, society, and reform. However, some aspects of preschool psychological and educational services lack empirical support, or are controversial. Thus, despite the long-standing promise of early intervention and prevention efforts, many programs remain vulnerable because of the possibility of modest or inconsequential gains, or even harmful outcomes. For these reasons, the analysis of intervention efforts is of crucial importance.

This chapter presents a framework for assessment and intervention design with preschool children. First, an overview of intervention issues is provided. Second, service delivery considerations are presented. Third, target behavior selection and intervention design principles are discussed. Last, the realities of practice are considered.

AN OVERVIEW OF INTERVENTION ISSUES AND ASSESSMENT PRACTICES

There have been several major reviews of early intervention research (Gallagher & Ramey, 1987; Guralnick & Bennett, 1987; White, 1985–86). The following summary comments can be made: early intervention demonstrates great promise; early intervention efforts also are likely to be limited in what they can achieve, but the limits are not well known, nor are results easily predicted for individual children; methodological difficulties plague many studies; and intervention research is in its infancy. Further, the goals of various programs are diverse, confounding the intervention and evaluation efforts. Although there has been documentation of gains in academic achievement, there are important long-term social outcomes that need to be studied (Schweinhart et al., 1986; Zigler & Trickett, 1978). The evaluation of early intervention efforts must eventually attend to effects of altering individual developmental trajectories with respect to a full range of personal and social adjustment indices over long time periods. Further, attention needs to be given to strategies for maintaining and extending the effects of early intervention.

There are many challenges within the context of preschool psychological services. Developmental constructs lead practitioners in diverse and often untested ways (Barnett, 1986). There are important limitations to many techniques used in evaluating young children (Bracken, 1987). Even for those techniques with adequate technical properties, difficult judgments are required for the development of professional practices plans. In addition, decisions concerning alternatives in service delivery strategies are necessary (Barnett & Paget, 1988).

Intervention design should be guided by factors that are likely to facilitate change, in addition to legal, ethical, and professional considerations. Thus, the targets of assessment and analysis might be different from those revealed by developmental theories or traditional measures because efforts are directed to altering or enhancing development, or reducing risk status, rather than understanding normal development or "defining" deviancy. The differences in emphases and especially their practical ramifications are significant. The time and resources required by assessments are substantial, and those assessment practices that possibly lack treatment utility (e.g., Hayes, Nelson, & Jarrett, 1987) should not detract from assessment efforts necessary for interventions.

Preschool assessment for intervention design should be guided by an idiographic understanding of the problem situation, parent and teacher collaboration and involvement, and intervention research. Ecological problem solving provides an important template for preschool assessment and intervention. In the next sections, several key ecological concepts are introduced.

Ecological Problem Solving

Ecological assessment includes a broad context for understanding adjustment and planning interventions by requiring multiple perspectives for each stage of problem solving (Bronfenbrenner, 1986; Cantrell & Cantrell, 1985) Environmental factors, behavior, and person variables all have potential importance in assessment and intervention design (Bandura, 1986). Thus, family and preschool environments need to be understood with respect to their impact on individual

children, and their potential for facilitating personal and social development.

A major contribution from the ecological or systems perspective is that problems can be resolved through a range of alternative strategies: by modifying the problem behavior, by changing the expectations of persons encountering the problem, and by altering the situation. In addition, attention is drawn to the analysis of system strengths—healthy adaptive mechanisms and coping strategies. The professional attempts to understand the network of relationships within and between settings. A general principle is that problems are shared by child, family, school, and community systems, and do not necessarily belong to individuals.

Ecological assessments for young children are guided by the following considerations: the identification of a parental, guardian or caregiver relationship characterized as warm, reciprocal, guiding, and supportive, or someone who can fulfill that role within the community; the determination of an adaptive "educational" environment within the family (Laosa & Sigel, 1982) and/or community whereby a wide range of learning experiences are provided; and, when necessary, the development of a continuum of flexible support services for children, parents, and teachers that stress essential skills and social adaptation as child-centered outcomes. Further, personal, social, and economic outcomes for caregivers require attention, as discussed in the following paragraphs.

The Parental Role

The assessment of the parental role requires careful consideration. Sometimes parents will not be able to fulfill responsibilities because of a range of complicated factors. Crucial dimensions necessary for the analysis of family and environmental risk for children are discussed by Magura and Moss (1986). Also, family environments have unique effects on individual children even within the same family that might be important to determine (Plomin & Daniels, 1987). Further, many interventions place increased demands on parents, but, for some parents, "respite may be more important and beneficial than increased involvment" (White, 1985–86, p. 413).

Thus, although much attention has been focused on the parental role, many factors mediate the effectiveness of parent-child interventions (Webster-Stratton, 1986). While often leading to successful outcomes, parental involvement in early intervention is not a panacea (Dumas & Albin, 1986), nor are the effects of parent based treatments well known (Casto, 1987; White, 1985–86).

An example of complexities in assessing the parental role for preschool interventions is suggested by the concept of *insularity*. The term "insular" is used to describe mothers that feel "'cut off' from social contact," and who view the limited contacts as "unsolicited," or aversive (Wahler, 1980, p. 208). Wahler and his associates (e.g., Panaccione & Wahler, 1986; Wahler, 1980; Wahler & Dumas, 1986) have examined the hypothesis that "extra-family contacts," especially when they are "few" or "aversive," significantly impact on child rearing practices. The demands of parenting can lead to neglect or coercive styles of interactions (Panaccione & Wahler, 1986; Patterson & Bank, 1986; Wahler & Dumas, 1986). Insular mothers also are at increased risk of treatment failure.

The findings by Wahler and his associates suggest that points of assessment must include more than child characteristics or those of the parent-child dyad. Interventions need to have positive outcomes for parents in terms of parent-child relationships, and potentially must contribute to their adult lives as well. There can be tremendous effort and conflict involved in child care efforts depending on child characteristics and parental circumstances.

The analysis of the "locus of intervention" and the development of "naturalistic interventions," discussed next, help guide practitioners in the face of challenging and complex realities. Further, the analyses are characterized as being tentative, and subject to revision. Thus "sequential decision-making" strategies are used to guide the assessment-intervention process.

The Locus of Intervention

The links between ecological assessment and behavioral assessment are expressed in the concept of locus of intervention (Bandura, 1969; Glenwick & Jason, 1984). This phrase is used to encompass questions including where to intervene (e.g., home versus school); when; with whom

(eg., parent(s), teacher(s), peer(s)); how; and toward what target behaviors. Basically, those who interact with the child through the most intensive contacts can act as the most powerful agents of change. However, there usually are many decision points depending on problem behaviors, intervention alternatives, and the realities of situations.

Naturalistic Interventions

Interventions vary greatly in the demands that are made upon participants. Research trends suggest that "naturalistic" interventions can be achieved by examining the roles, routines, skills and interests of caregivers. Assessment plans can be directed to the identification of a range of treatment options based on research; naturally occurring parent or teacher intervention strategies that are likely to be successful with changes, guidance, and feedback; or interventions that can be adapted to evident styles of parenting or teaching. For example, interviews and observations can reveal that caregivers use techniques that are consistent at least in some ways with empirically based interventions. However, they might not be aware of the importance and logical extensions of their behaviors. Therefore, a role of the professional might be to evaluate emerging skills of caregivers that can be further enhanced through consultation, practice, and feedback.

Naturalistic interventions also include those that can be easily incorporated into the routines of caregivers. For example, language development is facilitated through peer and adult interactions, and is a primary concern in high risk and handicapped preschool populations. Relatively straightforward procedures such as the use of a brief (e.g., 5 second) delay (Halle, et al., 1981) and incidental teaching (Hart & Risley, 1980) have been demonstrated to be effective. In the first procedure, the delay is used as a nonverbal cue to respond. For example, the caregiver holds a glass of juice, is oriented towards the child, and waits for the child's vocal initiation (Halle, et al., 1981). Incidental teaching capitalizes on natural, brief, "comfortable," and unstructured learning situations through the use of attention, assistance, and practice to reinforce and expand language usage. Incidental teaching is dependent upon a "child-selected" situation based on either a verbal or nonverbal request. The adult focuses "close attention'' on the child, and asks for (or helps with) elaborated language related to the topic.

For behavior problems, an example of a naturalistic strategy easily adapted to routines is that of contingent observation. Contingent observation involves both incidental teaching and ''mild'' time out from active participation in an activity (Porterfield et al., 1976). The following conditions are included in response to disruptive behavior: a brief description of the inappropriate and appropriate behavior is given; the child is removed to the periphery of the play activity where he or she observes the appropriate behavior of other children (usually less than 1 minute); the child is asked whether he or she is ready to rejoin the activity and behave appropriately. Based on the child's response, the child either returns to play or remains sitting quietly while watching the activity for a brief period. The child is subsequently queried until ready to return. Positive attention is given for appropriate behavior after the child rejoins the group.

Sequential Decisions

In contrast to diagnostic or classification decisions, the development of ecologically based helping strategies typically involves sequential decisons (Bandura, 1969). Target behavior selection and intervention involves a progressive process (Kanfer, 1985), where plans are maintained, modified, or refined over time. A process of sequential decisions is used to revise plans as needed. Plans can be made to monitor troublesome behaviors even when decisions are made *not* to intervene at the present time. The results of well-conducted interventions directly assist with decisions concerning subsequent changes in educational programs. For young children, there is an increased likelihood that successful interventions can alter an impending diagnostic category.

In summary, this section presented ecological problem solving as a broad strategy for preschool assessment and intervention design. Although preschools offer important learning contexts, and despite potential difficulties, beneficial outcomes are likely to be associated with parents gaining or maintaining status as key problem solvers (Dunst & Trivette, 1987; Guralnick & Bennett, 1987). Factors that facilitate or impede this capability are important points of assessment.

In the next section, the following frameworks for service delivery are introduced: organizational development, curriculum-based assessment and intervention, and parent and teacher consultation. Assessment practices should be placed within the context of psychological and educational services provided to children and families.

SERVICE DELIVERY ISSUES

The philosophy, availability, and quality of preschool and family services directly impact upon assessment and intervention decisions. Therefore, a first step in establishing screening, assessment, and preschool educational and psychological services is organizational development (Adelman, 1982; Barnett, 1984).

Organizational Development

With respect to young children, personnel preparation for child care workers is extremely variable, and, for many, intervention-related training can be minimal or nonexistent. Therefore, a likely initial focus of educational consultations is on the provision of effective instructional strategies that encompass a wide range of functional developmental skills (Bricker, 1986). Functional skills emphasize the ''usefulness of learned responses'' (Bricker, 1986, p. 302). The goals of a functional approach to curriculum development are to expand opportunities and to facilitate independence and adaptabilty (Bricker, 1986; LeBlanc et al., 1978). Serving the mental health needs of preschool children is facilitated through successful participation in well functioning social groups established in preschool classrooms.

In the following paragraphs, two interrelated service delivery systems are discussed: curriculum-based assessment and intervention, and parent and teacher consultation.

Curriculum-Based Assessment and Intervention

The most reasonable approach to preschool educational and developmental screening and assessment is the systematic evaluation of children in a well-constructed curriculum (Bagnato et al., 1986; Neisworth & Bagnato, 1986) where children who are not progressing adequately, given teacher attempts at intervention, are referred for consultative, or ultimately, special services. An ecologically based curriculum for young children includes the continuous assessment of skill development in ways that are linked to teacher and peer behavior. Thus, professionals must have a thorough knowledge of the curriculum in use (i.e., rationale, organization, and methods for evaluation) to match the assessment to the child's educational programming (Bagnato & Neisworth, 1979). By utilizing a competency-based ecological assessment, psychologists, teachers, and parents can develop programming goals, instructional strategies, and educational strategies that will enable a child to progress.

An assessment of the classroom ecology (Fuchs & Fuchs, 1986) enables observations of children's performance in academic, social, and other developmental areas in ways that help delineate the environmental conditions necessary for competent performance (LeBlanc et al., 1978). Through on-going curriculum-based assessment procedures children receive instruction at the appropriate level, and progress is monitored. A range of empirically based teaching strategies should be available throughout the process that match instruction to the level of skill development and needs of individual children. Continuous assessment of the child's progress through the curriculum allows for evaluation of the effectiveness of the instructional strategies and available materials.

The assessment of the classroom environment and curriculum-based assessment provides information concerning the conditions necessary for learning to occur. Children who remain at a particular level of a skill sequence, and who are unable to complete a task, might need a change in instructional strategies to progress to the next curriculum step. By measuring current performance, and altering and adapting materials for a child, goals and instructional strategies can be devised that allow the child to develop competencies within a specific target area. Thus, curriculum-based assessment information includes: a child's current level of functioning, how rapidly a child learns skills, what strategies were necessary for the child to learn the skill, how long the child retained the skill, the generalization of previously taught skill sequences to new tasks, behaviors that the child displayed which could deter learning, the

environmental context needed by the child to learn skills (i.e., one-to-one, large group, peer mediated instruction), the motivational method used for the acquisition of skills, and individual skill development in relationship to peers (LeBlanc et al., 1978).

For many children, *preattending* skills might be an important focal point of assessment and intervention. Preattending skills involve looking at the materials, listening to instructions, and sitting quietly during instruction (Etzel et al., 1981).

There are currently many alternative preschool curricula (Bricker, 1986). An example is the HICOMP Preschool Curriculum (Willoughby-Herb & Neisworth, 1982). HICOMP is based on developmental and behavioral principles and includes 800 objectives appropriate for both handicapped and nonhandicapped children from birth to age 5. The objectives are organized by communication, "own-care," motor, and problem-solving domains. The materials also include behavioral strategies for teaching related developmental skills.

In summary, curriculum-based assessment provides information about a child's educational and developmental levels, as does traditional test-based assessment. However, curriculum-based assessment further provides information about the learning environment and the effects of instructional interventions. A well-developed curriculum includes a wide range of functional, developmentally sequenced tasks; enables ongoing measurment; and facilitates the use of a variety of teaching and learning strategies. Curriculum-based assessment is fundamental to preschool service delivery and facilitates both screening and assessment for intervention purposes.

Parent and Teacher Consultation

The nature of professional practice often requires unique, tentative, and ongoing problem solving, rather than technical responses to "given" questions (Schön, 1983). Strategies include the systematic appraisal of child systems, and a mutual and reciprocal partnership with the child, parents, and school personnel. A consultation-based problem-solving model is consistent with the approach taken throughout the chapter.

An underlying assumption of consultation-based services is the importance of providing needed assistance to children's caregivers rather than direct services to children (Gutkin & Curtis, 1982). The relationships are based on openness and trust, and participants are give equal (or coordinate) status. Parents and teachers are thus "experts" concerning their observations, interactions, and knowledge concerning a child, while professionals demonstrate expertise in the process of problem solving. The active involvement of caregivers is crucial to the success of problem solving.

Consultation involves the determination of goals and intervention strategies developed through joint problem solving efforts. Steps in problem solving typically entail: problem definition and clarification; solution generation and analysis; mutually agreed upon assessment/intervention plans and roles; trial periods for interventions; evaluation; replanning; or the termination of the intervention based on successful outcomes. Strategies to support consultation-based services are discussed next.

Prereferral interventions

The goals of prereferral interventions are to reduce the number of inappropriate referrals for multifactored evaluations and subsequent placements through consultation-based services. The process involves structured support and assistance to teachers to provide instructional programs to meet a broad range of children's needs. The principles also can be applied to assist parents and other caregivers. Following unsuccessful attempts at resolution by the caregivers, assistance can be offered through consultation with a specialist, using the problem-solving steps outlined in the previous section.

Relatedly, Intervention Assistance Programs (IAPs) are school-based problem solving groups (Graden et al., 1985). Their purpose is to assist teachers (and parents) with the design and implementation of intervention strategies in regular school programs for children who are having learning and/or behavior problems. IAPs are employed before a referral for special services eligibility, but after formal attempts at problem resolution based on independent interventions by the teacher, and interventions established collaboratively through the services of a consultant. Members of the team work together to clarify the problem, review prior steps at problem resolution, generate and select further intervention strategies, and discuss strategies for implementation and evaluation. Team meetings are used to monitor the effectiveness of interventions and to revise strategies as needed.

In summary, service delivery alternatives are fundamentally related to assessment and intervention decisions. In the next section, the focus is on specific assessment and intervention guidelines.

FRAMEWORKS FOR TARGET BEHAVIOR SELECTION AND INTERVENTION DESIGN

Many excellent sources exist on behavioral assessment and interventions (e.g., Paget, 1988). Earlier, curriculum-based assessment was described within the context of organizational approaches to preschool service delivery. Although related, in this section the emphasis is on basic concepts that guide assessment and intervention decisions for young children experiencing problem behaviors. Following a brief review of reliability and validity issues, the section summarizes interrelated views especially relevant for decisions concerning target behavior selection.

Reliability and Validity of Target Behavior Assessment

Reliability issues have received considerable attention (Page & Iwata, 1986). There are controversies as to whether traditional categories of reliability and validity should be extended or adapted to encompass behavioral assessment (Barrios & Hartmann, 1986), or whether new frameworks are needed (Hayes et al., 1986). Overall, a wide range of factors influence behavioral measurement (Foster & Cone, 1986), and the quality of the assessment must be established for the individual case. The present trend is to use procedures to estimate "agreement" and "accuracy."

Agreement stresses the consistency between raters while accuracy shifts the emphasis more stringently to the relationship of observations to objective indices of actual performance. The assessment of observer agreement provides an estimate of accuracy. Strategies to estimate agreement are necessary to examine the effects of observers, and the adequacy of target behavior definitions or observational systems. Estimates of agreement also are important over different occasions of measurement, and across settings.

A major challenge to the validity of behavioral assessment is that there might not be a direct correspondence between the accurate description of behavior and the intervention implications of the behavior (Kanfer, 1985). Content validity pertains to the adequacy of assessment procedures in the sampling of a behavioral domain and has been termed the "cornerstone" of behavioral assessment (Strosahl & Linehan, 1986). Criterion-related validity has been examined by Kazdin (1985). Questions pertaining to concurrent validity include the analysis of the relationships between the target behavior and other measures of the presenting problem, other behaviors related to possible syndromes, and the potential impact of the target behavior on the client's daily functioning. Predictive validity questions are relevant in considering potential differences in the effectiveness of alternative target behaviors over long time periods.

Further, construct validity has increasing relevance to target behavior assessment. Many constructs (e.g., conduct disorders, social skills) now appear in the behavioral literature (Mash, 1987). It is important to select multiple measures of a problem area—an issue of construct validity (Hayes & Nelson, 1986).

Target Behavior Assessment

Behavioral assessments do not automatically reveal targets for intervention. Important decisions are necessary (Hawkins, 1986; Kratochwill, 1985). Target behaviors can include: changes in parent, teacher, peer, sibling, and child behaviors; new or enchanced skills; and strategies for increased self-control. In the following paragraphs, frameworks for target behavior assessment are presented.

Determine Physically Dangerous Behaviors

Behaviors that threaten lives, either the child's or others', have the highest priority. With children, one of the initial goals should be to ensure that a safe environment is provided while behaviors of concern are being monitored and interventions planned. Aspects can involve abusive and neglectful parental relationships (Wolfe &

Bourdeau, 1987), or elements of home and community safety (Peterson, 1988; Yeaton & Bailey, 1978). For example, in a recent consultation with parents concerning an aggressive 4-year-old boy, initial assessment targets involved the parental monitoring of play behaviors, baths, and stair behaviors (to eliminate pushing and shoving on concrete steps) to protect a toddler sister. Other examples include health related behaviors, fire safety, and injury prevention (Jones & Kazdin, 1980; Mori & Peterson, 1986) which might receive high priority depending on parental situations, motivation, skills, and stressors—all of which can effect monitoring and responsiveness to child care needs.

Evaluate Other Behaviors with Potentially Severe and Damaging Impact

Behaviors that severely interfere with functioning through potentially damaging social or economic (i.e., for parents) consequences also receive high priority (Kanfer, 1985). For example, target behavior selection for severely disruptive child behavior can suggest the evaluation of the impact of the behavior on the caregiver's economic and social realities. Thus, initial consultations might be directed to day care settings based on the parents' employment considerations. Also, some behaviors (e.g., conduct disorders) have been linked to later difficulties in adjustment (Rutter, 1984), and these factors also contribute to setting priorities in target behavior selection.

Plan for Expanding Positive and Reducing Maladaptive Behaviors

Whenever possible, target behaviors should specify desirable goals, rather than inappropriate behaviors. Target behavior selection thus leads to the evaluation of resources and plans for action (Hawkins, 1986; Mash & Terdal, 1981). Further, because of the time-consuming process involved in sequential decisions, attention should be given to "enabling" behaviors that are likely to have powerful overall effects on adjustment. One strategy for target behavior selection is the evaluation of "keystone behaviors," where response classes based on research with specific disorders are considered for interventions (Nelson & Hayes, 1986). For example, compliance might be a likely "keystone behavior" for conduct disordered children (Loeber & Schmaling, 1985; McMahon, 1987; Patterson & Bank, 1986; Wahler, 1975). Compliance training has a broad base of support with respect to effective practices and implications for adjustment (Matson et al., 1978; Roberts, et al., 1978; Russo et al., 1981; Strain et al., 1982; Wahler & Fox, 1980). Selecting an appropriate "keystone" behavior can have beneficial "side effects." For example, Firestone (1976) found reductions in verbal aggression and teacher attention, and increases in cooperative play, following a brief intervention for aggressive behaviors.

Children's play and social behaviors can be crucial assessment targets for intervention design with broad implications for development. Guralnick (1987) writes: "Establishing successful relationships with one's peers is one of the most important accomplishments of early childhood" (p. 93). Potential targets for assessment include facility with functional social routines (e.g., turn taking), strategies for gaining access to play, communications skills, and toy play skills. Research that has examined the effectiveness of peer mediated (Hecimovic et al., 1985; Hendrickson et al., 1982), teacher mediated (e.g., Fox et al., 1986), and sibling mediated (James & Egel, 1986) strategies to extend play and social behaviors has been promising, although more research is needed particularly with respect to generalization effects.

As another example, "template matching" (Cone & Hoier, 1986; Hoier et al., 1987) involves the assessment of behavior in the current (e.g., special, preschool) and transition (e.g., mainstream, classroom) environments. "Index children" (i.e., those who are moderately successful) are identified in the receiving classroom to help evaluate child and teacher-child behaviors necessary for successful adaptation in the new setting. "Template matching" helps with the identification of probable transition settings, and the selection of target behaviors to help with transitions. Planning for educational transitions is a critical aspect of assessment and intervention design.

Plan for Sequences of Behavior Change

Some target behaviors can be prerequisite to other changes primarily because they are likely to influence later, more significant or "pivotal" behaviors (Kanfer, 1985). Behaviors that are viewed as aspects of a normal developmental progression, and that can result in "cumulative deficits" if not mastered, also are given high priority (Mash &

Terdal, 1981). Sequences of behaviors are established through developmental studies, task analysis, and through comparisons of skilled versus nonskilled performances on specific tasks.

Intervention Decisions

Intervention design is a complicated and changing topic (Haynes, 1986). Generally, interventions are selected based on a combination of strategies including the analysis of situations, through problem solving steps, and the consideration of the research base for interventions.

Strategies that stem from single case research designs (Barlow, et al., 1984; Tawney & Gast, 1984) are fundamental to the process of intervention design. They generally have three facets: measures of stability, level, and trend of behavior; an introduction of the intervention while maintaining the measurement procedures; and the evaluation of the intervention over substantial time periods with respect to intervention goals. The outcomes of observations are graphically represented. The visual presentation of data is used as a technical aid to help overcome the natural limitations of interpreting complex assessment information.

Further, interventions require data based modifications. Time-series methods based on single case research designs are appropriate for this function. Time-series methods can be used to monitor trends in behavior, and the effects of interventions. They have broad applicability with respect to philosophically different interventions and can be used to track behaviors when decisions are made not to intervene. The following paragraphs describe salient but interrelated points of assessment for preschool intervention decisions.

Assess the Research Base

Despite the difficulties, consumers (e.g., parents, teachers, administrators) generally expect that intervention decisions are guided by available and pertinent research. First, the correspondence between the child's behavior and syndromes that have research support should be determined (Achenbach & McConaughy, 1987; Kazdin, 1985; Powers, 1984). Kazdin (1985) refers to "constellations of behaviors" or "multiple characteristics that co-occur and encompass different behaviors, affect, cognitions, and physiological responses"

(p. 36). The practical importance of the identification of syndromes is in helping to determine the adequacy of assessment and intervention plans. As examples, parental behaviors and roles in addition to child characteristics often should be a focus of assessment and intervention plans for conduct disordered children (MacMahon, 1987; Patterson & Bank, 1986).

Second, behavioral consultants should be aware of valid and replicated intervention strategies that have been applied successfully to specific behavior problems of interest. The process involves making "logical generalizations" (Barlow & Hersen, 1984; Edgington, 1967) whereby child and setting characteristics, treatment components and alternatives, the magnitude of expected changes, and the observation systems and measures all can be logically evaluated for their potential relevance for individual cases. Numerous gaps exist in the research base for interventions with certain child behaviors and these also are of crucial importance to professionals and consumers. In such circumstances, accountability procedures are necessary (Barlow et al., 1984).

Assess the Availability of Resources for Reaching Treatment Goals

Interventions for target behaviors require the availablity of a range of caregivers and specialized personnel. Teachers can require planning time and support services. Baby sitters and extended family members all can contribute to intervention plans. Assessing the reasonableness of treatment plans is essential.

Assess the Acceptability of a Range of Intervention Alternatives

Acceptability refers to broad-base judgments by consumers (e.g., participants, caregivers) concerning "whether the treatment is appropriate for the problem, whether treatment is fair, reasonable, or intrusive, and whether treatment meets with conventional notions about what treatment should be" (Kazdin, 1980, p. 259; see also Wolf, 1978). The general premise is that for many problem behaviors, a range of alternative interventions is likely to be effective. Those viewed as more acceptable are more likely to be "sought, . . . initiated, and adhered to" (Kazdin, 1980, p. 260). Wolf (1978) wrote: ". . . if the participants don't

like the treatment then they may avoid it, or run away, or complain loudly" (p. 206). Unless participants view the intervention as acceptable, important technological advances will not be used.

Acceptability research is rapidly expanding (Reimers et al., 1987) with consumer groups such as parents (Calvert & McMahon, 1987), teachers (Witt et al., 1984), and children as focal points of various studies. One of the major issues is how acceptability ratings can be altered through planned sequences of interventions (Walle et al., 1984). Witt and Elliott (1985) hypothesize that acceptability, use, integrity, and effectiveness of the intervention are sequentially and reciprocally related.

Assess for Multiple and Broad-based Motivational Issues

Motivational issues of the caregivers in addition to those of the child need to be considered. Within the context of behavioral intervention, the construct refers to "the probability of an individual emitting the behaviors necessary for successful intervention" (Haynes, 1986, pp. 400–401). Joint or collaborative participation can enhance acceptance of the plans, and is a crucial requirment for intervention design (Kanfer, 1985).

Reducing rather than increasing caregivers' demands can be an important assessment and intervention goal in some situations. For problem children, caregivers can spend a considerable amount of time monitoring and responding to behavior. Preschool consultants need to assess the impact of interventions on caregiver–child interactions, and the caregiver's other roles and responsibilities. Successful interventions should "lighten" burdens for conscientious, effective, but harassed caregivers when possible, in addition to other planned outcomes.

Estimate Probable Success of the Possible Interventions

The behavior(s) selected for change must be realistically appraised with respect to methods, the behavior change agent's capabilities, resources of the client(s), and their impact on other members of the social community. Probable success rates also are determined through a review of interventions found in the literature. The relative efficiency and cost effectiveness (Yates,

1985) of the potential interventions are additional considerations.

Assess for Self-regulation and Regulation by the Natural Environment

Artificial means of control are often linked to difficulties with long-term success (Kanfer, 1985). Strategies for self-regulation, and "entry into the natural reinforcement community of the child" (Baer & Wolf, 1970; Stokes & Osnes, 1986) should be a part of assessment-intervention plans (Mash & Terdal, 1981). Preschool environments have considerable potential for establishing the generality of skill development (Baer & Wolf, 1970).

Self-directed change strategies currently have an uneasy status (Billings & Wasik, 1985; Bornstein, 1985). In large part, this is because of experimental design considerations and difficulties with ascertaining the extent of self versus other "directedness" (Gross & Wojnilower, 1984). Despite the controversies, however, a number of methods can be employed to encourage and facilitate self-regulation and independent problem solving including modeling, prompting, and reinforcing behaviors. As one example, Stokes and associates (1978) successfully taught preschoolers to judge the quality of their work, and to appropriately elicit teacher praise. Overall, external means are important in developing self-regulation (Poth & Barnett, 1983; Gross & Wojnilower, 1984).

An example of a "self-mediated" technique is that of "correspondence training" (Guevremont et al., 1986; Osnes et al., 1986). The method involves giving reinforcement contingent "on both promising to engage in a target response and then actually doing so, or on truthfully reporting past actions" (Baer et al., 1985, p. 479). A number of studies have demonstrated the effectiveness of reinforcing children's verbalizations to control behavior (C. F., Baer et al., 1988).

Assess Treatment Integrity

Treatment integrity refers to whether or not an intervention is being conducted as intended (Peterson et al., 1982; Salend, 1984; Sechrest et al., 1979). Treatment integrity is of major significance and casts doubt over intervention efforts if not evaluated. "Real treatments are often complex, are sometimes delivered by poorly trained or un-

motivated people, and can be totally disrupted by events in the real world" (Sechrest et al., 1979, pp. 15–16). Interventions as carried out in practice often are intentionally or unintentionally altered, or are not carried out as planned. Threats to treatment integrity include: person variables that affect the individual implementing and maintaining the intervention; the complexity and demands of the intervention; and the length of the intervention.

Although changes in plans frequently are required to ensure that the child receives an appropriate treatment, the needed changes should be identified, planned, and mutually agreed upon. It is important not to base decisions concerning more restrictive (e.g., special classes) or intrusive interventions on intervention outcomes that appeared ineffective, but which instead lacked treatment integrity. The intervention might have not failed, rather, it might not have been adequately attempted.

To help control for potential threats to treatment integrity, several strategies are available. First, using ecological- and consultation-based approaches when designing interventions enables the identification of likely change agents, and allows the individual with responsibility for implementation to be knowledgeable of the conditions necessary for adequately conducting the interventions. Second, through training, modeling, role playing, and guided practice, the individual can become competent in the intervention techniques prior to their actual implementation. The intervention can be evaluated and revised as necessary. Third, using a standardized protocol and simplifying procedures as much as possible also can help with threats to treatment integrity. Observers also can help by collecting data on the intervention procedures administered in the natural environment.

In summary, compliance with the planned intervention is a significant problem in outcome research. Further, potential difficulties with compliance underscores the possible need to identify a range of intervention alternatives and change agents for individual children.

Assess "Side Effects"

Interventions can have positive and/or negative outcomes (Willems, 1977). Factors within the social environment can be altered unintentionally, for better or worse, in addition to specified target behaviors. It is important to evaluate potential negative outcomes for children, families, and teachers. Although there are no standard procedures for measuring unplanned outcomes, general procedures involve extending measurements or "probes" into longer time periods, measuring multiple behaviors, and assessing the behaviors of others in the social environments.

Other Professional Considerations

Behavioral consultants should be aware of their own value systems, behaviors, and competencies. Further, they should adhere to well-established conventions for assessment and intervention design, and practice within ethical principles of major professional organizations associated with educational and mental health services to children and adolescents. Beyond the technical considerations, the major principles of intervention design are mutually agreed upon plans and the evaluation of the effectiveness of interventions.

There are numerous complexities in assessment and intervention design with young children. In the final section, the cognitive activities (Kendall, 1987) of the psychologist in planning assessments and interventions are the focal point of discussion.

THE REALITIES OF PRACTICE AND PROFESSIONAL JUDGMENT

Professional (or clinical) judgment is the traditional term used to describe practitioner decisions in difficult and ambiguous circumstances. In many, perhaps most, situations, decisions are made in less than ideal circumstances. Professional learn to practice "on-the-fly." However, the outcomes of professional judgment are quite vulnerable to both internal and external processes (Hogarth, 1987; Nisbett & Ross, 1980) even under ideal circumstances. The analysis of assessment and intervention decisions related to effective practice is essential.

Professional judgment has been widely analyzed with respect to diagnostic functions, and has recently been discussed with respect to intervention design (Barnett, 1988; Kanfer, 1985; Kendall, 1987; Rekers, 1984). The following is a summary of key issues.

First, many professional practices are simply not well-researched or properly evaluated (Barlow et al., 1984). Second, professional judgments can vary considerably by the information generated through the use of alternative assessment techniques (Poth & Barnett, 1988). Rather than leading to a "converging picture" of a child and situation, instrument selection and sources of information can have "diverging" effects on the professional's concept of the child and problem situation when all information is taken into account. Simply increasing the amount of information can actually reduce accuracy and at the same time increase professional confidence (see the review by Mash, 1985). Normal cognitive processes on the part of the professional simplify and structure information in known ways, in ways that "fit" favorite personal theories, and also possibly in ways that are "out of awareness." Further, even information from "objective" or empirically based assessments often leads to divergent findings that still need to be integrated into a valid and acceptable treatment plan or "case formulation" (Achenbach & McConaughy, 1987). Decision reliability for the diagnosis of childhood disorders can be surprisingly low, even when instruments have adequate psychometric characteristics (Barnett & Macmann, 1990).

Professional judgments are directly linked to ethical issues: ". . . the adoption of a decision frame is an ethically significant act" (Tversky & Kahneman, 1984, p. 40). Issues involve decisions regarding which assessment procedures should be used, a determination of what behavior pattern should be conceptualized as deviant, a professional judgment regarding the child's prognosis with and without assessment intervention, and the formulation of specific intervention strategies based on the data collected" (Rekers, 1984, p. 254).

Because of the difficulties and the need for further research, the most promising strategies involve those related to decision analysis (e.g., Hogarth, 1987). They include the self-questioning and cognitive appraisals of the representation of child systems (Cantrell & Cantrell, 1985; Evans, 1985); the development of assessment and intervention plans based on an interactive research-based model; and the evaluation of outcomes (Barlow et al., 1984).

CONCLUSION

Overwhelming interest in early intervention now exists. Although full of promise, the research base is surprisingly meager and controversial. This chapter reviewed the conceptual foundations of assessment practices related to intervention design. Emphasis was given to the assessment of a broad range of factors, service delivery systems oriented to enhancing the skills of caregivers, and on methods of improving intervention decisions. The concepts have applicability for multidisciplinary services to high-risk and handicapped children.

Many factors impact upon intervention decisions. Although typically practitioners rely on developmental scales, interviews, and observations, the technical adequacy of various instruments and techniques raises many concerns. The simple number of alternative developmental assessment devices thwarts efforts to study their relative merits and intervention implications. The most important and least understood process is one of integrating information into a professional practices plan.

An alternative to traditional assessment practices is to plan assessments based on principles of intervention design. Rather than being guided by various scales or domains, practitioners can be guided by research and concepts related to facilitating development. Through a shift in emphasis, new assessment tasks and roles emerge related to program planning, treatment evaluation, and parent consultation (Bagnato et al., in press).

The sources for evaluating early intervention effectiveness stem from large scale research projects and from single case experimental designs. Although both are important, single case designs are of special relevance because of the many unknowns in efficacy research. These designs are well suited for the study of individual change. The increasing amount of research is likely to lead to many new empirically based interventions for diverse problem situations, and new decision aids to guide the assessment-intervention process.

ACKNOWLEDGMENT

Appreciation is extended to Ed Lentz, Beth Berlager, Steve Coolahan, and Cathy Hardin for their editorial suggestions.

REFERENCES

Achenbach, T. M., & McConaughy, S. H. (1987). *Empirically Based Assessment of Child and Adolescent Psychopathology: Practical Applications*. Newbury Park, CA: Sage.

Adelman, H. S. (1982). Identifying learning problems at an early age: A critical appraisal. *Journal of Clinical Child Psychology, 11*, 255–261.

Baer, D. M., & Wolf, M. M. (1970). The entry into natural communities of reinforcement. In R. Ulrich, T. Stachnik, & J. Mabry (Eds.). *Control of Human Behavior: Vol 11. From Cure to Prevention* (pp. 319–324). Glenview, IL: Scott, Foresman.

Baer, R. A., Detrich, R., & Weninger, J. M. (1988). On the functional role of the verbalization in correspondence training procedures. *Journal of Applied Behavior Analysis, 21*, 345–356.

Baer, R. A., Williams, J. A., Osnes, P. G., & Stokes, T. F. (1985). Generalized verbal control and correspondence training. *Behavior Modification, 9*, 477–489.

Bagnato, S. J., & Neisworth, J. T. (1979). Between assessment and intervention: Forging an assessment/curriculum linkage for the handicapped preschooler. *Child Care Quarterly, 8*, 179–195.

Bagnato, S. J., Neisworth, J. T., & Capone, A., (1986). Curriculum-based assessment for the young exceptional child: Rationale and review. *Topics in Early Childhood Special Education, 6*, 97–110.

Bagnato, S. J., Neisworth, J. T., Paget, K. D., & Kovaleski, J. F. (in press). The developmental school psychologist: Professional profile of an emerging early childhood specialist. *Topics in Early Childhood Special Education, 7*, 75–89.

Bandura. A. (1969). *Behavior Modification*. Englewood Cliffs, NJ: Prentice-Hall.

Bandura, A. (1986). *The Social Foundations of Thought and Action: A Social Cognitive Theory*. Englewood Cliffs, NJ: Prentice-Hall.

Barlow, D. H., Hayes, S. C., & Nelson, R. O. (1984). *The Scientist–Practitioner: Research and Accountability in Clinical and Educational Settings*. New York: Pergamon.

Barlow, D. H., & Hersen, M. (1984). *Single Case Experimental Designs: Strategies for Studying Behavioral Change* (2nd ed.). New York: Pergamon.

Barnett, D. W. (in press) Professional judgment: A critical appraisal. *School Psychology Review*.

Barnett, D. W. (1984). An organizational approach to preschool services: Psychological screening, assessment, and intervention. In C. A. Maher, R. J. Illback, & J. E. Zins (Eds.). *Organizational Psychology in the Schools: A Handbook for Professionals* (pp. 55–82). Springfield, IL: Thomas.

Barnett, D. W. (1986). School psychology in preschool settings: A review of training and practice issues. *Professional Psychology: Research and Practice, 17,* 58–64.

Barnett, D. W., & Macmann, G. M. (in press). Personal and social assessment: Critical issues for research and practice. In C. R. Reynolds & R. W. Kamphaus (Eds.). *Handbook of Psychological and Educational Assessment of Children (Vol 2): Personality, Behavior, and Context.* New York: Guilford Press.

Barnett, D. W., & Paget, K. D. (in press) Alternative service delivery in preschool settings: Practical and conceptual foundations. In J. Graden, J. Zins, & M. Curtis (Eds.). *Alternative Educational Delivery Systems: Enhancing Instructional Options for All Students.* Washington, DC: National Association of School Psychologists.

Barrios, B., & Hartmann, D. P. (1986). The contributions of traditonal assessment: Concepts, issues, and methodologies. In R. O. Nelson & S. C. Hayes (Eds.). *Conceptual Foundations of Behavioral Assessment* (pp. 81–110). New York: Guilford.

Billings, D. C., & Wasik, B. H. (1985). Self-instructional training with preschoolers: An attempt to replicate. *Journal of Applied Behavior Analysis, 18,* 61–67.

Bornstein, P. H. (1985). Self-instructional training: A commentary and state-of-the-art. *Journal of Applied Behavior Analysis, 18,* 69–72.

Bonfenbrenner, U. (1986). Ecology of the family as a context for human development: Research perspectives. *Developmental Psychology, 22,* 723–742.

Bracken, B. A. (1987). Limitations of preschool instruments and standards for minimal levels of technical adequacy. *Journal of Psychoeducational Assessment, 5,* 313–326.

Bricker, D. D. (1986). *Early Education of At-risk and Handicapped Infants, Toddlers, and Preschool Children.* Glenview, IL: Little, Brown.

Calvert, S. C., & McMahon, R. J. (1987). The treatment acceptability of a parent training program and its components. *Behavior Therapy, 2,* 165–179.

Cantrell, M. L. & Cantrell, R. P. (1985). Assessment of the natural environment. *Education and Treatment of Children, 8,* 275–295.

Casto, G. (1987). Plasticity and the handicapped child: A review of efficacy research. In J. J. Gallagher & C. T. Ramey (Eds.). *The Malleability of Children* (pp. 103–113). Baltimore: Brookes.

Cone, J. D., & Hoier, T. S. (1986). Assessing children: The radical behavior perspective. In R. Prinz (Ed.). *Advances in Behavioral Assessment of Children and Families, Vol. 2* (1–27). Greenwich, CT: JAI Press.

Dumas, J. E., & Albin, J. B. (1986). Parent training outcome: Does active parental involvement matter? *Behavioral Research and Therapy, 24,* 227–230.

Dunst, C. J., & Trivette, C. M. (1987). Enabling and empowering families: Conceptual and intervention issues. *School Psychology Review, 16,* 443–456.

Edgington, E. S. (1967). Statistical inference from N = 1 experiments. *Journal of Psychology, 65,* 195–199.

Etzel B. C., LeBlanc, J. M., Schilmoeller, K. J., & Stella, M. E. (1981). Stimulus control procedures in the education of young children. In S. W. Bijou & R. Ruiz (Eds.). *Behavior Modification: Contribution to Education* (pp.3–37). Hillsdale, NJ: Erlbaum.

Evans, I. M. (1985). Building systems models as a strategy for target behavior selection in clinical assessment. *Behavior Assessment, 7,* 21–32.

Firestone, P. (1976). The effects and side effects of time-out on an aggressive nursery school child. *Journal of Behavior Therapy and Experimental Psychiatry, 6,* 79–81.

Foster, S. L., & Cone, J. D. (1986). Design and use of direct observation. In A. R. Ciminero, K. S. Calhoun, & H. E. Adams (Eds.). *Handbook of Behavioral Assessment* (2nd ed., pp. 253–324). New York: Wiley.

Fox, J., Shores, R., Lindeman, D., & Strain, P. (1986). Maintaining social initiations of withdrawn handicapped and nonhandicapped preschoolers through a response-dependent fading tactic. *Journal of Abnormal Child Psychology, 14,* 387–396.

Fuchs, L. S., & Fuchs, D (1986). Linking assessment to instructional interventions: An overview. *School Psychology Review, 15,* 318–323.

Gallagher, J. J., & Ramey, C. T. (Eds.). (1987). *The malleability of children.* Baltimore: Brookes.

Glenwick, D. S., & Jason, L. A. (1984). Locus of intervention in child cognitive behavior therapy: Implications of a behavioral community psychology perspective. In A. W. Meyers & W. E. Craighead (Eds.). *Cognitive Behavior Therapy with Children* (pp. 129–162). New York: Plenum.

Graden, J. L., Casey, A., & Christenson, S. L. (1985). Implementing a prereferral intervention system: Part I: The model. *Exceptional Children, 51,* 377–384.

Gross, A. M., & Wojnilower, D. A. (1984). Self-directed behavior change in children: Is it self-directed. *Behavior Therapy, 15,* 501–514.

Guevremont, D. C., Osnes, P. G., & Stokes, T. F. (1986a). Programming maintenance after correspondence training interventions with children. *Journal of Applied Behavior Analysis, 19,* 215–219.

Guevremont, D. C., Osnes, P. G., & Stokes, T. F. (1986b). Preparation for effective self-regulation:

The development of generalized verbal control. *Journal of Applied Behavior Analysis, 19,* 99–104.

Guralnick, M. J. (1987). The peer relationships of young handicapped and nonhandicapped children. In P. S. Strain, M. J. Guralnick, & H. M. Walker (Eds.). *Children's Social Behavior: Development, Assessment, and Modification* (pp. 49–91). New York: Academic Press.

Guralnick, M. J., & Bennett, F. C. (Eds.) (1987). *The Effectiveness of Early Intervention for At-risk and Handicapped Children.* New York: Academic Press.

Gutkin, T. B., & Curtis, M. J. (1982). School-based consultation: Theory and techniques. In C. R. Reynolds & T. B. Gutkin (Eds.). *Handbook of School Psychology* (pp. 796–828). New York: Wiley.

Halle, J. W., Baer, D. M., & Spradlin, J. E. (1981). Teachers' generalized use of delay as a stimulus control procedure to increase language use in handicapped children. *Journal of Applied Behavior Analysis, 14,* 389–409.

Hart, B., & Risley, T. R. (1980). In vivo language interventions: Unanticipated general effects. *Journal of Applied Behavior Analysis, 13,* 407–432.

Hawkins, R. P. (1986). Selection of target behaviors. In R. O. Nelson & S. C. Hayes (Eds.). *Conceptual Foundations of Behavioral Assessment* (pp. 331–385). New York: Guilford.

Hayes, S. C., & Nelson, R. O. (1986). Assessing the effects of therapeutic interventions. In R. O. Nelson & S. C. Hayes (Eds.). *Conceptual Foundations of Behavioral Assessment* (pp. 430–460). New York: Guilford.

Hayes, S. C., Nelson, R. O., & Jarrett, R. B. (1986). Evaluating the quality of behavioral assessment. In R. O. Nelson & S. C. Hayes (Eds.). *Conceptual Foundations of Behavioral Assessment* (pp. 461–503). New York: Guilford.

Haynes, S. N. (1986). The design of intervention programs. In R. O. Nelson & S. C. Hayes (Eds.). *Conceptual Foundations of Behavioral Assessment* (pp. 386–429). New York: Guilford.

Hecimovic, A., Fox, J. J., Shores, R. E., & Strain, P. S. (1985). An analysis of developmentally integrated and segregated free play settings and the generalization of newly acquired social behaviors of socially withdrawn preschoolers. *Behavioral Assessment, 7,* 367–388.

Hendrickson, J. M., Strain, P. S., Tremblay, A., & Shores, R. E. (1982). Interactions of behaviorally handicapped children: Functional effects of peer social initiations. *Behavior Modification, 6,* 323–353.

Hogarth, R. (1987). *Judgement and Choice* (2nd ed.). New York: Wiley.

Hoier, T. S., McConnell, S., & Pallay, A. G. (1987). Observational assessment for planning and evaluating educational transitions: An initial analysis of template matching. *Behavioral Assessment, 9,* 5–19.

James, S. D., & Egel, A. L. (1986). A direct prompting strategy for increasing reciprocal interactions between handicapped and nonhandicapped siblings. *Journal of Applied Behavior Analysis, 19,* 173–186.

Jones, R. T., & Kazdin, A. E. (1980) Teaching children how and when to make emergency telephone calls. *Behavior Therapy, 11* 509–521.

Kanfer F. H. (1985). Target selection for clinical change programs. *Behavioral Assessment, 7,* 7–20.

Kazdin, A. E. (1980). Acceptability of alternative treatments for deviant child behavior. *Journal of Applied Behavior Analysis, 13,* 259–273.

Kazdin A. E. (1985). Selection of target behaviors: The relationship of treatment focus to clinical dysfunction. *Behavior Assessment, 7,* 33–47.

Kendall P. C. (1987). Ahead to basics: Assessments with children and families. *Behavioral Assessment, 9,*321–332.

Kratochwill, T. R. (Guest editor) (1985). Mini-series on target behavior selection. *Behavioral Assessment, 7*(1).

Laosa, L. M., & Sigel, I. E. (1982). (Eds.). *Families as Learning-environments for Children.* New York: Plenum.

LeBlanc, J. M. Etzel, B. C., & Domash, M. A. (1978). A functional curriculum for early intervention. In K. E. Allen, V. A. Holm, & R. L. Schiefelbusch (Eds.). *Early Intervention-A Team Approach* (pp. 331–381). Baltimore: University Park Press.

Loeber, R., & Schmaling, K. B. (1985). Empirical evidence for overt and covert patterns of antisocial conduct problems: A metaanalysis. *Journal of Abnormal Child Psychology, 13,* 337–352.

Magura, S., & Moses, B. S. (1986). *Outcome Measures for Child Welfare Services: Theory and Applications.* Washington, DC: Child Welfare League of America.

Mash, E. J. (1985). Some comments on target selection in behavior therapy. *Behavioral Assessment, 7,* 63–78.

Mash E. J. (Guest editor) (1987). Behavioral assessment of child and family disorders. *Behavioral Assessment, 9*(3).

Mash, E. J., & Terdal, L. G. (1981). *Behavioral Assessment of Childhood Disorders* (2nd ed. in press). New York:. Guilford.

Matson, J. L., Horne, A. M., Ollendick, D. G., & Ollendick, T. H. (1978). Overcorrection: A further evaluation of restitution and positive practice. *Journal of Behavior Therapy and Experimental Psychiatry, 10,* 295–298.

McMahon, R. J. (1987). Some current issues in the behavioral assessment of conduct disordered children and their families. *Behavioral Assessment, 9,* 235–252.

Mori, L., & Peterson, L. (1986). Training preschoolers in safety skills to prevent inadvertent injury. *Journal of Clinical Child Psychology, 15,* 106–114.

Neisworth, J. T., & Bagnato, S. J. (1986). Curriculum-based developmental assessment: Congruence of testing and teaching. *School Psychology Review, 15,* 180–199.

Nelson, R. O., & Hayes, S. C. (1986). The nature of behavioral assessment. In R. O. Nelson & S. C. Hayes (Eds.). *Conceptual Foundations of Behavior Assessment* (1–40). New York: Guilford Press.

Nisbett, R. & Ross, L. (1980). *Human Inference: Strategies and Shortcomings of Social Judgement.* Englewood Cliffs, NJ: Prentice-Hall.

Osnes P. G., Guevremont, D. C., & Stokes, T. F. (1986). If I say I'll talk more, then I will: Correspondence training to increase peer-directed talk by socially withdrawn children. *Behavior Modification, 10,* 287–299.

Page, T. J., & Iwata, B. A. (1986). Interobserver agreement: History, theory, and current methods. In A. Poling & R. W. Fuqua (Eds.). *Research Methods in Applied Behavior Analysis* (pp. 99–126). New York: Plenum.

Paget, K. D. (in press). Early behavioral interventions:. Grasping the complexities. In J. C. Witt, S. N. Elliott, & F. M. Gresham (Eds.). *Handbook of Behavior Therapy in Education.* New York: Plenum.

Panaccione, V. F., & Wahler, R. G. (1986). Child behavior, maternal depression, and social coercion as factors in the quality of child care. *Journal of Abnormal Child Psychology, 14,* 263–278.

Patterson, G. R., & Bank, L. (1986). Bootstrapping your way in the nomological thicket. *Behavioral Assessment, 8,* 49–73.

Peterson L. (1988). Preventing the leading killer of children: The role of the school psychologist in injury prevention. *School Psychology Review, 17,* 593–600.

Peterson, L., Homer, A. L., & Wonderlich, S. A. (1982). The integrity of independent variables in behavior analysis. *Journal of Applied Behavior Analysis, 15,* 477–492.

Plionis, E. M. (1977). Family functioning and childhood accident occurrence. *American Journal of Orthopsychiatry, 47,* 250–263.

Plomin R. & Daniels, D. (1987). Why are children in the same family so different from one another? *Behavioral and Brain Sciences, 10,* 1–16.

Poche, C., Brouwer, R., & Swearingen, M. (1981). Teaching self-protection to young children. *Journal of Applied Behavior Analysis, 14,* 169–176.

Porterfield, J. K., Herbert-Jackson, E., & Risley, T. R. (1976). Contingent observation: An effective and acceptable procedure for reducing disruptive behavior of young children in a group setting. *Journal of Applied Behavior Analysis, 9,* 55–64.

Poth, R. L., & Barnett, D. W. (1983). Reduction of a behavioral tic with a preschooler using relaxation and self-control techniques across settings. *School Psychology Review, 12,* 472–475.

Poth, R. L. & Barnett, D. W. (1988). Establishing the limits of interpretive confidence: A validity study of two preschool developmental scales. *School Psychology Review, 17,* 322–330.

Powers, M. D. (1984). Syndromal diagnosis and the behavioral assessment of childhood disorders. *Child & Family Behavior Therapy, 6,* 1–15.

Reimers, T., Wacker, D., & Koeppl, G. (1987). Acceptability of behavioral interventions: A review of the literature. *School Psychology Review, 16,* 212–227.

Rekers, G. A. (1984). Ethical issues in child behavior assessment. In T. H. Ollendick & M. Hersen (Eds.). *Child Behavior Assessment: Principles and Procedures* (pp. 244–262). New York: Pergamon.

Roberts, M. W., McMahon, R. J., Forehand, R., & Humphreys, L. (1978). The effect of parental instruction-giving on child compliance. *Behavior Therapy, 9,* 793–798.

Russo, D. C., Cataldo, M. F., & Cushing, P. J. (1981). Compliance training and behavioral covariation in the treatment of multiple behavior problems. *Journal of Applied Behavior Analysis, 14,* 209–222.

Rutter, M. (1984). Continuities and discontinuities in socioemotional development: Empirical and conceptual perspectives. In R. M. Emde & J. R. Harmon (Eds.). *Continuities and Discontinuities in Development* (pp. 41–68). New York: Plenum.

Salend, S. (1984). Therapy outcome research: Threats to treatment intergrity. *Behavior Modification, 8,* 211–222.

Sechrest, L., West, S. G., Phillips, M. A., Redner, R., & Yeaton, W. (1979). Some neglected problems in evaluation research: Strength and integrity of treatments. In L. Sechrest, S. G. West, M. A. Phillips, R. Redner, & R. Yeaton (Eds.). *Evaluation Studies Annual Review* (pp. 15–35). Beverly Hills: Sage.

Schon, D. A. (1983). *The Reflective Practitioner: How Professionals Think in Action.* New York: Basic Books.

Schweinhart, L. J., Weikart, D. P., & Larner, M. B. (1986). Consequences of three preschool curriculum models through age 15. *Early Childhood Research Quarterly, 1,* 15–45.

Stokes T. F. Fowler, S. A., & Baer, D. M. (1978). Training preschool children to recruit natural communities of reinforcement. *Journal of Applied Behavior Analysis, 11,* 285–303.

Stokes, T. F., & Osnes, P. G. (1986). Programming the generalization of children's social behavior. In P. S.

Strain, M. J. Guralnick, & H. M. Walker (Eds.). *Children's social behavior: Development, assessment, and modification* (pp. 407–443). Orlando, FL: Academic Press.

Strain, P. S., Steele, P., Ellis, T., & Timm, M. A; (1982). Long-term effects of oppositional child treatment with mothers as therapists and therapist trainers. *Journal of Applied Behavior Analysis, 15,* 163–169.

Strosahl, K. D., & Linehan, M. M. (1986). Basic issues in behavioral assessment. In A. R. Ciminero, K. S. Calhoun, & H. E. Adams (Eds.). *Handbook of Behavioral Assessment* (2nd ed., pp. 12–46). New York: Wiley.

Tawney, J. W., & Gast, D. L. (1984). *Single Subject Research in Special Education.* Columbus, OH: Merrill.

Tversky, A., & Kahneman, D. (1984). The framing of decisions and the psychology of choice. In G. Wright (Ed.). *Behavioral Decision Making* (pp. 25–41). New York: Plenum.

Wahler R. G. (1975). Some structural aspects of deviant child behavior. *Journal of Applied Behavior Analysis, 8,* 27–42.

Wahler R. G. (1980). The insular mother: Her problems in parent-child treatment. *Journal of Applied Behavior Analysis, 13,* 207–219.

Wahler, R. G., & Dumas, J. E. (1986). "A chip off the old block": Some interpersonal characteristics of coercive children across generations. In P. S. Strain, M. J. Guralnick, & H. M. Walker (Eds.). *Children's Social Behavior: Development, Assessment, and Modification* (pp. 49–91). New York: Academic Press.

Wahler, R. G., & Fox, J. J. (1980). Solitary toy play and time out: A family treatment package for children with aggressive and oppositional behavior. *Journal of Applied Behavior Analysis, 13,* 23–39.

Walle, D. L., Hobbs, S. A., & Caldwell, H. S. (1984). Sequencing of parent training procedures: Effects on child noncompliance and treatment acceptability. *Behavior Modification, 8,* 540–552.

Webster-Stratton, C. (1986). Predictors of treatment outcome in parent training for conduct disordered children. *Behavior Therapy, 16,* 223–243.

White, K. R. (1985–86) Efficacy of early intervention. *Journal of Special Education, 19,* 401–416.

Willems, E. P. (1977). Steps toward an ecobehavioral technology. In A. Rogers-Warren & S. F. Warren (Eds.). *Ecological Perspectives in Behavior Analysis* (pp. 39–61). Baltimore: University Park Press.

Willoughby-Herb, S. J., & Neisworth, J. T. (1982). *HICOMP Preschool Curriculum.* Columbus, OH; Merrill.

Witt, J. C., & Elliott, S. N. (1985). Acceptability of classroom management strategies. In T. R. Kratochwill (Ed.). *Advances in School Psychology* (Vol. 4, pp. 251–288). Hillsdale, NJ: Erlbaum.

Witt, J. C., Martens, B. K., & Elliott, S. N. (1984). Factors affecting teachers' judgements of the acceptability of behavioral interventions: Time involvement, behavior problem severity, and type of intervention. *Behavior Therapy, 15,* 204–209.

Wolf, M. M. (1978). Social validity: The case for subjective measurement or how applied behavior analysis is finding its heart. *Journal of Applied Behavior Analysis, 11,* 203–214.

Wolfe, D. A., & Bourdeau, P. A. (1987). Current issues in the assessment of parent-child conflict. *Behavioral Assessment, 9,* 271–290.

Yates, B. T. (1985). Cost-effectiveness analysis and cost-benefit analysis: An introduction. *Behavioral Assessment, 7,* 207–234.

Yeaton, W. H., & Bailey, J. S. (1978). Teaching pedestrian safety skills to young children: An analysis and one-year follow up. *Journal of Applied Behavior Analysis, 11,* 315–329.

Zigler E. & Trickett, P. (1978). IQ, social competence and evaluation of early childhood intervention programs. *American Psychologist, 33,* 789–798

NAME INDEX

SUBJECT INDEX